ACI Advanced Monitoring and Troubleshooting

Sadiq Memon (CCIE No. 47508)

Joseph Ristaino (CCIE No. 41799)

Carlo Schmidt (CCIE No. 41842)

I0028694

Cisco Press

221 River St.

Hoboken, NJ 07030 USA

ACI Advanced Monitoring and Troubleshooting

Sadiq Memon, Joseph Ristaino, Carlo Schmidt

Copyright© 2021 Cisco Systems, Inc.

Published by: Cisco Press

Library of Congress Control Number: 2020941959

ISBN-13: 1-58714-528-6

ISBN-10: 978-158714-528-5

ScoutAutomatedPrintCode

Warning and Disclaimer

This book is designed to provide information about in-depth monitoring and troubleshooting techniques related to Cisco's Application Centric Infrastructure (ACI) to guide readers in learning to design, deploy, and maintain the ACI fabric. This book can also help in preparing and attaining advanced certification such as CCIE Data Center. This book was written based on ACI Release 3.2(-) as that release was the preferred long-lived release over the course of developing the content. Therefore, the vast majority of features and examples covered in the book reference ACI Release 3.2(-), and they can still be applied to later releases. However, newer features are identified where applicable, along with the supported version in order to provide more in-depth information. Every effort has been made to make this book as complete and as accurate as possible, but no warranty or fitness is implied.

The information is provided on an "as is" basis. The authors, Cisco Press, and Cisco Systems, Inc. shall have neither liability for nor responsibility to any person or entity with respect to any loss or damages arising from the information contained in this book or from the use of the discs or programs that may accompany it.

The opinions expressed in this book belong to the author and are not necessarily those of Cisco Systems, Inc.

Microsoft and/or its respective suppliers make no representations about the suitability of the information contained in the documents and related graphics published as part of the services for any purpose. All such documents and related graphics are provided "as is" without warranty of any kind. Microsoft and/ or its respective suppliers hereby disclaim all warranties and conditions with regard to this information, including all warranties and conditions of merchantability, whether express, implied or statutory, fitness for a particular purpose, title and non-infringement. In no event shall Microsoft and/or its respective suppliers be liable for any special, indirect or consequential damages or any damages whatsoever resulting from loss of use, data or profits, whether in an action of contract, negligence or other tortious action, arising out of or in connection with the use or performance of information available from the services. The documents and related graphics contained herein could include technical inaccuracies or typographical errors. Changes are periodically added to the information herein. Microsoft and/or its respective suppliers may make improvements and/or changes in the product(s) and/or the program(s) described herein at any time. Partial screen shots may be viewed in full within the software version specified.

Microsoft® and Windows® are registered trademarks of the Microsoft Corporation in the U.S.A. and other countries. Screenshots and icons reprinted with permission from the Microsoft Corporation. This book is not sponsored or endorsed by or affiliated with the Microsoft Corporation.

Trademark Acknowledgments

All terms mentioned in this book that are known to be trademarks or service marks have been appropriately capitalized. Cisco Press or Cisco Systems, Inc., cannot attest to the accuracy of this information. Use of a term in this book should not be regarded as affecting the validity of any trademark or service mark.

Special Sales

For information about buying this title in bulk quantities, or for special sales opportunities (which may include electronic versions; custom cover designs; and content particular to your business, training goals, marketing focus, or branding interests), please contact our corporate sales department at corpsales@pearsoned.com or (800) 382-3419.

For government sales inquiries, please contact governmentsales@pearsoned.com.

For questions about sales outside the U.S., please contact intlcs@pearson.com.

Feedback Information

At Cisco Press, our goal is to create in-depth technical books of the highest quality and value. Each book is crafted with care and precision, undergoing rigorous development that involves the unique expertise of members from the professional technical community.

Readers' feedback is a natural continuation of this process. If you have any comments regarding how we could improve the quality of this book, or otherwise alter it to better suit your needs, you can contact us through email at feedback@ciscopress.com. Please make sure to include the book title and ISBN in your message.

We greatly appreciate your assistance.

Editor-in-Chief: Mark Taub

Alliances Manager, Cisco Press: Ron Fligge

Product Line Manager: Brett Bartow

Executive Editor: James Manly

Managing Editor: Sandra Schroeder

Development Editor: Christopher A. Cleveland

Senior Project Editor: Lori Lyons

Copy Editor: Kitty Wilson

Technical Editors: Mioljub Jovanovic, Joe LeBlanc

Editorial Assistant: Cindy Teeters

Cover Designer: Chuti Prasertsith

Production Manager: Aswini Kumar, codeMantra

Composition: codeMantra

Indexer: Cheryl Ann Lenser

Proofreader: Gill Editorial Services

CISCO.

Americas Headquarters
Cisco Systems, Inc.
San Jose, CA

Asia Pacific Headquarters
Cisco Systems (USA) Pte. Ltd.
Singapore

Europe Headquarters
Cisco Systems International BV Amsterdam,
The Netherlands

Cisco has more than 200 offices worldwide. Addresses, phone numbers, and fax numbers are listed on the Cisco Website at **www.cisco.com/go/offices.**

Cisco and the Cisco logo are trademarks or registered trademarks of Cisco and/or its affiliates in the U.S. and other countries. To view a list of Cisco trademarks, go to this URL: www.cisco.com/go/trademarks. Third party trademarks mentioned are the property of their respective owners. The use of the word partner does not imply a partnership relationship between Cisco and any other company. (1110R)

About the Authors

Sadiq Memon, CCIE No. 47508, is a Lead Solutions Integration Architect (Automotive) with Cisco Customer Experience (CX). He has over 30 years of diversified experience in information technology with specialization and expertise in data center and enterprise networking. Sadiq joined Cisco in 2007, and as a Cisco veteran of over 13 years, he has worked with various large enterprise customers, including automotive, financials, manufacturing, and government in designing, implementing, and supporting end-to-end architectures and solutions. Sadiq was part of the Cisco Advanced Services Tiger Team during the early ACI incubation period. He has published a series of short videos covering ACI configuration on YouTube and has presented ACI/Cloud-related topics at Cisco Live! Sadiq was the technical editor for the Cisco Press book *Deploying ACI* and possesses multiple IT industry certifications from leading companies such as Cisco (CCIE, CCNA), VMware (VCP-DCV), Microsoft, and Citrix. Sadiq holds a bachelor's degree in computer systems engineering from NED University of Engineering & Technology, Karachi, Pakistan.

Joseph Ristaino, CCIE No. 41799, is a Technical Leader with the ACI Escalation Team in RTP, North Carolina. He joined Cisco in 2011 after graduating from Wentworth Institute of Technology with a bachelor's degree in computer networking. Joseph started with Cisco on the Server Virtualization TAC team, specializing in UCS and virtualization technologies. He has in-depth knowledge of compute/networking technologies and has been supporting customers for over eight years as they implement and manage data center deployments around the globe. Joseph now works closely with the ACI Technical Support teams to provide assistance on critical customer issues that go unsolved and has been working on ACI since its inception in 2014. Joseph lives with his wife in Durham, North Carolina.

Carlo Schmidt, CCIE No. 41842, is a Data Center Solutions Architect. He works with global enterprises, designing their next-generation data centers. Carlo started at Cisco in 2011, on the Data Center Switching TAC team. In that role, he focused on Nexus platforms and technologies such as FCoE, fabric path, and OTV. In 2016, he migrated to the ACI TAC team, where he specialized in customer problem resolution as well as improving product usability. In 2019 Carlo decided to take his knowledge and lessons learned from his eight years in Cisco TAC to a presales role as a Solutions Architect. Carlo is based out of Research Triangle Park, North Carolina.

About the Technical Reviewers

Mioljub Jovanovic, CCIE No. 17631, is certified in Routing & Switching and in Data Center. He is a Principal Engineer at Cisco Systems, working for Customer Experience organization, with more than 20 years of professional experience with Cisco networking products in solutions. Among other responsibilities, Mio's role included training and support for initial ACI global deployments. Between 2015 and 2019, he presented ACI training and troubleshooting sessions at multiple Cisco Live conferences and other technical seminars.

As a Data Center Technical Leader in the CX DC EMEAR group, Mio coached and mentored Cisco support engineers on ACI, HyperFlex, CNAE, Tetration, FlexPod, vBlock and solutions involving Cisco UCS and Nexus and MDS platforms. Prior to his TL role in the DC Solutions team, Mio worked as Network Management senior TAC engineer, specializing in SNMP and network services platforms. Mio's passions are Service Assurance, Day-2 Operations, Model-Driven Telemetry, Linux, Angular, and Python.

Joe LeBlanc, CCIE No. 41523, is a Technical Leader in the Intent-Based Networking Group at Cisco Systems. He has been supporting ACI customer escalations in the engineering group since FCS of the solution in 2014. Prior to that role, Joe worked in the Technical Assistance Center on the Server Virtualization team, supporting UCS and Nexus 1000v products.

Dedications

Sadiq H Memon:

This book is dedicated to my parents, Abdul Majeed Memon and Saeeda Memon, for their day and night gracious prayers. My beloved wife, Nazish Memon, and my kids, Nibras Memon, Ali Memon, and Ahmed Memon, for their utmost support and encouragement throughout the extended period of writing this book. My management at Cisco for their continuous support in excelling my career. And last but not least, the trust and support from all my auto customers, especially from Tony Cataldo (Manager Network Engineering from a renowned U.S.-based auto company). Without all their support, I don't think I would have been able to propose and author this book successfully.

Joseph Ristaino:

This book is dedicated to my wife, Katie, for her endless support, and to all the friends I've made at Cisco. Because of them, this book has become a reality.

Carlo Schmidt:

I dedicate this book to all the amazing mentors, managers, and coworkers who have supported me during my time at Cisco. Without their encouragement, and their countless after-work hours teaching me how to become a better engineer, I would have never had the ability to co-author this book with Sadiq and Joey. I also dedicate this book to my wife, Ally, who supported me through many late nights of researching, writing, and reviewing.

Acknowledgments

We would like to specially thank the technical editors Mioljub Jovanovic and Joe LeBlanc for providing their expert-level technical knowledge in editing the book. Being well-known for their subject matter expertise in Cisco and outside with ACI technology, both of the technical editors paid close attention in reviewing the material and were very blunt in identifying our mistakes and shortcomings; they helped make the content accurate and valuable for readers.

We would also like to acknowledge and appreciate Cisco Data Center Business Unit (DCBU) for the guidance and knowledge sharing. As the owner and developer of ACI, Cisco DCBU has empowered us to learn and excel this technology since the day of its inception, and this helped us successfully finish up this book. Cisco DCBU included us as part of Cisco Tiger Team in learning and developing the initial content of ACI before it was even publicly announced.

Big applause goes out to the production team for this book. James Manly and Christopher Cleveland have been incredibly professional and a pleasure to work with. This book could not have been completed successfully without their constant push and support.

Last but not least, we would like to acknowledge the services and support of our beloved friend and coworker Andy Gossett, whose in-depth technical expertise has not only helped in writing this book but has in general been a great help to Cisco teams and the extended customer base.

Contents at a Glance

Contents

Reader Services

Register your copy at www.ciscopress.com/title/9781587145285 for convenient access to downloads, updates, and corrections as they become available. To start the registration process, go to www.ciscopress.com/register and log in or create an account*. Enter the product ISBN 9781587145285 and click Submit. When the process is complete, you will find any available bonus content under Registered Products.

*Be sure to check the box indicating that you would like to hear from us to receive exclusive discounts on future editions of this product.

Command Syntax Conventions

The conventions used to present command syntax in this book are the same conventions used in the IOS Command Reference. The Command Reference describes these conventions as follows:

- **Boldface** indicates commands and keywords that are entered literally as shown. In actual configuration examples and output (not general command syntax), boldface indicates commands that are manually input by the user (such as a **show** command).

- *Italic* indicates arguments for which you supply actual values.

- Vertical bars (|) separate alternative, mutually exclusive elements.

- Square brackets ([ ]) indicate an optional element.

- Braces ({ }) indicate a required choice.

- Braces within brackets ([{ }]) indicate a required choice within an optional element.

Foreword by Yusuf Bhaiji

ACI Advanced Monitoring and Troubleshooting is an excellent self-study material for the latest blueprint of CCIE Data Center certification exam (v3.0). Whether you are studying to attain CCIE certification or are just seeking to gain a better understanding of Cisco ACI technology in designing, implementing, maintaining, and troubleshooting, you will benefit from the information presented in this book.

The authors have used a unique approach in explaining concepts and the architecture of the ACI technology carefully crafted into an easy-to-follow guide. The book provides readers a comprehensive and all-inclusive view of the entire range of Cisco ACI solutions in a single binder.

As an early-stage exam-preparation guide, this book presents a detailed and comprehensive introduction to the technologies used to build scalable software-defined networks and also covers the topics defined in the CCIE exam blueprint.

Cisco Press books are designed to help educate, develop, and excel the community of IT professionals in not only traditional networking technologies but also in today's state-of-the-art software-defined networking techniques.

Most networking professionals use a variety of learning methods to keep them up to the mark with the latest technologies. Cisco Press titles are a prime source of content for some individuals and can also serve as an excellent supplement to other forms of learning. Training classes, whether delivered in a classroom or online, are a great way to quickly acquire knowledge on newer technologies. Hands-on practice is essential for anyone seeking to build or acquire new skills.

The author (Sadiq Hussain Memon) and his co-authors have a very distinct style and have proven their skills by writing on a difficult subject using real-world examples and use cases. A must-read and an essential part of your exam preparation toolkit and a valuable addition to your personal library.

Yusuf Bhaiji
Director of Certifications
Cisco Systems

Foreword by Ronak Desai

When Cisco built the Application Centric Infrastructure (ACI), it expanded the influence of Data Center operators by providing them with an agile and accessible framework on which they could build and operate their networks. My own journey with Cisco Data Center began soon after I joined the company in 2002, when it acquired Andiamo, where I was a lead engineer. After joining Cisco, I worked on building the MDS 9000 and Nexus 7000 series, which evolved into the first line of products for Cisco's then-new Data Center business unit. After successfully delivering MDS and Nexus I was asked to be founding employee on the ACI team and have been driving engineering there since day one.

In the past eight years, I have seen the ACI products mature and become part of the critical infrastructure for hospitals, emergency systems, banks, mobile networks, and large-scale enterprises. "ACI Anywhere" is recognized as the best SDN solution for private and public cloud.

So, I am honored to be the one to introduce you to this book, which will help you take the best advantage of this powerful networking platform.

Throughout my years at Cisco, I have pleasure to work with Sadiq Memon, Joey Ristaino, and Carlo Schmidt countless occasions. As invaluable members of the Data Center Networking Group, and their collective experience with the ACI solution, makes them incredible resources to anyone who wants to learn about the ins and outs of the infrastructure.

This book is accessible to network professionals just beginning with ACI, as well as to ACI veterans looking for insight and advanced tips. Readers seeking a deeper analysis can opt to dive into later chapters where the authors collaborate with technical engineers to effectively communicate key technical concepts. Here, readers can build upon their foundational knowledge with more hands-on application-based learning.

Readers will also find valuable the advice based on personal experiences and challenges our authors faced in the data center field. These vignettes provide readers with in-depth examinations into real-world cases with step-by-step instructions and troubleshooting advice. Even readers familiar with the ACI fabric will find that they can extend their knowledge with these critical insights into ACI monitoring and troubleshooting.

By the end of this book, engaged readers will be proficient with ACI technology and have an in-depth understanding of troubleshooting and monitoring best practices for the ACI fabric, giving them the competitive edge to grow their business.

Ronak Desai
VP of Engineering for the Data Center Networking Business Unit
Cisco Systems

Introduction

Application Centric Infrastructure (ACI) is a software-defined network offering from Cisco that addresses the challenges of application agility needs in data centers. ACI was announced on November 6, 2013, and it has been widely deployed on large number of customer data centers globally since then. The demand to monitor and troubleshoot this unique and modern form of network infrastructure has increased exponentially from every corner of the world. This book was written with the goal of helping guide data center professionals understand the crucial topics of ACI with real-world examples from field experiences. The Cisco Data Center Business Unit and industry leaders were consulted for technical accuracy of the content of this book.

Who Should Read This Book?

This book is intended for data center architects, engineers, software developers, network and virtualization administrators, and, most importantly, operations team members striving to better understand and manage this new form of software-defined networking.

The content of the book will help you confidently deploy, support, monitor, and troubleshoot ACI fabric and its components. It also introduces some of the newer concepts in this technology by relating them to traditional networking terminology and experiences. The readers should be at the intermediate to expert level. This book assumes common knowledge of Cisco NX-OS and network switching and routing concepts. A typical reader should at least possess a Cisco CCNA certification and be responsible for day-to-day operations of networks and applications. Because of its in-depth and advanced subject matter, this book can also be used as a reference guide for CCIE Data Center certification.

This book is also a good preparatory reference for those taking the Cisco DCACIA (300-630) exam toward the Cisco Certified Specialist—ACI Advanced Implementation certification. Where applicable, portions of some chapters are marked with a Key Topic icon to highlight concepts you should know for the exam. Chapters 1, 2, 4, 5, 7, 8, 9, 12, and 13 also provide some review questions to help you prepare for this exam. This book can also help you prepare for the CCIE Data Center (v3.0) exam.

How This Book Is Organized

This book is divided into three major sections:

Part I, "Introduction to ACI": This section includes the following chapters:

- **Chapter 1, "Fundamental Functions and Components of ACI":** This chapter provides a high-level overview of the core functions and components of Cisco Application Infrastructure (ACI). This chapter also covers key concepts of control and data plane protocols used in ACI fabric, such as IS-IS, MP-BGP EVPN, COOP, and VXLAN, along with logical constructs in configuring application-hosting infrastructure, such as tenants, VRF instances, application profiles, endpoint groups, bridge domains, external routed or bridge networks, and contracts.

■ **Chapter 2, "Introduction to the ACI Policy Model":** Cisco ACI is a policy-based object model, and it is important to understand how this model works. This chapter outlines the physical and logical constructs of ACI and their relationships in developing the overall application framework through software-defined policies.

■ **Chapter 3, "ACI Command-Line Interfaces":** Traditionally, network engineers have been comfortable in using command-line interfaces (CLIs) on network devices. This chapter describes the different CLIs that can be used to monitor and troubleshoot both APICs and ACI fabric switches.

■ **Chapter 4, "ACI Fabric Design Options":** To monitor and troubleshoot the ACI fabric and its components, it is important to understand ACI fabric design. This chapter explains in detail various design options, starting from physical designs such as stretching ACI fabric using transit leafs, multi-pod, multi-site, and remote leafs. The chapter also demonstrates logical designs, covering Kubernetes using Calico CNI, ERP SAP HANA, and vBrick Digital Media Engine.

■ **Chapter 5, "End Host and Network Connectivity":** This chapter describes compute, storage, and service device (load balancer and firewall) connectivity to ACI leaf switches using either Access ports, port channel, or virtual port channel. The chapter also covers switch and router connectivity between external networks and the ACI fabric. Finally, it also covers connectivity between ACI pods, sites, and remote leafs.

■ **Chapter 6, "VMM Integration":** Virtual Machine Manager (VMM) provides visibility into the virtualization layer. This chapter explains the integration of various hypervisors and container platforms into ACI to extend the networking stack up to the end-host level.

■ **Chapter 7, "L4/L7 Service Integration":** Layer 4 to Layer 7 services such as load-balancing and firewall services are essential components between application tiers for efficient and secure service delivery. Cisco ACI offers seamless integration of L4/L7 services, and these services can be stitched using service chaining or through policy-based routing and service graphs.

■ **Chapter 8, "Automation and Orchestration":** ACI technology enables automation and orchestration for speedy deployment of ACI. This chapter explains the difference between automation and orchestration and how the REST API works in ACI. It provides examples of automation scripts using JSON and XML. It explains Ansible, which is widely used as a data center automation tool, and provides examples for ACI- and non-ACI-based infrastructure. This chapter also provides details about UCS Director and examples for orchestrating various components of application-hosting infrastructure.

Part II, "Monitoring and Management Best Practices": This section includes the following chapters:

■ **Chapter 9, "Monitoring ACI Fabric":** Proper monitoring solutions can enable businesses to run their operations smoothly by minimizing service downtime and providing immediate ROI on software-defined application hosting infrastructure, such as

Cisco ACI. This chapter outlines the key concepts of ACI monitoring, such as using faults and health scores, built-in and external tools, and the REST API to monitor ACI.

■ **Chapter 10, "Network Management and Monitoring Configuration":** This chapter covers the configuration of ACI management, such as in-band and out-of-band management and AAA, along with monitoring protocols such as syslog, SNMP, SPAN, and NetFlow. Network management and monitoring configurations are provided, along with verification steps.

Part III, "Advanced Forwarding and Troubleshooting Techniques": This section includes the following chapters:

■ **Chapter 11, "ACI Topology":** To help lay a foundation for the following chapters, this chapter describes the lab infrastructure used for the rest of the Part III chapters.

■ **Chapter 12, "Bits and Bytes of ACI Forwarding":** The book covers many aspects of ACI, but to truly understand how the fabric works, you have to deep dive into the bits and bytes of forwarding. This chapter builds a strong foundation for VXLAN forwarding and the additional bits used in the iVXLAN header to enable policy enforcement and other ACI features. This chapter provides a variety of forwarding examples that demonstrate the packet life cycle through the ACI fabric.

■ **Chapter 13, "Troubleshooting Techniques":** This chapter highlights a variety of troubleshooting techniques that can be used to manage ACI fabric. The chapter begins by explaining system logs, such as fault, event, and audit logs, and then it dives deeper into specific components in the fabric to help build additional confidence for troubleshooting critical events.

■ **Chapter 14, "The ACI Visibility & Troubleshooting Tool":** The Visibility & Troubleshooting tool has been part of the APIC for many ACI releases. This chapter provides an overview of how the tool works and examples of how it can ease the troubleshooting process.

■ **Chapter 15, "Troubleshooting Use Cases":** This book demonstrates many ways to manage, monitor, and troubleshoot the ACI fabric. This chapter provides focused troubleshooting scenarios, illustrating problems and resolutions based on real-world issues seen in customer deployments. Each scenario outlines the problem faced, as well as how to troubleshoot the type of problem to isolate the issue using ACI tools.

Figure Credits

Figure	Selection Title	Attribution/Credit Line
Figure 8-6	Creating Tenant t01 Using Postman	Screenshot © 2020 Postman, Inc.
Figure 9-8	Fabric Node Unreachable System Message	Screenshot © 2005-2020 Splunk Inc.
Figure 9-11	Viewing NetFlow Information from the Border Leaf 201 CLI	Screenshot © 2020 Zoho Corp.
Figure 9-12	Viewing NetFlow Information in NetFlow Analyzer - 1	Screenshot © 2020 Zoho Corp.
Figure 9-13	Viewing Top Conversation	Screenshot © 2020 Zoho Corp.
Figure 9-14	Viewing NetFlow Information in NetFlow Analyzer - 2	Screenshot © 2020 Zoho Corp.
Figure 9-39	Tetration Software Agent in Windows	Screenshot © Microsoft 2020
Figure 9-40	Attaching a Datastore ISO File to a CD/DVD Drive	Screenshot © Microsoft 2020
Figure 9-41	Mapping Alert Types to Publisher Types	Screenshot © Microsoft 2020
Figure 9-42	Email Alerts	Screenshot © Microsoft 2020
Figure 9-43	Configuring Syslog in Tetration	Screenshot © Microsoft 2020
Figure 9-44	Enabling Alert Types	Screenshot © Microsoft 2020
Figure 15-46	JSON Syntax Error	Screenshot © 2020 Postman, Inc.
FIG15-47	JSON Syntax, Including the attributes Tag	Screenshot of JSON Syntax, Including the attributes Tag © 2020 Postman, Inc.

Chapter 1

Fundamental Functions and Components of Cisco ACI

This chapter covers the following topics related to Cisco Application Centric Infrastructure (ACI):

- High-level overview of ACI

- Major components and building blocks of ACI

- Key concepts of ACI

Data centers have been hosting business applications for many years, and computer networks have been integral in providing fast communication links for application traffic flows. Applications are driving these growing networks; they are the building blocks that consume and provide the data and are close to the heart of the business life cycle. Organizations must nurture and maintain these expanding networks with large amounts of data flows that are critical for application consumption.

Traditionally, companies have managed the plumbing of application data flow through network devices, and these devices have been managed individually. In the past, application deployment was handled manually, and the process was very slow. The initial application deployment compute, storage, and network requirements were requested by the application team and then by the subsequent infrastructure teams acting on fulfilling a request. With multiple teams working in their own silos, there was often tremendous delay in overall application deployment. The following are some of the granular tasks for application deployment processes hosted through a static infrastructure:

- Physical infrastructure (switches, ports, cables, and so on)

- Logical topology (VLANs, L2/L3 interfaces and protocols, and so on)

- Access control configuration (permit/deny ACLs) for application integration and common services

- Services integration (load balancing, firewalls, and so on)

- Connecting application workloads (physical servers, VMs, containers, and so on)

- Quality of service (QoS) configuration

- Multicast configuration

- Management and device access control protocol configuration

With this statically defined process, the application hosting cycle could take six months or more; although that was often acceptable to organizations in the past, it does not work well today. One of the roadblocks in application deployment was physical bare-metal servers. Server virtualization was a natural evolution in the effort to decouple workloads from hardware and to make the compute platform scalable and more agile; cramming many virtual machines onto a single physical server also provided huge cost savings. Server virtualization enables an organization to increase utilization of its server hardware to as much as 80%, which is a substantial increase over the 10% to 15% utilization available with bare-metal servers. Despite the advantages of server virtualization, large enterprises still face some challenges as teams often still work in silos in a typical application deployment cycle workflow, as depicted in Figure 1-1.

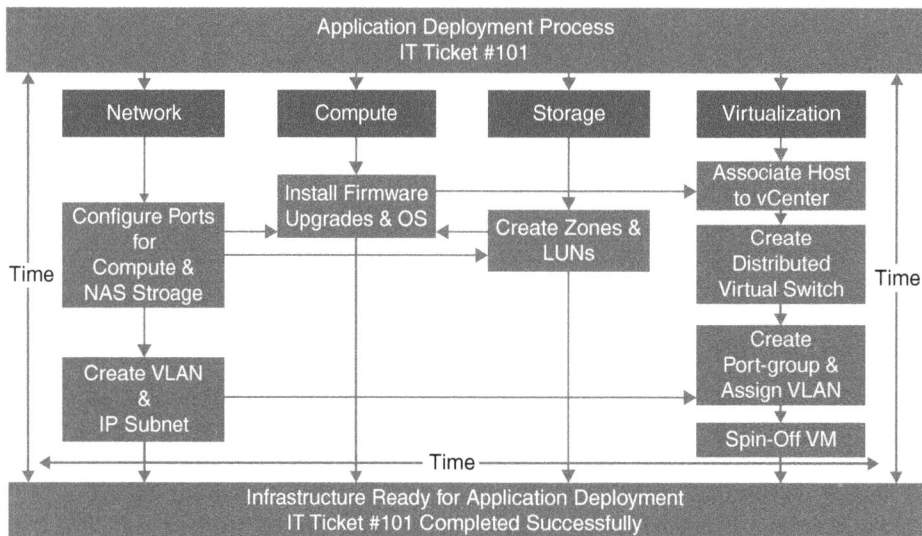

Figure 1-1   *Application Deployment Tasks Flow*

Server virtualization has brought challenges related to workload mobility as excessive east–west traffic in a traditional three-tier (core, aggregation, edge) network infrastructure results in instability for traditional data center networks as they scale. In addition, businesses have become highly dependent on applications hosted in data centers as e-commerce and cloud are becoming more and more critical to businesses. With the legacy way of deploying networks, compute and storage end up delaying overall application deployment and become pain points for business growth. Companies that provide service offerings to customers through application agility enable those customers to survive in this fast-paced and challenging global economy.

Cloud computing offers organizations the opportunity to increase competitiveness and improve agility. Organizations in all industry-specific market segments are therefore turning to cloud solutions to accelerate innovation, expand market reach, and reduce IT costs. However, embracing cloud solutions presents some challenges. End users often demand that IT departments quickly and flexibly offer services that can help them get their jobs done. Many IT teams struggle to maintain the business services needed to help ensure that end users remain productive and on time. Some of the challenges they face in helping ensure the uptime of critical business services include the following:

- A manual service mapping process that can take weeks or months, depending on service complexity

- Lack of correlation between infrastructure changes and the business services they support

- Disconnected infrastructure tools and portals for change management and troubleshooting

- Insufficient monitoring capabilities, which results in inefficient root-cause analysis and extended service outages

Cisco sought to innovate how this infrastructure is governed. It accomplished this by introducing a new paradigm based on an automated policy-based model. Using a policy-based model allows an organization to define a policy and the infrastructure to automate the implementation of the policy into the hardware components. This holistic systems-based approach to infrastructure management speeds up the application development and deployment process with efficient use of infrastructure.

Because application agility is critical for business growth, Cisco named its innovative new paradigm *Application Centric Infrastructure (ACI)*. ACI is a holistic systems-based approach to infrastructure management with new ways of operating the network fabric and the devices that provides application services within it. ACI uses a horizontally elongated leaf/spine architecture with one hop to every end host in a fully meshed ACI fabric in place of the traditional three-tier (core, aggregation, edge) architecture. Highly scalable data forwarding methods are incorporated into ACI fabric to deploy a large number of network segments for virtualized endpoints. Aside from ensuring the physical connectivity (such as port, VLAN, and IP address) of endpoints on network devices, ACI also applies the application logic by grouping these endpoints together to apply security and QoS policies and organizing them in application profiles. In this way, the physical infrastructure is decoupled from application logic, regardless of any kind of workload connectivity requirements. Another efficient forwarding mechanism that ACI initially employed is the Anycast Gateway feature. Each endpoint group carrying the specific subnet when attached to a physical port of the ACI leaf switch programmed the Anycast Gateway feature for that application subnet. This helped tremendously during virtual machine moves anywhere in the ACI fabric. Figure 1-2 illustrates this topology.

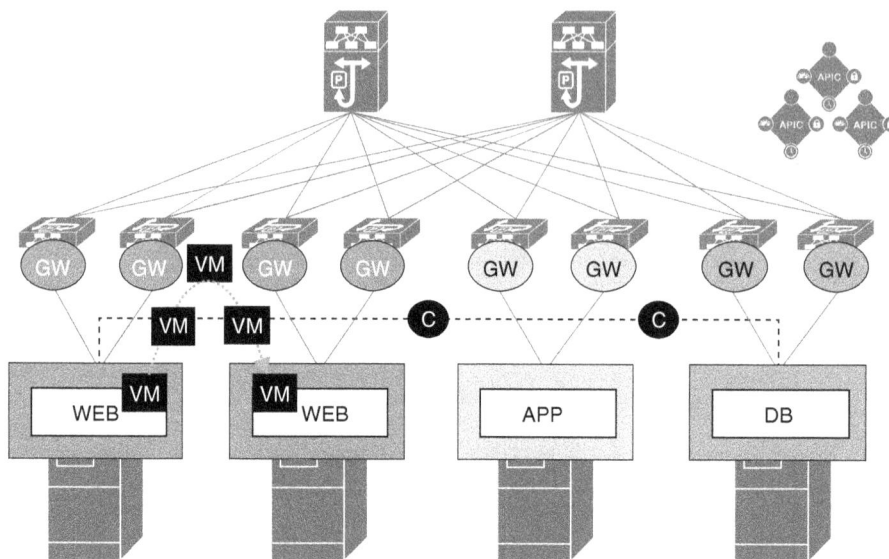

Figure 1-2   *ACI Application Logic*

Old-school network engineers initially resisted this cultural change of defining network logic created, but then the ease of configuration and availability provided by Cisco ACI won over even the holdouts. Immediate knowledge of the state of the network for a specific application is key to minimizing return-to-service timeframes, ensuring proactive maintenance, and eliminating the once-common help desk "Why is my application response time so slow?" calls. With ACI, the integration goes to the virtualization layer and thus provides full visibility into the workload running on a virtual machine. IT staff with appropriate access can determine if there is a fault in the fabric all the way up to the endpoint, and they can see what type of fault it is and when it occurred. They can then either remediate the issue quickly or emphatically state that the issue is not in the ACI fabric. Let's consider an example of a three-tier application running on a virtual machine hosted on multiple hypervisors. Figure 1-3 compares the connectivity of hosts in a legacy network and in the ACI fabric.

As shown on the left side of Figure 1-3, in a legacy network, you need to monitor the performance statistics on each network hop between hosts to check any network bottlenecks. A network engineer was limited to seeing the switches at the edge of the network through which physical hosts were connected and was not allowed to go further down into the virtual networking layer, as another team maintained it. Therefore, in such cases the network engineer had to rely on the performance data from the virtualization team. This lack of integration and visibility between the network infrastructure and the virtual compute infrastructure often resulted in unnecessary finger pointing and conflicts between silo teams, as well as lengthy outages and performance degradation.

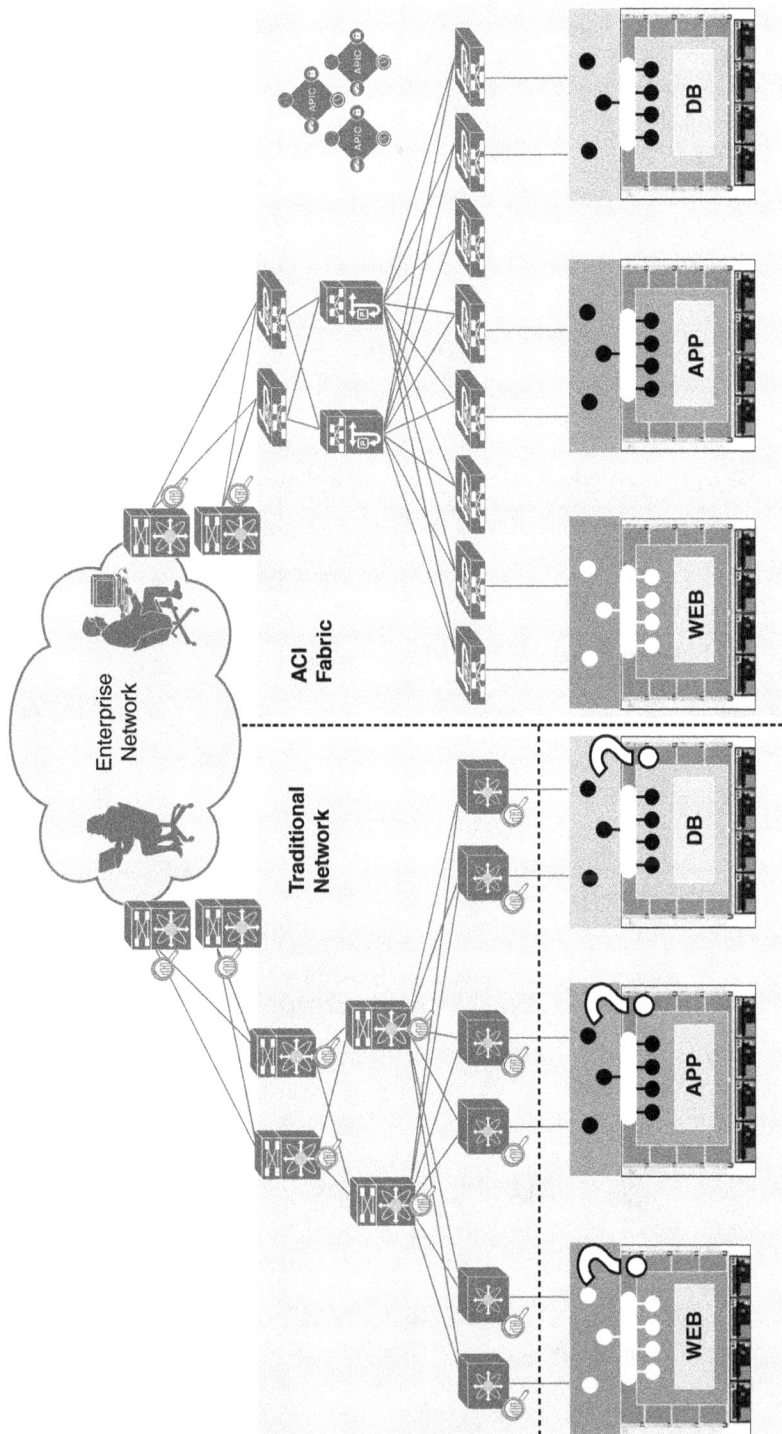

Figure 1-3 *Three-Tier Application Hosted in ACI Fabric*

Hosting the same three-tier application in ACI through virtual machine manager (VMM) integration provides the benefit of speedy application deployment and end-to-end visibility of the workload when performance or connectivity issues surface. (VMM integration in ACI is explained in detail in Chapter 6, "VMM Integration," and end-to-end workload visibility and troubleshooting are explained in detail in Chapter 14, "The ACI Visibility & Troubleshooting Tool.")

The goal and objective of ACI is to enable business growth and rapid application development by providing the following:

- Application-driven policy modeling

- Centralized policy management

- Visibility into infrastructure and application health

- Automated infrastructure configuration

- Integrated physical and virtual infrastructure workloads

- An open interface to enable flexible software and ecosystem partner integration

- Seamless communication between endpoints, using optimized forwarding and security enforcement

- Multi-cloud networks built with a consistent policy model

Key Topic

When deploying ACI, two design philosophies can be implemented individually or together:

- **Network centric:** With a network-centric design, full understanding of application interdependencies is not critical; instead, the legacy model of a network-oriented design is maintained by mapping each VLAN to an endpoint group (EPG) and a bridge domain (BD). This can take one of two forms:

   - **L2 fabric:** The L2 fabric leverages the Application Policy Infrastructure Controller (APIC) to automate provisioning of network infrastructure based on L2 connectivity between connected network devices and hosts.

   - **L3 fabric:** The L3 fabric leverages the APIC to automate provisioning of network infrastructure based on L3 connectivity between connected network devices and hosts.

- **Application centric:** An application-centric design takes full advantage of all the ACI objects to build out a flexible and completely automated infrastructure that includes L2 and L3 reachability, physical and virtual machine connectivity, service node integration, and full policy object manipulation and security.

Security is always a major concern in company networks. Cisco ACI addresses security concerns through a whitelist policy model. This means nothing can communicate unless policy allows it. This might prompt you to think a firewall is involved, but although the ACI whitelist model does change the paradigm, it is only analogous to access control lists within a switch or router. However, there is still a need to have protocol inspection and monitoring, which firewalls and intrusion prevention systems (IPSs) do very well. ACI handles the forwarding and ACL-based security and leaves protocol inspection and monitoring to the firewalls and IPSs. Security devices such as firewalls, IPSs, and detection systems (IDSs) can still be implemented within ACI via a services graph, even in Network Policy mode.

The manual configuration and integration work that used to be required are now automated in ACI based on policy, therefore making the infrastructure team more efficient and agile. Instead of manually configuring VLANs, ports, and access lists for every device connected to the network, the team can create the policy and allow the infrastructure itself to resolve and provision the relevant configuration either on demand or immediately, depending on the requirements.

Cisco ACI follows a model-driven approach to configuration management. This model-based configuration is disseminated through the managed nodes using the concept of promise theory, which Mark Burgess proposed in 2004 as a way to resolve issues in obligation-based computer management schemes for policy-based management. (Burgess later wrote the book *Promise Theory: Principles and Applications* in collaboration with Jan Bergstra.) Promise theory is a management model in which a central intelligence system declares a desired configuration "end state," and the underlying objects act as autonomous intelligent agents that can understand the declarative end state and either implement the required change or send back information on why it could not be implemented.

In ACI, the intelligent agents are specially built elements of the infrastructure that are active in its management by fulfilling promises. A management team can create an abstract end state model and the system to automate the configuration. The configuration is defined on the ACI controller, which resolves to hardware-level programming on the ACI fabric switches. The idea is that if the configuration could not be deployed, the APIC would be notified of this for reporting purposes. With this model, it is easier to build and manage networks of all sizes with less effort.

Many new ideas, concepts, and terms come with the coupling of ACI and the declarative model. When it comes to automated policy-based network architectures, it is very common to hear about declarative and imperative models, and it is good to understand them:

- **Declarative model:** The declarative model is the orchestration model in which control is distributed to intelligent devices based on centralized policies. It focuses on what the desired state of the network would be. Consider an example of declarative model architecture using the OpFlex protocol, as in the case of ACI or any other modern DevOps IT automation tool: A controller would instruct the network devices to set high priority on traffic while dropping certain traffic. The controller does not need to know how the devices actually fulfill these instructions.

- **Imperative model:** The imperative model focuses on how to achieve the desired state. For example, a controller would explicitly tell a switch how to handle network traffic.

This book is intended to provide advanced-level monitoring and troubleshooting guidelines and best practices.

ACI Building Blocks

Cisco ACI is a software-defined networking (SDN) solution that integrates with both software and hardware. Whereas Cisco competitors offer SDN solutions that work only in software, ACI allows for creating policies in software and using hardware for forwarding, which is an efficient and highly scalable approach that offers better performance. The hardware for ACI is based on the Cisco Nexus 9000 platform product line. The software is driven through the APIC centralized policy controller, which stores all configuration and statistical data. To provide high scalability and deal with excessive east–west traffic flows, Cisco created the Clos architecture. ACI constitutes a two-tier leaf/spine fabric where each end host is one hop away from another host in a full mesh topology, as illustrated in Figure 1-4.

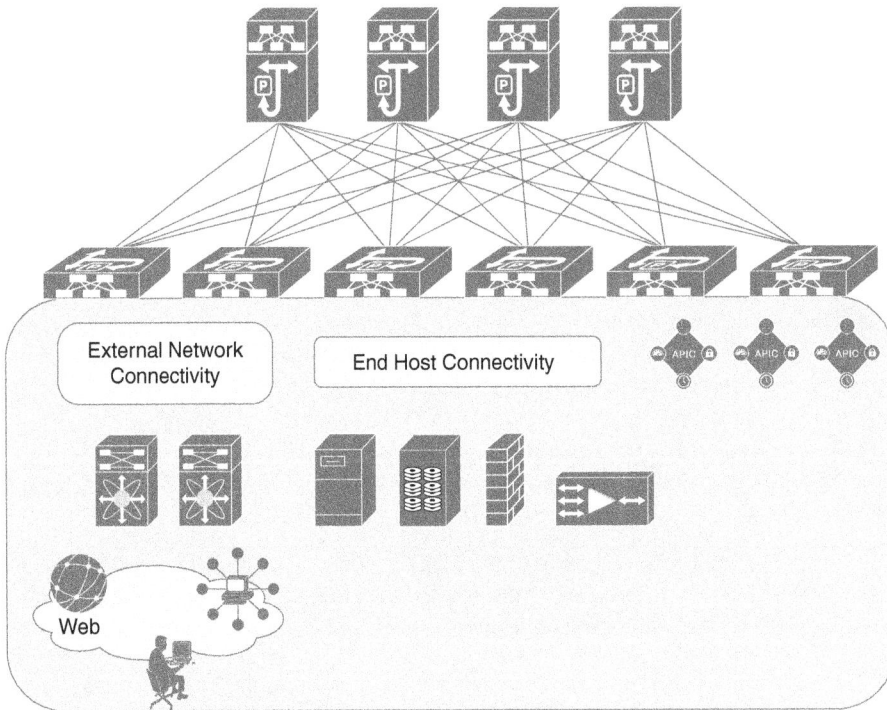

Figure 1-4 *ACI Topology*

Hardware Specifications

Hardware is the foundation of any computer system technology. Cisco ACI relies heavily on hardware, using state-of-the-art ASICs specifically designed to outperform its competitors in SDN. The hardware that the ACI fabric is built on is the Nexus 9000 product line.

Nexus 9000 Platform

The Nexus 9000 Series delivers proven high performance, port density, low latency, and exceptional power efficiency in a range of form factors. The switches are highly programmable for industry-leading SDN and data center automation. The Nexus 9000 Series provides investment protection with a range of multi-speed ports, such as 1/10/25/50/100/400 Gbps and also unified port capabilities supporting 10/25 Gbps and 8/16/32 Gbps fiber channel, RDMA over converged Ethernet (RoCE), and IP storage. The Nexus 9000 platform delivers industry-standard security and visibility with streaming telemetry, advanced analytics, and line-rate encryption (MACsec). Application performance is 50% faster in terms of completion time, with intelligent buffers and lossless Ethernet capabilities. The Nexus 9000 product line can operate in standalone NX-OS mode and ACI mode. The newer cloud-scale ASIC enables ACI leaf/spine architecture and NX-OS Virtual Extensible LAN (VXLAN) fabrics with a diverse modular and fixed portfolio. In ACI, the Nexus 9000 product line consists of the Nexus 9500 and Nexus 9300 platforms.

Note In this book, only the cloud-scale Nexus 9000 platform is covered in examples of monitoring and troubleshooting scenarios.

Nexus 9500

Nexus 9500 devices are primarily used as spines (except for the Nexus 9336PQ and Nexus 9364C devices, which can also be used as spines in smaller-scale environments). The Cisco Nexus 9500 Series switches have a modular architecture that comes in 4-, 8-, and 16-slot models and consists of switch chassis, supervisors, system controllers, fabric modules, line cards, power supplies, and fan trays. Among these parts, supervisors, system controllers, line cards, and power supplies are common components that can be shared among the entire Nexus 9500 product family.

The Cisco Nexus 9500 fabric modules and line cards are physically interconnected through direct attachment with connecting pins. Line cards are inserted horizontally, and fabric modules are inserted vertically, giving line cards and fabric modules orthogonal orientations in the chassis so that each fabric module is connected to all line cards and vice versa. This direct attachment of line cards to fabric modules alleviates the need for a switch chassis midplane and is a unique design that Cisco came up with in the Nexus 9500 platform for proper air cooling and circulation. Figure 1-5 shows the orthogonal interconnection of line cards and fabric modules and the midplane-free chassis of a Cisco Nexus 9500 platform switch.

Fabric Module

Line Card

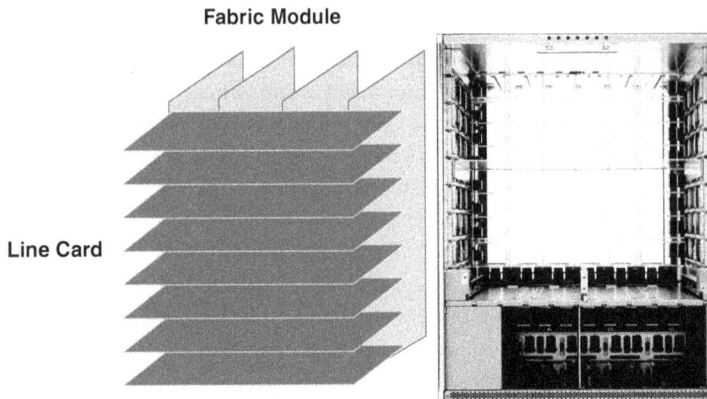

Figure 1-5   *Cisco Nexus 9500 Line Card and Fabric Module Interconnection*

Line cards include physical ports based on twisted-pair copper for 1/10 Gbps and on SFP and QSFP for 1/10/25/40/50/100 Gbps port speeds. All ports are at line rate, and there are no feature dependencies by card type other than the software code they operate under. Some (94xx, 95xx, 96xx, 97xx Series) are NX-OS only, some (97xx Series) are ACI spine only; at this writing, the newest cards are the 97xx (EX and FX) Series, which supports both software modes (NX-OS and ACI) but not simultaneously. There are also three different models of fabric modules, based on scale: FM, FM-S, and FM-E. If your design requires 100 Gbps support, FM-E is the fabric module for your chassis. The latest cloud-scale modules (EX/FX) in the Nexus 9500 platform supporting ACI mode are as follows:

■ The N9K-X9736C-FX 36-port 100 Gigabit Ethernet Quad Small Form-Factor Pluggable 28 (QSFP28) line card is shown in Figure 1-6.

Figure 1-6   *Cisco Nexus 9736C-FX Line Card for the Nexus 9500 Platform*

■ The N9K-X9732C-EX 32-port 100 Gigabit Ethernet QSFP28 line card is shown in Figure 1-7.

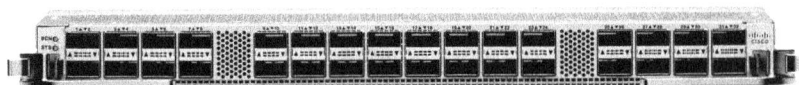

Figure 1-7   *Cisco Nexus 9732C-EX Line Card for the Nexus 9500 Platform*

Nexus 9300

Nexus 9300 platform devices are primarily used as leaf switches; however, the Nexus 9336PQ, Nexus 9364C, and Nexus 9332C devices can be used as only spines in smaller-scale environments. The Nexus 9300 is a fixed-chassis form factor. Nexus 9300 devices are capable of forwarding L2/L3 at line rate and support VTEP operations for VXLAN and IGP routing protocols such as BGP, OSPF, EIGRP, Multicast, anycast gateways, and so on. The Nexus 9300 comes with different flavors of 1/10 Gbps port speeds with twisted-pair and 1/10/25/40/50/100 Gbps port speeds with SFP/QSFP. The latest cloud-scale models of Nexus 9300 are as follows:

- The 93180LC-EX 1 RU with 24 × 40/50 Gbps Quad Small Form-Factor Pluggable Plus (QSFP+) ports and 6 × 40/100 Gbps QSFP28 uplink ports is shown in Figure 1-8.

Figure 1-8   *Cisco Nexus 93180LC-EX*

- The 93180YC-EX 1 RU with 48 × 1/10/25 Gbps Small Form Pluggable Plus (SFP+) ports and 6 × 40/100 Gbps QSFP28 uplink ports is shown in Figure 1-9.

Figure 1-9   *Cisco Nexus 93180YC-EX*

- The 93108TC-EX 1 RU with 48 × 1/10GBASE-T Ethernet ports, which can operate at 100 Mbps, 1 Gbps, and 10 Gbps speeds, and 6 × 40/100 Gbps QSFP28 uplink ports is shown in Figure 1-10.

Figure 1-10   *Cisco Nexus 93108TC-EX*

- The 93180YC-FX 1 RU with 48 downlink ports, which can work as 1/10/25 Gbps Ethernet or FCoE ports or as 8/16/32 Gbps Fiber Channel ports, and 6 × 40/100 Gbps QSFP28 uplink ports is shown in Figure 1-11.

Figure 1-11   *Cisco Nexus 93180YC-FX*

■ The 93108TC-FX 1 RU with 48 downlink ports that can work as 100 Mbps or 1/10 Gbps TP Ethernet ports, and 6 × 40/100 Gbps QSFP28 uplink ports is shown in Figure 1-12.

Figure 1-12   *Cisco Nexus 93108TC-FX*

■ The 9348GC-FXP 1 RU with 48 downlink ports, which can work as 100 Mbps or 1 Gbps TP Ethernet ports, and four 1/10/25 Gbps SFP28 ports and two 40/100 Gbps QSFP28 uplink ports, is shown in Figure 1-13.

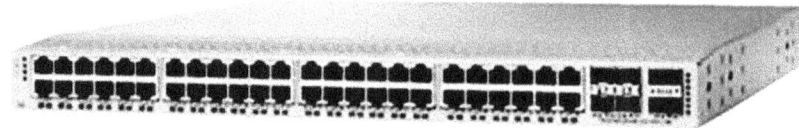

Figure 1-13   *Cisco Nexus 9348GC-FXP*

■ The 9336C-FX2 1 RU with 30 downlink ports, which can work as 10/40/100 Gbps QSP28 ports, and 6 × 40/100 Gbps QSFP28 uplink ports, is shown in Figure 1-14.

Figure 1-14   *Cisco Nexus 9336C-FX2*

Note   The details provided here are current as of this writing. For the latest updates on Nexus 9000 platform specifications, visit cisco.com.

APIC Controller

The Cisco APIC is the brain of the ACI solution. It is a software controller in the ACI fabric that runs on a Cisco UCS C220 1 RU standalone server. APICs are grouped together to form a cluster with a minimum of three controllers that can be extended to up to seven controllers, depending on the fabric scale. Typically high availability is established with an even number of hardware devices rather than odd. However, with ACI, all policies, logs, and statistical data are stored in a database on APIC controllers. That database breaks up the elements of a policy into data blocks called *shards*. The APIC distributes the shards into multiples of three copies to other APICs in the cluster.

The APIC controller is built on a Representational State Transfer (REST) architecture-based programmatic interface that is fully exposed northbound to end-users and set through Extensible Markup Language (XML) and JavaScript Object Notation (JSON), providing consumers with a rich set of tools to configure and operate an ACI fabric. The command-line interface (CLI) and web user interface (UI) operate as a wraparound on top of REST. An APIC provides the following benefits:

- A single pane of glass for application-centric network policies

- Fabric image management and inventory

- Application, tenant, and topology monitoring

- Troubleshooting

Unlike most industry SDN solutions, where a controller takes part in data forwarding by configuring flow forwarding rules, an APIC is not on the data path in ACI. This means the fabric network devices are fully capable of making traffic-forwarding decisions even when direct communication with the APIC is lost. The Cisco UCS C-Series server on which an APIC runs comes in two Large (L1 or L2) and Medium (M1 or M2) device specifications to cater to various ACI fabric sizes. An APIC consists of a VIC 1225 CNA PCIe card that has 2 × 10 Gbps interfaces (SFP+ or twisted-pair). These interfaces are part of the ACI fabric through which all policies get pushed to nodes (leafs/spines). A Cisco APIC is connected to two different leafs for redundancy using these interfaces. Aside from the VIC 1225 card, the APIC controller also consists of two 1 Gbps (twisted-pair) management ports, which must be connected to an out-of-band management network. The APIC is accessed through these management interfaces for managing the ACI fabric. Both the VIC 1225 and management interfaces at the back of the chassis function as a bond interface with active/standby status inside APIC software.

Note The first and second generation of APICs (L1 and L2 or M1 and M2) are end of sale. They have been replaced with third-generation APIC controllers (L3 or M3), each of which contains a VIC 1445 quad-port 10/25 Gbps SFP28 CNA PCIe card. Note that third-generation L3/M3 APICs require APIC code 4.x or later.

An APIC has two power supplies, display, and USB KVM and console ports at the back. An APIC is a server, and Cisco UCS servers use Cisco Integrated Management Controller (CIMC) to remotely manage an APIC without being physically present in the data center. The front of the chassis has a power button, status LEDs, hard disks, and a KVM port that can be used via a dongle (see Figure 1-15).

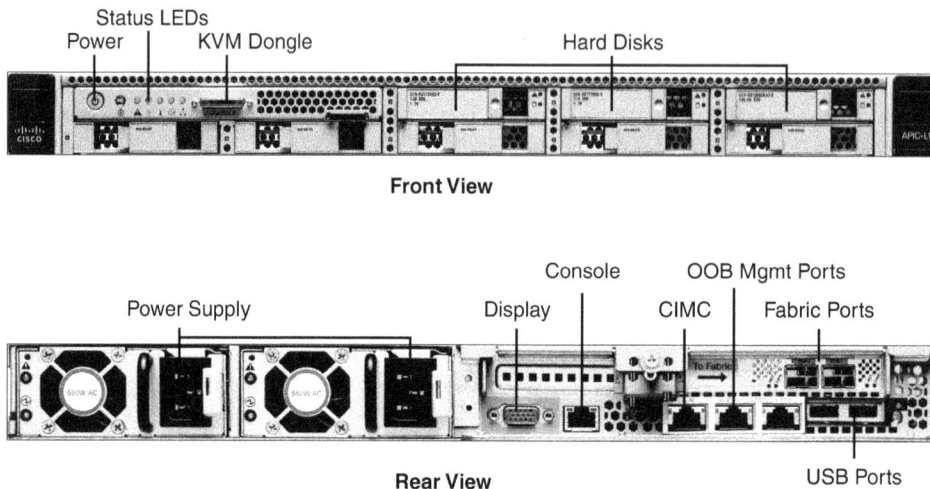

Figure 1-15 *Cisco APIC Front and Rear Views*

ACI Key Concepts

For the most part, the network concepts for Cisco ACI are the same as for other solutions deployed over the past several years in corporate data centers. ACI is different, however, in the management and policy framework, along with the protocols used in the underlying fabric.

Leaf switches provide end-host connectivity, and spines act as a fast non-blocking Layer 3 forwarding backplane that supports equal-cost multipathing (ECMP) between any two endpoints in the network but uses overlay protocols such as VXLAN under the hood to allow any workload to exist anywhere in the network. Supporting overlay protocols enables the fabric to have workloads, either physical or virtual, in the same logical network (Layer 2 domain), even while running Layer 3 routing down to the top of each rack. The VXLAN overlay is deployed on an Intermediate System-to-Intermediate System (IS-IS) underlay, where each ACI switch advertises reachability to each of the other VXLAN-enabled interfaces. This underlay is specifically built to be scalable as more links are added to the Cisco Clos topology, as well as resilient to failure when links are brought down. In addition, ACI switches dynamically build a multicast distribution tree (MDT) that is used to send flood traffic for certain protocols. The MDT ensures that this can be done without creating a loop in the overlay network.

From a management perspective, the APIC manages and configures the policy on each of the switches in the ACI fabric. Hardware becomes stateless with Cisco ACI. This means no configuration is tied to the network device (leaf or spine). The APIC acts as a central repository for all policies and has the capability to rapidly deploy and redeploy hardware, as needed, by using this stateless computing model.

Cisco ACI also serves as a platform for other services that are required within the data center or cloud environment. Through the use of the APIC, third-party services can be integrated for advanced security, load balancing, and monitoring. Vendors and products such as Cisco ASA, Cisco Firepower, F5, Palo Alto, and Citrix can integrate natively into the ACI fabric and be part of the policy framework defined by the administrator. Through the use of northbound APIs on the APIC, ACI can also integrate with different types of cloud environments.

ACI is an SDN architecture from Cisco that uses a policy-based approach to abstract traditional network constructs such as VLANs, VRF instances, and IP subnets and build an application tier with security policies. This chapter describes various basic concepts of ACI at a high level. For in-depth understanding of each of the components of ACI, refer to the Cisco Press book *Deploying ACI: The Complete Guide to Planning, Configuring, and Managing Application Centric Infrastructure.*

Control Plane

For control plane protocols, ACI uses standard protocols that have been used in the industry for many years, such as IS-IS and MP-BGP EVPN. As an ACI fabric is instantiated, each new leaf or spine attached to the fabric uses a specific Type-Length-Value (TLV) setting in an LLDP PDU to discover the remaining fabric members. This allows the ACI administrator to join the newly connected switches to the ACI fabric.

ACI uses VXLAN as the data plane protocol, so each node (leaf/spine) is assigned a unique IP address called the VXLAN Tunnel Endpoint (VTEP) address. This address is added dynamically via the APIC controller. Forwarding across VTEPs is achieved via a single-area IS-IS configuration, which enables massive scale as well as simplicity.

For the control plane protocol, as mentioned earlier, ACI uses IS-IS, and it also uses MP-BGP to advertise prefixes inside and outside the ACI fabric via special leafs called border leafs. To configure BGP, you just need to assign one or more spines as BGP route reflectors to establish an iBGP mesh inside the fabric.

ACI also uses Council of Oracle Protocol (COOP) for efficient endpoint learning and optimized forwarding inside the fabric. All spines within the ACI fabric store endpoint information and synchronize with their fellow spines to track elements attached to the fabric via the leaf. COOP uses ZeroMQ to achieve this control plane communication and leverages MD5 authentication to protect from malicious attacks.

OpFlex is another new control plane protocol used in ACI designed to communicate policy intent from the APIC controller. It is used to communicate policy between the APIC and the end devices that support that protocol. OpFlex also allows for ACI policy to reach into the fabric hardware (leaf/spine) to enforce policy defined on the APIC.

Next we will look at the control plane protocols IS-IS and COOP to better understand the basics of how ACI forwards traffic between endpoints. (For more details on ACI forwarding, see Chapter 12, "Bits and Bytes of ACI Forwarding.")

Figure 1-16 shows an example of a simple ACI topology with two leafs, two spines, and a APIC controller.

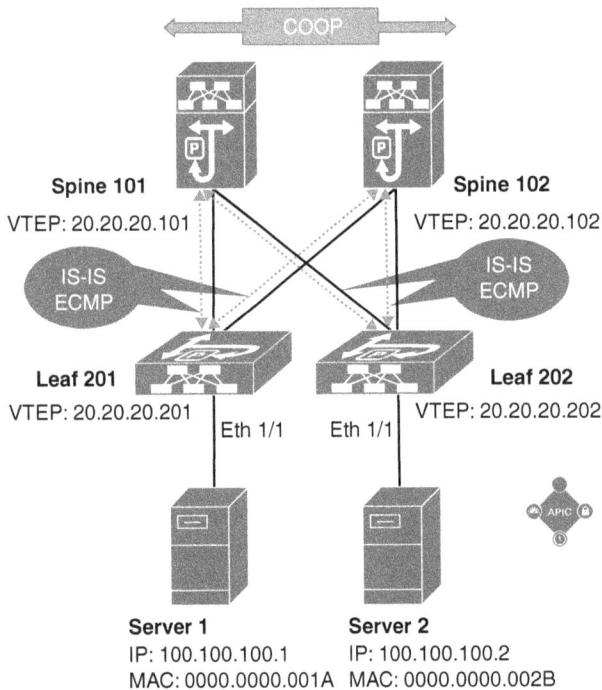

Figure 1-16 *ACI Control Plane Sample Topology*

This sample topology has two leafs, two spines, and an APIC connected in the Clos architecture forming ACI fabric. Spine 101 has VTEP address 20.20.20.101. Spine 102 has VTEP address 20.20.20.102. Leaf 201 and Leaf 202 have VTEP addresses 20.20.20..201 and 20.20.20.202. There are two end hosts connected to Leafs 201 and 202. Server 1, with MAC address 0000.0000.001A and IP address 100.100.100.1, is connected to Leaf 201 port Eth1/1. Similarly, Server 2 with MAC address 0000.0000.002B and IP address 100.100.100.2 is connected to Leaf 202 port Eth1/1.

Say that Server 1 wants to talk to Server 2. Server 1 sends an ARP request to its directly connected Leaf 201, in search of Server 2's location (the MAC address of Server 2). Leaf 201 then knows that Server 1 is connected to its local port Eth1/1 with MAC address 0000.0000.001A and, *most importantly*, IP address 100.100.100.1. It stores this information in its local station table (LST) and forwards the information to one of the two equally cost connected spines (randomly picked) using COOP. The spine that is picked with this information stores it in its global proxy table and shares that information with other spines in the fabric. Similarly, on the Server 2 side, the same processes have resulted in learning the MAC and IP addresses of Server 2 at some point through ARP. Hence, COOP stores the information of all endpoints connected in the entire ACI fabric on all spines; this information is provided by leafs. This setup provides optimized communication between endpoints without the need for the traditional ARP flooding in the fabric (although that is also available if enabled in the configuration for legacy network connectivity).

VTEPs are used to reach every node (leaf and spine), and these VTEP addresses are distributed by a very lightweight routing protocol under the hood. This protocol is instantiated as soon as a fabric node (leaf/spine) joins the fabric. IS-IS provides this capability to every leaf as it has equal-cost paths to reach other leafs via spines. (Cisco used the same IS-IS protocol to distribute fabric path IDs in fabric path configuration on Nexus 7000/5000 platform devices in the past.)

Data Plane

The IETF standard VXLAN is commonly used as data plane protocol in modern data centers where scalability is an issue. Cisco ACI has adopted VXLAN as its data plane protocol with the modification of leveraging the reserved bits for intelligent forwarding inside the fabric; and the ACI version of VXLAN is called iVXLAN (based on the earlier product name Insieme). In ACI, VXLAN is programmed in hardware on the Nexus 9000 platform for efficient performance and throughput. VXLAN offers the ability to provide L2 and L3 separation using a shared physical medium.

The use of VXLAN is prevalent across the ACI fabric, within the spines and leafs and even within various virtual switch elements attached to the fabric, such as the Cisco ACI Virtual Edge.

VXLAN

VXLAN is designed to provide the same Ethernet Layer 2 network services as a VLAN does today but with greater extensibility and flexibility. Compared to a traditional VLAN, VXLAN offers the following benefits:

- **Flexible placement of multitenant segments throughout the data center:** It provides a solution to extend Layer 2 segments over the underlying shared network infrastructure so that the tenant workload can be placed across physical pods in the data center.

- **Higher scalability to address more Layer 2 segments:** VLANs use a 12-bit VLAN ID to address Layer 2 segments, which limits scalability of only 4094 VLANs. VXLAN uses a 24-bit segment ID known as the VXLAN network identifier (VNID), which enables up to 16 million VXLAN segments to coexist in the same administrative domain.

- **Better utilization of available network paths in the underlying infrastructure:** VLANs require Spanning Tree Protocol for loop prevention, which ends up not using half of the network links in a network by blocking redundant paths. In contrast, VXLAN packets are transferred through the underlying network based on its Layer 3 header and can take advantage of Layer 3 routing and ECMP routing to use all available paths.

VXLAN is a Layer 2 overlay scheme over a Layer 3 network. It uses MAC-in-UDP encapsulation to provide a means to extend Layer 2 segments across the data center network. VXLAN uses MAC-in-UDP encapsulation instead of MAC-in-GRE because Cisco's other overlay technologies, such as OTV and LISP, also use MAC-in-UDP instead of MAC-in-GRE. In reality, the vast majority of (if not all) switches and routers do not parse deeply into GRE packets for applying policies related to load distribution (port channel and ECMP load spreading) and security (ACLs). VXLAN is a solution that supports a flexible, large-scale multitenant environment over a shared common physical infrastructure. IP and UDP are the transport protocols over the physical data center network.

VXLAN defines a MAC-in-UDP encapsulation scheme in which the original Layer 2 frame has a VXLAN header added and is then placed in a UDP/IP packet. With this MAC-in-UDP encapsulation, VXLAN tunnels a Layer 2 network over a Layer 3 network. Figure 1-17 illustrates the VXLAN packet format.

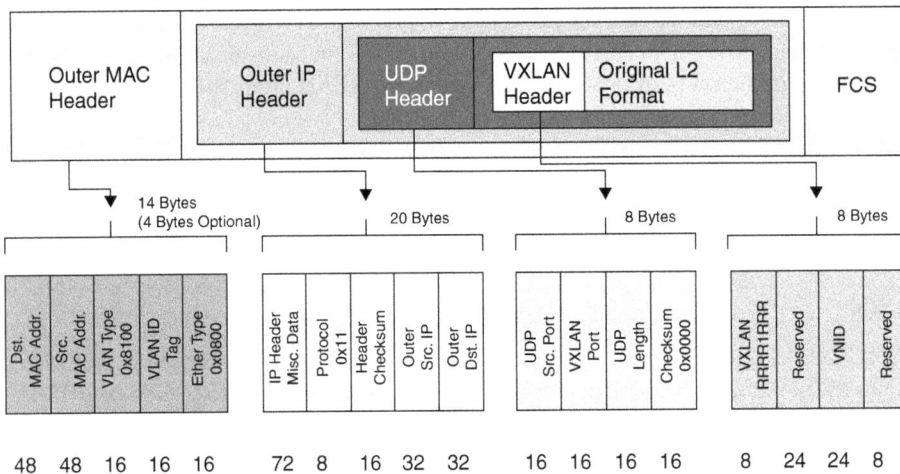

Figure 1-17   *VXLAN Packet Format*

Tenant

A tenant is a logical container that houses all application-related policies and constructs. It enables an administrator to exercise domain-based access control within an organization. A tenant represents a unit of isolation from a policy perspective, but it does not represent a private network. A tenant can represent a customer in a service provider environment, a department or division in an enterprise, or just a convenient grouping of policies. Figure 1-18 provides an overview of a tenant object and its relationship with other objects.

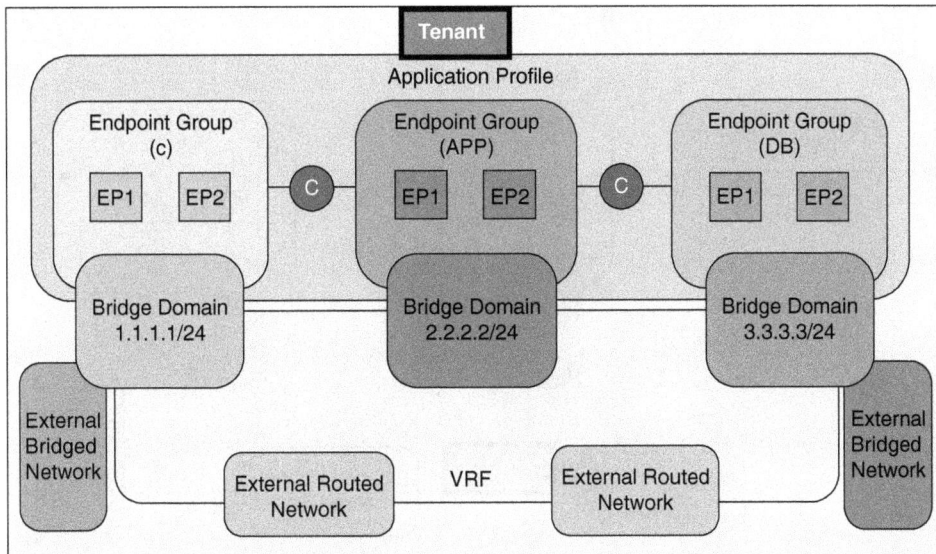

Figure 1-18   *Tenant*

Tenants can be isolated from one another or can share resources. The primary elements that a tenant contains are filters, contracts, outside networks, bridge domains, virtual routing and forwarding (VRF) instances, and application profiles that contain endpoint groups (EPGs). Entities in the tenant inherit the tenant's policies.

In an ACI fabric, you can create multiple tenants based on your business requirements. You must configure a tenant before you can deploy any other application-related configuration.

VRF

A VRF instance, also known as a context, is a tenant network (called a private network in the APIC GUI). A tenant can have multiple VRF instances. A VRF instance is a unique Layer 3 forwarding and application policy domain. Figure 1-19 shows the relationship of a VRF instance to other objects under the tenant configuration.

A VRF instance defines a Layer 3 address domain. One or more bridge domains are associated with a VRF instance. All the endpoints within the Layer 3 domain must have unique IP addresses because it is possible to forward packets directly between these devices if the policy allows it.

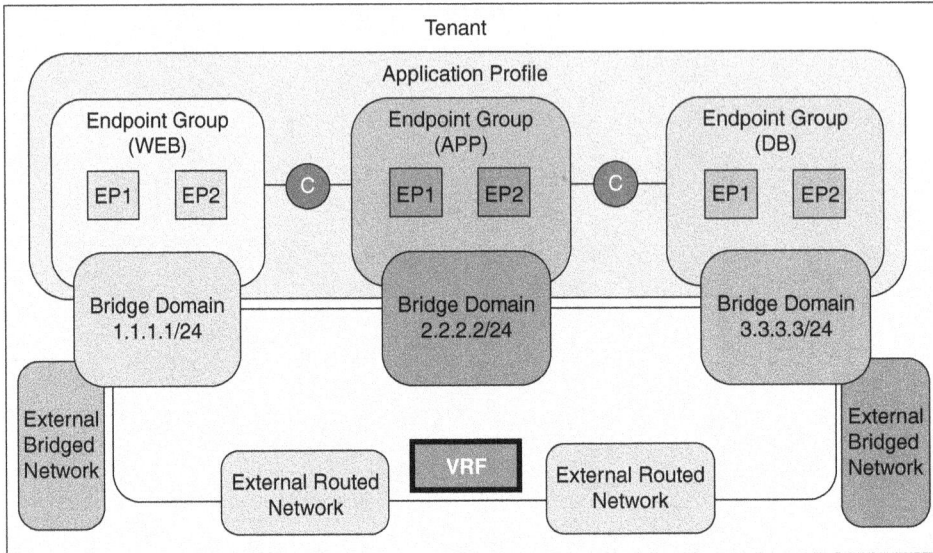

Figure 1-19   *VRF Instance*

Application Profile

An application profile defines the policies, services, and relationships between EPGs. Figure 1-20 shows the relationship of the application profile to other objects in the tenant configuration.

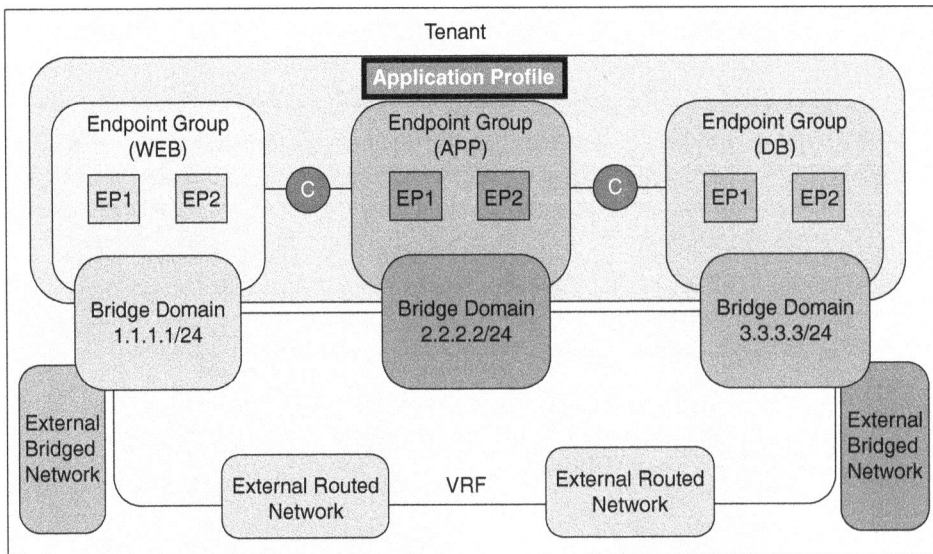

Figure 1-20   *Application Profile*

An application profile acts as a folder that contains one or more EPGs. Modern applications contain multiple components. For example, an e-commerce application could require a web server, a database server, data located in a storage area network, and access to outside resources that enable financial transactions. The application profile contains as many (or as few) logically related EPGs as necessary to provide the capabilities of an application.

EPGs can be organized according to one of the following:

- The application they provide, such as a DNS server or SAP application

- The function they provide (such as infrastructure)

- Where they are in the infrastructure of the data center (such as DMZ)

- Whatever organizing principle a fabric or tenant administrator chooses to use

Endpoint Group

The most commonly asked question related to ACI is "What is an EPG, and how is it used within ACI?" The basic idea is that you define groups of servers, virtual machines, IP storage, or other devices that have common policy requirements. Once those devices are grouped together, it becomes much easier to define and apply policy to the group rather than to individual endpoints.

ACI EPGs provide a new model for mapping applications to the network. Rather than using VLANs or subnets to apply connectivity and policy, policy is defined on an EPG, and ports are assigned to it. Using this concept, an administrator no longer needs to statically apply networking requirements such as ACLs or QoS on a per-port basis. Instead, the policy is applied once at the EPG level, and then interfaces are added to that EPG. The APIC then ensures that the policy is pushed to those interfaces, which decreases deployment time and change control dramatically. EPGs are then associated with a bridge domain to provide the Layer 2 forwarding boundary for the connected devices. Now the security and forwarding are automated by the APIC, which simplifies the deployment process.

Imagine that you have a standard three-tiered application like the one depicted in Figure 1-21.

Within each of the application tiers, a number of endpoints can be either bare-metal or virtualized workloads. The important thing is that these endpoints all require the same policy to be applied. If you can identify which group these endpoints need to be part of, you can create the corresponding EPGs within ACI (refer to Figure 1-18).

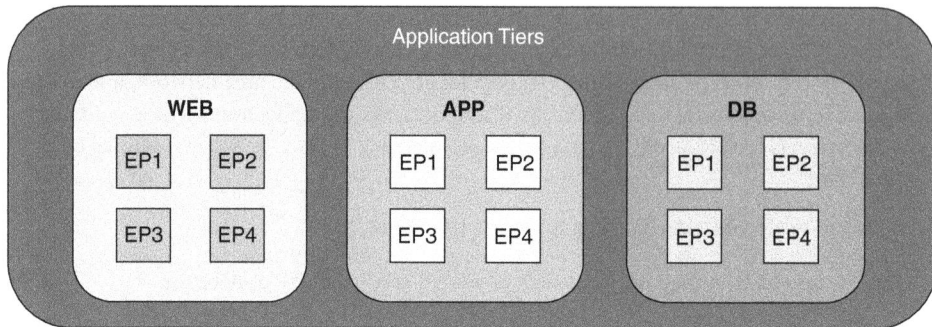

Figure 1-21   *Standard Three-Tiered Application*

How do you define which endpoints reside in which EPG? You can do so by either statically or dynamically attaching to an EPG with either physical or virtual domains, depending on the computer characteristics. If these are VMs, then ACI can integrate closely with
the VMM (such as vCenter), and the process of attaching a VM to a network results in
that VM becoming part of the desired EPG. When you have EPGs defined and endpoints
residing within them, what comes next? At this point, there are two important concepts
to understand:

- Within an EPG, communication is free-flowing by default. An endpoint can communicate freely with another endpoint within the same EPG, regardless of where those
  endpoints reside.

- Between EPGs, no communication is permitted by default. If you do nothing else at
  this point, an EP residing in the Web EPG will not be able to communicate with an
  EP in the App EPG.

Now that you know these rules, you need to understand how traffic is allowed to flow
between endpoints that are in different EPGs. This is where contracts and filters come
into the picture; you will learn more about in the next section. Figure 1-22 illustrates the
EPGs and how endpoints communicate via contracts.

Contracts

In addition to EPGs, contracts are key objects in the policy model. EPGs can only communicate with other EPGs according to contract rules. Figure 1-23 highlights the locations of contracts and their relationships to other objects in the tenant configuration.

An administrator uses a contract to select the type(s) of traffic that can pass between
EPGs, including the protocols and ports allowed. If there is no contract, inter-EPG communication is disabled by default. There is no contract required for intra-EPG communication; intra-EPG communication is always implicitly allowed, with the exception of
micro-segmentation use cases.

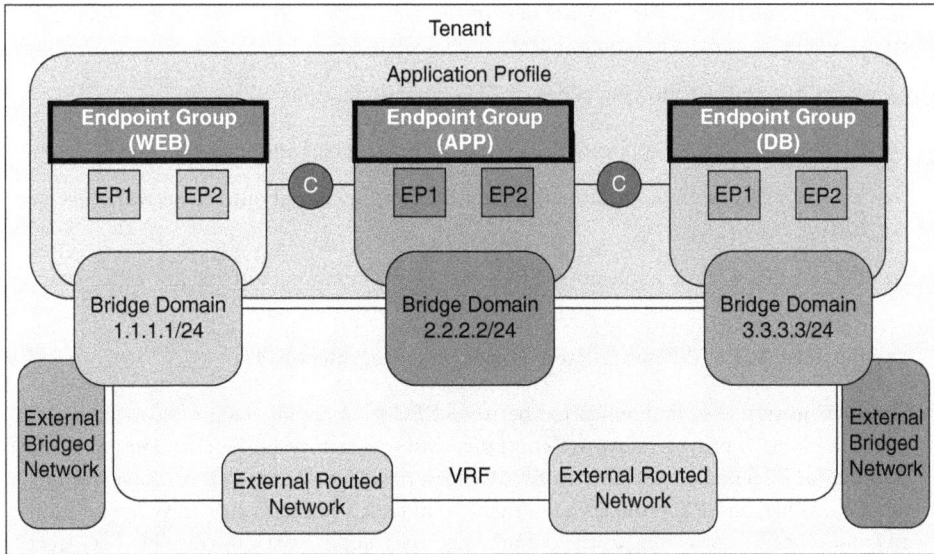

Figure 1-22 *Endpoint Group*

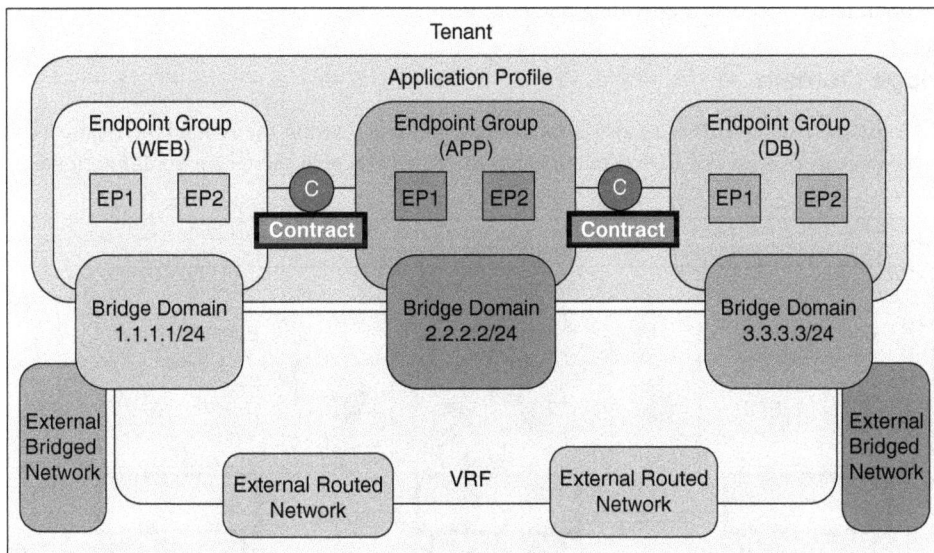

Figure 1-23 *Contract*

You can also configure contract preferred groups that enable greater control of communication between EPGs in a VRF. If most of the EPGs in a VRF should have open communication, but a few should have only limited communication with other EPGs, you can configure a combination of a contract preferred group and contracts with filters to control communication precisely. Contract preferred groups allow two or more EPGs to communicate freely, as if they are part of the same EPG. EPGs outside the preferred group require a contract to communicate.

Contracts govern the following types of EPG communications:

■ Between ACI fabric application EPGs, both intra-tenant and inter-tenant

■ Between ACI fabric application EPGs and Layer 2 external outside network instance EPGs

■ Between ACI fabric application EPGs and Layer 3 external outside network instance EPGs

■ Between ACI fabric out-of-band or in-band management EPGs

Contracts govern the communication between EPGs that are labeled providers, consumers, or both. EPG providers expose contracts with which a would-be consumer EPG must comply. An EPG and a contract can have either a provider relationship or consumer relationship. When an EPG provides a contract, communication with that EPG can be initiated from other EPGs, as long as the communication complies with the provided contract. If you were to compare a contract to a traditional access list, the consumer would be the source, and the provider would be the destination. However, when an EPG consumes a contract, the endpoints in the consuming EPG may initiate communication with any endpoint in an EPG that is providing that contract.

Bridge Domain

A bridge domain (BD) is a Layer 2 forwarding construct within the ACI fabric. Figure 1-24 shows the locations of BDs in relationship to other objects in the tenant configuration.

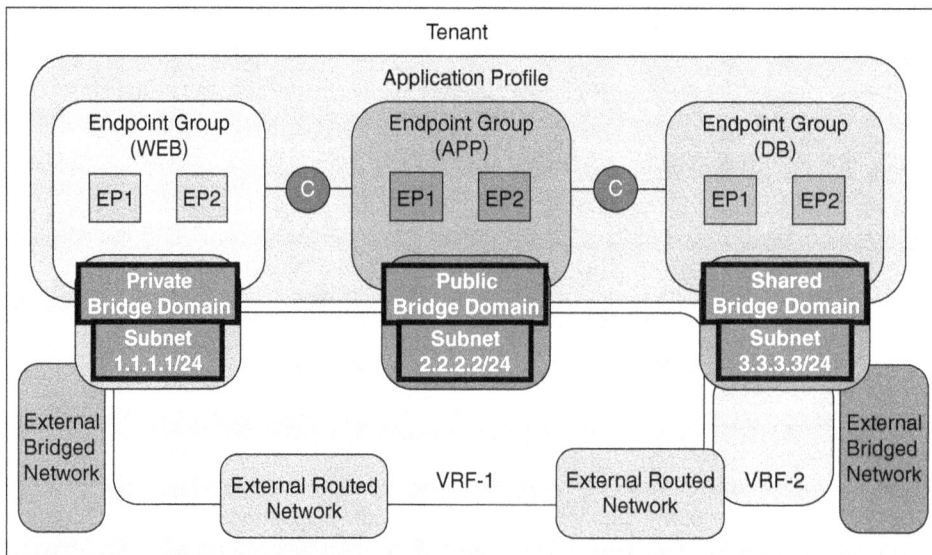

Figure 1-24 *Bridge Domain*

A BD must be linked to a VRF instance, even if only operating at Layer 2. The BD defines the unique Layer 2 MAC address space and a Layer 2 flood domain, if such flooding is enabled. While a VRF defines a unique IP address space, that address space can consist of multiple subnets. Those subnets are defined in one or more BDs that reference the corresponding VRF.

The options for a subnet under a BD or under an EPG are as follows:

- **Public:** The subnet can be advertised via a routed connection using a dynamic routing protocol.

- **Private:** The subnet applies only within its tenant.

- **Shared:** The subnet can be shared with and exported to multiple VRF instances in the same tenant or across tenants as part of a shared service. An example of a shared service is a routed connection to an EPG present in another VRF in a different tenant. This is sometimes referred to as a "shared L3-out," and it enables traffic to pass in both directions across VRF instances.

External Routed or Bridged Network

An external routed network extends a Layer 3 construct from ACI to the external network. This configuration is commonly done on a pair of leafs for redundancy; this pair of leafs, called *border leafs*, is preferably a dedicated leaf pair. The interfaces that connect from border leafs to external routers can be either routed interfaces, routed subinterfaces, or switch virtual interfaces (SVIs). All commonly used routing protocols—such as OSPF, EIGRP, and BGP—along with static routes are supported with external routed network configuration.

Once network adjacency is established between border leafs and external routers, externally learned prefixes are advertised into MP-BGP so that they can be reflected to non-border leafs. This ensures that devices can be connected to any leaf in the fabric, and the route to these prefixes will point to the border leaf.

An external bridged network is sometimes referred to as a Layer 2 outside connection in various Cisco documents. It is one of the options to provide Layer 2 extension from the ACI fabric to an outside network. With an external bridged network you can define policy between your ACI fabric and the external Layer 2 domain.

Outside network policies control connectivity to external networks from ACI fabric. A tenant can contain multiple outside network objects. Figure 1-25 shows the locations of outside networks and their relationships to other objects in the tenant configuration.

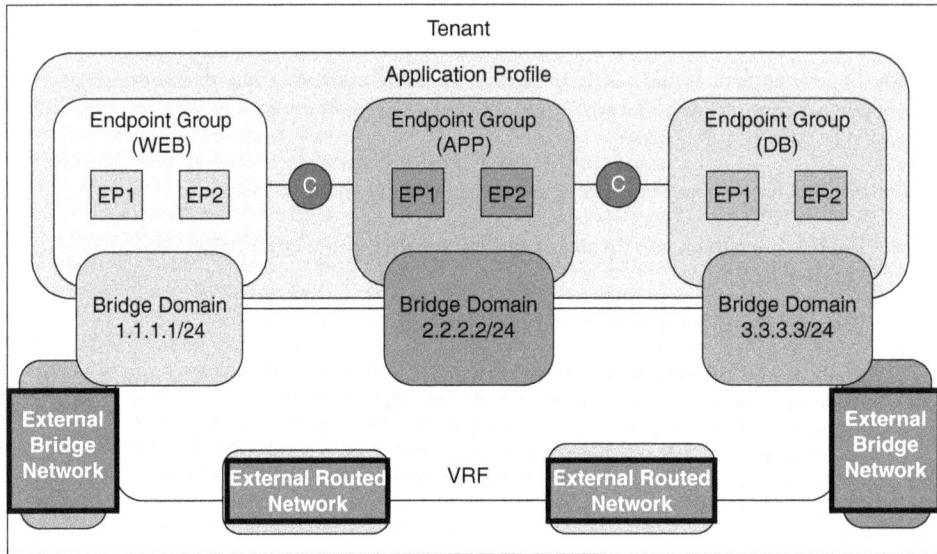

Figure 1-25   *Outside Network*

Outside network policies specify the relevant Layer 2 or Layer 3 properties as well as security policies that control communications between an outside public or private network and the ACI fabric. External devices could be routers such as data center cores or WAN cores or Layer 2 switches during the workload migration phase from a legacy network to ACI. These external devices connect to the front panel interfaces of a leaf switch. A leaf switch that provides such connectivity is known as a *border leaf*. The border leaf switch interface that connects to an external device can be configured as either a bridged or routed interface. In the case of a routed interface, static or dynamic routing can be used. The border leaf switch can also perform all the functions of a normal leaf switch; however, Cisco's recommendation is to at least have a pair of dedicated border leafs for redundancy.

Summary

After reading this chapter, you should have a better understanding of ACI technology, its foundation and building blocks, and key concepts of its various components. Without proper understanding of these key concepts of ACI technology, it would be really hard for you to monitor and troubleshoot ACI. In the next chapter you will learn about the ACI policy model.

Review Key Topics

If you are preparing to take the Implementing Cisco Application Centric Infrastructure - Advanced (300-630 DCACIA) exam to attain the Cisco Certified Specialist—ACI

Advanced Implementation certification, be sure to review the key topics marked in this chapter as outlined in Table 1-1.

Table 1-1 *Key Topics*

Key Topic Element	Description	Page Number
Bulleted list	Network-centric and application-centric design philosophies when deploying ACI.	6

Review Questions

The questions that follow are designed to help you prepare for the Implementing Cisco Application Centric Infrastructure - Advanced (300-630 DCACIA) exam if you are planning on acquiring the Cisco Certified Specialist: ACI Advanced Implementation certification.

1. What are the key benefits of ACI compared to traditional networking for hosting applications in data centers? (Choose three options that collectively answer these questions.)

    a. Achieving business agility through rapid deployment of application-hosting infrastructure using automation and orchestration

    b. Filling gaps between various application infrastructure siloed teams (such as network, storage, and virtualization teams)

    c. Rapidly deploying network devices in the data center through automation

    d. Easing virtual machine workloads through the Clos architecture without compromising performance

    e. Eliminating bare-metal servers and increase virtualized compute platforms in Datacenter for high scalability

2. What are the two logical design philosophies ACI uses to efficiently deploy and consume application infrastructure? How can they be adopted? Choose three options that collectively answer these questions.

    a. Multi-pod and multi-site.

    b. Network centric and application centric.

    c. Start your ACI deployment with VLAN-to-EPG mapping through the application centric design model and move down the path of the network centric design model.

    d. The application centric design model provides efficient use of the entire application infrastructure through policy object manipulation and security.

    e. Start your ACI deployment with VLAN-to-EPG mapping through the network centric design model and move down the path of the application centric design model.

    f. Full meshed design and partial meshed design.

3. What protocol does ACI use to discover fabric nodes?

   a. Cisco Discovery Protocol (CDP)

   b. Link Layer Discovery Protocol (LLDP)

   c. Border Gateway Protocol (BGP)

   d. Interior Gateway Protocol (IGP)

4. What are the control plane and data plane protocols used in ACI fabric? What functions do they provide in ACI fabric? Choose two options that collectively answer these questions.

   a. The use of VXLAN protocol provides higher scalability in application workloads through a large number of network segments.

   b. For the control plane, ACI uses IS-IS, MP-BGP EVPN, and VXLAN, and for the data plane, ACI uses COOP and OpFlex.

   c. IS-IS is used to learn endpoints throughout the fabric.

   d. MP-BGP EVPN distributes VXLAN Tunnel Endpoint (VTEP) addresses inside the fabric.

   e. COOP is used to redistribute external routes inside the ACI fabric through a border leaf.

   f. For the control plane, ACI uses IS-IS, MP-BGP EVPN, COOP, and OpFlex, and for the data plane, ACI uses VXLAN.

   g. OpFlex is a Cisco-proprietary protocol used to communicate with APICs.

5. What are the key characteristics of the Cisco ACI VXLAN protocol? (Choose two.)

   a. ACI uses the IETF VXLAN standard (RFC 7348) as the data plane protocol.

   b. VXLAN provides a Layer 3 extension between geographically dispersed data centers.

   c. ACI uses a slightly modified version of the IETF VXLAN standard by using the reserved bits for intelligent forwarding inside the fabric.

   d. VXLAN is a data plane protocol that provides high scalability of network segments using 12-bit IDs.

   e. VXLAN is a Layer 2 overlay mechanism over a Layer 3 network in which an Ethernet frame is encapsulated in a UDP packet.

   f. The ACI VXLAN version uses the MAC-in-MAC method to build a Layer 2 overlay on Layer 3 networks.

   g. VXLAN requires proper configuration of Spanning Tree Protocol for efficient use of redundant fabric links.

6. What is the ACI application logical construct, and how do each of its components relate to each other? (Choose three.)

a. An application profile is a container that houses application endpoint groups (EPGs).

b. Security policies are applied on an application profile container to allow traffic flow between multiple applications.

c. An endpoint group is a collection of endpoints that require similar policies.

d. A tenant is a Layer 3 forwarding construct inside the ACI fabric.

e. A contract preferred group further restricts communication between endpoints located in different EPGs.

f. VRF is used to securely host multiple organization application-hosting infrastructures.

g. A bridge domain is a Layer 2 forwarding construct in ACI that can contain a subnet that can be local or advertised externally.

## Chapter 2

Introduction to the ACI Policy Model

This chapter covers the following topics related to Cisco Application Centric Infrastructure (ACI):

- Policy model overview and key characteristics

- Management information tree

- Benefits of the ACI policy model

- Logical constructs

- Physical constructs

- Managed object relationships and policy resolution

- Tags

- Default policies

- How the policy model helps in diagnosis

The ACI policy model provides a convenient way of building application logic based on required policies. APIC automatically renders policies inside the fabric infrastructure. When an administrator or a process initiates a change in the configuration, the APIC actually executes it by changing the state of the objects in the ACI policy model. This policy model change then triggers a change to the actual physical infrastructure within the fabric. In ACI, everything is an *object*, whether it is a configuration, a fault, an event, or a fabric node. These objects are organized in a hierarchical policy model, and this approach is called a *model-driven architecture*.

ACI uses logical network provisioning of stateless hardware. It defines network-related application profiles, which are similar to service profiles in Cisco Unified Computing System (UCS).

Key Characteristics of the Policy Model

The following are the key characteristics of the ACI policy model:

- As a model-driven framework, the APIC software maintains a complete representation of the administrative and operational state of the entire system. This means that when you make configuration changes, you are creating or modifying objects. Furthermore, if a configuration is incorrect and a fault is raised, that fault is represented as an object as well. Thus, everything in ACI is an object. ACI uses objects to represent and store the configuration, operational, and statistical data fabric-wide.

- There are different types of objects, depending on where the configuration is deployed in the ACI fabric:

  Logical: A logical object is a managed object such as AEPg (application EPG), BrCP (contract), or Filter (filter) that the user manipulates from the APIC through the GUI, the CLI, or API calls.

  Resolved: Resolved managed objects are objects that the APIC automatically instantiates after resolving the logical model managed object.

  Concrete: A concrete object is a managed object that delivers the actual configuration to each fabric node, based on the resolved model and attached endpoint.

- Even if a configuration is defined for devices, that configuration is not deployed until a device is registered in the fabric.

- No configuration can be done on an individual ACI physical infrastructure. All configuration is defined on the APIC in the form of policies and commanded through it for execution.

- The APIC converts logical objects into concrete objects that the fabric hardware uses to configure the various network components. Each switch in the fabric validates these concrete objects and translates them into hardware-level programming.

How does the policy model work in ACI? Well, the interaction of the user with an ACI controller (APIC) happens through an application programming interface (API) to create or modify the objects in the policy model with an objective of creating and allocating resources in hardware. This is illustrated in the sequential flow process shown in Figure 2-1.

As Figure 2-1 shows, the user interacts with the APIC through an API to create or modify objects. This can be through a native REST API or through a Python SDK such as Cobra. The APIC runs a process called *NGINX* that creates logical managed objects such as fvTenant (tenant), fvCtx (VRF instance/context), fvAp (application profile), fvAEPg (application endpoint group), fvBD (bridge domain), and fvBDSubnet (subnet).

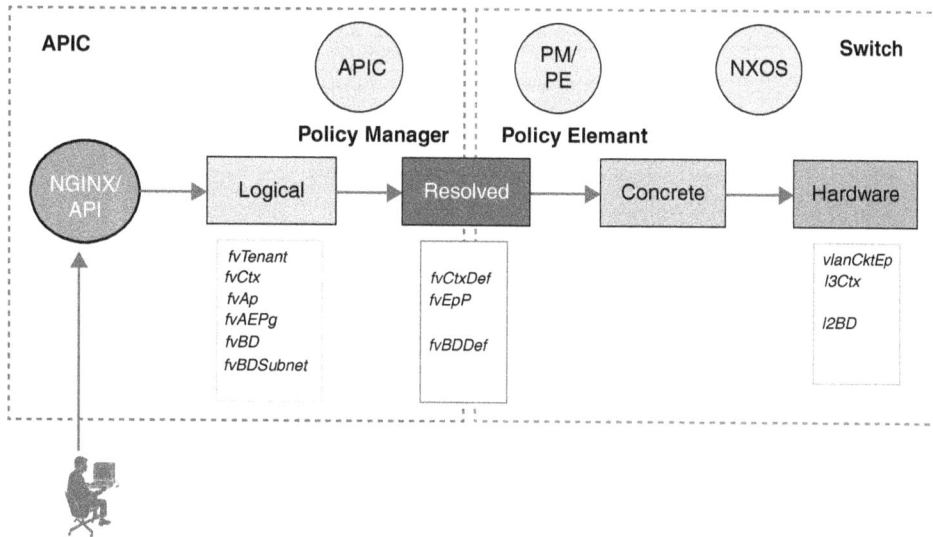

Figure 2-1 *ACI Policy Model Flow*

Note The fv (fabric virtualization) represents a logical grouping of object classes.

Once the APIC creates or modifies the logical managed objects, it resolves the managed objects—such as fvCtxDef (context definition), fvEpP (endpoint profile), fvBDDef (bridge domain definition)—through the Policy Manager process and sends the instructions to switches to program them. The fabric switches running the object model operating system code understand the instructions from the APIC, and by using the Policy Element process, the APIC creates or modifies concrete objects—such as vlanCktEp (VLAN circuit endpoint), l3Ctx (Layer 3 context), l2BD (Layer 2 bridge domain)—and hence fabric switches finally program the instructions in their hardware.

These objects are organized in a hierarchical tree structure called the *management information tree (MIT)*, as discussed in the following section.

Management Information Tree (MIT)

The fabric is composed of physical and logical components that are recorded in the Management Information Model (MIM) and can be represented in a hierarchical management information tree (MIT). You might have worked on X.500 network directory services (such as Microsoft Active Directory or Novell Directory Services) or SNMP MIB structure; the concept of MIT is similar. The MIM is stored and managed by processes that run on the fabric controller APIC. The APIC enables the control of resources by presenting their manageable attributes as object properties that can be inherited according to the location of the object within the hierarchical structure of the MIT.

Each node in the MIT represents a managed object (MO) or group of objects. MOs are abstractions of fabric resources. A MO can represent a concrete object, such as a switch, or a logical object, such as an application profile, an endpoint group, or a fault. Figure 2-2 provides an overview of the MIT.

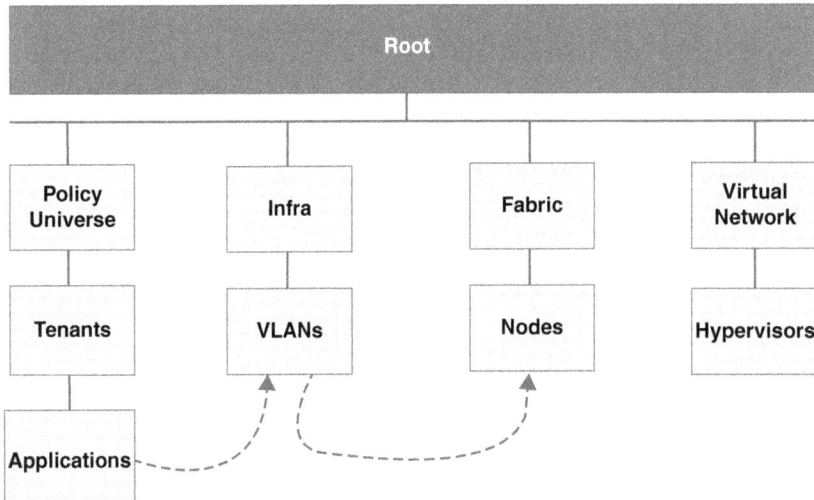

Figure 2-2 *Cisco ACI Policy Management Information Tree*

The logical hierarchical structure of the object model starts with the policy universe (polUni) at the top and contains child objects. Additional objects contain parent objects and can contain child objects, as shown in Figure 2-3.

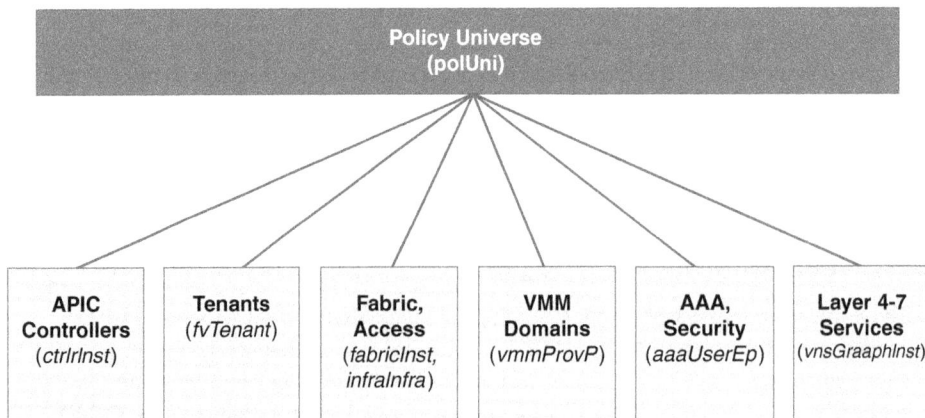

Figure 2-3 *Cisco ACI Logical Policy Model*

Each object in the tree is a MO that has a class, a globally unique relative name (RN), and a distinguished name (DN) that describe the object and its location in the tree. All the configurable entities and the structure of a managed object are represented as a class. For example, *fvBD* represents a class of bridge domain managed objects and all the configurable attributes in the system. All classes have a single parent and can contain multiple children, except the root of the tree, which is a special class called *topRoot*. Within the policy model, there are different packages that act as logical groupings of classes with similar entities for easier navigation in the MIT. Each class has a name, which is composed of the package name and a class name. For example, in the class called *topRoot*, *top* is the package, and *Root* is the class name. Similarly in the class called *fvTenant*, *fv* is the package, and *Tenant* is the class name.

MOs are identified by RNs. An RN is a prefix that is prepended by some sort of naming properties. For example, an object class *fvTenant* has the RN prefix *tn-* followed by the name of the MO, such as *AMT*; in this example, the managed object RN of class *fvTenant* would be *tn-AMT*. A relative name is unique in its namespace, which means that within the local scope of a MO, there can only ever be one RN using that name. To locate this unique managed object in the tree, the policy model uses a DN that tracks the entire path in the tree. In this example, the DN would be *uni/tn-AMT*. Note that *topRoot* is always implied and does not appear in the distinguished name.

The following managed objects contain the policies that govern the operation of the system:

- The ACI policy model is stored in an object-oriented database that is synchronized throughout the cluster (comprising multiple APICs) to ensure that the configuration is sustained in the event of APIC failures. Different portions of the tree are stored in *shards*. Database sharding is a mechanism of splitting a large chunk of data into smaller units. One of the APICs in the cluster is a leader for a particular shard. If the leader goes down, another APIC takes over leadership. Configuration can be done from any APIC, but the leader for the shard is always what is updated. Once the leader is updated, the policy is synchronized to the remaining members in the cluster.

- The tenant MO acts as a container or parent MO for policies that enable an administrator to exercise domain-based access control. Therefore, the tenant is the administrative boundary of the ACI system. The system provides the following four kinds of tenants:

    - *User* tenants are defined by the administrator according to the needs of the organization's application-hosting requirements. They contain policies that govern the operation of resources such as applications, databases, web servers, network-attached storage, virtual machines, and so on. If you are a service provider, you might have one tenant per customer. Or, depending on how your organization is structured, you might need only a single tenant. A common deployment is to have a production tenant and a development tenant; another common deployment is to have a tenant named after each business entity.

    - The *Common* tenant is provided by the system but can be configured by the fabric administrator. It contains policies that govern the operation of resources that can be shared and consumed between all tenants, such as firewalls, load balancers, and intrusion detection appliances. The *Common* tenant cannot be deleted.

- The *Infra* tenant is provided by the system but can be configured by the fabric administrator for certain needs. It contains policies that govern the operation of infrastructure resources such as the fabric Virtual Extensible Local Area Network (VXLAN) overlay. Examples of those policies exist in cases of multi-pod, multi-site, and remote leaf deployment (discussed in detail in Chapter 4, "ACI Fabric Design Options"). The *Infra* tenant cannot be deleted.

- The *Mgmt* tenant is provided by the system but can be configured by the fabric administrator. It contains policies that govern the operation of fabric management functions used for in-band and out-of-band management configuration of fabric nodes. The out-of-band and in-band addresses, when configured, provide management access to the ACI fabric and also are used when connecting to external data collectors, orchestrators, and other managed devices.

- Access policies define the configuration of switch specific parameters. Access policies include policies such as Control Plane Policing (COPP) or virtual port channel (VPC) domains and interface-specific parameters such as Cisco Discovery Protocol (CDP), Link Layer Discovery Protocol (LLDP), Link Aggregation Control Protocol (LACP), and interface speed. An administrator must configure these policies to enable tenant administrators with the capability to deploy endpoint groups (EPGs) on these ports.

- Fabric policies govern the operation of the switch fabric ports, including such functions as Network Time Protocol (NTP) server synchronization, Intermediate System-to-Intermediate System (IS-IS) Protocol, Border Gateway Protocol (BGP) route reflectors, and Domain Name System (DNS). The fabric MO contains objects such as power supplies, fans, chassis, and so on.

- Virtual machine manager (VMM) policies group virtual machine (VM) controllers in a domain with similar networking policy requirements. VM controllers can share VLAN or VXLAN space and application endpoint groups. The APIC communicates with the VM controller to publish network configurations such as port groups that are then applied to the virtual workloads. These network configurations map to EPGs in the ACI fabric to ensure consistent policy between virtual and physical workloads.

- Authentication, authorization, and accounting (AAA) policies govern user privileges, roles, and security domains of the Cisco ACI fabric.

- The Layer 4 to Layer 7 service integration automation framework enables the system to dynamically respond when a service comes online or goes offline. Policies provide service device package, inventory management functions, and traffic redirection to L4/L7 service devices using policy-based routing.

The hierarchical policy model fits well with the REST API interface. When invoked, the API reads from or writes to objects in the MIT. These objects are logically grouped into various classes. Your browser URLs map directly into distinguished names that identify the locations of the managed objects in the MIT. You can also query on a tree level to discover all members of an object. The data in the MIT can be described as a self-contained structured object encoded in XML or JSON natively.

Benefits of a Policy Model

The benefits of a policy-driven model are as follows:

- **Abstraction:** Instead of deploying configurations directly into hardware, using a policy-driven model, you can abstract the control layer or policy from actual configuration. This allows you to replicate the policies for future use and provides ease in deployment on a large number of hardware infrastructure devices.

- **Flexibility:** Defined policies can be modified as network capabilities and requirements change.

- **Reuse:** Policies can be reused on future end hosts requiring the same settings.

- **Agility:** It is possible to rapidly deploy a large number of application-hosting infrastructure devices.

Logical Constructs

The ACI policy model manages the entire fabric, including the infrastructure, authentication, security, services, applications, and diagnostics. Logical constructs in the policy model define how the fabric meets the needs of any of the functions of the ACI fabric. Figure 2-4 provides an overview of the ACI policy model logical constructs.

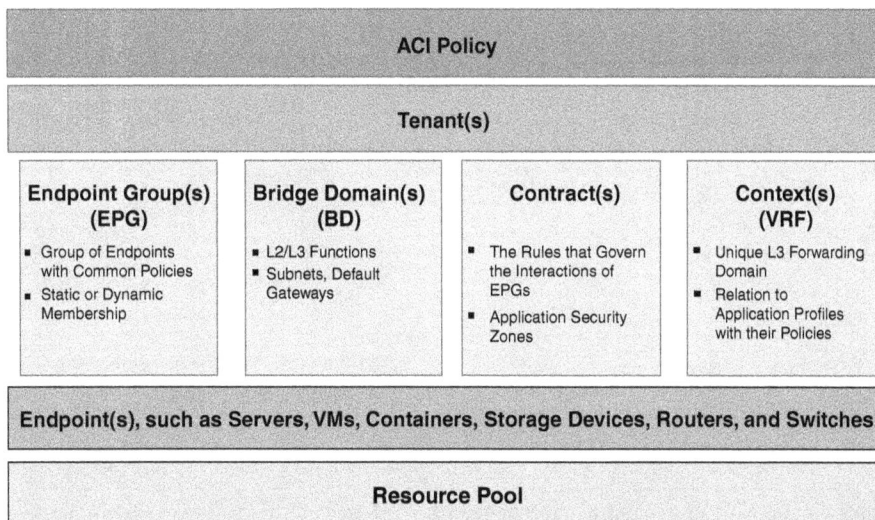

Figure 2-4 *ACI Policy Model Logical Constructs*

Administrators create predefined policies, either fabric-wide or tenant based, that contain application logic or shared resources that will be consumed by applications. These policies automate the provisioning of applications, network-attached services, security policies, and tenant subnets, which puts administrators in the position of approaching the resource pool in terms of applications rather than infrastructure building blocks. The application needs to drive the networking behavior—not the other way around.

The following sections provide details on the MOs in the ACI policy model.

Tenant Objects

A tenant object is represented in the MIT by the class *fvTenant*. It is a logical container that houses all application-related policies and allows for granular role-based access control (RBAC). Forwarding constructs created within a tenant are by default accessible only by the specific tenant they were created in, unless route leaking is used or forwarding constructs are created in the *common* tenant for shared resources. Within the tenant, you still need to create a VRF instance as your Layer 3 boundary, and you create bridge domains as the Layer 2 boundary that the EPG object consumes. A tenant can represent a customer in a service provider environment, an organization or a domain in an enterprise setting, or just a convenient grouping of policies. Figure 2-5 provides an overview of the tenant portion of the MIT.

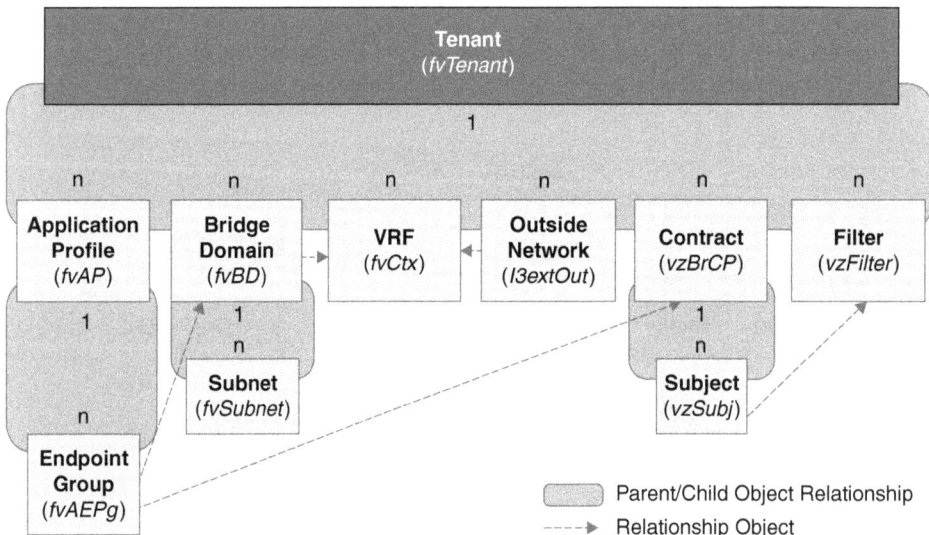

Figure 2-5   *Tenant Object*

Tenants can be isolated from one another for administrative reasons; however, interactions between tenants are possible through route leaking and contract exporting. You must configure a tenant object first before creating any child objects for it, such as VRF instances, bridge domains, application profiles, or endpoint groups. Starting with Release 2.3(1), the Cisco APIC introduced a quota policy, which allows the ACI administrator to define limits to what objects can be configured. This ensures that scalability can be enforced for each user-defined tenant. This feature is useful when you want to prevent any tenant or group of tenants from exceeding ACI maximums per leaf or per fabric or unfairly consuming the majority of available resources and potentially affecting other tenants on the same fabric.

Deletion of a user-defined tenant deletes all the subsequent application policies underneath. Cisco ACI provides three default tenants that users cannot delete: *Common*, *Infra*, and *Mgmt*.

VRF Objects

A virtual routing and forwarding (VRF) object, also known as a context, is a child object of a tenant object in the MIT. It is represented by the class *fvCtx*. A tenant object is the parent object, and you can create multiple VRF objects in it, based on your design requirements.

A VRF instance is a unique Layer 3 forwarding domain. Figure 2-6 shows the locations of VRF instances in the MIT and their relationships to other objects in the tenant object.

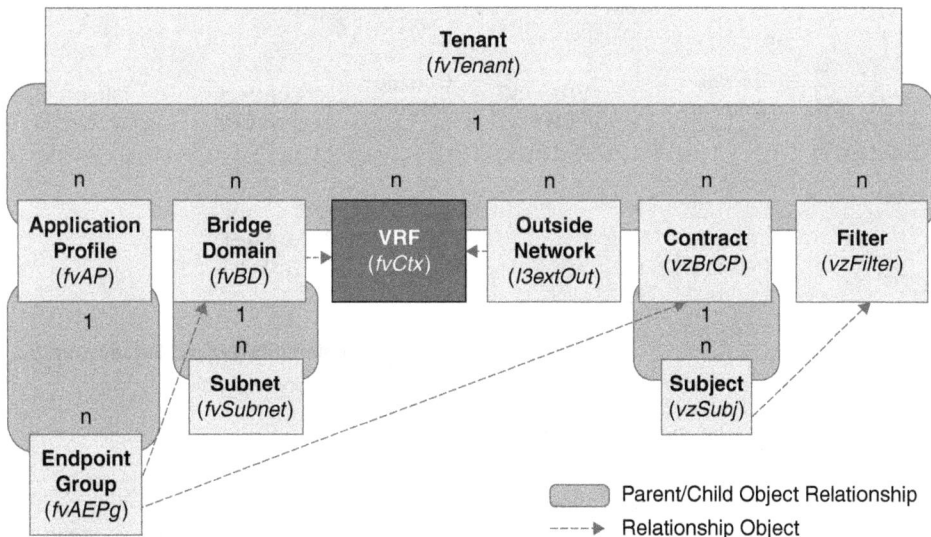

Figure 2-6 *VRF Object*

A VRF object defines a Layer 3 address domain. One or more bridge domains and external routed networks are associated with a VRF instance. All of the endpoints within the Layer 3 domain must have unique IP addresses because it is possible to forward packets directly between these devices if the policy allows it. Furthermore, all subnets defined under bridge domains that map to a VRF instance must be unique so that there is no overlapping IP space. One additional configuration of the VRF object in ACI allows the administrator to define whether the contract enforcement model should be used (whitelisting) or whether policy enforcement should be turned off for all hosts inside the VRF instance by configuring the Policy Control Enforcement Preference parameter.

Each VRF object is dynamically allocated a unique VXLAN VNID to be used when traffic is routed in the VRF. The VNID will be used to segment the Layer 3 traffic into unique L3 forwarding domains.

Application Profile Objects

An application profile object is a child object of a tenant object in the MIT and is represented by the class *fvAp*. It defines the policies, services, and relationships between EPGs. Figure 2-7 shows the locations of application profiles in the MIT and their relationships to other objects in the tenant object.

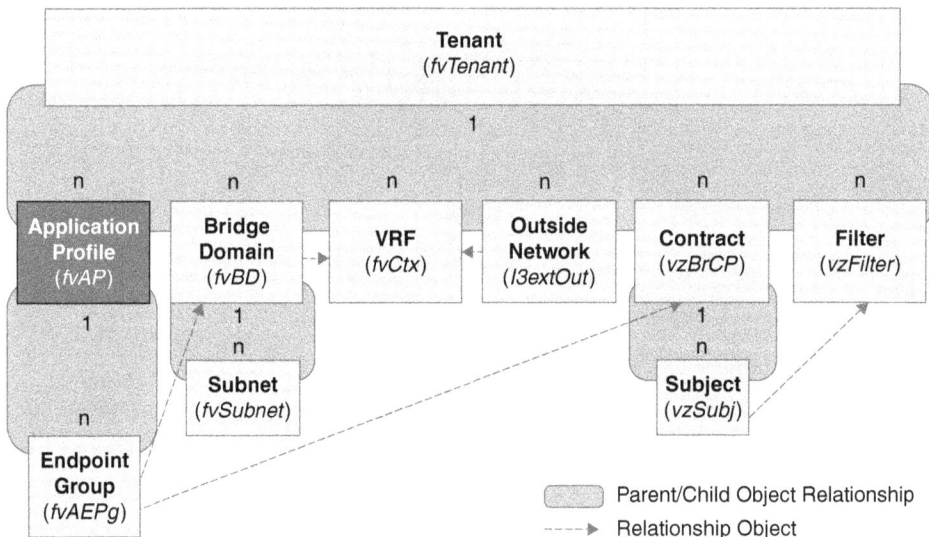

Figure 2-7   *Application Profile Object*

An application profile object is a logical container that houses one or more EPGs. Modern applications contain multiple components. For example, a three-tier e-commerce application could require a web server, an application server, a database server, data located in a storage area network, and access to outside resources that enable financial transactions. An application profile object contains as many (or as few) EPGs as necessary that are logically related to providing the capabilities of running an application. Keep in mind that an application profile object is just for organizational purposes; it is a logical container for grouping EPGs.

Endpoint Group Objects

An endpoint group object is a child object of an application profile object in the MIT. It is represented by the class *fvAEPg*. The EPG object is the most important object in the policy model because it is where you define the security policies that allow endpoints to communicate in the fabric. Figure 2-8 shows where application EPGs are located in the MIT and their relationships to other objects in the tenant object.

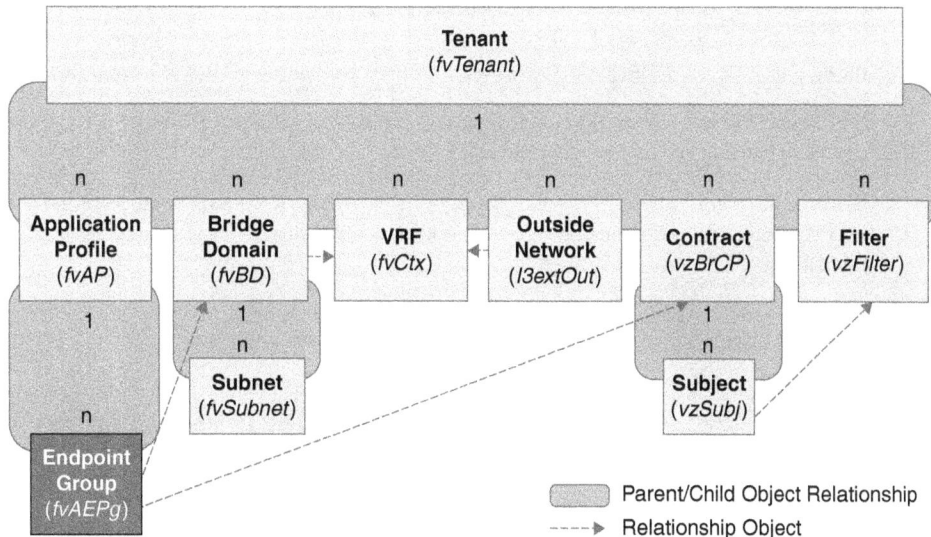

Figure 2-8 *Endpoint Group Objects*

An EPG is a managed object that contains a collection of endpoints. EPGs are designed to contain endpoints that have common policy requirements, such as security, VMM, QoS, or Layer 4/Layer 7 services. Rather than configure and manage endpoints individually, you place them in an EPG and manage them as a group. Why do we need EPGs? Say that your security team asks that all web traffic be switched to an intrusion detection system (IDS) for security and auditing purposes. To accomplish this, you would have to identify all web servers, configure a SPAN session on all switches to which the web servers connect, and plan for workload mobility. This would require hours of planning, and time on the weekend implementing change control—and it would be error prone.

EPGs simplify how new policy requirements are deployed in a data center network. You configure a policy on an EPG and then attach endpoints to that EPG by deploying VLANs on specific interfaces or extending VXLAN VNIDs to hypervisors. Within an EPG, the VLAN tag and the interface on which a host connects define the EPG to which the endpoint belongs. In the previous example, say that your security team wants to mirror all the web server traffic. You group all web servers to an EPG called Web-Servers. These web servers would attach to the fabric by using either an untagged VLAN or a tagged VLAN on the physical interfaces for which they attach. Now, the SPAN configuration needs to be defined in one place: the EPG. As devices move around, or as new web servers get added to the network, the APIC ensures that their SPAN configurations are pushed automatically to the leafs where these servers attach. This drastically decreases the time invested to deploy the requirements and brings a more positive feeling to the term *change control*.

There are a few ways that you can extend the EPG down to connected devices and begin classifying that traffic within the EPG:

■ Binding the EPG to an entire leaf switch (static leafs) by statically mapping a VLAN to the node

■ Binding an EPG to an individual port (static ports) by adding a VLAN to that port

■ Binding an EPG to a grouping of ports across multiple switches by adding a VLAN to the attachable access entity profile (AAEP)

■ Binding an EPG to a VMM domain, which pushes network policies to an external VMM controller, and ensuring that traffic in that virtual network is associated to the EPG

Note   If a leaf switch is configured for static leafs under an EPG, the following restrictions apply:

■ The static binding cannot be overridden with a static port since the static leaf deployment was deployed first.

■ Interfaces in that switch cannot be used for routed external network (L3Out) configurations using routed interfaces or subinterfaces, since the port mode is set to switchport.

The ACI fabric can contain the following types of EPGs:

■ Application endpoint group (*fvAEPg*)

■ Layer 2 external outside network instance endpoint group (*l2extInstP*)

■ Layer 3 external outside network instance endpoint group (*l3extInstP*)

■ Management endpoint groups for out-of-band (*mgmtOoB*) or in-band (*mgmtInB*) access

Layer 2 external EPGs were created to simplify the integration of legacy Layer 2 environments with the ACI fabric. All traffic entering from the legacy network is classified in the external EPG, and contracts are again used to define which endpoints inside ACI the legacy network can communicate with at Layer 2. The same can be achieved by using two different application endpoint groups by associating them to the same bridge domain. This is preferred by many users since they are more familiar with *fvAEPg* than with external bridged networks. If no contracts are required, and all traffic should be allowed by default between the devices in this Layer 2 boundary, simply extending the application EPG to the external switch would be the best path.

A Layer 3 external network EPG is used to classify endpoints or prefixes that exist outside the fabric and apply consistent policy as traffic enters or leaves the fabric. This allows you to classify traffic coming from an internal campus subnet differently than traffic coming from an internet-facing router and to use contracts to define what resources inside the data center external users have access to.

Virtual machine management connectivity to VMware vCenter is an example of a configuration that uses a dynamic EPG. Once the virtual machine management domain is configured in the fabric, policy can be pushed to the leaf switches as VMs dynamically connect in the ACI fabric. If VMs are powered on, migrated, or powered off, the policy can get added, moved, or deleted.

Further endpoint isolation can be accomplished by using microsegmentation. Microsegmentation associates endpoints from multiple EPGs into a microsegmented EPG according to virtual machine attributes such as IP address or MAC address. Virtual machine attributes include vNIC domain name, VM identifier, VM name, hypervisor identifier, VMM domain, data center, operating system, vSphere attribute tag, and custom attributes.

Advantages of microsegmentation include the following:

- Stateless whitelist network access security with line rate enforcement

- Per-microsegment granularity of security automation through dynamic Layer 4 through Layer 7 service insertion and chaining

- Hypervisor-agnostic microsegmentation in a broad range of virtual switch environments

- ACI policies that easily move problematic VMs into a quarantine security zone

For any EPG, the ACI fabric ingress leaf switch classifies packets into an EPG according to the policies associated with the ingress port. Microsegmented EPGs apply policies to individual virtual or physical endpoints that are derived based on the VM attribute, MAC address, or IP address specified in the microsegmented EPG policy.

Intra-EPG endpoint isolation policies provide full isolation for virtual or physical endpoints; no communication is allowed between endpoints in an EPG that is operating with isolation enforced. Isolation-enforced EPGs reduce the number of EPG encapsulations required when many clients access a common service but are not allowed to communicate with each other.

An EPG is isolated for all ACI network domains or none. While the ACI fabric implements isolation directly to connected endpoints, switches connected to the fabric are made aware of isolation rules according to a primary VLAN (PVLAN) tag.

Bridge Domain and Subnet Objects

A bridge domain represents a Layer 2 forwarding construct within the fabric. Figure 2-9 shows the locations of bridge domains (BDs) in the MIT and their relationships to other objects in the tenant object. It is represented by the class *fvBD*.

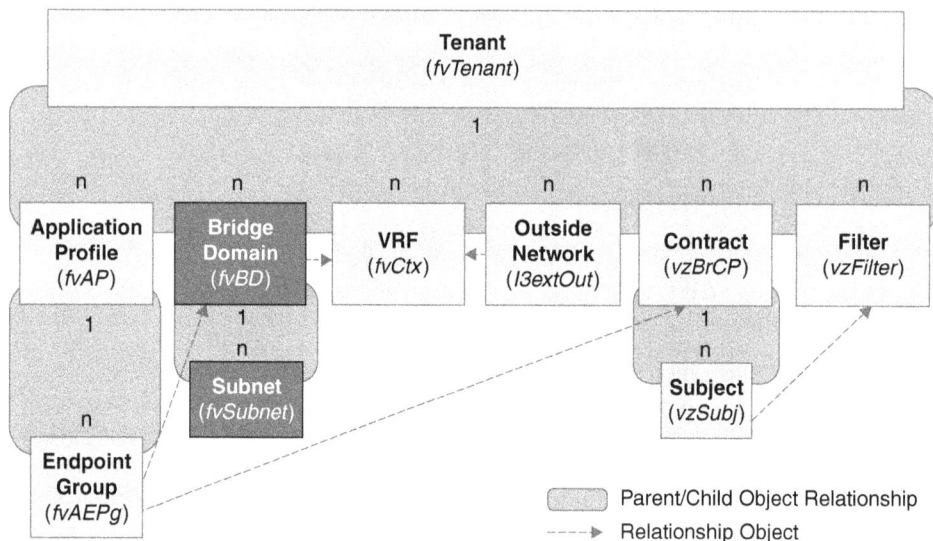

Figure 2-9   *Bridge Domain and Subnet Objects*

A BD must be linked to a VRF instance, even if the bridge domain is operating in a Layer 2–only mode. A BD can have one or more subnets associated with it. The BD defines the unique Layer 2 MAC address space and a Layer 2 flood domain if such flooding is enabled. Different options are available to define how Layer 2 traffic should be forwarded in the bridge domain. While a VRF instance defines a unique IP address space, that address space can consist of multiple subnets. Those subnets are defined in one or more BDs that reference the corresponding VRF instance.

The options for a subnet under a BD or under an EPG are as follows:

- **Public:** The subnet can be advertised externally via a routed connection, using a dynamic routing protocol.

- **Private:** The subnet applies only within its VRF instance.

- **Shared:** The subnet can be shared with and exported to multiple VRF instances in the same tenant or across tenants as part of a shared service. An example of a shared service is a routed connection to an EPG present in another VRF instance in a different tenant. This is sometimes referred to as a *shared L3Out*. For more details on shared L3Out, please refer to the Cisco website.

Note   Shared subnets must be unique across the VRF instance involved in a communication. When a subnet under an EPG provides a Layer 3 external network shared service, the subnet must be globally unique within the entire ACI fabric.

Bridge Domain Options

A bridge domain can be configured to operate as a pure Layer 2 domain, or it can have unicast routing enabled. The Layer 3 routing capability is configured by enabling the Unicast Routing option on the bridge domain. The Layer 3 Configurations tab of the bridge domain panel allows an administrator to configure the following parameters:

- **Unicast Routing:** If this setting is enabled and a subnet address is configured, the fabric provides the default gateway function and routes the traffic. Enabling unicast routing also instructs the mapping database to learn the endpoint IP-to-VTEP mapping for this bridge domain. The IP learning is not dependent on having a subnet configured under the bridge domain unless the setting Limit IP Learning to Subnet is configured.

- **Subnet Address:** This option configures the SVI IP address(es), the default gateway for the bridge domain, which acts as an anycast address on all leafs where the bridge domain is deployed.

Table 2-1 outlines how the forwarding behavior for various scenarios is affected by the different settings on a bridge domain.

Table 2-1   *Controlling BD Packet Behavior*

BD Setting	Description
ARP Optimization	When enabled, ARP packets are sent to the spine proxy, or to the leaf where the Target-IP endpoint resides.
	When disabled, ARP frames are flooded in the BD.
L2 Unknown Unicast	When set to Flood, unknown unicast frames are flooded in the BD.
	When set to Hardware Proxy, unknown unicast frames are sent to the spine proxy for a lookup.
	Note: Modifying the L2 Unknown Unicast setting causes the BD to get redeployed on the leaf switches. This means there is a slight disruption in service when making this change.
Unknown L3 Multicast	When set to Flood, if an L3 multicast packet is received, the packet is flooded to all interfaces in the BD, even if there are no receivers.
	When set to Optimized, if an L3 multicast packet is received, the packet is sent only to router ports. If there are no router ports, the packet is dropped.
Multi-Destination Flooding	When set to Flood in BD, floods the packet in the BD.
	When set to Flood in Encapsulation, floods the packet only in the VLAN encapsulation it was received in.
	When set to Drop, drops the packet.

Bridge domains can span multiple switches because the EPG can exist anywhere in the fabric. If the bridge domain (*fvBD*) has the Limit IP Learning to Subnet property set to yes (which is the default setting in ACI Release 2.3 and later code), endpoint learning occurs in the bridge domain only if the IP address of the endpoint is within any of the configured subnets for the bridge domain or within an EPG subnet when the EPG is a shared service provider. Subnets can span multiple EPGs; one or more EPGs can be associated with one bridge domain. In hardware proxy mode, ARP traffic can be forwarded to an endpoint in a different bridge domain when that endpoint has been learned as part of the Layer 3 lookup operation.

Each BD gets dynamically allocated a unique VXLAN VNID to be used when traffic is switched or flooded in the BD. The VNID is used to segment the Layer 2 traffic into unique L2 forwarding domains.

Contract Objects

ACI involves the idea of the policy-driven network. ACI refers to security policies as *contracts*. Contracts are in some ways similar to access control lists (ACLs), but there are a few differences. First of all, ACLs can be applied only at Layer 2, such as in VLANs, or Layer 3, such as in IP address or subnets; in contrast, ACI contracts can be applied on an EPG where multiple endpoints are grouped together, regardless of their Layer 2 or Layer 3 attributes. Also, contracts can be easily applied bidirectionally, meaning you can apply the same policy from your *WEB* EPG, for example, to your *APP* EPG and vice versa. You can make it bidirectional by simply clicking a checkbox in contract configuration on an APIC instead of writing several more ACLs to make it work.

Let's now look at some of the configuration components that go along with contracts:

- **Filter:** The filter applies to the traffic you want to manage or, more specifically, the ports or protocols you want to permit or deny. Filter depends on intent or action. Usually, the action is to permit traffic. However, other actionable items are also allowed, including the following:

  - **Deny (taboo):** This could be for a specific use case, such as during a migration from legacy networks to ACI. In this case, you may specify to allow all traffic in a contract but set up taboos to deny certain traffic.

  - **Redirect:** This may be useful for sending traffic from an EPG to a Layer 4 through Layer 7 device such as a firewall, load balancer, or IPS/IDS.

  - **Mark:** You might want to mark traffic for quality of service reasons.

- **Label:** A label is an identifier in a filter to specify a more complex relationship between endpoints.

- **Subject:** A subject, also called a label, contains a filter with an action.

A contract contains one or more subjects that each contain one or more filters. Let's consider an example of an Apache web server that requires HTTPS access for external clients, along with ICMP. The Apache web server talks to the app server on TCP port 2500 that then talks to the database server on UDP port 1100, as shown in Figure 2-10.

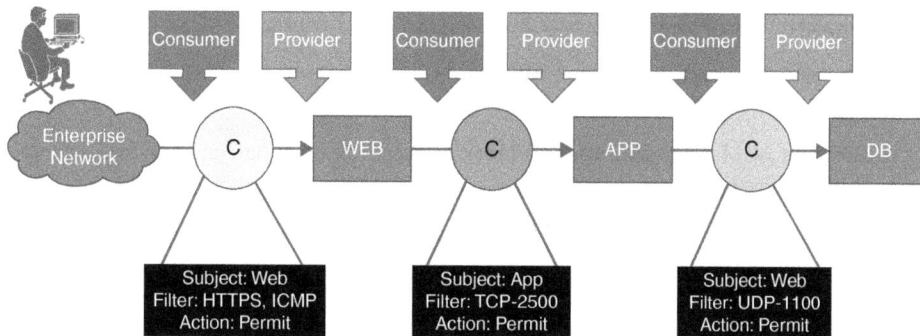

Figure 2-10 *Contracts, Subjects, and Filters*

In this example, an external user that is part of an external EPG consumes a contract that has a filter action to allow ports HTTPS and ICMP. The *WEB* EPG in this transaction is providing this contract. During the communication between *WEB* and *APP* EPGs, the *WEB* EPG consumes a contract that has a filter action of allowing TCP port 2500. The *APP* EPG is the provider for the contract. Similarly, the communication from the *WEB* EPG to the *DB* EPG is allowed via a contract with a filter permitting UDP port 1100. This contract is consumed by the *APP* EPG and is provided by the *DB* EPG.

In addition to EPGs, contracts (vzBrCP) are key objects in the policy model. EPGs can communicate with other EPGs only according to contract rules. Figure 2-11 shows the locations of contracts in the MIT and their relationships to other objects in the tenant object.

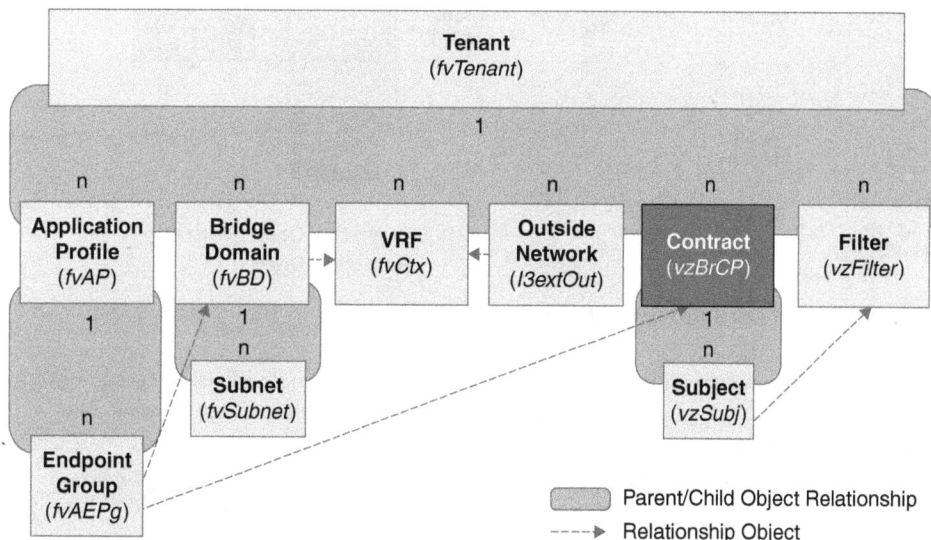

Figure 2-11 *Contract Objects*

Contracts govern the following types of EPG communications:

- Between ACI fabric application EPGs (*fvAEPg*), both intra-tenant and inter-tenant

- Between endpoints in the same EPG using intra-EPG contracts

- Between ACI fabric application EPGs and Layer 2 external outside network instance EPGs (*l2extInstP*)

- Between ACI fabric application EPGs and Layer 3 external outside network instance EPGs (*l3extInstP*)

- Between ACI fabric out-of-band (*mgmtOoB*) or in-band (*mgmtInB*) management EPGs and external users

Labels, Filters, and Aliases

Subjects, filters, labels, and aliases are managed objects that are the components governing EPG communications. These managed objects enable mixing and matching among EPGs and contracts to satisfy various applications or service delivery requirements. Figure 2-12 shows the locations of application subjects and filters in the MIT and their relationships to other objects in the tenant object.

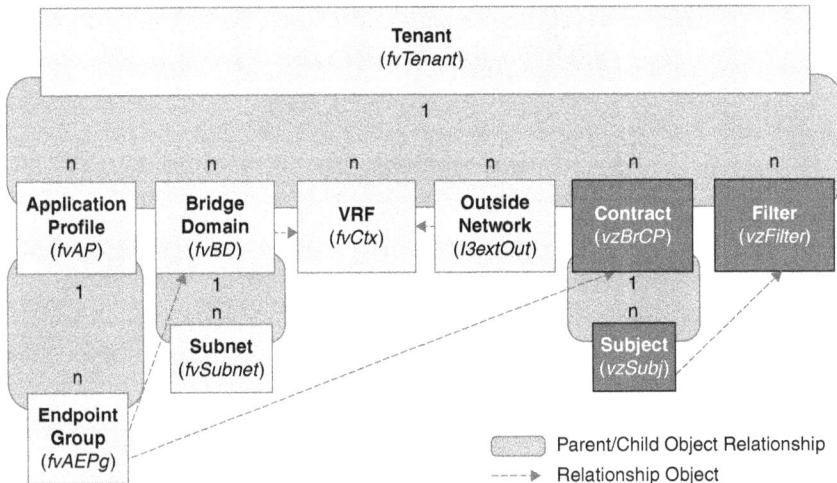

Figure 2-12   *Subject and Filter Objects*

Contracts can contain multiple communication rules for multiple EPGs. EPGs can both consume and provide multiple contracts. Labels control which rules apply when communicating between a specific pair of EPGs. A policy designer can compactly represent complex communication policies and reuse those policies across multiple instances of an application. For example, suppose you have multiple EPGs, five that would like to communicate ICMP with each other, and a separate five with the same requirements. However, one group should not be able to send ICMP to the other group. At first, you might think that you need to create two separate contracts, each with a subject and filter that allows ICMP. Instead, you can create a single contract and reuse that contract by defining labels. Labels allow you to selectively choose which EPGs will consume and provide a contract.

Contract Inheritance

To streamline the process of associating contracts to new EPGs, you can enable an EPG to inherit all provided and consumed contracts associated directly to another EPG in the same tenant. Contract inheritance can be configured for application, microsegmented, L2Out, and L3Out EPGs.

With Cisco ACI Release 3.0 and later, you can also configure contract inheritance for inter-EPG contracts as both provided and consumed. Inter-EPG contracts are supported on Cisco Nexus 9000 Series switches, including the EX and FX platforms.

You can enable an EPG to inherit all the contracts associated directly to another EPG by using the APIC GUI, NX-OS style CLI, and the REST API. In Figure 2-13, EPG A is configured to inherit Provided Contracts 1 and 2 and Consumed Contract 3 from EPG B (the contract master for EPG A).

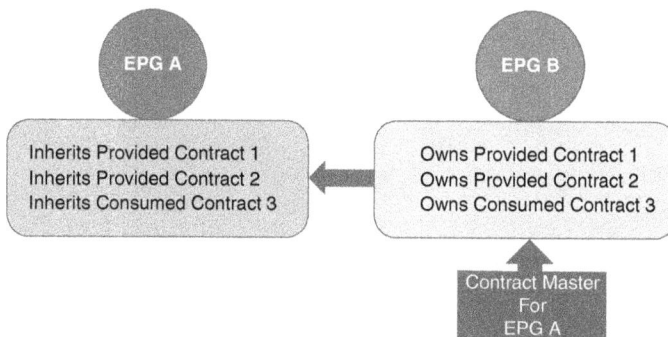

Figure 2-13   *Contract Inheritance*

Contract Preferred Groups

Contract preferred groups enable greater control of communication between EPGs in a VRF instance. If most of the EPGs in a VRF instance should have open communication but a few should have only limited communication with the other EPGs, you can configure a combination of a contract preferred group and contracts with filters to control inter-EPG communication precisely.

Two types of policy enforcements in a VRF instance are available for EPGs with a contract preferred group configured:

- **Included EPGs:** EPGs can freely communicate with each other without contracts if they have membership in a contract preferred group. This is based on the source-any-destination-any-permit default rule.

■ **Excluded EPGs:** EPGs that are not members of preferred groups require contracts to communicate with each other. Otherwise, the default source-any-destination-any-deny rule applies.

EPGs that are excluded from the preferred group can communicate with other EPGs only if there is a contract in place to override the source-any-destination-any-deny default rule. Figure 2-14 illustrates this behavior.

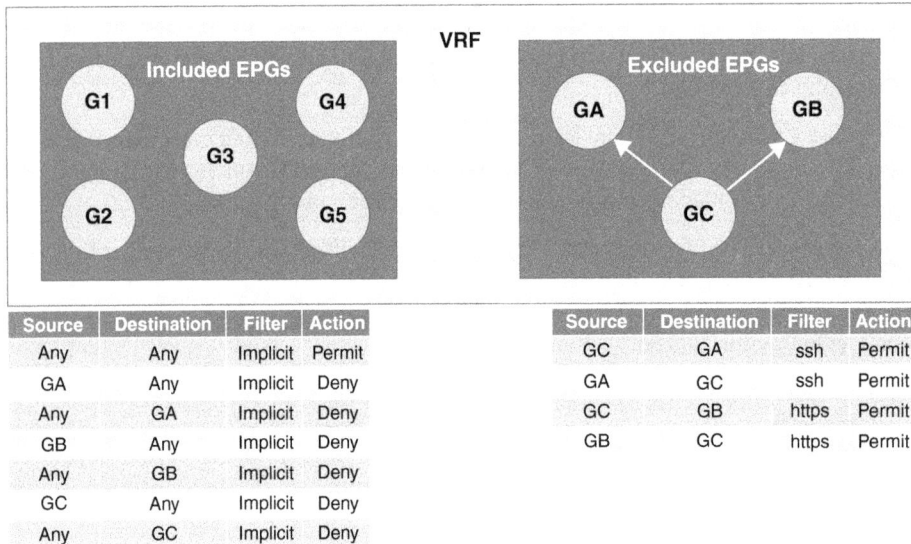

VRF

Included EPGs

G1   G4

G3

G2   G5

Excluded EPGs

GA   GB

GC

Source	Destination	Filter	Action
Any	Any	Implicit	Permit
GA	Any	Implicit	Deny
Any	GA	Implicit	Deny
GB	Any	Implicit	Deny
Any	GB	Implicit	Deny
GC	Any	Implicit	Deny
Any	GC	Implicit	Deny

Source	Destination	Filter	Action
GC	GA	ssh	Permit
GA	GC	ssh	Permit
GC	GB	https	Permit
GB	GC	https	Permit

Figure 2-14 *Contract Preferred Group*

Contract preferred groups do have some limitations. In topologies where L3Out and application EPGs are configured in a contract preferred group and the EPG is deployed only on a VPC, you may find that only one leaf switch in the VPC has the prefix entry for the L3Out. In this situation, the other leaf switch in the VPC does not have the entry, and it therefore drops the traffic.

To resolve this issue, you can do one of the following:

■ Disable and reenable the contract group in the VRF

■ Delete and re-create the prefix entries for the L3Out EPG

vzAny

The vzAny managed object allows you to efficiently associate all EPGs in a VRF instance to one or more contracts (*vzBrCP*) instead of creating a separate contract object relationship for each EPG.

In the Cisco ACI fabric, EPGs can only communicate with other EPGs according to contract rules in Enforced mode. A relationship between an EPG and a contract specifies whether the EPG provides the communications defined by the contract rules, consumes them, or both. By dynamically applying contract rules to all EPGs in a VRF, vzAny automates the process of configuring EPG contract relationships. Whenever a new EPG is added to a VRF, vzAny contract rules automatically apply and control the traffic forwarding. The vzAny contract consumes less TCAM memory of fabric physical infrastructure and is the most efficient way of applying security policies in ACI. TCAM entries are generally specific to each EPG pair. In other words, even if the same contract is reused, new TCAM entries are installed for every EPG pair group that requires restrictive communication.

Outside Network Objects

Outside network policies control connectivity from ACI fabric to the external networks. This connectivity from ACI fabric to outside networks can occur at either Layer 2 or Layer 3. Outside network policies specify the relevant Layer 2 (*l2extOut*) or Layer 3 (*l3extOut*) properties that govern communications between an outside public or private network and the ACI fabric. A tenant can contain multiple outside network objects. Figure 2-15 shows the locations of outside networks in the management information tree (MIT) and their relationships to other objects in the tenant object.

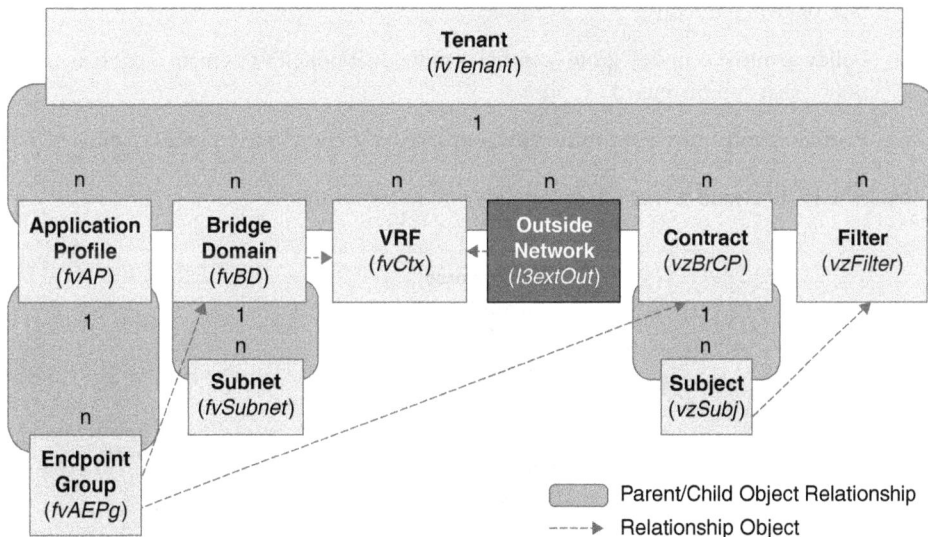

Figure 2-15   *Outside Network Objects*

External devices, such as routers that connect to the WAN and data center core or existing Layer 2 switches, all connect to the front panel interfaces of a leaf switch. The leaf switch that provides such connectivity is known as a *border leaf*. As the name implies, the border leaf is the demarcation point of all traffic coming in and going out of the fabric from external networks. The border leaf switch interface that connects to an external device can be configured as either a bridged or routed interface. In the case of a routed interface, static or dynamic routing can be enabled. The border leaf switch can also perform all the functions of a normal leaf switch.

Physical Construct

ACI decouples the physical infrastructure from the logical construct to provide application agility. In the past, application deployment was often delayed because of unavailability of physical infrastructure to service applications. Provisioning a physical infrastructure separately and building application logic on top of it is a free and efficient way of hosting business applications. The physical construct in ACI governs the infrastructure-related configuration, as explained in the following sections.

Access Policies

Access policies in ACI control the configuration of port-level policies such as CDP, LLDP, and LACP as well as features such as storm control and how they are programmed on physical hardware. For fabric policies, three building blocks make up the access policy workflow:

- **Policies:** A policy defines a specific characteristic without being applied to an interface or switch directly.

- **Policy groups:** A policy group combines individual policies to create a consistent policy that can be reused.

- **Profiles:** Profiles are used to tie policy groups to specific interfaces and switches.

Figure 2-16 illustrates a fabric access policy and its workflow.

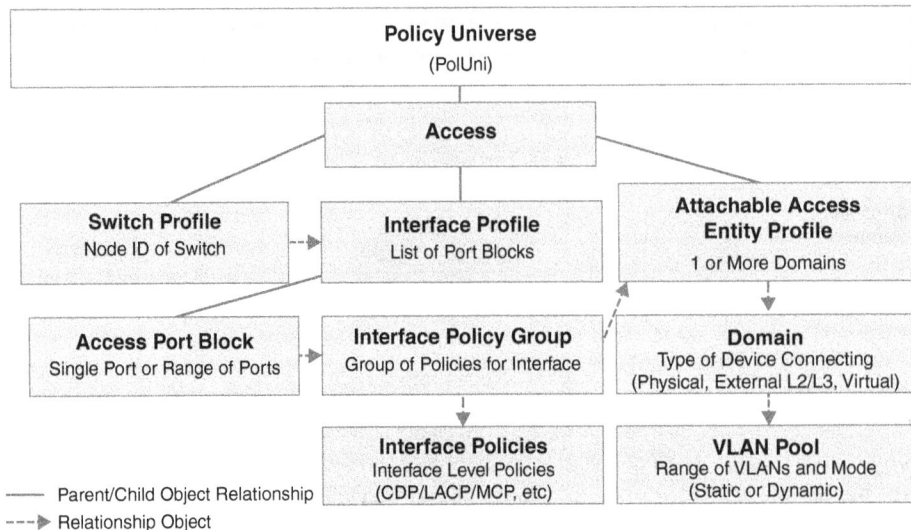

Figure 2-16 *Fabric Access Policy*

Switch Policies

Switch policies are used to configure switch-specific parameters in ACI fabric. These policies govern switch-wide configurations that can be grouped together for common functionalities and applied to specific switch nodes. For ease and flexibility of configuration changes, these policies function through the following three main categories:

- **Policy:** Switch policies are used to define switch-wide settings such as COPP policies or to define the VPC domain. The default policies work well in most environments and do not need to be customized in most instances.

- **Policy group:** A policy group is used to tie different policies together and acts as an updating policy, so that if a change is made to a policy group, any switch profile using the policy group will be updated.

- **Profile:** A switch profile is used to tie a fabric node (leaf or spine switch) to a specific switch policy group. A more critical function of a switch profile is the ability to tie a switch or range of switches to an interface profile. A recommended way to configure switch profiles is to create a one-to-one mapping of physical nodes to switch profiles and one switch profile that contains two switches per VPC domain. For example, if you had four switches in your fabric with node IDs 101 through 104, you would create four leaf profiles named Leaf101, Leaf102, Leaf103, and Leaf104. Each one of these profiles would contain only the corresponding node. If two VPC domains existed, one containing nodes 101 and 102 and the other containing 103 and 104, two additional switch profiles, named vPC101-102 and vPC103-104 and containing the corresponding nodes, could be created.

Figure 2-17 shows the relationships between switch policies and the interface policies.

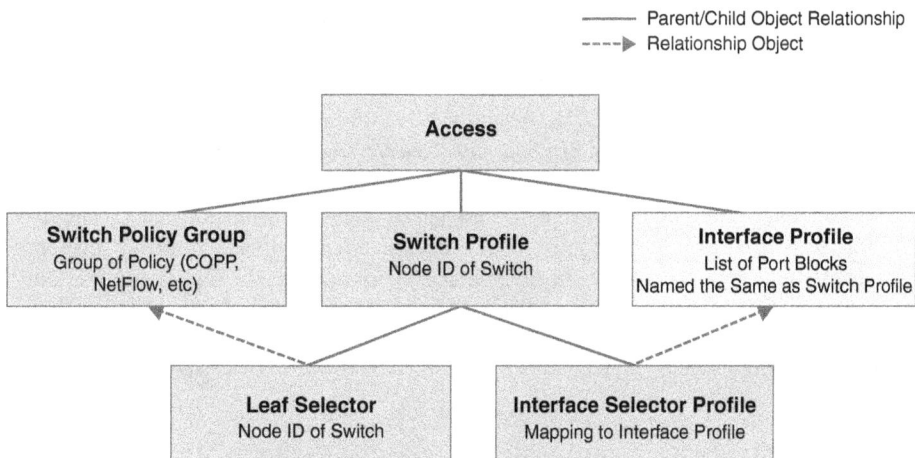

Figure 2-17 *Object Relationship in Fabric Access Policy*

Interface Policies

Interface policies are part of the Access Policies main tab in the APIC user interface. These policies are grouped together for common functionality of end-host connectivity and are assigned to the interfaces of your choice and requirement. For ease and flexibility of configuration changes, these policies function through the following three main categories:

- **Policy:** Interface policies are used to configure interface-specific parameters, which range from enabling or disabling CDP or LLDP to specifying how LACP should react if PDUs are no longer received.

- **Policy group:** The policy group is used to tie different policies together and acts as an updating policy, so that if a change is made to a policy group, any interface profile using this policy group will be updated. Policy groups can be created for a set of similar servers such as a hypervisor farm or a firewall cluster. It is recommended that you determine your balance of policy reuse versus flexibility. In many cases, a handful of policy groups can be created to meet the needs of most servers, but this severely restricts the ability to make a configuration change for one specific device. The interface policy group is also used to tie back into an AAEP (as discussed in the following section).

- **Profile:** The interface profile is used to map Ethernet interfaces to an interface selector, which is mapped to a policy group. The interface profile is also mapped back to a switch profile. With an interface profile, you create a link between an interface policy group and a leaf switch on which you want to deploy the policy. To simplify the profiles and policies, you can create a single interface profile per switch in the fabric and a single profile per VPC domain. For example, if you had four switches in your fabric with node IDs 101 through 104, you would create four interface profiles named Leaf101, Leaf102, Leaf103, and Leaf104. Each one of these profiles will be mapped to the corresponding switch profile. If two VPC domains existed, one containing nodes 101 and 102 and the other containing 103 and 104, two additional switch profiles, named vPC101-102 and vPC103-104 and containing the corresponding nodes, could be created. If you follow this naming convention, you maintain a one-to-one mapping between switch profile and interface profile. This means that when you need to configure a new interface, all you need to do is create the appropriate port block under the interface profile. The interface profile is already mapped back to the switch profile, so these policies do not need to be created or modified every time.

Figure 2-18 demonstrates the relationships between interface policies and the AAEP.

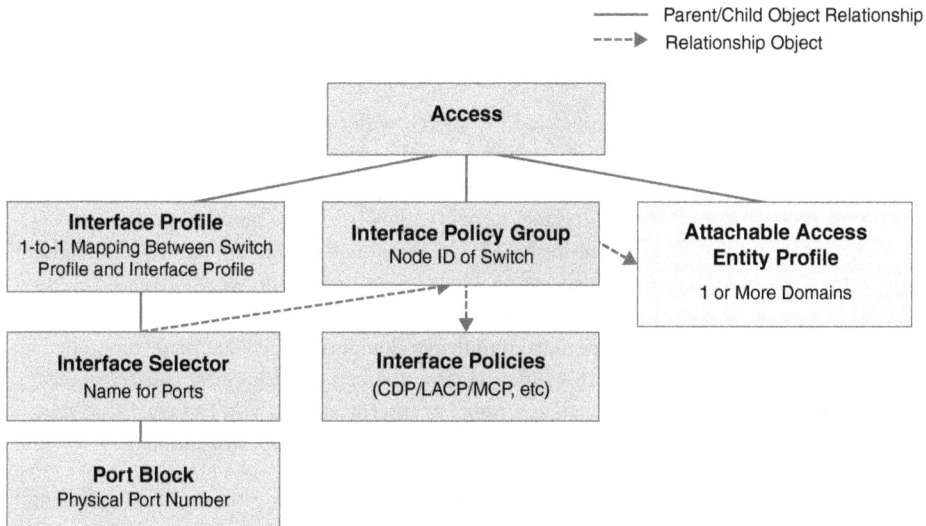

Figure 2-18 *Object Relationship Between Interface Policies and AAEP*

Global Policies

Global policies configure VLAN pools, domains, and AAEP, as explained in the following sections.

VLAN Pools

A VLAN pool is used to define a range of VLANs that are allowed to be deployed on an ACI fabric. These VLANs will inevitably be trunked on an interface to map an endpoint to an EPG. Mapping a VLAN pool to an interface is similar to configuring the Switchport Trunk Allowed VLAN A-Z setting on a Nexus or Catalyst switch. These VLANs aren't extended on the interface until the VLAN is created. With ACI, the pool creates a list of potential VLANs that can be extended on the physical interface.

The secondary role of a VLAN pool is to create a VNID range to assign to each VLAN. Features such as flooding in encapsulation or spanning tree require that BPDUs be flooded only within a specific VLAN and not the bridge domain or every EPG/VLAN associated with it. This is accomplished by using the encapsulation VNID instead of the BD VNID when sending traffic via the fabric.

A third use case of the VLAN pool is for VPC switches. When two switches are in a VPC domain, VPC and orphan port learned endpoints are synchronized between the two switches, and the VNID must be the same in order for the synchronization to be successful. Therefore, when a VLAN is mapped to an EPG that is deployed on a VPC pair, the domain from which that EPG is deployed must not have an overlapping VLAN pool.

Domains

ACI is built for a multitenancy environment where tenant administrators can have full access to deploying EPGs within the fabric. When deploying an EPG to a switch port, that VLAN is reserved for the specific EPG switch-wide. This could create a problem in which a single tenant uses up all VLANs available on a switch. To prevent this from happening, you can limit the VLANs a tenant can deploy on an interface. VLAN pools are not directly mapped to an interface; rather, VLAN pools are mapped to domains, and these domains are mapped to an AAEP. On the domain itself, the fabric administrator can restrict which tenant has access to which specific domain, which gives access to the VLAN pool. This means that in a single interface policy group, there is a relationship to a single AAEP. This AAEP can map to multiple domains, which can map to one or more VLAN pools. Because of this functionality, you can provide the server team a list of VLANs that they can use as well as a range of interfaces, and you can trust that they won't use resources reserved for other tenants. There are five types of domains:

- **Physical (*physDomP*)**: Physical domains are used to deploy static path attachments to an EPG.

- **Virtual (*vmmDomP*)**: VMM domains are used when integrating virtual domains with the Cisco APIC.

- **External bridged (*l2extDomP*)**: External bridged domains are used when creating an external bridged network.

- **External routed (*l3extDomP*)**: External routed domains are used when creating an external routed network.

- **Fibre Channel (*fcDomP*)**: Fiber Channel domains are used when connecting Fibre Channel devices to the ACI fabric.

Attachable Access Entity Profile

In order to restrict what interfaces have access to what domains and, consequently, what VLAN ranges, an AAEP is needed. An AAEP is an object that acts as a filter for one or more domains on a particular interface. In order to create this mapping, an AAEP is associated to an interface policy group. The domain is then associated to the AAEP. Therefore, an interface on a switch has a given set of policies. Those policies are grouped on a policy group, and an AAEP is tied to the group, allowing access to certain domains. The interface is then allowed access to the VLAN pools that the domains provide. This allows an ACI admin to restrict access to certain VLANs so that they are not allowed to overlap. This is critical in a shared infrastructure where there are multiple tenants.

In most cases, a single AAEP for each domain type (physical, VMM, external L2, external L3) is sufficient. The physical and external domains map to a VLAN pool with static allocation ranges, and the VMM domain maps to a VLAN pool with dynamic allocation ranges. Figure 2-19 demonstrates the relationships of global policies and the interface and EPG.

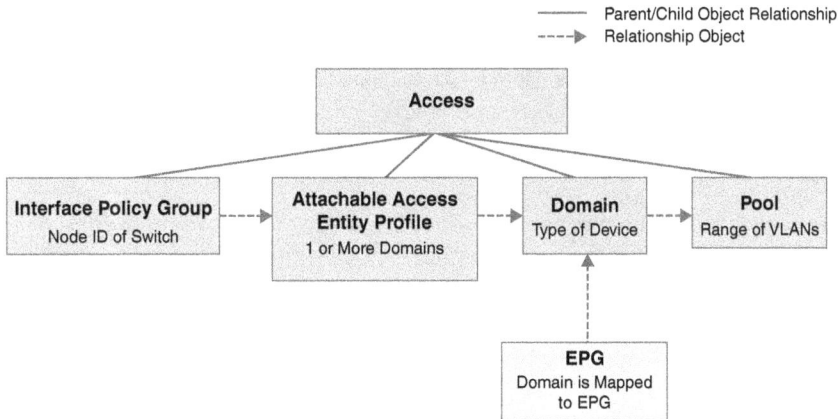

Figure 2-19 *Object Relationship Between Global Policies and Interface Policy Group to an EPG*

Managed Object Relationships and Policy Resolution

A managed object relationship outlines the relationship between managed object processes that do not share the parent/child relationship. MO relationships are established between the source MO and a target MO in one of the following two ways:

- An explicit relationship (*fvRsPathAtt*) defines a relationship based on the target MO distinguished name (DN).

- A named relationship defines a relationship based on the target MO name.

The dotted lines in Figure 2-20 show examples of common MO relationships.

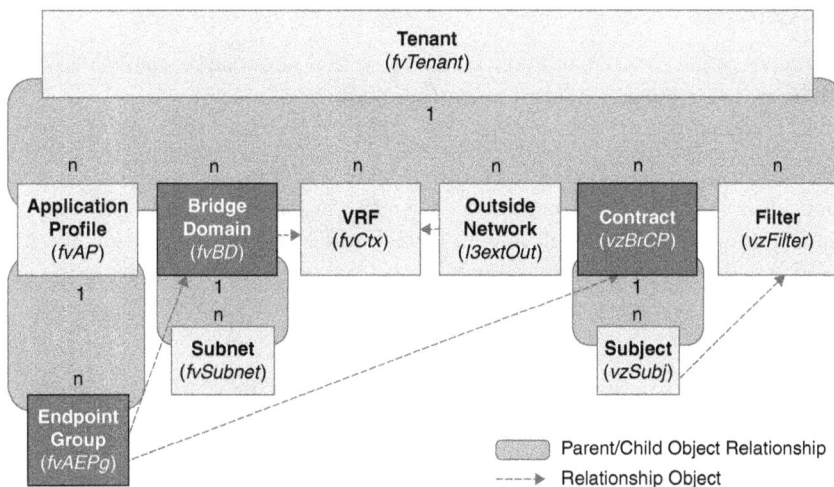

Figure 2-20 *Managed Object Relationship*

In Figure 2-20, the dotted line between the EPG and the bridge domain defines the relationship between those two managed objects. In this figure, the EPG *fvAEPg* contains the relationship MO *fvRsBD* that is named with the name of the target bridge domain MO (*fvBD*). For example, if **production** is the bridge domain name (*fvBD*=**production**), the relationship object name is *tnFvBDName*=**production**. There is a similar managed object relationship between the EPG *fvAEPg* and contract *vzBrCP*.

In the case of policy resolution based on named relationships, if a target MO with a matching name is not found in the current tenant, the ACI fabric tries to resolve in the common tenant. For example, if the user tenant EPG contains a relationship MO targeted to a bridge domain that does not exist in the tenant, the system tries to resolve the relationship in the common tenant. If a named relationship cannot be resolved in either the user-defined tenant or the common tenant, the ACI fabric attempts to resolve to a default policy. If a default policy exists in the current tenant, it is used. If it does not exist, the ACI fabric looks for a default policy in the common tenant. Bridge domain, VRF, and contract (security policy) named relationships do not resolve to a default.

Tags

A tag MO provides simplification in API operations. While executing an API operation, an object or a group of objects can be referenced by the tag name instead of by the DN. Tags are child objects of the item they tag; besides the name, they have no other properties.

You can use a tag to assign a descriptive name to a group of objects. The same tag name can be assigned to multiple objects. Multiple tag names can be assigned to an object. For example, to enable easy searchable access to all web server EPGs, assign a web server tag to all such EPGs. Web server EPGs throughout the fabric can be located by referencing the web server tag.

Default Policies

The initial values of the APIC default policies are taken from the concrete model that is loaded in the switch. A fabric administrator can modify default policies.

Warning   Default policies can be modified or deleted. Deleting a default policy can result in a policy resolution process completing abnormally. Be sure there are no current or future configurations that rely on a default policy before deleting a default policy. For example, deleting a default firmware update policy could result in a problematic future firmware update.

The ACI fabric includes default policies for many of its core functions. Examples of default policies include the following:

- Bridge domain (in the common tenant)
- Layer 2 and Layer 3 protocols

- Fabric initialization, device discovery, and cabling detection

- Storm control and flooding

- VPC

- Endpoint retention for caching and aging of learned endpoints in switch buffers

- Loop detection

- Monitoring and statistics

When the ACI fabric is upgraded, the existing policy default values persist, even if the default value changes in the newer release. When a node connects to an APIC for the first time, the node registers itself with the APIC, which pushes all the default policies to the node. Any subsequent change in the default policy is pushed to the node.

A default policy allows a fabric administrator to override the default values in the policy model by using explicit policy. In addition, if an administrator does not provide an explicit policy, the APIC applies the default policy. An administrator can create a default policy, which the APIC uses unless the administrator provides an explicit policy. For example, based on the actions the administrator does or does not take, the APIC will do the following:

- Because the administrator does not specify the LLDP policy for the selected ports, the APIC applies the default LLDP interface policy for the ports specified in the port selector.

- If the administrator removes a port from a port selector, the APIC applies the default policies to that port. In this example, if the administrator removes port 1/15 from the port selector, the port is no longer part of the port channel, and the APIC applies all the default policies to that port.

The following scenarios describe common policy resolution behavior:

- **A configuration explicitly refers to the default policy:** If a default policy exists in the current tenant, it is used; otherwise, the default policy in the common tenant is used.

- **A configuration refers to a named policy (not the default policy) that does not exist in the current tenant or in tenant common:** If the current tenant has a default policy, it is used; otherwise, the default policy in the common tenant is used.

Note   This does not apply to a bridge domain or a VRF instance in a tenant.

- **A configuration does not refer to any policy name:** If a default policy exists in the current tenant, it is used; otherwise, the default policy in the common tenant is used.

Note   For bridge domains and VRF instances, this applies only if the connectivity instrumentation policy (*fvConnInstrPol*) in the common tenant has the appropriate bridge domain or VRF flag set. This prevents unintended EPGs from being deployed in common tenant subnets.

How a Policy Model Helps in Diagnosis

Now that you understand the policy model in ACI, let's dive into a failure scenario and observe how you can leverage the ACI policy model concepts in diagnosing and resolving problems.

Say that you have received a complaint that your application servers hosted in ACI fabric are not reachable. The external network connectivity from ACI leafs is by route peering using OSPF, as shown in Figure 2-21.

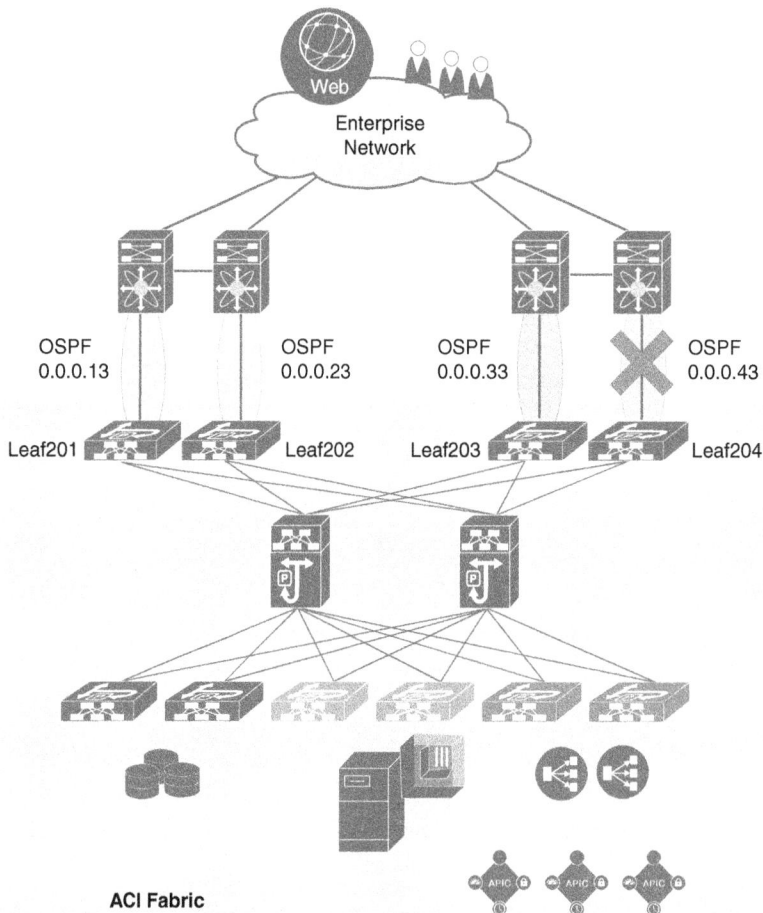

Figure 2-21   *Diagnosis Use Case*

For this kind of issue, typically you need to check the following:

- Are your border leafs up and running?

- Is your OSPF neighbor relationship up?

- Is any fault generated?

Checking this manually on each of the border leafs is time-consuming and extends your service downtime unnecessarily. In ACI, you can run a short query against your entire fabric to get all this information at once, as demonstrated in Example 2-1.

Example 2-1   *Checking External Network Connectivity from ACI Leafs via Route Peering Using OSPF*

```
https://{{apic}}/api/node/class/ospfAdjEp.json?query-target=self&rsp-subtree-
  include=faults
{
    "totalCount": "4",
    "imdata": [
        {
            "ospfAdjEp": {
                "attributes": {
                    "area": "0.0.0.13",
                    "dn": "topology/pod-1/node-201/sys/ospf/inst-default/
  dom-t01:standard/if-[eth1/1]/adj-50.88.193.130",
                    "operSt": "full",
                    "peerIp": "50.88.192.30",
                }
            }
        },
        {
            "ospfAdjEp": {
                "attributes": {
                    "area": "0.0.0.23",
                    "dn": "topology/pod-1/node-202/sys/ospf/inst-default/
  dom-t02:mainframe/if-[eth1/1]/adj-60.88.152.130",
                    "operSt": "full",
                    "peerIp": "60.88.152.2",
                }
            }
        },
        {
            "ospfAdjEp": {
                "attributes": {
                    "area": "0.0.0.33",
                    "dn": "topology/pod-1/node-203/sys/ospf/inst-default/
  dom-t03:hadoop/if-[eth1/1]/adj-70.88.172.130",
```

```
                                "operSt": "full",
                                "peerIp": "70.88.172.2",
                        }
                    }
                },
                {
                    "ospfAdjEp": {
                        "attributes": {
                            "area": "0.0.0.43",
                            "dn": "topology/pod-1/node-204/sys/ospf/inst-default/
dom-t01:standard/if-[vlan48]/adj-80.88.143.4",
                            "operSt": "full",
                            "peerIp": "80.88.143.104",
                        },
                        "children": [
                            {
                                "faultInst": {
                                    "attributes": {
                                        "ack": "no",
                                        "cause": "protocol-ospf-adjacency-down",
                                        "changeSet": "operSt (New: full)",
                                       "code": "F1385",
                                        "created": "2020-05-01T04:53:37.931-04:00",
                                        "descr": "OSPF adjacency is not full, current state
Exchange",
                                        "domain": "external",
                                        "highestSeverity": "warning",
                                        "lastTransition": "2020-05-01T04:53:38.093-04:00",
                                        "lc": "soaking-clearing",
                                        "occur": "1",
                                        "origSeverity": "warning",
                                        "prevSeverity": "warning",
                                        "rn": "fault-F1385",
                                        "rule": "ospf-adj-ep-failed",
                                        "severity": "warning",
                                        "subject": "oper-state-failed",
                                        "type": "operational"
                                    }
                                }
                            }
                        ]
                    }
                }
            ]
        }
```

Note   The output in Example 2-1 is truncated to include only necessary values for explanation.

From Example 2-1, you can observe that the REST query provides quick feedback of the issue you are encountering. Out of four border leafs, one of the OSPF route peer relationships from Border Leaf ID 204 to external router is down and in OSPF EXSTART state. The REST query is calling an object class *ospfAdjEp* (an OSPF adjacency endpoint) fabric-wide, including the fault *F1385* associated with the object class.

Summary

ACI is a policy-based object model in which configurations are stored as managed objects in a hierarchical fashion. All configuration management to fabric devices called *nodes* is carried out via a set of controllers in a replicated and synchronized cluster fashion. Traffic forwarding is still conducted directly by nodes called leafs and spines that constitute the ACI fabric. The Cisco ACI policy model is a top-down model based on promise theory that is meant to control a scalable architecture of defined network and service objects. This model provides robust repeatable controls, multitenancy, and minimal requirements for detailed knowledge by the Cisco APIC control system. The model is designed to scale beyond current requirements and to satisfy the needs of private clouds, public clouds, and software-defined data centers.

The policy enforcement model within the fabric is built from the ground up in an application-centric object model. This provides a logical model for laying out applications, which will then be applied to the fabric by the Cisco APIC. This helps to bridge the gaps in communication between application requirements and the network constructs that enforce them. The Cisco ACI model is designed for rapid provisioning of applications on the network that can be tied to robust policy enforcement while maintaining a workload-anywhere approach with single-pane-of-glass management.

In the next chapter, you will learn about ACI command-line interfaces.

Review Key Topics

If you are preparing to take the Implementing Cisco Application Centric Infrastructure - Advanced (300-630 DCACIA) exam to attain the Cisco Certified Specialist—ACI Advanced Implementation certification, be sure to review the key topics marked in this chapter as outlined in Table 2-2.

Table 2-2   *Key Topics*

Key Topic Element	Description	Page Number
Paragraph	Description of VLAN Pools	55

Review Questions

The questions that follow are designed to help you prepare for the Implementing Cisco Application Centric Infrastructure - Advanced (300-630 DCACIA) exam if you are planning on acquiring the Cisco Certified Specialist: ACI Advanced Implementation certification.

1. What is the ACI policy model? How does it help in building application logic? (Choose two.)

   a. The ACI policy model is a convenient model for building application logic through required policies.

   b. Spine switches render the ACI policy model in the fabric with admin instructions.

   c. In ACI, faults and events are not part of the policy model as they are generated as system logs.

   d. The ACI policy model only deals with the configuration of stateful devices.

   e. Policies are rendered automatically by APICs inside the fabric infrastructure.

2. How does the policy model work in ACI? How does it help in expediting the application deployment process? (Choose three.)

   a. Configuration is applied through a centralized APIC system to fabric switches. This method ensures consistent changes and avoids human errors.

   b. A user interacts with an APIC through the REST API to create and modify objects in the policy model, which ultimately results in the allocation of hardware resources.

   c. An APIC only maintains the configuration of the fabric. For faults, an external server is required.

   d. Switches must register to the fabric first before they can be configured by an APIC.

   e. Everything in ACI is an object that is represented in a logical model only.

3. What are the benefits of using the ACI policy model? (Choose two.)

   a. Policies that are programmed in hardware cannot be reused.

   b. It slows down the deployment process as the fabric infrastructure scales.

   c. Control policy is abstracted from the configuration in hardware.

   d. It provides flexibility in modifying the defined policies as service requirements change.

4. What are contracts, and how are they used in ACI? (Choose four.)

    a. Contracts are mapped to bridge domains for Layer 2 isolation.

    b. Contracts are used to enforce security policies in ACI.

    c. A contract allows or denies specific ports and protocols.

    d. In ACI, contracts are applied on application EPGs to enforce security policies on endpoints, regardless of their Layer 2 or Layer 3 attributes.

    e. Contract inheritance allows for modified filters on new EPGs.

    f. A contract preferred group allows certain EPGs with full communication within a VRF instance while restricting others through a contract with restrictive filters.

    g. A taboo contract allows all traffic but denies certain traffic. It is useful during migration cases.

5. What are switch policies? How does a switch policy work in ACI? (Choose four.)

    a. Switch policies govern switchwide configurations, which can be grouped together for common functionalities and applied to specific switch nodes.

    b. A VPC domain is defined under a switch policy group.

    c. A COPP policy is defined under a switch policy.

    d. A switch profile is used to tie a fabric node (leaf or spine switch) to a specific switch policy group.

    e. The recommended configuration is to always create a one-to-one mapping between physical switches and the corresponding switch profile.

    f. Switch policies are part of the Inventory tab in the Access Policies main menu bar.

6. What are interface policies? How do they work in ACI? (Choose three.)

    a. Interface policies are part of Admin tab in main menu bar of the APIC GUI.

    b. Interface policies govern the interface-related policies that are grouped together for common functionality of end-host connectivity.

    c. CDP, LLDP, and LACP protocols are configured under an interface policy group.

    d. To configure interface policies, first you need to configure policies, and then you include those policies in a policy group, and finally you create a profile with an interface selector and assign a policy group to it.

    e. An attachable access entity profile is tied to an interface profile.

    f. Interface policies are directly configured on a switch profile.

    g. An interface profile associates the Ethernet interfaces through the interface selector and maps it to a switch profile.

7. What is an attachable access entity profile (AAEP)? What are the benefits of an AAEP? (Choose three.)

 a. If multitenancy is not required, a single AAEP is sufficient for each domain type, such as physical, VMM, External L2, or External L3.

 b. An AAEP restricts admins to access certain VLANs that are part of the domain on a particular interface to avoid overlap.

 c. An AAEP is tied to an interface policy group and associated with a domain.

 d. An AAEP is mapped to an application EPG to enforce interface policy.

 e. An AAEP does not help in a shared infrastructure situation where there are multiple tenants.

Chapter 3

ACI Command-Line Interfaces

This chapter covers the following topics related to ACI command-line interfaces (CLIs):

- APIC CLIs

- ACI fabric switch CLIs

With the implementation of a REST API, ACI offers the ability to configure and manage a data center network as never before. With a fully function GUI written on top of the API, an ACI administrator has many options when it comes to managing, monitoring, and troubleshooting the ACI data center. Not all interactions with the APIC and switches require use of a REST client or GUI, however. Built into each node in the ACI fabric is a CLI that can be used to leverage existing knowledge of Cisco NX-OS with many common commands and a few new additions. Because the APIC and switches serve different purposes in an ACI solution, each provides unique CLI functionality that can be leveraged.

Throughout the book, you will see references to many different commands and the shell in which they are run. This chapter does the following:

- Introduces the different CLI shells that exist within ACI

- Shows how to access the different shells

- Describes why certain shells should be used over the others

- Shows how the different shells differ from traditional Cisco CLIs

APIC CLIs

The APIC provides two CLIs that can be used to monitor and troubleshoot the ACI fabric. This section describes in detail the CLIs available when a remote terminal session (either via Secure Shell [SSH] or Telnet) is initiated on an APIC controller. For security reasons, SSH is recommended, and it is the remote terminal session protocol of choice throughout this book.

NX-OS–Style CLI

Along with a GUI and REST API, an APIC also offers an NX-OS–style CLI built on top of a Bash shell that allows you to navigate and configure the ACI fabric as if you were on a traditional NX-OS device. Almost every configuration option that is exposed via the REST API is also configurable via the NX-OS–style CLI. Before diving into how to access the NX-OS CLI, you will find that there are some differences in operating the APIC NX-OS CLI versus the traditional NX-OS CLI on any other Nexus platform. The usage of the NX-OS–style CLI for an APIC differs from the traditional NX-OS CLI in these ways:

- With the NX-OS–style CLI for an APIC, to make changes to a particular leaf switch, you must first navigate to that switch by using the **leaf** command followed by node ID.

- The command syntax in certain cases is slightly different. For example, while specifying an Ethernet port in the NX-OS–style CLI for an APIC, you should type **eth x/y** instead of **ethx/y**.

- With the NX-OS–style CLI for an APIC, when a configuration field consists of user-defined text, such as a password, special characters such as $ or ! should be escaped with a backslash (for example, **\$**), or the entire word or string should be wrapped in single quotes to avoid misinterpretation by the Bash shell.

- Some command shortcuts with the NX-OS–style CLI for an APIC are different due to Bash behavior:

  - Ctrl+D exits a session.

  - Ctrl+Z suspends a job.

  - Ctrl+C stops a command.

After initiating an SSH session to an APIC, the first shell you are dropped into is the NX-OS CLI (see Example 3-1).

Example 3-1 *Accessing the APIC NX-OS CLI by Using SSH*

```
terminal$ ssh username@apic-address-or-hostname
apic1#
```

Table 3-1 lists and describes the most commonly used NX-OS CLI modes—the EXEC and global configuration modes—and provides examples of submodes. The table shows how to enter and exit the modes and the resulting system prompts, which help identify which mode you are in and the commands that are available to you in that mode.

Table 3-1 *NX-OS CLI Modes with Prompts and Exit Methods*

Mode	Access Method	Prompt	Exit Method
EXEC	From the APIC prompt, enter **execsh**.	apic#	To exit to the login prompt, use the **exit** command.
Global configuration	From EXEC mode, enter the **configure** command.	apic(config)#	To exit from a configuration submode to its parent mode, use the **exit** command.
DNS configuration	From global configuration mode, enter the **dns** command.	apic(config-dns)	To exit from any configuration mode or submode to EXEC mode, use the **end** command.

Just as on any NX-OS device, with the NX-OS–style CLI for an APIC, the **?** character allows you to see what options are available, and the <TAB> character allows you to auto-complete commands. For example, to see the list of **show** commands, you could run **show ?** as shown in Example 3-2.

Example 3-2 *Using the **show** Command to See a List of Command Options*

```
apic1# show ?
 aaa Show AAA information
 access-list Show Access-list Information
 accounting Show accounting information
 acllog Show acllog information
 analytics Show analytics cluster configuration
 application Show Application Profiles Information
 audits Show audit-log information
 bridge-domain Show Bridge-domain Information
 callhome Show command for callhome
 catalog Show catalog information
 cli Show All Commands
 clock Show clock information
 <output omitted for brevity>
```

To see a list of commands that begin with a particular character sequence, type those characters followed by a question mark (**?**). Do not include a space before the question mark, as shown in Example 3-3.

Example 3-3   *Using the show Command to See a List of Command Options Matching a Character Sequence*

```
apic1# sh a?
aaa          Show AAA information
access-list  Show Access-list Information
accounting   Show accounting information
acllog       Show acllog information
analytics    Show analytics cluster configuration
application  Show Application Profiles Information
audits       Show audit-log information
```

To auto-complete a command after you begin typing, type **<TAB>**, as demonstrated in Example 3-4.

Example 3-4   *Using <TAB> to Auto-Complete Commands*

```
apic1# sh<TAB>
apic1# show
```

From here, you can select a more specific option to view the contents. A good example of this would be viewing audit log entries on the fabric. You can type **show audits** to get the contents of the current audit log, which can be used to review all changes that have happened in the environment, as demonstrated in Example 3-5.

Example 3-5   *Viewing Audit Log Entries by Using the NX-OS–Style CLI*

```
apic1# show audits
Creation Time : 2018-09-24T15:33:27.785-04:00
ID : 4295033379
User : admin
Action : deletion
Affected Object : uni/fabric/outofsvc/rsoosPath-[topology/pod-1/paths-101/pat
 hep-[eth1/27]]
Description : RsOosPath topology/pod-1/paths-101/pathep-[eth1/27] deleted

Creation Time : 2018-09-24T15:33:24.074-04:00
ID : 4295033378
User : admin
Action : creation
Affected Object : uni/fabric/outofsvc/rsoosPath-[topology/pod-1/paths-101/pat
 hep-[eth1/27]]
Description : RsOosPath topology/pod-1/paths-101/pathep-[eth1/27] created
```

Along with **show** commands, a variety of other tools are exposed via the NX-OS CLI. Because the CLI is on the APIC, you can use it to run commands against one or more switches in the fabric by using the **fabric** command, which has the following syntax: **fabric** *<nodeId> <show command>. nodeId* can be a comma-separated list of more than one node ID to run the command against multiple switches at one time. Example 3-6 shows an example of output from the **fabric** command.

Example 3-6 *Using the fabric Command to Execute a Command on Nodes 101 and 102*

```
apic1# fabric 101,102 show interface mgmt 0
------------------------------------------------------------------
 Node 101 (leaf101)
------------------------------------------------------------------
mgmt0 is up
admin state is up,
 Hardware: GigabitEthernet, address: 002a.100e.2054 (bia 002a.100e.2054)
 Internet Address is 192.168.4.12/24
 MTU 1500 bytes, BW 1000000 Kbit, DLY 10 usec
 reliability 255/255, txload 1/255, rxload 1/255
 Encapsulation ARPA, medium is broadcast
 Port mode is routed
 full-duplex, 1000 Mb/s
 Beacon is turned off
 Auto-Negotiation is turned on
 Input flow-control is off, output flow-control is off
 Auto-mdix is turned off
 EtherType is 0x0000
 30 seconds input rate 1000 bits/sec, 1 packets/sec
 30 seconds output rate 848 bits/sec, 1 packets/sec
 Rx
 386298 input packets 297387 unicast packets 13417 multicast packets
 75494 broadcast packets 32067345 bytes
 Tx
 296292 output packets 296276 unicast packets 8 multicast packets
 8 broadcast packets 23768146 bytes


------------------------------------------------------------------
 Node 102 (leaf102)
------------------------------------------------------------------
mgmt0 is up
admin state is up,
 Hardware: GigabitEthernet, address: 002a.100e.22d4 (bia 002a.100e.22d4)
 Internet Address is 192.168.4.13/24
 MTU 1500 bytes, BW 1000000 Kbit, DLY 10 usec
 reliability 255/255, txload 1/255, rxload 1/255
```

```
Encapsulation ARPA, medium is broadcast
Port mode is routed
full-duplex, 1000 Mb/s
Beacon is turned off
Auto-Negotiation is turned on
Input flow-control is off, output flow-control is off
Auto-mdix is turned off
EtherType is 0x0000
30 seconds input rate 1152 bits/sec, 1 packets/sec
30 seconds output rate 616 bits/sec, 0 packets/sec
Rx
760965 input packets 585204 unicast packets 26324 multicast packets
149437 broadcast packets 63823992 bytes
Tx
585152 output packets 585136 unicast packets 8 multicast packets
8 broadcast packets 49255940 bytes
```

In order to apply the configuration, you need to enter configuration mode, just as you do on any other Cisco platform. This is done by entering **configure** at the prompt, as shown in Example 3-7.

Example 3-7   *Entering the Configuration Mode of the NX-OS CLI on an APIC*

```
apic1# configure
apic1(config)#
```

For many configuration commands, you can precede the command with the **no** keyword to remove a setting or to restore a setting to the default value. Example 3-8 shows how to create a blacklist policy to shut down an interface and how to remove the blacklist policy to restore the interface to its original state. It also demonstrates how to remove a previously configured DNS server from the configuration.

Example 3-8   *Restoring a Configuration to the Default State by Using no*

```
apic1# configure
apic1(config)# leaf 101
apic1(config-leaf)# interface ?
 ethernet Ethernet IEEE 802.3z
 fc FC Interface
 port-channel Port Channel interface
 vfc Virtual Fiber Channel interface
 vfc-po VFC Port Channel interface
 vlan Vlan interface
```

```
apic1(config-leaf)# interface ethernet 1/27
apic1(config-leaf-if)# shutdown
apic1(config-leaf-if)# no shutdown
apic1(config-leaf-if)# end
apic1#
apic1# config
apic1(config)# dns
apic1(config-dns)# address 192.0.20.123 preferred
apic1(config-dns)# show dns-address
Address         Preferred
-------------   ---------
192.0.20.123    yes
apic1(config-dns)# no address 192.0.20.123
apic1(config-dns)# show dns-address
Address         Preferred
-------------   ---------
```

In configuration mode, all configuration options are exposed. At any time, you can issue the **where** command to see your exact tree location, as shown in Example 3-9.

Example 3-9 *Displaying the Current Working Path by Using the **where** Command*

```
apic1(config-leaf-if)# where
configure t; leaf 101; interface ethernet 1 / 27
```

Using the NX-OS–style CLI, you can use SSH to access any ACI switch connected in the fabric. This is achieved by initiating an SSH session to the TEP address of the leaf or spine or by using the hostname, as demonstrated in Example 3-10.

Example 3-10 *Initiating an SSH Session to a Fabric Node via an APIC NX-OS–Style CLI*

```
apic1# ssh admin@leaf101
Password:
Last login: Thu Feb 14 13:38:44 2019 from 10.0.0.1
Cisco Nexus Operating System (NX-OS) Software
TAC support: http://www.cisco.com/tac
Copyright (c) 2002-2018, Cisco Systems, Inc. All rights reserved.
The copyrights to certain works contained in this software are
owned by other third parties and used and distributed under
license. Certain components of this software are licensed under
the GNU General Public License (GPL) version 2.0 or the GNU
Lesser General Public License (LGPL) Version 2.1. A copy of each
such license is available at
http://www.opensource.org/licenses/gpl-2.0.php and
http://www.opensource.org/licenses/lgpl-2.1.php
leaf101# whoami
admin
```

If you do not know the TEP address or hostname, you can view the details for each node by using the **show switch** command, as demonstrated in Example 3-11.

Example 3-11   *Using the show switch Command to Retrieve Information About the Fabric Nodes*

```
apic1# show switch detail
ID                  : 101
Role                : leaf
Name                : leaf101
Pod Id              : 1
Address             : 10.0.64.68
In-Band V4 Address  : 0.0.0.0
In-Band V6 Address  : ::
OOB V4 Address      : 192.168.4.12
OOB V6 Address      : ::
Serial Number       : FDO202711U6
Version             : n9000-13.2(3i)
Up Time             : 02:03:00:59.000
Fabric State        : active
State               : in-service
Valid Certificate   : yes
Validity Start      : 2016-07-28T19:39:02.000-05:00
Validity End        : 2026-07-28T19:49:02.000-05:00...
```

Bash CLI

Along with the NX-OS CLI, an APIC also offers a Linux Bash shell. The Bash shell exposes, but is not limited to, the following functionality:

- Native Linux command set

- File system and directory navigation

Originally, the Bash CLI was the only available CLI. When the NX-OS–style CLI was introduced in ACI Release 2.0, many commands that were offered in the Bash CLI were deprecated and added to the NX-OS CLI. However, because the Bash shell is a portal into the Linux operating system on which the APIC is built, the bash CLI can provide convenience under a variety of circumstances.

In order to access the Bash shell, type the command **bash** at the NX-OS CLI prompt, as shown in Example 3-12.

Example 3-12   *Accessing the APIC Bash Shell*

```
apic1# bash
admin@apic1:~>
```

Once in the Bash shell, you have access to the native Linux environment, which exposes commands that would otherwise be unavailable in the NX-OS CLI shell. An example of this is the use of the **route** command, as shown in Example 3-13.

Example 3-13 *Using the route Command to View the Linux Routing Table*

```
admin@apic1:~> route
Kernel IP routing table
Destination     Gateway       Genmask           Flags Metric Ref    Use  Iface
default         192.168.4.1   0.0.0.0           UG    16     0      0    oobmgmt
10.0.0.0        10.0.0.30     255.255.0.0       UG    0      0      0    bond0.3093
10.0.0.30       0.0.0.0       255.255.255.255   UH    0      0      0    bond0.3093
10.0.32.65      10.0.0.30     255.255.255.255   UGH   0      0      0    bond0.3093
10.0.32.66      10.0.0.30     255.255.255.255   UGH   0      0      0    bond0.3093
169.254.1.0     0.0.0.0       255.255.255.0     U     0      0      0    teplo-1
169.254.254.0   0.0.0.0       255.255.255.0     U     0      0      0    lxcbr0
172.17.0.0      0.0.0.0       255.255.0.0       U     0      0      0    docker0
192.168.4.0     0.0.0.0       255.255.255.0     U     0      0      0    oobmgmt
```

The command **route** is not recognized by the NX-OS–style CLI as it is only available as a Linux command. Furthermore, any time a command that includes a **?** needs to be run, the NX-OS CLI interprets this as a need to view the available command options. For instance, maybe you want to query the API for audit logs by using the iCurl functionality that is built into the APIC. iCurl is discussed in detail in Chapter 13, "Troubleshooting Techniques," but for now just know that you can achieve this by running the following command:

```
icurl 'http://localhost:7777/api/class/aaaModLR.xml?order-by=aaaModLR.
created'
```

If you run this command via the NX-OS–style CLI, when the **?** is entered, the CLI interprets it as a need to see all available commands. This sort of command should be executed in the Bash shell.

Bash shell commands can also be executed directly from the NX-OS–style CLI. In order to do this, you type **bash -c** "*path/command*" into the NX-OS CLI from any prompt, as shown in Example 3-14.

Example 3-14 *Executing a Bash Command from the NX-OS CLI*

```
apic1# bash -c "route"
Kernel IP routing table
Destination     Gateway       Genmask           Flags Metric Ref    Use  Iface
default         192.168.4.1   0.0.0.0           UG    16     0      0    oobmgmt
10.0.0.0        10.0.0.30     255.255.0.0       UG    0      0      0    bond0.3093
10.0.0.30       0.0.0.0       255.255.255.255   UH    0      0      0    bond0.3093
```

```
10.0.32.65     10.0.0.30     255.255.255.255   UGH   0     0        0   bond0.3093
10.0.32.66     10.0.0.30     255.255.255.255   UGH   0     0        0   bond0.3093
169.254.1.0    0.0.0.0       255.255.255.0     U     0     0        0   teplo-1
169.254.254.0  0.0.0.0       255.255.255.0     U     0     0        0   lxcbr0
172.17.0.0     0.0.0.0       255.255.0.0       U     0     0        0   docker0
192.168.4.0    0.0.0.0       255.255.255.0     U     0     0        0   oobmgmt
```

The Bash shell can also be useful for navigating the file system. For example, after a firmware upgrade, you might see the fault shown in Figure 3-1.

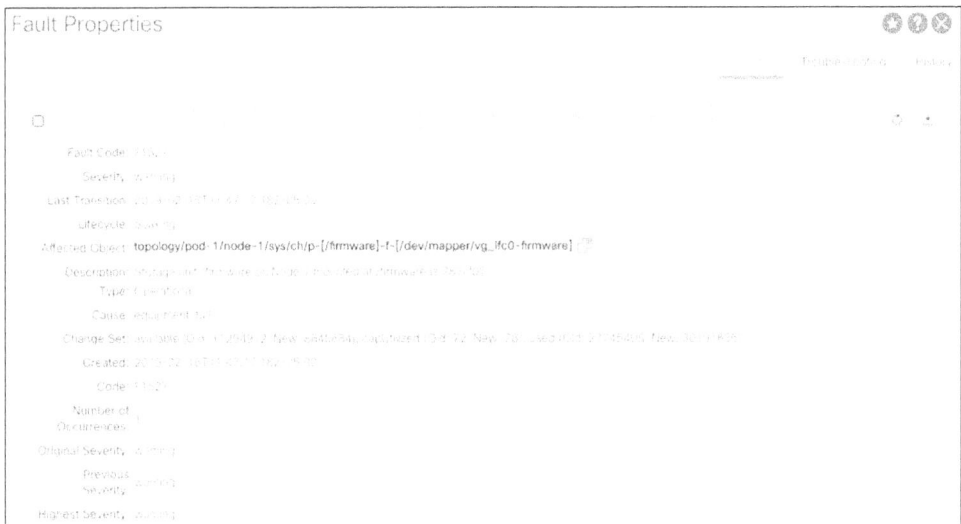

Figure 3-1   *Fault Illustrating That the /firmware Directory Is Low on Space*

You can leverage traditional Linux commands such as **df** (disk free) or **du** (disk usage) to determine the contents of the directory that is full. This is very helpful when determining what is eligible for removal to free up some used space, as demonstrated in Example 3-15.

Example 3-15   *Finding Directory Sizes and Navigating the File System on an APIC by Using the Bash Shell*

```
admin@apic1:~> df -h
Filesystem                    Size  Used Avail Use% Mounted on
/dev/mapper/vg_ifc0-boot       40G  8.8G   29G  24% /bin
/dev/mapper/vg_ifc0_ssd-data  175G  6.1G  160G   4% /var/log/dme
devtmpfs                       63G     0   63G   0% /dev
tmpfs                         4.0G  140M  3.9G   4% /dev/shm
/dev/mapper/vg_ifc0-firmware   40G   29G  8.5G  78% /firmware
/dev/mapper/vg_ifc0-scratch    40G  103M   38G   1% /home
```

```
tmpfs                              63G     0   63G   0% /sys/fs/cgroup
/dev/mapper/vg_ifc0-techsupport    40G   3.3G   34G   9% /data/techsupport
tmpfs                              16G   136K   16G   1% /tmp
tmpfs                             2.0G   320M  1.7G  16% /var/log/dme/log
/dev/mapper/vg_ifc0-logs           40G   300M   37G   1% /var/log/dme/oldlog
/dev/mapper/vg_ifc0-data2         493G   8.6G  461G   2% /data2
/dev/mapper/vg_ifc0-dmecores       50G    52M   47G   1% /var/log/dme/core
tmpfs                              63G   4.1G   59G   7% /var/run/utmp

admin@apic1:~> cd /firmware
admin@apic1:firmware> du | sort -rn | more
30142636        .
27309904        ./fwrepos
27309836        ./fwrepos/fwrepo
```

Keep in mind that when you are operating in a Bash shell, you can write Bash scripts to automate certain tasks or monitor your ACI fabric. For example, Example 3-16 shows a simple Bash script to monitor the size of the /firmware directory every two seconds.

Example 3-16 *Using a Bash Script to Check the /firmware Directory Every Two Seconds*

```
admin@apic1:~> cat check_firmware_directory.sh
#!/bin/bash

while true; do
    time=$(date)
    echo $time
    cmd=$(df -h | grep firmware)
    echo $cmd
    sleep 2
done

admin@apic1:~> bash check_firmware_directory.sh
Mon Feb 18 13:54:19 EST 2019
/dev/mapper/vg_ifc0-firmware 40G 29G 8.5G 78% /firmware
Mon Feb 18 13:54:21 EST 2019
/dev/mapper/vg_ifc0-firmware 40G 29G 8.5G 78% /firmware
Mon Feb 18 13:54:23 EST 2019
/dev/mapper/vg_ifc0-firmware 40G 29G 8.5G 78% /firmware
...
```

Finally, the **history** command allows you to view all commands that have previously been run (see Example 3-17).

Example 3-17   *Using the history Command to View Previously Run Commands*

```
admin@apic1:~> history
1  route
2  fd -h
...
```

ACI Fabric Switch CLIs

For ACI fabric switches, three different CLIs can be used to view different aspects of the platform: iBash, VSH, and VSH_LC. The following sections describe the CLIs available when you use SSH to connect directly to an ACI spine or leaf switch.

iBash CLI

After initiating an SSH session to an APIC, the first shell you are dropped into is the iBash CLI, as shown in Example 3-18.

Example 3-18   *Accessing the Switch NX-OS iBash CLI by Using SSH*

```
terminal$ ssh username@node-address-or-hostname
leaf101#
```

iBash is a unique implementation of the Linux Bash shell as it adds NX-OS–like functionality on top of the normal shell. The idea behind the iBash shell was to allow access to native Linux commands but also offer a full NX-OS–style CLI in one shell. The NX-OS commands leverage the REST API to fetch data and display it in an NX-OS–style format. Whenever a command is run from iBash, an HTTP GET request is sent to the API. The same applies for the NX-OS CLI on APIC when running **show** commands: The query is processed and returned, and the output is displayed to the user in a format that is representative of NX-OS.

There are no **configure** commands on any of the ACI switches because all configuration is managed and pushed by the APIC. In addition, because much of the configuration may be spread out across multiple security domains and tenants, you must authenticate to the switch by using an account with administrative access in order to access the iBash shell. This ensures that users who access the switch have the right to view all configuration, regardless of which security domain it belongs to. There is no way to limit the output of a command run via iBash based on security domain.

There are a few more differences that you need to be aware of when using the iBash shell on an ACI switch for the first time. The first difference is that when attempting to use the Tab key to complete commands, the first word in the command must be fully completed. This is because the first word dictates whether to interpret the command as a Bash command or an NX-OS command. Once the first word is completed, normal NX-OS functionality exists. Commands can be Tab-completed and abbreviated. If more than one option exists for an abbreviated command, the command is logged as ambiguous, just as in the traditional NX-OS CLI. Example 3-19 demonstrates the use of the iBash shell.

Example 3-19   *Using Abbreviations and Command Syntax in the Switch iBash Shell*

```
leaf102# sho clock
bash: sho: command not found

leaf102# show c
Ambiguous command: "show c"

leaf102# show clo
13:49:54.098469 EDT Tue Oct 23 2018

leaf102# show clock
13:49:32.143976 EDT Tue Oct 23 2018
```

Another major difference is in how you view available commands. Traditionally, you rely on the **?** character to list all available command options. In iBash, however, the **?** can be used in a normal Bash command like *icurl*, as demonstrated in the "Bash CLI" section, earlier in this chapter. In order to list all available command options in iBash, you use two Esc keystrokes, as shown in Example 3-20.

Example 3-20   *Using <ESC><ESC> to Display All Available Command Options*

```
leaf102# show <ESC><ESC>
 <CR> Carriage return
 all-ports Show all ports on VLAN
 brief All VLAN status in brief
 extended VLAN extended info like encaps
 fcoe FCOE Configuration
 id VLAN status by VLAN id
 internal Show VLAN manager internal
 reserved Internal reserved VLANs
 summary VLAN summary information
```

Because the switch CLI is now running in a Bash shell, you can use useful Bash commands directly on the switches as you would in any other Bash shell. A great example of this is the **watch** command. Suppose you want to monitor an interface for errors or other attributes. You can leverage the **watch** command to print the output of **show interface** at a given interval, as demonstrated in Example 3-21.

Example 3-21   *Using the* **watch** *Command to Refresh Command Output on a One-Second Interval*

```
leaf101# watch -n 1 "show interface ethernet 1/1"
Every 1.0s: show interface ethernet 1/1                  Mon Feb 18 10:55:07 2019

[?1034hEthernet1/1 is up
admin state is up, Dedicated Interface
  Hardware: 1000/10000/25000/auto Ethernet, address: 002a.100e.2055 (bia 002a.
  100e.2055)
  MTU 9216 bytes, BW 10000000 Kbit, DLY 1 usec
  reliability 255/255, txload 1/255, rxload 1/255
  Encapsulation ARPA, medium is broadcast
  Port mode is trunk
  full-duplex, 10 Gb/s, media type is 10G
  FEC (forward-error-correction) : disable-fec
  Beacon is turned off
  Auto-Negotiation is turned on
  Input flow-control is off, output flow-control is off
  Auto-mdix is turned off
  Rate mode is dedicated
  Switchport monitor is off
  EtherType is 0x8100
  EEE (efficient-ethernet) : n/a
  Last link flapped 2d01h
  Last clearing of "show interface" counters never
  1 interface resets
  30 seconds input rate 0 bits/sec, 0 packets/sec
  30 seconds output rate 272 bits/sec, 0 packets/sec
  Load-Interval #2: 5 minute (300 seconds)
    input rate 0 bps, 0 pps; output rate 272 bps, 0 pps
  RX
    0 unicast packets  5944 multicast packets  0 broadcast packets
    5944 input packets  1491944 bytes
    0 jumbo packets  0 storm suppression bytes
    0 runts  0 giants  0 CRC  0 no buffer
    0 input error  0 short frame  0 overrun   0 underrun  0 ignored
    0 watchdog  0 bad etype drop  0 bad proto drop  0 if down drop
    0 input with dribble  0 input discard 0 input total drop
    0 Rx pause
  TX
    0 unicast packets  7386 multicast packets  122 broadcast packets
    7508 output packets  2137474 bytes
    0 jumbo packets
    0 output error  0 collision  0 deferred  0 late collision
    0 lost carrier  0 no carrier  0 babble  0 output discard 0 output total drops
    0 Tx pause
```

This makes gathering output more hands free compared to rerunning the command(s) manually.

Bash also allows you to alias commands to avoid having to type commands that are repetitive or that might contain very long names, as demonstrated in Example 3-22.

Example 3-22   *Setting Bash Environment Variables to Define Aliases*

```
leaf101# v1="longVrfName:longVrfName"

leaf101# show ip route vrf $v1
IP Route Table for VRF "longVrfName:longVrfName"
'*' denotes best ucast next-hop
'**' denotes best mcast next-hop
'[x/y]' denotes [preference/metric]
'%<string>' in via output denotes VRF <string>

0.0.0.0/0, ubest/mbest: 1/0
    *via 10.10.27.3, vlan34, [110/1], 2d03h, ospf-default, type-2
10.10.20.0/24, ubest/mbest: 1/0, attached, direct, pervasive
    *via 10.0.32.66%overlay-1, [1/0], 2d03h, static, tag 4294967295
10.10.20.1/32, ubest/mbest: 1/0, attached, pervasive
    *via 10.10.20.1, vlan27, [1/0], 2d04h, local, local
```

The other switch CLIs—VSH and VSH_LC—are accessed via iBash. Some command shortcuts are also different due to the behavior of the iBash shell:

- Ctrl+D exits a session.
- Ctrl+C stops a command.

VSH CLI

Because the iBash CLI relies on querying the API to return data to the user, there might be times when you would like to query the NX-OS software directly to get access to command output that isn't stored in the management information tree (MIT). In such cases, you can use the VSH shell.

The VSH shell exposes no Linux Bash functionality but rather provides direct access to the traditional NX-OS shell. Once you have used SSH to connect to an ACI switch, you can enter the VSH shell by typing **vsh** into the iBash CLI, as demonstrated in Example 3-23.

Example 3-23   *Entering the Switch VSH Shell from iBash*

```
leaf102# vsh
Cisco iNX-OS Debug Shell
This shell should only be used for internal commands and exists
for legacy reasons. User should use ibash infrastructure as this
will be deprecated.
leaf102#
```

Notice the message stating that the shell might be deprecated in the future. It is important to understand that the iBash shell was intended to supersede the traditional NX-OS shell, and therefore development efforts to maintain the traditional NX-OS shell are not always prioritized. However, it is safe to run **show** commands in this environment, and in most cases, doing so can provide great value.

You can also run any **vsh** command directly from iBash. This is helpful in the event that you want to redirect the output to a file and store it somewhere in the Linux file system, as demonstrated in Example 3-24.

Example 3-24   *Running VSH Commands from iBash and Redirecting to a File*

```
leaf101# vsh -c "show clock"
14:05:58.838 EDT Thu Oct 25 2018

leaf101# vsh -c "show clock" > /tmp/clock.txt
leaf101# cat /tmp/clock.txt
14:06:19.226 EDT Thu Oct 25 2018
```

If you are unsure of what commands are available, you can leverage the **show cli list** command and **grep** for certain keywords. For example, suppose you want to see all available commands that start with **show ip**. You can find these commands by using **show cli list**, as demonstrated in Example 3-25.

Example 3-25   *Using show cli list in the VSH Shell to Find a List of Available Commands*

```
leaf101# show cli list | grep "show ip"
show ip interface <if> vrf <str>
show ip interface <if> vrf <str>
show ip interface <if> vrf all
show ip interface vrf <str>
show ip interface vrf <str>
show ip interface vrf all
...
```

To get back into the iBash CLI from VSH, you simply type **exit**.

VSH_LC CLI

Both the iBash and VSH shells can be used to check the software state of an ACI switch. However, to run hardware-level commands, you use the VSH_LC shell.

For nonmodular switches, you can enter the VSH_LC shell by typing **vsh_lc** into the iBash shell, as shown in Example 3-26.

Example 3-26   *Accessing the VSH_LC Shell from iBash*

```
leaf101# vsh_lc
vsh_lc
module-1#
```

For modular switches like spines, each line card and fabric module has its own shell. In order to access it, you need to issue the **attach module** *<X>* command from the VSH shell, as shown in Example 3-27.

Example 3-27   *Accessing the VSH_LC Shell of a Particular Module*

```
spine201# vsh
Cisco iNX-OS Debug Shell
This shell should only be used for internal commands and exists
for legacy reasons. User should use ibash infrastructure as this
will be deprecated.

spine201# attach module 1
Attaching to module 1 ...
To exit type 'exit', to abort type '$.'
module-1#
```

Just like VSH commands, VSH_LC commands can be run directly from iBash, as shown in Example 3-28.

Example 3-28   *Running VSH_LC Commands from iBash and Redirecting to a File*

```
leaf101# vsh_lc -c "show clock"
14:07:06.419 EDT Thu Oct 25 2018

leaf101# vsh_lc -c "show clock" > /tmp/clock.txt
leaf101# cat /tmp/clock.txt
14:07:14.092 EDT Thu Oct 25 2018
```

Just like in the VSH shell, you can use **show cli list** in the VSH_LC shell, as shown in Example 3-29.

Example 3-29   *Using show cli list in the VSH_LC Shell to Find a List of Available Commands*

```
module-1# show cli list | grep forwarding | grep trace
show system internal forwarding l2 multicast binlog traces
show forwarding trace clear module <int>
show forwarding trace clear
show forwarding trace module <int>
show forwarding trace
...
```

To get back into the iBash CLI from VSH_LC, you simply type **exit** from the base prompt. You can quickly get back to the base prompt by entering the command **end**.

Summary

For both the APIC and ACI fabric switches, there are a variety of command-line interfaces you can leverage to configure, monitor, and troubleshoot an ACI deployment. On an APIC, the NX-OS–style CLI can be used to configure the fabric, just as with the API or GUI, and the Bash shell allows you to access the Linux operating system of the APIC. For each switch in the ACI fabric, the iBash shell allows you to run read-only commands that leverage the API for the result. VSH can be used to access an NX-OS–style CLI directly, and VSH_LC allows you to run commands that poll the software and hardware that run on the line card(s) of the device. With the knowledge of all the CLI options available, many new doors open into the world of ACI. This chapter covers CLI usage of ACI; however, for overall application infrastructure provisioning, more sophisticated automation and orchestration techniques should be used to achieve application agility, as described in Chapter 8, "Automation and Orchestration."

Reference

Cisco, *APIC NX-OS Style Command-Line Interface Configuration Guide.*

Note   There are no Key Topics or Review Questions for this chapter.

Chapter 4

ACI Fabric Design Options

Monitoring and troubleshooting in ACI require you to have good knowledge of its architectural background. Without a clear understanding of different ways of plumbing ACI fabric and hardware components together, it is difficult to understand on what and how to proactively monitor the fabric to help expedite resolution during troubleshooting sessions. In this chapter, you will learn various design options offered by the Cisco Application Centric Infrastructure (ACI):

- Physical design
  - Single- versus multiple-fabric design
  - Multi-pod
  - Multi-site
  - Remote leaf
- Logical design
  - Kubernetes using Calico CNI
  - ERP SAP-HANA
  - vBrick digital media engine

Physical Design

ACI works in the Clos architecture, also referred to as a fully meshed fabric network, where every leaf is physically connected to every spine for traffic forwarding through nonblocking links. This architecture, shown in Figure 4-1, yields excellent throughput and convergence.

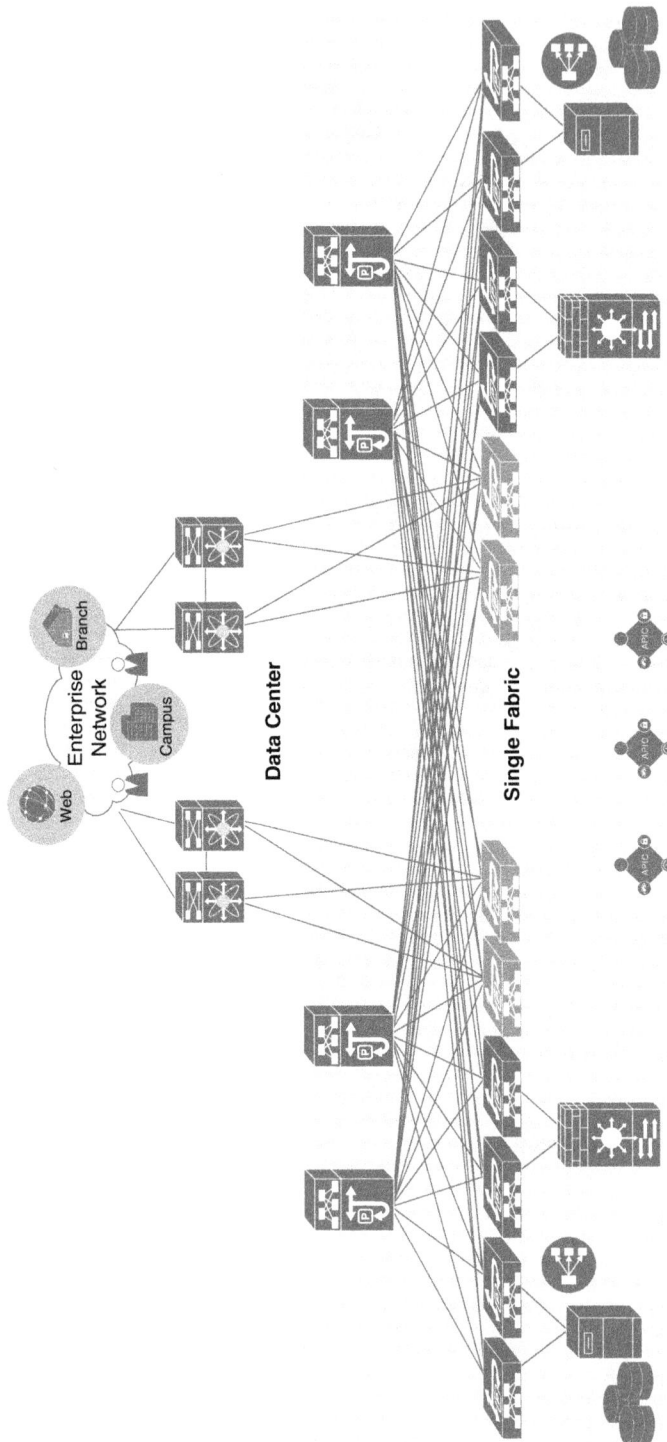

Figure 4-1 *Fully Meshed ACI Fabric*

This kind of architectural design is good for a single data center or site. However, companies and enterprises often have two or more separate data centers or sites to provide overall application resiliency. This separation is important for business continuance and disaster avoidance, which are key to the success of every organization. In multiple-data center or multi-site scenarios, full-mesh connectivity may not be possible or may not be cost-effective. Multiple sites, buildings, or rooms can span distances that are not serviceable by enough fiber connections, or it may be too costly to connect each leaf switch to each spine switch across the sites. Due to various network environment variances, customers face challenges in how to extend a fully meshed ACI fabric to multiple locations and still keep the same policies throughout.

Cisco has provided various design options in ACI to stretch a single fabric between multiple data centers or have multiple fabrics in each of two or more data center locations.

As highlighted above and illustrated in Figure 4-2, there are two separate families of physical design solutions in ACI:

- Single-fabric design
- Multiple-fabric design

Single- Versus Multiple-Fabric Design

With *single-fabric* design, Cisco provides the early offering of ACI stretched fabric, using a dedicated leaf at each site, followed by its predecessor design option, multi-pod. Both design models leverage a single APIC cluster representing the single point of management and policy definition for the entire network plugged into a single fabric.

Single-fabric design options fulfill the requirements for interconnecting data centers deployed in active/active fashion, offering the freedom of deploying various application tiers within a single point of delivery (pod) or across separate pods. The entire network runs as a single large fabric from an operational perspective. ACI multi-pod design introduces extra enhancements to isolate as much as possible the failure domains between pods, contributing to increased overall design resiliency. At the same time, the change management plane is common for all the pods since a configuration or policy definition applied to any of the APIC nodes gets propagated to all the pods managed by the single APIC cluster. This behavior greatly simplifies the operational aspects of the solution and provides a common policy model across the entire fabric.

Multiple-fabric design is categorized by an independent APIC cluster managing each interconnected ACI fabric separately. This design provides complete resiliency to application infrastructure hosted on ACI fabrics as configuration and policy definitions can be managed independently. The typical use case for this type of solution is disaster recovery, where a secondary data center site is deployed in order to recover applications after a major failure of a primary site(s) where the applications were initially hosted.

One possible multiple-fabric design option is dual-fabric design (see Figure 4-3). This deployment model leverages more traditional Layer 2 and Layer 3 Data Center Interconnect (DCI) technology options to connect disjoint ACI fabrics.

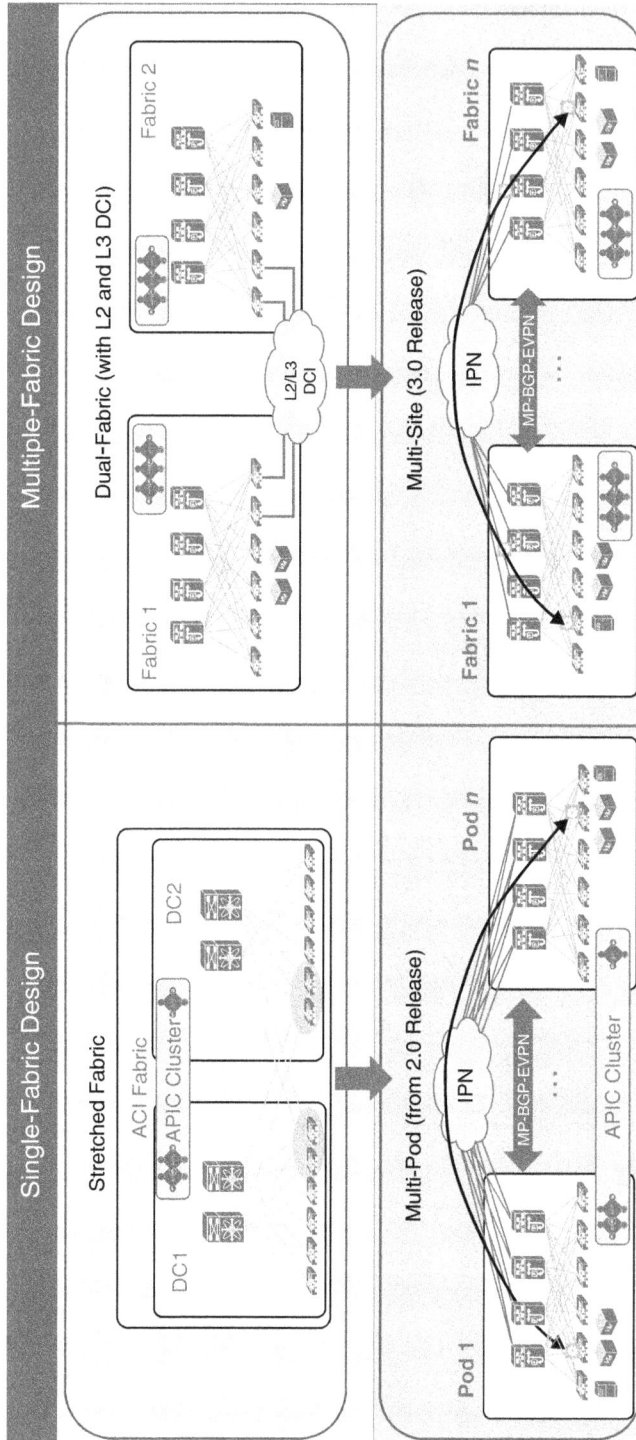

Figure 4-2   *ACI Fabric Design Solution*

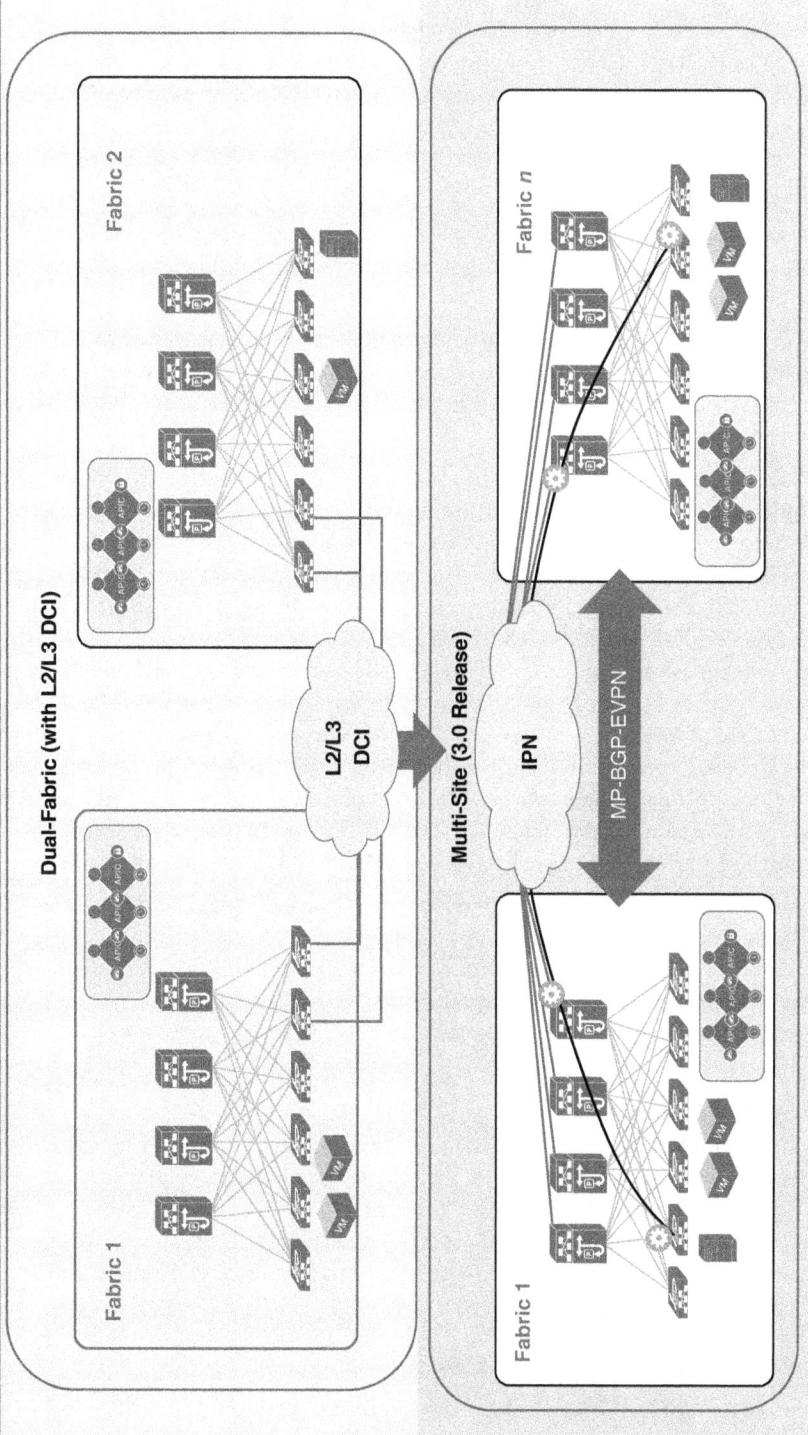

Figure 4-3 *Multiple-Fabric Design Solution*

However, a dual-fabric design represents a disjointed domain from a policy perspective, as there is a requirement to reclassify endpoint traffic (Layer 2 or Layer 3) at the entry point of each ACI fabric. This move ensures that the same configuration is created in each APIC domain to provide a consistent end-to-end policy-based application construct. In order to overcome some of the challenges of the dual-fabric design, in ACI Release 3.0, Cisco delivered another architecture representing the evolution of the dual-fabric design option, called multi-site.

Next, you will see some of the details of each of these design options and identify a few pros and cons that you can weigh in making the right decision based on your business requirements.

For stretching a single ACI fabric between multiple data centers, Cisco's initial design included a dedicated leaf called a *transit leaf* (TL) at each site to provide a path between the sites. For redundancy, it is recommended to use a pair of leafs at each site, as shown in Figure 4-4.

This design offers simplicity in the sense that you do not need to configure anything on the TLs after initially registering them into the ACI fabric. The only requirement of the ACI fabric is to have physical connectivity through uplink ports to all the spines, providing a path for traffic flow between the two locations. The stretched fabric using TLs is a single ACI fabric design. The data centers or sites are one *administration domain* (AD) and one *availability zone* (AZ). With an AD, administrators can manage the data centers or sites as one entity; configuration changes made on any APIC controller node are applied to devices across the data centers or sites. An AZ, on the other hand, is an isolated area of resources, such as network, compute, and storage, connected through high-speed links to provide resiliency within a data center into multiple data halls; an AZ can span multiple data centers within a metropolitan area. The stretched ACI fabric preserves live virtual machine (VM) migration capability across the data centers or sites. Currently, stretched fabric designs have been validated with three data centers or sites.

The site-to-site connectivity options for ACI stretched fabric using TLs includes dark fiber, dense wavelength-division multiplexing (DWDM), and Ethernet over MPLS (EoMPLS) pseudowire. The beauty of these technologies is that they are transparent to the underlying protocols. It is important that you understand these inter-site connectivity technologies, which are explained next.

Dark Fiber

Fiber-optic cables are used to transmit data at high speeds using light signals. Optical cable that is available to send light signals but is not yet used (that is, unlit) is called *dark fiber*. Large enterprises use dark fiber to connect their data center facilities that are closely located within a metropolitan area. Short-range transceivers can be used, and ACI transit leafs can be connected to spines using the following supported long-reach QSFP transceivers:

- Cisco QSFP-40G-LR4 (10 km supported distance)
- Cisco QSFP-40GE-LR4 (10 km supported distance)
- Cisco QSFP-40G-LR4L (2 km supported distance)
- Cisco QSFP-40G-ER4 (40 km supported distance)

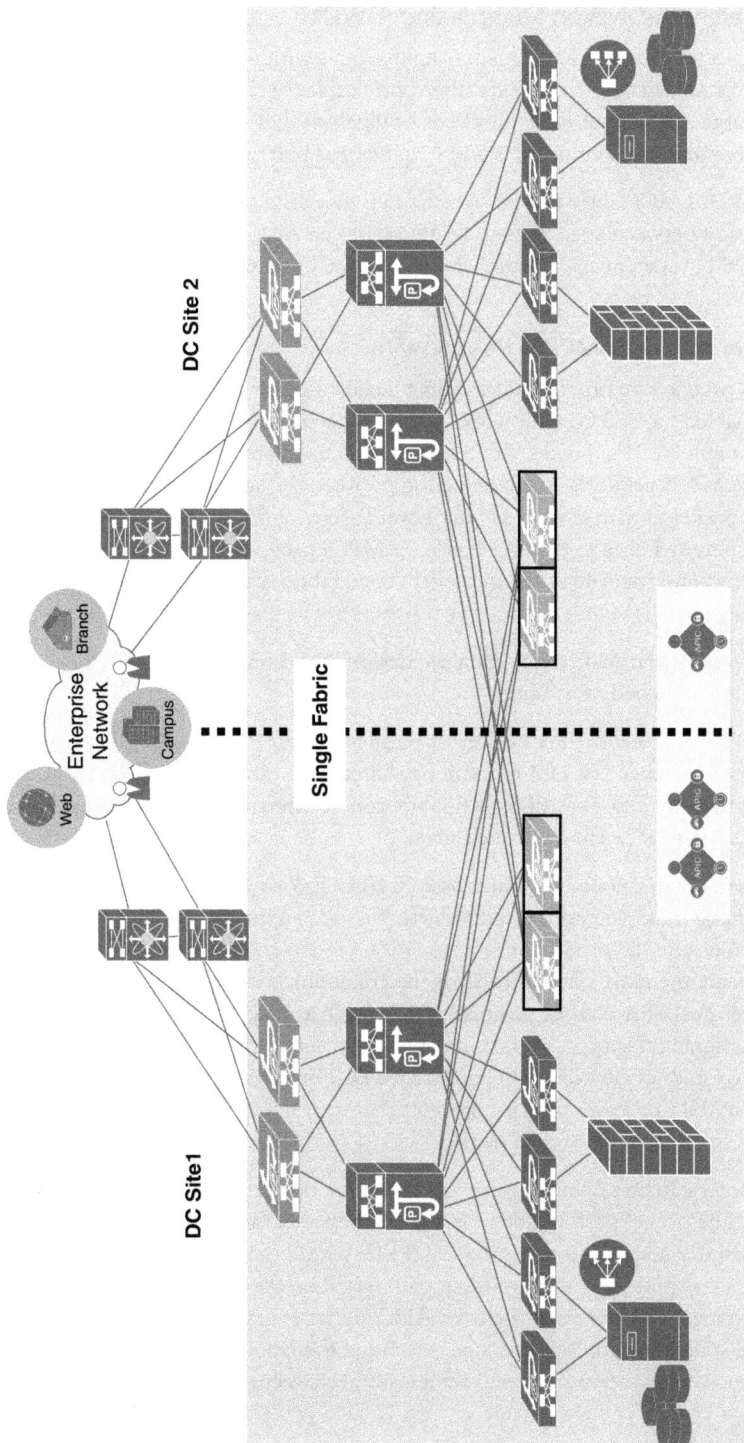

Figure 4-4   *Partially Meshed Stretched ACI Fabric*

Dense Wavelength-Division Multiplexing (DWDM)

DWDM is a technology that transmits light signals with different wavelengths, called *channels* or *lambdas*, over a single fiber-optic cable. Because it has the capability to transfer large amounts of data (hundreds of gigabytes), it is very popular among telecommunications and cable companies and is an integral part of today's modern DCI option.

Using DWDM, ACI fabric can be stretched up to a distance of 800 km with up to 10 msec latency between sites. Figure 4-5 illustrates an ACI leaf or spine switch connected to a DWDM system using short-reach (or long-reach) transceivers.

Ethernet over MPLS (EoMPLS) Pseudowire

EoMPLS pseudowire provides a tunneling mechanism for Ethernet traffic through an MPLS-enabled Layer 3 core network. EoMPLS pseudowire encapsulates Ethernet protocol data units (PDUs) inside MPLS packets and uses label switching to forward them across the MPLS network. The connection between the sites must support some sort of link-level packet exchange such as Link Level Discovery Protocol (LLDP) between the leaf and spine switches in the ACI fabric. EoMPLS pseudowire can provide connectivity between leaf and spine switches in the stretched fabric when a dedicated 40/100 Gbps long-distance DWDM link between two sites is not available.

Figure 4-6 shows an ACI stretched fabric design with EoMPLS pseudowire connectivity between the stretched fabric sites.

An EoMPLS pseudowire link between two sites can be 10 Gbps, 40 Gbps, or 100 Gbps, and the long-distance DWDM link can be shared with other types of services as well. As with DWDM, with EoMPLS, ACI fabric can be stretched up to a distance of 800 km with up to 10 msec latency between sites.

When there is a low-speed link such as a 10 Gbps link or when there is a link that is shared among multiple types of data traffic flows, an appropriate QoS policy must be enabled to ensure the protection of critical ACI fabric control traffic. In an ACI stretched fabric design, the most critical traffic is the communication between the APIC controllers in a cluster. Also, the control protocol traffic (such as IS-IS or MP-BGP) needs to be protected. Assigning this type of traffic to a priority queue ensures that it is not impacted when congestion occurs on the long-distance DCI links. Assigning other types of traffic (such as SPAN) to a lower priority prevents that traffic from jamming bandwidth consumption from production data traffic.

A single inter-site link failure has no impact on the operation of the ACI fabric, but it does degrade overall performance throughput between the two sites. The Intermediate System-to-Intermediate System Protocol (IS-IS) within the ACI fabric reacts to the link failure and computes a new forwarding path based on the topology change. As long as there is connectivity between sites, the APIC cluster is maintained, and the controller nodes are synchronized. Best practice is to bring the failed link(s) back up to avoid system performance degradation or to prevent a split fabric scenario from developing.

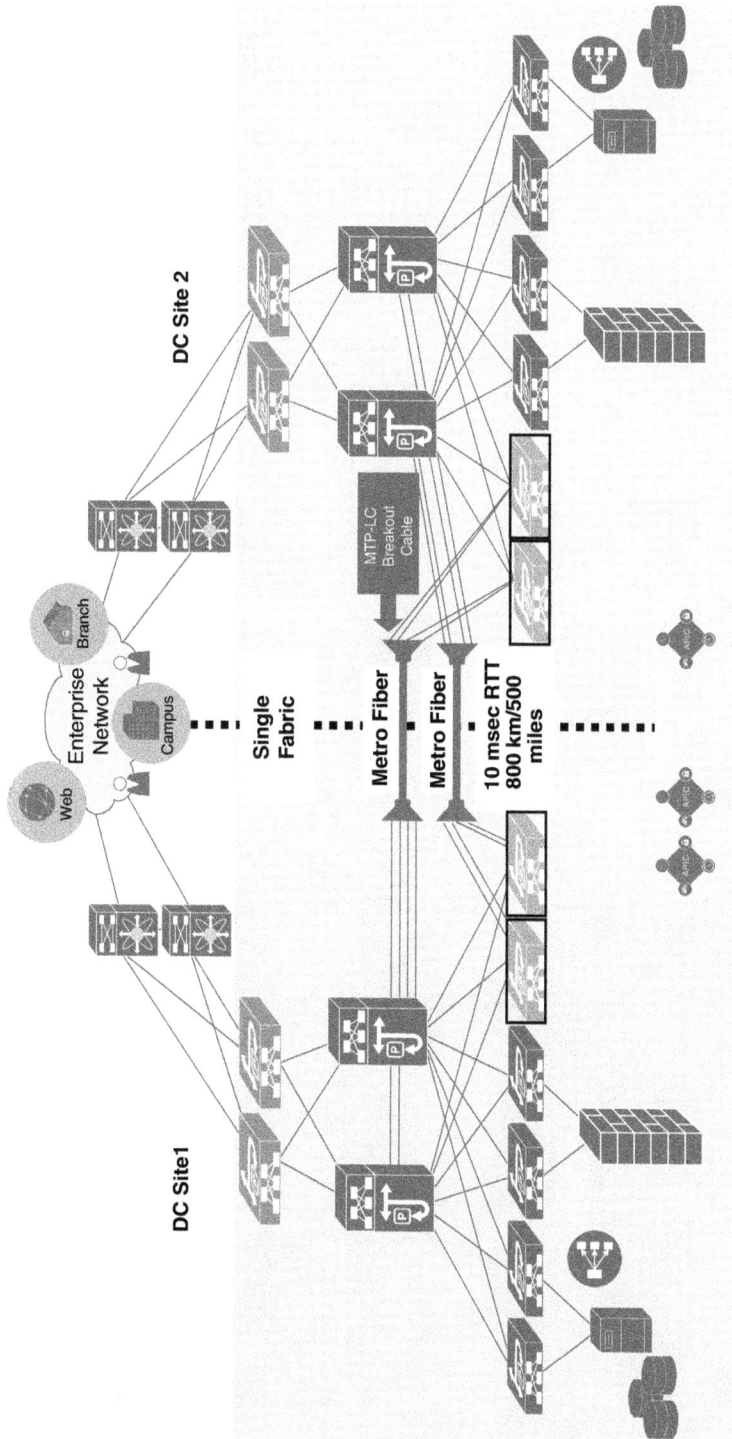

Figure 4-5   *DWDM Connectivity Between Sites in a Single ACI Fabric*

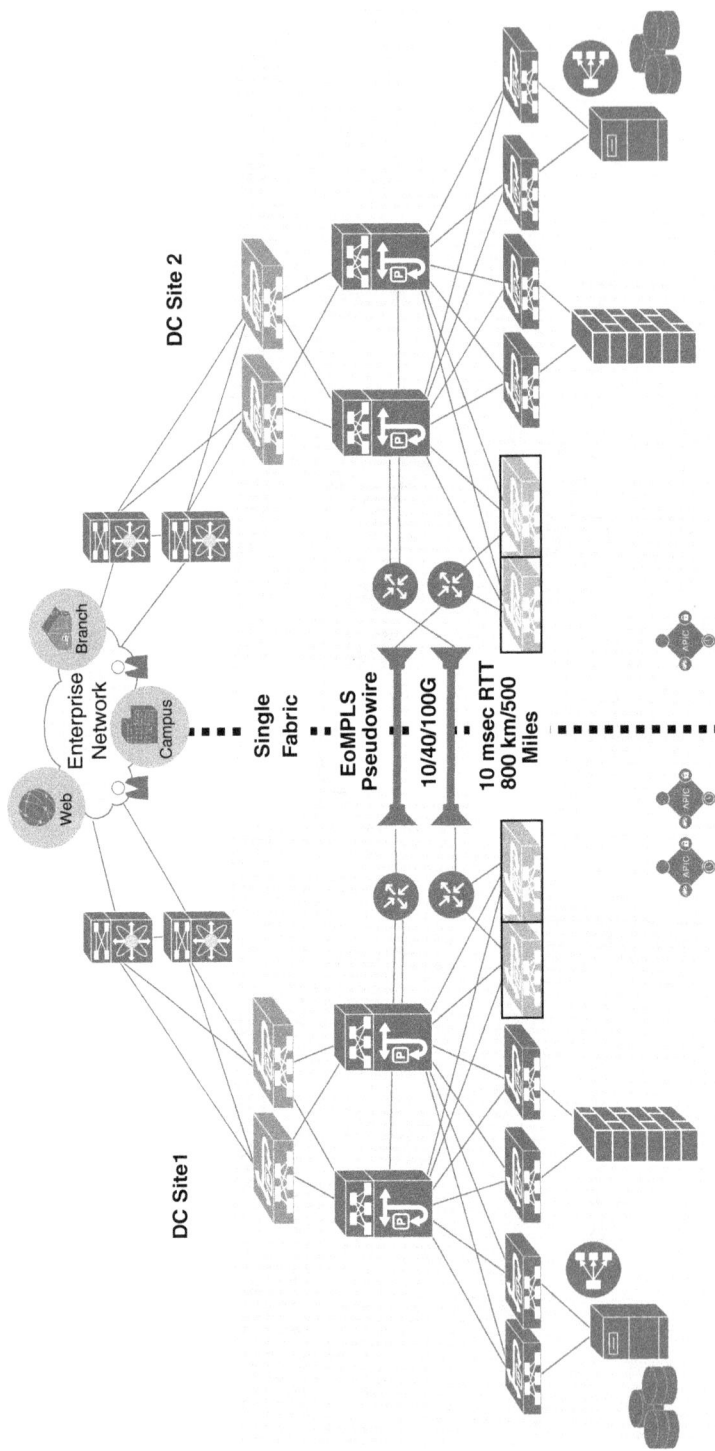

Figure 4-6   *EoMPLS Pseudowire Connectivity Between Sites in a Single ACI Fabric*

When all connections between sites are lost, the single fabric splits into two fabrics. This scenario is referred to as *split-brain*. In Figure 4-7, the APIC controller in Site 2 is no longer able to communicate with the rest of the cluster.

In this situation, the split fabrics continue to operate independently. Traffic forwarding is not affected within the site, but it may be impacted between the sites in some cases. The two fabrics can learn the new endpoints through the data plane. At the site containing the VMM controller, endpoints are learned by the control plane as well. Upon learning new endpoints, leaf switches update the spine proxy via the Council of Oracle Protocol (COOP).

As mentioned in Chapter 1, "Fundamental Functions and Components of ACI," COOP provides a mapping database to keep track of all the endpoints throughout the fabric. This information is sent from leaf to spine (and endpoints are always attached to leafs) using ZeroMQ. The spines then share that information among themselves to keep consistent information.

After the connections between sites are restored, the spine proxy databases from the two sites merge, and all spine switches have complete and identical proxy mapping databases.

In terms of management plane, the split fabric site with two APIC controller nodes (DC Site 1 in Figure 4-7) has a cluster quorum (two working nodes out of a cluster of three) and hence can execute policy read and write operations to the fabric. An administrator can log in to either APIC controller node in DC Site 1 and make policy changes. After the link between the two sites recovers, the APIC cluster synchronizes configuration changes across the stretched fabric, pushing configuration changes to all the switches throughout the fabric.

When the connection between two sites is lost, the site with one APIC controller (Site 2 in Figure 4-7) is in the *minority state*. When a controller is in the minority state, it cannot be the leader for any shards. This limits the controller in DC Site 2 to read-only operations; administrators cannot make any configuration changes through the controller in DC Site 2. However, the Site 2 fabric still responds to network events such as workload migration, link failure, node failure, and switch reload. When a leaf switch learns a new endpoint, it not only updates the spine proxy via COOP but also sends notifications to the controller so that an administrator can view the up-to-date endpoint information from the single controller in DC Site 2. Updating endpoint information on the controller is a write operation. While the links between the two sites are lost, leaf switches in DC Site 2 try to report the newly learned endpoints to the shard leader (which resides in DC Site 1 and is not reachable). When the links between the two sites are restored, the learned endpoints are reported to the controller successfully. Table 4-1 and Table 4-2 show best practices for deploying APIC controllers at multiple sites (scalable up to three) in a stretched fabric design that helps prevent ACI fabric from being in the minority state during single-site failure scenarios. More details on an APIC cluster sizing scheme and the behavior it exhibits during failures are provided in the next section.

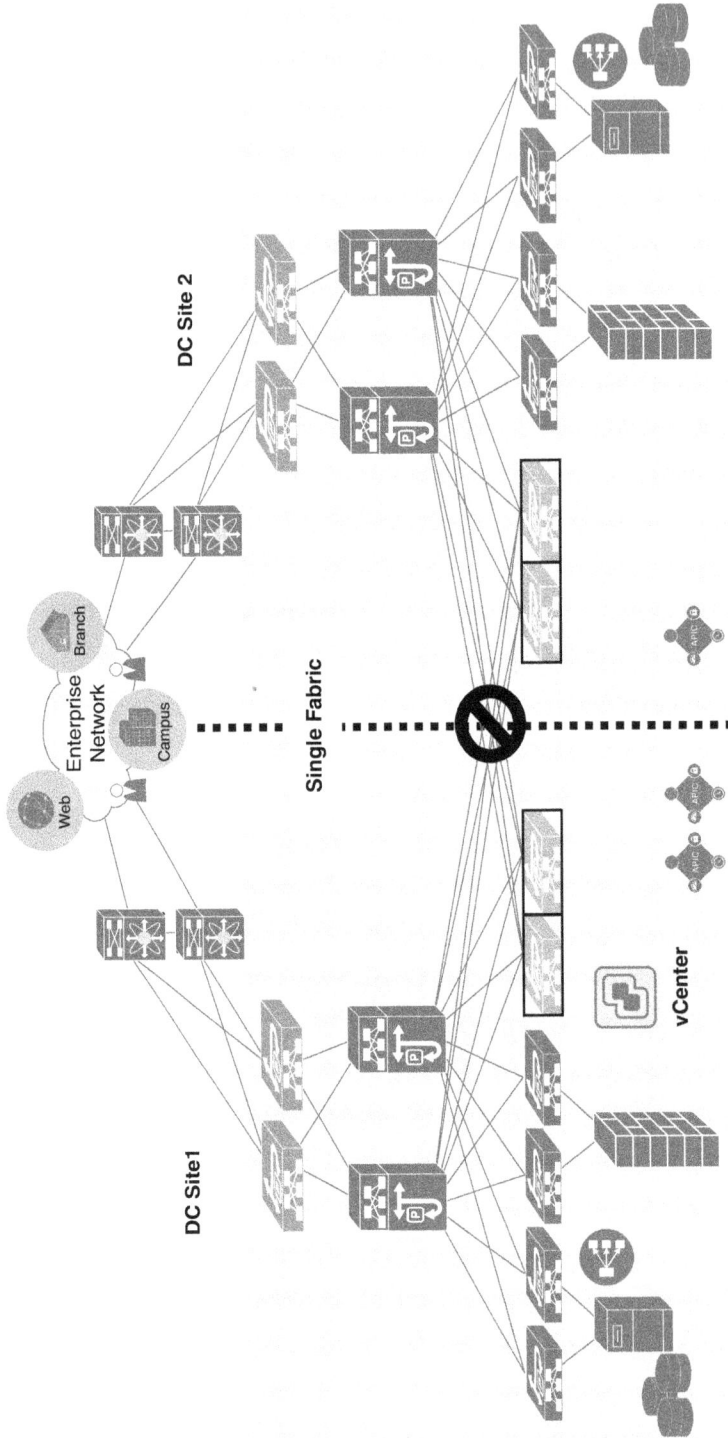

Figure 4-7   *Split Fabric Due to Total Link Failure Between Sites*

Note Stretched fabric is a single-pod fabric that allows up to 200 leafs with up to 5 APIC controllers per cluster.

Table 4-1 *APIC Deployment in Two-Site Stretch Fabric*

APIC Cluster Size	DC Site 1	DC Site 2
APIC cluster (3)	2	1 + 1 (standby)
APIC cluster (5)	3 + 1 (standby)	2 + 1 (standby) + 1 (spare). Contact Cisco for special handling of data restoration.

Table 4-2 *APIC Deployment in Three-Site Stretch Fabric*

APIC Cluster Size	DC Site 1	DC Site 2	DC Site 3
APIC cluster (3)	1	1	1
APIC cluster (5)	2	2	1 + 1 (standby)

Note Since ACI Release 4.0(1), it has been possible to deploy a four-node APIC cluster to support up to 200 leaf nodes per pod. This prevents data loss in certain cases of five-APIC-cluster-node deployments, as explained in detail in the following section. Please see the Cisco website for more details on four-APIC-cluster-node deployments in Release 4.0(1) as this book only covers scenarios up to ACI Release 3.2.x.

In short, ACI fabric design using transit leafs is the simplest way of stretching multiple data centers (with a three-site recommended limit) without any extra configuration required. This is a single-pod design where the single control plane and data plane is extended between data centers or sites.

The second design option for a single ACI fabric stretched between multiple data centers or sites is called *multi-pod*. This option is discussed in the following section.

Multi-Pod

Key Topic

A naturally evolved stretched fabric design using transit leafs is ACI multi-pod design. This architecture further enhances multilocation fabric design by isolating each site as much as possible. ACI multi-pod creates separate failure domains between pods, contributing to increased overall application resiliency during failures. It is achieved by running separate instances of fabric control planes (IS-IS, COOP, MP-BGP) across pods.

Multi-pod design requires you to have an IP network for stretching a single ACI fabric between multiple data centers or sites. An ACI multi-pod-like stretched fabric design also allows you to interconnect and centrally manage separate ACI networks with a single APIC cluster, as shown in Figure 4-8.

As discussed in the previous section, ACI multi-pod is part of the single APIC cluster/ single domain family of design solutions, with a single stretched APIC cluster deployed to manage all the different ACI networks that are interconnected with each other. Those separate ACI networks are called pods, and each of them looks like a regular two-tier spine/leaf topology. To increase the resiliency of the solution, the various APIC controller nodes that make up the cluster can be deployed across different pods.

The deployment of a single APIC cluster simplifies the management and operational aspects of the solution because all the interconnected pods essentially function as a single ACI fabric. The logical construct of ACI—the tenant's configuration policies, such as application profiles, endpoint groups (EPGs), virtual routing and forwarding (VRF) instances, and bridge domains—is made available across all the pods, providing a high degree of freedom for connecting endpoints to the fabric. For example, different work-loads that are part of the same functional group (EPG), such as app servers, web servers, or DB servers, can all be connected to or moved across different pods without concern for provisioning configuration or policy in the new location. At the same time, seamless Layer 2 and Layer 3 connectivity services can be provided between endpoints independently from the physical location where they are connected and without requiring any specific functionality from the network interconnecting these various pods.

Multi-pod not only offers ease of managing and operating different pods as a single distributed fabric but also provides the capability of increasing failure domain isolation across pods through separation of the fabric control plane protocols. As highlighted in Figure 4-8, different instances of IS-IS, COOP, and MP-BGP protocols run inside each pod so that faults and issues with any of those protocols are contained within the single pod and not spread across the entire ACI fabric. This is a property that clearly differentiates multi-pod from the stretched fabric using transit leaf approach and makes it the recommended Cisco single-fabric design option.

From a physical perspective, the different pods are interconnected by leveraging an inter-pod network (IPN). Each pod connects to the IPN through the spine nodes; the IPN can be as simple as a single Layer 3 device or can be built with a larger Layer 3 network infrastructure provided by carrier services or through private links. In any case, the IPN is simply a basic Layer 3 connectivity service that allows for the establishment of spine-to-spine and leaf-to-leaf VXLAN tunnels across pods. The use of the VXLAN overlay technology in the data plane provides seamless Layer 2 and Layer 3 connectivity between endpoints, independent of the physical location (pod) where they are connected.

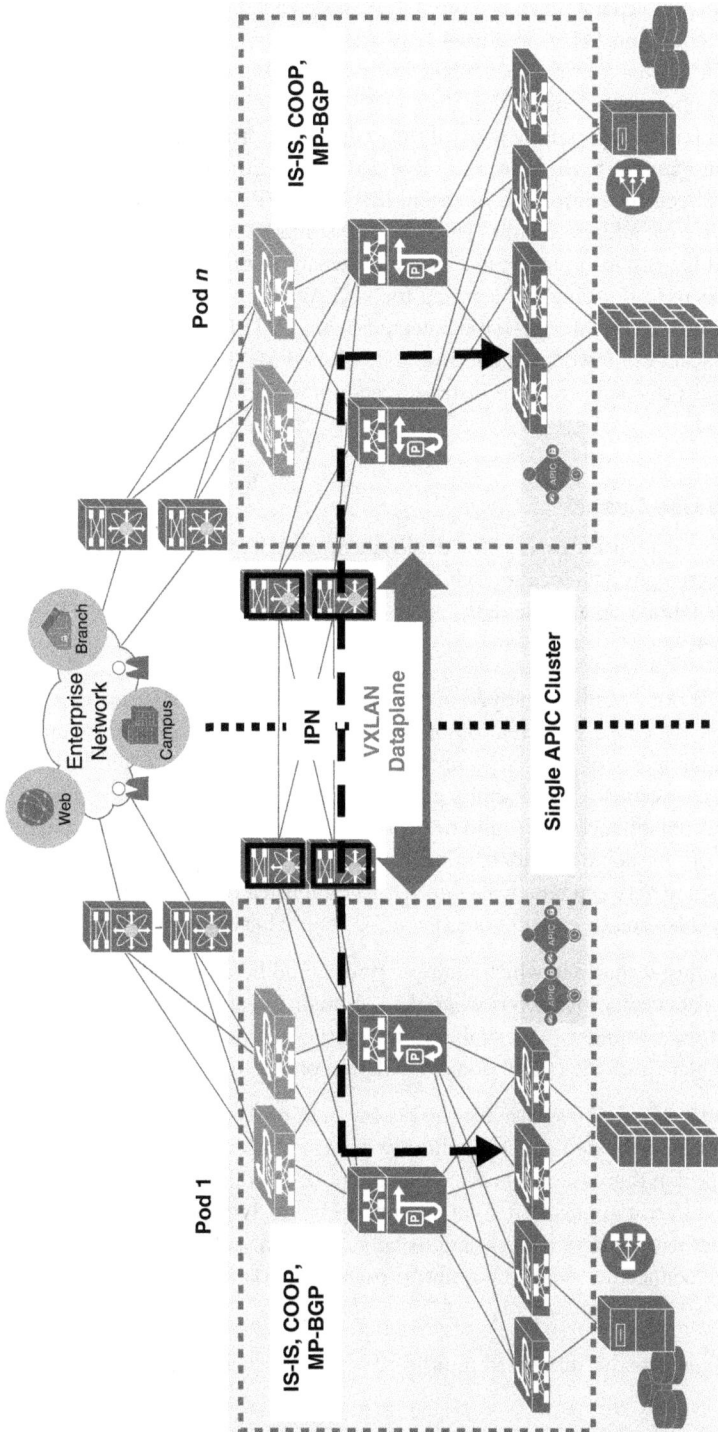

Figure 4-8 *ACI Multi-pod Solution*

Finally, running a separate instance of COOP inside each pod implies that information about local endpoints (MAC and IPv4/IPv6 addresses and their locations) is stored only in the COOP database of the local spine nodes. Since ACI multi-pod functions as a single fabric, it is important to ensure that the COOP database implemented in the spine nodes across pods has a consistent view of all the endpoint information throughout the fabric. As shown in Figure 4-8, Multiprotocol BGP (MP-BGP) Ethernet Virtual Private Network (EVPN) has been chosen for this function. MP-BGP EVPN is flexible and scalable, and it supports different address families (such as EVPN and VPNv4), allowing the exchange of Layer 2 and Layer 3 information in a true multitenant fashion. In the past, VXLAN overlay networks used flooding and learning for VXLAN Tunnel Endpoint (VTEP) discovery and endpoint location information connected behind VTEPs. However, to build more robust and scalable networks, the industry developed MP-BGP EVPN under RFC 7342, and then multi-pod adopted it to distribute endpoint reachability information between multiple pods.

ACI Multi-Pod Use Cases

There are two main use cases for the deployment of ACI multi-pod, and their substantial difference is the physical location where the multiple pods are deployed, depending on whether the fabric is in a single data center or expanded between multiple data centers (see Figure 4-9):

- Multiple pods can be deployed in the same physical data center location between multiple data halls. The creation of multiple pods could be driven, for example, by the requirements of a specific cabling layout within the data center. Let's say you have a data center (or availability zone) with multiple data halls providing separate power, cooling, rack space, and network/virtualization resources for your application workload. In such conditions, it is physically not possible to connect every leaf to every spine between data halls in order to establish a fully meshed ACI fabric. Multi-pod enables you to extend your single ACI fabric between multiple data halls.

  - Another scenario in which multiple pods could be deployed in the same physical data center location is when the requirement is to create a very large fabric. In that case, it might be desirable to divide the large fabric into smaller pods to get the benefit of the failure domain isolation provided by the multi-pod approach.

- The most common use case for the deployment of ACI multi-pod is to interconnect different pods hosted at geographically dispersed data centers. The deployment of multi-pod in this case meets the requirement of building active/active data centers, where different application components can be freely deployed across pods. The different data center networks are usually deployed within a metropolitan area and are interconnected leveraging point-to-point links (dark fiber connections or DWDM circuits).

Figure 4-10 depicts the supported multi-pod topologies based on these use cases.

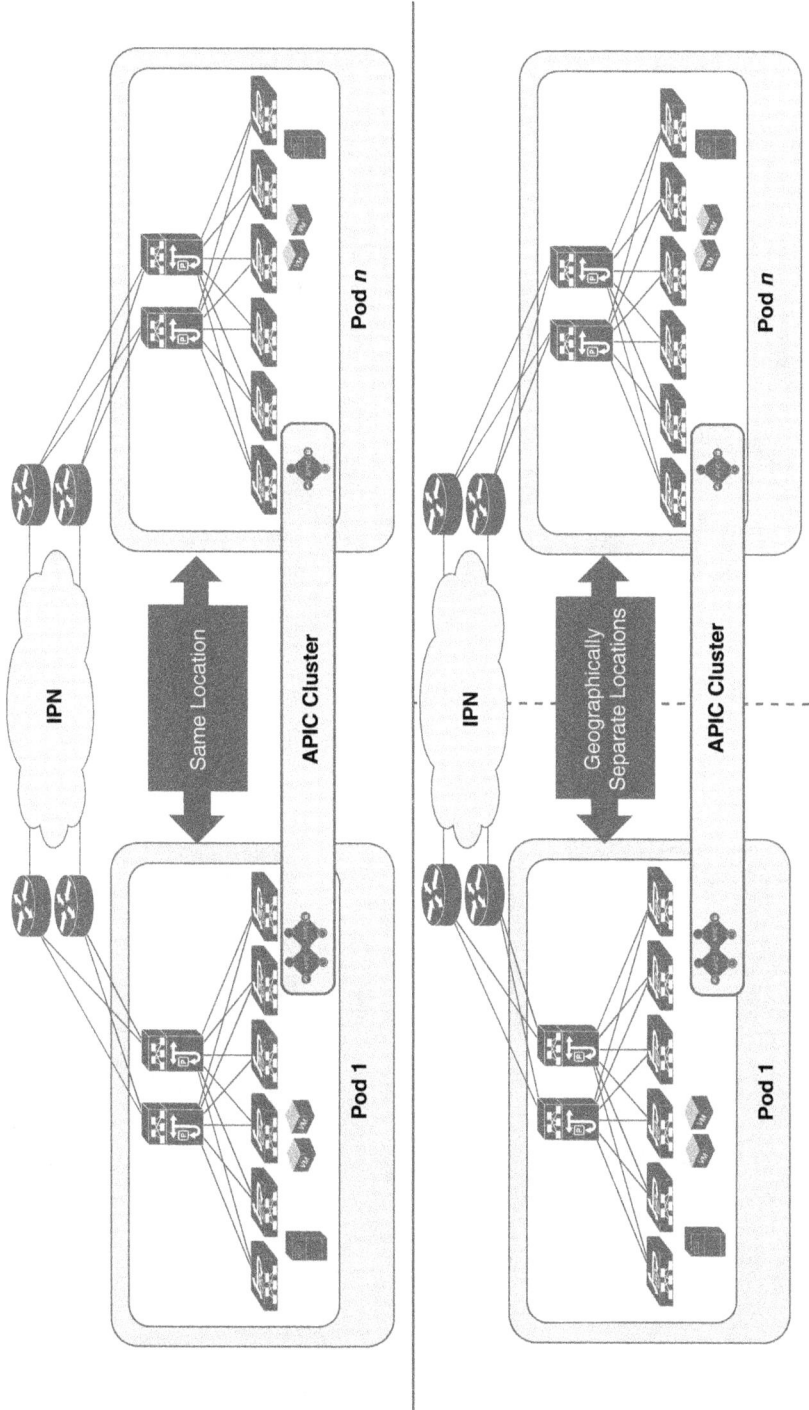

Figure 4-9 *Multi-pod Topology*

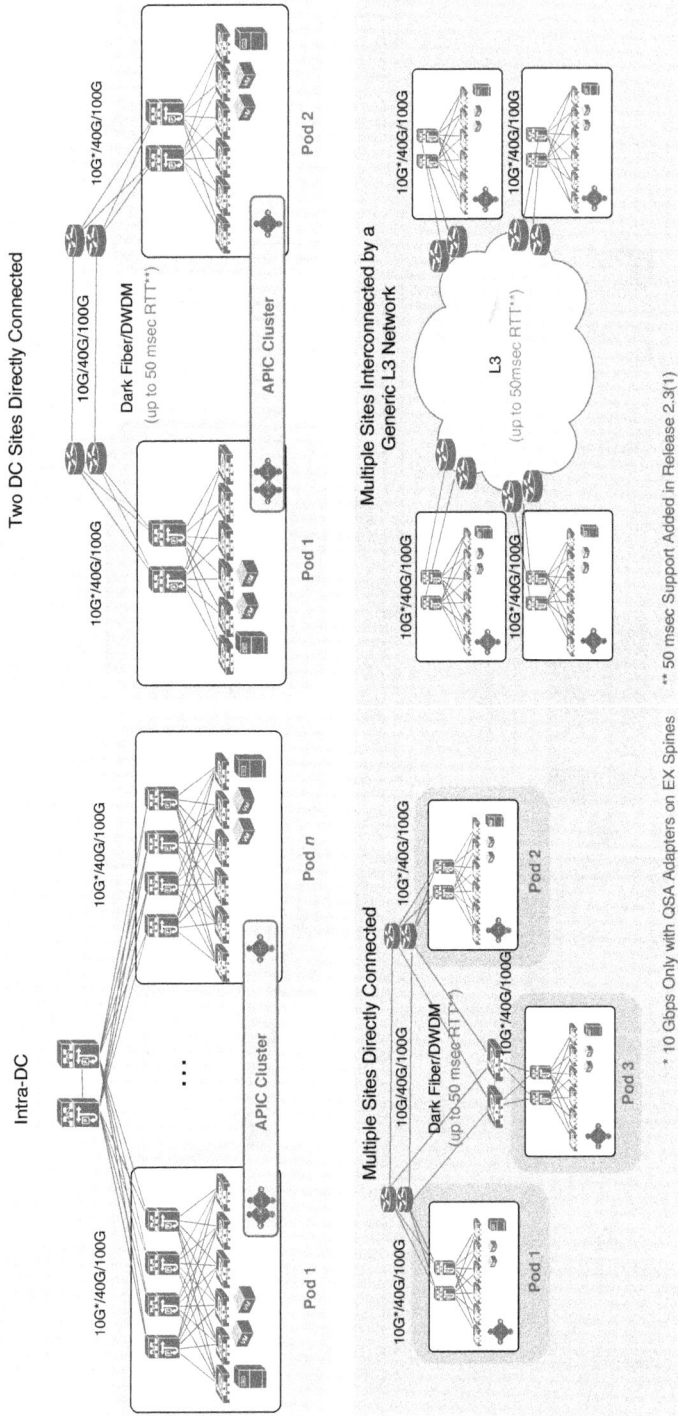

Figure 4-10   *Multi-pod Supported Topologies*

In the top-left corner of Figure 4-10, because the pods are locally deployed (in the same data center location), a pair of centralized IPN devices can be used to interconnect the different pods. Those IPN devices must potentially support a large number of 40/100 Gbps interfaces, so a couple of modular switches (non-ACI) could be chosen for that role.

Starting with ACI Release 2.3, the maximum latency supported between pods is 50 msec RTT, which roughly translates to a geographic distance of up to 4200 km. Also, an IPN is often represented by point-to-point links (dark fiber or DWDM circuits); in specific cases, a generic Layer 3 infrastructure (for example, an MPLS network) can also be leveraged as an IPN if it satisfies the Cisco-provided requirements.

ACI Multi-Pod Scalability

Before looking in detail at the various components of an ACI multi-pod solution, it is important to reiterate that this design option addresses the challenges faced in a single fabric with respect to cable management and location. In addition, it enforces some scalability limits since all the deployed nodes must be managed by a single APIC controller cluster.

The list that follows describes the scalability figures for ACI multi-pod, based on what was supported in ACI Release 3.0:

- Maximum number of pods: 12

Note Support for 12 pods is available from ACI Release 3.0 when deploying a 7-node APIC cluster.

- Maximum number of leaf nodes across all pods:
  - 400 with a 7-node APIC cluster (from ACI Release 3.0)
  - 300 with a 5-node APIC cluster
  - 200 with a 4-node APIC cluster (from ACI Release 4.0)
  - 80 with a 3-node APIC cluster
- Maximum number of leaf nodes per single pod: 200
- Maximum number of spine nodes per single pod: 6

Note These are not configuration limits but rather Cisco verified performance scalability limits. It is recommended to refer to the latest ACI software release notes for updated scalability figures and also for information on other scalability parameters that are not listed here.

Inter-Pod Connectivity Deployment Considerations

An IPN is an IP network that connects different ACI pods and allows communication between pods for east–west traffic flows. In this function, the IPN basically represents an extension of the ACI fabric underlay infrastructure.

In order to perform those connectivity functions, the IPN must support a few specific functionalities, such as Multicast PIM Bidirectional (Bidir), DHCP Relay, OSPF, maximum transmission unit (MTU), Dot1q, and QoS, as detailed in the sections that follow.

Multicast Support

Between multiple pods, apart from unicast communication, east–west traffic is also composed of Layer 2 multi-destination flows belonging to bridge domains that are extended across pods. This type of traffic is usually referred to as BUM (broadcast, unknown unicast, and multicast), and it is exchanged by leveraging VXLAN data plane encapsulation between leaf nodes.

Inside a pod, BUM traffic is encapsulated into a VXLAN multicast frame and is forwarded to all leaf nodes that are part of the same EPG/BD. A unique multicast group is associated with each BD when it is configured. This multicast group is assigned from the pool of Group IP outer (GIPo) addresses that you define during the initial setup of an APIC. Once the frame arrives at the leaf node, it is forwarded to connected devices that are part of the EPG/BD or dropped, depending on the type of the BUM frame. This is depicted in Figure 4-11.

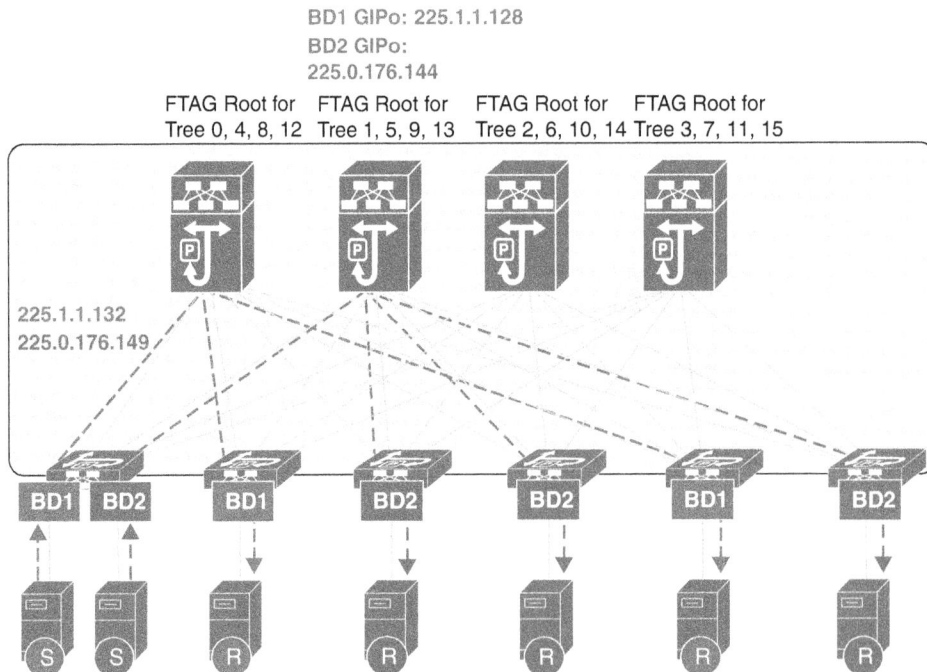

Figure 4-11 *Multi-pod Multicast*

In a case where the same EPG/BD is stretched between multiple pods, the same multi-cast group associated with the bridge domain is extended across the IPN using Platform Independent Multicast Bidirectional (PIM Bidir). IPN devices must support PIM Bidir for a range of at least /15. This is the reason Nexus 9000 Generation 1 hardware cannot function as IPN devices as it only supports a maximum PIM Bidir range of /24.

Why do you need to run PIM Bidir in an IPN? The following points explain the reasons for configuring PIM Bidir:

- Because BUM traffic can be originated by all the leaf nodes deployed across pods that are associated with EPG/BD, the use of a different PIM mode such as Any-Source Multicast (ASM) would result in the creation of multiple individual (S, G) entries on the IPN devices that may exceed the specific platform capabilities. Using PIM Bidir, a single (*, G) entry is created for a given BD, independent of the overall number of leaf nodes. This ensures that the scale of the multicast routing table on the IPN does not increase exponentially as the ACI fabric grows.

- The (*, G) entries are created in the IPN as soon as a BD is activated and extended in the ACI multi-pod fabric, independently from forwarding BUM traffic across pods for that given BD. This implies that when the need for BUM traffic arises, the network will be ready to perform those duties, avoiding longer convergence time for the application. If PIM ASM is used instead, it would have required data-driven multicast state creation.

- Cisco recommends using PIM Bidir in an IPN based on its regression testing and field experiences.

One important thing you need to consider when designing PIM Bidir in an IPN is the deployment of the rendezvous point (RP). Unlike PIM Sparse mode, where RP works in the control plane, building the shortest path tree, in a PIM Bidir setup, the RP runs in the data plane, where all data traffic flows through the rendezvous point. Therefore, it is important to have proper redundancy and placement of the RP in an IPN. A possible design choice to balance the workload across different RPs could be achieved by splitting the default multicast address pool range into multiple subranges and configuring RP on each IPN device, as shown in Figure 4-12.

However, when deploying PIM Bidir using this design logic, at any given time, it is only possible to have an active RP on a single IPN router for a given multicast group range; for example, IPN 1 is the only active RP handling the 225.0.0.0/17 multicast range shown in Figure 4-12. To avoid this issue, you can use a more efficient RP redundancy method for PIM Bidir called *Phantom RP*. With Phantom RP, a single rendezvous point handles all the multicast flows, and in the event of a failure, another RP takes over. This methodology is achieved by configuring different subnet masks on the loopback interface addresses for each IPN router, which allows the use of the longest-prefix-match logic in the routing protocol, as shown in Example 4-1.

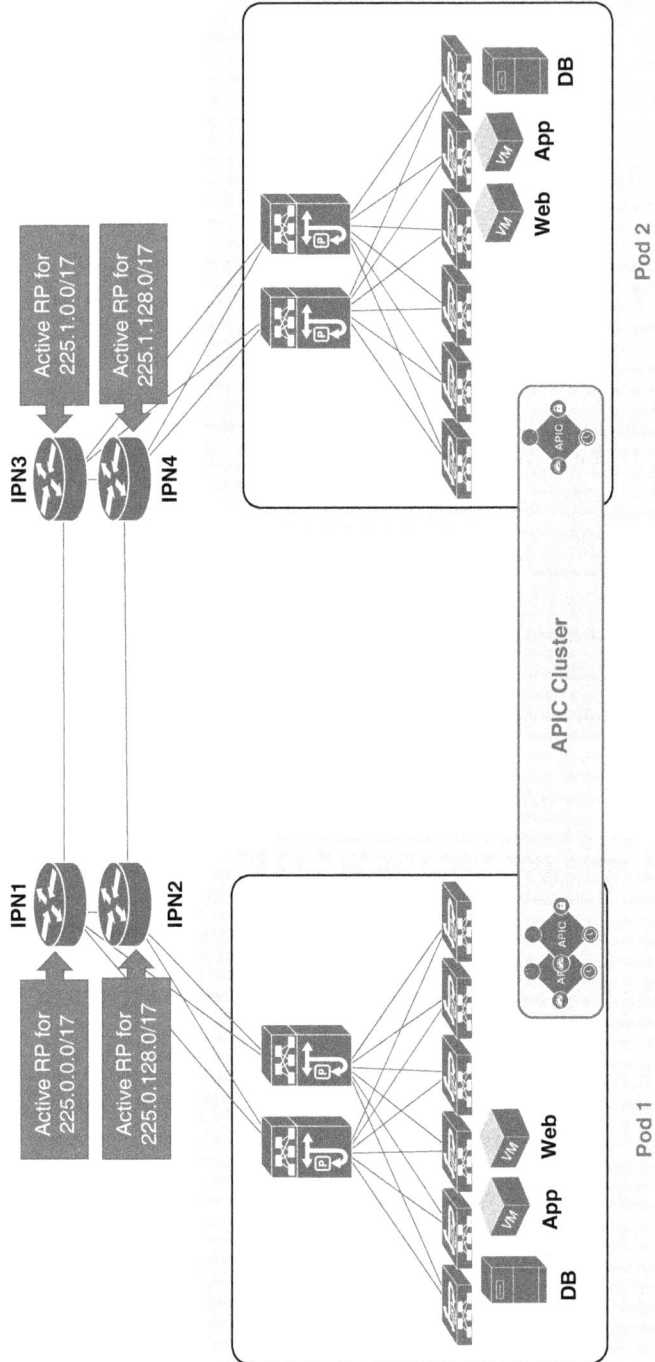

Figure 4-12 *Deployment with Multiple Active RPs*

Example 4-1 *Configuring Phantom RP*

IPN 1, Pod 1	IPN 3, Pod 2
| ```
interface loopback1
  description PIM Bidir Phantom RP
  vrf member IPN-VRF
  ip address 100.100.100.1/30
  ip ospf network point-to-point
  ip router ospf IPN area 0.0.0.0
  ip pim sparse-mode

vrf context IPN-VRF
  ip pim rp-address 100.100.100.2
group-list 225.0.0.0/8 bidir
  ip pim rp-address 100.100.100.2
group-list 239.0.0.0/8 bidir
``` | ```
interface loopback1
  description PIM Bidir Phantom RP
  vrf member IPN-VRF
  ip address 100.100.100.1/29
  ip ospf network point-to-point
  ip router ospf IPN area 0.0.0.0
  ip pim sparse-mode

vrf context IPN-VRF
  ip pim rp-address 100.100.100.2
group-list 225.0.0.0/8 bidir
  ip pim rp-address 100.100.100.2
group-list 239.0.0.0/8 bidir
``` |
| **IPN 2, Pod 1** | **IPN 4, Pod 2** |
| ```
interface loopback1
  description PIM Bidir Phantom RP
  vrf member IPN-VRF
  ip address 100.100.100.1/28
  ip ospf network point-to-point
  ip router ospf IPN area 0.0.0.0
  ip pim sparse-mode

vrf context IPN-VRF
  ip pim rp-address 100.100.100.2
group-list 225.0.0.0/8 bidir
  ip pim rp-address 100.100.100.2
group-list 239.0.0.0/8 bidir
``` | ```
interface loopback1
  description PIM Bidir Phantom RP
  vrf member IPN-VRF
  ip address 100.100.100.1/27
  ip ospf network point-to-point
  ip router ospf IPN area 0.0.0.0
  ip pim sparse-mode

vrf context IPN-VRF
  ip pim rp-address 100.100.100.2
group-list 225.0.0.0/8 bidir
  ip pim rp-address 100.100.100.2
group-list 239.0.0.0/8 bidir
``` |

For the complete and latest multi-pod and IPN configuration, please refer to the Cisco website.

DHCP Relay Support

When a new node joins the fabric, the APIC assigns a unique IP address known as a VTEP through the DHCP process. So how do new fabric nodes (leafs/spines) get provisioned in a newly instantiated pod that is physically separated through an IPN? To accomplish that, you need to enable DHCP Relay in the IPN to forward the DHCP handshake traffic between the APIC and newly provisioned nodes in different pods. Enabling DHCP Relay in the IPN allows those remote pods to join the multi-pod fabric with zero-touch configuration, as it normally happens to fabric nodes part of the fully meshed ACI fabric. When a new spine in a new pod (such as Pod 2) is powered up, it sends the DHCP request to the APIC located in Pod 1. This DHCP request is relayed by the IPN router connected to the newly instantiated spine in Pod 2. The DHCP request is then forwarded to the IPN router connected to the spine in Pod 1, where the APIC resides. When the DHCP process is complete, the spine can get its configuration from APIC and hence fully joins the fabric. Likewise, other new fabric nodes can also join the newly deployed Pod 2.

At this writing, OSPF is the only routing protocol supported on the spine interfaces connecting to the IPN routers. As previously mentioned, IPN represents an extension of the ACI infrastructure network, ensuring that VXLAN tunnels are established across pods to allow intra-EPG/BD communication between endpoints.

During the initial auto-provisioning process of the fabric node, the APIC assigns a unique IP address called a VTEP from the TEP pool to the loopback interfaces of the leaf and spine nodes that are part of the same pod. IS-IS is the routing protocol that fabric nodes use to advertise their unique VTEP addresses.

In a multi-pod deployment, each pod is assigned a separate and not overlapping TEP pool, as shown in Figure 4-13.

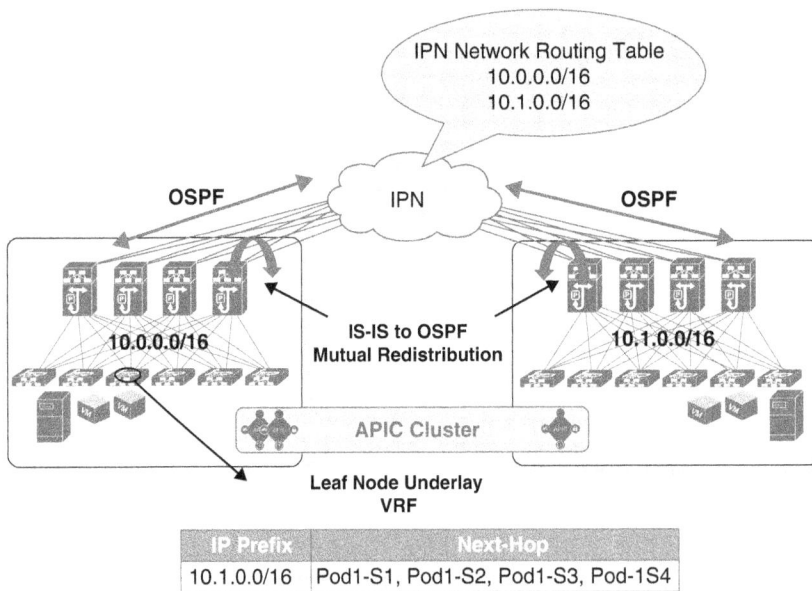

Figure 4-13 *ACI Multi-pod IPN Control Plane*

The spines in each pod establish OSPF neighbor relationships with the directly connected IPN devices to be able to send out the TEP pool prefix for the local pod. As a result, the IPN devices install in their routing tables equal-cost routes for the TEP pools that are valid in different pods. At the same time, the TEP pool prefixes relative to remote pods received by the spines via OSPF are redistributed into the IS-IS process of each pod so that the leaf nodes can install them in their routing tables. (Those routes are part of the *overlay-1* VRF part of the *Infra* tenant.)

Note   The spines also send to the IPN a few /32 host route addresses that are associated with specific loopback addresses of spines. This ensures traffic symmetry and prevents following of equal-cost paths that may lead to choosing different spines for traffic forwarding. No /32 host routes for leaf node loopback interfaces should ever be sent into the IPN to keep the routing table of the IPN devices very thin and independent from the total number of deployed leaf nodes.

Just because the spines require OSPF to connect to the IPN does not mean that the transport between IPN routers must also be OSPF. Figure 4-14 highlights this design point. There could be a case in which the IPN is a generic Layer 3 infrastructure interconnecting the pods using carrier services such as MPLS or private links such as dark fiber or DWDM; a separate routing protocol for that static route (depending on the use case) could be used inside that Layer 3 network. Mutual redistribution would then be needed with the process used toward the spines.

Maximum Transmission Unit (MTU) Support

As explained earlier, VXLAN is used to forward packets inside an ACI fabric. VXLAN adds an extra 50 bytes to a frame. Prior to ACI Release 2.2, spines were hard-coded to generate 9150-byte full-size frames for exchanging MP-BGP control plane traffic with spines in different pods. Therefore, it was mandatory to configure IPN routers with an MTU size of 9150 bytes on the interfaces connecting to spines in their respective pods and among each other. With ACI Release 2.2 and later, a global configuration knob has been added in an APIC to allow proper tuning of the MTU size. This essentially means that the MTU size required on IPN routers is solely dependent on the maximum frame size generated by the endpoints connected to the ACI leaf nodes plus an additional 50 bytes for VXLAN.

Dot1q Support

In multi-pod, the connectivity between the spine and an IPN router requires a point-to-point Layer 3 interface to forward ACI control and data plane traffic over an IP network. However, because the spine always tags this traffic flow with the vlan-4 value in the code, there is a need to create Layer 3 subinterfaces on both the spine and its directly connected IPN router. This requirement does not apply on IPN router interfaces that connect to each other.

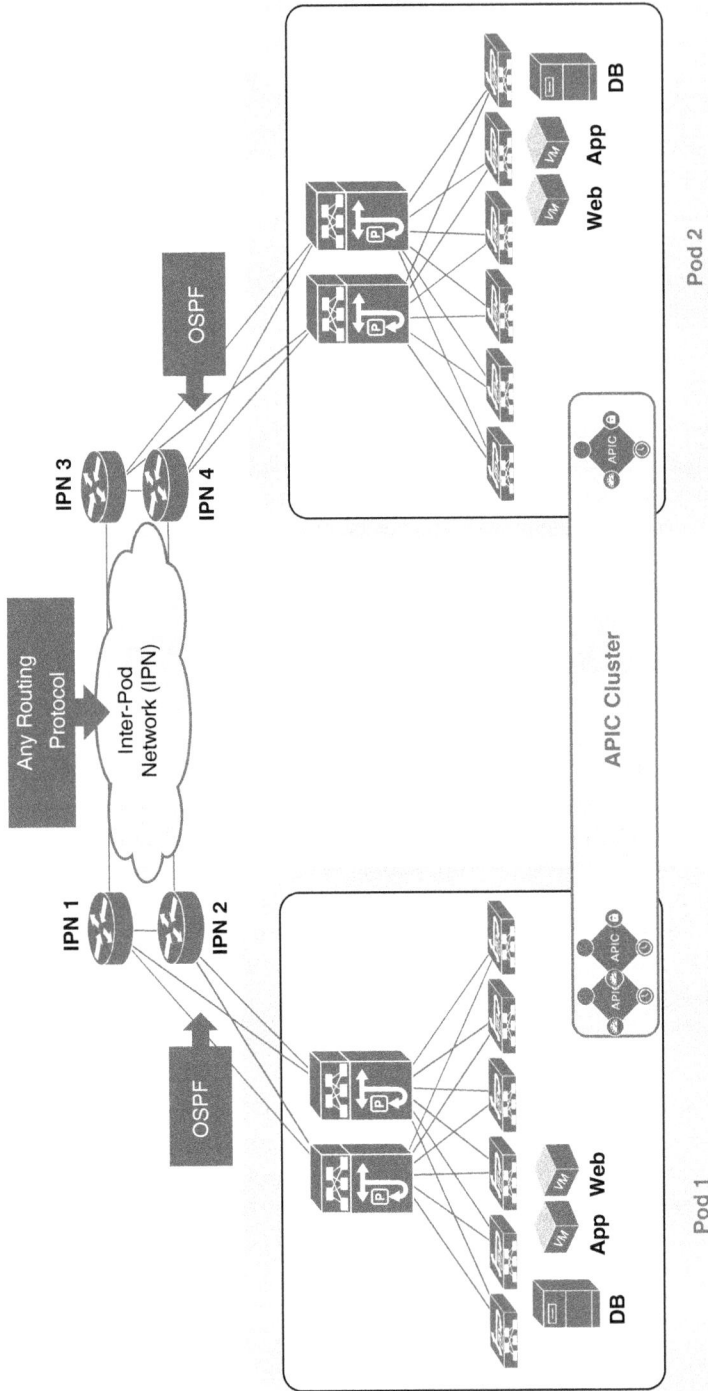

Figure 4-14 *Support for Any Routing Protocol in IPN*

QoS Support

As highlighted in Figure 4-15, traffic inside an ACI pod can be separated into different classes of service.

Class of Service / QoS Group	Traffic Type	Dot1p Marking in VXLAN Header
0	Level 3 User Data	0
1	Level 2 User Data	1
2	Level 1 User Data	2
3	APIC Control Traffic	3
4	SPAN Traffic	4
5	Control Traffic	5
5	Traceroute	6

Figure 4-15 *Intra-pod Classes of Traffic*

Each QoS class of service (CoS) is marked with a specific value in the outer Layer 2 header of the VXLAN-encapsulated frame forwarded inside the pod. This information allows the spine and leaf nodes inside the pod to perform proper classification and prioritization of the traffic.

In a multi-pod deployment, two important considerations arise when discussing end-to-end QoS behavior:

■ Because IPN routers are outside an ACI fabric and are not managed by an APIC, in many cases it may not be possible to assume that the 802.1p values are properly preserved across the IPN. By default, traffic received by the spines on the interfaces connecting to the IPN routers is classified to one of the classes of service shown in Figure 4-15, based on the CoS value in the outer IP header of inter-pod iVXLAN traffic. This may lead to unexpected handling of traffic flows received from IPN routers entering the ACI fabric. Therefore, it is highly recommended to configure proper CoS-to-DSCP mapping in ACI to ensure that traffic received on the spine in a remote pod can be reassigned its proper CoS value, based on the Differentiated Services Code Point (DSCP) value in the outer IP header of the inter-pod iVXLAN frame, as shown in Figure 4-16.

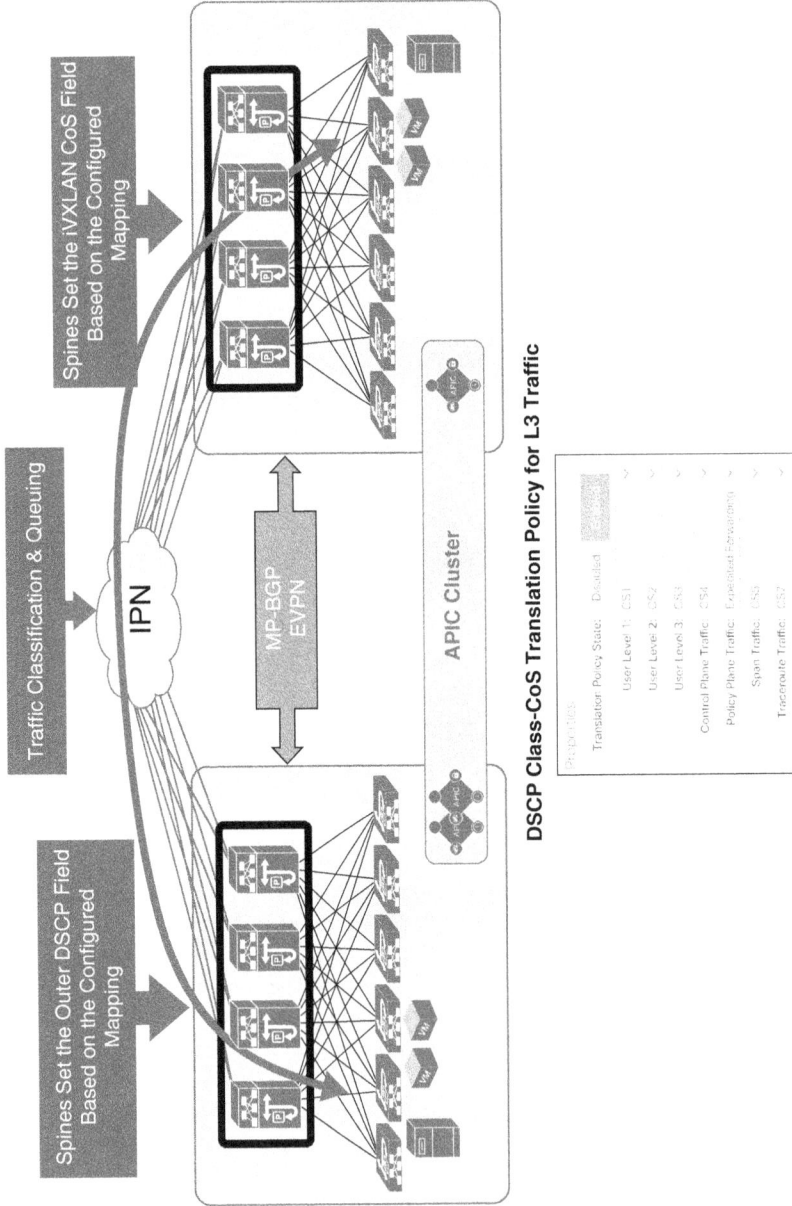

Figure 4-16 *CoS-to-DSCP Mapping*

■ The DSCP values set by the spine before forwarding traffic into the IPN can then be used to classify and prioritize the different types of traffic. In Figure 4-16, policy plane traffic between APIC nodes deployed in separate pods is marked as expedited forwarding (EF), whereas control plane traffic such as OSPF and MP-BGP is marked as CS4. The IPN routers should be configured separately to classify and prioritize these two types of traffic flows to ensure smooth fabric operation even during times when large amounts of east–west user data traffic are required to flow between pods.

APIC Cluster Deployment Considerations

APIC cluster deployment considerations in multi-pod design options are similar to those in stretch fabric design at multiple locations using transit leafs, where the APIC cluster nodes must be physically present in each location to avoid complete cluster failure or a cluster minority state situation. Remember that an APIC does not play any role in the control plane or data plane, and only the management plane is affected during the minority state. Traffic forwarding continues to happen even when the APIC in a cluster fails.

An APIC stores data in blocks called *shards* (the database units in a data repository), and a shard is replicated three times, with each copy assigned to a specific APIC node. Figure 4-17 shows the distribution of shards across clusters of three and five APIC nodes.

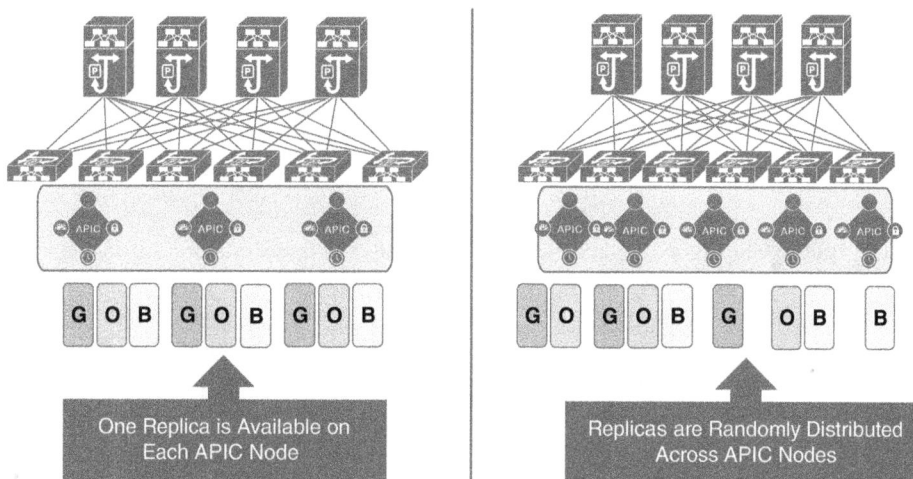

Figure 4-17   *Shard Replication Across APIC Nodes*

With three-node APIC cluster deployments, one replica for each shard is always available on every APIC node, but this is not the case when deploying five- or seven-node cluster deployments. This behavior implies that increasing the number of APIC nodes from three to five or seven does not improve the overall resiliency of the cluster but only makes it possible to support a higher number of leaf nodes in a single fabric. In order to better understand this, let's consider what happens if two of the APIC nodes fail at the same time (see Figure 4-18).

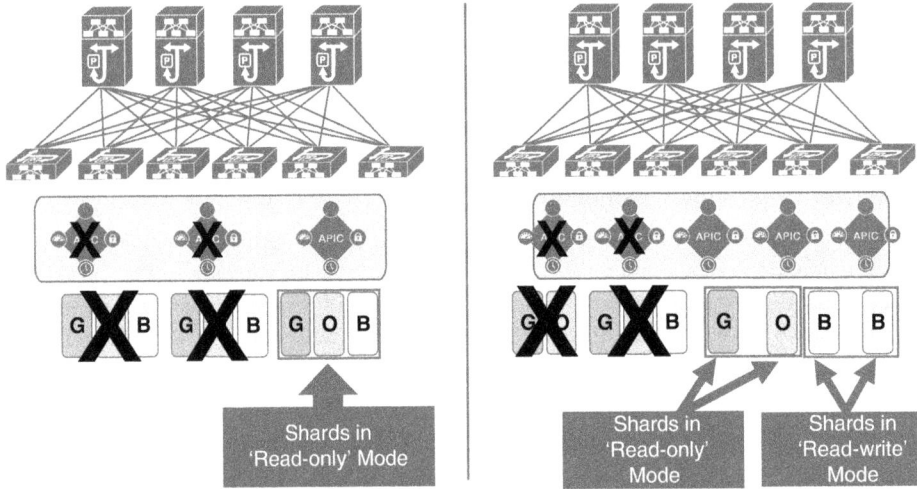

Figure 4-18   *Two-APIC-Node Failure Scenario*

With the failure of two APIC nodes in a three-node cluster, as shown on the left side of Figure 4-18, the third APIC still possesses a copy of all the shards. However, because it does not have the replica of shards anymore, the quorum is broken. Therefore, all the shards are in read-only mode, and this is known as the *cluster minority state*. In this state, while connecting to the remaining APIC, no configuration changes are allowed in the fabric.

In the example shown on the right side of Figure 4-18, a two-node failure scenario is demonstrated for a five-node cluster. In this case, some shards on the remaining APIC nodes are in the *cluster minority state*, which is a read-only mode (for example, shards G and O), whereas the others are in a quorum, which is a read/write mode (for example, shard B). This implies that connecting to one of the three remaining APIC nodes in this situation would lead to nondeterministic behavior across shards, as configuration change is allowed for shard B but not for shards G or O.

In multi-pod design, although it is not necessary, it is recommended to deploy APIC nodes in separate pods whenever possible. This addresses two main failure scenarios:

- The first failure scenario is a split-brain case where the connectivity between the pods is interrupted because of link failures in the IPN, as shown in Figure 4-19.

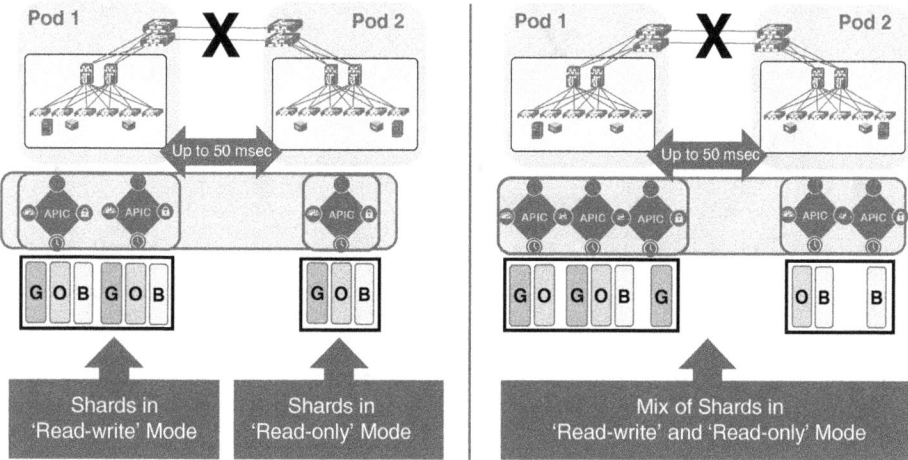

Figure 4-19   *IPN Link Failure Causing APIC Split-Brain*

■ In the second failure scenario, an entire site goes down because of a disaster event, as shown in Figure 4-20.

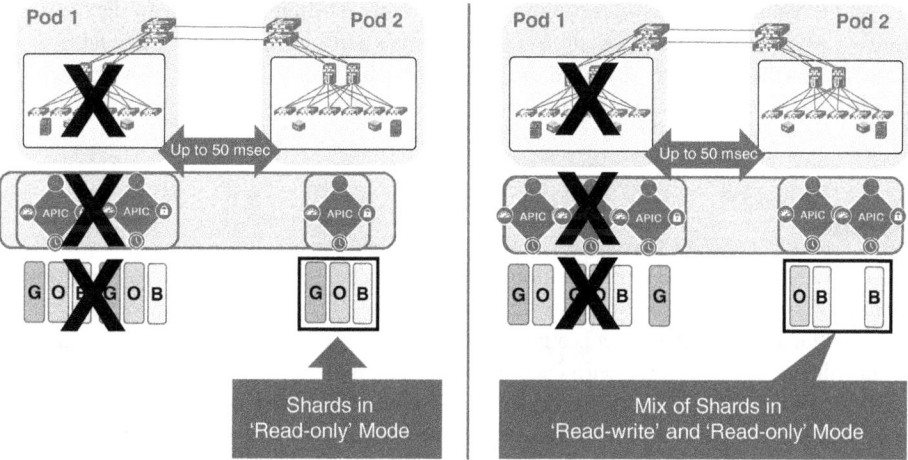

Figure 4-20   *Site Failure Causing APIC Split-Brain*

In the event of these failure events, a specific procedure is required to bring up the stand-by APIC node, as shown in Figure 4-21. More details and configuration steps for bringing up the standby APIC node can be found on the Cisco website.

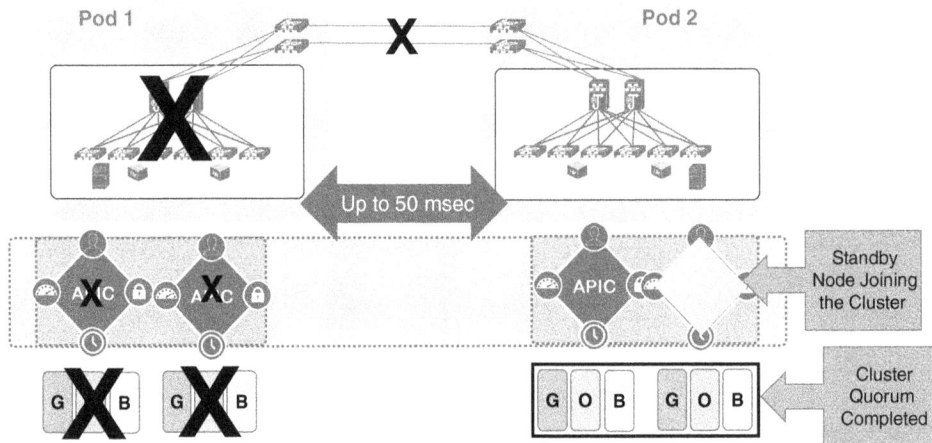

Figure 4-21   *Standby APIC Node Joining the Cluster*

Note   The situation just described does not happen if, for example, you have a two-pod deployment with a seven APIC nodes cluster. In that case, you can deploy four APICs in Pod 1 and three in Pod 2. Also, starting with ACI Release 4.0(1), it is possible to deploy a four-node APIC cluster to support up to 200 leaf nodes across all pods in a single fabric. (Please refer to the Cisco website for more details on deploying a four-node APIC cluster as this book only covers scenarios up to ACI Release 3.2.x.)

Multi-Site

So far we have examined design options within a data center and spread across multiple data centers using a single fabric with a single APIC cluster providing a single availability zone within a region. A *region* is a geographically separate area composed of multiple availability zones connected with each other through high-speed links. ACI multi-site makes it possible to connect separate fabrics that are considered availability zones geographically located apart into regions. Furthermore, it provides complete isolation both at the network and management plane levels across separate ACI fabrics, as shown in Figure 4-22. ACI multi-site architecture was introduced in ACI Release 3.0.

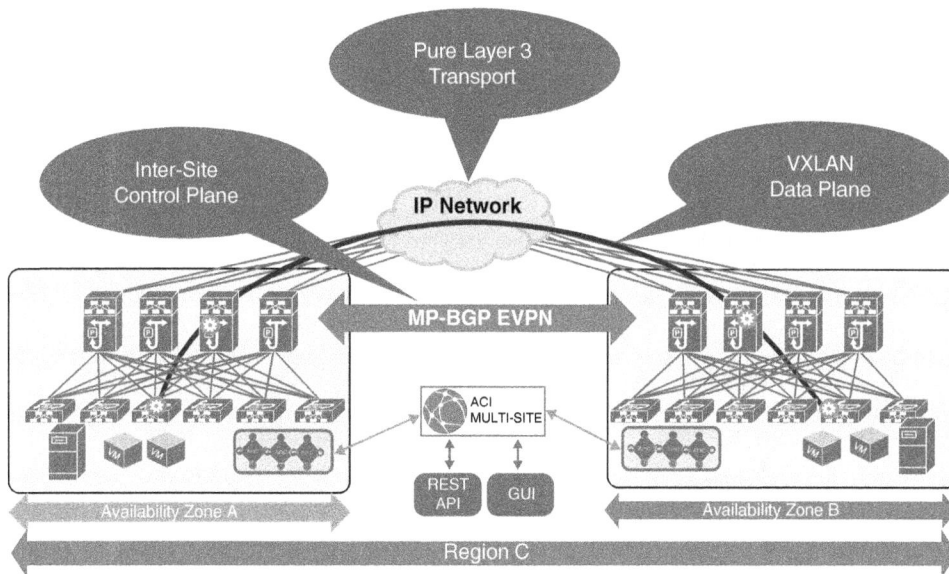

Figure 4-22   *ACI Multi-Site Architecture*

The architecture allows you to interconnect separate Cisco ACI APIC clusters (fabrics), each representing a different availability zone. Doing so helps ensure multitenant Layer 2 and Layer 3 network connectivity across sites, and it also extends the policy domain end to end across the hosting infrastructure. This design is achieved by using the following functional components:

- **Multi-Site Orchestrator:** ACI Multi-Site Orchestrator, commonly known as MSO, is the inter-site policy manager in the multi-site architecture. It provides a single pane of glass for managing and monitoring multiple ACI fabrics. MSO enables you to monitor the health score state for all the interconnected sites and also allows you to define all the inter-site policies that can be pushed to different APIC clusters to be rendered on the physical switches. Using Multi-Site Orchestrator, you can achieve greater control over when and where to push those policies; this means complete freedom on tenant configuration and yet preserves domain isolation.

- **Inter-site control plane:** The control plane protocol used between sites is MP-BGP EVPN for endpoint reachability. This approach allows the exchange of MAC and IP address information for the endpoints that would like to communicate across sites. MP-BGP EVPN sessions are established between the spines deployed in separate fabrics through the IPN.

■ **Inter-site data plane:** Layer 2 and Layer 3 traffic forwarding between endpoints connected to different sites is achieved by establishing site-to-site VXLAN tunnels across a generic IP network that interconnects various sites. Unlike multi-pod, this IP network has no specific functional requirements other than the requirement of simple IP reachability and increased MTU size due to the extra 50 bytes from the VXLAN encapsulation. The use of head-end replication for BUM traffic greatly simplifies the configuration and functions required for a multi-site IPN. It also allows network and policy information (metadata) to be carried across sites, as shown in Figure 4-23.

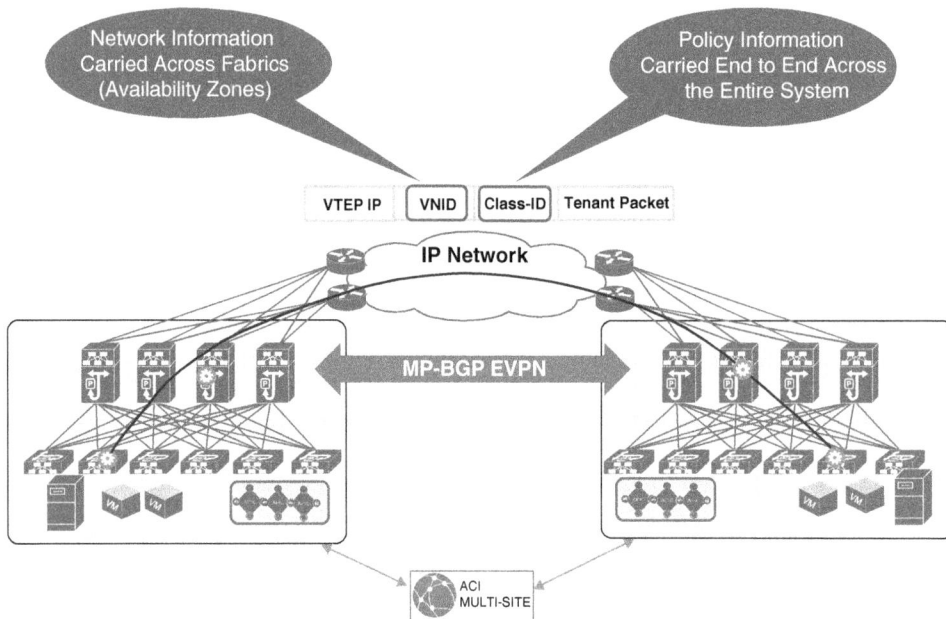

Figure 4-23   *Network and Policy Information Across Multiple Sites*

In a single ACI fabric, if the traffic sourced from an endpoint is Layer 2 traffic, the VXLAN network identifier (VNID) identifies the bridge domain (BD) from which it originated. On the other hand, if the traffic sourced from an endpoint is Layer 3 traffic, the VRF instance identifies the origin. Similarly, for endpoint group (EPG) identification, a unique class ID is used. With multi-site deployment, because each fabric is separate, a translation function must be applied before the traffic is forwarded and enters the receiving site, ensuring that the original values such as EPG, bridge domain, and VRF instance remain intact. This is depicted in Figure 4-24, where the spines located on the destination site are responsible for performing this namespace translation function.

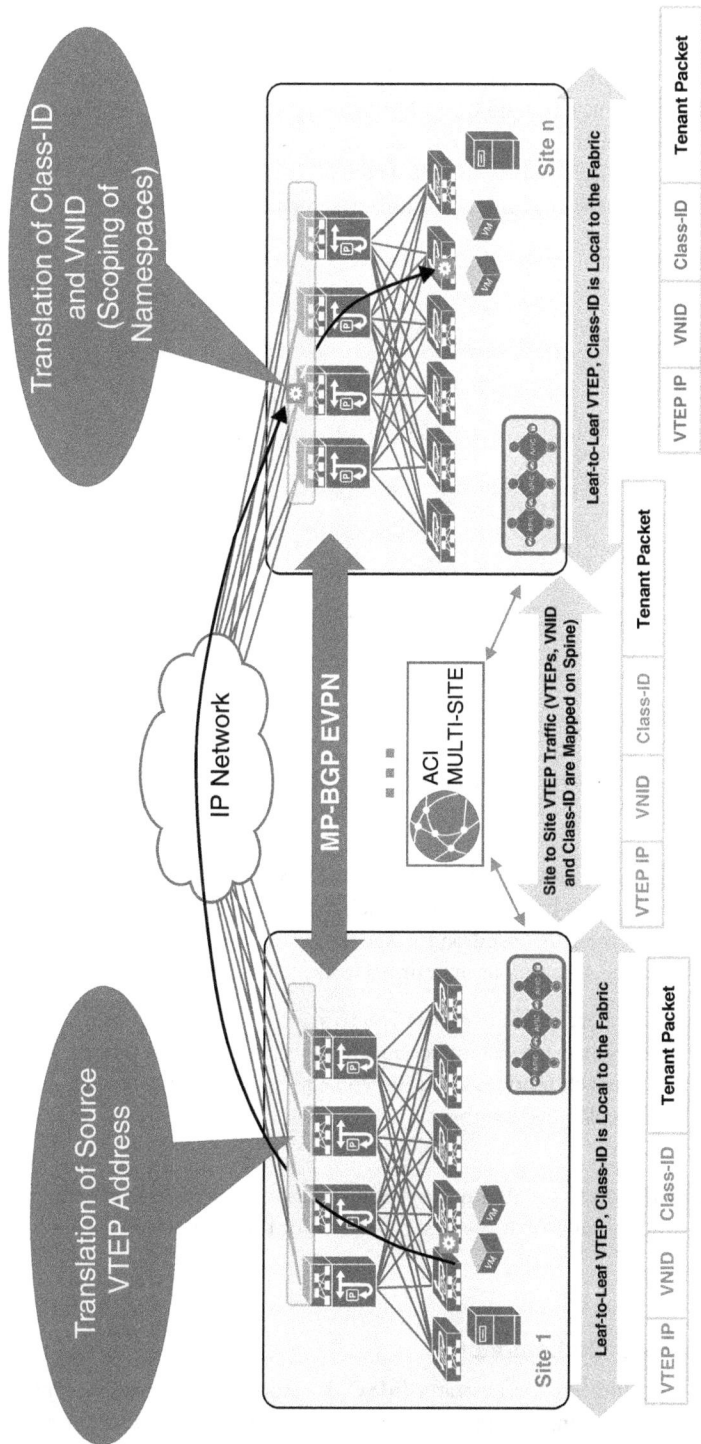

Figure 4-24   *Namespace Translation Function on Receiving Spine Nodes*

Now the spines responsible for this namespace translation should perform the function at the device line rate to avoid any performance degradation of inter-site communication. To ensure this, you must use specific hardware for the spines deployed in the Cisco ACI multi-site deployment. Only the Cisco Nexus cloud-scale EX/FX spine switches are supported in a multi-site architecture. First-generation spine switches can coexist with the cloud-scale spine switch models, as long as the latter are the only ones connected to the IPN and used for inter-site communication, as shown in Figure 4-25.

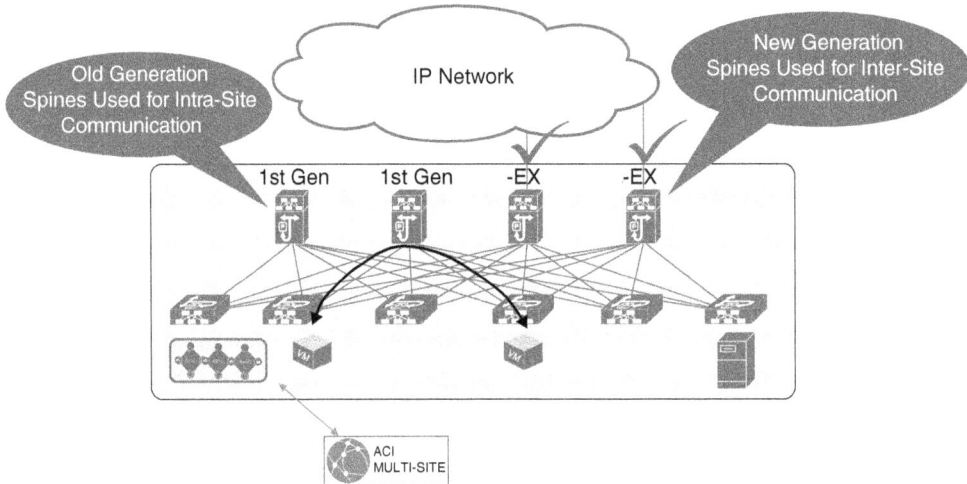

Figure 4-25 *Coexistence of First-Generation Spines with Second-Generation (EX/FX) Spines*

The spine model coexistence scenario in Figure 4-25 also clarifies the fact that not every deployed spine needs to be connected to the IPN. You should plan the connection of the spines and links to the IPN based on the specific hardware availability, your desired level of resiliency, and the throughput in your network.

Cisco ACI multi-site architecture allows you to scale up the total number of leaf and spine nodes deployed across the interconnected fabrics, as well as the total number of endpoints. Because each fabric is separate, you can have multi-pod running, which provides overall high scalability numbers.

Note   When planning a Cisco ACI deployment, you should always refer to the ACI verified scalability guides available at the Cisco website for the latest figures.

Cisco ACI Multi-Site Orchestrator

The Cisco ACI Multi-Site Orchestrator (MSO) is responsible for provisioning, health monitoring, and managing complete ACI networking and stretched tenant policies across

Cisco ACI sites that can be geographically located around the globe. MSO allows you to do the following:

- Create and manage multi-site users (administrative and generic users) and applications based on specific role-based access control (RBAC) rules.

- Use the Health dashboard to monitor the health, faults, and logs of inter-site policies for each of the Cisco ACI fabrics interconnected using the multi-site architecture. The health score information is retrieved from each APIC cluster domain and presented through a single pane of glass, as shown in Figure 4-26.

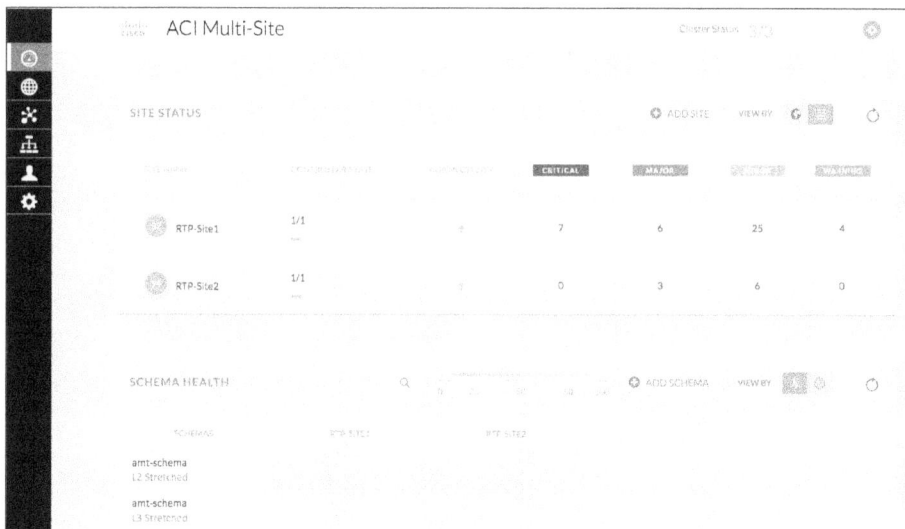

Figure 4-26   *ACI Multi-Site Policy Manager Dashboard*

- Add, delete, and modify Cisco ACI sites in the multi-site architecture.

- Provision and configure the initial infrastructure to allow the spine switches at all Cisco ACI sites to peer and connect with each other. This establishes MP-BGP EVPN control plane reachability and makes it possible to exchange endpoint host information (MAC and IPv4/IPv6 addresses) throughout the entire multi-site architecture.

- Create inter-site tenants with policy profiles, deploy them across sites, and define and provision scoped policies for change management. When you create inter-site policies, the MSO also properly programs the required namespace translation rules on the spine switches connecting via IPN across sites.

- Define multi-site policy templates. Each template can be associated with and pushed to a specific set of ACI fabrics.

- Import tenant policies from an already deployed and running ACI fabric (brownfield deployment) and stretch them to a newly deployed ACI fabric (greenfield deployment).

The MSO uses the out-of-band (OOB) management network to connect to the APIC clusters deployed in different sites. It also provides northbound access through the REST API or the MSO GUI, so you can manage the full life cycle of networking and tenant policies required to be stretched across multiple sites.

An important thing to note here is that the Cisco ACI Multi-Site Orchestrator is not responsible for configuring Cisco ACI fabric local site policies. This task still remains the responsibility of the APIC cluster of the fabric at each site. The policy manager can import the local site policies relevant to the APIC cluster of each fabric and associate them with stretched objects. For example, it can import a site's locally defined VMM domains and associate them with stretched EPGs.

Multi-site design is based on a microservices architecture in which three virtual machines are clustered together in an active/active fashion. Each of these three virtual machines internally has a Docker daemon installed with multi-site application services. Those services are managed and orchestrated by a Docker swarm that load balances all of the job transactions across all multi-site containers in concurrent active/active fashion for high availability.

A stable data plane connection (TCP) must exist between the Cisco ACI multi-site cluster virtual machines when they are deployed across a wide-area network (WAN). The virtual machines in a Cisco ACI multi-site cluster communicate with each other over a TCP connection, so if any packet drop occurs in the WAN, the packet will be retransmitted. Keep in mind that it is important to appropriately mark the DSCP value of virtual machine traffic in a VMware port group to allow smooth communication even during WAN link congestion. The recommended approach is to mark the DSCP as Expedited Forwarding (EF).

The recommended connection bandwidth between virtual machines in a Cisco ACI multi-site cluster is from 300 Mbps to 1 Gbps. These numbers are based on Cisco's internal regression testing.

Cisco ACI Multi-Site Deployment Considerations

There are two customer-focused use cases for Cisco ACI multi-site deployments:

- Centralized data center at a local facility, which requires the creation of separate availability zones due to cable management or high scalability.

- Geographically located data centers across cities, countries, or continents, in which case each data center is an availability zone and requires a common platform for provisioning, monitoring, and managing stretched policies across availability zones.

Cisco ACI Multi-Site Deployment Within a Local Data Center or Site

A locally deployed centralized data center use case for multi-site design is to help customers in a building or a local campus with high scalability requirements such as an increased port count for bare-metal servers, virtual machines, or container connectivity. An increased quantity of leaf nodes can be deployed across separate Cisco ACI fabrics to scale out the application hosting infrastructure and yet limit the scope of the failure domains and manage everything though a single pane of glass.

In the example shown in Figure 4-27, four Cisco ACI fabrics, each containing 200 leafs, are deployed in a data center, with one ACI fabric in each data hall. The Cisco ACI Multi-Site Orchestrator cluster virtual machines are deployed on their own separate ESXi host so that there is no single point of failure. All tenant policies can be stretched across all four Cisco ACI sites through the Cisco ACI multi-site interface.

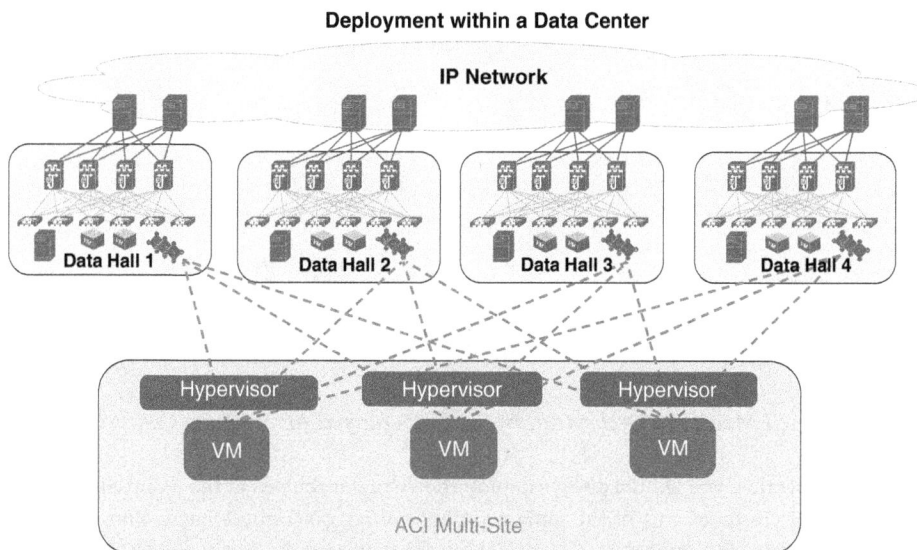

Figure 4-27   *ACI Multi-Site Orchestrator Cluster Deployed Within a Data Center*

Cisco ACI Multi-Site Data Centers Interconnected over a WAN

The WAN use case is common in scenarios where geographically separated data centers are interconnected across cities in different countries or on different continents. Each data center is fully contained in an availability zone consisting of a Cisco ACI fabric at a site. All inter-data center policies and connectivity over the WAN are owned and managed through the Cisco ACI Multi-Site Orchestrator.

In the example shown in Figure 4-28, three Cisco ACI fabrics are deployed—in Frankfurt, Cologne, and Boston—and all of them are managed from the Cisco ACI Multi-Site Orchestrator cluster deployed in Frankfurt and Cologne. An interesting point to note is that the Boston site is managed remotely by the Multi-Site Orchestrator cluster deployed in Germany (and the maximum RTT support between the MSO cluster and the ACI managed site is 1 second).

Interconnecting Data Centers Over the WAN

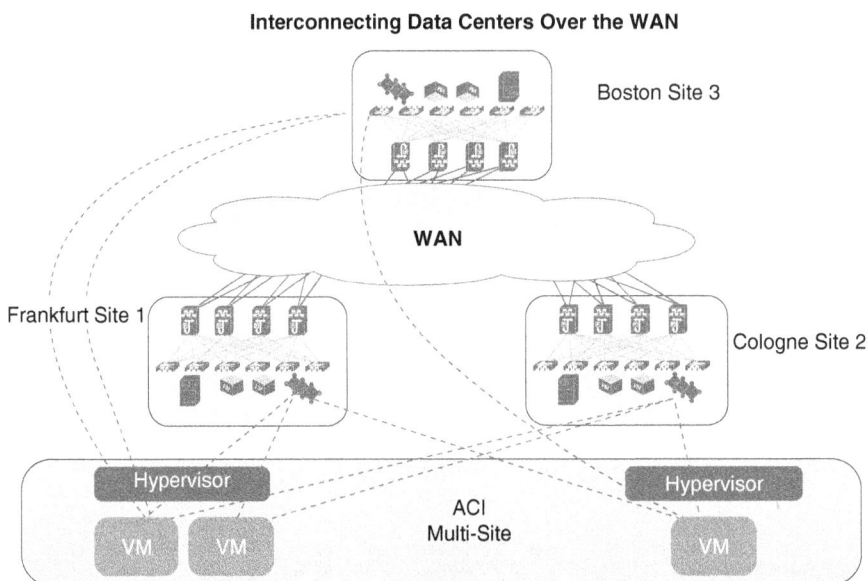

Figure 4-28 *ACI Multi-Site Orchestrator Cluster Deployed Across Data Centers*

As a best practice, you should always deploy the virtual machines in the Multi-Site Orchestrator cluster as part of the same geographical region (United States, Europe, Asia, and so on), even when managing Cisco ACI fabrics that span the world due to the maximum RTT dependency of 150 msec.

Migration Scenarios

For migration, you can choose between two common scenarios: either create new policies in the Cisco ACI Multi-Site Orchestrator or import existing APIC policies into Cisco ACI Multi-Site Orchestrator.

Creating New Policies in the Cisco ACI Multi-Site Orchestrator

In this migration scenario, say that you deploy the Multi-Site Orchestrator to start creating and pushing new policies to separate Cisco ACI fabrics, as shown in Figure 4-29.

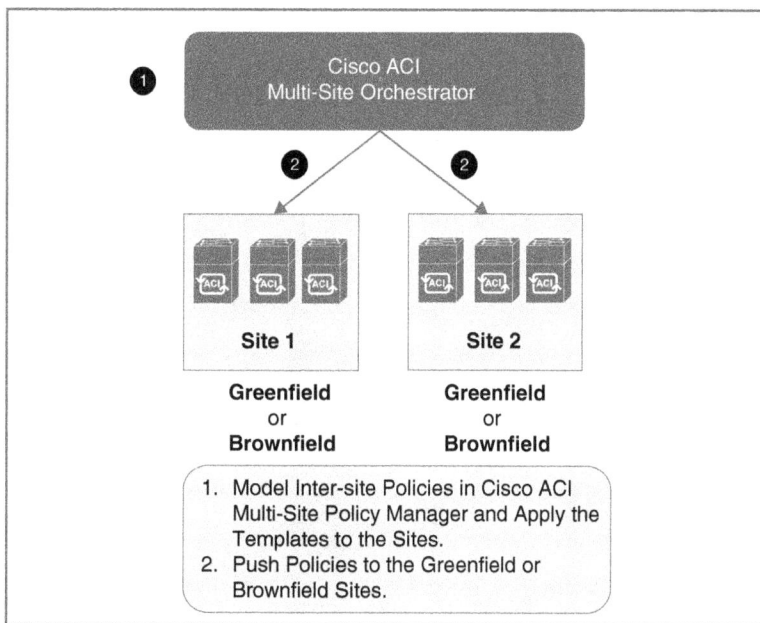

Figure 4-29 *Deploying New Policies in ACI Multi-Site Orchestrator*

In this case, the existing Cisco ACI fabrics may be completely new (greenfield) ones, or already deployed (brownfield) ones. The important point is that you deploy Multi-Site Orchestrator and use it to create new policies that must be pushed to those fabrics. In other words, you are not importing any existing configuration (tenants and other policies) from the Cisco ACI fabric APIC controllers into the Multi-Site Orchestrator. Figure 4-30 demonstrates those two typical use cases.

The migration scenario at the top of Figure 4-30 is straightforward because it consists of adding one (or more) Cisco ACI fabric(s) to an existing one. Of course, as explained earlier, this use case requires you to connect the spines in the existing ACI fabric to the IPN that connects to the new ACI fabric(s) at different sites. The assumption here is that new policies will be deployed in the Multi-Site Orchestrator and subsequently pushed to all the interconnected ACI fabrics.

The migration use case at the bottom of Figure 4-30 involves converting an existing multi-fabric design to a Cisco ACI multi-site design. In this scenario, you need to not only deploy Multi-Site Orchestrator but also change the way the already existing ACI fabric is deployed; this means connecting the multi-fabrics using spines via the IPN instead of connecting border leafs together. Because only new policies are created and pushed, this approach helps prevent conflicts with imported policies.

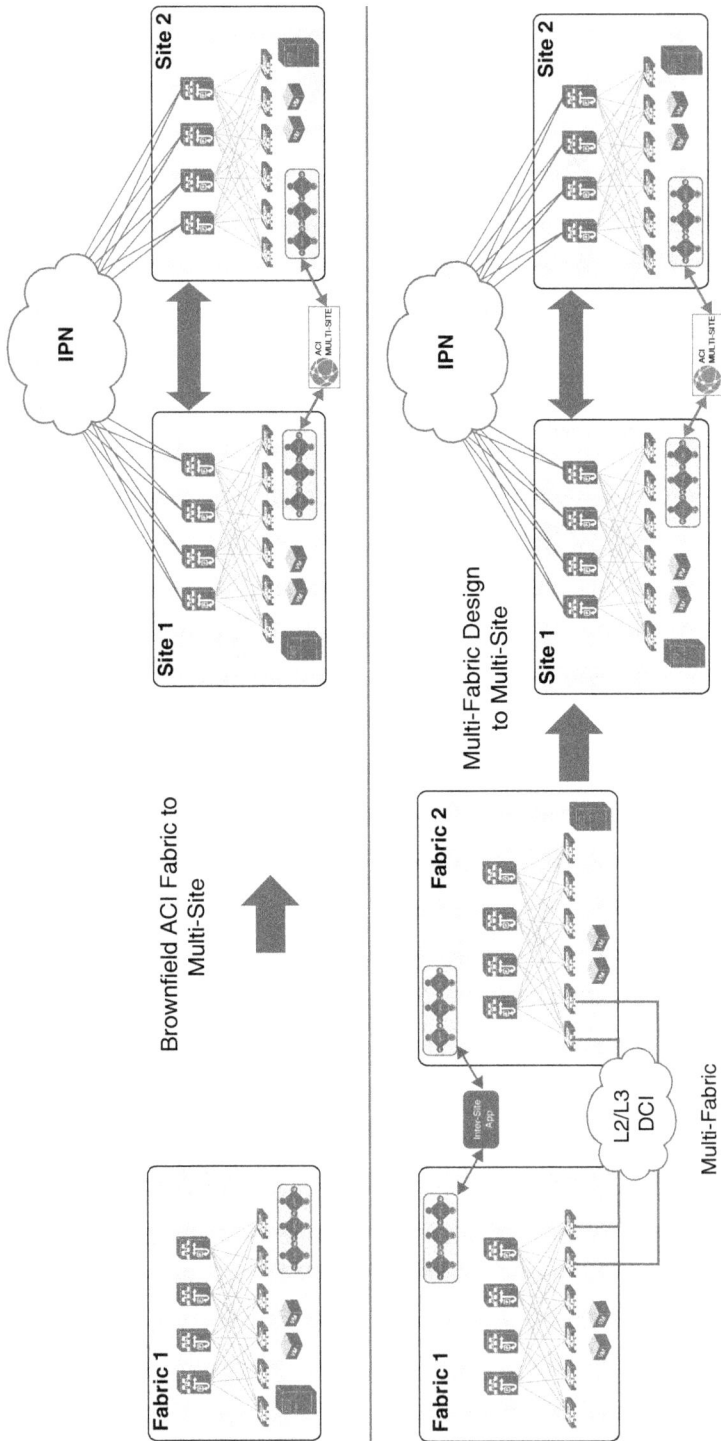

Figure 4-30   *ACI Multi-Site Migration Scenarios*

Note   Warnings are displayed in the Cisco ACI Multi-Site Orchestrator if the new policies conflict with policies already implemented in the Cisco ACI fabric APIC controller.

Importing Existing APIC Policies into the ACI Multi-Site Orchestrator

In this migration use case, existing policies for a tenant are imported from one or more ACI fabrics located at a site or sites. The imported policies thus become part of a new template in the Cisco ACI Multi-Site Orchestrator policy manager that can then be deployed to multiple fabrics located at a different site or sites, as shown in Figure 4-31.

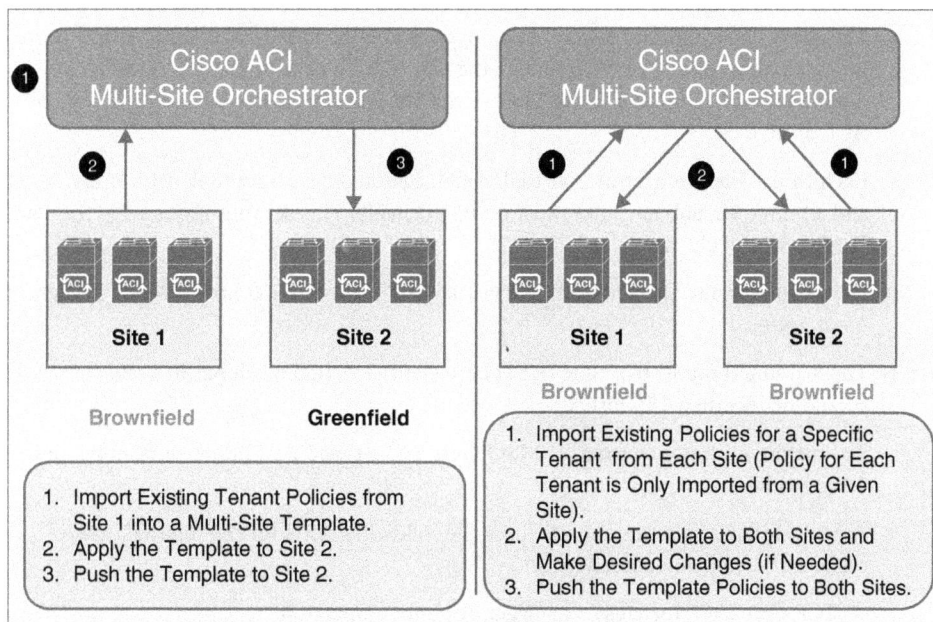

Figure 4-31   *Importing Policies into ACI Multi-Site Orchestrator*

The use case shown on the left of Figure 4-31 is pretty straightforward: Existing policies for each tenant are imported only from one Cisco ACI fabric and then pushed to one or more different fabrics. For the scenario shown on the right side of Figure 4-31, the assumption in ACI Release 3.0 is that policies for a given tenant are only imported from a fabric that is stretched to other fabrics. This means that for each tenant, the site from which the policy is imported can be considered brownfield, and the other fabrics where the policies are stretched are considered greenfield. Note that these two scenarios can apply to both migration use cases shown in Figure 4-30.

Deployment Best Practices

This section provides a summary of best practices and hints to help you easily and smoothly deploy a Cisco ACI multi-site design. These recommendations are based on thorough lab testing and experiences in deploying real Cisco ACI multi-site designs at customer sites from the proof-of-concept (PoC) phase through actual deployment in the production networks.

In order to deploy a Cisco MSO cluster successfully, consider the following recommendations:

- Connect the MSO cluster to each fabric APIC controller cluster by using the OOB management network.

- The MSO cluster should never be deployed inside the Cisco ACI fabric part of a site. It should always be deployed outside the Cisco ACI fabric in the IPN. Otherwise, double failures can occur if the Multi-Site Orchestrator cluster fails or if the Cisco ACI fabric fails.

- Each Multi-Site Orchestrator virtual machine should have a routable IP address, and all three virtual machines must be IP reachable. This setup is required to form a Docker swarm cluster.

- Deploy one Multi-Site Orchestrator virtual machine per ESXi host for high availability at a site.

- The maximum round-trip time (RTT) between the virtual machines in a cluster should be less than 150 msec.

- The maximum distance from an MSO cluster to a Cisco ACI fabric site can be up to 1 second RTT.

- A Multi-Site Orchestrator cluster uses the following ports for the internal control plane and data plane communication:

  - TCP port 2377 for cluster management communication

  - TCP and UDP port 7946 for communication among nodes

  - UDP port 4789 for overlay network traffic

  - TCP port 443 for the multi-site policy manager user interface (UI)

  - IP port 50 for Encapsulating Security Protocol (ESP) for encryption

  In the case of an access control list configuration or a firewall deployment, ensure that your underlay network has these ports open.

- IPsec is used to encrypt all intra-MSO cluster communication (control plane and data plane traffic) to provide security because the virtual machines can be placed at distant locations with up to 150 msec RTT.

- The minimum specifications for Multi-Site Orchestrator virtual machines are ESXi 5.5 or later, four vCPUs, 8 GB of RAM, and a 5 GB disk.

General Best Practices for Cisco ACI Multi-Site Design

Besides the border leaf option to connect WAN and external networks, Cisco also offers WAN connectivity using the GOLF feature, which uses the BGP EVPN protocol over OSPF for WAN routers that are connected to spine switches. If you have WAN connectivity over GOLF, you need to consider two scenarios:

- **Scenario 1 (non-stretched BD/subnet between sites):**

    - Site 1 contains a non-stretched BD 1 and Subnet 1.

    - BD 1 and Subnet 1 are associated with the GOLF L3Out-1 connection in Site 1.

    - Site 2 contains a non-stretched BD 2 and Subnet 2.

    - BD 2 and Subnet 2 are associated with the GOLF L3Out-2 connection in Site 2.

    - Each GOLF L3Out connection advertises its own bridge domain subnet to its own GOLF router, so host routing is not required.

- **Scenario 2 (stretched BD/subnet between sites):**

    - BD 1 and Subnet 1 are stretched to Site 1 and Site 2.

    - The Layer 2 stretch flag is enabled.

    - InterSiteBUMTrafficAllow can be enabled or disabled per your requirement.

    - Each site has its own local GOLF L3Out connection, which advertises the subnet through its GOLF L3Out connection toward its GOLF router.

    - The Subnet 1 in the WAN has an equal-cost multipathing (ECMP) path to the two GOLF routers.

    - For optimal routing of traffic across sites, host routing /32 can be used for stretched bridge domain BD 1 and Subnet 1 in this case.

    - Suboptimal routing of GOLF traffic over IPN is not supported. This means that traffic cannot be delivered from the GOLF router to a specific site and then redirected to a separate site to reach a remote destination endpoint.

- Inter-site VXLAN tunnels must be established over IPN and cannot use another site for transit. As a consequence, you must build enough resiliency into the IPN to help ensure that multiple ACI fabrics located at different sites are always connected through the IPN in any spine node or link failure scenarios.

- Each site must deploy its own local L3Out connection:

    - A site cannot provide transit routing services for a different site.

    - A pair of WAN edge routers can be shared across sites (traditional L3Out connection on border leaf nodes).

    - Shared WAN edge routers across sites are not supported in the first Cisco ACI–supported release for multi-site when GOLF L3Out connections are deployed.

- A multi-pod fabric is not supported as a site in the initial Cisco ACI-supported release for multi-site. However, newer ACI releases now support multi-pod in a multi-site deployment. Check and verify the latest ACI release notes on the Cisco website for a support matrix.

- Domain (physical and virtual) definition and association are performed at the site level.

- Policies pushed to a site from a multi-site deployment can be modified locally in the fabric APIC cluster. A warning appears in the Multi-Site Orchestrator if the policy implemented for a site is different from the policy specified in the multi-site template.

- QoS marking in the WAN is not supported when intra-EPG isolation or microsegmentation is configured.

- Without any proper QoS policies configured at a site, the default DSCP value of the outer IP address of the VXLAN packet in the IPN is set to 0. You should configure a QoS DSCP marking policy on the spine node to help ensure proper QoS treatment as a packet traverses the IPN.

- Each tenant or VRF instance must have its own L3Out connection configured. Shared L3Out connections are not supported.

- A multi-site deployment can be enabled only when at least one spine interface is connected to the IPN.

  - If a spine port is connected to the IPN and route peering is disabled, only the data plane is enabled on that spine.

  - If a spine port is connected to the IPN and route peering is enabled, control plane BGP EVPN sessions are formed across spines and across sites that have route peering enabled through control plane TEPs.

- BGP EVPN convergence for route reflector (RR) or full-mesh scenarios with iBGP, eBGP, or a hybrid (iBGP plus eBGP) is typically less than or equal to 1 second in lab environments for medium-size deployments. However, for convergence in real medium-size deployments, typically less than or equal to 5 seconds is common due to external factors such as the WAN.

- The multi-site fabric discovers pods and spine EX/FX line card information from the APIC and updates the *Infra* tenant configuration.

- All available *Infra* tenant configurations are retrieved from the APIC of the site being created from the managed objects, and the multi-site configuration is auto-populated.

- The multi-site L3Out connection under the *Infra* tenant is named *intersite* in the APIC, as shown in Figure 4-32.

- When a site is deleted from a Cisco ACI multi-site deployment, its control plane and data plane functionalities are disabled. However, the Multi-Site Orchestrator retains the *Infra* configuration and auto-populates it if that site is added again.

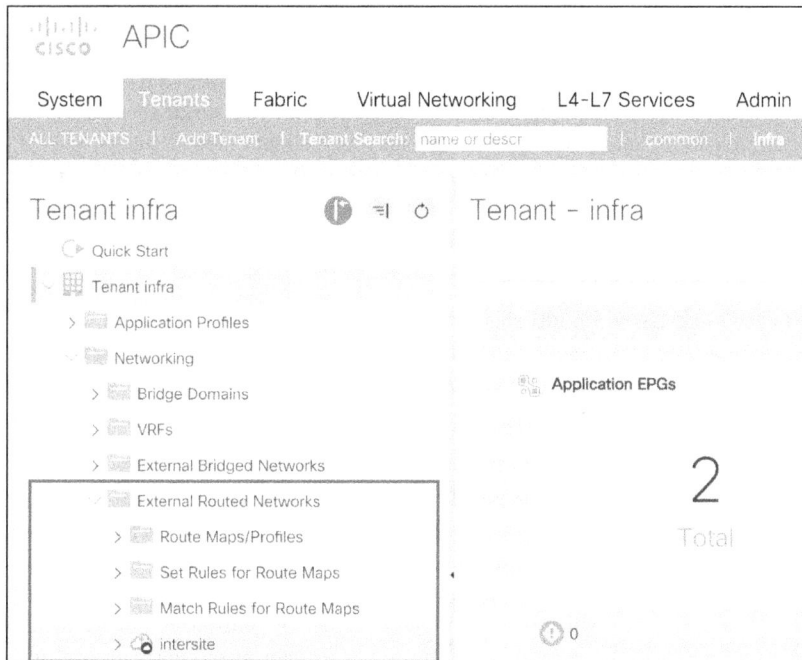

Figure 4-32 *Creation of Inter-Site L3Out in APIC*

Remote Leaf

As ACI fabrics are more commonly being deployed at large customer bases, accommodating various single- and multiple-site scenarios using single-fabric stretch between multiple sites or having multiple single fabrics at each site all connected together to have the same policy model, customers have started asking how to extend their application workloads to remote locations without investing a lot on extra fabric infrastructure.

Customers also ask Cisco how to achieve the same policy definitions and security rules; what they have applied on their application-hosting infrastructure in their data centers can be extended to workloads that needs to be deployed with limited rackspace, power, and cooling. To address such issues, the remote leaf design option was created. With this design option, a regular Nexus 9300 leaf switch can be deployed at a remote location registered to the same ACI fabric deployed in the data center over the existing IPN. With such a setup, you do not have to spend extra money buying a full-fledged ACI fabric, yet you can build and deploy your applications through the common policy model at colocation facility or by renting data center floor space.

The following are some of the use cases for remote leaf deployment:

■ **Satellite/colocation hosting facility:** Due to critical business growth needs, customers often have main data centers and many small satellite data centers and colocation hosting facilities distributed across multiple locations. There is a constant demand from Cisco's large customer base for centralized management of all these data centers to simplify operations. Customers also often want to ensure that satellite data centers and colocation hosting facilities have the same networking, security, monitoring, telemetry, and troubleshooting policy as the main data centers. The ACI remote leaf option provides a solution for these demands. Customers can use remote leaf switches at satellite data centers and colocation facilities to manage and apply policies in the same way as they do in their data centers.

■ **Data center extension and migration:** Remote leaf deployment simplifies the extension of Layer 2 and Layer 3 multitenant connectivity between main data center and remote locations with consistent ACI policy. It also helps during the migration phase, when workloads (physical or virtual) are required to move from Data centers to remote locations.

■ **Telco 5G distributed data centers:** Typically, companies build data centers at their central locations to fulfill the demands of their business application end users. However, due to increasing demands and the need to provide a better experience to subscribers, some services are now moving close to end users. Therefore, in some business use cases, data centers are becoming smaller but more numerous and spread across multiple locations, which results in high demand for centralized management and consistent policy. Cisco remote leaf solutions offer centralized management of these data centers by providing full automation, consistent Day 2 policy, and end-to-end troubleshooting across locations.

■ **Disaster recovery:** With recent enhancement in ACI code, a remote leaf deployment can even function normally and forward traffic between locally connected and learned endpoints/prefixes during a complete failure of network connectivity to the main data center ACI fabric.

In a remote leaf solution, APIC controllers, spines, and local leafs remain at the main data center (DC), and some leaf switches are extended to remote locations that logically connect to spines in the main data center over a backbone IPN. Leaf node discovery, configuration, and pushing policies at remote locations are handled by the APIC cluster at the main data center. A remote leaf connects to the spine of one of the pods in the main data center over VXLAN tunnels. Just like a local leaf solution, a remote leaf solution can be used to connect any compute workloads, such as virtual servers, physical servers, and containers. Traffic to the endpoints connected to the remote leaf is locally forwarded instead of traversing the main data center in most cases. Remote location firewalls, routers, load balancers, and other service devices can be connected to remote leaf switches much as they would be connected to local leaf switches, as depicted in Figure 4-33.

For application load balancing and security needs, customers can use ACI service graphs to perform service chaining using an ACI remote leaf solution. At this writing, only unmanaged service graph mode is supported when connecting service nodes (for the load balancer and firewall, for instance) to remote leaf switches. Local L2Out or L3Out can also be used to connect external network devices at remote locations using a remote leaf solution.

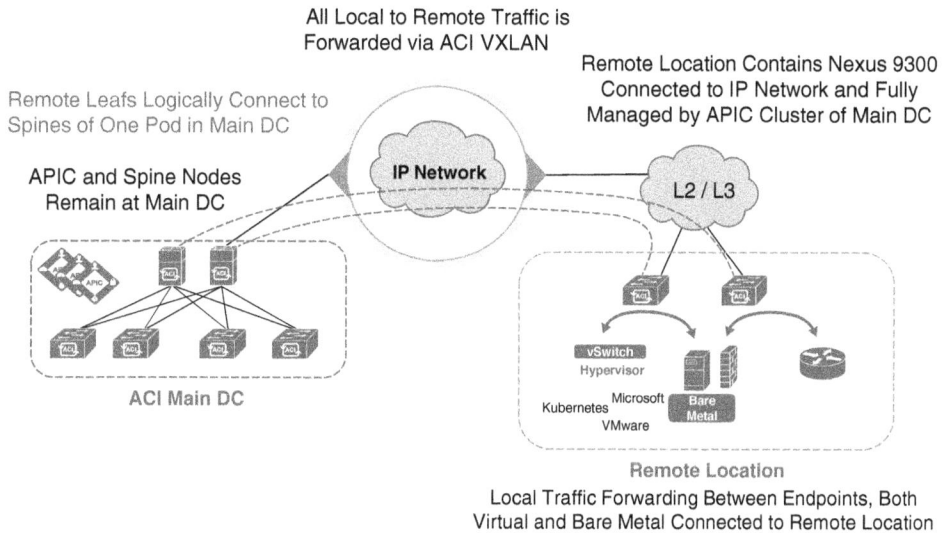

Figure 4-33 *Remote Leaf Architecture*

In a multi-pod ACI fabric deployment, a remote leaf node gets logically associated with one specific pod. In Figure 4-34, the remote leaf pair is associated with ACI Pod 1.

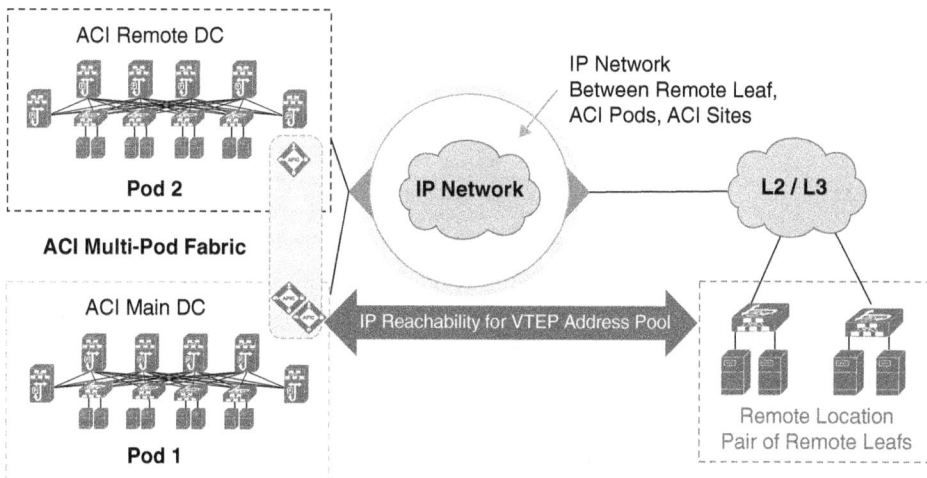

Figure 4-34 *Remote Leaf Connectivity in a Multi-pod ACI Fabric*

The remote leaf nodes require IP reachability to the APIC controller for allowing zero-touch provisioning. Remote leafs also need connectivity to the VTEP pool of the associated pod (Pod 1 in the example shown in Figure 4-34) to make sure remote endpoints can leverage the L3Out connection in the ACI main data center when the local L3Out fails.

Hardware and Software Support

The remote leaf solution is supported starting from ACI Release 3.1(1) on cloud-scale (EX/FX) ASICs. Table 4-3 provides a list of hardware that supports remote leaf solutions, as of this writing. Please check the latest release notes for hardware support on the Cisco website.

Table 4-3   *Remote Leaf Hardware Support*

Spine	Leaf
Fixed spine:	N93180YC-EX
N9364C	N93180YC-FX
N9332C	N93108TC-EX
	N93108TC-FX
Modular spine with following line card:	N93180LC-EX
N9732C-EX	N9348GC-FXP
N9736C-FX	N9336C-FX2
N9736Q-FX	N93240YC-FX2
	N9358GY-FXP
	N93360YC-FX2
	N93216TC-FX2

Note   Check the Cisco website for the latest hardware support matrix.

You might already be using first-generation spines that do not support a remote leaf solution. As with multi-site, first-generation and second-generation (cloud-scale) spines can be part of the same ACI fabric. However, only second-generation spines, as shown in Figure 4-25, should connect to the IPN to support remote leaf functionality.

Recommended QOS Configuration for a Remote Leaf Solution

What happens to the CoS value that comes out of the endpoint connected to a remote leaf? Often there may be a requirement to preserve this COS value from remote endpoints connected to EPGs and carry it over to the ACI main data center pod. To achieve this goal, it is possible to enable the preservation of the CoS value (via the Dot1p Preserve flag) as part of the External Access Policies section in the APIC GUI, as shown in Figure 4-35. With this configuration, the CoS value of the original frame received from the endpoint connected to the remote leaf node is translated to a corresponding DSCP value that is then copied to the outer IP header of the VXLAN-encapsulated frame.

This value can then be propagated across the IPN and converted back to the original CoS value before the traffic is sent to the endpoints connected in the main ACI build data center and vice versa.

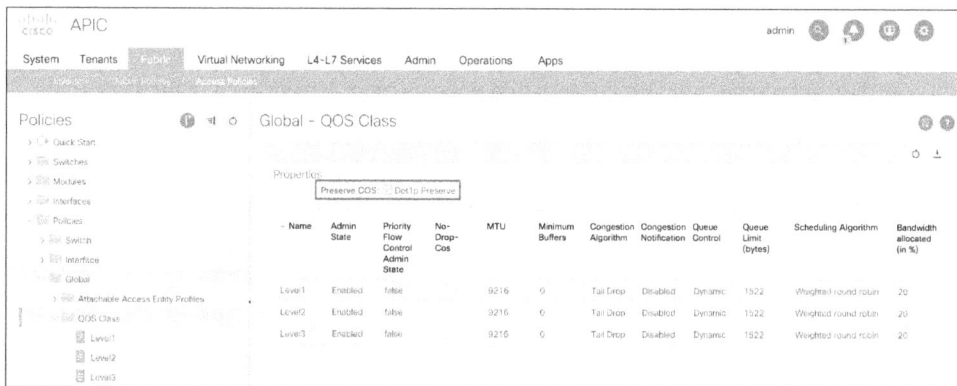

Figure 4-35 *Preserving CoS Values Between the Remote Location and the Main Data Center*

Customers also often want to classify ACI fabric classes (QoS levels) to a DSCP value within the IPN. To do this, you should enable the setting DSCP class-cos translation policy for L3 traffic in your ACI fabric, as shown in Figure 4-36.

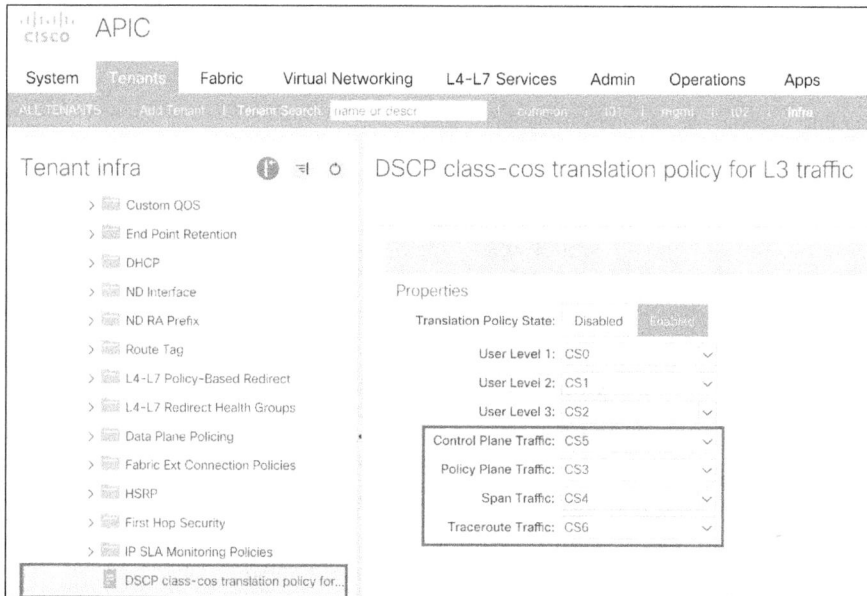

Figure 4-36 *Mapping DSCP Values to CoS for Layer 3 Traffic*

To configure QoS policies in the ACI fabric for the remote leaf, keep in mind the following key points:

- Retain the DSCP value inside the IPN because the ACI fabric is expecting the DSCP value coming from the remote leaf to the main data center spine over the IPN to be the same.

- Dot1p preserve and DSCP translation policies cannot be enabled at the same time.

Table 4-4 explains the CoS values that are used within the ACI fabric and recommended actions for those CoS values in the IPN.

Table 4-4   *CoS Values and Recommendations for the ACI Fabric*

Traffic Class	COS Value	Recommendation
Control plane	COS5	Prioritize in the IPN
Policy plane	COS3	Prioritize in the IPN
Traceroute	COS6	Prioritize in the IPN
SPAN	COS4	Deprioritize in the IPN

Discovery of a Remote Leaf

A remote leaf gets discovered and configured automatically as soon as it gets powered up at a remote location; this is similar to the local leaf functionality. The APIC controller at the ACI main data center pod and IPN needs to be preconfigured to achieve this task. Two steps take place during the discovery of a remote leaf (see Figure 4-37):

1. IP address allocation to uplink interfaces and configuration push to the remote leaf

2. TEP IP address allocation to the remote leaf

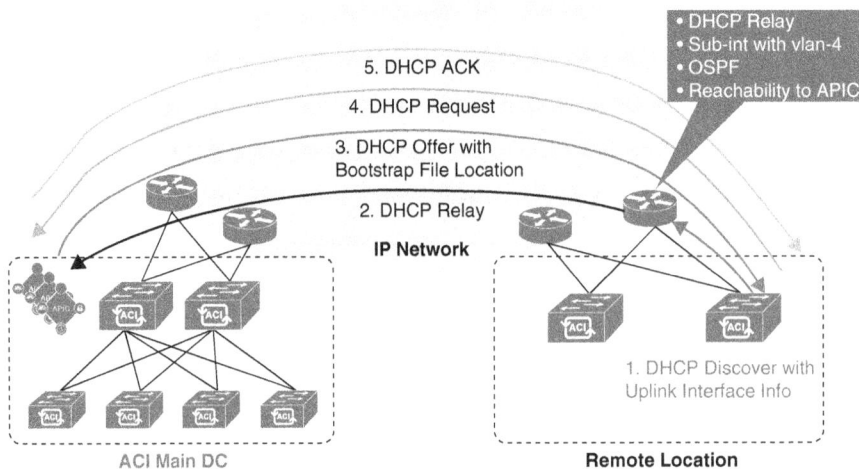

Figure 4-37   *IP Address Assignment for Remote Leaf Uplink Ports*

The following steps are involved in the complete remote leaf discovery process shown in Figure 4-38:

1. When the remote leaf is powered up, it sends a broadcast DHCP discover message out its uplink interfaces connected to the IPN router.

2. When the DHCP discover message is received by the upstream IPN router, that router relays the DHCP discover message to the APIC controller in the main data center. It is important to ensure that the IPN router's interfaces toward the remote leaf are configured with the DHCP relay message.

3. APIC controllers send DHCP offer messages for the uplink interface of the remote leaf along with the bootstrap configuration file location in the DHCP Offer message.

4. The remote leaf picks up one of the APIC controllers and sends a DHCP request for the uplink interface of the remote leaf to the APIC controller.

5. The APIC controller sends a DHCP ACK to complete the IP address allocation for the uplink IP address.

This process is repeated for all the uplink addresses. To get the bootstrap configuration file from the APIC controller, the remote leaf automatically configures a static route with the next hop of the upstream router. After receiving the configuration file, this static route is removed from the system, and the remote leaf is configured according to the configuration file.

The next step in remote leaf discovery is the assignment of the TEP address to the remote leaf switches. Figure 4-38 and the steps that follow explain the assignment on the TEP address to the remote leaf.

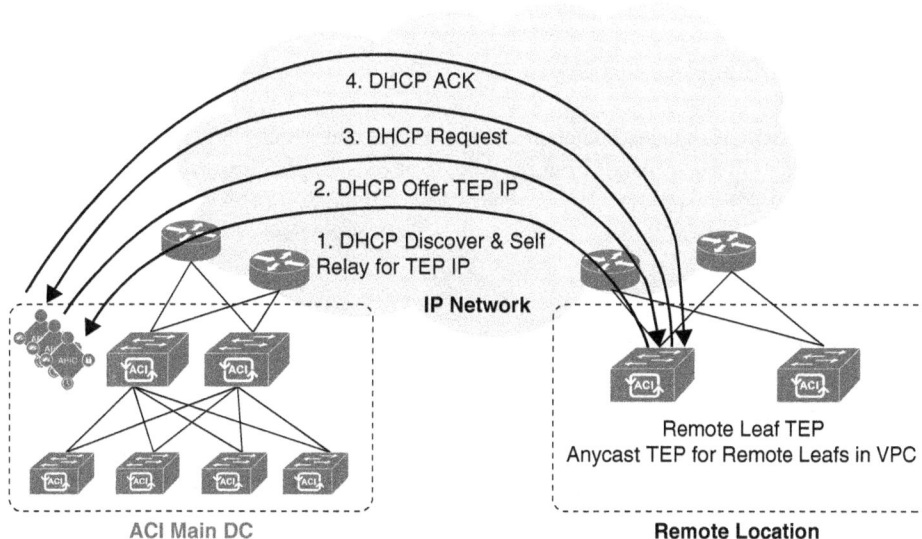

Figure 4-38 *TEP Address Assignment to a Remote Leaf*

1. The remote leaf gets full IP reachability to the APIC controllers. Once its uplink interfaces get IP addresses, it sends a DHCP discover message to APICs to receive the TEP address.

2. The APIC controllers send the DHCP offer message to the remote leaf for the TEP IP address.

3. The remote leaf picks up one of the APIC controllers and sends the DHCP request message for the TEP IP address.

4. The APIC controller sends a DHCP ACK to the remote leaf to complete the DHCP discovery process.

When this process is over, the remote leaf becomes active in the fabric, as shown in Figure 4-39.

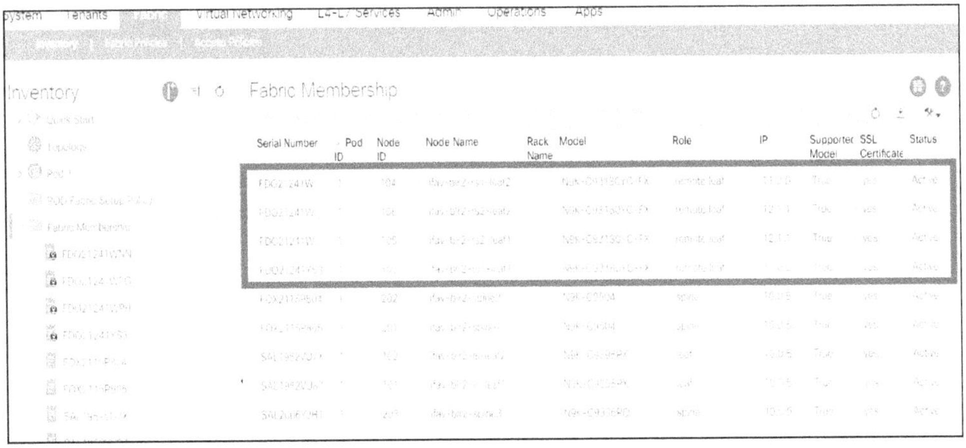

Figure 4-39 *Discovered Remote Leaf in the ACI Fabric (Single Pod)*

Remote leaf switches can also be connected in an ACI multi-pod fabric deployment. Figure 4-40 shows a screenshot from the APIC controller, highlighting the ACI fabric with two pods (Pod 1 and Pod 2). The remote leaf with node ID 105 is part of Pod 1. An important thing to note here is that a remote leaf can be part of one specific pod in a multi-pod environment.

Remote Leaf Control Plane and Data Plane

As you have learned by now, in a Cisco ACI fabric, information about all the endpoints connected to leaf switches is stored in the COOP database running on spines. Every time an endpoint is discovered and learned as being locally connected to a given leaf, that leaf node originates a COOP control plane message to communicate the endpoint information (IPv4/IPv6 and MAC addresses) to a given spine. This information is further replicated between spines using COOP.

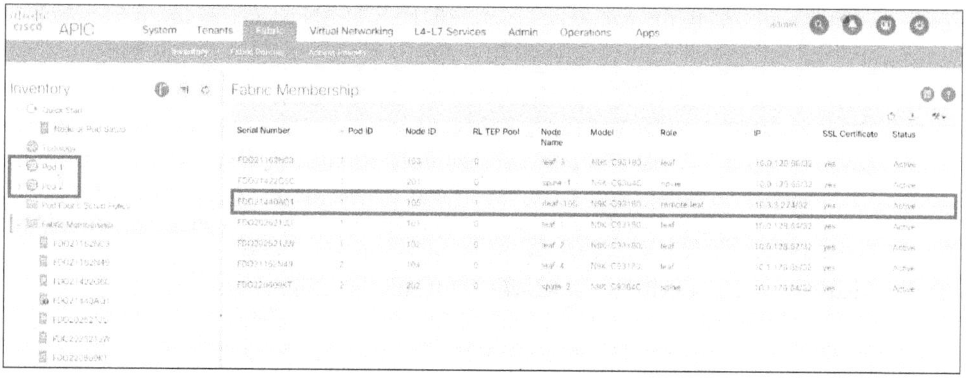

Figure 4-40 *Discovered Remote Leaf in ACI Fabric (Multi-pod)*

Similarly, in a Cisco ACI remote leaf deployment, host information for newly discovered and learned endpoints must be exchanged with spines in the main data center. A remote leaf builds a COOP session with the spines and updates the spines with the information of locally attached hosts.

Specific TEP IP address pools are defined on the spine and remote leaf to exchange control plane and data plane information, but before diving into this topic, it would be beneficial to become familiar with the acronyms you'll see throughout the examples that follow:

LL: local leaf

RL: remote leaf

EP: endpoint

TEP: tunnel endpoint

Ucast: unicast

Mcast: multicast

VPC: virtual port channel

HREP: head-end replication (multicast)

The TEP IP address pools that are defined on spine and remote leafs to exchange control plane and data plane information are as follows:

- **RL-DP-TEP (remote leaf data plane tunnel endpoint):** This is a unique IP address that is automatically assigned to each remote leaf switch from the TEP address pool that is allocated to the remote location. The VXLAN packets from a remote leaf node are originated using this TEP address as the source IP address when the remote leaf nodes are not part of a VPC domain.

- **RL-vPC-TEP (remote leaf VPC tunnel endpoint):** This is an anycast TEP address that is automatically assigned to the VPC pair of remote leafs from the TEP pool that is allocated to the remote location. All the VXLAN packets sourced from both remote leaf switches are originated from this TEP address if the remote leaf switches are part of a VPC domain.

■ **RL-Ucast-TEP (remote leaf unicast tunnel endpoint):** This is an anycast TEP address that is part of the local TEP pool automatically assigned to all the spines to which the remote leaf switches are being associated. When unicast packets are sent from endpoints connected to the remote leaf nodes to the ACI main data center pod, VXLAN-encapsulated packets are sent with the destination RL-Ucast-TEP address and the source RL-DP-TEP or RL-vPC-TEP. Any spine in the ACI main data center pod can therefore receive the traffic, decapsulate it, perform the required L2 or L3 lookup, and re-encapsulate it and forward it to the final destination (a leaf in the local pod or in a different pod in case of multi-pod fabric deployments).

■ **RL-Mcast-TEP (remote leaf unicast tunnel endpoint):** This is another anycast TEP address part of the local TEP pool automatically assigned to all the spines to which the remote leaf switches are being associated. When BUM traffic is generated by an endpoint connected to a remote leaf node, packets get encapsulated with VXLAN by the remote leaf node and sent with the destination RL-Mcast-TEP address and the source RL-DP-TEP or RL-vPC-TEP. Any of the spines in the ACI pod can receive the BUM traffic and forward it inside the fabric.

Figure 4-41 shows the endpoint learning process on a spine through the COOP session. It also shows the TEP addresses present on remote leafs and spines.

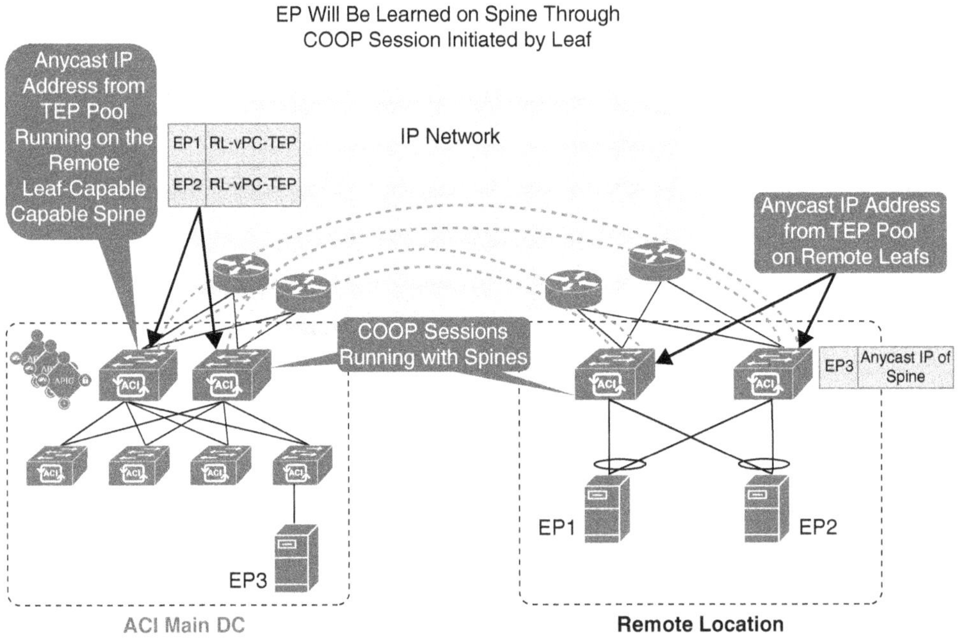

Figure 4-41   *TEP Addresses on Remote Leaf and Main Data Center Spine Connected via IPN*

Remote Leaf Design Considerations

When it comes to remote leaf design options, you should clearly understand traffic forwarding patterns in certain scenarios where two endpoints connected at the same satellite data center or colocation facility through a pair of remote leafs are required to communicate with each other but traverse the main data center spines. This unique behavior in a remote leaf is illustrated in Figure 4-42. For more details on packet forwarding in ACI, refer to Chapter 12, "Bits and Bytes of ACI Forwarding."

Note   The packet-forwarding behavior in remote leafs is different in ACI Release 4.x. This book only covers up to ACI Release 3.2.x and its feature sets. Please check the Cisco website for the latest updates on remote leaf packet forwarding behavior.

Multiple Remote Leafs at a Remote Location

Say that there is a business requirement to have more than one remote leaf switch at a remote location. In such a case, traffic between the remote leaf pair gets forwarded through the spines in the ACI main data center pod, as shown in Figure 4-42.

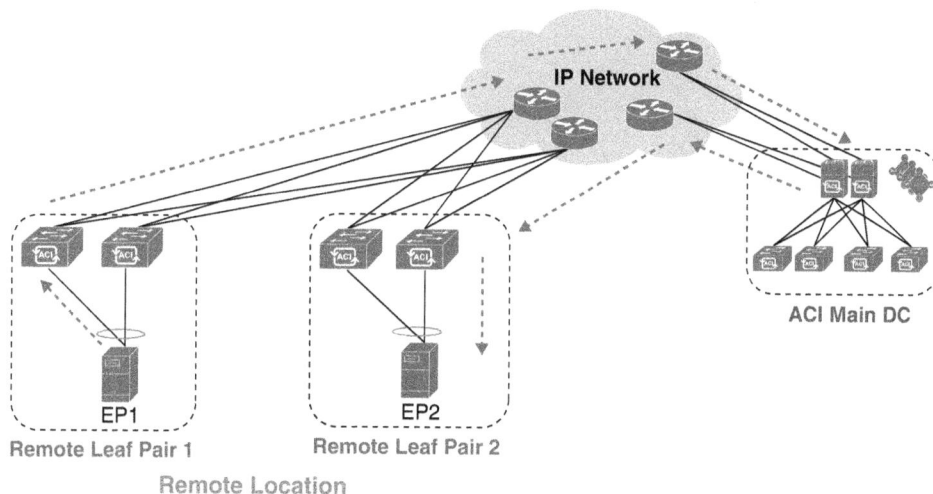

Figure 4-42   *Traffic Flow Between Multiple Remote Leafs*

When EP1 wants to talk to EP2, the packet is received by Remote Leaf Pair 1, which forwards it to Spine since it has no clue where EP2 is located. The packet source would be Remote Leaf Pair 1 Anycast VPC TEP (RL-vPC-TEP), and the packet destination would be Spine Anycast IP (RL-Ucast-TEP). Assuming that the spine has EP2 location information through the COOP session, it forwards the packet to Remote Leaf Pair 2 to be delivered to EP2. This information is sent by using Spine Anycast IP (RL-Ucast-TEP) as the source and Remote Leaf Pair 2 Anycast VPC TEP (RL-vPC-TEP) as the destination. Hence, communication between EP1 and EP2 will always flow via the spine through RL-Ucast-TEP.

Inter-VRF Traffic Between Remote Leafs

In the ACI fabric, inter-VRF-instance traffic always gets forwarded to the spine proxy because there is no remote learning that occurs with shared services in remote leaf deployments. When endpoints are connected to remote leaf nodes in different VRF instances that require communication, the inter-VRF-instance traffic gets forwarded through the spines in the main data center. This is the behavior in the older ACI releases, as illustrated in Figure 4-43. However, an enhancement introduced in ACI Release 4.x allows inter-VRF-instance traffic between endpoints connected to remote leaf switches to be locally forwarded, as illustrated in Figure 4-44.

Note   This book only covers ACI Release 3.2.x and its feature set.

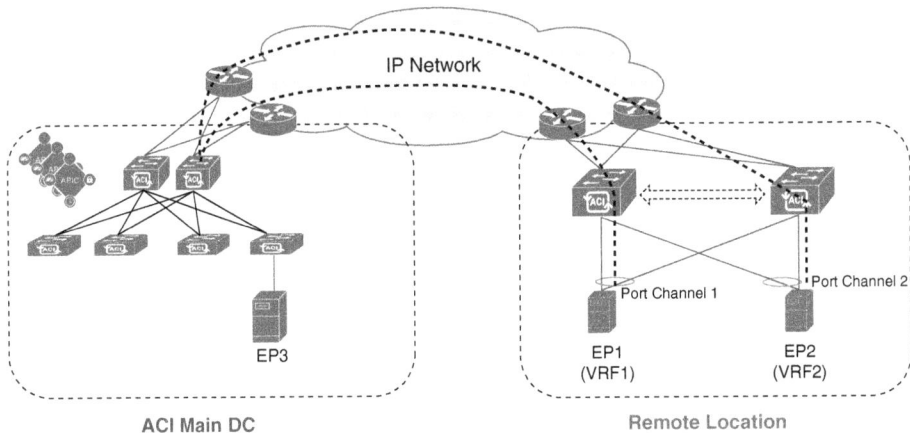

Figure 4-43   *Inter-VRF Traffic with Remote Leafs Before ACI Release 4.0*

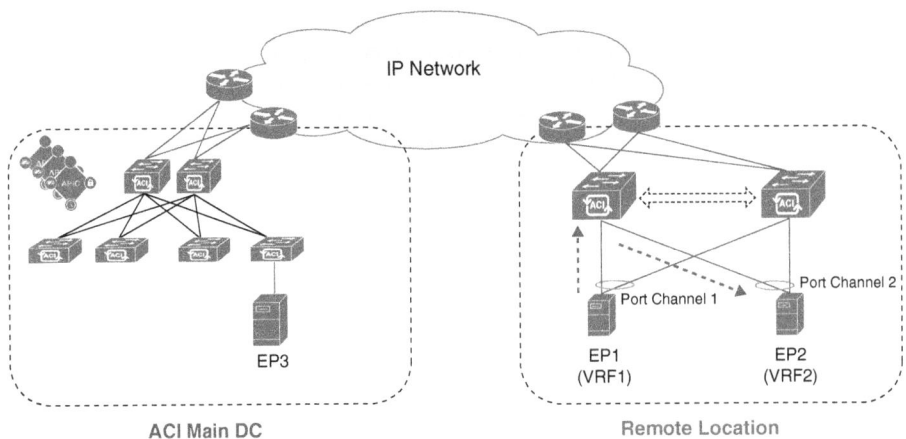

Figure 4-44   *Inter-VRF Traffic with Remote Leafs After ACI Release 4.0*

ACI Multi-Pod and Remote Leaf Integration

ACI remote leaf switches support integration with an ACI multi-pod fabric. In such a deployment, the remote leaf switches logically become part of one of the ACI pods. In the following example, the ACI main data center has two pods: Pod 1 has one remote location, and Pod 2 has two remote locations that are logically connected to it, as illustrated in Figure 4-45.

The following sections describe the considerations involved in integrating remote leafs with ACI multi-pod.

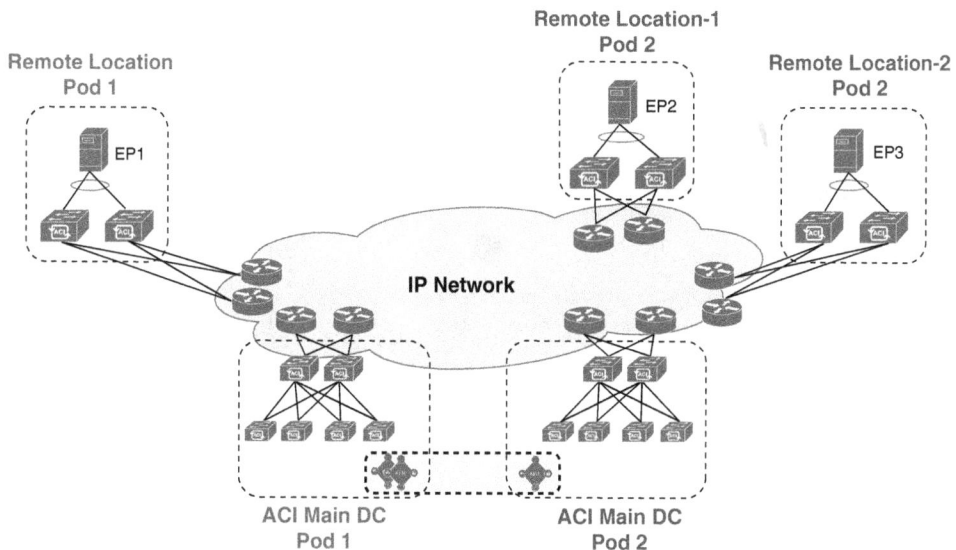

Figure 4-45   *Remote Leaf with ACI Multi-pod*

Separate Subinterface and VRF for Spine/IPN Connectivity

When remote leaf switches are deployed in a multi-pod solution, there is a need to configure separate subinterfaces and VRF instances for spine/IPN connectivity. You need to ensure that unicast and multicast traffic takes the same path and to avoid endpoint next-hop address flapping.

To understand the reason for this requirement, consider these two traffic scenarios:

- Unicast traffic between a remote leaf endpoint and a multi-pod local leaf endpoint in a different pod.

- L2 multicast traffic from a multi-pod local leaf endpoint in a different pod and a remote leaf endpoint.

In the example that follows, the remote leaf is associated to Pod 1 where EP1 is connected. EP2 is connected to the local leaf in Pod 2.

Unicast Traffic Between a Remote Leaf Endpoint and a Multi-Pod Local Leaf Endpoint in a Different Pod

Figure 4-46 highlights the unicast traffic flow initiated from endpoint EP1 connected to the remote leaf switches to endpoint EP2 in the ACI multi-pod fabric but connected in a different pod (Pod 2 in this example). The following sequence of events establishes a unicast traffic flow between EP1 and EP2. The assumption here is that EP1 and EP2 are part of the same BD and IP subnet.

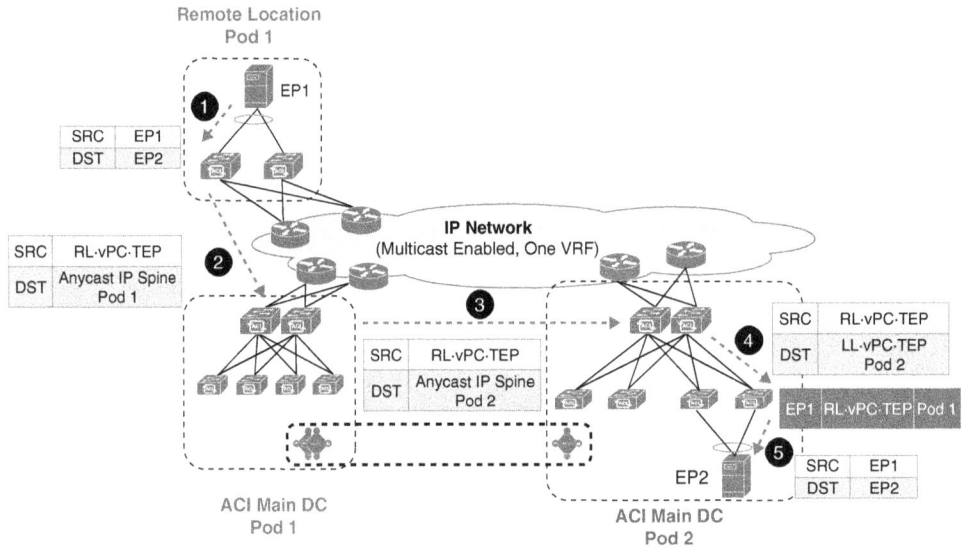

Figure 4-46 *Unicast Traffic from a Remote Leaf Endpoint to a Multi-pod Local Leaf Endpoint in a Different Pod*

1. EP1 sends a unicast packet to EP2, which is part of the same BD and subnet with the source MAC address of EP1 and the destination MAC address of EP2.

2. The packet is received by one of the remote leaf switches, which performs a Layer 2 lookup for EP2's MAC address in its hardware table. Of course, it finds no matching entry for EP2 since it is not connected locally, and it is the first conversation between EP1 and EP2. Therefore, the remote leaf switch uses the hardware proxy method to encapsulate this packet with the VXLAN header and forwards it toward the spine in Pod 1 (since the remote leaf is associated with Pod 1) with the source IP address being the anycast TEP address of the remote leafs (RL-vPC-TEP), and the destination IP address being the anycast TEP address of the spines in Pod 1 (RL-Ucast-TEP).

3. One of the spines in Pod 1 receives the packet. The spine performs a lookup in the COOP database and finds that EP2 is part of Pod 2 through EVPN control plane learning updates. As a consequence, it changes the destination IP address to the anycast TEP address of the spines in Pod 2.

4. One of the spines in Pod 2 receives this packet, performs the lookup in the COOP database, and forwards the packet to the local leaf where EP2 is located. While doing that, it changes the destination IP address to the TEP address of the local leaf (LL-vPC-TEP) of Pod 2 where EP2 is located.

5. The local leaf of Pod 2 receives the packet and updates the hardware table with EP1 information with the next hop of RL-vPC-TEP, based on the source TEP address of the packet, and forwards traffic to EP2.

This is the normal packet forwarding behavior in ACI. On the return path from EP2 to EP1, the local leaf of Pod 2 knows the location of EP1 in its hardware table to be reachable via RL-vPC-TEP, and because the remote leaf and multi-pod are sharing the same IP network in the same VRF instance, it can directly send the packet to remote leaf switches over the IP network without going through the Pod 1 spines. Once the return packet is received, the remote leaf adds an entry for EP2 to its hardware table to be reachable via LL-vPC-TEP of Pod 2, as shown in Figure 4-47.

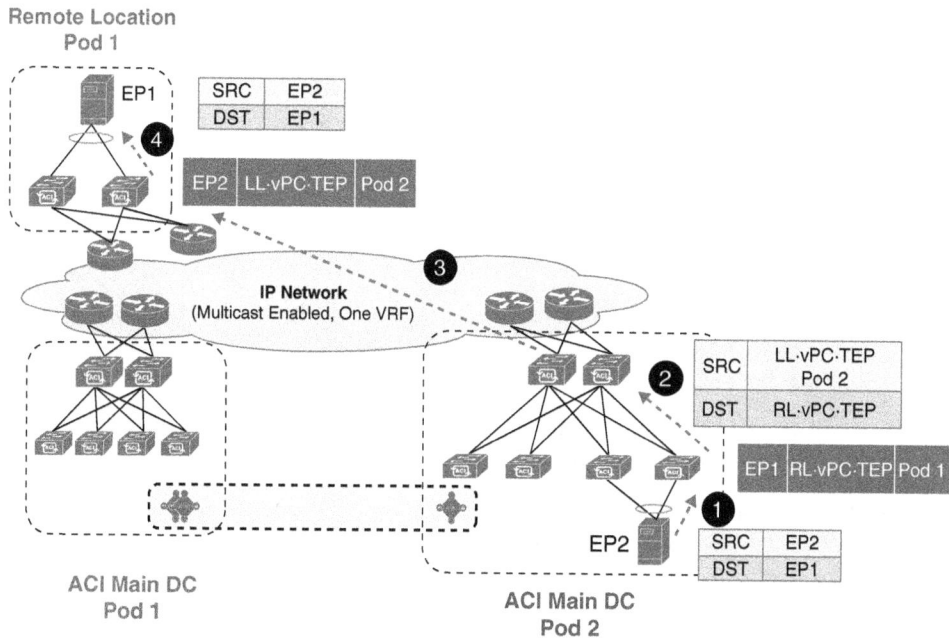

Figure 4-47 *Return Unicast Traffic from the Multi-pod Local Leaf Endpoint in a Different Pod to a Remote Leaf Endpoint*

L2 Multicast Traffic from a Multi-Pod Local Leaf Endpoint in a Different Pod to a Remote Leaf Endpoint

Figure 4-48 shows what happens when a multicast traffic flow is sent from EP2 to EP1 without configuration of a separate subinterface and separate VRF instance in the IPN, assuming that EP1 and EP2 are part of the same BD and IP subnet.

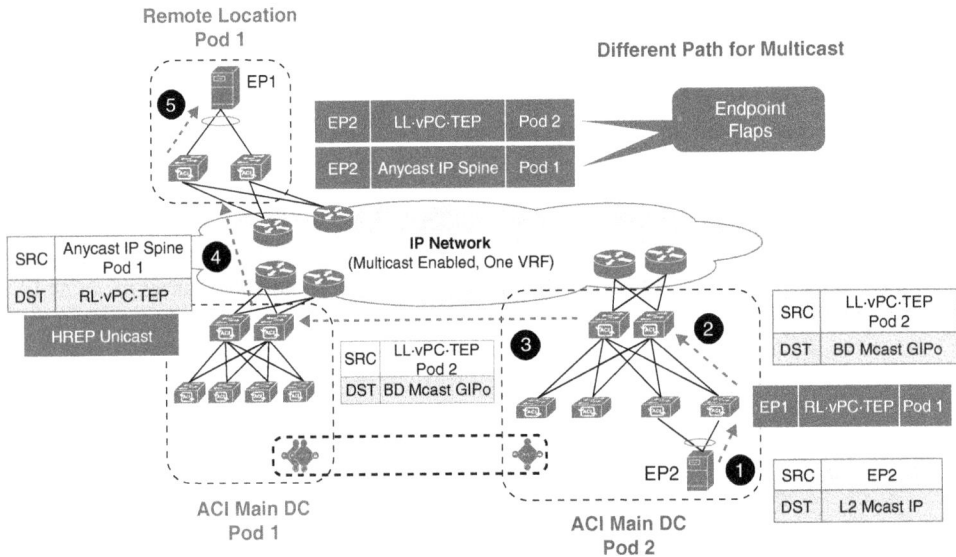

Figure 4-48 *L2 Multicast Traffic from Multi-pod Local Leaf Endpoint in Different Pod to Remote Leaf Endpoint*

1. EP2 sends multicast traffic with the source MAC address of EP2 and the destination MAC address of the L2 multicast group.

2. The multi-pod local leaf in Pod 2 receives this packet, checks for the BD of EP2, and forwards the packet to the GIPo multicast IP address of the BD. In ACI, multicast trees are built on spines.

3. Local spines in Pod 2 receive the packet and forward it to spines of Pod 1 (assuming that the BD resides in that pod as well) with the BD multicast group as the destination.

4. In an ACI remote leaf deployment, PIM multicast routing is not supported, and hence the packet is forwarded from the Pod 1 spine directly to the remote leaf by using head-end replication (HREP). The spine in Pod 1 forwards the packet to the remote leaf after encapsulating the multicast packet in a unicast VXLAN packet with the anycast IP address of Pod 1 spines as the source and the anycast IP address of remote leafs (RL-vPC-TEP) as the destination.

5. The remote leaf now learns that EP2 is the next-hop anycast IP address of the Pod 1 spine from its hardware table. It had previously learned about EP2 from the multi-pod local leaf TEP (LL-vPC-TEP) of Pod 2 during the unicast traffic flow.

In this example, unicast and multicast traffic take different paths because separate sub-interfaces and separate VRF instances in the IPN are not configured, which ultimately results in endpoint information flapping on the remote leaf, as Figure 4-48 illustrates.

To avoid this condition, Figure 4-49 highlights the configuration needed to support the integration of remote leaf switches with an ACI multi-pod fabric by creating a separate vlan-5 interface and a separate VRF instance between spines in multiple pods and the IPN. It is critical to highlight that this configuration is *not* required in a single-pod design (full or partially meshed fabric).

Note Starting with Cisco ACI Release 4.1(2), there is no longer a need to deploy a separate vlan-5 subinterface for integrating remote leaf nodes with multi-pod, as outlined in the steps that follow. This book covers up to ACI Release 3.2.x and its features. Always check the latest release notes at the Cisco website for any functional or configuration changes.

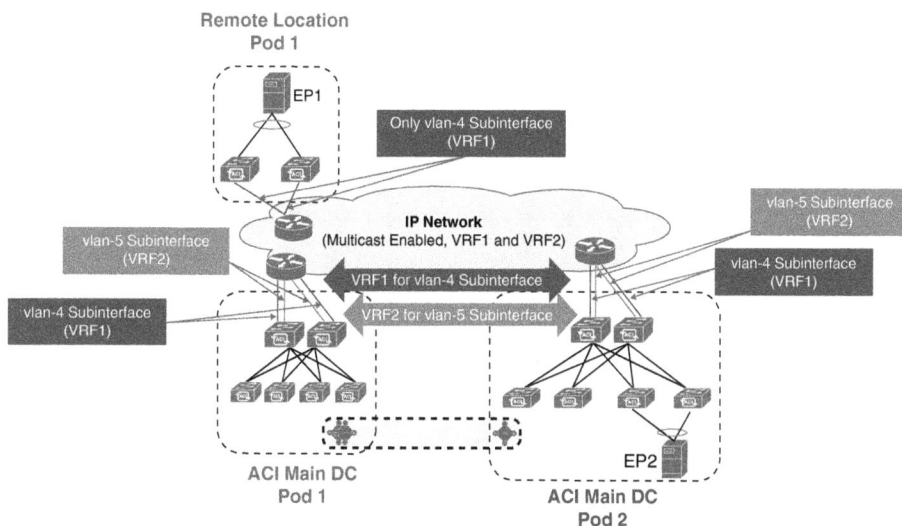

Figure 4-49 *Configuration Details for Remote Leaf with Multi-pod*

As shown in Figure 4-49, the following measures are required to deploy a remote leaf in the ACI multi-pod fabric:

■ In a regular ACI multi-pod configuration, an L3Out in the tenant *Infra* is required to leverage the vlan-4 subinterfaces on the spines to peer via OSPF with the IPN routers. For integrating remote leaf switches with a multi-pod fabric, it is also necessary to create a separate L3Out in the tenant *Infra* to leverage vlan-5 subinterface peering via OSPF as well with IPN routers in ACI code 3.2.x and earlier code.

■ The corresponding vlan-5 subinterfaces on the upstream IPN routers are configured in a different routing domain (such as VRF2) than the one used by vlan-4 subinterfaces (such as VRF1) for east–west multi-pod traffic.

- The IPN must extend connectivity across pods for this second VRF instance (VRF2 in the example) to which the vlan-5 subinterfaces are connected. This can be achieved in multiple ways, such as with MPLS VPN, VXLAN, or VRF-Lite.

- The remote leaf switches remain configured with only vlan-4 subinterfaces used to peer OSPF with the IPN. As mentioned earlier, vlan-4 subinterfaces on upstream routers are configured in VRF1. As a consequence, reachability information for the remote leaf TEP pool is propagated across the IPN only in the VRF1 context.

- The APIC controller configures spines in Pod 1 to automatically advertise the remote leaf TEP pool address (as the remote leaf is associated to Pod 1) on the vlan-5 subinterface and in VRF2.

- Similarly, APIC also automatically configures a route map on spines in Pod 2 to reject the remote leaf TEP pool address on its vlan-4 subinterface and in VRF1 and only allows it to be learned on its vlan-5 subinterface and in VRF2, as shown in Figure 4-50. Therefore, packets always flow through spines of Pod 1 since Pod 2 does not have a direct connection to the remote leaf because of the separation of the vlan-5 subinterface and a separate VRF instance.

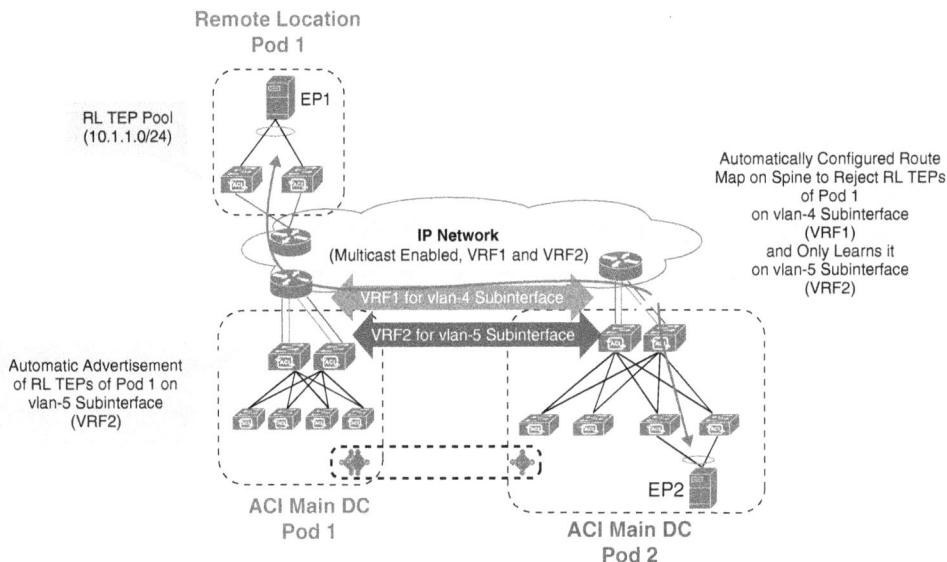

Figure 4-50 *Automatic Configuration by the APIC for a Remote Leaf in Multi-pod*

Now the traffic path is the same for both unicast and multicast traffic from the multi-pod local leaf to the remote leaf; hence, there is no endpoint information flapping on the remote leaf. Again, as a reminder the additional vlan-5 configuration for a remote leaf is only required in ACI code 3.2.x or earlier. Starting with ACI code 4.1(2), this extra configuration for the vlan-5 subinterface is not required anymore. Always check the Cisco website for the latest information and modified configurations with respect to the software code you want to run in your data center.

Logical Design

Now that you have learned about various design options for the physical build-out of ACI fabrics, it's time to go over some of the logical design aspects of ACI. As discussed earlier, ACI works in the Clos architecture, also referred to as a fully meshed fabric network, where leafs are connected to spines for traffic forwarding through nonblocking links. On top of this physical infrastructure, you construct your application logic. Multiple application tiers reside on this physical fabric architecture, which is discussed in this section in the context of a few real-world logical design scenarios.

Design 1: Container-as-a-Service Using the OpenShift Platform and Calico CNI

Key Topic

Before we dive into the design details, let's look at why customers might want to use container as a service (CaaS) and why they might choose OpenShift. Much like virtual machines (VM), containers allow you to package applications together with libraries and other dependencies and provide isolation for running your application services. However, whereas a VM virtualizes the hardware stack, the container approach involves virtualizing the operating system running on top of an OS kernel. In this way, it is lightweight, consumes less memory, and offers fast operation on a large scale. A container platform offers application development teams the ability to move fast, deploy their software efficiently, and operate at an unprecedented scale. OpenShift, a next-generation container-hosting platform offered by Red Hat, enables developers to create, deploy, and manage their applications using Kubernetes with a complete automation suite of tools. OpenShift is gaining a lot of momentum in the industry. ACI provides seamless integration of the OpenShift platform using its own Container Network Interface (CNI). The benefit of this integration is that you get the same policy model and segmentation you use on your bare-metal and virtualized application workloads. (The OpenShift integration with ACI is explained in detail in Chapter 6, "VMM Integration.")

Business Case

In this case, the customer wants to use industry open standard Calico CNI with its OpenShift platform. The company wants to connect rack loads of bare-metal servers with a single ACI fabric's two top-of-rack (ToR) leafs with 10 Gbps connectivity in each data center. These servers are required to load the operating system using Preboot Execution Environment (PXE). The other business requirement is to stretch the OpenShift cluster to multiple data centers over an IPN. The OpenShift pod and services IPN needs to be floated between the two data centers in active/active fashion to provide service uptime even during any failures in one of the data centers. Proper route filtering and network segmentation techniques must be used in the design to protect the customer's overall network. In this case, it is important to design application logic to accommodate this customer's needs.

Design Solution

Figure 4-51 shows the design logic for this example: a simple ACI topology with a single rack of OpenShift servers in each data center.

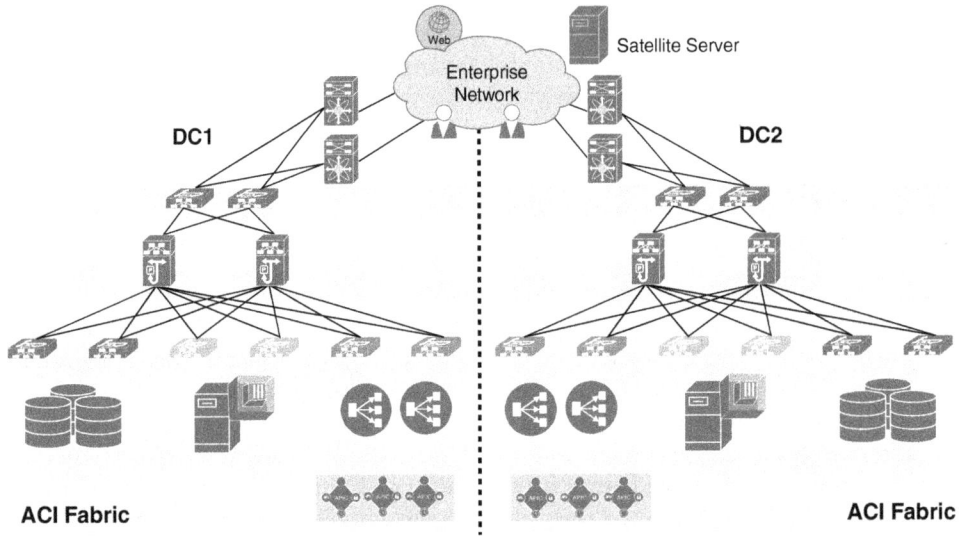

Figure 4-51   *OpenShift Design with ACI Using Calico*

Figure 4-51 shows a single rack unit (42-RU) of bare-metal servers connected to two ToR leafs using Nexus 93180YC-EX (48 host ports) for 1/10 Gbps connectivity. Each of the 2RU standalone servers is connected via two 10 Gbps VPCs: one for data and one for storage connectivity. Server management ports (for console and other server management operations) have 1 Gbps connectivity to the same ToR leaf pair. You can have roughly 18 × 2RU servers per rack deployed with OpenShift Container Platform. NAS devices are connected via another VPC to a separate pair of ToR leafs, and so are the load balancer active/standby pair as shown in Figure 4-52.

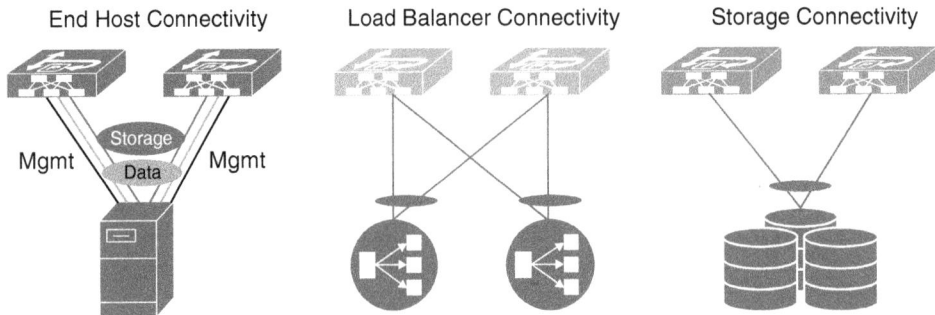

Figure 4-52   *Server, Storage, and Load Balancer Connectivity with ACI*

With servers, storage, and load balancers physically connected to ACI leafs, let's now talk about how to put this all together in a logical configuration. In order to extend the OpenShift cluster within a rack, between racks in the same data center, and between racks in separate data centers, Kubernetes node and services networks need to be advertised out via BGP.

Before going into BGP configuration for CaaS, let's first elaborate the load balancer configuration required to distribute the traffic load of the OpenShift pod and services network. Load balancers are connected to a separate leaf pair via a separate L3Out using an OSPF not-so-stubby area (NSSA) to advertise the virtual IP (VIP) and source NAT (SNAT) subnets. This load balancer pair enables internal users to access container-based applications. For external user access, a separate pair of load balancers is required to be connected to the DMZ layer of the network. Finally, a separate pair of leafs is connected to a pair of routers for external network connectivity from ACI via another L3Out, using OSPF NSSA advertising prefixes into and out of the ACI fabric. Figure 4-53 shows the sample ACI configuration for the load balancer L3Out using the OSPF routing protocol.

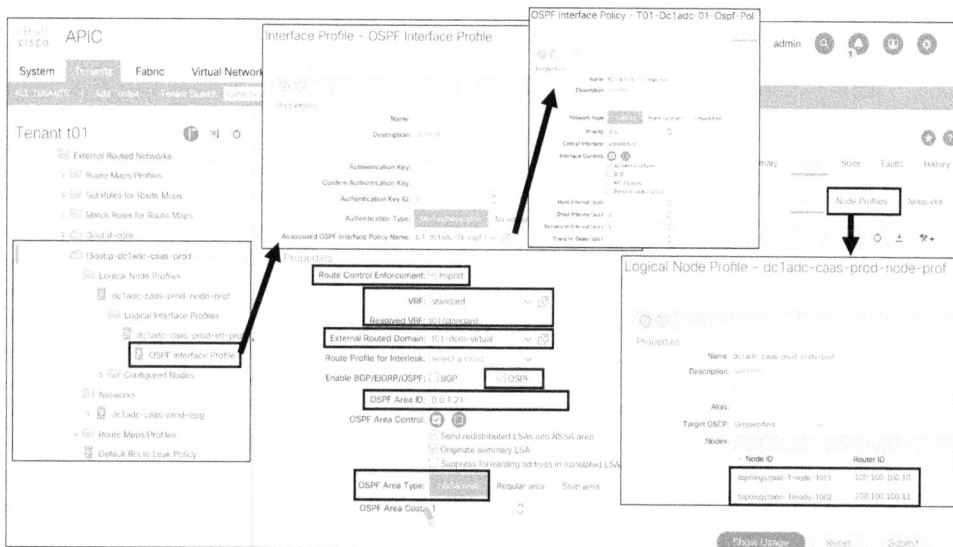

Figure 4-53 *Load Balancer L3Out Configuration in ACI (OSPF)*

As shown in Figure 4-54, first you need to configure the L3Out routing policy. In this case, it is OSPF with NSSA 0.0.1.1. Select the appropriate VRF (in this case, standard) and external routed domain (in this case, t01-dom-virtual). To protect your network with any route anomalies from peering with load balancers, you should apply the *Import* route control enforcement policy to allow only certain prefixes in the ACI fabric from this L3Out route peering. You can then configure the logical node profile and select the leaf node IDs that you are planning to peer with the load balancer and configure the router IDs for each. Ensure that the OSPF interface profile with network type broadcast is created and associated to the load balancer L3Out. For security, it is advisable to use MD5 authentication.

Now, you need to configure the logical interface profiles. The load balancers in this example are virtualized, so a switch virtual interface (SVI) needs to be configured as a transport link between the load balancer and ToR leafs. Figure 4-54 demonstrates this configuration for the active load balancer with route peering transport addresses 151.151.151.1/28 (leaf node ID 1001) and 151.151.151.2/28 (leaf node ID 1002). The VLAN used for this sample SVI configuration is 1072. You need to repeat a similar configuration for the standby load balancer as well, with different route peering transport addresses and a different VLAN. It is preferable to connect the standby load balancer to another pair of leafs for redundancy.

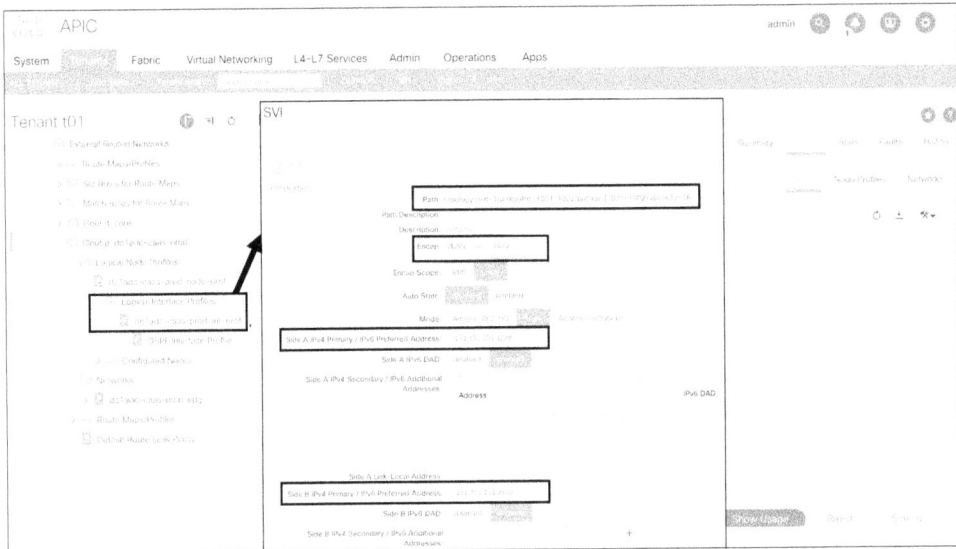

Figure 4-54   *Load Balancer L3Out Configuration in ACI: Logical Interface Profile*

Next, you need to classify the load balancer VIP and SNAT subnets under the Networks tab to apply a contract for traffic forwarding between the load balancer L3Out, CaaS L3Out, and data center core L3Out, as shown in Figure 4-55. Ensure that the contract (in this case, l3out:p-dc1adc-caas-prod-c01) is created for load balancer traffic forwarding.

In order to protect the rest of the network with route anomalies coming in from load balancer networks, you need to configure route map profiles. To do so, you need to match the prefixes (in this case VIP subnet 1.1.1.0/24 and SNAT subnet 2.2.2.0/24) and then apply this route map profile to load balancer L3Out as an import, as shown in Figure 4-56.

Make sure to create the default route leak policy because this OSPF connectivity is using an NSSA. Figure 4-57 shows this configuration.

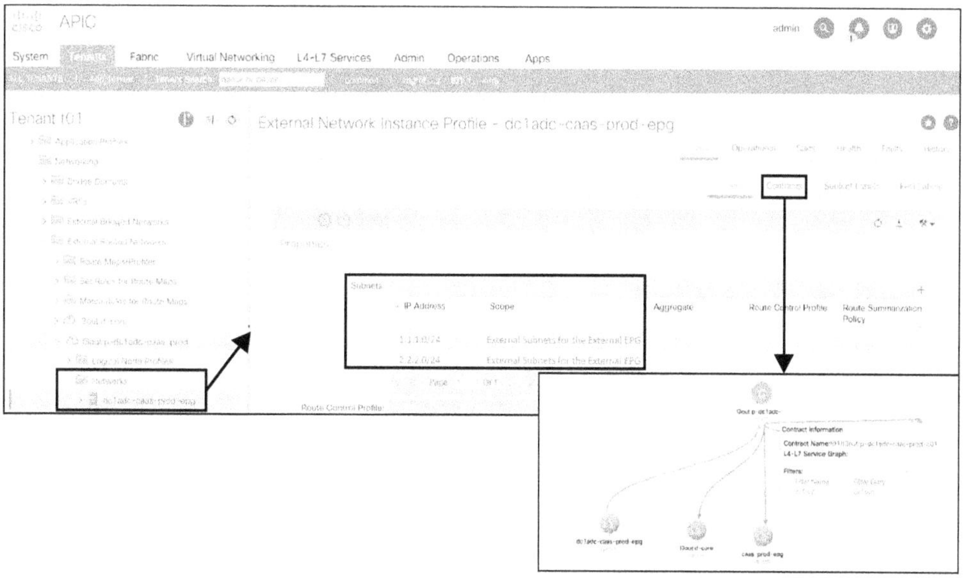

Figure 4-55   *Load Balancer L3Out Configuration in ACI: Networks*

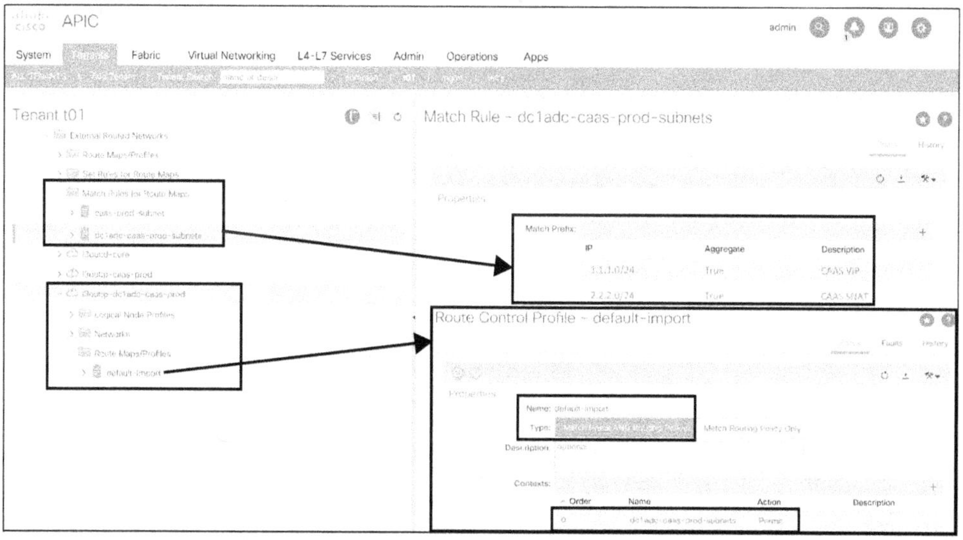

Figure 4-56   *Load Balancer L3Out Configuration in ACI: Route Map Profile*

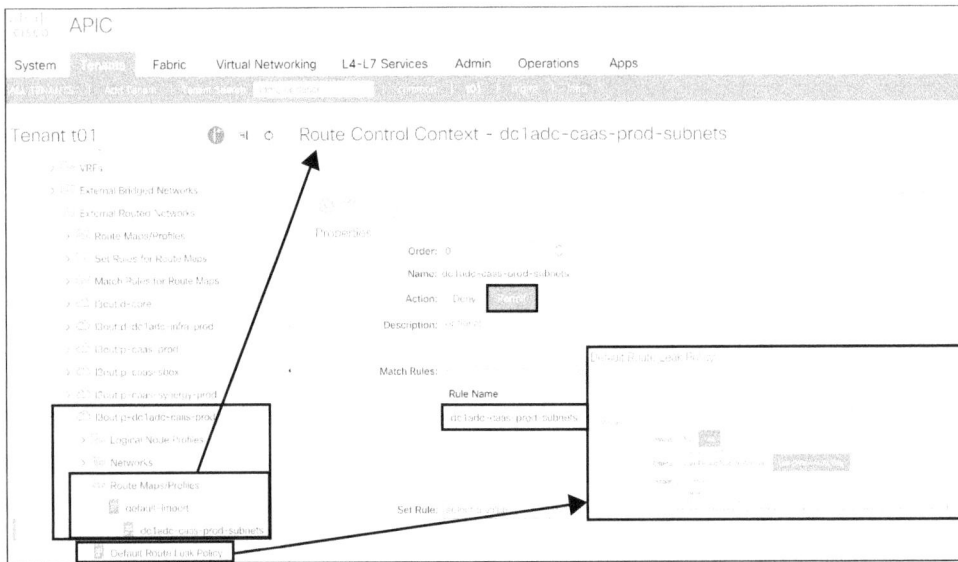

Figure 4-57   *Load Balancer L3Out Configuration in ACI: Route Map Profile and Default Route Leak*

After configuring the load balancer L3Out, you can move on to the CaaS L3Out configuration. As suggested earlier for CaaS cluster connectivity, you can use BGP to peer each of the OpenShift servers to its respective ToR leafs. An open-source BGP daemon called BIRD can be used for this purpose. The way you do is by assigning a BGP autonomous system (AS) to each OpenShift server Calico CNI, along with a BGP local AS to each ToR leaf pair. ACI uses MP-BGP within the fabric with a BGP AS assigned that you can use to build a full-mesh iBGP peering extending into an OpenShift cluster as well. However, for better control of route distribution from each of the OpenShift nodes, it is recommended to use eBGP peering from the ACI ToR leaf pair to each of the OpenShift nodes. You can use private AS numbers ranging from 64512 to 65535 (a total of 1023) for this purpose. You would require 19 BGP AS numbers per rack (18 for servers and 1 for the leaf pair). BGP configuration is executed via a single extended routed network commonly known as L3Out through eBGP peering with 18 OpenShift servers per rack.

You need to assign two subnets in this case (with size depending on usage): one for the OpenShift pod network and the other for the services network that will float between the two data centers over the IPN to extend the OpenShift cluster. It is important to ensure that proper route filtering is in place for each of these L3Out configurations. This can be done through route maps with matching criteria of the OpenShift pod and services subnets you assign. Use the *Import* route control enforcement policy in this CaaS L3Out to filter route ingress to ACI. You can create route map *Import* and *Export* policies by associating those pod and service subnets. In this way, only the networks you allow from OpenShift servers get into ACI.

Much as in the load balancer L3Out configuration, you need to configure the L3Out routing policy. In the CaaS L3Out configuration, it is BGP. Select the appropriate VRF (in this case, standard) and external routed domain (in this case, t01-dom-phys). To protect your network with any route anomalies from peering with OpenShift nodes, you should apply the *Import* route control enforcement policy to only allow certain prefixes in the ACI fabric from this L3Out route peering. Then you configure the logical node profile and select the leaf node IDs that you are planning to peer with OpenShift nodes and configure the router IDs for each. Ensure that the BGP protocol profile with the proper BGP timers is created and associated to the CaaS L3Out. For security, it is advisable to use a password for BGP route peering. Figure 4-58 shows an example of an ACI configuration of CaaS L3Out.

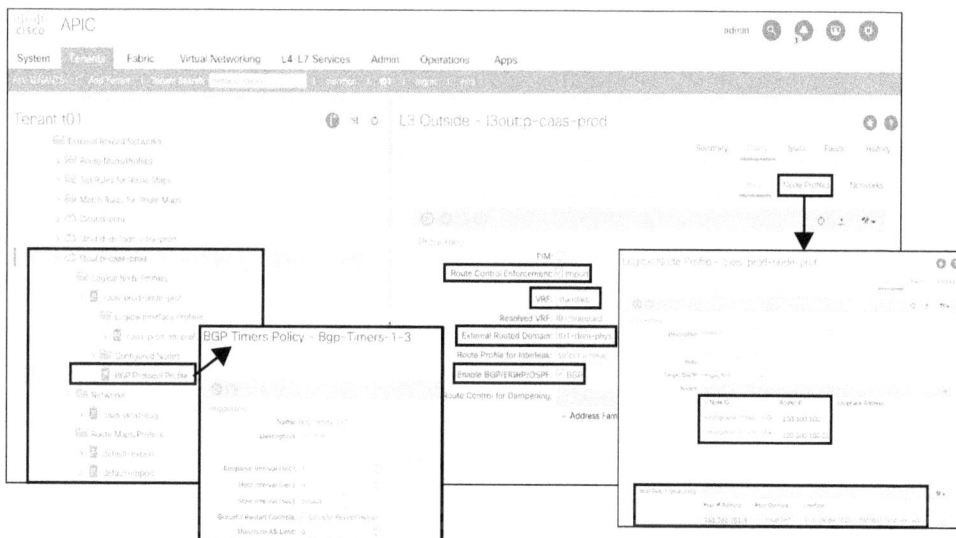

Figure 4-58   *CaaS L3Out Configuration in ACI (BGP)*

Now you need to configure the logical interface profiles. As mentioned earlier, CaaS nodes are connected via a VPC called Data, which is used for both L3Out configuration and EPG staging, which means an SVI needs to be configured as a transport link between CaaS nodes and ToR leafs. Figure 4-59 demonstrates this configuration for the single CaaS node with route peering transport addresses 161.161.161.1/29 (leaf node ID 1001) and 161.161.161.2/29 (leaf node ID 1002). In CaaS L3Out SVI configuration, you should use the secondary IP address (in this case, 161.161.161.3/29) as a default gateway for OpenShift nodes prior to establishing eBGP peering for OpenShift software installation. The BGP peer IP address in this sample configuration for the CaaS node is 161.161.161.4. The VLAN used for this sample SVI configuration is 102. You need to do a similar configuration for other OpenShift nodes as well, with different route peering transport and secondary addresses and VLANs.

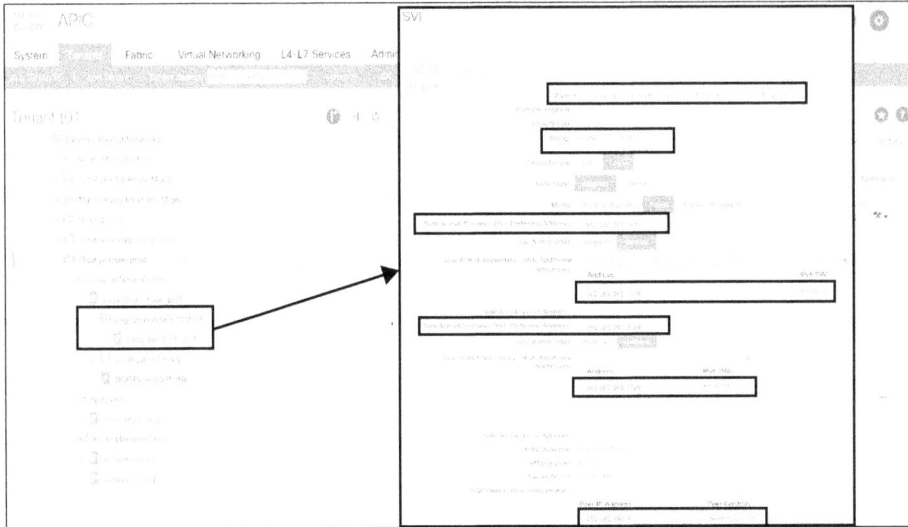

Figure 4-59 *CAAS L3Out Configuration in ACI: Logical Interface Profile*

You also need to create the eBGP peer configuration, as shown in Figure 4-60.

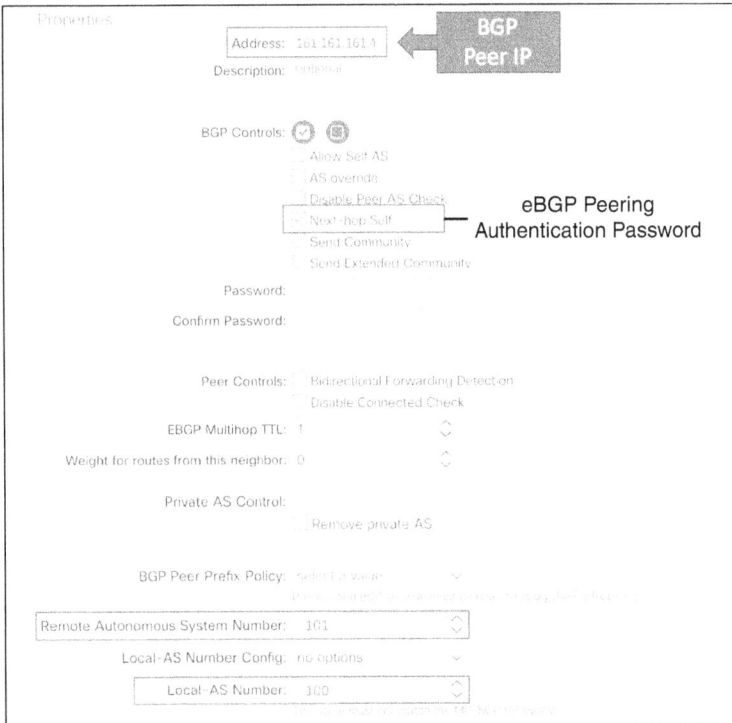

Figure 4-60 *CAAS eBGP Peer Configuration*

Example 4-2 shows a sample Calico manifest file for BGP peering with ACI leafs.

Example 4-2   *Calico Manifest Files for BGP Peering with ACI Leafs*

```
node.yaml:

apiVersion: projectcalico.org/v3
kind: Node
metadata:
      name: master0.caas.dc1.cisco.com
spec:
      bgp:
         asNumber: 101
         ipv4Address: 161.161.161.4

leaf1003.yaml:

apiVersion: projectcalico.org/v3
kind: BGPPeer
metadata:
      name: leaf1003
spec:
      peerIP: 161.161.161.1
      node: master0.caas.dc1.cisco.com
      asNumber: 100

leaf1004.yaml:

apiVersion: projectcalico.org/v3
kind: BGPPeer
metadata:
      name: leaf1004
spec:
      peerIP: 161.161.161.2
      node: master0.caas.dc1.cisco.com
      asNumber:  100
```

Next, you need to classify the OpenShift pod and services subnets under the Networks tab to apply a contract for traffic forwarding between the CaaS L3Out, data center core L3Out, and load balancer L3Out, as shown in Figure 4-61. Ensure that the contract (in this case, l3out:p-caas-prod-c01) has been created for CaaS traffic forwarding.

In order to protect the rest of the network from route anomalies coming in from CaaS networks, you need to configure route map profiles. To do so, you need to match the prefixes (in this case, OpenShift pod subnet 50.50.50.0/24 and services subnet 60.60.60.0/24) and then apply this route map profile to CaaS L3Out as *Import* and *Export*, as shown in Figure 4-62.

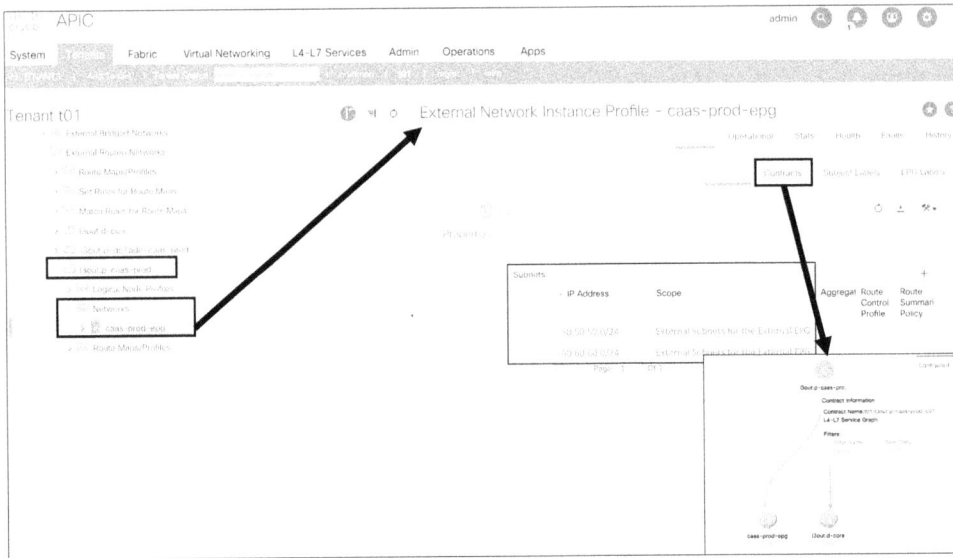

Figure 4-61   *CAAS L3Out Configuration in ACI: Networks*

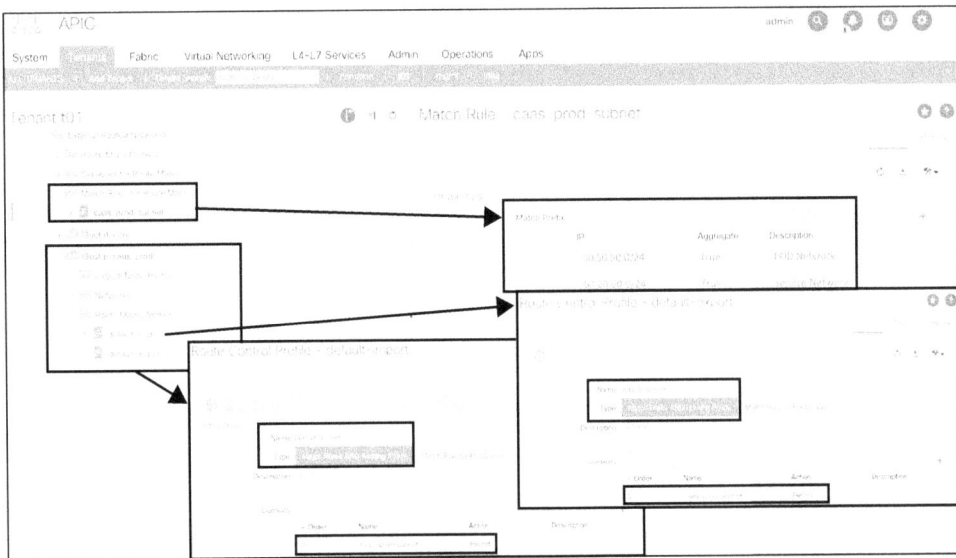

Figure 4-62   *CAAS L3Out Configuration in ACI: Route Map Profile*

As you know by now, ACI uses a whitelist policy model in which traffic forwards only when you allow it via contract. You can use ACI contracts between these separate L3Outs for further protection of your network. Remember that ACI provides a physical infrastructure on top of which you deploy your various application tiers, and hence it is important to protect each one of them from others. Figure 4-63 shows application traffic flow.

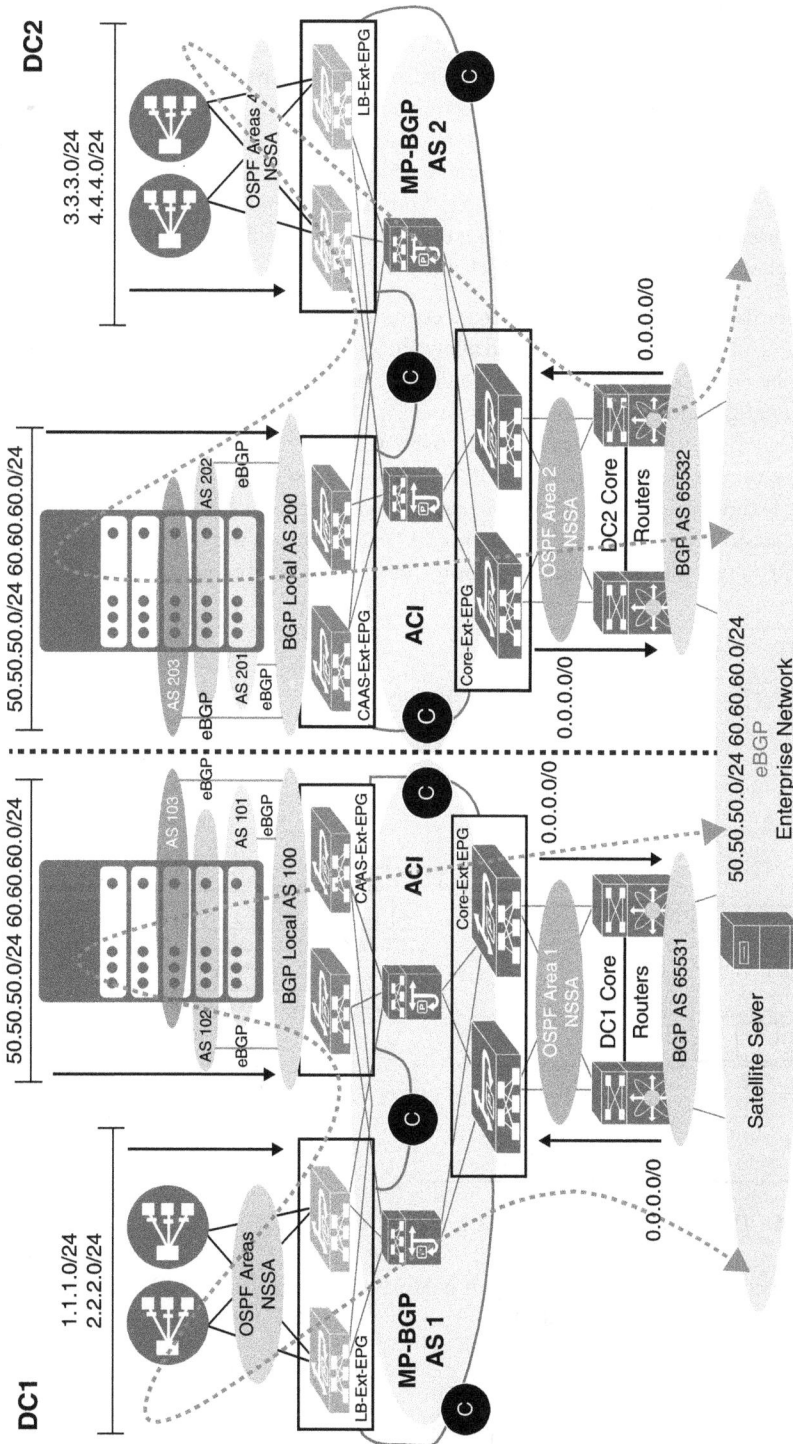

Figure 4-63   *OpenShift Cluster with ACI Extended Between Data Centers*

Notice in Figure 4-63 and preceding configuration examples that 1.1.1.0/24 and 2.2.2.0/24 are only allowed to be advertised into ACI from load balancers in EDC1, and 3.3.3.0/24 and 4.4.4.0/24 are only allowed to be advertised into ACI from load balancers in EDC2, which are the VIP and SNAT subnets for internal user access in each of the data centers (DC1 and DC2, respectively). Similarly, only 50.50.50.0/24 from the OpenShift pod network subnet and 60.60.60.0/24 from the OpenShift services network subnet are allowed to be advertised out into the ACI fabric in both data centers. Ensure that the transport subnets used for route peering in L3Out are included in the match criterion in route maps; otherwise, they will not be reachable.

At the border leaf connecting to the data center core router side, you can use the *Export* route control enforcement policy and allow all networks (0.0.0.0/0) since you are already protecting on the edge of the application layer through route filtering and contracts in L3Out configurations for load balancers and CaaS. Figure 4-64 shows a sample ACI configuration of a border leaf connecting to the data center core router. OSPF is used as the routing protocol for data center core L3Out; hence, most of the configuration is similar to what is shown earlier for the load balancer L3Out—except that the transport links used here are Layer 3 interfaces instead of SVI. Therefore, in the OSPF interface profile, the OSPF network type should be point-to-point instead of broadcast.

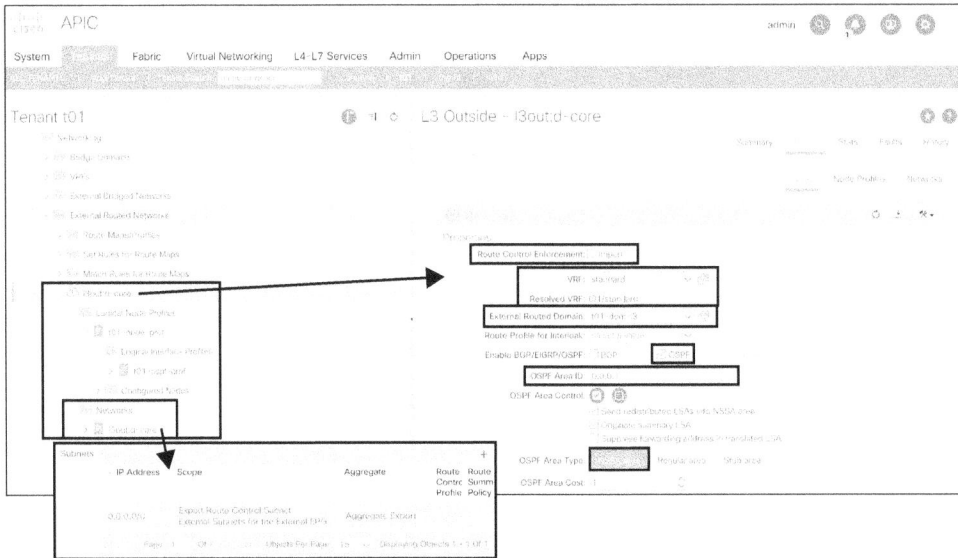

Figure 4-64   *Data Center Core L3Out Configuration in ACI*

The data center core routers peering with ACI border leafs using OSPF use the sample configuration shown in Example 4-3.

Example 4-3   *Sample Configuration of Data Center Core Routers Peering with ACI Border Leaf Using OSPF*

```
DC1-Core ←→ ACI Border Leaf (OSPF):
interface Ethernet1/6
  description Link Connecting DC1-BL201 on Eth1/16
  no switchport
  mtu 9000
  ip address 150.150.150.0/31
  ip ospf authentication message-digest
  ip ospf message-digest-key 1 md5 3 1d7b031bc9c9bb77
  ip ospf dead-interval 15
  ip ospf hello-interval 5
  ip ospf network point-to-point
  no ip ospf passive-interface
  ip router ospf 1 area 0.0.0.1
  no shutdown

ip prefix-list CAAS-SUBNETS seq 10 permit 50.50.50.0/24 le 32          ← CAAS pod
  Subnet
ip prefix-list CAAS-SUBNETS seq 20 permit 60.60.60.0/24 le 32          ← CAAS Ser-
  vices Subnet
ip prefix-list CAAS-SUBNETS seq 30 permit 161.161.161.0/24 le 32      ← CAAS eBGP
  Peering Transport Subnet

route-map Redistr_65531_BGP permit 10           ← Creating route-map to match CAAS
  Subnets
  match ip address prefix-list CAAS-SUBNETS

router ospf 1
  router-id 100.100.100.1
  area 0.0.0.1 nssa no-summary
  redistribute bgp 65531 route-map Redistr_65531_BGP ← Redistributing routes into
  DC1 ACI fabric learned from DC2 via BGP
  log-adjacency-changes
  area 0.0.0.1 authentication message-digest
  timers throttle spf 5000 10000 10000
  timers lsa-group-pacing 240
  auto-cost reference-bandwidth 100000 Mbps
  passive-interface default
```

The data center core routers running NX-OS are connected to each other via eBGP. For proper router filtering between data centers DC1 and DC2, you need to define CaaS subnets by using a prefix list and apply them through route maps. Example 4-4 shows the sample configuration on the data center core routers.

Example 4-4 *Sample Configuration of Data Center Core Routers Filtering CaaS Subnets Between Them via* eBGP

```
DC1-Core ↔ DC2-Core (eBGP):
interface Ethernet1/1
  description Link Connecting to DC2 Core
  no switchport
  mtu 9000
  ip address 200.200.200.1/31

ip prefix-list CAAS-SUBNETS seq 10 permit 50.50.50.0/24 le 32      ← CaaS pod
  subnet
ip prefix-list CAAS-SUBNETS seq 20 permit 60.60.60.0/24 le 32      ← CaaS ser-
  vices subnet
ip prefix-list CAAS-SUBNETS seq 30 permit 161.161.161.0/24 le 32   ← CaaS eBGP
  peering transport subnet

route-map FROM-DC2-CORE permit 5         ← Creating route map to match CaaS subnets
  match ip address prefix-list CAAS-SUBNETS


route-map Redistr_1_OSPF deny 5
  match tag 65532
route-map Redistr_1_OSPF permit 10
  match route-type internal external type-1 type-2 nssa-external


router bgp 65531
  router-id 100.100.100.1
  timers bgp 5 15
  log-neighbor-changes
  address-family ipv4 unicast
    redistribute ospf 1 route-map Redistr_1_OSPF      ← Redistributing OSPF learned
  routes from DC1 ACI fabric into BGP
    maximum-paths 4


  template peer DC2-AS65532
    remote-as 65532
    description DC2-AS65532
    password 3 1d7b031bc9c9bb99
    address-family ipv4 unicast
      route-map FROM-DC2-CORE in         ← Applying route map to allow CaasS Sub-
  nets between DC1 and DC2
      soft-reconfiguration inbound always
  neighbor 200.200.200.2
    inherit peer DC2-AS65532
    description eBGP Peering to DC2-Core
    no shutdown
```

You have now configured all three required L3Outs—the load balancer L3Out, CaaS L3Out, and data center core L3Out—so it's time to look into server staging configuration. The servers are required to load the OS using PXE. For that, you can install a Red Hat Enterprise (RHEL) satellite server either inside or outside the ACI fabric running DHCP and FTP services. On ACI, you can create an application profile with an EPG for staging the OpenShift servers. This OpenShift staging EPG must be associated to a BD with a publicly advertised subnet. You need to create DHCP relay on the BD to get IP address leases from the DHCP server running on the RedHat satellite server in order to download and install the OS on the servers where you will run the OpenShift Container Platform. Initially, the staging EPG is bound statically to the VPC named Data (refer to Figure 4-65) for OS installation, and then the same Data VPC is used to create eBGP peering with the server. For storage connectivity, a Storage EPG is bound statically to the VPC named Storage (refer to Figure 4-67). This process can be automated using Ansible or any other tool of your choice. Figure 4-65 and Figure 4-66 show the sample ACI configuration for the staging EPG along with DHCP relay. In this example, the DHCP server is located outside the ACI fabric, and hence the data center core L3Out external EPG is used to reach out.

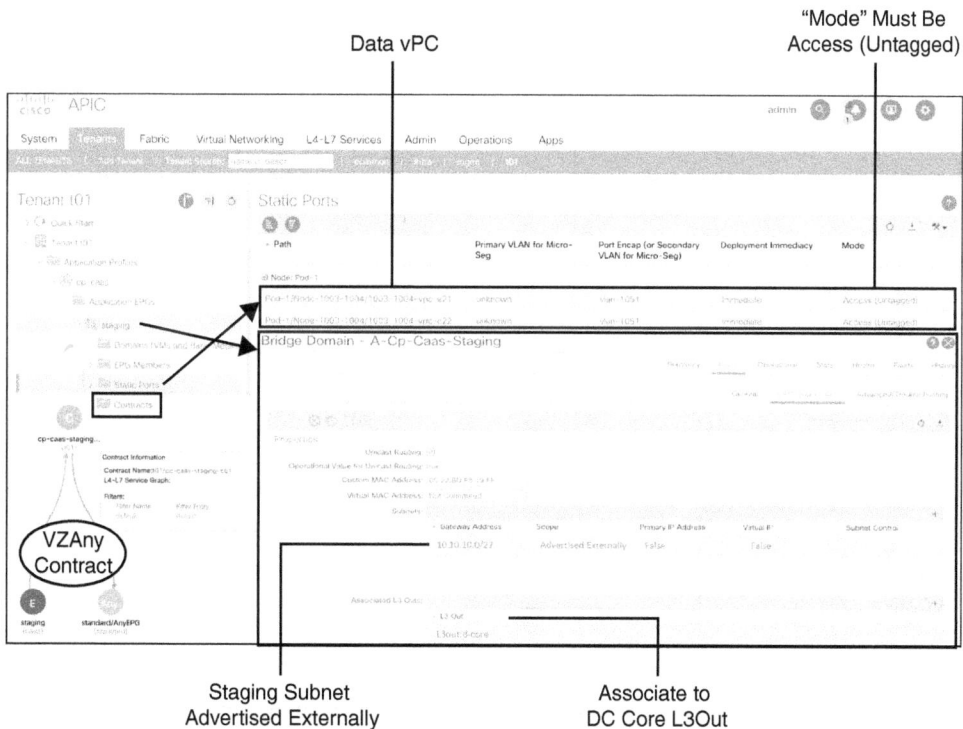

Figure 4-65 *Staging EPG Configuration in ACI*

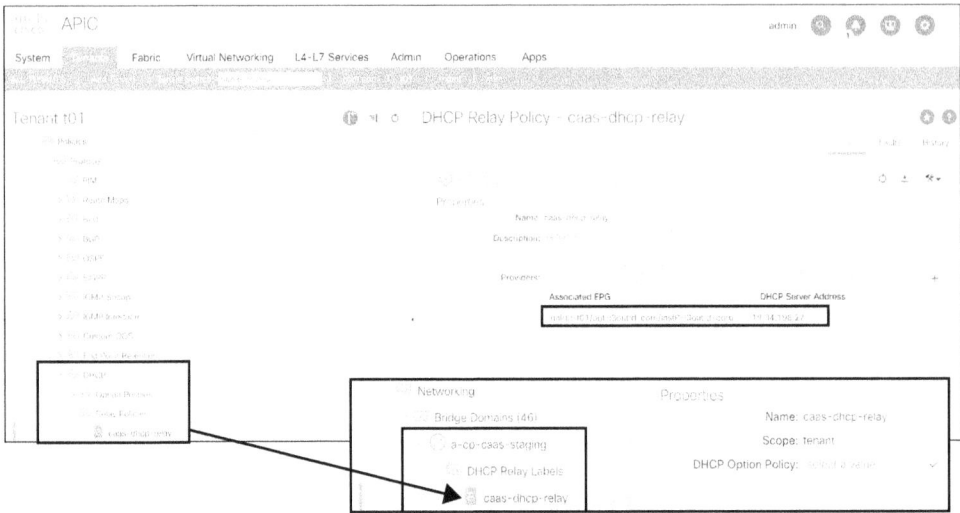

Figure 4-66   *DHCP Relay Configuration in ACI for Staging EPG Configuration*

Figure 4-67 shows a sample ACI configuration for the Storage EPG.

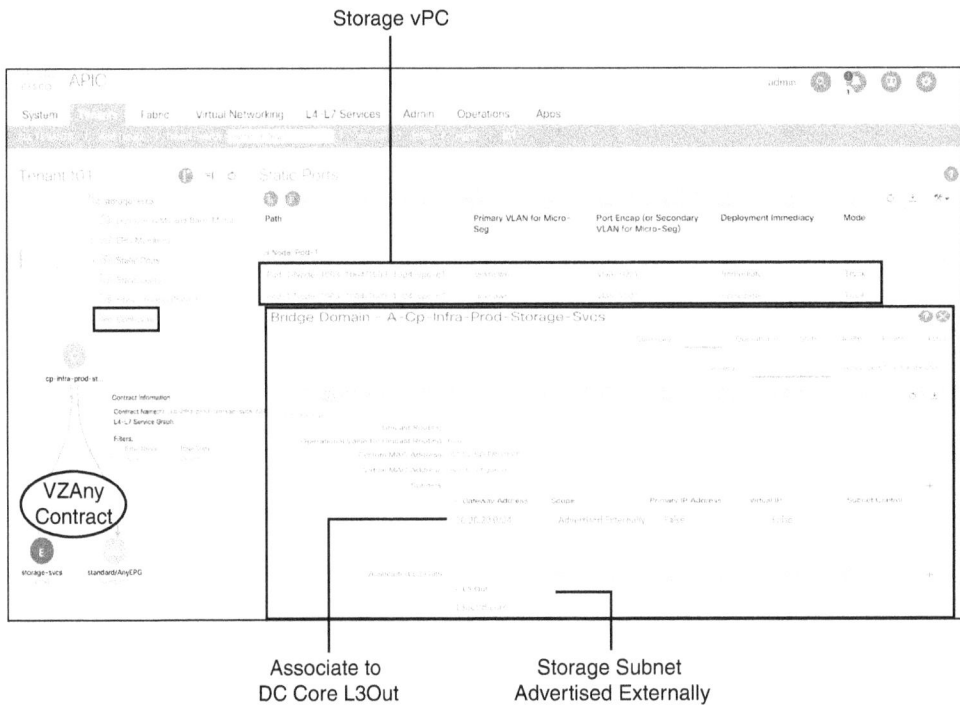

Figure 4-67   *Storage EPG Configuration in ACI*

Note   This design solution can be used for a Kubernetes system of any flavor.

Design 2: Vendor-Based ERP/SAP Hana Design with ACI

Companies are using an increasing number of vendor-based application-hosting solutions, either hosted locally at their on-premises data center and still managed and run by a cloud service provider (commonly known as a *hybrid cloud*) or full-fledged public cloud services hosted elsewhere. ACI's open architecture allows the application workload to be located anywhere and allows full automation and network segmentation. Enterprise resource planning (ERP) application suites provide centralized management of various business functions, such as human resources, accounting, sales and marketing, purchasing, and customer support, through automation that streamlines processes and information across the entire organization. The core component of ERP systems is a shared in-memory database that supports multiple functions consumed by various business units. ERP systems are commonly used by companies in a supply chain to keep track of all the moving parts in manufacturing and distribution. However, other business, such as construction, healthcare, and disaster relief organizations, can also benefit from ERP systems.

Business Case

The customer in this example has contracted a vendor to provide an on-premises cloud service to host its ERP system in its data center. This ERP system infrastructure must be connected to a separate single ACI fabric in each of the customer's two enterprise data centers that service clients globally. Multiple racks of blade system compute platforms run on hypervisors and host ERP front-end applications that need to be connected to ACI fabric. The ERP system in-memory database is hosted on standalone pizza boxes that are also required to be connected to ACI fabric in separate racks. For storage needs, a dedicated separate rack is populated with a flash storage system that provides block, file, and object access. Since this is a vendor-based on-premises solution, proper network segmentation techniques must be used in the design to protect the customer's overall network. The customer wants to use firewall clusters to apply security policies.

Design Solution

Figure 4-68 shows the design solution for this example. As you can see, the ACI topology has a single rack of ERP system compute and storage in each data center.

In Figure 4-68, a single rack unit (42-RU) of bare-metal servers servicing a SAP HANA in-memory database is connected to two ToR leafs using Nexus 93180YC-EX (48 host ports) for 1/10 Gbps connectivity. Each of these 5RU standalone servers houses four interface cards with 2 × 10 Gbps NICs each and one interface card with 2 × 1 Gbps NICs each. These two NICs on each 10 Gbps interface card form a VPC with several ToR leafs: one for backup, one for data, one for Hana-rep, and one for user. The two NICs on the 1 Gbps interface card form another VPC called admin that has two ToR leafs. Figure 4-69 shows the physical connectivity details for this SAP HANA in-memory database.

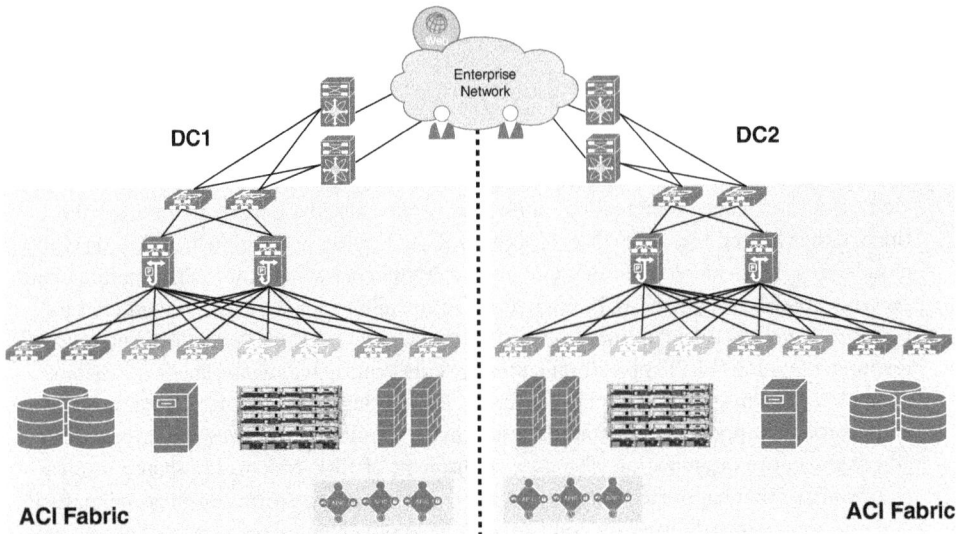

Figure 4-68   *Vendor-Based ERP Design with ACI*

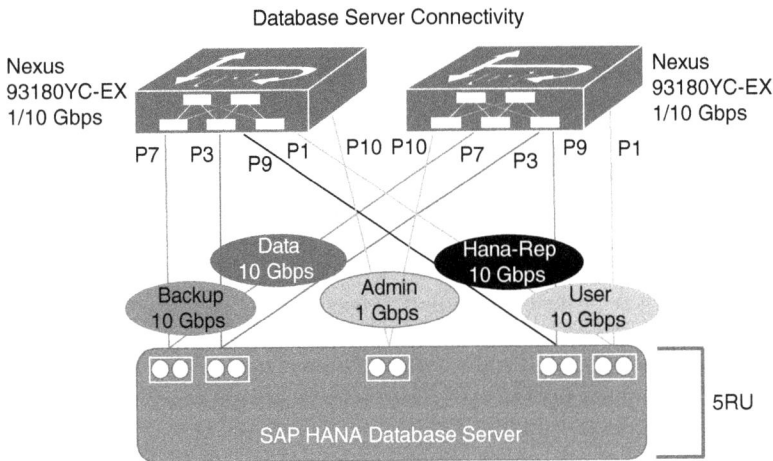

Figure 4-69   *End Host Physical Connectivity of a SAP HANA In-Memory Database Rack*

The VPCs are statically bound with an encapsulation VLAN to EPGs named backup, data, Hana-rep, user, and admin, as shown in Figure 4-70.

Note   Figure 4-70 shows only one of the EPG configurations.

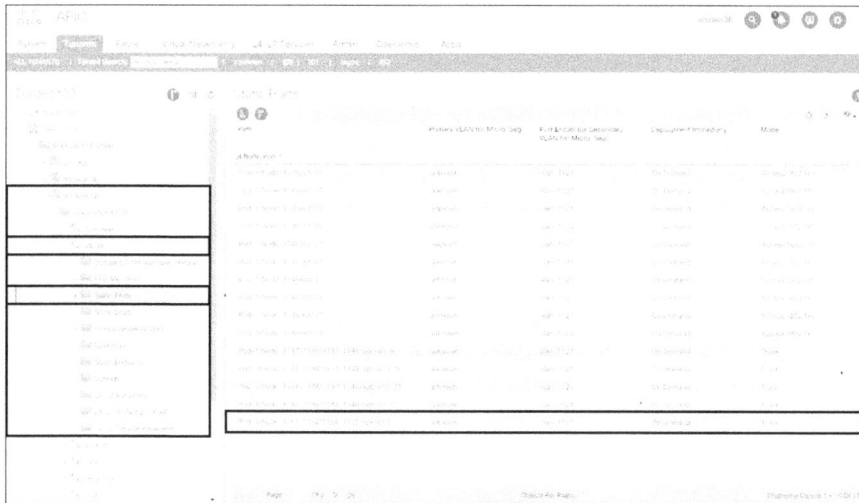

Figure 4-70 *Statically Binding a VPC to an EPG with an Encapsulation VLAN in a SAP HANA In-Memory Database Rack*

The next rack is hosting a virtualized compute for a front-end application running on a blade system. Blade server switches are connected to two ToR leaf switches (Nexus 93180LC-EX) via 10 × 40 Gbps links using a VPC, as shown in Figure 4-71.

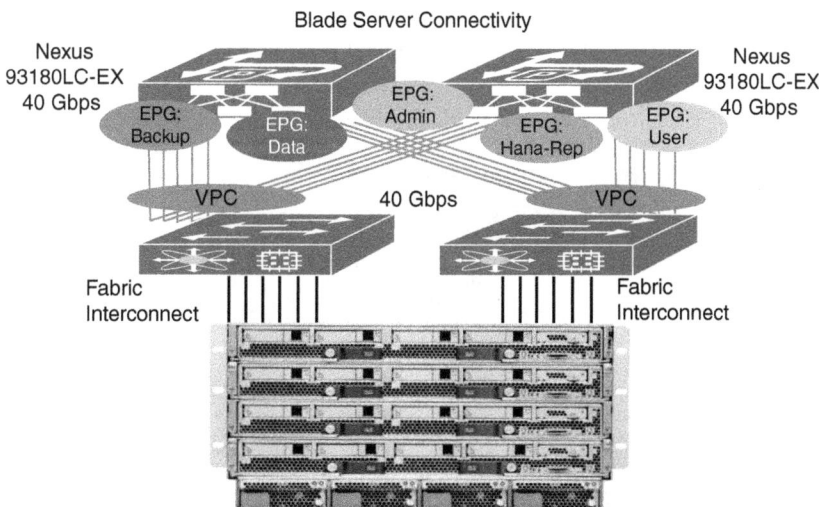

Figure 4-71 *End Host Physical Connectivity of SAP HANA Virtualized Compute Rack*

Notice here that all the EPGs are mapped with encapsulation VLANs to these VPCs as all the VLANs are trunked down toward the blade system that will be used by VMs. This is done by associating the EPGs to the virtual attachable access entity profile (AAEP), as shown in Figure 4-72.

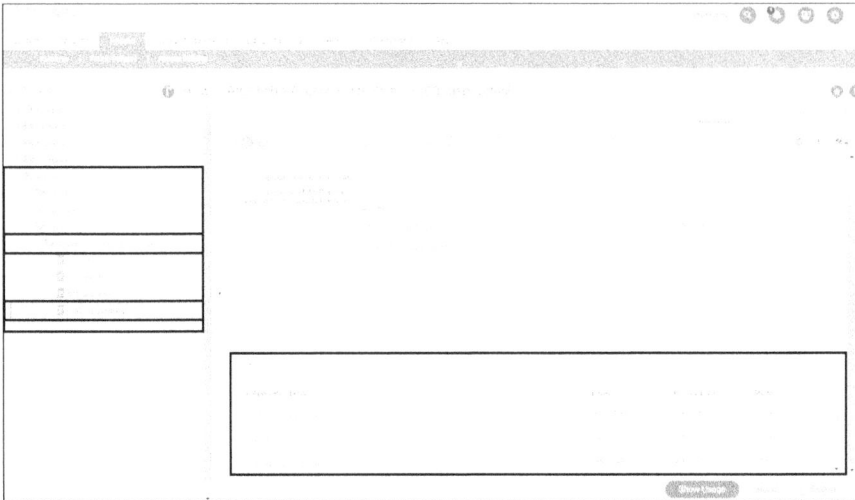

Figure 4-72   *Mapping EPGs with Encapsulation VLANs to the AAEP for a SAP HANA Virtualized Compute Rack*

The third rack houses a flash storage system to provide block, file, and object access. This rack uses two end-of-row (EoR) leaf switches with 1/10 Gbps connectivity (Nexus 93180YC-EX). Two 1 Gbps links from each leaf switch are used to connect to the flash storage system as access ports and are statically mapped with the encapsulation VLAN to admin. Similarly, two 10 Gbps links from each leaf switch are used to connect to the flash storage system as access ports and are statically mapped with the encapsulation VLAN to data, as shown in Figure 4-73.

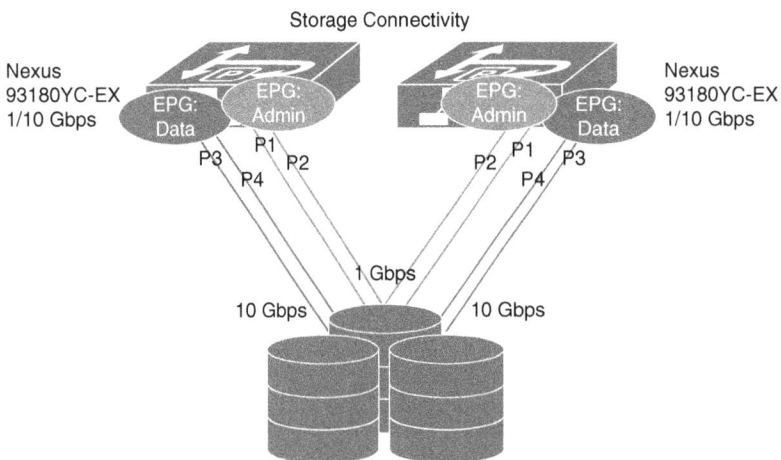

Figure 4-73   *Physical Connectivity of the SAP HANA Storage Rack*

Figure 4-74 shows the admin EPG configuration with static access port binding to the encapsulation VLAN.

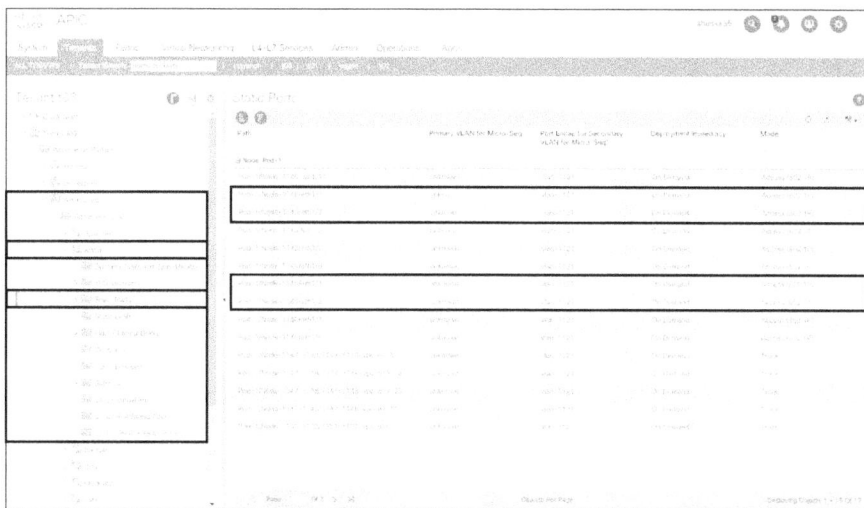

Figure 4-74 *Statically Binding an Access Port to an EPG with an Encapsulation VLAN in a SAP Storage Rack*

Finally, you need to connect a pair of firewalls to ACI leafs that will run in a cluster. For that, you can use the same pair of 1/10 Gbps leafs (Nexus 93180YC-EX) that you used for EoR flash storage connections. You can house the firewalls in that rack as well. For firewall connectivity to the ACI leaf pair, you need to create 3 × 10 Gbps VPCs: one for the firewall cluster-control link (CCL), one for the firewall inside interface, and one for the firewall DMZ interface (see Figure 4-75). For firewall management, 1 Gbps links are used as an access port to the ACI leaf pair.

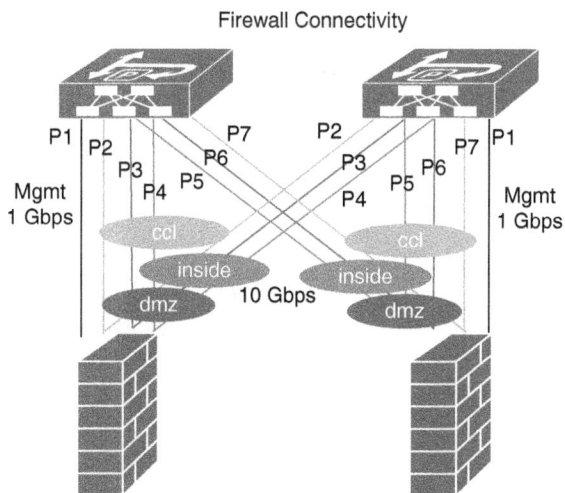

Figure 4-75 *Firewall Connectivity to ACI Leafs*

The firewall CCL is a Layer 2 cluster heartbeat between firewalls to maintain cluster state. For that, you need to create an EPG with a Layer 2 BD, as shown in Figure 4-76.

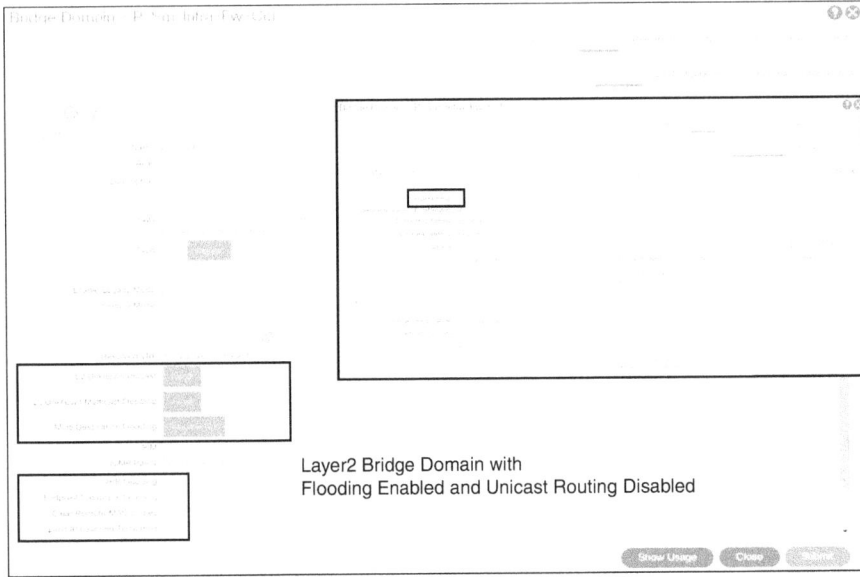

Figure 4-76   *Firewall CCL Configuration in ACI*

You need to statically bind the CCL VPC to the EPG, with the encapsulation VLAN providing Layer 2 connectivity for firewall cluster heartbeat traffic to flow through the ACI leaf pair. Similarly, for firewall management traffic, you need to create an EPG with a BD and a subnet. You can statically bind the firewall management ports to this EPG with the encapsulation VLAN as the access port.

Now you can move on to logical configuration required for redirecting all ERP SAP HANA traffic toward the firewall cluster using the policy-based routing (PBR).

NOTE   PBR is explained in detail in Chapter 6.

In order to use PBR, you need to carry out the following configuration steps:

Step 1.   Create the L4–L7 device.

Step 2.   Create a policy-based redirect.

Step 3.   Create a service graph template.

Step 4.   Deploy a service graph.

In this case, you need to create the L4–L4 device (in this case, a firewall) in routed mode (GoTo). The customer does not want to manage this device through the device package, so you uncheck the Managed selection box. Since this is a physical firewall, you can choose Physical as the device type. Select the physical domain and assign device interfaces. Select the VPC you created earlier to be used as firewall DMZ and inside interfaces. Apply the necessary encapsulation VLAN to these interfaces. Figure 4-77 shows these configurations.

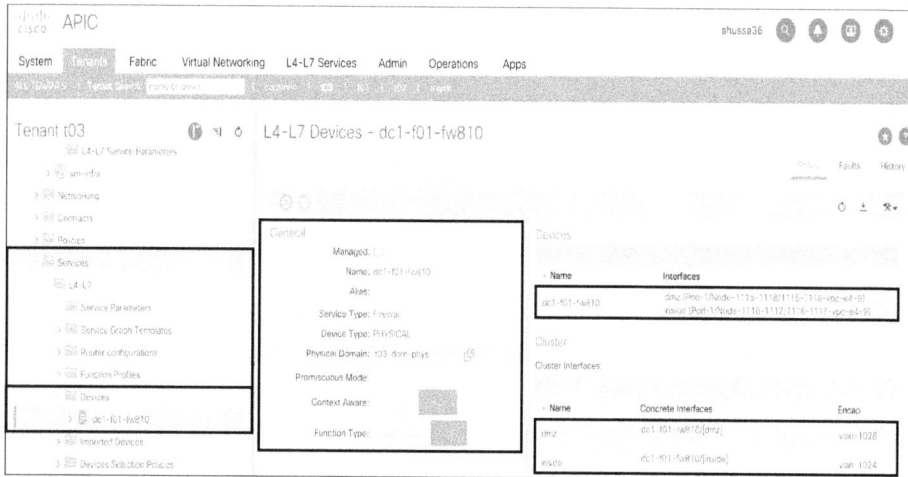

Figure 4-77   *Creating an L4–L7 Device*

Once the L4–L7 device is created, you can create the policy-based redirect configuration, as shown in Figure 4-78.

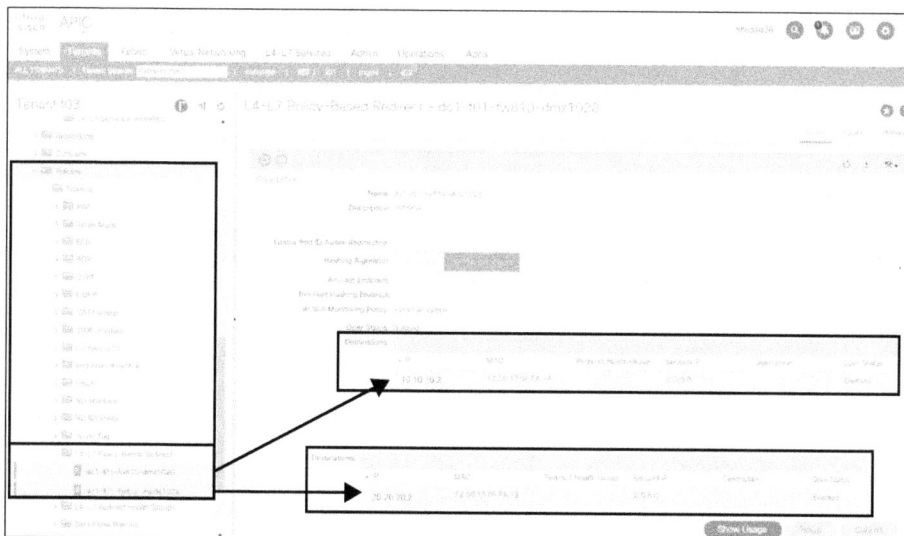

Figure 4-78   *Creating a Policy-Based Redirect Configuration*

Because this is a two-arm-mode PBR, you need to create a policy-based redirect toward the DMZ interface and toward the inside interface. The IP addresses should be taken from the service BD subnets. ACI provides the policy configuration to monitor the reachability of these IP addresses as being the next hop for policy-based redirect, but most customers want to be able to periodically check the status through their external enterprise monitoring tools. Therefore, you need to advertise the service BD subnets (from which the next-hop IP addresses are been carved out) outside through L3Out for reachability, as shown in Figure 4-79.

Note   Figure 4-79 shows only the service BD **a-sm-infra-fw-dmz**. You would use the same method to create the service BD **a-sm-infra-fw-inside**.

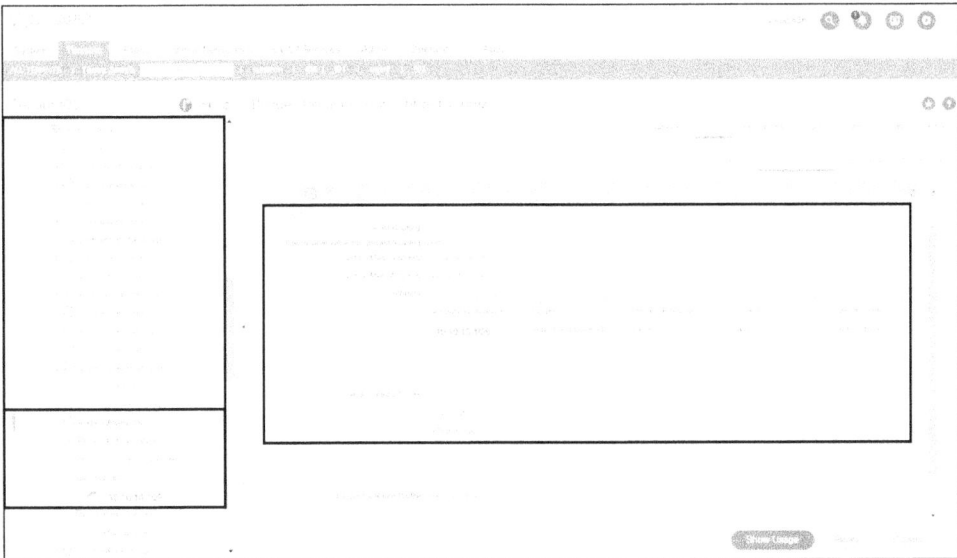

Figure 4-79   *Service BD Configuration*

Next, you have to create the service graph template. Ensure that you enable Direct Connect in order to ping the next-hop IP addresses from the service BD, as shown in Figure 4-80.

This service graph template can be used to deploy the service graph, as shown in Figure 4-81.

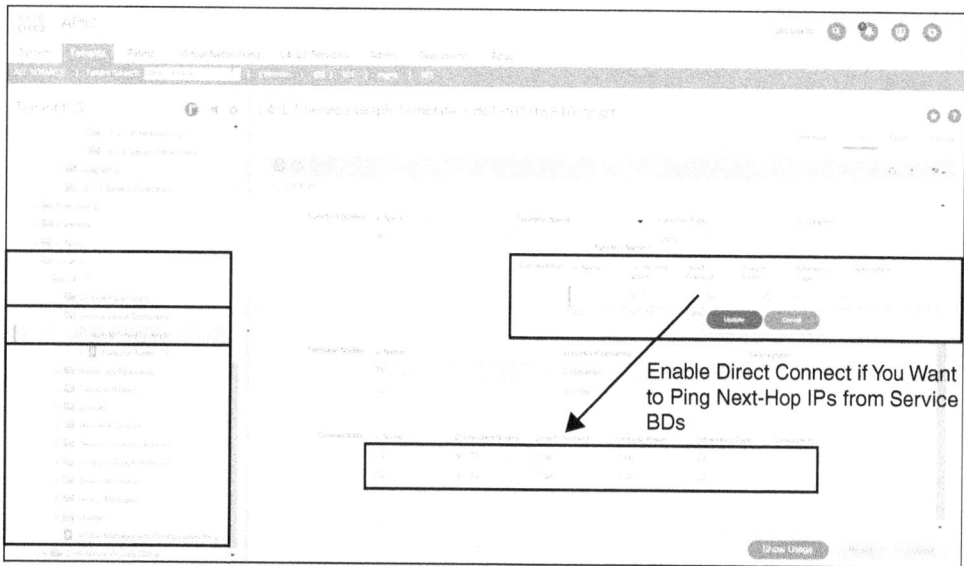

Figure 4-80 *Service Graph Template Configuration*

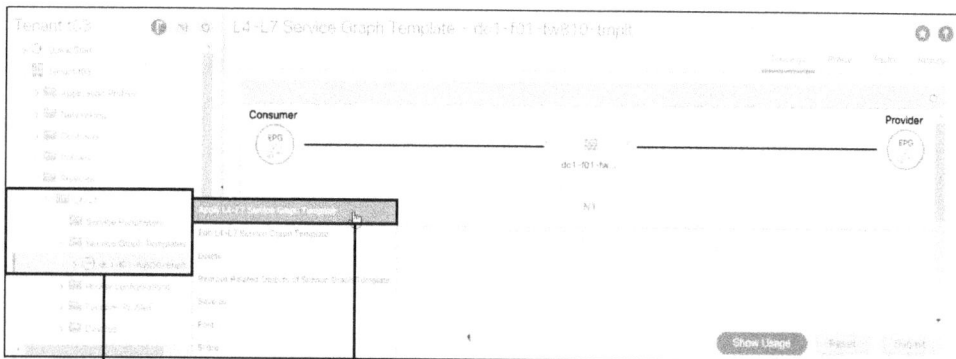

Service Graph Template   Apply Service
                                Graph Template

Figure 4-81 *Applying the Service Graph Template Configuration*

Note Figure 4-82 shows only one service graph configuration. In it, vendor traffic (coming from outside) destined to the EPG admin for administering the ERP on-premises cloud system deployed at the customer data center is redirected toward the firewall cluster where security policy is defined.

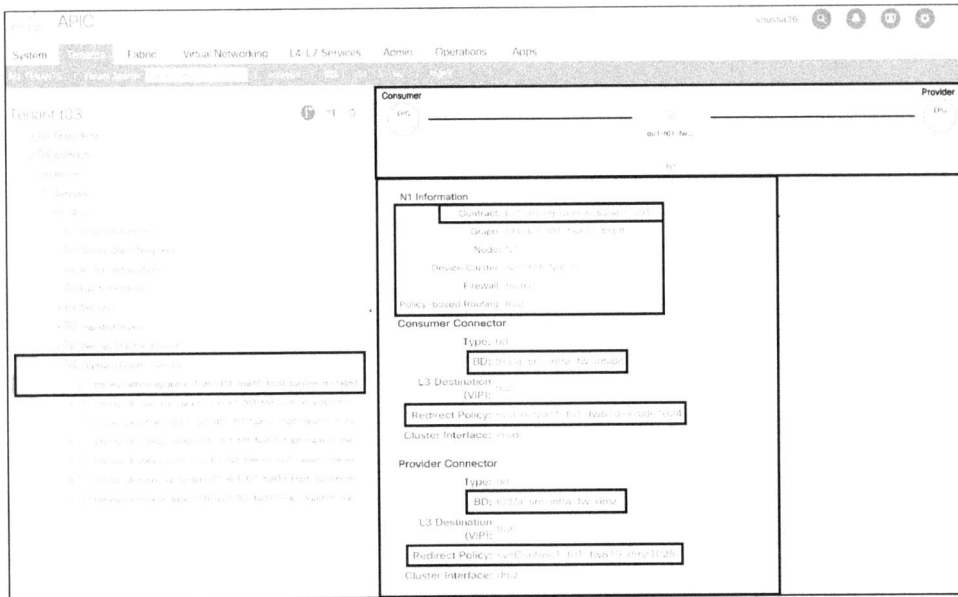

Figure 4-82 *Admin EPG Service Graph Configuration*

The contract **sm-erp-admin-sgraph-c01** is used as the vzAny contract where the consumer is the VRF supplier-managed, and the provider is the admin EPG, as shown in Figure 4-83.

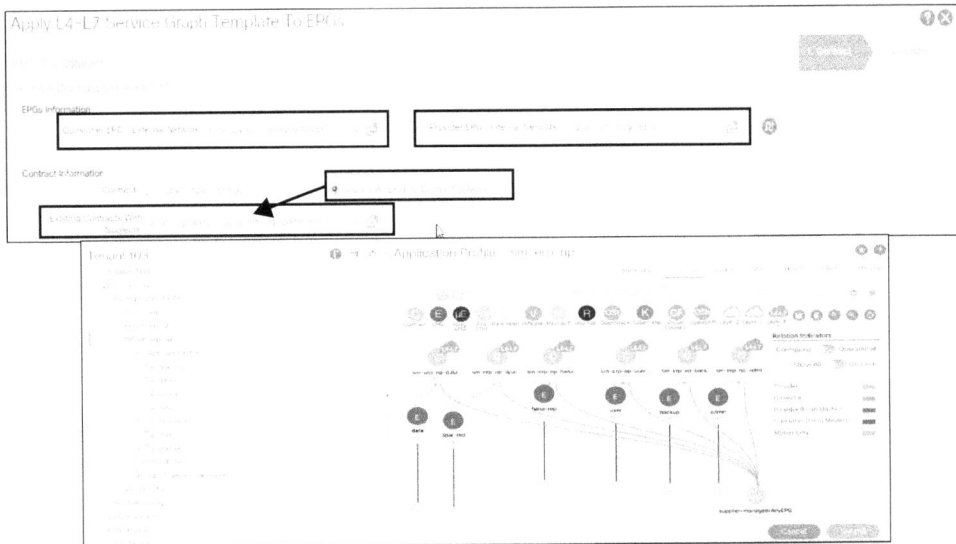

Figure 4-83 *Service Graph Contract Configuration*

As you can see in Figure 4-83, the subject of the contract a-sm-erp-admin-s01, where filters are defined, is mapped to a PBR service graph. You can create the contract and its associated subject/filter while creating the service graph, or you can use an existing one, as shown for this example in Figure 4-83. The service graph configuration will map the contract to the appropriate EPGs and/or VRF instances for the vzAny configuration, as shown in Figure 4-84.

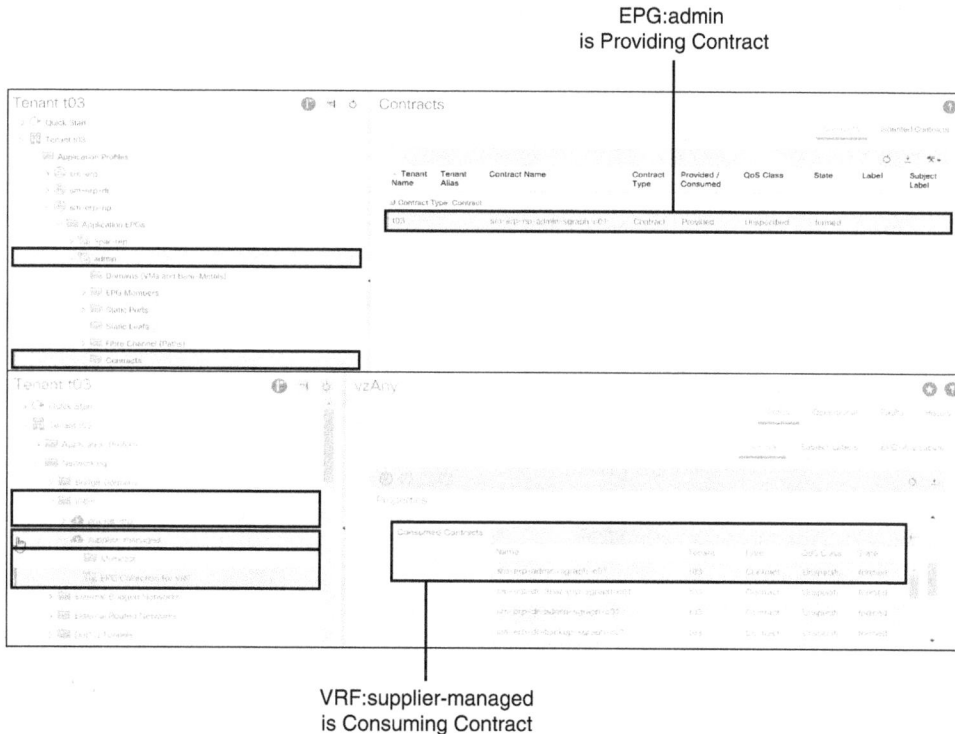

Figure 4-84   *Service Graph Contract (Consumer/Provider) Mapping Configuration*

Design 3: vBrick Digital Media Engine Design with ACI

Most large enterprises have a business requirement to enable the leadership to periodically address the widely dispersed employees using media streaming to update them about the company's business growth, financial challenges, rules of conduct, and so on. Personally visiting and meeting each employee would be impossible in most large enterprises. Cisco, with its partner vBrick, offers a media streaming management solution using unicast and multicast video streaming.

Business Case

In this example, management wants to deploy the vBrick Digital Media Engine (DME) in the company's data center hosting applications running over an ACI fabric. The requirement is to enable Protocol Independent Multicast (PIM) in ACI with a rendezvous point (RP) running outside the ACI fabric. The company wants to configure Auto-RP Listen and Forward mode as part of its global multicast design standards.

The company's executives should be able to do real-time video streaming any time by using vBrick DME appliances, and employees located anywhere in the corporate network should be able to view that video stream.

Design Solution

Figure 4-85 shows a design solution for this example that involves an ACI topology with vBrick DME connecting using 10 Gbps interfaces to ToR leafs.

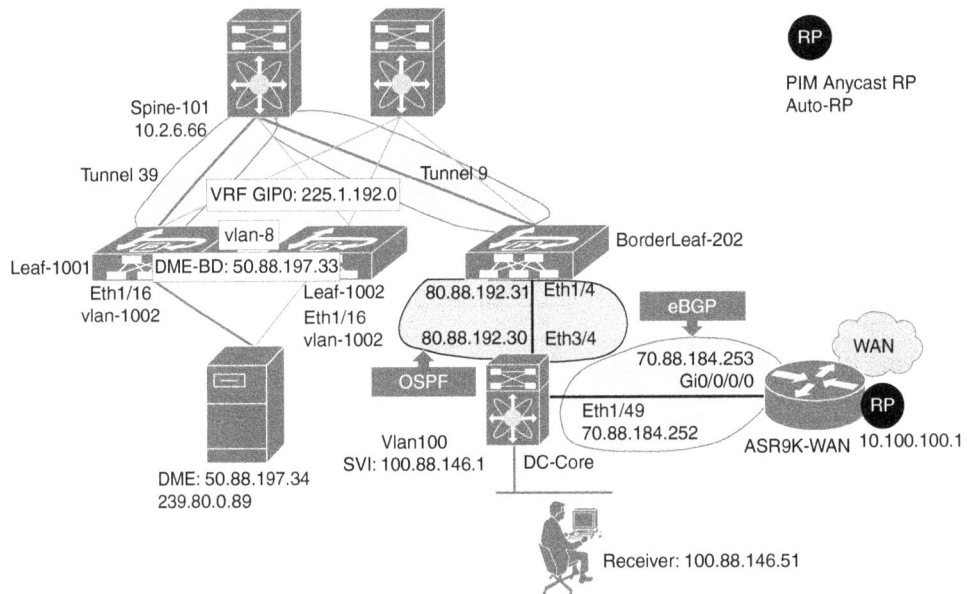

Figure 4-85   *vBrick DME Design Topology Using ACI*

As shown in the design topology in Figure 4-85, a vBrick DME appliance running ESXi is connected to two ToR ACI leaf nodes (1001 and 1002) on port Eth1/16. The vBrick DME hypervisor configuration dictates the use of regular access ports configured on ACI leaf nodes. It is necessary to create the access port configurations for 10 Gbps DME interfaces and statically bind them to an EPG (in this example, the DME EPG) with the encapsulation VLAN (vlan-1002). It is also necessary to associate the DME EPG to a BD (in this example, the DME BD) with subnet 50.88.197.32/28. The pervasive gateway of the DME BD subnet is 50.88.197.33, with the platform-independent vlan-8 and the DME VMkernel port IP address 50.88.197.34. The DME BD subnet must be advertised externally to have unicast IP reachability of the multicast source, which in this case is the vBrick DME inside the ACI fabric from multicast receivers outside the ACI fabric. The vBrick DME is streaming video on multicast group 239.80.0.89. The multicast RP is running on an ASR9K WAN core router with anycast RP address 10.100.100.1.

After you are done configuring the physical interfaces of the DME on the ACI leafs and associating them with the EPG BD with IP reachability, you need to enable PIM in ACI, as shown in Figure 4-86.

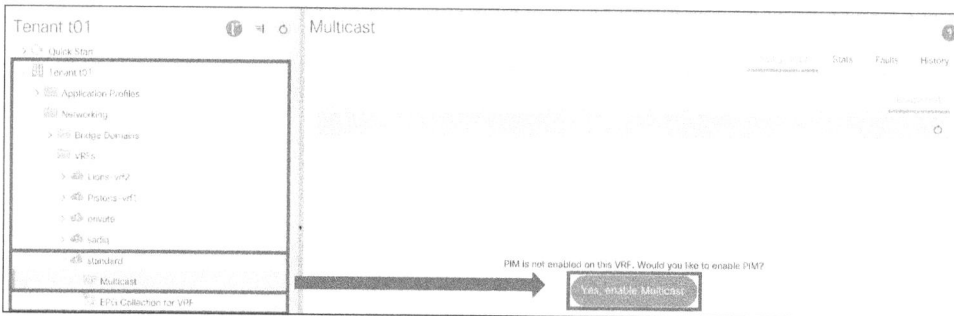

Figure 4-86   *Enabling PIM Multicast in ACI*

As shown in Figure 4-86, you need to go to your defined tenant policy, where you select the VRF for which you want to enable multicast (in this example, tenant t01 with the standard VRF instance). After you enable multicast on the VRF instance, the APIC assigns a unique multicast address from the GIPo address pool, as shown in Figure 4-87. ACI uses this multicast address encapsulated in VXLAN to forward multicast traffic inside the fabric. Ensure that you enable Fast Convergence Control State because the multicast stream only flows through one border leaf, and in the event of the failure of this border leaf, you would like another border leaf to take over as quickly as possible. This setting quickly converges the multicast stream to the other border leaf part of the L3Out.

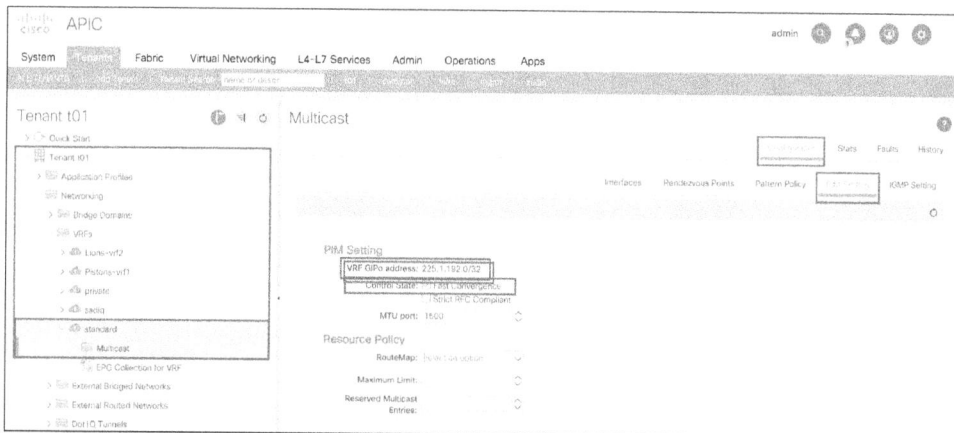

Figure 4-87   *VRF GIPo Multicast Address and Fast Convergence Settings*

Enable PIM on the DME BD and on the border leaf 202 interface Eth1/4 connecting to the external core router, as shown in Figure 4-88. This ensures that the vBrick DME can send PIM register messages to an RP sitting outside the ACI.

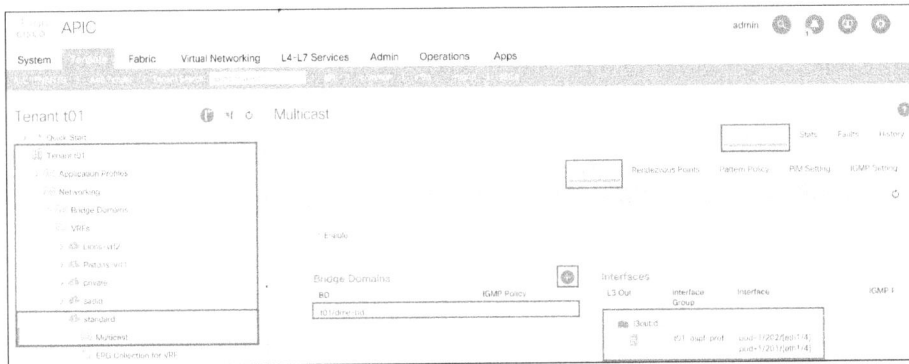

Figure 4-88   *Enabling PIM Multicast on the BD and Border Leaf Interfaces*

Next, you have to configure PIM Auto-RP Listen and Forward mode to ensure that the multicast source residing in ACI can reach the RP sitting outside the ACI fabric, as shown in Figure 4-89.

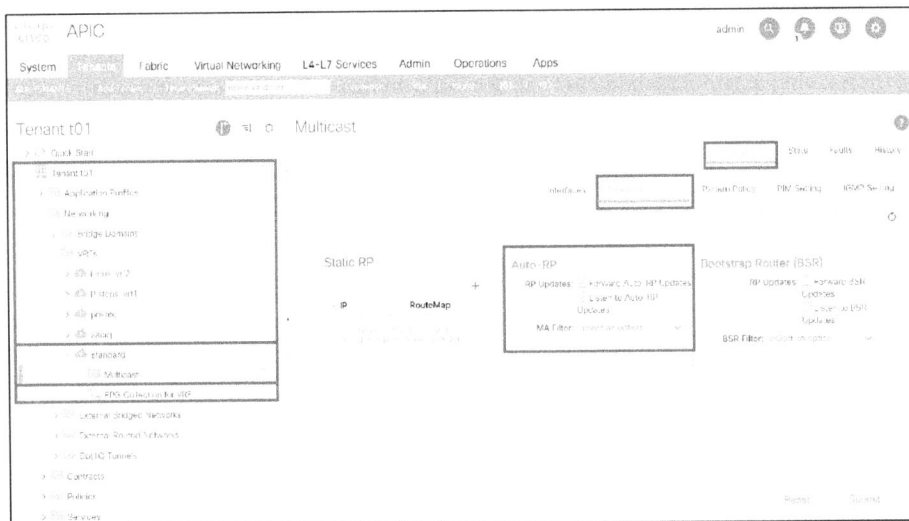

Figure 4-89   *Enabling PIM Auto-RP Listen and Forward Mode*

You are now done with all the necessary multicast-related configuration on the ACI fabric.

Next, you need to ensure that the external core router that is connected to the ACI border leaf has PIM Sparse mode enabled on the interfaces connecting to ACI border leaf and toward the WAN core router running RP. Also make sure that Auto-RP Listen and Forward mode is enabled on the data center core router. Example 4-5 shows a sample configuration for the data center core router.

Example 4-5 *Configuring PIM and Auto-RP Settings on a Data Center Core Router (NX-OS)*

```
DC-Core ↔ Border Leaf 202:


feature pim
ip pim auto-rp forward listen


interface Ethernet3/4
  description Link Connecting to ACI Border Leaf 202
 ip pim sparse-mode


interface Ethernet1/49
  description Link Connecting to WAN Core ASR9K
 ip pim sparse-mode
```

Next, you need to ensure that the WAN core ASR9K router on which RP is running has PIM enabled on all interfaces connecting to the data center core router and toward the downstream router connecting to the multicast receiver known as the last-hop router (LHR). Also make sure proper RP configuration is done on ASR9K WAN core router. Example 4-6 shows a sample configuration for the ASR9K WAN core router.

Example 4-6 *Configuring PIM and RP Settings on a WAN Core Router (IOS XR)*

```
WAN-Core ↔ DC Core:


ipv4 access-list 10
 10 permit ipv4 any host 224.0.1.39  ← Required for Auto-RP
 20 permit ipv4 any host 224.0.1.40  ← Required for Auto-RP
 30 permit ipv4 any 239.1.0.0 0.0.0.255  ← Only this multicast group range is
   allowed


interface Loopback0
 ipv4 address 10.138.211.1 255.255.255.255
!
interface Loopback9
 ipv4 address 10.100.100.1 255.255.255.255  ← Anycast RP address


multicast-routing
 address-family ipv4
  interface Loopback0
   enable
  !
```

```
  interface Loopback9
    enable
    !
  interface HundredGigE0/1/0/1  ← toward the data center core router
    enable
    !
  interface GigabitEthernet0/0/0/0  ← toward the multicast receiver (LHR)
    enable

router pim
 address-family ipv4
  register-source Loopback0
  auto-rp mapping-agent Loopback9 scope 20 interval 60
  auto-rp candidate-rp Loopback9 scope 16 group-list 10 interval 60
  old-register-checksum
  interface Loopback0
    enable
    !
  interface Loopback9
    enable
    !
  interface HundredGigE0/1/0/1
    enable
    !
  interface GigabitEthernet0/0/0/0
    enable
```

Make sure that IGMP snooping is enabled on the multicast receiver switch interface. In most switch platforms, it is enabled by default. Also enable PIM on the SVI connected to the multicast receiver (in this case, VLAN 100). After completing all these steps, management can start streaming multicast video using the vBrick DME connected to the ACI fabric.

Summary

As you learned in this chapter, Cisco ACI operates in the Clos fabric architecture, which is a fully meshed leaf/spine network connected through nonblocking links. For various customer use cases and business requirements, Cisco offers various design options, such as splitting a single ACI fabric into two or more physical locations (within the same data center or between multiple data centers) by using either transit leaf or multi-pod.

Cisco also makes it possible to combine discrete ACI fabrics (fully meshed or partially meshed) together via a single policy model called multi-site. In this design, the Multi-Site Orchestrator is used to manage policies across multiple ACI fabrics.

The third design option, called remote leaf, involves stretching leafs to remote locations. This option allows management by an APIC cluster hosted in the main data center. It consumes a consistent policy model but does not require an investment in a full-fledged ACI fabric.

In addition to learning about the physical connectivity design options of ACI, you have also learned a few logical design options based on real-world business use cases.

In the next chapter, you will learn about end host and network connectivity in ACI.

Review Key Topics

If you are preparing to take the Implementing Cisco Application Centric Infrastructure - Advanced (300-630 DCACIA) exam to attain the Cisco Certified Specialist—ACI Advanced Implementation certification, be sure to review the key topics marked in this chapter as outlined in Table 4-5.

Table 4-5 *Key Topics*

Key Topic Element	Description	Page Number
Section	Multi-pod	97
Section	Multi-site	116
Section	Logical Design - Kubernetes using Calico CNI	149

Review Questions

The questions that follow are designed to help you prepare for the Implementing Cisco Application Centric Infrastructure - Advanced (300-630 DCACIA) exam if you are planning on acquiring the Cisco Certified Specialist: ACI Advanced Implementation certification.

1. What are the different connectivity options available for stretching a single ACI fabric to multiple locations using leaf switches? (Choose three.)

   a. Stretch a single ACI fabric to multiple locations by connecting leaf switches in each location to an external IP network.

   b. Stretch a single ACI fabric to multiple locations by connecting leaf switches in each location through dark fiber to every spine switch in the fabric.

   c. A single ACI fabric cannot be stretched to multiple locations due to limitations in the underlay IS-IS protocol.

   d. ACI fabric with a single APIC cluster can be stretched using transit leafs connected through EoMPLS.

   e. Stretch a single ACI fabric using GOLF routers.

   f. A single ACI fabric can be stretched using transit leafs connected through DWDM.

2. What are the limitations of a single stretched ACI fabric using a transit leaf design? (Choose three.)

  a. The verified latency between sites is up to 10 milliseconds.

  b. The verified distance between sites is up to 500 miles, or 800 kilometers.

  c. A single ACI fabric can be stretched between up to six sites.

  d. The verified latency between sites is up to 150 milliseconds.

  e. A single ACI fabric can be stretched between up to three sites.

3. Which two of the following design options will work between multiple ACI fabrics for applications requiring Layer 2 extensions hosted at distant locations?

  a. ACI fabric can be stretched to multiple locations by using transit leafs for Layer 2 extension.

  b. ACI fabrics can be connected together using a multi-site design through ISN for applications requiring Layer 2 extension.

  c. Using a service graph design, ACI fabrics can be connected together to provide Layer 2 extension for applications.

  d. ACI fabrics can be extended at Layer 2 by using special routers called border leafs.

  e. Multiple ACI fabrics can be connected together using a multi-pod design for applications requiring Layer 2 extension.

  f. ACI fabrics can be connected together using a dual-fabric design through DCI to provide Layer 2 extension for applications.

4. What are the benefits of a multi-pod design over a single stretched ACI fabric using a transit leaf design? (Choose three.)

  a. It provides fabric scalability for up to 400 leafs.

  b. Multi-pod uses separate control plane protocol instances in different pods deployed at different locations.

  c. It extends the same control plane protocol instances to multiple locations.

  d. It does not require any extra configuration.

  e. Multi-pod provides better design resiliency than the stretched fabric using the transit leaf design.

  f. It provides pod scalability for up to 400 leafs.

5. How are multiple pods connected through IPN in a multi-pod design? (Choose four.)

  a. Any routing protocol can be used between spines and IPN routers.

  b. Spines in each POD are connected to the IPN router with either 40 Gbps or 100 Gbps interfaces.

  c. The routed interface is configured on a spine in each pod to connect to the IPN router.

  d. The routing protocol used between spines and IPN routers must be OSPF.

  e. PIM Bidir must be enabled in the IPN router.

  f. DHCP Relay must be enabled in the IPN router for fabric node registration in other pods.

6. Why is the maximum transmission unit (MTU) size required to be increased in the IPN router? How much increase in the MTU size is required? (Choose two.)

  a. The COOP protocol on spines requires a larger MTU size to store endpoint information.

  b. The data plane protocol VXLAN requires a larger MTU size.

  c. VXLAN requires an extra 50 bytes in MTU size.

  d. The control plane protocol IS-IS requires larger MTU size.

  e. MP-BGP requires a larger MTU size for external prefix advertisements.

7. What are the requirements for ISN connectivity in a multi-site design? (Choose three.)

  a. Cloud-scale spines are required to connect to ISN routers.

  b. OSPF is required to connect ISN routers.

  c. PIM Bidir must be enabled in the ISN router.

  d. Maximum transmission unit (MTU) size is required to be increased an additional 50 bytes in the ISN router for VXLAN.

  e. Spines in each site are connected to the ISN router with either 40 Gbps or 100 Gbps interfaces.

  f. DHCP Relay must be enabled in the ISN router.

8. What migration strategies are used in a multi-site design? (Choose two.)

  a. Create brand-new policies in Multi-Site Orchestrator to be deployed at multiple ACI fabric sites.

  b. Create the same existing APIC policies in Multi-Site Orchestrator.

  c. Export new policies from Multi-Site Orchestrator into existing fabric APICs for policy synchronization.

  d. Import existing APIC policies into Multi-Site Orchestrator.

9. What are the requirements for implementing a remote leaf in an ACI fabric? (Choose four.)

  a. In a multi-pod fabric deployment, a remote leaf is registered with one specific pod only.

  b. An APIC can be connected to a remote leaf.

  c. Only cloud-scale leaf switches are supported for remote leaf deployments.

  d. Remote leafs can only connect to compute endpoints at co-location facilities for application hosting.

  e. The ACI fabric expects the DSCP value coming from the remote leaf to the main DC spine over the IPN router to be the same.

  f. Only cloud-scale spine switches are supported for IPN connectivity.

  g. A remote leaf does not allow service graph connectivity to service nodes such as firewalls and load balancers.

## Chapter 5

End Host and Network Connectivity

Now that you have read the first four chapters, you should be well acquainted with the various design options in Cisco Application Centric Infrastructure (ACI). This chapter delves into end host and network connectivity options offered by ACI:

- End host connectivity
  - Access policies and configuring virtual port channels (VPCs), port channels, and access ports
  - Compute and storage connectivity
  - L4/L7 service device connectivity
- Network connectivity
  - External bridge network connectivity
  - External routed network connectivity
  - Network connectivity between pods, sites, and remote leafs
- Diagnosing connectivity problems

End Host Connectivity

Thanks to the openness of the ACI architecture, a wide variety of end host and network connectivity options are available, with all sorts of combinations of speed, transceiver, cabling, protocol, and redundancy, in compliance with industry standards. ACI has a connectivity option available for you whether you want to connect bare-metal or virtual compute using standard pizza boxes or blade chassis, connect storage (IP, FCoE), connect a wide range of Layer 2/3 devices such as switches and routers and a variety of Layer 4/7 devices such as load balancers, IP address management devices, firewall devices, and so on.

Because ACI is a policy-based demand and consume model, to provide efficient usage of your application hosting infrastructure, you need to understand some key object components and a defined sequence of steps in creating each of the configuration policies for end host and network connectivity. As mentioned earlier in the book, ACI was designed with multitenancy in mind, and an APIC needs to provide an administrator with a way to restrict which tenants can deploy what resources. The way this is accomplished is by configuring access policies, which define domains (types of end device), pools (VLAN ranges), and who has access to deploy them on the ACI switch interfaces. These components are explained in Chapter 2, "Introduction to the ACI Policy Model," and this chapter goes over some of the key concepts of access policies and their workflows again as this information is crucial for end host and network connectivity.

VLAN Pool

A VLAN pool contains a VLAN or range of VLANs that are associated with a single or multiple domains and consumed by the endpoint groups (EPGs). VLANs are instantiated on leaf switches based on attachable access entity profile (AAEP) configuration. Allow/deny forwarding decisions are based on contracts and the policy model rather than subnets and VLANs, as was traditionally the case in legacy networks.

Domain

A domain identifies the type of device that will be connecting to the ACI fabric, such as bare-metal, virtualized compute, or any other Layer 2–Layer 7 device. VLAN pools are mapped to domains to specify what VLAN ranges each type of device will have access to. A domain is associated with a single VLAN pool. EPGs are configured to use one or more domains, allowing the EPGs access and mapping to VLANs. Hence, a domain could be physical, virtual, external (bridged or routed), or Fibre Channel.

Attachable Access Entity Profiles (AAEPs)

An AAEP is a conduit between the logical and physical constructs of the ACI fabric configuration and is used to group domains with similar requirements. AAEPs are tied to interface policy groups. One or more domains can be added to an AAEP to allow multiple types of devices to connect on a single interface (such as a blade switch). Grouping domains into AAEPs and associating them enables the fabric to know where the various devices in the domain live, and the APIC can push the VLANs and policy where they need to be. AAEPs are configured in the Global Policies section of the APIC interface.

EPGs are considered the *who* in ACI, contracts are considered the *what/when/why*, AAEPs can be considered the *where*, and domains can be thought of as the *how* of the fabric. Different domain types are created, depending on how a device is connected to the leaf switch. There are five different domain types:

- **Physical domains:** These domains are generally used for bare-metal servers or virtualized compute, where VMM integration with ACI is not an option.

- **External bridged domains:** These domains are used for Layer 2 connections. For example, an external bridged domain could be used to connect an existing legacy NX-OS switch to an ACI leaf switch.

- **External routed domains:** These domains are used for Layer 3 connections. For example, an external routed domain could be used to connect a WAN router to an ACI leaf switch.

- **VMM domains:** These domains are used when integrating virtual machine controllers or container orchestration tools with the ACI fabric.

- **Fibre Channel domains:** These domains are used for connecting Fibre Channel– and Fibre Channel over Ethernet (FCoE)–enabled devices to the ACI fabric.

Let's look at some switch and interface policy concepts and configuration. These policies are grouped into two top-level categories: switch policy and interface policy. Furthermore, these policies have subcategories for efficient consumption of resources on the hardware. For example, under interface policy are the subcategories policies, policy groups, and profiles.

Switch Policies

There are certain unique policies for switches, such as policies for configuring VPC domains, which are explicitly called *VPC protection groups* in the APIC. Ideally, policies should be created once and reused when connecting new devices to the fabric. Maximizing reusability of policy and objects makes Day 2 operations exponentially faster and easier to manage.

Switch Policy Groups

Switch policy groups allow leveraging of existing switch policies such as spanning-tree and monitoring policies.

Switch Profiles

Switch profiles enable the selection of one or more leaf switches and associate interface profiles to configure the ports on a specific node. This association pushes the configuration to the interface and creates an access port, a port channel, or a virtual port channel (VPC) if one has been configured in the interface policy.

Figure 5-1 depicts the workflow between various policies.

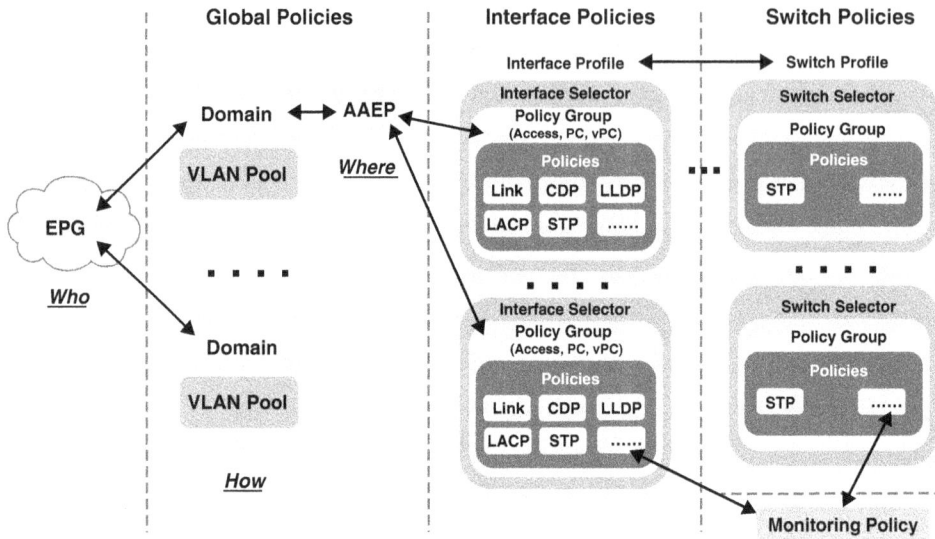

Figure 5-1 *Relationship Between Logical and Physical Construct in ACI*

Interface Policies

Interface policies dictate interface behavior such as link speed, link discovery, port channel, and so on and are also tied to interface policy groups. For example, there could be a policy that dictates whether virtual port channel should use the LACP mode active, passive, or so on or whether an interface should have CDP enabled or disabled; such policies can be reused as new devices are connected to the leaf switches.

Interface Policy Groups

Interface policy groups are templates that dictate port behavior and are associated to an AAEP. Interface policy groups use policies to specify how links should behave. These are also reusable objects, as many devices are likely to be connected to ports that require the same port configuration. There are three types of interface policy groups: access port, port channel, and VPC. The policy group used depends on the link type.

The ports on the leaf switches default to 10 Gigabit Ethernet, and a Gigabit Ethernet link-level policy must be created for devices connected at that speed. Regarding port channels and VPCs, the policy group is what defines the logical identifier (poX) on the switch. Therefore, if you want to create 10 PCs/VPCs, you must create 10 policy groups. Access port policy groups can be reused (which is recommended) between interfaces because there is no logical interface defined. Policy groups do not actually specify where the protocols and port behavior should be implemented. The *where* happens by associating one or more interface profiles to a switch profile, as discussed in the following section.

Interface Profiles

Interface profiles help glue the pieces together. An interface profile contains blocks of ports called *interface selectors* and is also tied to the interface policy groups described in the previous section. Again, this is just an arbitrary port, such as e1/1; the profile must be associated with a specific switch profile to configure the ports.

While many policies are reusable, it is important to understand the implications of deleting policies from the ACI fabric. Policy usage can be viewed by clicking the Show Usage button in the APIC GUI when viewing a given object. The information provided can help you determine what objects are using what policy so you can understand the impact when making changes and evaluate whether changes would impact production services.

Access policies enable an administrator to configure port channels and VPCs; protocols such as LLDP, CDP, or LACP; and features such as monitoring and diagnostics. To apply a configuration across a potentially large number of switches, an administrator defines switch profiles that associate interface configurations in a single policy group. In this way, large numbers of interfaces across the fabric can be configured at once. Switch profiles can contain symmetric configurations for multiple switches or unique special-purpose configurations. Figure 5-2 shows the process for configuring access to the ACI fabric.

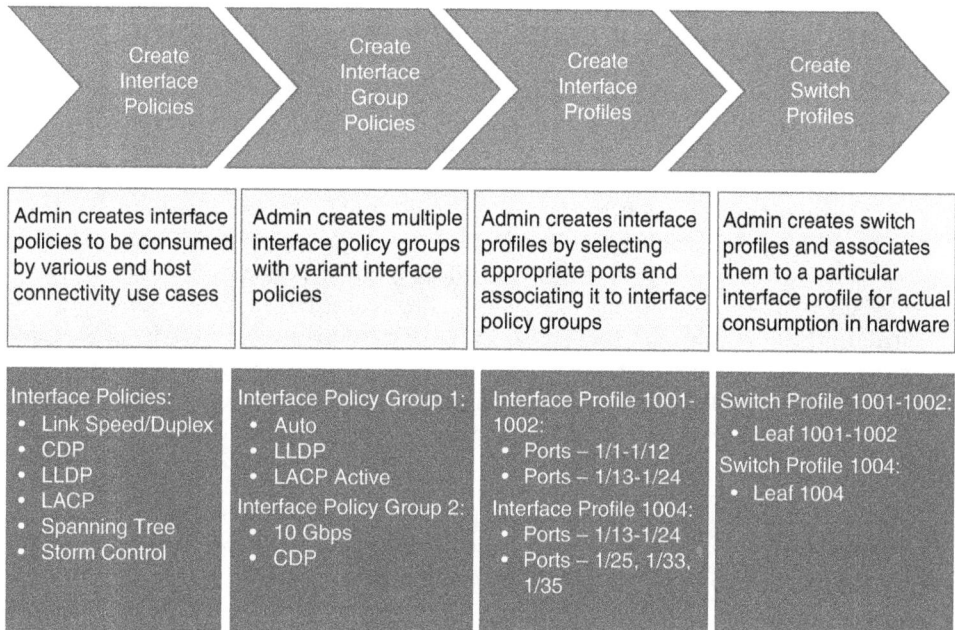

Create Interface Policies	Create Interface Group Policies	Create Interface Profiles	Create Switch Profiles
Admin creates interface policies to be consumed by various end host connectivity use cases	Admin creates multiple interface policy groups with variant interface policies	Admin creates interface profiles by selecting appropriate ports and associating it to interface policy groups	Admin creates switch profiles and associates them to a particular interface profile for actual consumption in hardware
Interface Policies: • Link Speed/Duplex • CDP • LLDP • LACP • Spanning Tree • Storm Control	Interface Policy Group 1: • Auto • LLDP • LACP Active Interface Policy Group 2: • 10 Gbps • CDP	Interface Profile 1001-1002: • Ports – 1/1-1/12 • Ports – 1/13-1/24 Interface Profile 1004: • Ports – 1/13-1/24 • Ports – 1/25, 1/33, 1/35	Switch Profile 1001-1002: • Leaf 1001-1002 Switch Profile 1004: • Leaf 1004

Figure 5-2 *ACI Access Policy Configuration Process*

Figure 5-3 shows the result of applying Switch Profile 1001–1002 and Switch Profile 1004 to the ACI fabric.

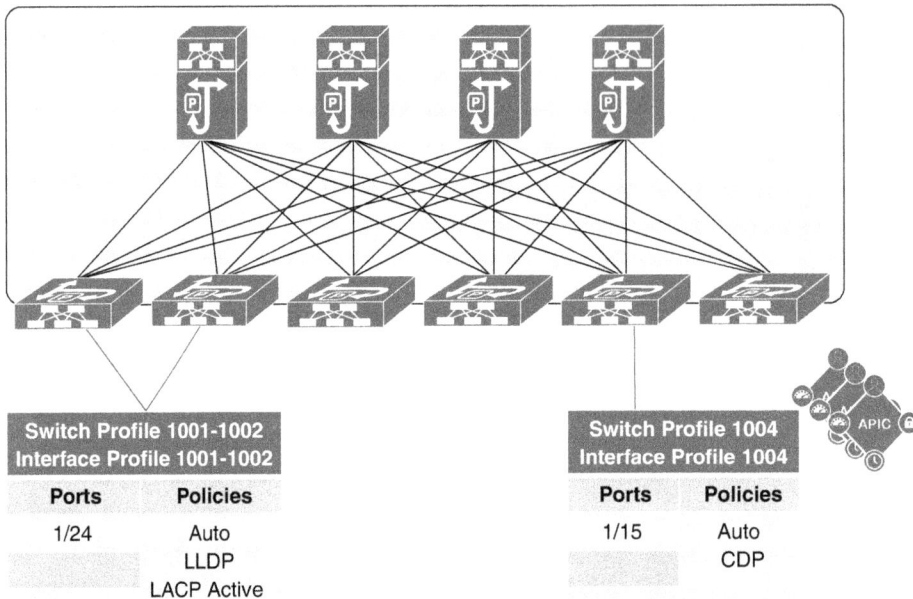

Figure 5-3   *Applying Access Policy Configuration*

Notice that the switch profile and interface profile are named in the same way. A recommended way to configure your switch profiles is to create a one-to-one mapping of physical nodes to switch profiles and one switch profile that contains two switches per VPC domain. Using the example in Figure 5-3, there could be four switch profiles created: 1001, 1002, 1004, and 1001–1002. The same interface profiles could be created and mapped to the matching switch profiles. Then, to enable and configure new interfaces on a given switch or VPC, you would simply need to allocate the port block under the interface profile, and the relationship to the appropriate switch or VPC domain would already be defined for you.

This combination of infrastructure and scope enables administrators to manage fabric configuration in a scalable fashion. These configurations can be implemented using the REST API, the CLI, or the GUI. The Quick Start interface in the GUI enables you to automatically create the underlying objects needed to implement such policies.

For physical connectivity of end hosts, you have the option of creating a nonbonded access port and bonded single-chassis or multi-chassis EtherChannel called a VPC. While using the wizards is an excellent way of deploying configuration quickly, it's always recommended to look at what objects are being created for you. This way, if an issue aris-es and you need to troubleshoot your configuration, you are familiar with the workflow and can validate the configuration on your own.

Virtual Port Channel (VPC)

VPC technology has been around in the industry for quite some time on Nexus switches. It allows you to create a Multichassis EtherChannel (MEC) where physical links are con-nected to two different ACI leaf switches to appear as a single logical switch and yet bundle them up for connecting to an end host. This end host could be a server, switch, router, Layer 4/Layer 7 device, or any other networking device that supports link aggre-gation group (LAG) or Ethernet bundling technology. Cisco developed VPC to pair two Nexus switches together to act as one logical node connecting to an end host and provide redundant links and prevent being blocked by Spanning Tree Protocol. VPC works by joining two switches together into a "VPC domain." In the VPC domain, one switch is referred to as primary and the other as secondary.

Due to the immense adoption of VPC in the industry today, Cisco ACI includes this technology. However, there are some unique differences in the way Cisco ACI configures VPC as compared to VPC on NX-OS–based switches:

■ **No dedicated peer link:** Traditionally, VPC is required to have a dedicated peer link between the pair of Nexus switches to synchronize state between the VPC peers. These links *must* be 10 Gbps interfaces. The VPC peer link also carries multicast and broadcast traffic and, in some failure cases, unicast traffic as well. In ACI, the fabric provides the transport or path to VPC peers to exchange that state, so this traffic can traverse from leaf to leaf using the Virtual Extensible LAN (VXLAN) overlay.

■ **VPC peer state protocol:** ACI VPC uses ZeroMQ instead of Cisco Fabric Services (CFS). ZeroMQ is an open-source messaging library that uses a TCP socket as the transport layer. Any application that requires synchronization of state on the peer, such as IGMP and Endpoint Manager (EPM), uses ZeroMQ.

■ **Peer keepalive:** In ACI VPC, peer keepalive is not handled via a physical link or peer link. Instead, routing triggers are used to detect peer reachability. Since the ACI fabric has a VXLAN tunnel built to each device in a pod, the members of the VPC domain have a unique tunnel interface that points to the members. This tunnel con-tains the destination physical VTEP of the peer switch. If for any reason the route to this VTEP is removed in the overlay-1 routing table (that is, if IS-IS goes down and so does the VPC peer), the VPC manager process brings down the ZeroMQ socket. When the route comes back, the tunnel comes up, and the socket is established again.

Figure 5-4 compares VPC between switches running NX-OS and ACI.

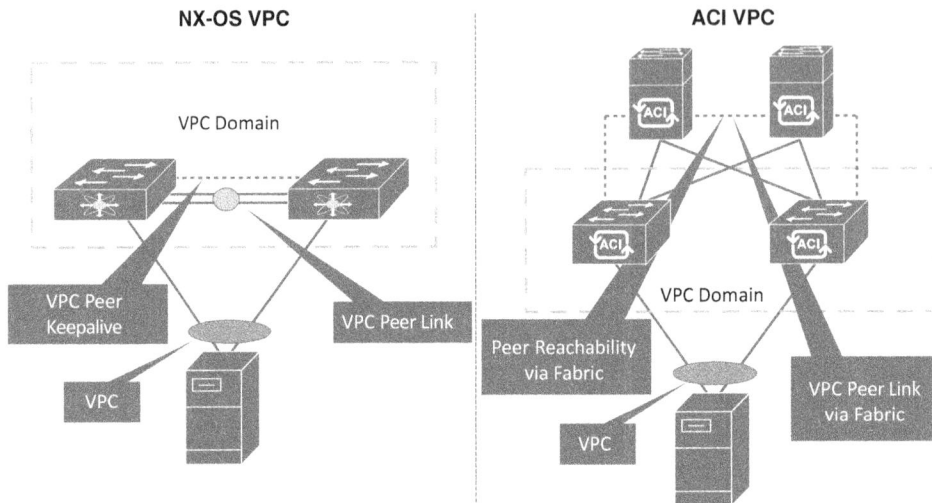

Figure 5-4   *VPC in NX-OS and ACI*

When creating a VPC domain between two leaf switches, both switches must be in the same switch generation in one of the following Nexus 9300 platform product lines:

■ **Generation 1:** Cisco Nexus 9000 switches without EX or FX at the end of the switch model name, such as 9372PX, 93120TX, or 9332PQ

■ **Generation 2:** Cisco Nexus 9000 switches with EX or FX at the end of the switch model name, such as 93180YC-EX, 93180YC-FX, 93108TC-EX, or 93108TC-FX

If you try to configure a VPC domain between two switches of different generations, a fault will be raised on the APIC, and the VPC configuration will not be pushed.

Configuring VPC

Configuring VPC requires a few simple steps that can be scripted and automated programmatically for rapid deployment of application infrastructure:

Step 1.   Define the VPC domain.

Step 2.   Create the interface policy:

   a. Create the interface policy, including LLDP, CDP, LACP, link speed/duplex, and so on.

   b. Create the VPC policy group, including consuming interface policies and associating an AAEP.

   c. Create the interface profile, including choosing the downlink ports and associating the VPC policy group.

Step 3.   Create the switch profile:

        a. Associate the interface profile.

Figure 5-5 provides a flow diagram that illustrates this process.

Note   Following a naming standard is important in the ACI policy model. Best practice is to use simple and meaningful object names.

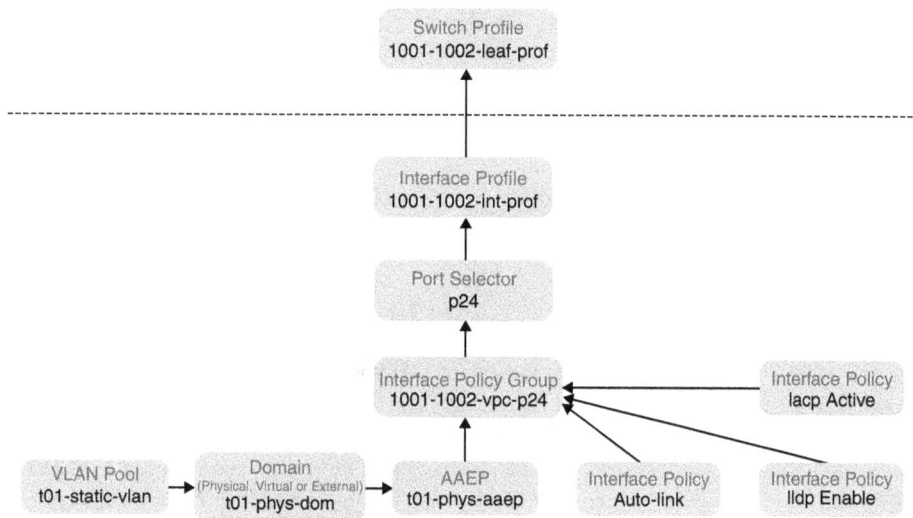

Figure 5-5   *VPC Logical Flow Diagram*

Defining the VPC Domain

To define a VPC domain, follow these steps (in ACI Release 3.2.5 and later):

Step 1.   Go to Fabric > Access Policies > Policies > Switch > Virtual Port Channel default.

Step 2.   Click the + sign to define VPC explicit protection group. The screen shown in Figure 5-6 appears.

Step 3.   Name the VPC explicit protection group (for example, 1001-1002-vpc-grp).

Step 4.   Define the VPC logical pair ID. The value has to be between 1 and 1000.

Step 5.   Select the two switches you want to group—in this case, 1001 for Switch 1 and 1002 for Switch 2.

Step 6.   Click Submit.

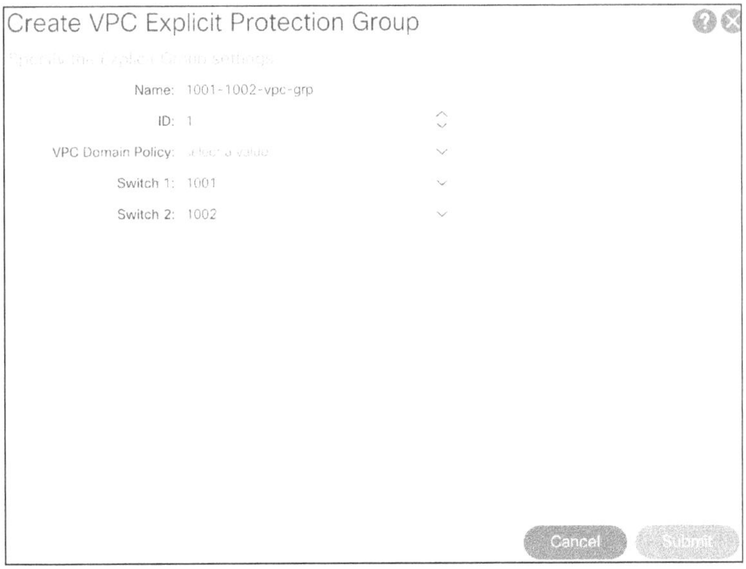

Figure 5-6   *Defining the VPC Domain*

As you can see in Figure 5-7, the VPC explicit protection group name you entered is shown (1001-1002-vpc-grp), as is the logical pair ID you entered (1) for the first vpc domain. The virtual IP address (10.34.20.67/32) is an auto-generated IP address from the system TEP pool that represents the virtual shared (anycast) TEP of the VPC switch pair leafs 1001 and 1002; in this case, packets destined to VPC-connected endpoints off Leafs 1001 and 1002 will use this anycast VTEP to send the packets. When it comes to creating VPC domains, ACI is an immense improvement over traditional NX-OS, as there is no need to manually configure the peer link and peer keepalive.

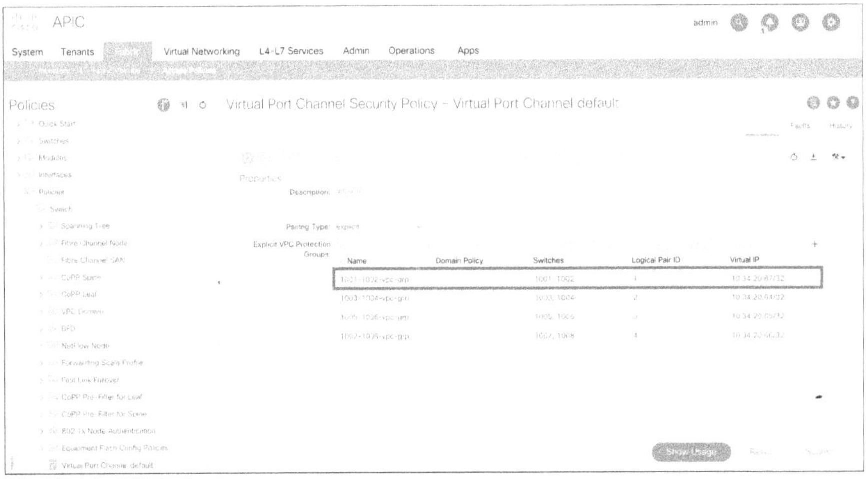

Figure 5-7   *VPC Domain Between a Leaf Pair*

Creating an Interface Policy

To create an interface policy, follow these steps (in ACI Release 3.2.5 and later):

Step 1.   Create the interface policy, such as link-level, CDP, LLDP, or LACP, per your interface use case by going to Fabric > Access Policies > Policies > Interface in the APIC GUI.

Step 2.   Create the interface policy group by going to Fabric > Access Policies > Interfaces > Leaf Interfaces > Policy Groups > VPC Interface in the APIC GUI. The screen shown in Figure 5-8 appears.

Step 3.   Name the VPC interface policy group (for example, 1001-1002-vpc-p24). Choose the appropriate interface policies and associate the AAEP. Click Submit.

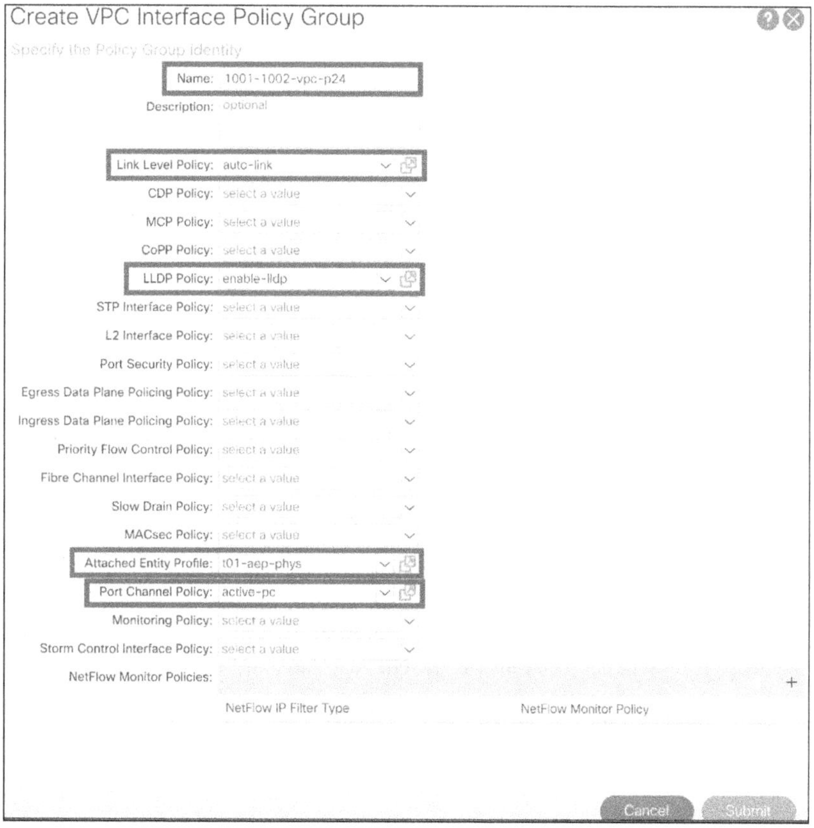

Create VPC Interface Policy Group

Specify the Policy Group identity

Name:	1001-1002-vpc-p24
Description:	optional
Link Level Policy:	auto-link
CDP Policy:	select a value
MCP Policy:	select a value
CoPP Policy:	select a value
LLDP Policy:	enable-lldp
STP Interface Policy:	select a value
L2 Interface Policy:	select a value
Port Security Policy:	select a value
Egress Data Plane Policing Policy:	select a value
Ingress Data Plane Policing Policy:	select a value
Priority Flow Control Policy:	select a value
Fibre Channel Interface Policy:	select a value
Slow Drain Policy:	select a value
MACsec Policy:	select a value
Attached Entity Profile:	t01-aep-phys
Port Channel Policy:	active-pc
Monitoring Policy:	select a value
Storm Control Interface Policy:	select a value
NetFlow Monitor Policies:	

NetFlow IP Filter Type   NetFlow Monitor Policy

Cancel   Submit

Figure 5-8   *Creating a VPC Interface Policy Group*

Step 4.   Create the leaf interface profile by going to Fabric > Access Policies > Interfaces > Leaf Interfaces > Profiles in the APIC GUI, as shown in Figure 5-9.

Step 5.   Name the leaf interface profile (for example, 1001-1002-int-prof).

Step 6.   Click the + sign to choose the interface selector.

Step 7.   Name the access port selector (for example, p24).

Step 8.   Select the interface ID 1/24.

Step 9.   Associate to the interface policy group 1001-1002-vpc-p24 and click OK.

Step 10.   Click Submit to finish creating the leaf interface profile.

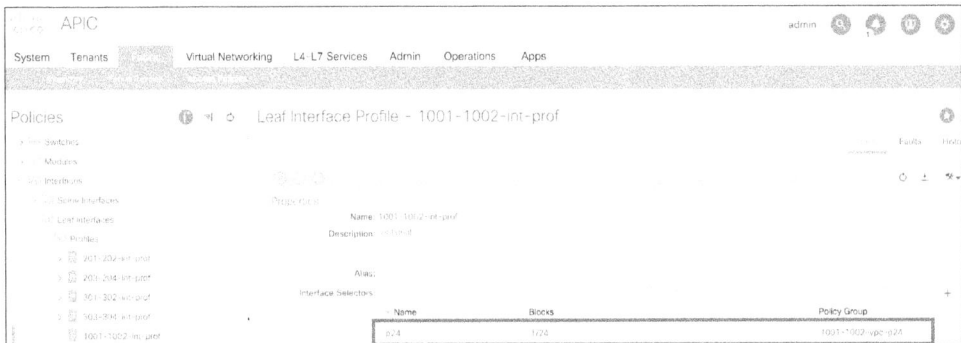

Figure 5-9   *Creating a Leaf Interface Profile*

Creating a Switch Profile

To create a switch profile, follow these steps (in ACI Release 3.2.5 and later):

Step 1.   Create the switch profile by going to Fabric > Access Policies > Switches > Leaf Switches > Profiles in the APIC GUI (see Figure 5-10).

Step 2.   Name the leaf profile (for example, 1001-1002-leaf-prof).

Step 3.   Choose leaf selectors by clicking the + sign.

Step 4.   Name the leaf selectors (for example, L1001-1002).

Step 5.   Choose leaf switches 1001 and 1002, click Update, and click Next.

Step 6.   Choose the leaf interface profile (in this example, 1001-1002-int-prof).

Step 7.   Click Finish.

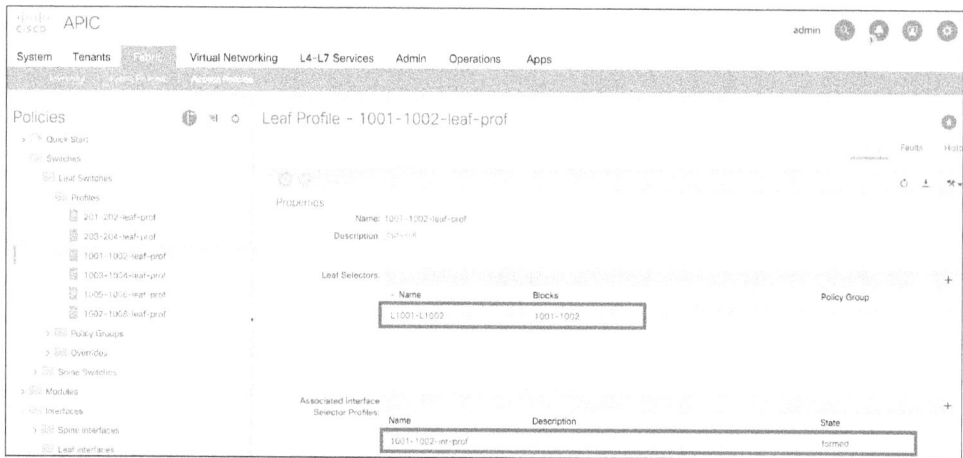

Figure 5-10   *Creating a Switch Profile*

Port Channel

A port channel allows multiple physical links bundled together with a single ACI leaf to appear as a single logical port for link redundancy and extra bandwidth (see Figure 5-11). Port channel configuration can use the active/passive LACP or the Static Channel mode.

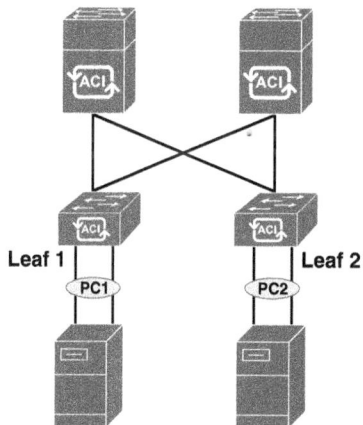

Figure 5-11   *Port Channel in ACI*

Configuring a Port Channel

Configuring a port channel is quite similar to configuring a virtual port channel aside from a few minor differences shown in the following steps. Again, as with VPC configuration, these steps can all be scripted and automated programmatically for rapid deployment of application infrastructure:

Step 1.   Define the VPC domain. (There is no need to create a VPC domain because this is just a single-chassis port channel.)

Step 2.   Create the interface policy:

   a. Create the interface policy, including LLDP, CDP, LACP, link speed/duplex, and so on.

   b. Create the PC policy group, including consuming interface policies and associating an AAEP.

   c. Create the interface profile by choosing downlink ports and associating a PC policy group.

Step 3.   Create the switch profile.

   a. Associate the interface profile.

Figure 5-12 provides a flow diagram that illustrates this process.

Note   Following a naming standard is important in the ACI policy model. Best practice is to use simple and meaningful object names.

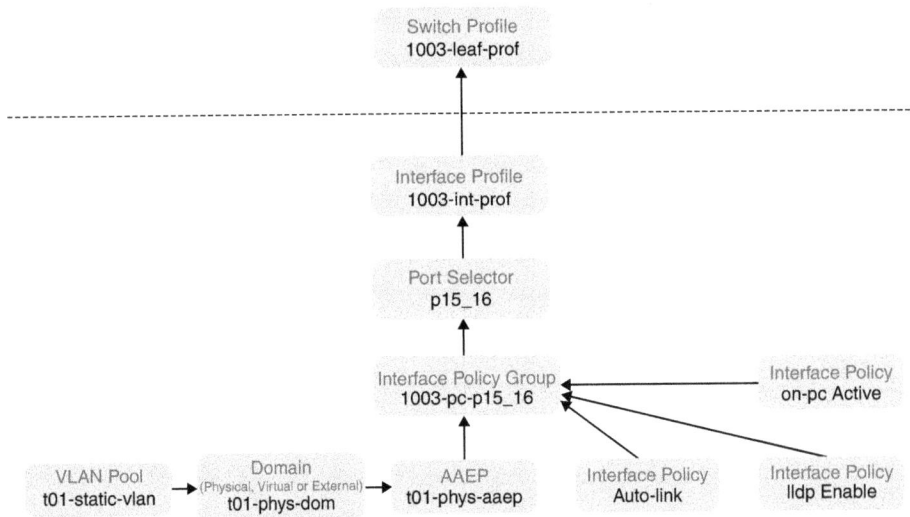

Figure 5-12   *Port Channel Logical Flow Diagram*

Creating an Interface Policy

To create an interface policy, follow these steps (in ACI Release 3.2.5 and later):

Step 1. Create the interface policy, such as link-level, CDP, LLDP, or LACP, per your interface use case by going to Fabric > Access Policies > Policies > Interface in the APIC GUI (see Figure 5-13).

Step 2. Create the interface policy group by going to Fabric > Access Policies > Interfaces > Leaf Interfaces > Policy Groups > PC Interface in the APIC GUI.

Step 3. Name the PC interface policy group (for example, 1003-pc-p15_16).

Step 4. Choose the appropriate interface policies and associate the AAEP. Click Submit.

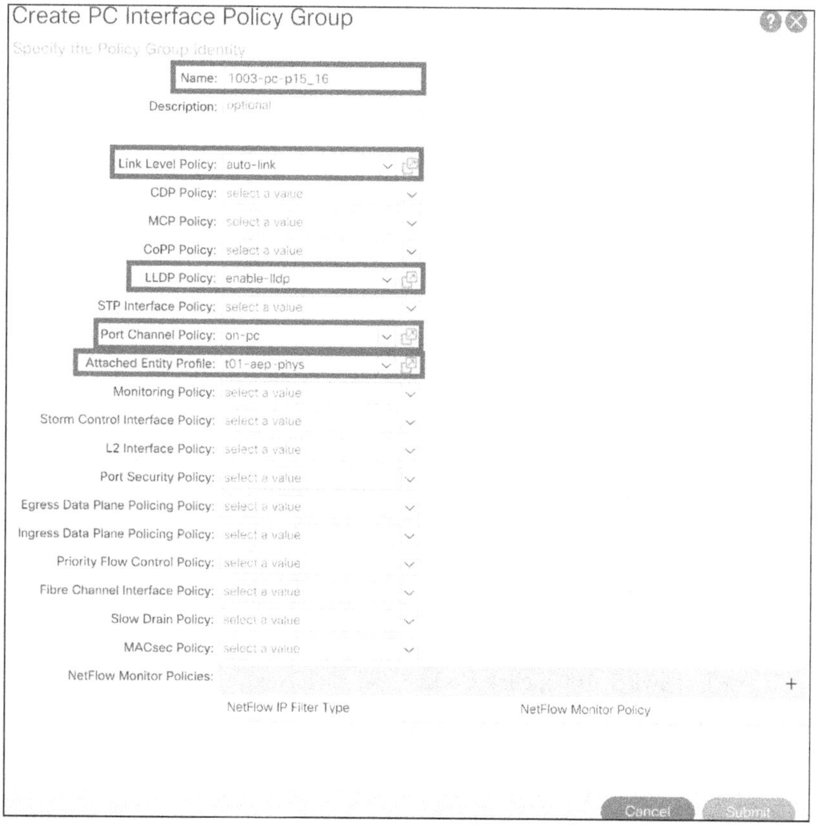

Create PC Interface Policy Group

Specify the Policy Group Identity

Name: 1003-pc-p15_16
Description: optional

Link Level Policy: auto-link
CDP Policy: select a value
MCP Policy: select a value
CoPP Policy: select a value
LLDP Policy: enable-lldp
STP Interface Policy: select a value
Port Channel Policy: on-pc
Attached Entity Profile: t01-aep-phys
Monitoring Policy: select a value
Storm Control Interface Policy: select a value
L2 Interface Policy: select a value
Port Security Policy: select a value
Egress Data Plane Policing Policy: select a value
Ingress Data Plane Policing Policy: select a value
Priority Flow Control Policy: select a value
Fibre Channel Interface Policy: select a value
Slow Drain Policy: select a value
MACsec Policy: select a value
NetFlow Monitor Policies: +

NetFlow IP Filter Type   NetFlow Monitor Policy

Cancel   Submit

Figure 5-13 *Creating a PC Interface Policy Group*

Step 5. Create a leaf interface profile by going to Fabric > Access Policies > Interfaces > Leaf Interfaces > Profiles in the APIC GUI (see Figure 5-14).

Step 6. Name the leaf interface profile (for example, 1003-int-prof).

Step 7.   Click the + sign to choose the interface selector.

Step 8.   Name the access port selector (for example, p15_16).

Step 9.   Select the interface IDs 1/15 and 1/16.

Step 10.   Associate to the interface policy group 1003-pc-p15_16 and click OK.

Step 11.   Click Submit to finish creating the leaf interface profile.

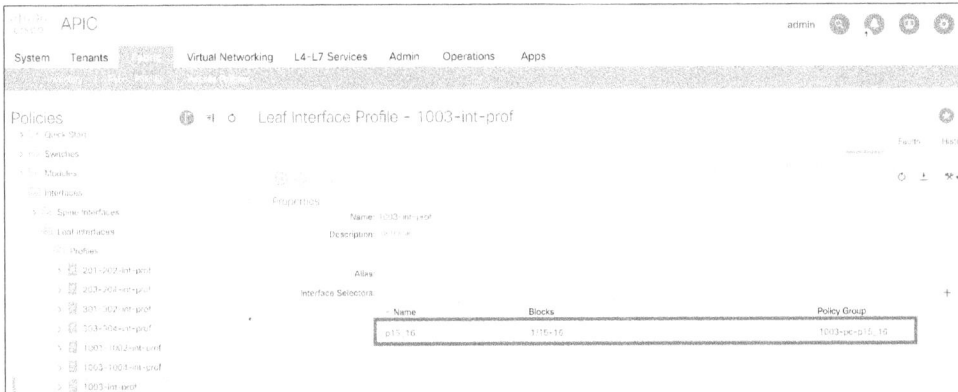

Figure 5-14   *Creating the Leaf Interface Profile*

Creating a Switch Profile

To create a switch profile, follow these steps (in ACI Release 3.2.5 and later):

Step 1.   Create the switch profile by going to Fabric > Access Policies > Switches > Leaf Switches > Profiles in the APIC GUI (see Figure 5-15).

Step 2.   Name the leaf profile (for example, 1003-leaf-prof).

Step 3.   Choose leaf selectors by clicking the + sign.

Step 4.   Name the leaf selectors (for example, L1003).

Step 2.   Choose leaf switch 1003, click Update, and click Next.

Step 5.   Choose the leaf interface profile (in this example, 1003-int-prof).

Step 6.   Click Finish.

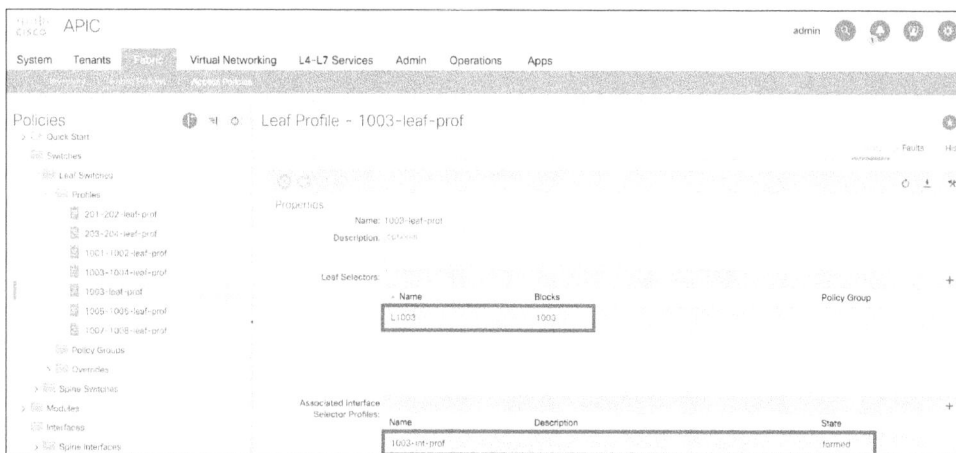

Figure 5-15 *Creating a Switch Profile*

Access Port

Access ports are the end host–facing ports such as server, IP storage, switch, router, and L4/L7 devices. In ACI, access ports can be defined as Trunk, Access (802.1P), or Access (untagged). Why are there two types of access port configurations in ACI, and what is the difference between them?

IEEE 802.1P refers to a QoS implementation using 802.1Q protocols, which basically means that the switch access port with an 802.1P setting should send and receive frames tagged with VLAN 0, whereas the switch access port with an Untagged setting should send and receive frames without any VLAN tag. Most modern operating systems should be able to manage frames tagged with VLAN 0 similar to Untagged frames. However, installing a server operating system using a Preboot Execution Environment (PXE) method across a Cisco ACI fabric switching infrastructure could lead to some issues because small BIOS/firmware cannot read VLAN 0 tagged frames.

ACI second-generation—and later—switches (EX/FX) do not distinguish between the Access (802.1p) and Access (Untagged) modes. When EPGs are deployed on second-generation switch ports configured with either 802.1p or Untagged mode, the traffic always egresses untagged. The port accepts ingress traffic that is untagged, tagged, or in 802.1p mode. Figure 5-16 illustrates this.

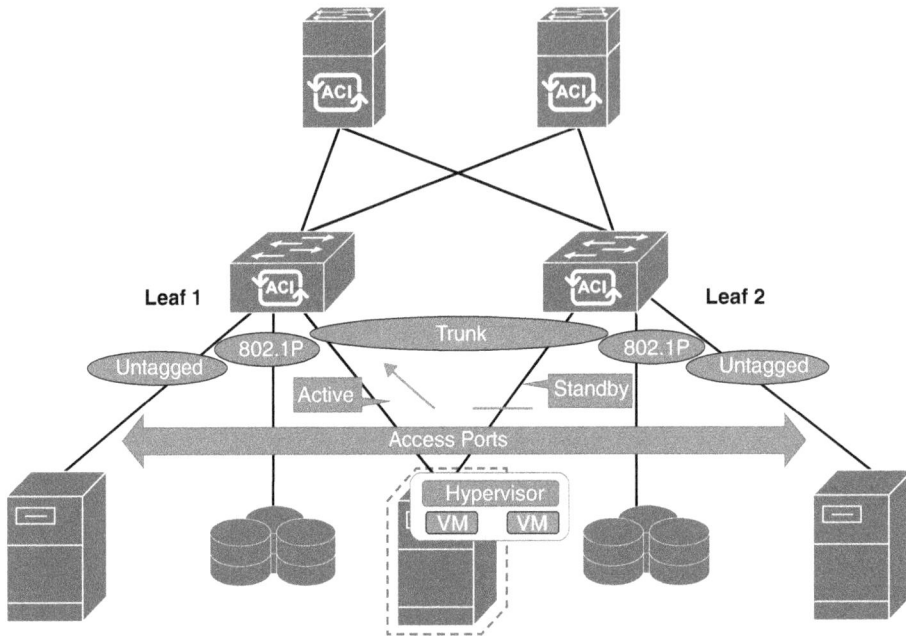

Figure 5-16 *Access Ports in ACI*

Configuring an Access Port

Except for some minor differences, configuration of access ports involves the same policy-driven workflow as configuration of VPCs or port channels, as shown in the following steps:

Step 1.   Create the interface policy:

   a. Create the interface policy, including LLDP, CDP, LACP, link speed/duplex, and so on.

   b. Create the access port policy group, including consuming interface policies and associating AAEP.

   c. Create the interface profile, including choosing downlink ports and associating the PC policy group.

Step 2.   Create the switch profile:

   a. Associate the interface profile.

Again, as with configuration of VPCs and single port channels, these steps can all be scripted and automated programmatically for rapid deployment of application infrastructure.

You can either go with a single physical link to a single leaf or dual physical links (active/ standby) to two top of the rack (ToR) leafs. Note that in both cases, just one access port policy group (in this example, t01-access-polgrp) is reused multiple times. Figures 5-17 and 5-18 are flow diagrams that illustrate the process.

Note   Following a naming standard is important in the ACI policy model. Best practice is to use simple and meaningful object names.

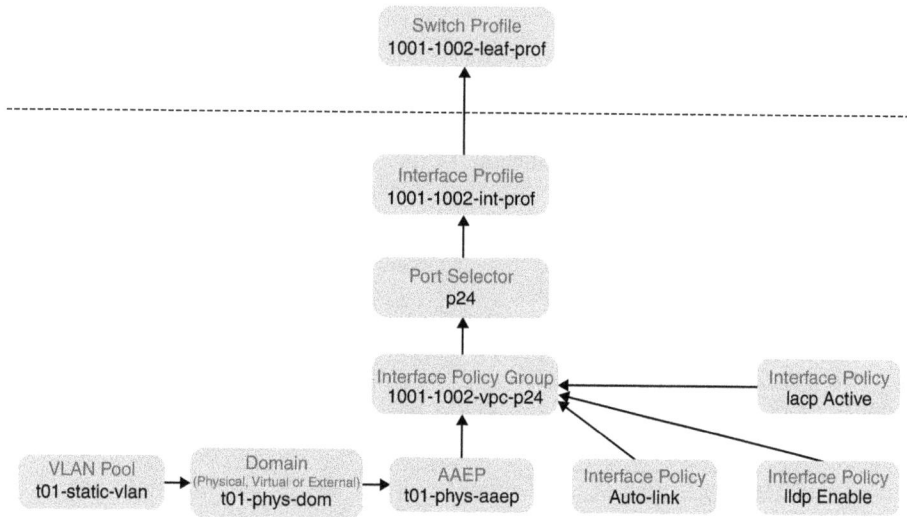

Figure 5-17   *Access Port Logical Flow Diagram (Single Link to Single Leaf)*

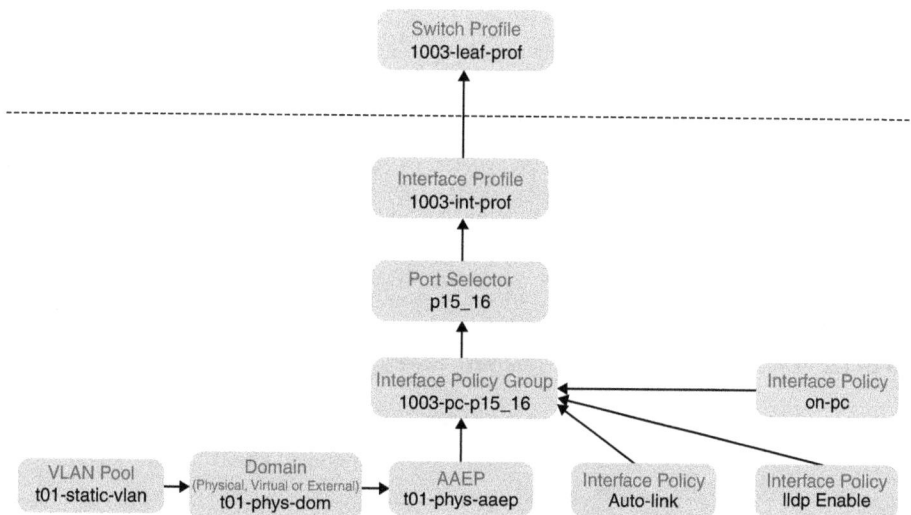

Figure 5-18   *Access Port Logical Flow Diagram (Dual Links to Two Leafs)*

Creating an Interface Policy

To create an interface policy, follow these steps (in ACI Release 3.2.5 and later):

Step 1.   Create an interface policy, such as link-level, CDP, LLDP, or LACP, per your interface use case, by going to Fabric > Access Policies > Policies > Interface in the APIC GUI.

Step 2.   Create an interface policy group by going to Fabric > Access Policies > Interfaces > Leaf Interfaces > Policy Groups > Leaf Access Port in the APIC GUI.

Step 3.   Name the leaf access port policy group (for example, t01-access-polgrp).

Step 4.   Choose the appropriate interface policies and associate the AAEP, as shown in Figure 5-19, and click Submit.

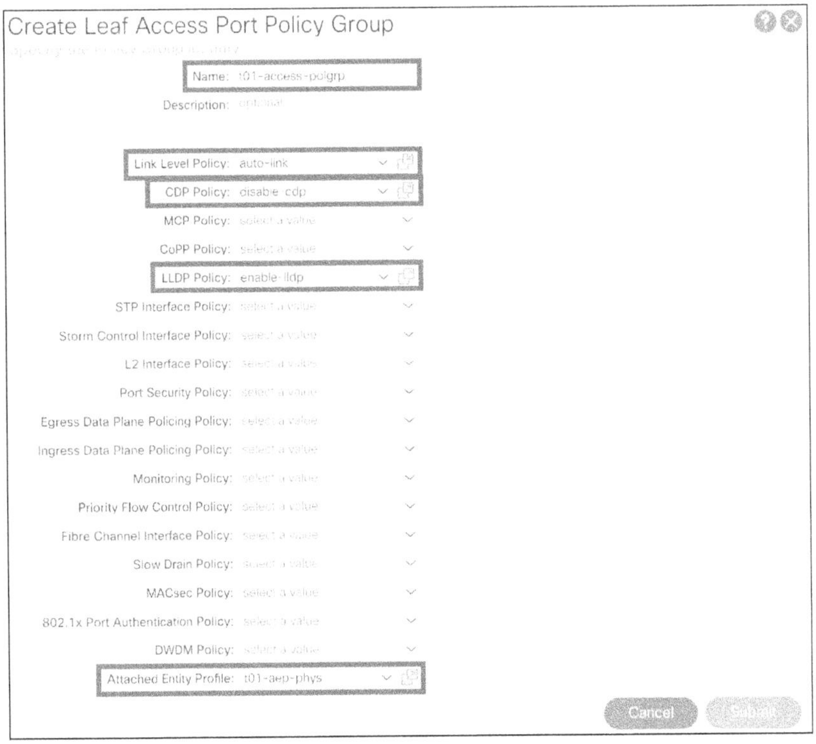

Figure 5-19   *Creating an Access Port Interface Policy Group*

Step 5. Create a leaf interface profile by going to Fabric > Access Policies > Interfaces > Leaf Interfaces > Profiles in the APIC GUI, as shown in Figure 5-20.

Step 6. Name the leaf interface profile (for example, 1004-int-prof).

Step 7. Click the + sign to choose the interface selector.

Step 8. Name the access port selector (for example, p15).

Step 9. Select the interface ID 1/15.

Step 10. Associate with the interface policy group t01-access-polgrp and click OK.

Step 11. Click Submit to finish creating the leaf interface profile.

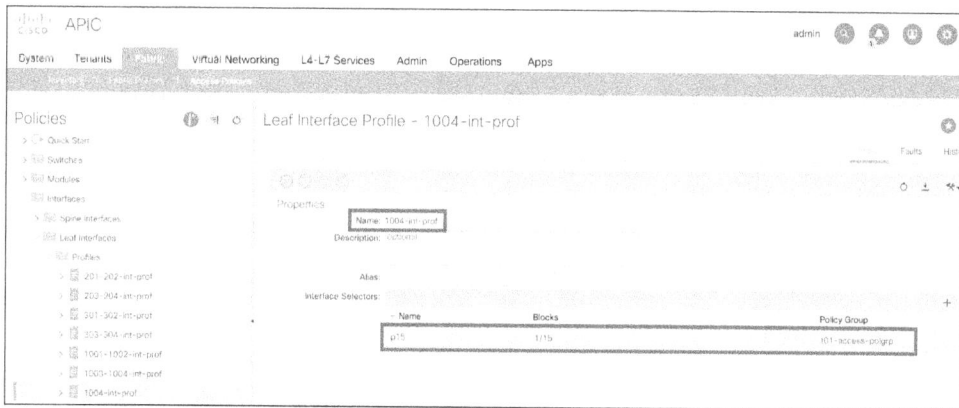

Figure 5-20 *Creating a Leaf Interface Profile*

Creating a Switch Profile

To create a switch profile, follow these steps (in ACI Release 3.2.5 and later):

Step 1. Create a switch profile by going to Fabric > Access Policies > Switches > Leaf Switches > Profiles in the APIC GUI, as shown in Figure 5-21.

Step 2. Name the leaf profile (for example, 1004-leaf-prof).

Step 3. Choose leaf selectors by clicking the + sign.

Step 4. Name the leaf selectors (for example, L1004). Choose leaf switch 1003, click Update, and click Next.

Step 5. Choose the leaf interface profile (in this example, 1004-int-prof).

Step 6. Click Finish.

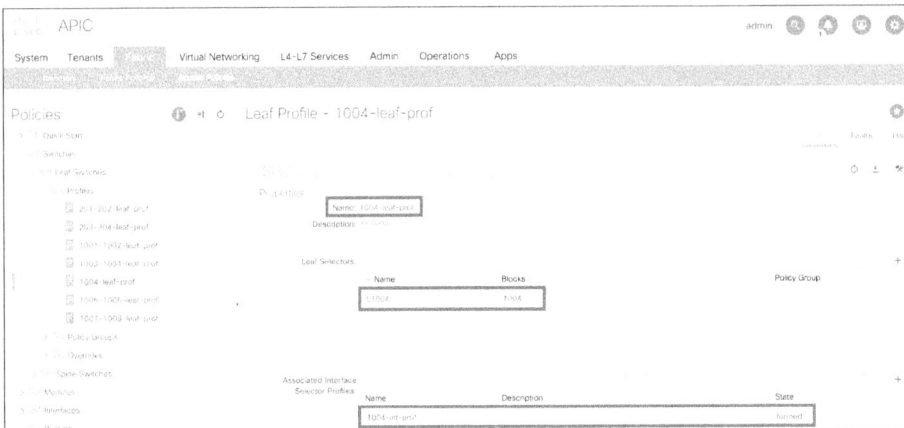

Figure 5-21   *Creating a Switch Profile*

Best Practices in Configuring Access Policies

Cisco has established several best practices for ACI fabric configuration based on field experiences and lab scale-out testing. These are not configuration-related requirements and might be different for different cases and for different customers, but following these best practices can help simplify Day 2 operations of the Cisco ACI fabric.

Policy Best Practices

Best practice is to reuse policies whenever possible for manageability and efficient usage. For example, there should be policies for 1/10/40/100 Gbps and auto port speeds, CDP, LLDP, LACP, and so on.

Following a naming standard is important in the ACI policy model. When naming policies, use names that clearly describe the configuration setting. For example, a policy that enables LACP in active mode could be called something like LACP-Active. There are many default out-of-the-box policies, but it is hard to remember all the default values, so policies need to be clearly named to avoid mistakes when making configuration changes in the fabric.

Create a switch profile individually for each leaf switch, and additionally create a separate switch profile for each VPC pair if VPC is configured.

Domain Best Practices

Create one physical domain per tenant for bare-metal servers that requires similar treatment, excluding the virtualized compute part of VMM integration with ACI.

Create one physical domain per tenant for external network connectivity.

If a VMM domain needs to be leveraged across multiple tenants, a single VMM domain can be created and associated with all leaf ports where virtualized compute is connected.

AAEP Best Practices

When possible, create one AAEP for physical bare-metal compute and another AAEP for virtualized compute. If a single interface needs access to both virtual and physical domains, multiple domains can be associated with a single AAEP. A good use case for this, as described earlier, would be if you had a blade switch connected to the ACI fabric. On a given leaf switch port, there might be several hosts connected, offering different functions and trunking different VLAN ranges. In such a case, the AAEP associated with the interfaces connecting to the blade switch would need access to multiple domains.

Compute and Storage Connectivity

Compute connectivity is key for all application workloads to function properly on the Cisco ACI fabric. Therefore, fabric connectivity requirements that are dictated by the server infrastructure team must be carefully considered. Different customers have different varieties of compute platforms. Platforms include blade systems such as Cisco UCS B-Series and standalone pizza boxes such as Cisco UCS C-Series servers as well as third-party blade system and standalone servers that all need to be connected to the ACI fabric. These compute platforms, whether they are baremetal or virtualized, can be connected to the ACI fabric using VPC, regular port channel, or access port configuration. These policies are all controlled by access policies in the Cisco APIC. The connection to a bare-metal compute platform can also be established via Cisco Fabric Extender (FEX). Let's look at FEX connectivity with ACI leafs and some of the limitations.

FEX Connectivity

FEX provides an alternative way to connect end host devices to the ACI fabric. However, there are restrictions to be aware of when using FEX connected to ACI leafs:

- There is no support for external router connectivity using L3Outs on FEX ports.

- FEX is supported in only a single home because FEX connects to one leaf only.

- There is no FCoE support on FEX ports except for N9K-C93180YC-FX and N9K-C93108TC-FX leaf switches running ACI Release 2.3(x) and later.

- 802.1P CoS values are not preserved when the outgoing interface is on the FEX port.

- With ACI Release 3.1(x) or later, multicast sources or receivers connected to FEX ports are supported.

- With ACI Release 3.2(x) or later, FEX is supported for connecting remote leafs.

Always check the Cisco website for the latest limitations related to feature such as FEX connectivity in the ACI software release notes. The ACI fabric supports FEX server-side VPCs, also known as FEX straight-through VPCs. In this configuration, as illustrated in Figure 5-22, FEX uplinks to leaf downlinks connect via regular port channel to a single leaf switch.

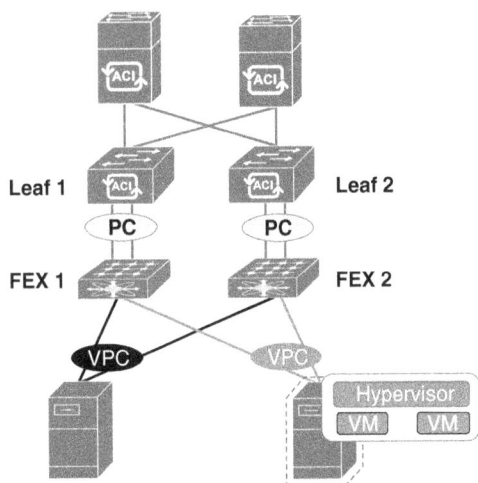

Figure 5-22   *ACI Topology Supporting FEX*

Cisco Blade Chassis Servers UCS B-Series

In order to connect a UCS B-Series blade chassis to ACI fabric, the type of Layer 2 connection needed on the fabric interconnect–facing ports must be determined first. You must ensure that VLANs that are required on UCS blades are trunked to uplink ports of fabric interconnects connecting to ACI leafs. You also need to make sure the link discovery protocol—either CDP or LLDP—is configured the same way on both UCS fabric interconnects and ACI leafs. A best practice is to leverage a VPC to connect the UCS fabric interconnects to create a MEC. In this scenario, individual link and fabric switch failures are mitigated to maintain a higher expected service uptime, as illustrated in Figure 5-23.

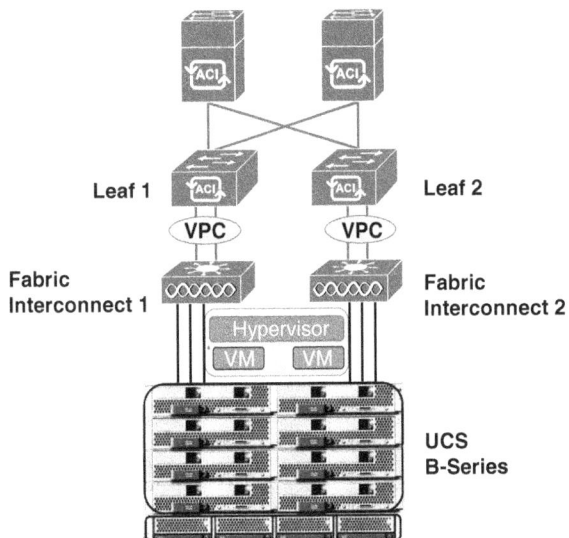

Figure 5-23   *Connecting a Blade Chassis Server to an ACI Leaf*

Standalone Rack-Mount Servers

Like blade systems, standalone rack-mount servers such as UCS C-Series can be connected to ACI leafs in the same three connection scenarios: VPC, regular port channel, and access port. For redundancy and better convergence during failures, VPC connection is highly recommended unless the compute platform does not support LAG or Ethernet bonding techniques such as in the case of VMWare vSphere 6.0 and earlier releases. When a server is being connected to the ACI fabric, the kind of traffic expected out of the server links needs to be considered for proper bandwidth determination. Standalone server connectivity can also be done via FEX port. Figure 5-24 shows the options for connecting servers directly to ACI leafs or through FEX.

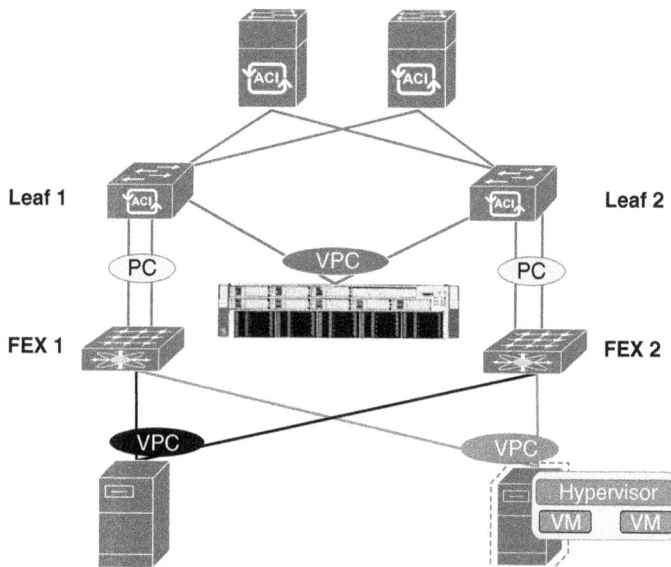

Figure 5-24   *Connecting a Bare-Metal Server to an ACI Leaf*

Connecting Storage in ACI

Cisco ACI provides storage connectivity using FCoE on a cloud-scale EX/FX platform. FCoE is a protocol that enables you to send Fibre Channel traffic over an Ethernet medium. This is useful for sending Fibre Channel traffic over high-speed Ethernet transport while preserving the Fibre Channel packets. The other benefit of using FCoE is to use a converged infrastructure for both Fibre Channel and Ethernet traffic.

With FCoE support in ACI, the hosts are connected through virtual fiber (F) ports deployed on an ACI leaf switch. The SAN storage switch and Fibre Channel network are connected through a Fibre Channel forwarding (FCF) bridge to the ACI fabric through a virtual network port (NP) deployed on the *same* ACI leaf switch where the host is connected as a virtual F port. The reason for this limitation is that the ACI leaf switch does not perform local switching between SAN accessing hosts, and the FCoE traffic is not forwarded to a spine switch. In Fibre Channel technology, virtual NP and virtual F ports are referred to as virtual Fibre Channel (VFC) ports. Figure 5-25 illustrates FCoE storage connectivity with ACI leafs.

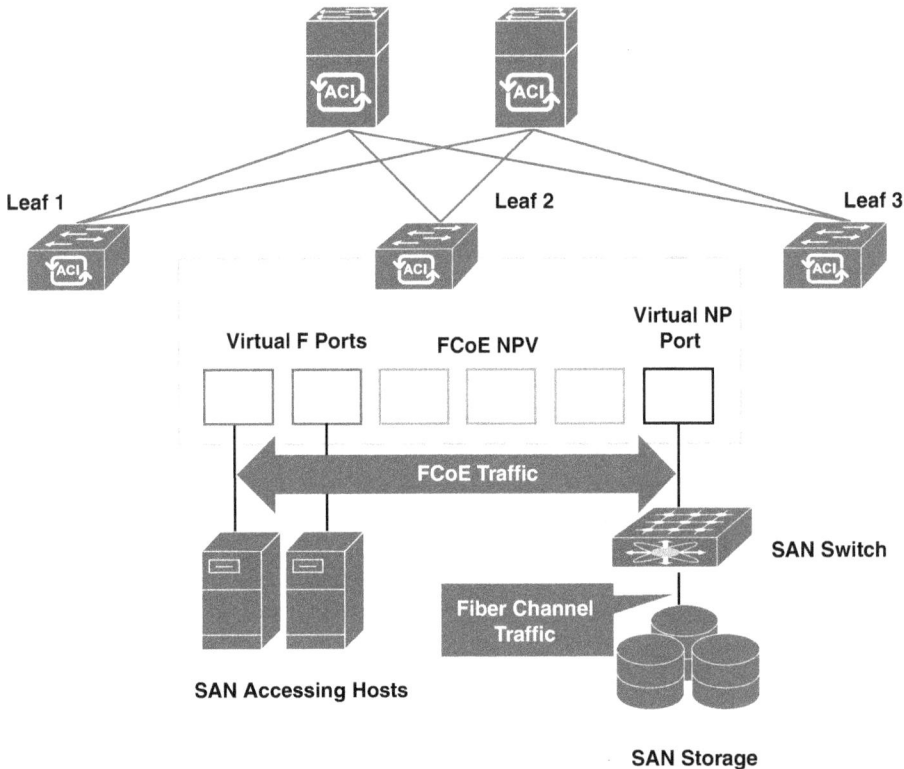

Figure 5-25 *ACI Topology Supporting FCoE*

FCoE traffic requires you to configure a separate VLAN connectivity over which SAN-accessing hosts broadcast FCoE Initialization Protocol (FIP) packets to discover the interfaces enabled as F ports. ACI allows one VSAN assignment per bridge domain. You must configure VSAN and VLAN pool allocations as static while configuring FCoE. (Only static allocation is allowed in VSAN configuration.) While configuring VFC interfaces in ACI, F port mode is the default mode on the interface. Therefore, you need to specifically configure NP port mode in access policies.

L4/L7 Service Device Connectivity

L4/L7 services are a critical component of application hosting infrastructure for all data center networks. Therefore, it is important to understand physical connectivity options for L4/L7 devices in ACI. Let's look at a few examples of firewall and load balancer connectivity with ACI.

Connecting Firewalls

Firewalls protect network segments from unauthorized access by users or miscreants while also enforcing security policies and posture. When discussing the networks connected to a firewall, the *outside* network is typically defined as being in front of the firewall (an unsecured area), while the *inside* network is protected (by default) and resides behind the firewall; a *demilitarized zone* (*DMZ*) allows limited access to outside (external) and inside (internal) users.

While ACI allows any vendor security platform to be connected to the fabric, the focus in this book is the Cisco product line. Cisco firewalls can be connected to a network in either Transparent mode (also called Bridge mode) or Routed mode. Firewalls can be deployed in Failover mode or Cluster mode for redundancy and high availability.

In active/standby failover mode, the heartbeat cable must be connected directly between the firewall pair (recommended) or via ACI leafs using a separate VPC if the two firewalls are not in the same rack. If you are establishing the failover heartbeat connections via ACI leafs, you need to create a private BD (with no subnet) and associate it with an EPG that you need to then statically bind to ACI leaf ports (in this example, the H-Beat VPC ports). Figure 5-26 illustrates the firewall connectivity with ACI leafs in active/standby mode.

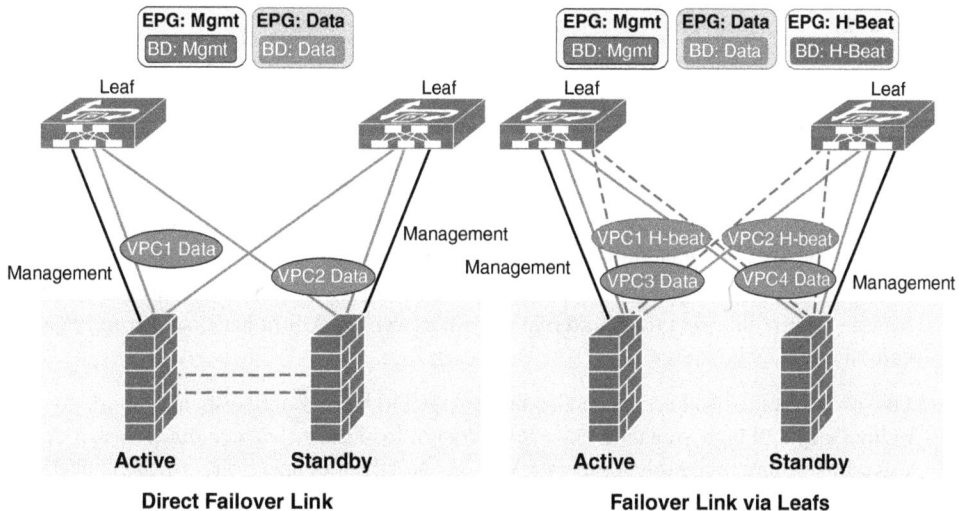

Figure 5-26 *ACI Connectivity with a Firewall in Active/Standby Failover Mode*

In Cisco Firewall Cluster mode for a two-node cluster, you need to have two separate VPCs for the cluster control link (CCL) as Access (untagged) ports connecting each of the firewall. You also need another separate VPC connecting both firewalls for data that you can Trunk and create Dot1q interfaces for your inside and outside interfaces on firewall cluster. On ACI leafs for firewall CCL traffic, you need to create a BD (with flooding, disable unicast routing and no subnet) and associate it with an EPG that you need to then statically bind to ACI leaf ports (in this example, the CCL VPC ports). Figure 5-27 illustrates firewall cluster connectivity with ACI leafs.

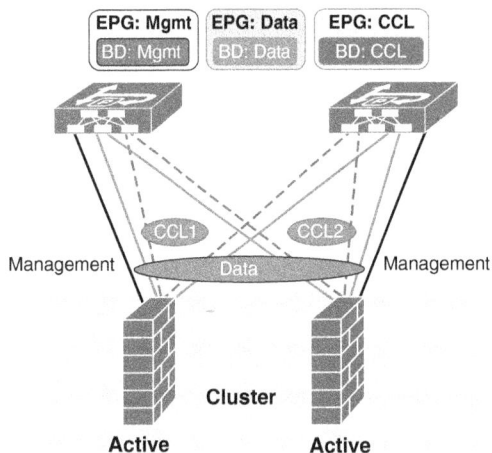

Figure 5-27   *ACI Connectivity with a Firewall in Cluster Mode*

Connecting Load Balancers

Load balancers provide high availability of applications by seamlessly balancing the load between a pool of servers. They also provide the capability of persisting the user connections to maintain the state of an application. Load balancers can be connected to networks in either Bridge mode or Routed mode to provide transparent inspection or router-like functionality. When operating in routed mode, the recommendation is to connect any router-like port to an external routed network in ACI rather than use an EPG/BD combination.

Like firewalls, load balancers can also be deployed in failover active/standby mode for redundancy and high availability. Most vendors of load balancers recommend using dedicated links—and preferably a separate VPC for heartbeat connection—when connecting to ACI. However, you can use a single VPC to traverse both data and heartbeat traffic by segmenting each function in a different VLAN and bridge domain, as shown in Figure 5-28.

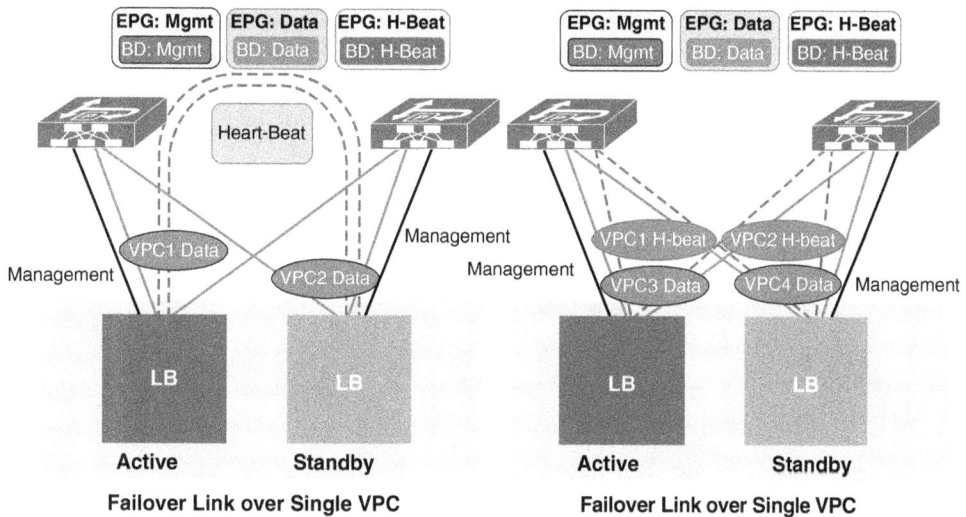

Figure 5-28 *ACI Connectivity with Load Balancers*

Network Connectivity

ACI has brought some new methodologies and terms to network connectivity. ACI uses traditional Layer 2 and Layer 3 constructs, but traffic forwarding requires additional steps, such as proper contracts between EPGs and physical connectivity on the interface level that is mapped to the logical construct under tenant configuration. In this section you will learn about various network connectivity options in ACI.

Connecting an External Bridge Network

Enterprises often need to extend their application network infrastructure between multiple data centers. Sometimes perhaps during the migration phase, they need to connect legacy network infrastructure to ACI in order to seamlessly move their workloads. Certain applications requires Layer 2 connectivity between application hosting facilities. This can be accomplished in Cisco ACI in two ways:

- Extending EPGs outside the ACI fabric

- Extending an ACI bridge domain outside the fabric

Extending EPGs Outside the ACI Fabric

The simplest way to extend Layer 2 connectivity to hosts residing outside ACI fabric is to extend an EPG outside the ACI fabric by statically assigning a leaf port and VLAN to an existing EPG. After doing so, all the traffic received on this leaf port with the configured VLAN is mapped to the EPG, and the configured policy for this EPG is enforced. This is a typical network-centric migration strategy, where a one-to-one mapping between legacy VLAN and EPG is desired. The endpoints do not need to be directly connected to the ACI leaf, as the traffic classification is based on the VLAN encapsulation received on a port, as shown in Figure 5-29.

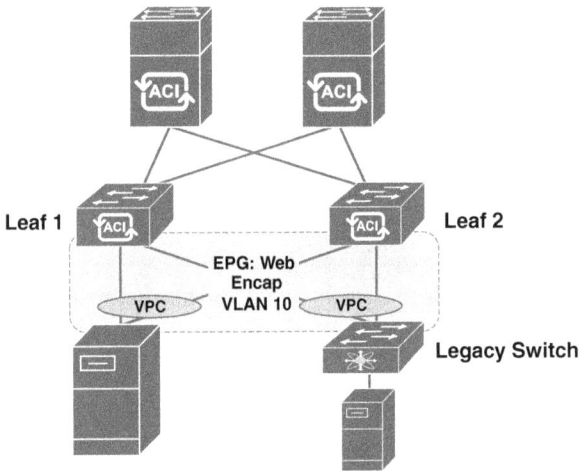

Figure 5-29 *Extending an EPG Outside the ACI Fabric*

To statically assign a Layer 2 connection on an ACI leaf port to an EPG, follow these steps:

Step 1. From the top main menu bar, choose Tenants > ALL TENANTS.

Step 2. In the navigation pane, select the user-defined tenant in which you want to extend EPG outside the ACI fabric.

Step 3. In the navigation pane, go to Application Profiles > App_Profile_Name > Application EPGs > EPG_Name > Static Bindings (Paths).

Step 4. In the work pane, choose Action > Deploy Static EPG on PC, vPC or Interface.

    a. In the Path field, specify a port as well as a VLAN ID.

    b. Click one of the Deployment Immediacy radio buttons. Deployment immediacy determines when the actual configuration will be applied on the leaf switch hardware. The immediacy also determines when the hardware resource, such as a VLAN resource and policy content-addressable memory (CAM) to support the related contract for this EPG, will be consumed on the leaf switch. The option Immediate means that the EPG configuration and its related policy configuration will be programmed in the hardware right away. The option On Demand instructs the leaf switch to program the EPG and its related policy in the hardware only when traffic matching this policy is received for this EPG.

    c. Click one of the Mode radio buttons to specify whether the ACI leaf
    expects incoming traffic to be tagged with a VLAN ID or not:

- Trunk: The Trunk option means that the leaf node expects incoming
traffic to be tagged with the specified VLAN ID previously established.
This is the default deployment mode. Choose this mode if the traffic
from the host is tagged with a VLAN ID. Multiple EPGs can be statically bound to the same interface as long as the encapsulation VLAN/
VXLAN ID is unique. This is similar to the **switchport trunk allowed
vlan** *vlan_ID* command.

- Untagged: The Untagged option means that the leaf expects untagged
traffic without a VLAN ID. Much as with the **switchport access
vlan** *vlan_ID* command, with this option you can assign the interface
to only one EPG. This option can be used to connect a leaf port to a
bare-metal server whose network interface cards (NICs) typically generate untagged traffic. A port can have only one EPG statically bound to
a port as untagged.

- 802.1P: The 802.1P option refers to traffic tagged with 802.1P headers.
802.1P mode is useful when it's necessary to handle the traffic on one
EPG as untagged to the interface (much as with the **switchport trunk
native vlan** *vlan_ID* command), but, unlike the untagged mode, 802.1P
allows other tagged EPGs to be statically bound to the same interface.

Figure 5-30 illustrates these steps in the APIC GUI.

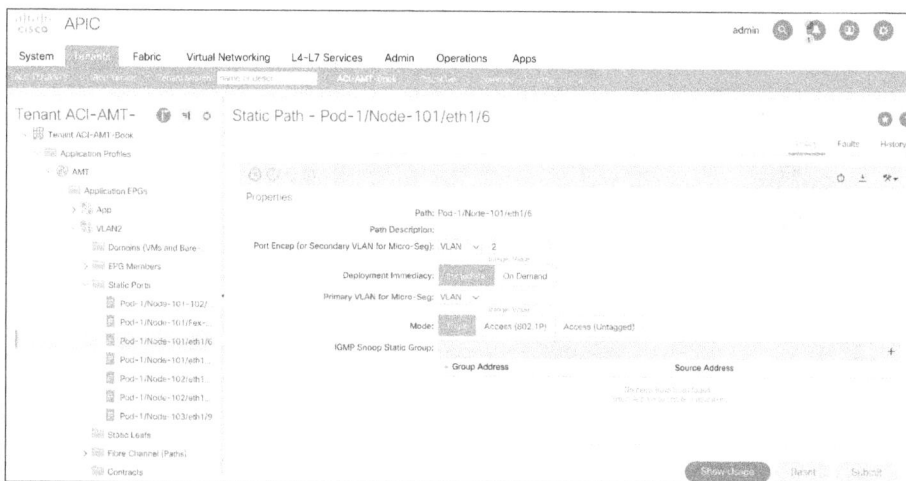

Figure 5-30 *Extending an EPG Outside in the APIC GUI*

In addition to completing the preceding configuration, the VLAN you are trying to
deploy must be provided from a VLAN pool. This means that the domain that provides

access to that pool must also be associated on the EPG. The domain can be associated by navigating to EPG > Domains > Add Physical Domain Association, as illustrated via Figure 5-31.

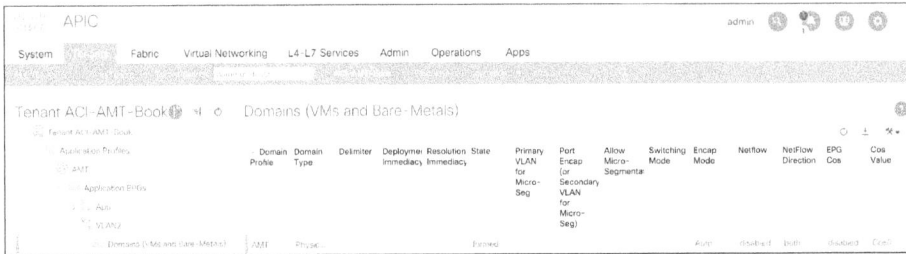

Figure 5-31   *Attaching a Domain to an EPG*

Extending an ACI Bridge Domain Outside the Fabric

An external bridge domain, also known as Layer 2 outside, helps you extend an entire bridge domain and not just an individual EPG under the bridge domain to the outside network, as illustrated in the earlier section "Extending EPGs Outside the ACI Fabric."

In ACI, Layer 2 extension can also be accomplished by creating an external bridge domain as an extension of the bridge domain to the outside network; a Layer 2 outside connection must be created for the bridge domain. During this process, create a new external EPG to classify this external traffic. This new EPG will be part of the existing bridge domain. Classify any outside connections or endpoints into this new external EPG. With two separate EPGs, you also need to select which traffic you would like to traverse the two EPGs. Much like the previous example of adding an endpoint to a pre-existing EPG, this method also allows the endpoints to share the same subnet and default gateway. Figure 5-32 illustrates the extension of an ACI bridge domain outside the fabric.

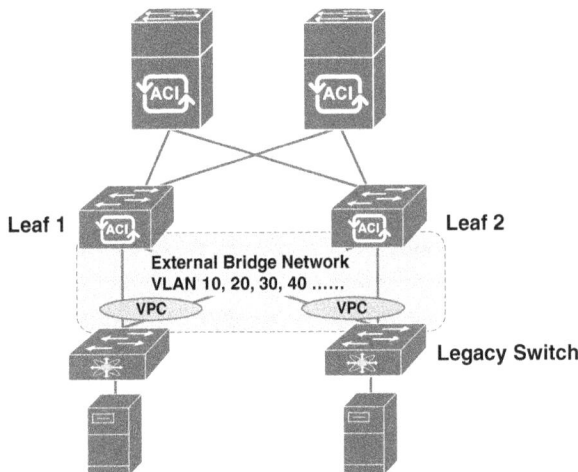

Figure 5-32   *Extending a Bridge Network Outside the ACI Fabric*

To create an external Layer 2 domain, follow these steps:

Step 1.   From the main menu bar, choose Tenants > ALL TENANTS.

Step 2.   In the navigation pane, select the user-defined tenant in which you want to configure external routed networks.

Step 3.   Browse through the menu tabs on the left side of the navigation pane and go to Networking > External Bridged Networks.

Step 4.   Right-click External Bridged Networks and choose Create Bridged Outside.

Step 5.   In the Create Bridged Outside dialog box, perform the following actions:

   a. Associate the bridge outside connection with the bridge domain and a VLAN. This VLAN must be configured on the external Layer 2 network. The bridge outside connection will put this VLAN and the bridge domain of the ACI fabric under the same Layer 2 domain. The VLAN must be part of the VLAN pool that is associated with the external bridge domain configuration.

   - From the External Bridged Domain drop-down list, create a Layer 2 domain if one does not already exist.

   - While creating the Layer 2 domain, if it does not already exist, create a VLAN pool to associate to the VLAN on the bridge outside connection. This is a way to specify the range of the VLAN IDs that will be used for creating a bridge outside connection, and it helps avoid overlap in the VLAN range between VLANs used for an EPG and those in use for a bridge outside connection.

   b. Add a Layer 2 border leaf node and Layer 2 interface for a bridge outside connection.

   c. Click Next and provide a name for the Layer 2 external EPG. All of the traffic entering the ACI fabric with the designated VLAN (the VLAN ID provided earlier) will be classified into this Layer 2 EPG.

   d. Configure a contract to allow communication between the existing endpoints in the existing EPG and the new external Layer 2 EPG. In the navigation pane, choose External Bridged Networks > Networks and specify a contract to govern this policy as the consumed contract. The communication between this external Layer 2 EPG and your existing internal EPG will then be allowed.

   e. Create an AAEP, which is a policy object that tells the APIC to allow certain encapsulation VLANs on selected ports.

After finishing the final step, you should have the desired reachability between the inside and outside Layer 2 segments. Figure 5-33 shows the configuration screen for extending an ACI bridge domain outside the fabric.

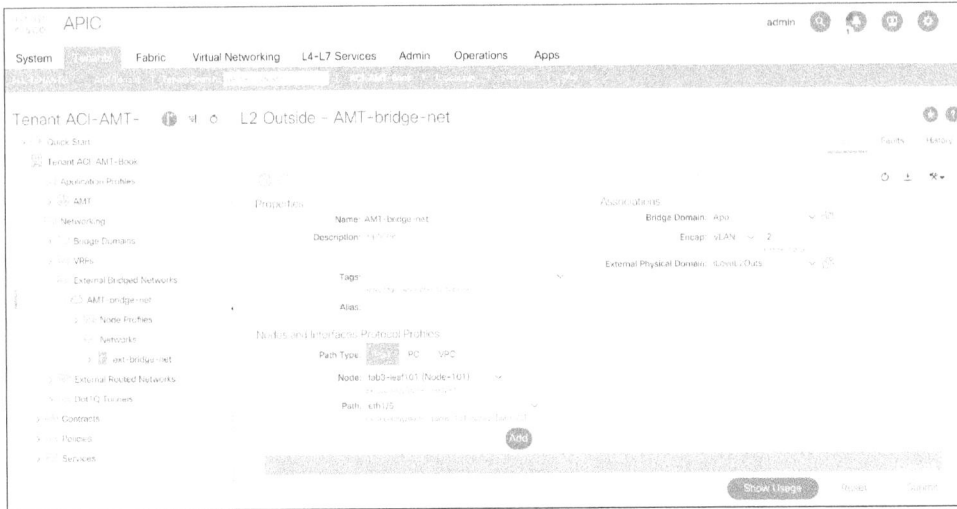

Figure 5-33 *Extending an ACI Bridge Domain Outside the ACI Fabric*

Connecting an External Routed Network

The most important consumer of any application is the end user, which generally does not directly attach to the fabric. Therefore, there must be connectivity to the external network from ACI fabric hosting applications. A company must be able to connect to both its internal corporate backbone network and to the Internet to provide access to the applications. This integration is possible with Cisco ACI at the tenant policy level. Layer 3 connectivity to a device such as a router is known in ACI as an *external routed network* or *L3Out*. The external routed network provides IP connectivity between tenant-associated networks and the external IP network. Each Layer 3 external connection is associated with one tenant network. The Layer 3 external network is only needed when a group of devices in the application profile require Layer 3 connectivity to a network outside the ACI fabric.

An application profile enables an operator to group different tiers of an application into EPGs. These application tiers might have requirements for external connectivity into them. Figure 5-34 shows a logical layout demonstrating this communication.

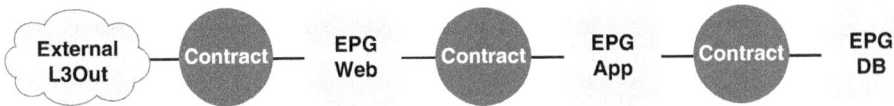

Figure 5-34 *Three-Tier Application with External Network Connectivity*

For example, web servers need a connection to the outside world for end-user consumption. With ACI, the communication is defined by a contract because of its whitelist model to a configured external Layer 3 endpoint group. As the operator of the fabric, you can provide the tenant administrator with the ability to interface to an external Layer 3 connection in various ways by using a uniquely defined Layer 3 outside configuration for the tenant application profile or via a shared common infrastructure.

External Layer 3 connections are usually established on leafs that are commonly known as *border leafs* in ACI. Any ACI leaf can become a border leaf, provided that it has an external routed network configured. In large-scale ACI designs, it might be efficient to have dedicated ACI leafs as border leafs to perform Layer 3 lookups and routing. It is not necessary to call border leafs when you only connect them to a physical external router. Other devices, such as servers performing routing functionality, can still connect to the border leafs, as in the case of Kubernetes nodes running on a RedHat Linux platform and peering to ACI border leafs via BGP. In the ACI fabric, the external Layer 3 connection can be one of the following types:

- Physical Layer 3 interface

- Subinterface with 8021.Q tagging

- Switch virtual interface (SVI)

Figure 5-35 depicts the logic of public and private networks.

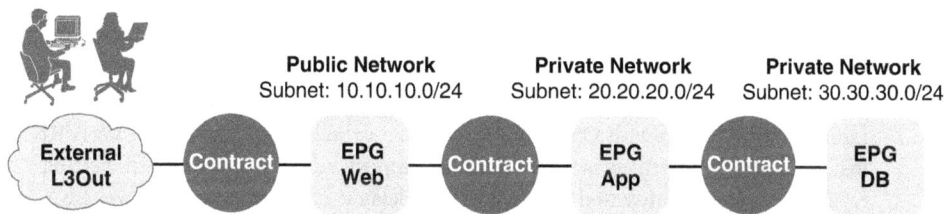

Figure 5-35   *Three-Tier Application with External Users Consuming Internal/External Applications*

With devices connecting through the external Layer 3 connection, the external network has learned of the internal ACI network 10.10.10.0/24, as it is advertised to the adjacent router through the Layer 3 external connection, as depicted in Figure 5-35. For the private networks, ACI does not advertise the networks through the routing protocol to the adjacent Layer 3 router, and the networks are not reachable to devices external to the fabric.

In older versions of ACI, routes learned externally from the fabric are not advertised through other ports. This behavior creates a non-transit fabric. In Release 1.1 and later, ACI is able to act as a transit network, and routes learned from one external Layer 3 connection can be advertised out to a different external Layer 3 connection—and not just to fabric internal prefixes.

The network team provides the external Layer 3 connectivity for the tenants. One common mechanism is to use subinterfaces on a router to create different Layer 3 domains since each tenant will likely not have its own external router for cost reasons.

External Layer 3–Supported Routing Protocols

The following routing options are supported for external Layer 3 network connectivity in ACI:

- **Static routes:** In ACI, you can define static routes to reach the external networks. Using static routes reduces the size and complexity of the routing tables in the leaf node(s) but increases administrator overhead. With static routes, you must also configure the static path back to the internal ACI network that you want to be reachable from the outside world.

- **OSPF:** Open Shortest Path First (OSPF) is a commonly used Interior Gateway Protocol in the industry today, and ACI has supported it since its first release. You can define OSPF area types such as regular, NSSA, and stub in ACI. Using a not-so-stubby area (NSSA) reduces the size of the OSPF database and the need to maintain the overhead of routing protocols with large route table sizes. With OSPF NSSA, the router learns only a summarization of routes, including a default path out of the fabric. OSPF NSSA advertises to the adjacent router the internal ACI public subnets part of the Layer 3 external. You enable OSPF by configuring an *ospfExtP* policy managed object under an *l3extOut* policy managed object.

- **EIGRP:** Enhanced Interior Gateway Routing Protocol (EIGRP) is similar to other routing protocols in the ACI fabric and supports features such as IPv4 and IPv6 routing, virtual routing and forwarding (VRF) and interface controls for each address family, redistribution with OSPF across nodes, a default route leak policy per VRF instance, passive interface and split horizon support, route map control for setting tags for exported routes, and bandwidth and delay configuration options via EIGRP interface policy. At this writing, only a few EIGRP features are not supported in ACI; among them are stub routing, EIGRP used for BGP connectivity, summary prefix, and per-interface distribution lists for imports and exports.

- **BGP:** ACI fabric supports Border Gateway Protocol (BGP) peering with external routers. BGP peers are associated with an *l3extOut* policy managed object. Multiple BGP peers can be configured per single *l3extOut* policy managed object. BGP can be enabled at the *l3extOut* level by defining the *bgpExtP* managed object under an *l3extOut* policy managed object. BGP peer reachability can occur through OSPF, EIGRP, a connected interface, static routes, or a loopback. Internal BGP (iBGP) or external BGP (eBGP) can be used for peering with external routers. The BGP route attributes from the external router are preserved because Multiprotocol Border Gateway Protocol (MP-BGP) is used for distributing the external routes in the fabric.

BGP enables IPv4 and/or IPv6 address families for the VRF associated with an *l3ext-Out* policy managed object. With iBGP, ACI supports only one autonomous system (AS) number, which has to match the one that is used for the internal MP-BGP route reflector. Without MP-BGP, the external routes (static, OSPF, or BGP) for the Layer 3 outside connections are not propagated within the ACI fabric. Given that the same AS number is used for both cases, the user must learn the AS number on the router to which the ACI border leaf will connect and use that AS number as the BGP AS number when using the ACI internal fabric.

Configuring MP-BGP Spine Route Reflectors

ACI uses MP-BGP to distribute external network prefixes inside the fabric. This requires a full mesh of iBGP peering between all leafs and spines fabric-wide or use of a more efficient way of configuring route reflectors on spine switches to avoid excessive route peering. To enable BGP route reflectors in the ACI fabric, the fabric administrator must select at least two spine switches (for redundancy) to act as a route reflector by assigning a BGP AS number for the fabric. After the BGP route reflectors are configured, it is possible to advertise external routes in the fabric.

To configure a BGP route reflector policy, you need to follow these steps:

Step 1. From the top menu bar, choose System > System Settings > BGP Route Reflector.

Step 2. On the right side of the work pane, perform the following actions:

a. Input the AS number of your choice. This is locally significant within the ACI fabric.

b. Add the two spine switch nodes that will be members of this BGP route reflector policy.

c. Click Submit.

Step 3. From the top menu bar, choose Fabric > Fabric Policies > Pods > Policy Groups.

Step 4. On the right side of the work pane, choose Actions > Create Pod Policy Group.

Step 5. In the Create Pod Policy Group dialog box, from the BGP Route Reflector Policy drop-down list, choose Default. Click Submit.

Step 6. From the top menu bar, choose Fabric > Fabric Policies > Pods > Profiles.

Step 7. On the right side of the work pane, choose Actions > Create Pod Profile. Choose the default pod profile and associate the previously created pod policy group. Click Submit.

Figure 5-36 shows the screen where these route reflector configuration steps occur.

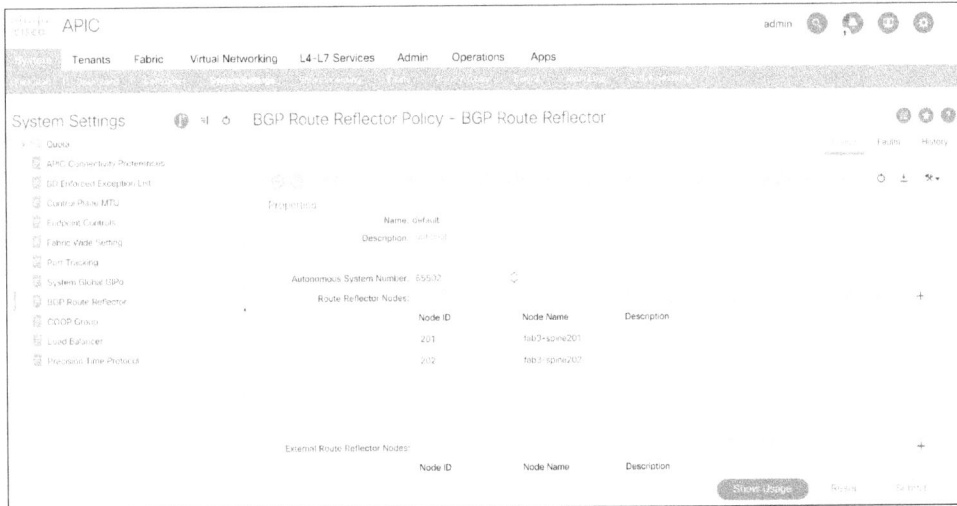

Figure 5-36   *Configuring a BGP Route Reflector*

Configuring External Routed Networks

In ACI, you can configure external routed networks on leafs called border leafs that can be reused for multiple tenants. If an external router is a network switch with a Layer 2 trunk interface, the external Layer 3 connection can be configured to route via SVI. Routers capable of using subinterfaces can be used to provide multiple external Layer 3 connections for multiple VRF instances and/or tenants. The fabric administrator can configure multiple external Layer 3 connections by using either a subinterface or SVI provided to each tenant. Layer 3 connectivity can be provided either using the routing protocol of your choice—such as OSPF, EIGRP, or BGP—or static routing.

Before diving into the actual configuration of an external routed network, it's important that you memorize the procedural steps workflow illustrated in Figure 5-37.

Let's look at an external routed network (also known as L3Out) configuration through a tenant network with an OSPF NSSA setup. Figure 5-38 shows a sample configuration for a Layer 3 external network into ACI using the OSPF routing protocol.

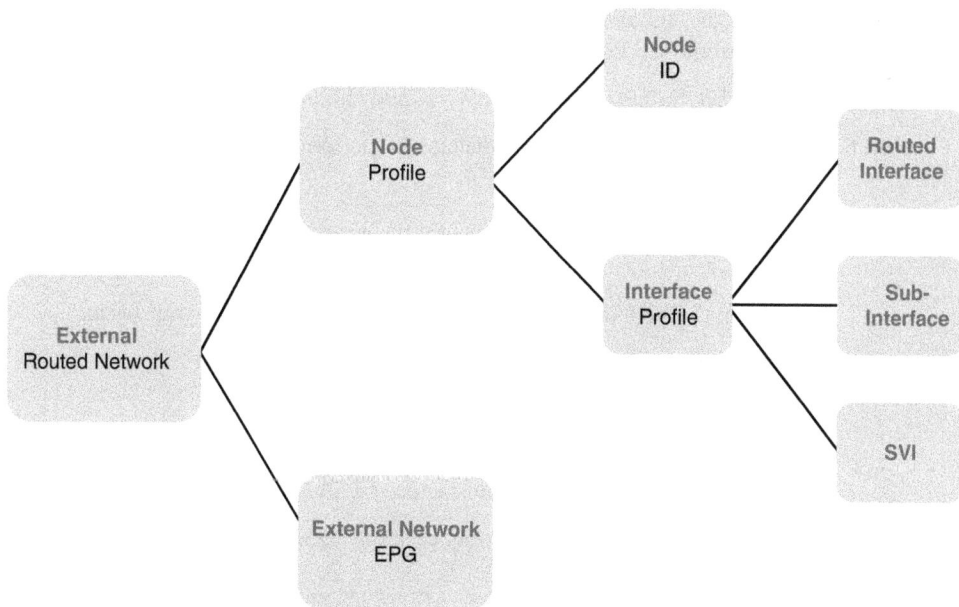

Figure 5-37   *Procedural Steps Workflow for Layer 3 Outside*

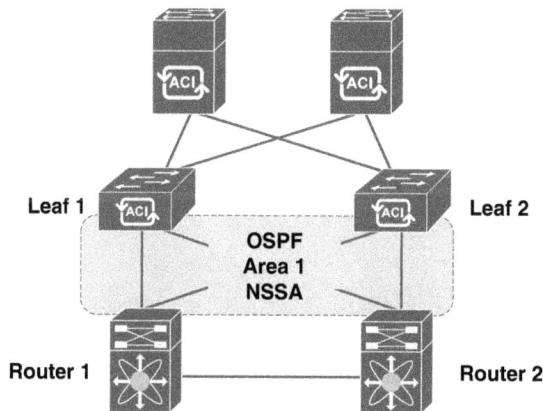

Figure 5-38   *L3Out Topology Using OSPF*

To integrate Layer 3 through a tenant network with OSPF/NSSA, follow these steps:

Step 1.   From the top menu bar, choose Tenants > ALL TENANTS.

Step 2.   In the navigation pane, select the user-defined tenant in which you want to configure external routed networks.

Step 3. Browse through the menu tabs on the left side of the navigation pane and go to Networking > External Routed Networks.

Step 4. Right-click External Routed Networks and choose Create Routed Outside.

Step 5. In the Create Routed Outside dialog box, perform the following actions (see Figure 5-39):

a. In the Name field, enter a name for the external routed networks policy object.

b. From the VRF drop-down list, choose a VRF option for your tenant.

c. Click the OSPF checkbox.

d. In the OSPF Area ID field, enter an OSPF area ID.

e. In the OSPF Area Control section, ensure that the Send redistributed LSAs into NSSA area and Originate summary LSA checkboxes are selected.

f. In the OSPF Area Type section, click the NSSA Area radio button.

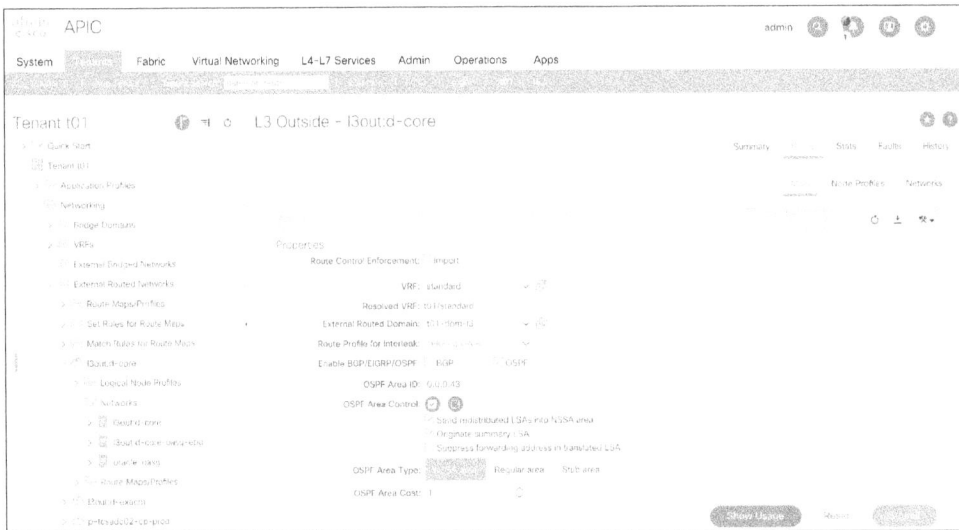

Figure 5-39   *Configuring L3Out Using OSPF*

g. In the Nodes and Interfaces Protocol Profiles section, click **+** to add a profile.

h. In the Create Node Profile dialog box, perform the following actions:

■ In the Name field, enter a name for the node profile policy object.

■ In the Nodes section, click **+** to add a node.

    i. In the Select Node dialog box, perform the following actions:

- From the Node ID drop-down list, choose a registered leaf node to use as the border leaf.

- In the Router ID field, enter the router's IP address.

- Uncheck the Router ID as Loopback Address checkbox if you want to use another IP address as your router's loopback address.

- In the Loopback Addresses section, click **+** to add a loopback address.

- Enter the loopback address of your choice and click Update.

- Click OK.

Step 6. In the OSPF Interface Profiles section, click **+** to create an OSPF interface profile.

Step 7. In the Create Interface Profile dialog box, perform the following actions:

    a. In the Name field, enter a name for the interface profile policy object and click Next.

    b. Choose the authentication type (MD5 authentication, no authentication, or simple authentication). Type the authentication key and confirm it.

    c. From the OSPF Policy drop-down list, choose Create OSPF Interface Policy. When defining the interaction with external adjacent OSPF router, you must specify the policy interaction.

    d. In the Create OSPF Interface Policy dialog box, perform the following actions:

- In the Name field, enter a name for the OSPF interface policy of your choice, such as OSPF-Point2Point.

- In the Network Type section, click the radio button that matches the external adjacent router, such as Point to Point.

- Complete the remainder of the dialog box as appropriate to your setup in terms of OSPF interface cost, controls, and timers settings.

- Click Submit.

Step 8. In the Interfaces section, click on the Routed Interfaces tab. You can also select SVI and Routed Subinterface as your choice.

Step 9. Click the **+** sign to select a routed interface.

Step 10. In the Select Routed Interface dialog box, perform the following actions:

    a. From the Node drop-down list, choose the node leaf router that you want to connect to the external adjacent router.

b. From the Path drop-down list, choose the interface on the leaf router that you want to connect to external adjacent router interfaces.

c. In the IP Address field, enter the IP address of the border leaf node from the transport network segment for which you want to establish OSPF peering with the external adjacent router (for example, 100.100.100.1/24).

d. In the MTU (bytes) field, enter the maximum MTU size that matches your external adjacent router settings. (The default is 9000.)

Complete the remainder of the dialog box as appropriate to your setup and click OK multiple times and then click Next to configure external EPG networks.

Step 11. In the External EPG Networks section, click + to create an external network.

Step 12. From the Create External Network dialog box, in the IP Address field, enter 0.0.0.0/0 to permit the learning of any subnet. Create and apply the appropriate contract and click OK.

Step 13. Click Finish.

Figure 5-40 shows the screens for completing steps 6 through 13.

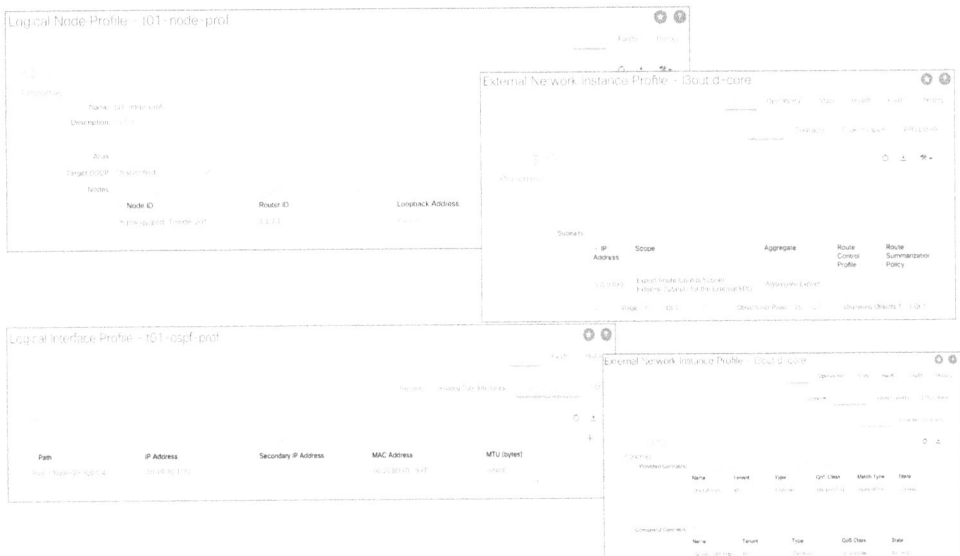

Figure 5-40 *Configuring the L3Out Node Profile, Interface Profile, and External EPG*

GOLF

As mentioned earlier, you ensure that traffic flows in and out of the Cisco ACI fabric to the external Layer 3 network domain by creating external routed networks, commonly known as L3Out. These external connections can either be via border leafs, as discussed earlier, or via connectivity through spines called GOLF.

As shown in Figure 5-41, the traditional ACI L3Out approach uses a VRF-Lite configuration to extend connectivity for each VRF instance toward the WAN edge routers. The data plane VXLAN encapsulation used within the Cisco ACI fabric is terminated on the border leaf nodes before the traffic is sent out toward the WAN edge routers.

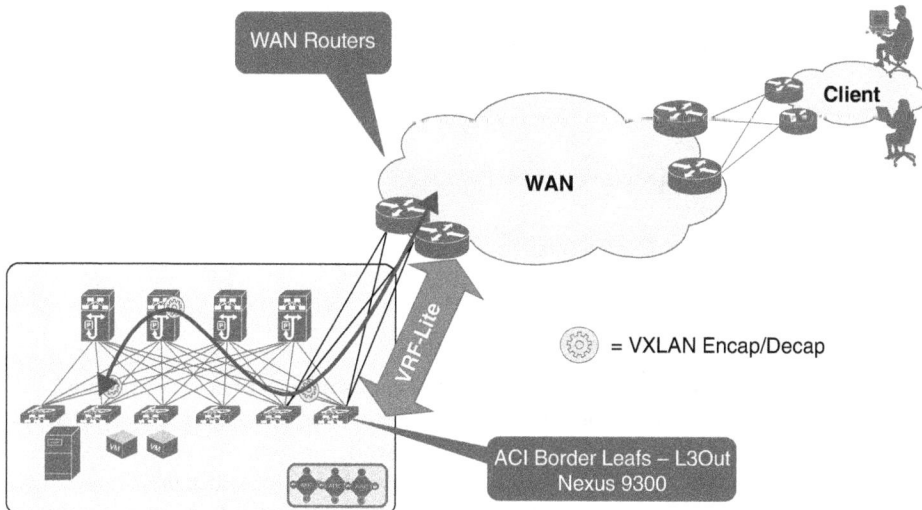

Figure 5-41   *Traditional L3Out Connections*

Figure 5-42 shows the EVPN-based L3Out, or GOLF, design option. The GOLF approach was originally introduced to scale up the number of VRF instances to be connected to the external Layer 3 network domain. (Cisco ACI supports 1000 VRF instances with GOLF.)

As shown in Figure 5-42, with GOLF, the connectivity to the WAN edge routers is not provided by the traditional ACI border leafs; rather, these external routers connect to the spine nodes. The MP-BGP EVPN control plane allows the exchange of routes for all the ACI VRF instances requiring external connectivity, the OpFlex control plane automates the fabric-facing VRF instance configuration on the GOLF router, and the VXLAN data plane enables north–south communication.

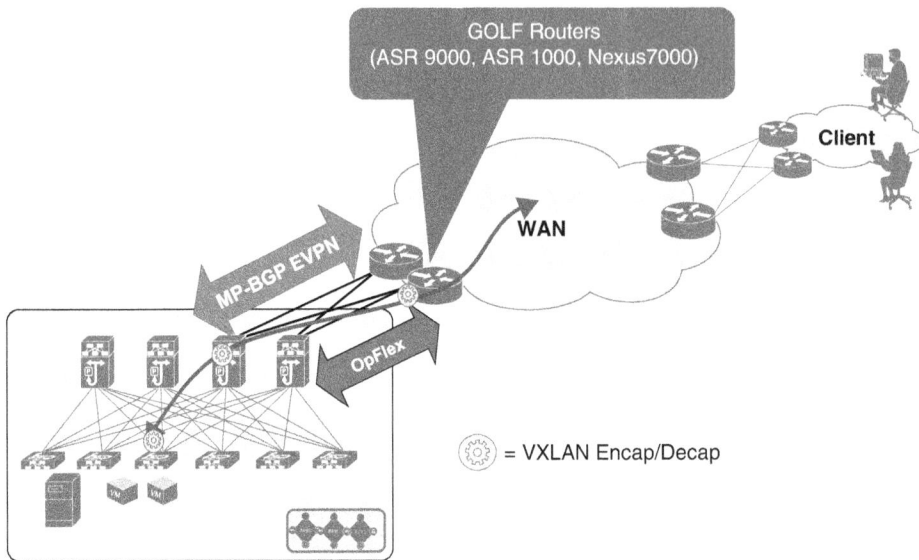

Figure 5-42   *GOLF L3Out Connections*

Network Connectivity Between Pods and Sites

In ACI, for network connectivity between multiple pods or sites or between the main pod in the data center and a remote site, you need to have an inter-pod network (IPN) connected through spines at each location. This network is also known as an inter-site network, but at the end of the day, it's just an IP network through which you are extending VXLAN for forwarding traffic with the common policy model. To take care of the overhead of the VXLAN encapsulation, it's important to increase by at least 50 bytes the supported MTU in the IPN network to allow data plane communication between endpoints at multiple locations. Let's discuss in more detail various options for this type of network connectivity requirement.

IPN Connectivity Considerations for Multi-Pod and Multi-Site

Numerous connectivity options might surface when you think of how to interconnect the spines deployed in a pod/site to the IPN devices and how the IPN devices deployed in separate pods/sites should be connected together.

You might wonder whether you need to connect all the spines to IPN devices in a pod. It is not a mandatory requirement to connect every spine deployed in a pod/site to the IPN devices. Figure 5-43 shows a scenario in which only two of the four spines are connected to the IPN devices in a multi-pod fabric.

Note   The spines *must* have EX/FX second-generation line cards in order to peer with IPN devices.

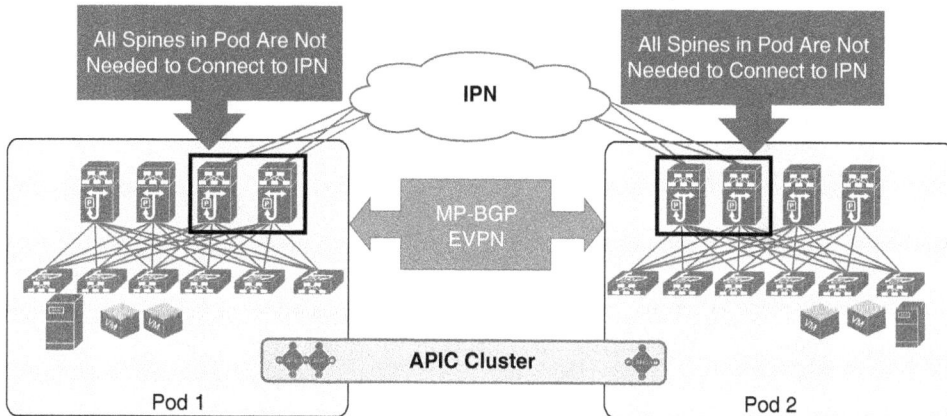

Figure 5-43   *Connectivity Between Spines and the IPN*

There are not functional implications for unicast communication across sites, as the local leaf nodes encapsulating traffic to a remote pod or site would always prefer the paths via the spines that are actively connected to the IPN devices based on the IS-IS routing metric. At the same time, there are also no implications either for the BUM traffic that needs to be sent to remote pods or sites, as only the spine nodes that are connected to the IPN devices are considered for the designated router position, which is responsible for sending/receiving traffic for a GIPo via IS-IS control plane exchange.

There are a few other potential IPN connectivity considerations. However, none of them are supported due to the reasons spelled out in the section "IPN Connectivity Considerations for Multi-Pod and Multi-Site," earlier in this chapter. The first option is to connect spines belonging to separate pods or sites with direct back-to-back links, as shown in Figure 5-44.

As illustrated in Figure 5-44, direct connectivity between spines may lead to potential issues in forwarding BUM traffic across pods/sites in scenarios where the directly con-nected spines in separate pods/sites have the potential of both not being selected as designated router (DR) for a given bridge domain. Therefore, the recommendation is to always deploy at least one Layer 3 IPN device (or a pair for redundancy) between pods with full-mesh connectivity links.

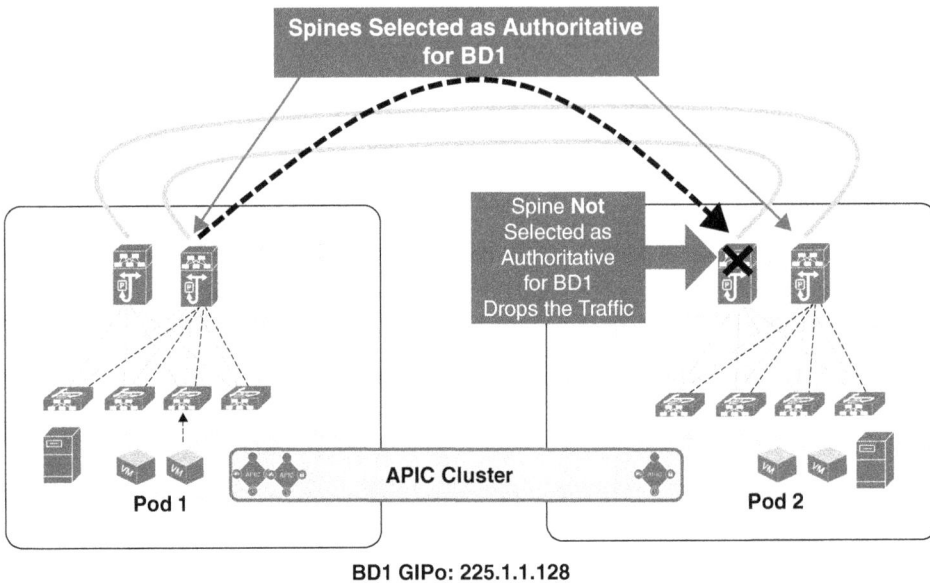

Figure 5-44   *Direct Back-to-Back Links Between Spines in Different Pods*

Figure 5-45 shows another IPN connectivity option, which could point out a similar situation when connecting the spines to the IPN devices.

Both of the depicted connectivity scenarios highlight an issue in which the designated spines in Pod 1 and Pod 2 for the bridge domain with GIPo address 225.1.1.128 send the BUM traffic and the IGMP join for that group to two different IPN nodes that do not have a physical path between them. As a consequence, the IPN devices don't have proper (*, G) state, and the BUM communication fails. To prevent this issue from happening, the recommendation is to always ensure that there is a physical path interconnecting all the IPN devices in a full-mesh connection, as shown in Figure 5-46.

The full-mesh connections in the scenario between multiple IPN devices could be replaced by a Layer 3 port channel connecting the local IPN devices. This would be useful for reducing the number of required geographic links, as shown in Figure 5-47.

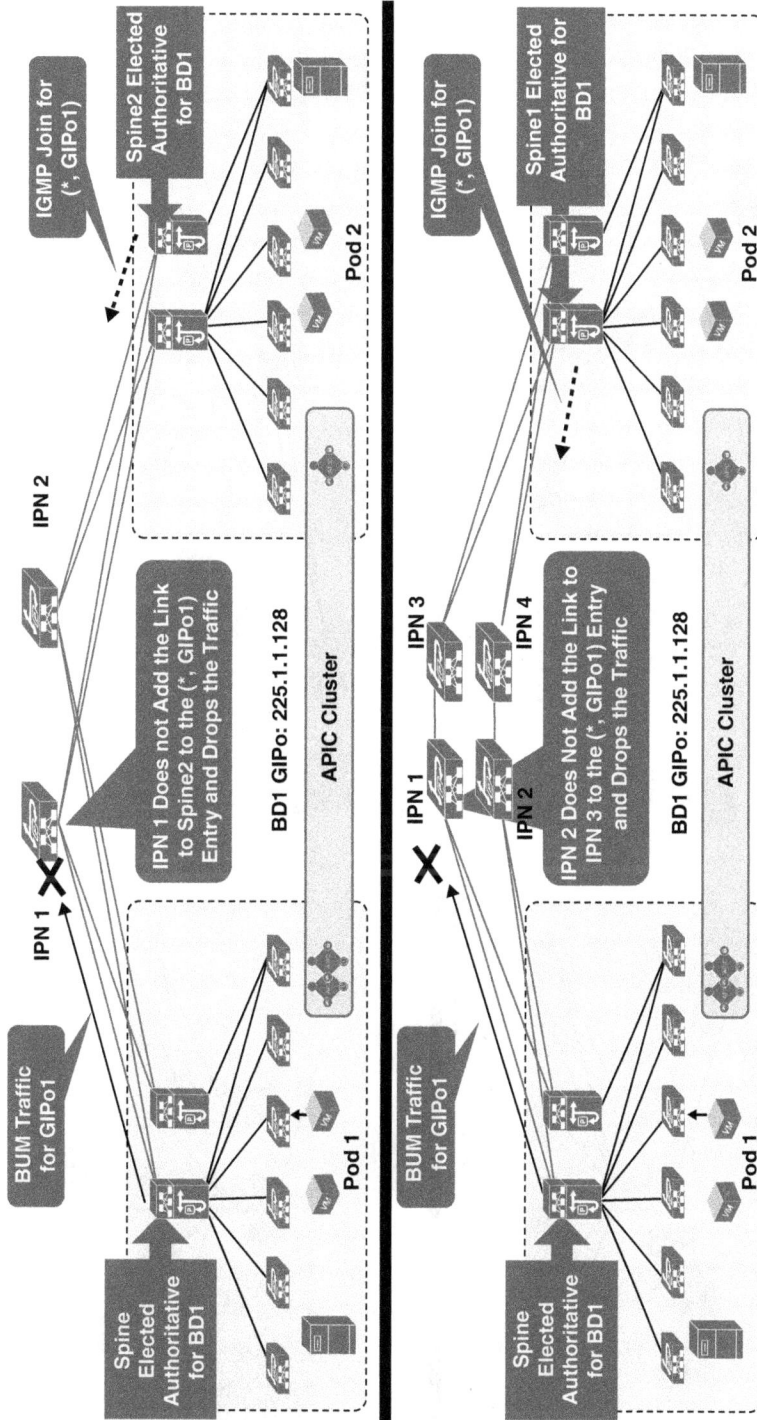

Figure 5-45 *Problems Sending BUM Traffic Across Pods*

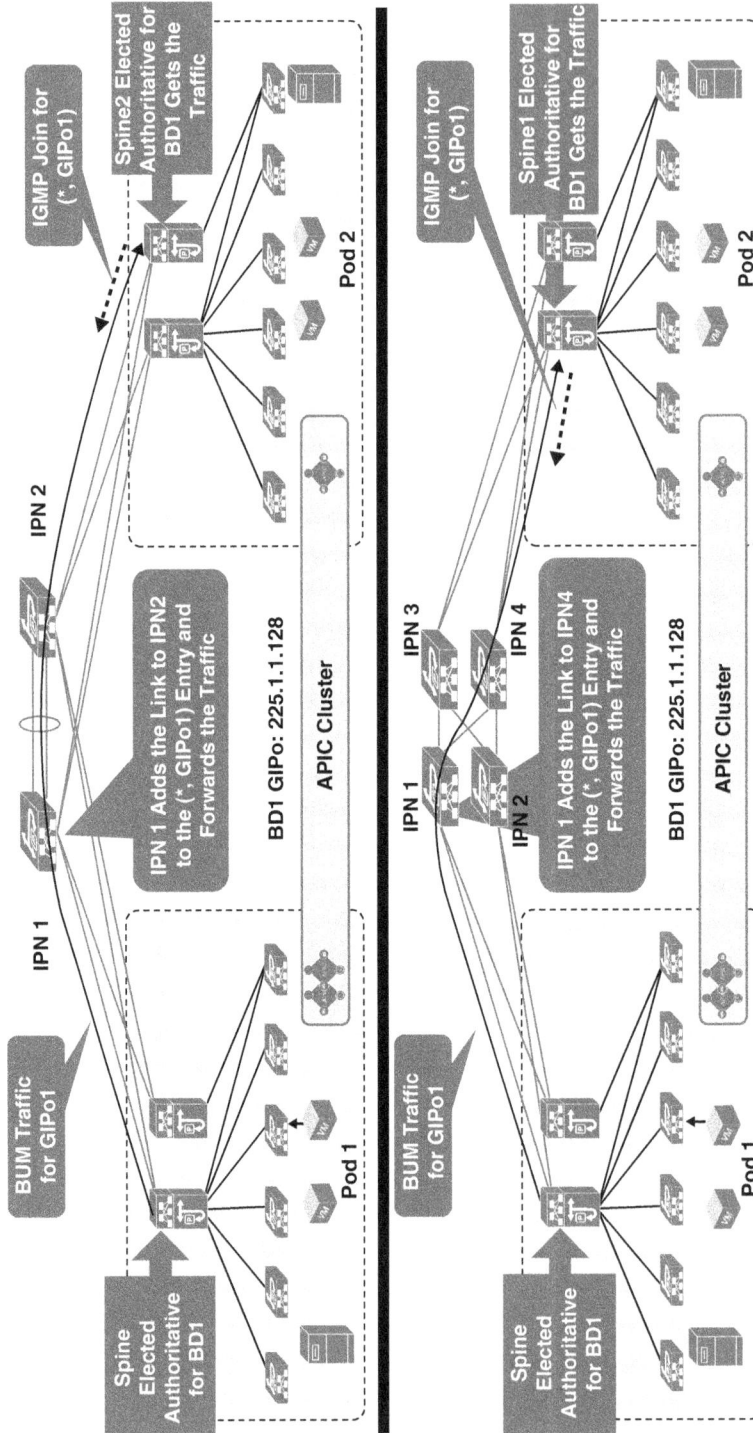

Figure 5-46 *Full-Mesh Connectivity to IPN Devices*

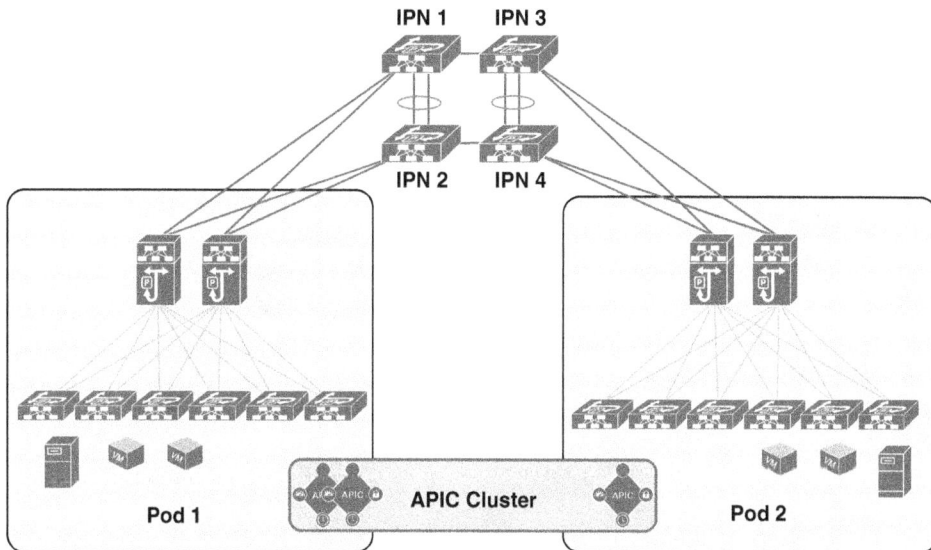

Figure 5-47 *Layer 3 Port Channel Connection to IPN Devices*

Having full-mesh physical connections between IPN devices, as shown in Figures 5-46 and 5-47, guarantees that each IPN router has a physical path toward the PIM Bidir active RP. There is another challenge you might run into if you have a lower-speed connection between two IPN devices than the speed at which you connect your IPN devices to spines in a pod. In our example of the Layer 3 port channel connecting the two IPN devices, if this is created by bundling 10 Gbps interfaces, the preferred OSPF metric for the path between IPN1 and IPN2 could indeed steer the traffic through one of the spines in Pod 1 because it is connected either via 40 Gbps or 100 Gbps. This issue could be solved by deploying links of consistent speed (10/40/100 Gbps) for connecting local IPN devices to each other and connecting each IPN device to its local spine nodes. Alternatively, it is possible to increase the OSPF cost of the IPN interfaces facing the spines to render that path less preferred from an OSPF metric point of view.

The other consideration is about the link speed support of the connections between the spines and the IPN devices, which depends on the hardware model of the deployed spine node in the ACI fabric. For first-generation spines (for example, modular Nexus 9500 switches with first-generation line cards or Nexus 9336-PQ fixed-chassis spines), only a 40 Gbps interface is supported on the spines, which implies the need to support the same link speed on the IPN devices, as shown in Figure 5-48.

The support of Cisco QSA modules (that convert a QSFP port into a SFP or SFP+ port) on a second-generation spine node (for example, modular Nexus 9500 switches with second-generation EX/FX line cards or Nexus 9364C fixed-chassis spines) allows the use of 10 Gbps link speeds between spines and IPN routers for a specific use case. Please refer to the latest ACI software release notes on the Cisco website to verify support for this connectivity option.

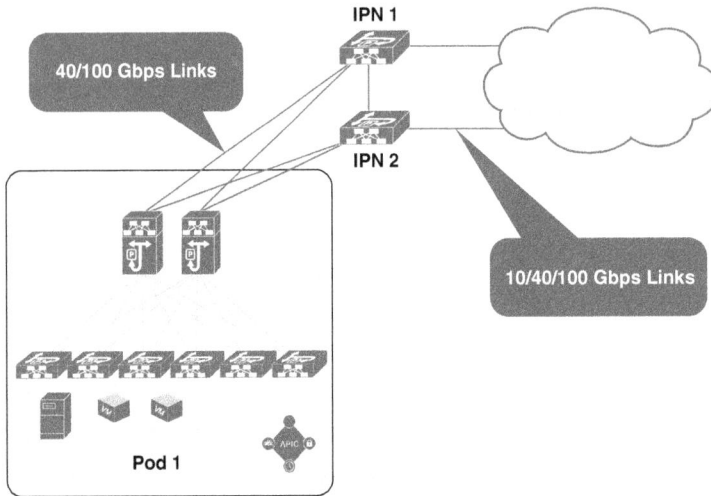

Figure 5-48 *Supported Interface Speed Between Spines and IPN Devices*

Notice that the links connecting the IPN devices at one location to the IPN devices at the other or, for that matter, to a generic Layer 3 network infrastructure do not need to have 40/100 Gbps link speeds. However, it is not recommended to use connection speeds less than 10 Gbps to avoid traffic congestion across pods/sites that may affect the communication of APIC nodes deployed in separate pods/sites.

Configuring an IPN

In order to configure an IPN, you need to follow the steps outlined in this section, which uses a simple IPN topology for multi-pod to help you understand the configuration steps (see Figure 5-49). However, for production deployment, please follow the detailed configuration guide from the Cisco website.

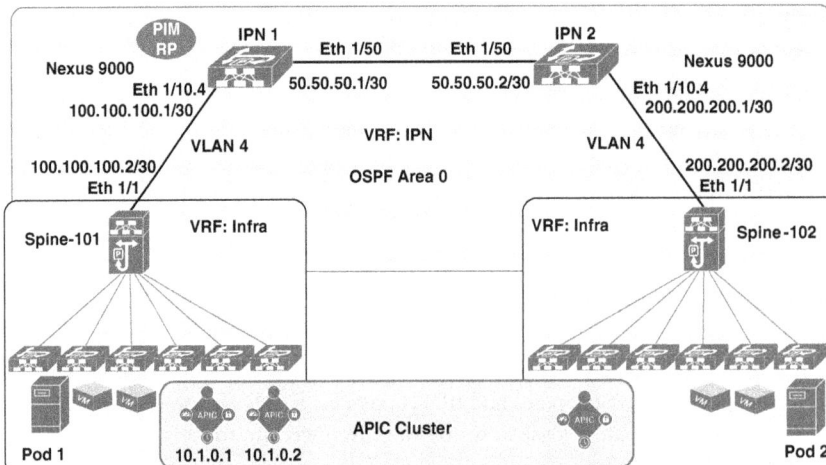

Figure 5-49 *Sample IPN Topology for Configuration*

To configure spine connectivity with the IPN router on an APIC, follow these steps:

Step 1. Create a VLAN pool and add VLAN 4. (VLAN 4 is the only VLAN used to peer with IPN devices.)

Step 2. Create an external routed domain. Associate the newly created VLAN pool with this domain.

Step 3. Create an AAEP and associate it with the external routed domain.

Step 4. Create interface and switch policies under the Access Policy tab in the APIC to program ports Eth1/1 on Spine-101 and Spine-102 to peer with IPN devices. Associate the AAEP to the spine interface policy groups.

Step 5. Create an external routed network (L3Out) under the *Infra* tenant:

   a. Associate the external routed domain.

   b. Select OSPF regular area 0. (The OSPF area could be other than area 0. OSPF is the only protocol supported while peering spines with IPN devices. Any routing protocol or static routes within the IPN are supported.)

   c. Create a routed sub-interface using VLAN 4 as the transport link to route peer with IPN devices using OSPF.

To configure an IPN device in route peering with the ACI spine, use the following steps:

Step 1. Enable the system features on a Nexus device by using the following commands:

```
feature ospf
feature pim
feature dhcp
feature lldp
!
```

Step 2. As a recommended (though not required) step, create a VRF instance for IPN traffic:

```
vrf context IPN
!
```

Step 3. Set the system and L3 interface MTU to 9150.

```
system jumbomtu 9216
! On Nexus, System Jumbo MTU size of 9216 is enabled by
default
!
interface Ethernet1/10
 description "Interface connected to Spine"
 no switchport
 mtu 9150
 no shutdown
```

Step 4.   Configure PIM BiDir:

```
! Dedicated loopback interface for PIM RP
!
interface loopback90
  description "Interface dedicated for PIM RP"
  vrf member IPN
  ip address 90.90.90.1/30
  ip ospf network point-to-point
  ip router ospf 1 area 0.0.0.0
  ip pim sparse-mode
!
! Increasing MTU under PIM
ip pim mtu 9000
vrf context IPN
  ip pim rp-address 90.90.90.2 group-list 225.0.0.0/8 bidir
  ip pim rp-address 90.90.90.2 group-list 239.255.255.240/28
bidir
!
```

Cisco ACI uses one multicast address per bridge domain to encapsulate BUM traffic to be sent to other TEPs (leaf switches) across the fabric. This concept is extended over the IPN for multi-pod deployments only. IPN for multi-site and remote leaf deployments *does not* require PIM BiDir. Multicast address 225.0.0.0/8 is the GIPo address range for bridge domains. The 239.255.255.240/28 address is used for fabric-specific purposes, such as ARP gleaning.

Step 5.   Enable DHCP Relay on IPN devices for ACI nodes in other pods or sites to get the TEP addresses from the APIC during the initial fabric registration:

```
service dhcp
ip dhcp relay
!
```

Step 6.   Create a subinterface with Dot1q by using VLAN-4 on IPN devices connecting to the spine:

```
interface Ethernet1/10.4
  description 40G link to pod1-SPINE-101(Eth1/1)
  mtu 9150
  encapsulation dot1q 4
  vrf member IPN
  ip address 100.100.100.1/30
  ip ospf network point-to-point
  ip ospf mtu-ignore
  ip router ospf 1 area 0.0.0.0
  ip pim sparse-mode
```

```
! DHCP relay pointing to APIC-1 and APIC2 TEP addresses
ip dhcp relay address 10.1.0.1
ip dhcp relay address 10.1.0.2
no shutdown
!
```

Step 7. Configure the interface between IPN devices:

```
interface Ethernet1/50
  description link between IPN devices
  mtu 9150
  vrf member IPN
  ip address 50.50.50.1/30
  ip ospf network point-to-point
  ip ospf mtu-ignore
  ip router ospf 1 area 0.0.0.0
  ip pim sparse-mode
  no shutdown
!
```

Step 8. Configure the OSPF routing process:

```
router ospf 1
  vrf IPN
    router-id 1.1.1.1
    log-adjacency-changes detail
!
```

IPN Connectivity Considerations for Remote Leafs

Remote leafs connect to the ACI main data center over an IPN, much like multi-pod and multi-site. However, there are a few different connectivity considerations with remote leafs and an IPN:

- A remote leaf is logically associated with one of the pods of the ACI main data center. Remote leaf nodes should have reachability to the VTEP pool of the logically associated pod. This could be achieved via the backbone network if the TEP pool addresses are enterprise routable or via a dedicated VRF instance or a tunneling mechanism.

- An APIC cluster's *Infra* IP addresses must be reachable. APIC nodes may have gotten IP addresses from a TEP pool that is different from the one used in the pod with which the remote leaf is associated. Figure 5-50 provides an example of the reachability requirement for a remote leaf.

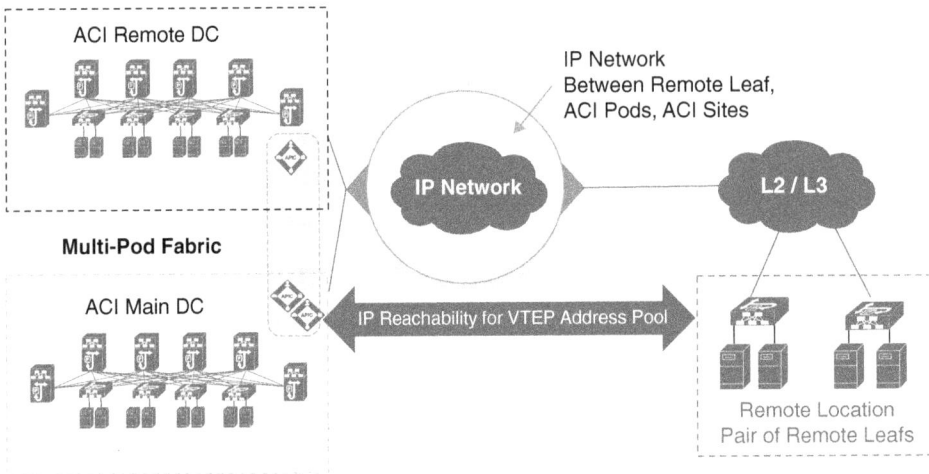

Figure 5-50   *Remote Leaf Reachability to TEP Pool on APIC*

There are two scenarios in which remote leafs are connected to an ACI fabric:

■ Remote leaf connectivity to single-pod fabric

■ Remote leaf connectivity to multi-pod fabric

Each scenario requires special configuration, as outlined in the sections that follow.

Remote Leaf Connectivity to Single-Pod Fabric

For remote leaf connectivity to single-pod fabric, you must configure the upstream IPN router to the remote leaf by using OSPF with the VLAN-4 subinterface under a separate VRF (in this example, *infra*), configured much like multi-pod or multi-site. You also need to have DHCP relay enabled to get VTEP address leases from the APIC in the main data center. (A separate TEP pool should be allocated for remote leafs.) Figure 5-51 illustrates this configuration.

Note that the three DHCP relay addresses belong to three APICs at the main data center. Also, at the main data center site, the IPN router needs to be configured using OSPF with the VLAN-4 subinterface connecting to spines, as illustrated in Figure 5-52. This configuration goes into the *Infra* tenant with L3Out as part of the *infra* VRF instance.

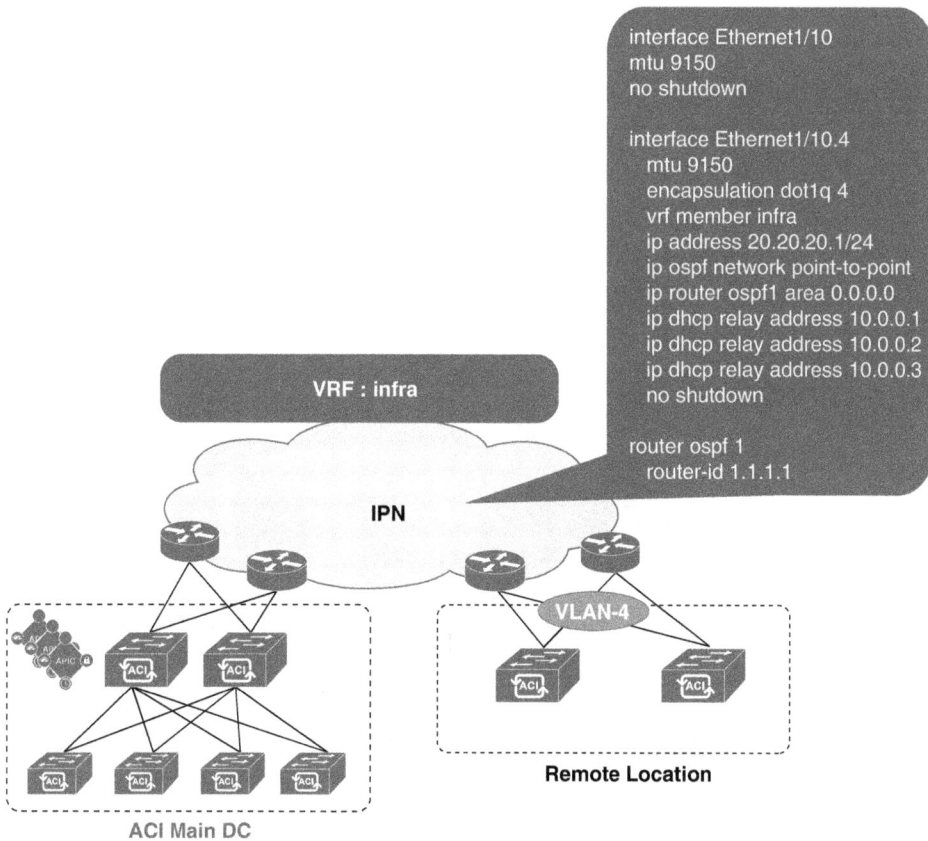

The configuration callout in the figure reads:

```
interface Ethernet1/10
mtu 9150
no shutdown

interface Ethernet1/10.4
  mtu 9150
  encapsulation dot1q 4
  vrf member infra
  ip address 20.20.20.1/24
  ip ospf network point-to-point
  ip router ospf1 area 0.0.0.0
  ip dhcp relay address 10.0.0.1
  ip dhcp relay address 10.0.0.2
  ip dhcp relay address 10.0.0.3
  no shutdown

router ospf 1
  router-id 1.1.1.1
```

Figure 5-51 *Configuration on an Upstream IPN Router at a Remote Location*

Remote Leaf Connectivity to Multi-Pod Fabric

For remote leaf connectivity to multi-pod fabric, you need to make a few more configurations. First, you must configure the upstream IPN router to a remote leaf by using OSPF with the VLAN-4 subinterface under a separate *infra* VRF instance. You need to do the same configuration between IPN routers and spines in each pod, much as you do with remote leaf connectivity to a single pod. Then you also need to configure another OSPF peering from IPN routers to spines with VLAN-5 under another separate VRF instance (in this example, *rl-mpod*) for each pod in the multi-pod fabric. Figure 5-53 illustrates this configuration.

interface Ethernet1/10
  mtu 9150
  no shutdown

interface Ethernet1/10.4
  mtu 9150
  encapsulation dot1q 4
  vrf member infra
  ip address 30.30.30.1/24
  ip ospf network point-to-point
  ip router ospf 1 area 0.0.0.0
  no shutdown

router ospf 1
  router-id 1.1.1.1

VRF : infra

IPN

VLAN-4

Remote Location

ACI Main DC

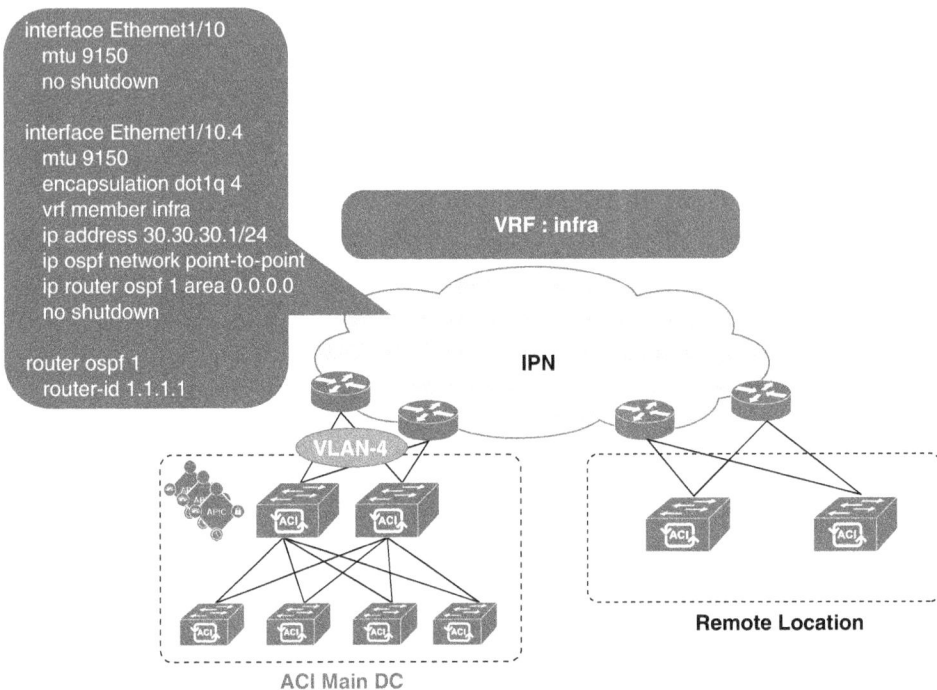

Figure 5-52   *Configuration on an Upstream IPN Router at a Main Data Center (Single Pod)*

Note   This extra configuration is needed for multicast flow symmetry between endpoints connected to remote leafs and the endpoints connected to any pod network in a multi-pod fabric. This scenario is explained in detail in Chapter 4, "ACI Fabric Design Options." There is no need to create extra OSPF peering with the VLAN-5 configuration with a separate VRF instance at the remote leaf.

1G or 10 Gbps Connectivity from Remote Leaf Switches to Upstream IPN Routers

IPN routers at remote locations may not have 40/100 Gbps link speed options. You might be cornered to connect remote leaf switches with upstream IPN routers using only 1 Gbps or 10 Gbps link speed. In such a case, a QSA adapter can be used to connect remote leaf switches to upstream IPN routers, as shown in Figure 5-54. Please check the latest optics compatibility matrix for QSA support at the Cisco website.

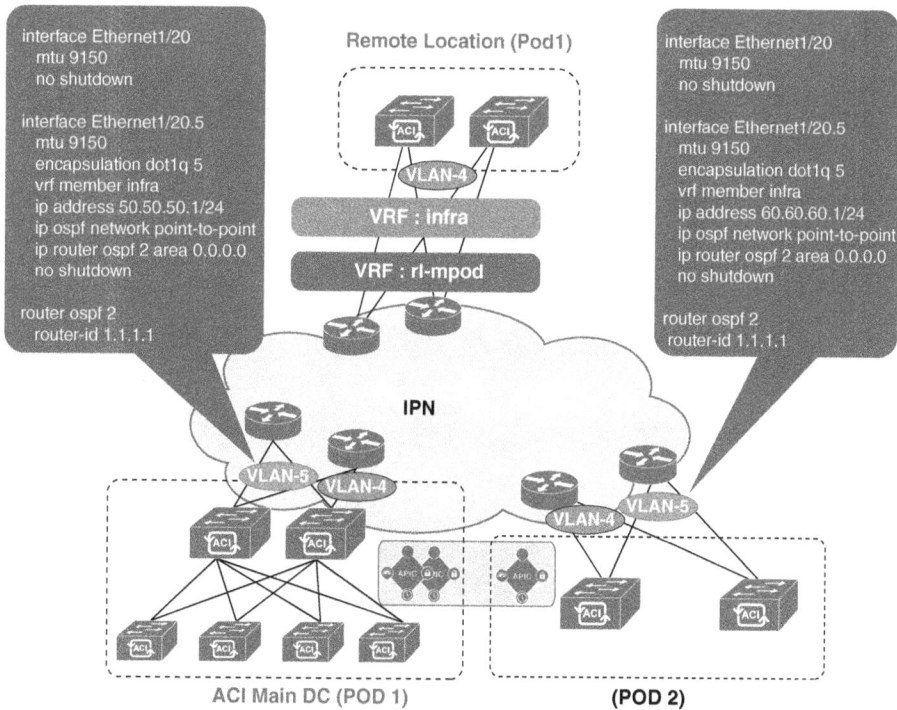

Figure 5-53   *Configuration on Upstream IPN Routers at Multiple Pods*

RL Node HW	10 Gbps Uplink	1 Gps Uplink
N93180YC-EX	Yes	Yes
N93108TC-EX	Yes	Yes
N93180LC-EX	Yes	No
N93180YC-FX	Yes	Yes
N9K-C93108TC-FX	Yes	Yes
N9K-C9348GC-FXP	Yes (use 4 10/25 Gbps Uplink Ports, no QSA Needed)	Yes (Convert One of the 4 SFP Downlink Ports to Uplink and Connect to the First-Hop Device)

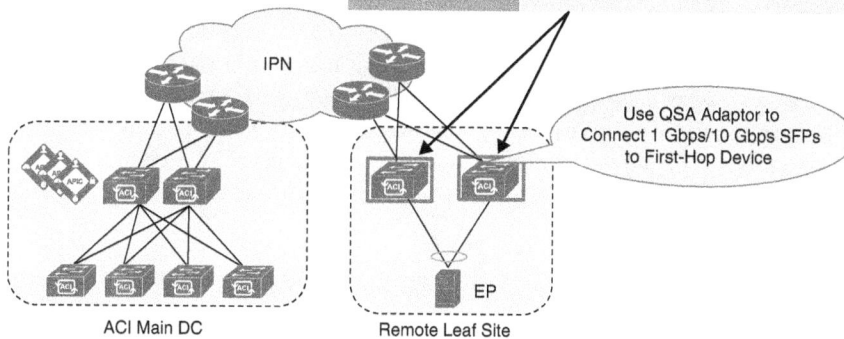

Figure 5-54   *Port Speed Options from Remote Leaf to Upstream Router Connectivity*

Diagnosing Connectivity Problems

Now that you have learned about various connectivity options in ACI, let's look at an example of a connectivity issue reported by an application team and how you would diagnose it. Say that members of your application team complain that they cannot access their application. In your initial checking, you find out that the server team has recently plugged in the application server to your ACI fabric. The team has provided you the MAC and IP addresses of the server. Figure 5-55 shows the connectivity problem. What should you do in this case?

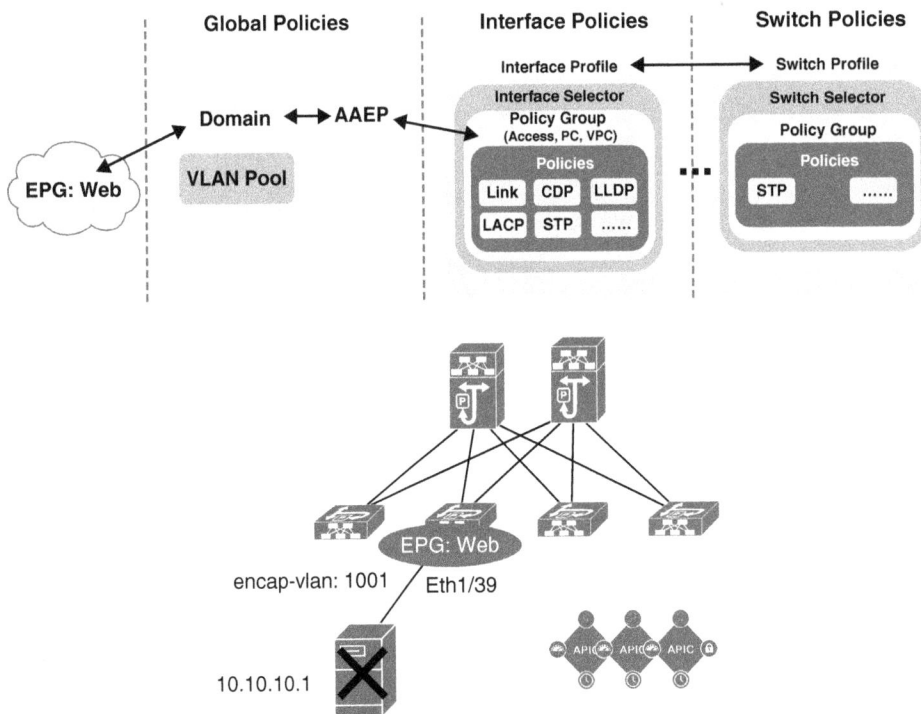

Figure 5-55 *Server Connectivity Problem*

Say that the server is up and sending traffic on a wire; you have confirmed this by examining a Wireshark packet capture on the server. You have also verified that the ACI fabric did not learn the MAC or IP address of the application server through the Endpoint Tracker tool in the APIC. In this case, you should start with physical connectivity or configuration issues.

Perform the following steps to troubleshoot connectivity issues:

Step 1.   Check that the server port on the ACI leaf is up.

Step 2.   Check the interface profile and ensure that the server port is selected and associated with the correct interface policy group.

Step 3.   Ensure that the interface policy group is created with the correct setting for your server (regular access port, port channel, or VPC).

Step 4.   Ensure that the AAEP is associated with the interface policy group.

Step 5.   Verify that the switch profile has been created.

Step 6.   Ensure that the VLAN pool has been created with the encapsulation VLAN that is required for the application server.

Step 7.   Ensure that the domain (physical or virtual) has been created and that the VLAN pool is associated.

Figure 5-56 illustrates these troubleshooting steps.

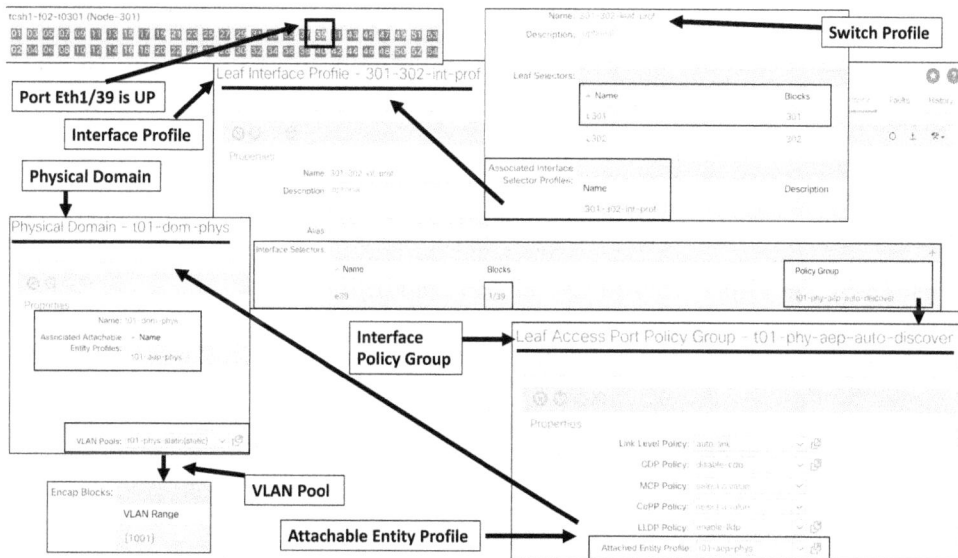

Figure 5-56   *ACI Leaf Switch Interface Configuration Verification*

Next, you need to look into the logical configuration of the application EPG under the Tenant menu. Follow these steps to ensure that your application server is connected:

Step 1.   Ensure that the server EPG is associated with the domain.

Step 2.   Ensure that the server port is statically bound with the encapsulation VLAN to server EPG (if it is a bare-metal configuration).

Figure 5-57 illustrates these steps.

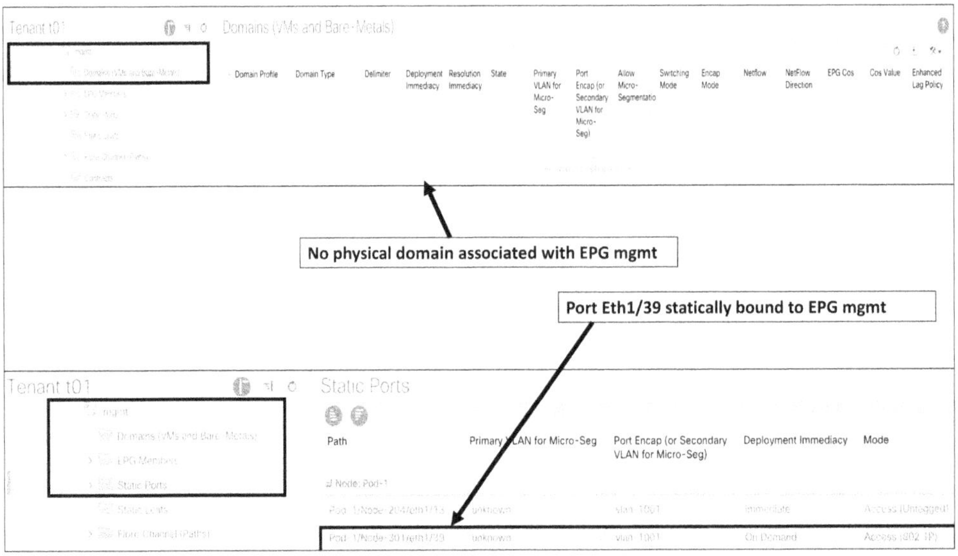

Figure 5-57   *ACI Application EPG Configuration Verification*

These steps can help you troubleshoot a service downtime problem. In Figure 5-57, notice that there is no physical domain with the *mgmt* EPG; this is your issue. It is the physical domain that is associated with a VLAN pool where the encapsulation VLAN is defined. The physical domain also gets associated with the AEP, which is part of your interface policies.

Note   Always check the faults and audit logs early in your troubleshooting. If there are any failure events, the fault log will show them. Also, most issues result from configuration changes that either did not go well or did not complete successfully, leaving the network in an unstable state.

Figure 5-58 shows the fault and audit log output.

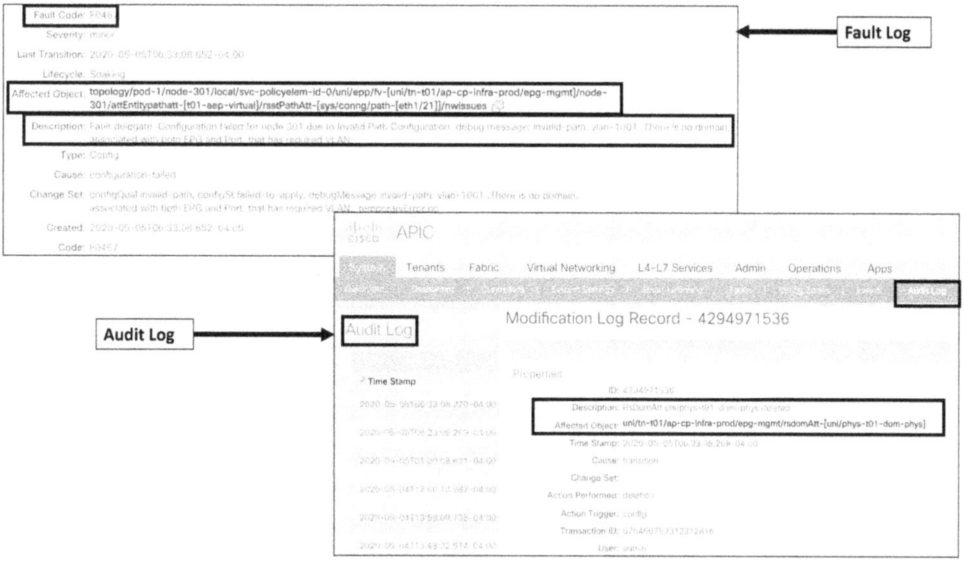

Figure 5-58 *ACI Fault Log and Audit Log*

Summary

ACI offers numerous end host connectivity options and supports multivendor compute, storage, and network platforms. These connectivity options use industry-standard protocols and allow you to have endpoints reside practically anywhere and everywhere.

In this chapter, you have learned how to connect different compute platforms, such as bare-metal or virtualized compute, in both standalone and blade system format, and you have learned about storage connectivity, L4/L7 service device connectivity, L2/L3 network connectivity, and how to connect multiple pods/sites or remote leafs via IPNs in ACI fabric.

In the next chapter, you will learn about VMM integration.

Review Questions

The questions that follow are designed to help you prepare for the Implementing Cisco Application Centric Infrastructure - Advanced (300-630 DCACIA) exam if you are planning on acquiring the Cisco Certified Specialist: ACI Advanced Implementation certification.

   1. How does VPC work in ACI? (Choose three.)

   a. VPC peer-keepalive messages pass through a peer link between two leafs in a VPC domain.

   b. Two leaf switches of any kind can be grouped together to form a VPC domain.

    c. VPC in ACI uses ZeroMQ for control messages.

    d. VPC in ACI does not require a separate physical peer link between leaf switches.

    e. An APIC assigns an auto-generated virtual IP address from the system TEP pool for a VPC leaf pair.

    f. VPC in ACI uses Cisco Fabric Service (CFS) for control messages.

2. What is an access port? What different modes are available for configuring access ports, and how do they differ? (Choose three.)

    a. An access port creates a link bundling for server connectivity.

    b. Access ports are the end host–facing ports, such as ports for servers, IP storage, switches, routers, and L4/L7 devices.

    c. An access port uses the ON mode to connect end hosts.

    d. Access ports can be configured as Trunk, Access (802.1P), or Access (untagged).

    e. Access (802.1P) sends traffic tagged with VLAN 0, whereas Access (untagged) sends traffic without tagging any VLAN.

3. What are the best practices for configuring access policies? (Choose three.)

    a. A clear and meaningful naming standard should be defined and used.

    b. There should be one switch profile individually for each leaf switch for access port configuration, and there should be a separate switch profile for each VPC pair configuration.

    c. A separate VMM domain is required for each tenant.

    d. ACI provides flexibility in using policy object names, and there is no need to define any naming standards.

    e. There should be one physical domain per tenant for bare-metal servers, one for virtual compute, and one for external network connectivity.

4. What is a FEX? What are the limitations of connecting a FEX in ACI? (Choose three.)

    a. A fabric extender (FEX) is a device used to extend switching capability for ease of cable management.

    b. There is no support for external router connectivity using L3Outs on FEX ports.

    c. A remote leaf connected to a FEX is not supported in ACI.

    d. A FEX can connect to only a single leaf.

    e. FCOE is supported on FEX ports connected to all ACI leafs.

5. How does Cisco ACI connect storage devices? What are the limitations? (Choose three.)

    a. ACI creates a Fibre Channel (FC) fabric on leafs using the FC protocol to connect storage.

    b. In ACI, storage-accessing hosts are connected using an F port, and a SAN switch is connected using an NP port configuration on the same leaf.

    c. FCoE traffic in ACI is not forwarded to spine switches.

d. ACI uses the FCoE protocol on leafs to connect to storage devices.

e. Storage connectivity is supported on all ACI leaf platforms.

f. ACI allows multiple VSAN assignments per bridge domain.

6. How does ACI fabric connect to an external bridge network? (Choose three.)

a. ACI connects to an external bridge network by using the VXLAN protocol.

b. An external bridge domain helps you extend the entire bridge domain.

c. ACI statically maps the traditional VLAN to an EPG to extend a bridge network externally.

d. ACI is a Layer 3 fabric and does not support bridge network connectivity.

e. In ACI, an EPG can be extended to an external bridge network during application server migration.

7. How does ACI fabric connect to an external routed network? (Choose three.)

a. External routed network connections support routed interfaces, routed subinterfaces, and SVIs.

b. An external routed network is configured under a tenant.

c. For external routed network connectivity, only access port configuration is allowed.

d. External routed network connectivity using L3Out configuration supports OSPF, BGP, and EIGRP protocols and static routes.

e. An external routed network is configured using a physical domain.

8. What is GOLF? How is it connected in ACI fabric? (Choose three.)

a. Only Nexus 9000 devices can be GOLF routers.

b. VXLAN encapsulation and decapsulation happen on spines in a GOLF solution.

c. GOLF is an EVPN-based external routed network connectivity solution for scaling VRF instances.

d. GOLF routers are connected through spines.

e. The OpFlex control plane automates the fabric-facing VRF configuration on a GOLF router.

9. How is an IPN router connected in an ACI fabric? (Choose three.)

a. Spine-to-IPN connectivity must be via 40/100 Gbps links.

b. Spine-to-IPN connectivity is configured under the *Infra* tenant, using the OSPF routing protocol only.

c. Spines can be directly connected back-to-back between pods and sites.

d. All spines are required to connect to IPN routers.

e. For remote leaf-to-upstream IPN router connectivity, a QSA adapter is required for 1/10 Gbps connections.

Note There are no Key Topics for this chapter.

Chapter 6

VMM Integration

Cisco ACI virtual machine (VM) networking supports hypervisors from multiple vendors. It allows for multivendor hypervisors along with programmable and automated access to high-performance scalable virtualized data center infrastructure. In this chapter, you will learn about Virtual Machine Manager (VMM) and its integration into Cisco Application Centric Infrastructure (ACI) from the following virtualization-supported products and vendors:

- VMware
- Microsoft
- OpenStack
- Kubernetes
- OpenShift

You will also learn about VMM integration with ACI at multiple locations.

Virtual Machine Manager (VMM)

VMM integration enables the ACI fabric to extend network policies and policy group definitions into the virtualization switching layer on end hosts. This integration automates critical network plumbing steps that typically create delays in the deployment of overall virtual and compute resources in legacy network environments. VMM integration into ACI also provides value in getting visibility up to the virtualization layer of the application, which is a perpetually conflicting factor between network and server virtualization teams.

VMM Domain Policy Model

VMM domain profiles (vmmDomP) specify connectivity policies that enable virtual machine controllers to connect to the ACI fabric. Figure 6-1 shows the general hierarchy of VMM configuration.

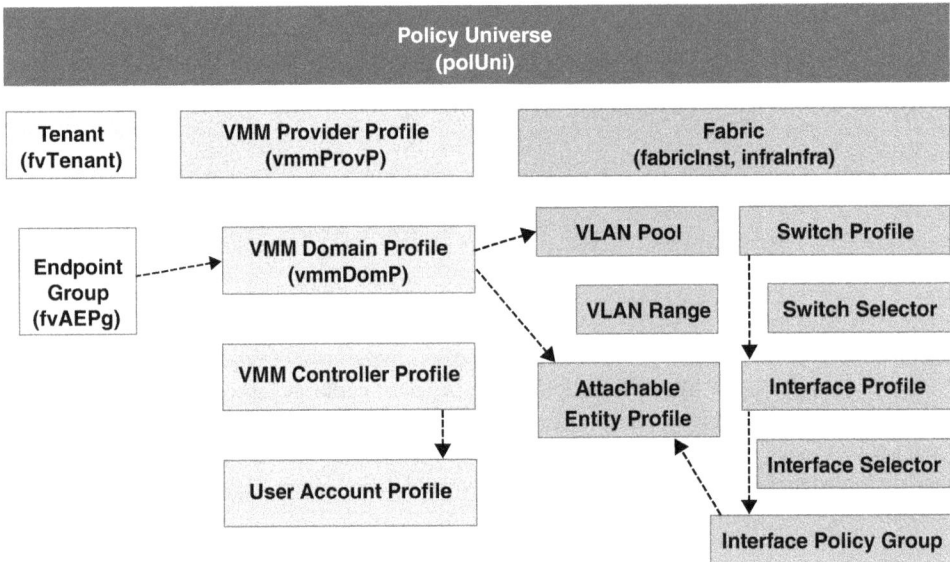

Figure 6-1   *VMM Policy Model*

VMM Domain Components

VMM domains enable an administrator to configure connectivity policies for virtual machine controllers in ACI. The essential components of an ACI VMM domain policy include the following:

- VMM domain
- VLAN pool association
- Attachable access entity profile association
- VMM domain endpoint group (EPG) association

VMM Domains

VMM domains make it possible to group VM controllers with similar networking policy requirements. For example, VM controllers can share VLAN pools and application EPGs. The Cisco Application Policy Infrastructure Controller (APIC) communicates with the VM controller to publish network configurations such as port groups, which are then applied to the virtual workloads. The VMM domain profile includes the following essential components:

■ **Credential:** Associates a valid VM controller user credential with an APIC VMM domain.

■ **Controller:** Specifies how to connect to a VM controller that is part of a policy enforcement domain. For example, the controller specifies the connection to a VMware vCenter instance that is part of a VMM domain.

Note A single VMM domain can contain multiple instances of VM controllers, but they must be from the same vendor (for example, VMware, Microsoft).

An APIC VMM domain profile is a policy that defines a VMM domain. The VMM domain policy is created on an APIC and pushed into the leaf switches. Figure 6-2 illustrates VM controllers of the same vendor as part of the same VMM domain.

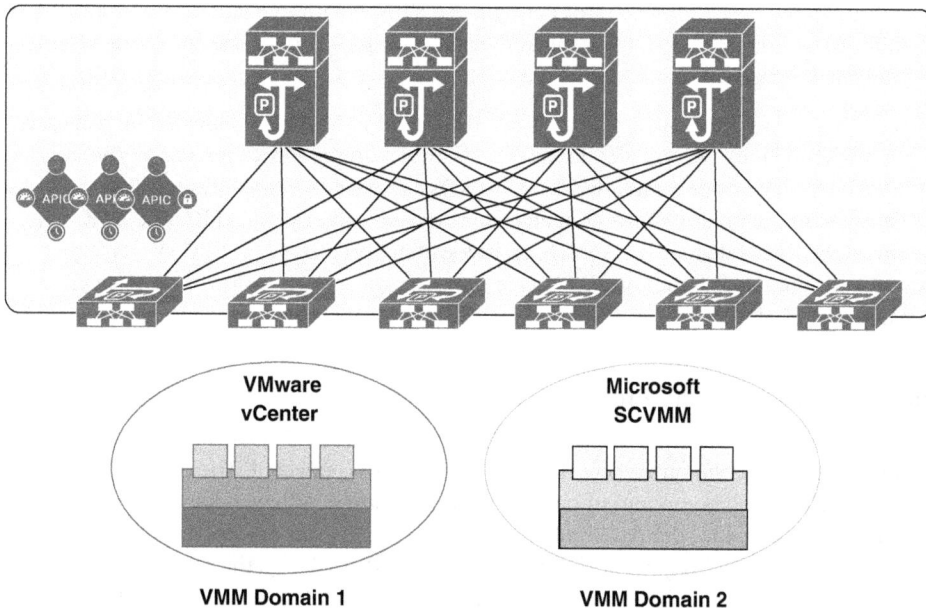

Figure 6-2 *VMM Domain Integration*

VMM domains provide the following:

■ A common layer in the ACI fabric that enables scalable fault-tolerant support for multiple VM controller platforms.

■ VMM support for multiple tenants within the ACI fabric.

VMM domains contain VM controllers such as VMware vCenter or Microsoft System Center Virtual Machine Manager (SCVMM) and the credentials required for the ACI API to interact with the VM controllers. A VMM domain enables VM mobility within the domain but not across domains. A single VMM domain can contain multiple instances of VM controllers, but they must be from the same vendor. For example, a VMM domain can contain many VMware vCenter instances managing multiple controllers, each running multiple VMs; however, it cannot contain Microsoft SCVMM instances. A VMM domain inventories controller elements (such as pNICs, vNICs, and VM names) and pushes policies into the controllers, creating port groups or VM networks and other necessary elements. The ACI VMM domain listens for controller events such as VM mobility events and responds accordingly.

VMM Domain VLAN Pool Association

A VLAN pool specifies a single VLAN ID or a range of VLAN IDs for VLAN encapsulation. It is a shared resource that can be consumed by multiple domains, such as physical, VMM, or external domains.

In ACI, you can create a VLAN pool with allocation type static or dynamic. With static allocation, the fabric administrator configures a VLAN; with dynamic allocation, the APIC assigns the VLAN to the domain dynamically. In ACI, only one VLAN or VXLAN pool can be assigned to a VMM domain.

A fabric administrator can assign a VLAN ID statically to an EPG. However, in this case, the VLAN ID must be included in the VLAN pool with the static allocation type, or the APIC will generate a fault. By default, the assignment of VLAN IDs to EPGs that are associated with the VMM domain is done dynamically by the APIC. The APIC provisions VMM domain VLAN IDs on leaf switch ports based on EPG events, either statically binding or based on VM events from controllers such as VMware vCenter or Microsoft SCVMM.

Attachable Access Entity Profile Association

An attachable access entity profile (AAEP) associates a VMM domain with the physical network infrastructure where the vSphere hosts are connected. The AAEP defines which VLANs will be permitted on a host-facing interface. When a domain is mapped to an endpoint group, the AAEP validates that the VLAN can be deployed on certain interfaces. An AAEP is a network interface template that enables the deployment of VM controller policies on a large set of leaf switch ports. An AAEP specifies which switches and ports are available and how they are configured. The AAEP can be created on-the-fly during the creation of the VMM domain itself.

VMM Domain EPG Association

Endpoint groups regulate connectivity and visibility among the endpoints within the scope of the VMM domain policy. VMM domain EPGs behave as follows:

- The APIC pushes these EPGs as port groups into the VM controller.

- An EPG can span multiple VMM domains, and a VMM domain can contain multiple EPGs.

The ACI fabric associates EPGs to VMM domains, either automatically through an orchestration component such as VMware vRealize suite (vRA/vRO) or Microsoft Azure, or when an APIC administrator creates such configurations. An EPG can span multiple VMM domains, and a VMM domain can contain multiple EPGs.

In Figure 6-3, endpoints (EPs) of the same color are part of the same EPG. For example, all the gray EPs are in the same EPG, even though they are in different VMM domains.

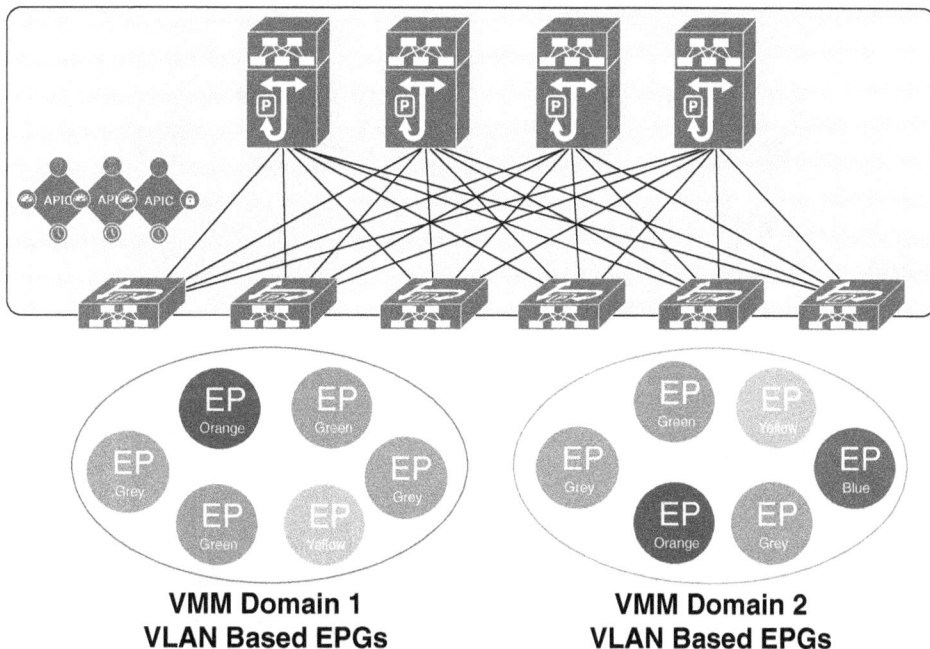

VMM Domain 1
VLAN Based EPGs

VMM Domain 2
VLAN Based EPGs

Figure 6-3   *VMM Domain EPG Association*

Note   Refer to the latest *Verified Scalability Guide for Cisco ACI* at the Cisco website for virtual network and VMM domain EPG capacity information.

Figure 6-4 illustrates multiple VMM domains connecting to the same leaf switch if they do not have overlapping VLAN pools on the same port. Similarly, the same VLAN pools can be used across different domains if they do not use the same port of a leaf switch.

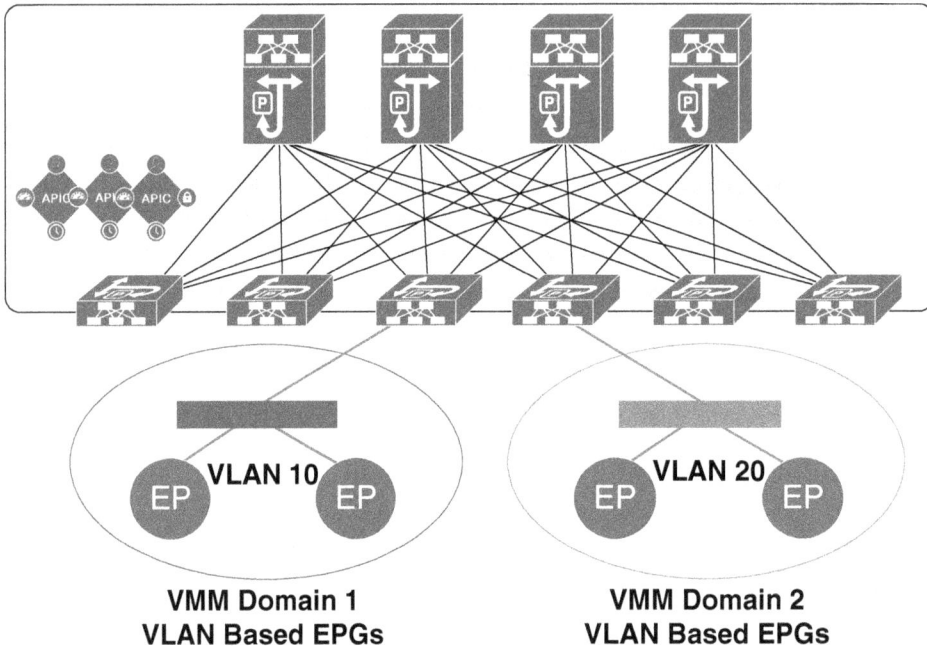

Figure 6-4 *VMM Domain EPG VLAN Consumption*

EPGs can use multiple VMM domains in the following ways:

■ An EPG within a VMM domain is identified by an encapsulation identifier that is either automatically managed by the APIC or statically selected by the administrator. An example for a VLAN is a virtual network ID (VNID).

■ An EPG can be mapped to multiple physical (for bare-metal servers) or virtual domains. It can use different VLAN or VNID encapsulations in each domain.

Note By default, an APIC dynamically manages the allocation of a VLAN for an EPG in a VMM integration. VMware vSphere Distributed Switch (VDS) administrators have the option of configuring a specific VLAN for an EPG. In that case, the VLAN is chosen from a static allocation block within the pool associated with the VMM domain.

Applications can be deployed across VMM domains, as illustrated in Figure 6-5. While live migration of VMs within a VMM domain is supported, live migration of VMs across VMM domains is not supported.

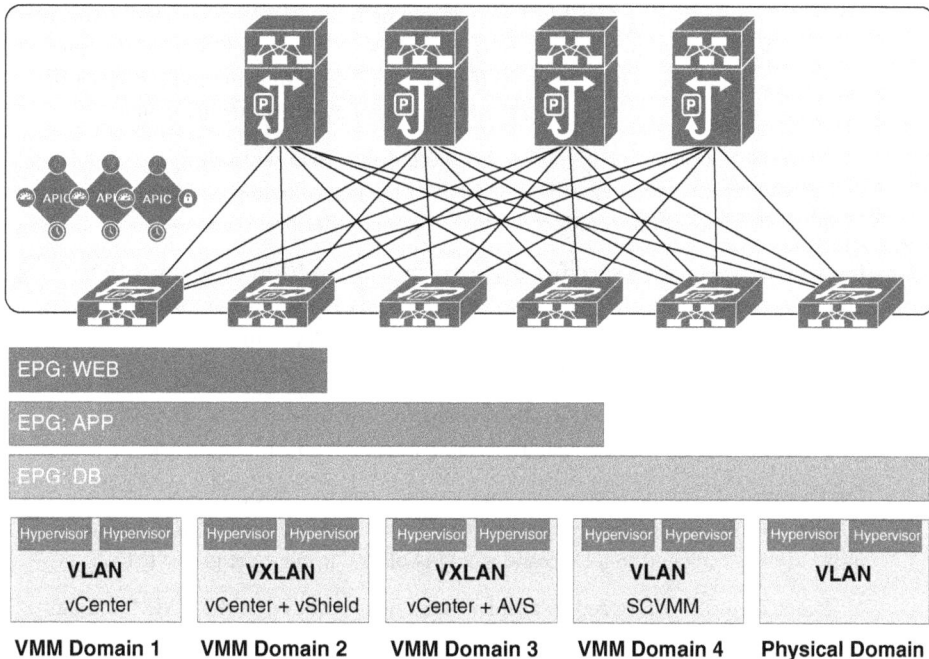

Figure 6-5   *Multiple VMM Domains and Scaling of EPGs in the ACI Fabric*

EPG Policy Resolution and Deployment Immediacy

Whenever an EPG associates to a VMM domain, the administrator can choose the policy resolution and deployment preferences to specify when it should be pushed and programmed into leaf switches. This approach provides efficient use of hardware resources because resources are consumed only when demanded. You should be aware of picking one option over the other, depending on the use case and scalability limits of your ACI infrastructure, as explained in the following sections.

Resolution Immediacy

The Resolution Immediacy option defines when policies are downloaded to the leaf software based on the following options:

■ **Pre-provision:** This option specifies that a policy (such as VRF, VLAN, VXLAN binding, contracts, or filters) is downloaded to the associated leaf switch software even before a VM controller is attached to the distributed virtual switch (DVS), such as a VMware (VDS), defined by an APIC through the VMM domain.

   ■ This option helps when management traffic between hypervisors and VM controllers such as VMware vCenter is also using the APIC-defined virtual switch.

   ■ When you deploy a VMM policy such as VLAN or VXLAN on an ACI leaf switch, an APIC must collect CDP/LLDP information from hypervisors through the VM controller and ACI leaf switch to which the host is connected. However, if the VM controller is supposed to use the same VMM policy to communicate with its hypervisors or even an APIC, the CDP/LLDP information for hypervisors can never be collected because the required policy is not deployed yet.

■ With the Pre-provision immediacy option, policy is downloaded to the ACI leaf switch software, regardless of CDP/LLDP neighborship and even without a hypervisor host connected to the VMM domain-defined DVS.

■ **Immediate:** This option specifies that a policy (such as VRF, VLAN, VXLAN binding, contracts, or filters) is downloaded to the associated leaf switch software upon ESXi host attachment to a DVS. LLDP or OpFlex permissions are used to resolve the VM controller to leaf switch attachments.

■ The policy is downloaded to a leaf when you add a host to the VMM domain-defined DVS. CDP/LLDP neighborship from host to leaf is required.

■ **On Demand:** This option specifies that a policy (such as VRF, VLAN, VXLAN binding, contracts, or filters) is pushed to the leaf node only when a host running hypervisor is attached to a DVS and a VM is placed in the port group (EPG).

■ The policy is downloaded to a leaf when a host is added to the VMM domain-defined DVS and a virtual machine is placed in the port group (EPG). CDP/LLDP neighborship from host to leaf is required.

With both the Immediate and On Demand options for resolution immediacy, if the hypervisor running on the host and leaf lose LLDP/CDP neighborship, the policies are removed from the leaf switch software.

Deployment Immediacy

After the policies are downloaded to the leaf software through the Resolution Immediacy option, you can use Deployment Immediacy to specify when the policy is pushed to the hardware policy content-addressable memory (CAM). Two options are available:

■ **Immediate:** This option specifies that the policy is programmed into the hardware policy CAM as soon as the policy is downloaded in the leaf software. You should be aware of your ACI infrastructure scalability limits when choosing this option.

■ **On Demand:** This option specifies that the policy is programmed in the hardware policy CAM only when the first packet is received through the data path. This process helps optimize the hardware resources.

Note When you use On Demand deployment immediacy with MAC-pinned VPCs, the EPG contracts are not pushed to the leaf ternary content-addressable memory (TCAM) until the first endpoint is learned in the EPG on each leaf. This can cause uneven TCAM utilization across VPC peers. (Normally, the contract would be pushed to both peers.)

VMware Integration

When integrating your VMware infrastructure into Cisco ACI, you have two options for deploying virtual networking:

- VMware vSphere Distributed Switch (VDS)
- Cisco Application Virtual Switch (AVS)

These two options provide similar basic virtual networking functionality; however, the AVS option provides additional capabilities, such as VXLAN and microsegmentation support.

Prerequisites for VMM Integration with AVS or VDS

The prerequisites for VMM integration with AVS or VDS are as follows:

- You need to decide whether to use VLAN or VXLAN encapsulation or multicast groups.
- A virtual machine manager must be already deployed, such as vCenter.
- The VMM must be accessible by the APIC through either the out-of-band or in-band management network.
- For Cisco AVS deployment, a vSphere Installation Bundle (VIB) must be installed on all hypervisor hosts to be added to the AVS.
- For a VXLAN deployment, you need to know whether intermediate devices have Internet Group Management Protocol (IGMP) snooping on or off by default.

Guidelines and Limitations for VMM Integration with AVS or VDS

The guidelines and limitations for VMM integration with AVS or VDS are as follows:

- When utilizing VLANs for VMM integration, whether with Cisco AVS or VMware VDS, the range of VLANs to be used for port groups must be manually allowed on any intermediate devices.
- For VMM integration with VLANs and the Resolution Immediacy setting On Demand or Immediate, there can be a maximum of one hop between a host and the compute node.
- For VMM integration with VXLAN, only the infrastructure VLAN needs to be allowed on all intermediate devices.
- For VMM integration with VXLAN, if the *Infra* bridge domain subnet is set as a querier, the intermediate devices must have IGMP snooping enabled for traffic to pass properly.

- To log in to the APIC GUI, choose Tenants > *Infra* > Networking > Bridge Domains > default > Subnets > 10.0.0.30/27.

- For VMM integration with VXLAN and UCS-B, IGMP snooping is enabled on the UCS-B by default. Therefore, you need to ensure that the querier IP address is enabled for the *Infra* bridge domain. The other option is to disable IGMP snooping on the UCS and disable the querier IP address on the *Infra* bridge domain.

ACI VMM Integration Workflow

Figure 6-6 illustrates the ACI VMM integration workflow steps.

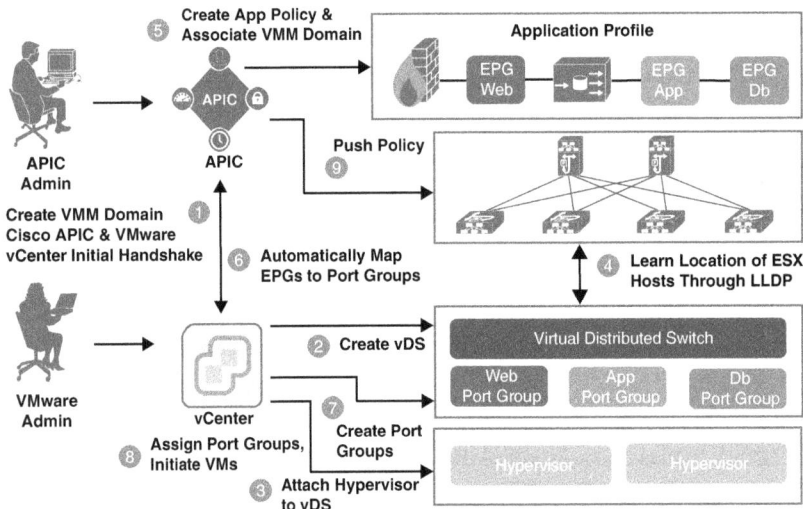

Figure 6-6   *ACI VMM Integration Workflow*

Publishing EPGs to a VMM Domain

This section details how to publish an existing EPG to a VMM domain. For an EPG to be pushed to a VMM domain, you must create a domain binding within the tenant EPG by following these steps:

Step 1.   From the menu bar, choose Tenants > All Tenants.

Step 2.   From the Work pane, choose the *Tenant_Name*.

Step 3.   From the Navigation pane, choose *Tenant_Name* > Application Profiles > *Application_Profile_Name* > Application EPGs > *Application_EPG_Name* > Domains (VMs and bare-metal servers).

Step 4.   From the Work pane, choose Actions > Add VM Domain Association.

Step 5.   In the Add VM Domain Association dialog box, choose the VMM domain profile that you created previously. For Deployment and Resolution

Immediacy, Cisco recommends keeping the default option, On Demand. This provides the best resource usage in the fabric by deploying policies to leaf nodes only when endpoints assigned to this EPG are connected. There is no communication delay or traffic loss when you keep the default selections.

Step 6.   Click Submit. The EPG is now available as a port group to your VMM.

Connecting Virtual Machines to the Endpoint Group Port Groups on vCenter

To connect virtual machines to the endpoint group port groups on vCenter, do the following:

Step 1.   Connect to vCenter by using the VMware VI Client.

Step 2.   From the Host and Clusters view, right-click on your virtual machine and choose Edit Settings.

Step 3.   Click on the network adapter and from the Network Connection drop-down box, choose the port group that corresponds to your EPG. It should appear in the format of TENANT | *APPLICATION_PROFILE* | EPG | *VMM_DOMAIN_PROFILE.*

If you do not see your Cisco ACI EPG in the Network Connection list, it means one of the following:

■ The VM is running on a host that is not attached to the distributed switch managed by the APIC.

■ There may be a communication between your APIC and vCenter either through the OOB or the INB management network.

Verifying VMM Integration with the AVS or VDS

The following sections describe how to verify that the Cisco AVS has been installed on the VMware ESXi hypervisor.

Verifying the Virtual Switch Status

To verify the virtual switch status, follow these steps:

Step 1.   Log in to the VMware vSphere client.

Step 2.   Choose Networking.

Step 3.   Open the folder for the data center and click the virtual switch.

Step 4.   Click the Hosts tab. The VDS Status and Status fields display the virtual switch status. Ensure that the VDS status is Up, which indicates that OpFlex communication has been established.

Verifying the vNIC Status

To verify the vNIC status, follow these steps:

Step 1.   In the VMware vSphere client, click the Home tab.

Step 2.   Choose Hosts and Clusters.

Step 3.   Click the host.

Step 4.   In the Configuration tab, select the Hardware panel and choose Networking.

Step 5.   In the View field, click the vSphere Distributed Switch button.

Step 6.   Click Manage Virtual Adapters. The vmk1 displays as a virtual adapter with an IP address.

Step 7.   Click the newly created vmk interface to display the vmknic status.

Note   Allow approximately 20 seconds for the vmk to receive an IP address through DHCP.

Microsoft SCVMM Integration

Figure 6-7 shows a representative topology for a Microsoft SCVMM integration with Cisco ACI. Hyper-V clustering connectivity between SCVMM virtual machines and the APIC can run over the management network.

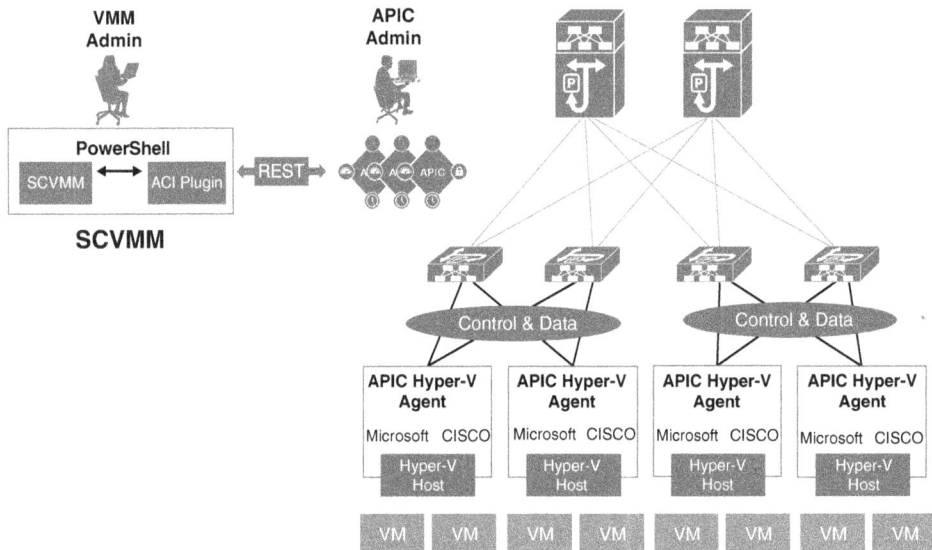

Figure 6-7   *Microsoft SCVMM Topology with ACI*

Figure 6-8 illustrates the workflow for integrating Microsoft SCVMM with Cisco ACI. The following sections describe the steps in this workflow.

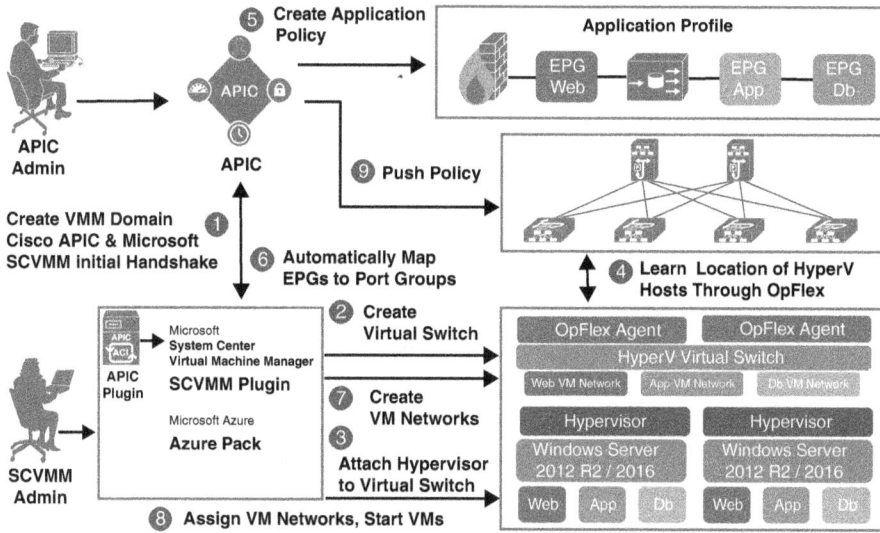

Figure 6-8   *Workflow for Integrating ACI and Microsoft SCVMM*

Mapping ACI and SCVMM Constructs

Figure 6-9 shows the mapping of Cisco ACI and the SCVMM constructs (SCVMM controller, cloud, and logical switches).

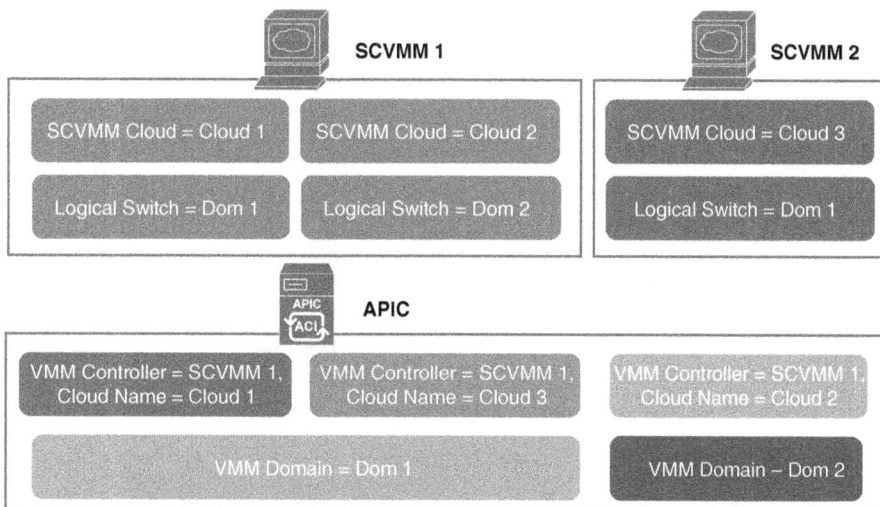

Figure 6-9   *Mapping ACI and SCVMM Constructs*

One VMM domain cannot map to the same SCVMM more than once. An APIC can be associated with up to five SCVMM controllers. For additional information on other limitations, see the *Verified Scalability Guide for Cisco ACI* on the Cisco website.

Mapping Multiple SCVMMs to an APIC

When multiple SCVMMs are associated with an APIC, the OpFlex certificate from the first SCVMM controller must be copied to the secondary controller and other controllers, as applicable. You use the **certlm.msc** command on the local SCVMM controller to import the certificate to the following location:

> Certificates - Local Computer > Personal > Certificates

The same OpFlex certificate is deployed on the Hyper-V servers that are managed by this SCVMM controller. You use the **mmc** command to install the certificate on the Hyper-V servers.

Verifying That the OpFlex Certificate Is Deployed for a Connection from the SCVMM to the APIC

You can verify that the OpFlex certificate is deployed for a connection from the SCVMM to the APIC by viewing the Cisco_APIC_SCVMM_Service log file, which is located in the C:\Program Files (x86)\ApicVMMService\Logs\ directory. In this file, ensure that the correct certificate is used and also check to make sure there was a successful login to the APIC (see Example 6-1).

Example 6-1   *Viewing the Cisco_APIC_SCVMM_Service Log File*

```
4/15/2017 2:10:09 PM-1044-13||UpdateCredentials|| AdminSettingsController:
  UpdateCredentials.
4/15/2017 2:10:09 PM-1044-13||UpdateCredentials|| new: EndpointAddress:
  Called_from_SCVMMM_PS,
  Username ApicAddresses 10.10.10.1;10.10.10.2;10.10.10.3 CertName: OpflexAgent
4/15/2017 2:10:09 PM-1044-13||UpdateCredentials|| ########
4/15/2017 2:10:09 PM-1044-13||UpdateCredentials|| oldreg_apicAddresses is
4/15/2017 2:10:09 PM-1044-13||UpdateCredentials|| Verifying APIC address 10.10.10.1
4/15/2017 2:10:09 PM-1044-13||GetInfoFromApic|| Querying URL https://192.168.10.10/
  api/node/class/infraWiNode.xml
4/15/2017 2:10:09 PM-1044-13||GetInfoFromApic|| HostAddr 10.10.10.1
4/15/2017 2:10:09 PM-1044-13||PopulateCertsAndCookies|| URL:/api/node/class/
  infraWiNode.xml
4/15/2017 2:10:09 PM-1044-13||PopulateCertsAndCookies|| Searching Cached Store
  Name: My
4/15/2017 2:10:09 PM-1044-13||PopulateCertsAndCookies|| Using Certificate
  CN=OpflexAgent, C=USA, S=MI, O=CX, E=aci@lab.local in Cached Store Name:My
```

```
4/15/2017 2:10:09 PM-1044-13||PopulateCertsAndCookies|| Using the following CertDN:
 uni/userext/user-admin/usercert-OpFlexAgent
4/15/2017 2:10:09 PM-1044-13||GetInfoFromApic|| IFC returned OK to deployment query
4/15/2017 2:10:09 PM-1044-13||GetInfoFromApic|| Successfully deserialize deployment
 query response
4/15/2017 2:10:09 PM-1044-13||UpdateCredentials|| ApicClient.Login(addr 10.10.10.1)
 Success.
```

Verifying VMM Deployment from the APIC to the SCVMM

You can verify that the OpFlex certificate is deployed on the Hyper-V server by viewing log files in the C:\Program Files (x86)\ApicHyperAgent\Logs directory. In this file, ensure that the correct certificate is used and ensure that the connection with the Hyper-V servers on the fabric leafs is established. In addition, ensure that a VTEP virtual network adapter is added to the virtual switch and an IP address is assigned to the VTEP adapter.

In the SCVMM, check for the following:

- Under Fabric > Logical Switches, verify that apicVswitch_VMMdomainName is deployed from the APIC to the SCVMM.

- Under Fabric > Logical Networks, verify that apicLogicalNetwork_ VMMdomainName is deployed from the APIC to the SCVMM.

- Under Fabric > Port Profiles, verify that apicUplinkPortProfile_VMMdomainName is deployed. If it is not deployed, right-click the host under Servers and choose Properties. Go to Virtual Switches and ensure that the physical adapters are attached to the virtual switches.

Note   In the APIC GUI, the Hyper-V servers and the virtual machines do not appear in the Microsoft SCVMM inventory until you ensure that these points for the SCVMM are satisfied.

OpenStack Integration

OpenStack defines a flexible software architecture for creating cloud-computing environments. The reference software-based implementation of OpenStack allows for multiple Layer 2 transports, including VLAN, GRE, and VXLAN. The Neutron project within OpenStack can also provide software-based Layer 3 forwarding. When OpenStack is used with ACI, the ACI fabric provides an integrated Layer 2/3 VXLAN-based overlay networking capability that can offload network encapsulation processing from the compute nodes to the top-of-rack or ACI leaf switches. This architecture provides the flexibility of software overlay networking in conjunction with the performance and operational benefits of hardware-based networking.

Extending OpFlex to the Compute Node

OpFlex is an open and extensible policy protocol designed to transfer declarative networking policies such as those used in Cisco ACI to other devices. By using OpFlex, you can extend the policy model native to ACI all the way down into the virtual switches running on OpenStack Nova compute hosts. This OpFlex extension to the compute host allows ACI to use Open vSwitch (OVS) to support common OpenStack features such as source Network Address Translation (SNAT) and floating IP addresses in a distributed manner.

The ACI OpenStack drivers support two distinct modes of deployment. The first approach is based on the Neutron API and Modular Layer 2 (ML2), which are designed to provide common constructs such as network, router, and security groups that are familiar to Neutron users. The second approach is native to the group-based policy abstractions for OpenStack, which are closely aligned with the declarative policy model used in Cisco ACI.

ACI with OpenStack Physical Architecture

A typical architecture for an ACI fabric with an OpenStack deployment consists of a Nexus 9000 spine/leaf topology, an APIC cluster, and a group of servers to run the various control and compute components of OpenStack. An ACI external routed network connection as a Layer 3 connection outside the fabric can be used to provide connectivity outside the OpenStack cloud. Figure 6-10 illustrates OpenStack infrastructure connectivity with ACI.

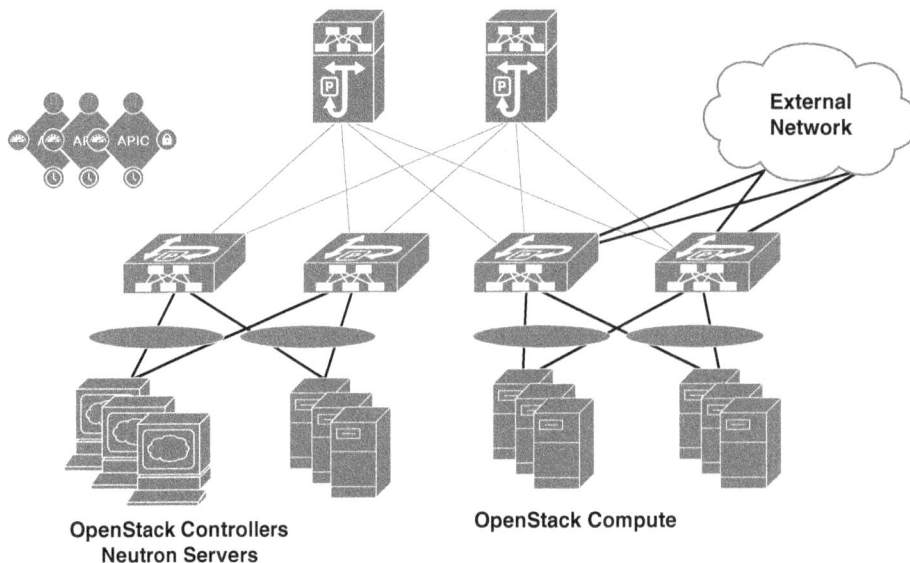

Figure 6-10 *OpenStack Physical Topology with ACI*

OpFlex Software Architecture

The ML2 framework in OpenStack enables the integration of networking services based on type drivers and mechanism drivers. Common networking type drivers include local, flat, VLAN, and VXLAN. OpFlex is added as a new network type through ML2, with an actual packet encapsulation of either VXLAN or VLAN on the host defined in the OpFlex configuration. A mechanism driver is enabled to communicate networking requirements from the Neutron servers to the Cisco APIC cluster. The APIC mechanism driver translates Neutron networking elements such as a network (segment), subnet, router, or external network into APIC constructs in the ACI policy model.

The OpFlex software stack also currently utilizes OVS and local software agents on each OpenStack compute host that communicates with the Neutron servers and OVS. An OpFlex proxy from the ACI leaf switch exchanges policy information with the agent OVS instance in each compute host, effectively extending the ACI switch fabric and policy model into the virtual switch. Figure 6-11 illustrates the OpenStack architecture with OpFlex in ACI.

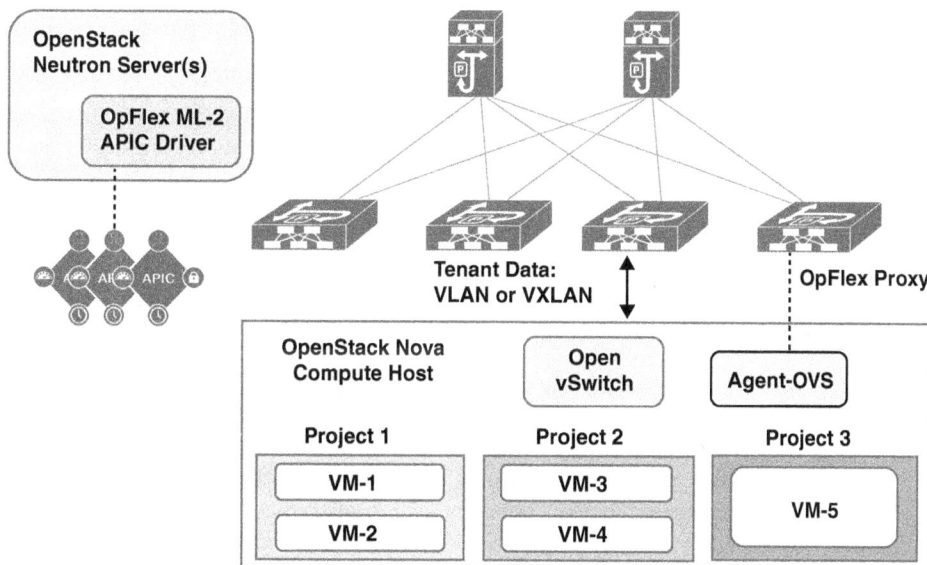

Figure 6-11 *OpenStack Architecture with OpFlex in ACI*

OpenStack Logical Topology

The logical topology diagram in Figure 6-12 illustrates the connections to OpenStack network segments from Neutron/controller servers and compute hosts, including the distributed Neutron services.

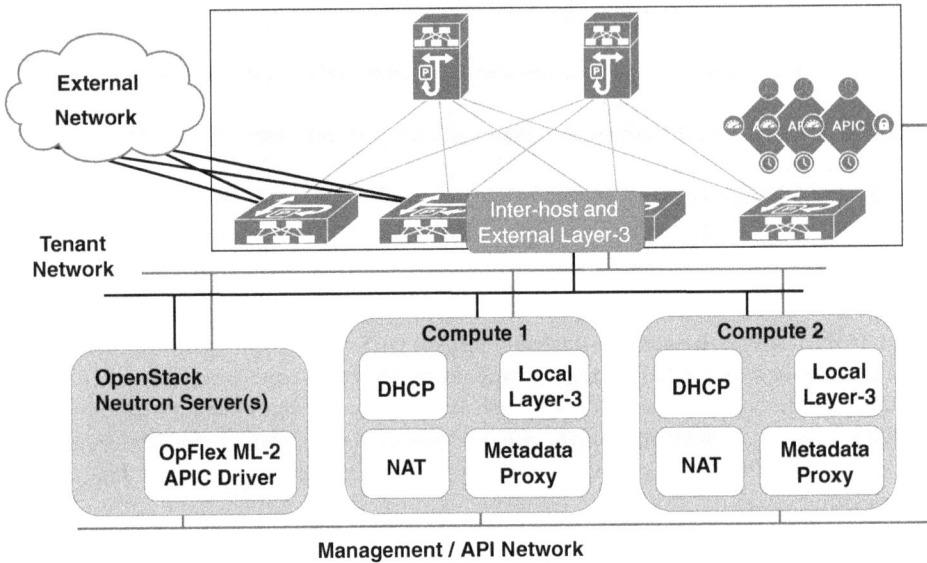

Figure 6-12 *OpenStack Logical Topology in ACI*

Note The management/API network for OpenStack can be connected to servers using an additional virtual NIC/subinterface on a common uplink with tenant networking to the ACI fabric, or by way of a separate physical interface.

Mapping OpenStack and ACI Constructs

Cisco ACI uses a policy model to enable network connectivity between endpoints attached to the fabric. OpenStack Neutron uses more traditional Layer 2 and Layer 3 networking concepts to define networking configuration. The OpFlex ML2 driver translates the Neutron networking requirements into the necessary ACI policy model constructs to achieve the desired connectivity. The OpenStack Group-Based Policy (GBP) networking model is quite similar to the Cisco ACI policy model. With the Cisco ACI unified plug-in for OpenStack, you can use both ML2 and GBP models on a single plug-in instance.

Note Only ML2 or GBP can be used for any given OpenStack project. A single project should not mix ML2 and GBP configurations.

Table 6-1 illustrates the OpenStack Neutron constructs and the corresponding APIC policy objects that are configured when they are created. In the case of GBP deployment, the policies have a direct mapping to the ACI policy model. Table 6-2 shows the OpenStack GBP objects and their corresponding ACI objects.

Table 6-1 *OpenStack Neutron Objects and Corresponding APIC Objects*

Neutron Object	APIC Object
(Neutron Instance)	VMM Domain
Project	Tenant + Application Network Profile
Network	EPG + Bridge Domain
Subnet	Subnet
Security Group + Rule	N/A (Iptables rules maintained per host)
Router	Contract
Network:external	L3Out/Outside EPG

Table 6-2 *OpenStack GBP Objects and Corresponding APIC Objects*

GBP Object	APIC Object
Policy Target	Endpoint
Policy Group	Endpoint Group (fvAEPg)
Policy Classifier	Filter (vzFilter)
Policy Action	--
Policy Rule	Subject (vzSubj)
Policy Ruleset	Contract (vzBrCP)
L2 Policy	Bridge Domain (fvBD)
L3 Policy	Context (fvCtx)

Prerequisites for OpenStack and Cisco ACI

Keep in mind the following prerequisites for OpenStack and Cisco ACI:

- **Target audience:** It is important to have working knowledge of Linux, the intended OpenStack distribution, the ACI policy model, and GUI-based APIC configuration.

- **ACI Fabric:** ACI fabric needs to be installed and initialized with a minimum APIC version 1.1(4e) and NX-OS version 11.1(4e). For basic guidelines on initializing a new ACI fabric, see the relevant documentation. For communication between multiple leaf pairs, the fabric must have a BGP route reflector enabled to use an OpenStack external network.

- **Compute:** You need to have a controller and servers connected to the fabric, preferably using NIC bonding and a VPC. In most cases the controller does not need to be connected to the fabric.

- **L3Out:** For external connectivity, one or more Layer 3 Outs (L3Outs) need to be configured on the ACI.

- **VLAN mode:** For VLAN mode, a non-overlapping VLAN pool of sufficient size should be allocated ahead of time.

Guidelines and Limitations for OpenStack and Cisco ACI

The following sections describes the guidelines and limitations for OpenStack and Cisco ACI.

Scalability Guidelines

There is a one-to-one correlation between the OpenStack tenant and the ACI tenant, and for each OpenStack tenant, the plug-in automatically creates ACI tenants named according to the following convention:

convention_*apic_system_id_openstack_tenant_name*

You should consider the scalability parameters for supporting the number of required tenants.

It is important to calculate the fabric scale limits for endpoint groups, bridge domains, tenants, and contracts before deployment. Doing so limits the number of tenant/project networks and routers that can be created in OpenStack. There are per-leaf and per-fabric limits. Make sure to check the scalability parameters for the deployed release before deployment. In the case of GBP deployment, it can take twice as many endpoint groups and bridge domains as with ML2 mode. Table 6-3 and Table 6-4 list the APIC resources that are needed for each OpenStack resource in GBP and ML2 configurations.

Table 6-3   *OpenStack GBP and ACI Resources*

GBP Resource	APIC Resources Consumed
L3 policy	One context
L2 policy	One bridge domain
	One endpoint group
	Two contracts
Policy group	One endpoint group
Ruleset	One contract
Classifier	Two filters (forward and reverse)
	Note: Five overhead classifiers are created

Table 6-4 *OpenStack ML2 and ACI Resources*

ML2 Resource	APIC Resources Consumed
Network	One bridge domain
	One endpoint group
Router	One contract
Security groups	N/A (no filters are used)

Availability Guidelines

For redundancy, you can use bonded interfaces (VPCs) by connecting two interfaces to two leaf switches and creating a VPC in ACI. You should deploy redundant OpenStack controller nodes to avoid a single point of failure. The external network should also be designed to avoid a single point of failure and service interruption.

NAT/External Network Operations

The OpFlex driver software can support external network connectivity and Network Address Translation (NAT) functions in a distributed manner using the local OVS instance on each OpenStack compute node. This distributed approach increases the availability of the overall solution and offloads the central processing of NAT from the Neutron server Layer 3 agent that is used in the reference implementation. You can also provide direct external connectivity without NAT or with a mix of NAT and non-NAT external connectivity.

Subnets Required for NAT

Unlike with the standard Neutron approach, three distinct IP subnets are required to take full advantage of external network functionality with the OpFlex driver:

- **Link subnet:** This subnet represents the actual physical connection to the external next-hop router outside of the fabric to be *assigned* to a routed interface, subinterface, or SVI.

- **Source NAT subnet:** This subnet is used for Port Address Translation (PAT), allowing multiple virtual machines to share an outside-routable IP address. A single IP address is assigned to each compute host, and Layer 4 port number manipulation is used to maintain unique session traffic.

- **Floating IP subnet:** With OpenStack, the term *floating IP* is used when a virtual machine instance is allowed to claim a distinct static NAT address to support inbound connections to the virtual machine from outside the cloud. The floating IP subnet is the subnet assigned within OpenStack to the Neutron external network entity.

Optimized DHCP and Metadata Proxy Operations

The OpFlex driver software stack provides optimized traffic flow and distributed processing to provide DHCP and metadata proxy services for virtual machine instances. These services are designed to keep processing and packet traffic local to the compute host as much as possible. The distributed elements communicate with centralized functions to ensure system consistency. You should enable optimized DHCP and metadata services when deploying the OpFlex plug-in for OpenStack.

Physical Interfaces

OpFlex uses the untagged fabric interface for an uplink trunk in VLAN mode. This means the fabric interface cannot be used for PXE because PXE usually requires an untagged interface. If you require PXE in a VLAN mode deployment, you must use a separate interface for PXE. This interface can be connected through ACI or an external switch. This issue is not present in VXLAN mode since tunnels are created using the tagged interface for an infrastructure VLAN.

Layer 4 to Layer 7 Services

Service insertion in OpenStack is done through a physical domain or device package. You should check customer requirements and the plug-in mode (GBP or ML2) to plan how service insertion/chaining will be done. The OpenStack Neutron project also defines Layer 4 to Layer 7 extension APIs, such as LBaaS, FWaaS, and VPNaaS. The availability of these extensions depends on the device vendor. Check the vendor for the availability of these extensions.

Blade Servers

When deploying on blade servers, you must make sure there is no intermediate switch between the fabric and the physical server interfaces. Check the OpenStack ACI plug-in release notes to make sure a particular configuration is supported. At this writing, there is limited support for B-Series blade servers, and the support is limited to VLAN mode only.

Verifying the OpenStack Configuration

Follow these steps to verify the OpenStack configuration:

Step 1.   Verify that a VMM domain was created for the OpenStack system ID defined during installation. The nodes connected to the fabric that are running the OpFlex agent should be visible under Hypervisors. The virtual machines running on the hypervisor should be visible when you select that hypervisor. All networks created for this tenant should also be visible under the DVS submenu, and selecting the network should show you all endpoints connected to that network.

Step 2.   Look at the health score and faults for the entity to verify correct operation. If the hypervisors are not visible or appear as being disconnected, check the OpFlex connectivity.

Step 3.   Verify that there is a tenant created for the OpenStack tenant/project. All the networks created in OpenStack should show up as endpoint groups and corresponding bridge domains. Choose the Operational tab for the endpoint group to see all of the endpoints for that endpoint group.

Step 4.   Check the Health Score tab and Faults tab to make sure there are no issues.

Configuration Examples for OpenStack and Cisco ACI

The following sections provide configuration examples for OpenStack and Cisco ACI.

Optimized Metadata and DHCP

In the configuration file, optimized DHCP is enabled by default in the OpFlex OpenStack plug-in. To disable optimized DHCP, add the following line:

```
enable_optimized_dhcp = False
```

In the configuration file, the optimized metadata service is disabled by default. To enable the optimized metadata, add the following line:

```
enable_optimized_metadata = True
```

External Network/NAT Configuration

You can define external network connectivity by adding an apic_external_network section to the configuration file, as in this example:

```
[apic_external_network:DC-Out]
preexisting=True
external_epg=DC-Out-EPG
host_pool_cidr=10.10.10.1/24
```

In this example, host_pool_cidr defines the SNAT subnet. You define the floating IP subnet by creating an external network in Neutron or an external policy in GBP. The name of the external network or policy should use the same name as apic_external_network that is defined in the file (in this case, DC-Out).

It is possible to disable NAT by adding enable_nat = False in the apic_external_network section. You can have multiple external networks using different Layer 3 Outs on ACI, and you can have a mix of NAT and non-NAT external networks.

In GBP deployment, network subnets for policy groups are carved out of the default_ip_pool setting defined in the plug-in configuration file, as in this example:

```
[group_policy_implicit_policy]
default_ip_pool = 192.168.10.0/16
```

This pool is used to allocate networks for created policy groups. You must make sure that the pool is large enough for the intended number of groups.

Kubernetes Integration

Kubernetes is a portable, extensible open-source platform that automates the deployment, scaling, and management of container-based workloads and services in a network. Beginning with Cisco APIC Release 3.0(1), you can integrate Kubernetes on bare-metal servers into Cisco ACI.

To integrate Kubernetes with Cisco ACI, you need to execute a series of tasks. Some of them you perform in the network to set up the Cisco APIC; others you perform on the Kubernetes server. Once you have integrated Kubernetes, you can use the Cisco APIC to view Kubernetes in the Cisco ACI.

Note   The following sections show the workflow for integrating Kubernetes and provide specific instructions for setting up the Cisco APIC. However, it is assumed that you are familiar with Kubernetes and containers and can install Kubernetes. Specific instructions for installing Kubernetes are beyond the scope of this book.

The following are the basic tasks involved in integrating Kubernetes into the Cisco ACI fabric:

Step 1.   Prepare for the integration and set up the subnets and VLANs in the network.

Step 2.   Fulfill the prerequisites.

Step 3.   To provision the Cisco APIC to integrate with Kubernetes, download the provisioning tool, which includes a sample configuration file, and update the configuration file with information you previously gathered about your network. Then run the provisioning tool with the information about your network.

Step 4.   Set up networking for the node to support Kubernetes installation. This includes configuring an uplink interface, subinterfaces, and static routes.

Step 5.   Install Kubernetes and Cisco ACI containers.

Step 6.   Use the Cisco APIC GUI to verify that Kubernetes has been integrated into Cisco ACI.

The following sections provide details on these steps.

Planning for Kubernetes Integration

Various network resources are required to provide capabilities to a Kubernetes cluster, including several subnets and routers. You need the following subnets:

■ **Node subnet:** This subnet is used for Kubernetes control traffic. It is where the Kubernetes API services are hosted. Make the node subnet a private subnet and make sure that it has access to the Cisco APIC management address.

■ **Pod subnet:** This is the subnet from which the IP addresses of Kubernetes pods are allocated. Make the pod subnet a private subnet.

Note   This subnet specifies the starting address for the IP pool that is used to allocate IP addresses to pods and your Cisco ACI bridge domain IP address. For example, if you define it as 192.168.255.254/16, this is a valid configuration from a Cisco ACI perspective. However, your containers will not get an IP address because there are no free IP addresses after 192.168.255.254 in this subnet. We suggest always using the first IP address in the pod subnet, which in this example would be 192.168.0.1/16.

- **Node service subnet:** This subnet is used for internal routing of load-balanced service traffic. Make the node service subnet a private subnet.

Note   Much as with the pod subnet, you should configure the service subnet with the first IP address of the allocated subnet.

- **External service subnets:** These subnets are pools from which load-balanced services are allocated as externally accessible service IP addresses.

Note   The externally accessible service IP addresses could be globally routable. You should configure the next-hop router to send traffic destined for these IP addresses to the fabric. There are two such pools: One is used for dynamically allocated IP addresses, and the other is available for services to request a specific fixed external IP address.

You need the following VLANs for local fabric use:

- **Node VLAN:** This VLAN is used by the physical domain for Kubernetes nodes.
- **Service VLAN:** This VLAN is used for delivery of load-balanced service traffic.
- **Infrastructure VLAN:** This is the infrastructure VLAN used by the Cisco ACI fabric.

Prerequisites for Integrating Kubernetes with Cisco ACI

Ensure that the following prerequisites are in place before you try to integrate Kubernetes with the Cisco ACI fabric:

- A working Cisco ACI installation
- An attachable entity profile (AEP) set up with interfaces that are desired for the Kubernetes deployment
- An L3Out connection, along with a Layer 3 external network to provide external access
- Virtual routing and forwarding (VRF)

Note   The VRF and L3Out connection in Cisco ACI that are used to provide outside connectivity to Kubernetes external services can be in any tenant. The most common usage is to put the VRF and L3Out in the common tenant or in a tenant that is dedicated to the Kubernetes cluster. You can also have separate VRFs—one for the Kubernetes bridge domains and one for the L3Out—and you can configure route leaking between them.

■ Any required route reflector configuration for the Cisco ACI fabric

■ A next-hop router that is connected to the Layer 3 external network and that is capable of appropriate external access and configured with the required routes

In addition, the Kubernetes cluster must be up through the fabric-connected interface on all the hosts. The default route should be pointing to the ACI node subnet bridge domain. This is not mandatory, but it simplifies the routing configuration on the hosts and is the recommend configuration. If you choose not to use this design, all Kubernetes-related traffic must go through the fabric.

Provisioning Cisco ACI to Work with Kubernetes

You can use the acc_provision tool to provision the fabric for the Kubernetes VMM domain and generate a .yaml file that Kubernetes uses to deploy the required Cisco ACI container components. The procedure to accomplish this is as follows:

Step 1.   Download the provisioning tool from

https://software.cisco.com/download/type.html?mdfid=285968390&i=rm and then follow these steps:

a. Click APIC OpenStack and Container Plugins.

b. Choose the package that you want to download.

c. Click Download.

Step 2.   Generate a sample configuration file that you can edit by entering the following command:

```
terminal$ acc-provision--sample
```

This command generates the aci-containers-config.yaml configuration file, which looks as follows:

```
#
# Configuration for ACI Fabric
#
aci_config:
  system_id: mykube          # Every opflex cluster must have a
                             distinct ID
```

```
  apic_hosts:                      # List of APIC hosts to connect for
                                   APIC API

    - 10.1.1.101
  vmm_domain:                      # Kubernetes VMM domain configuration
    encap_type: vxlan             # Encap mode: vxlan or vlan
    mcast_range:                  # Every opflex VMM must use a distinct
                                   range

      start: 225.20.1.1
      end: 225.20.255.255
  # The following resources must already exist on the APIC,
  # they are used, but not created by the provisioning tool.
  aep: kube-cluster               # The AEP for ports/VPCs used by this
                                   cluster

  vrf:                             # This VRF used to create all
                                   Kubernetes EPs

    name: mykube-vrf
    tenant: common               # This can be system-id or common
  l3out:
    name: mykube_l3out           # Used to provision external IPs
    external_networks:
    - mykube_extepg              # Used for external contracts
#
# Networks used by Kubernetes
#
net_config:
  node_subnet: 10.1.0.1/16       # Subnet to use for nodes
  pod_subnet: 10.2.0.1/16        # Subnet to use for Kubernetes Pods
  extern_dynamic: 10.3.0.1/24    # Subnet to use for dynamic external IPs
  extern_static: 10.4.0.1/24     # Subnet to use for static external IPs
  node_svc_subnet: 10.5.0.1/24   # Subnet to use for service graph ←This
                                   is not the same as the
                 Kubernetes service-cluster-ip-range: Use different
subnets.
  kubeapi_vlan: 4001             # The VLAN used by the physdom for
                                   nodes

  service_vlan: 4003             # The VLAN used by LoadBalancer
                                   services

  infra_vlan: 4093               # The VLAN used by ACI infra
#
# Configuration for container registry
# Update if a custom container registry has been setup
#
registry:
  image_prefix: noiro                    # e.g: registry.example.com/
                                         noiro

  # image_pull_secret: secret_name      # (if needed)
```

Note   Do not modify the Cisco ACI bridge domain configuration that is pushed by the acc-provisioning tool. Setting the bridge domain to flood results in a broken environment.

Step 3.   Edit the sample configuration file, providing information from your network, and save the file.

Step 4.   Provision the Cisco ACI fabric by using the following command:

```
acc-provision -c aci-containers-config.yaml -o
aci-containers.yaml -f kubernetes-<version> -a -u
[apic username] -p [apic password]
```

This command generates the file aci-containers.yaml, which you use after installing Kubernetes. It also creates the files user-[system id].key and user-[system id].crt, which contain the certificate used to access the Cisco APIC. Save these files in case you change the configuration later and want to avoid disrupting a running cluster because of a key change.

Note   The file aci-containers.yaml is security sensitive. It contains keys necessary for connecting to the Cisco APIC administration API.

Note   Currently, the provisioning tool supports only the installation of a single Kubernetes cluster on a single or multi-pod Cisco ACI fabric. However, you can run the tool as often as needed to install multiple Kubernetes clusters. A single Cisco ACI installation can support more than one Kubernetes cluster.

Step 5.   (Optional) Configure advanced optional parameters to adjust to custom parameters other than the ACI default values or base provisioning assumptions. For example, if your VMM's multicast address for the fabric is different from 225.1.2.3, you can configure it by using the following:

```
aci_config:
  vmm_domain:
    mcast_fabric: 225.1.2.3
```

If you are using VLAN encapsulation, you can specify the VLAN pool for it, as follows:

```
aci_config:
  vmm_domain:
    encap_type: vlan
```

```
      vlan_range:
        start: 10
        end: 25
```

If you want to use an existing user, key, certificate, add the following:

```
aci_config:
  sync_login:
    username: <name>
    certfile: <pem-file>
    keyfile: <pem-file>
```

If you are provisioning in a system nested inside virtual machines, enter the name of an existing preconfigured VMM domain in Cisco ACI into the aci_config section under the vmm_domain of the configuration file:

```
nested_inside:
    type: vmware
    name: myvmware
```

Preparing the Kubernetes Nodes

When you are done provisioning Cisco ACI to work with Kubernetes, you can start preparing the networking construct for the Kubernetes nodes by following this procedure:

Step 1.   Configure your uplink interface with or without NIC bonding, depending on how your AAEP is configured. Set the MTU on this interface to 1600.

Step 2.   Create a subinterface on your uplink interface on your infrastructure VLAN. Configure this subinterface to obtain an IP address by using DHCP. Set the MTU on this interface to 1600.

Step 3.   Configure a static route for the multicast subnet 224.0.0.0/4 through the uplink interface used for VXLAN traffic.

Step 4.   Create a subinterface (for example, kubeapi_vlan) on the uplink interface on your node VLAN in the configuration file. Configure an IP address on this interface in your node subnet. Then set this interface and the corresponding node subnet router as the default route for the node.

Note   Many Kubernetes installer tools look specifically for the default route to choose interfaces for API server traffic and other traffic. It's possible to install with the default route on another interface. To accomplish this, you set up a number of static routes into this interface and override your installer configuration. However, we recommend setting up the default route through the node uplink.

Step 5.   Create the /etc/dhcp/dhclient-eth0.4093.conf file with the following content, inserting the MAC address of the Ethernet interface for each server on the first line of the file:

Note   If you have a single interface, you could name the file dhclient.conf without the added interface name, as in dhclient-eth0.4093.conf.

```
send dhcp-client-identifier 01:<mac-address of infra VLAN
interface>;
request subnet-mask, domain-name, domain-name-servers,
host-name;
send host-name <server-host-name>;

option rfc3442-classless-static-routes code 121 = array of
unsigned integer 8;
option ms-classless-static-routes code 249 = array of
unsigned integer 8;
option wpad code 252 = string;

also request rfc3442-classless-static-routes;
also request ms-classless-static-routes;
also request static-routes;
also request wpad;
also request ntp-servers;
```

The network interface on the infrastructure VLAN requests a DHCP address from the APIC infrastructure network for OpFlex communication. Make sure the server has a dhclient configuration for this interface to receive all the correct DHCP options with the lease.

Note   The infrastructure VLAN interface in your environment may be a basic Linux-level subinterface, such as eth0.4093.

Step 6.   If you have a separate management interface for the node being configured, configure any static routes that you need to access your management network on the management interface.

Step 7.   Ensure that OVS is not running on the node.

Here is an example of the interface configuration (in /etc/network/interfaces):

```
# Management network interface (not connected to ACI)
auto ens160
iface ens160 inet static
    address   192.168.66.17
    netmask 255.255.255.0
    up route add -net 10.0.0.0/8 gw 192.168.66.1
    dns-nameservers  192.168.66.1
```

```
# Interface connected to ACI
auto ens192
iface ens192 inet manual
    mtu 1600

# ACI Infra VLAN
auto ens192.3095
iface ens192.3095 inet dhcp
    mtu 1600
    up route add -net 224.0.0.0/4 dev ens192.3095
    vlan-raw-device ens192

# Node Vlan
auto ens192.4001
iface ens192.4001 inet static
    address  12.1.0.101
    netmask 255.255.0.0
    mtu 1600
    gateway 12.1.0.1
    vlan-raw-device ens192
```

Installing Kubernetes and Cisco ACI Containers

After you provision Cisco ACI to work with Kubernetes and prepare the Kubernetes nodes, you can install Kubernetes and ACI containers. You can use any installation method you choose, as long as it is appropriate to your environment. This procedure provides guidance and high-level instruction for installation; for details, consult Kubernetes documentation.

When installing Kubernetes, ensure that the API server is bound to the IP addresses on the node subnet and not to management or other IP addresses. Issues with node routing table configuration and API server advertisement addresses are the most common problems during installation. If you have problems, therefore, check these issues first.

Install Kubernetes so that it is configured to use a Container Network Interface (CNI) plug-in, but do not install a specific CNI plug-in configuration through your installer. Instead, deploy the CNI plug-in. To install the CNI plug-in, use the following command:

```
kubectl apply -f aci-containers.yaml
```

Note   You can use this command wherever you have kubectl set up—generally from a Kubernetes master node. The command installs the following:

- ACI container host agent and OpFlex agent in a daemon set called aci-containers-host

- Open vSwitch in a daemon set called aci-containers-openvswitch

- ACI containers controller in a deployment called aci-containers-controller

- Other required configurations, including service accounts, roles, and security context

Verifying the Kubernetes Integration

After you have performed the steps described in the preceding sections, you can verify the integration in the Cisco APIC GUI. The integration creates a tenant, three EPGs, and a VMM domain. The procedure to do this is as follows:

Step 1.   Log in to the Cisco APIC.

Step 2.   Go to Tenants > *tenant_name*, where *tenant_name* is the name you specified in the configuration file that you edited and used in installing Kubernetes and the ACI containers.

Step 3.   In the tenant navigation pane, expand the following: *tenant_name* > Application Profiles > *application_profile_name* > Application EPGs. You should see three folders inside the Application EPGs folder:

- **kube-default:** The default EPG for containers that are otherwise not mapped to any specific EPG.

- **kube-nodes:** The EPG for the Kubernetes nodes.

- **kube-system:** The EPG for the kube-system Kubernetes namespace. This typically contains the kube-dns pods, which provide DNS services for a Kubernetes cluster.

Step 4.   In the tenant navigation pane, expand the Networking and Bridge Domains folders. You should see two bridge domains:

- **node-bd:** The bridge domain used by the node EPG

- **pod-bd:** The bridge domain used by all pods

Step 5.   If you deploy Kubernetes with a load balancer, go to Tenants > common, expand L4-L7 Services, and perform the following steps:

- Open the L4-L7 Service Graph Templates folder; you should see a template for Kubernetes.

- Open the L4-L7 Devices folder; you should see a device for Kubernetes.

- Open the Deployed Graph Instances folder; you should see an instance for Kubernetes.

Step 6.   Go to VM Networking > Inventory, and in the Inventory navigation pane, expand the Kubernetes folder. You should see a VMM domain, with the name you provided in the configuration file, and in that domain you should see folders called Nodes and Namespaces.

OpenShift Integration

OpenShift is a container application platform that is built on top of Docker and Kubernetes that makes it easy for developers to create applications and provides a platform for operators that simplifies deployment of containers for both development and production workloads. Beginning with Cisco APIC Release 3.1(1), OpenShift can be integrated with Cisco ACI by leveraging the ACI CNI plug-in.

To integrate Red Hat OpenShift with Cisco ACI, you must perform a series of tasks. Some tasks are performed by the ACI fabric administrator directly on the APIC, and others are performed by the OpenShift cluster administrator. After you have integrated the Cisco ACI CNI plug-in for Red Hat OpenShift, you can use the APIC to view OpenShift endpoints and constructs within the fabric.

Note   This section describes the workflow for integrating OpenShift with ACI. However, it is assumed that you are familiar with OpenShift and containers and have knowledge of installation. Specific instructions for installing OpenShift are beyond the scope of this book.

The following is a high-level look at the tasks required to integrate OpenShift with the Cisco ACI fabric:

Step 1.   To prepare for the integration, identify the subnets and VLANs that you will use in your network.

Step 2.   Perform the required Day 0 fabric configurations.

Step 3.   Configure the Cisco APIC for the OpenShift cluster. Many of the required fabric configurations are performed directly with a provisioning tool (acc-provision). The tool is embedded in the plug-in files from www.cisco.com. Once downloaded and installed, modify the configuration file with the information from the planning phase and run the tool.

Step 4.   Set up networking for the node to support OpenShift installation. This includes configuring an uplink interface, subinterfaces, and static routes.

Step 5.   Install OpenShift and Cisco ACI containers.

Step 6.   Update the OpenShift router to use the ACI fabric.

Step 7.   Use the Cisco APIC GUI to verify that OpenShift has been integrated into the Cisco ACI.

The following sections provide details on these steps.

Planning for OpenShift Integration

The OpenShift cluster requires various network resources, all of which are provided by the ACI fabric integrated overlay. The OpenShift cluster requires the following subnets:

- **Node subnet:** This is the subnet used for OpenShift control traffic. This is where the OpenShift API services are hosted. The acc-provisioning tool configures a private subnet. Ensure that it has access to the Cisco APIC management address.

- **Pod subnet:** This is the subnet from which the IP addresses of OpenShift pods are allocated. The acc-provisioning tool configures a private subnet.

Note   This subnet specifies the starting address for the IP pool that is used to allocate IP addresses to pods as well as your ACI bridge domain IP address. For example, if you define it as 192.168.255.254/16, which is a valid configuration from an ACI perspective, your containers do not get IP addresses as there are no free IP addresses after 192.168.255.254 in this subnet. We suggest always using the first IP address in the pod subnet, which in this example is 192.168.0.1/16.

- **Node service subnet:** This is the subnet used for internal routing of load-balanced service traffic. The acc-provisioning tool configures a private subnet.

Note   Much as with the pod subnet, you should configure the node service subnet with the first IP address in the subnet.

- **External service subnets:** These are pools from which load-balanced services are allocated as externally accessible service IP addresses.

The externally accessible service IP addresses could be globally routable. Configure the next-hop router to send traffic destined for IP addresses to the fabric. There are two such pools: One is used for dynamically allocated IPs, and the other is available for services to request a specific fixed external IP address.

All of the aforementioned subnets must be specified on the acc-provisioning configuration file. The node pod subnets are provisioned on corresponding ACI bridge domains that are created by the provisioning tool. The endpoints on these subnets are learned as fabric endpoints and can be used to communicate directly with any other fabric endpoint without NAT, provided that contracts allow communication. The node service subnet and the external service subnet are not seen as fabric endpoints but are instead used to manage the cluster IP address and the load balancer IP address, respectively, and are programmed on Open vSwitch via OpFlex. As mentioned earlier, the external service subnet must be routable outside the fabric.

OpenShift nodes need to be connected on an EPG using VLAN encapsulation. Pods can connect to one or multiple EPGs and can use either VLAN or VXLAN encapsulation. In addition, PBR-based load balancing requires the use of a VLAN encapsulation to reach the OpFlex service endpoint IP address of each OpenShift node. The following VLAN IDs are therefore required:

- **Node VLAN ID:** The VLAN ID used for the EPG mapped to a physical domain for OpenShift nodes

- **Service VLAN ID:** The VLAN ID used for delivery of load-balanced external service traffic

- **The fabric infrastructure VLAN ID:** The infrastructure VLAN used to extend OpFlex to the OVS on the OpenShift nodes

Prerequisites for Integrating OpenShift with Cisco ACI

Ensure that the following prerequisites are in place before you try to integrate OpenShift with the Cisco ACI fabric:

- A working Cisco ACI fabric running a release that is supported for the desired OpenShift integration

- An attachable entity profile (AEP) set up with the interfaces desired for the OpenShift deployment (When running in nested mode, this is the AEP for the VMM domain on which OpenShift will be nested.)

- An L3Out connection, along with a Layer 3 external network to provide external access

- VRF

Note   The VRF and L3Out connection in Cisco ACI that are used to provide outside connectivity to OpenShift external services can be in any tenant. The most common usage is to put the VRF and L3Out in the common tenant or in a tenant that is dedicated to the OpenShift cluster. You can also have separate VRFs—one for the OpenShift bridge domains and one for the L3Out—and you can configure route leaking between them.

- Any required route reflector configuration for the Cisco ACI fabric

In addition, ensure that the subnet used for external services is routed by the next-hop router that is connected to the selected ACI L3Out interface. This subnet is not announced by default, so either static routes or appropriate configuration must be considered.

In addition, the OpenShift cluster must be up through the fabric-connected interface on all the hosts. The default route on the OpenShift nodes should be pointing to the ACI node subnet bridge domain. This is not mandatory, but it simplifies the routing configuration on the hosts and is the recommend configuration. If you do not follow this design, ensure that the OpenShift node routing is correctly used so that all OpenShift cluster traffic is routed through the ACI fabric.

Provisioning Cisco ACI to Work with OpenShift

You can use the acc_provision tool to provision the fabric for the OpenShift VMM domain and generate a .yaml file that OpenShift uses to deploy the required Cisco ACI container components. This tool requires a configuration file as input and performs two actions as output:

- It configures relevant parameters on the ACI fabric.

- It generates a YAML file that OpenShift administrators can use to install the ACI CNI plug-in and containers on the cluster.

Note   We recommended that when using ESXi nested for OpenShift hosts, you provision one OpenShift host for each OpenShift cluster for each ESXi server. Doing so ensures that, in the event of an ESXi host failure, a single OpenShift node is affected for each OpenShift cluster.

The procedure to provision Cisco ACI to work with OpenShift is as follows:

Step 1.   Download the provisioning tool from https://software.cisco.com/download/
type.html?mdfid=285968390&i=rm and then follow these steps:

   a. Click APIC OpenStack and Container Plugins.

   b. Choose the package that you want to download.

   c. Click Download.

Step 2.   Generate a sample configuration file that you can edit by entering the following command:

```
terminal$ acc-provision--sample
```

Note   Take note of the values if you are provisioning OpenStack to work with OpenShift.

This command generates the aci-containers-config.yaml configuration file, which looks as follows:

```
#
# Configuration for ACI Fabric
#
aci_config:
  system_id: mykube          # Every opflex cluster must have a
                             distinct ID
  apic_hosts:                # List of APIC hosts to connect for
APIC API - 10.1.1.101
  vmm_domain:                # Kubernetes VMM domain configuration
```

```
    encap_type: vxlan          # Encap mode: vxlan or vlan
    mcast_range:               # Every opflex VMM must use a distinct
                                 range

      start: 225.20.1.1
      end: 225.20.255.255
  # The following resources must already exist on the APIC,
  # they are used, but not created by the provisioning tool.
  aep: kube-cluster            # The AEP for ports/VPCs used by this
                                 cluster
  vrf:                         # This VRF used to create all
                                 kubernetes EPs

    name: mykube-vrf
    tenant: common             # This can be system-id or common
  l3out:
    name: mykube_l3out         # Used to provision external IPs
    external_networks:
    - mykube_extepg            # Used for external contracts
#
# Networks used by Kubernetes
#
net_config:
  node_subnet: 10.1.0.1/16     # Subnet to use for nodes
  pod_subnet: 10.2.0.1/16      # Subnet to use for Kubernetes Pods
  extern_dynamic: 10.3.0.1/24  # Subnet to use for dynamic external
                                 IPs

  node_svc_subnet: 10.5.0.1/24 # Subnet to use for service graph<-
                                 This is not the same as openshift_
                                 portal_net: Use different subnets.
  kubeapi_vlan: 4001           # The VLAN used by the physdom for
                                 nodes
  service_vlan: 4003           # The VLAN used by LoadBalancer
                                 services
  infra_vlan: 4093             # The VLAN used by ACI infra
#
# Configuration for container registry
# Update if a custom container registry has been setup
#
registry:
  image_prefix: noiro                 # e.g: registry.example.com/
                                        noiro
  # image_pull_secret: secret_name  # (if needed)
```

Note The APIC administrator must not modify the Cisco ACI bridge domain configuration that is pushed by the acc-provisioning tool.

Note   Make sure to remove the following line from the **net_config** section:

```
extern_static: 10.4.0.1/24     # Subnet to use for static external IPs
```

This subnet is not used for OpenShift.

Step 3.   Edit the sample configuration file with the relevant values for each of the subnets, VLANs, and so on, as appropriate to your planning, and then save the file.

Step 4.   Provision the Cisco ACI fabric by using the following command:

```
acc-provision -f openshift-<version> -c aci-containers-
config.yaml -o aci-containers.yaml \

-a -u [apic username] -p [apic password]
```

This command generates the file aci-containers.yaml, which you use after installing OpenShift. It also creates the files user-[system id].key and user-[system id].crt, which contain the certificate that is used to access the Cisco APIC. Save these files in case you change the configuration later and want to avoid disrupting a running cluster because of a key change.

Note   The file aci-containers.yaml is security sensitive. It contains keys necessary for connecting to the Cisco APIC administration API.

Note   Currently, the provisioning tool supports only the installation of a single OpenShift cluster on a single or multi-pod ACI fabric. However, you can run the tool as often as needed to install multiple OpenShift clusters. A single ACI installation can support more than one OpenShift cluster.

Step 5.   (Optional) Configure advanced optional parameters to adjust to custom parameters other than the ACI default values or base provisioning assumptions. For example, if your VMM's multicast address for the fabric is different from 225.1.2.3, you can configure it by adding the following:

```
aci_config:
  vmm_domain:
     mcast_fabric: 225.1.2.3
```

If you are using VLAN encapsulation, you can specify the VLAN pool for it, as follows:

```
aci_config:
  vmm_domain:
    encap_type: vlan
```

```
    vlan_range:
      start: 10
      end: 25
```

If you want to use an existing user, key, certificate, add the following:

```
aci_config:
  sync_login:
    username: <name>
    certfile: <pem-file>
    keyfile: <pem-file>
```

If you are provisioning in a system nested inside virtual machines, enter the name of an existing preconfigured VMM domain in Cisco ACI into the aci_config section under the vmm_domain of the configuration file:

```
nested_inside:
    type: vmware
    name: myvmware
```

Preparing the OpenShift Nodes

After you provision Cisco ACI, you prepare networking for the OpenShift nodes by following this procedure:

Step 1.   Configure your uplink interface with or without NIC bonding, depending on how your AAEP is configured. Set the MTU on this interface to 1600.

Step 2.   Create a subinterface on your uplink interface on your infrastructure VLAN. Configure this subinterface to obtain an IP address by using DHCP. Set the MTU on this interface to 1600.

Step 3.   Configure a static route for the multicast subnet 224.0.0.0/4 through the uplink interface that is used for VXLAN traffic.

Step 4.   Create a subinterface (for example, kubeapi_vlan) on the uplink interface on your node VLAN in the configuration file. Configure an IP address on this interface in your node subnet. Then set this interface and the corresponding node subnet router as the default route for the node.

Note   Many OpenShift installer tools look specifically for the default route to choose interfaces for API server traffic and other traffic. It's possible to install with the default route on another interface. To do this, you set up static routes into this interface and override your installer configuration. However, we recommend setting up the default route through the node uplink.

Step 5.   Create the /etc/dhcp/dhclient-eth0.4093.conf file with the following content, inserting the MAC address of the Ethernet interface for each server on the first line of the file:

```
send dhcp-client-identifier 01:<mac-address of infra VLAN
interface>;
request subnet-mask, domain-name, domain-name-servers,
host-name;
send host-name <server-host-name>;

option rfc3442-classless-static-routes code 121 = array of
unsigned integer 8;
option ms-classless-static-routes code 249 = array of
unsigned integer 8;
option wpad code 252 = string;

also request rfc3442-classless-static-routes;
also request ms-classless-static-routes;
also request static-routes;
also request wpad;
also request ntp-servers;
```

Note   If you have a single interface, you could name the file just dhclient.conf and not include the interface name, as in dhclient-eth0.4093.conf.

The network interface on the infrastructure VLAN requests a DHCP address from the Cisco APIC infrastructure network for OpFlex communication. The server must have a dhclient configuration for this interface to receive all the correct DHCP options with the lease.

Note   The infrastructure VLAN interface in your environment may be a basic Linux-level subinterface, such as eth0.4093.

Step 6.   If you have a separate management interface for the node being configured, configure any static routes required to access your management network on the management interface.

Step 7.   Ensure that OVS is not running on the node.

Here is an example of the interface configuration (in /etc/network/interfaces):

```
# Management network interface (not connected to ACI)
# /etc/sysconfig/network-scripts/ifcfg-eth0
NAME=eth0
DEVICE=eth0
ONBOOT=yes
BOOTPROTO=none
TYPE=Ethernet
```

```
IPADDR=192.168.66.17
NETMASK=255.255.255.0
PEERDNS=no
DNS1=192.168.66.1

# /etc/sysconfig/network-scripts/route-eth0
ADDRESS0=10.0.0.0
NETMASK0=255.0.0.0
GATEWAY0=192.168.66.1

# Interface connected to ACI
# /etc/sysconfig/network-scripts/ifcfg-eth1
NAME=eth1
DEVICE=eth1
ONBOOT=yes
BOOTPROTO=none
TYPE=Ethernet
IMTU=1600

# ACI Infra VLAN
# /etc/sysconfig/network-scripts/ifcfg-4093
VLAN=yes
TYPE=Vlan
PHYSDEV=eth1
VLAN_ID=4093
REORDER_HDR=yes
BOOTPROTO=dhcp
DEFROUTE=no
IPV6INIT=yes
IPV6_AUTOCONF=yes
IPV6_DEFROUTE=yes
IPV6_FAILURE_FATAL=no
IPV6_ADDR_GEN_MODE=stable-privacy
NAME=4093
DEVICE=eth1.4093
ONBOOT=yes
MTU=1600

# /etc/sysconfig/network-scripts/route-4093
ADDRESS0=224.0.0.0
NETMASK0=240.0.0.0
METRIC0=1000

# Node Vlan
# /etc/sysconfig/network-scripts/ifcfg-node-vlan-4001
VLAN=yes
TYPE=Vlan
PHYSDEV=eth1
```

```
VLAN_ID=4001
REORDER_HDR=yes
BOOTPROTO=none
IPADDR=12.1.0.101
PREFIX=24
GATEWAY=12.1.0.1
DNS1=192.168.66.1
DEFROUTE=yes
IPV6INIT=no
NAME=node-vlan-4001
DEVICE=eth1.4001
ONBOOT=yes
MTU=1600
```

Installing OpenShift and Cisco ACI Containers

After you provision Cisco ACI and prepare the OpenShift nodes, you can install OpenShift and ACI containers. You can use any installation method appropriate to your environment. We recommend using this procedure to install the OpenShift and Cisco ACI containers.

When installing OpenShift, ensure that the API server is bound to the IP addresses on the node subnet and not to management or other IP addresses. Issues with node routing table configuration, API server advertisement addresses, and proxies are the most common problems during installation. If you have problems, therefore, check these issues first.

The procedure for installing OpenShift and Cisco ACI containers is as follows:

Step 1.   Install OpenShift by using the following command:

```
git clone https://github.com/noironetworks/openshift-ansible/
tree/release-3.9
git checkout release-3.9
```

Follow the installation procedure provided at https://docs.openshift.com/container-platform/3.9/install_config/install/advanced_install.html. Also consider the configuration overrides listed at https://github.com/noironetworks/openshift-ansible/tree/release-3.9/roles/aci.

Step 2.   Install the CNI plug-in by using the following command:

```
oc apply -f aci-containers.yaml
```

Note   You can use this command wherever you have oc set up—generally from an OpenShift master node. The command installs the following:

- ACI containers host agent and OpFlex agent in a daemon set called aci-containers-host
- Open vSwitch in a daemon set called aci-containers-openvswitch
- ACI containers controller in a deployment called aci-containers-controller
- Other required configurations, including service accounts, roles, and security context

Updating the OpenShift Router to Use the ACI Fabric

To update the OpenShift router to use the ACI fabric, follow these steps:

Step 1.   Remove the old router by entering the commands such as the following:

```
oc delete svc router
oc delete dc router
```

Step 2.   Create the container networking router by entering a command such as the following:

```
oc adm router --service-account=router --host-network=false
```

Step 3.   Expose the router service externally by entering a command such as the following:

```
oc patch svc router -p '{"spec":{"type": "LoadBalancer"}}'
```

Verifying the OpenShift Integration

After you have performed the steps described in the preceding sections, you can verify the integration in the Cisco APIC GUI. The integration creates a tenant, three EPGs, and a VMM domain. The procedure to do this is as follows:

Step 1.   Log in to the Cisco APIC.

Step 2.   Go to Tenants > *tenant_name*, where *tenant_name* is the name you specified in the configuration file that you edited and used in installing OpenShift and the ACI containers.

Step 3.   In the tenant navigation pane, expand the following: *tenant_name* > Application Profiles > *application_profile_name* > Application EPGs. You should see three folders inside the Application EPGs folder:

- **kube-default:** The default EPG for containers that are otherwise not mapped to any specific EPG.

- **kube-nodes:** The EPG for the OpenShift nodes.

- **kube-system:** The EPG for the kube-system OpenShift namespace. This typically contains the kube-dns pods, which provide DNS services for a OpenShift cluster.

Step 4.   In the tenant navigation pane, expand the Networking and Bridge Domains folders, and you should see two bridge domains:

- **node-bd:** The bridge domain used by the node EPG

- **pod-bd:** The bridge domain used by all pods

Step 5.   If you deploy OpenShift with a load balancer, go to Tenants > common, expand L4-L7 Services, and perform the following steps:

   a. Open the L4-L7 Service Graph Templates folder; you should see a template for OpenShift.

   b. Open the L4-L7 Devices folder; you should see a device for OpenShift.

   c. Open the Deployed Graph Instances folder; you should see an instance for OpenShift.

Step 6.   Go to VM Networking > Inventory, and in the Inventory navigation pane, expand the OpenShift folder. You should see a VMM domain, with the name you provided in the configuration file, and in that domain you should see folders called Nodes and Namespaces.

VMM Integration with ACI at Multiple Locations

In a single ACI fabric with a single APIC cluster located at a single site or stretched between multiple sites using transit leaf, multi-pod, or remote leaf design options, individual VMM integration can be leveraged using the same policy model in any of the locations where the ACI fabric is stretched. This is because a single control and data plane has been stretched between multiple data center locations. In a dual ACI fabric or multi-site environments, separate APIC clusters are deployed in each location and, therefore, a separate VMM domain is created for each site.

Multi-Site

In order to integrate VMM domains into a Cisco ACI multi-site architecture, as mentioned earlier, you need to create separate VMM domains at each site because the sites have separate APIC clusters. Those VMM domains can then be exposed to the ACI multi-site policy manager in order to be associated to the EPGs defined at each site.

Two deployment models are possible:

   ■ Multiple VMMs can be used across separate sites, each paired with the local APIC cluster.

   ■ A single VMM can be used to manage hypervisors deployed across sites and paired with the different local APIC clusters.

The next two sections provide more information about these models.

Multiple Virtual Machine Managers Across Sites

In a multi-site deployment, multiple VMMs are commonly deployed in separate sites to manage the local clusters of hypervisors. Figure 6-13 shows this scenario.

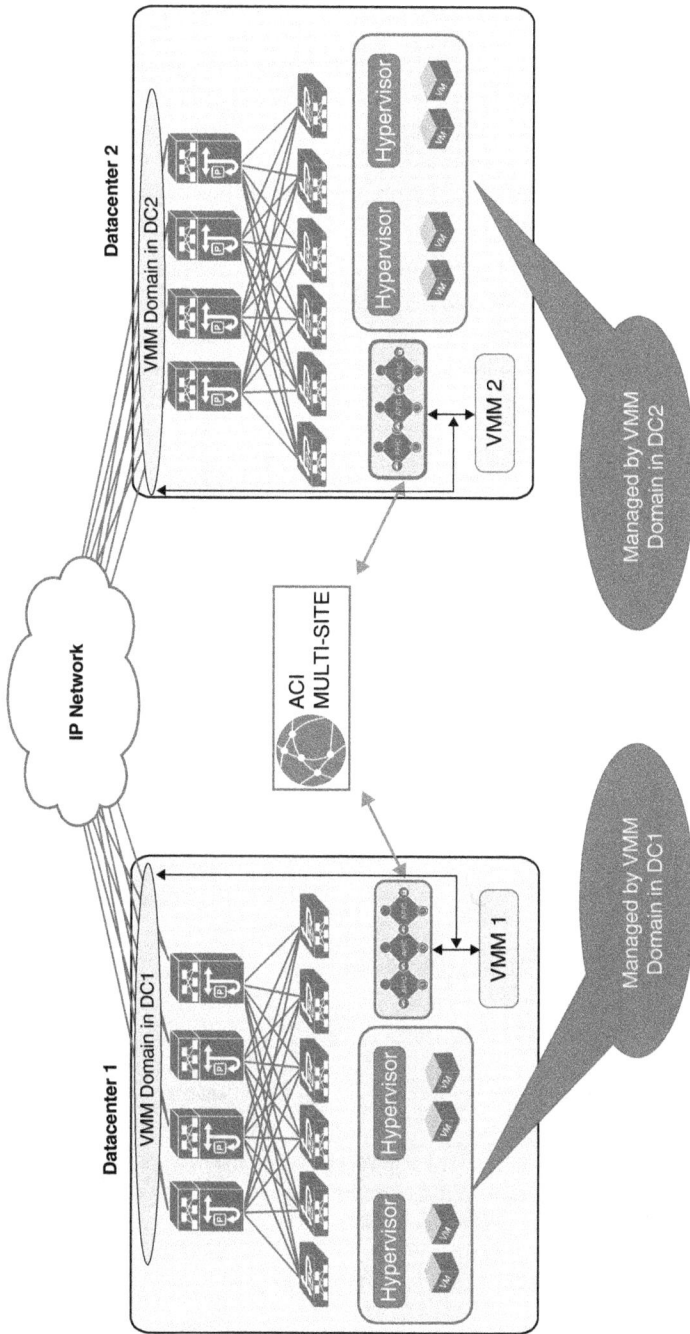

Figure 6-13   *Multiple VMM Domains Across Multiple Sites*

The VMM at each site manages the local hosts and peers with the local APIC domain to create a local VMM domain. This model is supported by all the VMM options supported by Cisco ACI: VMware vCenter Server, Microsoft SCVMM, and OpenStack controller.

The configuration of the VMM domains is performed at the local APIC level. The created VMM domains can then be imported into the Cisco ACI multi-site policy manager and associated with the EPG specified in the centrally created templates. If, for example, EPG 1 is created at the multi-site level, it can then be associated with VMM domain DC 1 and with VMM domain DC 2 before the policy is pushed to Sites 1 and 2 for local implementation.

The creation of separate VMM domains across sites usually restricts the mobility of virtual machines across sites to cold migration scenarios. However, in specific designs using VMware vSphere 6.0 and later, you can perform hot migration between clusters of hypervisors managed by separate vCenter servers. Figure 6-14 and the list that follows demonstrate and describe the steps required to create such a configuration.

Note   At this writing, vCenter Server Release 6.0 or later is the only VMM option that allows live migration across separate Cisco ACI fabrics. With other VMMs (such as vCenter releases earlier than 6.0, SCVMM, and OpenStack deployments), if you want to perform live migration, you must deploy the VMMs in a single Cisco ACI fabric (single pod or multi-pod). Please check Cisco.com for the latest updates.

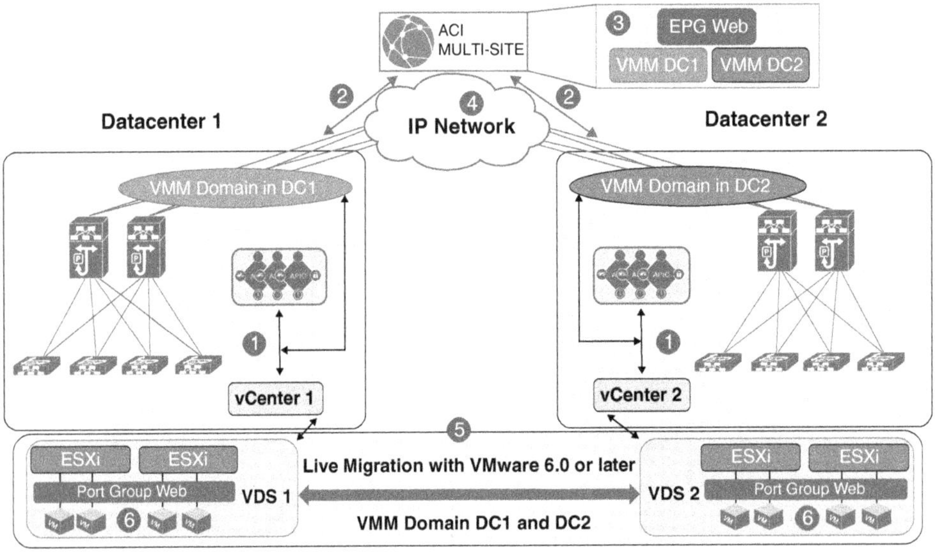

Figure 6-14   *Live Migrations Across VMM Domains with vCenter 6.0 and Later*

Step 1.   Create a VMM domain in each fabric by peering the local vCenter server and the APIC. This peering results in the creation of local vSphere distributed switches (VDS 1 at Site 1 and VDS 2 at Site 2) in the ESXi clusters.

Step 2.   Expose the created VMM domains to the Cisco ACI multi-site policy manager.

Step 3.   Define a new *Web* EPG in a template associated with both Sites 1 and 2. The EPG is mapped to a corresponding *Web* bridge domain, which must be configured as stretched with flooding across sites enabled. At each site, the EPG then is associated with the previously created local VMM domain.

Step 4.   Push the template policy Sites 1 and 2.

Step 5.   Create the EPGs in each fabric, and because they are associated with VMM domains, each APIC communicates with the local vCenter server, which pushes an associated Web port group to each VDS.

Step 6.   Connect the Web virtual machines to the newly created Web port groups. At this point, live migration can be performed across sites.

Single Virtual Machine Manager Across Sites

Figure 6-15 depicts the scenario in which a single VMM domain is used across sites.

In this scenario, a VMM is deployed in Site 1 but manages a cluster of hypervisors deployed within the same fabric and also in separate fabrics. Note that this configuration still leads to the creation of different VMM domains in each fabric, and different VDSs are pushed to the ESXi hosts that are locally deployed. This scenario essentially raises the same issues as discussed in the previous section about the support for cold and hot migration of virtual machines across fabrics.

Remote Leaf

ACI fabric allows for integration with multiple VMM domains. With this integration, the APIC pushes the ACI policy configuration—such as networking, telemetry monitoring, and troubleshooting—to switches based on the locations of virtual instances. The APIC can push the ACI policy in the same way as a local leaf. A single VMM domain can be created for compute resources connected to both the ACI main DC pod and remote leaf switches. VMM/APIC integration is also used to push a VDS to hosts managed by the VMM and to dynamically create port groups as a result of the creation of EPGs and their association to the VMM domain. This allows you to enable mobility ("live" or "cold") for virtual endpoints across different compute hypervisors.

Note   It is worth noting that mobility for virtual endpoints can also be supported if a VMM domain is not created (that is, if VMs are treated as physical resources).

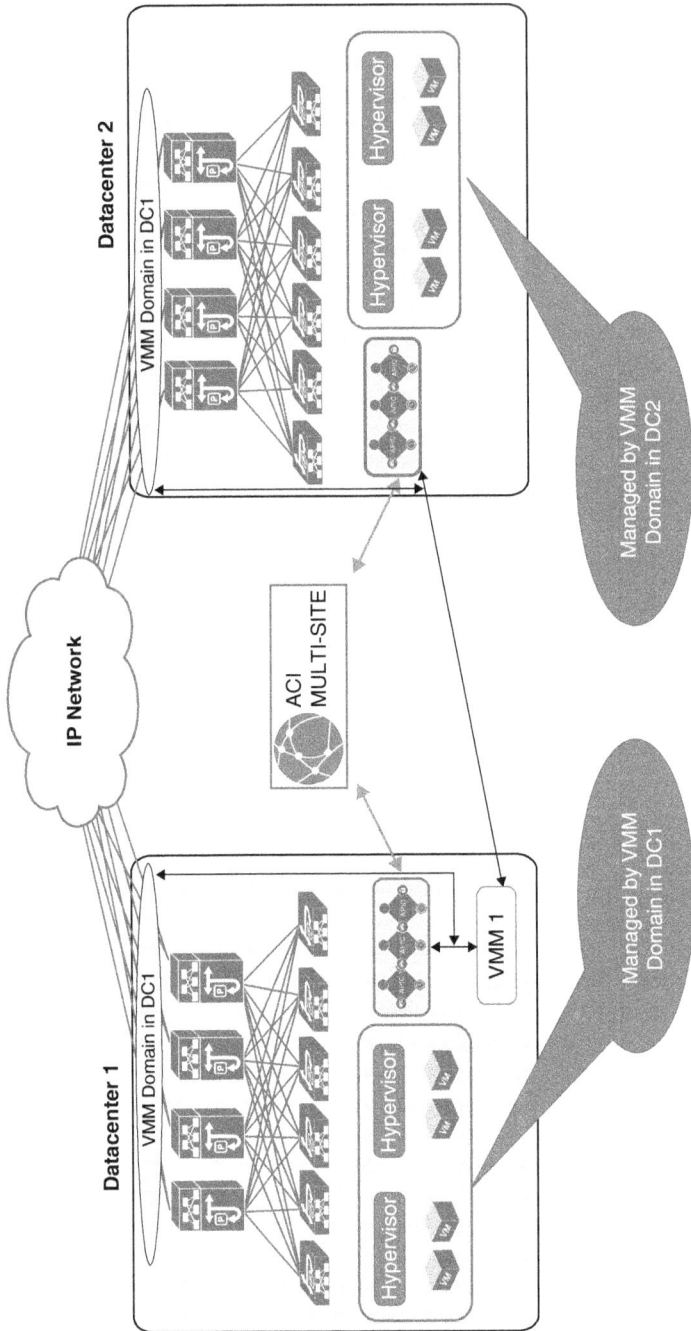

Figure 6-15 *Single VMM Domain Managing VMs Across Multiple Sites*

Virtual instances in the same EPG or Layer 2 domain (VLAN) can be behind the local leaf as well as the remote leaf. When a virtual instance moves from the remote leaf to the local leaf or vice versa, the APIC detects the leaf switches where virtual instances are moved and pushes the associated policies to new leafs. All VMM and container domain integration supported for local leafs is supported for remotes leaf as well.

Figure 6-16 shows the process of vMotion with the ACI fabric.

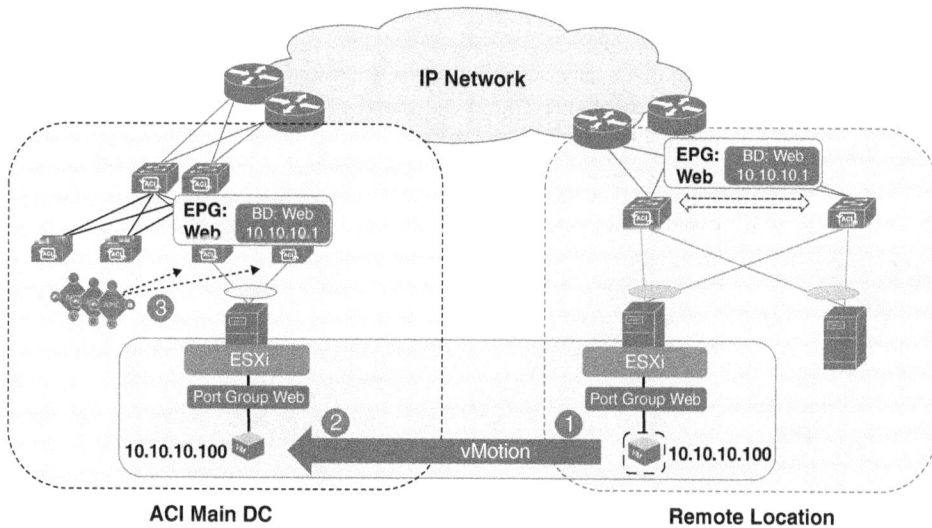

Figure 6-16   *vMotion Between Remote Leaf to ACI Fabric in the Main Data Center*

The following events happen during a vMotion event:

Step 1.   The VM has IP address 10.10.10.100 and is part of the *Web* EPG and the *Web* bridge domain with subnet 10.10.10.1/24. When the VM comes up, the ACI fabric programs the encapsulation VLAN (vlan-100) and the switch virtual interface (SVI), which is the default gateway of the VM on the leaf switches where the VM is connected. The APIC pushes the contract and other associated policies based on the location of the VM.

Step 2.   When the VM moves from a remote leaf to a local leaf, the ACI detects the location of the VM through the VMM integration.

Step 3.   Depending on the EPG-specific configuration, the APIC may need to push the ACI policy on the leaf for successful VM mobility, or a policy may already exist on the destination leaf.

Summary

Integrating the virtual compute platform into ACI extends the policy model down and provides deep visibility into the virtualization layer. As discussed in this chapter, due to the open architecture of Cisco ACI, any hypervisor or container-based platform vendor—such as VMware, Microsoft, OpenStack, Kubernetes, or OpenShift—can be integrated into ACI.

In a single ACI fabric located at a single site or stretched between multiple sites using transit leaf, multi-pod, or remote leaf, individual VMM integration can be leveraged using the same policy model in any of the locations where the ACI fabric is stretched because a single control and data plane has been stretched between multiple data center locations. In a dual ACI fabric or multi-site environment, separate APIC clusters are deployed in each location; therefore, a separate VMM domain is created for each site.

Note   There are no Key Topics or Review Questions for this chapter.

## Chapter 7

L4/L7 Service Integration

In this chapter, you will learn about L4/L7 service integration in Cisco Application Centric Infrastructure (ACI). This chapter covers the following topics:

- Service insertion
- The service graph
- Policy-based redirect
- L4/L7 service integration in multi-pod and multi-site

Service Insertion

The data center is the most critical floor space of any organization today, as it hosts business-critical applications. For better application performance, uptime, and security, service devices such as load balancers and firewalls play a key role in application traffic flows. Traditionally, service devices were connected in Layer 2 Transparent/Bridge mode or Layer 3 Routed mode, depending on the customer use case.

In ACI, service devices can also be connected in traditional Layer 2 Transparent/Bridge mode or Layer 3 Routed mode by a front-end and back-end endpoint group (EPG); this is commonly known as a *sandwich design* in ACI (see Figure 7-1).

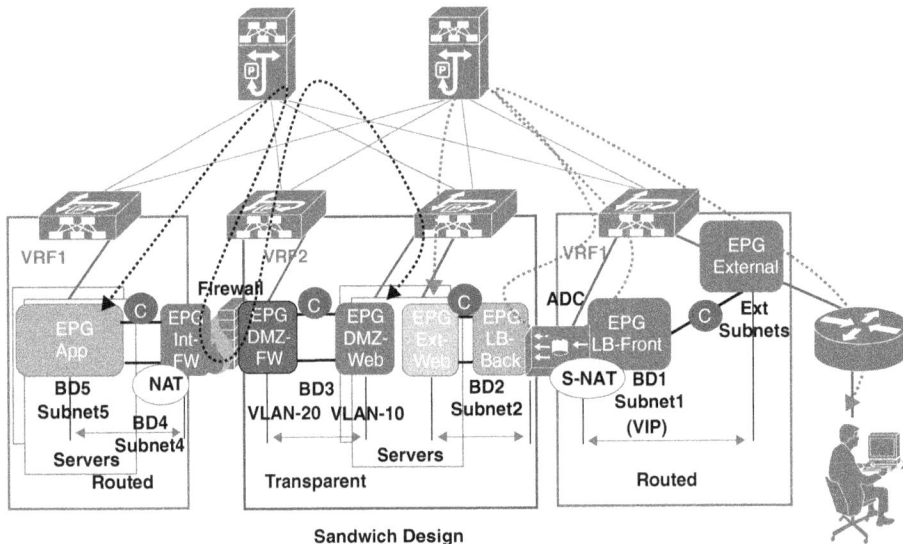

Figure 7-1   *Services Sandwich Design*

This type of service integration is called *service insertion* or *service chaining*. In the logical service insertion design, the web application is front-ended by a load balancer VIP subnet (Subnet1) associated with the EPG *LB-Front*. The traffic is then load balanced from the application delivery controller (ADC) to one of the back-end real servers connected to another subnet (Subnet2) associated with the EPG *LB-Back* and the EPG *Ext-Web*, which are part of the same BD2 and Subnet2. For return traffic, the ADC is configured with source NAT. The web servers that need to communicate with app servers go through the firewall in Transparent/Bridged mode using the EPG *DMZ-Web* encapsulated with VLAN-10 and EPG *DMZ-FW* encapsulated with VLAN-20 as a trunk. Both of these EPGs are part of the same BD, BD3. Web servers have their default gateway pointing to the firewall. On the firewall, the Dot1q interface can be created with an IP address that is used as the default gateway for the web server. The other leg of the firewall is part of the EPG *Int-FW*, which is associated with BD4 and Subnet4, to forward traffic to the EPG *App* with BD5 and Subnet5. NAT is configured on the firewall for return traffic back to the web servers. You can see that this is quite complex in terms of configuration of network and service devices.

The Service Graph

The concept of a service graph differs from the concept of service insertion. The service graph specifies that the path from one EPG (the source) to another EPG (the destination) must pass through certain functions by using a contract and internal and external EPGs, also known as "shadow EPGs," to communicate to service nodes. The sample application traffic flow shown in the service insertion design in Figure 7-1 can be stitched using the service graph in ACI for additional benefits. The service graph introduces innovations at both the data plane and management plane levels, providing you with the capabilities of not only service stitching the application traffic flows but also leveraging the specific configuration on a service node for you. Using the ACI service graph, application traffic can be redirected between security zones to a firewall or load balanced to an ADC, without the need for these service devices to be the default gateway for the application servers. With the use of the service graph, firewall and ADC administrators can define service policies using the management tool of their preferred vendor. The Cisco Application Policy Infrastructure Controller (APIC) administrator can then associate these policies with the traffic path defined in Cisco ACI. This process is called *rendering*. The service graph in ACI introduces changes in the operation model in the sense that configuration not only contains the network connectivity parameters such as VLANs, subnets, and routing but also access lists, firewall rules, load balancing policies, and so on. The service graph seamlessly stitches the service policies through a contract defined between two EPGs, as illustrated in Figure 7-2.

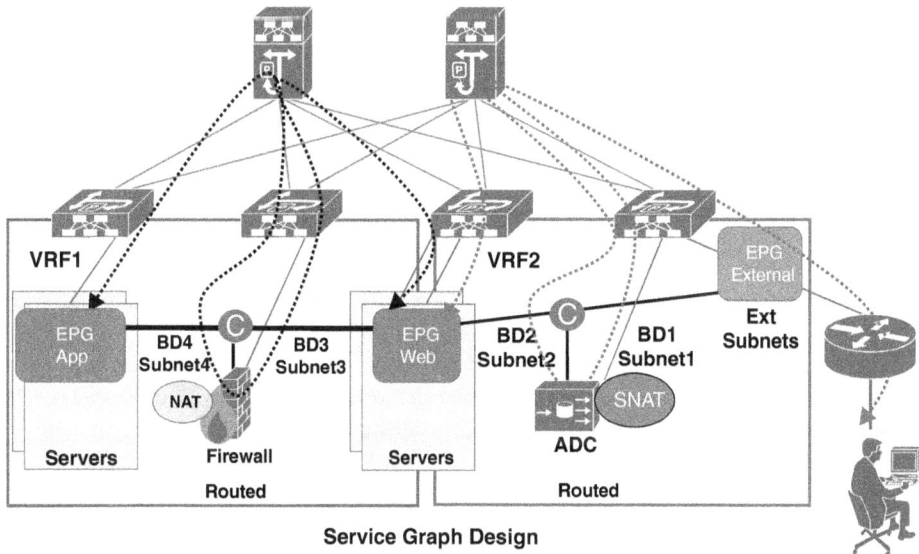

Figure 7-2   *Services Deployed Using the Service Graph*

As you can see in Figure 7-2, there is no need to sandwich front-end and back-end EPGs in the service graph. In ACI, the service graph seamlessly stitched the service node(s) in application flows by creating the shadow EPGs and contract for forwarding the traffic.

Managed Mode Versus Un-Managed Mode

The Cisco ACI service graph supports three different operational modes:

■ **Managed mode:** This mode provides a single pane of glass for centralized management of L2–L7 configuration and service automation using a Cisco APIC. During the configuration of the network infrastructure, you also need to consider the security and load balancing rules, which are part of the configuration workflow in the service graph. Managed mode is also called Service Policy mode. Because all necessary service device configurations, such as interface settings, L2/L3 constructs, policies/rules, and so on, are carried out through the APIC, there is no need to log on to the service device console or GUI interface. However, the device package must be installed on an APIC before you can understand and provision the configuration parameters of the service device. A device package is a collection of XML files that provides device properties (model, vendor, version), device function (load balancing, SSL termination), network connectivity information, device configuration parameters, and Python scripts that provide connectivity to the service node from APIC using REST or SSH.

■ **Un-Managed mode:** In this mode, only the network portion of the service graph configuration is carried out by the APIC on the Cisco ACI fabric. The configuration to the service device is done in the console or GUI. The benefit of this mode is that you do not lock yourself with code alignment between your ACI infrastructure and service device; this means you do not need to worry about keeping ACI to a certain code release in order to support the service device packages. Also, in large enterprises, which often have silo teams, this mode is quite popular because ACI infrastructure and services infrastructure teams may be separated. No device package is required in Un-Managed mode, which is also called Network Policy mode.

■ **Hybrid mode:** In this mode, all the network configuration (such as creating EPGs, BDs, subnets, contracts, and so on) L4–L7 device configuration (such as VLANs, VIP pool, and so on) are carried out by the service graph workflow through the APIC, which is still in Managed mode with the device package installed. The more granular L4–L7 configuration is carried out by templates using an intermediate controller commonly known as a *device manager*; for example, with the F5 load balancer it is called iWorkflow. These fine-tuned configuration parameter templates are then pushed to service devices. Hybrid mode, also known as Service Manager mode, works with most load-balancing device vendors. In the case of firewalls such as Cisco ASA and Firepower, the Managed and Un-Managed operational modes are valid.

L4–L7 Integration Use Cases

To decide whether you should use the service graph feature in ACI, you need to understand the problem that it solves. Cisco designed the service graph technology to automate the deployment of L4–L7 services in the network. Cisco ACI does not provision the service device separately as a physical device, but it can configure it as part of the same application logical construct that creates tenants, bridge domains, EPGs, and so on.

You might find the service graph useful and handy if you want to create a service portal for administrators in which they can create and decommission network infrastructure, including firewalls and load balancers. In such a case, Cisco ACI can help automate the configuration of the firewalls and load balancers as long as they already exist (as either physical or virtual devices). For this use case, you might want to use Managed mode or Hybrid mode. With the service graph in Managed mode, the configuration of the L4–L7 device is part of the configuration of the entire network infrastructure, so you need to consider the security and load balancing rules at the time of executing the configuration change. This approach is different from that of traditional service insertion in that if you don't use the service graph, you can configure the security and load balancing rules at a later time directly on the service devices. With Hybrid mode, the interactions with the L4–L7 device depend on the vendor management tool. Cisco ACI references a policy defined on the vendor management tool through configuration templates. This tool enables you to make changes to the firewall or load balancer configurations without the need to redeploy the service graph. With a service graph, if you have an existing firewall deployed in a graph and you want to replace it with another, you simply need to define to which ACI leaf the new firewall is connected and how it should be managed. Cisco ACI then configures the new firewall just like the existing one, and the graph now points to the new firewall.

In cases where all you need is an application-hosting infrastructure with an already deployed perimeter firewall that controls access to the data center, you should consider using an Un-Managed mode deployment. Also, the service graph is an extension of a contract between two EPGs that requires communication, so by default it operates with the model of shadow EPGs.

In the case of using the service graph for a firewall with multiple security zones or DMZs, you need to reuse the service graph multiple times between each pair of interfaces. Therefore, for this type of deployment, you might find it more convenient to integrate your firewall without using the service graph.

How Contracts Work in ACI

You know that the service graph works by using a contract that stitches the application flow between two EPGs with a service node in between. It is important to also understand how policy enforcement using contracts works in ACI. This section details how contracts work in ACI.

When you create an EPG, it is represented in ACI by a numeric value known as a policy control tag, or PCTag. When a VRF instance is created, APIC assigns a scope or segment ID. Figure 7-3 illustrates this process.

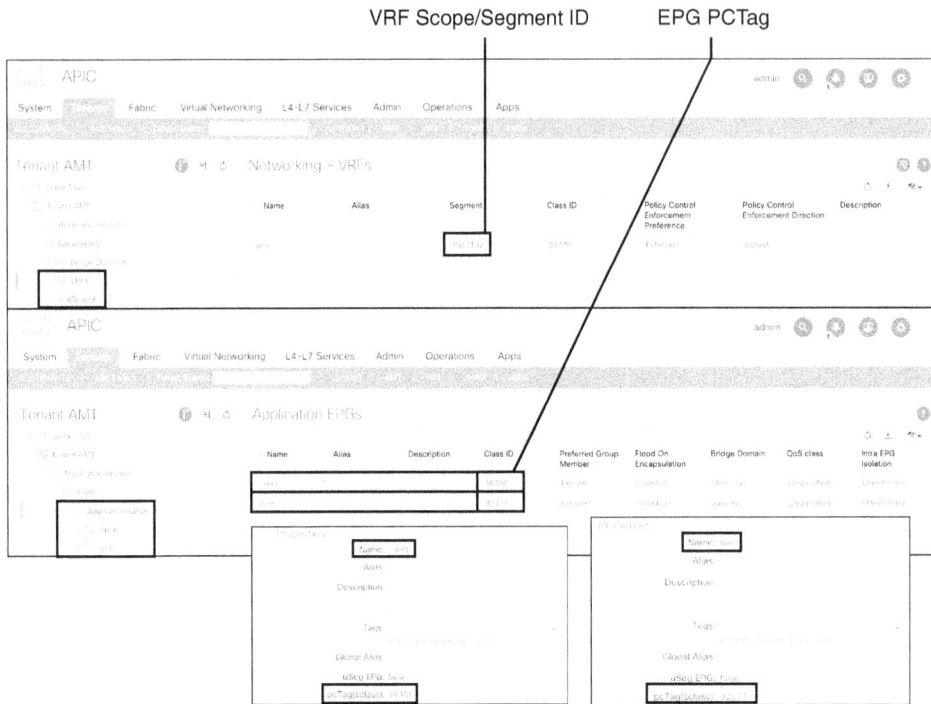

Figure 7-3 *EPG PCTag Value and VRF Scope/Segment ID*

From the switch's (ASIC) perspective, the traffic initiated from the source EPG is assigned a source PCTag and is represented by the *sClass* (source class) that gets encapsulated in the Virtual Extensible LAN (VXLAN) header. Similarly, the destination EPG is represented by a PCTag. So, if an endpoint in the source EPG wants to talk to an endpoint in the destination EPG, ACI uses these PCTags and applies policies instead of using source and destination IP addresses, as in traditional access control lists. The benefit of programing the hardware infrastructure using this method is that you don't need to identify IPv4 and IPv6 access control entities (ACE) separately, which consumes more TCAM space in hardware.

Figure 7-4 illustrates this concept, where an endpoint part of the EPG *client* is communicating with the web server endpoint part of the EPG web. The EPG *client* is assigned the PCTag value 49163, and the EPG *web* is assigned the PCTag value 32776. The zoning rule in ACI, which is equivalent to an access list in traditional networking, clearly shows that the endpoint in the EPG *client* is allowed to talk to the endpoint in the EPG *web*. The endpoints are part of the VRF instance with scope 2949120.

```
Leaf1# show vlan id 3 extended
VLAN     Name                          Encap        Ports
----     ----                          -----        -----
3        t01:prod: client             vlan-1002    Eth1/1, Eth 1/2,

Leaf2# show vlan id 10 extended
VLAN     Name                          Encap        Ports
----     ----                          -----        -----
10       t01:prod:web                 vlan-1008    Eth1/21, Eth1/22,

Leaf1# vsh_lc-c "show system internal eltmc info vlan 3" | egrep sclass
sclass: 49163          : : :                    scope: 2949120
Leaf2# vsh_lc-c "show system internal eltmc info vlan 10" | egrep sclass
sclass: 32776          : : :                    scope: 2949120
```

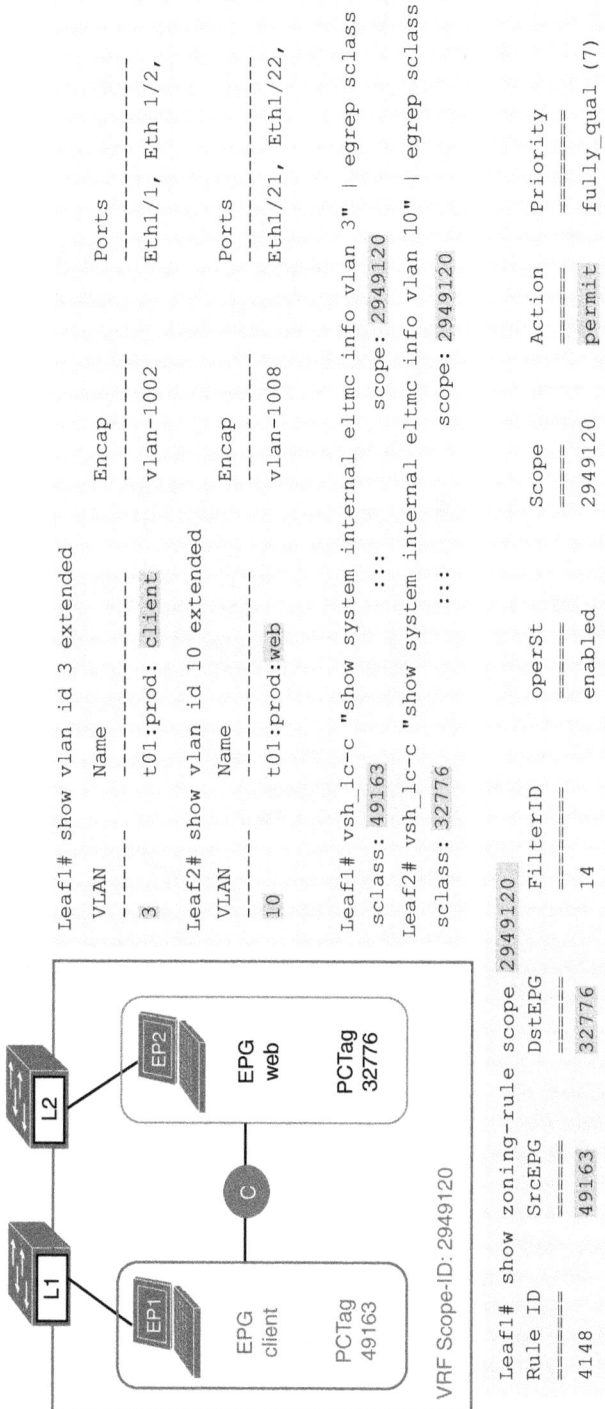

```
VRF Scope-ID: 2949120

Leaf1# show zoning-rule scope 2949120
Rule ID   SrcEPG   DstEPG   FilterID   operSt    Scope     Action   Priority
=======   ======   ======   ========   ======    =====     ======   ========
4148      49163    32776    14         enabled   2949120   permit   fully_qual (7)
```

Figure 7-4 *Policy Enforcement in ACI Using Contracts*

In Figure 7-4, notice that Leaf1 is receiving traffic with encapsulation vlan-1002 on ingress ports Eth1/1 and Eth1/2 bound to the EPG *client*. The APIC allocates an internal VLAN called a platform-independent (PI) VLAN to each EPG and BD that is locally significant to that leaf switch. The PI VLAN is randomly allocated, and it is different on each leaf switch. In this case, for the EPG *client*, the PI VLAN is 3. Similarly, on Leaf2, the PI VLAN on the EPG *web* is 10.

The Shadow EPG

As explained earlier in this chapter, that service graph stitches traffic flow between two application EPGs to a service node by using a contract. The connection to the service node is established by using external and internal interfaces. The external interface is called the consumer connector, and the internal interface is called the provider connector. These interfaces are assigned special EPGs called *shadow EPGs* with VLAN IDs and specific PCTags, as shown in Figure 7-5.

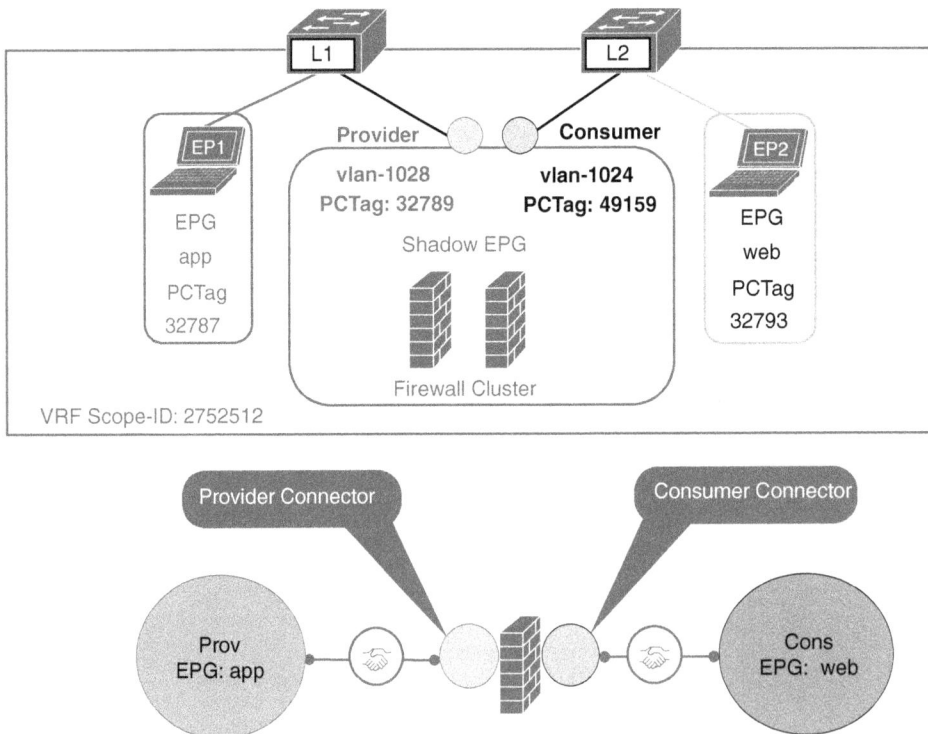

Figure 7-5   *Shadow EPGs and PCTags*

In Figure 7-5, the EPG *app* and the EPG *web* are called *terminal nodes* in the service graph and are connected together with the contracts to the *function node*, which is a firewall in this case. Once connected, traffic between the consumer EPG *web* and the provider EPG *app* of the contract is redirected to the service graph.

Configuring the Service Graph

To configure the service graph in ACI, perform the following steps:

Step 1.   Create an L4–L7 device.

Step 2.   Create a service graph template.

Step 3.   Deploy the service graph from the template.

Step 4.   Configure L4–L7 parameters (Managed mode only).

These configuration steps are explained in the sections that follow.

Step 1: Create an L4–L7 Device

In step 1, you create the L4–L7 device, which involves the following settings (see Figure 7-6):

- Define what kind of L4–L7 device you want to use in your service graph: firewall or load balancer.

- Choose the operation mode: Managed or Un-Managed.

- Enter the object name of the L4–L7 device.

- Select the service type: firewall or ADC.

- Select the device type: physical or virtual.

- Choose the physical or virtual domain.

- Select Single or Multiple Context and the function type (either GoThrough [Transparent mode] or GoTo [Routed mode]).

- Define the internal and external interfaces of the service node and associate it with the physical ports of ACI leafs connecting to the service node.

- Create a cluster interface and assign the VLAN IDs to each of the internal and external interfaces (shadow EPGs).

If Managed mode is used, configure several more configuration parameters, such as choosing the device package, selecting a management network (oob or inb), inserting credentials to access the service node from the APIC, and defining the management IP and port of your service node.

L4-L7 Device Physical Interfaces

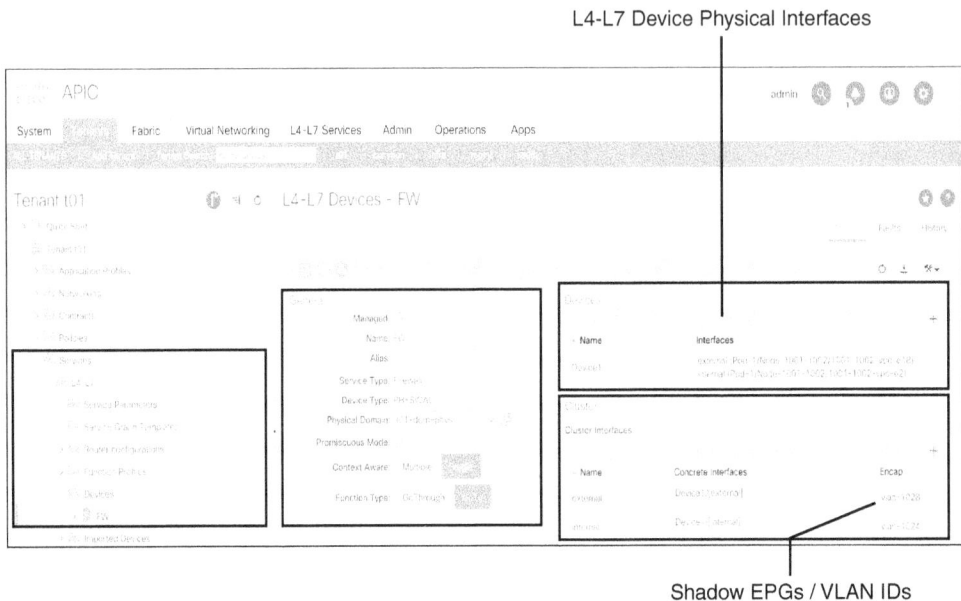

Figure 7-6   *Create L4–L7 Device*

Step 2: Create a Service Graph Template

The service graph template is a representation of expected traffic flow. It defines functional nodes, which are the service type you want to use (firewall or ADC); terminal nodes, which are the application EPGs that want this communication (consumer or provider EPGs); and connections, which refer to service node connectivity (Layer2 or Layer3). The service graph template can be applied to multiple contracts for future use. In step 2, you do the following (see Figure 7-7):

- Enter the object name of the service graph template.

- Drag and drop the L4–L7 device that you created in step 1 between the consumer and provider EPGs.

- In the case of a firewall, select the connection type: routed or transparent. One thing to note here is that with only Routed mode, the Route Redirect option is available for selection. This means the policy-based redirect service graph requires Routed mode.

- In the case of an ADC, choose the mode: one-arm or two-arm.

Step 3: Deploy the Service Graph from the Template

In step 3, you apply the service graph from the template that you created in step 2. This is a two-step process in which you first define the consumer and provider EPGs that require service stitching. You can create a new contract or choose an existing contract subject. Then you define the consumer and provider BDs and choose the cluster interfaces.

Figure 7-8 illustrates this step.

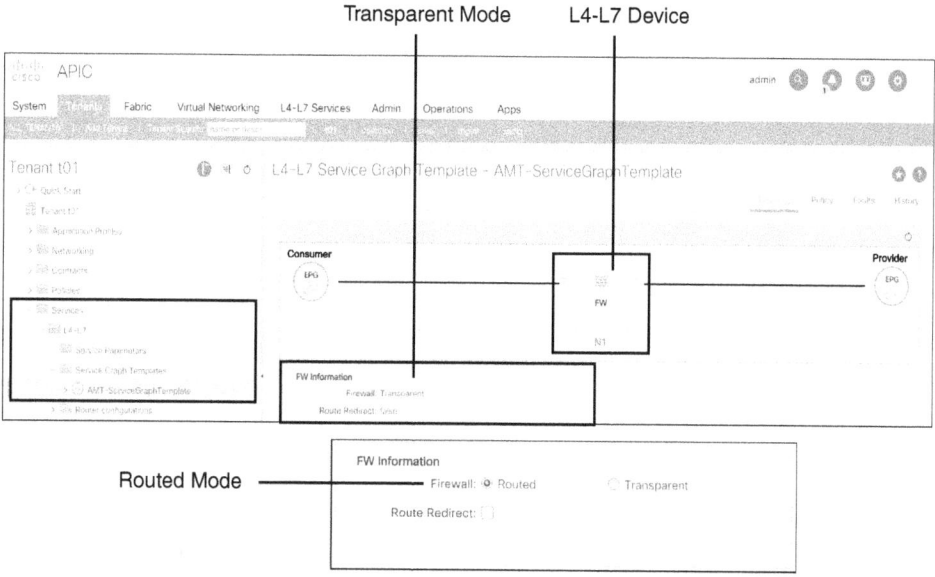

Figure 7-7 *Creating a Service Graph Template*

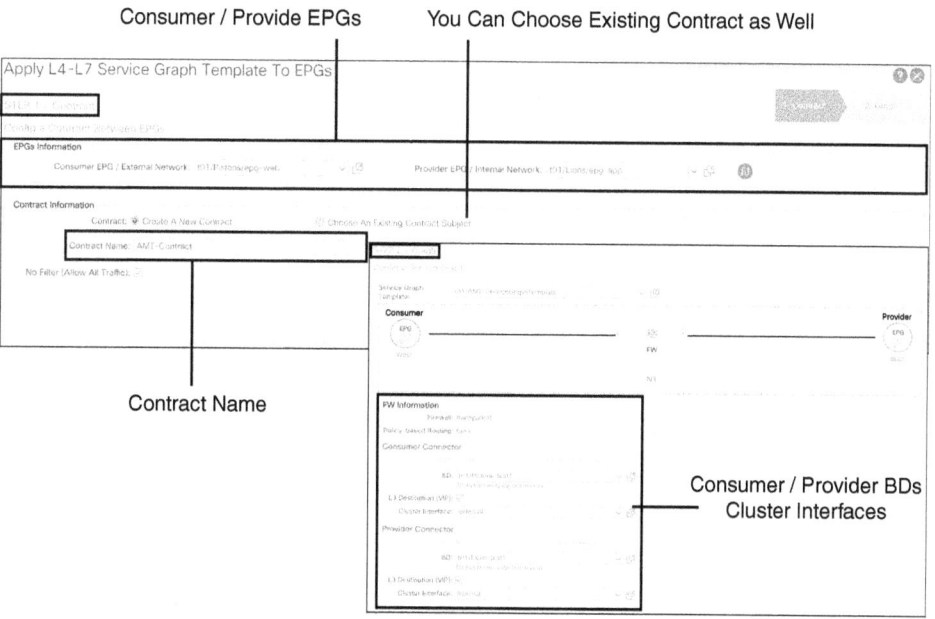

Figure 7-8 *Deploying a Service Graph from a Template*

Step 4: Configure the L4–L7 Parameters (Managed Mode Only)

With Cisco ACI, the provisioning of services is not limited to network connectivity on the Cisco ACI fabric side; it also includes the capability to configure the firewall and the load balancers with all the necessary rules for application security and load balancing needs. This configuration is performed either through REST API calls to the APIC or from the APIC GUI. The configurations required to be pushed to the L4–L7 devices are called *L4–L7 parameters*.

The L4–L7 parameters include the following:

- Interfaces (access ports, port channels)
- Interface IP addresses and subnet masks
- Routing configuration
- Virtual IP (VIP) configuration
- Server farm configuration
- ACL configuration

These parameters do not assign VLANs to physical interfaces and virtual interfaces (vNICs); rather, ACI dynamically allocates them. The device package defines which L4–L7 parameters can be configured from the APIC. The vendor of the firewall or ADC appliance dictates the syntax of these L4–L7 parameters, and this syntax reflects the syntax used by the firewall or ADC administrator when the device is configured.

The configuration of L4–L7 parameters from the APIC can be time-consuming, particularly if you want to decommission a device and redeploy it in a different way. Therefore, Cisco ACI provides the function profile feature, which allows you to define a collection of L4–L7 parameters that you can use when you apply a service graph template. Function profiles can also be prepopulated by the management system of the L4–L7 device vendor.

In Managed mode, the APIC communicates with the L4–L7 device to configure it as part of the rendering of the graph. The APIC communicates with the firewalls or load balancers to render the graph defined by the user. For Cisco ACI to be able to talk to firewalls and load balancers, it needs to speak their language: application programming interfaces (APIs). Therefore, administrators are required to install plug-ins called *device packages* on the APIC to enable this communication and then configure L4–L7 parameters.

Verifying the Service Graph Configuration

To verify the service graph configuration steps, first you check to see if there are any faults associated with this configuration. Then you execute the **show system internal policy-mgr stats** command, as shown in Figure 7-9.

EPG Pistons-Test1
PCTag: 32793

Provider

Shadow EPG Internal
PCTag: 49159

Contract

Shadow EPG External
PCTag: 32789

Consumer

EPG Pistons-Test1
PCTag: 32787

VRF Scope-ID: 2752512

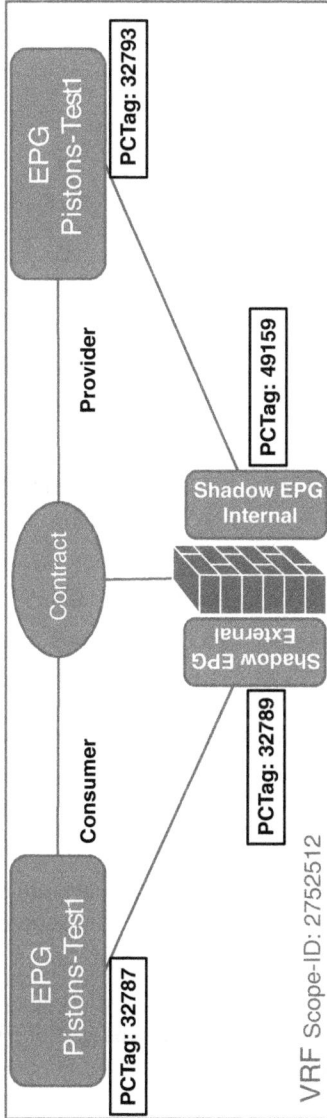

```
Before Service Graph Policy

Leaf1# show system internal policy-mgr stats | grep 2752512 ← VRF Scope ID

Rule (4178) DN (sys/actrl/scope-2752512/rule-2752512-s-32787-d-32793-f-default) Ingress: 0, Egress: 0, Pkts: 8339     RevPkts: 0
Rule (4179) DN (sys/actrl/scope-2752512/rule-2752512-s-32793-d-32787-f-default) Ingress: 0, Egress: 0, Pkts: 14564792  RevPkts: 0
```

```
After Service Graph Policy

Leaf1# show system internal policy-mgr stats | grep 2752512 ← VRF Scope ID

Rule (4180) DN (sys/actrl/scope-2752512/rule-2752512-s-49159-d-32793-f-default) Ingress: 0, Egress: 0, Pkts: 13785728  RevPkts: 0
Rule (4162) DN (sys/actrl/scope-2752512/rule-2752512-s-32787-d-32787-f-default) Ingress: 0, Egress: 0, Pkts: 23366860  RevPkts: 0
```

Figure 7-9 *Service Graph Verification*

Service Graph Design and Deployment Options

When deploying an L4–L7 service graph, you can choose the following deployment methods:

- **Transparent mode:** Deploy the L4–L7 device in Transparent mode when the L4–L7 device is bridging the two bridge domains. In Cisco ACI, this mode is called *Go-Through mode*.

- **Routed mode:** Deploy the L4–L7 device in Routed mode when the L4–L7 device is routing between the two bridge domains. In Cisco ACI, this mode is called *Go-To mode*.

- **One-Arm mode:** Deploy the L4–L7 device in One-Arm mode when a load balancer is located on a dedicated bridge domain with a single interface.

- **Two-Arm mode:** Deploy the L4–L7 device in Two-Arm mode when a load balancer is located on a dedicated bridge domain with two interfaces.

- **Policy-based redirect (PBR):** Deploy the L4–L7 device on a separate bridge domain from the clients or the servers, and redirect traffic to it based on protocol and port number.

The sections that follow provide various service graph design and deployment options that suit different business requirements.

Firewall as Default Gateway for Client and Server (Routed Mode)

In the simplest service graph design, your clients and servers are pointing to your firewall as your default gateway. In this design, you just need BDs without any subnets at all in the same VRF instance. Figure 7-10 shows the recommended settings for these BDs. This kind of design is well suited for a proof-of-concept scenario in a lab to test the service graph feature.

Firewall Not the Default Gateway for Clients (Routed Mode)

While the preceding scenario is simple, it is not always a choice in real production networks. In a real production network, the clients are always on different subnets and locations than the servers.

In this design scenario, you can still use your server to point to the firewall as the default gateway. The other leg of the firewall, toward the client side, can be part of a Layer 3 BD with a subnet, as shown in Figure 7-11. This design does not work until you enable NAT on the external leg of the firewall because the ACI leafs have no clue about the server subnet behind the firewall and hence cannot advertise it out via L3Out toward the client side. Therefore, the client cannot reach the server.

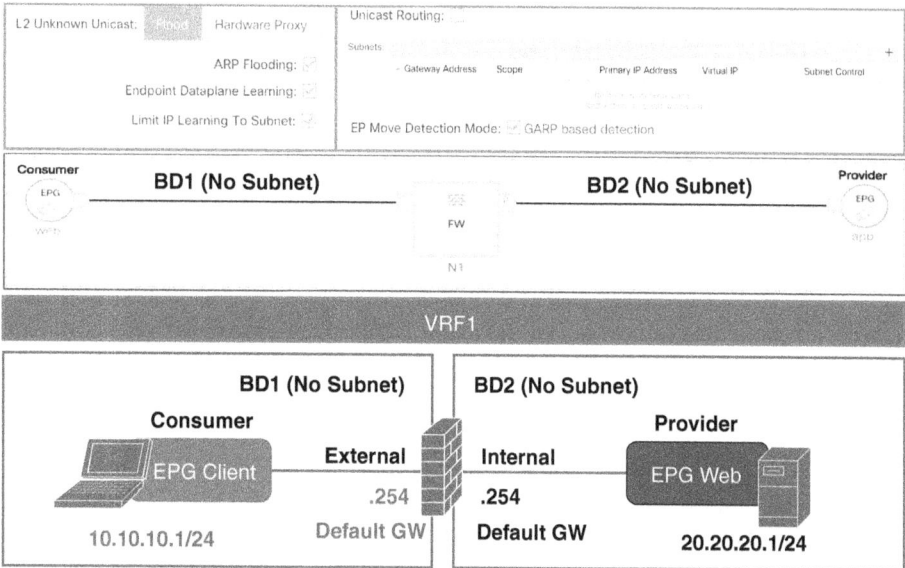

Figure 7-10 *Firewall as Default Gateway in a Service Graph*

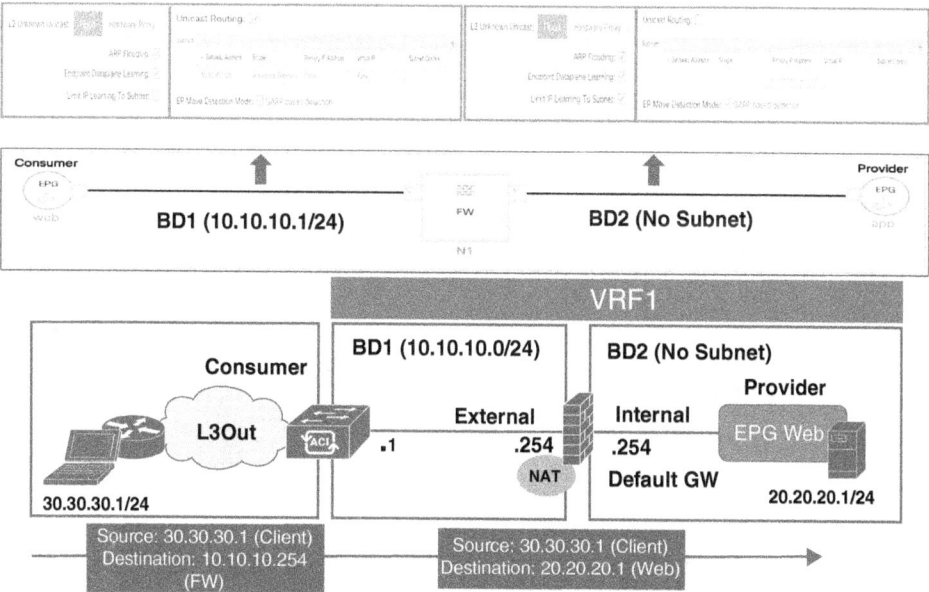

Figure 7-11 *Firewall Not the Default Gateway for Clients (NAT)*

For some operation team members, resolving NAT is a nightmare, especially during failures such as with traffic forwarding issues between client and server with a service device in between (such as a firewall with NAT configured, as in this case). To eliminate NAT and be able to use the design in Figure 7-11, the only option left is to route peer your firewall with the ACI leaf, as shown in Figure 7-12. In that way, you can advertised the server subnet out toward the client side.

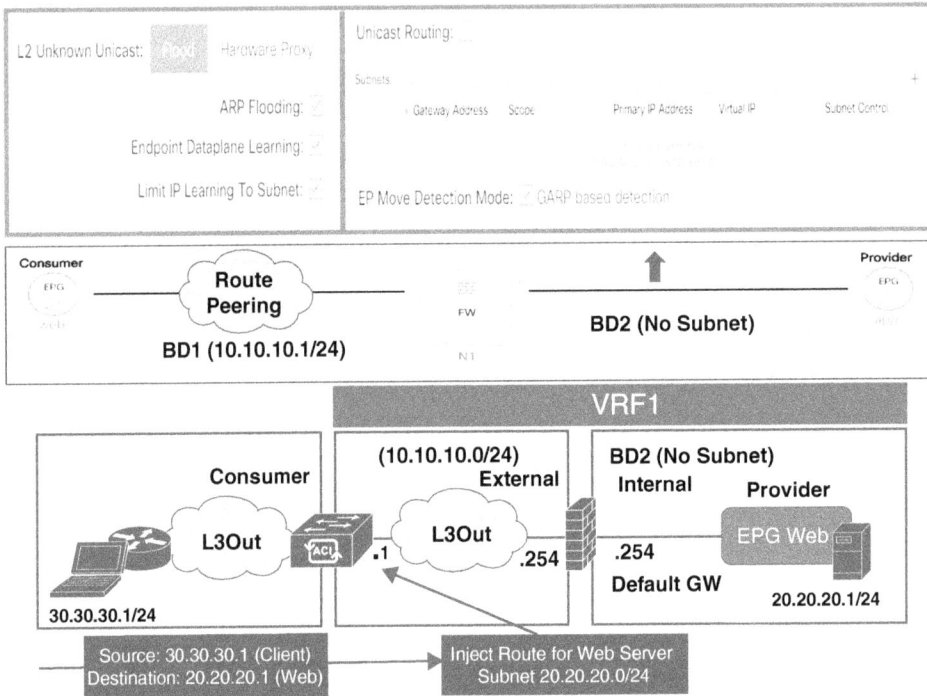

Figure 7-12   *Firewall Not the Default Gateway for Clients (No NAT)*

Route Peering with a Firewall (Routed Mode)

In general security designs, firewalls are placed in different VRF instances for Layer 3 isolation between different security zones, such as the DMZ, and are internal unless you have your firewall acting as a default gateway for your client and server, as in the earlier example. Firewalls are usually connected in Routed mode, which requires either static routes or some sort of route peering with other network devices. If you attach firewalls with a BD and subnet in ACI, the endpoint cannot use the firewall address as the next hop. The endpoint uses the subnet pervasive gateway as its default gateway, whereas a firewall consumes one of the IP addresses in that subnet.

The ACI service graph supports route peering with firewalls. Traffic flows through firewalls, which perform stateful inspection and forward the traffic toward the destination endpoint, as shown in Figure 7-13.

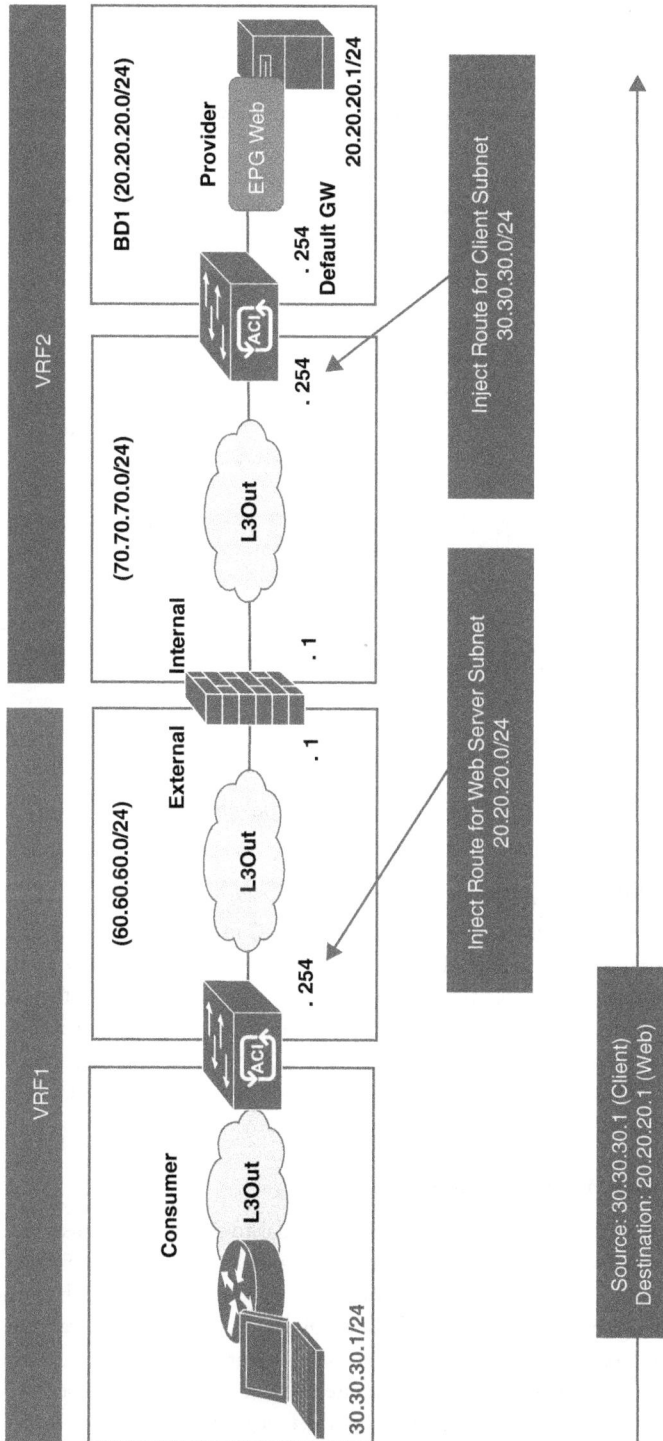

Figure 7-13 *Route Peering Firewall in the Service Graph*

Service Graph with Firewall (Transparent Mode)

In Transparent/Bridge mode, the firewall acts as a Layer 2 device, bridging traffic flows between client and server. This is illustrated in the two examples shown in Figure 7-14; in the first example, the client and server are using the firewall as their gateway, and in the second example, the client is on a different subnet.

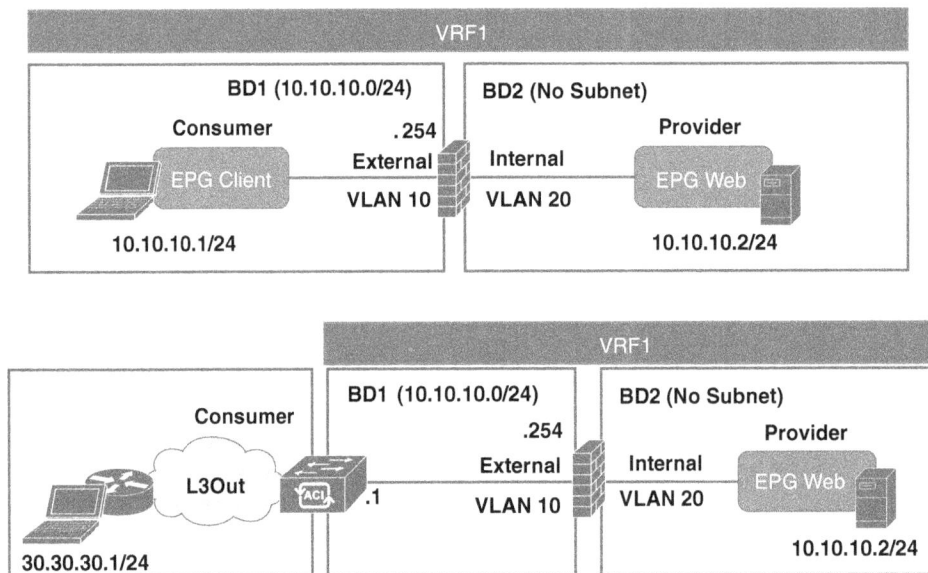

Figure 7-14 *Service Graph with a Firewall in Transparent Mode*

Service Graph with ADC (One-Arm Mode with S-NAT)

When you want to perform a service graph with ADC in One-Arm mode, you need to configure source NAT on the ADC. This brings the return traffic back to the ADC; otherwise, the traffic bypasses the ADC and reaches the client directly through routing. The incoming traffic from the client hitting the VIP is through regular routing, as VIP is advertised out by the ADC, as illustrated in Figure 7-15. To avoid using source NAT, you need to use PBR with the service graph, as explained later in this chapter, in the section "Policy-Based Redirect (PBR)."

Service Graph with ADC (Two-Arm Mode)

A service graph with ADC in two-arm mode is similar to the design of a service graph with the firewall being the default gateway of the client and server, as shown in Figure 7-16. The BDs do not need to have subnets unless you want to use the service graph feature Dynamic Attach Endpoint. This feature gives you the capability to dynamically attach an endpoint as part of your server pool as soon as the endpoint is learned by the fabric. Also with Dynamic Attach Endpoint, in order to do route peering with ADC, you need to install the device package for routing exchange between the fabric and the ADC.

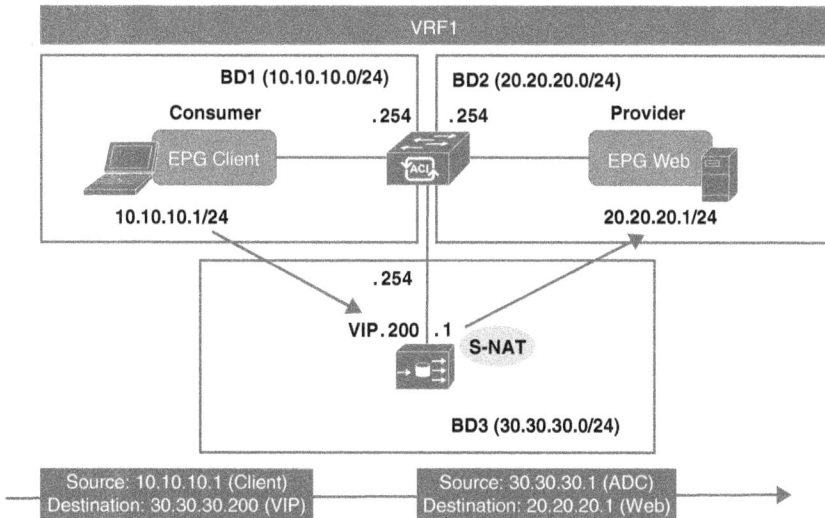

Figure 7-15 *Service Graph with ADC in One-Arm Mode*

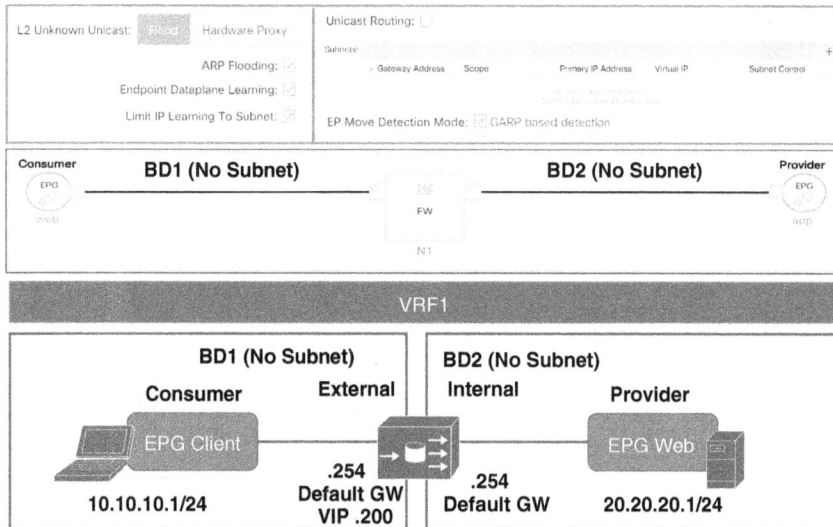

Figure 7-16 *Service Graph with ADC in Two-Arm Mode*

Service Graph with Two Service Nodes (Firewall with NAT and ADC in Two-Arm Mode)

With this service graph design, you can have two service nodes, such as a firewall and an ADC in Two-Arm mode. The ADC can be your server default gateway; otherwise, you need to enable source NAT on the ADC. The firewall needs NAT, as the ACI leaf does not know about the web server VIP behind the firewall. Figure 7-17 illustrates this design.

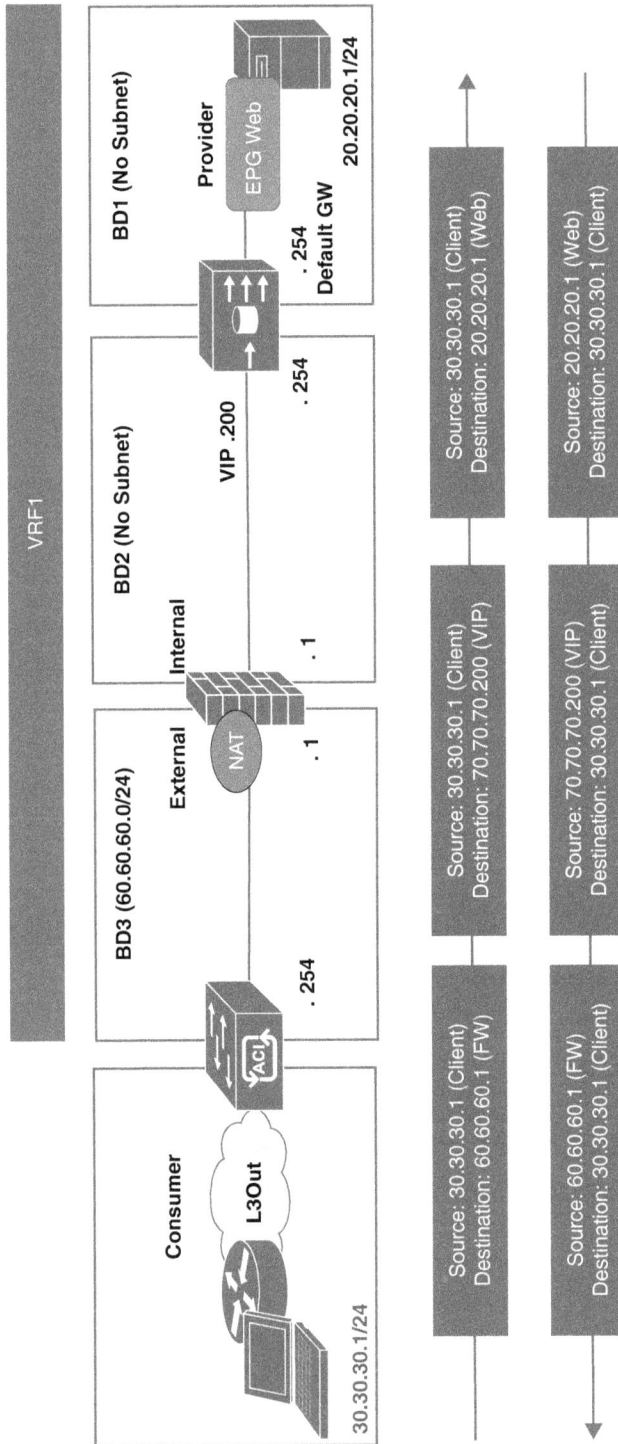

Figure 7-17   *Service Graph with Two Service Nodes (Firewall with NAT and ADC in Two-Arm Mode)*

Service Graph with Two Service Nodes (Firewall with No NAT and ADC in Two-Arm Mode)

With this service graph design, you can have two service nodes, such as a firewall and an ADC in Two-Arm mode. The ADC can be your server default gateway; otherwise, you need to enable source NAT on the ADC. The firewall does not need NAT because it is route peering with the ACI leaf that will reach the VIP behind the firewall through regular routing. Figure 7-18 illustrates this design.

Service Graph with Two Service Nodes (Firewall with No NAT and ADC in One-Arm Mode)

With this service graph design, you can have two service nodes, such as a firewall and an ADC in One-Arm mode. The ADC can be your server default gateway; otherwise, you need to enable source NAT on the ADC. The firewall does not need NAT because it is route peering with the ACI leaf that will reach the VIP behind the firewall through regular routing. The only thing you need to consider is that you need two VRF instances instead of just one because the return traffic is not going through a firewall. ACI fabric in VRF1 knows the client subnet as the direct connect route. Figure 7-19 illustrates this design.

Service Graph with an Intrusion Prevention System (IPS)

For IPS service integration, you can use a service graph in Un-Managed mode only. At this writing, there is no device package available for IPS in service graph Managed mode for device-level configuration. When connecting IPS with a service graph in Un-Managed mode, you need to ensure that the IPS device connects to two different leafs because each leg of the IPS device uses the same encapsulation VLAN to pass Layer 1 traffic, and the service graph in Un-Managed mode does not support per-port VLANs. Figure 7-20 illustrates this design.

For IPS integration, you can also use the Copy Service feature of the service graph. Copy Service is similar to SPAN, in that traffic gets copied and sent over to the service node, such as an IPS. With SPAN configuration, all traffic gets copied and sent to the SPAN destination. On the other hand, with the service graph Copy Service feature, only specific traffic can be copied and stitched to the service node. To use the Copy Service feature for the service graph, you need to create the copy device.

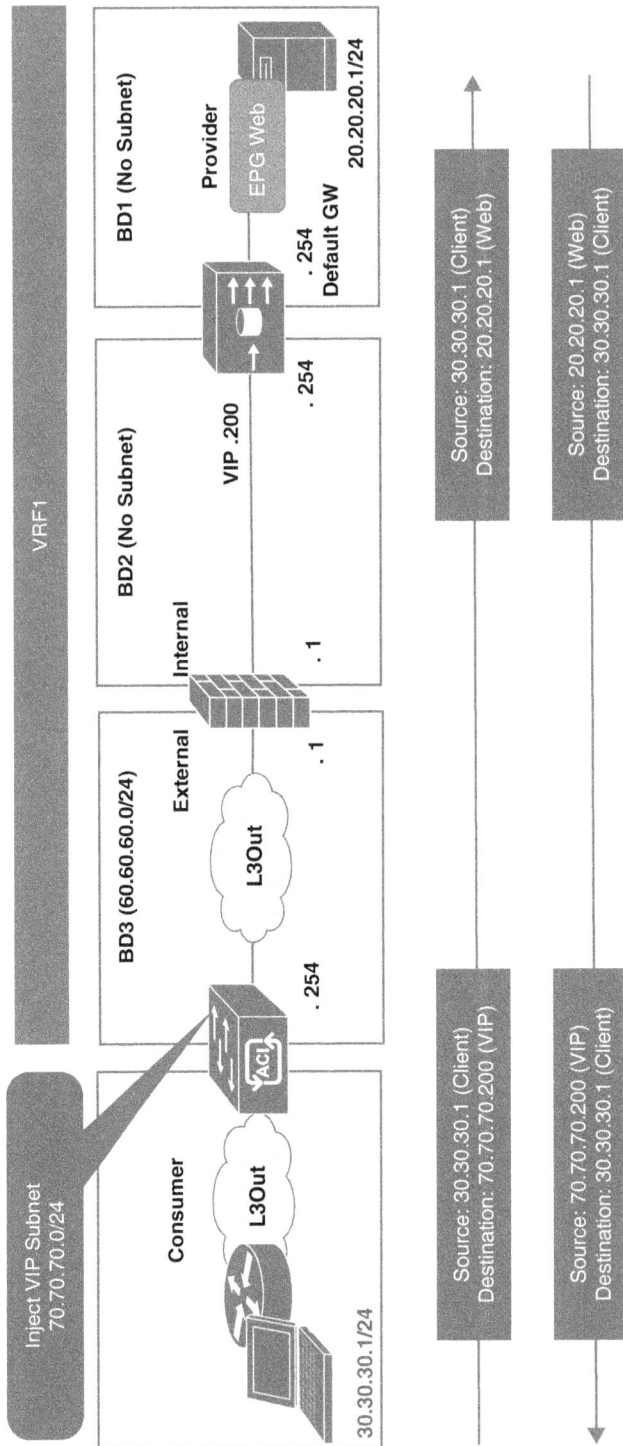

Figure 7-18 *Service Graph with Two Service Nodes (Firewall with No NAT and ADC in Two-Arm Mode)*

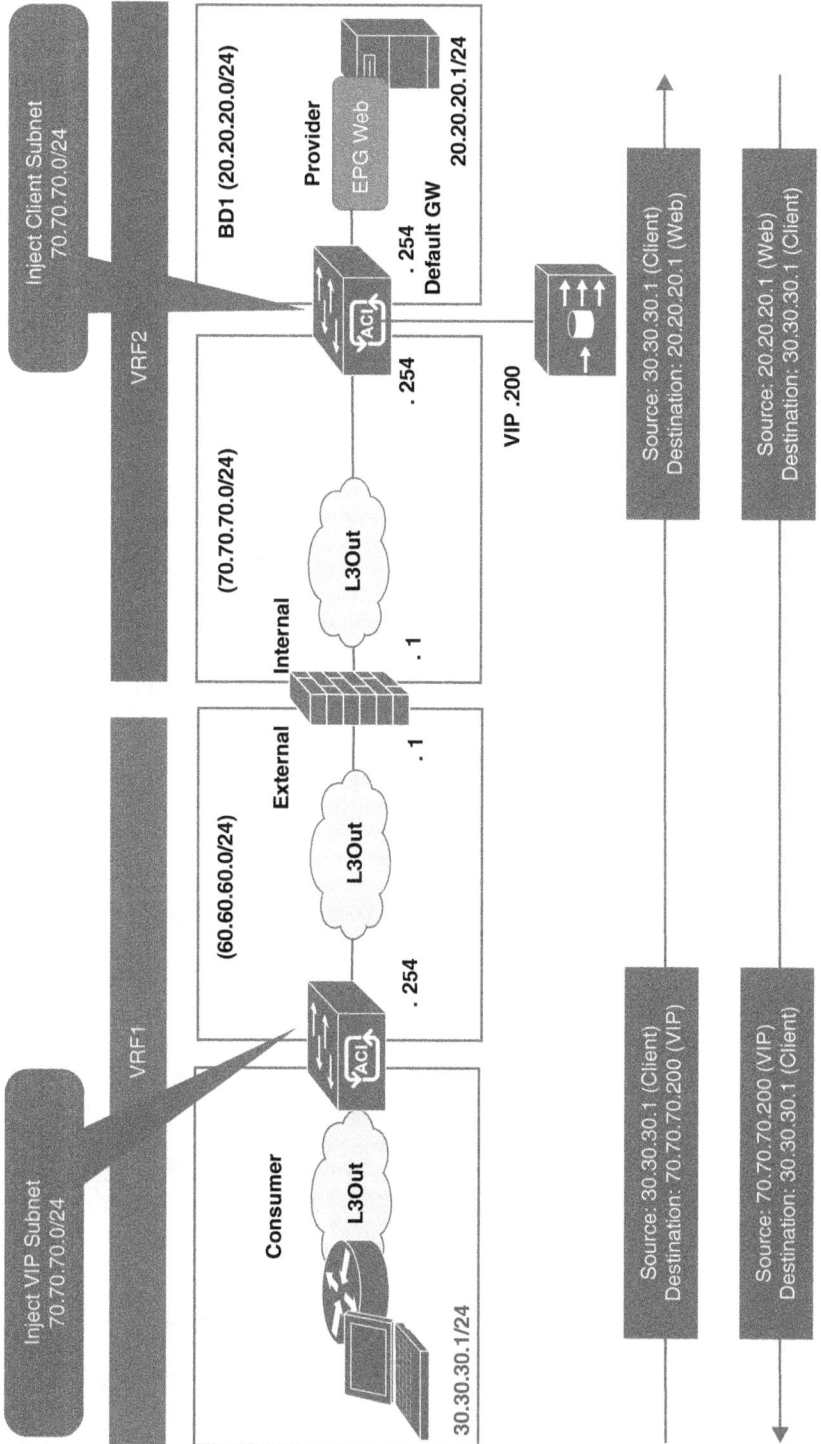

Figure 7-19 *Service Graph with Two Service Nodes (Firewall with No NAT and ADC in One-Arm Mode)*

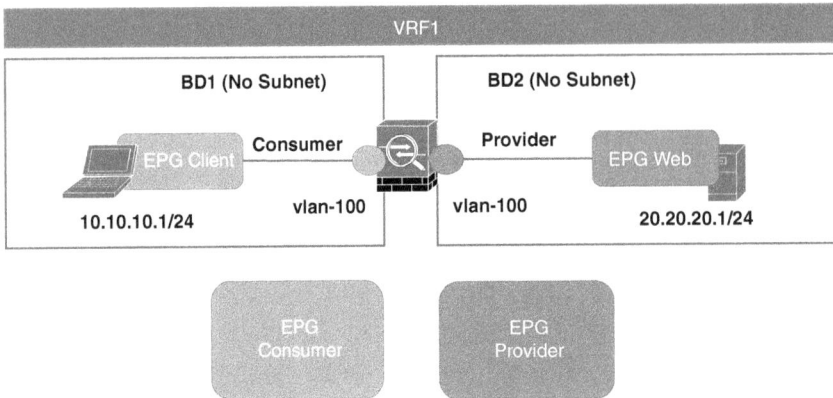

Figure 7-20 *Service Graph with IPS*

Policy-Based Redirect (PBR)

The ACI L4–L7 policy-based redirect (PBR) concept (see Figure 7-21) is similar to policy-based routing in traditional networking. Policy-based routing in traditional networking was a method to classify the traffic and steer that desired traffic from its actual path to a network device as the next-hop route (NHR). The feature was used in networking for decades to redirect traffic to service devices such as firewalls, load balancers, IPSs/IDSs, and Wide Area Application Services (WAAS). In ACI, the PBR concept is similar: You classify certain traffic to steer to service node by using a subject in a contract. Other traffic follows the regular forwarding path, using another subject in the same contract without the PBR policy applied.

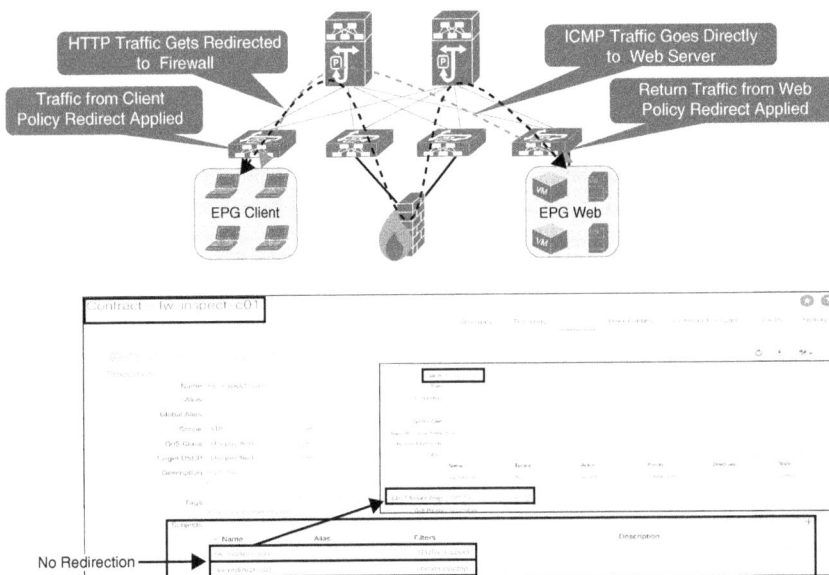

Figure 7-21 *Policy-Based Redirect*

PBR is available in ACI Release 2.0(1m) and later. Before PBR, all the traffic forwarding decisions in ACI were based on IP or MAC addresses. With the PBR feature, you have the leverage to steer certain desired traffic off-path and redirect to a service node by using a subject in a contract.

PBR Design Considerations

When using PBR, you need to consider the following:

■ The service node has to be connected to a BD called Service BD with a subnet. Unicast Routing should be enabled. The subnet can be private to a VRF instance or advertised externally, depending on the use case. For example, some customers use external monitoring tools to constantly ping the service node interface for availability. However, PBR does offer the tracking and probing capabilities discussed later in this section. In PBR, the service node cannot be connected via L3Out.

■ Endpoint Dataplane Learning *must* be disabled on service BDs in PBR. In ACI, endpoints are learned not only via ARP but also through conversational learning in the data plane. With PBR, because traffic is steered toward the service nodes, you do not want the same source endpoint that is learned via an ACI leaf to be learned via the service node.

■ Service nodes cannot be connected to first-generation leafs if either the source or the destination endpoint is also connected to the same leaf. In this situation, you need to connect your service nodes to dedicated leafs. This restriction does not apply in second-generation (cloud-scale) leafs.

Note   First-generation leafs are Nexus 9300 leaf switches such as N9K-9372PX, N9K-93128TX, and N9K-9332PQ with dual ASICs. One of the ASIC is the Broadcom merchant silicon chip for front panel downlink ports connecting end hosts, and the other one is the Cisco-branded Northstar ASIC for uplink fabric nodes connectivity. First-generation leafs are being phased out and are therefore not part of the book's focus.

■ In the case of active/standby service node deployment, you should assign the same virtual MAC address. This process is called *MAC masquerade*.

■ Only the Routed mode of deploying the service node is supported with PBR.

■ The PBR service graph supports both Managed and Un-Managed service device modes.

■ PBR can only be enabled on one node in a multi-node service graph.

PBR Design Scenarios

The following sections provide a few design scenarios for using the PBR service graph.

PBR Service Graph with an ADC (One-Arm Mode and No S-NAT)

As mentioned earlier, whenever you want to use the service graph with ADC in One-Arm mode, you need to configure source NAT on the ADC. This brings the return traffic back to the ADC; otherwise, the traffic bypasses the ADC and reaches the client directly through routing. The incoming traffic from the client hitting the VIP occurs through regular routing because the VIP is advertised by the ADC. To avoid using source NAT, you need to use PBR with the service graph that takes care of return traffic. Figure 7-22 illustrates this design.

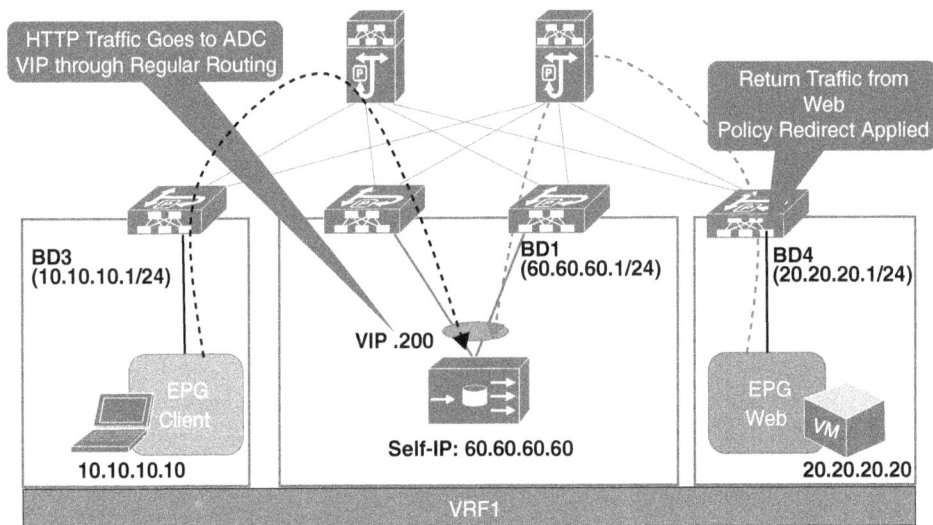

Figure 7-22   *PBR Service Graph with an ADC in One-Arm Mode*

PBR Service Graph with a Firewall (Two-Arm Mode and Routed)

There could be a situation in which you do not want your client and server to point their default gateway to your firewall. In this case, your client and server are placed in different subnets, and you want your HTTP traffic from the client toward the web server to be redirected to the firewall for screening, and management traffic such as SSH should flow directly toward the web server. This can be done using the PBR service graph in Two-Arm Routed mode, as shown in Figure 7-23. You can also achieve this task by using One-Arm Routed mode.

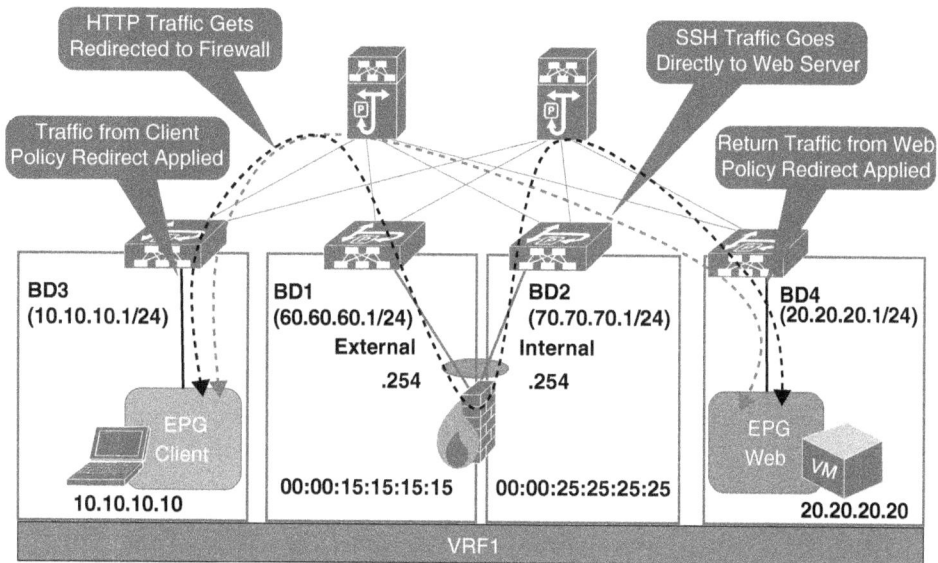

Figure 7-23 *PBR Service Graph with a Firewall in Two-Arm Mode*

Configuring the PBR Service Graph

The steps to configure the PBR service graph are quite similar to the regular service graph configuration steps described earlier in this chapter, in the section "Configuring the Service Graph," with few additional considerations:

- PBR requires the services BD with the subnet as internal and external interfaces of the service node. You need to create the services BD with the settings shown in Figure 7-24. Note that Endpoint Dataplane Learning is disabled for the services BD in PBR.

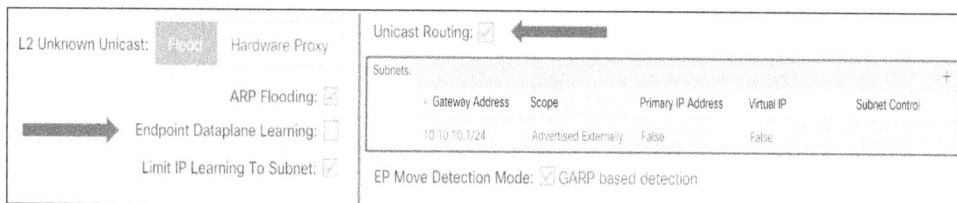

Figure 7-24 *Services BD Settings*

- While configuring the service graph template, you need to select the Route Redirect tab to use PBR feature, as shown in Figure 7-25.

FW Information

           Firewall: ◉ Routed   ◯ Transparent

   Route Redirect: ☑

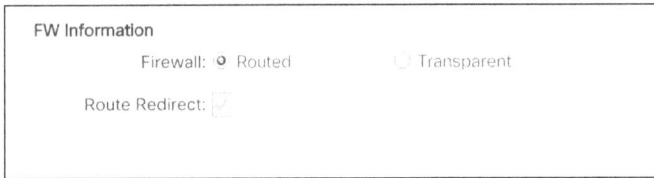

Figure 7-25 *PBR Service Graph Setting*

Service Node Health Check

In PBR, it is important to ensure that your service node is available. This is because you are dictating that the regular traffic flow be redirected to the service node through ACI policy. If the service node is not available, the fabric will have no place to forward the traffic and hence may drop the packet if other necessary measurements are not taken care of, as explained in the sections that follow.

L4–L7 PBR Tracking

When you enable L4–L7 PBR Tracking, the leaf through which the service node(s) is connected tracks its availability by using the IP SLA monitoring policy. The leaf switch periodically probes the service node(s) connected to it to check for availability. If for some reason the service node loses connectivity to the leaf switch or is not available (that is, is down), the leaf switch informs all the other fabric leaf switches not to redirect the traffic toward it. In case of service node redundancy using either clustering or active/standby mode techniques, losing one service node does not disrupt the service as other service nodes take over and start serving the application traffic flows.

To configure the L4–L7 PBR Tracking feature, you need to go to Tenant > user-tenant > Policies > Protocol > L4–L7 Policy Based Redirect and right-click to create the PBR policy. While creating this policy, you can create an IP SLA monitoring policy as well. Figure 7-26 illustrates this process.

L4–L7 PBR Threshold

Firewalls provide clustering capabilities for better throughput and efficient convergence during failures. Say that you have a firewall cluster with two service nodes, based on your throughput requirements. If one of the firewalls goes down, it reduces the overall throughput to half. Of course, firewall clustering seamlessly transfers the load to the other working firewall, but overall, throughput of services is impacted. In that case, ACI offers you a choice to stop redirecting the traffic and forward it through the regular path to continue service or deny the traffic altogether for security reasons.

To configure the L4–L7 PBR Threshold feature, you need to go to Tenant > *user-tenant* > Policies > Protocol > L4–L7 Policy Based Redirect and right-click to create the PBR policy. Enable Threshold, define the minimum and maximum Threshold values, and select the Threshold action (forward traffic normally or deny and drop it). Figure 7-27 illustrates this process.

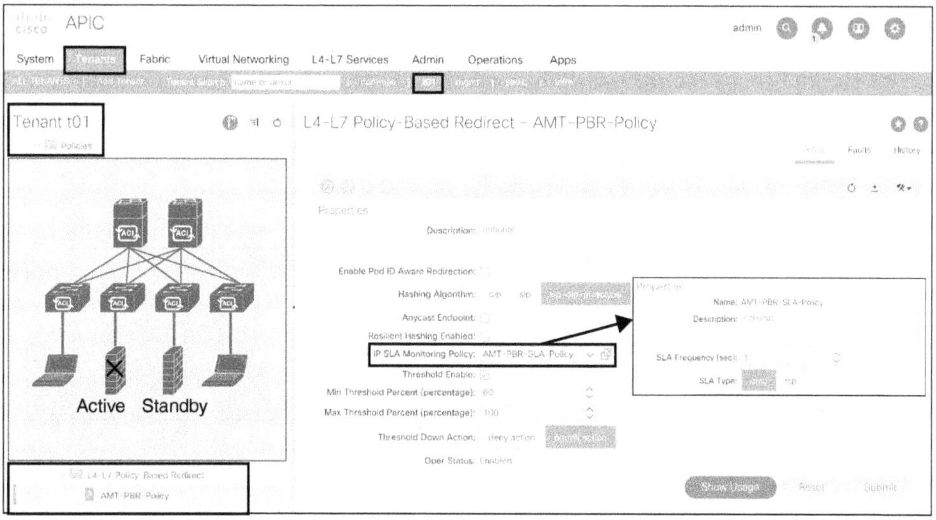

Figure 7-26 *Service Node Tracking*

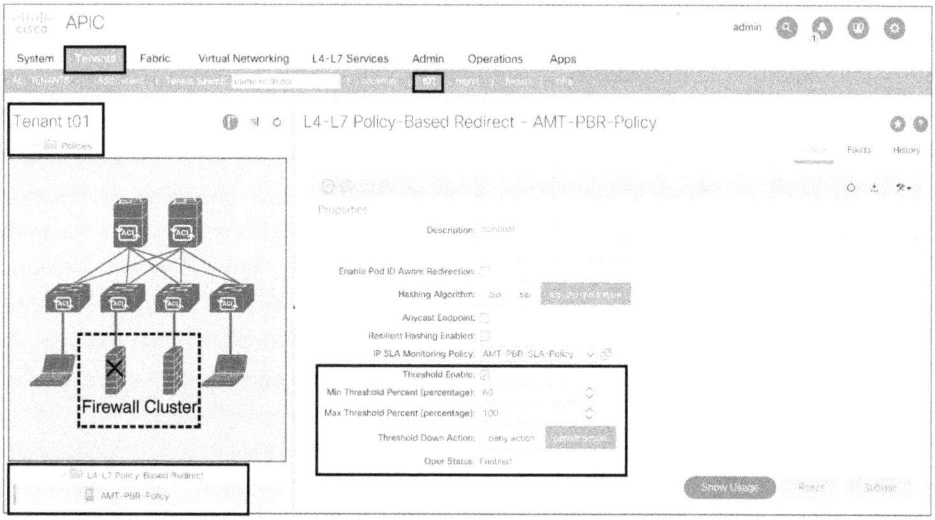

Figure 7-27 *Service Node Threshold*

L4–L7 PBR Health Groups

The L4–L7 PBR Health Groups feature helps you in Two-Arm mode service node deployments in which one interface is dedicated to internal traffic flows and the other interface is for external traffic flows. Suppose that one of the interfaces is down. In that case, you do not want the other leg of the traffic to be redirected to the service node. That is why you group those services BD interfaces together. To configure the L4–L7 PBR Health Groups feature, you need to go to Tenant > *user-tenant* > Policies > Protocol > L4–L7 PBR Health Groups and right-click to create the policy. In the L4–L7 redirect policy where you have defined the IP addresses of both internal and external interfaces of the services BD, attach the health groups policy. Figure 7-28 illustrates this process.

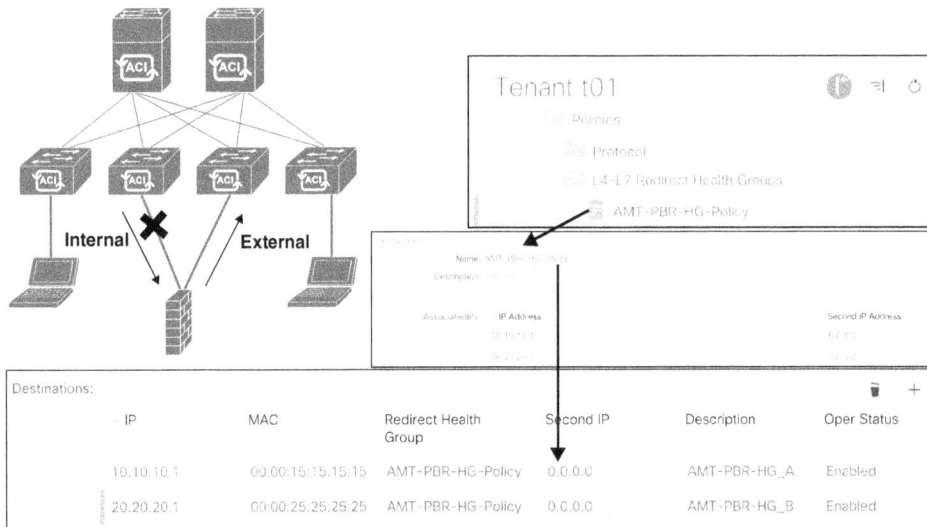

Figure 7-28   *Service Node Health Group*

Common Issues in the PBR Service Graph

Some of the common issues in the PBR service graph that you need to understand and remember are as follows:

- Unnecessary Layer 2 traffic redirection toward the service node
- Inability to ping the consumer connecter
- Routing on the service node

The following sections provide details on each of these common issues in the PBR service graph.

Unnecessary Layer 2 Traffic Redirection Toward the Service Node

As you have learned by now, the PBR service graph is executed using a subject in a contract. In the event that a service node is a firewall, the intention is to redirect traffic toward the firewall for security enforcement rather than to apply a specific filter on the subject used for traffic redirection in the ACI service graph. This leads to unintentional use of the default contract for the *common* tenant, which allows everything, causing Layer 2 forwarding issues (in some cases VPC links flaps between leaf and end host due to LACP PDUs) being redirected to service node. Similarly, you do not want ARP, CDP, LLDP, and other Layer 2 traffic to be unnecessarily redirected toward the service node. The PBR service graph is used to redirect IP or Layer 3 traffic only. Therefore, it is important to specify a filter in the subject with a minimum of **permit ip an any**, as shown in Figure 7-29.

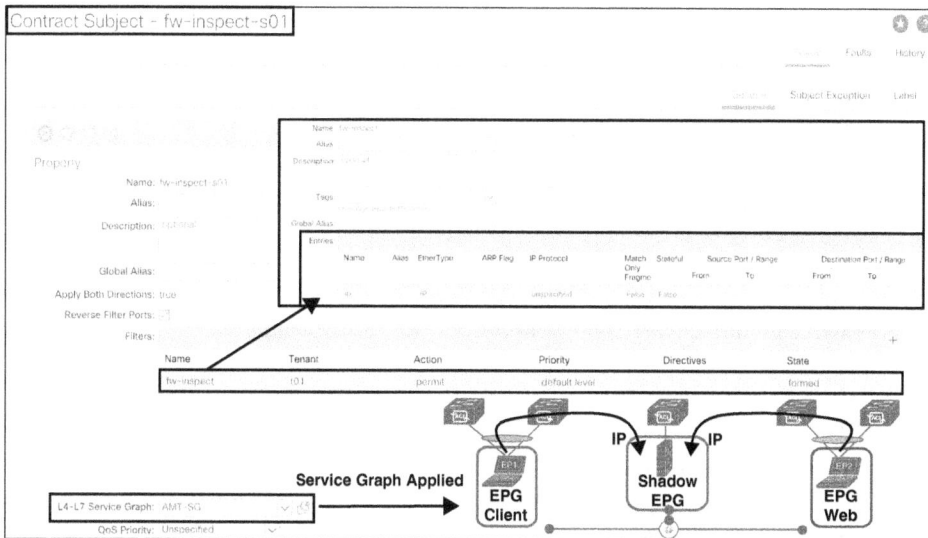

Figure 7-29 *PBR Service Graph Minimum Required Filter*

Inability to Ping the Consumer Connector

Customers always want to ensure that their service nodes are alive by running some sort of constant probing. This is achieved either by leveraging the L4–L7 PBR Tracking feature or using an outside monitoring tool to constantly ping the service node consumer connector (that is, the shadow EPG) IP addresses. With the PBR service graph, by default ACI does not allow this direct communication from either the consumer or provider side toward the service node shadow EPGs. The filter between a shadow EPG and a consumer or provider is unidirectional by default. The purpose of the PBR service graph is to redirect traffic from the consumer to provider EPG toward a service node. To be able to probe the consumer connector from client side, you need to enable Direct Connect on the service graph template, which you can then use to apply the PBR service graph, as illustrated in Figure 7-30.

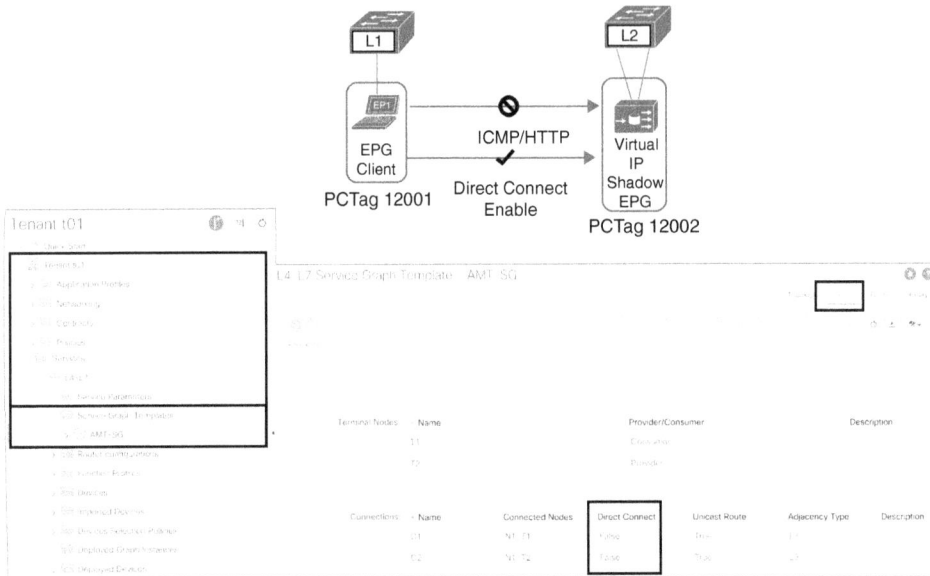

Figure 7-30 *Enabling Direct Connect in the Service Graph Template*

Routing on a Service Node

You might come across a situation in which an engineer has configured routes on a service node to send all the traffic out toward the consumer connecter or the outside interface. This might lead to an issue if the traffic is destined toward the provider EPG via the provider connector or inside interface. This happens because the fabric does not have a contract between the consumer connector and provider EPG. This issue cannot be fixed by enabling Direct Connect in the service graph template.

One solution is to create a One-Arm mode PBR service graph policy in which on your service node you define a default route that points to the anycast gateway IP address of the service BD residing on the leaf to which the service node is connected. The benefit of using this design is that it gives you the capability of redirecting traffic to the service node—which we'll say in this case is a firewall. The firewall, upon receiving traffic, decides based on its security rules to either permit or deny the traffic and return the traffic to the ACI fabric, which then forwards it based on its policy. Figure 7-31 illustrates this process.

L2 — Shadow EPG 12003 12004

L1 — EP1 EPG Web 12002 / EP1 EPG Client 12001

L2 — Shadow EPG 12003

L1 — EP1 EPG Web 12002 / EP1 EPG Client 12001

```
fw# show route
Codes: L - local, C - connected, S - static, R - RIP, M - mobile, B - BGP
       D - EIGRP, EX - EIGRP external, O - OSPF, IA - OSPF inter area
       N1 - OSPF NSSA external type 1, N2 - OSPF NSSA external type 2
       E1 - OSPF external type 1, E2 - OSPF external type 2, V - VPN
Gateway of last resort is 200.100.60.1 to network 0.0.0.0

S*    0.0.0.0 0.0.0.0 [1/0] via 200.100.60.1, inside
S     172.18.1.0 255.255.255.0 [1/0] via 200.100.50.1, outside
S     172.18.2.0 255.255.255.0 [1/0] via 200.100.50.1, outside
```

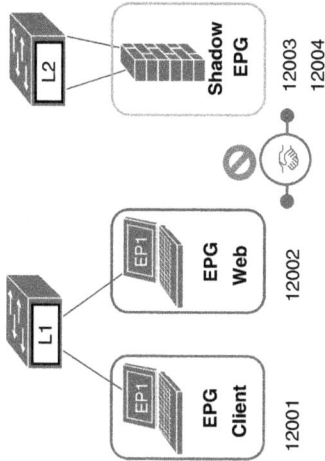

With One Arm-Mode Only Default Route Needed to Point Back to Fabric

```
fw # show route
Codes: L - local, C - connected, S - static, R - RIP, M - mobile, B - BGP
Gateway of last resort is 200.100.60.1 to network 0.0.0.0

S*    0.0.0.0 0.0.0.0 [1/0] via 200.100.60.1, inside
```

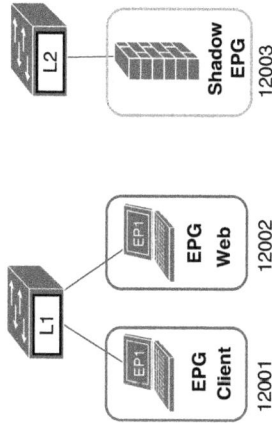

```
Leaf 1# show zoning-rule scope 2561263
```

Rule ID	SrcEPG	DstEPG	FilterID	Dir	operSt	Scope	Name	Action	Priority
4269	12003	12001	16	uni-dir	enabled	2561263		permit	fully_qual(7)
4561	12001	12002	15	bi-dir	enabled	2561263		redir(destgrp-24)	fully_qual(7)
4537	12002	12001	16	uni-dir-ignore	enabled	2561263		redir(destgrp-24)	fully_qual(7)
4536	12003	12002	default	uni-dir	enabled	2561263		permit	src_dst_any(9)

Figure 7-31 *Routing on the Service Node*

L4/L7 Service Integration in Multi-Pod and Multi-Site

As explained earlier, the integration of network services with ACI can be done in multiple ways, such as the following:

- Using service insertion

- Using the service graph in Un-Managed mode

- Using service graph in Managed mode

- Using service graph in Hybrid mode

- Using service graph with PBR mode

The decision of which approach to follow depends on several factors, such as operational model choice and availability of a device package for the service device of your choice.

Let's now discuss the various design scenarios for integrating service nodes in multi-pod and multi-site environments.

Multi-Pod

As explained in detail in Chapter 4, "ACI Fabric Design Options," Cisco ACI multi-pod is a design option that evolved from the stretch fabric design using transit leafs. Multi-pod provides a more efficient way of extending a single ACI fabric into multiple pods with complete isolation of the control plane and data plane between pods. Starting from Cisco ACI Release 3.2(2), the deployment options available for integrating L4–L7 service nodes with Cisco ACI multi-pod are as follows:

- **Active/standby load balancer pair stretched across pods:** This deployment model can be applied to both north–south and east–west traffic flows between pods. Since the active service node is only on one side in Pod 1, this option has certain traffic-path inefficiencies as by design some traffic flows will hair-pin across the inter-pod network (IPN). Therefore, it is important to ensure that you have proper bandwidth available across pods and consider the possible latency impact on application components (such as application hosts) connected to separate pods. The active/standby model is supported with service nodes deployed in Layer2 Bridged mode or Layer3 Routed mode. In Routed mode, both the border leaf nodes and the GOLF router options are supported for L3Out connectivity.

Note   In the case of a firewall service node, the traffic path must be symmetric, or else it could lead to communication drops on the firewall.

- **Active/active firewall cluster stretched across pods:** Using firewall clusters is an efficient way then to deploy active/standby service nodes. This is because they provide better convergence and do not impact service during failures. Starting with ACI

Release 3.2(1), an active/active firewall cluster can be stretched across pods. Firewall clustering can be achieved on both physical Cisco ASA and Firepower appliances. Virtual firewalls are not supported with firewall clustering. This deployment model, which is referred to as *split spanned EtherChannel*, ensures that all the nodes of the cluster own the same MAC/IP address values. The stretched firewall cluster therefore appears as a single logical entity to the entire ACI multi-pod fabric. This deployment model eliminates any concern of asymmetric traffic paths for both north–south and east–west traffic flows. With firewall clustering, the connection states of flows are synced between firewalls; therefore, the return traffic is always sent to the firewall that received the initial packet of the traffic flow and established the connection state.

- **Separate active/standby firewall pair in each pod:** This model mandates that symmetric traffic flows through each of these separate active/standby service node pairs be maintained because the connection state is not synchronized between them. This is a critical requirement to avoid any connection drops and can be achieved with the following approaches:

  - You can deploy PBR for both north–south and east–west security policy enforcement to achieve traffic symmetry. Using PBR is the recommended solution because it can include multiple active service node pairs in the policy. ACI cloud-scale leaf switches that support PBR would then apply the symmetric PBR policy, selecting one of the available service node for the two directions of each given traffic flow, based on hashing.

  - To achieve traffic flow symmetry, PBR mandates that the service nodes be deployed in Routed mode only. This model can use border leaf nodes or GOLF nodes for external Layer 3 connectivity.

If deployment of PBR is not possible, such as in the specific case of perimeter-screening firewall deployments (requiring only north–south traffic flows), granular host route advertisement toward the external Layer 3 domain should be enabled to ensure that ingress traffic paths are always delivered in the right pod, where the destination endpoint is connected. Up until ACI Release 3.x, host route advertisement is supported only on GOLF L3Out connections. Firewall service nodes can then be deployed in Routed mode and must be physically connected northbound of the GOLF routers to apply security policy on the traffic when it is not encapsulated by VXLAN.

Note Support for host route advertisement is extended to regular L3Outs deployed on border leafs from ACI Release 4.0 onward. This enables the connection of screening firewall nodes deployed in Routed mode between the border leafs and the external WAN edge routers.

Figure 7-32 illustrates the deployment options for L4–L7 in multi-pod.

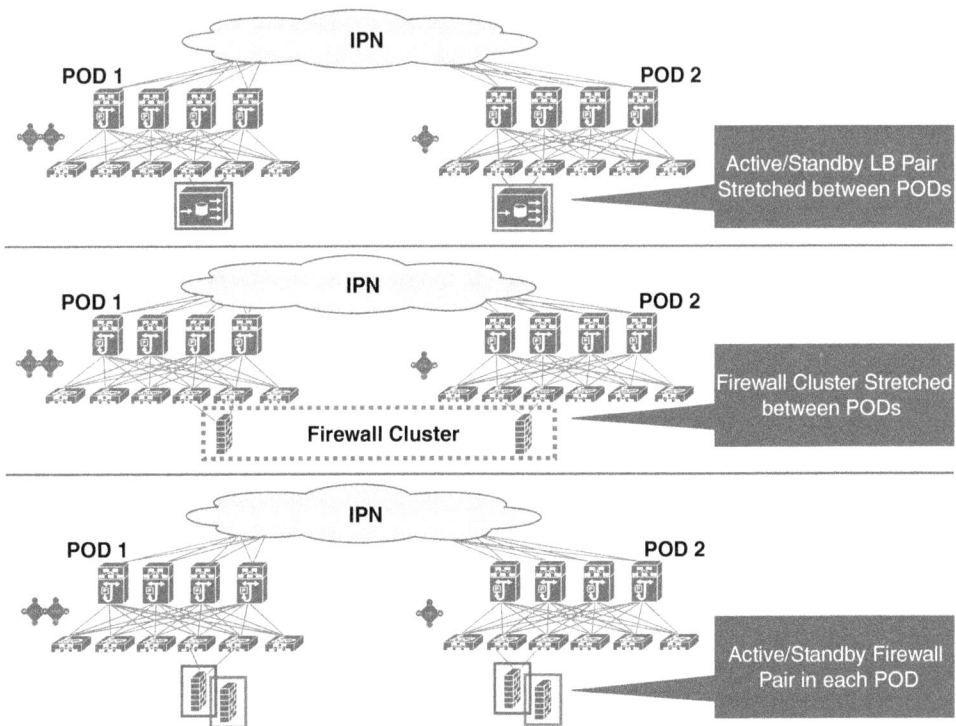

Figure 7-32 *L4–L7 Services Deployment in Multi-pod*

Anycast Services in Multi-Pod

By using anycast services in the data center, an enterprise can deploy an active/active service in a single ACI fabric stretched between multiple pods. ACI started supporting anycast services with ACI Release 3.2(1). However, the anycast services using the PBR service graph have been supported since Release 3.2(4). Anycast services are supported only from the cloud-scale (EX/FX) leaf platform and cannot be executed on legacy first-generation hardware. With anycast services, a single IP and MAC address is floated between multiple service nodes to provide active/active service availability throughout the fabric.

Anycast services in multi-pod provide the advantage of maintaining traffic symmetry within each pod. In a multi-pod deployment with anycast services, each leaf through which L4–L7 devices are connected in a pod installs the anycast MAC and IP addresses as a proxy route to the spine in that pod. This means that if the anycast services have been learned on a leaf located in Pod 1, then COOP installs the entry on the spine to point to the service node that is local to Pod 1. The same goes for anycast services deployed in Pod 2. The spines located in the opposite pods receive the route information for the anycast service through BGP-EVPN over the IPN. With anycast services in multi-pod, all local service nodes (which are members of one service) must be connected to the same single virtual port channel (VPC) leaf pair in each pod.

There are three ways to configure anycast services in Cisco ACI:

- Behind an EPG subnet

- As part of an L4/L7 service graph with PBR

- As part of an L4/L7 service graph without PBR

With anycast services, a typical use case is to support Cisco firewalls in each pod of a multi-pod fabric. However, anycast can also be used to enable other services, such as anycast DNS or printing services. Let's look at an example of deploying anycast in a firewall cluster stretched between multiple pods using the PBR service graph deployment.

In this example, you will install at least one firewall in Pod 1, connected to a single VPC leaf pair. Similarly, in Pod 2, you will install another firewall connected to a single VPC leaf pair. For the firewall cluster control link (CCL), another VPC is created in each pod between firewalls and the leaf pair, using an EPG and BD stretched between pods, as shown in Figure 7-33.

As mentioned earlier, anycast services in multi-pod provide the advantage of keeping traffic symmetry within each pod. In this example, the leaf pair through which these firewalls are connected in their respective pods installs the anycast MAC and IP addresses as a proxy route to the spine in the pod. In this way, a COOP entry is installed on spines in respective pods pointing to the service node local to that pod. The spines located in opposite pods receive the route information for the anycast service (in this case the firewall) through BGP-EVPN over IPN.

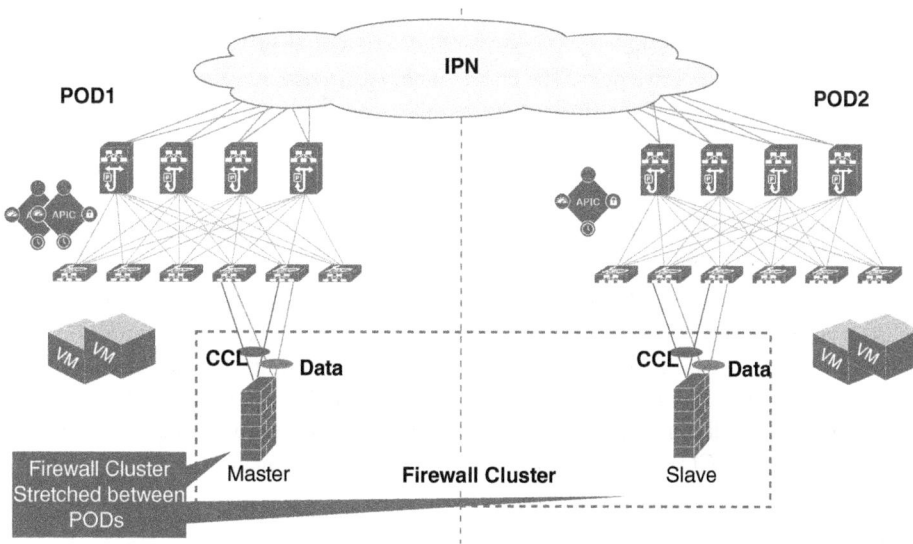

Figure 7-33 *Firewall Cluster Deployment in Multi-pod*

Figure 7-34 shows the ACI configuration of the VPCs and L4–L7 device.

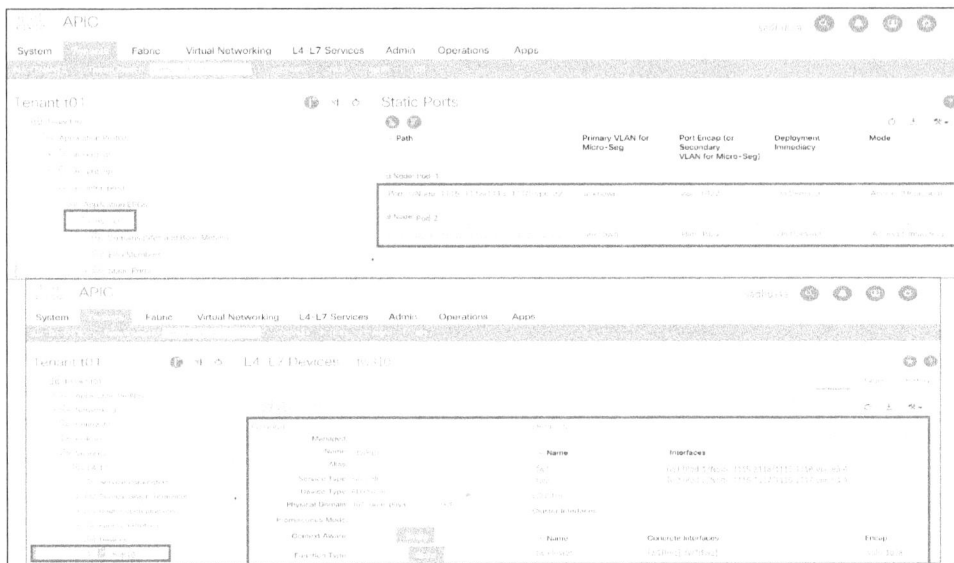

Figure 7-34   *ACI Configuration of the Firewall VPC and L4–L7 Device*

Figure 7-34 indicates successful creation of the EPG *fw-ccl* to pass firewall cluster heart-beats between the firewall (master) in Pod 1 and firewall (slave) in Pod 2. This is a pure Layer 2 connection using VPC with the access mode Untagged. The EPG and BD (with no subnet and with unicast routing disabled) is extended between Pod 1 and Pod 2. As part of the L4–L7 service configuration, the devices—physical firewalls in this case—are also created. In addition, the two firewalls are defined, with their VPC connections to leaf pairs in their respective pods. The cluster interface (*fw-cluster* in this case) is defined and added to both firewall physical interfaces (VPC connections to leaf pairs) with encapsulation VLAN 1028 (the shadow EPG).

The traffic from the EPG *web* and the EPG *app* will be redirected toward this firewall cluster anycast MAC/IP address using the PBR service graph in a simple One-Arm mode, as shown in Figure 7-35.

Notice in Figure 7-35 that the Anycast IP address (30.30.30.1) created on the firewall cluster is part of the service BD subnet (30.30.30.0/24). The anycast MAC address is 00:00:15:15:15:15. On the service BD, remember to enable flooding for ARP and unknown L2 unicast. Also, ensure that IP Data-Plane Learning is disabled and Unicast Routing is enabled. On firewalls, only the default route is created in the cluster configuration to point back to the ACI service BD anycast gateway IP address (30.30.30.254).

In ACI, you need to create the L4–L7 redirect policy with the anycast MAC/IP address, as shown in Figure 7-36.

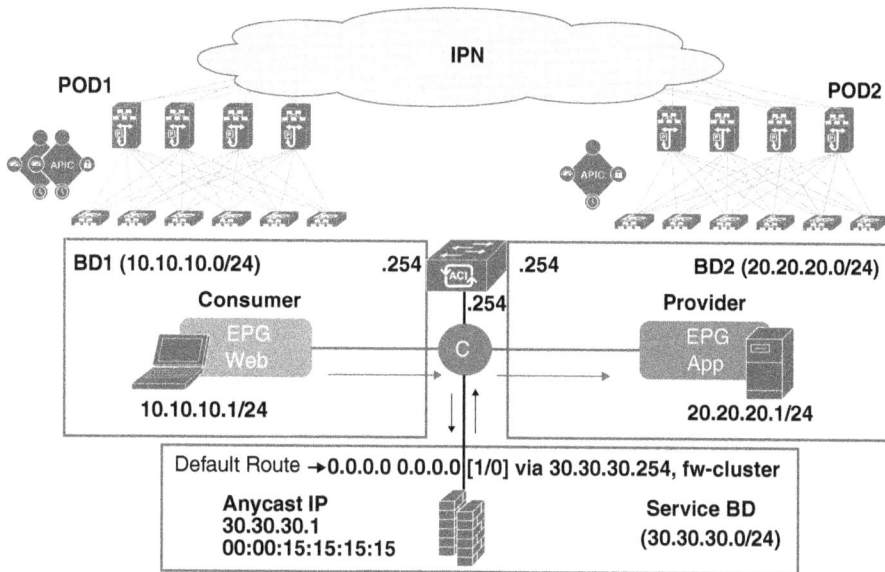

Figure 7-35 *One-Arm PBR Service Graph Toward a Firewall Cluster*

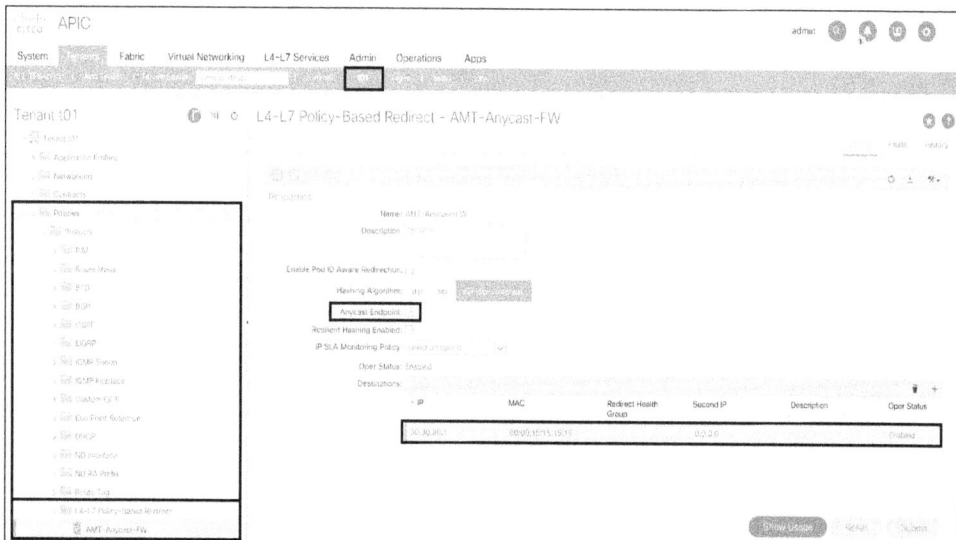

Figure 7-36 *L4–L7 Redirect Policy with the Anycast MAC/IP Address*

Note   Make sure you do not configure the IP SLA Monitoring Policy and Redirect Health Groups features because they are not supported with PBR anycast services.

Now you need to create the service graph template with PBR by using the service device you created earlier (refer to Figure 7-34). After creating the service graph template, you have to apply the service graph, as shown in Figure 7-37.

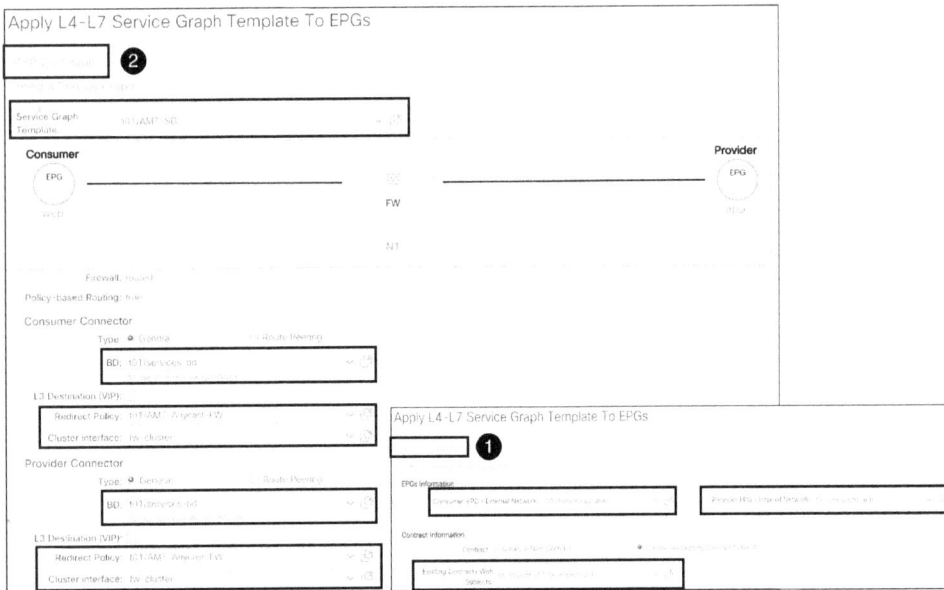

Figure 7-37   *Applying the PBR Service Graph with the Anycast MAC/IP Address*

As you can see in Figure 7-37, the same service BD, redirect policy, and cluster interface are used for both consumer and provider connectors because this is a One-Arm mode PBR service graph deployment.

Multi-Site

Starting with ACI Release 3.0(1), Cisco offers a design option called multi-site, which allows you to interconnect multiple separate single Cisco ACI fabrics together if they are either physically located in the same data center between multiple data halls to resolve cable management issues or in different locations or sites for high availability or disaster recovery.

As explained earlier, for L4–L7 services, such as firewalls, load balancers, and IPSs, Cisco ACI offers a service stitching function called a service graph. The service graph feature can be further enhanced by using PBR policies that enable you to steer certain types of traffic toward service nodes, while the rest of the traffic follows the regular forwarding path.

The Cisco ACI multi-site architecture offers some design options to integrate network services in between application traffic flows, including the following:

■ **Active/standby pair:** Active in Site 1 and standby in Site 2 (limited support)

■ **Active/standby pair:** One pair each site (recommended option)

■ **Separate firewall cluster:** One cluster in each site (recommended option)

The Cisco ACI multi-site architecture does not support an active/active pair (active in Site 1 and another active in Site 2).

Of these design options, the recommended option for integrating L4–L7 services in a Cisco ACI multi-site architecture calls for the deployment of independent service nodes in each site, whether an active/standby pair or separate firewall clusters, as shown in Figure 7-38. This is due to the fact that the ACI multi-site architecture has been designed to interconnect separate ACI fabrics, providing complete network fault domain and management level isolation.

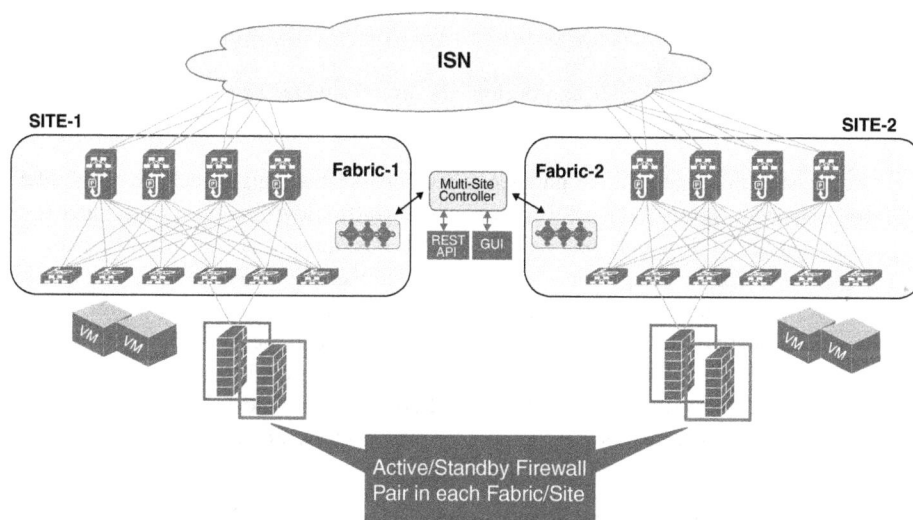

Figure 7-38 *Recommended L4–L7 Services Deployment in Multi-Site*

Because the connection state is not synchronized between independent service nodes deployed in different sites, this design option mandates that traffic flow symmetry through the service nodes be maintained. Otherwise, a connection could potentially be dropped by the firewall during some trombone situation. This requirement can be achieved with the following approaches:

■ Use a host route /32 advertisement for north–south traffic flows with stateful firewall nodes connected through L3Out for route peering with ACI leafs. Support for host route /32 advertisement is extended to regular L3Outs deployed on border leafs in ACI Release 4.0(1) and later. This capability allows for connecting independent firewall nodes deployed between the border leafs and the external WAN routers. The inbound traffic is always optimally steered toward the site where the destination endpoint resides, and the outbound traffic usually goes back through the same site-local L3Out connection. This approach, while fully supported and useful in many cases, relies on a more traditional routing design and only applies to north–south traffic flows.

- To leverage the advanced service insertion capabilities offered by ACI, using the service graph with PBR for both north–south and east–west communication is the preferred and recommended solution. It consists of defining a PBR policy in each site that specifies at least a local active service node. It is also possible to deploy multiple active service nodes in the same site to leverage symmetric PBR. Once PBR policy is applied, the traffic steers through one of the available service nodes for the two directions of each given flow, based on hashing. Prior to ACI Release 4.1(1), the use of PBR mandated that the service nodes be deployed in Layer 3 Routed mode only. However, after ACI Release 4.1(1), the service nodes can be deployed in Layer 1/Layer 2 Inline/Transparent mode as well. This allows you to use IPS/IDS devices as service nodes.

Now let's talk about the other design options for inserting network services into application traffic flows in an ACI multi-site environment:

- **Active/standby service node pair stretched across sites:** This model can be applied to both north–south and east–west application traffic flows between sites. Since the active service node is only on one side in Site1, this option has certain traffic-path inefficiencies as by design some traffic flows will hair-pin across the inter-site network (ISN). Therefore, it is important to ensure proper bandwidth across sites and to consider the possible latency impact on application components (such as application hosts) connected to separate sites. The active/standby model is supported with service nodes deployed in Layer 2 Bridged or Layer 3 Routed mode. In Routed mode, both the border leaf nodes and the GOLF router options are supported for L3Out connectivity.

- **Active/active clustered service nodes stretched across sites:** This model cannot be applied in multi-site architecture.

Figure 7-39 illustrates these design options.

ACI multi-pod remains the recommended architectural approach for the deployment of active/standby service node pairs across data centers and active/active clustered service nodes across data centers.

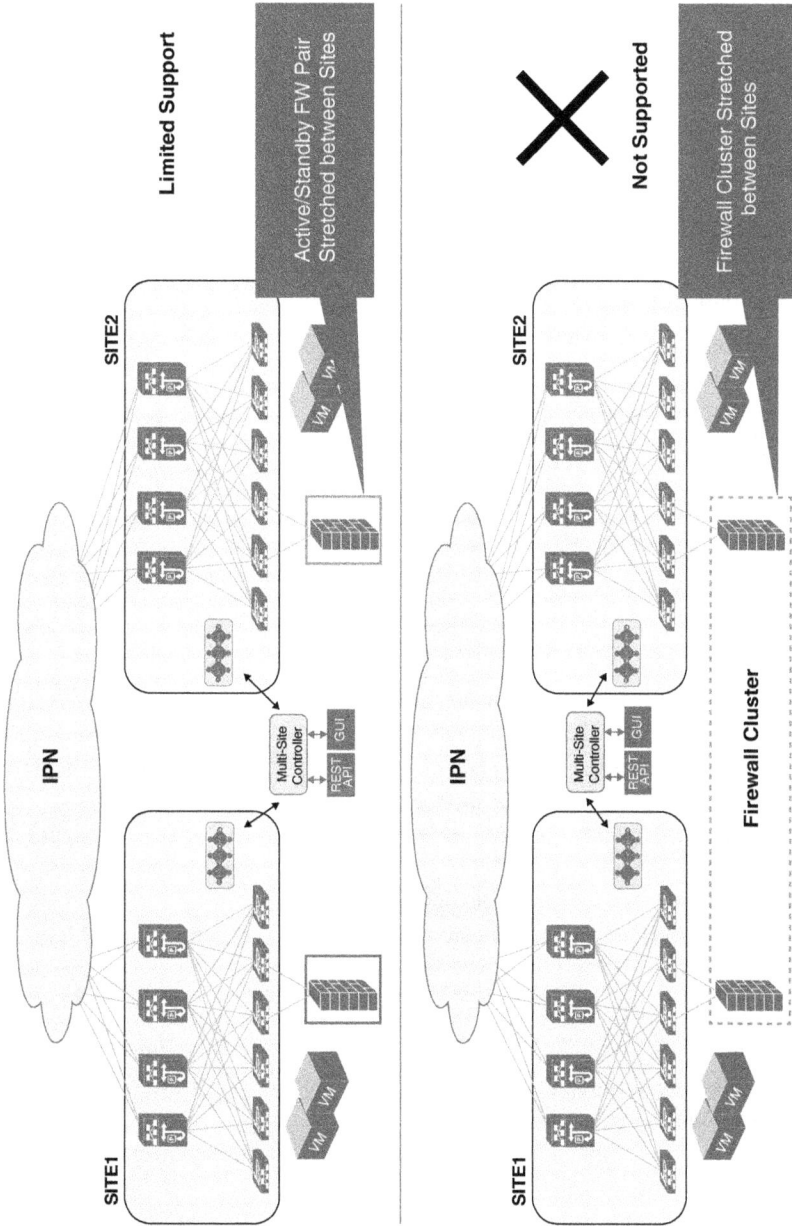

Figure 7-39 *L4–L7 Services Deployment in Multi-Site with Limited to Unsupported Options*

Review Questions

1. What is Service Insertion in ACI? How can you configure it? (Choose two.)

   a. Service Insertion is configured in ACI through external routed network connectivity.

   b. With ACI Service Insertion, service nodes such as firewalls or application delivery controllers (ADCs) can be connected in either Transparent mode or Routed mode.

   c. Using Service Insertion, the return traffic back to the service nodes is achieved through bridging.

   d. In ACI, Service Insertion is configured by creating front-end and back-end EPGs in a sandwich design.

   e. ACI Service Insertion allows you to stitch together storage services to virtualize computing.

2. What is a service graph? What additional value does a service graph provide over other service insertion techniques? (Choose three.)

   a. An ACI service graph, unlike other service insertion techniques, requires the provider and consumer EPGs to communicate through a contract.

   b. In a service graph, service nodes are attached using shadow EPGs.

   c. Using a service graph, the service nodes do not necessarily need to be the default gateways for application servers.

   d. A service graph requires a sandwich design, like service insertion, but with a contract.

   e. In a service graph, service nodes are attached using IP-based EPGs.

3. What are Managed and Unmanaged modes in a service graph? (Choose three.)

   a. Unmanaged mode requires all configuration to be executed manually.

   b. Managed mode provides a single pane of glass for centralized management of all the L2–L7 configuration and service automation using a Cisco APIC.

   c. In Unmanaged mode, the network infrastructure portion of the service graph configuration is carried out by the APIC, and service node configuration is done by non-Cisco service device vendors.

   d. With Unmanaged mode, there are no software code alignment restrictions between your ACI infrastructure and service nodes.

   e. Unmanaged mode requires a device package to be installed on an APIC.

4. What are the use cases for L4–L7 integration in ACI? (Choose three.)

   a. ACI uses service graph technology for speedy deployment of L4–L7 services in a network.

   b. With the service graph configuration in Hybrid mode, the interactions with L4–L7 devices depends on the device package.

   c. A service graph is useful for creating service portals for end users to insert L4–L7 services as they require.

   d. Unmanaged mode requires manual configuration of L4–L7 services.

   e. An ACI service graph offers three modes of configuration: Managed, Unmanaged, and Hybrid.

Chapter 8

Automation and Orchestration

In this chapter, you will learn about Cisco Application Centric Infrastructure (ACI) automation and orchestration. This chapter covers the following topics:

- The difference between automation and orchestration

- The REST API

- Automating tasks using the native REST API: JSON and XML

- Automating tasks using Ansible

- Orchestration through UCS Director

The Difference Between Automation and Orchestration

The key business growth enabler in the industry today is the speedy provisioning of the application-hosting infrastructure. Companies cannot survive if their applications are not available to provide services to their customers. Application developers have therefore adopted a model commonly known as DevOps, which is a combination of processes and tools that increase an organization's ability to deliver applications at a rapid pace, yielding improved end products and services. In the past, it took up to six months to bring a critical business application online due to the siloed approach and the bureaucratic red tape between the application, compute, storage, and network teams within an organization.

The application team taking an Agile path exerts tremendous pressure on other teams to create the underlying infrastructure as quickly as possible so that applications can be hosted on top of it. Instantiating the underlying compute, storage, and network infrastructure manually can lead to errors and service downtime. Therefore, companies like Cisco came up with the software-defined networking approach to cope with the pace of the application development cycle. This overall Agile method enables companies to better serve their customers and compete more efficiently in this fast-paced economy.

Two processes—automation and orchestration—can improve efficiency and speed. *Automation* involves running various processes, executing configuration changes, collecting statistics, and so on using tools and scripts as a single task on a single device or platform. *Orchestration*, on the other hand, executes multiple tasks as a workflow, speeding up the overall provisioning of a business application. Running a script to enable certain ports on network devices is an example of automation, whereas enabling ports on network devices connecting to servers, installing an operating system, and deploying and running an application through a single workflow are examples of orchestration.

Benefits of Automation and Orchestration

Automating one task may impress one team by expediting a particular task. An example might be automating a task to assign a port with encapsulation VLAN on an ACI leaf so that virtual machine (VM) traffic can be initiated; this task automation might get you some applause from a small group of individuals, but it will not make a perceivable difference in the overall rapid application development process. When automation is built into a series of processes and workflows, which are then orchestrated to run automatically, there can be endless benefits.

Some of the commonly observed benefits of automation and orchestration include the following:

- Rapid and consistent changes
- Simplicity
- Reducing human error
- Making changes on the fly
- Service catalog offerings for end users
- Quick recovery after disaster
- Cost reduction

In an ideal DevOps culture, both automation and orchestration are used in real-world environments to achieve application agility. Automation is the first step toward orchestration. As automation takes care of technical tasks, orchestration takes care of IT workflows that are composed of multiple technical tasks. Using both of these methods means streamlining workflows and accurately executing them, which results in speedier and successful application deployment. Thanks to automation and orchestration, IT staff can be engaged to work on other business-critical projects while the application-hosting infrastructure runs smoothly and efficiently.

Automation in traditional networks was mainly carried out through the command-line interface (CLI), using shell scripts, TCL scripts, and legacy languages such as Perl. However, with the evolution of software-defined networking (SDN) as networks continue to become more scalable and complex, newer open-source programming languages, such as Python and Ruby using the REST API, have grown in popularity due to their ease of use and flexibility.

With ACI, you have the option of using a graphical user interface (GUI), the CLI, and Representational State Transfer (REST) to provision the fabric. REST gives you the option of making native REST calls using the Extensible Markup Language (XML) and JavaScript Notation (JSON) formats. Native REST API calls are the simplest and easiest method for those who do not come from a developer background; therefore, this chapter focuses mainly on these calls. Besides using native REST API calls with raw XML and JSON formats, you also have the option of using a programming language such as Python. Cisco ACI offers the Python Software Development Kit (SDK), also known as Cobra, to make API calls to the Cisco Application Policy Infrastructure Controller (APIC) without having to post raw XML and JSON formats. If you are a creative developer, creating Python programs is not an issue. However, if you do not know about Python, you can still use the Cobra SDK by converting the native XML or JSON code into the Python program using the Arya tool, which is available on GitHub. The other REST API option is ACI Toolkit. Calling native REST APIs using raw XML or JSON and the Cobra SDK tool requires you to have some familiarity of the ACI object model. The ACI Toolkit is essentially a set of Python libraries built on top of the ACI object model that abstracts the model into a simplified version.

Almost everyone who gets to know about ACI starts by configuring tasks using the APIC GUI. Cisco ACI is a demand-and-consume model, where you need to create policies, combine them into policy groups, and assign them to profiles for consumption of the hardware resource. Therefore, for a simple task that you used to configure on a traditional network device, you now need to perform multiple steps in the APIC GUI to achieve the same outcome. This presents Day 2 operational challenges and means additional time is needed to diagnose issues, as outlined here:

- One configuration change requires many subconfiguration changes.

- It can be difficult to remember the sequence of steps.

- The process is prone to human error.

- It takes extra time to diagnose missing configuration steps.

- There is a risk of not completing a change successfully in the allotted time.

The following sections provide two examples to help you see these challenges in action.

Example 1

Configuring a simple route peering using OSPF in a traditional NX-OS router requires a few CLI commands, as shown in Example 8-1.

Example 8-1   *Route Peering Configuration Using OSPF in NX-OS*

```
router ospf 521
  router-id 10.10.10.10
  area 0.0.3.112 nssa no-summary
  redistribute static route-map NEXUS-STATIC-ROUTES
  area 0.0.3.112 authentication message-digest
  passive-interface default

interface Vlan11
  ip ospf message-digest-key 1 md5 3 f4d8a88ca5b42ef5ce8839184f9a1f5c
  ip ospf dead-interval 15
  ip ospf hello-interval 5
  ip ospf network point-to-point
  no ip ospf passive-interface
  ip router ospf 521 area 0.0.3.112
```

To configure the same route peering using OSPF in ACI through the GUI, you need to follow these steps:

Step 1.   Under Access Policies, create a VLAN in the VLAN pool and associate it with the external routed domain. (Note that you need to create an external routed domain if there is not already such a domain in the policy.)

Step 2.   Create an attachable access entity profile (AAEP) and associate it to the external routed domain.

Step 3.   Create an access policy with the interfaces you are planning to use, and associate it with the AAEP.

Step 4.   Create a switch profile and associate it with the interface profile.

Step 5.   Under Tenant Policies, create an L3Out configuration by choosing the routing protocol and associating the external routed domain and VRF instance.

Step 6.   Create a logical node profile by selecting the leaf nodes to be border leafs and assigning the necessary router IDs and loopback addresses.

Step 7.   Assign the interfaces of leaf nodes that you are planning to peer with the external routers.

Step 8.   If OSPF is in use, create an interface policy and assign it to the OSPF interface profile.

Skipping any of these steps could result in a failed configuration. In some cases, an APIC generates a fault, as shown in Figure 8-1, where a missing external routed domain in the L3Out configuration generated a fault.

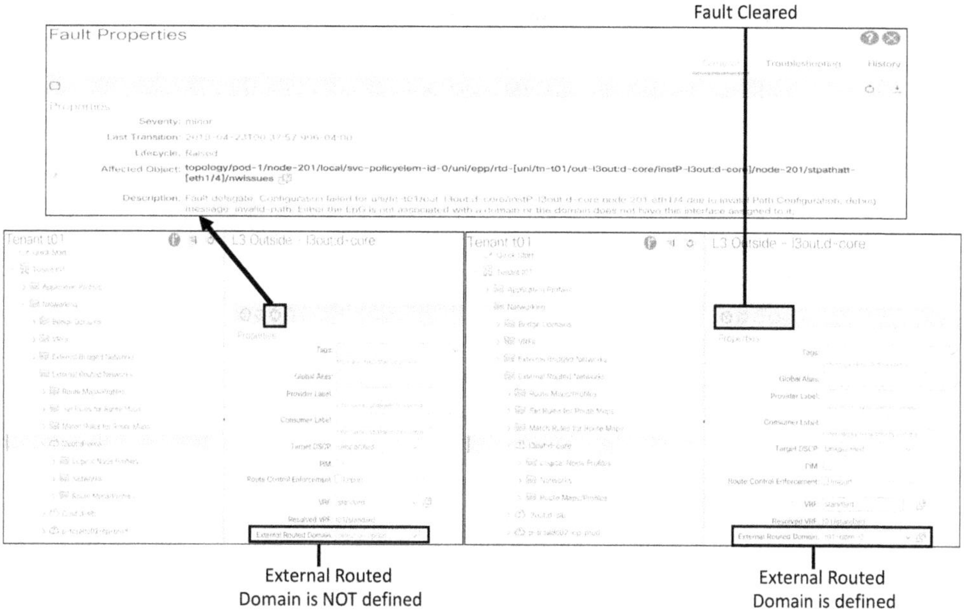

Figure 8-1 *L3Out Configuration Failure Fault*

Example 2

Configuring a simple virtual port channel (VPC) in a traditional NX-OS switch requires a few CLI commands, as shown in Example 8-2.

Example 8-2 *VPC Configuration in NX-OS*

```
vpc domain 1
  peer-switch
  role priority 8192
  peer-keepalive destination 10.10.10.2 source 10.10.10.1 vrf default
  peer-gateway exclude-vlan 11
  ip arp synchronize

interface port-channel1
  vpc peer-link

interface port-channel5
  vpc 5
```

To configure the same VPC in ACI through GUI, you need to follow these steps:

Step 1.   Under Access Policies, create a VLAN in the VLAN pool and associate it with the physical domain. (Note that you need to create a physical domain if there is not already such a domain in the policy.)

Step 2.   Create an AAEP and associate it to the physical domain.

Step 3.   Create a VPC interface policy group and associate access policies and the AAEP with it.

Step 4.   Create a leaf interface profile with interfaces you want to use for VPC, and associate it with the VPC interface policy group.

Step 5.   Under Switch Policies, create a VPC switch policy by combining two leaf nodes and assigning a VPC logical pair ID.

Step 6.   Create a switch profile by selecting two leaf nodes and associating them with the leaf interface profile.

In this example, the APIC does not generate a fault when you apply the missing configuration (if you forgot to associate the interface policy group with the interface profile). The configuration is accepted, but you don't get the desired results, as shown in Figure 8-2.

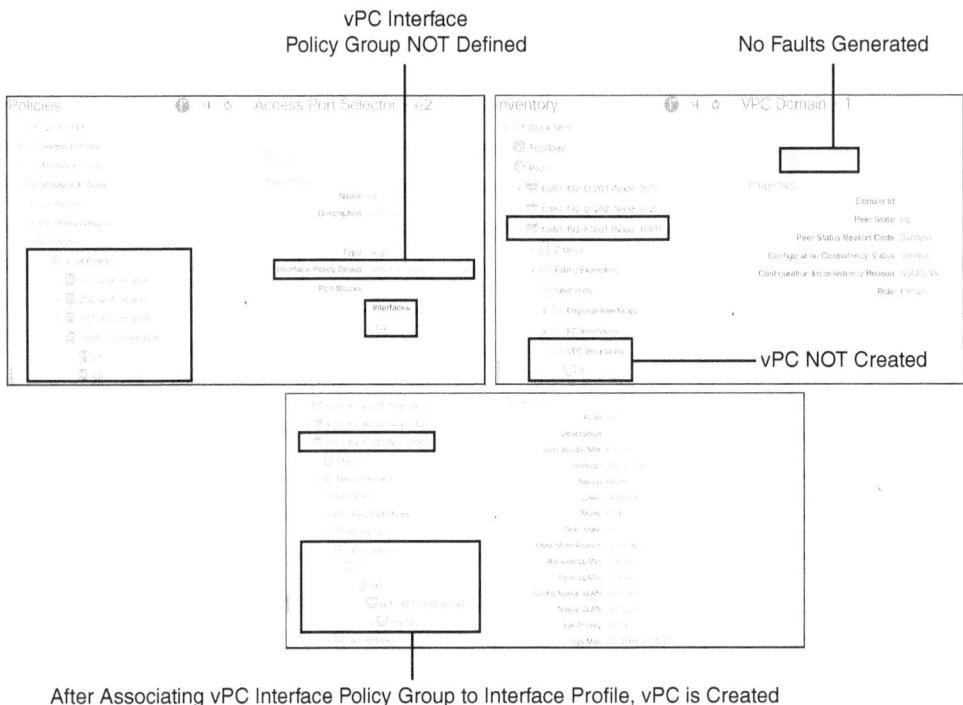

Figure 8-2   *VPC Missing Configuration Example*

These examples show that provisioning ACI using the GUI is a good way to start. However, it is definitely not an efficient way of provisioning. In fact, it could add extra time to diagnosing configuration issues in certain cases.

REST API

Representational State Transfer, commonly known as *REST*, is a client/server communication method that uses a TCP-based HTTP or HTTPS protocol where the client makes a resource request to a server, and in response, the server transfers to the client a representation of the state of the requested resource. The REST application programming interface (API) natively accepts and returns HTTP or HTTPS messages that contain JSON or XML documents. A request generally consists of the following:

- **HTTP(S) method:** Defines what kind of operation to perform

- **Header:** Allows the client to pass along the request information

- **Path:** Identifies the location of a resource

- **Message body:** Contains data

Three HTTP(S) methods are used in requests to interact with resources in an ACI-based REST system:

- **GET:** Retrieves a specific resource or a collection of resources

- **POST:** Creates or updates a resource

- **DELETE:** Removes a specific resource

POST and DELETE methods are *idempotent*, meaning that there is no additional effect if they are called multiple times with the same input parameters. However, the GET method is *nullipotent*, meaning that no matter how many times it is executed, there is no change in the MIT object model (read-only operation), regardless of any input parameter.

Note   The PUT method is a valid REST API method that is used primarily to modify an existing resource; however, it is not supported in ACI.

Before we get into performing a read-only GET request to pull statistical data from an APIC, it is important to understand the format of the URL used in the call, as shown in Figure 8-3.

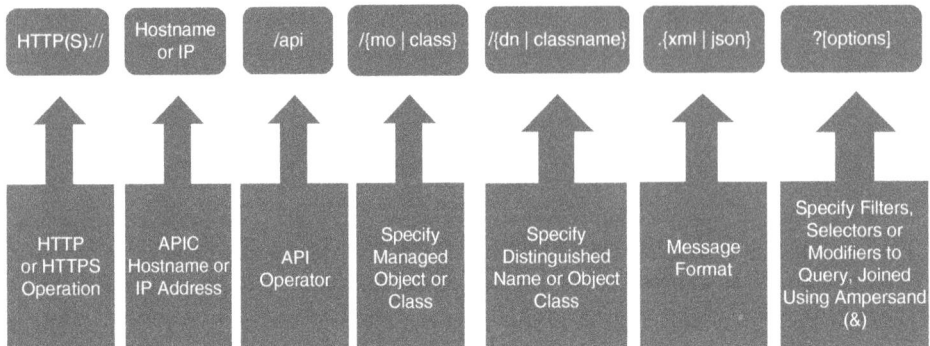

HTTP(S)://	Hostname or IP	/api	/{mo | class}	/{dn | classname}	.{xml | json}	?[options]
HTTP or HTTPS Operation	APIC Hostname or IP Address	API Operator	Specify Managed Object or Class	Specify Distinguished Name or Object Class	Message Format	Specify Filters, Selectors or Modifiers to Query, Joined Using Ampersand (&)

Figure 8-3   *REST API URL Format*

There is a slight difference in the URI resource path when running a REST query against a regular managed object than when running a REST query against a specific object node (or object instance) or an object class. For example, to get information about the tenant managed object named t01, you use the following URL, where the resource path contains the DN of the managed object (/uni/tn-t01):

https://{{*apic-host-or-ip*}}/api/mo/uni/tn-t01.json

If you want to pull some statistics from a node managed object, you use the following URL, where the resource path contains the DN of the managed object (/topology/pod-ID/node-ID/sys/ch/ftslot-number):

https://{{*apic-host-or-ip*}}/api/mo/topology/pod-1/node-1001/sys/ch/ftslot-1.json

To retrieve information about a class of objects, you use the following URL, where the resource path is /class/*class-name*:

https://{{*apic-host-or-ip*}}/api/class/fvTenant.json

The REST API offers a wide range of filter options to help narrow down the scope of a query in the URI to locate the intended resource quickly. You can apply the filters in your URI by starting with the ? symbol. If you want to join multiple queries, you use the & symbol.

For example, to pull the operational status of leaf node 1001, you can run the following REST query against the node 1001 MO containing DN topology/pod-1/node-1001/sys and filter a child object class eqptCh by using the filters query-target=children and target-subtree-class. Note that the filter section starts with the ? symbol, and the filters are joined with the & symbol.

https://{{*apic-host-or-ip*}}/api/mo/topology/pod-1/node-1001/sys.json?query-target=children&target-subtree-class=eqptCh

Automating Tasks Using the Native REST API: JSON and XML

With the evolution of SDN technology such as ACI, how can a modern network be provisioned programmatically. For many years, networks have been configured and deployed in some automated fashion, but mostly with the CLI. Therefore, network engineers are not typically equipped with software programming skills. With the industry shifting gears toward SDN, many vendors are providing tools to help automate infrastructure, but it can be difficult to know where to start.

Cisco ACI can help you develop basic automation tasks with its built-in tools such as API Inspector, Object Save As, Visore, and MOQuery, shown in Figure 8-4.

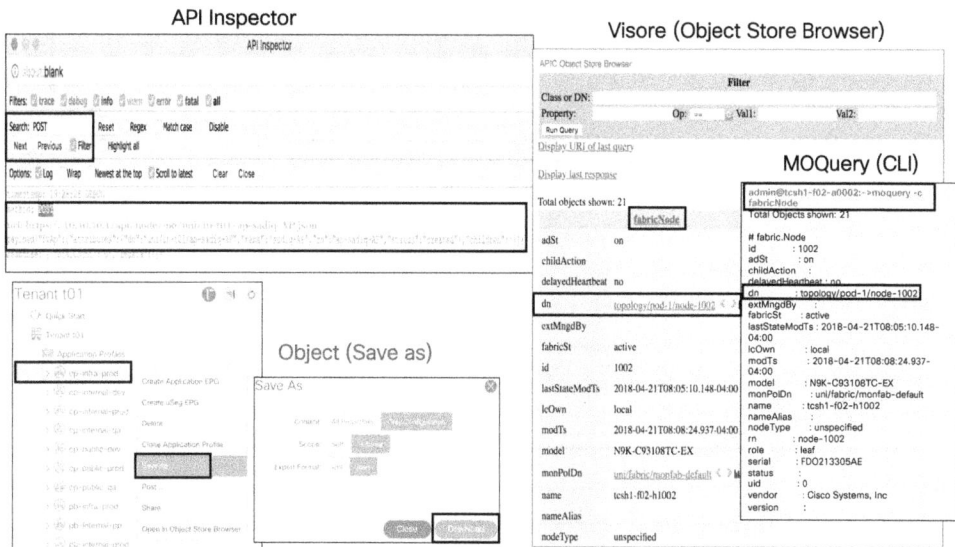

Figure 8-4 *ACI Automation Support Tools*

The following sections explore these built-in tools to help you build scripts to automate ACI configuration tasks.

API Inspector

API Inspector is like a network test access point (TAP), where every packet is captured as it flows through the wire. When any task is performed on the APIC, the GUI creates and sends internal API messages to the operating system to execute that task. The API

Inspector built-in tool can let you view and copy these API messages. You can replicate these API messages in order to automate key operations tasks in ACI. API Inspector displays an API message only in JSON format. The benefit of using API Inspector is that it provides not only the payload of the REST call but also the complete URL.

To open the API Inspector tool, you need to log on to the APIC GUI. In the top-right corner of the window, right-click on the circular Help and Tools button and click the Show API Inspector tab to open the API Inspector window. Then you can create a new tenant through the APIC GUI. Next, you can switch to the API Inspector window, where you can see the timestamp for the operation task executed in APIC GUI, the HTTP(S) method used, the URL, and the payload of the REST call, as illustrated in Figure 8-5.

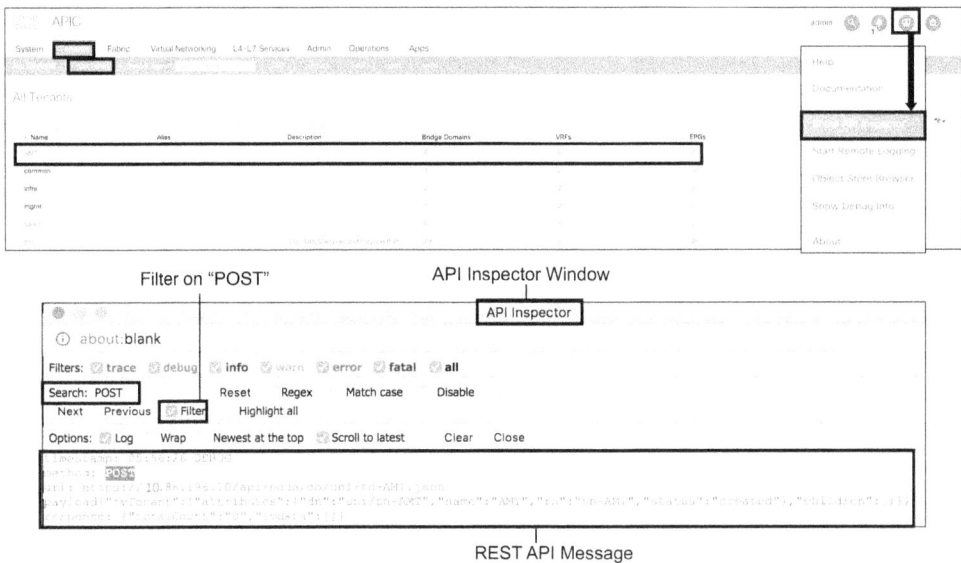

Figure 8-5   *API Inspector*

Figure 8-5 shows that after the new tenant AMT was created, the API Inspector indicates that the HTTP(S) method used is POST, and the URL is https://10.88.196.10/api/node/ mo/uni/tn-AMT.json. The API Inspector also displays the following API message payload:

```
{"fvTenant":{"attributes":{"dn":"uni/tn-AMT","name":"AMT",
"rn":"tn-AMT","status":"created"},"children":[]}}
```

Note   API Inspector displays all API messages running on the APIC. Therefore, it is advisable to filter on a particular task, as shown in Figure 8-5.

You need to understand the JSON format before you can start using it in your scripts. The API message payload output of the managed object includes the JSON format shown in Example 8-3.

Example 8-3   *JSON Format in ACI*

```
{"Parent-Object-Class": {"attributes": {"Property1":"value","Property2":"value"},
     "children": [
             {"Child-Object-Class1":
  {"attributes":{"Property1":"value","Property2":"value"},"children":[]}},
             {"Child-Object-Class2":
  {"attributes":{"Property1":"value","Property2":"value"},"children":[]}}
                  ] }}
```

The JSON format in ACI starts with a curly bracket ({), followed by "*Parent-Object-Class*" with double quotes and a colon (:). Then, **"attributes"** of "*Parent-Object-Class*" starts with double quotes and a colon followed by each of the object property key/value pairs, in the form {"*property1*":"**value**", "*property2*":"**value**"}. The properties of the child object class start with the key word **"children"** in double quotes and a colon followed by a square bracket ([). Then the properties of each "*Child-Object-Class*" start with a curly bracket in double quotes and a colon. The **"attributes"** of "*Child-Object-Class*" start with double quotes and a colon followed by each of the object property key/value pairs in the form {"*property1*":"**value**", "*property2*":"**value**"},"**children**":[]}}. The last child object class does not have a comma at the end but rather a closing square bracket and curly brackets for the top-level parent object class(es).

You can use the API message payload data collected from API Inspector, massage it by using any text editor, and POST it by using any REST client such as Postman in order to create more tenants in your fabric. For example, you create tenant **t01** by using the JSON script posted via Postman, as shown in Figure 8-6.

With the approach described in this section, you can also create other configuration tasks. For example, you could create an application profile, an endpoint group (EPG), a bridge domain, or a contract.

Object (Save As)

As mentioned in the preceding section, API Inspector can only display API message payload in JSON format. If you want to use the other supported native REST API format, XML, for automating configuration tasks in ACI, you need to use the Object (Save As) method to download the payload, as shown in Figure 8-7.

Paste URL Here   Click Send

| POST ▼ | https://10.58.198.10/api/node/mo/uni/tn-t01.json | | Send ▼ | Save ▼ |

Params   Authorization   Headers (8)   **Body ●**   Pre-request Script   Tests   Settings   Cookies Code

○ none   ○ form-data   ○ x-www-form-urlencoded   ● raw   ○ binary   ○ GraphQL   JSON ▼   Beautify

1 `{"fvTenant" : {"attributes" :{"dn":"uni/tn-t01","name":"t01","rn":"tn-t01","status":"created"},"children": []}}`

Body   Cookies (1)   Headers (12)   Test Results   Status: 200 OK   Time: 1025 ms   Size: 581 B   Save Response ▼

Pretty   Raw   Preview   Visualize   JSON ▼

```
1  {
2      "totalCount": "0",
3      "imdata": []
4  }
```

Paste Payload Here   POST Operation Executed
                                        Successfully With Status Code "200"

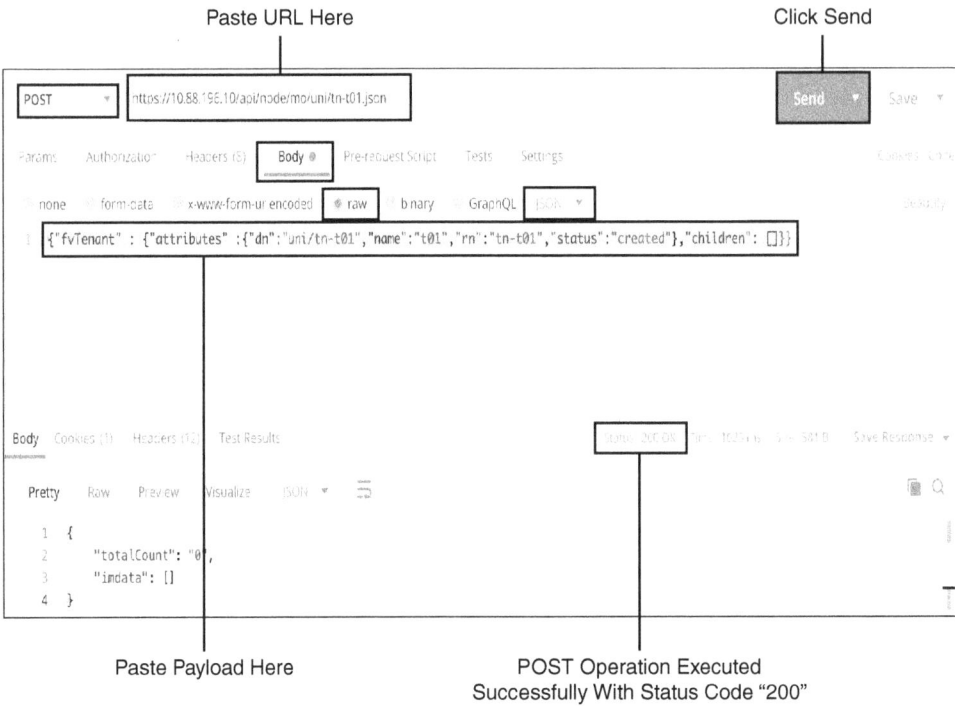

Figure 8-6   *Creating Tenant t01 Using Postman*

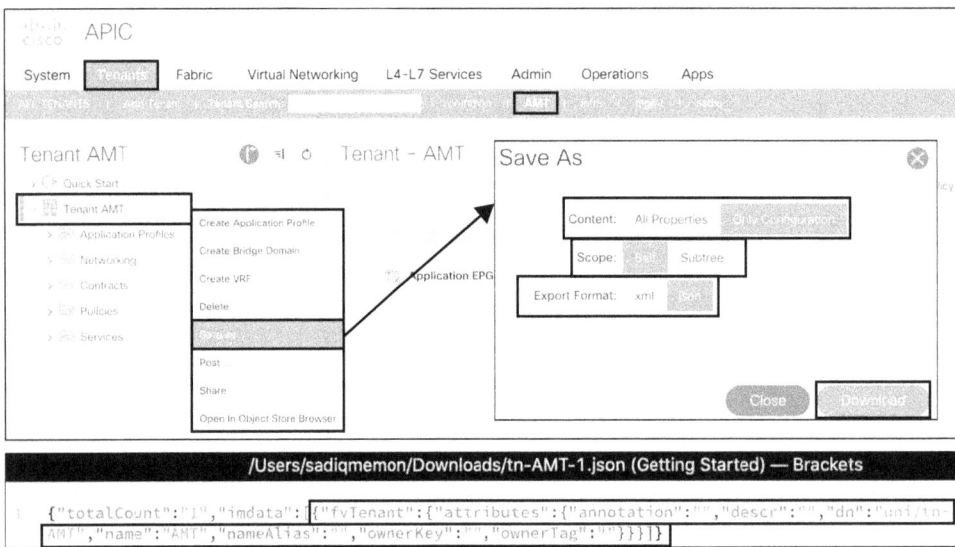

Figure 8-7   *ACI Object (Save As)*

You can right-click any object whose payload you want to download to your workstation and then select Save As. A window that pops up gives you various options to choose from before you download the payload. You can select All Properties or Only Configuration. You can select just the object attribute by selecting Self, or you can select Subtree to include all its child objects as well. Finally, you have the option to choose either XML or JSON format. After selecting the necessary options, click Download to save the API payload on your workstation.

One thing you may have noticed is that the Save As method does not give you the URL. This means you need to build the URL. For a managed object (MO), the URL starts with the following syntax:

https://<apic_IP>/api/node/mo/

You can collect the actual path of the MO location in the management information tree (MIT) through the distinguished name (dn) in the payload. In the example shown in Figure 8-7, "dn":"uni/tn-AMT needs to be concatenated to the common URL syntax for a MO followed by the APIC format (XML or JSON) used. Therefore, the complete URL for this example of a tenant creation API call is as follows:

https://<apic_IP>/api/node/mo/uni/tn-AMT.json

Note that you can use this method to post an API payload using APIC as a REST client. This can be useful when backing up and restoring during a simple configuration change on that particular object's properties.

Visore (Object Store Browser)

Visore (from the Italian word for *viewer*) provides a view of an entire MIT. You can use this tool to directly query a MO or class of objects when you point your web browser to the out-of-band management IP address of the APIC:

https://<apic_IP>/visore.html

You can also open it via the APIC GUI by clicking the circular icon in the top-right corner of the window and selecting Object Store Browser. You are then prompted to log in using the APIC credentials. By default, when you log in to the APIC Object Store Browser, it displays the result of a search for all managed objects of class fabricNode. Figure 8-8 illustrates this process.

From Figure 8-8, you can see that with Visore, you can query any class of object or the DN of a managed object in the entire MIT. In the example on the left side of Figure 8-9, you can see that when you query the bridge domain class fvBD, Visore pulls out 44 managed objects and their properties. In the example on the right side of Figure 8-9, you can see that when you query the DN of the MO epg-client, Visore pulls out all its properties.

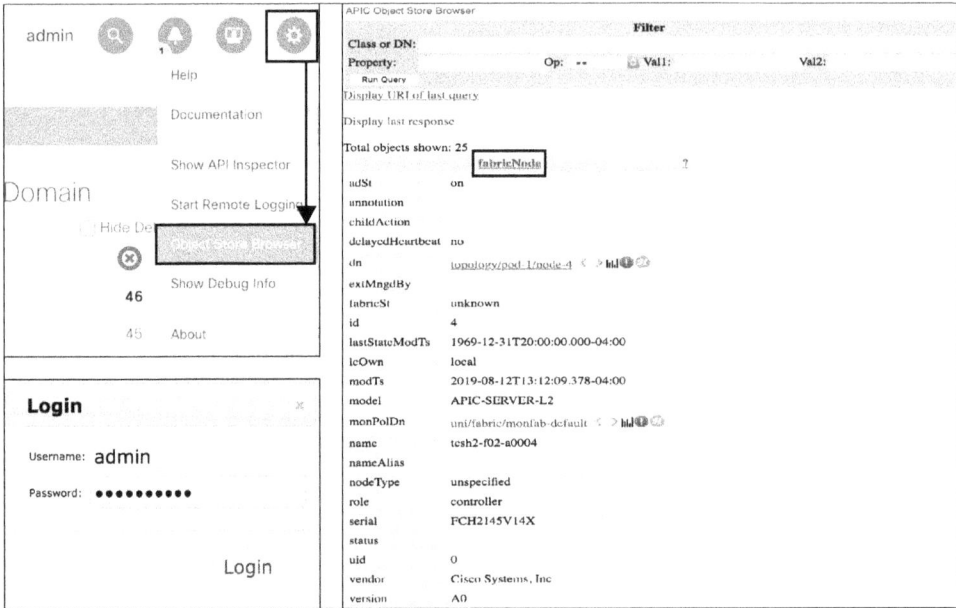

Figure 8-8 *Visore (Object Store Browser)*

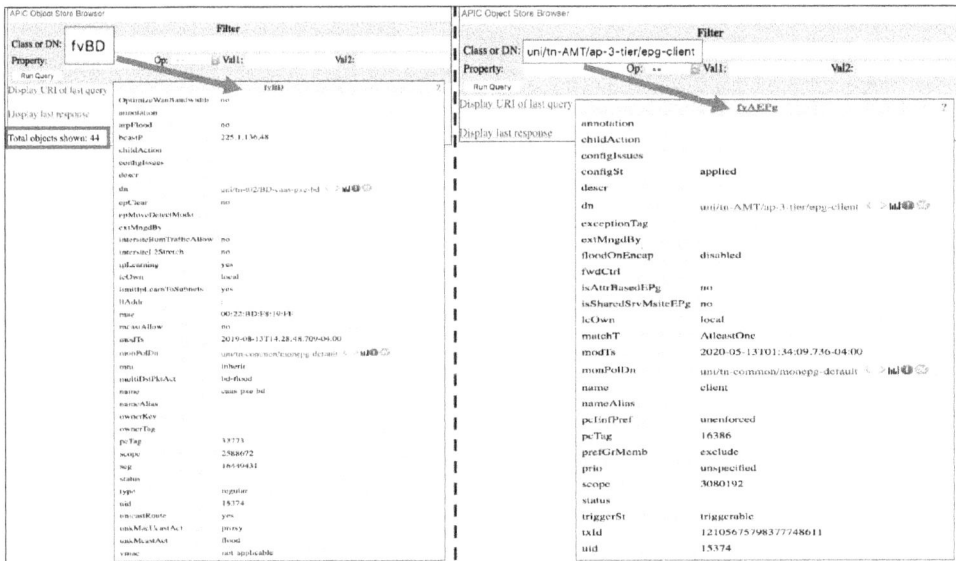

Figure 8-9 *Class- or DN-Based Query Using Visore (Object Store Browser)*

You can further filter a query by using the property of an object of a certain class, as in the example shown in Figure 8-10. In this example, let's say you want to pull all the objects that contain "test" in the name of the object of EPG class fvAEPg.

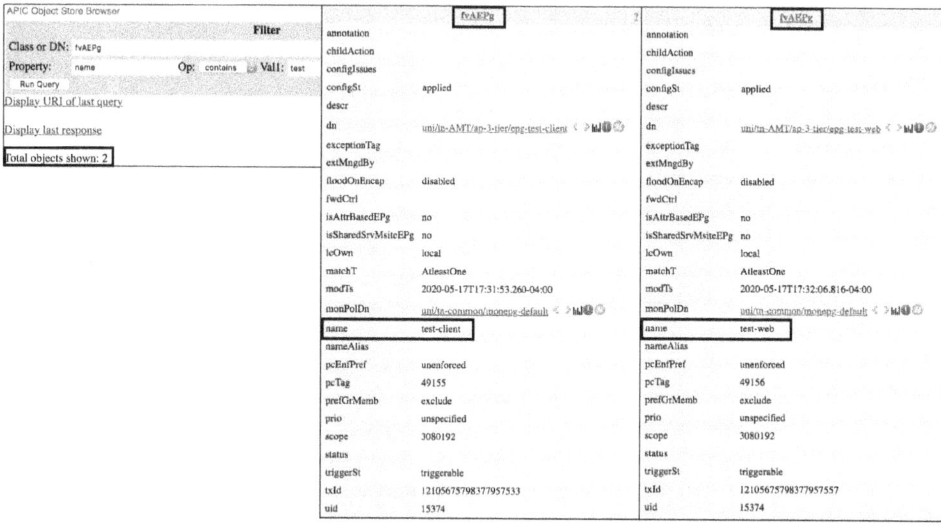

Figure 8-10   *Filter Options in Visore (Object Store Browser)*

You have already seen that you can use the API Inspector and Object (Save As) tools to find the class and DN of an object. There are two additional ways to find this information: by using a web browser URL and the Debug method. While navigating the APIC GUI through a web browser, when you click on an object, the browser URL is updated to reflect the location of the object, and everything after the vertical bar (|) in the URL is the object DN. Similarly, when you enable Show Debug Info in the APIC GUI by clicking the circular icon at the top-right corner of the window, you get the DN of the object at the bottom of the window after you click the mouse on any object. Figure 8-11 illustrates this process.

MOQuery

MOQuery is another tool you can use to browse objects in the MIT. It is quite similar to Visore, although whereas Visore is GUI based, MOQuery is CLI based. It is used to build automation scripts and more extensively, is used during troubleshooting events.

To get MOQuery command-line help, you can use the command in Example 8-4, which also provides information about all the filtering options you can use with the tool.

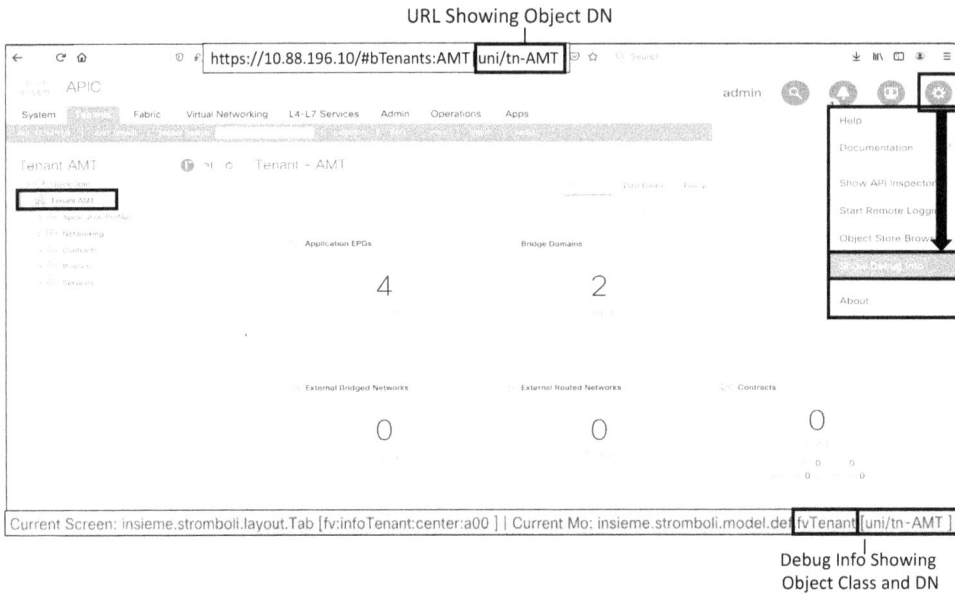

Figure 8-11 *Finding the Class or DN of an Object by Using the URL and Debug Methods*

Example 8-4 *MOQuery Command-Line Help*

```
apic1# moquery -h
usage: Command line cousin to visore [-h] [-i HOST] [-p PORT] [-d DN]
                                     [-c KLASS] [-f FILTER] [-a ATTRS]
                                     [-o OUTPUT] [-u USER]
                                     [-x [OPTIONS [OPTIONS ...]]]


optional arguments:
  -h, --help            show this help message and exit
  -i HOST, --host HOST  Hostname or ip of apic
  -p PORT, --port PORT  REST server port
  -d DN, --dn DN        dn of the mo
  -c KLASS, --klass KLASS
                        comma seperated class names to query
  -f FILTER, --filter FILTER
                        property filter to accept/reject mos
  -a ATTRS, --attrs ATTRS
                        type of attributes to display (config, all)
```

```
 -o OUTPUT, --output OUTPUT
                    Display format (block, table, xml, json)
 -u USER, --user USER  User name
 -x [OPTIONS [OPTIONS ...]], --options [OPTIONS [OPTIONS ...]]
                    Extra options to the query
```

Examples 8-5 and 8-6 provide examples of querying objects based on class and DN.

Example 8-5 *Using MOQuery to Find a Class (-c)*

```
apic1# moquery -c fvAp
Total Objects shown: 2


# fv.Ap
name         : pb-public-pp
annotation   :
childAction  :
descr        :
dn           : uni/tn-t01/ap-pb-public-pp
extMngdBy    :
lcOwn        : local
modTs        : 2019-08-13T14:28:46.647-04:00
monPolDn     : uni/tn-t01/monepg-default
nameAlias    :
ownerKey     :
ownerTag     :
prio         : unspecified
rn           : ap-pb-public-pp
status       :
uid          : 15374


# fv.Ap
name         : cp-internal-dev
annotation   :
childAction  :
descr        :
dn           : uni/tn-t01/ap-cp-internal-dev
extMngdBy    :
lcOwn        : local
modTs        : 2019-08-13T14:28:46.647-04:00
monPolDn     : uni/tn-t01/monepg-default
```

```
nameAlias    :
ownerKey     :
ownerTag     :
prio         : unspecified
rn           : ap-cp-internal-dev
status       :
uid          : 15374
```

Example 8-6   *Using MOQuery to Find a DN (-d)*

```
apic1# moquery -d uni/tn-AMT/ap-3-tier
Total Objects shown: 1


# fv.Ap
name          : 3-tier
annotation    :
childAction   :
descr         :
dn            : uni/tn-AMT/ap-3-tier
extMngdBy     :
lcOwn         : local
modTs         : 2020-05-13T01:34:09.636-04:00
monPolDn      : uni/tn-common/monepg-default
nameAlias     :
ownerKey      :
ownerTag      :
prio          : unspecified
rn            : ap-3-tier
status        :
uid           : 15374
```

Examples 8-7 and 8-8 provide examples of using the MOQuery tool with filtering options.

Example 8-7   *Using MOQuery to Find an EPG Class and Filtering on a Name Containing "test"*

```
tcsh1-f02-a0001# moquery -c fvAEPg -f 'fv.AEPg.name*"test"'
Total Objects shown: 2


# fv.AEPg
name            : test-client
annotation      :
childAction     :
configIssues    :
```

```
configSt             : applied
descr                :
dn                   : uni/tn-AMT/ap-3-tier/epg-test-client
exceptionTag         :
extMngdBy            :
floodOnEncap         : disabled
fwdCtrl              :
isAttrBasedEPg       : no
isSharedSrvMsiteEPg  : no
lcOwn                : local
matchT               : AtleastOne
modTs                : 2020-05-17T17:31:53.260-04:00
monPolDn             : uni/tn-common/monepg-default
nameAlias            :
pcEnfPref            : unenforced
pcTag                : 49155
prefGrMemb           : exclude
prio                 : unspecified
rn                   : epg-test-client
scope                : 3080192
status               :
triggerSt            : triggerable
txId                 : 12105675798377957533
uid                  : 15374


# fv.AEPg
name                 : test-web
annotation           :
childAction          :
configIssues         :
configSt             : applied
descr                :
dn                   : uni/tn-AMT/ap-3-tier/epg-test-web
exceptionTag         :
extMngdBy            :
floodOnEncap         : disabled
fwdCtrl              :
isAttrBasedEPg       : no
isSharedSrvMsiteEPg  : no
lcOwn                : local
matchT               : AtleastOne
modTs                : 2020-05-17T17:32:06.816-04:00
monPolDn             : uni/tn-common/monepg-default
nameAlias            :
pcEnfPref            : unenforced
```

```
pcTag                 : 49156
prefGrMemb            : exclude
prio                  : unspecified
rn                    : epg-test-web
scope                 : 3080192
status                :
triggerSt             : triggerable
txId                  : 12105675798377957557
uid                   : 15374
```

Example 8-8 *Using MOQuery to Find a BD Class and Filtering on a Name Containing "test" with ARP Flooding Enabled*

```
apic1# moquery -c fvBD -f 'fv.BD.name*"test" and fv.BD.arpFlood=="yes"'
Total Objects shown: 2


# fv.BD
name                     : test-bd1
OptimizeWanBandwidth     : no
annotation               :
arpFlood                 : yes
bcastP                   : 225.0.30.128
childAction              :
configIssues             :
descr                    :
dn                       : uni/tn-t02/BD-test-bd1
epClear                  : no
epMoveDetectMode         :
extMngdBy                :
intersiteBumTrafficAllow : no
intersiteL2Stretch       : no
ipLearning               : yes
lcOwn                    : local
limitIpLearnToSubnets    : yes
llAddr                   : ::
mac                      : 00:22:BD:F8:19:FF
mcastAllow               : no
modTs                    : 2019-08-13T14:28:48.709-04:00
monPolDn                 : uni/tn-common/monepg-default
mtu                      : inherit
multiDstPktAct           : bd-flood
nameAlias                :
ownerKey                 :
ownerTag                 :
```

```
pcTag                    : 49156
rn                       : BD-test-bd1
scope                    : 2588672
seg                      : 15007705
status                   :
type                     : regular
uid                      : 15374
unicastRoute             : no
unkMacUcastAct           : flood
unkMcastAct              : flood
vmac                     : not-applicable


# fv.BD
name                     : test-bd2
OptimizeWanBandwidth     : no
annotation               :
arpFlood                 : yes
bcastP                   : 225.1.21.96
childAction              :
configIssues             :
descr                    :
dn                       : uni/tn-t02/BD-test-bd2
epClear                  : no
epMoveDetectMode         :
extMngdBy                :
intersiteBumTrafficAllow : no
intersiteL2Stretch       : no
ipLearning               : yes
lcOwn                    : local
limitIpLearnToSubnets    : yes
llAddr                   : ::
mac                      : 00:22:BD:F8:19:FF
mcastAllow               : no
modTs                    : 2019-08-13T14:28:48.709-04:00
monPolDn                 : uni/tn-common/monepg-default
mtu                      : inherit
multiDstPktAct           : bd-flood
nameAlias                :
ownerKey                 :
ownerTag                 :
pcTag                    : 49157
rn                       : BD-test-bd2
scope                    : 2588672
seg                      : 15564693
status                   :
```

```
type                    : regular
uid                     : 15374
unicastRoute            : no
unkMacUcastAct          : flood
unkMcastAct             : flood
vmac                    : not-applicable
```

Automation Use Cases

This section goes over some of the automated ACI configuration tasks that are possible using JSON scripts. You can also use XML format. Software developers tend to prefer JSON with the native REST API as a wide range of network devices are supported.

In the preceding sections, you have learned about the ACI built-in tools and created basic automation script to create a tenant object. In this section we dive into more advanced automation scripts and look at how to create multiple objects located in different places in the hierarchical MIT.

Let's look at an example of registering a new ACI leaf node into the fabric and assigning an out-of-band (OOB) management address to it by using an automation script. This involves two configuration tasks: (1) Register the leaf node to the fabric and (2) assign the OOB management address. Say that you have registered an ACI leaf node to the fabric in your lab and have assigned an OOB management address by using the APIC GUI. While executing these configuration tasks, you captured API messages by using API Inspector tool, as shown in Example 8-9.

Example 8-9 *API Messages for Leaf Node Registration and an OOB Address*

```
API Message for Leaf Node registration to ACI fabric
{"fabricNodeIdentP": {"attributes": {"dn":"uni/controller/nodeidentpol/nodep-FDO
  213409YV","fabricId":"1","podId":"1","serial":"FDO213409YV","name":"Leaf-302",
  "nodeId":"302"} }}
API Message for assigning out-of-band management address to Leaf Node
{"mgmtRsOoBStNode": {"attributes": {"addr":"10.88.196.43/26","dn":"uni/tn-mgmt/
  mgmtp-default/oob-default/rsooBStNode-[topology/pod-1/node-302]", "tDn":"topology/
  pod-1/node-302","gw":"10.88.196.1"} }}
```

In order to combine these configuration tasks together into one script, you need to determine the location of the object classes fabricNodeIdentP and mgmtRsOoBStNode in the MIT. To do this, you can use Visore, as explained earlier in this chapter.

For the first configuration task of registering a leaf node, you perform the following steps to find the complete path of object class fabricNodeIdentP, which is further illustrated in Figure 8-12:

Step 1.   Copy the fabric registration object class fabricNodeIdentP from the API message text and paste it under the Class or DN field in the APIC Object Store Browser window.

Step 2.   Click the < next to the object class fabricNodeIdentP to move it up one level in the hierarchy, to the parent object class fabricNodeIdentPol.

Step 3.   Click the < next to the object class fabricNodeIdentPol to move it up one level in the hierarchy, to the parent object class ctrlrInst.

Step 4.   Click the < next to the object class ctrlrInst to move it up one level in the hierarchy, to the parent object class polUni.

Step 5.   At the top level, polUni, note the complete path with the object class names. Also note that the DN for object class polUni is uni, which you can use in the URL when executing (posting) the script.

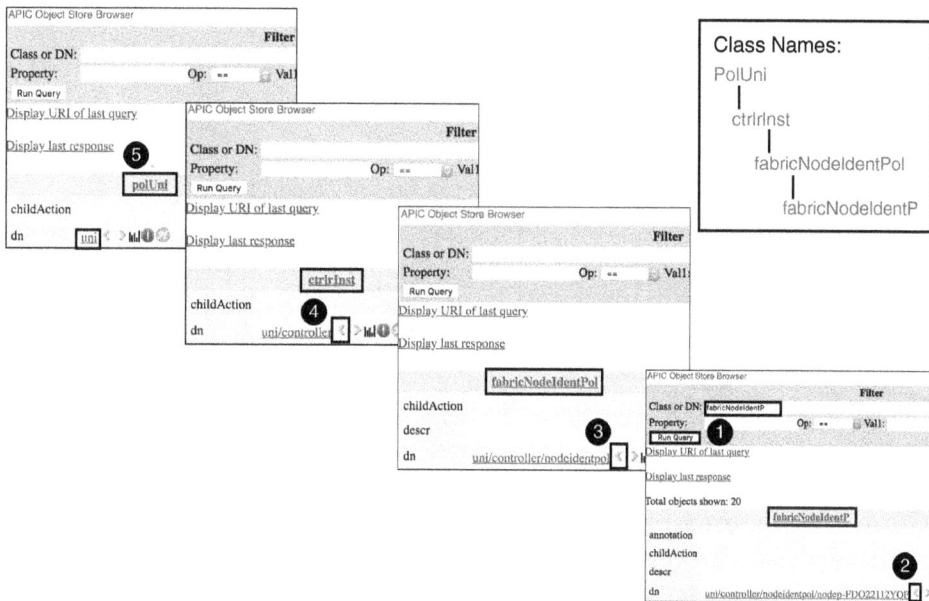

Figure 8-12   *Steps to Find the Path of the Node Registration Object Class*

For the second configuration task, assigning the OOB address to the leaf node, perform the steps that follow to find out the complete path of object class mgmtRsOoBStNode, which is further illustrated in Figure 8-13:

Step 1.   Copy the fabric registration object class mgmtRsOoBStNode from the API message text and paste it under the Class or DN field in the APIC Object Store Browser window.

Step 2.   Click the < next to the object class mgmtRsOoBStNode to move it up one level in the hierarchy, to the parent object class mgmtOoB.

Step 3.   Click the < next to the object class mgmtOoB to move it up one level in the hierarchy, to the parent object class mgmtMgmtP.

Step 4.   Click the < next to the object class mgmtMgmtP to move it up one level in the hierarchy, to the parent object class fvTenant.

Step 5.   Click the < next to the object class fvTenant to move it up one level in the hierarchy, to the parent object class polUni.

Step 6.   At the top level, polUni, note the complete path with the object class names. Also note that the DN for object class polUni is uni, which you can use in the URL when executing (posting) the script.

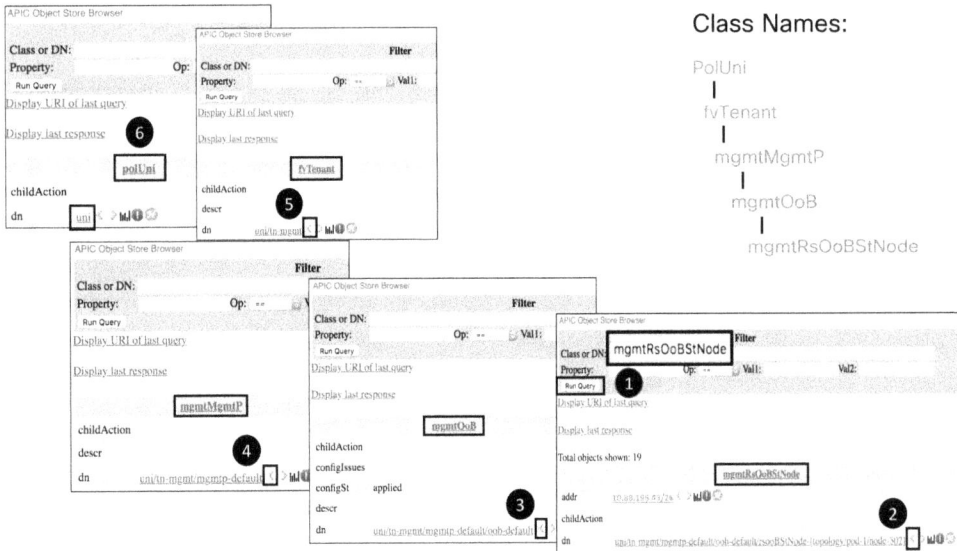

Figure 8-13   *Steps to Find the Path of the Node OOB Object Class*

Now that you know the complete paths for both the configuration tasks and have documented the object class names, you can build the URL and the script using JSON. Because both the object classes end up at the top-level polUni with uni, you can use the following URL:

https://*<apic_IP>*/api/node/mo/uni.json

It is recommended to always use this common URL whether configuring a single managed object or multiple managed objects, because the managed objects branch out from polUni at the top. For this configuration example, the tree looks as shown in Figure 8-14.

Using the JSON format, as explained earlier in Example 8-3 and the tree shown in Figure 8-14, the script looks as shown in Example 8-10.

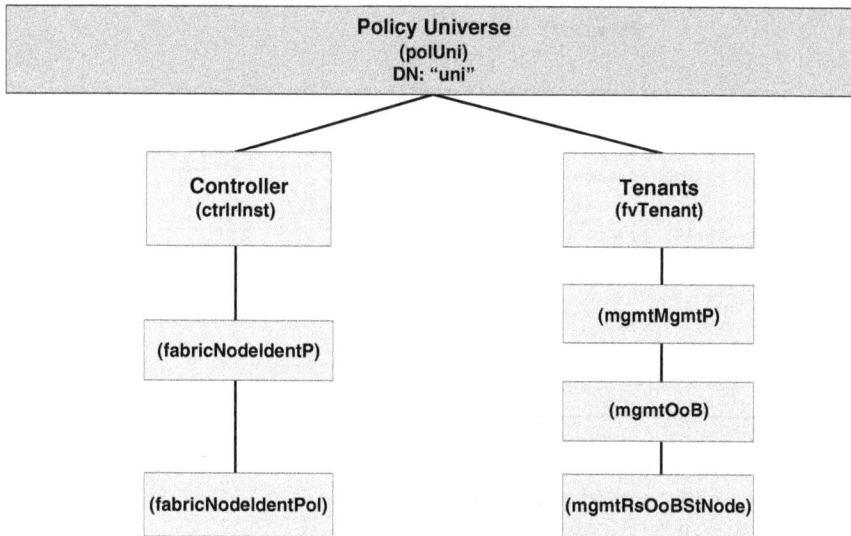

Figure 8-14 *Object Tree for Node Registration and OOB Management*

Example 8-10 *JSON Script to Configure Leaf Node Registration and OOB Address*

```json
{"polUni": {"attributes": {"dn":"uni"},
    "children": [

        {"ctrlrInst": {"attributes": {"dn":"uni/controller"},
            "children": [
                {"fabricNodeIdentPol": {"attributes":
{"dn":"uni/controller/nodeidentpol"},
                    "children": [
                        {"fabricNodeIdentP": {"attributes":
{"dn":"uni/controller/nodeidentpol/nodep-
                            FDO213409YV","fabricId":"1","podId":"1","serial":"FDO213
409YV","name":"leaf302",
                            "nodeId":"302"} }}
                        ] }}
                    ] }},

        {"fvTenant": {"attributes": {"dn":"uni/tn-mgmt","name":"mgmt"},
            "children": [
                {"mgmtMgmtP": {"attributes":
{"dn":"uni/tn-mgmt/mgmtp-default","name":"default"},
                    "children": [
                        {"mgmtOoB": {"attributes":
{"dn":"uni/tn-mgmt/mgmtp-default/oob-default","name":
```

```
                                    "default"},
                                        "children": [
                                            {"mgmtRsOoBStNode": {"attributes":
{"addr":"10.88.196.43/26","dn":"uni/tn-
                                            mgmt/mgmtp-default/oob-default/
rsooBStNode-[topology/pod-1/node-302]",
                                            "tDn":"topology/pod-1/node-
302","gw":"10.88.196.1"} }}
                                                    ] }}
                                        ] }}
                            ] }}

                    ] }}
```

You have successfully created your first ACI script using JSON format with multiple objects. You can use this method to create JSON scripts or even XML scripts for any configuration task in ACI.

Example 8-10 shows the single leaf node ID 302 registered to the fabric using its serial number FDO213409YV with leaf node name Leaf302 and assignment of the OOB address 10.88.196.43/26 with default gateway address 10.88.196.1, which is good if only single leaf configuration is required. However, in real-world use cases, you always end up having multiple leaf nodes requiring fabric registration and OOB addresses for management. Therefore, it is recommended to always use variables instead of using the exact values in the script, as shown in Example 8-11.

Example 8-11 *JSON Script to Configure Leaf Node Registration and OOB Address Using Variables*

```
{"polUni": {"attributes": {"dn":"uni"},
    "children": [

        {"ctrlrInst": {"attributes": {"dn":"uni/controller"},
            "children": [
                {"fabricNodeIdentPol": {"attributes":
{"dn":"uni/controller/nodeidentpol"},
                    "children": [
                        {"fabricNodeIdentP": {"attributes":
{"dn":"uni/controller/nodeidentpol/nodep-
                            {{serial-no}}","fabricId":"1","podId":"1","serial":
"{{serial-no}}",
                            "name":"{{node-name}}","nodeId":"{{node-id}}"} }}
                                ] }}
                        ] }},

        {"fvTenant": {"attributes": {"dn":"uni/tn-mgmt","name":"mgmt"},
            "children": [
```

```
            {"mgmtMgmtP": {"attributes": {"dn":"uni/tn-mgmt/mgmtp-default",
  "name":"default"},
                    "children": [
                        {"mgmtOoB": {"attributes":
  {"dn":"uni/tn-mgmt/mgmtp-default/oob-default","name":
                        "default"},
                            "children": [
                                {"mgmtRsOoBStNode": {"attributes":
  {"addr":"{{oob-ip}}","dn":"uni/tn-
                                mgmt/mgmtp-default/oob-default/rsooBStNode-
  [topology/pod-1/node-{{node-
                                id}}]","tDn":"topology/pod-1/node-{{node-
  id}}","gw":"{{oob-gw}}"} }}
                                        ] }}
                        ] }}
                ] }}

        ] }}
```

You can see that in Example 8-11, all exact values have been replaced by variables within double curly brackets. You can call these variables from the JSON script into a comma-separated values (CSV) file as table headings with exact vales from multiple objects, as shown in Table 8-1.

Note   The variable name is case sensitive, and you need to ensure that it matches exactly the name in the JSON script. Also, in Windows, make sure the carriage return is removed at the end. This can be done by opening up the CSV file in Notepad.

Table 8-1   *JSON Script Sample Variable CSV File*

serial-no	node-name	node-id	oob-ip	oob-gw
FDO213409YV	leaf302	302	10.88.196.43/26	10.88.196.1
FDO222574XY	leaf303	303	10.88.196.44/26	10.88.196.1

Now, you can do multiple iterations of these configuration tasks by using the REST client of your choice. In this case, let's look at the Postman Collection Runner tool as an example. Perform the following steps, which are further illustrated in Figure 8-15:

Step 1.   In Postman, open the Collection Runner tool.

Step 2.   Select the JSON script you created and collected in Postman (in this case, Script1-Fabric Discovery & OOB Management).

Step 3.   Select the Postman environment that you created to log on to the APIC from your REST client.

Step 4.   Type the number of iterations over which you want to input the variable's exact values into the script (in this case, 2). (In new Postman code, you do not need to add this information because Postman automatically selects the number of iterations based on your CSV input file.)

Step 5.   Insert your CSV input file (in this case, Scritp1-InputFile.csv).

Step 6.   Preview the script to ensure that all the variables' exact values are correct.

Step 7.   Click Run to execute the script.

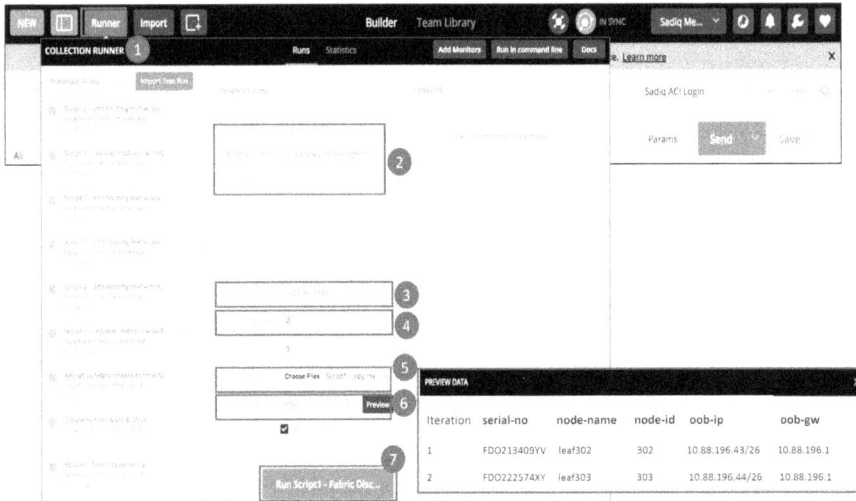

Figure 8-15   *Postman Collection Runner Tool*

In this way, you can create any configuration automation script by using JSON or XML in ACI. You can verify a configuration by using the MOQuery tool, as shown in Example 8-12.

Example 8-12   *Verifying the JSON Script to Configure Leaf Node Registration and OOB Address*

```
apic1# moquery -c mgmtRsOoBStNode -f 'mgmt.RsOoBStNode.tDn*"30"'
Total Objects shown: 2


# mgmt.RsOoBStNode
tDn            : topology/pod-1/node-302
addr           : 10.88.196.43/26
annotation     :
childAction    :
dn             : uni/tn-mgmt/mgmtp-default/oob-default/rsooBStNode-[topology/pod-1/
                 node-302]
extMngdBy      :
forceResolve   : yes
```

```
gw             : 10.88.196.1
lcOwn          : local
modTs          : 2019-08-13T14:28:54.975-04:00
rType          : mo
rn             : rsooBStNode-[topology/pod-1/node-302]
state          : unformed
stateQual      : none
status         :
tCl            : fabricNode
tType          : mo
uid            : 15374
v6Addr         : ::
v6Gw           : ::


# mgmt.RsOoBStNode
tDn            : topology/pod-1/node-303
addr           : 10.88.196.44/26
annotation     :
childAction    :
dn             : uni/tn-mgmt/mgmtp-default/oob-default/rsooBStNode-[topology/pod-1/
                 node-303]
extMngdBy      :
forceResolve   : yes
gw             : 10.88.196.1
lcOwn          : local
modTs          : 2019-08-13T14:28:54.975-04:00
rType          : mo
rn             : rsooBStNode-[topology/pod-1/node-303]
state          : unformed
stateQual      : none
status         :
tCl            : fabricNode
tType          : mo
uid            : 15374
v6Addr         : ::
v6Gw           : ::
apic1# moquery -c fabricNodeIdentP -f 'fabric.NodeIdentP.nodeId*"30"'
Total Objects shown: 2


# fabric.NodeIdentP
serial         : FDO213409YV
annotation     :
childAction    :
descr          :
dn             : uni/controller/nodeidentpol/nodep-FDO213409YV
```

```
extMngdBy      :
extPoolId      : 0
fabricId       : 1
lcOwn          : local
modTs          : 2019-08-12T13:08:46.842-04:00
monPolDn       : uni/fabric/monfab-default
name           : leaf302
nameAlias      :
nodeId         : 302
nodeType       : unspecified
podId          : 1
rn             : nodep-FDO213409YV
role           : unspecified
status         :
uid            : 15374


# fabric.NodeIdentP
serial         : FDO222574XY
annotation     :
childAction    :
descr          :
dn             : uni/controller/nodeidentpol/nodep-FDO222574XY
extMngdBy      :
extPoolId      : 0
fabricId       : 1
lcOwn          : local
modTs          : 2019-08-12T13:07:50.037-04:00
monPolDn       : uni/fabric/monfab-default
name           : leaf303
nameAlias      :
nodeId         : 303
nodeType       : unspecified
podId          : 1
rn             : nodep-FDO222574XY
role           : unspecified
status         :
uid            : 15374
```

Automating Tasks Using Ansible

Ansible can be used to automate certain tasks in the data center. For quite some time, it has been a tool of choice for application and server teams, who used it to orchestrate application-hosting tasks in the data center. Ansible is now commonly used in the network community as well. Initially, Ansible was developed as an open-source tool. However, Red Hat acquired it and started supporting a commercial version, called Ansible Tower. Unlike its competitors, such as Chef and Puppet, Ansible is an agentless tool that runs in a push model using modules developed in Python. It runs on a system called a control node that pushes these automation scripts securely using SSH connection to end hosts called managed nodes contained in an inventory file. The automation script comprises sets of instructions in a *playbook* (see Figure 8-16).

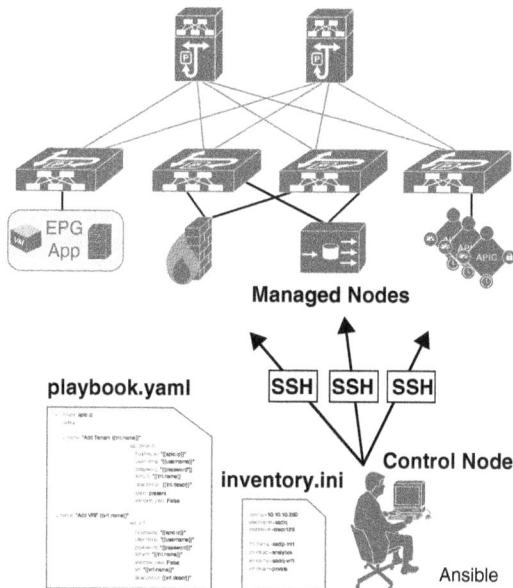

Figure 8-16 *Ansible Automation Tool Architecture*

The control node can run on an operating system (OS) such as Red Hat Enterprise Linux (RHEL), CentOS, Ubuntu, Debian, Fedora, or macOS, and a managed node can be a physical or virtual server, network device, or L4–L7 device. The core of the automation in Ansible is the playbook, which is a YAML file with the extension .yaml. YAML (which stands for "YAML Ain't Markup Language") is a human-readable data serialization language. It is mainly used for configuration files and is also commonly used in applications where data is being stored or transmitted. YAML is similar to the XML and JSON formats in that it contains various key/value pairs in the syntax. An Ansible playbook is a set of instructions that contains multiple plays for configuring managed nodes. Example 8-13 shows a sample playbook YAML file.

Example 8-13 *Playbook YAML File*

```
---
    - name: play1
      hosts: webservers
      tasks:
          - name: install apache
            Yum:
                  Name: apache
                  State: present
          - name: start apache
            Service:
                  Name: apache
                  State: start


    - name: play 2
      hosts: appservers
      tasks:
          - name: install exim email server
            Yum:
                  Name: exim
                  State: present
          - name: start apache
            Service:
                  Name: exim
                  State: start
...
```

In Example 8-13, you can see that the YAML file starts with three hyphens (---), followed by three tags: name, which identifies the name of the play (in this case, play1); hosts, which identifies a single node or a group of managed nodes on which these instructions will be executed (in play1 it is webservers); and tasks, which is a set of instructions executed by using Ansible modules. In this example, there are two tasks in play1: install the Apache server and then run it. These are executed using Yum and Service Ansible modules. Similarly, play2 installs and runs a free email server on a group of managed nodes' app servers. The YAML file optionally ends with three dots (...).

A playbook fetches the information about the managed nodes through inventory files, also known as host files. A playbook is used to organize managed nodes into groups. Running a playbook against a single device does not provide a huge efficiency gain. However, by using an inventory file, a single playbook can automate hundreds of end-host devices (managed nodes) with a single command. In Ansible, the inventory file can be in one of many formats, depending on the inventory plug-ins you have. The most common formats are INI and YAML. Inventory files are stored in the folder where you store all your playbooks. A sample inventory file with an .ini extension might look as shown in Example 8-14.

Example 8-14   *Inventory INI File*

```
mail.cisco.com

[webservers]
amt.cisco.com
sad.cisco.com

[appservers]
app1.cisco.com
app2.cisco.com
app3.cisco.com
```

In Example 8-14, the headings in square brackets ([webservers] and [appservers]) are group names that are used in classifying hosts and deciding what hosts you are controlling at what times and for what purposes.

Example 8-15 shows the same sample inventory file from Example 8-14 but in YAML format.

Example 8-15   *Inventory YAML File*

```
all:
  hosts:
    mail.cisco.com:
  children:
    webservers:
      hosts:
        amt.cisco.com:
        sad.cisco.com:
    appservers:
      hosts:
        app1.cisco.com:
        app2.cisco.com:
        app3.cisco.com:
```

Ansible Support in ACI

Cisco has developed Ansible modules for ACI as part of standard Ansible packages starting from Ansible Release 2.4 to automate various configuration tasks for creating single or multiple objects. Additional Ansible modules for ACI can be found at https://docs.ansible.com/ansible/latest/modules/list_of_network_modules.html.

The Ansible modules for ACI provide automation support for a broad set of data center application-hosting use cases, including the following:

- **Day 0 (ACI fabric installation and setup):** Initial configuration of ACI generic policies, such as those related to switch registration, VLAN pool creation, domains, AAEPs, user access management, monitoring policies, configuration import/export policies, and firmware updates.

- **Day 1 (initial configuration and operation):** Initial configuration of ACI logical constructs, such as creating tenant, VRF, L3Out, and other instances, and building physical construct such as creating interface and switch policies.

- **Day 2 (new/updated configuration and optimization):** Adding, modifying, and deleting policies related to ACI logical and physical constructs, such as tenants, VRF instances, APs, BDs, EPGs, contracts, and L3Outs, and associating domains and binding physical ports to EPGs.

Example 8-16 shows a simple example of creating a tenant AMT by using the Ansible module for ACI.

Example 8-16 *Sample Ansible Playbook to Create a Tenant in ACI*

```
---                                            ← Start of YAML File.
# Demo Ansible Playbook to create Tenant in ACI  ← Playbook Comment.
  - name: Creating a Tenant                    ← Name of the Playbook.
    hosts: apics                               ← Managed Nodes Group Name.
    connection: local                          ← Local connection.
    gather_facts: no                           ← Do not collect information
                                                 about Managed Nodes.

    tasks:
      - name: Configure a New Tenant           ← Name of the Task.
        aci_tenant:                            ← ACI "Tenant" Ansible
                                                 Module.

          hostname: "{{ inventory_hostname }}"  ← Host from Inventory.
          username: "{{ username }}"           ← Username to access APIC.
          password: "{{ password }}"           ← Password to access APIC.
          tenant: AMT                          ← Name of the "Tenant".
          description: "Tenant for Cisco Press Book"  ← Description of Tenant
                                                 Object.
          validate_certs: no                   ← Validate Certs.
          state: present                       ← Create Tenant Object if
                                                 does not exist.
```

Ansible modules are developed to run on target devices known as managed nodes. However, the Ansible modules developed for ACI run on neither fabric switches nor on the fabric controller (the APIC). Rather, they communicate directly with the APIC's REST interface. Therefore, Ansible modules for ACI either run locally on the Ansible control node or are delegated to other systems that have secure connections to the APIC. Collecting information about target devices does not work, and it is mandatory to disable it in Ansible modules for ACI, as shown in Example 8-16 (gather_facts: no). You can disable it globally in your ansible.cfg file or under each play.

There are many Ansible modules available for ACI automation, and most common configurations can be executed through them. However, some configuration tasks, such as assigning the OOB address to switches, cannot be executed using those built-in over-the-counter modules. Therefore, your best bet is to use the aci_rest Ansible module, which provides direct access to the APIC REST API and fills any gaps in automating the configuration tasks that are not currently available using regular Ansible modules for ACI. This may seems like extra effort and complexity, but generating native REST API payload is pretty simple and straightforward, as described earlier in this chapter. The other benefit of using the aci_rest module is that the REST API is idempotent in nature and reports the state of a configuration change (whether successful or failed).

The aci_rest module accepts native REST API payloads using XML and JSON formats. In addition, it accepts inline YAML payload that is structured much like JSON format and uses the .json extension. Example 8-17 shows an example of assigning the OOB address to fabric leaf node ID 302 by using the Ansible aci_rest module for ACI.

Example 8-17 *Sample Ansible Playbook Using the aci_rest Module to Assign the OOB Address in ACI*

```
---
# Demo Ansible Playbook to Configure OOB Management in ACI
  - name: Configuring OOB Management
    hosts: apics
    connection: local
    gather_facts: no
    tasks:
      - name: Assigning OOB Address
        aci_rest:                              ← ACI "REST" Ansible Module.
          hostname: "{{ inventory_hostname }}"
          username: "{{ username }}"
          password: "{{ password }}"
          validate_certs: no
          path: /api/node/mo/uni.json          ← Path of Object in the MIT.
          method: post                         ← REST method "POST" is
                                                 used.
          content: |                           ← REST API Payload.
                      {"fvTenant": {"attributes": {"dn":"uni/tn-mgmt","name":
"mgmt"},
                "children": [
```

```
                    {"mgmtMgmtP": {"attributes":
{"dn":"uni/tn-mgmt/mgmtp-default","name":"default"},
                        "children": [
                            {"mgmtOoB": {"attributes":
{"dn":"uni/tn-mgmt/mgmtp-default/oob-default",
                            "name":"default"},
                            "children": [
                                {"mgmtRsOoBStNode": {"attributes":
{"addr":"10.88.196.43/26",
                                "dn":"uni/tn-mgmt/mgmtp-default/oob-default/
rsooBStNode-[topology/
                                pod-1/node-302]","tDn":"topology/pod-1/node-
302","gw":"10.88.196.1"} }}
                                        ] }}
                            ] }}
                    ] }}
```

In Example 8-17, you can see the JSON payload with actual values of the OOB management address, gateway address, and node ID. These values can be replaced with variables much as if you were using a native REST API call. For example, instead of inserting the actual OOB address 10.88.196.43/26, you could use the variable {{oob-ip}} in the payload and add OOB addresses by using this variable in the inventory file to call out the actual values in the Ansible playbook. Similarly, the gateway address and node ID actual values can be replaced by variables as well.

Installing Ansible and Ensuring a Secure Connection

As mentioned earlier in this chapter, an Ansible local machine node or control node can run on operating systems such as RHEL, CentOS, Ubuntu, Debian, Fedora, and macOS.

The following steps provide an example of installing Ansible on an Ubuntu machine:

Step 1. Update the repository on the Ansible control node by using the following command:

```
root@ansible:/home/sadhussa# sudo apt-get update
```

Step 2. Install the common software properties on the Ansible control node by using the following command:

```
root@ansible:/home/sadhussa# sudo apt-get install
software-properties-common
```

Step 3. Add the Personal Package Archive (PPA) for Ansible to the repository by using the following command:

```
root@ansible:/home/sadhussa# sudo apt-add-repository
ppa:ansible/ansible
```

Press Enter to continue.

Step 4. Update the repository once again on the Ansible control node by using the following command:

```
root@ansible:/home/sadhussa# sudo apt-get update
```

Step 5. Install Ansible on the control node by using the following command:

```
root@ansible:/home/sadhussa# sudo apt-get install ansible
```

Press Y to continue.

Once Ansible is installed properly and with the right version supported by ACI modules (Ansible version 2.4.4.0 and Python version 2.7.6 or later), you need to ensure that the SSH connectivity from the Ansible control node to the managed nodes (in this case, APICs) is functioning normally.

To check the Ansible and Python version running on a control node, you use the **ansible --version** command, as shown in Example 8-18.

Example 8-18 *Checking Ansible and Python Software Version*

```
root@ansible:/home/sadhussa# ansible --version
ansible 2.4.4.0
 config file = /etc/ansible/ansible.cfg
 configured module search path = [u'/root/.ansible/plugins/modules', u'/usr/share/
  ansible/plugins/modules']
 ansible python module location = /usr/lib/python2.7/dist-packages/ansible
 executable location = /usr/bin/ansible
 python version = 2.7.6 (default, Nov 23 2017, 15:49:48) [GCC 4.8.4]
```

To ensure the secure connection from the Ansible control node to the managed nodes (APICs), you use the **ansible -m ping apics** command, as shown in Example 8-19.

Example 8-19 *Checking the Secure SSH Connection to the Ansible Managed Nodes*

```
root@ansible:/home/sadhussa# ansible -m ping apics
10.10.10.1 | UNREACHABLE! =>{
  "changed": false,
  "msg": "Failed to connect to the host via ssh: WARNING! THIS IS A PRIVATE COM-
  PUTER SYSTEM. USAGE MAY BE MONITORED AND UNAUTHORIZED ACCESS OR USE MAY RESULT IN
  CRIMINAL OR CIVIL PROSECUTION.\nPermission denied (publickey,password).\r\n",
  "unreachable": true
}
```

The output in Example 8-19 shows that the Ansible control node cannot reach the group of managed nodes (**apics**), as defined in the inventory file. This is most likely to be an issue with SSH configuration. To configure SSH on an Ansible control node, you need to perform the following steps:

Step 1. Generate an SSH key on the Ansible control node.

Step 2. Copy the SSH key to the managed nodes.

To generate an SSH key on an Ansible control node, you need to use the command shown in Example 8-20.

Example 8-20   *Generating an SSH Key on an Ansible Control Node*

```
root@ansible:/home/sadhussa# ssh-keygen -t rsa
Generating public/private rsa key pair.
Enter file in which to save the key (/root/.ssh/id_rsa): ← Directory where SSH Key
  is stored
Enter passphrase (empty for no passphrase): ← Type passphrase and Press Enter OR
  Just Enter for no passphrase
Enter same passphrase again:   ← Repeat the same as above
Your identification has been saved in /root/.ssh/id_rsa.
Your public key has been saved in /root/.ssh/id_rsa.pub.
The key fingerprint is:
78:7a:a0:2a:b1:bf:39:38:67:8c:70:7a:04:96:a7:79 root@time
The key's randomart image is:
+--[ RSA 2048]----+
|                 |
|                 |
|                 |
|     o           |
|. . o S          |
|=o.. O           |
|=@. . .          |
|XEB. .           |
|+*++             |
+----------------+
```

To copy the recently generated SSH key from the Ansible control node to an Ansible managed node (in this case, the APIC with IP address 10.10.10.1), you need to run the **ssh-copy-id** command, as shown in Example 8-21.

Example 8-21   *Copying the SSH Key to an Ansible Managed Node*

```
root@ansible:~/.ssh# ssh-copy-id 10.10.10.1
/usr/bin/ssh-copy-id: INFO: Source of Key(s) to be installed: "/root/.ssh/id_rsa"
The authenticity of host 10.10.10.1 can't be established.
ECDSA key fingerprint is SHA256:abcdef!
Are you sure you want to continue connecting (yes/no)? yes  ← Type "yes"
/usr/bin/ssh-copy-id: INFO: attempting to log in with the new key(s), to filter out
  any that are already installed
/usr/bin/ssh-copy-id: INFO: 1 key(s) remain to be installed -- if you are prompted
  now it is to install the new keys
```

```
WARNING!

THIS IS A PRIVATE COMPUTER SYSTEM. USAGE MAY BE MONITORED. UNAUTHORIZED ACCESS OR
  USE MAY RESULT IN CRIMINAL OR CIVIL PROSECUTION, DISCIPLINE UP TO AND INCLUDING
  TERMINATION OF EMPLOYMENT, TERMINATION OF ASSIGNMENT, OR LOSS OF ACCESS.

Number of key(s) added: 1

Now try logging into the machine, with: "ssh '10.10.10.1'"

and check to make sure that only the key(s) you wanted were added.
```

You can verify the SSH connection by entering the **ansible –m ping apics** command, as shown in Example 8-22.

Example 8-22 *Verifying the Secure SSH Connection to an Ansible Managed Node*

```
root@ansible:/home/sadhussa# ansible -m ping apics
10.10.10.1 | SUCCESS =>{
   "changed": false,
   "ping": "pong"
}
```

Example 8-22 shows that you have successfully connected to the APIC from your Ansible control node. Now you can proceed with writing your playbooks and inventory file and executing them as you desire.

To execute an Ansible playbook, you use the syntax shown in Example 8-23.

Example 8-23 *Executing an Ansible Playbook*

```
"ansible-playbook -i {inventory-file} {playbook-file}"  ← -v, -vvv, -vvvv knobs can
  be used to get more output during playbook execution.
root@ansible:/home/sadhussa# ansible-playbook -i apics tenant.yaml
PLAY [Creating a Tenant] **********************************************************
  ****
TASK [Configure a New Tenant] ****************************************************
  ****
changed: [10.10.10.1]
PLAY RECAP ***********************************************************************
  ****
10.10.10.1         : ok=1    changed=1    unreachable=0    failed=0    skipped=0
    rescued=0     ignored=0
```

Example 8-23 shows that a play creating a tenant has successfully executed a single task to configure a new tenant. ok=1 in the output indicates that one task has executed successfully. changed=1 in the output indicates that the one task has changed its configuration status.

APIC Authentication in Ansible

APIC authentication in Ansible can be done by using *username* and *password* tags in a playbook. However, this is not a secure authentication method. In addition, large playbooks with lots of tasks having multiple iterations could result in HTTP 503 errors and login failures due to the Nginx throttling introduced with ACI Release 3.1 and later.

To mitigate this issue, two workarounds are to disable APIC session throttling or add a pause in the tasks in the playbook. However, the recommended method is to use *signature-based authentication*, which is available in Ansible version 2.5 and later. To enable signature-based authentication in Ansible using certificates instead of passwords, you need to perform the following steps.

Step 1.   Generate a self-signed certificate by using the **openssl** command:

```
root@ansible:/home/sadhussa# openssl req -new -newkey
rsa:1024 -days 36500 -nodes -x509 -keyout ansible.key -out
ansible.crt - subj '/CN=ansible/O=Cisco Systems/C=US'
```

Step 2.   Create a local user on the APIC with the appropriate role and privileges.

Step 3.   Associate the self-signed X.509 certificate with the local user.

Example 8-24 shows how to complete these steps using the sample Ansible playbook.

Example 8-24   *Ansible Playbook to Configure Signature-Based Authentication in ACI*

```
---
# Demo Ansible Playbook for Signature Based Authentication in ACI
  - name: Generate a Self-Signed Certificate
    command: "openssl req -new -newkey rsa:1024 -days 36500 -nodes -x509 -keyout
ansible.key -out ansible.crt - subj '/CN=ansible/O=Cisco Systems/C=US'"


  - name: Creating Local User w-Certificate in ACI
    hosts: apics
    connection: local
    gather_facts: no
    tasks:
      - name: Configure a Local User
        aci_aaa_user:
          hostname: "{{ inventory_hostname }}"
          username: "{{ username }}"
          password: "{{ password }}"
          aaa_user: ansible
          aaa_password: C!sco123
          expiration: never
          expires: no
          email:amt@cisco.com
```

```
            first_name: Sadiq
            last_name: Memon
            validate_certs: no
               state: present

     - name: Assigning Admin Role/Priv to Local User
        aci_rest:
           hostname: "{{ inventory_hostname }}"
           username: "{{ username }}"
           password: "{{ password }}"
           validate_certs: no
           path: /api/node/mo/uni/usertext/user-ansible/userdomain-all.json
           method: post
           content: |
             {"aaaUserDomain": {"attributes":{"name":"all","rn":"userdomain-all"},
                 "children":[
                     {"aaaUserRole": {"attributes":{"name":"admin",
                       "privType":"writePriv","rn":"role-admin"} }}
                          ] }}

     - name: Associate a Certificate to Local User
        aci_aaa_user_certificate:
           hostname: "{{ inventory_hostname }}"
           username: "{{ username }}"
           password: "{{ password }}"
           aaa_user: ansible
           certificate_name: ansible
           certificate_data: "{{ lookup('file', 'ansible.crt') }}"
           validate_certs: no
               state: present
```

When you are finished with the preceding steps, you can use the signature-based authentication in your Ansible playbooks, as shown in Example 8-25.

Example 8-25   *Ansible Playbook Using Signature-Based Authentication in ACI*

```
---
# Demo Ansible Playbook to create VRF in ACI
  - name: Creating a VRF
    hosts: apics
    connection: local
    gather_facts: no
    tasks:
      - name: Configure a New VRF
        aci_vrf:
```

```
        hostname: "{{ inventory_hostname }}"
          username: ansible
          private_key: ansible.key
          tenant: AMT
          vrf: PUBLIC
          description: "VRF for Cisco Press Book"
          validate_certs: no
          state: present
```

Automation Use Cases

The following sections examine a few automation use cases of configuring various tasks in ACI with Ansible.

Use Case 1

Use Case 1 shows how to create an application profile (AP), an endpoint group (EPG), a bridge domain (BD), a subnet, a contract, a subject, and a filter in ACI by using the available Ansible modules, as shown in Example 8-26.

Example 8-26 *Use Case 1 Ansible Playbook*

```
---
# Demo Ansible Playbook to create AP/EPG/BD/Contract in ACI
  - name: Creating AP/EPG/BD/Contract
    hosts: apics
    connection: local
    gather_facts: no

    vars:

    vars_prompt:
        - name: "my_status"
          prompt: "Press 'c' to create or modify an object. Press 'd' to delete
    object."
          private: no
          default: 'c'

    tasks:
        - name: Setting ACI Object State
          set_fact:
            the_status: 'present'
          when: my_status == 'c'
        - name: Setting ACI Object Status as Deleted
          set_fact:
            the_status: 'absent'
          when: my_status == 'd'
```

```
- name: Configure an AP
  aci_ap:
    hostname: "{{ inventory_hostname }}"
    username: ansible
    private_key: ansible.key
    tenant: "{{ tenant_name }}"
    ap: "{{ ap_name }}"
    validate_certs: no
    state: "{{ the_status }}"

- name: Configure a BD
  aci_bd:
    hostname: "{{ inventory_hostname }}"
    username: ansible
    private_key: ansible.key
    tenant: "{{ tenant_name }}"
    vrf: "{{ vrf_name }}"
    bd: "{{ bd_name }}"
    enable_routing: "{{ routing_state }}"
    validate_certs: no
    state: "{{ the_status }}"

- name: Configure a BD Subnet
  aci_bd_subnet:
    hostname: "{{ inventory_hostname }}"
    username: ansible
    private_key: ansible.key
    tenant: "{{ tenant_name }}"
    bd: "{{ bd_name }}"
    gateway: "{{ gw_ip }}"
    mask: "{{ gw_mask }}"
    scope: "{{ subnet_scope }}"
    validate_certs: no
    state: "{{ the_status }}"

- name: Configure an EPG
  aci_epg:
    hostname: "{{ inventory_hostname }}"
    username: ansible
    private_key: ansible.key
    tenant: "{{ tenant_name }}"
    ap: "{{ ap_name }}"
    epg: "{{ epg_name }}"
    bd: " {{ bd_name }}"
```

```
          validate_certs: no
          state: "{{ the_status }}"


    - name: Configure a Contract
      aci_contract:
          hostname: "{{ inventory_hostname }}"
          username: ansible
          private_key: ansible.key
          tenant: "{{ tenant_name }}"
          contract: "{{ contract_name }}"
          scope: "{{ contract_scope }}"
          validate_certs: no
          state: "{{ the_status }}"


    - name: Configure a Contract Subject
      aci_contract_subject:
          hostname: "{{ inventory_hostname }}"
          username: ansible
          private_key: ansible.key
          tenant: "{{ tenant_name }}"
          contract: "{{ contract_name }}"
          subject: "{{ subject_name }}"
          reverse_filter: "{{ reverse_fltr }}"
          validate_certs: no
          state: "{{ the_status }}"


    - name: Configure a Filter
      aci_filter:
          hostname: "{{ inventory_hostname }}"
          username: ansible
          private_key: ansible.key
          tenant: "{{ tenant_name }}"
          filter: "{{ filter_name }}"
          validate_certs: no
          state: "{{ the_status }}"


    - name: Configure a Filter Entry
      aci_filter_entry:
          hostname: "{{ inventory_hostname }}"
          username: ansible
          private_key: ansible.key
          tenant: "{{ tenant_name }}"
```

```
        filter: "{{ filter_name }}"
        entry: "{{ filter_entry_name }}"
        ether_type: "{{ eth_type }}"
        ip_protocol: "{{ ip_prot }}"
        dst_port: "{{ dst_prt }}"
        validate_certs: no
        state: "{{ the_status }}"

    - name: Associating a Filter to Contract Subject
      aci_contract_subject_to_filter:
        hostname: "{{ inventory_hostname }}"
        username: ansible
        private_key: ansible.key
        tenant: "{{ tenant_name }}"
        contract: "{{ contract_name }}"
        subject: "{{ subject_name }}"
        filter: "{{ filter_name }}"
        validate_certs: no
        state: "{{ the_status }}"

    - name: Associating a Contract to EPG
      aci_epg_to_contract:
        hostname: "{{ inventory_hostname }}"
        username: ansible
        private_key: ansible.key
        tenant: "{{ tenant_name }}"
        ap: "{{ ap_name }}"
        epg: "{{ epg_name }}"
        contract: "{{ contract_name }}"
        contract_type: "{{ cont_type }}"
        validate_certs: no
        state: "{{ the_status }}"
```

Example 8-26 creates an AP, a BD, a subnet, an EPG, a contract, a subject, and a filter, and it also associates the filter to the contract subject and the contract to the EPG. You can see in the example that all this configuration can be created or deleted by using the vars_prompt tag and by using set_fact in the first two tasks in Ansible Playbook.

Example 8-27 shows a sample Ansible inventory file for automation Use Case 1.

Example 8-27   *Use Case 1: Ansible Inventory File*

```
[apics]
10.10.10.1


[apic:vars]
ap_name=web-app
epg_name=web-epg
bd_name=web-bd
routing_state=yes            ← "no" to disable routing
gw_ip=20.20.20.1
gw_mask=26
subnet_scope=public          ← Subnet Scope can be "public", "private" and
                               "shared"
contract_name=web-contract-c01
contract_scope=context       ← Contract Scope can be "context", "application-
                               profile", "global" and "tenant"
subject_name=web-subject-s01
reverse_fltr=yes             ← "no" to disable reverse filter
filter_name=allow-https
filter_entry_name=https
eth_type=ip                  ← Ether Type can be "ip" "arp", "fcoe", "trill", and
                               so on
ip_prot=tcp                  ← IP Protocol can be "tcp" "udp", "icmp", "igmp",
                               "pim" and so on
dst_prt=443
cont_type=provider           ← Contract Type can be "provider" and "consumer"
```

Use Case 2

Customers often ask how to automate the configuration of Inter-Pod Network (IPN) devices since it is done outside ACI. This section shows how to create the necessary configuration for this use case on an IPN router (in this case a Nexus 9000 device) for multi-pod. Example 8-28 shows the Ansible playbook for Use Case 2.

Example 8-28   *Use Case 2: Ansible Playbook*

```
---
# Demo Ansible Playbook to create Multi-POD IPN Configuration on N9K
  - name: Creating Multi-POD IPN Config on N9K
    hosts: nxos
    connection: local
    gather_facts: no


    vars_files:
        - ipn1-var.yml
        - ipn2-var.yml
```

```
    vars:
      nxos_provider:
        - host: "{{ inventory_hostname }}"
        - username: ansible
        - password: *Cisco123*
        - transport: cli

    Tasks:

      - name: Base Config on IPN Devices
        nxos_config:
          provider: "{{ nxos_provider }}"
          src: "~/sadiq/network/configs/ipn1-config.txt"


        nxos_config:
          provider: "{{ nxos_provider }}"
          src: "~/sadiq/network/configs/ipn2-config.txt"

      - name: Base Interface Config on IPN Devices
        nxos_config:
          provider: "{{ nxos_provider }}"
          lines:
              - encapsulation dot1q 4
              - ip router ospf 1 area 0.0.0.0
              - ip ospf network point-to-point
              - ip ospf mtu ignore
              - ip pim sparse-mode
              - ip dhcp relay address 10.0.0.1
          Parent: ['interface Ethernet1/1.4']

        nxos_config:
          provider: "{{ nxos_provider }}"
          lines:
              - ip router ospf 1 area 0.0.0.0
              - ip ospf network point-to-point
              - ip ospf mtu ignore
              - ip pim sparse-mode
          Parent: ['interface Ethernet1/2']

      - name: Configure Interfaces
        nxos_interfaces:
          config:
            - name: "{{ interface_1 }}"
              description: 'IPN1 connected to Spine1-POD1'
```

```
        mode: layer3
        mtu: 9150
        enabled: True
      - name: "{{ interface_1 }}".4
        description: 'IPN1 connected to Spine1-POD1'
        mtu: 9150
        enabled: True
      - name: "{{ interface_2 }}"
        description: 'IPN1 connected to IPN2'
        mode: layer3
        mtu: 9150
        enabled: True
    state: merged

- name: Configure Interfaces IPs
  nxos_l3_interfaces:
    config:
      - name: "{{ interface_1 }}".4
        ipv4:
          - address: "{{ address_1 }}"
      - name: "{{ interface_2 }}"
        ipv4:
          - address: "{{ address_2 }}"
    state: merged

- nxos_ospf_vrf:
    provider: "{{ nxos_provider }}"
    ospf: 1
    log_adjacency: log
    router_id: "{{ router_id }}"
    timer_throttle_spf_start: 50
    timer_throttle_spf_hold: 1000
    timer_throttle_spf_max: 2000
    timer_throttle_lsa_start: 60
    timer_throttle_lsa_hold: 1100
    timer_throttle_lsa_max: 3000
    state: present
```

Example 8-29 and Example 8-30 show the external variable files called out in
Example 8-28 as vars_files.

Example 8-29 *IPN1 Variable File (ipn1-var.yml)*

```
---
   router_id: 1.1.1.1

   address_1: 10.10.10.1/31
   address_2: 20.20.20.1/31

   interface_1: Ethernet1/1
   interface_2: Ethernet1/2
```

Example 8-30 *IPN2 Variable File (ipn2-var.yml)*

```
---
   router_id. 2.2.2.2

   address_1: 30.30.30.1/31
   address_2: 20.20.20.2/31

   interface_1: Ethernet1/1
   interface_2: Ethernet1/2
```

Example 8-31 shows a sample Ansible inventory file for automation Use Case 2.

Example 8-31 *Use Case 2: Ansible Inventory File*

```
[nxos]
100.100.100.1          ← IPN1 management address
100.100.100.2          ← IPN2 management address
```

Example 8-32 shows the NX-OS configuration baseline file for the IPN1 router.

Example 8-32 *Use Case 2: IPN Router Baseline Configuration File (NX-OS)*

```
! < ipn1-config.txt >
!
hostname IPN1
!
feature nxapi
feature ospf
feature pim
feature interface-vlan
feature dhcp
feature lldp
```

```
!
ip name-server 61.61.61.1
!
system jumbomtu 9216
!
service dhcp
ip dhcp relay
!
ntp server 51.51.51.1
logging server 111.111.111.1
!
ip pim mtu 9000
ip pim rp-address 90.90.90.1 group-list 225.0.0.0/8 bidir
ip pim rp-address 90.90.90.1 group-list 239.255.255.240/28 bidir
!
interface loopback90
  description "Interface dedicated for PIM RP"
  ip address 90.90.90.1/32
  ip router ospf 1 area 0.0.0.0
  ip pim sparse-mode
! < You can add any other baseline configuration parameters in this file >
```

Orchestration Through UCS Director

Cisco Unified Computing System (UCS) is a server platform offering composed of computing hardware, virtualization support, switching fabric, and management software. UCS Director, one of the tools in the UCS family, is a full end-to-end management, orchestration, and automation solution with built-in security components for a wide range of converged infrastructure platforms from Cisco and other vendors.

Cisco UCS Director is a 64-bit appliance that uses the standard virtualization template formats such as VMWare vSphere Open Virtualization Format (OVF) and Microsoft Hyper-V Virtual Hard Disks (VHD).

Management Through Cisco UCS Director

Cisco UCS Director extends the capabilities you experience when combining your compute, network, and storage components by providing comprehensive visibility into and management of your entire application-hosting infrastructure in your data center. You can use Cisco UCS Director to configure, administer, and monitor Cisco and other supported vendor-specific platforms. You can perform the following tasks using Cisco UCS Director:

- Create, clone, and deploy service profiles and templates for all Cisco UCS servers and applications.

- Monitor organizational usage, trends, and capacity across a converged infrastructure any time of the day. For example, you can view heat maps that show VM utilization across all your data center locations whenever needed.

- Deploy and add capacity to converged infrastructures in a consistent and repeatable manner.

- Manage, monitor, and report on data center components, such as Cisco UCS domains or Cisco Nexus network devices running in NX-OS or ACI mode.

- Extend virtual service catalogs, including services for your physical infrastructure.

- Manage secure multitenant environments, accommodating both physical and virtualized workloads.

Automation and Orchestration with Cisco UCS Director

Cisco UCS Director enables you to build workflows that provide service automation and to publish these workflows in extending the services to your end users when needed. You can collaborate with other subject matter experts in your company to quickly and easily create the policies. By following these policies, you can then build Cisco UCS Director workflows to automate simple or complex provisioning tasks.

Once the workflows are built and validated, they are executed and run the same way every time, no matter who runs them. A data center administrator can run workflows, or you can implement role-based access control (RBAC) to enable your end users and customers to execute them on a self-service basis.

As mentioned earlier, with Cisco UCS Director, you can automate and orchestrate an extended range of tasks and use cases across a wide variety of Cisco and other vendor-specific platforms. The following are some examples of automation and orchestration use cases:

- VM provisioning and life cycle management

- Configuration and life cycle management of network resources

- Configuration and life cycle management of storage resources

- Infrastructure and tenant configuration

- Provisioning of application infrastructure

- Self-service catalogs and VM provisioning

- Physical compute provisioning, including installation of an operating system

Cisco UCS Director replaces manual management of compute, network, storage, and virtualization layers with automated workflows that remove silos from IT teams and resources. IT can manage the data center support workforce as a single team with unified management across physical and virtual resources.

The two key components of UCS Director are tasks and workflows.

A task in UCS Director is a single action or operation that requires inputs and outputs (with the exception, in some rare cases, of task operations that do not require any inputs or outputs). Cisco UCS Director contains a task library comprising hundreds of predefined tasks covering many of the actions that could be included in infrastructure orchestration. New tasks are periodically added to the UCS Director task library. In cases where there is no suitable predefined task available for your desired use case, you can create a custom task. To see the available tasks in the task library, you need to log on to UCS Director and select the Orchestration tab on the left side of the menu bar. Then click on the book icon under the Workflows tab to see the list of all available tasks in the task library. Figure 8-17 illustrates this process.

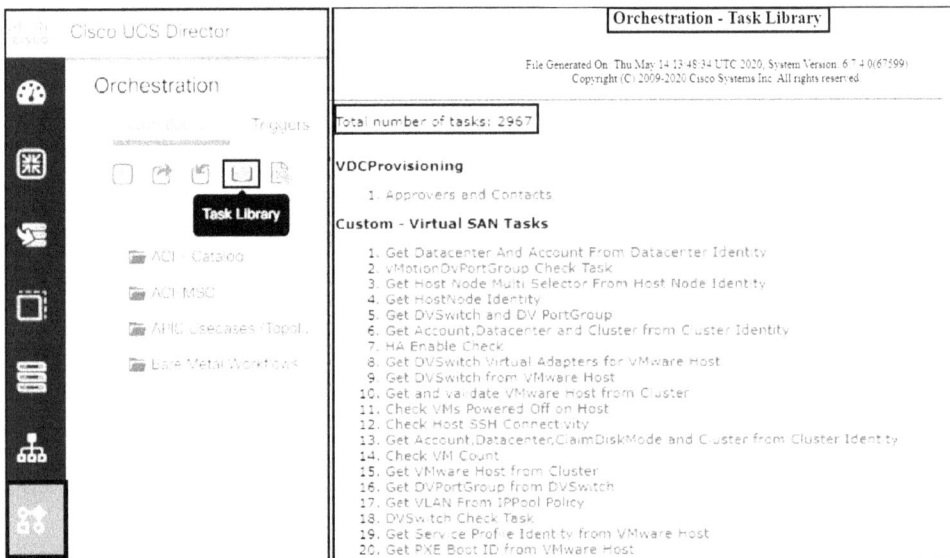

Figure 8-17   *UCS Director Task Library*

A workflow in UCS Director is a series of tasks arranged to orchestrate data center network operation. The simplest possible workflow contains a single task, but a workflow can contain any number of tasks. Workflows are the heart of the Cisco UCS Director orchestrator; they enable you to automate processes of any level of complexity on the physical and virtual infrastructure in your data center. You can build workflows using the Workflow Designer in UCS Director by simply dragging and dropping a task in the work plane. In the Workflow Designer, you arrange tasks in sequence and define inputs and outputs to those tasks. Outputs from earlier tasks can be used as inputs to any subsequent task.

A service request is a process under the control of UCS Director that is closely related to workflows. Every time you execute a workflow in Cisco UCS Director, a service request is generated. A workflow can be executed right away or can be scheduled to run at a later time. Therefore, a service request can have one of several states, depending on its execution status, such as scheduled, running, blocked, completed, or failed. In UCS Director, a workflow goes through an approval process. A workflow can be rolled back to a state identical to or similar to its original state before it was executed.

Automation Use Cases

This section considers an orchestration task that involves creating an EPG, associating a domain, and provisioning a VM (see Figure 8-18).

Note   Installing UCS Director is beyond the scope of this chapter, but you can find instructions on how to install it at Cisco.com.

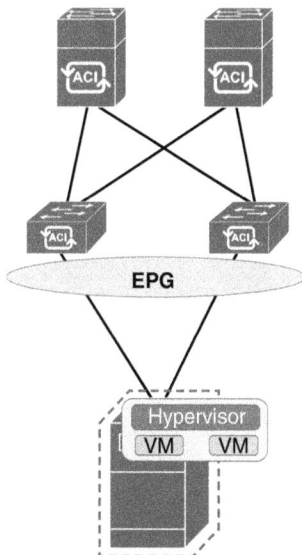

Figure 8-18   *Orchestration Use Case Using UCS Director*

This example shows how to configure the following tasks using UCS Director workflows:

- ACI:
    - Create an EPG and associate a BD for an application server.
    - Add a domain to an EPG.
- Server:
    - Provision a VM.

To orchestrate these tasks, log in to UCS Director and follow these steps:

Step 1.   Select the Orchestration tab and clone the Provision VMware VM workflow from the Default/VMware folder by right-clicking on the workflow and clicking Clone (see Figure 8-19).

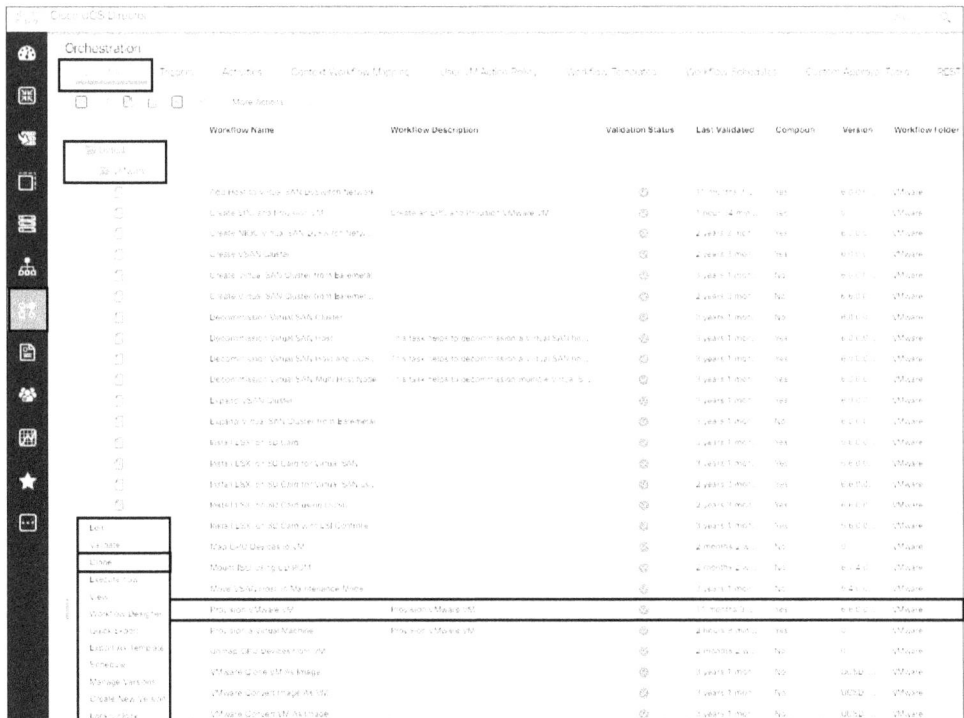

Figure 8-19   *Cloning a Workflow in UCS Director*

Step 2.   Define the name of the workflow as Create EPG and Provision VM, select the folder where you want to store the workflow, change the version label number, and click Next (see Figure 8-20).

Step 3.   Check the Select VDC option, click Next, and then click Next again (see Figure 8-21).

Step 4.   Click Submit to finish provisioning the VM task. To add another task for creating an EPG, browse through the Available Tasks list, click the Create APIC EPG task (under EPG Operations), and drag and drop it to the workflow designer pane (see Figure 8-22).

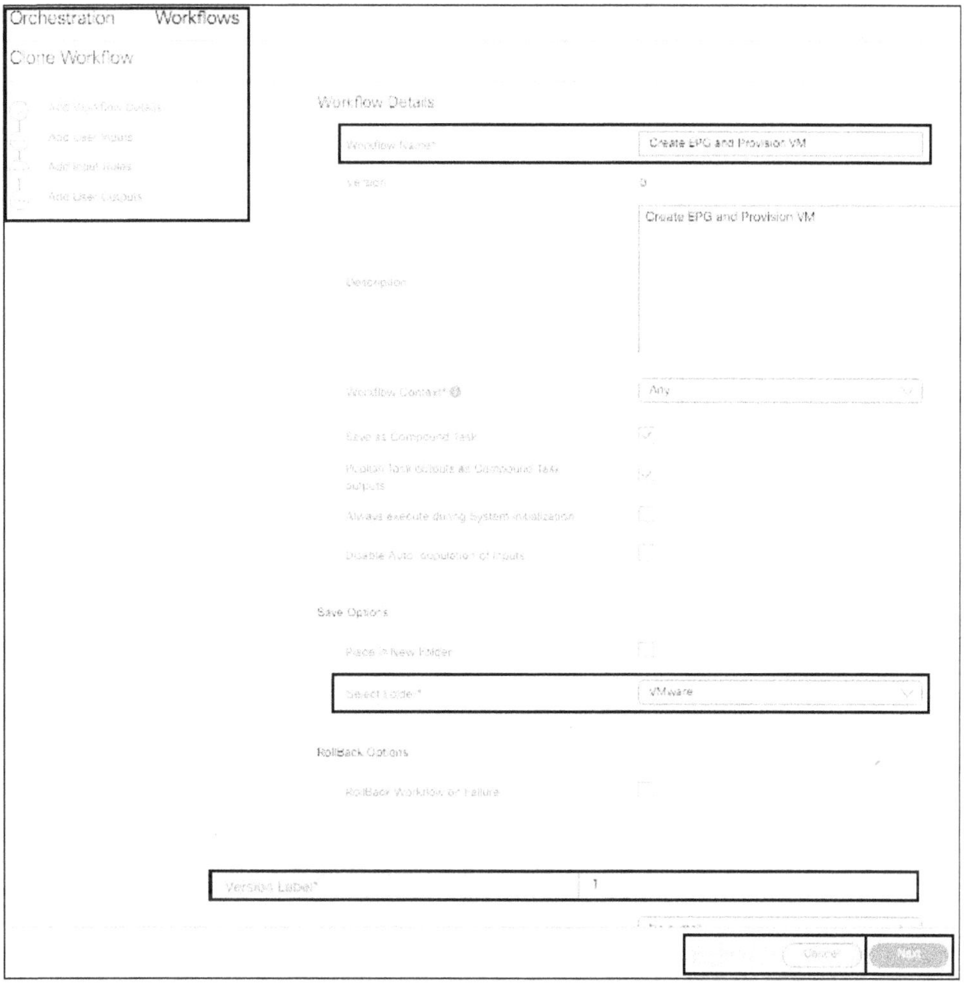

Figure 8-20 *Cloning a Workflow in UCS Director: Defining the Workflow Name*

Step 5. In the new workflow steps process that UCS Director initiates, click Next to proceed to the next step. For the mandatory items, select Application Profile Name and EPG Name from the User Input drop-downs and click Next (see Figure 8-23).

Figure 8-21   *Cloning a Workflow in UCS Director: Selecting the VDC*

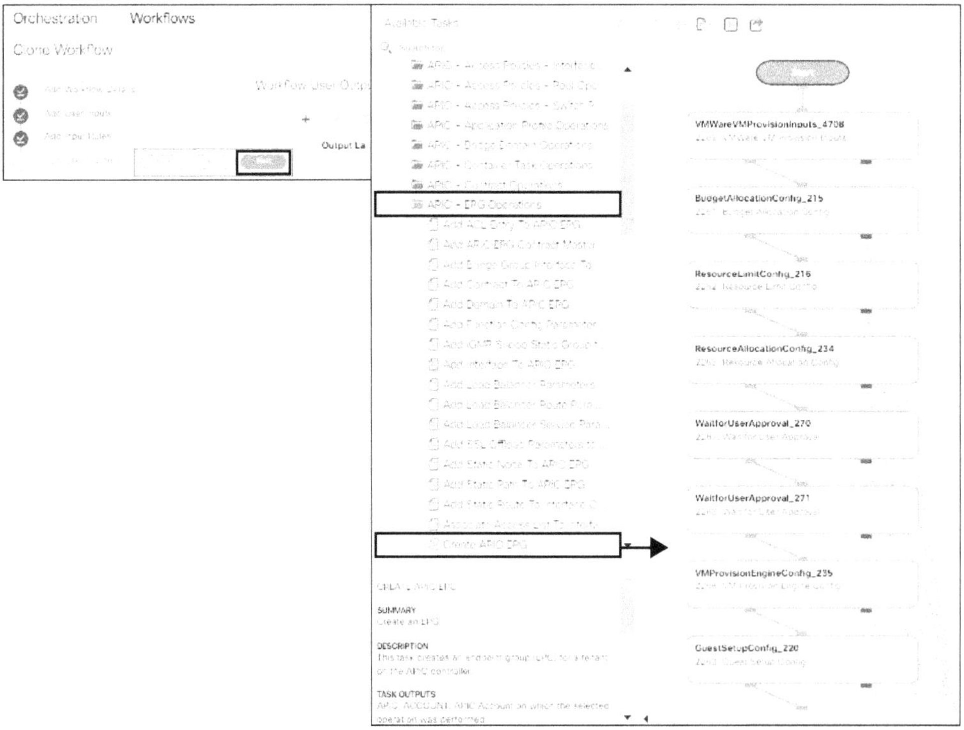

Figure 8-22   *Cloning a Workflow and Adding Another Task in UCS Director*

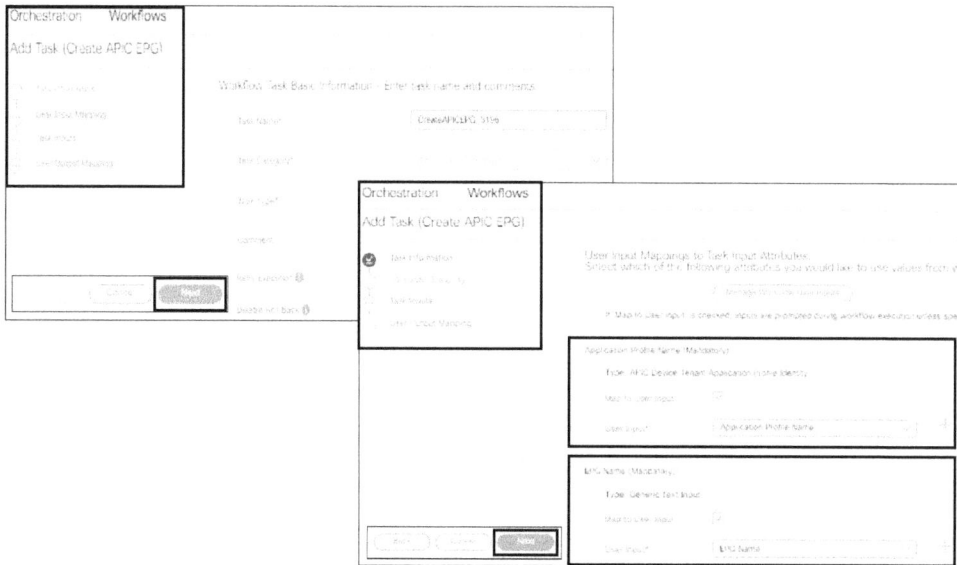

Figure 8-23 *Creating the APIC EPG Workflow Task in UCS Director*

Step 6.   As shown in Figure 8-24, select PXE_BD as the BD and click Next. Then click Submit.

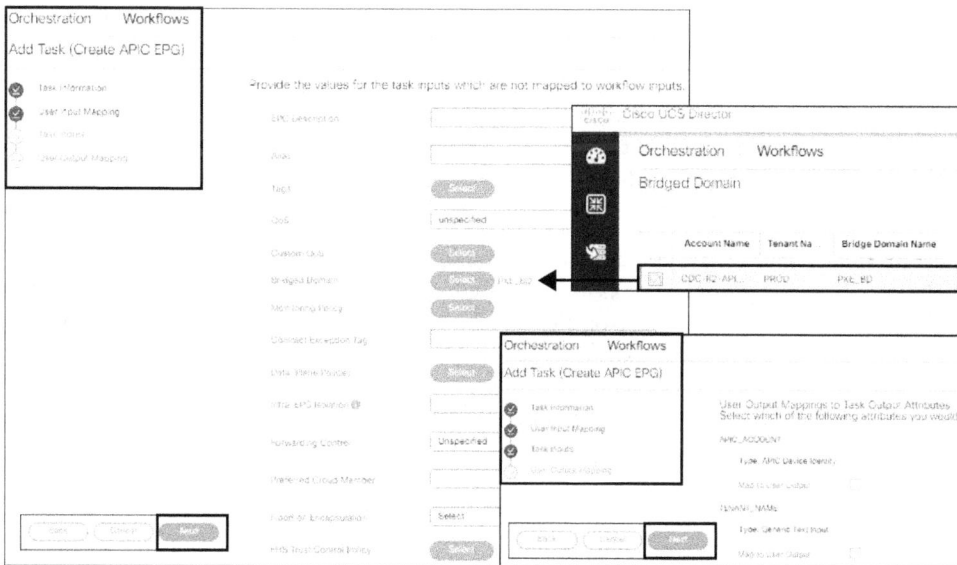

Figure 8-24 *Creating the APIC EPG Workflow Task in UCS Director: Selecting the BD*

Step 7. To add a task for adding a domain to the EPG, drag and drop the task to the workflow designer pane much as you did when creating the APIC EPG task. When UCS Director initiates a new workflow steps process, click Next. Then, for the mandatory items, select EPG and Domain Profile from the User Input drop-downs and click Next (see Figure 8-25).

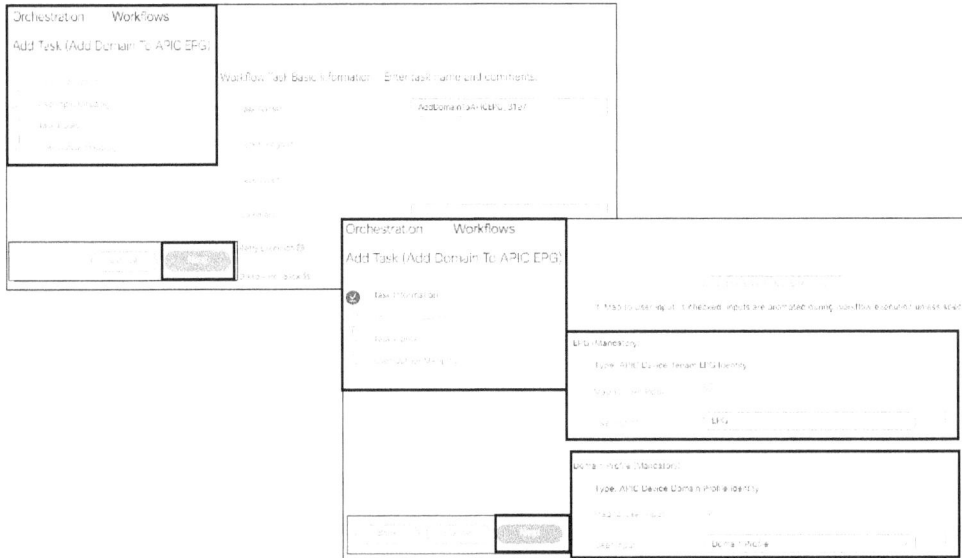

Figure 8-25   *Adding a Domain to the APIC EPG Workflow Task in UCS Director*

Step 8. As shown in Figure 8-26, select Dynamic Binding (because the server is a virtual machine that is part of the VMM domain) and click Next to proceed to next step. Click Submit. You have now added all three tasks to a single workflow in UCS Director.

Step 9. Ensure that you connect the appropriate success (green) and failure (red) links to each of the tasks in the workflow and click the Validate Workflow icon to ensure that your workflow is functioning. You can also use the Play icon to execute the workflow (see Figure 8-27).

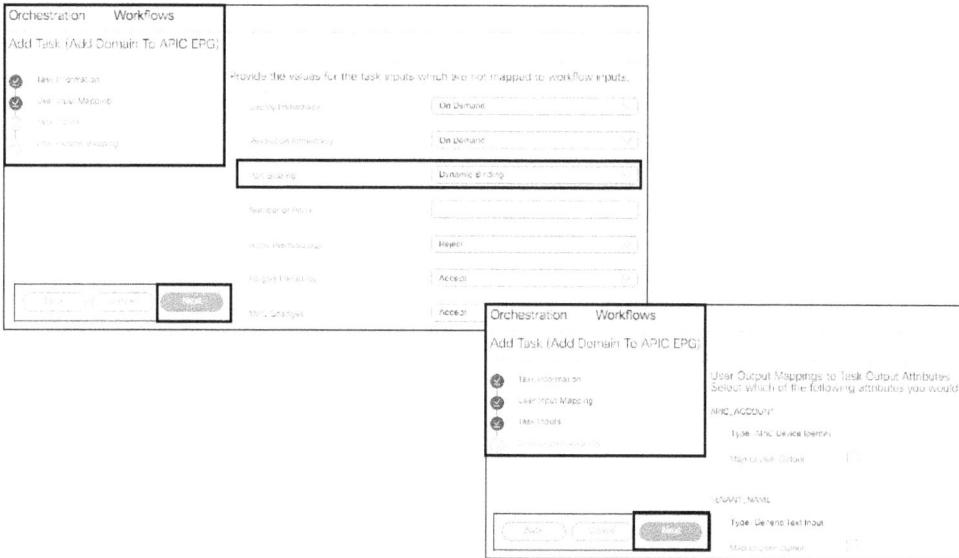

Figure 8-26 *Adding a Domain to the APIC EPG Workflow: Dynamic Binding*

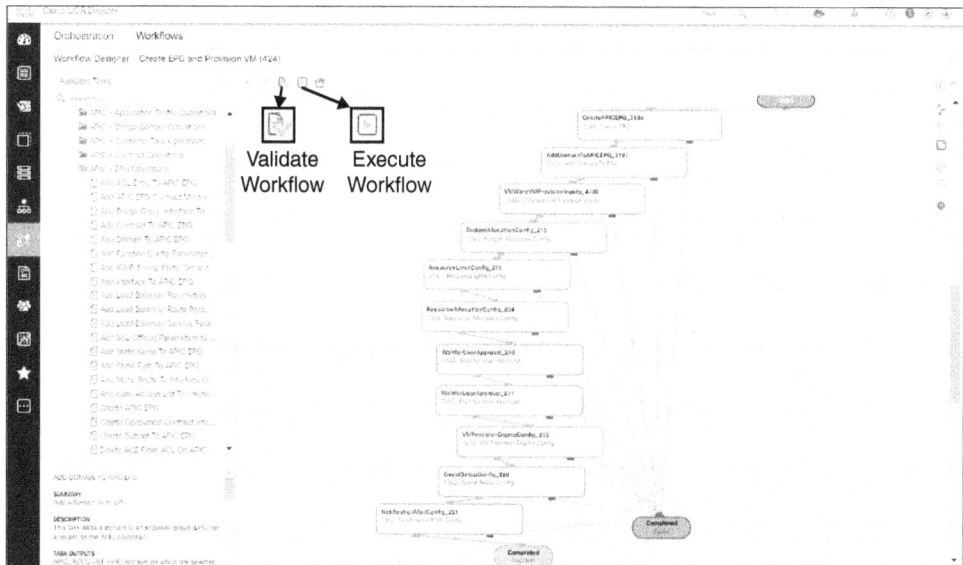

Figure 8-27 *UCS Director Create EPG and Provision VM Workflow*

For further details and more workflow examples, see cisco.com/go/ucsdirector.

Summary

In this chapter, you have learned the difference between automation and orchestration—which is commonly misunderstood by general IT community members. This chapter explores the benefits of automation and orchestration through examples. The chapter also talks about the REST API and how ACI configuration can be executed through automation scripts using native REST API calls with JSON and XML formats. ACI provides tools that help you create scripts easily, without any prior knowledge of coding. This chapter also covers Ansible, a tool that has been widely used by application and server teams and is now gaining popularity with the networking community. This chapter ends by discussing how to use UCS Director as an orchestration tool to automate multiple workflow tasks. UCS Director helps you in various workflow tasks, such as spinning off a VM, installing an OS, creating EPGs and BDs, and associating a port with an assigned encapsulation VLAN to bring up an application online.

Review Questions

The questions that follow are designed to help you prepare for the Implementing Cisco Application Centric Infrastructure - Advanced (300-630 DCACIA) exam if you are planning on acquiring the Cisco Certified Specialist: ACI Advanced Implementation certification.

1. What is the difference between automation and orchestration? (Choose two.)

    a. Automation is a process that involves executing multiple tasks as a workflow, which speeds up the overall provision of a business application.

    b. Orchestration can be achieved by making multiple configuration changes via APIC GUI workflows.

    c. Automation involves executing configuration changes, collecting statistics, and so on using tools and scripts as a single task on a single device.

    d. Orchestration is a process that involves executing configuration changes, collecting statistics, and so on using tools and scripts as a single task on a single device.

    e. Orchestration involves executing multiple tasks as a workflow for faster deployment of a business application.

2. What options are available for automation and orchestration? How do automation and orchestration help expedite the application deployment process? (Choose three.)

    a. With automation and orchestration methods, configuration changes are consistent and avoid human errors.

    b. With orchestration techniques, network changes can be made more quickly, but you still need to wait for the virtualization team to complete its changes.

    c. Automation reduces the use of the APIC GUI.

    d. Changes can be quickly backed out when an applied configuration fails or causes service downtime.

    e. Rapid and consistent configuration changes are possible.

3. What are the preferred options for automating ACI configurations? (Choose three.)

    a. Use the command-line interface (CLI) on an APIC.

    b. Use the native REST API with JSON and XML formats.

    c. Use the Cobra SDK.

    d. Use the ACI Toolkit.

    e. Use Visore.

4. What is the REST API? What is supported in the ACI REST API? (Choose three.)

    a. POST and DELETE methods are nullipotent.

    b. JSON and XML formats are used for native REST API calls.

    c. REST is a client/server communication method that uses the UDP-based SNMP protocol.

    d. REST is a client/server communication method that uses the TCP-based HTTP/HTTPS protocol.

    e. HTTPS supports the GET, POST, DELETE, and PUT operations.

    f. HTTPS supports the GET, POST, and DELETE operations.

5. What built-in tools are available in ACI that simplify and help you in automating configuration tasks using the native REST API? (Choose four.)

    a. Visore

    b. Visibility & Troubleshooting tool

    c. Saving a particular object configuration by using the Object (Save as) tab

    d. Using the MOQuery tool via the CLI

    e. Using an audit log to check what configuration is made and then copying and pasting it into the Tenant tab

    f. ACI configuration Import and Export

    g. Running the API Inspector tool while making configuration changes in ACI

6. What is Ansible, and how does it work? What platforms are supported with Ansible? (Choose three.)

    a. Ansible is a data center automation tool that manages network devices using Telnet.

    b. Ansible is an agent-based tool, like Chef and Puppet.

    c. Ansible runs on a computer system called a control node that pushes automation scripts to end devices called managed nodes by using an SSH connection.

    d. Ansible uses a YAML file, and YAML is a form of XML.

    e. The inventory file in Ansible stores information about all control nodes.

    f. Ansible is an agentless tool, unlike its competitors Chef and Puppet.

    g. Ansible is a data center automation tool that manages application, compute, network, and virtualization.

7. What is UCS Director, and how does it work? What platforms are supported with UCS Director? (Choose three.)

   a. UCS Director is a data center automation, orchestration, and monitoring tool that manages the entire application hosting infrastructure.

   b. Cisco UCS Director enables you to build workflows that provide service automation and to publish these workflows in Service Catalog for end users.

   c. Only the UCS Director administrator is allowed to run workflows.

   d. UCS Director does not allow automation of storage devices.

   e. Using UCS Director, you can configure and monitor only Cisco devices.

   f. ACI tenant and infrastructure configuration can be automated using UCS Director.

   g. UCS Director is a blade system offering from Cisco Systems.

Note   There are no Key Topics for this chapter.

Chapter 9

Monitoring ACI Fabric

In this chapter, you will learn about how proper monitoring solutions can enable businesses to run their network operations smoothly. Network monitoring can help companies minimize service downtime and get immediate return on investment on their software-defined application-hosting network infrastructure, such as Cisco ACI. The following topics related to monitoring ACI are covered in this chapter:

- Importance of monitoring

- Faults and health scores

- ACI internal monitoring tools (including SNMP, syslog, and NetFlow)

- ACI external monitoring tools (including Network Insights, Network Assurance Engine, and Tetration)

- Monitoring through the REST API

Importance of Monitoring

Today's businesses are highly dependent on applications that must be deployed on a network at a fast pace. This shift in doing business gave birth to software-defined networking, thus providing application agility. Many applications need to be up and running all the time, with minimal service disruptions for business continuity.

Another challenge is network scalability. With the adoption of virtualization techniques and an increase in the number of endpoints on IP networks, companies need to have highly scalable and continuously changing network infrastructure. Network monitoring is therefore necessary for a business to run smoothly and successfully. The main objective of monitoring the network is to constantly analyze system failures, network performance, and security threats and get automatic alerts before any real service outage occurs.

A great deal of IT time (up to 42%, according to Sirkin Research report in 2019) is spent in troubleshooting issues across the entire network. In addition, it's often very hard to reproduce issues; therefore, it is very hard to conclude root cause analyses (RCAs). Spending extra time troubleshooting the network extends service outage periods and leads to business loss and sometimes even complete business meltdowns. The problem is that IT teams often take reactive rather than proactive approaches. For example, when it comes to system failures, network administrators tend to jump straight to troubleshooting the issue. For issues related to change management, they might quickly undo the change to bring the service back to operational state. In the event of security breaches, network administrators often scramble to prevent risk. When it comes to compliance, they might dig into the audit logs. Thus, all their actions are reactionary. Proactively taking the appropriate measures can be much more effective. Proactive monitoring is an important piece of a network administrator's job. However, it is often neglected because solving critical issues in the network usually takes priority, and proactive monitoring tasks languish on the back burner.

Proactively monitoring your network infrastructure provides the following benefits:

- **Staying ahead of outages:** Having a proper monitoring solution helps keep you ahead of the game and prevents outages. Monitoring can give you a complete view of your network that will help you fix issues fast during troubleshooting and reduce service downtime.

- **Easing management in large and changing networks:** Software-defined networking infrastructure such as Cisco ACI provides scalability and flexibility to constantly make changes on the fly. With a proper monitoring solution in place, you can easily achieve these goals without disrupting service. Also, continuously making successful changes in the network builds trust within management, and getting maintenance window approval in the data center becomes much easier.

- **Identifying security threats:** One of the most important tasks of a network administrator is to keep the company's data secure. Network monitoring provides information about security breaches and anomalies happening in the network that might potentially compromise the company's confidential data.

- **Achieving service-level agreements (SLAs):** Keeping network operations up and running all the time helps you achieve SLAs with your end users and builds trust.

- **Providing immediate return on investment (ROI):** With increased service uptime, you more quickly realize ROI on the application-hosting infrastructure that is running your business.

Cisco ACI is a policy-driven object-oriented infrastructure that is managed by a centralized controller called the Cisco Application Policy Infrastructure Controller (APIC). The fabric infrastructure configuration and statistics are stored on an APIC rather than on each individual network device. This forces network administrators to adapt to a new way of managing, monitoring, and troubleshooting their infrastructure and makes it easier to deal with new technologies introduced in the industry.

Faults and Health Scores

Faults and health scores are key components of ACI monitoring, and it is critical to understand these concepts and their importance for smooth operation of your fabric.

Faults

As you have learned in this book, ACI is deployed and managed using a policy-based object model. In this policy-based model, the APIC not only provisions the entire network infrastructure but also provides centralized storage for all telemetry data, including faults, events, statistics reported by the fabric switches, virtual switches, and integrated L4/L7 devices. Much as configurations are stored as managed objects in ACI, faults, events, and statistics are also represented as a collection of managed object in the management information tree (MIT). All objects in ACI can be queried, including faults. In this policy model, a fault is represented as a mutable, stateful, and persistent managed object (MO) of class **faultInst** or **faultDelegate**.

When a specific condition occurs, such as a component failure or an alarm, the system creates a fault as a child object to the MO that is primarily associated with the fault. For a fault object class, the fault conditions are defined by the fault rules of the parent object class. Fault MOs are similar to other MOs in the MIT, as they have a parent, a distinguished name (DN), a relative name (RN), and so on. The fault code is an alphanumerical string in the form F*XXX* that uniquely identifies the type of fault being raised.

A fault is visible only if it affects an object in the MIT. The lower an object in the tree, the more specific the faults are to the object's failure. System faults list all the faults in the ACI fabric. In most cases, a fault MO is automatically created, escalated, de-escalated, and deleted by the system as specific conditions are detected. There can be at most one fault with a given code under a managed object. If the same condition is detected multiple times while the corresponding fault MO is active, no additional instances of the fault MO are created. In other words, if the same condition is detected multiple times for the same affected object, only one fault is raised, and a counter for the recurrence of that fault is incremented.

Faults are triggered based on fault rules, counters crossing thresholds, task/state failures, and object resolution failures. A fault is always raised on the node where the condition was detected (either a fabric node or controller). Users are not allowed to define new faults.

As illustrated in Figure 9-1, in ACI, faults go through a life-cycle process to avoid false positives. In that process, when a fault is generated due to a failure event, the system detects the fault, adds the fault object in the MIT, and goes into soaking state. When the soaking timer expires (the default is 120 seconds) and the target severity is reached, the fault transitions to a raised state. It retains the fault in this state until the error is resolved automatically by the system or by the network operator. Once the error is resolved, the system detects that and goes into clearing state. When the clearing timer expires (the default is 120 seconds), the system clears the fault. However, it still keeps the fault in the system until the retention timer expires (the default is 3600 seconds), and finally the fault is removed from the system completely. These timers are configurable within the range from 0 to 3600 seconds for the soaking and clearing intervals and from 0 to 31,536,000 seconds for the retention interval.

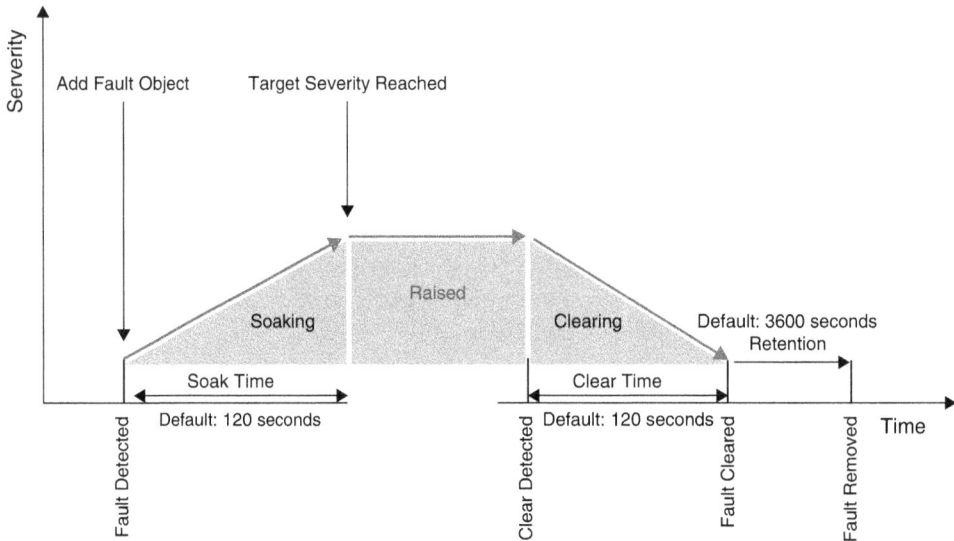

Figure 9-1 *Fault Life Cycle*

The fault severity provides an indication of the estimated impact on the system and its capability to provide further service. Some of the severity values are as follows:

- Warning (potential issue but possibly no immediate impact to the system)
- Minor
- Major
- Critical (system or component completely unusable)

Let's look at some useful NX-OS CLI commands for viewing system faults.

To view all system faults, use this command:

```
apic1# show faults details
```

Example 9-1 shows some specific subcommands for querying system faults.

Example 9-1 *show faults Subcommands*

```
apic1# show faults ?
 ack          Acknowledgment status
 cause        Cause
 code         Fault code
 controller   Show controller information
 detail       Detailed faults information
 end-time     Fault activity in time interval
 history      Historical information
 id           Fault ID
 l417-cluster Show L4 L7 Device information
 l417-graph   Show L4 L7 Graph information
 last-days    Fault activity in time interval
 last-hours   Fault activity in time interval
 last-minutes Fault activity in time interval
 lc           Lifecycle state
 leaf         Show command for leaf
 microsoft    Show Microsoft information
 min-severity Minimum severity
 quota        Show Quotas Information
 redhat       Show Redhat information
 severity     Severity
 spine        Show command for spine
 start-time   Fault activity in time interval
 tenant       Show Tenants Information
 type         Type
 vmware       Show VMware information
```

Also, you can query faults raised on fabric nodes through the REST API. Example 9-2 shows a REST query to fabric leaf node 201 that returns the fault with code F1543, along with details about the fault, such as fabric status inactive, Node 201 inactive and not reachable, and severity critical.

Example 9-2 *REST Query to Check Faults*

```
GET :  https://apic-hostname-or-IP/api/node/mo/topology/pod-1/node-201.json?query-
  target=self&rsp-subtree-include=faults
{
   "totalCount": "1",
   "imdata": [
       {
           "fabricNode": {
               "attributes": {
                   "adSt": "off",
```

```
                    "annotation": "",
                    "childAction": "",
                    "delayedHeartbeat": "no",
                    "dn": "topology/pod-1/node-201",
                    "extMngdBy": "",
                    "fabricSt": "inactive",
                    "id": "201",
                    "lastStateModTs": "2019-11-05T16:50:07.568-05:00",
                    "lcOwn": "local",
                    "modTs": "2019-11-05T16:50:21.889-05:00",
                    "model": "N9K-C93180LC-EX",
                    "monPolDn": "uni/fabric/monfab-default",
                    "name": "leaf-201",
                    "nameAlias": "",
                    "nodeType": "unspecified",
                    "role": "leaf",
                    "serial": "FDO212225QJ",
                    "status": "",
                    "uid": "0",
                    "vendor": "Cisco Systems, Inc",
                    "version": ""
                },
                "children": [
                    {
                        "faultInst": {
                            "attributes": {
                                "ack": "no",
                                "cause": "node-inactive",
                                "changeSet": "",
                                "childAction": "",
                                "code": "F1543",
                                "created": "2020-01-18T08:26:59.968-05:00",
                                "delegated": "no",
                                "descr": "Node 201 is inactive and not reachable.",
                                "domain": "infra",
                                "highestSeverity": "critical",
                                "lastTransition": "2020-01-18T08:29:13.714-05:00",
                                "lc": "raised",
                                "occur": "1",
                                "origSeverity": "critical",
                                "prevSeverity": "critical",
                                "rn": "fault-F1543",
                                "rule": "fabric-node-inactive",
                                "severity": "critical",
                                "status": "",
```

```
                                        "subject": "fabric-node-inactive",
                                        "type": "environmental"
                                }
                        }
                    }
                ]
            }
        }
    ]
}
```

Health Scores

Network operations teams are constantly asked to answer basic questions regarding the current status, performance, and availability of the networks they are operating. Answering such questions might be easy as they often relate to independent devices or links. However, this information by itself is of little to no value without additional data on the overall health of the network. Manually collecting and correlating information about the entire network is a time-consuming and laborious task. In the past, network operators had to search for the right tool to provide a model of the infrastructure that described the relationship between the various devices and links. ACI automates data collection and correlation of information about the network and provides a health score based on data collected, computed, and correlated throughout the fabric in real time.

The single consolidated health score shows the current status of all the objects in the network, including links and devices, their relationships, the real-time status of their utilization, and a quick at-a-glance assessment of the current status of the entire system. This visibility has a number of practical use cases, and later in this chapter we will classify these use cases as proactive or reactive. ACI also provides the flexibility to monitor some aspects of how the health score is calculated and how various faults impact the calculation of the health score. The health score ranges from 0 to 100%, with 100% indicating a fully fit and functional ACI fabric. Ideally, the health of all application and infrastructure components should always be 100%. However, this is not always realistic, given the dynamic nature of data center environments. Links, equipment, and endpoints experience failures. The health score should be seen as a metric that changes over time, and the goal should be to increase the average health score of a given set of components over time. Furthermore, a decrease in the health score does not always necessarily mean there is an issue in the network. For example, say that you have been given a task to preprovision all the ToR leaf ports and map them to EPGs. However, no application server has been physically connected to these ports. In this case, ACI generates faults, and the health score decreases, but in reality, this is a predetermined reduction in the health score based on decisions by the fabric administrator.

The majority of objects in ACI have associated health scores, which can be found in the APIC GUI's System Dashboard tab or the Policy tab for an object. To check the overall fabric health in the APIC GUI, go to System > Dashboard. In this tab, you can view the APIC, node (leaf/spine), and tenant health scores that are less than 99%. You can also examine a graph depicting the health score of the system over a period of time. The health graph provides a good indication of any system issues. If the system is stable, the graph shows a constant value; otherwise, it fluctuates.

The health score is corelated to faults. A fault generated in the system reduces the health score. On the other hand, remediating a fault normalizes the health score. All health scores are instantiated from the **healthInst** class in the MIT and can be extracted through the REST API. System and pod health scores are calculated based on average weighted health scores of leafs, spines, and the number of endpoints in the fabric. Similarly, tenant health scores are calculated based on logical components contained in each tenant. From a fabric administration perspective, there is no need to know the formula by which health score are calculated because the system automatically does the calculations. Basically, health scores are directly linked with faults associated to a managed object. Each fault is weighted based on the fault's severity level. For example, a critical fault might weigh 100%, whereas a warning might weigh only 20%.

Almost every object has a Health tab. For example, to check whether a specific EPG has faults, in the APIC GUI, you can go to Tenants > Application Profile > EPG. On the right-hand side of the work pane, look for the Health tab. You can also access the Health tab under History > Health. This tab shows information on the affected object and how it is tied within the larger model. By clicking on the health score, you can explore the health tree of any affected object or policy to reveal the faults (see Figure 9-2).

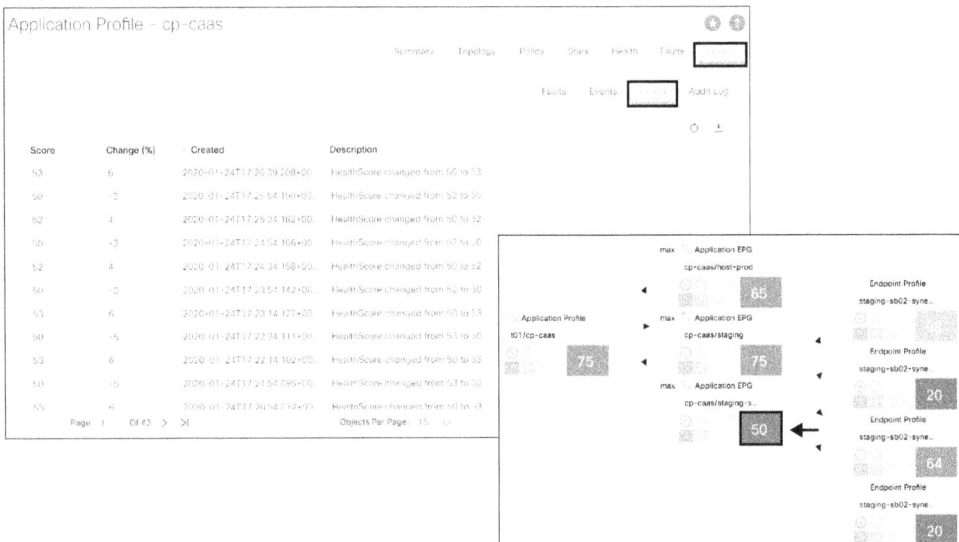

Figure 9-2 *Navigating the Health Score of an Object*

Let's look at some useful NX-OS CLI commands to view the health of specific objects.

To view the health of a tenant, enter the following command:

```
apic1# show health tenant tenant-name
```

To view the health of a bridge domain within a tenant, enter the following command:

```
apic1# show health tenant tenant-name bridge domain bd-name
```

To view the health of an endpoint group of an application within a tenant, enter the following command:

```
apic1# show health tenant tenant-name application app-name epg
epg-name
```

To view the health of a leaf, enter the following command:

```
apic1# show health leaf node-ID
```

Also, you can query health scores through the REST API. The following example is a REST query to the fabric that returns the health score for a tenant named t01:

```
GET :  https://apic-hostname-or-IP/api/node/mo/uni/
tn-t01.json?query-target=self&rsp-subtree-include=health
```

As mentioned earlier, there is really no need to understand the calculations of the health scores as ACI does them for you, but you do need to have a basic understanding of whether faults should have high, medium, low, or "none" fault levels. Although faults in ACI are initially set at default values, it is possible to change these values to better match your environment. Keep in mind that because of role-based access control, not all administrators can see all of the health scores. For example, a fabric administrator can see all health scores, but tenant administrators can only see the health scores that pertain to the tenants to which they have access.

The following sections dive into some proactive and reactive health score use cases.

Health Score Used in Proactive Monitoring

Health scores identify faults, and they essentially provide baselines to which you can make comparisons of your system later. If you see that a leaf switch is at 100% one week, and the next week the leaf is showing a warning, you can drill down to see what has changed. In such a scenario, it is possible that the links might be oversubscribed; hence, it could be time to either move some of the workload to another leaf or to add more bandwidth by connecting more cables. When you are facing only a warning, you have time to resolve the issue before any bottleneck on the network is noticeable.

Health scores can be used to proactively monitor your ACI environment in a number of other ways, such as providing visibility of certain components to other groups in your company. Because you can export health scores and faults, it is possible to send notifications to application owners, VMware administrators, database administrators, and so on to provide monitoring of the environment across the entire network that has not previously been easily available.

Health Score Used in Reactive Monitoring

Health scores can provide assistance in diagnosing problems and resolving immediate issues. Upon notification that a health score has been degraded, an operator can use the APIC GUI to easily navigate the relationships and faults that are contributing to the health score degradation. When the faults causing a poor health score have been identified, you can look at the faults to find information about possible remediation steps. For most objects there is a Health tab that can be used to explore the relationship between objects and their associated faults; the information on this tab could potentially help identify the root cause of the issue and provide remediation guidance.

Health Score with Interface Errors

Health scores enable you to monitor faults and the general health of your ACI fabric. However, in certain cases, such as with interface cyclic redundancy check (CRC) errors, if the interface does not flap, then no fault will be generated, and there will be no deviation in the health score result.

In order to monitor CRC errors through the health score, you need to take the following configuration steps in the APIC GUI:

Step 1.   Go to Fabric > Fabric Policies > Policies > Monitoring > default > Stats Collection Policies, and on the right-hand side of the navigation pane, select Layer 1 Physical Interface Configuration from the Monitoring Object drop-down and then select Ingress Drop Packets from the Stats Type drop-down.

Step 2.   Under Config Thresholds, click the + sign to open the Config Threshold window.

Step 3.   Click the Edit Threshold checkbox next to Ingress Errors Drop Packets rate.

Step 4.   In the Edit Stats Threshold box, modify the Rising values based on your environment and needs. Click Submit. Click Close.

Figure 9-3 illustrates these configuration steps, where the system counts the packets drop (CRC) at a five-minute interval and raises a fault when the threshold is hit. This affects the health score accordingly. In this example, if there are 5 CRC errors in a five-minute interval, a fault with severity warning is raised; if the count increases over 250, a minor fault is raised; and so on.

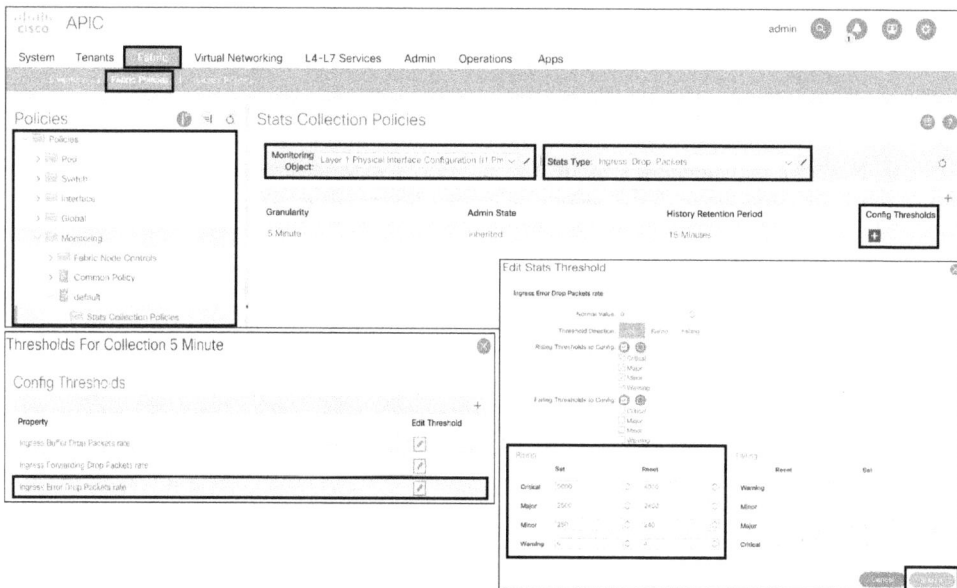

Figure 9-3 *Configuring Statistics Thresholds for Monitoring CRC Errors*

ACI Internal Monitoring Tools

ACI offers some monitoring tools and protocols out of the box, such as SNMP, syslog, and NetFlow. These tools, which companies have been using since early in the computer networking era, are part of the ACI software, but you need to enable and configure the necessary parameters before you can use them.

Note   Chapter 10, "Network Management and Monitoring Configuration," provides detailed configuration steps for SNMP, syslog, and NetFlow.

SNMP

Simple Network Management Protocol (SNMP), which has been in use for decades, is a mechanism for managing and monitoring network devices. SNMP runs on the UDP protocol with port numbers 161 and 162. SNMP works in both push and pull models. When you run an SNMP query against a network device, you are *pulling* the stats out from the network device. In this case, SNMP uses UDP port 161. On the other hand, when an event occurs on a network device, SNMP *pushes* the stats toward a management station and uses UDP port 162. (This push operation is called a *trap*.)

SNMP has three basic components:

- **Managed device:** The hardware device to be monitored

- **Agent:** The SNMP daemon running on the managed device

- **Network management system:** The monitoring system that enables the SNMP client to communicate with the agent running on the managed device

SNMP is supported on a wide range of networking devices, and you need to enable and configure an agent to be able to communicate to a network management system (NMS). The agent maintains an information database that describes the network parameters of a managed device. The network management system refers to this database to ask the agent for specific information and further translates it as needed. This commonly shared information database between the agent and the network management system is called the Management Information Base (MIB). This is similar to the ACI concept in which a configuration and its statistical data are stored as an object, and the objects are organized in a hierarchical fashion under the MIT. SNMP also stores the information as an object with an object ID (OID), and these objects are organized in a hierarchy under the MIB.

For example, Figure 9-4 shows that .1.3.6.1.2.1.1.1 is the OID for the system description sysDescr for a network device.

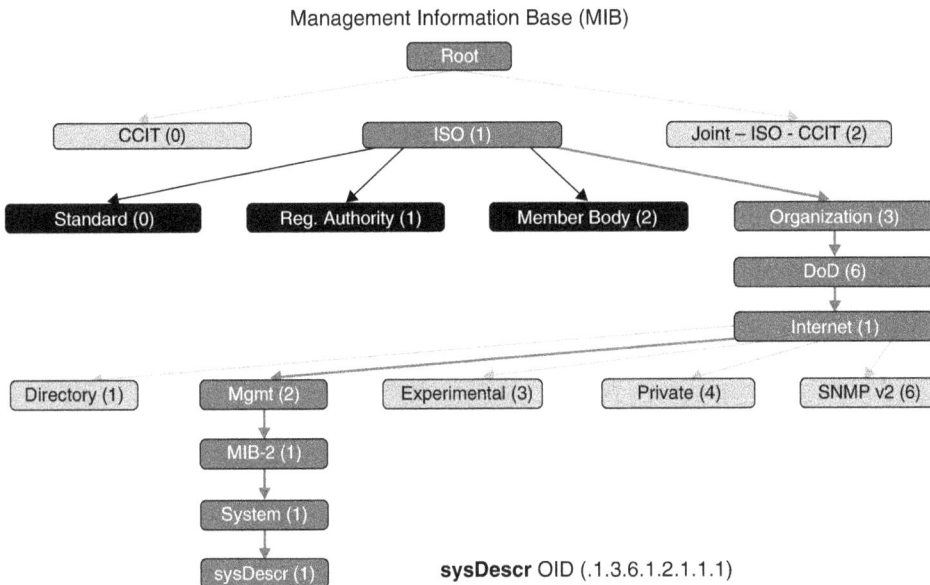

Figure 9-4 *SNMP MIB Hierarchy for the sysDescr OID*

Over time, SNMP has evolved into various versions (v1, v2c, and v3) for additional functionality but mainly focuses on security enhancements.

SNMP uses some of the following basic commands:

- **GET:** A request sent by the management system to the managed device. It is performed to pull one or more values from the managed device.

- **GET NEXT:** A similar operation to **GET**. The major difference is that the **GET NEXT** command retrieves the value of the next OID in the MIB.

- **GET BULK:** Used to retrieve a large volume of data from the MIB.

- **SET:** An operation used to modify or assign the value of a managed device.

- **TRAPS:** A command initiated by an agent (unlike the preceding SNMP operational commands, which are executed from the management system), which is a signal to the management system when an event occurs on the managed device.

- **INFORM:** A command initiated by an agent that includes confirmation from the management system on receiving the message.

- **RESPONSE:** A command used to carry back the value(s) or signal of actions directed by the management system.

Since ACI Release 1.2(1), SNMP has been supported on both the APIC and the switches (leafs/spines) of the ACI fabric. In ACI, SNMP agents run independently on the APIC and on switches, providing separate network statistics to the management station. ACI supports numerous SNMP MIBs on switches. However, only a subset of SNMP MIBs are available on the APICs.

Table 9-1 outlines the SNMP-supported MIBs and TRAPs.

Table 9-1   *SNMP MIB and Traps Supported in ACI*

MIBs	Traps
System	coldstart
Cisco-IF-Extension-MIB	cefcFRUInserted, cefcFRURemoved
Entity-MIB	cefcFanTrayStatusChange, cefcModuleStatusChange
Cisco-Entity-FRU-Control-MIB	entSensorThresholdNotification
Cisco-Entity-Sensor-MIB	cefcPowerStatusChange
Cisco Process MIB	cpmCPURisingThreshold, cpmCPUFallingThreshold
IF-MIB	ospfIfStateChange, ospfNbrStateChange
OSPF v2, OSPFv3	cieLinkUp, cieLinkDown (though only on downlink host ports)
BGP	
Cisco-BGP	
Cisco-IETF-ISIS	
Cisco-BFD-MIB	

Note   For the latest SNMP MIB and TRAP support in ACI, see Cisco.com.

All SNMP protocol versions (v1, v2c, and v3) are supported in ACI. SNMP in ACI can only perform **GET**, **GET NEXT**, **GET BULK**, and **WALK** operations. SNMP write queries using the **SET** command are not allowed. As you have already learned, ACI only allows the APIC to make configuration changes through REST APIs. ACI also supports SNMP traps, but only 10 traps destination management stations can be used in a configuration. SNMP traps is enabled based on policy configuration in the Access, Fabric, and Tenant tabs in the APIC GUI. SNMP traps are generated based on the events or faults that occurred on a managed object. On the APIC, a managed object is translated to an SNMP object. SNMP in ACI requires an explicit "out-of-band (OOB) contract" on the APIC by permitting the SNMP port (UDP port 161); otherwise, SNMP packets are dropped.

The SNMPd daemon running on an APIC has two components:

- **Agent:** The SNMP agent is an open-source net-snmp agent (version: 5.7.6). The SNMP agent handles SNMP sessions from the SNMP clients and also handles the SNMP protocol processing.

- **DME:** The SNMP Data Management Engine (DME) handles the MIT interface to read the MOs and translate the information into the SNMP object format.

Interface Failures Example

Let's consider an example of shutting down an interface of a leaf with OOB address (10.88.196.130). In this example, interface Eth1/30 is shut down. An SNMP trap is sent out to the destination IP address of the management station (10.88.146.197). The SNMP OID value included in the trap is .1.3.6.1.4.1.9.9.276.0.1. You can use the following URL to browse the OID details:

> https://snmp.cloudapps.cisco.com/Support/SNMP/do/BrowseOID.do?local=en

Figure 9-5 illustrates the interface down SNMP trap.

When you bring up the interface, another SNMP trap is sent out to the management station with a different OID value (.1.3.6.1.4.1.9.9.276.0.2), as shown in Figure 9-6.

Let's consider another example of interface failure. In this case, let's say the interfaces are bundled with a virtual port channel (VPC). In this example, VPC 2 is shut down. An SNMP trap is sent out to the destination IP address of the management station (10.88.146.197). The OID included in the trap is (.1.3.6.1.2.1.2.2.1.8). You can use the following URL to browse the OID details:

> https://snmp.cloudapps.cisco.com/Support/SNMP/do/BrowseOID.do?local=en

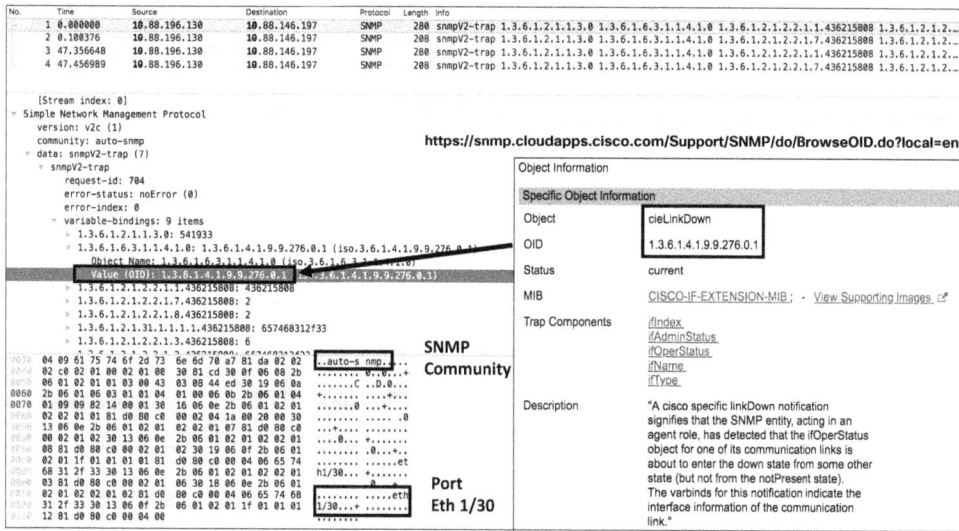

Figure 9-5 *Server Interface Down SNMP Trap*

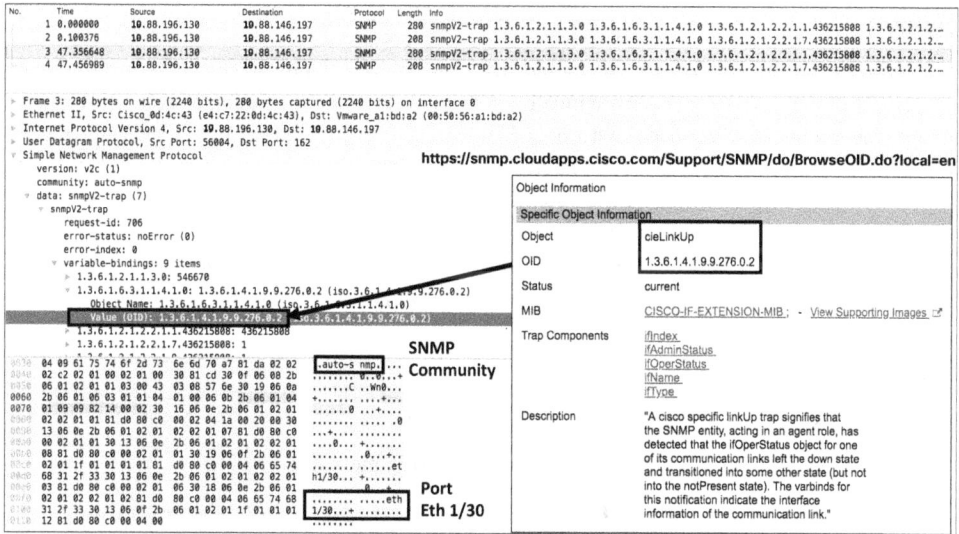

Figure 9-6 *Server Interface Up SNMP Trap*

As shown in Figure 9-7, the value of the first OID (1.3.6.1.2.1.2.2.1.8) in the SNMP trap is 2, which indicates "down" according to the IF-MIB details. The next OID (1.3.6.1.2.1.31.1.1.1.1) in the SNMP trap is the hex value 706f32, which converts to the ASCII value Po2. The third OID (1.3.6.1.2.1.2.2.1.3) in the SNMP trap shows the value 53, which is propVirtual according to the IF-MIB details and tells you that VPC 2 is down. Similarly, when the VPC comes back online, another SNMP trap with the same OID (1.3.6.1.2.1.2.2.1.8) shows the value 1, which is up according to the IF-MIB details.

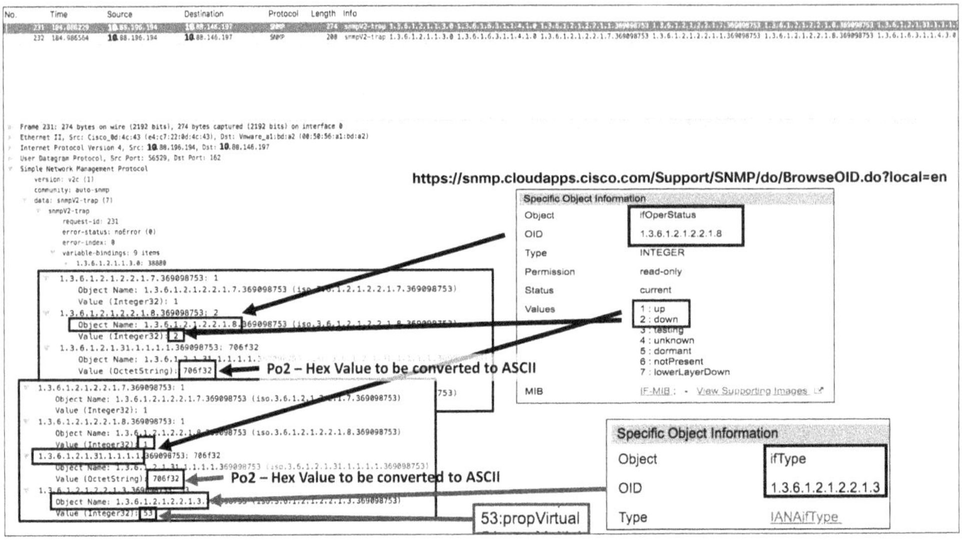

Figure 9-7   *Server VPC Interface Down/Up SNMP Traps*

Syslog

Syslog makes it possible to collect and store system logs (faults, events, audits, and sessions) of network devices either locally or to an external host running a syslog process. It runs on the UDP protocol with port 514. Faults or events in the ACI fabric can trigger the sending of a syslog message. Fault-generated system messages are triggered by a fault rule, a threshold crossing, or a failure of a task or finite state machine (FSM) sequence. Event-generated system messages are triggered by an event rule or an event in NX-OS on a leaf or the spine. Not all syslog messages indicate problems. Some of them are informational, and others help in diagnosing an issue during a troubleshooting session.

The syslog message structure in ACI is as follows:

```
timestamp host %LOG_LOCAL(1-7)-severity-SYSTEM_MSG [code][lifecycle
state][rule][severity text] [DN of affected MO] Message-text
```

The following is an example of a fault-related syslog message:

```
Apr 10 12:28:21 apic1 %LOG_LOCAL7-2-SYSTEM_MSG [F0321][soaking]
[unhealthy][critical][topology/pod-1/ node-1/av/node-1/fault-F0321]
Controller 1 is unhealthy because: Data Layer Partially Degraded
```

This system message conveys the following information:

- The timestamp of the message is Apr 10 12:28:21.

- **apic1** is the host and indicates that this message is generated by the controller.

- **2** (Major) is the severity level and indicates a critical condition.

- **F0321** is the fault code, which is **fltInfraWiNodeHealth.**

- **soaking** is the current fault life cycle state.

- **unhealthy** is the cause of the fault.

- **critical** is the fault severity.

- **topology/pod-1/node-1/av/node-1** is the DN of the affected MO, which is Node 1 in Pod 1.

- **fault-F0321** is the fault object.

- The message text **is Controller 1 is unhealthy because: Data Layer Partially Degraded.**

The following is an event-related syslog message:

```
Apr 10 02:18:16 leaf1 %LOG_LOCAL7-6-SYSTEM_MSG [E4205126] [port-down]
[info][sys/phys-[eth1/3]/phys] Port is down. Reason: adminCfgChng
```

This system message conveys the following information:

- The timestamp of the message is **Apr 10 02:18:16**

- **leaf1** is the host, which generated this message.

- **6 (Info)** is the severity level and indicates an informational condition.

- **E4205126** is the event code.

- **port-down** is the cause of the event.

- **info** is the fault severity.

- **sys/phys-[eth1/3]/phys** is the DN of the affected MO.

- The message text is **Port is down. Reason: adminCfgChng.**

The syslog severity level is a single-digit code that reflects various severity conditions. The lower the severity level of the system message, the more serious the condition of the system. Unlike NX-OS, ACI follows the International Telecommunication Union (ITU) standards for syslog severity levels described in RFC 5674. Table 9-2 maps the severity levels of system messages between NX-OS and ACI.

Table 9-2   *Syslog Severity Levels*

	Severity Level (NX-OS)	ITU Level (ACI)	Description
0	Emergency	—	System is unusable
1	Alert	Critical	Immediate action required
2	Critical	Major	Critical condition

	Severity Level (NX-OS)	ITU Level (ACI)	Description
3	Error	Minor	Error condition
4	Warning	Warning	Warning condition
5	Notification	Cleared	Normal but significant condition
6	Informational	Info	Informational messages only
7	Debugging	—	Messages that appear during debugging only

Table 9-3 lists some of the system messages that are critical enough to generate alerts and trouble tickets.

Table 9-3 *Critical System Messages*

Fault Number	Fault Object Name	Description
F1543	fltFabricNodeInactive	Fabric node is unreachable
F0532	fltEthpmIfPortDownInfraEpg	Host interface is down and is in use by the EPG
F1385	fltOspfAdjEpFailed	OSPF adjacency is down
F0299	fltBgpPeerEntryFailed	BGP peer is not established
F1296	fltVpcIfIfDown	VPC interface is down, and peer interface is down as well
F2705	fltVpcIfIfImpaired	VPC interface is down, and peer interface is up
F1262	fltInfraServiceOptimalLeadership	APIC reports that some services do not have ideal replica leaders of shards
F0321	fltInfraWiNodeHealth	APIC reports that the distributed internal database (data layer) of the controller cluster is not fully functional
F1394	fltEthpmIfPortDownFabric	Fabric port is down
F0475	fltTunnelIfDestUnreach	Tunnel destination is unreachable
F0360	fltIsisFmcastTreeTreeInactive	Operational state of an Mcast tree changes to inactive in the fabric
F1360	fltCoopAdjEpCoopAdjEpDown	Coop adjacency is down
F0411	fltEqptPsuFailed	Power supply unit is failed in the fabric node
F0412	fltEqptPsuFanFailed	Power supply unit fan is failed in the fabric node

Fault Number	Fault Object Name	Description
F0413	fltEqptPsuSlotPsuMissing	Power supply unit is missing/removed from the fabric node
F1317	fltEqptPsgPNonRedun	Power supply unit is nonredundant in the fabric node
F1318	fltEqptPsgPZeroPwr	Power supply unit is not detected correctly in the fabric node
F1321	fltEqptFtFanTrayFailed	Fan tray failed in the spine (Nexus 9500)
F1322	fltEqptFanFanFailed	Fan failed in the spine (Nexus 9500)
F1323	fltEqptFtSlotFanTrayMissing	Fan tray is missing/removed from the spine (Nexus 9500)
F1451	fltEqptPsuShut	No power in the power supply unit
F1526	fltEqptSlotFailed	Fabric module or line card failed in the spine (Nexus 9500)
F0101	fltEqptStorageFailed	Storage device on the APIC failed
F2992	fltSvcredirRsDestAttOperStFailed	PBR service destination goes to failed state

Note   For a complete and up-to-date list of all system messages for the ACI code you are running on your network, see Cisco.com.

Example: Leaf Membership Failure

Let's consider an example of a leaf node, Node 201, with an OOB management address (10.88.196.108) becoming unreachable by the APIC cluster due to a problem (likely due to fabric link, transceiver, or LLDP failure). A syslog message is generated as a fault with fault ID F1543. The incident went through the fault life cycle and now is in a raised state with a critical severity level. The system message states that Node 201 is inactive and not reachable, as shown in Figure 9-8.

Example: Spine/IPN Failure

Say that you have recently extended your single-pod ACI fabric to multiple pods for leaf scalability. Multi-pod requires an interpod network (IPN) to provide connectivity between multiple pods. This communication channel is established by connecting spines in each pod to IPN routers. Because an IPN glues together multiple pods in a single fabric, it is important to have proper network resiliency and proactive monitoring for this transport medium to ensure smooth operation of your application-hosting infrastructure hosted between multiple pods.

Figure 9-8 *Fabric Node Unreachable System Message*

Figure 9-9 shows a sample multi-pod topology.

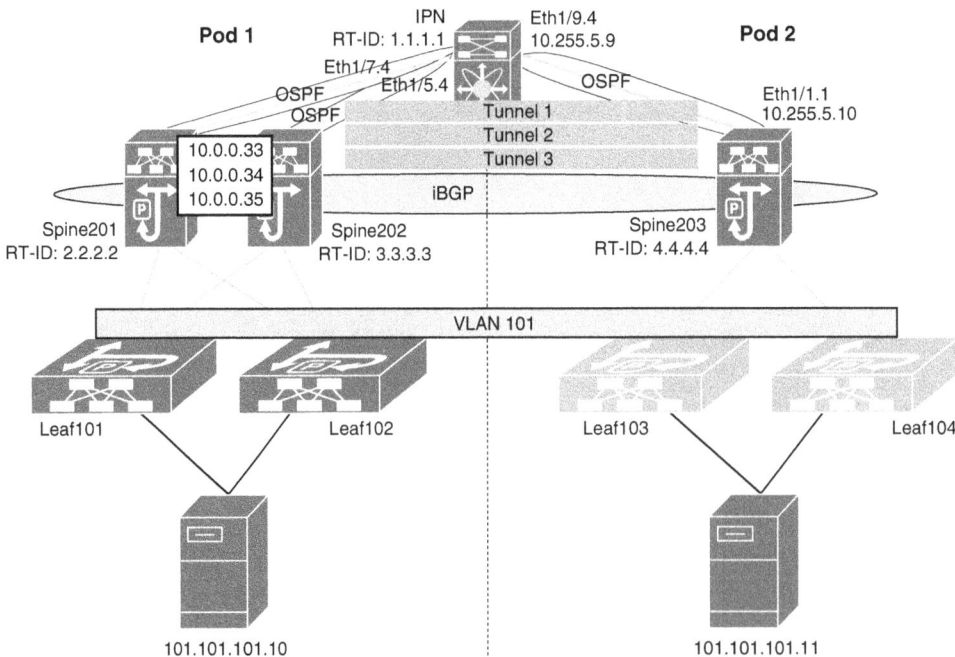

Figure 9-9 *Sample Multi-pod Topology for Monitoring*

The sample topology shown in Figure 9-9 has only one IPN router, which is not a best practice. The goal with this sample topology is to simplify the message and help you develop a proactive monitoring and alerting mechanism for your IPN. Say that you notice that the link from Spine203 loses connectivity to the IPN router and knocks off Pod 2 and its associated ACI fabric infrastructure, as shown in Figure 9-10.

You have configured syslog data collectors to send system logs to an external syslog server. However, in order to forward these logs to an external server, you need to enable the syslog source in tenant, fabric, and access policies and associate it with the syslog destination—the external server. The spine/IPN connectivity is configured in the *Infra* tenant, and so it is important to define the syslog sources in the *Infra* tenant. (Chapter 10 describes the configuration of syslog and other monitoring and management protocol and tools.)

After losing the link between Spine203 and the IPN router, as shown in Figure 9-10, you start receiving the logs. These are critical logs that you should proactively monitor and generate trouble tickets against to remediate the issue rapidly.

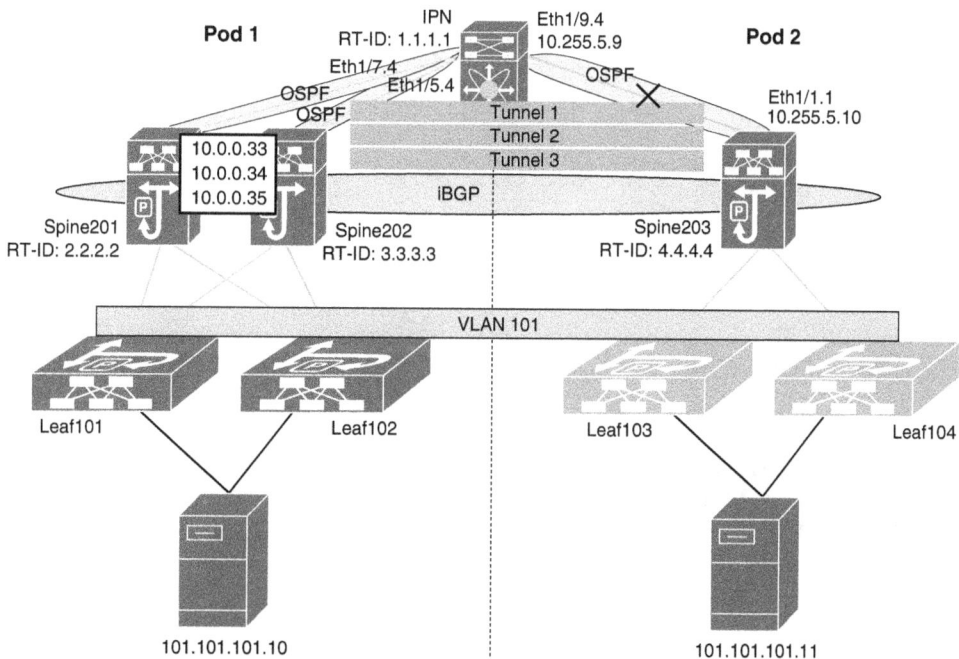

Figure 9-10 *Spine/IPN Link Failure in Multi-pod*

First, the OSPF adjacency between Spine203 and the IPN went down. ACI Spine203 in Pod 2 generates the following log:

```
Feb 18 14:26:30 s1-pod2-spine203 %LOG_LOCAL7-6-SYSTEM_MSG [F1385]
[deleted] [protocol-ospf-adjacency-down] [cleared] [sys/ospf/inst-default/
dom-overlay-1/if-[eth1/1.1]/adj-1.1.1.1/fault-F1385] OSPF adjacency is
not full
```

The IPN router generates the same OSPF adjacency down state log:

```
2020 Feb 18 14:26:29.869 IPN %ETHPORT-5-IF_DOWN: Interface
Ethernet1/9.4 is down
2020 Feb 18 14:26:29.274 IPN %OSPF-5-ADJCHANGE: ospf-aci [31054]  Nbr
10.255.5.9 on Ethernet1/9.4 went DOWN
```

Second, the tunnel interfaces go down from Spine203 in Pod 2 to Spine201 and Spine202 in Pod 1:

```
Feb 18 14:26:30 s1-pod2-spine203 %LOG_LOCAL7-3-SYSTEM_MSG [F0475]
[soaking] [interface-tunnel-down] [major] [sys/tunnel-[tunnel1]/
fault-F0475] Tunnel destination to ip: 10.0.0.33/32 for tunnel1 is
not reachable.\n
Feb 18 14:26:30 s1-pod2-spine203 %LOG_LOCAL7-6-SYSTEM_MSG [E4208070]
[oper-state-change] [info] [sys/tunnel-[tunnel1]] Interface tunnel1 is
down reason Destination unreachable\n
Feb 18 14:26:30 s1-pod2-spine203 %LOG_LOCAL7-3-SYSTEM_MSG [F0475]
[soaking] [interface-tunnel-down] [major] [sys/tunnel-[tunnel2]/
fault-F0475] Tunnel destination to ip: 10.0.0.34/32 for tunnel2 is
not reachable.\n
Feb 18 14:26:30 s1-pod2-spine203 %LOG_LOCAL7-6-SYSTEM_MSG [E4208070]
[oper-state-change] [info] [sys/tunnel-[tunnel2]] Interface tunnel2 is
down reason Destination unreachable\n
Feb 18 14:26:30 s1-pod2-spine203 %LOG_LOCAL7-3-SYSTEM_MSG [F0475]
[soaking] [interface-tunnel-down] [major] [sys/tunnel-[tunnel3]/
fault-F0475] Tunnel destination to ip: 10.0.0.35/32 for tunnel3 is
not reachable.\n
Feb 18 14:26:30 s1-pod2-spine203 %LOG_LOCAL7-6-SYSTEM_MSG [E4208070]
[oper-state-change] [info] [sys/tunnel-[tunnel3]] Interface tunnel3 is
down reason Destination unreachable\n
```

Finally, the iBGP peer relationship goes down from Spine203 in Pod 2 to Spine201 and Spine202 in Pod 1:

```
Feb 18 14:26:50 s1-pod2-spine203 %LOG_LOCAL7-6-SYSTEM_MSG [E4208055]
[oper-state-change] [info] [sys/bgp/inst/dom-overlay-1/peer-[2.2.2.2]/
ent-[2.2.2.2]] BGP peer operational state is changed to Closing\n
Feb 18 14:26:53 s1-pod2-spine203 %LOG_LOCAL7-6-SYSTEM_MSG [E4208055]
[oper-state-change] [info] [sys/bgp/inst/dom-overlay-1/peer-[3.3.3.3]/
ent-[3.3.3.3]] BGP peer operational state is changed to Closing\n
```

NetFlow

NetFlow is a protocol that Cisco developed and introduced in the industry in the 1990s, mainly to collect IP traffic entering and leaving a router or switch interface, depending on where it was enabled. The protocol has since evolved into various versions, but the commonly used ones are v5 and v9. Other network vendors have also developed flow technologies, but NetFlow is the industry's de facto protocol standard for network flow analysis. With NetFlow, IP flow information is collected and sent out as NetFlow records toward an analysis system called a NetFlow collector. The NetFlow collector processes the data, performs traffic analysis, and presents the information in a user-understandable format.

Many organizations use NetFlow primarily as a network monitoring tool, and others use it for network usage billing and forensics. Monitoring and analyzing flows using NetFlow provides a holistic view of the network, bandwidth utilization, traffic patterns between application users and servers, data security, and compliance, and it helps in resolving application performance issues. In addition to the many advantages NetFlow has provided to companies, there are a few drawbacks in using the protocol. One major one has to do with network devices keeping up with today's faster interface speeds while not over-loading system processing. It is really hard for a network device to capture every flow through high-speed interfaces. To deal with this shortcoming, network devices collect only sample flows, which makes it tough to provide full network visibility, as intended by network administrators. The industry is therefore adopting more efficient ways to monitor today's complex high-speed networks through tools using telemetry data such as Network Insights and Cisco Tetration (discussed later in this chapter).

A typical NetFlow monitoring system has three main components:

- **Flow exporter:** Aggregates packets into flow records and exports them toward one or more flow collectors.

- **Flow collector:** Responsible for receiving, storing, and preprocessing flow data received from a flow exporter.

- **Application analysis system:** Analyzes the received flow data in the context of intrusion detection, traffic profiling, billing, and other use cases.

Cisco ACI supports NetFlow v9. NetFlow support in ACI started with the second-generation cloud-scale platform (for leaf switches only; spines are not supported), with the following code releases:

- **EX leaf:** Release 2.2(1)

- **FX leaf:** Release 2.3(1)

- **Remote leaf:** Release 4.0(1)

The Nexus 9300 platform in ACI can be configured for either NetFlow or Tetration Analytics through a hardware agent to provide flow information. NetFlow policies in ACI can be configured under the following:

- Access policies (leaf downlink ports: access, VPC, and port channel)

- Tenant policies (bridge domain, L3Out)

NetFlow can be enabled on a VMware vSphere Distributed Switch (VDS) if integrated with ACI. (In-band management is required.) NetFlow in ACI does not support active/inactive timers, as do NX-OS and IOS. Flow records are exported to collectors every min-ute. As mentioned earlier, NetFlow can be tough on resource consumption. With ACI, the filter TCAM has no labels for bridge domain or interfaces. If a NetFlow monitor is added to two bridge domains, the NetFlow monitor uses two rules for IPv4 or eight rules for IPv6. The scale is very limited with the 1K filter TCAM in the Nexus 9300 platform. Therefore, you should keep a close eye on your ACI fabric TCAM utilization when configuring NetFlow on leaf interfaces.

Example: Network Visibility on a Border Leaf

Say that your management has tasked you with ensuring visibility of network traffic entering and leaving your newly deployed ACI fabric in your company's data center. You start researching various protocols and tools and hear that one of your best options is to enable NetFlow on your border leaf in order to monitor all the flows coming into and going out of the ACI fabric. How can you do that?

First, you have to enable the NetFlow feature on your leafs (in this case, your border leaf). Remember that in ACI you can either run NetFlow *or* Tetration Analytics on your Nexus 9300 leaf platforms. You can enable all your leafs with NetFlow or Tetration, or you can enable some with NetFlow and some with Tetration. However, a single leaf cannot run both features at the same time.

When configuring NetFlow in ACI, you need to follow four simple steps under Access Policies or Tenant Policies, depending on where you need to do the configuration:

Step 1.   Configure the flow record using either IPv4 or IPv6. The parameters you can select are the source/destination IP address and the source/destination port.

Step 2.   Configure the flow exporter by providing the IP address of your NetFlow Analyzer machine.

Step 3.   Configure the flow monitor by combining the flow record and flow exporter.

Step 4.   Attach the flow monitor to the leaf interface that you intend to use to collect NetFlow information.

Note   Chapter 10 provides details on NetFlow configuration.

After configuring NetFlow on your border leaf, you start receiving network flows. You can view NetFlow information on your border leaf by using the CLI command shown in Figure 9-11. In this example, you can see that you are receiving TCP (protocol 6) and UDP (protocol 17) flows between multiple hosts with packet and byte counts.

```
Bleaf-0201# show flow cache ipv4
IPV4 Entries
SIP            DIP            BD ID   S-Port   D-Port   Protocol   Byte Count   Packet Count   TCP FLAGS   if_id       flowStart
10.88.146.51   10.88.197.48   4611    53       37779    17         144          1              0x0         0x1a003000  28365088   28365088
10.88.150.154  2.2.2.2        4611    28570    1967     17         98           1              0x0         0x1a003000  28367890   28367890
10.88.144.73   10.88.197.53   4611    5640     59228    6          70           1              0x10        0x1a003000  28365680   28365680
10.88.194.7    10.88.193.14   4611    58282    4353     6          10456        98             0x18        0x1a003000  28365917   28367549
```

Figure 9-11   *Viewing NetFlow Information from the Border Leaf 201 CLI*

To view NetFlow information in more detail, you can use the NetFlow Analyzer software of your choice. The example in Figure 9-12 shows that you are receiving NetFlow traffic on border leaf Node ID 201 with SNMP interface index IfIndex 436219904. You can run the command **show interface snmp-ifindex** on the leaf via the CLI, as shown in Figure 9-12, to get the actual port number, which is Eth1/4 in this case. The NetFlow Analyzer software can provide much more detailed information, such as top N applications, top N protocols, top talkers, traffic usage, and so on.

Note   Figure 9-12 shows the limited free trial version of NetFlow Analyzer.

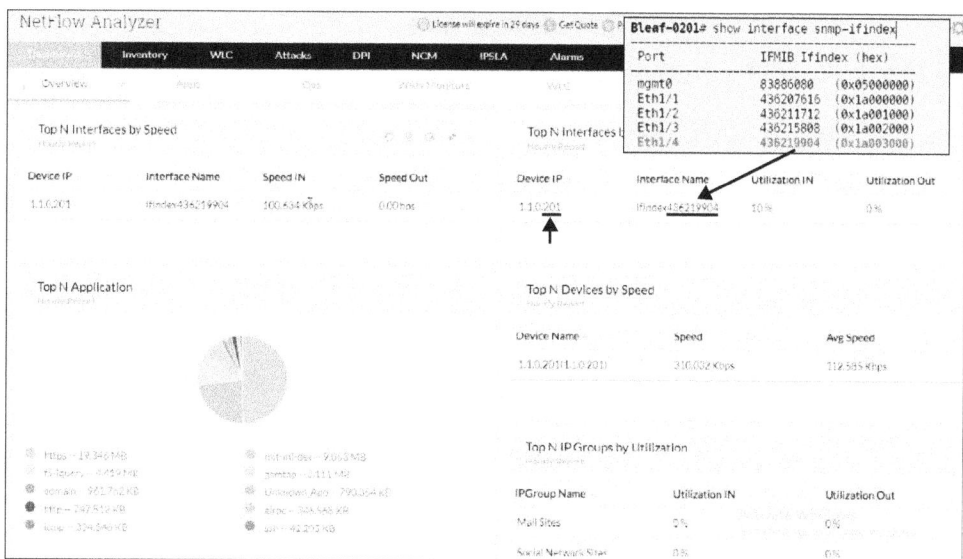

Figure 9-12   *Viewing NetFlow Information in NetFlow Analyzer*

The example shown in Figure 9-13 illustrates the top conversations between hosts with source/destination IP, application, and traffic usage information.

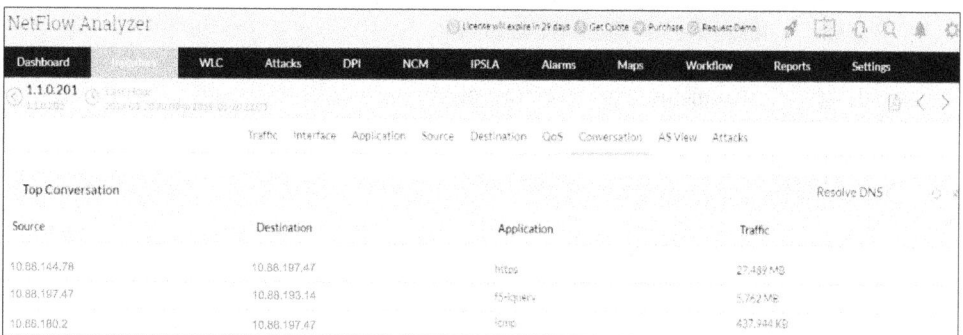

Figure 9-13   *Viewing Top Conversation*

The example shown in Figure 9-14 illustrates the top N protocol information between hosts with source/destination IP, application, DSCP, and traffic usage information.

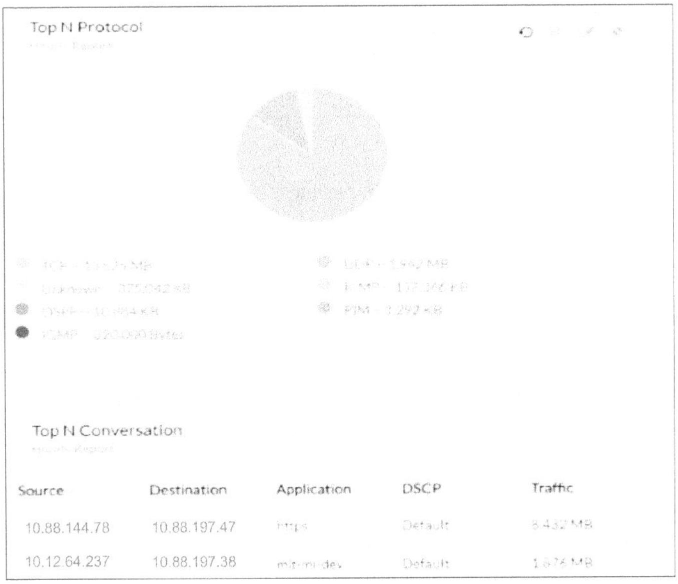

Figure 9-14 *Viewing NetFlow Information in NetFlow Analyzer*

ACI External Monitoring Tools

Besides internal monitoring tools and protocols that are packaged as part of ACI software, Cisco also offers external tools such as Network Insights, Network Assurance Engine, and Tetration for proactively monitoring your application-hosting infrastructure running over ACI. The following sections describe these tools.

Network Insights

Cisco Network Insights tool is for monitoring and analyzing your fabric, whether ACI fabric or a standalone VXLAN fabric running on NX-OS in real time to identify anomalies and to provide root-cause analysis and enable capacity planning. Network Insights is a suite of tools that includes Network Insights for Resources (NIR) and Network Insights Advisor (NIA). It functions by collecting and processing telemetry data and correlating it with the existing network infrastructure deployment by leveraging Cisco's extensive knowledge and experiences from the field. Let's dive in to each one of these tool sets.

Note   Cisco Network Insights is supported in ACI Release 4.2 and later. This book's main focus is on ACI Release 3.2, but it also includes new features and tools in newer releases that benefit readers. Due to the great benefits and value that Network Insights provides for monitoring ACI fabric, it is included in this book.

Network Insights for Resources (NIR)

NIR is a tool that helps with troubleshooting, monitoring, auditing, and capacity planning. It is integrated as a plug-in into the Cisco ACI APIC and Data Center Network Manager (DCNM) for NX-OS support. NIR performs of the following functions:

- **Anomaly detection:** This involves understanding the behavior of each fabric component by using different machine-learning algorithms. When the resource behavior deviates from an expected pattern, anomalies are detected and raised.

- **Endpoint analytics:** NIR monitors the availability, location, and health of endpoints. It also analyzes the impact to these endpoints of any events or changes in the network infrastructure and helps derive potential root causes and reduce mean time to restore (MTTR).

- **Resource utilization:** NIR offers early detection of resources that are exceeding capacity thresholds. These analytics include monitoring of software and hardware resources such as CPU, memory, and VRF instances to ensure optimal usage. NIR identifies anomalies by observing parameters such as CPU, memory, temperature, power draw, and fan speed.

- **Statistics:** NIR monitors and detects anomalies related to interface utilization, errors, protocol stats, and state machines. It helps detect, locate, and determine root causes of issues. Correlation with endpoint analytics provides impact analysis data.

- **Flow analytics:** NIR helps identify, locate, and analyze root causes of data path issues such as latency and packet drops for specific traffic flows.

The NIR dashboard enables quick action on specific issues that need swift attention, as shown in Figure 9-15.

In this dashboard, you can use the time range and filter anomalies based on category, nodes, description, and so on for a quick run of problems you are encountering. You can also examine anomalies based on health score and top nodes with a specific timeline view.

NIR collects both software and hardware telemetry data and processes it for further analysis. For software telemetry, it provides visibility into resource utilization, environmental data, interface counters, and control plane protocol stats and events. For hardware telemetry, it provides visibility into data plane flow information and shows the flow path and statistics. You need a Cisco Services Engine (SE) appliance to store hardware flow telemetry data. For further details and the latest information, see Cisco.com.

Timeline View
With Anomalies

Inventory With Health
Score

Clicking On Any New Node
Gives a 360 Node View

Top Nodes by Anomalies

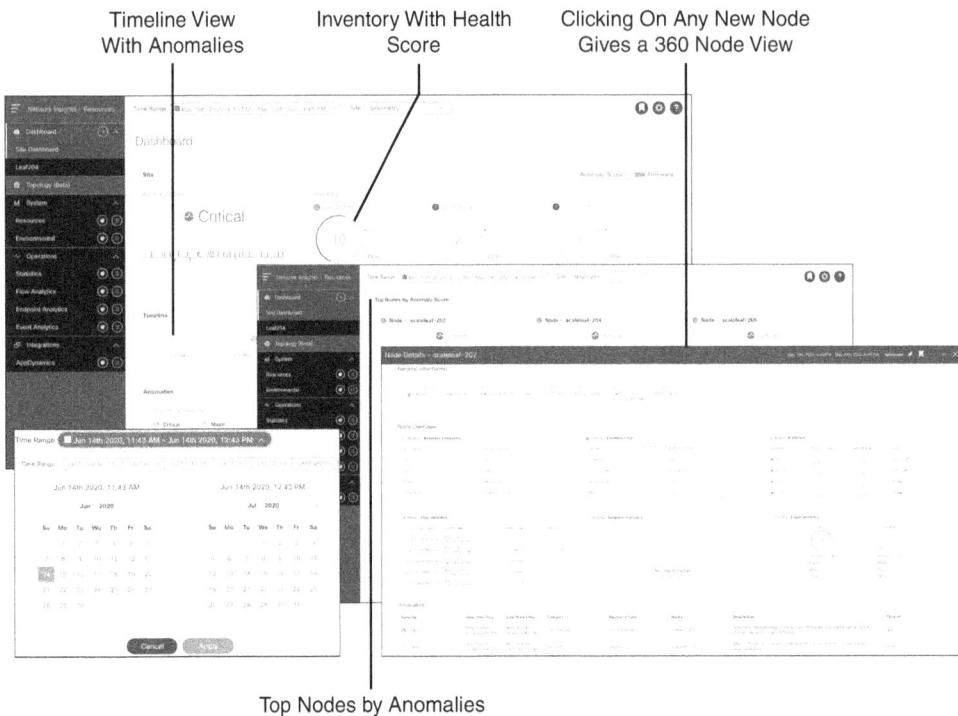

Figure 9-15   *NIR Dashboard View*

Network Insights Advisor (NIA)

NIA is a tool that provides deployment-relevant supportability information and advisories. It is focused on actionable recommendations based on known issues and Cisco common best practices. Many people have the misconception that this tool is a replacement for Cisco Advanced Services, but it is not. NIA efficiently provides information about software caveats, security alerts, configuration best practices, and so on, enabling Cisco Advanced Services engineers to focus on design and architecture support, lab setup and build-out, knowledge transfer, and so on for their customers. NIA performs the following functions:

- **Advisories:** NIA provides deployment-specific recommendations and best practices and upgrade impact analysis and experience.

- **Notices:** NIA provides an inbox function, proactive end-of-life and end-of-sale announcements, new field notices, and new software maintenance updates.

- **Anomalies:** NIA alerts users about known software defects and PSIRTs through the Anomalies Flow State Validator.

- **Compliance:** NIA conducts system hardening checks, ensures version-specific scale limits, and provides monitoring to generate advisory.

- **Diagnostics:** NIA offers diagnostics through Cisco TAC, cloud technical support, and Diagnostics Fast Start.

The NIA dashboard view is intended for quick action on specific issues that need swift attention, as shown in Figure 9-16.

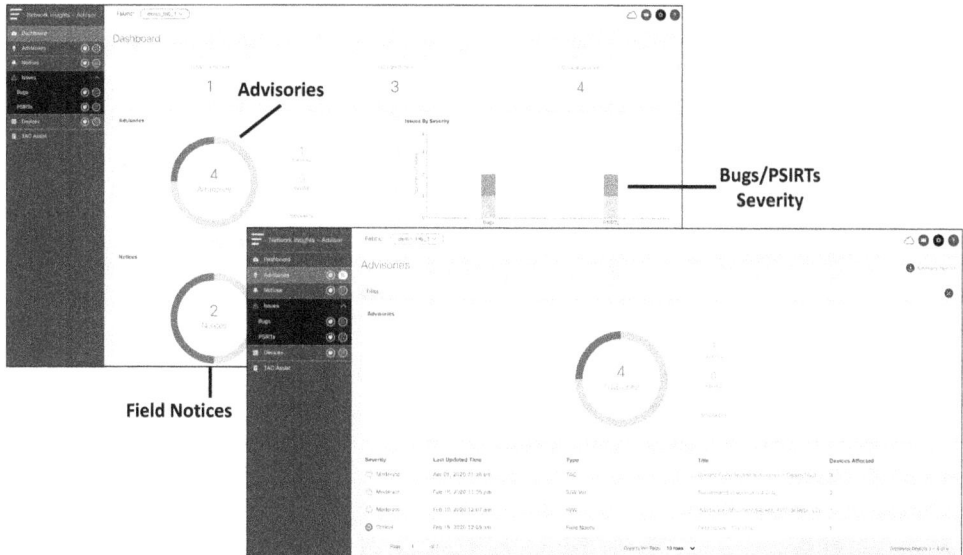

Figure 9-16 *NIA Dashboard View*

The NIA dashboard provides advisories, field notices, and bugs and PSIRTs (with severity). For further details and the latest information, see Cisco.com.

Example: Application Intermittent Disconnect Issue (Standalone Compute)

Say that your application team complains of experiencing performance issues. The application is running on a standalone Linux host. The application server with IP address 10.10.10.10 was functioning normally, but for the past week or so it has gotten intermittent disconnects. You check Endpoint Tracker in the APIC and find that 10.10.10.10 is connected to Leaf 201 on interface Eth1/1, as illustrated in Figure 9-17.

You have NIR installed in your network. After gathering the initial data of the incident, you select the past week as the timeframe and filter the anomalies by category, nodes, and cleared in the NIR dashboard. As shown in Figure 9-18, NIR indicates that DOM and CRC errors have resulted in Layer 2 LLDP flaps and traffic disruption.

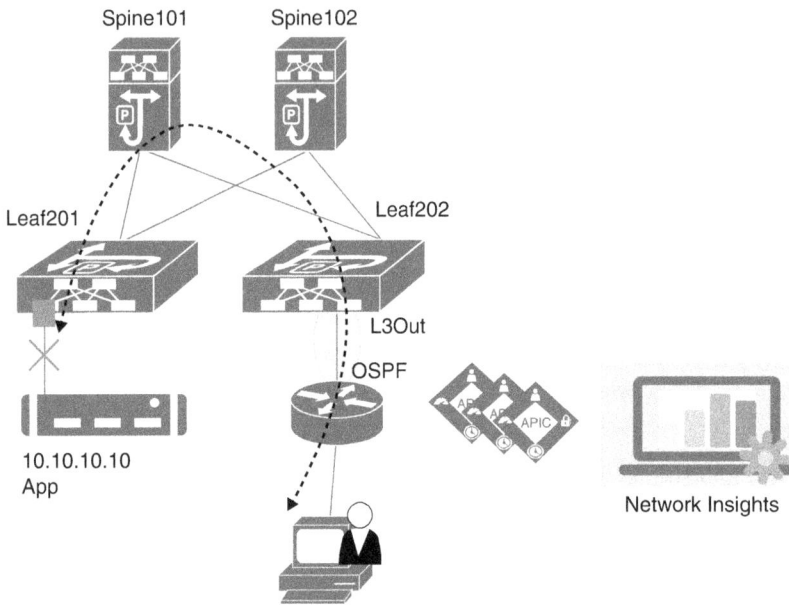

Figure 9-17 *Application Intermittent Disconnect Issue (Standalone Compute)*

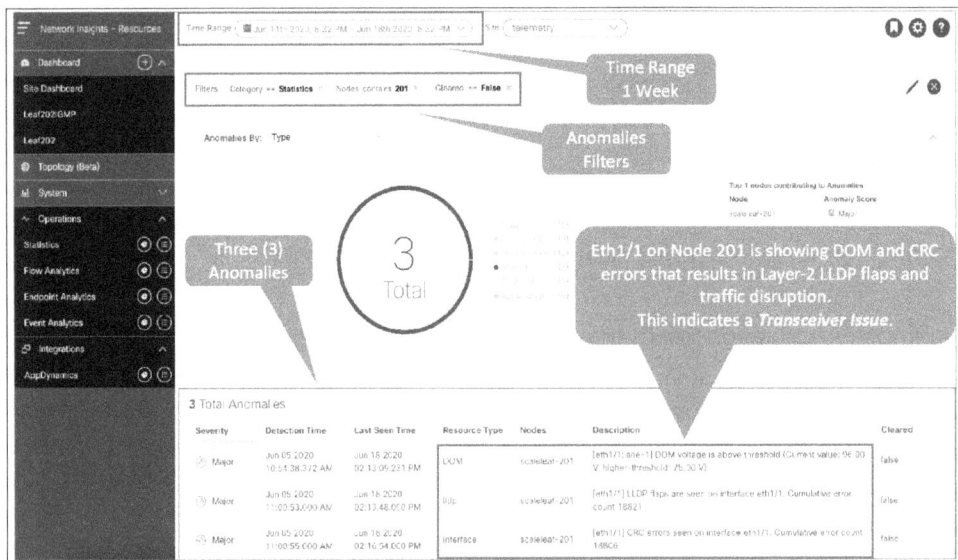

Figure 9-18 *NIR Dashboard Showing Anomalies*

This clearly indicates that the transceiver in interface Eth1/1 is bad. You replace the transceiver, and this fix ultimately resolves the application intermittent disconnect issue.

Example: Application Connectivity Issue (Virtual Compute)

Say that your virtualization team complains of experiencing performance issues on applications hosted on a virtual machine (VM) under VMware NSX. You have designed and implemented VMware NSX to run on top of ACI with an NSX edge gateway connected to an ACI leaf using eBGP peering. Figure 9-19 illustrates this scenario.

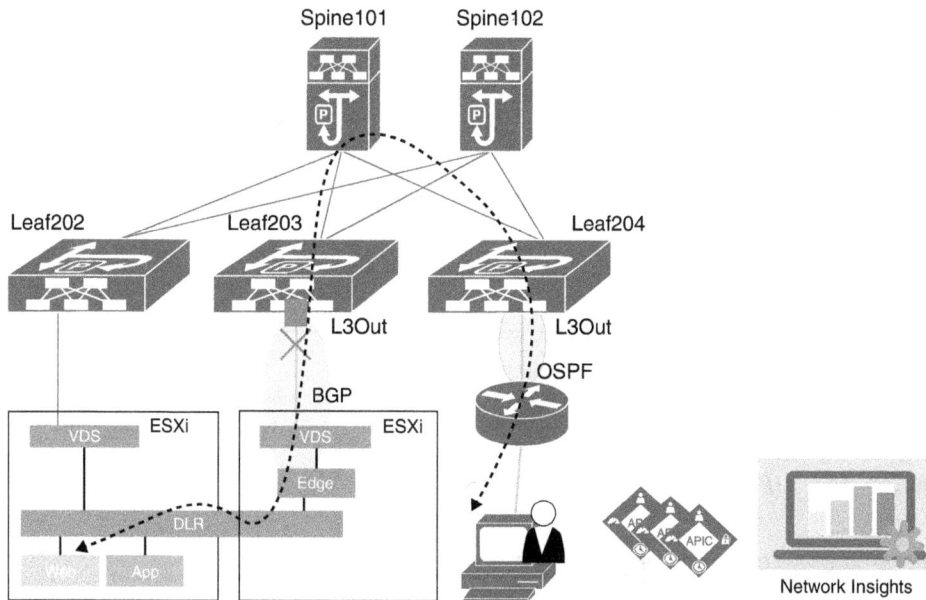

Figure 9-19   *NIR Dashboard Showing Anomalies*

NIR is deployed and running in the network, so you select the past one hour as the timeframe and filter the anomalies by category, nodes, description, and cleared. Figure 9-20 shows that BGP peer 12.37.81.3 is the NSX edge gateway connected to ACI Leaf 203 and is idle.

You double-click on the displayed anomaly in the NIR dashboard to get more details and recommended steps to troubleshoot the issue, as shown in Figure 9-21.

On further investigation, you find out that the NSX edge gateway VM got moved to another ESXi host connected to different leaf, which has not yet been configured for L3Out with BGP. In traditional networking without proper monitoring tools, such an issue could take hours to troubleshoot and fix.

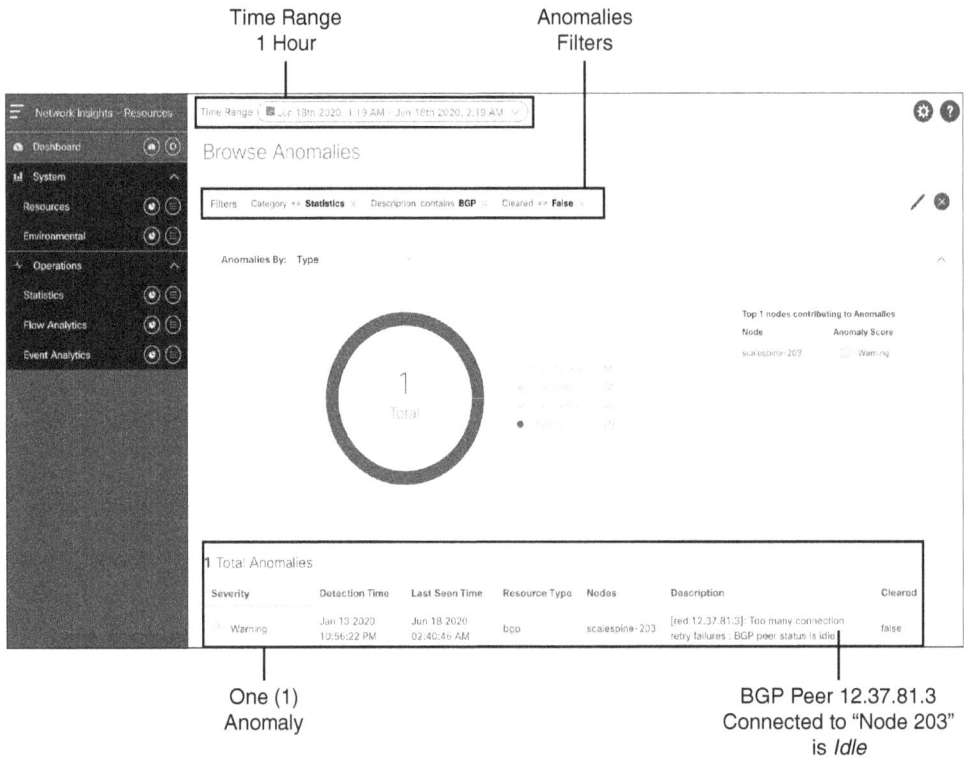

Figure 9-20 *NIR Dashboard Showing Anomalies*

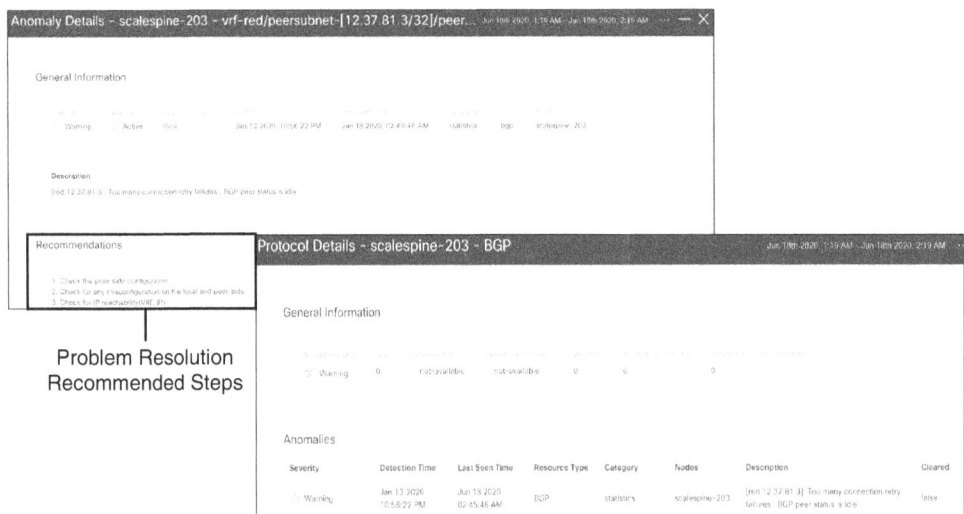

Figure 9-21 *NIR Dashboard Showing Anomalies*

Network Assurance Engine

With the software-defined networking (SDN) approach, adaptations have been made to address the challenges companies face in today's fast-paced economy through rapid provisioning of hosting infrastructures at a large scale. Having layers of virtualization and switching in next-generation data center networks makes these networks complex to manage and maintain. These modern intent-based networks that are built on policies come with unique challenges.

If you make any change in your network by modifying some high-level policies, how can you guarantee that you will not break something else? Many network outages occur after configuration changes. Even if you have done all the configuration steps right, remember that your network state is changing dynamically. For example, in ACI, external prefixes are learned via border leafs. Suppose you configure a BD with a subnet that has a more specific route coming in from outside the fabric, and the configuration is causing internal application traffic to divert in different direction. Intent-based networking through programmability is an efficient way of provisioning the network, but what happens when you realize that your network doesn't quite behave as you intended? How do you troubleshoot the network without having a complete view of the topology? Where are your VLANs, bridge domains, and endpoints sitting? How is connectivity being established between Endpoint A and Endpoint B?

To mitigate such challenges, you can use Cisco Network Assurance Engine (NAE), which provides a holistic view of your network and correlates it to the ACI policy model, helping you to troubleshoot issues rapidly. NAE encompasses everything you do in data center network operations, so when you use it, you can be confident in your changes and configurations, knowing your routing and forwarding state is consistent and ensuring that your security policies meet the segmentation goals and compliance requirements, pass audits easily, and so on. NAE brings formal verification techniques into networking, helping close the assurance gap. It mathematically verifies and validates an entire data center network for correctness, giving operators the confidence that their network is always operating consistently with their intent, even if it is dynamically changing. NAE does its magic through the methodology building blocks illustrated in Figure 9-22 and described in the list that follows.

Network Assurance Engine: How it Works

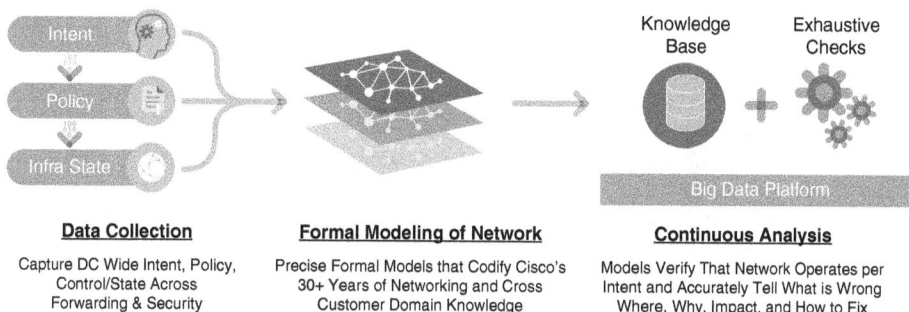

Data Collection	Formal Modeling of Network	Continuous Analysis
Capture DC Wide Intent, Policy, Control/State Across Forwarding & Security	Precise Formal Models that Codify Cisco's 30+ Years of Networking and Cross Customer Domain Knowledge	Models Verify That Network Operates per Intent and Accurately Tell What is Wrong Where, Why, Impact, and How to Fix

Figure 9-22 *Building Blocks of NAE*

- **Data collection:** The data collection framework periodically ingests all non-packet data—such as the operator's intent, policy configurations from the controller, software configurations, and traffic forwarding state—from each device and stores it in a platform-agnostic format.

- **Comprehensive modeling:** NAE performs formal modeling of a data center network through mathematically accurate representations of the network's actual behavior, based on the real-time state and policy. For instance, NAE models all the security contracts, the forwarding state across all the switches, the configurations of all the endpoints across the network, and so on.

- **Analytical engine:** Built on a big data architecture, NAE continuously runs thousands of failure scenarios against mathematical models of the network. More than 5000 failure scenarios have been considered in the product, based on more than 30 years of Cisco's network operational knowledge. These failure patterns are continuously being enhanced in the product through field-related knowledge collected from thousands of customers.

The analysis runs continuously every few minutes. NAE polls the entire policy and network state, updates the formal model, and runs the checks against the model. When a discrepancy is found, the tool generates a smart event, which pinpoints deviations from intended behavior and provides expert-level remediation suggestions. The Cisco Network Assurance Engine models multiple behavioral aspects of the network, including a tenant's endpoint mobility, policy configuration, security, forwarding, and resource utilization.

To understand how NAE can dramatically improve your network operations, consider these use cases:

- **Predicting the impact of changes:** Making changes to a network has traditionally been an uncertain process that is prone to failure (sometimes even days later). When errors occur, you drop everything and rush to find the root causes and fix them. Using Cisco Network Assurance Engine, you can quickly verify in advance whether particular changes might result in errors. The built-in checks are used to analyze the network model, helping you quickly pinpoint errors and fix them before they disrupt your network.

- **Conducting root-cause analysis:** Identifying a problem is the first step in problem resolution. You need to fully troubleshoot the network error state and understand its root cause before proper corrective action can be taken. This can be a very time-consuming process and extends service downtime. Cisco Network Assurance Engine leverages decades of accumulated networking experience. It applies thousands of checks to a network in real time. When it detects problems, NAE triggers smart events, which pinpoint the problems and offer suggested remediation.

- **Assuring Security compliance:** Achieving regulatory compliance and passing security audits is a labor-intensive process that must be repeated periodically. Using Cisco Network Assurance Engine, you can complete the auditing process with just a few mouse clicks. Because NAE stores the full network state, you can easily scroll back in the past to find answers to questions such as "What was the state of my network a few weeks back? Did I have any security issues? Were my policies correctly configured?" Cisco Network Assurance Engine runs such checks every few minutes, so it actually provides continuous compliance checking. There is no more need to scramble your network every time you have a security audit.

■ **Understanding resource utilization:** One of the challenges network administrators face is optimizing the use of network device level resources such as ternary content-addressable memory (TCAM), which is a critical component on switches. Cisco Network Assurance Engine analyzes how policies are mapped into each TCAM space. It provides a detailed multidimensional understanding of utilization, identifies policy redundancies, and reports hit counts at a rule level. This capability allows you to optimize your policies and tighten your security aperture.

NAE Installation

To install Cisco NAE, you need to consider some prerequisites. Three appliance size models are currently shipping with Cisco NAE: small, medium, and large. Table 9-4 identifies the system requirements for installing the Cisco NAE on each of these models.

Table 9-4 *NAE System Requirements*

Requirement	Appliance Model		
	Small	**Medium**	**Large**
Model	NAE-V500-S	NAE-V1000-M	NAE-V2000-L
Number of VMs	3	3	3
Number of CPU vCores per VM	8	12	24
Memory (GB per VM)	40 GB	64 GB	96 GB
Disk space per VM	1 TB	2 TB	4 TB
Storage	SSD	SSD	SSD
APIC fabric size	50 leaf switches for a 3-VM cluster	100 leaf switches for a 3-VM cluster	400 leaf switches for a 3-VM cluster

The hypervisor requirements for NAE are VMware vSphere versions 5.5, 6.0, 6.5, or 6.7.

Some important notes regarding NAE installation are as follows:

■ Starting from Release 3.0(1), HDD storage for the small appliance is not supported. Before upgrading to Release 3.0(1), ensure that you have SSD storage installed.

■ In a production environment, the supported and required configuration for virtual disks is to use thick provisioning. In a lab environment, if you have configured the

Cisco NAE appliance using thin provisioning, you must not use the same appliance in the production environment.

■ The recommended Intel processor for vCPUs mentioned in the table system requirements is Intel Xeon CPU E5-2697A v4 with 2.60 GHz or later.

■ For a particular Cisco NAE model, the disk space required depends on the retention period of the epoch data. To increase the disk size, check out the NAE documentation at Cisco.com.

■ The IOPS performance numbers for storage system SSDs tested are as follows:

■ Sequential read up to 550 Mbps

■ Sequential write up to 500 Mbps

■ Random read (100% span) 84000 IOPS

■ Random write (100% span) 27000 IOPS

■ The supported browser is Google Chrome.

Table 9-5 lists the compatibility information for Cisco ACI and NAE.

Table 9-5 *ACI/NAE Compatibility Versions*

Cisco ACI Release	Cisco ACI Mode NX-OS Switch Software Release for Cisco Nexus 9000 Series ACI Mode Switches
4.0	14.0
3.2	13.2
3.1	13.1
3.0	13.0
2.3	12.3
2.2	12.2
2.1	12.1
2.0	12.0
1.3	11.3
1.2	11.2

NAE Configuration and Initial Setup

Before you can configure NAE itself, you need to perform the following prerequisite steps:

Step 1. Install Python Version 2.7.11 or later to perform offline analysis.

Step 2. Reserve IP addresses, a subnet mask, and gateways for the Cisco NAE appliance.

Step 3.   Reserve IP addresses for the primary and secondary DNS servers.

Step 4.   Reserve IP addresses for the primary and secondary NTP servers.

Step 5.   Ensure that you have credentials for the SMTP server.

Step 6.   Ensure that TCP ports 443 and 22 are open for HTTPS and SSH communication between the Cisco NAE and the APIC.

Step 7.   Ensure that Cisco NAE appliance VMs (three in a cluster) have unrestricted communication between them, preferably in the same VLAN.

Step 8.   Ensure that you have administrator privileges to connect to VMware vSphere or vCenter.

Step 9.   Ensure that you have a Cisco NAE OVA image. The OVA image contains a set of OVAs for the different appliance flavors. You will receive the OVA for the appliance flavor based on the license you purchased.

When you are done with the prerequisite steps, follow these installation steps:

Step 1.   Log in to VMware vCenter.

Step 2.   In the Navigation pane, choose the data center for deployment.

Step 3.   Choose File > Deploy OVF Template. The Deploy OVF Template window appears.

Step 4.   In the Source pane, browse to the location, choose the file, and click Open to choose your OVF source location.

Step 5.   In the OVF Template Details pane, verify the details and click Next.

Step 6.   In the End User License Agreement pane, read the license agreement and click Accept.

Step 7.   In the Name and Location pane, perform the following steps:

   a. In the Name field, enter the VM name (optional).

   b. Choose the inventory location where the Cisco NAE is being deployed and click Next.

Step 8.   In the Host/Cluster pane, choose the required cluster and click Next.

Step 9.   In the Storage pane, choose the location in which to store virtual machine files.

Step 10.   In the Disk Format pane, enter the datastore and the required space for the appliance, click the Thick Provision button, and click Next.

Step 11.   In the Properties pane, provide the IP address, subnet mask, and gateway information for the NAE appliance and click Next.

Step 12.   In the Ready to Complete pane, verify the options selected and click Finish.

Step 13.   Reserve all the memory allocated to each virtual machine to avoid performance issues.

Step 14.   Edit VM settings to set up Disk 1 on a different physical datastore than Disk 2.

Step 15.   Power on the VM. The Cisco NAE virtual appliance is deployed as a cluster of three virtual machines.

Step 16.   Repeat steps 3 through 15 to deploy the remaining virtual machines in the cluster.

Note   You must perform the installation on one VM at a time. Do not perform the installation on all three VMs simultaneously.

After configuring the three virtual machines and powering them up, use the IP address or hostname of one of the NAE appliances to log on. Then perform the initial setup: Configure the administrator profile, add the remaining two virtual machines in the cluster, and configure the DNS, NTP, and SMTP servers. Use the following procedure to perform these tasks:

Step 1.   Log in to the Cisco NAE. The Appliance Setup form appears.

Step 2.   Complete the following fields for the administrator profile:

    a. Enter the email address.

    b. Enter the password and reenter it for confirmation.

Step 3.   Complete the following fields for cluster configuration:

Note   You must add at least three virtual machines to the cluster. The IP address of Virtual Machine 1 is prepopulated. Ensure that each of these VMs is reachable before clicking Submit and ensure that power remains on during installation.

    a. Click the **+** sign to add Virtual Machine 2 to the cluster and enter the IP address of the virtual machine.

    b. Click the **+** sign to add Virtual Machine 3 to the cluster and enter the IP address of the virtual machine.

Step 4. DNS servers are configured for hostname resolution. Cisco NAE validates the reachability of the DNS servers. You must specify at least one DNS server. Complete the following fields for the DNS servers (see Figure 9-23):

    a. Enter the IP address of the primary DNS server.

    b. Enter the IP address of the secondary DNS server (optional).

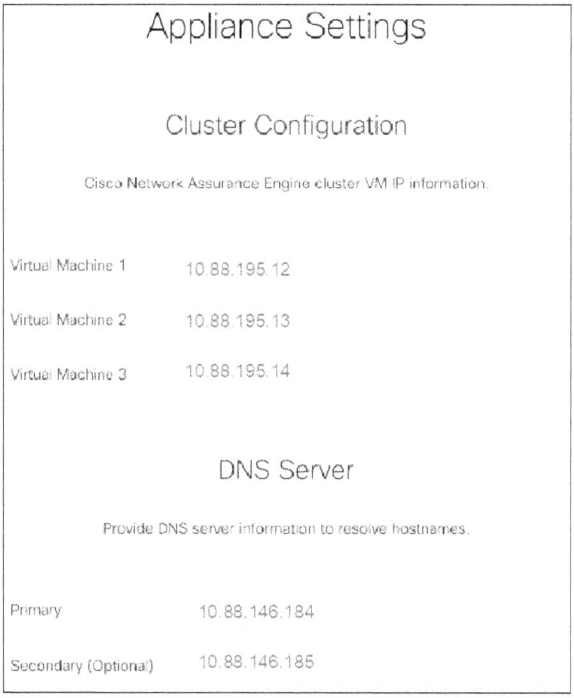

Appliance Settings

Cluster Configuration

Cisco Network Assurance Engine cluster VM IP information.

Virtual Machine 1	10.88.195.12
Virtual Machine 2	10.88.195.13
Virtual Machine 3	10.88.195.14

DNS Server

Provide DNS server information to resolve hostnames.

Primary	10.88.146.184
Secondary (Optional)	10.88.146.185

Figure 9-23 *NAE Cluster and DNS Configuration*

Step 5. Complete the fields for the NTP server and SMTP server, as shown in Figure 9-24, and click Submit.

Note Uncheck Use External NTP Server to create a local NTP server configuration. Use proper email credentials to access the SMTP server.

Now it's time to create assurance groups in NAE. An assurance group provides intent assurance for a group of entities at the same time. Assurance group configuration allows you to configure the entities that need to be analyzed together. Performing online analysis allows the Cisco NAE to collect data from an assurance group, build a model with the collected data, and generate results. The results are displayed on the dashboard as epochs. Use the following procedure to perform the online analysis.

NTP Server

Network Assurance Engine software uses local NTP service to ensure all the VMs in its cluster have synchronized time. The time source for local NTP service can be an external NTP server or the local VM time of the primary VM in the cluster. We recommend that you use the external NTP server option in a production environment as time source rather than local VM time of primary VM. It is highly recommended that you set time correctly during the installation of the appliance via external NTP server or at the host of the VM used for installation. Setting time back or in future in the appliance VMs or in the host post installation is not supported and can result in unpredictable behavior including but not limited to loss of data in some scenarios. If you need to set time back post installation then the supported method is to re-install the appliance and set time correctly.

☑ Use external NTP server

Primary   time.lab.cisco.com

Secondary (Optional)   time2.lab.cisco.com

SMTP Server

Provide SMTP server information.

Hostname   labsmtpgw.cisco.com

Port   25

Figure 9-24   *NAE NTP and SMTP Configuration*

Note   You must have admin credentials to access ACI in configuring assurance groups and export policy.

Step 1.   From the gear icon, select Assurance Groups, as shown in Figure 9-25.

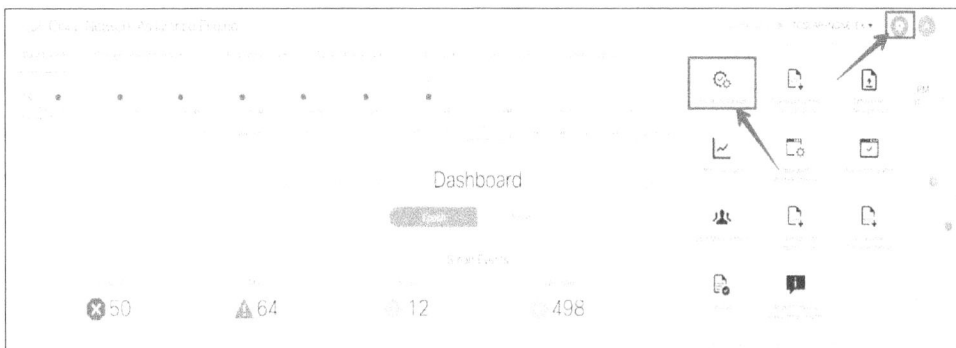

Dashboard

❌50   ⚠64   12   498

Figure 9-25   *Configuring an NAE Assurance Group*

Step 2. Click Create New Assurance Group, as shown in Figure 9-26.

Figure 9-26 *Creating a New Assurance Group*

Step 3. Complete the following fields to create the new assurance group (see Figure 9-27):

a. In the Name field, enter the name.

b. In the Description field, enter the description.

c. Select the Switch to Online Mode checkbox to automatically analyze the assurance group in real time.

d. In the Username field, enter the username to use for accessing the APIC hosts.

e. In the Password field, enter the password to use for accessing the APIC hosts.

f. From the Analysis Interval drop-down list, choose the interval at which to run the analysis. The analysis interval includes the time to collect data from the APIC and the switches, analyze the data to build a model, generate results, and display the results on the dashboard. For production environments, the recommended analysis interval is a minimum of 15 minutes. An interval below 15 minutes should be used only in lab environments or for testing.

g. From the Analysis Timeout drop-down list, choose the time the system needs to wait before terminating the analysis. This value should be greater than the Analysis Interval setting.

h. Check the Start Immediately checkbox to start the analysis of the selected assurance group immediately.

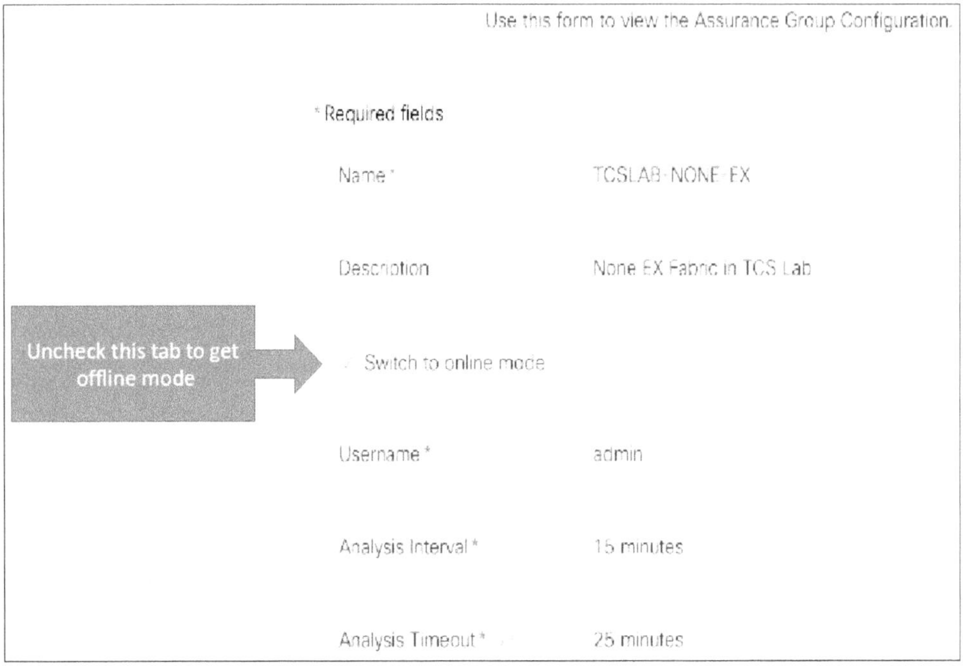

Figure 9-27 *New Assurance Group Configuration*

Step 4.   Complete the following fields for APIC hosts (see Figure 9-28):

   a. In the APIC Hostname 1 field, enter the APIC hostname in the format *apic1.example*.com.

   b. Click the + sign to add another APIC hostname. (We recommend adding all the APIC hosts to the assurance group.)

Step 5.   Complete the following fields for the collection settings, which are required for NAT and epoch delta analysis:

   a. Select the Use APIC Configuration Export Policy checkbox to export the configuration policy for the policy delta.

   b. Click Show.

   c. Select the export format.

   d. In the Export Policy Name field, enter the policy name.

Step 6.   Click Save.

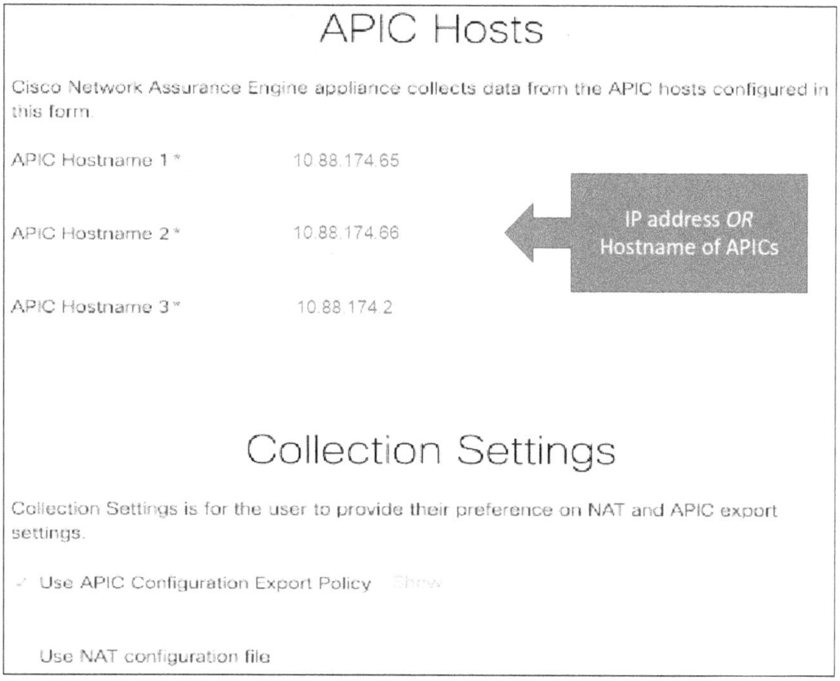

APIC Hosts

Cisco Network Assurance Engine appliance collects data from the APIC hosts configured in this form.

APIC Hostname 1 *   10.88.174.65

APIC Hostname 2 *   10.88.174.66   IP address *OR*
                                               Hostname of APICs

APIC Hostname 3 *   10.88.174.2

Collection Settings

Collection Settings is for the user to provide their preference on NAT and APIC export settings.

✓ Use APIC Configuration Export Policy   Show

   Use NAT configuration file

Figure 9-28 *APIC Host Configuration*

Step 7.   To start the analysis of a fabric, click the Play button. To stop the analysis, click the Stop button.

Note   The status of the analysis is displayed in the Data Collection form. Cisco NAE performs analysis on only one fabric at a time. To perform analysis on another fabric, you must stop the analysis on the current fabric and then start the analysis on another fabric. In a future NAE release, you should be able to run analyses on multiple ACI fabrics at the same time.

Step 8.   To view the results of the analysis, click Dashboard. To ensure that you have the correct assurance group selected to view the results, click Assurance Group and select the appropriate assurance group from the drop-down list.

Step 9.   To export data, select an epoch dot on the timeline and click Export Data.

Besides real-time analysis, Cisco NAE can also perform offline analysis of your fabric. It can be helpful to perform analysis of your production ACI fabric in a lab or preproduction environment. If something unusual is found in your production ACI fabric, you can plan your change accordingly. In order to perform NAE offline analysis, you need to run a Python script on a workstation or laptop running one of the following operating systems:

- Ubuntu 14.04/16.04 or later

- macOS X El Capitan 10.11.6 or later

- CentOS 7.x or later

Note   Windows OS is *not* supported.

- Python version 2.7.11 or later

To run the Python script, follow these steps:

Step 1.   Ensure that the Python package manager **pip** is installed by running the following command:

```
shussa36@eco:~> which pip
/usr/bin/pip
```

Step 2.   If the location of **pip** is not returned, follow the instructions for your operating system to install **pip**:

- For Ubuntu:

```
sudo apt-get install python-pip
sudo apt-get install build-essential libssl-dev
libffi-dev python-dev
```

- For CentOS:

```
sudo yum install python-pip
```

- For macOS:

```
sudo easy_install pip
```

Step 3.   Ensure that **wget** is installed by running the following command:

```
shussa36@eco:~> which wget
/usr/bin/wget
```

If the location of **wget** is not returned, follow the instructions for your operating system to install **wget**:

- For Ubuntu:

```
sudo apt-get install wget
```

■ For CentOS:

```
sudo yum install wget
```

■ For macOS, ensure that the package manager **brew** is installed in order to install **wget**. To install **brew**, run the following command:

```
/usr/bin/ruby -e "$(curl -fsSL
https://raw.githubusercontent.com/Homebrew/install/
master/install)"
```

Then install **wget** by running this command:

```
brew install wget
```

Step 4.   Ensure that **openssl** is installed by running the following command:

```
shussa36@eco:~> which openssl
/usr/bin/openssl
```

Step 5.   If the location of **openssl** is not returned, follow the instructions for your operating system to install **openssl**:

■ For Ubuntu:

```
sudo apt-get install openssl
```

■ For CentOS:

```
sudo yum install openssl
```

■ For macOS:

```
brew install openssl
```

Step 6.   Verify the Python version by running the following command:

```
shussa36@eco:~> python -V
Python 2.7.13
```

After performing the preceding prerequisite steps, perform the following procedure to run an NAE offline analysis:

Step 1.   Select Settings > Download Offline Collection Script to download the Python script.

Step 2.   Execute the following downloaded script to collect the data for assurance:

```
sudo python ./cnae_data_collection.py -APIC apic1.nglab.
cisco.com -clusterName NGLAB -user nae -targetDir .
```

Step 3.   Select Settings > Offline File Management to upload the collected data.

Step 4.   Click Create New Upload.

Step 5.   In the Create New Upload form, complete the following fields:

    a. Click Browse to upload the collected data to provide one-time assurance.

    b. In the Name field, enter the name of the file.

    c. In the Description field, enter the description.

Step 6.   Click Submit. After the file has been uploaded successfully, it is displayed in the Upload table.

Step 7.   Select Settings > Offline Analysis.

Step 8.   In the New Offline Analysis form, complete the following fields:

    a. In the Analysis Name field, enter the name of the offline analysis.

    b. From the File drop-down list, choose the file with the collected data.

    c. From the Assurance Group drop-down list, choose the assurance group.

    d. Optionally click the **+** sign to add another assurance group. Use this form if you want to define a new assurance group.

    e. From the Analysis Timeout drop-down list, choose the time the system needs to wait before terminating the analysis. You can also enter the time the system needs to wait before terminating the analysis.

Step 9.   Click Run to initiate the offline analysis. When the offline analysis is complete, the status is displayed in the New Offline Analysis form.

Step 10.   To view the results of the analysis, click Dashboard.

Example: Subnet Reachability Issue

Say that you have been informed that your application EPG subnet 10.88.179.16/29 is not reachable. You verify the issue by pinging the subnet's pervasive gateway 10.88.179.17 from your laptop and get no response, as demonstrated in Example 9-3.

Example 9-3   *Confirming a Nonresponsive Subnet*

```
laptop:~ sadiq$ ping 10.88.179.17
PING 10.88.179.17 (10.88.179.17): 56 data bytes
Request timeout for icmp_seq 0
Request timeout for icmp_seq 1
Request timeout for icmp_seq 2
^C
--- 10.88.179.17 ping statistics ---
4 packets transmitted, 0 packets received, 100.0% packet loss
```

To troubleshoot this particular issue in ACI, you need to manually validate the following configurations in the APIC:

- The BD with the subnet is advertised outside and attached to an L3Out.

- An EPG is associated with the BD and statically bound to an interface using the encapsulation VLAN.

- The VLAN is part of the VLAN pool that is part of the physical domain.

- The physical domain is associated with an attachable access entity profile (AAEP) that is part of interface policy group, which is part of the interface profile with a port connected to an end host.

- The route reflector is configured and functioning on spines.

- A contract is created between the internal application EPG and the external L3Out EPG.

- The L3Out is functioning properly, and external network route peering is established.

Figure 9-29 illustrates this configuration check.

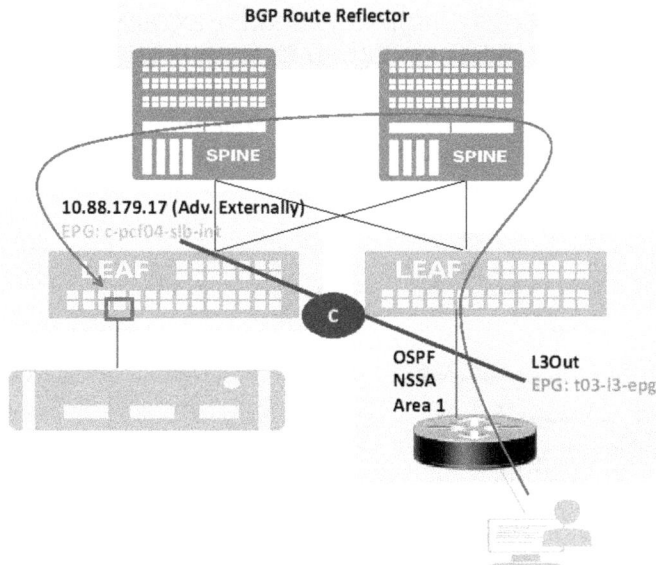

Figure 9-29 *BD Subnet Configuration Steps*

Manually verifying that all of this configuration is in place is time-consuming and can delay problem resolution and extend a service outage. With Cisco NAE, you can run an epoch delta analysis by selecting a time range. NAE provides meaningful error messages in the smart events dashboard to help you identify that the issue lies with the contract, as shown in Figure 9-30.

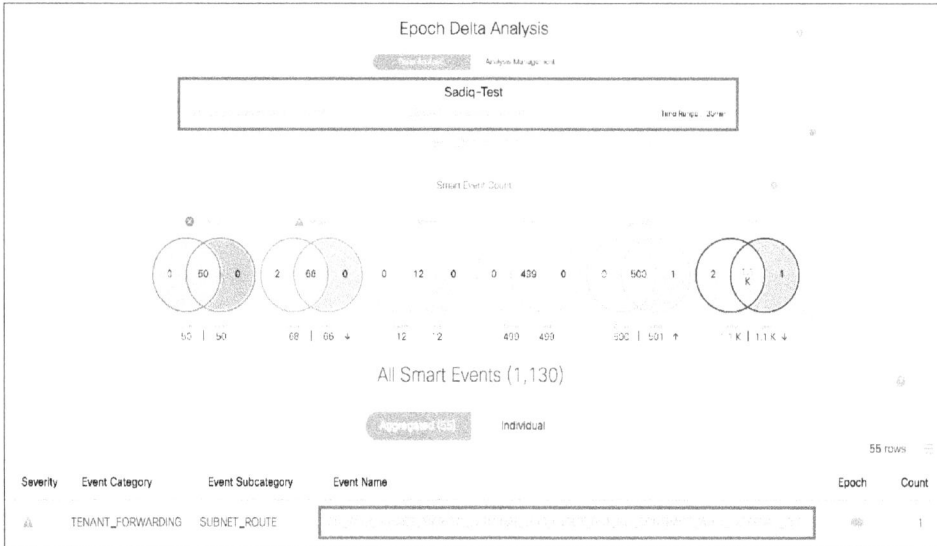

Figure 9-30 *Subnet Inaccessible Error Message*

If you click the error message BD_WITH_SUBNET_MARKED_EXTERNAL_HAS_
L3OUT_BUT_NO_CONTRACT_WITH_EXTERNAL_EP, NAE provides complete details
about the affected subnet and the BD associated to an EPG, a tenant, or a VRF instance,
along with L3Out information. You can quickly verify the symptoms identified by NAE
in your ACI fabric and confirm that there is no contract defined under the EPG c-pcf04-
slb-int that belongs to the BD (see Figure 9-31).

Figure 9-31 *Verifying an Error Message in an ACI Fabric*

After applying the appropriate contracts, you can reach out to the problematic subnet, as illustrated in Figure 9-32.

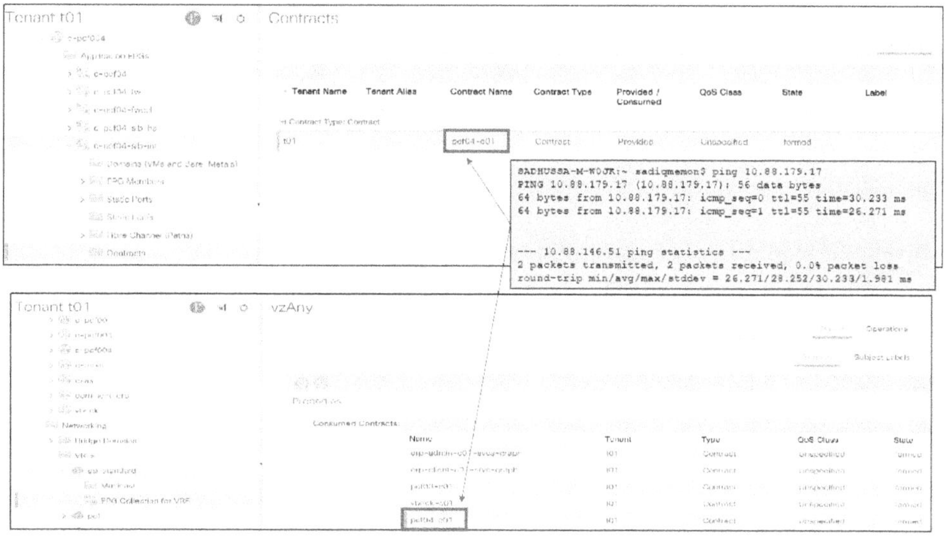

Figure 9-32 *Rectifying a Subnet Reachability Issue*

Tetration

Today's modern data centers are equipped with various virtualization techniques, using hypervisors and container platforms that come with their own switching layer. For example, in the hypervisor world, a virtual switch (vSwitch) or a Distributed Virtual Switch (DVS) is deployed. In the container world, a container bridge (CBR) provides the switching layer for pod and service networks. Furthermore, application services are hosted on blade systems that each come with at least a pair of switches. The story does not end there. Application workloads running as a VM or as a container can be moved anywhere at any time. This is great because it provides business agility and flexibility to grow and prosper, but it also creates lots of challenges when it comes to network operations, visibility, and security.

The Cisco Tetration analytics platform addresses these data center challenges by providing comprehensive workload-protection capability and unprecedented insights across a multi-cloud infrastructure. Tetration does this by collecting data from various entry and exit points of your application-hosting infrastructure, using software/hardware sensors and third-party sources. This data then gets fed into the Tetration analytics engine for running big data. You can pull in this information either via the Tetration web GUI, the REST API, or the Event Notification or Tetration apps, as shown in Figure 9-33.

Cisco Tetration Platform
Architecture Overview

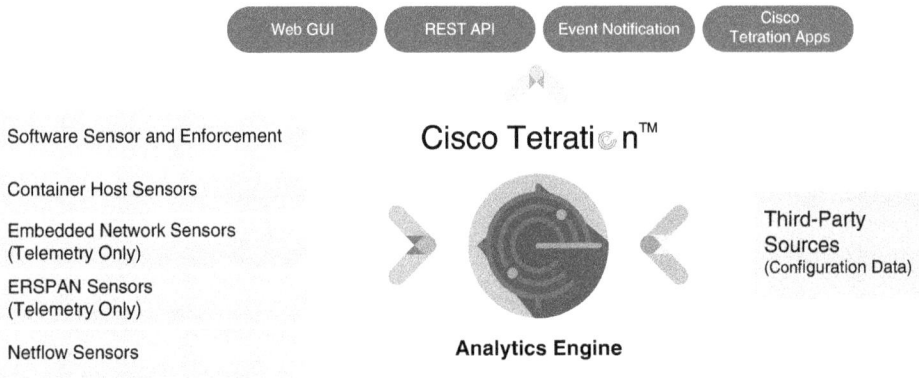

Figure 9-33 *Tetration Architecture*

Tetration is similar to NetFlow, but Tetration captures only the metadata of the flow. This way, all flows are captured, even in today's high-speed networks, and there is no sampling of flows, as in the case of NetFlow captures on high-speed links. Tetration collects the network flow information and reduces device processing overhead and network consumption compared to NetFlow, and it still achieves full visibility of your network. With Tetration deep visibility software sensors, you have the ability to view per-packet flow metadata, including the following:

- Application response time, SRTT, TCP resets, retransmits, window size issues, TCP performance, and bottlenecks

- Open used and unused ports

- Hostname, interface, and OS version

- Process name, launch string, PID, life cycle data, and SHA 256 hash

- Parent/child processes and privilege escalations

- Installed packages and CVE exposure

Tetration can also collect third-party sources of data traffic, including the following:

- Cisco AnyConnect agents

- NetFlow agents

- F5 agents

- AWS (Amazon Web Services) agents

- NetScaler agents

- SPAN (ERSPAN) agents

Software Agents

Software agents are software components running on the host operating system (Linux or Windows). An agent monitors and collects network flow metadata. It also collects host information such as network interfaces, active processes, and other analytical items. The information collected by the agents is exported to the Cisco Tetration collectors running in the cluster. In addition to the telemetry data, agents have the capability to enforce security policies using firewall rules on the installed hosts.

Hardware Agents

Hardware sensors are built into the cloud-scale Nexus 9000 Series switches—EX (for ingress flows), FX, and GX switches—which capture full network flow data at very fast export intervals and without performance penalties to the normal data traffic. Like software agents, hardware agents also export data to the Cisco Tetration analytics engine. Hardware agents only provide telemetry data and cannot be used to apply security policy enforcement.

Tetration Installation and Configuration

Setup and initialization of a Tetration cluster is done by Cisco's Advanced Services team onsite as part of the purchase agreement. The process takes roughly about a day, and you are required to provide the following details:

- Site name (for example, tcslabtetration)
- SSH key from a Linux machine (for example, ssh-keygen -t rsa -b 4096)
- Three email addresses:
  - The user interface (UI) administration email (for example, tcstetrationadmin@ cisco.com)
  - The UI primary customer support email (for example, tcstetrationsupport@ cisco.com)
  - The sentinel alert email (for example, tcstetrationalert@cisco.com)
- IP addresses:
  - Tetration requires two /30 subnets for point-to-point uplink to your core network.
  - Tetration does not support routing, so you must have a static route to the external subnet.
- For the external subnet for a cluster, a /26 subnet that is reachable via the static route on the point-to-point connection
- DNS resolvers
- DNS domain

- NTP server

- SMTP server IP address/FQDN and port

- SMTP username/password

- Syslog server IP/FQDN and port

- Syslog severity

- UI FQDN (for example, tcslabtetration.tcslab.cisco.com)

Tetration Agent Download

The following procedure describes the software agent download process:

Step 1.   Log in to Tetration, click the gear icon in the top-right corner, and select Agent Config.

Step 2.   Select Software Agent Download, select the platform, select the agent type, and click Download.

Step 3.   Select specific platforms for software agents, if needed:

a. Click Show Classic Agent Packages in the top-right corner of the Software Agent pane.

b. Click Download Action for the specific platform and agent type.

Step 4.   Select Hardware Agent Download and click Download under Correct Version.

Tetration Hardware Agent Installation

The prerequisites for the hardware agent installation are as follows:

- In-band management on ACI fabric

- Downloading the agent

To install the hardware agent, follow these steps:

Step 1.   To upload the agent to the ACI APIC, select Admin > Firmware > Firmware Repository, click Upload Firmware to APIC, and select the Tetration agent RPM (for example, tet-agent-3.1.1.53-tcslabtetration.rpm).

Step 2.   To create the analytics policy, select Fabric > Fabric Policies > Policies, right-click Analytics, and select Create Analytics Policy. Type the object name of your choice (for example, **tet-policy**). Type the name of the Tetration cluster that you used while setting up the Tetration analytics engine (for example, **Tcslabtetration**). Figure 9-34 illustrates this step.

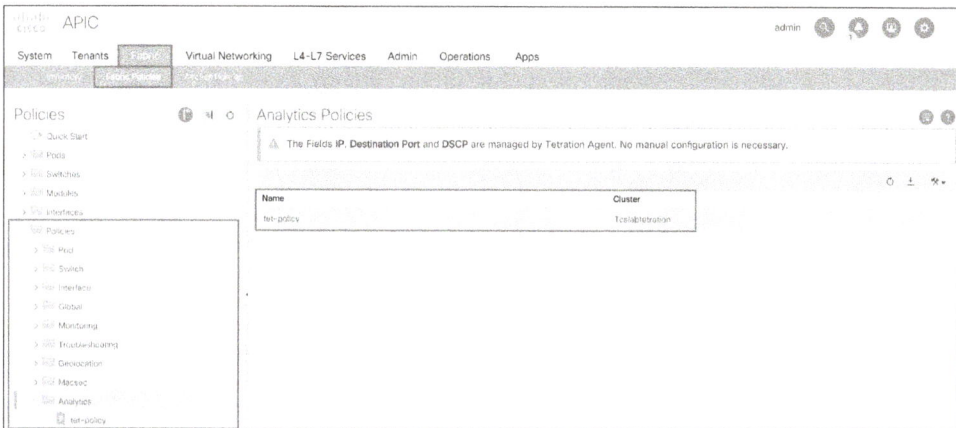

Figure 9-34 *Creating an Analytics Policy*

Step 3. To enable leaf switches for analytics, follow these steps:

   a. As shown in Figure 9-35, select Fabric > Fabric Policies > Policies > Monitoring, right-click Fabric Node Controls, and select Create Fabric Node Control. Type the object name of your choice (for example, **analytics**). Select Analytics Priority and click Submit.

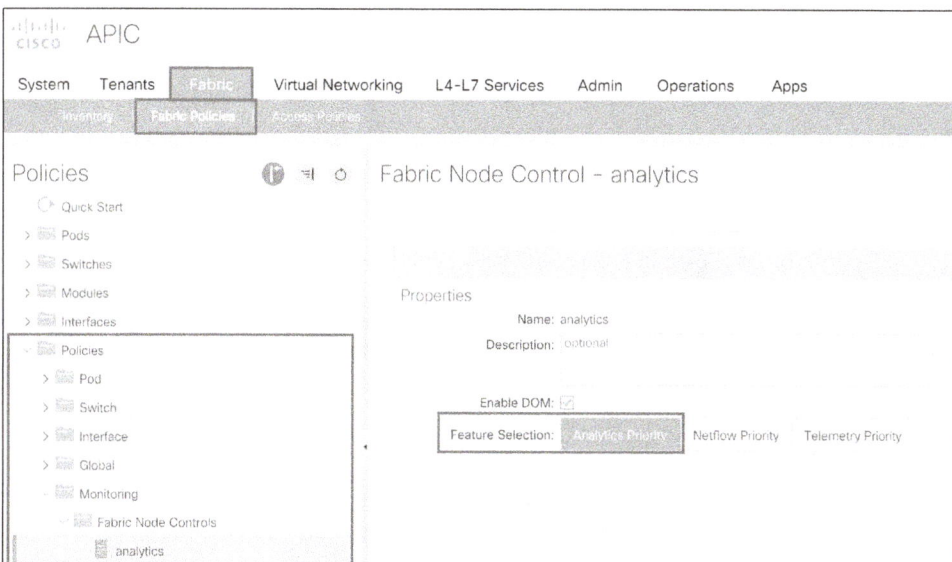

Figure 9-35 *Creating a Fabric Node Control Policy*

b. As shown in Figure 9-36, select Fabric > Fabric Policies > Switches > Leaf Switches, right-click Policy Groups, and select Create Leaf Switch Policy Group. Type the object name of your choice (for example, **analytics-sw-polgrp**). Select the analytics policy that you created in the previous step (that is, tet-policy) and also select analytics from the Node Control Policy drop-down. Click Submit.

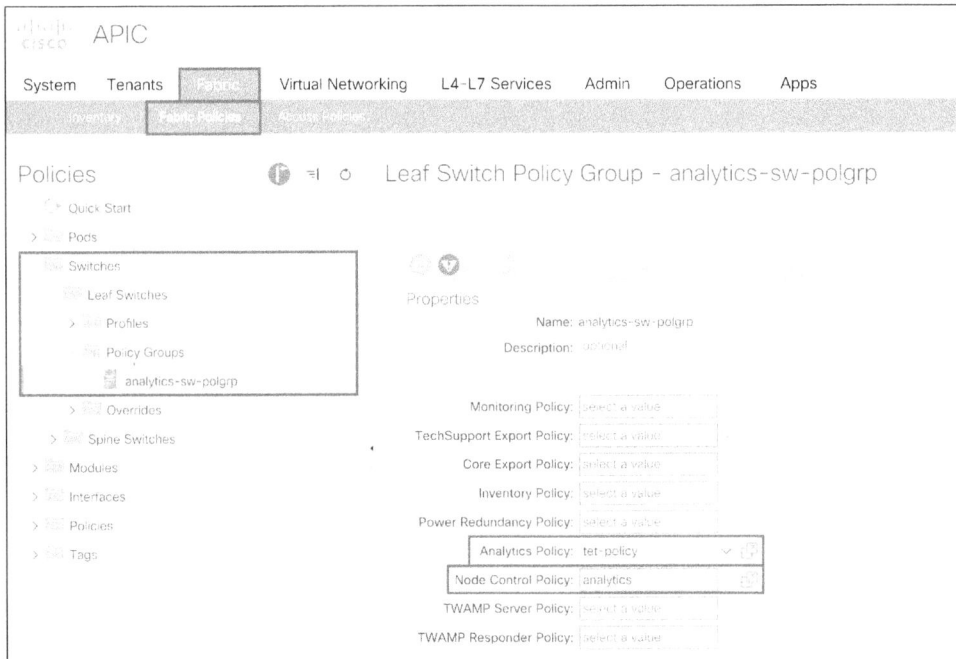

Figure 9-36   *Creating an Analytics Policy Group*

c. As shown in Figure 9-37, select Fabric > Fabric Policies > Switches > Leaf Switches, right-click Profile, and select Create Leaf Switch Profile. Type the object name of your choice (for example, **leaf-sw-prof**). On the right-hand side of the pane, under Switch Association, click the + sign. Type the name of your choice (for example, **all**) and select the leaf switches that you would like to enable for Tetration analytics. Choose the Policy Group you created earlier. Click Submit.

Step 4.   As shown in Figure 9-38, verify the hardware agents for the ACI fabric in Tetration by selecting the Monitoring drop-down in the top-right corner and then selecting Agents > Hardware Switch and verifying that your fabric is in the inventory.

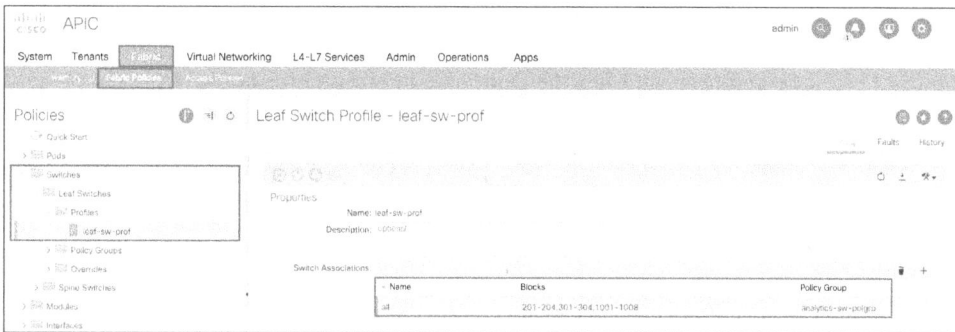

Figure 9-37 *Create Analytics Profile*

Serial	IP Address	Name	Switch SW Ver	Agent SW Ver	Bootup Time	Last Check-in	First Check-in
FDO212225F9	10.88.149.158	tcsh1-f02-b0202	n9000-13.2(4d)	3.1.1.53	Dec 6, 2:25 PM	9:45 AM	Feb 13, 4:10 PM
FDO212225HE	10.88.149.157	tcsh2-f02-b0203	n9000-13.2(4d)	3.1.1.53	Dec 6, 2:26 PM	9:43 AM	Feb 13, 4:10 PM
FDO212225QJ	10.88.149.159	tcsh1-f02-b0201-test	n9000-13.2(4d)	3.1.1.53	Dec 7, 11:25 AM	9:44 AM	Feb 13, 4:10 PM
FDO212225TP	10.88.149.140	tcsh2-f02-b0204	n9000-13.2(4d)	3.1.1.53	Dec 6, 2:54 PM	9:44 AM	Feb 13, 4:10 PM
FDO213305BE	10.88.149.180	tcsh1-f02-h1002	n9000-13.2(4d)	3.1.1.53	Dec 6, 2:26 PM	9:43 AM	Feb 13, 4:10 PM
FDO213317KK	10.88.149.176	tcsh2-f02-h1004	n9000-13.2(4d)	3.1.1.53	Dec 6, 5:07 PM	9:44 AM	Feb 13, 4:10 PM
FDO213317QB	10.88.149.162	tcsh2-f02-h1003	n9000-13.2(4d)	3.1.1.53	Jan 3, 4:19 PM	9:45 AM	Feb 13, 4:10 PM
FDO213317SU	10.88.149.143	tcsh1-f02-h1001	n9000-13.2(4d)	3.1.1.53	Dec 6, 2:54 PM	9:45 AM	Feb 13, 4:10 PM
FDO21332E6T	10.88.149.182	tcsh2-f02-t0304	n9000-13.2(4d)	3.1.1.53	Dec 6, 2:54 PM	9:43 AM	Feb 13, 4:10 PM

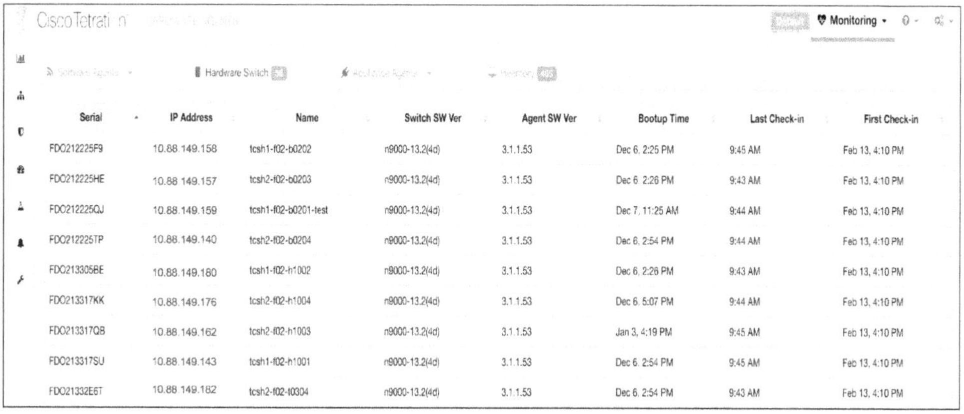

Figure 9-38 *Verifying Tetration Hardware Agents*

Tetration Software Agent Installation (Linux)

To install the Tetration software agent on Linux, the following dependencies are required:

- lsof
- ps
- whoami
- The default shell available in the platform (sh, ksh, or bash)
- unzip

To install the software agent in Linux, follow these steps:

Step 1. Click the Settings menu in the top-right corner.

Step 2. Select Agent Config. The Agent Config page displays.

Step 3.   Click the Software Agent Download tab and, in the Select Platform section, choose Linux. In the Select Agent Type section, choose either Deep Visibility or Enforcement. Click the Download Installer button and save the file to the local disk.

Step 4.   Copy the installer shell script to all the Linux hosts for deployment and execute the script with root privilege:

- **chmod u+x tetration_installer_sensor_linux.sh**

- **sudo ./tetration**

Verifying the Linux Tetration Installation

To verify the Tetration installation, use the following commands:

- **ps -ef**

- **netstat -an | grep 5640**

Software Agent Installation (Windows)

To install the Tetration software agent on Windows, the following dependencies are required:

- Administrator privileges (both installation and service execution)

- Npcap version 0.94 (or later)

Note   If the Npcap driver is not already installed, it will be installed silently.

- PowerShell Version 4.0 or later if the agent is installed via an installer script

- The latest service packs available for the Windows platforms (provided by Microsoft)

The steps for installing the software agent in Windows are as follows:

Step 1.   Click the Settings menu in the top-right corner.

Step 2.   Select Agent Config. The Agent Config page displays.

Step 3.   Click the Software Agent Download tab and, in the Select Platform section, choose Windows. In the Select Agent Type section, choose either Deep Visibility or Enforcement. Click the Download Installer button and save the file to the local disk.

Step 4.   Right-click the PowerShell script to run it in PowerShell.

The agent is downloaded and installed.

Verifying the Windows Tetration Installation

To verify the Tetration installation, use the following command:

```
netstat | findstr 5640
```

Figure 9-39 shows the Tetration software agent running in Windows.

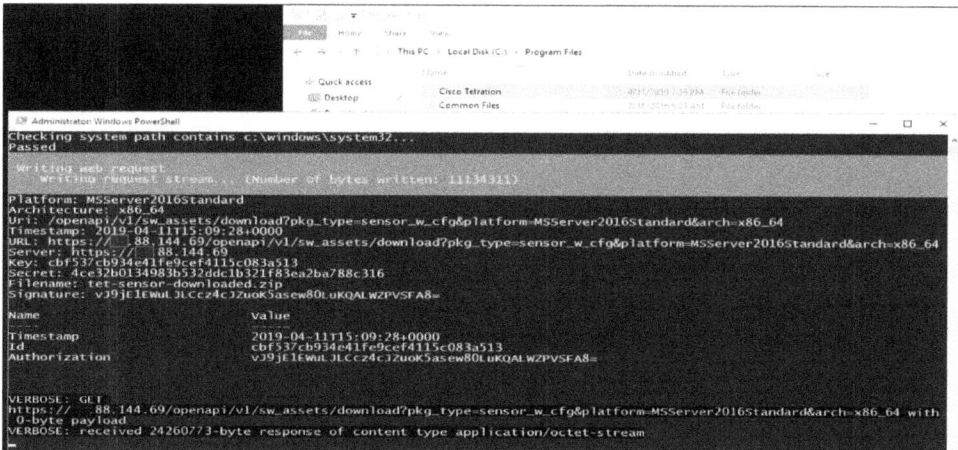

Figure 9-39 *Tetration Software Agent in Windows*

Tetration System Monitoring

In order to use alerting in the Tetration platform, you must use the Tetration Alerts Notification (TAN) agent. In order to install the TAN agent, perform the following steps:

Step 1.   Download the OVA file from cisco.com and download the TAN agent (by selecting Alerts > Configuration > Notifiers > Download).

Step 2.   On a local Linux machine, create the cfg directory by entering the following command:

```
mkdir mon_cfg
```

Then create the file ip_config in this directory and add the IP address to the file in <CIDR> <GATEWAY IP> format such as (172.30.20.10/24 172.30.20.1). Create the file host_name and include the hostname in this file. Copy the TAN agent file tet-alerts-notifier.tar.gz to the cfg directory.

Step 3.   Create an ISO file of the directory by running the following command:

```
mkisofs -r -o monitortet.iso mon_cfg
```

Step 4.   Create a virtual machine from the OVA that has at least the following specs:

  ▪ 8 single-threaded cores

  ▪ 8 GB of memory

   ■ 40 GB disk space

   ■ 1 interface in bridge mode

Step 5.   Upload the ISO file to a datastore and attach it to the VM's CD/DVD drive, as shown in Figure 9-40. Boot the VM.

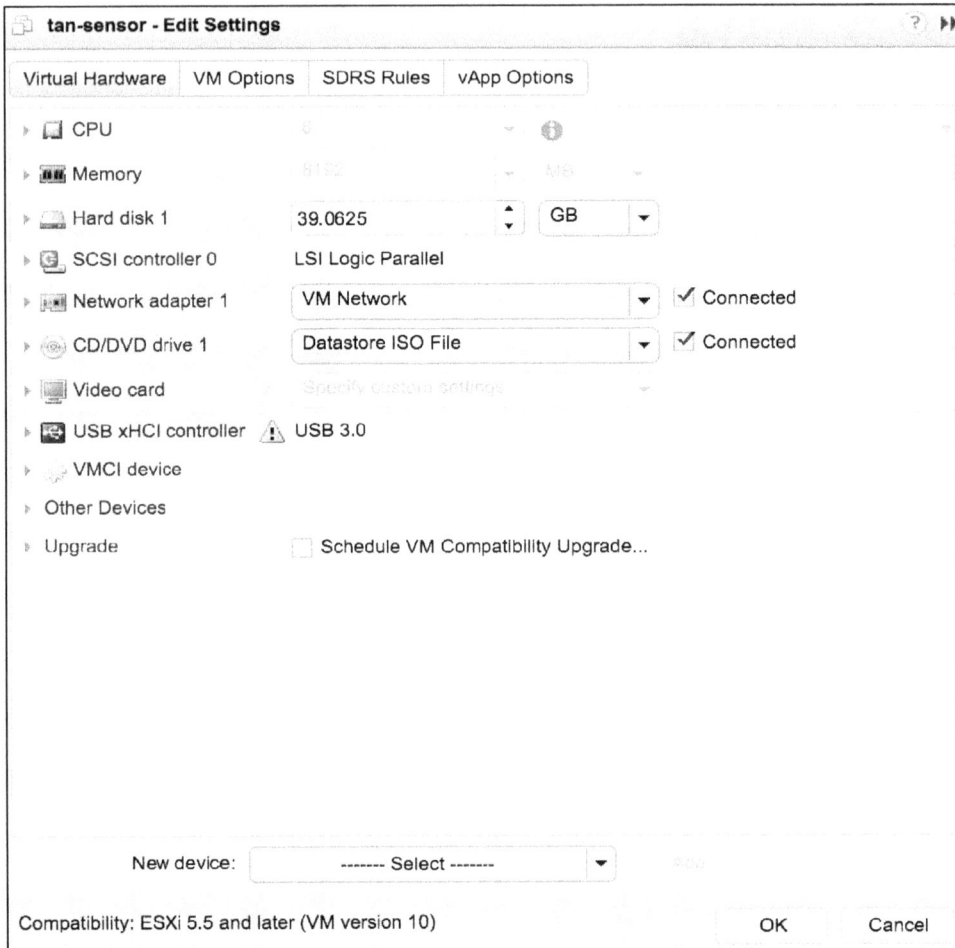

Figure 9-40   *Attaching a Datastore ISO File to a CD/DVD Drive*

When the TAN agent is installed, you see the notification Active under Publishers. You can now map alert types to publisher types, as shown in Figure 9-41.

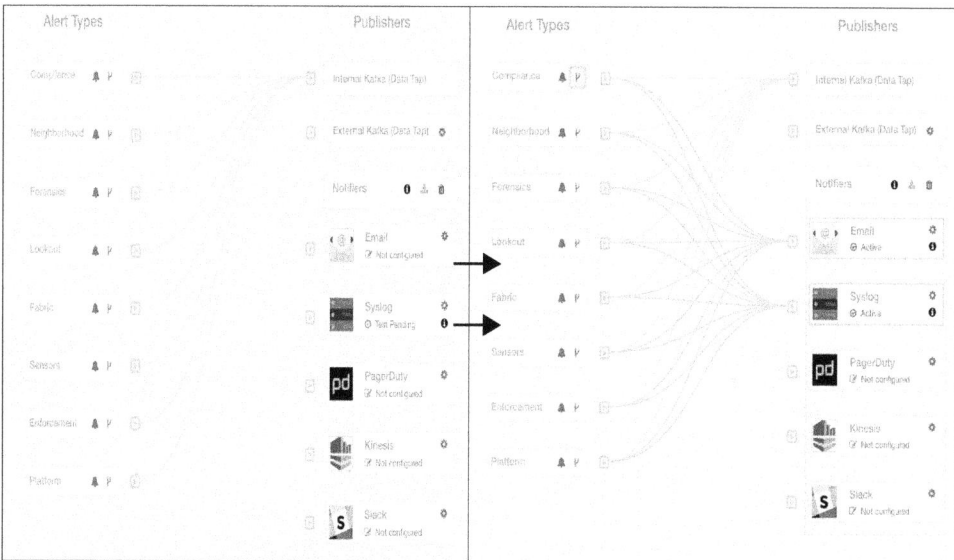

Figure 9-41   *Mapping Alert Types to Publisher Types*

Configuring Email Alerts

Email alerts from a cluster come from the alert email you set up during the initial configuration of the Tetration cluster. You can send to either default recipients or distribution groups. You need the TAN agent and the SMTP server/relay.

Go to Alerts > Configuration, select the gear icon, and configure the SMTP parameters as shown in Figure 9-42.

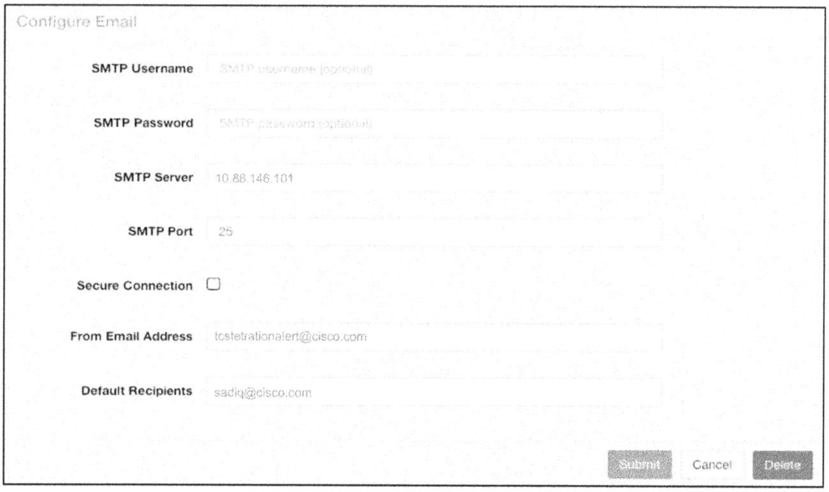

Figure 9-42   *Email Alerts*

Enabling Syslog

To enable syslog, you must have the TAN agent configured. If the TAN agent is installed, then you can configure to send messages to a syslog server.

Go to Alerts > Configuration, select the gear icon, and configure your syslog protocol, server address, and port number, as shown in Figure 9-43.

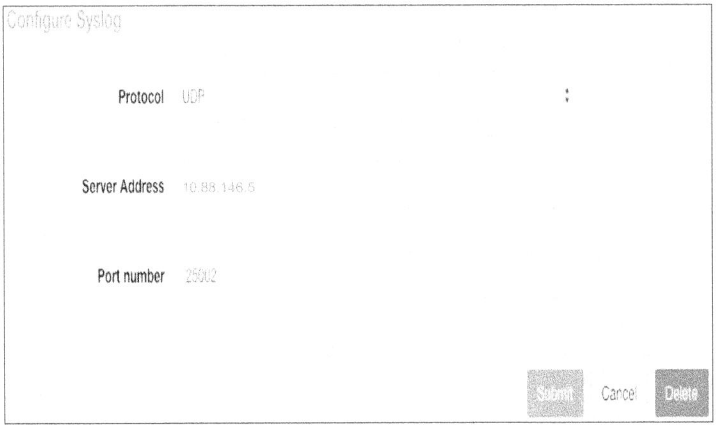

Figure 9-43 *Configuring Syslog in Tetration*

Next, select the alert types of your choice and configure the recipient to send alerts to the publisher of your choice. Be sure to select the appropriate alert severity level, as shown in Figure 9-44.

Figure 9-44 *Enabling Alert Types*

Tetration Scopes

Scopes are used to group data center applications and roles. They give you fine-grained control for management in Cisco Tetration. Scopes are organized in a hierarchical fashion as a set of trees with the root corresponding VRF instance. Each scope tree hierarchy represents disjointed data that does not overlap, as illustrated in Figure 9-45.

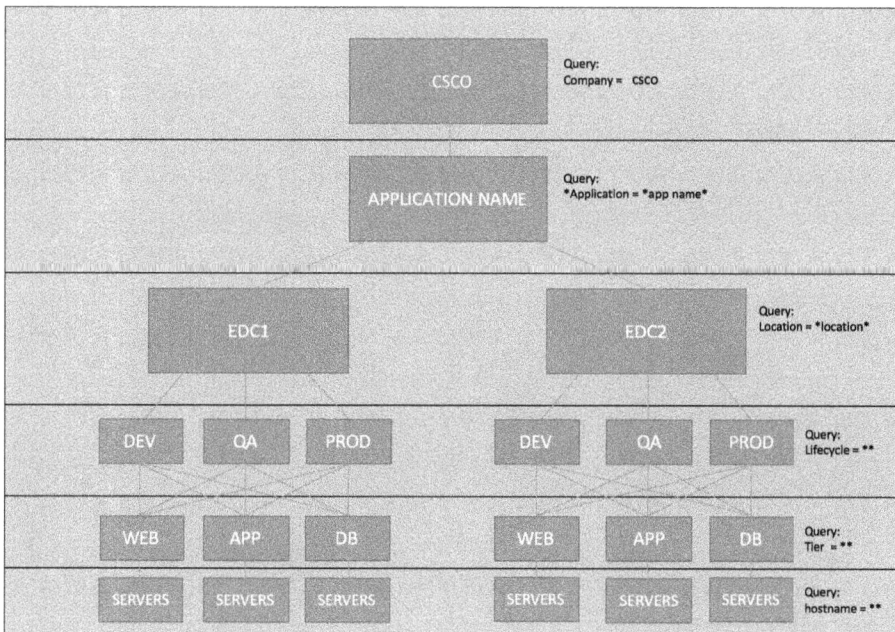

Figure 9-45   *Scope Tree*

To create a new scope, you need to perform the following procedure in the Tetration GUI:

Step 1.   Click on the gear icon in the top-right corner and select Scopes.

Step 2.   Go to the parent scope CSCO.

Step 3.   Click Create New Scope, enter the application name, and enter the query (from the CMDB app name column EX:*Application = CaaS). Then click Create.

Step 4.   Click the newly created scope and continue creating the layers of the tree shown in Figure 9-45.

Tetration Applications

Applications play a central role in Cisco Tetration, providing features such as policy enforcement, application dependency mapping (ADM), and visibility.

To create an application, follow these steps:

Step 1.   Log in to Tetration and, in the left pane, select Applications > Create New Application Workspace.

Step 2.   In the Create New Application Workspace window, type the application name and description. Select the scope and uncheck Dynamic Mode (because you don't want cluster queries to overlap). Then click Create Application, as shown in Figure 9-46.

Figure 9-46   *Creating an Application*

Once an application is created, you can enter it. You do not see any policies until ADM is run against the application with the desired start and end times. After the agents see enough Tetration flows for a few days or weeks, ADM should be run.

Application Dependency Mapping (ADM)

ADM runs groups of similar endpoints of a workspace into clusters and generates security policies (whitelists) among the clusters. To run (or rerun) ADM, you select the time range for gathering data on the endpoints (for computing similarities and policies), and you can change other run parameters (the run configuration). After this, you can launch a run and explore, modify, and approve the results.

External Orchestrators

External orchestrators, such as vCenter and Kubernetes, provide a user interface to the Tetration analytics engine. Orchestrators provide inventory learning for Cisco Tetration in the form of annotations.

To create an external orchestrator, follow these steps:

Step 1.   In the left pane of the Tetration GUI, select Visibility > External Orchestrators.

Step 2.   Select Create New Configurations on the External Orchestrator page.

Step 3. Fill in the information for the specific orchestrator that is being added, as shown in Figure 9-47.

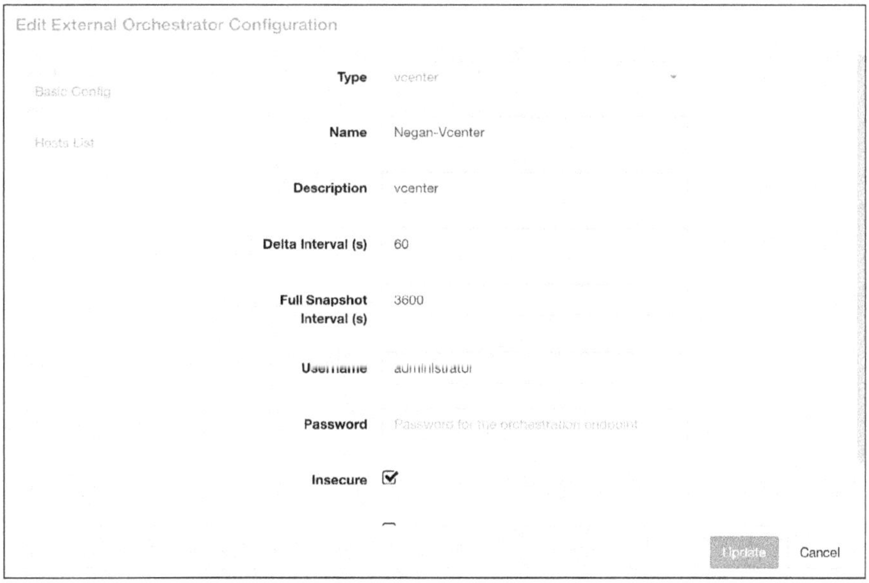

Edit External Orchestrator Configuration

Basic Config	**Type**	vcenter
Hosts List	**Name**	Negan-Vcenter
	Description	vcenter
	Delta Interval (s)	60
	Full Snapshot Interval (s)	3600
	Username	administrator
	Password	Password for the orchestration account
	Insecure	☑

Update   Cancel

Figure 9-47 *Adding an External Orchestrator*

Tetration Code Upgrades

Tetration code upgrades are completed through the Tetration GUI. To update the Tetration code, follow these steps:

Step 1. Click the wrench icon in the left pane and select Upgrade.

Step 2. Select Send Upgrade Link, and an email goes out to the administrative account with the upgrade link.

Step 3. Upload the specified files and click Continue, as shown in Figure 9-48.

Tetration Patch Upgrade

Tetration patching is completed through the Tetration GUI. To update the Tetration code, follow these steps:

Step 1. Click the wrench icon in the left pane and select Upgrade.

Step 2. Select Send Patch Upgrade Link, and an email goes out to the administrative account with the upgrade link (see Figure 9-49).

Step 3. In the message that goes to the administrative account, click Patch upgrade Tcslabtetration, and a browser window opens.

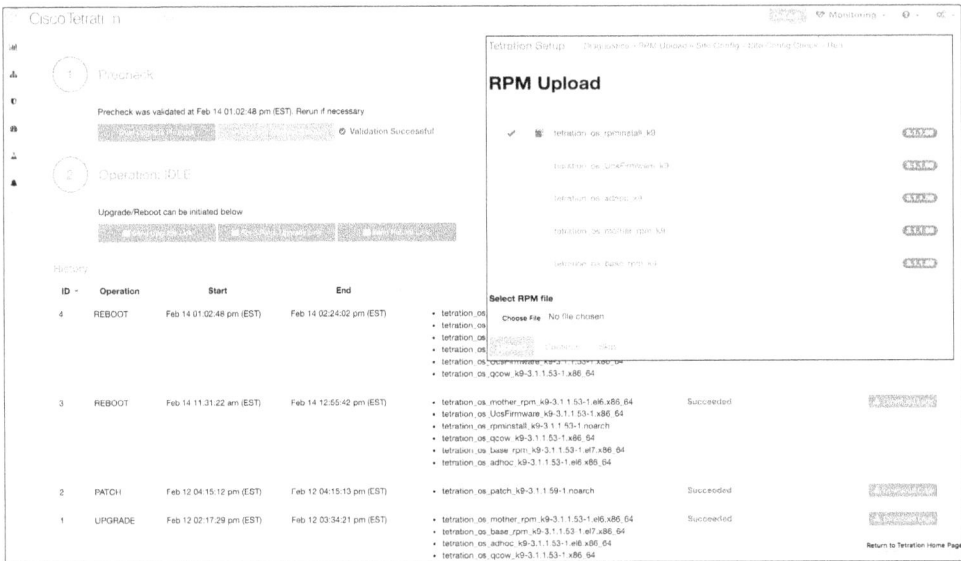

Figure 9-48 *Tetration Code Upgrade*

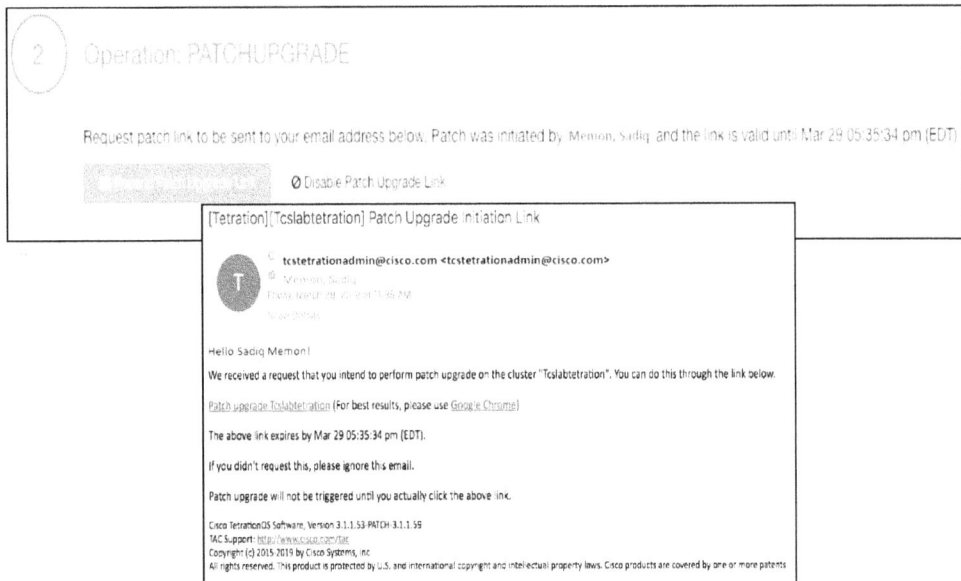

Figure 9-49 *Tetration Patch Upgrade*

Step 4.   In the browser window, select the patch RPM file and click Upload, as shown in Figure 9-50.

Figure 9-50 *RPM Upload*

Tetration Cluster Reboot

Use the following process to reboot a Tetration cluster:

Step 1.   Click the wrench icon in the left pane and select Upgrade.

Step 2.   Select Send Reboot Link, and an email goes out to the administrative account with the reboot link.

Step 3.   In the message that goes to the administrative account, click the reboot link. Tetration takes you to the setup UI.

From this point, the process is the same as for upgrades.

Tetration Cluster Shutdown

To shut down a Tetration cluster, you must use a POST operation in the GUI. Cluster shutdown stops all running Tetration processes and powers down all individual bare-metal servers. Follow these steps to shut down a cluster:

Step 1.   Click the wrench icon in the left pane and select Explore.

Step 2.   Choose the POST action.

Step 3.   Enter **orchestrator.service.consul** as the snapshot host.

Step 4.   Enter **cluster_powerdown?args=--start** as the snapshot path.

Step 5.   Click Send.

Figure 9-51 illustrates this process.

Figure 9-51 *Tetration Cluster Shutdown*

Example: Workload Security with Tetration

Say that you have received a call from a customer, who says that her web application has been performing slowly for the past few days. You examine the ACI infrastructure and find that the leaf interface through which the web server is connected is showing congestion. Figure 9-52 shows the network topology for this example.

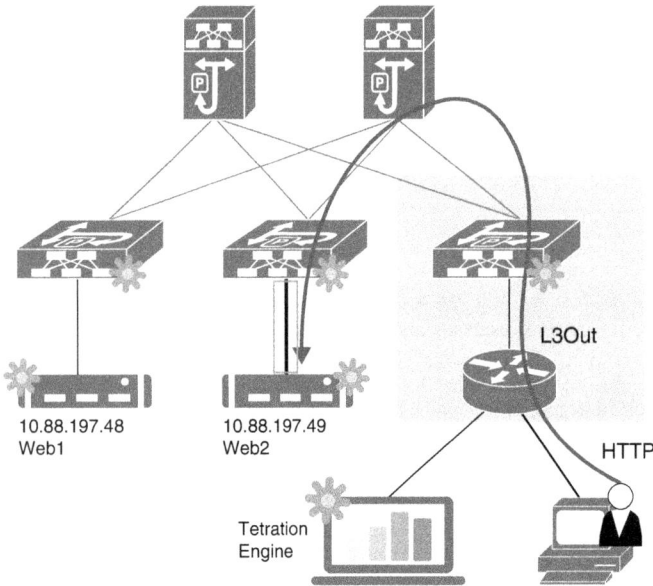

Figure 9-52 *Web Application Hosting Network Topology*

Your company has recently deployed Cisco Tetration for network visibility and workload security. You log in to the Tetration engine and run a flow search for a specific time range. You observe a spike in traffic flow on May 31, at around 9 p.m. Upon further investigation, you discover that another web server, web1, is pulling SNMP data from the impacted web server, web2, as shown in Figure 9-53.

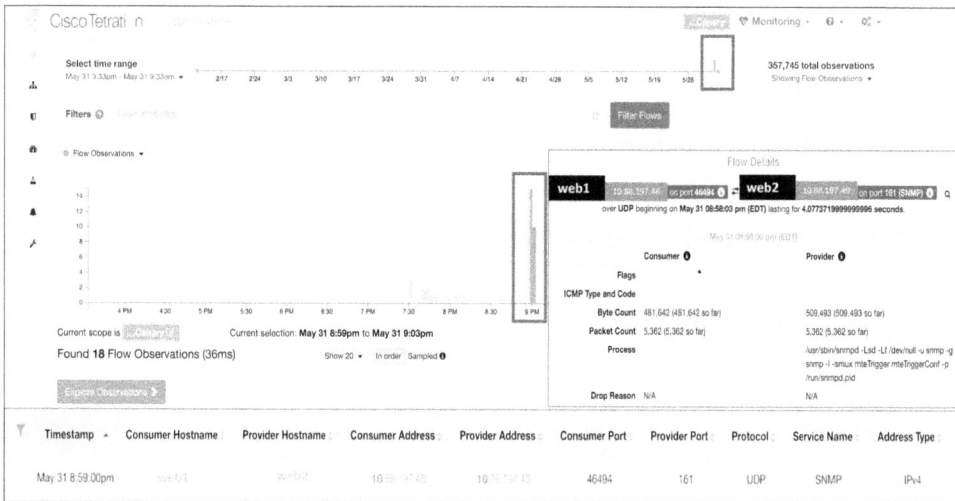

Figure 9-53 *Traffic Flow Analysis*

This is indeed suspicious behavior because you only run web services on your web server providing services to customers and nothing else. So how is it possible that the SNMP daemon is running on web2, and web1 is pulling data using SNMP? When you check the workload profile of web2, you find that on May 31, 2019, at 07:29:38pm (EDT), someone installed the SNMP daemon on web2, indicating the process binary hash. Luckily, web2 has the Tetration Enforcement agent installed, as shown in Figure 9-54.

You create a security policy to allow only ICMP and HTTPS traffic and apply the Enforcement agent to a scope that includes all web servers. When Tetration enforces the policy, web2 stops responding to any SNMP queries and starts performing normal application web serving for your customers, as shown in Figure 9-55.

Web2 Got Hacked; SNMP Daemon Got Installed and Running

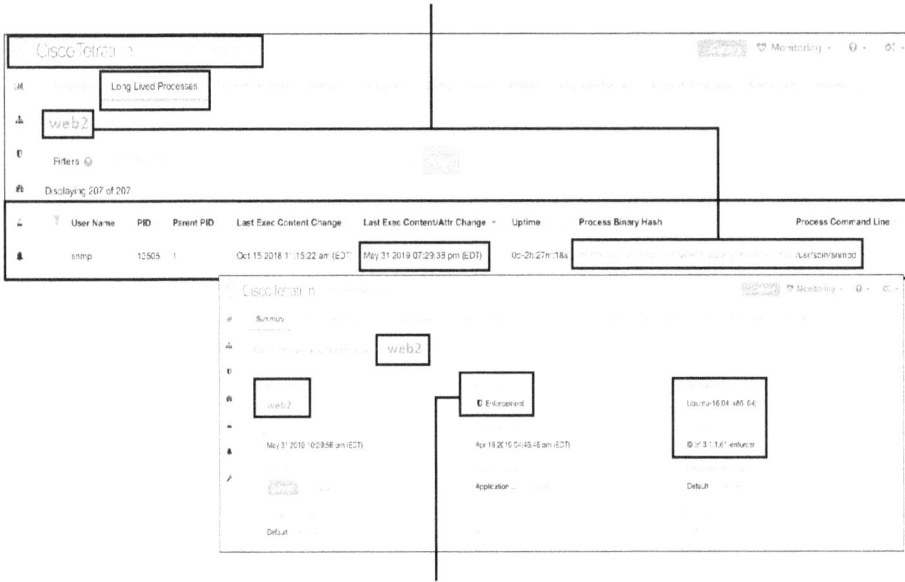

Luckily, Enforcement Agent is Installed on Web2

Figure 9-54   *SNMP Daemon Process Binary Hash*

Enforcement Policy Applied to Only *ALLOW* HTTP / ICMP

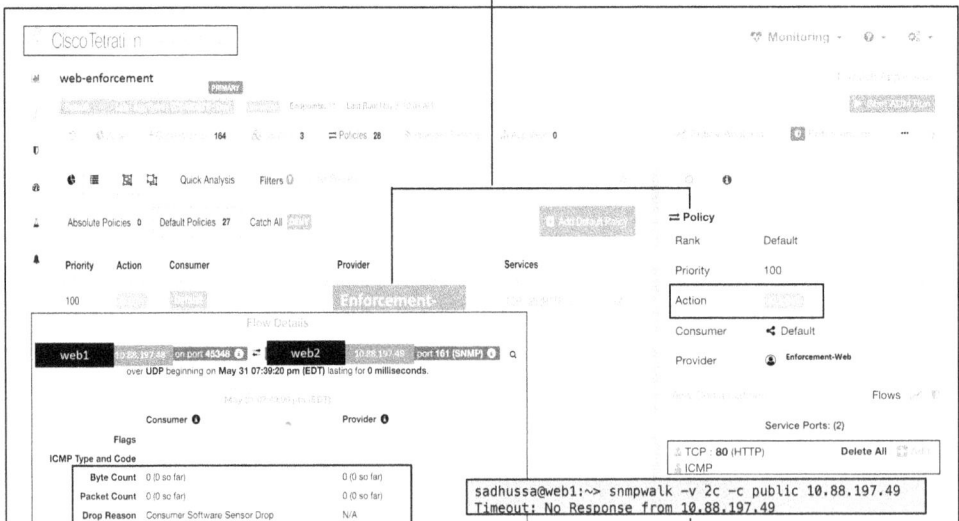

Web2 (10.88.197.49) *NOT* Responding on SNMP

Figure 9-55   *Tetration Policy Enforcement*

This example clearly shows the benefit of Tetration providing network visibility and workload security.

Monitoring Through the REST API

With the industry boom in SDN, where network infrastructure is now provisioned and managed programmatically through the Representational State Transfer (REST) application programming interface (API), network engineers can use the REST interface for monitoring their software-defined network infrastructure as well. As explained in the previous chapters, in ACI, all the configuration, statistical data, faults, events, and audit logs are stored on an APIC, which provides a suitable foundation for REST calls to send this data to external devices for further analysis and alerting. SNMP and syslog are two monitoring protocols that have been used on network devices for decades; they both work on UDP, which is a connectionless protocol and does not guarantee traffic flow all the time. SNMP sends traps to an external management station, and syslog sends system messages to an external logging server during failure events. Both of these cases involve push operations using the connectionless protocol UDP; in contrast, the REST API pulls data from an APIC. Likewise, an SNMP query is a pull operation. However, running SNMP queries from multiple management stations and especially pulling full routing tables may result in CPU spikes on traditional switches such as the Cisco Catalyst 6500. The REST method is a much lighter operation on network devices. Until SDN is prevalent in the industry, there will continue to be debate about which option is the best.

REST is a client/server communication method based on TCP using HTTP or HTTPS, where the client makes a resource request to a server and, in response, the server transfers to the client a representation of the state of the requested resource. The REST API accepts and returns HTTP or HTTPS messages that contain documents in JavaScript Object Notation (JSON) or Extensible Markup Language (XML) format. A request generally consists of the following:

- **HTTP(S) method:** Defines what kind of operation to perform

- **Header:** Allows the client to pass along the request information

- **Path:** Identifies the location of a resource

- **Message body:** Contains data

Three HTTP(S) methods are used in requests to interact with resources in an ACI-based REST system:

- **GET:** Retrieves a specific resource or a collection of resources

- **POST:** Creates or updates a resource

- **DELETE:** Removes a specific resource

POST and DELETE methods are *idempotent*, meaning that there is no additional effect if they are called multiple times with the same input parameters. However, the GET method is *nullipotent*, meaning that no matter how many times it is executed, there is no change in the MIT object model (read-only operation), regardless of the input parameter.

Note   The PUT method is a valid REST API method that is used primarily to modify an existing resource; however, it is not supported in ACI.

Before we get into performing a read-only GET request to pull statistical data from an APIC, it is important to understand the format of the URL used in the call, as shown in Figure 9-56.

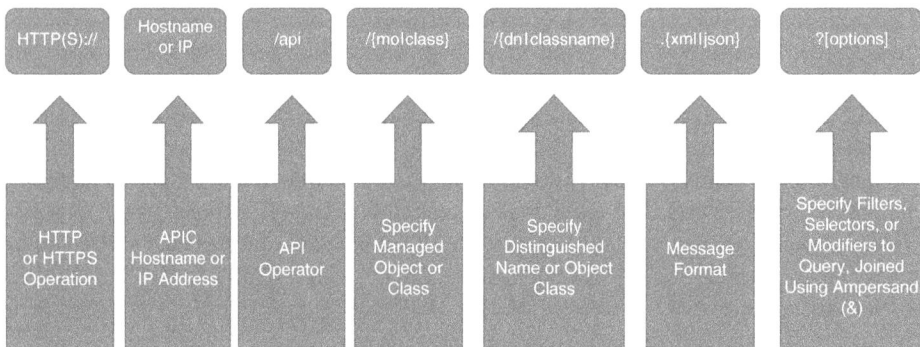

Figure 9-56   *REST API URL Format*

There is a slight difference in the URI resource path when running a REST query against a regular managed object than when running a REST query against a specific object node (or object instance) or an object class. For example, to get information about the tenant managed object named t01, you use the following URL, where the resource path contains the DN of the managed object (/uni/tn-t01):

https://{{*apic-host-or-ip*}}/api/mo/uni/tn-t01.json

If you want to pull some statistics from a node managed object, you use the following URL, where the resource path contains the DN of the managed object (/topology/pod-ID/node-ID/sys/ch/ftslot-number):

https://{{*apic-host-or-ip*}}/api/mo/topology/pod-1/node-1001/sys/ch/ftslot-1.json

To retrieve information about a class of objects, you use the following URL, where the resource path is /class/*class-name*:

https://{{*apic-host-or-ip*}}/api/class/fvTenant.json

The REST API offers a wide range of filter options to help narrow down the scope of a query in the URI to locate the intended resource quickly. You can apply the filters in your URI by starting with the ? symbol. If you want to join multiple queries, you use the & symbol.

For example, to pull the operational status of leaf node 1001, you can run the following REST query against the node 1001 MO containing DN topology/pod-1/node-1001/sys and filter a child object class eqptCh by using the filters query-target=children and target-subtree-class. Note that the filter section starts with the ? symbol, and the filters are joined with the & symbol.

https://{{*apic-host-or-ip*}}/api/mo/*topology/pod-1/node-1001/sys.json*?query-target=children&target-subtree-class=*eqptCh*

> **Note**   The REST API and other programmability techniques are discussed in Chapter 8, "Automation and Orchestration." This section just provides a refresher for you to understand the examples shown below for monitoring the ACI fabric using REST.

Let's now dive in to some examples of monitoring an APIC, network nodes such as leafs and spines, and applications by using REST API.

Monitoring an APIC

This section demonstrates monitoring of APIC-related components using the REST API.

Monitoring CPU and Memory

An APIC provides information regarding the health status of a CPU as well as memory utilization by creating instances of the process entity class **procEntity**. The **procEntity** object class contains the following useful properties:

- **cpuPct:** CPU utilization
- **maxMemAlloc:** The maximum memory allocated for the system
- **memFree:** The maximum amount of memory available for the system

To retrieve information about APIC CPU and memory usage, you can use the REST API call shown in Example 9-4.

Example 9-4   *Retrieving Information About APIC CPU and Memory Usage*

```
GET Operation
URL: https://{{apic-host-or-ip}}/api/class/procEntity.json
{
    "totalCount": "3",
    "imdata": [
        {
            "procEntity": {
                "attributes": {
                    "adminSt": "enabled",
                    "childAction": "",
                    "cpuPct": "3",
                    "dn": "topology/pod-1/node-1/sys/proc"
```

```
                "maxMemAlloc": "21941292",
                 "memFree": "109550112",
                 "modTs": "2019-12-09T01:04:33.268-05:00",
                 "monPolDn": "uni/fabric/monfab-default",
                 "name": "",
                 "operErr": "",
                 "operSt": "enabled",
                 "status": ""
            }
        }
    },
    {
        "procEntity": {
            "attributes": {
                "adminSt": "enabled",
                "childAction": "",
                "cpuPct": "4",
                "dn": "topology/pod-1/node-2/sys/proc",
                "maxMemAlloc": "19891584",
                "memFree": "111525332",
                "modTs": "2019-12-09T01:04:32.971-05:00",
                "monPolDn": "uni/fabric/monfab-default",
                "name": "",
                "operErr": "",
                "operSt": "enabled",
                "status": ""
            }
        }
    },
    {
        "procEntity": {
            "attributes": {
                "adminSt": "enabled",
                "childAction": "",
                "cpuPct": "4",
                "dn": "topology/pod-1/node-3/sys/proc",
                "maxMemAlloc": "16422600",
                "memFree": "115001260",
                "modTs": "2019-12-09T01:04:38.641-05:00",
                "monPolDn": "uni/fabric/monfab-default",
                "name": "",
                "operErr": "",
                "operSt": "enabled",
                "status": ""
```

```
                }
            }
        }
    ]
}
```

Monitoring Disk Utilization

An APIC is a server with several disks and file systems present. The REST API provides easy access to disk space utilization of all partitions on the system. The output is similar to the output you get when you run the **df** (diskfree) command on an APIC in the Bash shell via the CLI.

To retrieve information about APIC disk utilization, you can use the REST API call shown in Example 9-5.

Example 9-5 *Retrieving Information About APIC Disk Utilization*

```
GET Operation
URL: https://{{apic-ip}}/api/class/eqptStorage.json
{
    "totalCount": "115",
    "imdata": [
        {
            "eqptStorage": {
                "attributes": {
                    "available": "2584188",
                    "blocks": "2817056",
                    "capUtilized": "3",
                    "childAction": "",
                    "device": "",
                    "dn": "topology/pod-1/node-1/sys/ch/p-[/boot]-f-[/dev/sda1]",
                    "failReason": "",
                    "fileSystem": "/dev/sda1",
                    "firmwareVersion": "",
                    "lcOwn": "local",
                    "mediaWearout": "100",
                    "modTs": "2019-10-15T12:30:54.694-05:00",
                    "model": "",
                    "monPolDn": "uni/fabric/monfab-default",
                    "mount": "/boot",
                    "name": "/boot",
                    "nameAlias": "",
                    "operSt": "ok",
                    "serial": "",
```

```
                        "status": "",
                        "used": "70052"
                }
            }
        },
        {
            "eqptStorage": {
                "attributes": {
                    "available": "37477520",
                    "blocks": "41153856",
                    "capUtilized": "5",
                    "childAction": "",
                    "device": "",
                    "dn": "topology/pod-1/node-1/sys/ch/p-[/logs]-f-
[/dev/mapper/vg_ifc0-logs]",
                    "failReason": "",
                    "fileSystem": "/dev/mapper/vg_ifc0-logs",
                    "firmwareVersion": "",
                    "lcOwn": "local",
                    "mediaWearout": "100",
                    "modTs": "2019-12-09T22:11:22.634-05:00",
                    "model": "",
                    "monPolDn": "uni/fabric/monfab-default",
                    "mount": "/logs",
                    "name": "/logs",
                    "nameAlias": "",
                    "operSt": "ok",
                    "serial": "",
                    "status": "",
                    "used": "1562800"
                }
            }
        },
        {
            "eqptStorage": {
                "attributes": { ........... Command output truncated.
```

Monitoring Interfaces

A Cisco APIC is recommended to connect to two leaf switches for redundancy. This involves using 10 Gbps interfaces. In addition, an APIC has two 1 Gbps interfaces for OOB management connectivity. An APIC configures these interfaces into two separate bonded interfaces:

- **Bond0:** This is the bond interface between the two 10 Gbps interfaces used to connect to the fabric via a pair of leaf switches.

■ **Bond1:** This is the bond interface between the two 1 Gbps interfaces used to connect to the OOB management network.

If you are using the in-band management network, the Bond0 fabric interface is carved into two subinterfaces: one for ACI fabric traffic (bond0.{infra-vlan}) and the other one for in-band management traffic (bond0.{Inband-vlan}).

To retrieve information about APIC interface status, you can use the REST API call shown in Example 9-6 with filter options to narrow down the search.

Example 9-6   *Retrieving Information About APIC Interface Status*

```
GET Operation
URL: https://{{apic-ip}}/api/mo/topology/pod-1/node-1/sys.json?query-
  target=subtree&target-subtree-class=l3EncRtdIf
{
    "totalCount": "3",
    "imdata": [
        {
            "l3EncRtdIf": {
                "attributes": {
                    "adminSt": "up",
                    "bw": "0",
                    "childAction": "",
                    "delay": "1",
                    "descr": "",
                    "dn": "topology/pod-1/node-1/sys/inst-bond1/encrtd-[po1.4093]",
                    "encap": "unknown",
                    "ethpmCfgFailedBmp": "",
                    "ethpmCfgFailedTs": "00:00:00:00.000",
                    "ethpmCfgState": "0",
                    "id": "po1.4093",
                    "ifConnDn": "",
                    "lcOwn": "local",
                    "linkLogEn": "default",
                    "modTs": "2019-08-12T10:08:36.569-05:00",
                    "monPolDn": "uni/tn-common/monepg-default",
                    "mtu": "1500",
                    "mtuInherit": "yes",
                    "name": "bond1",
                    "routerMac": "00:A3:8E:E2:CF:2E",
                    "status": ""
                }
            }
        },
```

```
{
    "l3EncRtdIf": {
        "attributes": {
            "adminSt": "up",
            "bw": "0",
            "childAction": "",
            "delay": "1",
            "descr": "",
            "dn": "topology/pod-1/node-1/sys/inst-bond0/encrtd-[po1.4093]",
            "encap": "vlan-4093",
            "ethpmCfgFailedBmp": "",
            "ethpmCfgFailedTs": "00:00:00:00.000",
            "ethpmCfgState": "0",
            "id": "po1.4093",
            "ifConnDn": "",
            "lcOwn": "local",
            "linkLogEn": "default",
            "modTs": "2019-08-12T10:08:36.569-05:00",
            "monPolDn": "uni/tn-common/monepg-default",
            "mtu": "1496",
            "mtuInherit": "yes",
            "name": "bond0.4093",
            "routerMac": "40:01:7A:B9:3B:0C",
            "status": ""
        }
    }
},
{
    "l3EncRtdIf": {
        "attributes": {
            "adminSt": "up",
            "bw": "0",
            "childAction": "",
            "delay": "1",
            "descr": "",
            "dn": "topology/pod-1/node-1/sys/inst-bond0/encrtd-[po1.51]",
            "encap": "vlan-51",
            "ethpmCfgFailedBmp": "",
            "ethpmCfgFailedTs": "00:00:00:00.000",
            "ethpmCfgState": "0",
            "id": "po1.51",
            "ifConnDn": "",
            "lcOwn": "local",
            "linkLogEn": "default",
```

```
                    "modTs": "2019-10-15T12:30:21.012-05:00",
                    "monPolDn": "",
                    "mtu": "1496",
                    "mtuInherit": "yes",
                    "name": "bond0.51",
                    "routerMac": "40:01:7A:B9:3B:0C",
                    "status": ""
                }
            }
        }
    ]
}
```

Monitoring the APIC Cluster State

ACI controllers run in a cluster of typically three, five, or seven APICs, depending on the number of leaf nodes supported in the fabric. It is important to monitor the state of a cluster. In order to do that, you can run the REST API call shown in Example 9-7.

Example 9-7 *REST API Call to Monitor the APIC Cluster State*

```
GET Operation
URL: https://{{apic-ip}}/api/mo/topology/pod-1/node-1/sys.json
{
"totalCount": "1",
    "imdata": [
        {
            "topSystem": {
                "attributes": {
                    "address": "10.2.0.1",
                    "bootstrapState": "none",
                    "childAction": "",
                    "configIssues": "",
                    "controlPlaneMTU": "9000",
                    "currentTime": "2019-12-09T23:45:39.337-05:00",
                    "dn": "topology/pod-1/node-1/sys",
                    "enforceSubnetCheck": "no",
                    "etepAddr": "0.0.0.0",
                    "fabricDomain": "f01",
                    "fabricId": "1",
                    "fabricMAC": "00:22:BD:F8:19:FF",
                    "id": "1",
                    "inbMgmtAddr": "100.100.100.1",
                    "inbMgmtAddr6": "fc00::1",
```

```
                    "inbMgmtAddr6Mask": "0",
                     "inbMgmtAddrMask": "26",
                     "inbMgmtGateway": "100.100.100.63",
                     "inbMgmtGateway6": "::",
                     "lcOwn": "local",
                     "modTs": "2019-08-13T13:28:56.006-05:00",
                     "mode": "unspecified",
                     "monPolDn": "uni/fabric/monfab-default",
                     "name": "apic1",
                     "nameAlias": "",
                     "nodeType": "unspecified",
                     "oobMgmtAddr": "200.200.200.1",
                     "oobMgmtAddr6": "fe80::2a3:8eff:fee2:cf2e",
                     "oobMgmtAddr6Mask": "0",
                     "oobMgmtAddrMask": "26",
                     "oobMgmtGateway": "200.200.200.63",
                     "oobMgmtGateway6": "2001:420:28e:2020:acc:68ff:fe28:b540",
                     "podId": "1",
                     "remoteNetworkId": "0",
                     "remoteNode": "no",
                     "role": "controller",
                     "serial": "FCH2113T1GY",
                     "siteId": "0",
                     "state": "in-service",
                     "status": "",
                     "systemUpTime": "55:11:17:22.000",
                     "tepPool": "0.0.0.0",
                     "unicastXrEpLearnDisable": "no"
                }
            }
        }
    ]
}
```

Monitoring Leafs and Spines

This section demonstrates monitoring of leafs and spines using the REST API.

Monitoring CPU Utilization

CPU utilization on leafs and spines can be monitored using the following object classes, depending on the desired sampling interval and update cycle:

- **procSysCPU5min:** Represents the most current statistics for system CPU in a 5-minute sampling interval and updates every 10 seconds.

- **procSysCPU15min:** Represents the most current statistics for system CPU in a 15-minute sampling interval and updates every 5 minutes.

- **procSysCPU1h:** Represents the most current statistics for system CPU in a 1-hour sampling interval and updates every 15 minutes.

- **procSysCPU1d:** Represents the most current statistics for system CPU in a 1-day sampling interval and updates every hour.

- **procSysCPU1w:** Represents the most current statistics for system CPU in a 1-week sampling interval and updates every day.

- **procSysCPU1mo:** Represents the most current statistics for system CPU in a 1-month sampling interval and updates every day.

- **procSysCPU1qtr:** Represents the most current statistics for system CPU in a 1-quarter sampling interval and updates every day.

- **procSysCPU1year:** Represents the most current statistics for system CPU in a 1-year sampling interval and updates every day.

In order to monitor CPU utilization on leafs and spines, you need to run the REST API call shown in Example 9-8, which shows CPU utilization on a 1-hour sampling interval.

Example 9-8 *Monitoring CPU Utilization on Leafs and Spines*

```
GET Operation
URL: https://{{apic-ip}}/api/class/procSysCPU1h.json
{
    "totalCount": "19",
    "imdata": [
        {
            "procSysCPU1h": {
                "attributes": {
                    "childAction": "",
                    "cnt": "1",
                    "dn": "topology/pod-1/node-1001/sys/procsys/CDprocSysCPU1h",
                    "idleAverage1mAvg": "93.407647",
                    "idleAverage1mLast": "93.407647",
                    "idleAverage1mMax": "93.407647",
                    "idleAverage1mMin": "93.407647",
                    "idleAverage1mSpct": "0",
                    "idleAverage1mThr": "",
                    "idleAverage1mTr": "0.000000",
                    "idleAverage1mTrBase": "93.513571",
                    "idleAverage1mTtl": "93.407647",
                    "idleAvg": "93.409271",
                    "idleLast": "93.409271",
```

```
                            "idleMax": "93.409271",
                            "idleMin": "93.409271",
                            "idleSpct": "0",
                            "idleThr": "",
                            "idleTr": "0.000000",
                            "idleTrBase": "93.512008",
                            "idleTtl": "93.409271",
                            "kernelAverage1mAvg": "3.027181",
                            "kernelAverage1mLast": "3.027181",
                            "kernelAverage1mMax": "3.027181",
                            "kernelAverage1mMin": "3.027181",
                            "kernelAverage1mSpct": "0",
                            "kernelAverage1mThr": "",
                            "kernelAverage1mTr": "0.000000",
                            "kernelAverage1mTrBase": "3.001924",
                            "kernelAverage1mTtl": "3.027181",
                            "kernelAvg": "3.025889",
                            "kernelLast": "3.025889",
                            "kernelMax": "3.025889",
                            "kernelMin": "3.025889",
                            "kernelSpct": "0",
                            "kernelThr": "",
                            "kernelTr": "0.000000",
                            "kernelTrBase": "3.002168",
                            "kernelTtl": "3.025889",
                            "lastCollOffset": "900",
                            "repIntvEnd": "2019-12-11T01:14:47.233-05:00",
                            "repIntvStart": "2019-12-11T00:59:47.231-05:00",
                            "status": "",
                            "userAverage1mAvg": "3.565172",
                            "userAverage1mLast": "3.565172",
                            "userAverage1mMax": "3.565172",
                            "userAverage1mMin": "3.565172",
                            "userAverage1mSpct": "0",
                            "userAverage1mThr": "",
                            "userAverage1mTr": "0.000000",
                            "userAverage1mTrBase": "3.484505",
                            "userAverage1mTtl": "3.565172",
                            "userAvg": "3.564840",
                            "userLast": "3.564840",
                            "userMax": "3.564840",
                            "userMin": "3.564840",
                            "userSpct": "0",
                            "userThr": "",
                            "userTr": "0.000000",
```

```
                    "userTrBase": "3.485824",
                    "userTtl": "3.564840"
               }
           }
        },
        {
            "procSysCPU1h": {   .......... Command output truncated.
```

Monitoring Memory Utilization

Much like CPU utilization, memory utilization on switches can be monitored using the following classes, depending on the desired sampling interval and update cycle:

- **procSysMem5min:** Represents the most current statistics for system memory in a 5-minute sampling interval and updates every 10 seconds.

- **procSysMem15min:** Represents the most current statistics for system memory in a 15-minute sampling interval and updates every 5 minutes.

- **procSysMem1h:** Represents the most current statistics for system memory in a 1-hour sampling interval and updates every 15 minutes.

- **procSysMem1d:** Represents the most current statistics for system memory in a 1-day sampling interval and updates every hour.

- **procSysMem1w:** Represents the most current statistics for system memory in a 1-week sampling interval and updates every day.

- **procSysMem1mo:** Represents the most current statistics for system memory in a 1-month sampling interval and updates every day.

- **procSysMem1qtr:** Represents the most current statistics for system memory in a 1-quarter sampling interval and updates every day.

- **procSysMem1year:** Represents the most current statistics for system memory in a 1-year sampling interval and updates every day.

In order to monitor memory utilization on leafs and spines, you need to run the REST API call in Example 9-9, which shows memory utilization for a 1-hour sampling interval.

Example 9-9 *Monitoring Memory Utilization on Leafs and Spines*

```
GET Operation
URL: https://{{apic-ip}}/api/class/procSysMem1h.json
{
{
    "totalCount": "19",
    "imdata": [
        {
            "procSysMem1h": {
                "attributes": {
```

```
                                     "childAction": "",
                                     "cnt": "0",
                                     "dn": "topology/pod-1/node-1001/sys/procsys/CDprocSysMem1h",
                                     "freeAvg": "0",
                                     "freeLast": "12935932",
                                     "freeMax": "0",
                                     "freeMin": "0",
                                     "freeSpct": "0",
                                     "freeThr": "",
                                     "freeTr": "0",
                                     "freeTrBase": "12920790",
                                     "freeTtl": "0",
                                     "lastCollOffset": "0",
                                     "repIntvEnd": "2019-12-11T01:59:47.232-05:00",
                                     "repIntvStart": "2019-12-11T01:59:47.232-05:00",
                                     "status": "",
                                     "totalAvg": "0",
                                     "totalLast": "24499860",
                                     "totalMax": "0",
                                     "totalMin": "0",
                                     "totalSpct": "0",
                                     "totalThr": "",
                                     "totalTr": "0",
                                     "totalTrBase": "24499860",
                                     "totalTtl": "0",
                                     "usedAvg": "0",
                                     "usedLast": "11563926",
                                     "usedMax": "0",
                                     "usedMin": "0",
                                     "usedSpct": "0",
                                     "usedThr": "",
                                     "usedTr": "0",
                                     "usedTrBase": "11579068",
                                     "usedTtl": "0"
                            }
                    }
            },
            {
                    "procSysMem1h": {  .......... Command output truncated.
```

Monitoring Power Supply Unit (PSU) Status

The power supply is a critical component of a network device. To ensure that the power supplies in a unit are functioning correctly, you can run the REST API call shown in Example 9-10.

Note Depending on the number of power supplies in a device that you would like to monitor, you can choose the appropriate PSU slot number in your REST calls.

Example 9-10 *Monitoring Power Supply Unit Status*

```
GET Operation
URL: https://{{apic-ip}}/api/mo/topology/pod-1/node-1001/sys/ch/psuslot-1.json
{
    "totalCount": "1",
    "imdata": [
        {
            "eqptPsuSlot": {
                "attributes": {
                    "cardOperSt": "unknown",
                    "childAction": "",
                    "descr": "PSU Slot N9K-PAC-3000W-B",
                    "dn": "topology/pod-1/node-101/sys/ch/psuslot-1",
                    "id": "1",
                    "loc": "front",
                    "modTs": "2019-10-09T17:21:14.709+00:00",
                    "monPolDn": "uni/fabric/monfab-default",
                    "operSt": "inserted",
                    "physId": "1",
                    "status": "",
                    "type": "psuslot"
                }
            }
        }
    ]
}
!! If the power is down or not connected, you will get the following output.
{
    "totalCount": "1",
    "imdata": [
        {
            "eqptPsuSlot": {
                "attributes": {
                    "cardOperSt": "unknown",
                    "childAction": "",
                    "descr": "PSU slot",
                    "dn": "topology/pod-1/node-101/sys/ch/psuslot-3",
                    "id": "3",
```

```
                    "loc": "front",
                    "modTs": "2019-10-09T17:21:14.709+00:00",
                    "monPolDn": "uni/fabric/monfab-default",
                    "operSt": "empty",
                    "physId": "3",
                    "status": "",
                    "type": "psuslot"
                }
            }
        }
    ]
}
```

Monitoring Fan Status

Fan assemblies in switches are required to dissipate the heat that is generated by power supplies. It's important to monitor fan assemblies in switches to prevent devices from powering down. In order to monitor fans in switches, you need to run the REST API call shown in Example 9-11.

Note   Example 9-11 shows the status of the fan in slot 1 of the Leaf 1001 chassis.

Example 9-11   *Monitoring FAN Status*

```
GET Operation
URL: https://{{apic-ip}}/api/mo/topology/pod-1/node-1001/sys/ch/ftslot-1.json
{
    "totalCount": "1",
    "imdata": [
        {
            "eqptFtSlot": {
                "attributes": {
                    "cardOperSt": "unknown",
                    "childAction": "",
                    "descr": "Fan slot NXA-FAN-30CFM-F",
                    "dn": "topology/pod-1/node-1001/sys/ch/ftslot-1",
                    "id": "1",
                    "loc": "rear",
                    "modTs": "2019-10-15T13:55:02.593-05:00",
                    "monPolDn": "uni/fabric/monfab-default",
                    "operSt": "inserted",
```

```
                        "physId": "1",
                        "status": "",
                        "type": "fantray"
                    }
                }
            }
        ]
}
```

Monitoring Module Status

The Nexus 9500 is a modular switch that consists of a supervisor module to process network traffic and line cards to forward network traffic. The device also uses a midplane fabric module for fast switching of packets between line cards. It is important to monitor the status of supervisor modules, line cards, and fabric modules for smooth functioning of the device. You can use the REST API call shown in Example 9-12 to determine the status of these peripherals in the switch.

Example 9-12 *Monitoring Supervisor Module, Line Card, and Fabric Module Status*

```
GET Operation
URL: https://{{apic-ip}}/api/mo/topology/pod-1/node-101/sys/ch/supslot-1/sup.json
{
    "totalCount": "1",
    "imdata": [
        {
            "eqptSupC": {
                "attributes": {
                    "childAction": "",
                    "descr": "Supervisor Module",
                    "dn": "topology/pod-1/node-101/sys/ch/supslot-1/sup",
                    "hwVer": "2.1",
                    "id": "1",
                    "macB": "18-80-90-93-9c-24",
                    "macL": "18",
                    "mfgTm": "2017-06-04T19:00:00.000-05:00",
                    "modTs": "2019-10-15T13:53:22.969-05:00",
                    "model": "N9K-SUP-B",
                    "monPolDn": "uni/fabric/monfab-default",
                    "numP": "0",
                    "operSt": "online",
                    "pwrSt": "on",
                    "rdSt": "active",
                    "rev": "B0",
```

```
                        "ser": "FOC21234SNF",
                        "status": "",
                        "swCId": "250",
                        "type": "supervisor",
                        "upTs": "2019-10-15T13:53:22.969-05:00",
                        "vendor": "Cisco Systems, Inc."
                    }
                }
            }
        ]
    }
}
```

GET Operation
URL: https://{{apic-ip}}/api/mo/topology/pod-1/node-101/sys/ch/lcslot-1/lc.json

```
{
    "totalCount": "1",
    "imdata": [
        {
            "eqptLC": {
                "attributes": {
                    "childAction": "",
                    "descr": "32p 40/100G Ethernet Module",
                    "dn": "topology/pod-1/node-101/sys/ch/lcslot-1/lc",
                    "hwVer": "1.4",
                    "id": "1",
                    "macB": "00-27-e3-45-13-a8",
                    "macL": "132",
                    "mfgTm": "2017-06-25T19:00:00.000-05:00",
                    "modTs": "2019-10-15T13:54:27.426-05:00",
                    "model": "N9K-X9732C-EX",
                    "monPolDn": "uni/fabric/monfab-default",
                    "numP": "32",
                    "operSt": "online",
                    "pwrSt": "on",
                    "rdSt": "active",
                    "rev": "B0",
                    "ser": "FOC2126018E",
                    "status": "",
                    "swCId": "270",
                    "type": "linecard",
                    "upTs": "2019-10-15T13:54:27.426-05:00",
                    "vendor": "Cisco Systems, Inc."
                }
            }
```

```
            }
        ]
    }
```

```
GET Operation
URL: https://{{apic-ip}}/api/mo/topology/pod-1/node-101/sys/ch/fcslot-1/fc.json
{
    "totalCount": "1",
    "imdata": [
        {
            "eqptFC": {
                "attributes": {
                    "childAction": "",
                    "descr": "Fabric Module",
                    "dn": "topology/pod-1/node-101/sys/ch/fcslot-1/fc",
                    "hwVer": "1.0",
                    "id": "1",
                    "macB": "00-00-00-00-00-00",
                    "macL": "0",
                    "mfgTm": "2017-02-12T19:00:00.000-05:00",
                    "modTs": "2019-10-15T13:54:38.428-05:00",
                    "model": "N9K-C9504-FM-E",
                    "monPolDn": "uni/fabric/monfab-default",
                    "numP": "0",
                    "operSt": "online",
                    "pwrSt": "on",
                    "rdSt": "active",
                    "rev": "A0",
                    "ser": "FOC21070SAZ",
                    "status": "",
                    "swCId": "267",
                    "type": "fabriccard",
                    "upTs": "2019-10-15T13:54:38.428-05:00",
                    "vendor": "Cisco Systems, Inc."
                }
            }
        }
    ]
}
```

Monitoring Leaf/Spine Membership Status in a Fabric

Leaf and spine nodes are registered and discovered by the ACI fabric during the initial joining state. It is important to monitor whether leaf and spine switches stay connected and remain registered with the ACI fabric all the time in order for the APIC to manage

and monitor them. You can use the REST API call shown in Example 9-13 to determine
the leaf and spine membership status in the fabric.

Example 9-13   *Monitoring Leaf and Spine Fabric Membership by Using the REST API*

```
GET Operation
URL: https://{{apic-ip}}/api/mo/topology/pod-1/node-202/sys.json
{
    "totalCount": "1",
    "imdata": [
        {
            "topSystem": {
                "attributes": {
                    "address": "10.2.44.64",
                    "bootstrapState": "done",
                    "childAction": "",
                    "configIssues": "",
                    "controlPlaneMTU": "9000",
                    "currentTime": "2020-01-03T06:13:38.080-05:00",
                    "dn": "topology/pod-1/node-202/sys",
                    "enforceSubnetCheck": "no",
                    "etepAddr": "0.0.0.0",
                    "fabricDomain": "f02",
                    "fabricId": "1",
                    "fabricMAC": "00:22:BD:F8:19:FF",
                    "id": "202",
                    "inbMgmtAddr": "50.50.50.202",
                    "inbMgmtAddr6": "::",
                    "inbMgmtAddr6Mask": "0",
                    "inbMgmtAddrMask": "0",
                    "inbMgmtGateway": "0.0.0.0",
                    "inbMgmtGateway6": "::",
                    "lcOwn": "local",
                    "modTs": "2019-11-05T17:01:54.468-05:00",
                    "mode": "unspecified",
                    "monPolDn": "uni/fabric/monfab-default",
                    "name": "leaf202",
                    "nameAlias": "",
                    "nodeType": "unspecified",
                    "oobMgmtAddr": "60.60.60.202",
                    "oobMgmtAddr6": "::",
                    "oobMgmtAddr6Mask": "0",
                    "oobMgmtAddrMask": "0",
                    "oobMgmtGateway": "0.0.0.0",
                    "oobMgmtGateway6": "::",
```

```
                    "podId": "1",
                    "remoteNetworkId": "0",
                    "remoteNode": "no",
                    "role": "leaf",
                    "serial": "FDO212225F9",
                    "siteId": "0",
                    "state": "in-service",
                    "status": "",
                    "systemUpTime": "58:13:19:16.000",
                    "tepPool": "10.2.0.0/18",
                    "unicastXrEpLearnDisable": "no"
                }
            }
        }
    ]
}
```

If a node is out of service and is no longer registered with the ACI fabric, you get the output shown in Example 9-14.

Note   In this example, Node 201 is out of service.

Example 9-14   *Fabric Node Out-of-Service Output Through the REST API*

```
GET Operation
URL: https://{{apic-ip}}/api/node/mo/topology/pod-1/node-201/sys.json
{
    "totalCount": "1",
    "imdata": [
        {
            "error": {
                "attributes": {
                    "code": "1",
                    "text": "the messaging layer was unable to deliver the stimulus
    (destination (node) is marked unavailable)"
                }
            }
        }
    ]
}
```

You can also run a more granular REST query that targets a specific object class, such as **fabricNode**, to get the membership status for every node in the ACI fabric, along with device serial and model numbers, as demonstrated in Example 9-15.

Example 9-15   *Pulling Fabric Node Status by Using the REST API*

```
GET Operation
URL: https://{{apic-ip}}/api/mo/topology/pod-1.json?query-target=children&target-
  subtree-class=fabricNode
{
    "totalCount": "25",
    "imdata": [
        {
            "fabricNode": {
                "attributes": {
                    "adSt": "on",
                    "annotation": "",
                    "childAction": "",
                    "delayedHeartbeat": "no",
                    "dn": "topology/pod-1/node-1005",
                    "extMngdBy": "",
                    "fabricSt": "active",
                    "id": "1005",
                    "lastStateModTs": "2019-10-15T14:00:21.324-05:00",
                    "lcOwn": "local",
                    "modTs": "2019-10-15T14:00:46.369-05:00",
                    "model": "N9K-C93180LC-EX",
                    "monPolDn": "uni/fabric/monfab-default",
                    "name": "leaf1005",
                    "nameAlias": "",
                    "nodeType": "unspecified",
                    "role": "leaf",
                    "serial": "FDO21462QHN",
                    "status": "",
                    "uid": "0",
                    "vendor": "Cisco Systems, Inc",
                    "version": ""
                }
            }
        },
        {
            "fabricNode": {
                "attributes": {
                    "adSt": "on",
                    "annotation": "",
```

```
                        "childAction": "",
                        "delayedHeartbeat": "no",
                        "dn": "topology/pod-1/node-102",
                        "extMngdBy": "",
                        "fabricSt": "active",
                        "id": "102",
                        "lastStateModTs": "2019-10-15T13:33:38.344-05:00",
                        "lcOwn": "local",
                        "modTs": "2019-10-15T13:34:11.481-05:00",
                        "model": "N9K-C9504",
                        "monPolDn": "uni/fabric/monfab-default",
                        "name": "spine102",
                        "nameAlias": "",
                        "nodeType": "unspecified",
                        "role": "spine",
                        "serial": "FOX2126PD4S",
                        "status": "",
                        "uid": "0",
                        "vendor": "Cisco Systems, Inc",
                        "version": ""
                }
        }
    },
    {
        "fabricNode": {
            "attributes": {
                "adSt": "on",
                "annotation": "",
                "childAction": "",
                "delayedHeartbeat": "no",
                "dn": "topology/pod-1/node-1",
                "extMngdBy": "",
                "fabricSt": "unknown",
                "id": "1",
                "lastStateModTs": "1969-12-31T19:00:00.000-05:00",
                "lcOwn": "local",
                "modTs": "2019-08-12T10:10:03.443-05:00",
                "model": "APIC-SERVER-L2",
                "monPolDn": "uni/fabric/monfab-default",
                "name": "apic1",
                "nameAlias": "",
                "nodeType": "unspecified",
                "role": "controller",
                "serial": "FCH2113V1GX",
```

```
                        "status": "",
                        "uid": "0",
                        "vendor": "Cisco Systems, Inc",
                        "version": "A0"
                    }
                }
            },
            {
                "fabricNode": {
                    "attributes": {
                        "adSt": "off",
                        "annotation": "",
                        "childAction": "",
                        "delayedHeartbeat": "no",
                        "dn": "topology/pod-1/node-201",
                        "extMngdBy": "",
                        "fabricSt": "inactive",
                        "id": "201",
                        "lastStateModTs": "2019-11-05T16:50:07.568-05:00",
                        "lcOwn": "local",
                        "modTs": "2019-11-05T16:50:21.889-05:00",
                        "model": "N9K-C93180LC-EX",
                        "monPolDn": "uni/fabric/monfab-default",
                        "name": "leaf201",
                        "nameAlias": "",
                        "nodeType": "unspecified",
                        "role": "leaf",
                        "serial": "FDO212225QJ",
                        "status": "",
                        "uid": "0",
                        "vendor": "Cisco Systems, Inc",
                        "version": ""
                    }
                }
            }
        ]
}
```

Monitoring Interface Status

Monitoring leaf and spine interface status is important especially when you face connectivity and performance issues. You can run the REST API call shown in Example 9-16 to retrieve that information.

Note   In Example 9-16, interface Ethernet1/1 on leaf Node 202 is being monitored.

Example 9-16   *Monitoring the Status of Leaf and Spine Interfaces*

```
GET Operation
URL: https://{{apic-ip}}/api/mo/topology/pod-1/node-202/sys/phys-[eth1/1]/
  dbgEtherStats.json
{
    "totalCount": "1",
    "imdata": [
        {
            "rmonEtherStats": {
                "attributes": {
                    "broadcastPkts": "40",
                    "cRCAlignErrors": "0",
                    "childAction": "",
                    "clearTs": "never",
                    "collisions": "0",
                    "dn": "topology/pod-1/node-202/sys/phys-[eth1/1]/dbgEtherStats",
                    "dropEvents": "0",
                    "fragments": "0",
                    "jabbers": "0",
                    "modTs": "never",
                    "multicastPkts": "3676300",
                    "octets": "7982783217",
                    "oversizePkts": "4726",
                    "pkts": "29858838",
                    "pkts1024to1518Octets": "2336916",
                    "pkts128to255Octets": "3625907",
                    "pkts256to511Octets": "7755066",
                    "pkts512to1023Octets": "444631",
                    "pkts64Octets": "10057075",
                    "pkts65to127Octets": "5634517",
                    "rXNoErrors": "16424455",
                    "rxGiantPkts": "0",
                    "rxOversizePkts": "2362",
                    "status": "",
                    "tXNoErrors": "13434383",
                    "txGiantPkts": "0",
```

```
                    "txOversizePkts": "2364",
                    "undersizePkts": "0"
            }
        }
      }
    ]
}
```

You can also run the REST calls in Example 9-17 to collect more interface-related information.

Example 9-17 provides the RX, or input-related, interface statistics.

Example 9-17   *Checking Interface Unicast Packets Received by Using the REST API*

```
GET Operation
URL: https://{{apic-ip}}/api/mo/topology/pod-1/node-202/sys/phys-[eth1/1]/
  dbgIfIn.json
{
    "totalCount": "1",
    "imdata": [
        {
            "rmonIfIn": {
                "attributes": {
                    "broadcastPkts": "19",
                    "childAction": "",
                    "clearTs": "never",
                    "discards": "0",
                    "dn": "topology/pod-1/node-202/sys/phys-[eth1/1]/dbgIfIn",
                    "errors": "0",
                    "modTs": "never",
                    "multicastPkts": "2301795",
                    "nUcastPkts": "2301814",
                    "octets": "2853600184",
                    "status": "",
                    "ucastPkts": "14376887",
                    "unknownProtos": "0"
                }
            }
        }
    ]
}
```

Example 9-18 provides the TX, or output-related, interface statistics.

Example 9-18   *Checking Interface Unicast Packets Transmitted by Using the REST API*

```
GET Operation
URL: https://{{apic-ip}}/api/mo/topology/pod-1/node-202/sys/phys-[eth1/1]/
  dbgIfOut.json
{
    "totalCount": "1",
    "imdata": [
        {
            "rmonIfOut": {
                "attributes": {
                    "broadcastPkts": "21",
                    "childAction": "",
                    "clearTs": "never",
                    "discards": "0",
                    "dn": "topology/pod-1/node-202/sys/phys-[eth1/1]/dbgIfOut",
                    "errors": "0",
                    "modTs": "never",
                    "multicastPkts": "1430409",
                    "nUcastPkts": "1430430",
                    "octets": "5252627292",
                    "qLen": "0",
                    "status": "",
                    "ucastPkts": "12208831"
                }
            }
        }
    ]
}
```

Monitoring Applications

This section provides application-related monitoring examples using the REST API.

Monitoring Application Traffic Status

To monitor network-related statistics for an application, you can investigate the aggregate amount of traffic flow to a specific application tier by executing the REST API query shown in Example 9-19.

Note   In Example 9-19, the application EPG *db* under application profile *3-tier* in tenant *t01* is being monitored.

Example 9-19   *Monitoring the Aggregate Amount of Traffic Flow to a Specific Application Tier*

```
GET Operation
URL: https://{{apic-ip}}/api/mo/uni/tn-t01/ap-3-tier/epg-db.json?query-
  target=self&rsp-subtree-include=stats
{
    "totalCount": "1",
    "imdata": [
        {
            "fvAEPg": { •
                "attributes": {
                    "annotation": "",
                    "childAction": "",
                    "configIssues": "",
                    "configSt": "applied",
                    "descr": "",
                    "dn": "uni/tn-t01/ap-3-tier/epg-db",
                    "exceptionTag": "",
                    "extMngdBy": "",
                    "floodOnEncap": "disabled",
                    "fwdCtrl": "",
                    "isAttrBasedEPg": "no",
                    "isSharedSrvMsiteEPg": "no",
                    "lcOwn": "local",
                    "matchT": "AtleastOne",
                    "modTs": "2019-08-13T13:28:48.008-05:00",
                    "monPolDn": "uni/tn-t01/monepg-default",
                    "name": "db",
                    "nameAlias": "",
                    "pcEnfPref": "unenforced",
                    "pcTag": "49159",
                    "prefGrMemb": "exclude",
                    "prio": "unspecified",
                    "scope": "2949120",
                    "status": "",
                    "triggerSt": "triggerable",
                    "txId": "6341068275337697100",
                    "uid": "15374"
                },
                "children": [
                {
                        "l2IngrBytesAgHist1h": {
                            "attributes": {
```

```
                            "childAction": "deleteNonPresent",
                            "cnt": "4",
                            "dropCum": "24564298",
                            "dropPer": "13192",
                            "dropRate": "3.643595",
                            "dropSpct": "0",
                            "dropThr": "",
                            "dropTr": "680",
                            "floodCum": "0",
                            "floodPer": "0",
                            "floodRate": "0.000000",
                            "floodSpct": "0",
                            "floodThr": "",
                            "floodTr": "0",
                            "index": "10",
                            "lastCollOffset": "3620",
                            "modTs": "never",
                            "multicastCum": "0",
                            "multicastPer": "0",
                            "multicastRate": "0.000000",
                            "multicastSpct": "0",
                            "multicastThr": "",
                            "multicastTr": "0",
                            "repIntvEnd": "2020-01-03T19:00:08.914-05:00",
                            "repIntvStart": "2020-01-03T17:59:48.314-05:00",
                            "rn": "HDl2IngrBytesAg1h-10",
                            "status": "",
                            "unicastCum": "41838460449",
                            "unicastPer": "23760234",
                            "unicastRate": "6562.512843",
                            "unicastSpct": "0",
                            "unicastThr": "",
                            "unicastTr": "15104"
                        }
                    }
                },
            {

                    "l2EgrBytesPartHist15min": {
                        "attributes": {
                            "childAction": "deleteNonPresent",
                            "cnt": "3",
                            "index": "88",
                            "lastCollOffset": "900",
                            "modTs": "never",
```

```
                                    "multicastAvg": "0",
                                    "multicastCum": "0",
                                    "multicastMax": "0",
                                    "multicastMin": "0",
                                    "multicastPer": "0",
                                    "multicastRate": "0.000000",
                                    "multicastSpct": "0",
                                    "multicastThr": "",
                                    "multicastTr": "0",
                                    "nodeId": "1006",
                                    "repIntvEnd": "2020-01-03T07:44:58.200-05:00",
                                    "repIntvStart": "2020-01-03T07:29:58.200-05:00",
                                    "rn": "HDl2EgrBytesPart15min-88-node-1006",
                                    "status": "",
                                    "unicastAvg": "271532",
                                    "unicastCum": "6282680533",
                                    "unicastMax": "272889",
                                    "unicastMin": "270136",
                                    "unicastPer": "814597",
                                    "unicastRate": "905.107778",
                                    "unicastSpct": "0",
                                    "unicastThr": "",
                                    "unicastTr": "-3200"
                                }
                            }
                        },
. . . . . . . . . . Output truncated
```

Monitoring External Network Connectivity

In ACI, any traffic that comes into and goes out of the fabric does so via a border leaf. As explained in Chapter 5, "End Host and Network Connectivity," you need to configure an external routed network or L3Out with a routing protocol or static route on the ACI border leaf. It is critical to monitor the status of external network connectivity from the ACI fabric; if there are problems, no traffic can flow in and out of the fabric.

To monitor external network connectivity status, you can execute the REST API query shown in Example 9-20.

Note   In Example 9-20, with the L3Out configuration, Border Leaf 202 has established an OSPF neighbor relationship with its peer router (ID 20.88.193.130) under tenant *t01* and the VRF instance *t01:standard*. Routed interface eth1/4 is used to establish the OSPF neighbor relationship. If you use a switch virtual interface (SVI), you can adjust your query with if-[vlanX] (where *X* is the VLAN number). If you use a routed subinterface, you can adjust your query with if-[eth1/4.X] (where *X* is the VLAN number).

Example 9-20 *Monitoring External Network Connectivity by Using the REST API*

```
GET Operation
URL: https://{{apic-ip}}/api/mo/topology/pod-1/node-202/sys/ospf/inst-default/
  dom-t01:standard/if-[eth1/4]/adj-20.88.193.130.json?query-target=subtree&target-
  subtree-class=ospfAdjStats,ospfAdjEp
{
    "totalCount": "2",
    "imdata": [
        {
            "ospfAdjEp": {
                "attributes": {
                    "area": "0.0.0.43",
                    "bdr": "0.0.0.0",
                    "bfdSt": "down",
                    "childAction": "",
                    "dbdOptions": "64",
                    "dn": "topology/pod-1/node-202/sys/ospf/inst-default/dom-
t01:standard/if-[eth1/4]/adj-20.88.193.130",
                    "dr": "0.0.0.0",
                    "flags": "",
                    "helloOptions": "8",
                    "id": "20.88.193.130",
                    "ifId": "0",
                    "modTs": "never",
                    "monPolDn": "uni/fabric/monfab-default",
                    "name": "",
                    "operSt": "full",
                    "peerIp": "30.88.192.30",
                    "peerName": "",
                    "prio": "1",
                    "status": ""
                }
            }
        },
        {
            "ospfAdjStats": {
                "attributes": {
                    "childAction": "",
                    "dbdSeqNum": "146976805",
                    "deadTimerExpTs": "2020-01-12T00:27:48.564-05:00",
                    "dn": "topology/pod-1/node-202/sys/ospf/inst-default/
dom-t01:standard/if-[eth1/4]/adj-20.88.193.130/adjstats",
                    "lastNonHelloPktTs": "2019-11-05T16:54:22.932-05:00",
                    "lastStChgTs": "2020-01-12T00:20:43.678-05:00",
```

```
                          "lsaReqRexmitCnt": "0",
                           "modTs": "never",
                           "outstandingLsaCnt": "0",
                           "reqLsaCnt": "0",
                           "stChgCnt": "4",
                           "status": ""
                      }
                  }
              }
          ]
      }
```

Monitoring the PBR Service Graph

Policy-based routing (PBR) is a method of redirecting IP traffic to a defined destination next-hop, based on the set criterion. This next-hop destination could be any L4/L7 device defined in the configuration. In ACI, PBR is done through service graph configuration.

It is important to monitor the state of the PBR service graph to prevent your traffic from black-holing. To monitor policy-based redirect status, you can execute the REST API query shown in Example 9-21.

Note   In Example 9-21, with PBR configuration, you can check that the policy is enforced on Leaf 201, which is redirecting the traffic firewall front-end interface with IP address 10.15.250.26 that is part of the service BD in the VRF instance with segment ID 2555904. The output shows that the operational state of the PBR service graph is enabled, and the state is formed.

Example 9-21   *Monitoring PBR Status by Using the REST API*

```
GET Operation
URL: https://{{apic-ip}}/api/mo/topology/pod-1/node-201/sys/svcredir/inst/
  destgrp-1/rsdestAtt-[topology/pod-1/node-201/sys/svcredir/inst/
  dest-[10.15.250.26]-[vxlan-2555904]].json
{
    "totalCount": "1",
    "imdata": [
        {
            "svcredirRsDestAtt": {
                "attributes": {
                    "childAction": "",
                    "destName": "",
```

```
                      "dn": "topology/pod-1/node-201/sys/svcredir/
inst/destgrp-1/rsdestAtt-[topology/pod-1/node-201/sys/svcredir/inst/
dest-[10.15.250.26]-[vxlan-2555904]]",
                      "forceResolve": "yes",
                      "lcOwn": "local",
                      "modTs": "2019-09-09T11:50:08.481-05:00",
                      "monPolDn": "uni/fabric/monfab-default",
                      "operSt": "enabled",
                      "rType": "mo",
                      "redirDestKey": "uni/tn-t03/svcCont/svcRedirectPol-dc1-f01-
fw810-dmz1028/RedirectDest_ip-[10.15.250.26]",
                      "state": "formed",
                      "stateQual": "none",
                      "status": "",
                      "svcredirCfgFailedBmp": "",
                      "svcredirCfgFailedTs": "00:00:00:00.000",
                      "svcredirCfgState": "0",
                      "tCl": "svcredirDest",
                      "tDn": "topology/pod-1/node-201/sys/svcredir/inst/
dest-[10.15.250.26]-[vxlan-2555904]",
                      "tType": "mo"
                  }
              }
          }
      ]
}
```

Summary

A proper monitoring solution is key to running your network operations smoothly. Monitoring can drastically reduce service downtime and provide rapid resolution of any issues you might encounter during normal business services. With the evolution of SDN in the industry requiring complex application deployment solutions, it is becoming mandatory to have a robust proactive monitoring solution for today's modern networks. ACI works with monitoring tools such as SNMP, syslog, and NetFlow, as discussed in this chapter. In addition, this chapter discusses Cisco tools such as Network Insights, Network Assurance Engine, and Tetration. By reading this chapter, you should now have a better idea of how to build a proper monitoring solution that suits your environment.

Review Questions

The questions that follow are designed to help you prepare for the Implementing Cisco Application Centric Infrastructure - Advanced (300-630 DCACIA) exam if you are planning on acquiring the Cisco Certified Specialist: ACI Advanced Implementation certification.

1. What is a fault? How does the fault cycle work? (Choose three.)
   a. A fault is a failure in ACI fabric that is represented by a managed object (MO).
   b. A fault managed object (MO) is unique in the MIT and does not have a distinguished name (DN).
   c. A fault code is an alphanumeric string that uniquely identifies the type of fault being raised.
   d. The fault life cycle transitions from Soaking to Raised to Clearing.
   e. The fault life cycle transitions from Raised to Soaking to Clearing.
   f. The fault severity levels are major, minor, and warning.

2. What is a health score? What benefit does a health score bring to overall monitoring of the ACI fabric? (Choose three.)
   a. A health score provides system audit logs of any change made in the fabric.
   b. Health scores enable you to monitor faults and the general health of the entire ACI fabric.
   c. To check the overall fabric health in the APIC GUI, go to System > Dashboard.
   d. Health scores range from 0 to 100%, with 100% indicating a fully fit and functional ACI fabric.
   e. Health scores enable you to monitor tenant configuration.

3. What built-in tools are available for ACI monitoring? (Choose three.)
   a. NTP
   b. TACACS+
   c. Syslog
   d. SNMP
   e. NetFlow

4. What is SNMP? How is it supported in ACI? (Choose three.)
   a. SNMP is a mechanism to manage and monitor computer networks.
   b. SNMP is supported only on fabric switches in ACI.
   c. SNMP in ACI can only perform GET, GET NEXT, GET BULK, and WALK operations.
   d. All SNMP protocol versions are supported in ACI.
   e. SNMP is a TCP-based protocol that uses port 123.

5. What is supported with SNMP in ACI? How is an SNMP trap configured in ACI? (Choose three.)

   a. ACI supports 10 trap destination servers.

   b. SNMP traps are generated based on the events or faults that occurred on a managed object (MO).

   c. SNMP trap is a mechanism for querying network devices by performing GET, GET NEXT, GET BULK, and WALK operations.

   d. SNMP traps are enabled under access, fabric, and tenant configuration on an APIC.

   e. An SNMP trap uses UDP port 161.

6. What is syslog? How is it supported in ACI? (Choose three.)

   a. Syslog is sent to an external server using an agent in ACI.

   b. Syslog is a mechanism for collecting and storing system logs.

   c. Fault, event, audit, and session logs can be collected and stored locally on an APIC and sent to an external logging server.

   d. ACI supports only critical, major, minor, and warning syslog severity-level messages.

   e. Faults or events in the ACI fabric can trigger the sending of a syslog message.

   f. Only fault and event logs can be collected and stored locally on an APIC and sent to an external logging server.

7. What is NetFlow? How is it supported in ACI? (Choose three.)

   a. NetFlow is a protocol used to collect IP traffic information.

   b. NetFlow policies are enabled with access and tenant configuration on an APIC.

   c. NetFlow is configured in ACI to provide telemetry data to Cisco Tetration.

   d. NetFlow is supported on all fabric switches.

   e. ACI supports only NetFlow Version 9.

8. How is NetFlow used? (Choose three.)

   a. NetFlow is used for network monitoring.

   b. NetFlow is used in network usage billing.

   c. NetFlow is used to boost application performance.

   d. NetFlow is used in forensics.

   e. NetFlow is used in the change management process.

Note   There are no Key Topics for this chapter.

## Chapter 10

Network Management and Monitoring Configuration

After reading Chapter 9, "Monitoring ACI Fabric," you should now be well versed in the various monitoring protocols and techniques that Cisco Application Centric Infrastructure (ACI) offers. Now, it's time to examine the configuration steps of each of these management and monitoring protocols and techniques. In ACI, although you can configure policies by using the GUI, the CLI, the REST API, and SDKs, this chapter covers only the GUI method of policy configuration and use of the APIC CLI for verifying configurations. This chapter covers the following topics::

- ACI management

  - Out-of-band management

  - In-band management

  - AAA

- ACI monitoring

  - Syslog

  - SNMP

  - SPAN

  - NetFlow

Out-of-Band Management

ACI offers out-of-band (OOB) management for managing the APICs and switches in a fabric. This is the preferred method because it enables efficient management and monitoring in the event of any failure in the fabric. ACI OOB management uses two RJ-45 management ports on APICs for redundancy; these ports can be connected to any OOB management network with 10/100/1000BASE-T connectivity options.

Note You can configure the OOB management addresses either by statically assigning them on fabric nodes of your choice individually or by defining the range of fabric nodes and letting the APIC assign the OOB addresses from the management subnet automatically. Our in-field recommendation is to configure static management addresses individually on each fabric node.

Configuring OOB management in ACI involves the follow basic steps:

Step 1. Create static OOB management addresses and associate them to the OOB node management EPG.

Step 2. Create an OOB contract.

Step 3. Choose the OOB contract as a provided contract under the OOB node management EPG.

Step 4. Create an external management entity instance (that is, an external management EPG) with external prefixes allowed to access and manage the ACI fabric infrastructure and use the OOB contract as a consumed contract.

The following sections describe the details of these steps.

Creating Static Management Addresses

To create a static OOB management address, in the APIC GUI you need to go to Tenants > mgmt > Node Management Addresses > Static Node Management Addresses and right-click Create Static Node Management Addresses. In the dialog box that appears (see Figure 10-1), you need to fill out the ACI node static management addresses individually (for APICs, leafs, and spines).

You need to create individual static node management addresses for all ACI fabric infrastructure (APICs, leafs, and spines). You can follow the process just outlined to create the rest of the addresses.

Creating the Management Contract

For an OOB management contract, you first create the filter with specific management ports and protocols. To do so, from the APIC GUI you need to go to Tenants > mgmt > Contracts, right-click Filters, and click Create Filter, as shown in Figure 10-2.

As shown in Figure 10-3, in the dialog that appears, type **mgmt-fil** as the filter name and then click the + sign to add the management ports and protocols (in this example, syslog).

This section has shown how to create a filter with just one syslog entry. However, based on field experience, it is recommended that you create a filter with the management ports and protocols listed in Table 10-1. You can follow the process just outlined to create the rest of the ports and protocols.

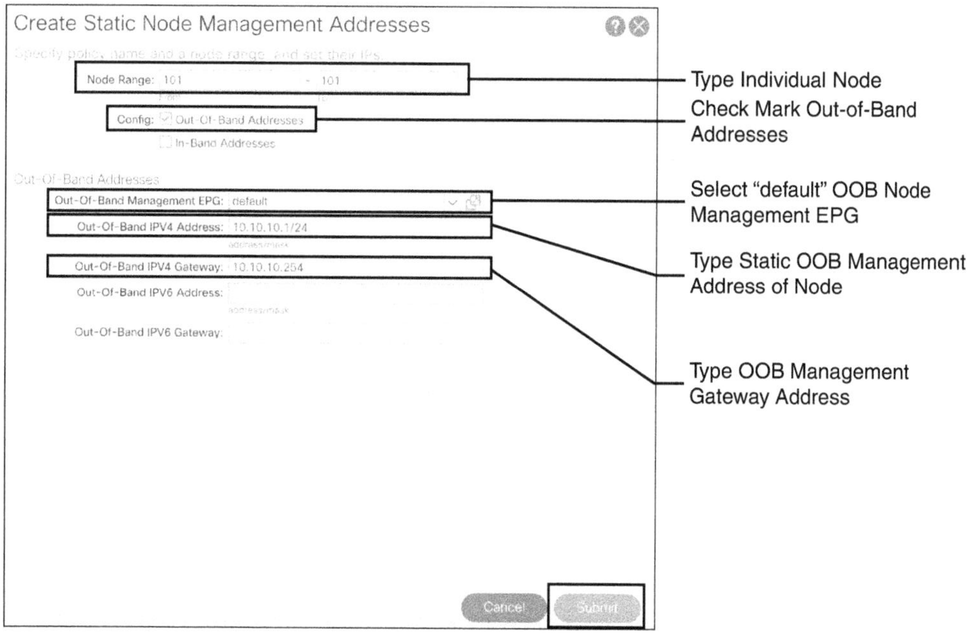

Figure 10-1   *Creating OOB Static Node Management Addresses*

Figure 10-2   *Creating a Management Filter*

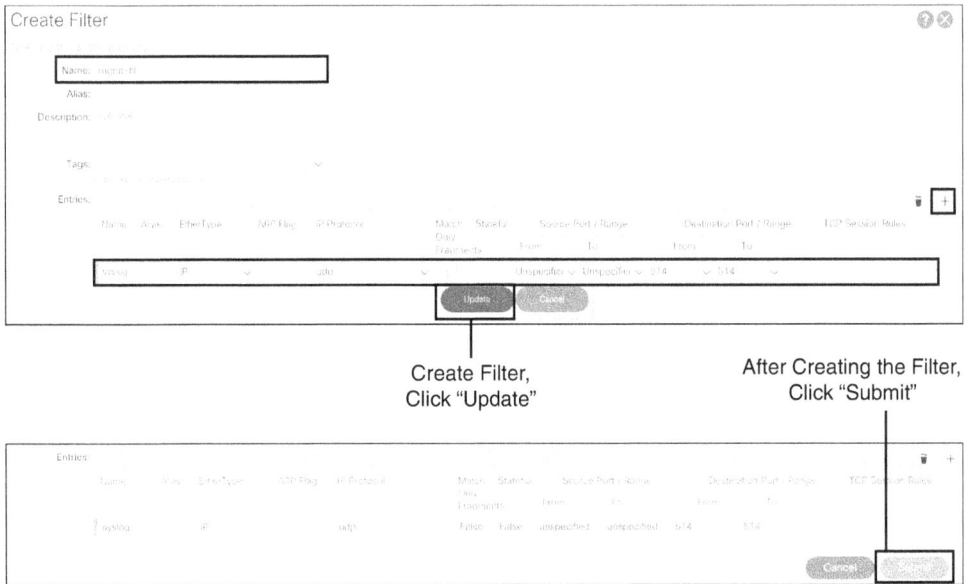

Figure 10-3 *Creating Management Filter Ports/Protocols*

Table 10-1 *Management Filter Ports/Protocols*

Name	EtherType	IP Protocol	Source Port/Range		Destination Port/Range	
			From	To	From	To
syslog	IP	UDP	Unspecified	Unspecified	514	514
snmp	IP	UDP	Unspecified	Unspecified	161	162
icmp	IP	ICMP	Unspecified	Unspecified	Unspecified	Unspecified
ntp	IP	UDP	123	123	123	123
https-in	IP	TCP	Unspecified	Unspecified	https	https
https-out	IP	TCP	https	https	Unspecified	Unspecified
ssh-in	IP	TCP	Unspecified	Unspecified	22	22
ssh-out	IP	TCP	22	22	Unspecified	Unspecified
dns-in	IP	TCP	Unspecified	Unspecified	dns	dns
dns-out	IP	TCP	Dns	dns	Unspecified	Unspecified
tacacs	IP	TCP	Unspecified	Unspecified	49	49

After creating a management filter, you need to create the OOB contract. On the left side of the policy navigation pane, expand Contracts, right-click the Out-of-Band Contracts tab, and click Create Out-of-Band Contract. In the dialog that appears (see Figure 10-4), you need to type **oob-cnt** as the contract name, choose VRF as the scope, and click the **+** sign to create the subject. In the new dialog that appears, enter **oob-sbj** as the subject name, click the **+** sign, and select mgmt-fil from the Filters drop-down menu.

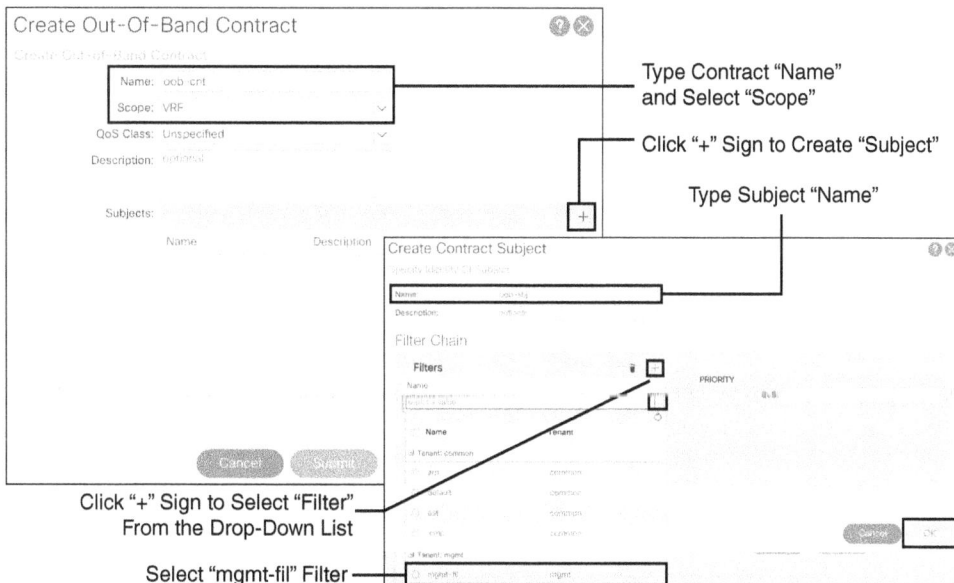

Figure 10-4 *Creating an OOB Contract*

Choosing the Node Management EPG

As you already know, ACI groups all endpoints (for all ACI infrastructure: APICs, leafs, and spines with management IP addresses) to endpoint groups (EPGs). An EPG is the object on which ACI applies policy enforcement. This concept remains intact even with management traffic. In order to create an OOB node management EPG, on the left side of the APIC GUI pane, navigate to Node Management EPGs > Out-of-Band EPG - default. On the right side of the pane, click the + sign to add the oob-cnt contract as a provided contract (see Figure 10-5).

Creating an External Management Entity EPG

For an OOB external management entity instance, also known as an out-of-band external management EPG, on the left side of the policy navigation pane in the APIC GUI, right-click External Management Network Instance Profiles and select Create External Management Network Instance Profile. Then, on the right side of the pane, type **oob-ext** as the object name, click the + sign to add the OOB contract as a consumed contract, and click Update. Click the + sign to add the subnets allowed to manage and access the ACI fabric from external networks (in this case, 0.0.0.0/0). Click Update and then click Submit. Figure 10-6 illustrates this process.

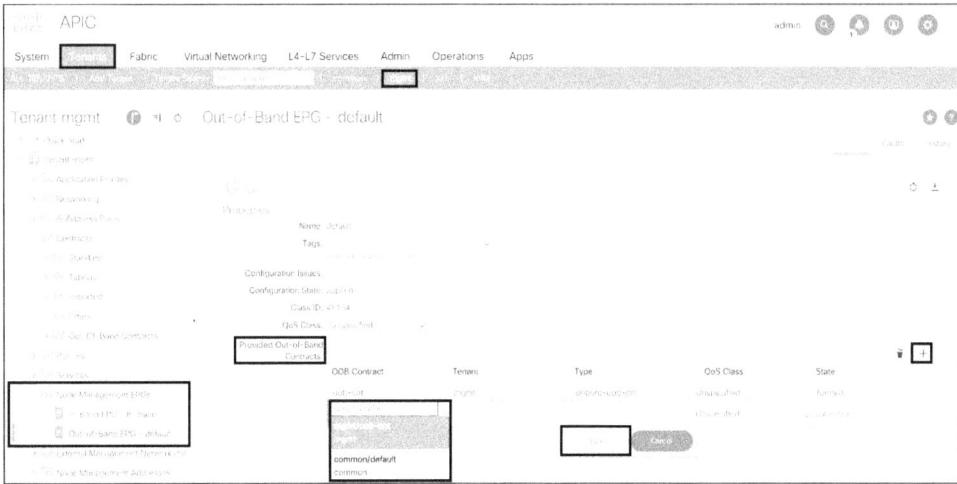

Figure 10-5 *Choosing the OOB Node Management EPG*

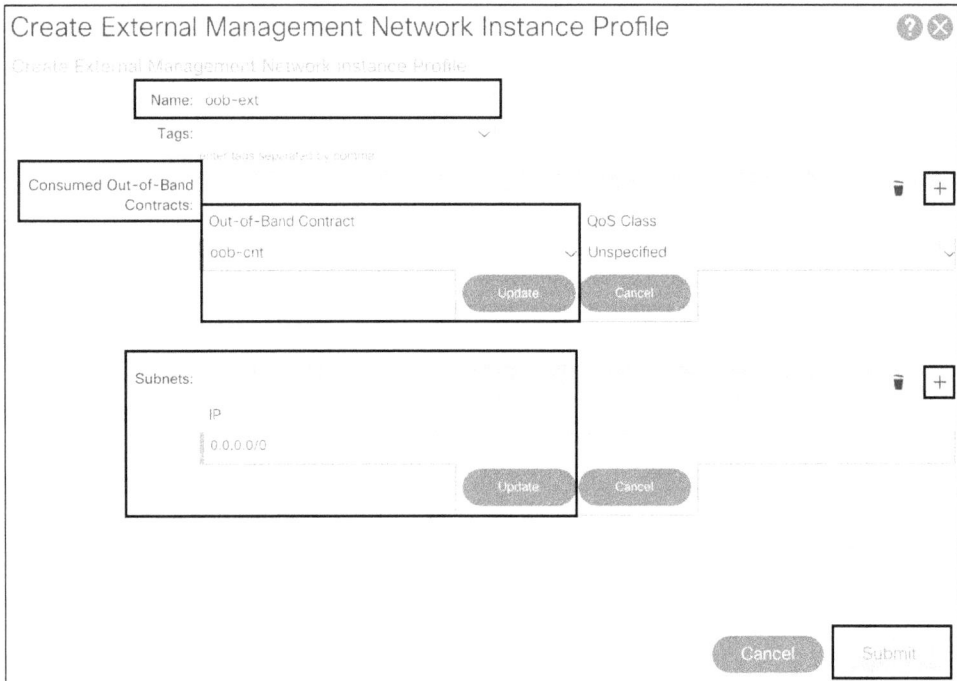

Figure 10-6 *Creating the OOB External Management Entity Instance*

You should now be able to use the OOB management network for managing and monitoring the ACI fabric.

Verifying the OOB Management Configuration

For verification, you can check various configuration items, but the main objective is to check the OOB management functionality. To do this, you can establish a Secure Shell (SSH) session to one of your ACI nodes by using its OOB management IP address, as shown in Example 10-1.

Example 10-1 *Connecting to an APIC by Using SSH*

```
Sadiq-laptop$ ssh admin@10.10.10.251
Application Policy Infrastructure Controller
admin@10.10.10.251's password:
Last login: 2019-11-05T16:35:13.000-05:00 UTC
apic1#
apic1#
```

To check the OOB configuration, you can run the commands shown in Example 10-2 on the APIC via the CLI.

Example 10-2 *Verifying the OOB Configuration*

```
apic1# show tenant mgmt contract oob-cnt
Tenant   Contract    Type       Qos Class    Scope  Subject  Access-group  Dir
  Description
------   --------    --------   -----------  -----  ------   ------------  ----
  ------
mgmt     oob-cnt     oob-mgmt   unspecified  vrf    oob-sbj  mgmt-fil      both


apic1# show tenant mgmt access-list mgmt-fil
Tenant      : mgmt
Access-List : mgmt-fil
    match icmp
    match tcp dest 22
    match tcp src 22
    match tcp src 443
    match tcp dest 443
    match udp src 123 dest 123
    match udp dest 161-162
    match udp dest 514
    match udp dest 53
    match udp src 53
        match tcp dest 49
```

```
apic1# show running-config tenant mgmt oob-mgmt
# Command: show running-config tenant mgmt oob-mgmt
# Time: Wed Nov 13 21:47:34 2019
  tenant mgmt
    oob-mgmt epg default
      contract provider oob-cnt
      exit
    exit

apic1 # show running-config tenant mgmt external-l3
# Command: show running-config tenant mgmt external-l3
# Time: Wed Nov 13 21:51:57 2019
  tenant mgmt
    external-l3 epg OOB-ext oob-mgmt
      match ip 0.0.0.0/0
      contract consumer oob-cnt
      exit

apic1# show oob-mgmt switch 1001

Table1 : OOB-Mgmt Node Details


 Type           Node ID  Ip Address    Gateway      OOB-EPG   Oper State
 ---------      -------  -----------   --------     -------   ----------
 Leaf-1001      1001     10.10.10.11/24 10.10.10.254 default    up

Table2 : OOB-Mgmt EPG Details


 Name            Qos             Tag             Nodes       Oper State
 --------------- --------------- --------------- ---------- ----------
 default         unspecified     49154           101         up
 default         unspecified     49154           102         up
 default         unspecified     49154           201         up
 default         unspecified     49154           202         up
 default         unspecified     49154           1001        up
 default         unspecified     49154           1002        up

Table3 : OOB-Mgmt EPG Contract Details


 Provider OOB-Mmgt-Epg  Contracts        Consumer OOB-Mgmt Ext-L3 Epg
 --------------         ---------------  -------------------------
 default                oob-cnt          OOB-ext
```

```
Table4 : OOB-Mgmt External L3 EPG Details


Name             Qos              Contract         IP Network
---------------  ---------------  ---------------  ----------
OOB-ext          unspecified      oob-cnt          0.0.0.0/0
```

In-Band Management

In addition to supporting OOB management, ACI offers in-band (INB) management, which is suitable for enterprises that do not want the extra expense of an OOB management infrastructure. Also, INB is a good choice for environments where a predefined row of racks with application servers are hosted in the data center and there is not much room available for extra switches aside from ACI ToR leafs. Furthermore, if you have Cisco Tetration deployed, you must use INB.

Note   You can configure the INB management addresses either by statically assigning them on fabric nodes of your choice individually or by defining the range of fabric nodes and letting the APIC assign the INB addresses from the management subnet automatically. Our in-field recommendation is to configure static management addresses individually on each fabric node.

Configuring INB management in ACI involves the following basic steps:

Step 1.   Create an INB contract.

Step 2.   Create access policies for the leaf(s) connected to APICs.

Step 3.   Create access policies for the border leaf(s) connected to the external router(s).

Step 4.   Create an INB management external routed network (L3Out) and choose a routing method.

Step 5.   Create networks (external management EPGs) under the INB L3Out and choose the INB contract as a consumed contract.

Step 6.   Create an INB BD with a subnet.

Step 7.   Under the INB node management EPG, type **encap-vlan**, choose the INB BD, and choose the contract as a provided contract.

Step 8.   Create static INB management addresses and associate them with the INB node management EPG.

The following sections describe the details of these steps.

Creating a Management Contract

For an INB management contract, you can use the same filter you created earlier for the OOB contract (refer to Figure 10-2 and Figure 10-3). After you create the INB management filter, you need to create the INB contract. On the left side of the policy navigation pane, expand Contracts, right-click Standard, and click Create Contract. In the dialog that appears, you need to type **inb-cnt** as the contract name, choose VRF as the scope, and click the + sign to create subject. Then type **inb-sbj** as the subject name, click the + sign, and select mgmt-fil from the Filters drop-down menu (see Figure 10-7).

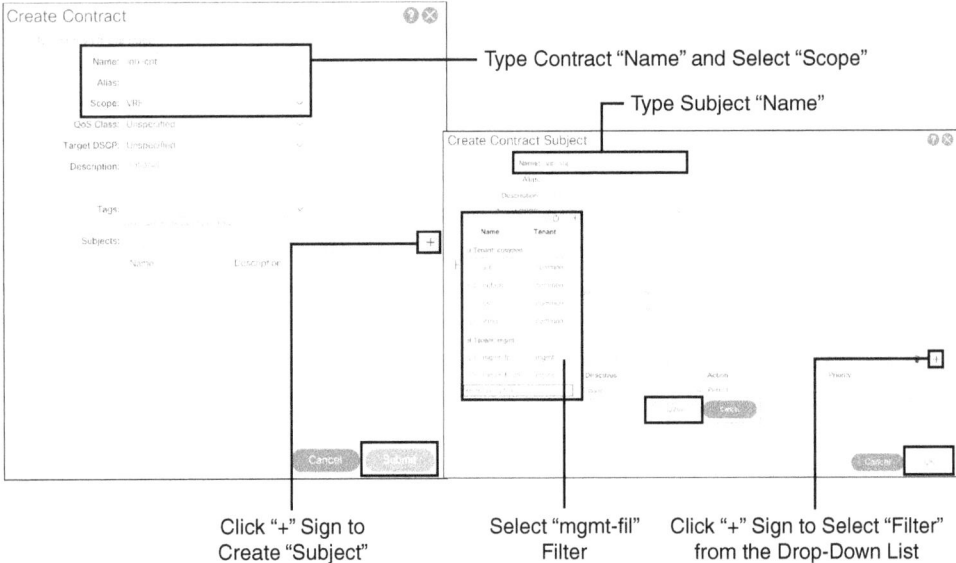

Figure 10-7   *Creating an INB Contract*

Creating Leaf Interface Access Policies for APIC INB Management

To perform INB management on an APIC, you need to create interface access policies for leafs connected to the APIC. In order to do that, you first create a leaf interface access port policy group: Go to Fabric > Access Policies > Interfaces > Leaf Interfaces > Policy Groups, right-click Leaf Access Port, and click Create Leaf Access Port Policy Group. In the dialog that appears, type **mgmt-inb-polgrp** as the name of the object and fill out the desired interface policies, as shown in Figure 10-8.

Next, you have to create the leaf interface profile. To do so, go to Fabric > Access Policies > Interfaces > Leaf Interfaces, right-click Profiles, and click Create Leaf Interface Profile. In the dialog that appears, type **301-302-int-prof** as the name of the object and click on the + sign to select the leaf interfaces that you connect to APIC. Fill out the desired access port selector policies and choose mgmt-inb-polgrp from the Interface Policy Group drop-down menu (see Figure 10-9).

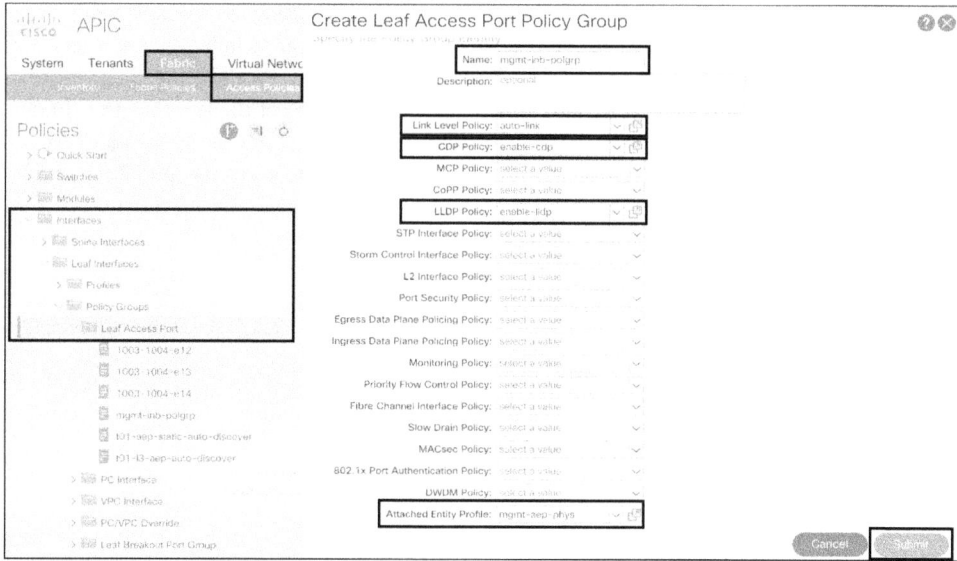

Figure 10-8 *Creating a Leaf Interface Access Port Policy Group (on an APIC)*

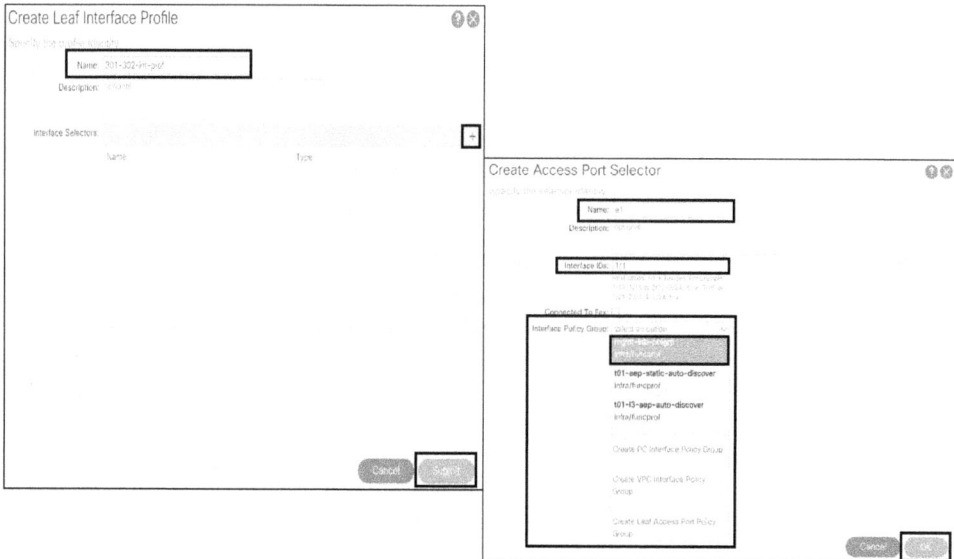

Figure 10-9 *Creating a Leaf Interface Profile (on an APIC)*

Follow the same procedure to add more leaf interfaces connecting to APICs. When you finish the leaf interface policies, you need to create the leaf switch policies. Select Fabric > Access Policies > Switches > Leaf Switches, right-click Profiles, and click Create Leaf Profile. As shown in Figure 10-10, click the + sign and select the leaf selectors. In the dialog that appears, type **L301-L302** as the object name and select the appropriate leaf block (in this example, leaf nodes **301** and **302**). Click Next to go to the Step 2 screen, where you can choose the previously created interface selector profile. Click Finish.

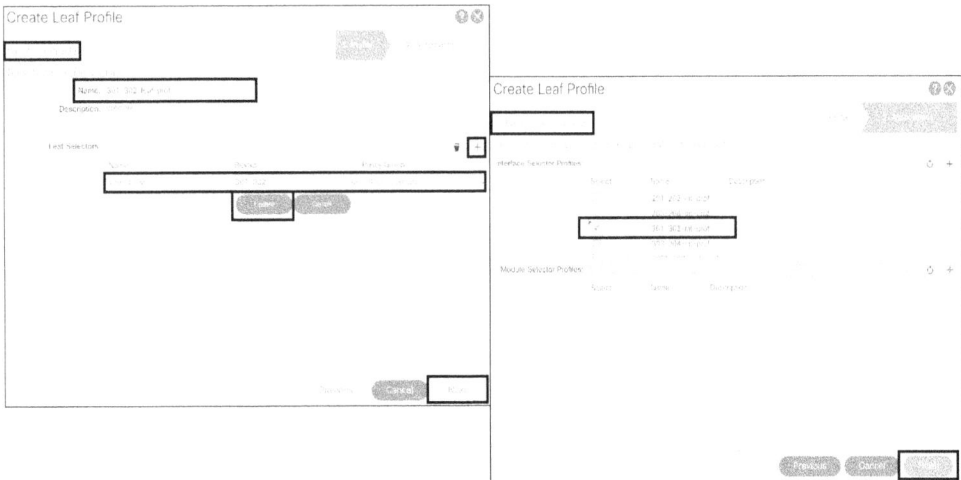

Figure 10-10   *Creating a Leaf Switch Profile (on an APIC)*

Creating Access Policies for the Border Leaf(s) Connected to L3Out

As mentioned earlier, the ACI fabric provides INB management capabilities through its infrastructure. INB management traffic requires a path to flow in and out of the fabric. This can be achieved by establishing an L3Out from ACI border leafs toward external routers. However, before you create the L3Out in the mgmt tenant, you need to first create border leaf interface access policies connecting to external routers. To do that, you first create a leaf interface access port policy group: Go to Fabric > Access Policies > Interfaces > Leaf Interfaces > Policy Groups, right-click Leaf Access Port, and click Create Leaf Access Port Policy Group. In the dialog that appears, type **l3-inb-polgrp** as the name of the object, and fill out the desired interface policies (see Figure 10-11).

Note   Ensure that the attached entity profile mgmt-aep-phys is part of external routed domain mgmt-dom-l3, which will be used while creating the INB management L3Out configuration shown in the next section.

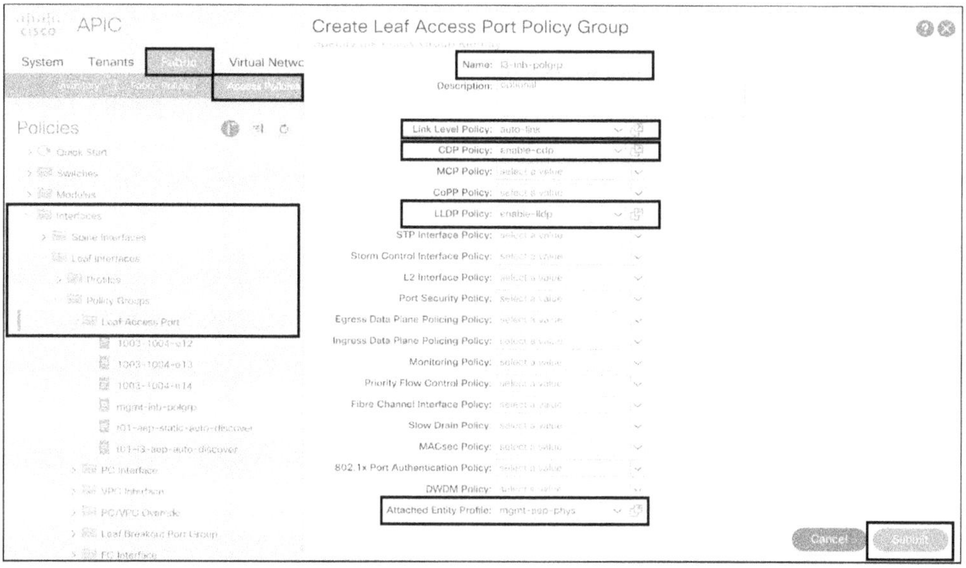

Figure 10-11   *Creating a Leaf Interface Access Port Policy Group (L3Out)*

Next, you have to create the border leaf interface profile. To do so, go to Fabric > Access Policies > Interfaces > Leaf Interfaces, right-click Profiles, and click Create Leaf Interface Profile. In the dialog that appears, type **201-202-int-prof** as the name of the object and click the **+** sign to select the leaf interfaces that you want to connect to APIC. Fill out the desired access port selector policies and choose l3-inb-polgrp from the Interface Policy Group drop-down menu (see Figure 10-12).

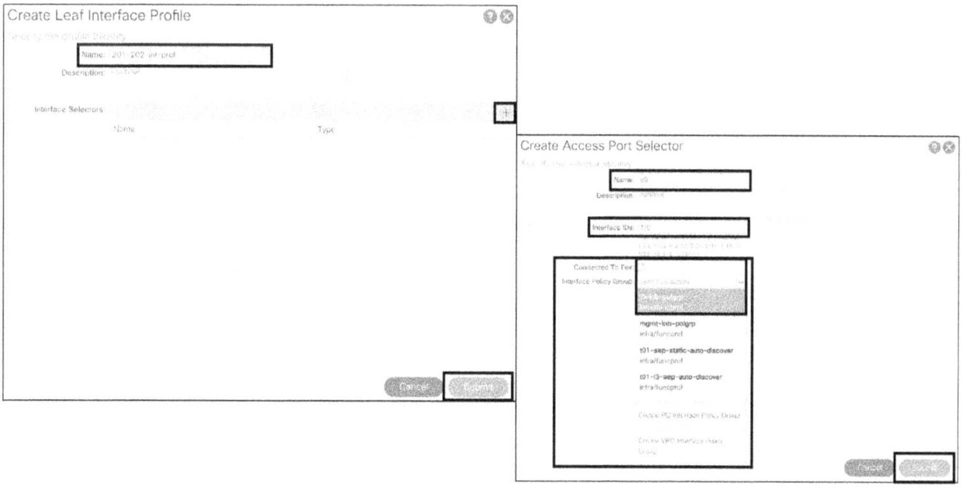

Figure 10-12   *Creating a Leaf Interface Profile (L3Out)*

Follow the same procedure to add more border leaf interfaces connecting to external routers. When you finish the leaf interface policies, you need to create the leaf switch policies. Select Fabric > Access Policies > Switches > Leaf Switches, right-click Profiles, and click Create Leaf Profile. As shown in Figure 10-13, click the + sign and select the leaf selectors. In the dialog that appears, type **L201-L202** as the object name and select the appropriate leaf block (in this example, border leaf nodes **201** and **202**). Click Next to go to the Step 2 screen, where you can choose the previously created interface selector profile. Click Finish.

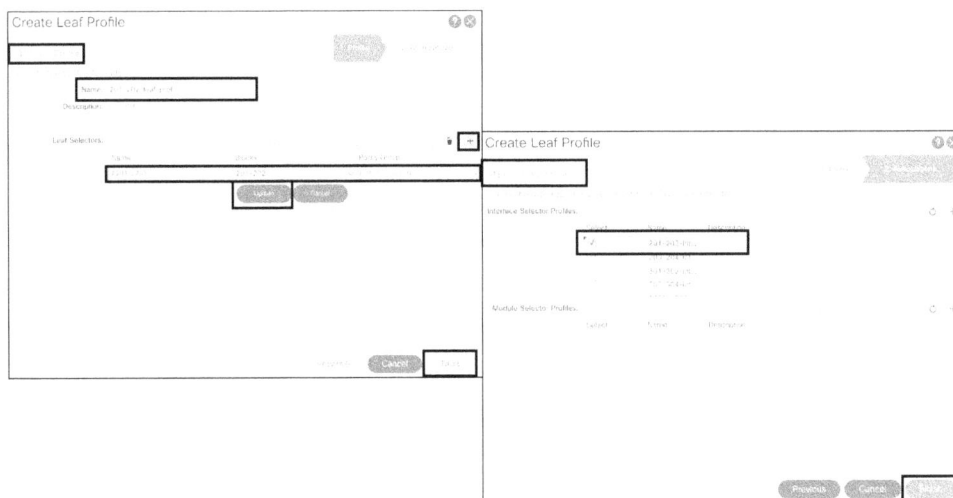

Figure 10-13 *Creating a Leaf Switch Profile (L3Out)*

Creating INB Management External Routed Networks (L3Out)

After you create the border leaf interface access port policies, you need to create the INB management external routed network, also known as L3Out. To do that, go to Tenant > mgmt > Networking, right-click External Routed Networks, and click Create Routed Outside. In the dialog that appears, fill out the attributes of the L3Out object policy: Enter **l3out:p-inband-mgmt** as the name of the object, keep the default route control enforcement policy, Export, select inb from the In-Band VRF drop-down menu, and select mgmt-dom-l3 from the External Routed Domain drop-down menu. Finally, choose OSPF with area ID 0.0.0.11 as the routing method and type **NSSA** for the area. You can use the OSPF area of your choice. Click Submit. Figure 10-14 illustrates these steps.

Expand the newly created external routed networks object l3out:p-inband-mgmt, right-click Logical Node Profiles, and click Create Node Profile. Type **inband-mgmt-node-prof** as the name of the object, click the + sign, and add the node ID and router ID. Click OK and then click Submit. Figure 10-15 illustrates this process.

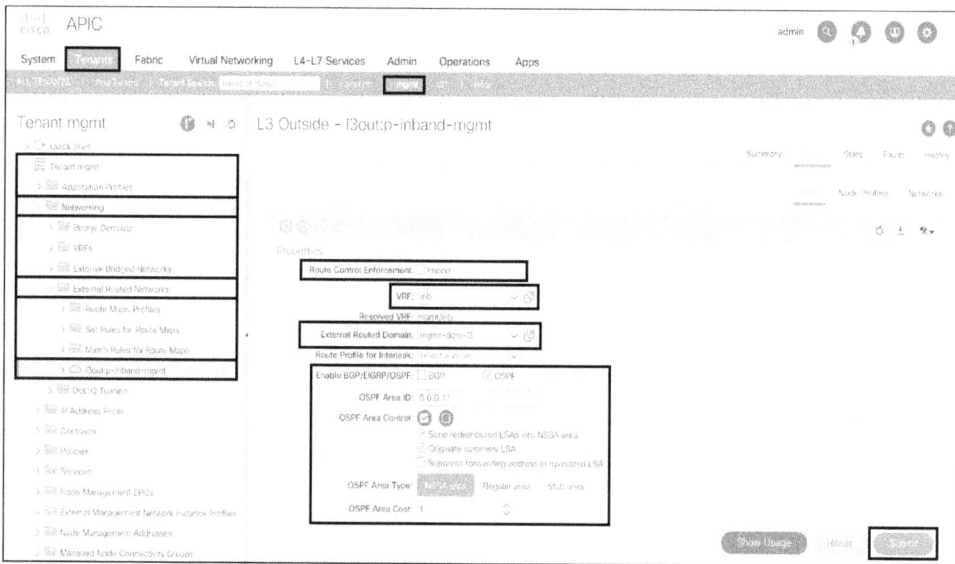

Figure 10-14 *Creating an INB Management L3Out*

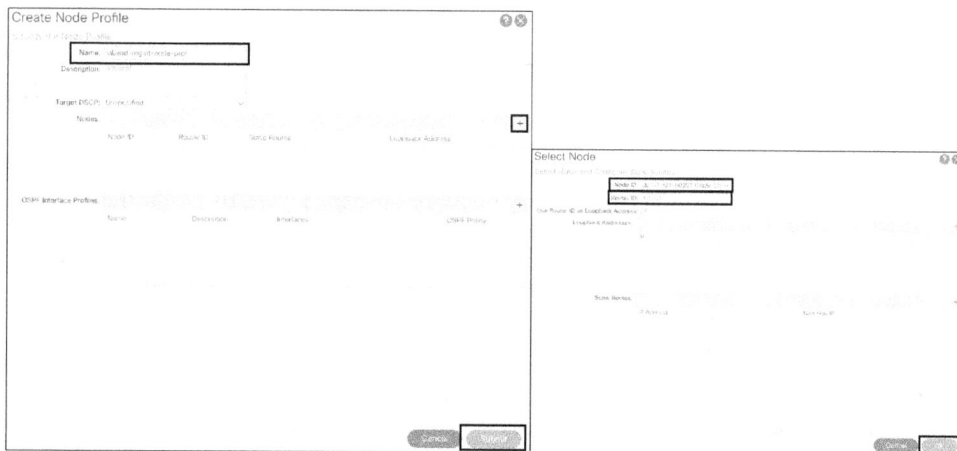

Figure 10-15 *Creating an INB Management L3Out Logical Node Profile*

You can add more node IDs and router IDs by following the same procedure, depending on how many border leafs you want to peer with external routers for INB management traffic flow.

Next, you need to expand the newly created logical node profile object inband-mgmt-node-prof, right-click Logical Interface Profiles, and click Create Interface Profile. As shown in Figure 10-16, a three-step configuration process begins. In the Step 1 dialog, type **inband-int-prof** as the name of the object and click Next.

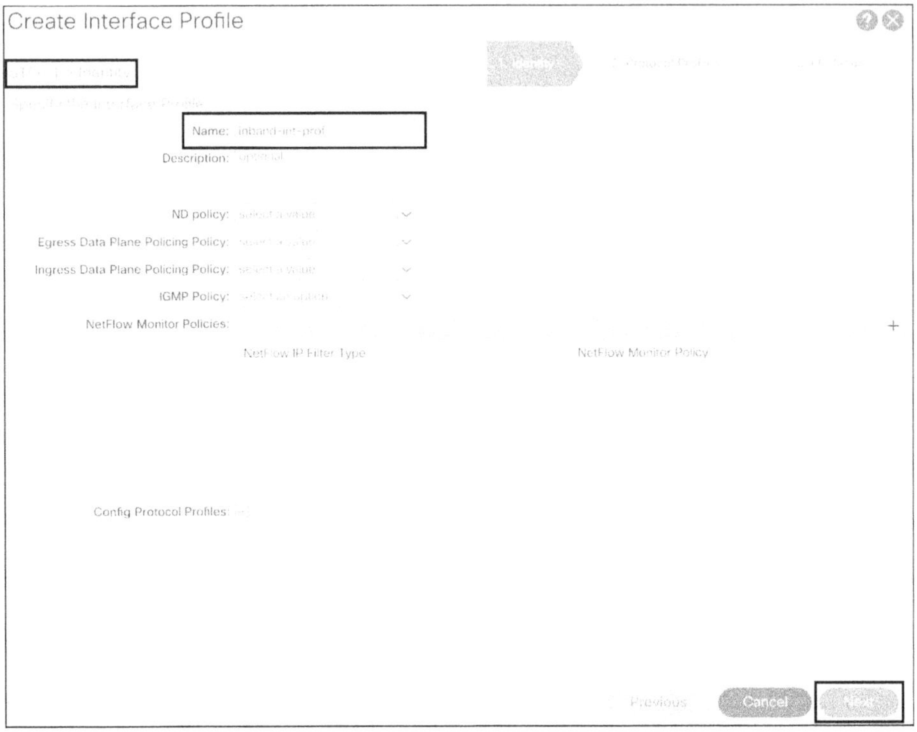

Figure 10-16   *Creating an INB Management L3Out Logical Interface Profile: Step 1*

From the Step 2 dialog, under the OSPF Policy drop-down menu, select Create OSPF Interface Policy and configure necessary OSPF parameters. Figure 10-17 illustrates this process.

Also in the Step 2 dialog, shown in Figure 10-18, choose the OSPF Authentication Type of your choice or choose no authentication and fill out other necessary configuration according to your requirements. Click Next to move to Step 3.

In the Step 3 dialog (see Figure 10-19), click the + sign to create a routed interface. Select the Port as the path type. From the Node drop-down menu, select node 201. Select eth1/9 as the interface path. Type **20.20.20.1/29** as the IPv4 address. Click OK and then click Finish. The node ID, interface path, and IPv4 address are sample values taken as an example. You should insert the values based on your environment.

Creating External Management EPGs

To create networks under INB management L3Out, navigate to Networking > External Routed Networks > l3out:p-inband-mgmt, right-click Networks, and click Create External Network. In the dialog that appears, type **inband-mgmt-epg** as the object name and click the + sign to create the subnet that you will allow to access your ACI infrastructure via INB management (see Figure 10-20).

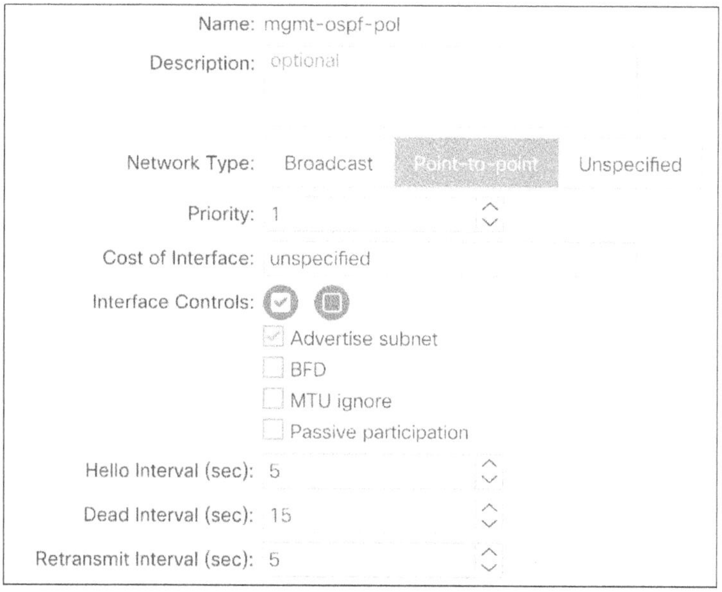

Figure 10-17 *Creating an OSPF Interface Policy*

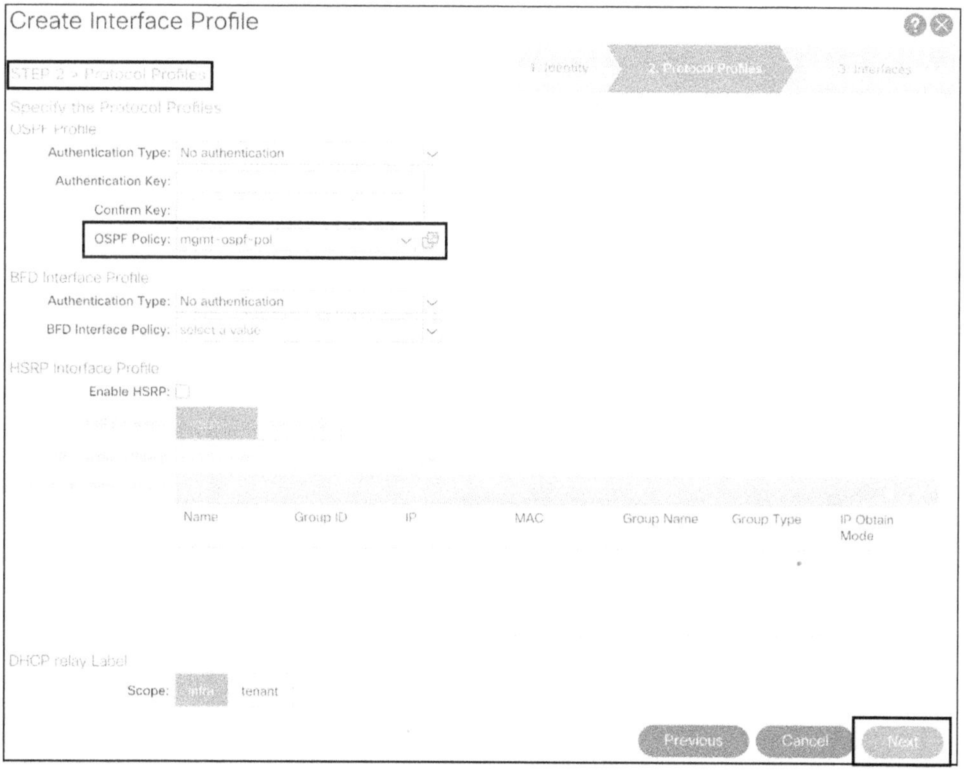

Figure 10-18 *Creating an INB Management L3Out Logical Interface Profile: Step 2*

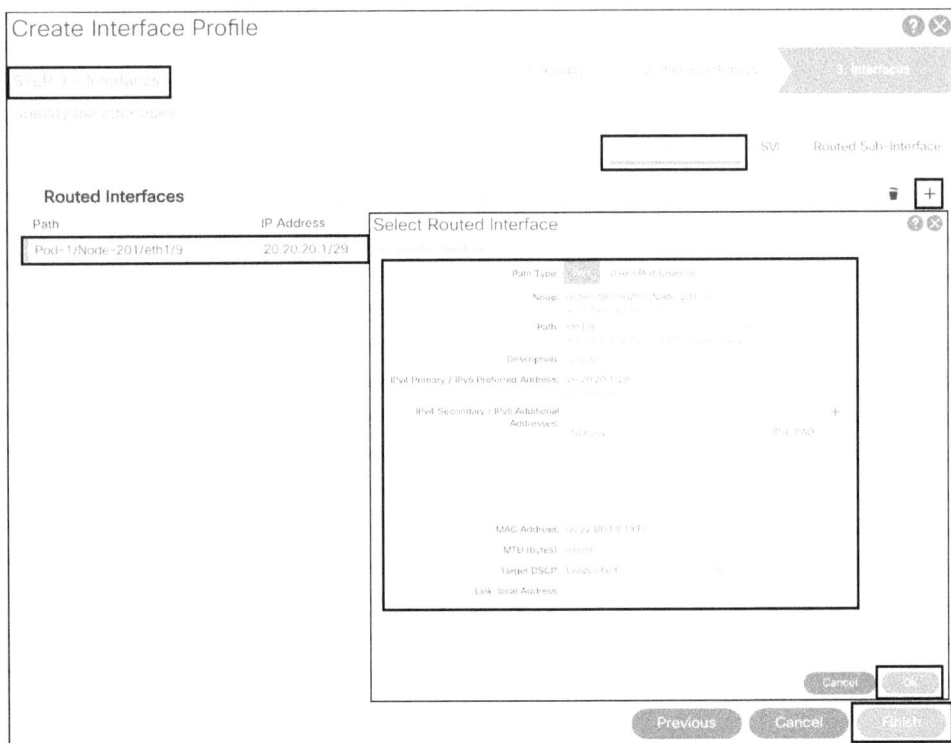

Figure 10-19 *Creating an INB Management L3Out Logical Interface Profile: Step 3*

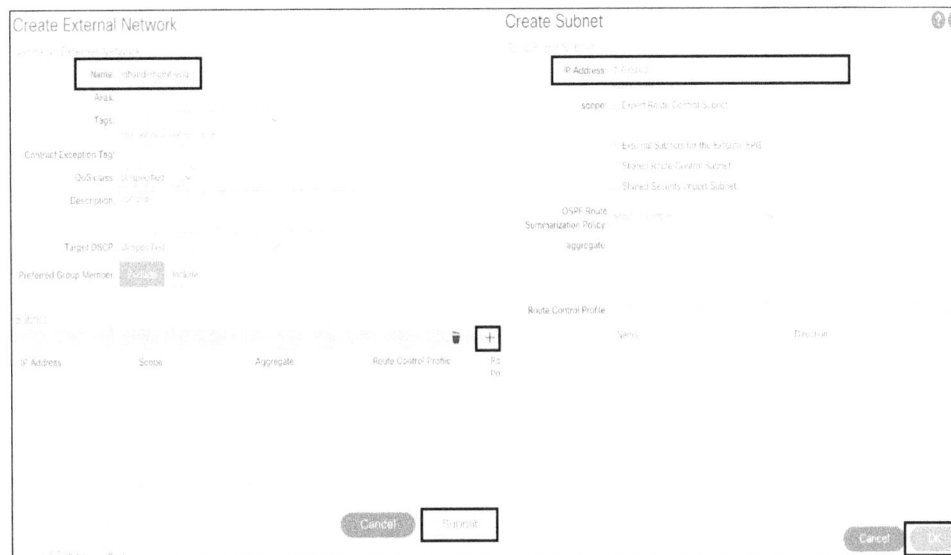

Figure 10-20 *Creating INB Management Networks (External Management EPG)*

Next, select the newly created INB management L3Out networks and select the Contracts tab. Navigate to Consumed Contracts, as shown in Figure 10-21, and click the + sign to add the inb-cnt contract as a consumed contract. Click Update.

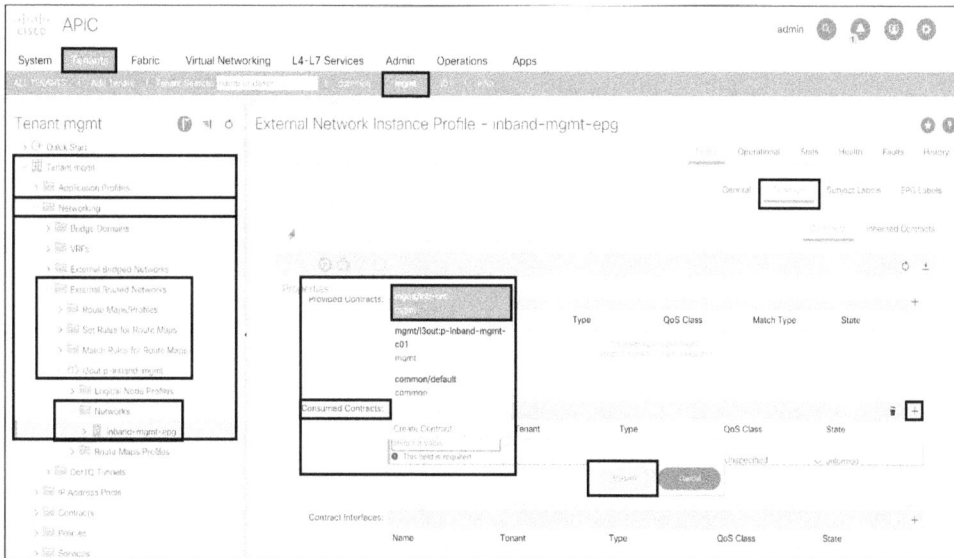

Figure 10-21 *Consuming an INB Contract in INB L3Out Networks*

Creating an INB BD with a Subnet

In ACI, the INB management BD object is already predefined in the policy. You just need to create a subnet under the inb INB management BD because the spine does not reply to ARP requests for the node's INB management IP address. To do this configuration, you need to go to Tenants > mgmt > Networking > Bridge Domains > inb. On the right-hand side of the window, click Policy and then click the L3 Configurations tab, as shown in Figure 10-22.

To create a subnet, click the + sign and type **20.20.20.1/24** as the gateway IP address, select Advertised Externally, and click Submit (see Figure 10-23). The subnet gateway IP address shown here is an example. You should insert the values based on your environment.

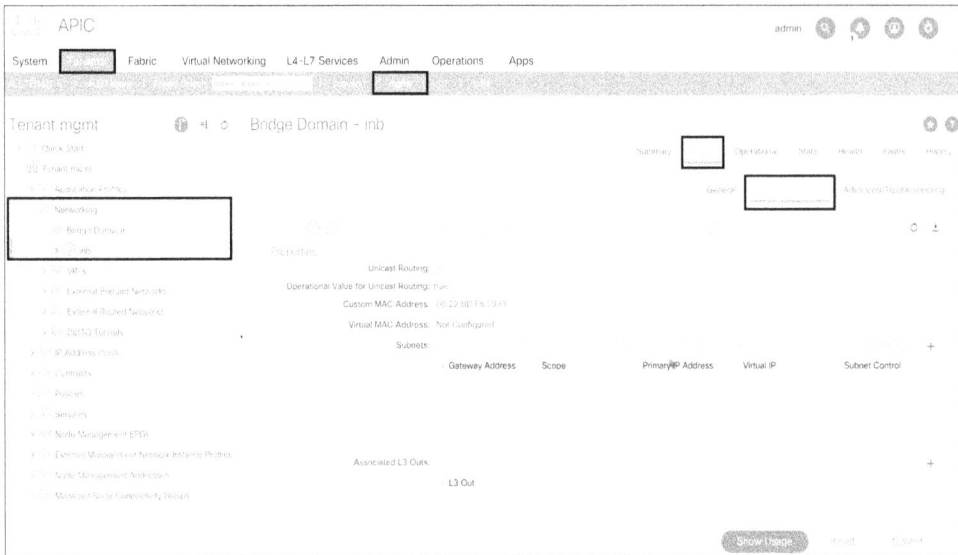

Figure 10-22 *Navigating the INB Management Bridge Domain Object*

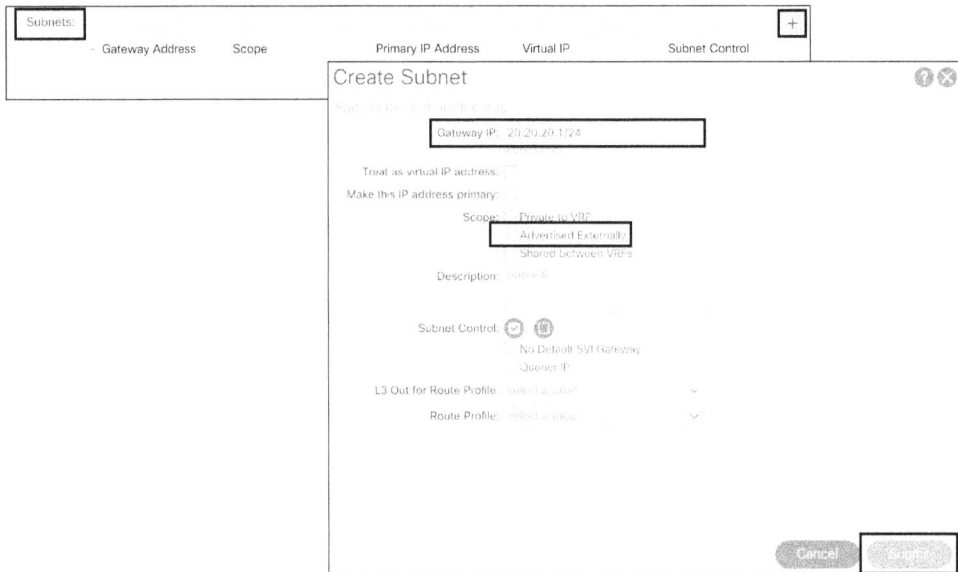

Figure 10-23 *Creating an INB Management BD Subnet*

Next, to associate this subnet to INB management L3Out, click on the + sign, select the l3out:p-inband-mgmt INB management L3Out, and click Update (see Figure 10-24). Finally, click Submit to finish creating the INB management BD subnet.

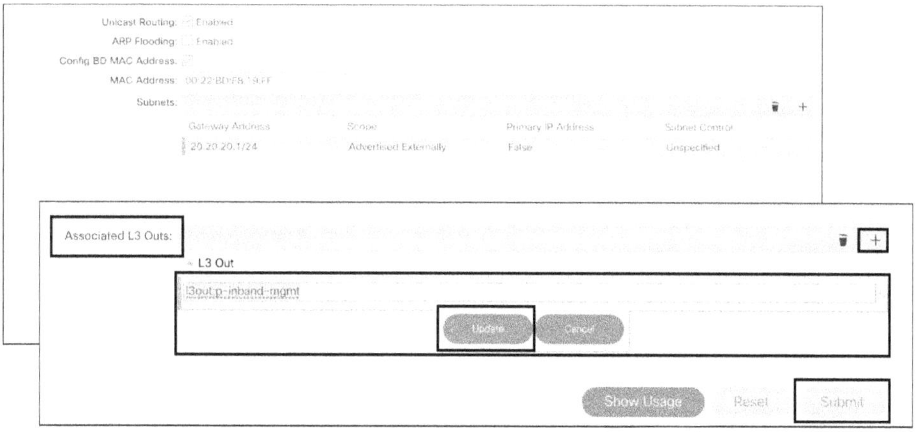

Figure 10-24 *Associating an INB Management BD Subnet to L3Out*

Configuring the Node Management EPG

To configure the INB node management EPG, as shown in Figure 10-25, navigate to Tenants > mgmt > Node Management EPGs > select In-Band EPG. In the dialog that appears, type **vlan-5** in the Encap field and select inb from the Bridge Domain drop-down menu. Click Submit. Next, you need to add the INB management contract in the INB node management EPG, so select the In-Band EPG - default object again and, on the right side of the screen, click the + sign and add the inb-cnt INB management contract as a provided contract. The values used here are shown as an example. You should insert the values based on your environment.

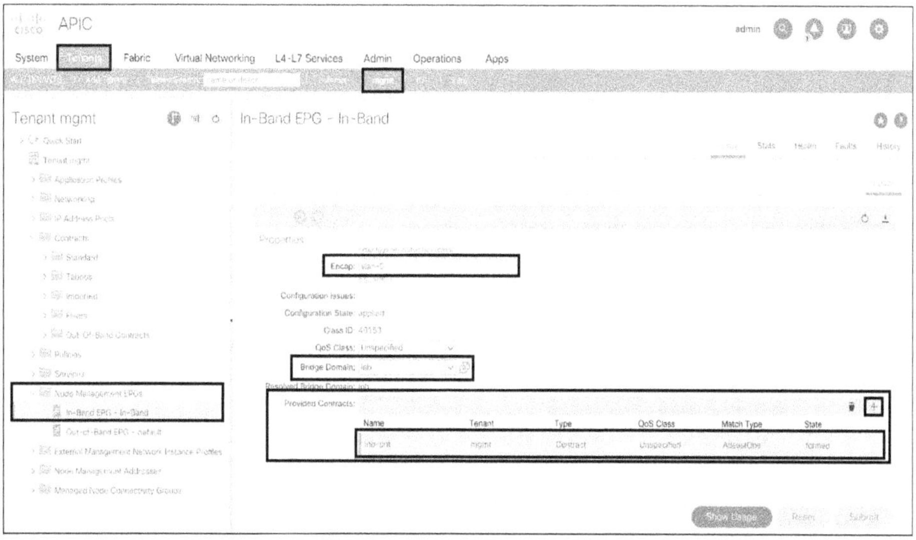

Figure 10-25 *Configuring the INB Node Management EPG*

Creating Static Management Addresses

To create a static INB management address, in the APIC GUI, go to Tenants > mgmt > Node Management Addresses, right-click Static Node Management Addresses, and click Create Static Node Management Addresses. In the dialog that appears, you need to fill out the ACI node (APIC, leaf, and spine) static management addresses individually, as shown in Figure 10-26.

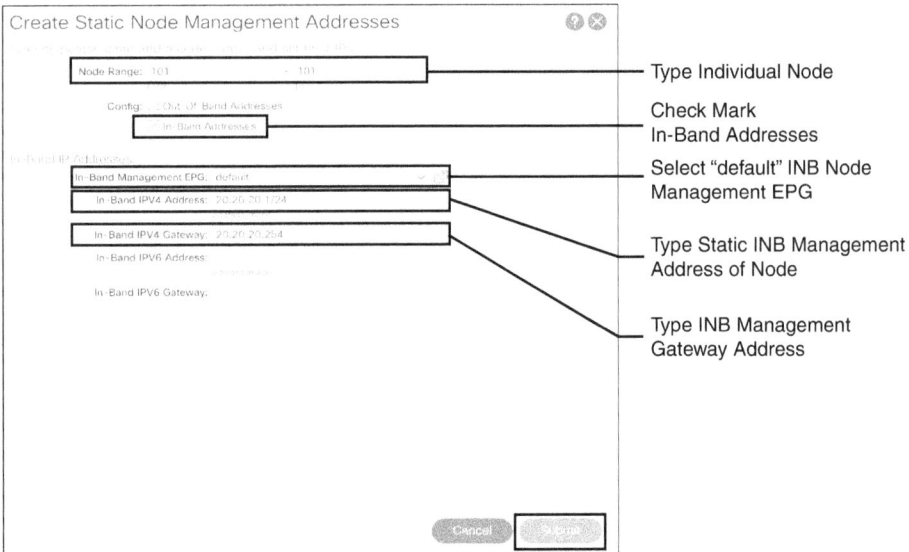

Figure 10-26 *Creating INB Static Node Management Addresses*

You should now be able to use the INB management network for managing and monitoring the ACI fabric.

Verifying the INB Management Configuration

To verify the INB management configuration, you can check various configuration items, but the main objective is to check the INB management functionality. To do this, you can establish an SSH session to one of your ACI nodes by using its INB management IP address, as shown in Example 10-3.

Example 10-3 *Connecting to an APIC by Using SSH*

```
Sadiq-laptop$ ssh admin@20.20.20.251
Application Policy Infrastructure Controller
admin@20.20.20.251's password:
Last login: 2019-11-05T23:31:19.000-05:00 UTC
apic1#
apic1#
```

Example 10-4 shows the commands you can run on the APIC to check the INB configuration.

Example 10-4 *Verifying the INB Configuration*

```
apic1# show tenant mgmt contract inb-cnt
 Tenant Contract Type      Qos Class  Scope Subject Access-group  Dir  Description
 ------ -------- -------- ----------- ----- ------- ------------  ---- ----------
 mgmt    inb-cnt  permit   unspecified vrf


apic1# show tenant mgmt access-list mgmt-fil
Tenant      : mgmt
Access-List : mgmt-fil
    match icmp
    match tcp dest 22
    match tcp src 22
    match tcp src 443
    match tcp dest 443
    match udp src 123 dest 123
    match udp dest 161-162
    match udp dest 514
    match udp dest 53
    match udp src 53
        match tcp dest 49

apic1# show running-config tenant mgmt inband-mgmt
# Command: show running-config tenant mgmt inband-mgmt
# Time: Mon Nov 25 08:14:18 2019
  tenant mgmt
    inband-mgmt epg In-Band
      contract provider inb-cnt
      bridge-domain inb
      vlan 5
      exit
    exit

apic1# show running-config tenant mgmt external-l3 epg inband-mgmt-epg
# Command: show running-config tenant mgmt external-l3 epg inband-mgmt-epg
# Time: Mon Nov 25 08:29:05 2019
  tenant mgmt
    external-l3 epg inband-mgmt-epg l3out l3out:p-inband-mgmt
      vrf member inb
      match ip 0.0.0.0/0
```

```
          contract consumer inb-cnt
        exit
      exit

apic1# show running-config tenant mgmt l3out
# Command: show running-config tenant mgmt l3out
# Time: Mon Nov 25 08:32:37 2019
  tenant mgmt
    l3out l3out:p-inband-mgmt
      vrf member inb
      exit
    exit

apic1# show inband-mgmt switch 1001

Table1 : INB-Mgmt Node Details


  Type         Node ID  Ip Address        Gateway        INB-EPG  Oper State
  ---------    -------  ----------------  ------------   -------  ----------

  Leaf-1001    1001     20.20.20.11/24    20.20.20.254   default  up


Table2 : INB-Mgmt EPG Details


  Name           Qos           Tag        Nodes      Vlan       Oper State
  -------        -----------   -----      ------     ----       ----------

  default        unspecified   49153      101        vlan-5     up
  default        unspecified   49153      102        vlan-5     up
  default        unspecified   49153      201        vlan-5     up
  default        unspecified   49153      202        vlan-5     up
  default        unspecified   49153      1001       vlan-5     up
  default        unspecified   49153      1002       vlan-5     up


Table3 : INB-Mgmt EPG Contract Details


  INB-MGMT-Epg    Contracts   App EPG    L3 External EPG    Oper State
  ------------    ---------   --------   ---------------    ----------

  default         inb-cnt                inband-mgmt-epg    up
```

Caution   If you have configured both OOB and INB management in ACI, INB management is preferred for packets sourced from the APIC by default. Therefore, ensure that you select OOB as your preferred method of management if that is what you selected in all ACI management-related configurations, such as for SNMP, syslog, NTP, TACACS+, and VMM. In order to do that, make the selections shown in Figure 10-27.

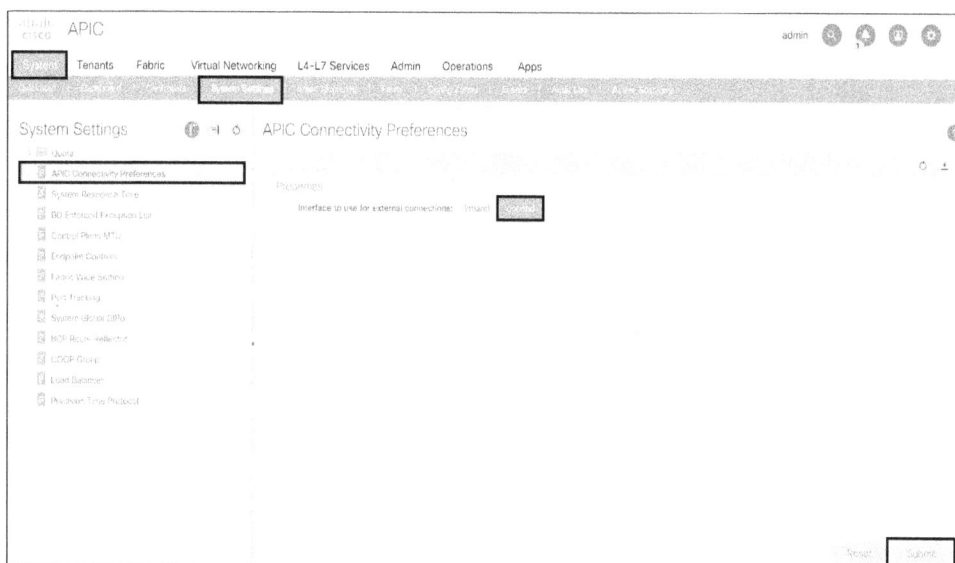

Figure 10-27 *Selecting OOB as the Preferred Management Method*

To verify this configuration, log in to the APIC via the CLI and run the command shown in Example 10-5.

Example 10-5 *Verifying OOB as the Preferred Management Method for an APIC*

```
apic1# bash
admin@apic1:~>
admin@apic1:~> ip route show 0.0.0.0/0
default via 10.10.10.1 dev oobmgmt  metric 16
default via 20.20.20.1 dev bond0.5  metric 32
```

From this output, you can see that the OOB management gateway is selected as the preferred next-hop route for all management traffic, with a metric of 16 followed; INB management is preferred next, with a higher metric of 32.

AAA

Authentication, authorization, and accounting (AAA) in ACI supports TACACS+, RADIUS, and LDAP protocols. However, because TACACS+ is the industry standard for network device control, this section covers only the TACACS+ protocol with respect to AAA configuration.

Configuring Cisco Secure ACS

Before configuring AAA in ACI, you need to first make the necessary configuration on Cisco Secure Access Control System (ACS) to provide the appropriate secure access control to the ACI fabric infrastructure. The high-level configuration steps on ACS server are as follows:

- Configure network device group location and type.

- Configure network devices and AAA clients.

- Create identity group.

- Configure read-only and read-write access users on ACS server.

- Create shell profile with AV pair.

- Configure device administration authorization policy.

Let's follow these high-level steps into more detail configuration steps as illustrated below.

Note   Only specific web browsers and versions work well with the Cisco ACS GUI. This section uses Mozilla Firefox version 63.0.1.

Step 1.   First, you need to create the Network Device Group Location and Device Types to group all of your ACI fabric infrastructure, which will be acting as TACACS+ clients. To configure the network device group location, navigate to the following ACS web GUI path as Network Resources > Network Device Groups > Location and click Create. Type the name of the location (in this case, NGLAB) and click Submit. Figure 10-28 illustrates this process.

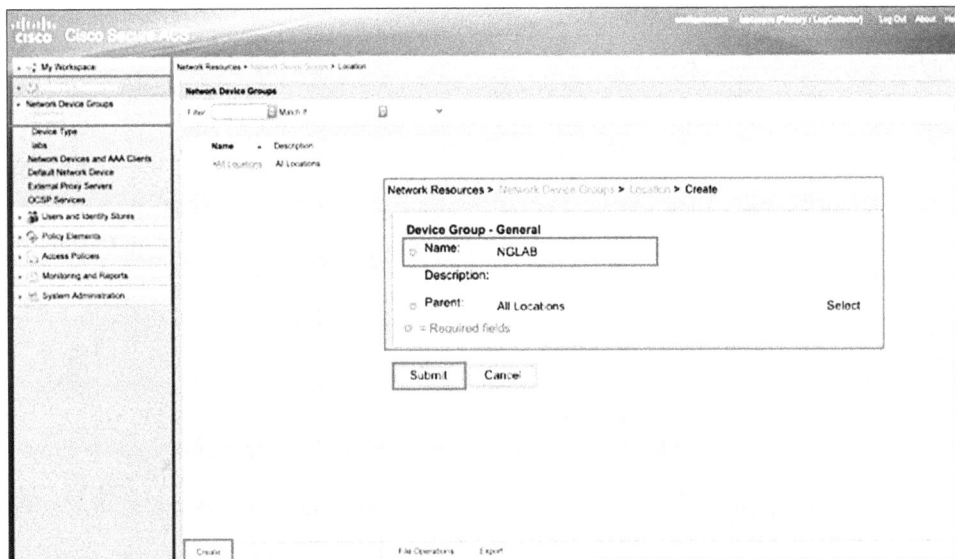

Figure 10-28   *Creating Network Device Groups Location in Cisco Secure ACS*

Step 2. For network device type configuration, navigate to Network Resources > Network Device Groups > Device Type and click Create. Type the name of the device type (in this case ACI Fabric) and click Submit. Figure 10-29 illustrates this process.

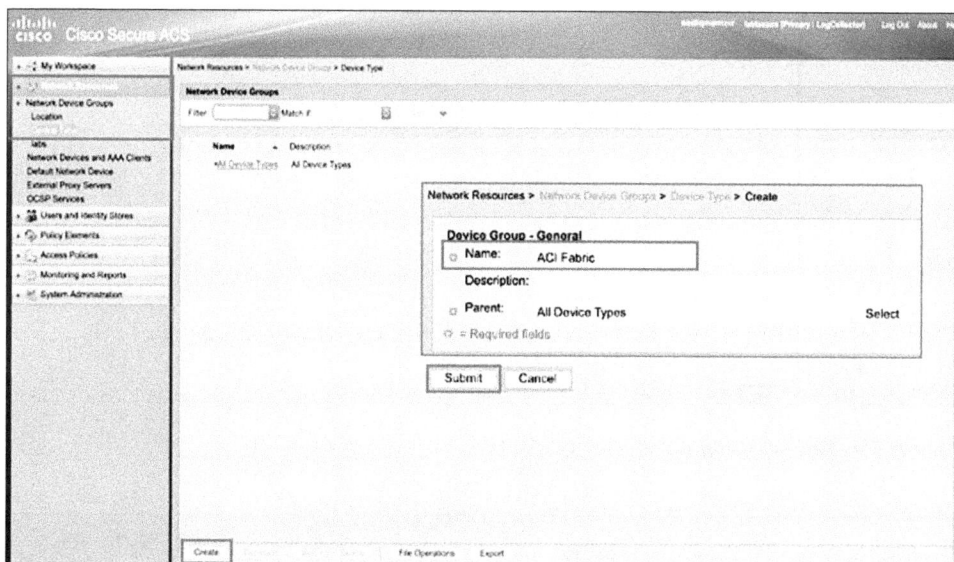

Figure 10-29 *Creating Network Device Type in Cisco Secure ACS*

Step 3. Configure the ACI fabric infrastructure devices (APICs, leafs, and spines) on the Cisco Secure ACS server. Navigate to Network Resources > Network Device Groups > Network Devices and AAA Clients and click Create. Figure 10-30 illustrates this process.

Step 4. As shown in Figure 10-31, enter **DC1-ACI-FAB1** as the client name and enter the description **ACI Fabric in DC1**. For the already created Location and Device Type, click Select. Choose the IP Range(s) radio button and type the Management IP addresses of all ACI fabric devices in the Add tab. (Note that management IP addresses can be either OOB or INB, depending on the management EPG you use while configuring TACACS+ in ACI, as discussed later in this chapter.) Expand TACACS+ under Authentication Options and type in **cisco123** as the shared secret key. This is the same shared secret key that you will use later in this chapter, when you configure TACACS+ in ACI. Click Submit. All the input values are shown as an example. You can use your own values based on your environment.

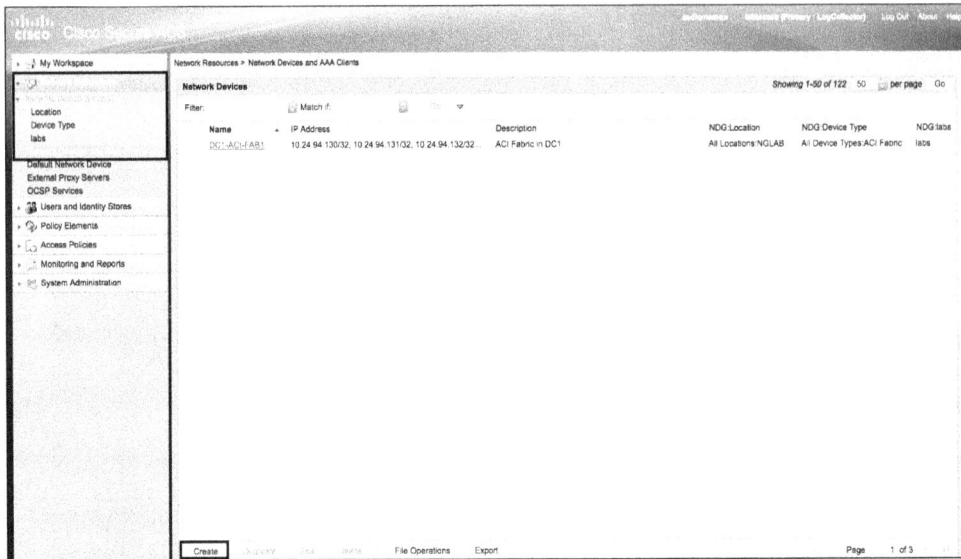

Figure 10-30   *Creating Network Devices in Cisco Secure ACS*

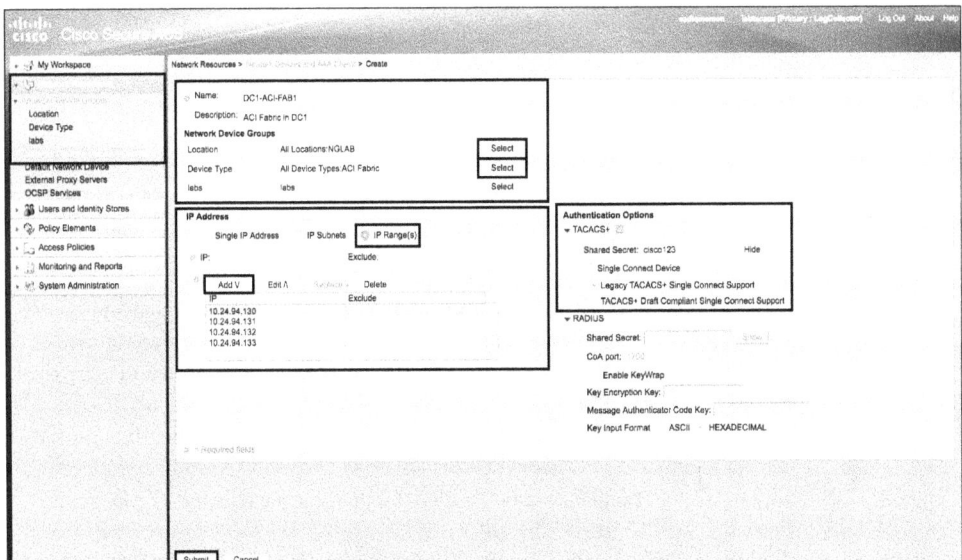

Figure 10-31   *Configuring the Network Device Group in Cisco Secure ACS*

Step 5.   Now you need to configure Cisco Secure ACS users and identity groups. Navigate to Users and Identity Stores > Identity Groups and click Create. Specify the name of an identity group and click Submit. Create at least the identity groups ACI-Admins and ACI-Read-Only for this example. Figure 10-32 shows the configuration for ACI-Admins.

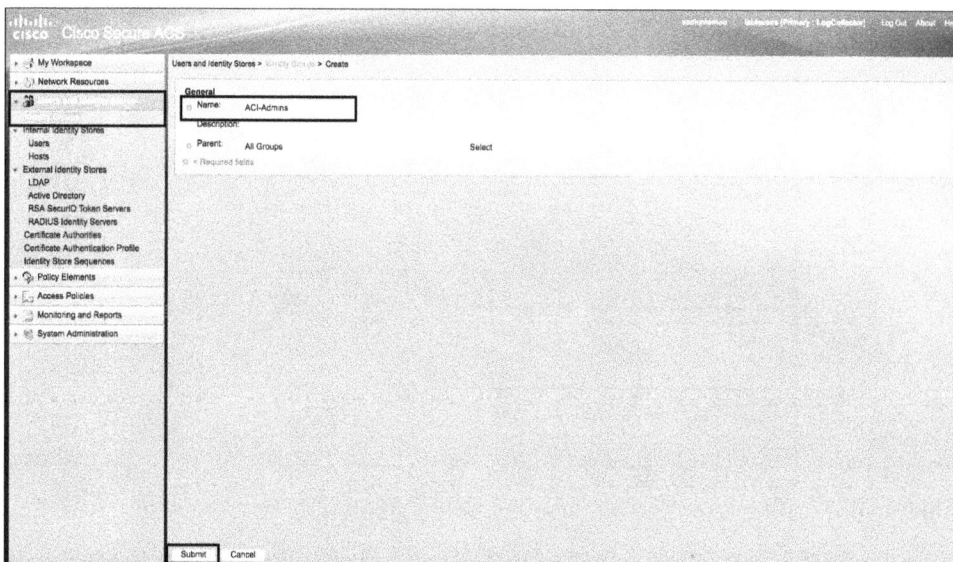

Figure 10-32   *Creating Identity Groups in Cisco Secure ACS*

Step 6.   Configure external users that will be used to access the ACI fabric infrastructure; these can be internal Cisco ACS users or external users, such as from Microsoft Active Directory. To do so, navigate to Users and Identity Stores > Internal Identity Stores > Users. Create admin user aci-rw as an example here, map this user to the identity group ACI-Admins created in the previous step, and configure a password. Similarly, create another user called aci-ro as an example with read-only privileges, map this user to the identity group ACI-Read-Only created in the previous step, and configure a password. Click Submit. Figure 10-33 illustrates the configuration steps for user aci-rw.

Note   Cisco Secure ACS can be integrated to external Identity Store such as LDAP; in that case, local users are not required to be created.

Step 7.   Create the policy elements. This is where you define the Cisco AV pair to specify the APIC required role-based access control (RBAC) roles and privileges for different users.

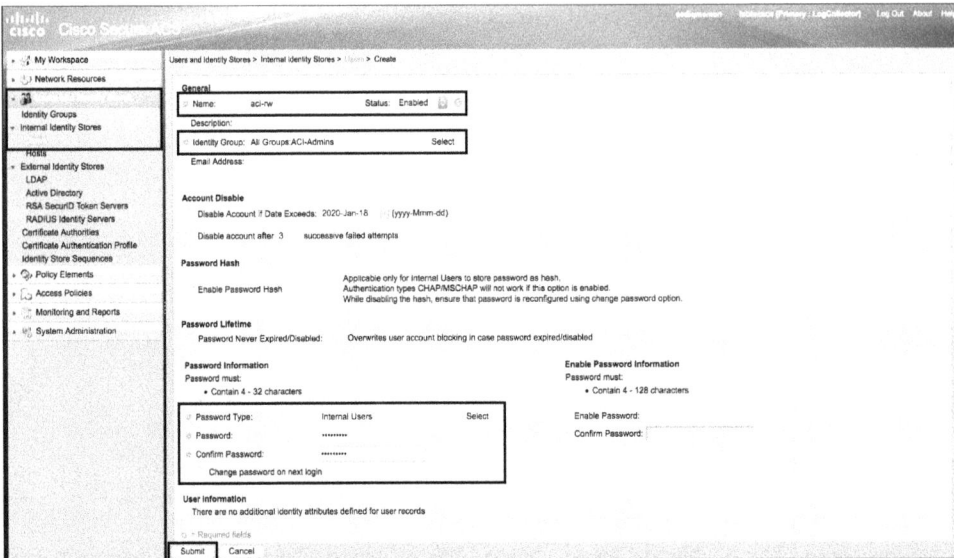

Figure 10-33   *Creating Users with Passwords and Mapping Them to Identity Groups*

You configure the AV pair in the following format:

```
shell:domains = domainA/writeRole1|writeRole2|writeRole3/
readRole1|readRole2,

domainB/writeRole1|writeRole2|writeRole3/readRole1|readRole2
```

The following are some examples of the AV pair strings for different types of user access:

Users with admin access to the entire fabric:

```
shell:domains = all/admin
```

Users with read-only access to the entire fabric:

```
shell:domains = all//admin
```

Users with admin access to tenants under the security domain cisco and read-only access to the rest of the tenants:

```
shell:domains = cisco/admin/,all//admin
```

Note   Starting with ACI Release 3.1(x), the AV pair shell:domains=all//admin allows you to assign read-only privileges to users and provide them access to the switches via the CLI.

Step 8.   Navigate to Policy Elements > Authorization and Permissions > Device Administration > Shell Profiles and click Create. Name the new shell profile aci-rw, as shown in Figure 10-34.

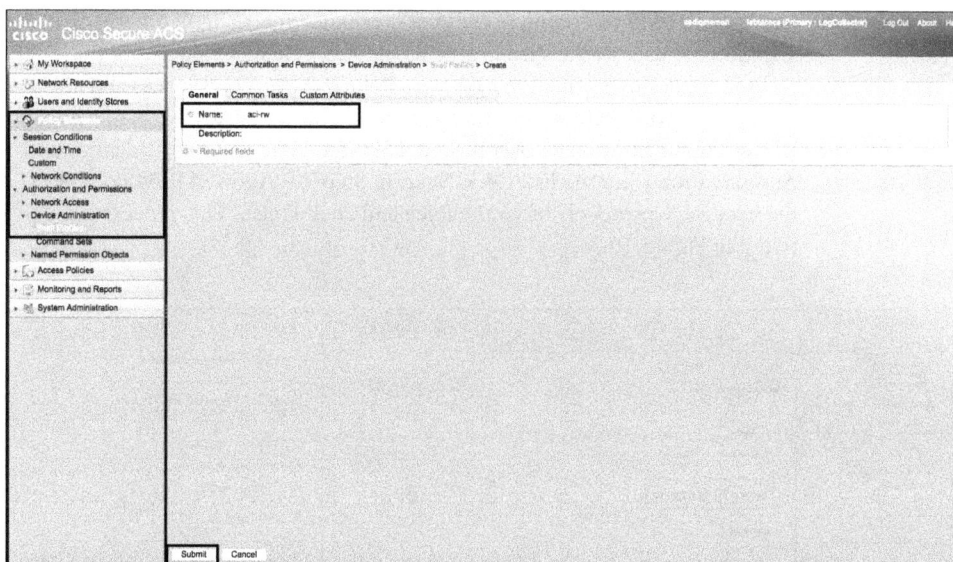

Figure 10-34   *Creating a Shell Profile*

Step 9.   Navigate to the Custom Attributes tab, add the AV pair string, and click Submit. Figure 10-35 illustrates this process. You can use the same procedure to create another shell profile for read-only access using AV pair shell:domains=all//admin in the Custom Attributes tab.

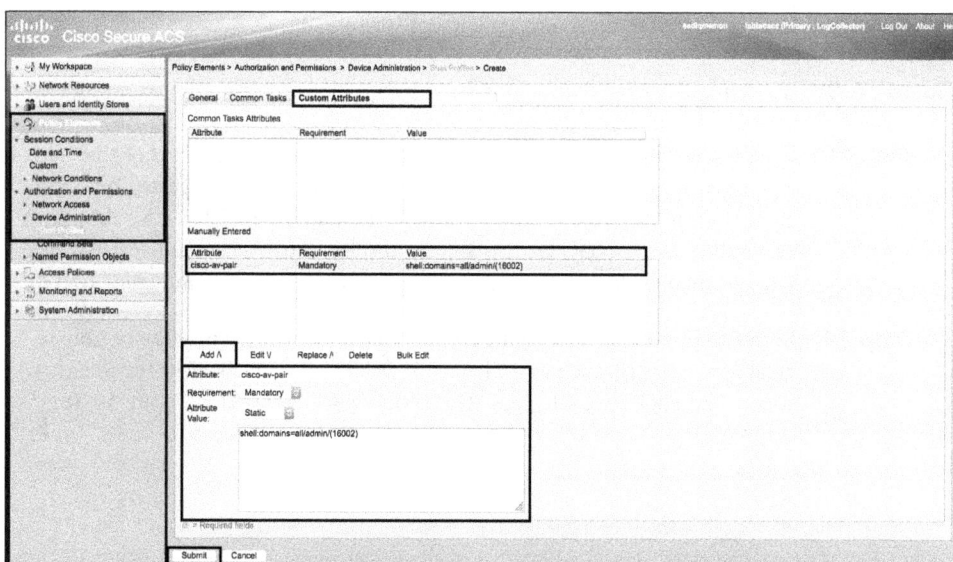

Figure 10-35   *Adding an AV Pair String in the Custom Attributes Tab*

Step 10. Finally, you need to configure the access policies and tie it all together by mapping the user to the shell profile to the AAA clients. First create the access services by navigating to Access Policies > Access Services and click Create. In Step 1 – General, type the name (in this case ACI Access). Choose Device Administration as User Selected Service Type and select Identity and Authorization from the list. Click Next. In Step 2 – Allowed Protocols, elect the necessary protocols of your choice and click Finish. This process is illustrated in Figure 10-36.

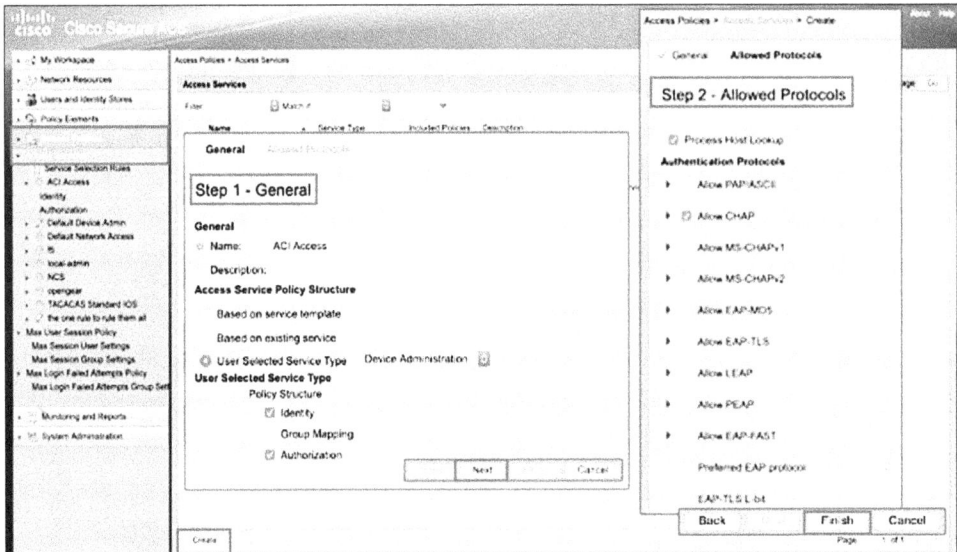

Figure 10-36   *Creating Access Services in Cisco ACS*

Step 11. In this step, you need to configure the Service Selection Rules. For that, navigate to Access Policies > Service Selection Rules and click Create. Type the name (in this case ACI). Select Protocol and match it to TACACS. Choose ACI Fabric as the NDG Device Type and select ACI Access as Service. Click OK and then click Save Changes. This process is illustrated in Figure 10-37.

Step 12. In this step, you need to configure Identity under the access service you created in Step 10, such as ACI Access. Select Internal Users as the Identity source and click Save Changes. This process is illustrated in Figure 10-38.

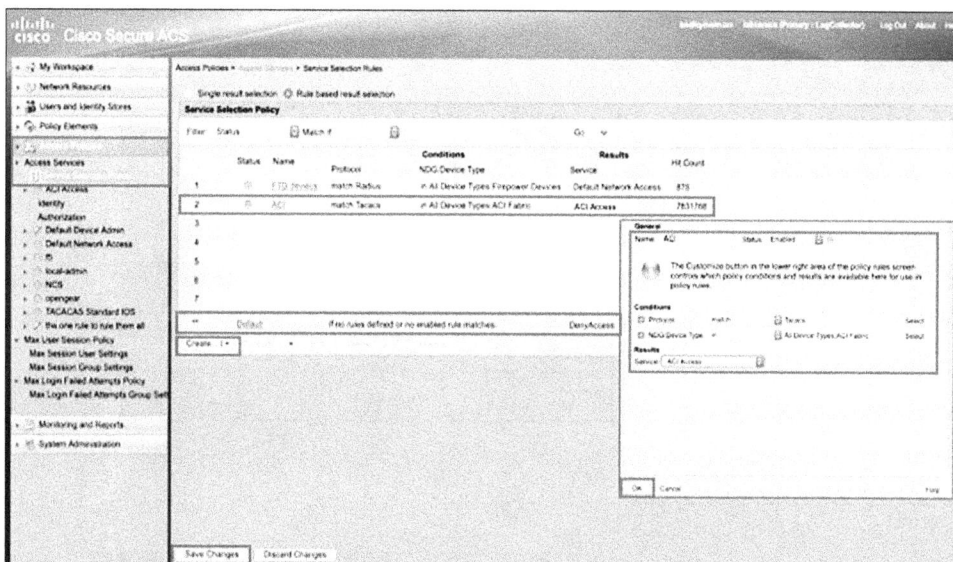

Figure 10-37   *Creating Service Selection Rules in Cisco ACS*

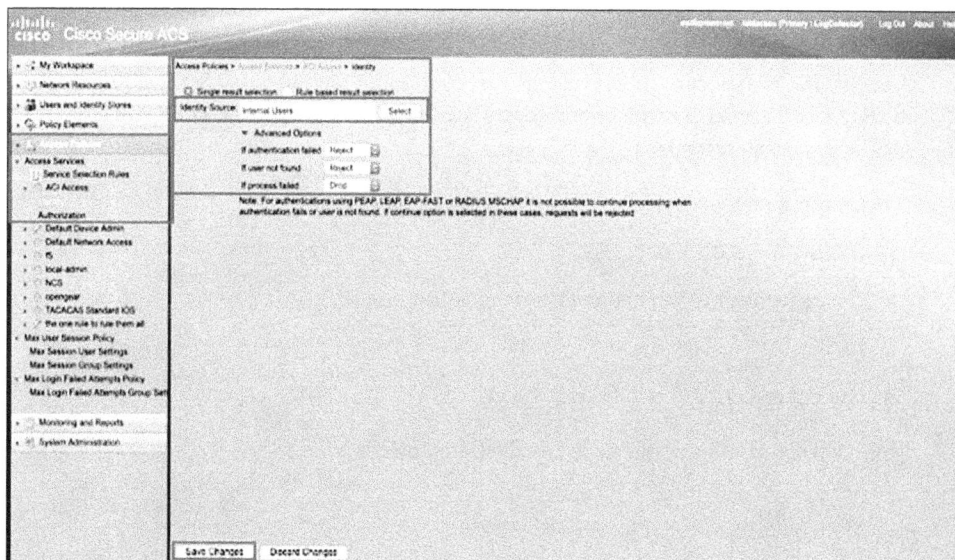

Figure 10-38   *Configure Identity in Cisco ACS*

Step 13.   In the final step, you need to configure the device administration authorization policy. Navigate to Access Policies > ACI Access > Authorization. Create a new rule that maps the identity group, device type, location, and shell profile, as shown in Figure 10-39. Click OK and Save Changes.

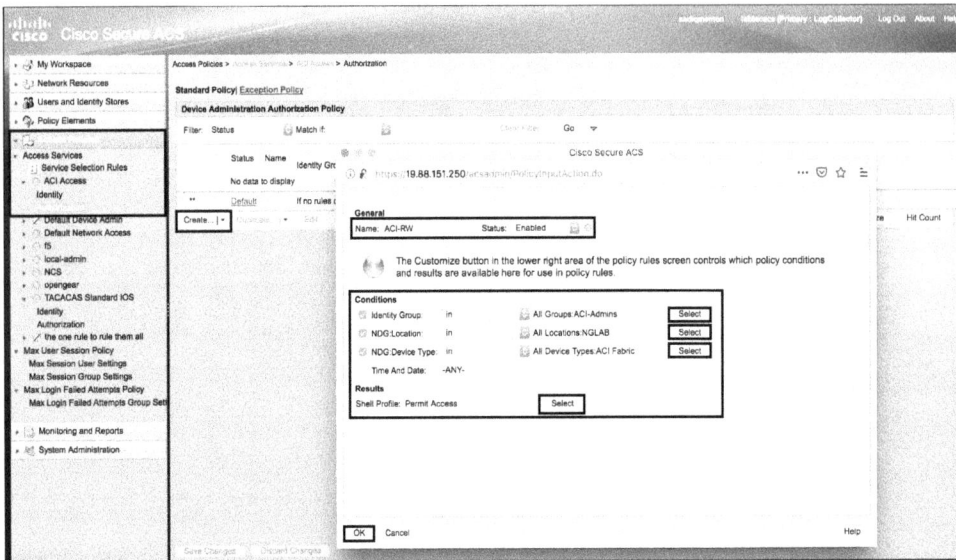

Figure 10-39 *Creating an Access Policy and Authorization*

Configuring Cisco ISE

Aside from Cisco Secure ACS, you can also configure Cisco Identity Service Engine (ISE) as an external access control system for the ACI fabric infrastructure. Following are the high-level configuration steps on ISE:

■ Configure network device group location and type.

■ Configure network devices.

■ Create identity group and configure identities in ISE.

■ Create TACACS profile with AV pair.

■ Configure TACACS admin policy set.

More detailed configuration steps are illustrated below.

Note   These configuration steps are for ISE version 2.x.

Step 1.   You first need to create the Network Device Groups Location and Device Types to group all your ACI fabric infrastructure acting as TACACS+ clients. To configure the network device groups location, navigate to Administration > Network Resources > Network Device Groups > Groups > All Locations and click Add. Type the name of the location (in this case, NGLAB) and click Submit. For Network Device type configuration, browse through

Administration > Network Resources > Network Device Groups > Groups > All Device Types and click Add. Type the name of the device type (in this case, ACI Fabric) and click Submit. Figure 10-40 illustrates the process.

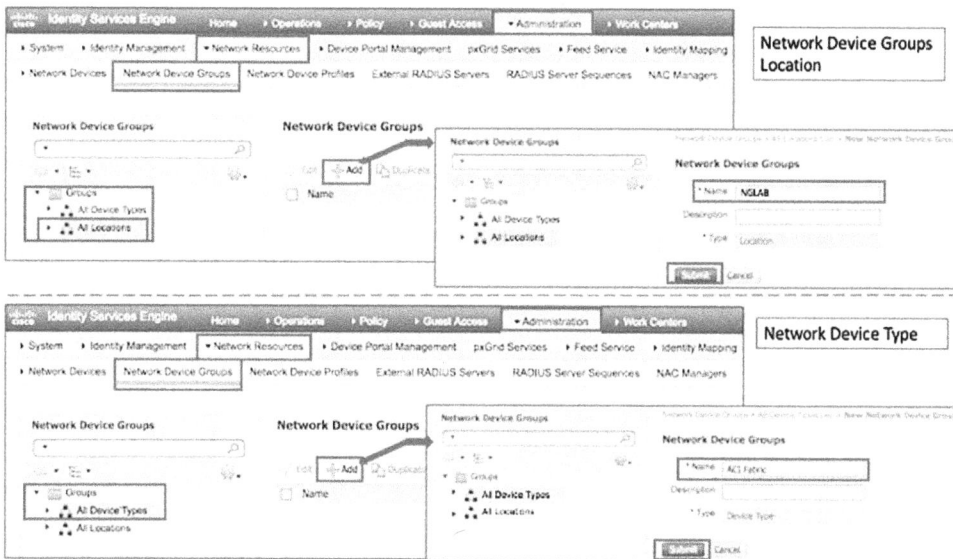

Figure 10-40   *Configuring Network Device Groups Location and Device Type in ISE*

Step 2.   Create your Network Devices where you will define ACI infrastructure for access control through TACACS+. To do this task, navigate to the following ISE web GUI path as Administration > Network Resources > Network Devices and click Add. From here, you can go ahead and assign a name to your Network Device, assign the Location and Device Type, enable TACACS+ authentication using the same Shared Secret as what you will assign in ACI AAA configuration, and assign the IP addresses of the APICs and fabric switches. In this example, the IP address of APIC1, which is 10.24.94.130, is demonstrated in Figure 10-41.

Step 3.   In this step, you will create an Identity Group to organize local users (called Identities in ISE). To create the Identity Group, navigate to Work Centers > Device Administration > User Identity Groups > User Identity Group and click Add. Type the name of the Identity Group. You can create at the minimum two groups—namely, ACI Admin and ACI Read-only groups are created. Now, create a local user such as aci-rw and assign it to the ACI Admin group. Similarly, for read-only access you can create another local user as aci-ro and assign it to the ACI Read-only group. For learning purposes, only aci-rw account is shown in Figure 10-42.

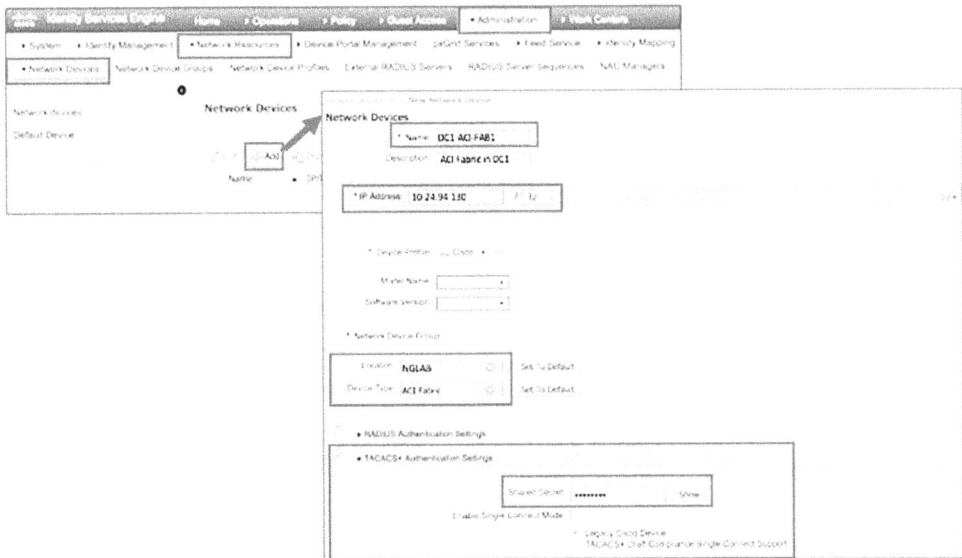

Figure 10-41 *Configuring Network Device in ISE*

Note   Cisco ISE can be integrated to an external Identity Store such as LDAP; in that case, local users are not required to be created.

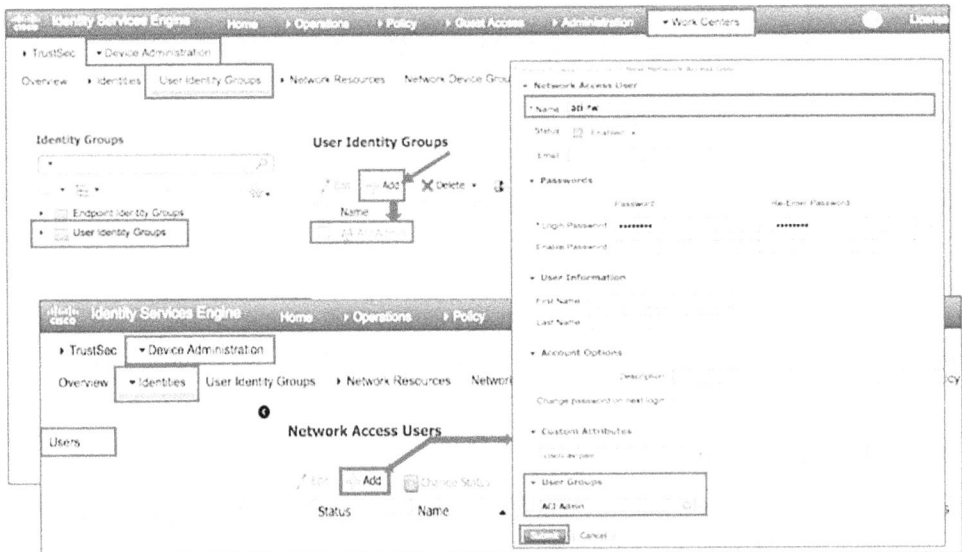

Figure 10-42 *Configuring Identity Group and Identities in ISE*

Step 4. Now create the TACACS Profiles containing the AV pair. The AV pair syntax for the ACI infrastructure is explained in detail in the earlier section "Configuring Cisco Secure ACS." To configure TACACS Profiles, navigate to the following ISE web GUI path as Work Centers > Device Administration > Policy Results > TACACS Profiles, and click Add. Type the name (in this case, **Read-Write**) and configure custom attributes as shown in Figure 10-43. You can follow this procedure to create another TACACS Profile for Read-Only access.

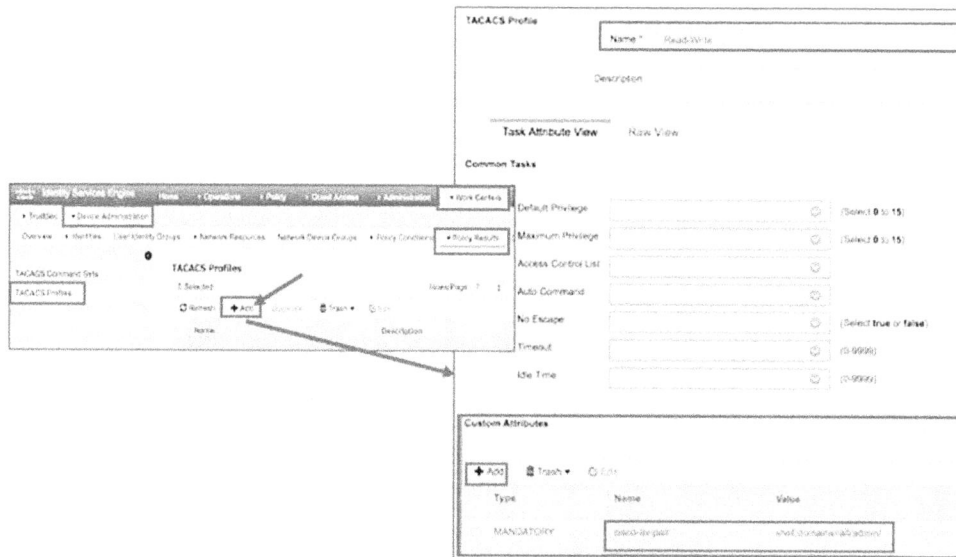

Figure 10-43 *Configuring TACACS Profiles with Custom Attributes in ISE*

Step 5. You now need to create a Device Admin Policy Set to gel together all the ISE policies. To create the Device Admin Policy Set, navigate to Work Centers > Device Administration > Device Admin Policy Sets and click the + sign to create a policy above the existing Default policy. Type the name of the policy set and click Create New Condition to set up access control conditions based on the policies shown in Figure 10-44.

Step 6. The next step in creating the device admin policy set is to define the Authentication Policy. You can select the Default Rule and apply the Allowed Protocols and Identity Source configurations. From the Allowed Protocols list, click Create a new Allowed Protocol, type the name, and choose the authentication protocol of your choice, as shown in Figure 10-45. This should match with ACI AAA configuration authentication protocol selection.

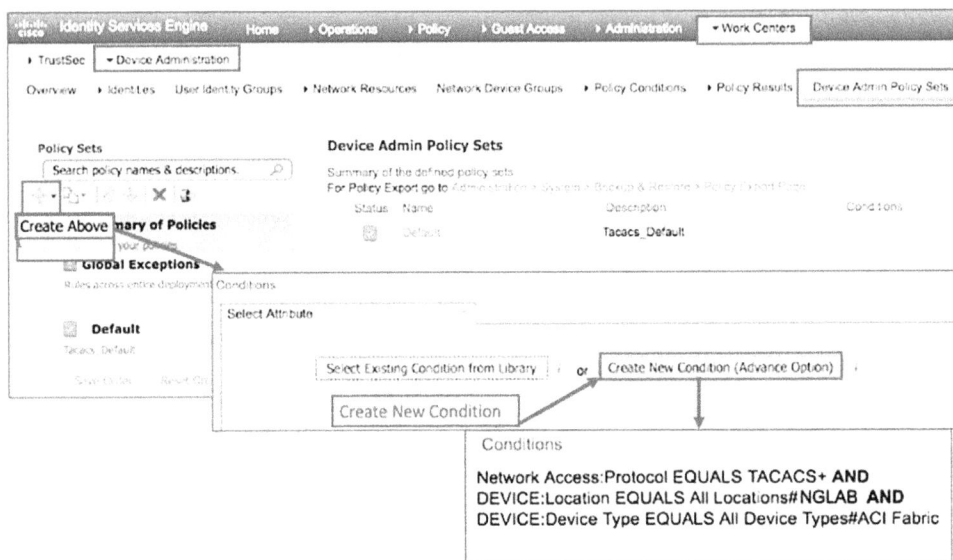

Figure 10-44   *Configuring Device Admin Policy Set with New Condition in ISE*

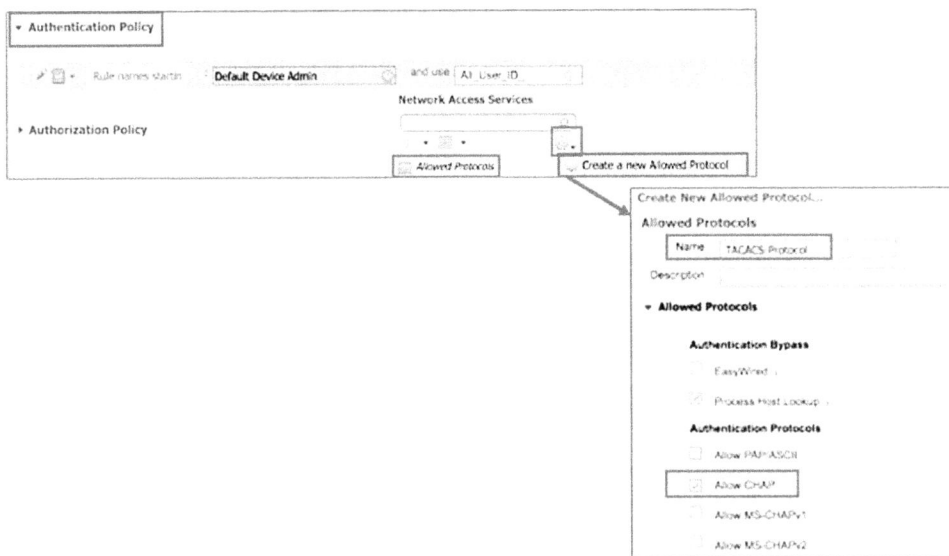

Figure 10-45   *Configuring Authentication Policy for Device Admin Policy Set*

Step 7.   Finally, in creating a device admin policy set, you now need to define the
Authorization Policy. For that you will need to create a new rule, which
you should place above the Default rule. Specify the Name, Identity Group,
and Shell Profile. For example, since you have already created two Identity

Groups, namely ACI Admin and ACI Read-Only, you should assign the correct Shell Profiles to each group, such as Read-Write and Read-Only. This process is illustrated in Figure 10-46.

In Figure 10-46, you can see that ACI-TACACS-Pol-Set is created with Default Authentication Policy Rule using TACACS-Protocol and Internal Users as external Identity Store along with Authorization Policy rules, ACI-Admins and ACI-Read-Only with respective shell profiles.

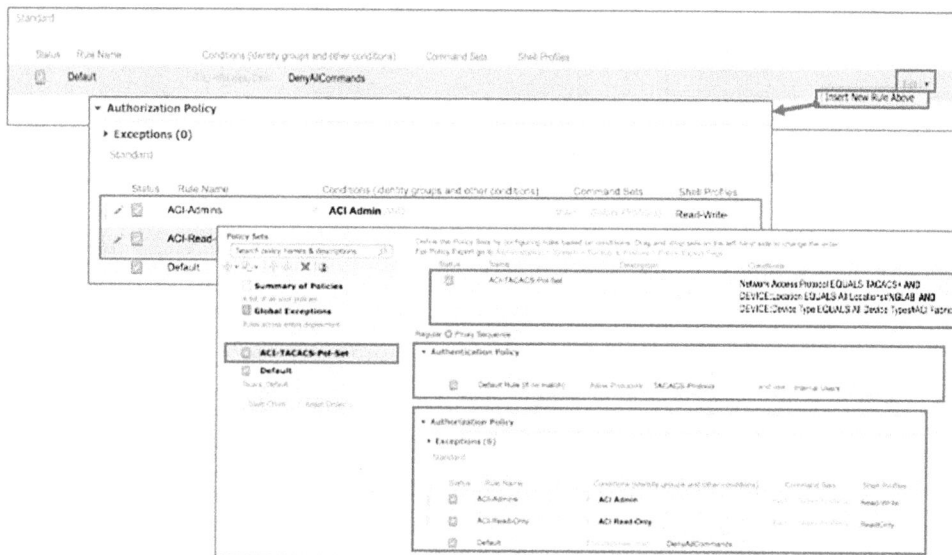

Figure 10-46   *Configuring Authorization Policy for Device Admin Policy Set*

Configuring AAA in ACI

Now that you have finished configuring a portion of the Cisco Secure ACS or Cisco ISE to provide secure access control to the ACI fabric infrastructure, it's time to start configuring AAA in ACI. To configure AAA in ACI, you need to perform the following steps:

Step 1.   Navigate to Admin > AAA > TACACS+ Management and right-click TACACS+ Providers. Specify the ACS server hostname (and ensure that DNS is set up in your fabric if you are using hostname) or IP address, the port (the default is TCP port 49), the authorization protocol (in this case CHAP, and it should match in the ACS/ISE configuration), the shared secret key (which should match the shared secret key configured on the ACS server shown earlier in this section), and the management EPG (INB or OOB). Figure 10-47 illustrates this process.

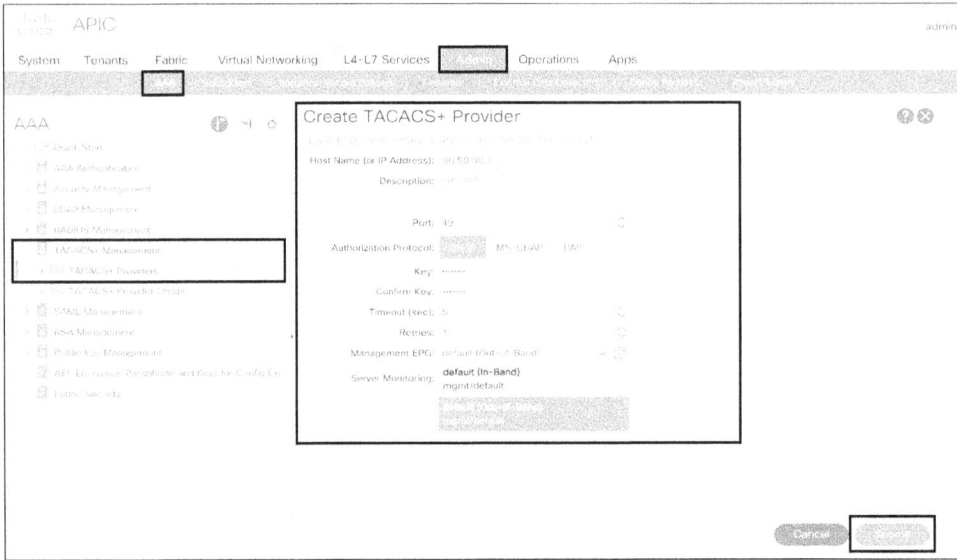

Figure 10-47   *Creating a TACACS+ Provider*

Step 2.   To create the TACACS+ provider group and map to the TACACS+ provider created in the previous step, navigate to Admin > AAA > the TACACS+ Management and right-click TACACS+ Provider Groups. Specify the name of the TACACS+ provider group and associate it with a previously created TACACS+ provider, as shown in Figure 10-48.

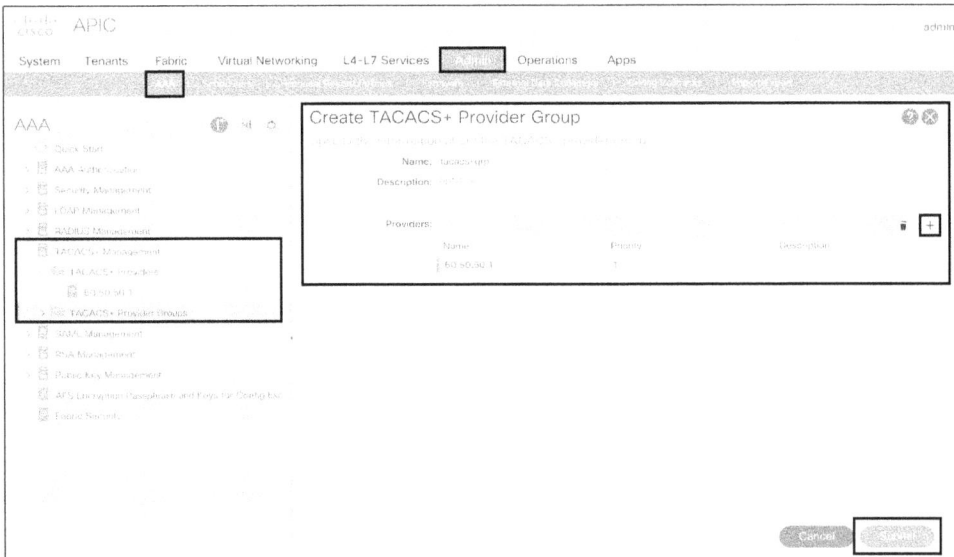

Figure 10-48   *Creating a TACACS+ Provider Group*

Step 3. To create the login domain and map to the TACACS+ provider group, navigate to Admin > AAA > AAA Authentication and right-click Login Domains. Specify the name of the login domain, select TACACS+ for the realm, and associate a previously created TACACS+ provider group, as shown in Figure 10-49.

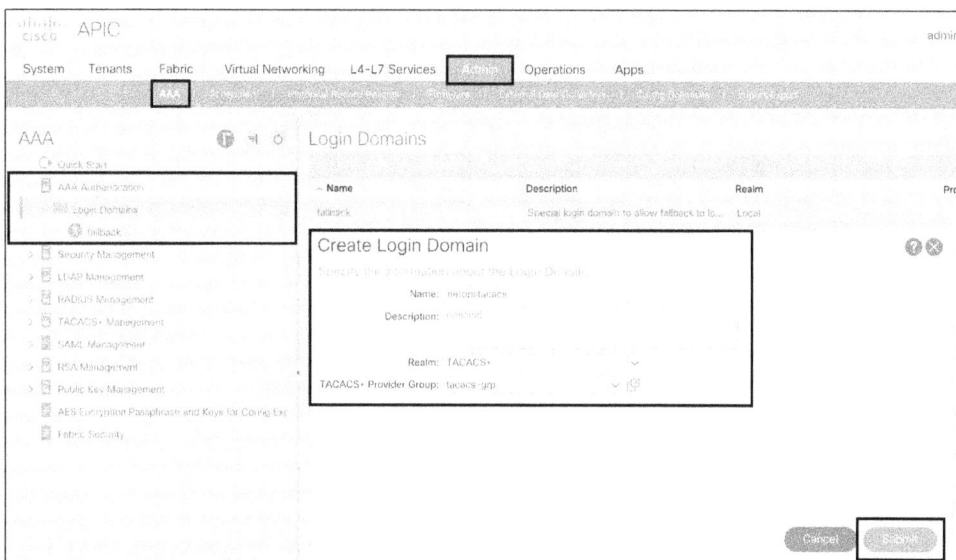

Figure 10-49 *Creating a Login Domain*

Note A fallback login domain is already created by default. This is the local domain for allowing local authentication in case you are locked out of your fabric if the default authentication settings are changed or misconfigured somehow.

Step 4. To change the default authentication method to TACACS+, click AAA Authentication in the navigation pane, select TACACS+ as the realm, and select the TACACS+ provider group, as shown in Figure 10-50.

Note Make sure Fallback Check is set to false under Default Authentication; otherwise, you will not be able to recover with local login credentials.

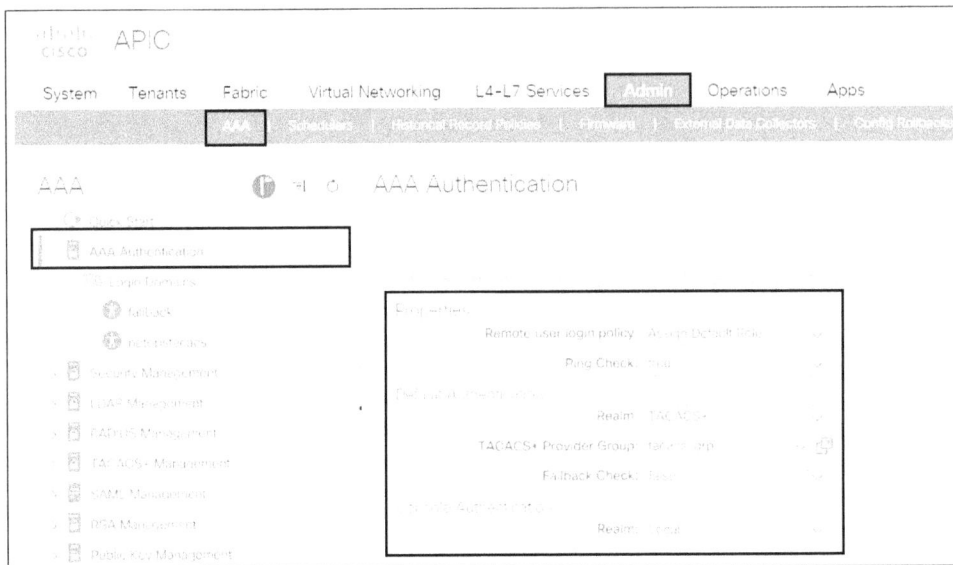

Figure 10-50 *Changing the Default Authentication Method to TACACS+*

Recovering with the Local Fallback User

In the event that connectivity to the TACACS+ server is lost and you are locked out of your fabric, you can use the local admin fallback user. To log in to ACI fabric as a local fallback user, you can use either of the following:

■ **From the GUI:** Use apic:fallback\\admin.

■ **From CLI:** Use ssh apic#fallback\\admin.

Verifying the AAA Configuration

You need to do a couple of checks to make sure your AAA configuration is correct. Follow these steps:

Step 1.   Make sure you can ping the TACACS+ server from both the APIC and the fabric nodes. Success with these pings can rule out any network issues.

Step 2.   Check to see if the configuration has been correctly pushed to the APICs and fabric nodes, as shown in Example 10-6.

Step 3.   Check the Nginx logs and search for the TACACS+ provider IP address to confirm reachability (see Example 10-7). These logs can sometimes give you clues about why TACACS connectivity is not working.

Example 10-6 *Verifying AAA Configuration*

```
apic1# show tacacs-server
timeout : 5
retries : 1


Total number of servers: 1


Hostname : 50.50.50.1
Port : 49
Protocol : chap
Timeout : 10
Retries : 1


Leaf101# show tacacs-server groups
total number of groups:1
following TACACS+ server groups are configured:
        group tacacs-grp:
                server: 50.50.50.1 on port 49
                deadtime is 0


Leaf101# show aaa authentication
        default: group tacacs-grp
        console: local
```

Example 10-7 *Verifying TACACS+ Server Reachability Through Nginx Logs*

```
leaf101# grep 50.50.50.1 /var/log/dme/log/nginx.log | less
34703||19-11-10 10:40:33.239+08:00||aaa||DBG4||||Received response from 50.50.50.1 -
  notifying callback handler (IPv4)||../dme/svc/extXMLApi/src/gen/ifc/app/./ping/
  lib_ifc_ping.cc||757
34703||19-11-10 11:29:23.239+08:00||aaa||DBG4||||Received update on status of
  50.50.50.1 (DN uni/userext/tacacsext/tacacsplusprovider-50.50.50.1) - status is
  \ ALIVE||../dme/svc/extXMLApi/src/gen/ifc/app/./pam/PamWorker.cc||1448
```

Syslog

As explained in detail in Chapter 9, syslog is a network monitoring protocol that has been used in the industry for quite some time. It runs on UDP port 514. During failures, ACI generates faults and events that get stored as system logs on an APIC or that can be sent out to a centralized syslog server, preferably connected outside the ACI fabric. Besides faults and events, an APIC can also send audit and session logs to an external syslog server.

In order to configure syslog in ACI, you need to follow these steps:

Step 1.   Create an external data collector as a syslog destination.

Step 2.   Create a syslog source at the access level, fabric level, or tenant level and associate the syslog source with a destination.

To create a syslog external data collector, from the APIC GUI, you need to go to Admin > External Data Collectors > Monitoring Destinations, right-click Syslog, and select Create Syslog Monitoring Destination Group, as shown in Figure 10-51.

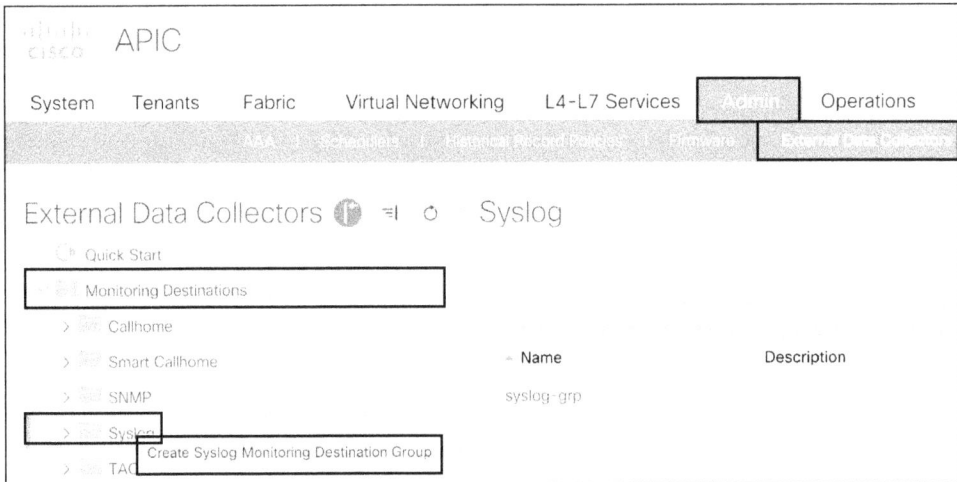

Figure 10-51   *Creating Syslog External Data Collectors*

You now need to follow this configuration process (see Figure 10-52). The input values are shown as an example.

Step 1.   Complete the profile:

  a. Type **syslog-gr**p as the object name.

  b. Type a description, if needed.

  c. Choose the syslog format to ACI.

  d. Set Admin State to enabled.

  e. Under Local File Destination, set Admin State to enabled and Severity to information.

  f. Under Console Destination, set Admin State to enabled and Severity to alerts.

  g. Click Next.

Step 2.   Specify the remote destinations:

a. Click the **+** sign to add a remote destination.

b. Type **30.30.30.1** as the IP address of the external syslog server.

c. Set Admin State to enabled.

d. Set Severity to information.

e. Set Port to 514.

f. Set Forwarding Facility to local7.

g. Set Management EPG to default (Out-of-Band).

h. Click OK and click Finish.

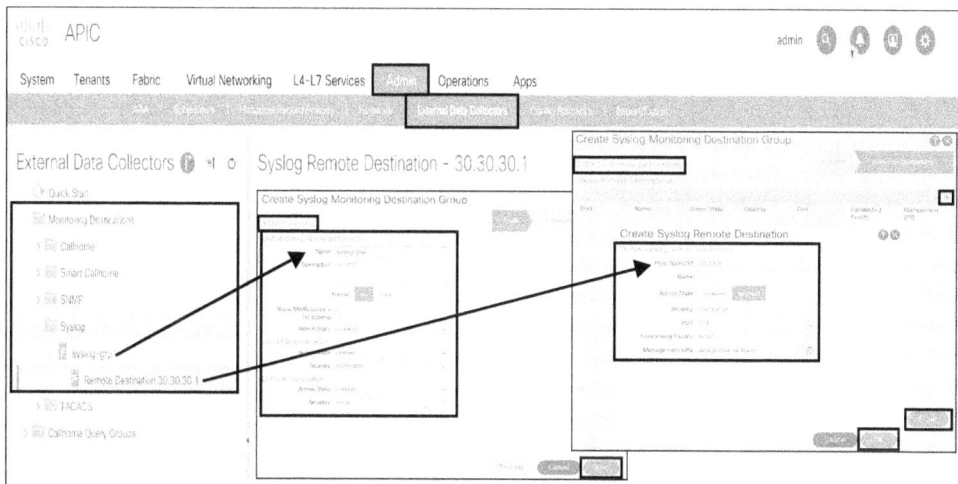

Figure 10-52   *Creating Syslog Monitoring Destination Servers*

After creating the syslog monitoring destination servers, you need to create the syslog sources. You can create syslog sources at three levels:

- Access level
- Fabric level
- Tenant level

Next we look at the syslog source configuration steps for each of these levels.

To create the syslog source policy at the access level, you need to go to Fabric > Access Policies > Policies > Monitoring > default > Callhome/Smart Callhome/SNMP/Syslog. On the right side of the screen, select Syslog and click the **+** sign. Enter **syslog-src** as the object name and include the logs shown in Figure 10-53. For Min Severity, select information. Associate syslog-src with syslog-grp.

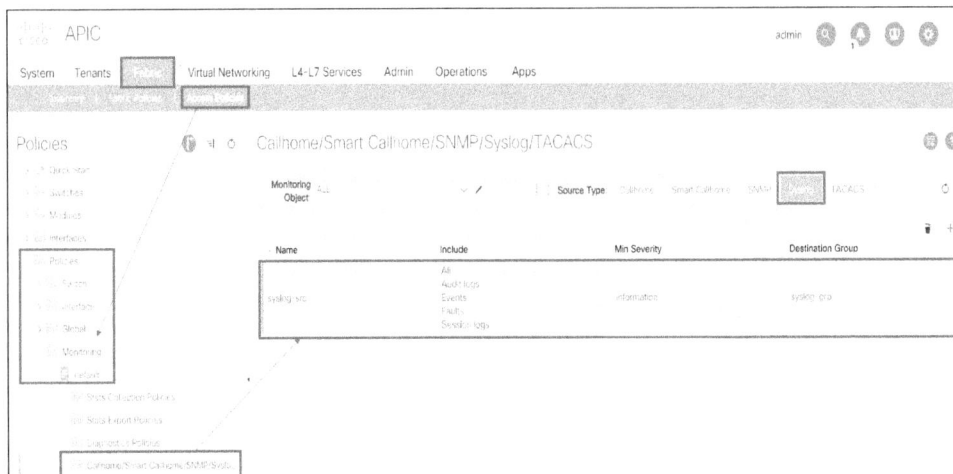

Figure 10-53   *Creating a Syslog Source at the Access Level*

To create a syslog source policy at the fabric level, you need to go to Fabric > Fabric Policies > Policies/Monitoring > default > Callhome/Smart Callhome/SNMP/Syslog. On the right side of the screen, select Syslog and click the + sign. Enter **syslog-src** as the object name and include the logs shown in Figure 10-54. For Min Severity, select information. Associate syslog-src with syslog-grp.

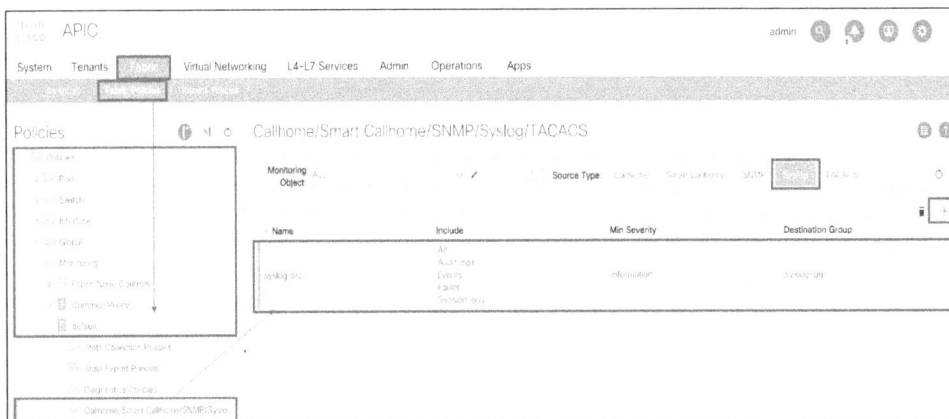

Figure 10-54   *Creating a Syslog Source at the Fabric Level*

To create a syslog source policy at the tenant level, you need to go to Tenants > t01 > Policies > Monitoring > default > Callhome/Smart Callhome/SNMP/Syslog. On the right side of the screen, select Syslog and click the + sign. Enter **syslog-src** as the object name and include the logs shown in Figure 10-55. For Min Severity, select information. Associate syslog-src with syslog-grp.

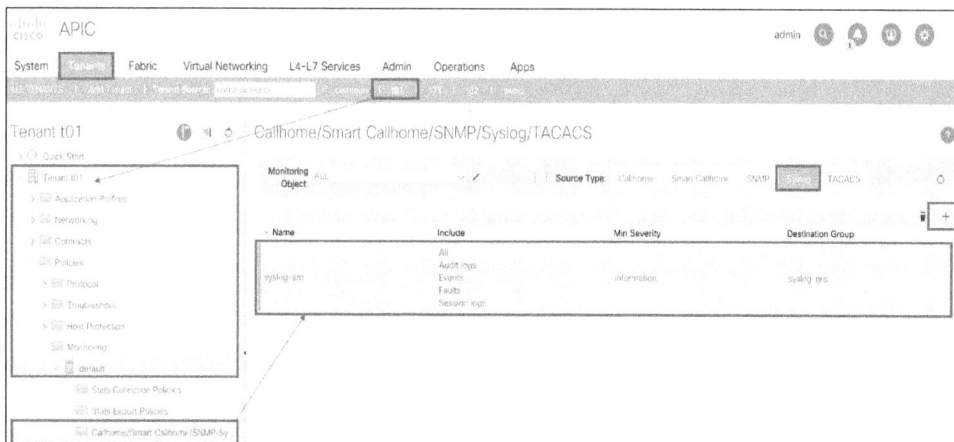

Figure 10-55 *Creating a Syslog Source at the Tenant Level*

ACI is a whitelist model in which traffic can only be forwarded when allowed by contracts. Management traffic can use either the OOB or the INB method to flow. Syslog traffic using OOB management does not require an explicit OOB contract on the APIC with UDP port 514. However, it is still a good practice to create a specific filter with UDP port 514 for syslog and add it to the filter list in your OOB contract subject configuration.

Syslog traffic using INB management requires an explicit INB contract on the APIC with UDP port 514. If this contract is not created, the syslog packets will be dropped by the border leaf, and the INB management L3Out will be used for management traffic.

Verifying the Syslog Configuration and Functionality

There are different ways to verify syslog configuration and functionality. The following examples show verification steps that should suffice for normal operation of your syslog configuration in ACI.

You can check the syslog configuration on the APIC as shown in Example 10-8.

Example 10-8 *Verifying Syslog Configuration on an APIC*

```
apic1# show running-config logging
# Command: show running-config logging
# Time: Sat Nov 16 17:59:14 2019
  logging server-group syslog-grp
    console
    server 100.100.100.1 severity warnings facility local7 mgmtepg oob port 514
    exit
```

Next, you can run the packet capture utility **tcpdump** on a leaf and capture only syslog traffic while shutting down a port (eth1/9 in this example on Leaf-201, which is part of an L3Out with OSPF peering to the external router) on the leaf via the APIC. You should see syslog generated by the leaf as soon as you shut down the port, as shown in Example 10-9.

Example 10-9   *Verifying Syslog Functionality Through tcpdump Utility on a Leaf*

```
Leaf-201# tcpdump -i eth0 -f port 514 -v

tcpdump: listening on eth0, link-type EN10MB (Ethernet), capture size 65535 bytes

19:16:56.022699 IP (tos 0x0, ttl 64, id 40817, offset 0, flags [none], proto UDP
  (17), length 274)
    Leaf-201.cisco.com.46672 > 100.100.100.1.syslog: SYSLOG, length: 246
      Facility local7 (23), Severity warning (4)
      Msg: Nov 16 19:16:56 Leaf-201 %LOG_LOCAL7-4-SYSTEM_MSG [F1385][deleted]
  [protocol-ospf-adjacency-down][warning][sys/ospf/inst-default/dom-mgmt:inb/if-
  [eth1/9]/adj-50.50.50.1/fault-F1385] OSPF adjacency is not full, current state
  Exchange\0x0a
^C
1 packets captured
1 packets received by filter
0 packets dropped by kernel
```

Note   In Example 10-9, the **tcpdump** utility is used with the interface filter **-i** knob and eth0, which represents the OOB management that you have used in your configuration to send all management traffic. If you want to use INB management to send out all management traffic, you use the interface filter **kpm_inb** with the **tcpdump** utility.

SNMP

Like syslog, SNMP is a network monitoring protocol that has been in the industry for quite some time. It uses UDP port 162 for sending out traps and UDP port 161 for read queries (walk, get, next, bulk) from a managed station. In Cisco ACI, much as in legacy networks, SNMP trap configuration is different from SNMP read query configuration. Therefore, you need to ensure that both are configured properly.

In order to configure SNMP trap configuration in ACI, you need to perform the following steps:

Step 1.   Create an external data collector as the SNMP trap destination.

Step 2.   Create an SNMP source at the access level, fabric level, or tenant level and associate the SNMP source with an SNMP trap destination.

To create an SNMP external data collector, you need to go to Admin > External Data Collectors > Monitoring Destinations, right-click SNMP, and select Create SNMP Monitoring Destination Group (see Figure 10-56).

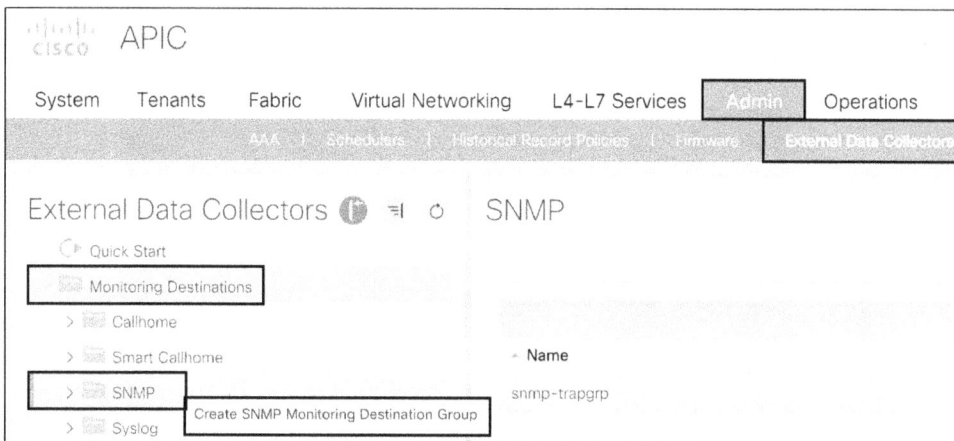

Figure 10-56   *Creating an SNMP External Data Collector*

As shown in Figure 10-57, you now need to follow this configuration process. The input values are shown as an example.

Step 1.   Complete the profile:

    a. Type **snmp-trpgrp** as the object name.

    b. Type a description, if needed.

    c. Click Next.

Step 2.   Specify the remote destinations:

    a. Click the **+** sign to add an SNMP trap destination.

    b. Type **10.10.10.1** as the IP address of the external SNMP management station receiving traps.

    c. Set Port to 162.

    d. Set Version to v2c.

    e. Set Community Name to auto-snmp.

    f. Set Management EPG to default (Out-of-Band).

    g. Click OK and click Finish.

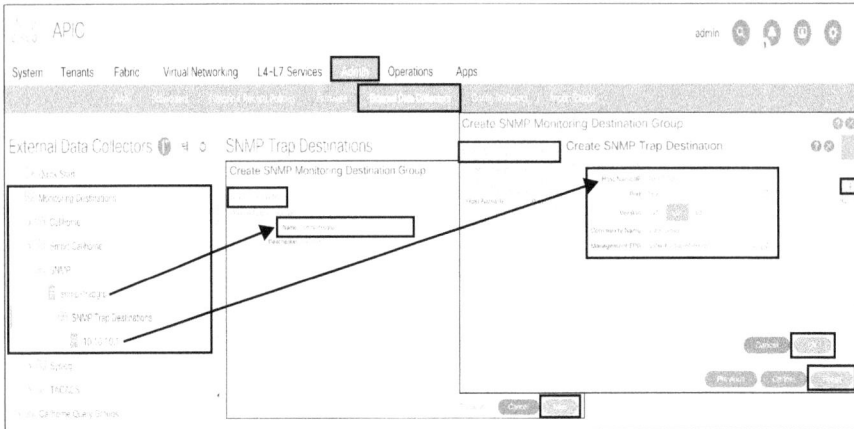

Figure 10-57   *Creating an SNMP Monitoring Destination*

After you create the SNMP monitoring destination servers, you need to create the SNMP trap sources. You can create SNMP trap sources at three levels:

- Access level
- Fabric level
- Tenant level

Next, we look at the SNMP trap configuration steps for each of these levels.

As shown in Figure 10-58, to create the SNMP trap source policy at the access level, you need to go to Fabric > Access Policies > Policies > Monitoring > default > Callhome/Smart Callhome/SNMP/Syslog. On the right side of the screen, select SNMP and click the + sign. Enter **snmp-src** as the object name. Associate snmp-src with snmp-trpgrp.

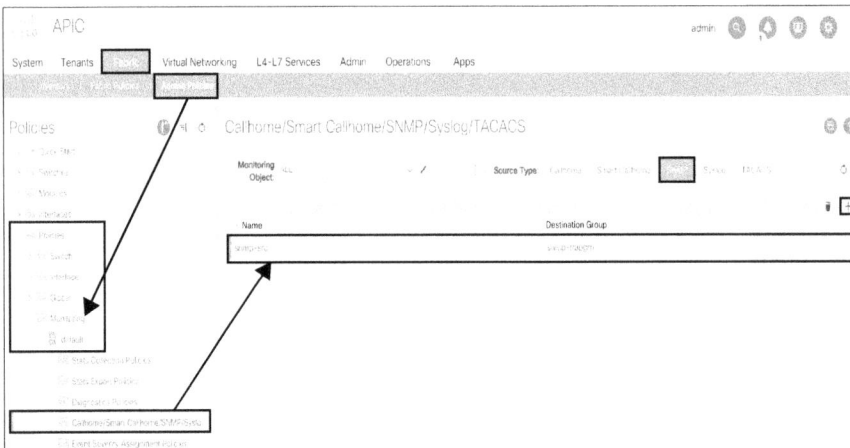

Figure 10-58   *Creating an SNMP Trap Source at the Access Level*

As shown in Figure 10-59, to create the SNMP trap source policy at the fabric level, you need to go to Fabric > Fabric Policies > Policies > Monitoring > default > Callhome/Smart Callhome/SNMP/Syslog. On the right side of the screen, select SNMP and click the + sign. Enter **snmp-src** as the object name. Associate snmp-src with snmp-trpgrp.

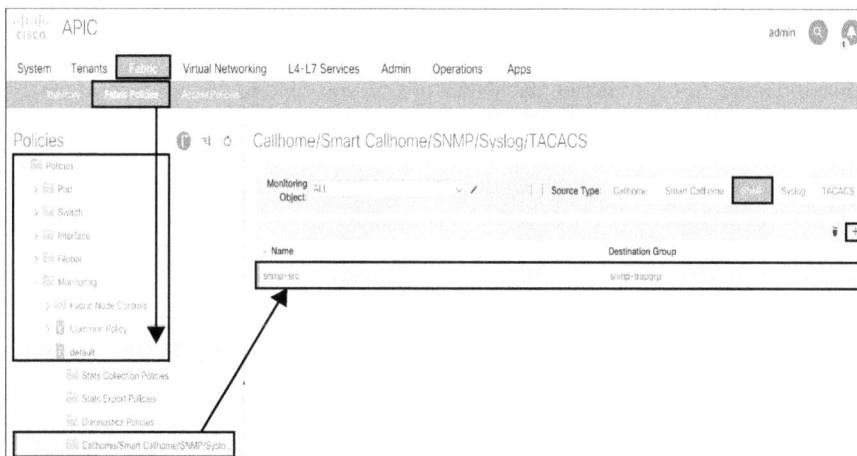

Figure 10-59 *Creating an SNMP Trap Source at the Fabric Level*

As shown in Figure 10-60, to create the SNMP trap source policy at the tenant level, you need to go to Tenants > t01 > Policies > Monitoring > default > Callhome/Smart Callhome/SNMP/Syslog. On the right side of the screen, select SNMP and click the + sign. Enter **snmp-src** as the object name. Associate snmp-src with snmp-trpgrp.

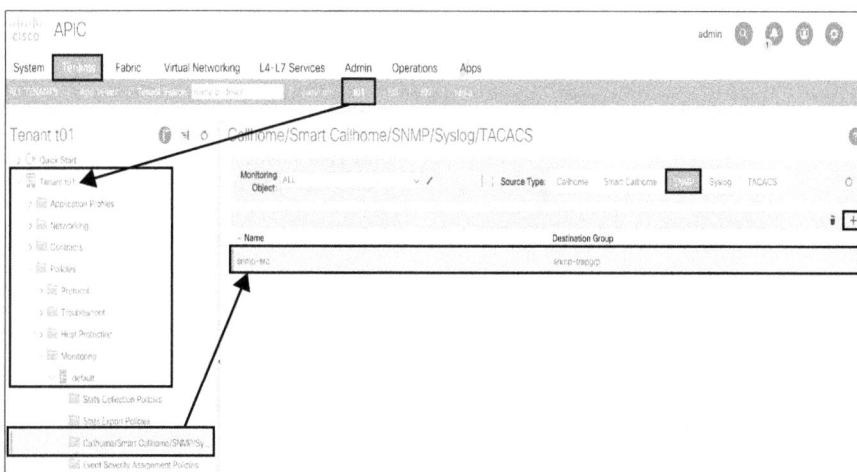

Figure 10-60 *Creating an SNMP Trap Source at the Tenant Level*

To do the SNMP read query configuration in ACI, you need to perform the following steps:

Step 1.   Define the SNMP policy.

Step 2.   Add an SNMP policy to the pod policy group.

Step 3.   Add the pod policy group to the pod profile.

As shown in Figure 10-61, to define the SNMP policy, you need to go to Fabric > Fabric Policies > Policies > Pod, right-click SNMP, and select Create SNMP Policy. On the right side of the screen, enter **snmp-policy** as the name of the object. Set Admin State to Enabled and enter contact and location information. Click the + sign to add client group policies. Add the IP addresses of the SNMP management stations for which you want to allow SNMP read queries against ACI fabric infrastructure. Finally, click the + sign to add community policies.

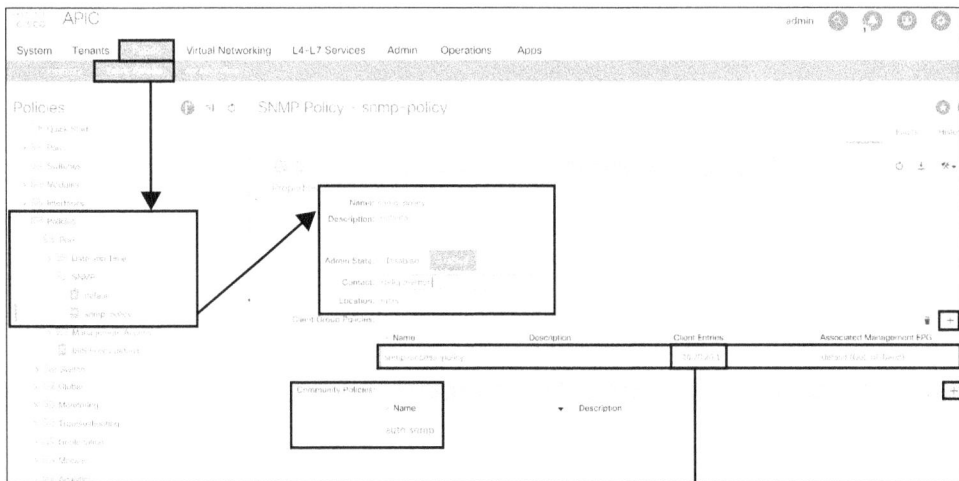

Only This Host Can Perform
Read Query to ACI Nodes

Figure 10-61   *Creating an SNMP Policy*

After you create the SNMP policy, the next step is to add this policy to the pod policy group. To do that, you need to go to Fabric > Fabric Policies > Pods and right-click Policy Groups to create a group with the name of your choice (in this case, pod-policy). On the right side of the screen, select the SNMP policy you created in the previous step and click Submit (see Figure 10-62).

Note   If your policy group is already created, you just need to click on that policy group and select SNMP Policy.

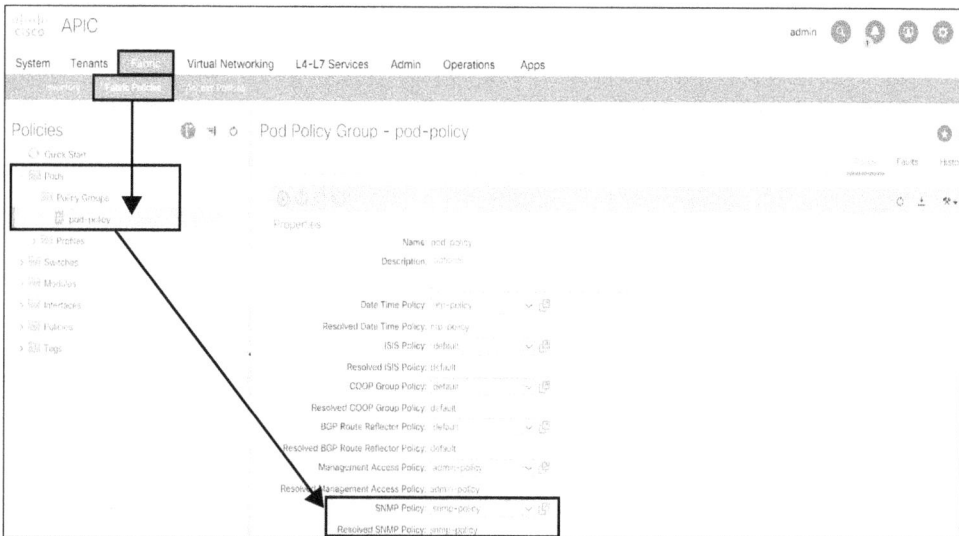

Figure 10-62 *Adding an SNMP Policy to the Pod Policy Group*

Finally, you need to add the pod policy group to a pod profile, as shown in Figure 10-63.

Note If you already added the pod policy group in the pod profile earlier, you do not need to execute this step.

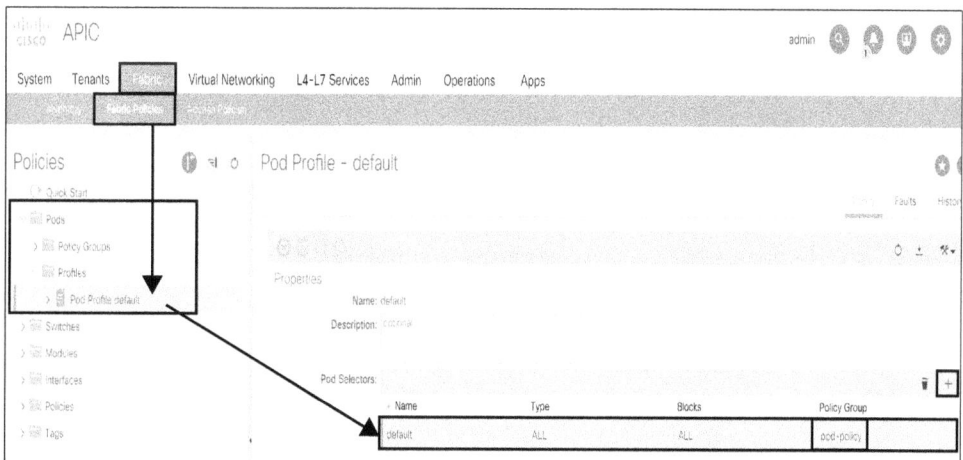

Figure 10-63 *Adding a Pod Policy Group to a POD Profile*

ACI is a whitelist model in which traffic can only be forwarded when allowed by contracts. Management traffic can use either the OOB or INB method to flow. SNMP traffic using OOB management does not require an explicit OOB contract on the APIC with UDP ports 161 (read queries) and 162 (traps). However, it is still a good practice to create a specific filter with UDP ports 161/162 for SNMP and add it to the filter list in your OOB contract subject configuration.

SNMP traffic using INB management requires an explicit INB contract on the APIC with UDP ports 161/162. If this contract is not created, the SNMP packets will be dropped by the border leaf, and the INB management L3Out will be used for management traffic.

Verifying the SNMP Configuration and Functionality

There are different ways to verify your SNMP configuration and functionality. The following examples show verification steps that should suffice for normal operation of your SNMP configuration in ACI.

You can check the SNMP configuration on the APIC as shown in Example 10-10.

Example 10-10 *Verifying SNMP Configuration on an APIC*

```
apic1# show snmp summary

Active Policy: snmp-policy, Admin State: enabled

Local SNMP engineID: [Hex] 0x800000098040e9b277fa3cec5a00000000


----------------------------------------
Community          Description
----------------------------------------
Public
Private


------------------------------------------------------------
User               Authentication      Privacy
------------------------------------------------------------


------------------------------------------------------------
Client-Group       Mgmt-Epg                 Clients
------------------------------------------------------------
snmp-access-policy  default (Out-Of-Band)    20.20.20.1


------------------------------------------------------------
Host               Port  Version  Level    SecName
------------------------------------------------------------
10.10.10.1         162   v2c      noauth    auto-snmp
```

Next, you need to verify that the configuration is pushed on one of the fabric nodes (APIC, leaf, or spine), as shown in Example 10-11.

Example 10-11 *Verifying SNMP Configuration on a Leaf/Spine*

```
Leaf-201# show snmp
sys contact: sadiq memon
sys location: mars


13 SNMP packets input
      0 Bad SNMP versions
      12 Unknown community name
      0 Illegal operation for community name supplied
      0 Encoding errors
      1 Number of requested variables
      0 Number of altered variables
      1 Get-request PDUs
      0 Get-next PDUs
      0 Set-request PDUs
      0 No such name PDU
      0 Bad value PDU
      0 Read Only PDU
      0 General errors
      0 Get Responses
      0 Unknown Context name
125 SNMP packets output
      124 Trap PDU
      0 Too big errors (Maximum packet size 0)
      0 No such name errors
      0 Bad values errors
      0 General errors
      0 Get Requests
      0 Get Next Requests
      0 Set Requests
      1 Get Responses
      0 Silent drops



Community             Group / Access       context    acl_filter
----------            --------------       -------     ----------
auto-snmp             network-admin


_____
                SNMP USERS
_____

User                          Auth  Priv(enforce) Groups
____                          ____  _____   _____
```

```
SNMP protocol : Enabled


-----------------------------------------------------------------
Context                         [Protocol instance, VRF, Topology,]
                                [vlan, MST]
-----------------------------------------------------------------



----------------------------------------------------------------------
Host                            Port Version  Level  Type   SecName
----------------------------------------------------------------------
10.10.10.1                      162  v2c       noauth trap   auto-snmp
Use VRF: management
```

Now that you have verified the configuration, it's time to verify the functionality of SNMP traps and read queries. Much as with syslog verification, you can run the packet capture utility **tcpdump** on a leaf and capture only SNMP trap traffic while shutting down a port (eth1/9 in this example on Leaf-201, which is part of an L3Out with OSPF peering to external router) on the leaf via the APIC. You should see the SNMP trap generated by the leaf as soon as you shut down the port, as shown in Example 10-12.

Note In Example 10-12, tcpdump -i eth0 sees the SNMP trap only if the trap destination is reachable over the OOB interface.

Example 10-12 *Verifying SNMP Trap Functionality Through the* tcpdump *Utility on a Leaf*

```
Leaf-201# tcpdump -i eth0 -f port 162 -v

tcpdump: listening on eth0, link-type EN10MB (Ethernet), capture size 65535 bytes

23:57:02.565989 IP (tos 0x0, ttl 64, id 35956, offset 0, flags [none], proto UDP
 (17), length 266)
   Leaf-201.cisco.com.46298 > 10.10.10.1.snmp-trap:  { SNMPv2c C=auto-snmp
 { V2Trap(218) R=116  system.sysUpTime.0=55950023 S:1.1.4.1.0=E:cisco.9.276.0.1
 interfaces.ifTable.ifEntry.ifIndex.436240384=436240384
 interfaces.ifTable.ifEntry.ifAdminStatus.436240384=2
 interfaces.ifTable.ifEntry.ifOperStatus.436240384=2 31.1.1.1.1.436240384=eth1/9
 interfaces.ifTable.ifEntry.ifType.436240384=6
 interfaces.ifTable.ifEntry.ifDescr.436240384=eth1/9 31.1.1.1.18.436240384= } }


23:57:02.666355 IP (tos 0x0, ttl 64, id 35980, offset 0, flags [none], proto UDP
 (17), length 194)
```

```
   Leaf-201.cisco.com.46298 > 10.10.10.1.snmp-trap:  { SNMPv2c C=auto-snmp
  { V2Trap(146) R=117  system.sysUpTime.0=55950033 S:1.1.4.1.0=S:1.1.5.3
  interfaces.ifTable.ifEntry.ifAdminStatus.436240384=2
  interfaces.ifTable.ifEntry.ifIndex.436240384=436240384
  interfaces.ifTable.ifEntry.ifOperStatus.436240384=2 S:1.1.4.3.0=S:1.1.5.3 } }

23:57:02.766708 IP (tos 0x0, ttl 64, id 35985, offset 0, flags [none], proto UDP
  (17), length 188)
   Leaf-201.cisco.com.46298 > 10.10.10.1.snmp-trap:  { SNMPv2c C=auto-snmp
  { V2Trap(140) R=118  system.sysUpTime.0=55950043 S:1.1.4.1.0=14.16.2.16
  14.1.1.0=29.34.92.236 14.7.1.1.50.50.50.1.0=50.50.50.1 14.7.1.2.50.50.50.1.0=0
  14.7.1.12.50.50.50.1.0=1 } }
^C
3 packets captured
3 packets received by filter
0 packets dropped by kernel
```

Note   In Example 10-12, the **tcpdump** utility is used with the interface filter **-i** knob and
eth0, which represents the OOB management that you have used in your configuration to
send all management traffic. If you want to use INB management to send out all management traffic, you use the interface filter **kpm_inb** with the **tcpdump** utility.

In the packet capture in Example 10-12, you can see that an SNMP trap from Leaf-201 is
sent to destination server 10.10.10.1 with community string snmp-auto. The packet capture output shows the ifAdminStatus value as 2, which means Down:

```
interfaces.ifTable.ifEntry.ifAdminStatus.436240384=2
```

In addition, the ifOperStatus value is 2, which means Down:

```
interfaces.ifTable.ifEntry.ifOperStatus.436240384=2
```

The integer value 436240384 is the snmp-ifindex of the eth1/9 interface, as shown in the
Leaf 201 command output in Example 10-13.

Example 10-13   *Verifying Interface Status Through SNMP IFMIB Value*

```
Leaf-201# show interface snmp-ifindex
-------------------------------------------
 Port             IFMIB Ifindex (hex)
-------------------------------------------
Eth1/9            436240384  (0x1a008000)
```

Next, you can try performing SNMP read queries as shown in Example 10-14.

Example 10-14   *Verifying SNMP Read Query Functionality Through the tcpdump Utility on a Leaf*

```
admin@user-laptop:~> snmpget -v2c -c auto-snmp Leaf-201.cisco.com SNMPv2-
  MIB::sysDescr.0
Leaf-201# tcpdump -i eth0 -f port 161 -v

tcpdump: listening on eth0, link-type EN10MB (Ethernet), capture size 65535 bytes

14:52:48.632453 IP (tos 0x0, ttl 55, id 36995, offset 0, flags [DF], proto UDP (17),
  length 74)
    20.20.20.1.52535 > Leaf-201.cisco.com.snmp:  { SNMPv2c C=auto-snmp { GetRequest
(28) R=1081746390  system.sysDescr.0 } }

14:52:48.632991 IP (tos 0x0, ttl 64, id 18250, offset 0, flags [none], proto UDP
  (17), length 239)
    Leaf-201.cisco.com.snmp > 20.20.20.1.52535:  { SNMPv2c C=auto-snmp { GetResponse
(191) R=1081746390  system.sysDescr.0=Cisco NX-OS(tm) aci, Software (aci-
n9000-system), Version 13.2(7k), RELEASE SOFTWARE Copyright (c) 2002-2015 by Cisco
Systems, Inc. Compiled 2019/08/15 11:29:24 } }
^C
2 packets captured
2 packets received by filter
0 packets dropped by kernel
```

From the packet capture output in Example 10-14, you can see that client machine 20.20.20.1 is making an SNMP GetRequest to Leaf-201 by using SNMPv2-MIB to pull system description information. Leaf-201 responds with the SNMP GetResponse.

SPAN

Switched Port Analyzer (SPAN) provides the capability to capture ingress/egress traffic flows from a switch interface. In traditional networking, in order to create a SPAN session, you define the source interface where you want the packets to be duplicated and sent out to your defined SPAN destination, such as a packet analyzer. With ACI, SPAN capabilities are extended further—such as where network admins do not have a packet analyzer available or in a virtualization scenario where, due to workload mobility, the application server VM is allowed to move anywhere. In such cases, ACI makes it possible to capture packets dynamically on the APIC as a SPAN destination and also defines SPAN sources based on the endpoint, regardless of their location.

SPAN in ACI can be configured in four different categories:

- **Access:** For monitoring traffic originating from access ports in leaf nodes
- **Fabric:** For monitoring traffic from fabric ports between leaf and spine nodes
- **Tenant:** For monitoring traffic from endpoint groups (EPGs) within a tenant
- **Visibility & Troubleshooting:** For initiating SPAN based on a defined endpoint to another endpoint

The following sections describe the configuration steps for each of these SPAN categories.

Access SPAN

Access SPAN is used to configure local SPAN or ERSPAN on leaf switches. These SPAN sessions can capture packet ingress, egress, or both directions. SPAN sources can be physical ports, port channels, or VPCs. The SPAN destination can be a local access port if the SPAN source is on the same leaf switch or ERSPAN if the SPAN source is on a different leaf switch. If a packet analyzer is running on a VM front-ended by a virtual switch, the SPAN destination must be ERSPAN, although the host running hypervisor is connected directly to the local leaf switch. For access SPAN, you can create filters based on EPG or L3Out. When routed outside or based on L3Out, SPAN filters based on the encapsulation VLAN used in the routed sub-interface or SVI.

To use access SPAN, you need to first create the SPAN destination. To do that, you go to Fabric > Access Policies > Policies > Troubleshooting > SPAN, right-click SPAN Destination Groups, and select Create SPAN Destination Group. Depending on the SPAN destination type you choose—ERSPAN or local SPAN—select either the EPG or Access Interface option.

For ERSPAN, enter **span-erspan-dst** as the name of the object. Select the EPG under the application profile in your defined tenant (in this case, t01/cp-infra-prod/mgmt). Type **10.10.10.1** as the destination IP address of the packet analyzer machine. Type **1.1.1.1** as the source IP/prefix. As explained in Chapter 9, SPAN traffic competes with data traffic. Therefore, you need to define the right QoS DSCP values (in this example, CS5). Click Submit.

For local SPAN, type **span-local-dst** as the name of the object. Select the leaf node and interface through which you are connecting your packet analyzer machine (in this example, 1003-eth1/5). Click Submit. The input values are for example only.

Figure 10-64 illustrates the previous configuration steps.

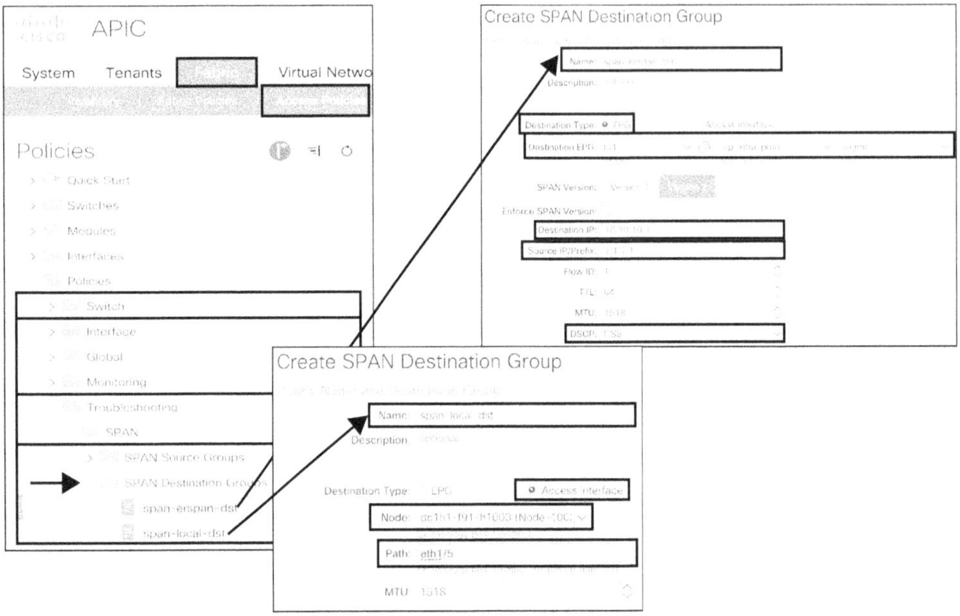

Figure 10-64 *Access SPAN Destination*

Next, you need to create the SPAN source with different filter options and associate it with the SPAN destination object created earlier. To configure an access SPAN source with no filter, go to Fabric > Access Policies > Policies > Troubleshooting > SPAN, right-click SPAN Source Groups, and select Create SPAN Source Group. Type **span-src-web** as the name of the object. Select span-local-dst from the Destination Labels drop-down menu. Click the + sign to create a source and specify **web-srv** as the source name. Keep the default Direction setting, Both, and specify no filter. Click the + sign to add source access paths. Choose Port as the interface path type. Select 1003 from the Node drop-down menu and eth1/55 from the Path menu. Click OK twice and then click Submit. Figure 10-65 illustrates this process.

To configure an access SPAN source with an EPG filter, go to Fabric > Access Policies > Policies > Troubleshooting> SPAN, right-click SPAN Source Groups, and select Create SPAN Source Group. Type **span-src-web** as the name of the object. Select span-erspan-dst from the Destination Labels drop-down menu. Click the + sign to create a source and specify **web-srv** as the source name. Keep the default Direction setting, Both, and set the filter type to EPG. From the Source EPG drop-down menu, select t01/c-inf/c-net-mgmt. Click the + sign to add source access paths. Choose Port as the interface path type. Select 1003 from the Node drop-down menu and eth1/55 from the Path menu. Click OK twice and then click Submit. Figure 10-66 illustrates this process.

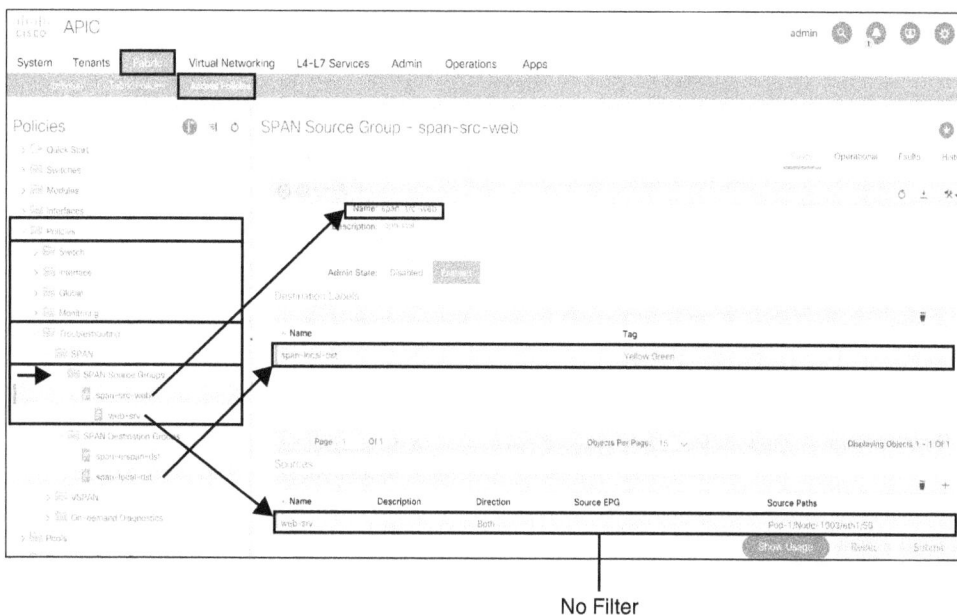

Figure 10-65 *Access SPAN Source with No Filter*

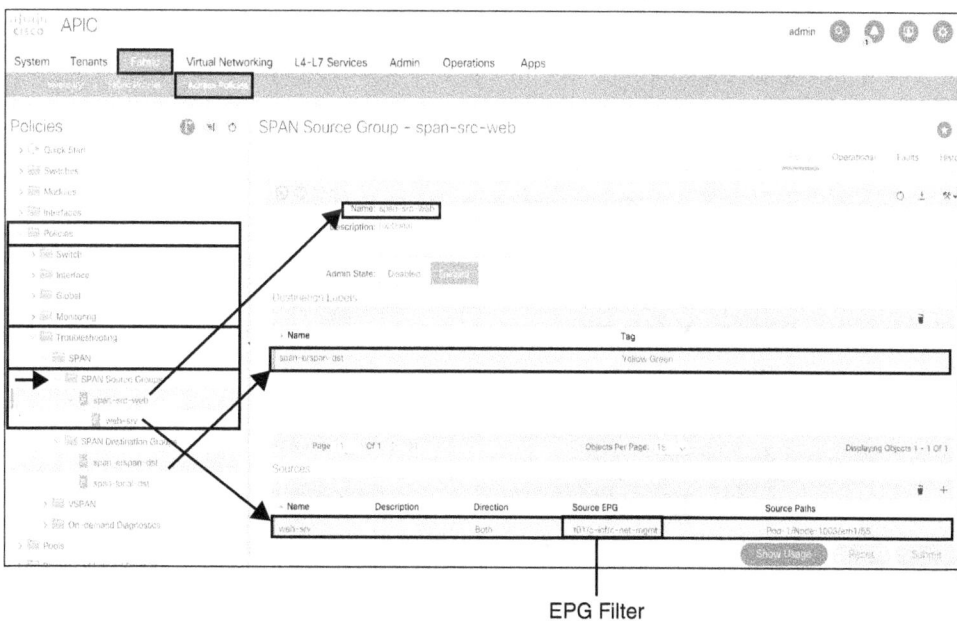

Figure 10-66 *Access SPAN Source with an EPG Filter*

To configure an access SPAN source with a routed outside filter, go to Fabric > Access Policies > Policies > Troubleshooting > SPAN, right-click SPAN Source Groups, and select Create SPAN Source Group. Type **span-src-web** as the name of the object. Select span-erspan-dst from the Destination Labels drop-down menu. Click the + sign to create a source and specify **web-srv** as the source name. Keep the default Direction setting, Both, and select the filter type Routed Outside. Choose l3out:d-core as the name of the routed outside object, and type **10.10.10.1/30** as the transport IP address of the border leaf for peering with the external router.

Note   Fault F1561 is raised if the IP address does not match the transport address of the border leaf connecting to the external router.

Type the encapsulation VLAN of the SVI or routed subinterface that you used in peering your border leaf with the external router (in this example, 50). Click the + sign to add a source access path. Choose Port as the interface path type. Select 1003 from the Node drop-down menu and eth1/55 from the Path drop-down menu. Click OK twice and then click Submit. Figure 10-67 illustrates this process.

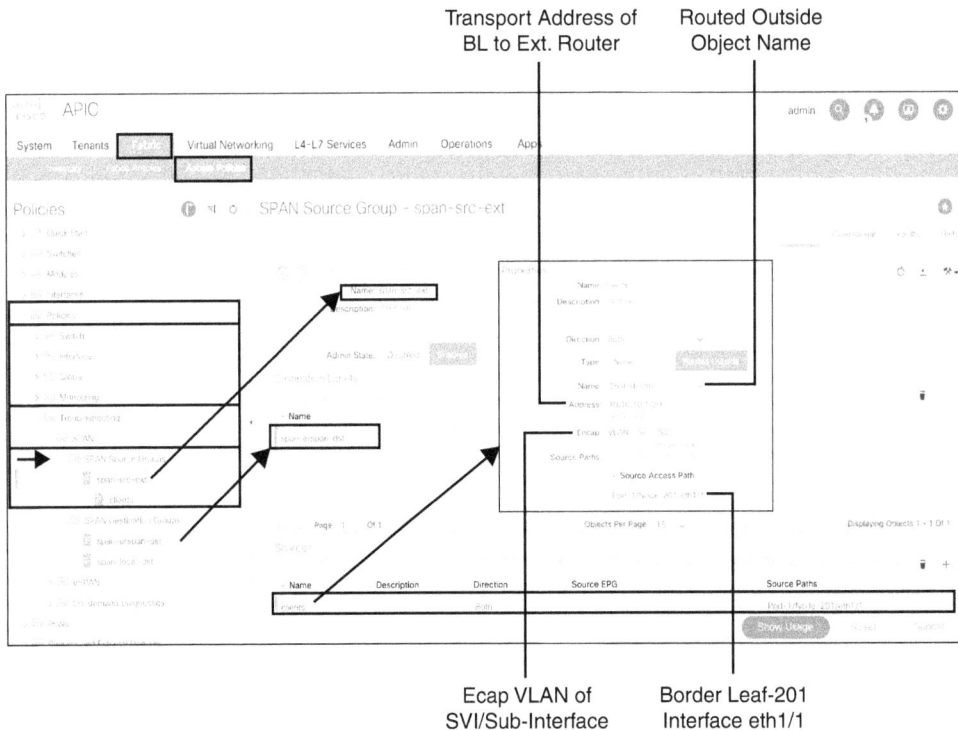

Figure 10-67   *Access SPAN Source with a Routed Outside Filter*

Fabric SPAN

Fabric SPAN is used to capture packets from fabric ports between leafs and spines. These SPAN sessions can capture packet ingress, egress, or both directions. SPAN sources can only be fabric ports between leafs and spines. The SPAN destination can only be an ERSPAN. For fabric SPAN, you can create filters based on a VRF instance or bridge domain.

To create a fabric SPAN, you need to first create the SPAN destination. To do that, you go to Fabric > Access Policies > Policies > Troubleshooting > SPAN, right-click SPAN Destination Groups, and select Create SPAN Destination Group. As mentioned earlier, the only Destination option in fabric SPAN is ERSPAN. Type **span-erspan-dst** as the name of the object. Select t01/c-inf/infra-mgmt as the EPG under the application profile in your defined tenant. Type **10.10.10.1** as the destination IP address of the packet analyzer machine. Type **1.1.1.1** as the source IP/prefix. As explained in Chapter 9, SPAN traffic competes with data traffic. Therefore, you need to define the right QoS DSCP values (in this example, CS5). Click Submit. Figure 10-68 illustrates these configuration steps. The input values are for example only.

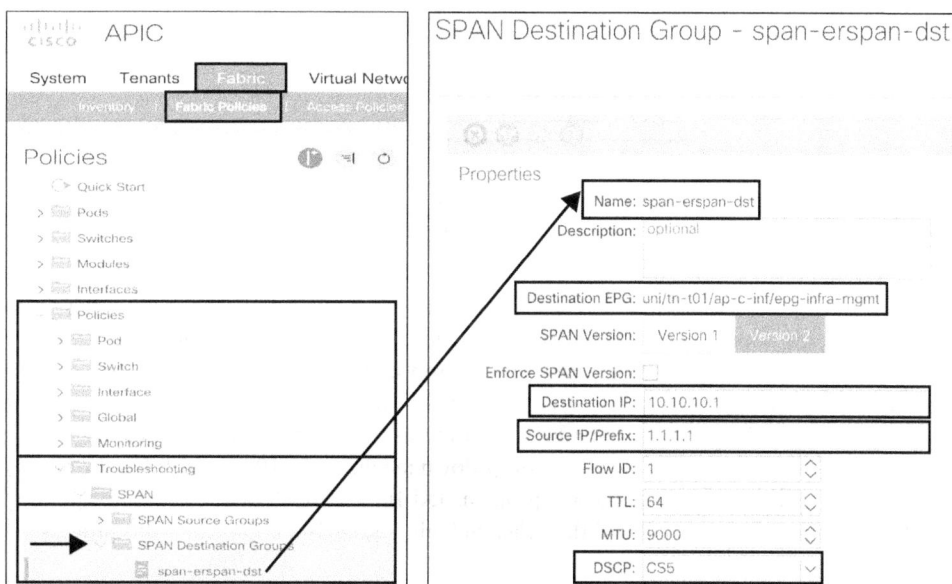

Figure 10-68 *Fabric SPAN Destination*

Next, you need to create a SPAN source with different filter options and associate it with the SPAN destination object created earlier. To configure a fabric SPAN source with a VRF filter, go to Fabric > Fabric Policies > Policies > Troubleshooting> SPAN, right-click SPAN Source Groups, and select Create SPAN Source Group. Type **span-fabric-src** as the name of the object. Select span-erspan-dst from the Destination Labels drop-down menu. Click the + sign to create a source. Specify **leaf-1004** as the source name. Keep the default direction, Both, set Association to VRF, and select cp-standard from the VRF drop-down menu. Click the + sign to add a source fabric path. From the drop-down menu, select 1004-eth1/97 as the fabric path and click Update. Click the + sign again, add 1004-eth1/98 as a source fabric path, and click Update. Click OK and then click Submit. Figure 10-69 illustrates this process.

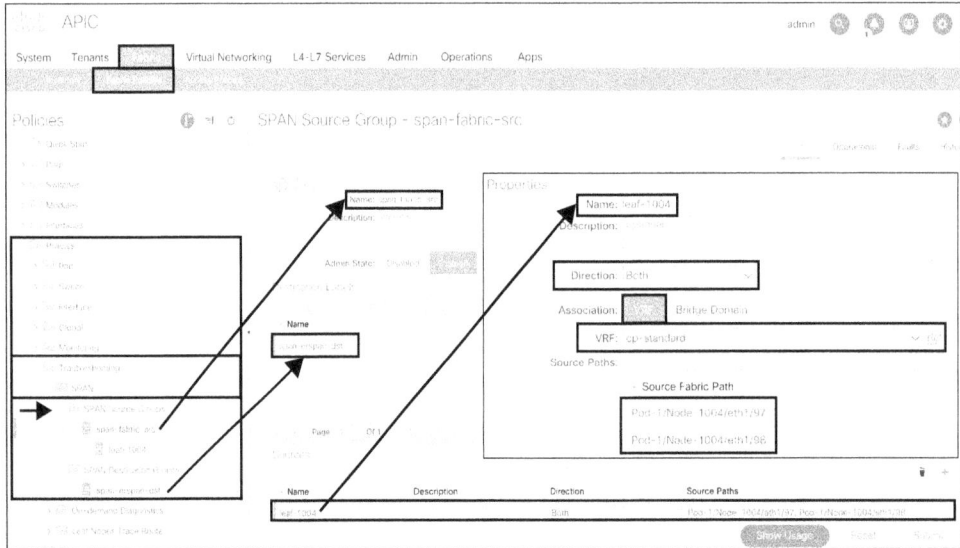

Figure 10-69 *Fabric SPAN Source with VRF Filter*

To configure a fabric SPAN source with a bridge domain filter, go to Fabric > Fabric Policies > Policies > Troubleshooting> SPAN, right-click SPAN Source Groups, and select Create SPAN Source Group. Type **span-fabric-src** as the name of the object. Select span-erspan-dst from the Destination Labels drop-down menu. Click the + sign to create a source. Specify **leaf-1004** as the source name. Keep the default direction, Both, set Association to Bridge Domain, and select a-tools as the bridge domain. Click the + sign to add a source fabric path. From the drop-down menu, select 1004-eth1/97 as the fabric path and click Update. Click the + sign again, add 1004-eth1/98 as a source fabric path, and click Update. Click OK and then click Submit. Figure 10-70 illustrates this process.

Tenant SPAN

Tenant SPAN is used to capture packets from an EPG that is part of an application profile contained in a tenant. These SPAN sessions can capture packets ingress, egress, or both directions. A SPAN source can only be an EPG. The SPAN destination can only be an ERSPAN. There are no SPAN filter options available for tenant SPAN.

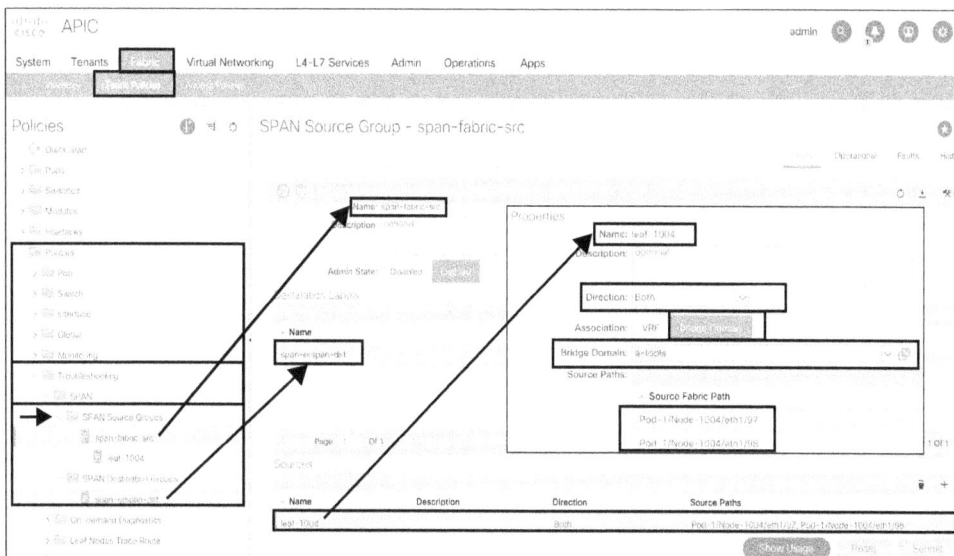

Figure 10-70 *Fabric SPAN Source with a Bridge Domain Filter*

To create a Tenant SPAN, you need to first create the SPAN destination. To do that, go to Tenant tab > t01 > Policies > Troubleshooting > SPAN, right-click SPAN Destination Groups, and select Create SPAN Destination Group. As mentioned earlier, the only destination option in tenant SPAN is ERSPAN. Type **span-erspan-dst** as the name of the object. Select t01/c-inf/infra-mgmt as the EPG under the application profile in your defined tenant. Type **10.10.10.1** as the destination IP address of the packet analyzer machine. Type **1.1.1.1** as the source IP/prefix. As explained in Chapter 9, SPAN traffic competes with data traffic. Therefore, you need to define the right QoS DSCP values (in this example, CS5). Click Submit. Figure 10-71 illustrates these configuration steps. The input values are for example only.

Next, you need to create a SPAN source and associate it with the SPAN destination object created earlier. To do so, go to Tenant > t01 > Policies > Troubleshooting > SPAN, right-click SPAN Source Groups, and select Create SPAN Source Group. Type **span-tenant-src** as the name of the object. Select span-erspan-dst from the Tenant Destination Labels drop-down menu. Click the + sign to create a source. Type **web-srv** as the source name. Choose the default direction, Both. Select c-tools from the Source EPG drop-down menu and click OK. Click Submit. Figure 10-72 illustrates this process.

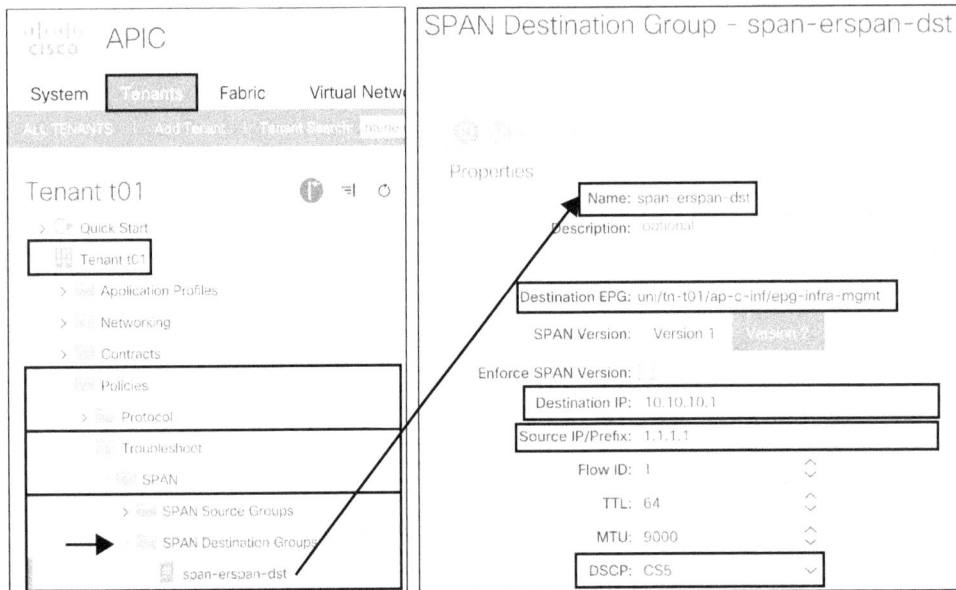

Figure 10-71   *Tenant SPAN Destination*

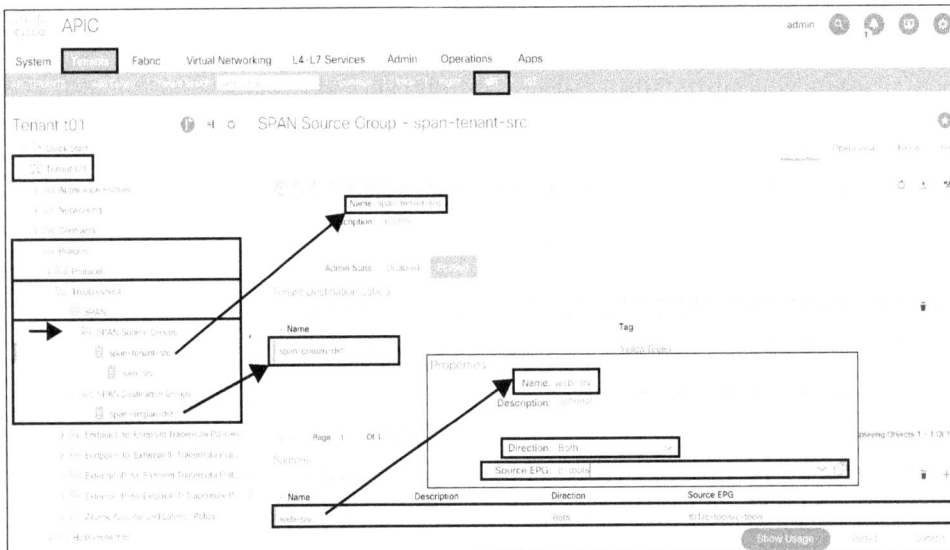

Figure 10-72   *Tenant SPAN Source*

Ensuring Visibility and Troubleshooting SPAN

ACI offers a unique SPAN capability in which you can use the APIC controller as the SPAN destination. This provides a useful capability to take a quick look at an endpoint connectivity issue remotely without the need for a packet-capturing host. It's important to note that the capture rate might be limited because you're capturing to the APIC.

Note   It is mandatory to have INB management in order to run a SPAN session in the Visibility & Troubleshooting tool. Without it, you get an error.

In order to create a SPAN session in the Visibility & Troubleshooting tool, you first need to create a session between two endpoints. To do that, go to Operations > Visibility & Troubleshooting. Type **sadiq-web** as the session name and select External IP to Endpoint as the session type. Under Source, type **50.50.50.1** as the external IP address. Under Destination, type **100.100.100.1** as the destination IP address and click Search. ACI locates the endpoint connected to one of its leaf switches; in this example, the destination endpoint belongs to EPG-mgmt, which is part of Application-cp-infra-prod, contained within Tenant-t01, and learned on virtual port-channel 1001-1002-vpc-e13-18. Click Start. Figure 10-73 illustrates these configuration steps. The input values are for example only.

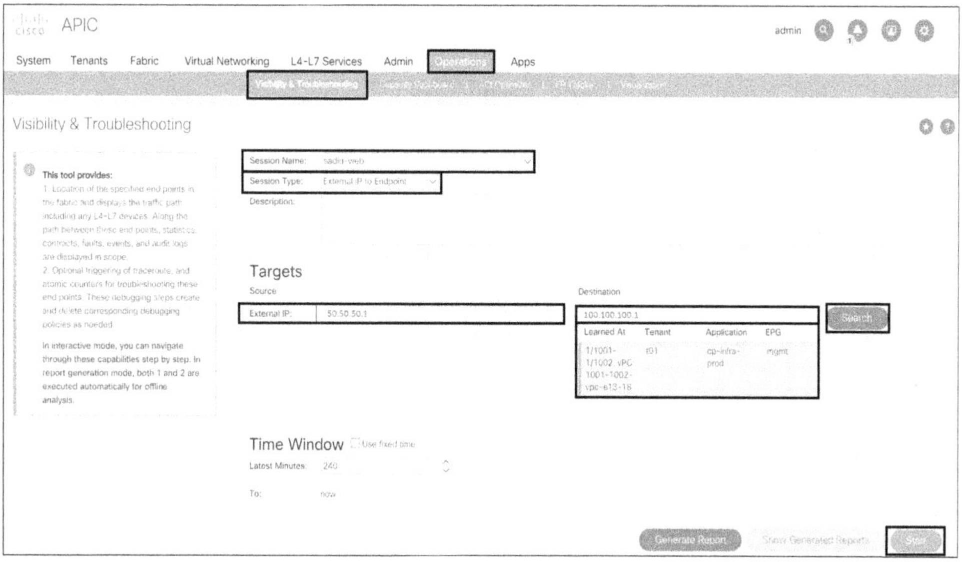

Figure 10-73   *Visibility & Troubleshooting Session*

After a few seconds, ACI uploads the full topology view of the two endpoints (External IP and Endpoint) that you already selected in the Visibility & Troubleshooting tool. Next, click the SPAN tab, and in the window that appears, select APIC as the destination type and type **172.168.1.0** as the source IP prefix (because this is the ERSPAN prefix). The last octet will be the node ID of the leaf from which the packets are captured. From the Flow ID drop-down menu select 1. From the Preferred Version drop-down menu select Version 2. Click the Play button. Run your traffic between endpoints for a short period and then click the Stop button. The capture stops, and the data is stored in a PCAP file. You can download the file for further analysis from the APIC to your local PC by clicking that file. Figure 10-74 illustrates this process.

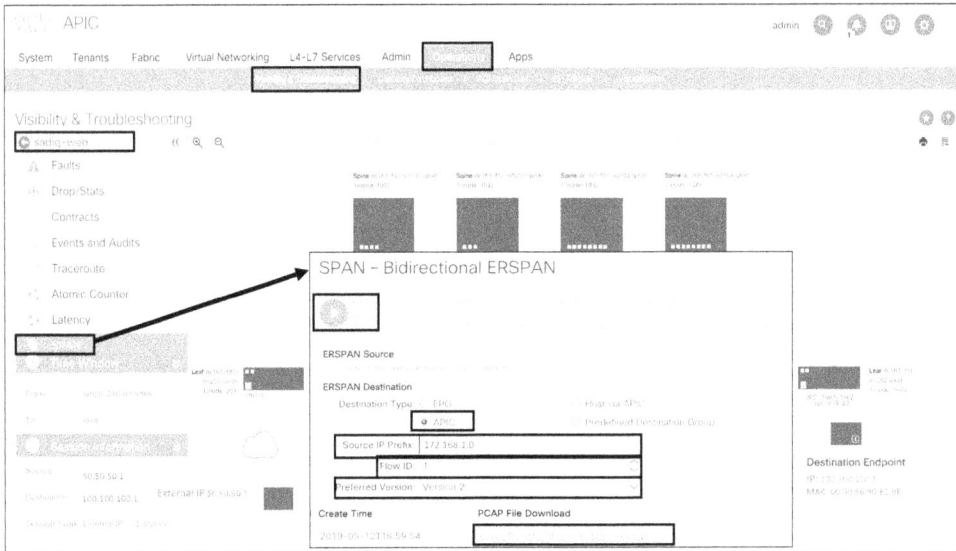

Figure 10-74   *Visibility & Troubleshooting SPAN*

Verifying the SPAN Configuration and Functionality

There are different ways to verify your SPAN configuration and functionality. Example 10-15 shows verification steps that should typically suffice for a SPAN configuration in ACI.

Example 10-15   *Verifying SPAN Configuration*

```
APIC2# show monitor access session leaf3
Type           : access
Session        : leaf3  *** Session not created by CLI ***
Node           : 303
Type           : local
Admin state    : enabled
Oper state     : up (active)
Dest Interface : eth1/21
```

```
Interface/Vlan/Vxlan     State    State Qualifier    Dir     Encap/BdEncap
  FabEncap/CtxEncap
---------------------    ------   ----------------   ------  --------------------
-----------------
po2                      up       active             both    vlan-811
  vxlan-15564700



Leaf3# show monitor session all
   session 3
---------------
description       : Span session 3
type              : local
state             : up (active)
mode              : access
source intf       :
    rx            : Po2
    tx            : Po2
    both          : Po2
source VLANs      :
    rx            :
    tx            :
    both          :
filter VLANs      : 76
filter L3Outs     : vlan74
destination ports : Eth1/21
```

NetFlow

NetFlow is a networking protocol for caching traffic flows passing through a router. These flows can then be exported out to a NetFlow collector for further analysis. NetFlow data is used for isolating application slowness and for bandwidth monitoring, cyber threat forensics, and network usage billing.

NetFlow has been supported since ACI Release 2.2(1), and it is available on the Nexus 9300 Gen-2 cloud-scale platform, such as EX and FX. In addition, NetFlow is also supported on remote leafs with ACI Release 4.0(1). In ACI, you can either enable NetFlow on Nexus 9300 cloud-scale platforms or enable Tetration Hardware Agent but not both.

To configure NetFlow, you need to first enable NetFlow on Nexus 9300 cloud-scale platforms. To do that, go to Fabric > Fabric Policies > Policies > Monitoring, right-click Fabric Node Control, and select Create Fabric Node Control. Type **netflow** as the object name, set Feature Selection to NetFlow Priority, and click Submit. Figure 10-75 illustrates this process. The input values are for example only.

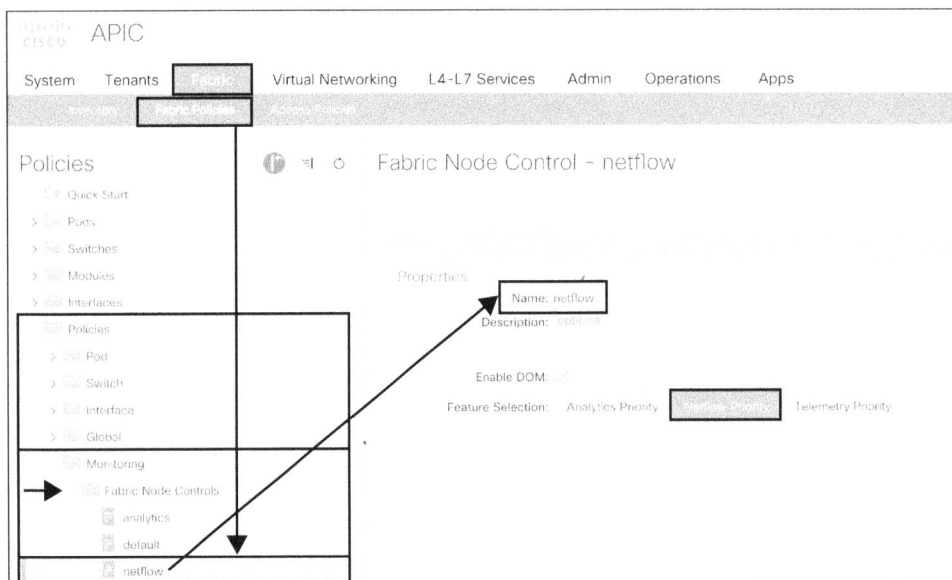

Figure 10-75   *Enabling NetFlow Policies*

Next, you create policy groups. To do this, go to Fabric > Fabric Policies > Switches > Leaf Switches, right-click Policy Groups, and select Create Policy Group. Type **netflow-sw-polgrp** as the object name. Choose netflow from the Node Control Policy drop-down menu. Click Submit. Figure 10-76 illustrates this process.

Finally, you need to create a profile. To do so, go to Fabric > Fabric Policies > Switches > Leaf Switches, right-click Profiles, and select Create Profile. Type **leaf-sw-prof** as the object name. Click the + sign to add switch associations. Type **L201** as the object name. Select 201 in the Blocks column to run NetFlow in this leaf node. Select netflow-sw-polgrp in the Policy Group column. Click Update and then click Submit. Figure 10-77 illustrates this process. You should now be able to run NetFlow on Leaf 201.

NetFlow policies can be configured as either of the following:

- Access policies (leaf downlink ports: access, VPC, port channel)
- Tenant policies (bridge domain, L3Out)

In order to configure NetFlow, you need to follow four basic steps:

Step 1.   Create a record (IPv4/IPv6).

Step 2.   Create an exporter.

Step 3.   Create a monitor and associate the record and exporter with it.

Step 4.   Apply the monitor on the leaf interface.

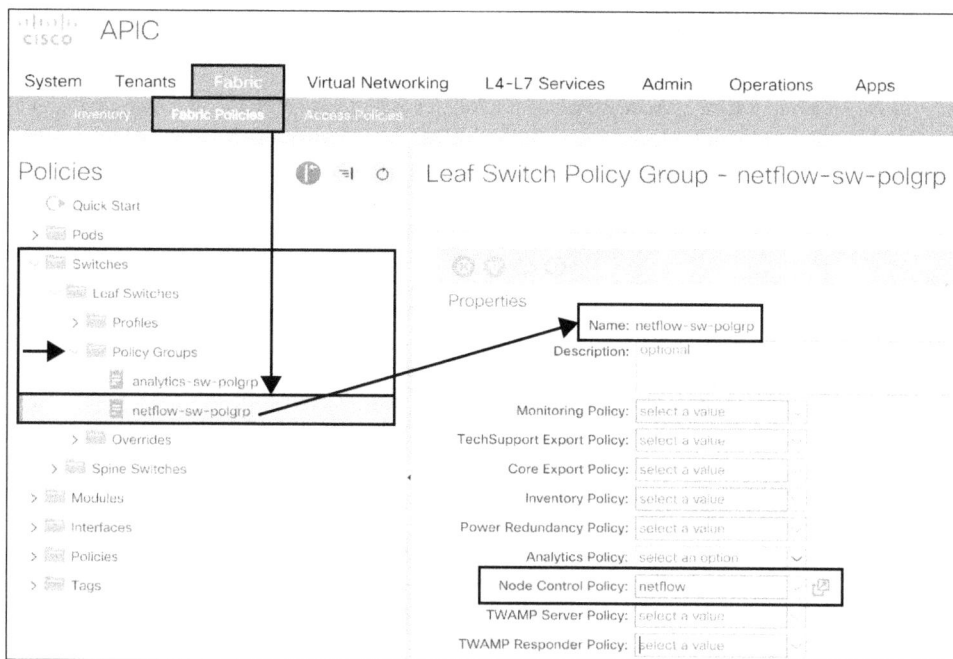

Figure 10-76   *Enabling NetFlow Policy Groups*

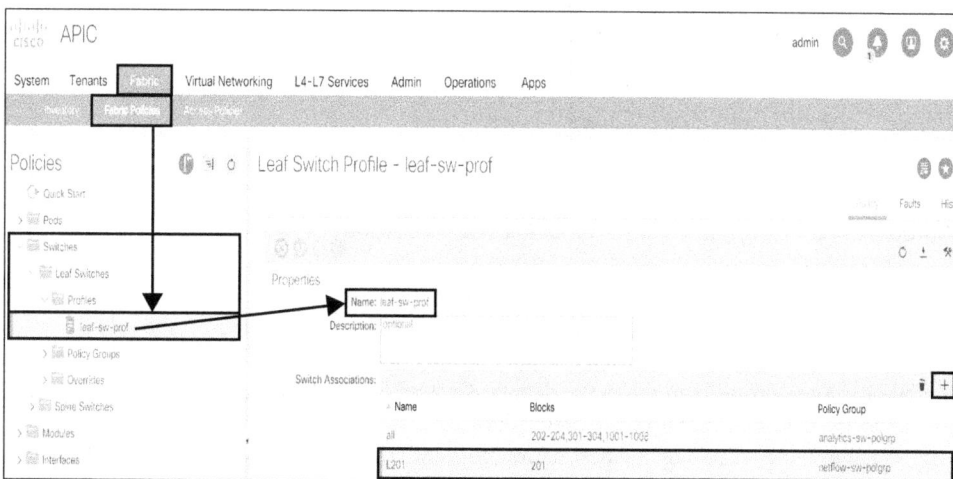

Figure 10-77   *Enabling a NetFlow Profile*

The following sections walk through these steps for NetFlow access policies and tenant policies.

NetFlow with Access Policies

To configure NetFlow with access policies, you first need to create a NetFlow record. To do so, go to Fabric > Access Policies > Policies > Interface > NetFlow, right-click NetFlow Records, and select Create Flow Record. Type **ipv4-record** as the object name. Keep the Collect Parameters drop-down set to the default, Source Interface. From the Match Parameters drop-down menu, select Source IPv4, Destination IPv4, Source Port, Destination Port, and IP Protocol. Click Submit. Figure 10-78 illustrates this process.

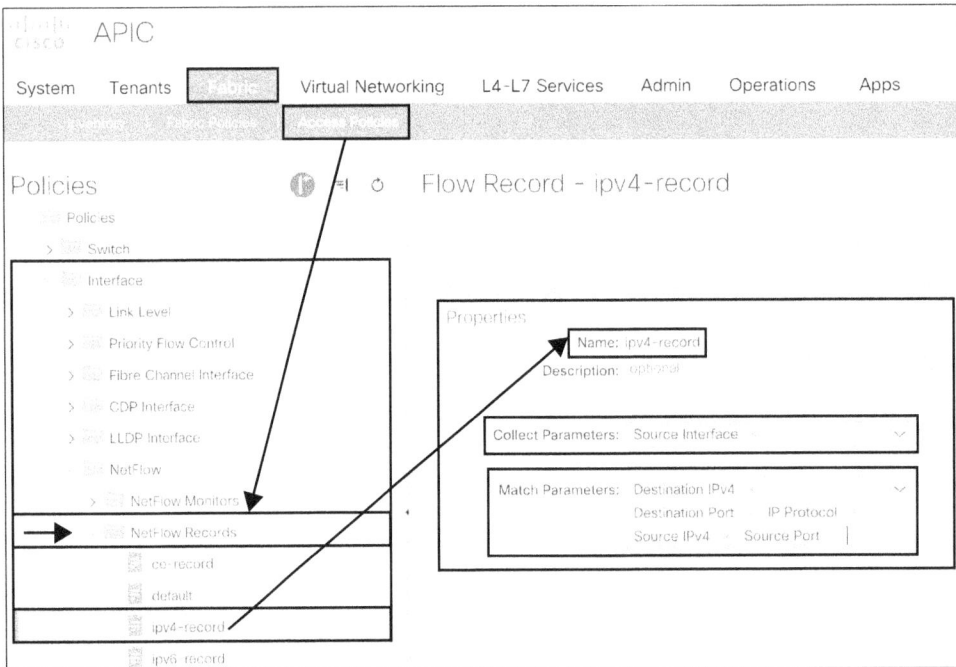

Figure 10-78 *Configuring a NetFlow Record with Access Policies*

Next, you need to create the NetFlow exporter. To do that, go to Fabric > Access Policies > Policies > Interface > NetFlow, right-click NetFlow Exporters, and select Create External Collector Reachability. Type **solarwinds** as the object name. Keep the Source Type drop-down set to the default, Custom Src IP. Type **1.1.0.0/24** as the source IP address. The last octet of the prefix shows the node ID of the leaf on which NetFlow is enabled. Type **2055** as the destination port and **20.86.84.111** as the destination IP address. As with SPAN, NetFlow traffic competes with data traffic, so you need to choose CS5 as the QoS DSCP value. Set NetFlow Exporter Version Format to Version 9 (as this is the only format that ACI supports). Depending on the location of the NetFlow collector, you need to pick the EPG Type—either App EPG or L3 EPG; in this case, choose L3 EPG. Set Tenant to t01, L3 EPG to l3out:d-core, and VRF to standard. Click Submit. Figure 10-79 illustrates this process.

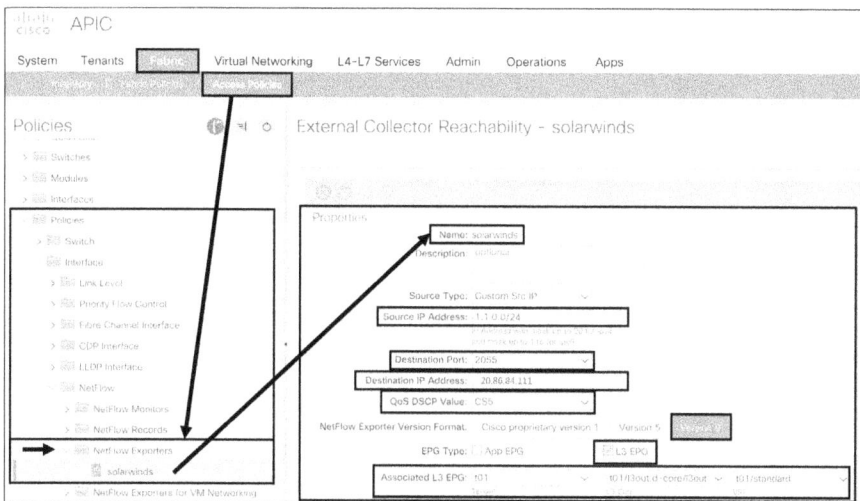

Figure 10-79 *Configuring the NetFlow Exporter with Access Policies*

Next, you now need to create the NetFlow monitor and associate the previously created NetFlow record and exporter with it. To do that, go to Fabric > Access Policies > Policies > Interface > NetFlow, right-click NetFlow Monitors, and select Create NetFlow Monitor. Type **ipv4-monitor** as the object name. Set Associated Flow Record to the previously created ipv4-record NetFlow record. Click the + sign and set Flow Exporter to the previously created solarwinds NetFlow exporter. Click Update and then click by Submit. Figure 10-80 illustrates this process.

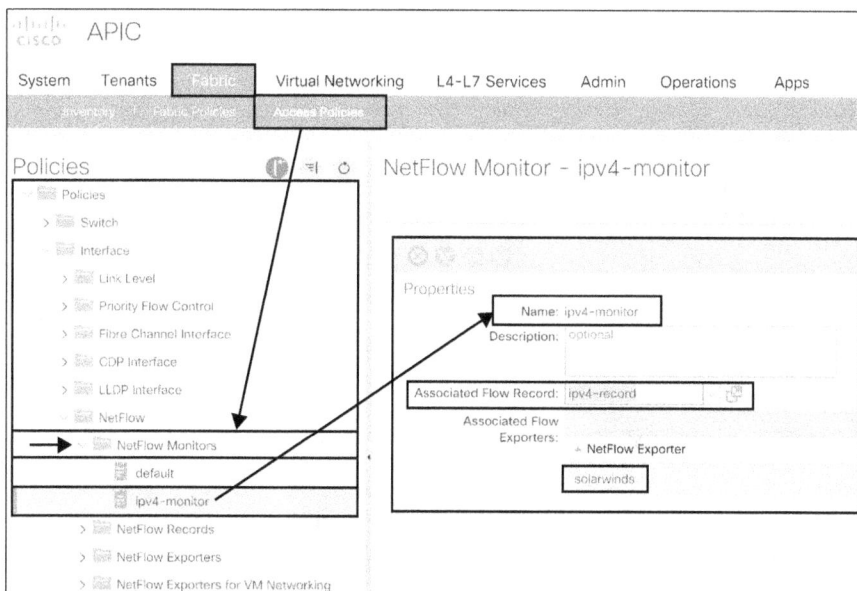

Figure 10-80 *Configuring the NetFlow Monitor with Access Policies*

Finally, you need to associate the NetFlow monitor with the leaf interface. To do that, go to Fabric > Access Policies > Interfaces > Leaf Interfaces > Leaf Access Port and select t01-l3-aep-auto-discover, the border leaf interface policy group that you configured for L3Out connectivity to the external router. In addition to a leaf access port, you can also use a port channel or a VPC, depending on how you have connected your border leaf to the external router. On the right side of the screen, click the + sign and set NetFlow Monitor Policies to the previously created ipv4-monitor policy. Click Update and then click Submit. Figure 10-81 illustrates this process.

Note   Border leaf interface eth1/4 is selected in the Profiles tab. This is the interface used to peer from the border leaf to the external router in this example.

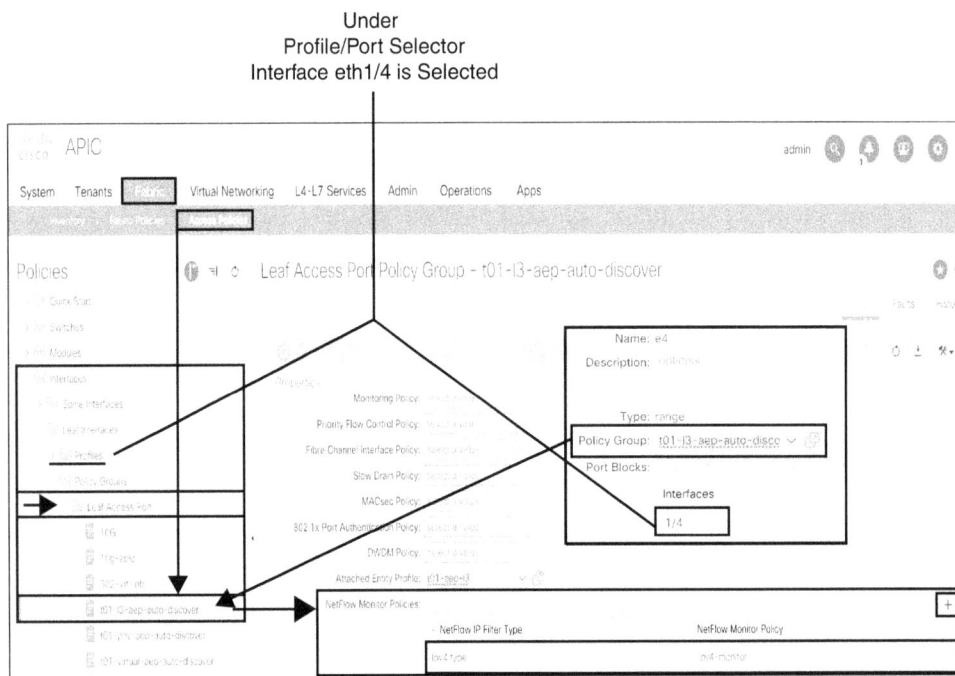

Figure 10-81   *Applying the NetFlow Monitor to a Leaf Interface with Access Policies*

NetFlow with Tenant Policies

To configure NetFlow with tenant policies, you first create the NetFlow Record. To do so, go to Tenant > t01 > Policies > NetFlow, right-click NetFlow Records, and select Create Flow Record. Type **ipv4-record** as the object name. Keep the Collect Parameters drop-down set to the default, Source Interface. From the Match Parameters drop-down menu, select Source IPv4, Destination IPv4, Source Port, Destination Port, and IP Protocol. Click Submit. Figure 10-82 illustrates this process.

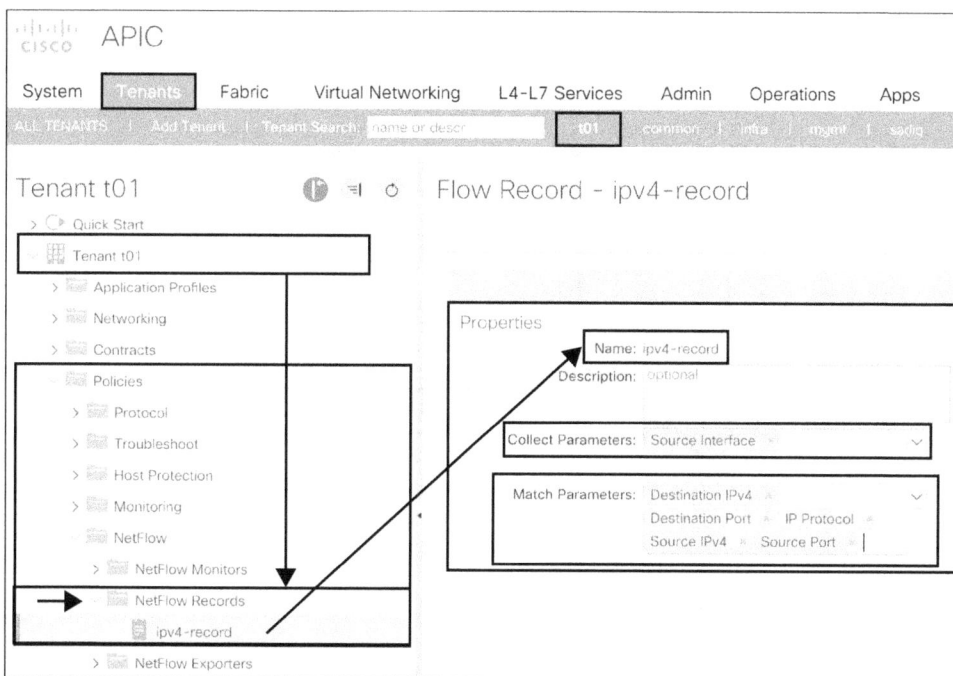

Figure 10-82 *Configuring a NetFlow Record with Tenant Policies*

Next, you need to create the NetFlow Exporter. To do that, go to Tenant > t01 >
Policies > NetFlow, right-click NetFlow Exporters, and select Create External Collector
Reachability. Type **flow-exporter** as the object name. Keep the Source Type drop-down
set to the default, Custom Src IP. Type **1.1.0.0/24** as the source IP address. The last octet
of the prefix shows the node ID of the leaf on which NetFlow is enabled. Type **2055**
as the destination port and **30.88.197.38** as the destination IP address. As with SPAN,
NetFlow traffic competes with data traffic, so you need to choose CS5 as the QoS DSCP
value. Set NetFlow Exporter Version Format to Version 9 (as this is the only format that
ACI supports). Depending on the location of the NetFlow collector, you need to pick the
EPG Type—either App EPG or L3 EPG; in this case, choose App EPG. Set Tenant to t01,
Application EPG to cp-infra-prod/services, and VRF to standard. Click Submit. Figure 10-83
shows this process.

Next, you need to create the NetFlow monitor and associate the previously created
NetFlow record and exporter with it. To do that, go to Tenant > t01 > Policies > NetFlow,
right-click NetFlow Monitors, and select Create NetFlow Monitor. Type **ipv4-monitor**
as the object name. Set Associated Flow Record to the previously created ipv4-record
NetFlow record. Click the + sign and set Flow Exporter to the previously created
flow-exporter NetFlow exporter. Click Update and then click by Submit. Figure 10-84
illustrates this process.

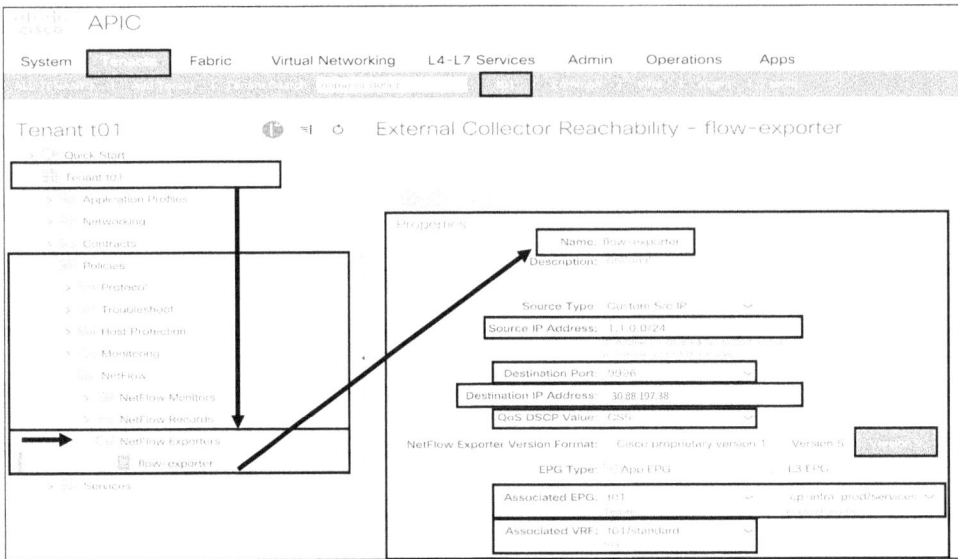

Figure 10-83 *Configuring the NetFlow Exporter with Tenant Policies*

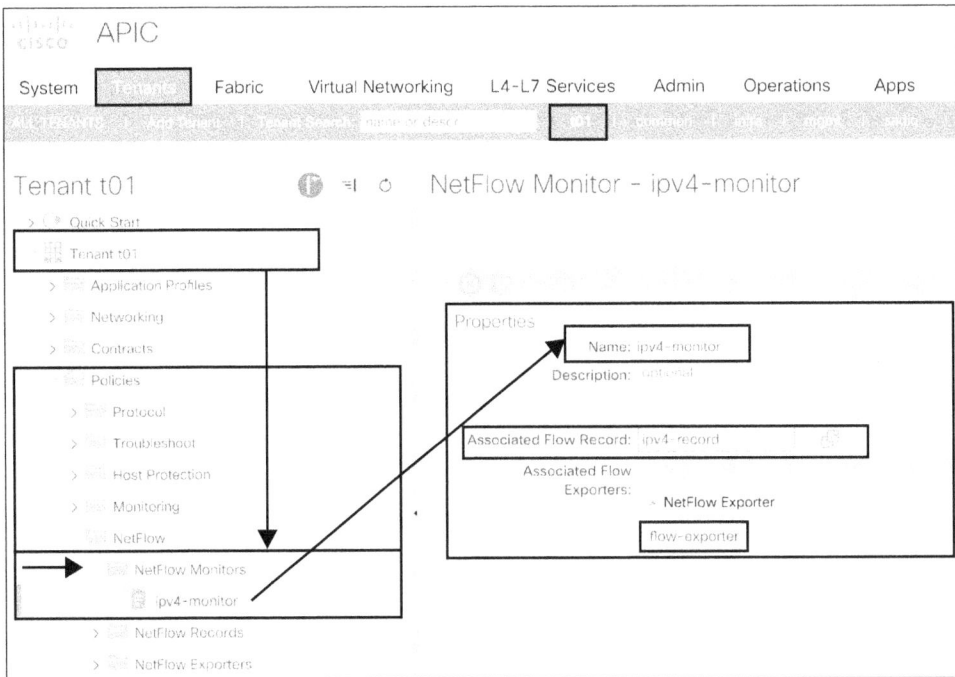

Figure 10-84 *Configuring the NetFlow Monitor with Tenant Policies*

Finally, you need to associate the monitor with the leaf interface. To do that, go to Tenant > t01 > Networking > External Routed Networks and select l3out:d-core as the L3Out policy object. Expand t01-node-prof and then example t01-ospf-prof. On the right side of the screen, click the + sign and set NetFlow Monitor Policies to the previously created ipv4-monitor policy. Click Update and then click Submit. Figure 10-85 illustrates this process.

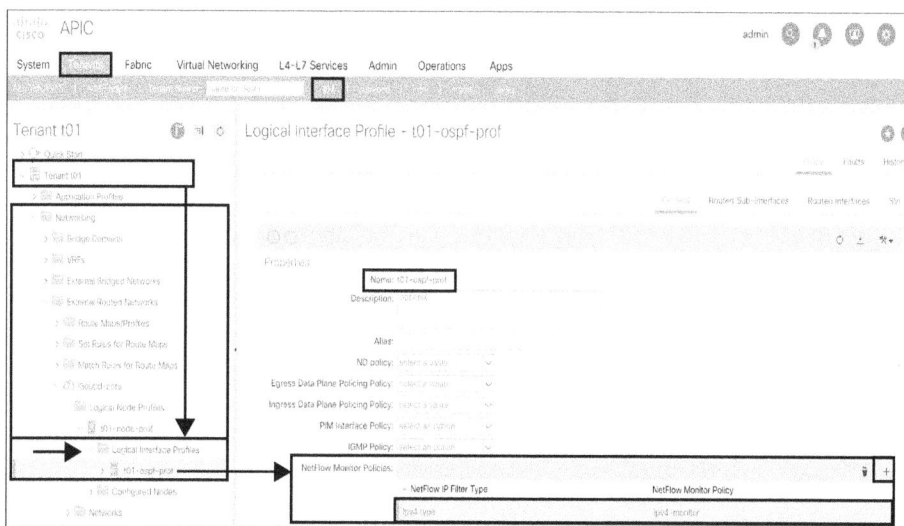

Figure 10-85 *Applying a NetFlow Monitor to a Leaf Interface with Tenant Policies*

You have finished configuring NetFlow in ACI, and you're ready to verify your configuration.

Verifying the NetFlow Configuration and Functionality

Example 10-16 shows verification steps that should typically suffice for a NetFlow configuration in ACI.

Example 10-16 *Verifying the NetFlow Configuration*

```
tcsh1-f02-b0201# show flow cache ipv4
IPV4 Entries
SIP              DIP              BD ID   S-Port   D-Port   Protocol   Byte Count
  Packet Count   TCP FLAGS   if_id          flowStart
10.88.146.51     10.88.197.48     4611     53       37779    17         144
  1          0x0         0x1a003000   28365088   28365088
10.88.150.154    2.2.2.2          4611     28570    1967     17         98
  1          0x0         0x1a003000   28367890   28367890
10.88.144.73     10.88.197.53     4611     5640     59228    6          70
  1          0x10        0x1a003000   28365680   28365680
10.88.194.7      10.88.193.14     4611     58282    4353     6          10456
  98         0x18        0x1a003000   28365917   28367549
```

```
tcsh1-f02-b0201# show flow exporter
Flow exporter solarwinds:
    Destination: 20.86.84.111
    VRF: t01:standard (1)
    Destination UDP Port 2055
    Source: 1.1.0.201
    DSCP 40
    Export Version 9
        Sequence number 2656
        Data template timeout 0 seconds
    Exporter Statistics
        Number of Flow Records Exported 8582
        Number of Templates Exported 9
        Number of Export Packets Sent 255
        Number of Export Bytes Sent 349040
        Number of Destination Unreachable Events 0
        Number of No Buffer Events 0
        Number of Packets Dropped (No Route to Host) 0
        Number of Packets Dropped (other) 0
        Number of Packets Dropped (Output Drops) 0
        Time statistics were last cleared: Never
Feature Prio: NetFlow

tcsh1-f02-b0201# show flow exporter
Flow exporter t01:flow-exporter:
    Destination: 30.88.197.38
    VRF: t01:standard (1)
    Destination UDP Port 9996
    Source: 1.1.0.201
    DSCP 44
    Export Version 9
        Sequence number 895
        Data template timeout 0 seconds
    Exporter Statistics
        Number of Flow Records Exported 30240
        Number of Templates Exported 30
        Number of Export Packets Sent 895
        Number of Export Bytes Sent 1229700
        Number of Destination Unreachable Events 0
        Number of No Buffer Events 0
        Number of Packets Dropped (No Route to Host) 0
        Number of Packets Dropped (other) 0
        Number of Packets Dropped (Output Drops) 0
        Time statistics were last cleared: Never
Feature Prio: NetFlow
```

Summary

Managing and monitoring are two extremely crucial subjects in the smooth execution and operation of any network. In this chapter, you have learned about key ACI management and monitoring protocols, such as OOB and INB management, AAA, syslog, SNMP, SPAN, and NetFlow, and their respective configurations. You have also learned how to verify and validate these configurations.

Note   There are no Key Topics or Review Questions for this chapter.

## Chapter 11

ACI Topology

For the remainder of the book, you will be learning about the bits and bytes of ACI forwarding, as well as various troubleshooting techniques and scenarios to help you learn to troubleshoot an ACI fabric. It's important to understand the physical topology that will be used in the coming sections and to understand the logical layout and software specifications for the devices in the fabric.

This chapter covers the following topics:

- Physical topology

- APIC initial setup

- Fabric access policies

- VMM domain configuration

- Hardware and software specifications

- Logical layout of EPGs, BDs, VRF instances, and contracts

Physical Topology

As we wrote this book, we used a basic topology to test, simulate, and create scenarios that explain ACI concepts. This chapter will give you an understanding of the base topology shown in Figure 11-1, including addressing, naming conventions, and hardware used. Chapter 12, "Bits and Bytes of ACI Forwarding," will continue to draw on this topology. This single-pod topology consists of two spines and four leafs, each with unique node IDs. There is a VPC-connected server on Leafs 101 and 102, and there is a single attached server on Leaf 103. There is also a VPC attached router on Leafs 101 and 102, and there is another VPC-attached router on Leafs 103 and 104.

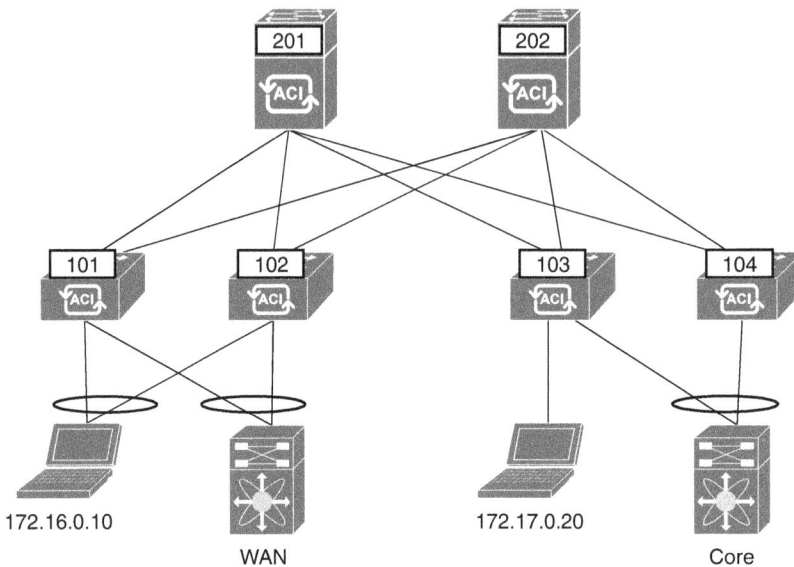

Figure 11-1 *Basic Topology for a Single Pod*

Table 11-1 shows the TEP addresses used for the devices in this single-pod topology. It includes the physical TEP addresses, as well as the VPC and Anycast TEP addresses. These addresses will be referenced throughout the forwarding examples and troubleshooting scenarios in this chapter and the next.

Table 11-1 *TEP Addresses Allocated in the Fabric*

Device	Physical TEP	Additional TEPs
101	10.0.128.70	VPC TEP: 10.0.184.70
102	10.0.128.71	VPC TEP: 10.0.184.70
103	10.0.128.64	VPC TEP: 10.0.184.69
104	10.0.128.67	VPC TEP: 10.0.184.69
201	10.0.128.65	MAC anycast: 10.0.184.65
		IPv4 anycast: 10.0.184.66
		IPv6 anycast: 10.0.184.64
202	10.0.128.66	MAC anycast: 10.0.184.65
		IPv4 anycast: 10.0.184.66
		IPv6 anycast: 10.0.184.64

In addition to discussing troubleshooting for a single pod, this chapter also presents multi-pod forwarding and troubleshooting scenarios. Figure 11-2 shows the physical topology used for multi-pod in the following chapters. The topology consists of two pods, each with two leafs and two spines. There is a VPC-connected server in Pod 1, and there are two single attached servers in Pod 2.

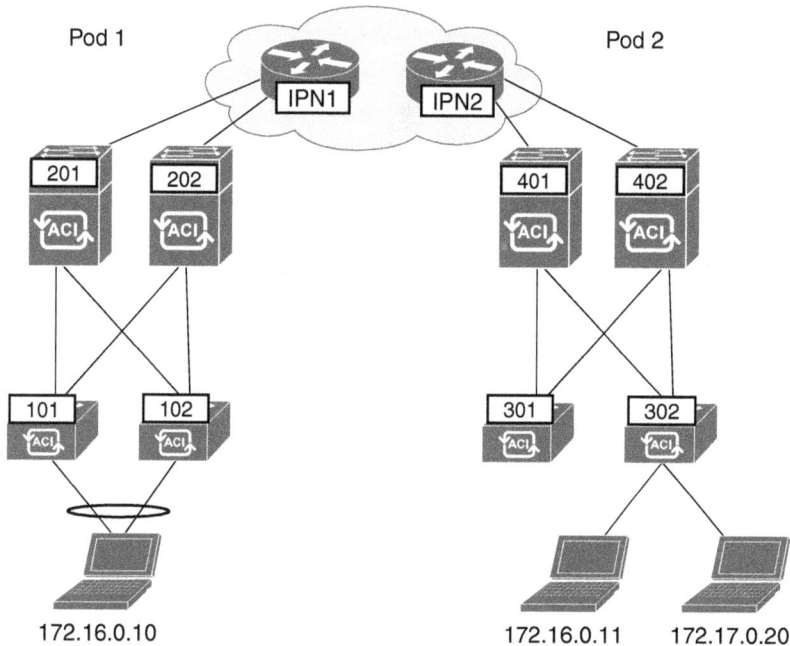

Figure 11-2 *Basic Topology for a Multi-pod Fabric*

Table 11-2 shows the important TEP addresses used for each device in this multi-pod topology. It includes the control plane and anycast TEP addresses used in a multi-pod solution. These TEP addresses will be discussed in further detail in Chapter 12.

Table 11-2 *TEP Addresses Allocated in the Multi-pod Fabric*

Device	Control Plane TEP	Data Plane TEP (E-TEP)	External MAC Proxy TEP	External IPV4 Proxy TEP	External IPV6 Proxy TEP
201	1.1.1.1	10.255.1.1	10.0.0.33	10.0.0.34	10.0.0.35
202	2.2.2.2	10.255.1.1	10.0.0.33	10.0.0.34	10.0.0.35
401	3.3.3.3	10.255.2.1	11.0.0.33	11.0.0.34	11.0.0.35
402	4.4.4.4	10.255.2.1	11.0.0.33	11.0.0.34	11.0.0.35

We will also examine multi-site scenarios in the following chapters, and they will be based on the physical topology shown in Figure 11-3. This topology consists of two sites with identical node IDs. There is a VPC-connected server in Site 1, and there are two single attached servers in Site 2.

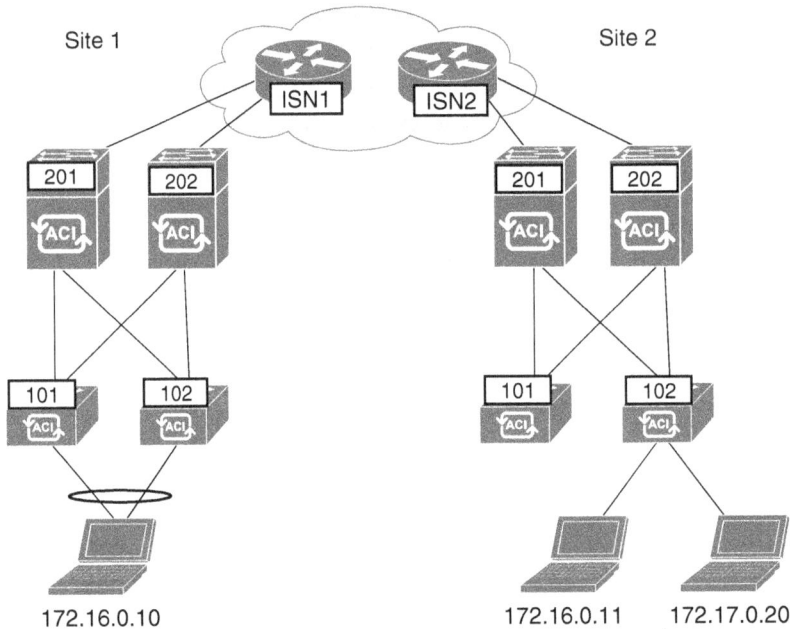

Figure 11-3 *Basic Topology for a Multi-Site Fabric*

Table 11-3 shows the important TEP addresses used for each device in this multi-site topology. It includes the control plane and anycast TEP addresses used in a multi-site solution. These TEP addresses will also be discussed in further detail in the next chapter.

Table 11-3 *TEP Addresses Allocated in the Multi-Site Fabric*

Device	Control Plane TEP	Data Plane TEP (E-TEP)	Data Plane Unicast TEP	Data Plane Multicast TEP
Site1-201	10.254.5.201	10.255.1.1	10.254.5.253	10.254.5.254
Site1-202	10.254.5.202	10.255.1.1	10.254.5.253	10.254.5.254
Site2-201	10.254.6.201	10.255.2.1	10.254.6.253	10.254.6.254
Site2-202	10.254.6.201	10.255.2.1	10.254.6.253	10.254.6.254

Figure 11-4 shows the physical topology used for remote leaf scenarios in the following chapters. The topology consists of a single pod and one remote leaf pair, where the node IDs are unique. There is a VPC-connected server in the main pod, there is a VPC-connected server on the remote leafs, and there is a single connected server on the remote leafs.

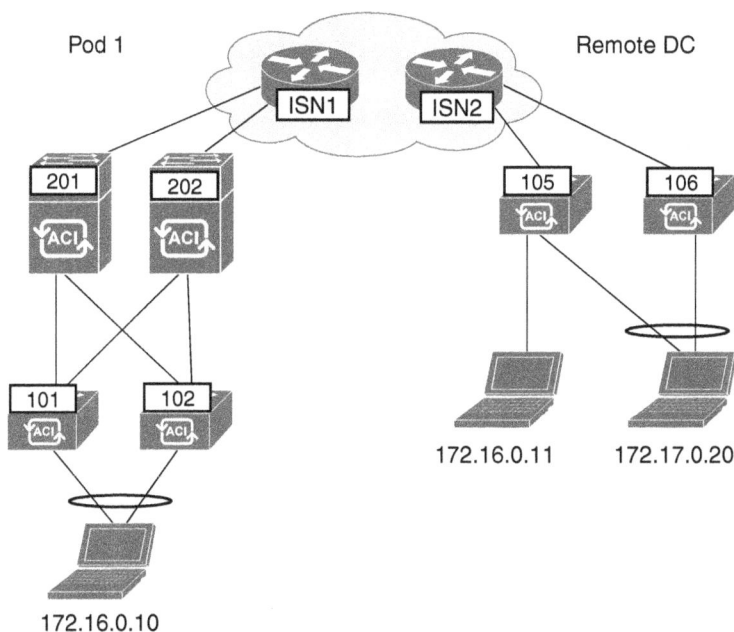

Figure 11-4   *Basic Topology for a Remote Leaf Fabric*

The TEP pool configured for the remote leaf is 10.100.0.0/22.

Table 11-4 shows the important TEP addresses used for the devices in this remote leaf topology. It includes the data plane, VPC, and anycast TEP addresses used in a remote leaf solution. These TEP addresses will also be discussed in further detail in the next chapter.

Table 11-4   *TEP Addresses Allocated in the Multi-site Fabric*

Device	RL-DP-TEP	RL-VPC-TEP	RL-Ucast TEP	RL-Mcast-TEP
201	N/A	N/A	10.0.0.36	10.0.0.37
202	N/A	N/A	10.0.0.36	10.0.0.37
105	10.100.1.128	10.100.0.96	N/A	N/A
106	10.100.2.128	10.100.0.96	N/A	N/A

APIC Initial Setup

Setting up the first APIC is the initial step in configuring the fabric, and it is a critical step. Many settings that are configured during the initial setup script cannot be changed after the initial configuration. It is also critical that these settings be consistent across the remaining APICs in the cluster. It is therefore recommended that you write down all required settings to keep them consistent while setting up a cluster. Table 11-5 shows all the required parameters used in the lab fabric.

Table 11-5 *APIC Initial Setup Parameters*

Setting	Description	Value
Fabric name	Fabric domain name	Prod-Fabric1
Fabric ID	Fabric ID	1
Number of active controllers	Cluster size	3
		Note: When setting up APIC in an active/standby mode, you must have at least three active APICs in a cluster.
POD ID	Pod ID	1
Standby controller	Set up standby controller.	No
Controller ID	Unique (per APIC) ID number for the active APIC instance	1
Controller name	Active controller name (unique per APIC)	apic1
IP address pool for TEP addresses	Tunnel endpoint address pool	10.0.0.0/16
VLAN ID for infrastructure network	Infrastructure VLAN for APIC-to-switch communication, including virtual switches	3967
	Note: Reserve this VLAN for APIC use only. The infrastructure VLAN ID must not be used elsewhere in the environment and must not overlap with any other reserved VLANs on other platforms.	
IP address pool for bridge domain multicast address (GIPo)	IP addresses used for fabric multi-destination traffic	225.0.0.0/15
	Note: For a Cisco APIC in a Cisco ACI multi-site topology, this GIPo address can be the same across sites.	
Enable IPv6 for Out of Band Mgmt Interface?	Enable IPv6 on management ports.	No
IPv4 addresses	IP address for APIC 1 (Unique per APIC)	192.168.4.11/24
IPv4 default gateway	Gateway address	192.168.4.1
Strong password check	Check for a strong password.	[Y]
Password	Password of the system administrator	—
	Note: This password must be at least 8 characters and must include at least 1 special character.	

APICs 1 and 2 are connected to Leafs 101 and 102, and APIC 3 is connected to Leafs 103 and 104.

Fabric Access Policies

Fabric access policies define not only port-level policies such as the administrative state of LLDP or CDP but also an overall naming convention that can help simplify the way ports are configured in the future. It is important to define a standard to follow early on to make it easier for new operators to understand what is going on. Naming schemes should be defined, as should the way to use pools, domains, and AAEPs. Users should decide early on how they want to carve out VLAN pools and whether overlap should or should not exist. Determining these conventions will greatly simplify the configuration of new ports in the future as well as troubleshooting access policies.

Switch Profiles, Switch Policies, and Interface Profiles

For the topology in Figure 11-1, Leaf Switches 101 and 102 are part of a VPC domain, and Leaf Switches 103 and 104 are part of another VPC domain. To configure a VPC in ACI, you have three choices in the Virtual Port Channel Default policy: Consecutive, Reciprocal, and Explicit. In this example, Explicit is used to give greater control over which switches are in a VPC domain. A VPC domain policy group can be created to modify the dead timer, but by default, it is set to the recommended value of 200 seconds.

For leaf switch profiles, a total of six policies were created, as shown in Figure 11-5. These switch profiles have a one-to-one mapping to the interface profiles.

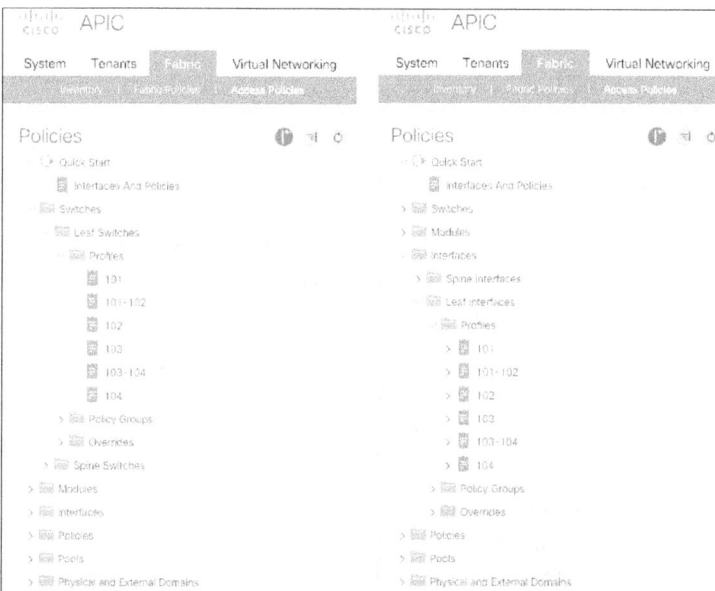

Figure 11-5   *Switch and Interface Profile Configuration*

Following this policy scheme gives you an easy overview of the interface configurations of different switches. Each access port selector is named after the Ethernet port that it configures. For example, a firewall is connected on eth1/14 on Leaf 104. Under Interface Profile 104, an access port selector named p14_firewall is created (see Figure 11-6).

Figure 11-6 *Access Port Selector Configuration on a Leaf Profile*

If the firewall had a VPC to 103–104, the 103–104 switch profile would be used instead of the one for only 104.

Interface Policies and Policy Groups

After defining switch profiles and interface profiles and creating access port selectors, you need to associate a policy group that contains the desired configuration of the individual interface or port channel. There are three types of policy groups:

- **Access port:** An access port policy group in ACI is not the same as an access port on a Catalyst switch, where only one VLAN is allowed. In ACI, an *access port* refers to the front panel port or an individual Ethernet interface. You use an access port policy group any time you don't plan on bundling multiple interfaces.

- **Port channel:** A port channel policy group is used to create a port channel and is switch significant. This means that if eth1/1 and eth1/10 on leaf 104 both use the same port channel policy group, they are bundled into the same port channel, even if different port selectors have been created. The same policy group can be reused on a different switch to create a new port channel.

■ **Virtual port channel (VPC):** Just as with the port channel policy, a VPC policy creates a port channel, but it also assigns a VPC ID to this port channel. This means the same VPC policy group cannot be used twice on the same switch pair to create two virtual port channels. Each VPC on the same switch pair requires a unique policy group to be created.

Note   If you need multiple port channels with the same configuration, you can right-click on the policy group and select Clone to use the clone functionality to easily replicate the policy group configuration.

Besides defining if the interface will be an access port or a port channel, a policy group also contains a collection of policies—hence the name *policy group*. When defining the different policies, it makes sense to give them descriptive names. For example, you might use the name *LLDP_Enable* for a policy that enables LLDP for transmitting and receiving. In addition, it makes sense to create port channel policies called *LACP_Active*, *Mode_On*, and *LACP_SuspendIndividual* so that when they are used in a policy group, you know what each policy does without having to examine it closely. A fabric administrator needs to find a balance between reusing the same policies for different workloads and creating a new one for each workload. One benefit and challenge with policies is that they are updating policies. This means that if multiple policy groups are all using an *LACP_Active* policy, and when you troubleshoot a new server where you have to change the policy to *Static Channel – Mode_On*, all other servers using this policy would see their bundle change from LACP to Mode On. A better way to accomplish this task would be to create a new port channel policy for this server specifically and reference the new policy in the policy group instead of editing the existing policy which multiple servers might be using.

Pools, Domains, and AAEPs

As described in Chapters 2, "Introduction to the ACI Policy Model," and 4, "ACI Fabric Design Options," pools, domains, and AAEPs are used to restrict what policy a tenant administrator can deploy on an interface. ACI was built from the ground up with multitenancy in mind. This means that either automation tools or different users can have administrative rights to a specific tenant and decide what static paths or L3Outs they want to deploy on an interface. To build a successful multitenancy environment, a fabric administrator needs to have a method to prevent others from using more resources than they should or deploying resources that were allocated for another tenant. This is done in three ways:

■ **VLAN pool:** The VLAN pool defines which VLANs will be made accessible. VLAN pools have two modes:

■ **Static:** The tenant administrator defines the VLAN ID to use.

■ **Dynamic:** A VMM controller or L4–L7 device can use a dynamic pool. This means the APIC chooses a VLAN, and you do not have to worry about VLAN mapping or stitching.

- **Domain:** The domain is linked to a single VLAN pool, and it defines what type of configuration can be deployed. It also defines which tenants have access to this VLAN pool by applying security domain configuration to it. There are four types of domains:

  - **Physical domain:** This domain type is used for static path deployments. It is linked to an EPG.

  - **External bridged domain:** These domains are not frequently used but are linked to external bridged networks (L2Outs).

  - **External routed domain:** VLANs from the VLAN pool that is tied to an external routed domain can be used to deploy an L3Out with SVIs or routed subinterface encapsulation.

  - **Fibre Channel domain:** Fibre Channel domains restrict the VSAN and VLAN IDs that can be used to deploy FCoE.

  The domain can be tied to a security domain. A security domain is created to provide users access to specific tenants.

- **AAEP:** The attachable access entity profile (AAEP) ties everything together and associates the domain, and therefore a VLAN pool, to an interface. This is accomplished by defining the AAEP in the interface policy group. Figure 11-7 shows an AAEP and its association to a domain.

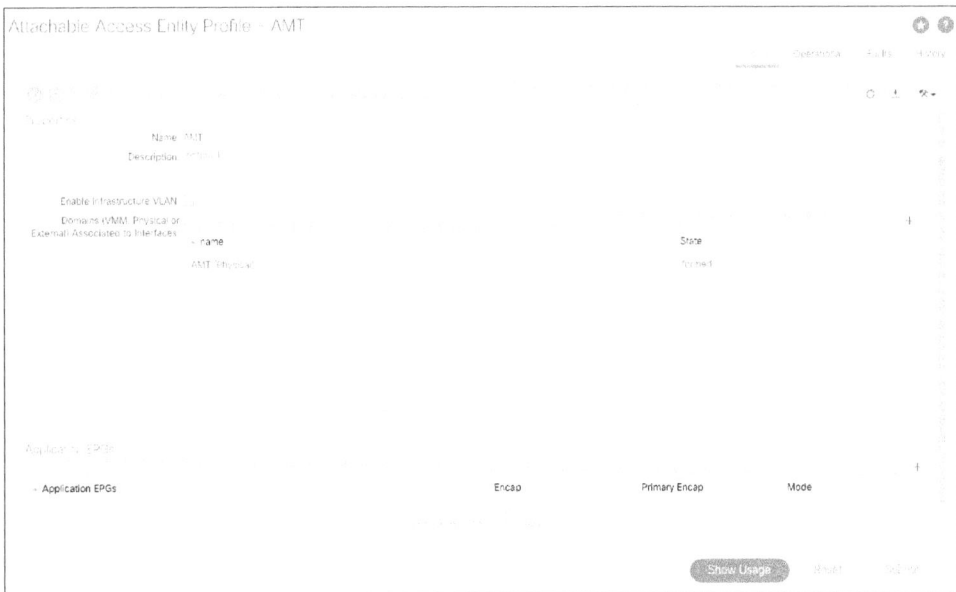

Figure 11-7 *Configuration with an Associated Physical Domain*

In Figure 11-7, you can see that the *AMT* AAEP is linked to a single physical domain, which is also called *AMT*. This means you can deploy static paths on any interface where the policy group references the *AMT* AAEP. The VLANs that can be deployed are part of the VLAN pool called *AMT-Static*, as shown in Figure 11-8.

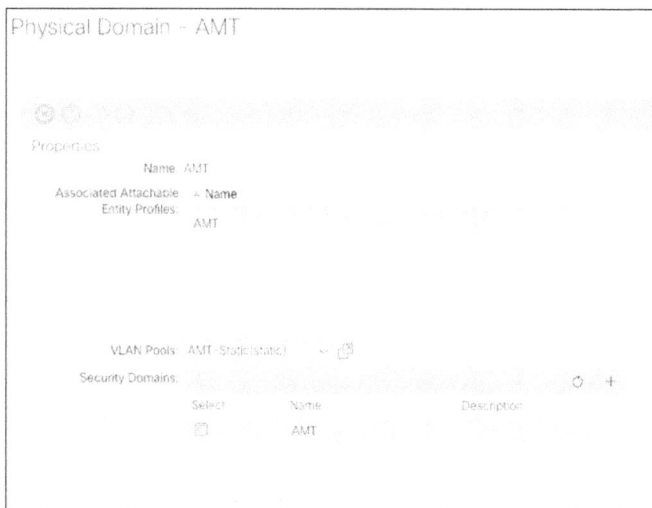

Figure 11-8 *Physical Domain Configuration with Associated AEP, VLAN Pool, and Security Domain*

The VLAN pool *AMT-Static* contains VLANs 1 through 200, which are the VLANs used in the lab's legacy environment, as well as VLANs that will be newly deployed. The security domain *AMT* is associated with the tenant *ACI-AMT-Book*.

When designing AAEPs, you should have a minimum of two AAEPs: one for static path bindings and another for external routed domains. If VMM integration is used, it's best practice to allocate a separate AAEP for VMM-attached servers as well so that the AAEP can be the boundary for where a VLAN gets deployed. One way to automatically deploy all VMM-enabled VLANs or EPGs on ports facing the ESX servers is by changing the resolution immediacy for a VMM domain to Pre-Provision. When this is configured, the VLAN gets pushed to every interface that is using the AAEP that is associated to the VMM domain. Another way to push the same VLAN to all ports is by deploying an EPG and an VLAN on the AAEP itself. When you do this, the VLAN is again pushed to every interface that has the AAEP associated. This can cause a major problem if the AAEP is also used for an L3Out and the L3Out is configured with a routed port. In this case, one configuration calls for the interface to be a routed port, and the other calls for it to be a switch port. After an upgrade or reload, the switch could have inconsistent configuration for this interface. To avoid this in our lab, the AAEP *AMT* is used for static and dynamic paths, and *AMT-L3-AAEP* is used to configure interfaces where L3Outs are deployed.

On top of the physical domain, the lab utilizes an external routed domain called *AMT-L3-Domain*. To extend EPGs into the legacy environment, static paths on the EPGs are used instead of an L2Out. Because of this, an external bridged domain is not created in our lab.

For the VLAN pool, a single pool called *AMT-Static* is used for deploying static paths and L3Outs. A second VLAN pool called *AMT-Dynamic* is used for VMM integration. Table 11-6 provides an overview of fabric access policies created for the lab.

Table 11-6   *Policy Overview*

Policy	Policy Number or Name	Notes
Switch profile	101	One switch profile per physical switch and one switch profile per VPC domain.
	102	
	103	
	104	
	101–102	
	103–104	
Interface profile	101	One interface profile per physical switch and one interface profile per VPC domain. Each is mapped to the corresponding switch profile.
	102	
	103	
	104	
	101–102	
	103–104	
Interface selector	*Px_Device*	*P* stands for port, and *x* is the numeric value of the Ethernet port that follows. *_Device* is a description of what is connected on the port.
Interface policy group	*unixServerFarm*	The interface policy group name should be descriptive of what is connected via these policies. Use the same policy group for interfaces that require identical configurations.
	windowsServerFarm	
	openStackServerFarm	
	loadBalancer	
Interface policies	*LLLDP-On*	Use descriptive names for policies so that it is easy to understand what the policy does. Keep in mind that these names should never be changed, and if a server requires an LACP policy that allows for individual ports, a new policy should be created.
	CDP-On	
	LACP-Sus-Individual	

Policy	Policy Number or Name	Notes
AAEP	*AMT* *AMT-L3-AAEP*	At minimum, one AAEP should be used for L3Outs. One or more can be created for static and dynamic paths.
Domain	*AMT* *AMT-L3-Domain*	
Pool	*AMT-Static* *AMT-Dynamic*	

VMM Domain Configuration

VMM domains simplify the process of connecting hypervisors and leaf switches. It is important to understand that these are domain-wide configurations, so if one server is configured with a port channel on the vSwitch, all remaining hosts in that domain have to be configured the same way. One common misconception is that the leaf configuration determine this. If a blade switch is between the host and the fabric, it does not matter if a VPC goes to the blade switch. The configuration of the server must match the capability and configuration of the blade switch.

VMM Topology

VMM domain integration needs to be configured, and a few troubleshooting scenarios for this are discussed in later chapters. In the topology shown in Figure 11-9, a UCS B-Series blade chassis and fabric interconnects are connected via a VPC to Leafs 101 and 102.

The VMM domain was configured using a dedicated vSphere user account called aciadmin@vsphere.local for the APIC that contains the following permissions:

- Alarms
- Distributed switch
- dvPort group
- Folder
- Network
- Host
- Virtual machine

This way, when the APIC pushes configuration to vCenter, these audits can be logged with the specific APIC user account. Furthermore, the APIC should be able to push and pull any information it needs to ensure a successful integration because the permissions are configured correctly.

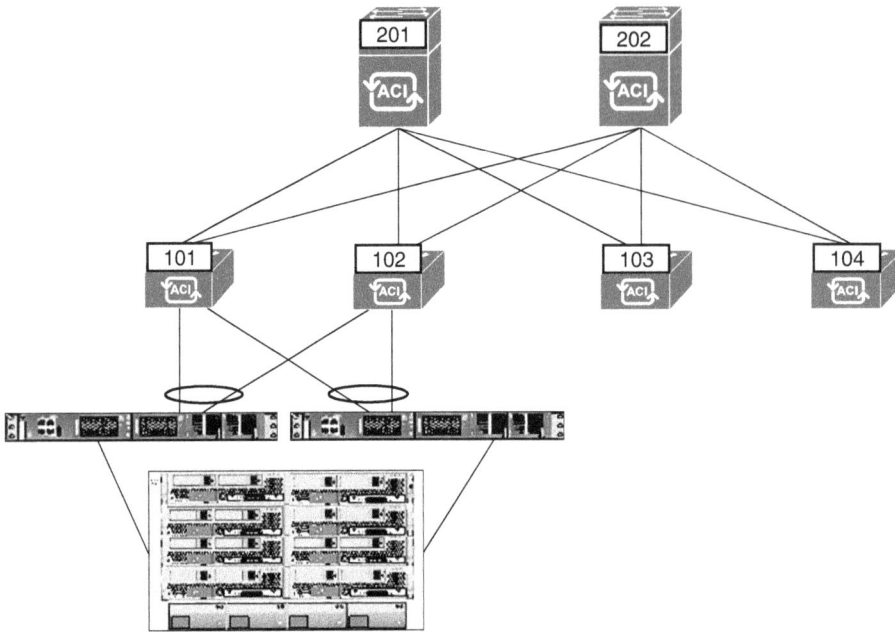

Figure 11-9   *Topology of VMM-Attached Servers*

After creating the VMM domain, you need to also create a vSwitch policy to ensure that the configuration on the APIC-managed VDS reflects best practices when integrating with Cisco UCS B-Series blades. The vSwitch policy for the lab has the following configuration:

- **Port channel policy: MAC Pinning:** Cisco UCS B-Series blades cannot be configured in a VPC toward the fabric interconnects. Because of this, in order to achieve an active/active workload with load balancing, the teaming method should either be "Route based on originating virtual port" or "Route based on physical NIC load." Both of these options are supported and can be configured via the APIC. "Route based on originating virtual port" is used in this deployment.

- **LLDP Policy: LLDP-On:** In this deployment, LLDP is the desired discovery protocol that will be pushed to the VDS.

- **CDP Policy: CDP-Off:** Only one discovery protocol should be enabled at a time to avoid issues with changes causing disruptions. Because LLDP is the desired protocol, CDP will be disabled.

Hardware and Software Specifications

The single-pod fabric in this deployment consists of two spines—one modular and one fixed chassis:

- **Spine 201:** 9504 with a N9K-X9736C-FX line card and C9504-FM-E fabric modules
- **Spine 202:** N9K-C9364C

In addition, four leaf switches are used, and two VPC domains are configured:

- **Leaf 101:** N9K-C93180YC-EX in VPC Domain 1
- **Leaf 102:** N9K-C93180YC-EX in VPC Domain 1
- **Leaf 103:** N9K-C9336C-FX2 in VPC Domain 2
- **Leaf 104:** N9K-C9336C-FX2 in VPC Domain 2

First-generation switches (those not ending in EX or FX) are not covered, and specific feature limitations for those platforms are omitted.

Most of the magic happens on the leaf switches. For the leafs to learn endpoints and routes and to enforce policy, a few different software and hardware components must interact together. On the supervisor module, there are four primary components that achieve this functionality:

- **Endpoint Manager (EPM):** EPM is responsible for managing MAC and IP endpoints, as well as for performing control plane–level functions, such as syncing endpoints to a VPC peer or publishing endpoints to the APIC for visibility.
- **Ethernet Lif Table Manager (ELTM):** ELTM is a component that programs the interfaces, VLANs, and VRF instances on an ACI switch. It gets configuration from the APIC when policy is pushed, translates that configuration to the appropriate constructs, and sends them to the hardware to be programmed.
- **Unicast Routing Information Base (uRib):** uRib is responsible for installing routes into the routing table on an ACI switch. Routes can be either BD routes defined in the APIC configuration or static/dynamic routes defined or learned through an L3Out.
- **Policy Manager:** Policy Manager is software that runs on the supervisor and is responsible for receiving contract configuration from the APIC and passing that configuration to the hardware.

Each of the four components in this list has one more matching software process that runs on the line card. These processes interact with the respective supervisor process to receive requests and program the hardware. This ensures that there is a full stack from software to hardware and enables the switch to perform forwarding and policy enforcement without penalty in hardware. On the line card, the processes are as follows:

- **Hardware Abstraction Layer (HAL):** HAL acts as a single point for all line card processes to communicate with the hardware. HAL understands how to program the cloud-scale ASICs, so multiple processes leverage HAL to configure their individual functions (endpoints, routes, contracts, and QoS) into the ASIC hardware.

- **Endpoint Manager Client (EPMC):** EPMC is responsible for learning MAC and IP endpoints from hardware and reporting the endpoint information to EPM. EPMC can also receive notifications from EPM to install endpoints based on control plane updates. EPMC also communicates with HAL to program endpoint information into the hardware.

- **Ethernet Lif Table Manager Client (ELTMC):** ELTMC is responsible for taking the configuration from ELTM and programming the hardware for interfaces, VLANs, and VRF instances. ELTMC uses HAL to interact with the hardware.

- **Unicast Forwarding Information Base (uFib):** uFib is responsible for installing routes into hardware. uFib receives updates from uRib and communicates routing updates to HAL to program the routes into hardware.

- **Access Control List and Quality of Service (ACLQOS):** ACLQOS is responsible for programming contracts and QoS configuration into hardware. Policy Manager sends requests to ACLQOS, which communicates with HAL to accomplish this.

Figure 11-10 provides a diagram of the logical configuration on the APIC and shows how the configuration gets programmed into the switch hardware, leveraging the processes on the supervisor and line card.

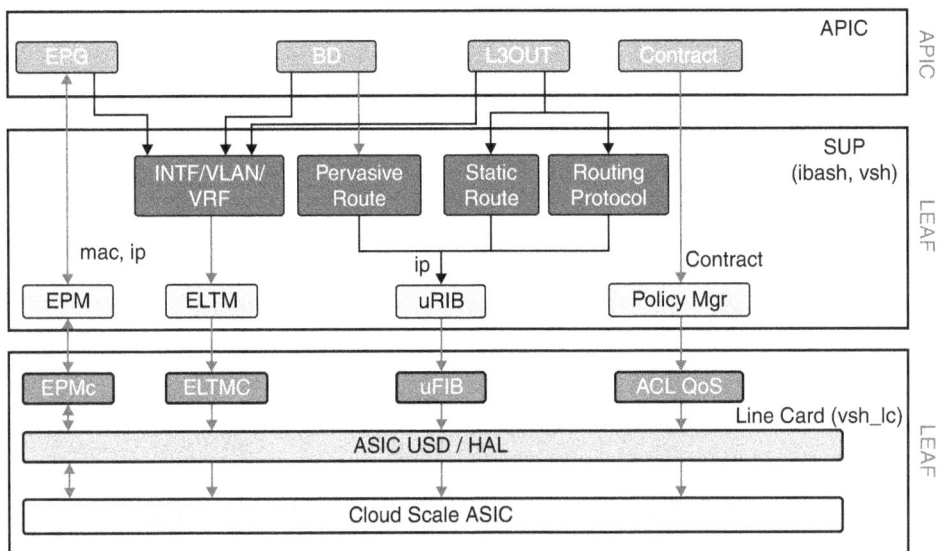

Figure 11-10 *The Software and Hardware Components of an ACI Cloud-Scale Leaf*

Throughout the following chapters, you will be hearing about each of these components in more detail. You will also learn when each component comes into play and what commands to run to see important information for troubleshooting purposes.

Logical Layout of EPGs, BDs, VRF Instances, and Contracts

Most forwarding examples in the following chapters use a single tenant called *ACI-AMT-Book*. Within this tenant, one application profile has been created for a network-centric design and another for an application-centric design. These two terms, network-centric and application-centric, are often talked about in a mutually exclusive way. However, there isn't a knob or a switch that you flip to go from one mode to the other; it is more of a naming scheme and design philosophy.

In this topology, a single VRF is used in tenant *ACI-AMT-Book* named *v1* (Short for VRF 1). To represent networks that exist outside ACI but that need to be extended into the fabric, an application profile named *NetCentric* has been created. The EPGs inside *NetCentric* use the naming scheme that combines the VLAN and the encapsulation VLAN ID. These EPGs map to the physical domain *AMT* to allow static paths to be deployed with the matching encapsulation. On top of this, a single bridge domain exists for each EPG that is part of the *NetCentric* application profile. A permit any contract is provided and consumed on all *NetCentric* EPGs to mimic the legacy environment where devices could communicate without having to whitelist the flows. Figure 11-11 illustrates this logical topology.

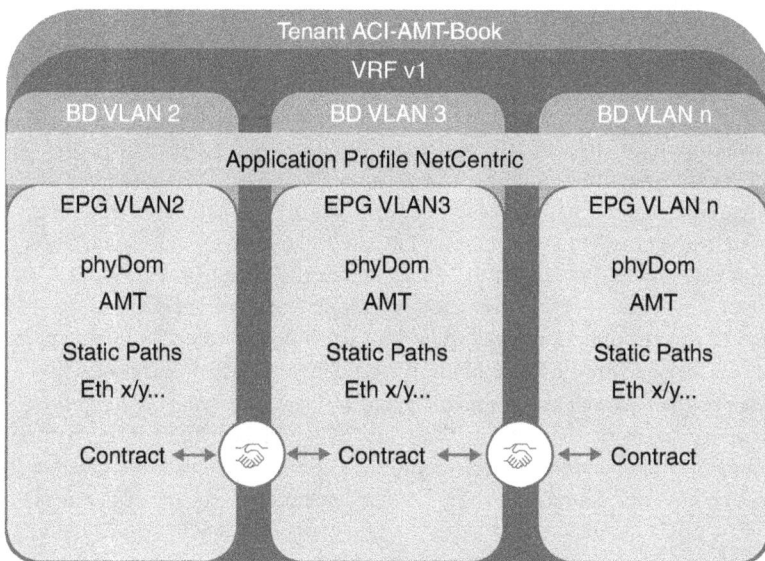

Figure 11-11 *Logical Topology for the Network-Centric Application Profile*

When creating bridge domains and EPGs for new services, it is important to understand what the application does and what contracts need to be consumed and provided. This is when you can start utilizing the application-centric approach of ACI and microsegment different applications. In the topology shown in Figure 11-12, a simple application is represented by an application profile named *AMT* with EPGs named *Web*, *App*, and *DB*. Based on the application requirements, you can create contracts specifically for the required traffic flows.

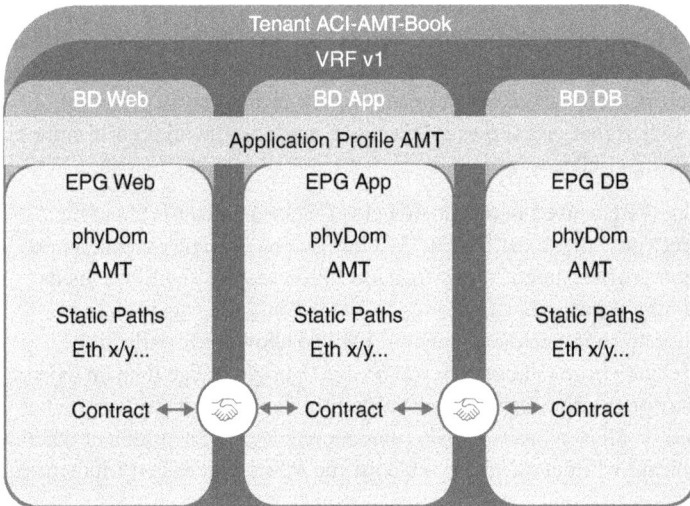

Figure 11-12   *Logical Topology for the Application-Centric Application Profile*

L3Out Logical Layout

The L3Out Logical topology contains two routers that will be used to gain access to external subnets: a core router that provides access to the 10.254.0.0/16 subnet range and a WAN router that connects the 10.255.0.0/16 network. The WAN router also advertises a default route into the fabric. When defining an L3Out, at the top level (*l3extOut*), you define the routing protocol that you want to use, as well as the VRF that the L3Out should be a part of. Furthermore, you must select which *external routed domain* the L3Out has access to so the configured encapsulation can be deployed on the physical interface. In the logical node profile (*l3extNodeP*), you define on which leaf nodes this L3Out should be deployed as well as the router ID and any static routes. BGP neighbor configuration is also defined via the node profile when BGP is the desired peering method. Under the node profile, the logical interface profile (*l3extLifP*) needs to be created; it defines the interface-level configuration. Under the interface profile, the physical path is created, along with the IP address(es) to use to create an adjacency to the external router. A routing protocol policy, such as an OSPF interface policy, can be defined as part of the logical interface profile if a dynamic routing protocol is used. This is where you specify the timers and authentication parameters. The logical node and interface profile configure the routing parameters, but the network (*l3extInstP*) designates how to treat data plane traffic and control the advertisement of routes. In this topology, all three subnets are used to classify data plane traffic, as shown in Figure 11-13.

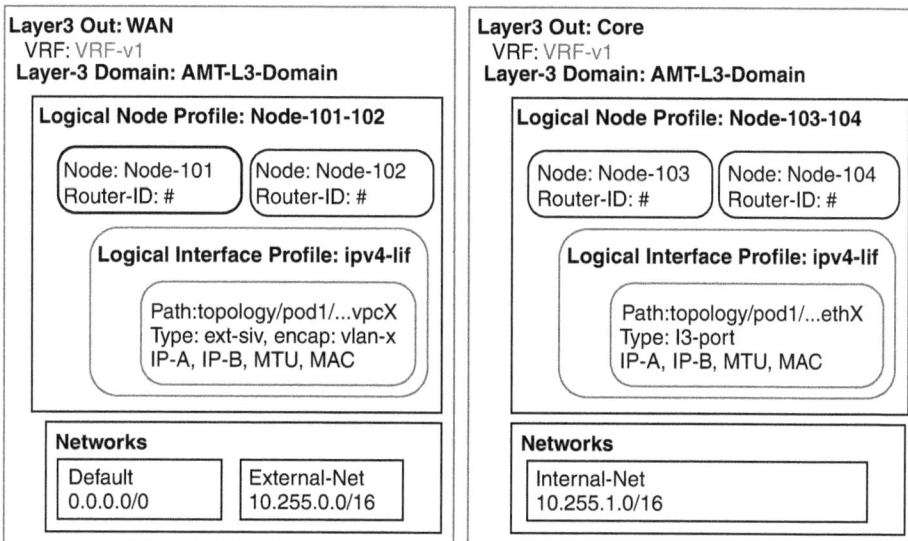

Layer3 Out: WAN
  VRF: VRF-v1
  Layer-3 Domain: AMT-L3-Domain

  Logical Node Profile: Node-101-102

    Node: Node-101   Node: Node-102
    Router-ID: #   Router-ID: #

      Logical Interface Profile: ipv4-lif

        Path:topology/pod1/...vpcX
        Type: ext-siv, encap: vlan-x
        IP-A, IP-B, MTU, MAC

  Networks

    Default   External-Net
    0.0.0.0/0   10.255.0.0/16

Layer3 Out: Core
  VRF: VRF-v1
  Layer-3 Domain: AMT-L3-Domain

  Logical Node Profile: Node-103-104

    Node: Node-103   Node: Node-104
    Router-ID: #   Router-ID: #

      Logical Interface Profile: ipv4-lif

        Path:topology/pod1/...ethX
        Type: l3-port
        IP-A, IP-B, MTU, MAC

  Networks

    Internal-Net
    10.255.1.0/16

Figure 11-13   *L3Out Logical Design*

To classify traffic coming from the WAN router into the *External-Net* EPG, 10.255.0.0/16 is defined within the external EPG, and the External Subnets for the External EPG flag is selected. A second external EPG called *Default* is created; it has 0.0.0.0/0 defined and External Subnets for the External EPG checked. This classifies all traffic where a more specific subnet isn't defined into the *Default* external EPG. Under the core L3Out, an external EPG called *Internal-Net* is created, and 10.254.0.0/16 is configured. This too acts as a prefix to classify traffic into this EPG when External Subnets for the External EPG is selected. An additional goal is to advertise *Internal-Net* to the WAN router. This is done by defining 10.254.0.0/16 along with only the Export Route Control Subnet flag under either the *Default* or *External-Net* external EPG. To allow traffic to flow between *Internal-Net* prefixes and *External-Net* prefixes, a provider/consumer contract relationship is created between the two EPGs (see Figure 11-14).

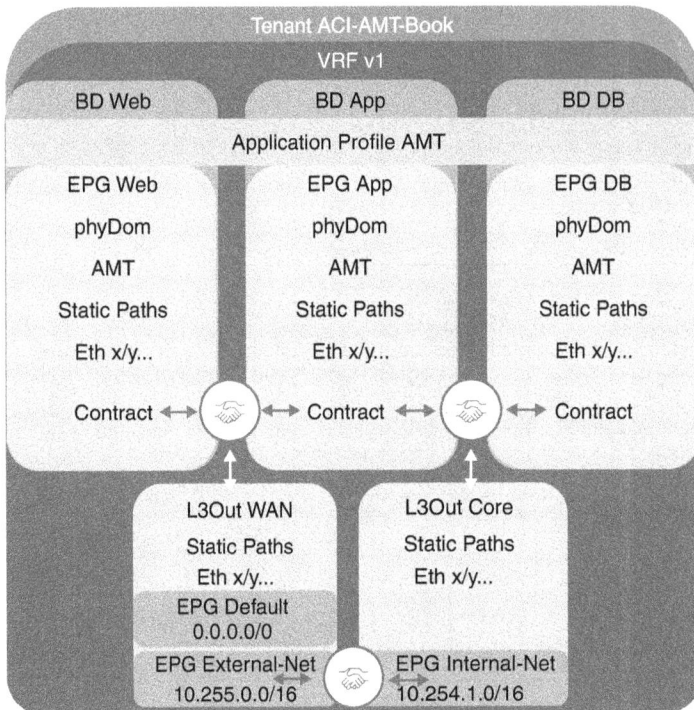

Figure 11-14 *Tenant with L3Out Design*

Summary

In this chapter, you have learned about the physical topology, fabric access policies, and logical layout of tenant policies and the software process on the switches that tie all this together. These base topologies are used in the following chapters to dive deeper into forwarding and troubleshooting of ACI. For certain scenarios, the topology might be slightly different to illustrate or highlight specific points.

Review Key Topics

If you are preparing to take the Implementing Cisco Application Centric Infrastructure - Advanced (300-630 DCACIA) exam to attain the Cisco Certified Specialist—ACI Advanced Implementation certification, be sure to review the key topics marked in this chapter as outlined in Table 11-7.

Table 11-7 *Key Topics*

Key Topic Element	Description	Page Number
Section	L3Out Logical Layout	606

References

Cisco, "Cisco APIC Getting Started Guide," Cisco.com

Cisco, "Mastering ACI Forwarding Behavior," CiscoLive.com

Note   There are no Review Questions for this chapter.

Chapter 12

Bits and Bytes of ACI Forwarding

At its core, ACI is a data center technology that provides a fully managed fabric with forwarding optimizations and performance enhancements. Using VXLAN, traffic can be tunneled to any node in the fabric, ensuring that workloads can exist anywhere without introducing complexity. This chapter describes how forwarding inside the fabric works. When you know how a packet moves through the ACI fabric, you can explore the details of the iVXLAN header, how multicast distribution trees (MDTs) are built, and what control plane protocols exist. This chapter presents forwarding scenarios that demonstrate how packets move inside the ACI fabric.

In this chapter, you will learn the following:

- Overview of overlay networking
- Introduction to iVXLAN
- IS-IS, TEP addressing, and the ACI underlay
- Endpoint learning
- Control plane protocols (such as COOP and BGP)
- Border leafs and external routes
- Policy enforcement
- Quality of service
- Forwarding scenarios

Limitations of Traditional Networks and the Evolution of Overlay Networks

To understand forwarding in an ACI fabric, it is important to first understand why overlay networks exist today and the challenges they try to overcome. Ethernet networks have existed for over 35 years, and engineers have spent their days trying to design stable networks in these decades. To overcome challenges of large Layer 2 networks, the Layer 3 boundary was pushed further and further to the edge so that Layer 3 networks using advanced routing protocols could handle failure scenarios and link redundancy. When virtualization became the standard in data centers and a virtual machine could exist on any host at a given time, Layer 2 had to again be extended to every switch within the data center to meet this requirement. In a large network, this meant that distribution or core switches would have to learn every MAC address for every flow that traversed it. Spanning Tree Protocol was used to block redundant links whenever they existed to avoid loops, but this reduced the available bandwidth. Virtual Switching System (VSS), virtual port channel (VPC), and other Multichassis EtherChannel (MEC) technologies could be used to avoid the blocking of a redundant link, but a misbehaving device, high CPU on a switch, or a unidirectional link could result in Spanning Tree Protocol not functioning correctly and causing bridging loops within the data center.

To overcome these challenges and take advantage of the convergence and stability and features available in Layer 3, overlay networks became popular simply by encapsulating traffic in a VXLAN header and forwarding it between VXLAN tunnel endpoints (VTEPs). By encapsulating traffic, a resilient Layer 3 network, the underlay, provides redundant paths through the use of equal-cost multipathing (ECMP) and fast-converging routing protocols to provide connectivity for the overlay.

The ACI fabric is built from the ground up to be a spine/leaf architecture, or a Clos fabric. In a basic fabric, every leaf switch is connected to every spine, and any endpoint is always the same distance, in terms of hops and latency, from every other endpoint inside the fabric. Figure 12-1 shows a 2-spine, 4-leaf ACI topology which in ACI Release 3.2 can scale to 200 leaf switches and 6 spines.

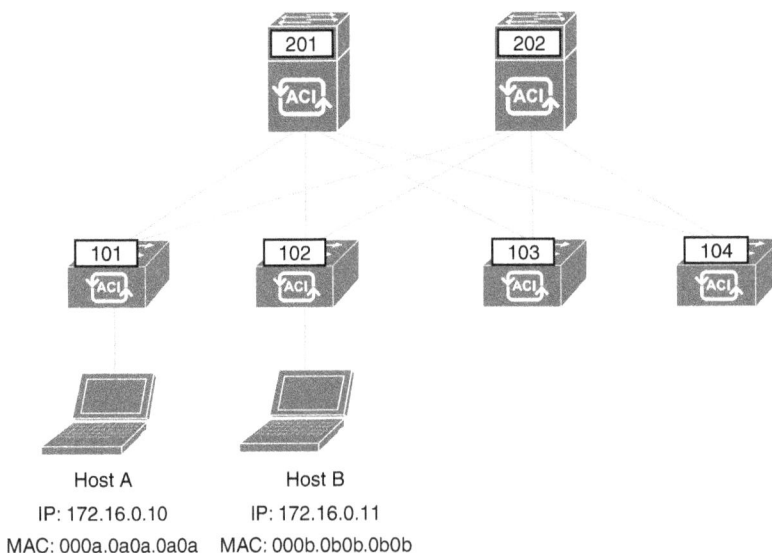

Figure 12-1 *Simple ACI Clos Topology*

High-Level VXLAN Overview

To highlight how a packet is forwarded in an ACI fabric, it is fitting to begin by examining the Ethernet, IPv4, and iVXLAN header used to encapsulate traffic traversing the ACI overlay. In Figure 12-1, Host A is connected to Leaf 101, and Host B is connected to Leaf 102. If Host A sends a unicast frame to Host B, Leaf 101 encapsulates this in an IP and iVXLAN header. To understand the forwarding process, let us examine the IP header shown in Figure 12-2.

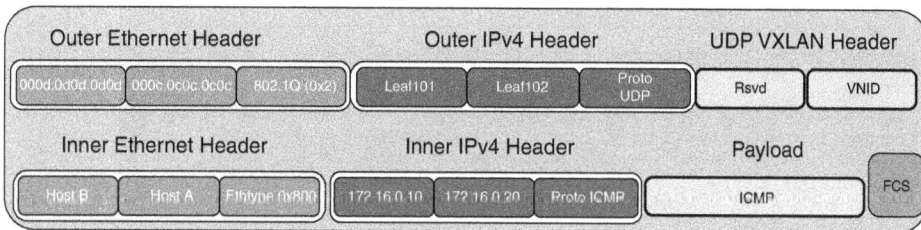

Figure 12-2   *iVXLAN Header Fields*

When Leaf 101 receives the packet from Host A and the destination MAC address, 000b.0b0b.0b0b, which is a learned unicast MAC address on a tunnel interface, it encapsulates the packet and uses the overlay to reach the destination. This means a new outer Ethernet header is populated, along with an IPv4 and iVXLAN header. When an endpoint isn't local, the next hop is always a spine switch, and the source MAC address is always 000d.0d0d.0d0d. The destination MAC address that the switch writes is always 000c.0c0c.0c0c. 000c.0c0c.0c0c is a MAC address that all spines treat as a router MAC address, and 0d0d.0d0d.0d0d is a MAC address that all leaf switches treat as a router MAC address. This simplifies the adjacency tables in ACI because the same source and destination are always used, no matter how many spines the leaf is connected to. This provides a significant advantage over non-ACI networks because after links flap or when bringing up new interfaces, the adjacency does not need to be updated.

The interfaces between a leaf and a spine are always point-to-point Layer 3 ports with subinterfaces. The subinterface ID is nondeterministic, but the encapsulation VLAN is always VLAN 2. In the IP header, the source IP address is set to the TEP address assigned by the APIC to the leaf switch. The TEP address is always assigned to a loopback on the leaf switches, and the Layer 3 ports do not have a unique IP address. This is similar to using an IP unnumbered configuration where the IP address for the subinterface is inherited from the loopback interface for the Layer 3 port connecting to the spine. If Leaf 101 has learned the MAC address of Host B via Leaf 102, the destination IPv4 address can be set to Leaf 102 in the IP header as well. The goal of the last step is to encapsulate the original frame from Host A to Host B in iVXLAN. The iVXLAN format calls for a UDP destination port 48879, and the source port is a hash of the inner packet. The inner packet is then encapsulated and followed by the FCS of the whole frame and not the original FCS that the host sent. If the original frame came in on a trunk interface and 802.1Q is present, the leaf switch removes the 802.1Q tag when encapsulating the frame. Table 12-1 provides an overview of the values that need to be set.

Table 12-1 *Overview of Fields in the Inner and Outer Headers*

Parameter	Value
Outer Source MAC	0d0d.0d0d.0d0d
Outer Destination MAC	000c.0c0c.0c0c
802.1Q	VLAN ID 2
Outer Source IP	Source TEP address
Outer Designation IP	Destination TEP
UDP Source Port	Hash of inner packet
UDP Destination Port	48879
VXLAN VNID	BD ID
VXLAN Source Group	EPG ID
Inner Destination MAC	Host B 000b.0b0b.0b0b
Inner Source MAC	Host A, 000a.0a0a.0a0a
Inner Source IP	172.16.0.10
Inner Destination IP	172.16.0.11

In the VXLAN header, the VNID field is used to identify the unique Layer 2 segment or bridge domain in which Hosts A and B reside. Bridge domain VNIDs are assigned by the APIC and are globally unique within a fabric. The source group, similar to the bridge domain, is a value assigned by the APIC to the EPG in which Host A resides. Source group IDs or policy control tags (PCTags) are not globally unique by default and can be reused across different VRF instances. Figure 12-3 shows the bits of the iVXLAN header in greater detail.

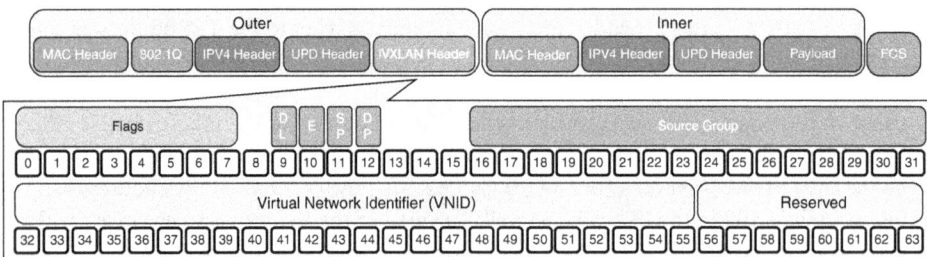

Figure 12-3 *The 64 Bits of the iVXLAN Header*

Now let's take a step back and review how the fabric knows how to reach each leaf using the underlay. In this section, the following terms are used often:

- **Underlay:** The underlay is the routing table that the ACI leaf switches use to determine how to traverse the fabric.

- **Overlay:** The overlay is the traffic that is encapsulated in VXLAN. All tenant traffic traverses the overlay.

- **Inner header:** When tenant traffic is encapsulated, the tenant headers are considered the inner headers.

- **Outer header:** When not encapsulated, a tenant traffic header is considered the outer header. When tenant traffic is encapsulated, the outer header is the header used by the underlay.

- **PTEP:** A physical tunnel endpoint (PTEP) is the IP address that identifies a single leaf and not a shared resource.

- **VPC TEP:** A VPC domain's tunnel endpoint (TEP) address is the address shared between two leaf switches.

IS-IS, TEP Addressing, and the ACI Underlay

For traffic to traverse the fabric, the leaf switches need to have TEP addresses configured. The leaf and spine switches also have to have a routing protocol running between them to exchange the TEP reachability information. This section provides information on TEP addressing and IS-IS and what NX-OS CLI commands to use to view more detail.

IS-IS and TEP Addressing

A critical component for a VXLAN overlay to function smoothly is a resilient underlay network. The underlay is responsible for advertising TEP routes between the leafs and spines within a fabric. Without reachability to TEP addresses, no VXLAN-encapsulated traffic can be sent to that TEP, which inevitably results in isolation of that TEP in the ACI fabric. Furthermore, when there is a link failure or some other physical change in the topology, you need the underlay infrastructure to converge quickly to prevent loss of connectivity. For this reason, IS-IS is the preferred routing protocol in the underlay network in ACI. In ACI, IS-IS is used as an underlay routing protocol to exchange reachability information of the TEP addresses as well as other TEP or IP ranges assigned for different purposes.

An ACI leaf switch is assigned a PTEP address when it joins the fabric. This address is always assigned to interface Loopback 0, which is always part of the VRF instance *overlay-1*. Example 12-1 shows the TEP address of Leaf 101.

Example 12-1 *TEP Address of Leaf 101*

```
leaf101# show interface loopback 0
loopback0 is up
admin state is up,
  Hardware: Loopback
  Internet Address is 10.0.128.70/32
  MTU 1500 bytes, BW 8000000 Kbit, DLY 5000 usec
  reliability 255/255, txload 1/255, rxload 1/255
  Encapsulation LOOPBACK, medium is broadcast
  Port mode is routed
  Auto-mdix is turned off
    0 packets input 0 bytes
    0 multicast packets 0 compressed
    0 input errors 0 frame 0 overrun 0 fifo
    0 packets output 0 bytes 0 underruns
    0 output errors 0 collisions 0 fifo
    0 out_carrier_errors
```

Once the leaf or spine node has received an IP address from the APIC, it begins sending IS-IS hello messages and exchanges routing information for each TEP address that it owns with other infrastructure neighbors in the fabric. The adjacency is established as a point-to-point adjacency, meaning that spines see leafs as neighbors and vice versa. In IS-IS, there is a system ID that is used when forming adjacencies with other neighbors. In ACI, the system ID is based on the PTEP address that is assigned to the node, and it is represented in reversed hexadecimal format. For example, you can view the IS-IS routing information for a given node, as demonstrated in Example 12-2.

Example 12-2 *System ID of Leaf 101*

```
leaf101# show isis protocol vrf overlay-1
ISIS process : isis_infra
VRF: overlay-1
  System ID : 46:80:00:0A:00:00  IS-Type :  L1
  SAP : 412  Queue Handle : 14
  Maximum LSP MTU: 1492
  Metric-style : advertise(narrow, wide), accept(narrow, wide)
  Area address(es) :
    01
  Process is up and running
  Interfaces supported by IS-IS :
    loopback0
    loopback1
    Ethernet1/50.63
    Ethernet1/49.62
```

```
Address family IPv4 unicast :
  Number of interface : 4
  Adjacency check disabled
   Distance : 115
```

Because the PTEP IP address of Leaf 101 is 10.0.128.70, the system ID is 46:80:00: 0A:00:00, as this represents the IP address with zeros appended to the last 2 bytes.

Once an IS-IS neighbor is established, TEP addresses that exist on those neighbors can be learned. Example 12-3 shows the spines as IS-IS neighbors to Leaf 101.

Example 12-3   *IS-IS Neighbors for Leaf 101*

```
leaf101# show isis adjacency vrf overlay-1
IS-IS process: isis_infra VRF:overlay-1
IS-IS adjacency database:
System ID         SNPA          Level  State  Hold Time  Interface
4180.000A.0000    N/A           1      UP     00:00:49   Ethernet1/49.62
4280.000A.0000    N/A           1      UP     00:00:57   Ethernet1/50.63
```

Routes to a neighboring switch are always learned via the same next hop, even if multiple physical paths exist. This is because IS-IS is a Layer 2 protocol but is advertising the IP address of the Loopback 0 interface. Example 12-4 shows the IPv4 underlay routing table built through IS-IS.

Example 12-4   *IPv4 Routing Table Built Through IS-IS*

```
leaf101# show ip route 10.0.128.65 vrf overlay-1
IP Route Table for VRF "overlay-1"
'*' denotes best ucast next-hop
'**' denotes best mcast next-hop
'[x/y]' denotes [preference/metric]
'%<string>' in via output denotes VRF <string>

10.0.128.65/32, ubest/mbest: 1/0
    *via 10.0.128.65, eth1/49.62, [115/2], 3d16h, isis-isis_infra, L1
    *via 10.0.128.65, eth1/53.64, [115/2], 3d16h, isis-isis_infra, L1
```

Note   In this example, there are two physical connections between leaf 101 and spine 201. Because of this, the path to the spine is reachable via two interfaces utilizing the same next hop. In the next example, the redundant interface via eth1/53 is removed.

In contrast, when viewing the route to a PTEP address of a device that is not directly connected, both neighbors can provide reachability if the topology is a full mesh.

Example 12-5 *IPv4 Next Hop Reachable Through Spines*

```
leaf101# show ip route 10.0.128.64 vrf overlay-1
IP Route Table for VRF "overlay-1"
'*' denotes best ucast next-hop
'**' denotes best mcast next-hop
'[x/y]' denotes [preference/metric]
'%<string>' in via output denotes VRF <string>


10.0.128.64/32, ubest/mbest: 2/0
    *via 10.0.128.65, eth1/49.62, [115/3], 3d16h, isis-isis_infra, L1
    *via 10.0.128.66, eth1/50.63, [115/3], 3d16h, isis-isis_infra, L1
```

Note   The path is advertised through two spines: 10.0.128.65 and 10.0.128.66.

As mentioned in Chapter 4, "ACI Fabric Design Options," IS-IS is always localized to a single pod. This means that in a multi-pod topology, there are separate instances of IS-IS running at each pod, which can decrease the size of the failure domain from an IS-IS perspective.

FTags and the MDT

On top of the unicast routing table, the ACI fabric switches build a multicast distribution tree (MDT), leveraging fabric tags (FTags) on top of IS-IS. This is another reason IS-IS was the obvious choice for the ACI underlay: It makes it possible to add extensions. FTags are added as extensions to the IS-IS frame and allow the switches to agree on the different paths through the fabric that a multidestination frame can use. This allows for a multidestination forwarding domain that is loop free and provides load sharing between all available links in the ACI fabric.

In ACI, there are 16 FTags, of which 12 are used in the fabric. Each FTag has a root that is anchored on a single spine switch. The roots for FTags 1 through 12 are determined by the APIC, and they are pushed automatically without any required user configuration. For example, say that the topology consists of two spine switches. The APIC would select six FTags to be rooted on Spine 1, and the other six to be rooted on Spine 2. They do not have to be anchored in sequential order. The roots for FTags 1 through 12 could look something like the topology in Figure 12-4.

Unlike with FTags 1 through 12, the root for FTag 0 is determined based on which spine has the lowest TEP address. If the root spine is reloaded, another spine is elected as the root, based on that same criteria. The root election does not have any preemption, which means that when the previous root becomes active again, the root does not move back. Once a spine is root for FTag0, it remains root until that device becomes inactive in the IS-IS topology, as illustrated in Figure 12-5.

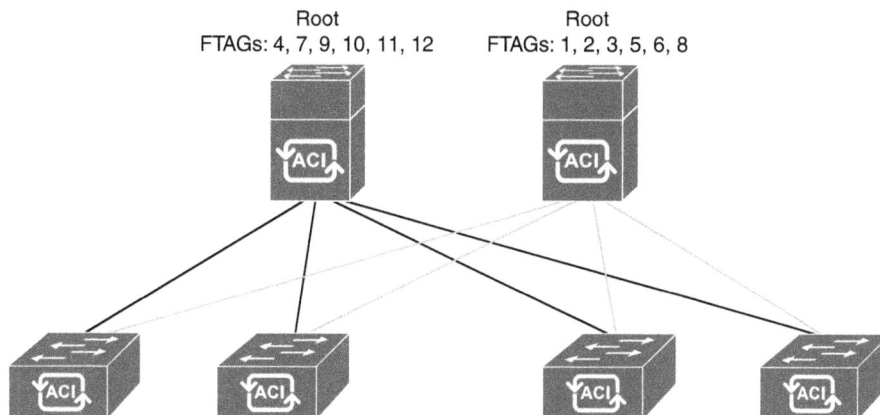

Figure 12-4 *FTag Root Placement Between Two Spines*

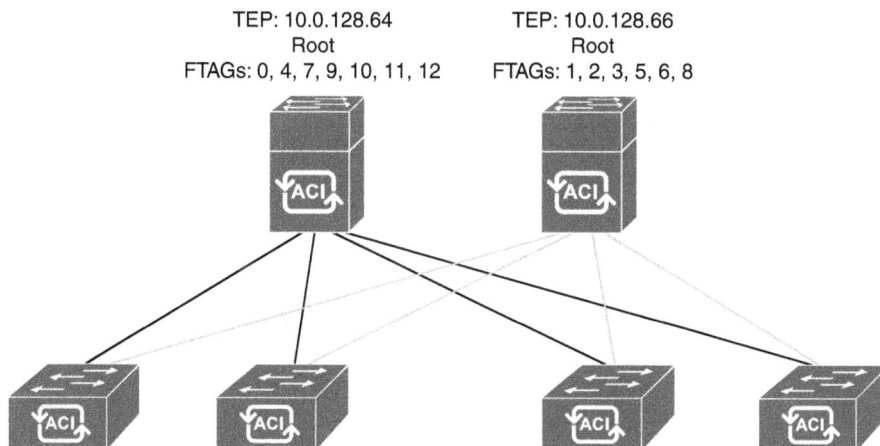

Figure 12-5 *TEP 10.0.0.128.64 as Root for FTag 0*

FTags are important because they allow the ACI fabric switches to utilize different trees on a per-flow basis. This means that for traffic in a given bridge domain, ACI can utilize different trees for load balancing multi-destination traffic while ensuring that the traffic is not looped in the routed underlay. FTag programming can be viewed via the CLI by running the command **show IS-IS internal mcast routes ftag** on a fabric switch, as illustrated in Example 12-6.

Example 12-6   *FTag Programming on Spine 201*

```
spine201# show isis internal mcast routes ftag
IS-IS process: isis_infra
  VRF : default
FTAG Routes
====================================
System ftag order: NEW
System ftag preference: 0
Max Fabric System ftag preference: 1
Phantom Spine Capable: NO
FTAG ID:    0 [Root] [Enabled] Cost:(   2/  13/   0)
-----------------------------------
    Root port: -
    OIF List:
      Ethernet1/1.1
      Ethernet1/5.83
      Ethernet1/6.84
      Ethernet1/53.86
      Ethernet1/54.85


FTAG ID:   1  [Enabled] Cost:(   2/   7/   0)
-----------------------------------
    Root port: Ethernet1/6.84
    OIF List:
      Ethernet1/1.1

FTAG ID:   2  [Enabled] Cost:(   2/   8/   0)
-----------------------------------
    Root port: Ethernet1/54.85
    OIF List:
      Ethernet1/1.1

FTAG ID:   3  [Enabled] Cost:(   2/   9/   0)
-----------------------------------
    Root port: Ethernet1/54.85
    OIF List:
      Ethernet1/1.1

FTAG ID:    4 [Root] [Enabled] Cost:(   0/   0/   0)
-----------------------------------
    Root port: -
    OIF List:
      Ethernet1/1.1
      Ethernet1/5.83
```

```
        Ethernet1/6.84
        Ethernet1/53.86
        Ethernet1/54.85


<Output intentionally omitted>


  FTAG ID:   13 [Disabled]
  FTAG ID:   14 [Disabled]
  FTAG ID:   15 [Disabled]
```

This output is important because it shows which FTags are operating as root when the output is run on a spine. For spines, the Root attribute can be seen on the FTag; furthermore, there is no root port, but there are outgoing interfaces (OIFs). If the spine were not root, there would be a root port representing the physical interface that provides the best path toward the root. Example 12-7 shows the same command as in Example 12-6, now run on one of the leaf switches.

Example 12-7   *FTags on a Leaf Switch*

```
leaf101# show isis internal mcast routes ftag
IS-IS process: isis_infra
  VRF : default
FTAG Routes
=====================================
System ftag order: NEW
Phantom Spine Capable: NO
FTAG ID:   0 [Enabled] Cost:(   1/   7/   0)
-----------------------------------
    Root port: Ethernet1/50.8
    OIF List:


FTAG ID:   1 [Enabled] Cost:(   1/   1/   0)
-----------------------------------
    Root port: Ethernet1/50.8
    OIF List:


FTAG ID:   2 [Enabled] Cost:(   1/   2/   0)
-----------------------------------
    Root port: Ethernet1/50.8
    OIF List:


FTAG ID:   3 [Enabled] Cost:(   1/   3/   0)
-----------------------------------
    Root port: Ethernet1/50.8
    OIF List:
```

```
FTAG ID:   4  [Enabled] Cost:(   1/   1/   0)
----------------------------------
    Root port: Ethernet1/49.7
    OIF List:


<Output intentionally omitted>

  FTAG ID:   8  [Enabled] Cost:(   1/   6/   0)
----------------------------------
    Root port: Ethernet1/50.8
    OIF List:
       Ethernet1/49.7


<Output intentionally omitted>

  FTAG ID:  13 [Disabled]
  FTAG ID:  14 [Disabled]
  FTAG ID:  15 [Disabled]
```

The leafs should always have a root port, which is the best path toward the root of the tree. Typically, a leaf always forwards to the root and then has the spine switch forward the packet to the remaining nodes. However, based on the current topology information, it's possible for a leaf to become "transit" for an FTag. This means that it has a path to the root, and it also has an OIF toward other spines. This is typically the case when multipod is in use and when the topology is not a full mesh. Figure 12-6 provides an example of a transit leaf scenario.

In this case, one of the leafs is not connected to all spines. Therefore, if the root of the FTag sends the frame on its tree, a leaf needs to send it to the other spine in order to get the frame to all leafs.

When a frame enters a leaf switch, and the forwarding decision is to flood that frame, the leaf encapsulates the frame in iVXLAN and sets the outer destination IP address to a multicast address (multicast Group IP outer [GIPo]) allocated to the bridge domain in which the frame was received. Based on the original frame content, a hash is run to determine the FTag the packet should follow. The FTag is then encoded in the 4 least significant bits of the outer IP address, which is why there is a maximum of 16. When the spine switches receive the iVXLAN packet, the FTag is checked, and the packet is sent on the tree. Table 12-2 provides a binary mapping of GIPo to FTag.

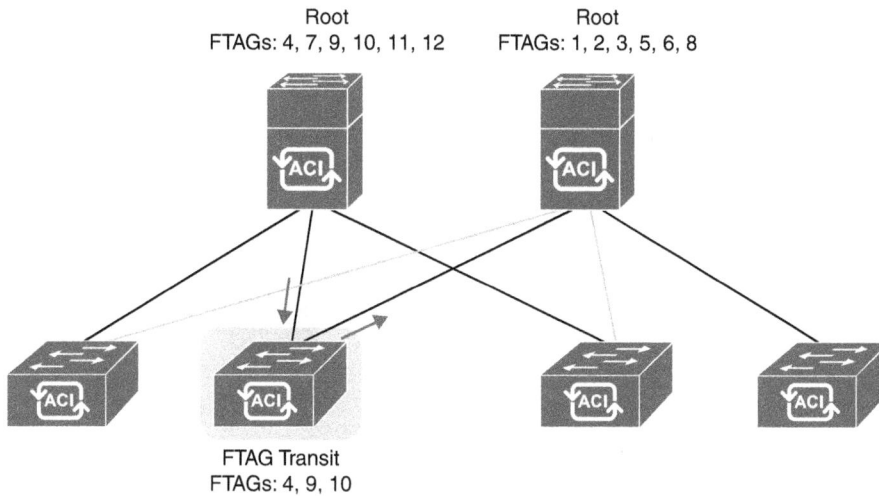

Root
FTAGs: 4, 7, 9, 10, 11, 12

Root
FTAGs: 1, 2, 3, 5, 6, 8

FTAG Transit
FTAGs: 4, 9, 10

Figure 12-6   *Leaf Acting as a Transit for FTags*

Table 12-2   *Binary Mapping of GIPo to FTag*

GIPo	Binary	FTag
225.0.96.144	11100001.00000000.01100000.10010000	0
225.0.96.145	11100001.00000000.01100000.10010001	1
225.0.96.156	11100001.00000000.01100000.10011011	11
225.0.96.157	11100001.00000000.01100000.10011100	12
225.0.96.160	11100001.00000000.01100000.10011111	15 (Disabled FTag)

If for any reason a frame is received on an interface that is not part of that FTag tree, the frame is dropped, preventing a loop.

In Figure 12-7, a bridge domain (BD) is deployed on Leafs 101 and 103. The BD has a GIPo of 225.0.96.144 assigned to it.

Because Leafs 101 and 103 have the bridge domain deployed, both of them advertise interest and create an mroute for 225.0.96.144. Example 12-8 demonstrates how to check the mroute state for a bridge domain GIPo address in overlay-1 on both Leafs 101 and 103.

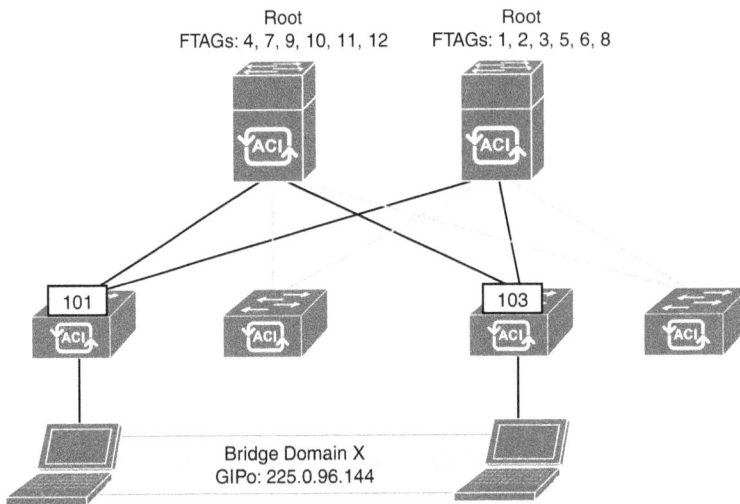

Figure 12-7 *GIPo mroute for BD*

Example 12-8 *GIPo mroute for BD in IS-IS*

```
leaf101# show isis internal mcast routes gipo
IS-IS process: isis_infra
  VRF : default


GIPo Routes
====================================
  System GIPo - Configured: 0.0.0.0
               Operational: 239.255.255.240
====================================
<Output intentionally omitted>
GIPo: 225.0.96.144 [LOCAL]
   OIF List:
       Ethernet1/49.62
       Ethernet1/50.63


leaf103# show isis internal mcast routes gipo


<Output intentionally omitted>


GIPo: 225.0.96.144[LOCAL]
   OIF List:
       Ethernet1/53.3
       Ethernet1/54.2


<Output intentionally omitted>
```

Figure 12-6 and Example 12-8 indicate that a loop exists for GIPo 255.0.96.144, which is true, but this can be prevented by using the FTag and MDT logic. The ingress leaf sends this traffic in an FTag. Let's assume that after running a hash against the multidestination packet received from the host, the ingress leaf chooses FTag 11 for this traffic and changes the multicast IP address to 225.0.96.156. It now uses the FTag table to prune the outgoing interface list (OIL), as shown in Example 12-9.

Example 12-9   *FTag 11 for Leaf 101*

```
leaf101# show isis internal mcast routes ftag
<Output intentionally omitted>
FTAG ID:  11  [Enabled] Cost:(  1/  5/  0)
----------------------------------
   Root port: Ethernet1/50.63
   OIF List:
```

When the spine receives this frame, it looks at the last 4 bits of the outer destination IP address (225.0.96.156), which are 0b1100. Based on this, the spine knows that it needs to forward the packet on FTag 12. It also knows that if it masks out the last 4 bits, the multicast base GIPo is 225.0.96.144. Only Leafs 101 and 103 advertised interest for this GIPo, so it only is forwarded to Leafs 101 and 103. Figure 12-8 depicts this scenario.

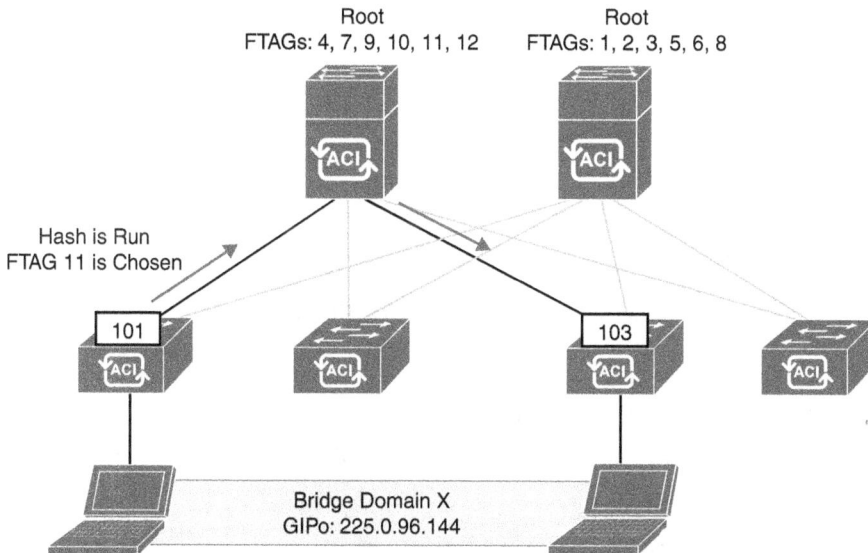

Figure 12-8   *Loop-Free Tree When Overlaying the FTag on Top of the mroute*

The combination of the FTag and mroute helps load balance traffic across all spines while keeping the mroute state to one GIPo per BD.

Endpoint Learning in ACI

You've learned about how the VXLAN underlay is built by assigning TEP addresses to leaf switches. Furthermore, you've seen that a loop-free multidestination topology is created using FTags and GIPos assigned to bridge domains. All this is done to forward traffic for endpoints that are attached to the fabric, but how does ACI learn the IP addresses and MAC addresses of the devices attached to the fabric?

Before you dive into the bits and pieces of ACI forwarding, it's important to think about how learning occurs in a traditional sense. In a legacy network, MAC addresses are learned through the data plane when a frame is received on a switch port. This allows a Layer 2 network to learn where all MAC addresses (endpoints) exist in the Layer 2 segment (VLAN). When a frame is sent to a MAC address that has not been learned yet, it is flooded out all interfaces in the VLAN that are in a spanning-tree forwarding state. If there are topology changes, a topology change notification (TCN) can inform the switch that all MAC addresses need to be flushed, which results in additional flooding. Additional flooding can cause performance impacts on the servers, which now have to process this traffic as well as output discards by overrunning the output buffer of an interface.

For a Layer 3 switch or router to learn IP addresses, it relies on sending ARP requests or gleaning the information from ARP frames received on its Layer 3 interface. In many cases, the Layer 3 identity of a host has not been learned, but routed traffic destined to this unknown host is received on the router. When this happens, the packet needs to be punted to the CPU for the glean process, which involves looking at the destination IP address and creating an ARP request for this host. If an ARP response is received, the MAC-to-IP binding is updated. Once the IP and MAC addresses of this host are learned in hardware, packet forwarding can resume.

As it has to process ARP frames in order to update IP-to-MAC bindings, a router can be susceptible to ARP storms caused by misbehaving servers or networking devices. When this happens, the CPU can become overloaded and may stop processing valid information. This can lead to a situation in which the production network is impacted by potentially only a few misbehaving devices. ACI tries to optimize this behavior by changing the way that IP-to-MAC bindings are learned, as well as providing a hardware proxy functionality to avoid the need to flood traffic in a Layer 2 segment to reach the destination.

To illustrate the behavior in ACI, the following sections discuss these details of endpoint learning:

- Endpoint learning in a Layer 2–only bridge domain

- Endpoint learning in a Layer 3–enabled bridge domain

- Remote learning (XR)

Endpoint Learning in a Layer 2–Only Bridge Domain

When a packet is received by a leaf switch, it needs to learn the source MAC address, and it also needs to determine the EPG to which this traffic belongs. Once the EPG is determined, the corresponding BD that defines the Layer 2 boundary for the endpoint can be determined. The EPG and BD learning attributes are highlighted in Figure 12-9.

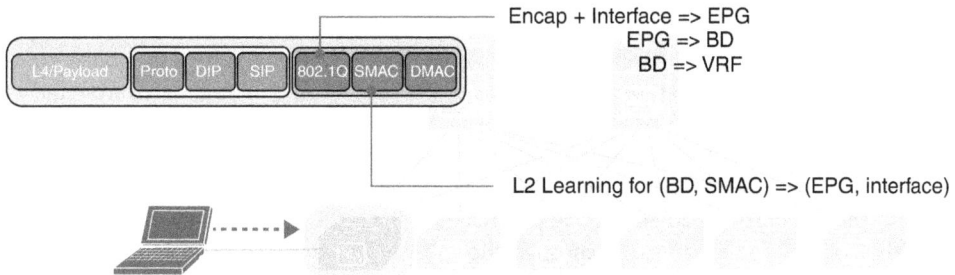

Figure 12-9 *Overview of Layer 2 Learning for an Endpoint*

As an example of Layer 2 learning, a single host is attached to Leaf 101 in EPG VLAN 2. The host is sending a unicast packet tagged with VLAN 2, which is set statically for the port under EPG VLAN 2. Figure 12-10 illustrates the logical and physical topology for this flow.

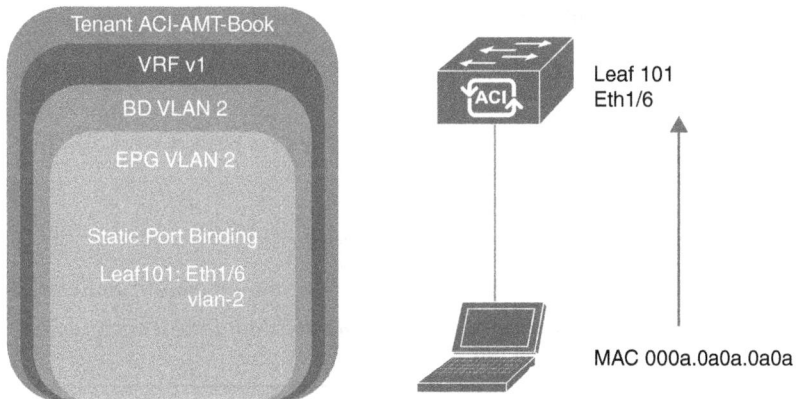

Figure 12-10 *Logical and Physical Topology of an Endpoint in EPG VLAN 2*

How does the leaf determine the bridge domain in which it should make a forwarding decision? Internally, the ASIC has a mapping of which encapsulation VLAN is deployed on an interface and which EPG this ties to. In the example in Figure 12-10, the leaf receives the traffic in encapsulation VLAN 2 on Eth1/6. Let's examine the VLANs deployed on Leaf 101 in Example 12-10.

Example 12-10   *Viewing the VLAN Name (EPG) Mapping to an Encap VLAN*

```
leaf101# show vlan extended | egrep "VLAN|vlan-2 "
VLAN Name                            Encap            Ports
27   ACI-AMT-Book:VLAN2              vxlan-15138760   Eth1/6
28   ACI-AMT-Book:AMT:VLAN2         vlan-2           Eth1/6
```

In Example 12-10 you can see that VLAN 28 is mapped to VLAN 2. So, what is the difference between VLAN 28 and encapsulation VLAN 2? In ACI, you have the ability to deploy any encapsulation for any EPG. Because of this, VLANs are translated from the platform-independent VLAN (PI VLAN) to an encapsulation VLAN. This allows you to still deploy encapsulation VLAN 28 on Leaf 101, and the leaf switch just chooses any available PI VLAN and configures a VLAN translation, or VLAN mapping. This means that the end hosts see an 802.1Q tagged frame in VLAN 28, but on the switch, VLAN 28 does not have to be mapped to encapsulation VLAN 28, so you have flexibility in how VLANs are used.

In ACI, the EPG VLAN ID does not define the Layer 2 boundary. The Layer 2 boundary is the bridge domain. So how does the leaf know the mapping of the EPG VLAN to the bridge domain? In hardware, there are three primary types of VLANs:

- **FD_VLAN:** FD_VLANs are VLANs deployed for EPGs and do not define the Layer 2 segment. FD_VLANs have an association to BD_VLANs to map them to the Layer 2 boundary. An FD_VLAN is also allocated an EPG VNID (fabric_encap) that is used when traffic should be flooded only in the encapsulation VLAN.

- **BD_VLAN:** A BD_VLAN is allocated for the whole bridge domain and is mapped to a VXLAN VNID (fabric_encap).

- **BD_EXT_VLAN:** BD_EXT_VLANs are VLANs deployed for L3Outs when the interface used is a switch virtual interface (SVI).

You can check the hardware component ELTMC to see what the VLAN mappings look like in hardware, as demonstrated in Example 12-11.

Example 12-11   *Viewing ELTMC Hardware Programming and Mapping from an EPG to a BD*

```
leaf101# vsh_lc -c 'show system internal eltmc info vlan access_encap_vlan 2' |
  egrep "vlan_id|type"
              vlan_id:          28   :::     hw_vlan_id:          34
            vlan_type:      FD_VLAN   :::        bd_vlan:          27
    access_encap_type:       802.1q   :::    access_encap:           2
    fabric_encap_type:        VXLAN   :::    fabric_encap:       10793
              vlan_id:          28   :::           isEpg:           1
           bd_vlan_id:          27   :::         hwEpgId:       11280
          accencaptype:          0   :::    fabencaptype:           2
            vlan_type:          13
```

After using ELTMC to determine what bridge domain EPG VLAN 2 is mapped to, you can confirm that the VLAN name and VXLAN VNID are what you expect. Example 12-12 shows how a BD is named on the leaf. BD VLANs are displayed in the format *Tenant:BridgeDomain*. Example 12-12 shows the PI VLAN and the name of the BD, which is mapped to EPG VLAN 2.

Example 12-12   *Viewing the PI VLAN and BD Mapped to EPG VLAN 2*

```
leaf101# show vlan id 27 extended
VLAN Name                              Encap             Ports
---- ------------------------------   ---------------   ----------------------
27   ACI-AMT-Book:VLAN2                vxlan-15138760    Eth1/6
```

EPG VLANs are always displayed in the format *Tenant:App_Profile:EPG*, as shown in Example 12-13.

Example 12-13   *PI VLAN Configured for EPG VLAN2*

```
leaf101# show vlan id 28 extended
VLAN Name                              Encap             Ports
---- ------------------------------   ---------------   ----------------------
28   ACI-AMT-Book:AMT:VLAN2            vlan-2            Eth1/6
```

Now that you understand how VLANs are programmed on switches for both EPGs and bridge domains, you can confirm that the endpoint is properly programmed on Leaf 101. As discussed in Chapter 11, "ACI Topology," Endpoint Manager (EPM) is responsible for processing the hardware interrupts from the ASIC when a new MAC address is learned. To confirm that an endpoint is learned properly, you start by querying the iBash NX-OS command line. Example 12-14 shows how to confirm that the MAC address 000a.0a0a.0a0a is learned on the supervisor.

Example 12-14   *Verifying That a MAC Address Is Learned on eth1/6 in the PI VLAN*

```
leaf101# show endpoint interface ethernet 1/6

Legend:
s - arp              H - vtep            V - vpc-attached     p - peer-aged
R - peer-attached-rl B - bounce          S - static           M - span
D - bounce-to-proxy  O - peer-attached   a - local-aged       m - svc-mgr
L - local            E - shared-service


+-------------------------+------------+-----------------+----------+-------------+
      VLAN/                    Encap       MAC Address       MAC Info/  Interface
```

```
      Domain                VLAN        IP Address       IP Info

+------------------------+-----------+--------------+--------------+-------------+


28/ACI-AMT-Book:v1          vlan-2      000a.0a0a.0a0a    L              eth1/6



+------------------------------------------------------------+
<Output intentionally omitted>
```

When you query the iBash NX-OS command line, you see that everything is properly learned, but if you are troubleshooting, it's important to understand how to verify the endpoint in more detail. By checking the status of EPMC by using the **vsh_lc** command line, you gain this additional insight. Example 12-15 highlights the command to get this information.

Example 12-15 *Viewing a MAC Endpoint from the EPMC Software on the Line Card of a Leaf*

```
leaf101# vsh_lc -c "show system internal epmc endpoint mac 000a.0a0a.0a0a"
vsh_lc -c "show system internal epmc endpoint mac 000a.0a0a.0a0a"


MAC : 000a.0a0a.0a0a ::: Num IPs : 0
Vlan id : 28 ::: Vlan vnid : 10793 ::: BD vnid : 15138760
Encap vlan : 802.1Q/2
VRF name : ACI-AMT-Book:v1  ::: VRF vnid : 2785280
phy if : 0x1a005000 ::: tunnel if : 0 ::: Interface : Ethernet1/6
Ref count : 4 ::: sclass : 49155
Timestamp : 01/05/1970 08:06:02.776214
::: Learns Src: Hal
EP Flags : local|MAC|sclass|timer|
Aging: Timer-type : HT ::: Timeout-left : 892 ::: Hit-bit : Yes ::: Timer-reset
  count : 0


PD handles:
[L2]: Hdl : 0x24865 ::: Hit: Yes
::::
```

Because BD VLAN 2 is a Layer 2–only bridge domain, you see that only the MAC address is learned, and no IP addresses are associated with this MAC address. VLAN ID 28 confirms what is expected after the previous steps of validating the VLAN programming. From a Layer 2 segment perspective, this MAC address is learned in BD VNID 15138760, which was mapped to BD ACI-AMT-BOOK:VLAN2. Later in this chapter, you will understand the use of the source class (sclass) for policy enforcement, but from a learning perspective, it is important to understand that traffic from this host will be tagged with the 49155 source group in the iVXLAN header.

The learning source is another important field to understand. In this case, HAL is the learning source, which informs you that hardware triggered this learning. If EPM is shown as the software component, it means another process informed EPM about this endpoint. An example of this would be a VPC sync happening, causing an endpoint to be installed on the peer, as shown in Example 12-16. If you compare the learning from Leaf 102, which is a VPC peer with Leaf 101, you notice that not only is the learning source different but the EP flags are different. In Example 12-16, the EP flags tell you that this MAC address exists on the peer, whereas in Example 12-15, the EP flags show that it is local.

From a troubleshooting perspective, the last important field to understand is the Aging information. In Example 12-15, you can see Timeout-left and Hit-bit entries. After learning an endpoint, software clears a hit bit in hardware for the specific MAC address query to the hardware every so often to see if the MAC address is seen again by the ASIC. If so, the hit bit is changed back to Yes, and the timer is reset to the local endpoint aging timer configured on the bridge domain. The Timer-reset count increments to show how many times hardware has refreshed this MAC address.

Example 12-16   *Viewing Endpoint Information Triggered by VPC Sync from Leaf 101 to Leaf 102*

```
leaf102# vsh_lc -c "show system internal epmc endpoint mac 000a.0a0a.0a0a"
vsh_lc -c "show system internal epmc endpoint mac 000a.0a0a.0a0a"

MAC : 000a.0a0a.0a0a ::: Num IPs : 0
Vlan id : 28 ::: Vlan vnid : 10793
::: BD vnid : 15138760
VRF name : ACI-AMT-Book:v1  ::: VRF vnid : 2785280
phy if : 0x1a005000 ::: tunnel if : 0x1801001b ::: Interface : Tunnel27
Ref count : 4 ::: sclass : 49155
Timestamp : 01/01/1970 17:04:49.042000
::: Learns Src: EPM
EP Flags : on-peer|MAC|sclass|
PD handles:
[L2]: Hdl : 0x1531f ::: Hit: No
::::

leaf101# show system internal epm endpoint mac 000a.0a0a.0a0a
MAC : 000a.0a0a.0a0a ::: Num IPs : 0
Vlan id : 28 ::: Vlan vnid : 10793 ::: VRF name : ACI-AMT-Book:v1
BD vnid : 15138760 ::: VRF vnid : 2785280
Phy If : 0x1a005000 ::: Tunnel If : 0
Interface : Ethernet1/6
Flags : 0x80004804 ::: sclass : 49155 ::: Ref count : 4
EP Create Timestamp : 08/08/2019 09:43:22.738214
EP Update Timestamp : 08/08/2019 09:43:22.738214
EP Flags : local|MAC|sclass|timer|

::::
```

Now that you are familiar with how a Layer 2 endpoint is learned in ACI, it's important to mention how the endpoint database is populated globally so that other leafs can reach this endpoint.

Council of Oracle Protocol (COOP)

In essence, the ACI fabric is composed of multiple smaller switches that act as a single large switch. When an endpoint is learned, it needs to be synced to multiple other locations to ensure proper forwarding throughout the entire fabric. The way this is achieved is by running a protocol called Council of Oracle Protocol (COOP). Each leaf maintains a ZeroMQ socket to each spine, where updates can be sent between leafs and spines as endpoint updates need to be generated. COOP is a control plane mechanism that syncs the endpoints, which has an impact on the data plane under certain scenarios. When local learning occurs, the leaf notifies the spine on the COOP ZeroMQ socket. The leaf, acting as a citizen, sends a COOP update to a single spine oracle. The spines sync the endpoint learning between them and send an ACK back to the leaf. All leafs send COOP updates for local learnings. As a result, the spines learn all endpoints within the fabric, which means they can act as proxies for unknown MAC/IP endpoints. Figure 12-11 illustrates this process.

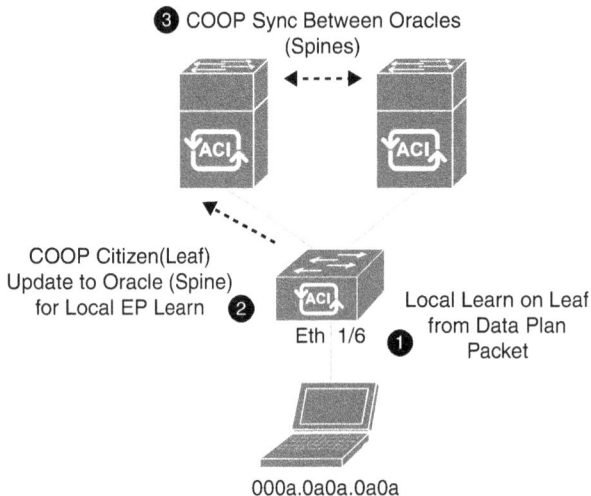

Figure 12-11 *Local Endpoint Learns Sent to COOP for Fabric-Wide Endpoint Consistency*

In the update from the leaf are a few key pieces of information which ensures that the fabric is consistent:

- **The MAC address or IP address of the endpoint:** In COOP, MAC addresses and IP addresses are stored as separate endpoints. Therefore, the total scale of the fabric is a combination of the total number of MAC addresses and IP addresses.

- **The VNID of the endpoint:** The BD VNID is used for the MAC address, and the VRF VNID is used for the IP address.

- **Current citizen:** This is the TEP address of where the endpoint resides. This could be a PTEP for a single attached host or a VPC TEP for a VPC-attached host.

Let's again use the previous example with the single attached host on Leaf 101 in EPG VLAN 2. This COOP state can be checked on the spines by running the **show coop internal info repo ep key** *<BD VNID>* *<MAC>* command, as demonstrated in Example 12-17.

Example 12-17 *Checking COOP State for an Endpoint by Using the MAC Address*

```
spine201# show coop internal info repo ep key 15138760 000a.0a0a.0a0a

Repo Hdr Checksum : 54141
Repo Hdr record timestamp : 08 08 2019 12:52:31 339018825
Repo Hdr last pub timestamp : 08 08 2019 12:52:31 339392345
Repo Hdr last dampen timestamp : 12 31 1969 19:00:00 0
Repo Hdr dampen penalty : 0
Repo Hdr flags : IN_OBJ ACTIVE
EP bd vnid : 15138760
EP mac :  00:0A:0A:0A:0A:0A
flags : 0x80
repo flags : 0x102
Vrf vnid : 2785280
Epg vnid : 0
EVPN Seq no : 0
Remote publish timestamp: 12 31 1969 19:00:00 0
Snapshot timestamp: 08 08 2019 12:52:31 339018825
Tunnel nh : 10.0.128.70
MAC Tunnel  : 10.0.128.70
IPv4 Tunnel : 10.0.128.70
IPv6 Tunnel : 10.0.128.70
ETEP Tunnel : 0.0.0.0
num of active ipv4 addresses : 0
num of anycast ipv4 addresses : 0
num of ipv4 addresses : 0
num of active ipv6 addresses : 0
num of anycast ipv6 addresses : 0
num of ipv6 addresses : 0
Primary Path:
Current published TEP : 10.0.128.70
Backup Path:
BackupTunnel nh : 0.0.0.0
Current Backup (publisher_id): 0.0.0.0
Anycast_flags : 0
```

```
Current citizen (publisher_id): 10.0.128.70
Previous citizen : 0.0.0.0
Prev to Previous citizen : 0.0.0.0
Synthetic Flags : 0x5
Synthetic Vrf : 477
Synthetic IP : 45.69.247.73
Tunnel EP entry: 0x1999e6a8
Backup Tunnel EP entry: (nil)
TX Status: COOP_TX_DONE
Hash: 933684246 owner: 10.0.128.66
```

10.0.128.70 is the PTEP address of Leaf 101. Based on this information, the spine has the correct view of where this endpoint exists in the ACI fabric.

Updating the Managed Object (MO) Tree

Besides updating COOP, the leaf also needs to update the API on the APIC and create a managed object that represents the endpoint. This is handled by a process called *policy element* that runs on the leaf switch. On the APIC CLI or in the GUI, you can view all endpoints. Example 12-18 shows how **moquery** can be used to view a specific endpoint.

Example 12-18   *Endpoint MO on an APIC*

```
fab3-apic1# moquery -c fvCEp -f 'fv.CEp.mac=="00:0A:0A:0A:0A:0A"' -x
  'rsp-subtree=full'
Total Objects shown: 4


# fv.CEp
name         : 00:0A:0A:0A:0A:0A
annotation   :
childAction  :
contName     :
dn           : uni/tn-ACI-AMT-Book/ap-AMT/epg-VLAN2/cep-00:0A:0A:0A:0A:0A
encap        : vlan-2
extMngdBy    :
id           : 0
idepdn       :
ip           : 0.0.0.0
lcC          : learned
lcOwn        : local
mac          : 00:0A:0A:0A:0A:0A
mcastAddr    : not-applicable
modTs        : 2019-08-08T12:53:00.775-04:00
monPolDn     : uni/tn-common/monepg-default
nameAlias    :
```

```
rn            : cep-00:0A:0A:0A:0A:0A
status        : modified
uid           : 0
uuid          :
vmmSrc        :


# fv.RsCEpToPathEp
  tDn         : topology/pod-1/paths-101/pathep-[eth1/6]
  childAction :
  dn          : uni/tn-ACI-AMT-Book/ap-AMT/epg-VLAN2/cep-00:0A:0A:0A:0A:0A/
                rscEpToPathEp-[topology/pod-1/paths-101/pathep-[eth1/6]]
  forceResolve : yes
  lcC         : learned
  lcOwn       : local
  modTs       : 2019-08-08T12:53:00.775-04:00
  rType       : mo
  rn          : rscEpToPathEp-[topology/pod-1/paths-101/pathep-[eth1/6]]
  state       : formed
  stateQual   : none
  status      :
  tCl         : fabricAPathEp
  tType       : mo
```

fvCEp is the classname for a MAC endpoint and a relational child object, *fvRsCEpToPathEp*, which has a relationship to the actual location in the fabric. In the APIC UI, you can automatically query this information by using Endpoint Tracker under the Operations tab or navigating to the EPG in the Tenant tab and viewing Operational > Client End-Points, as shown in Figure 12-12.

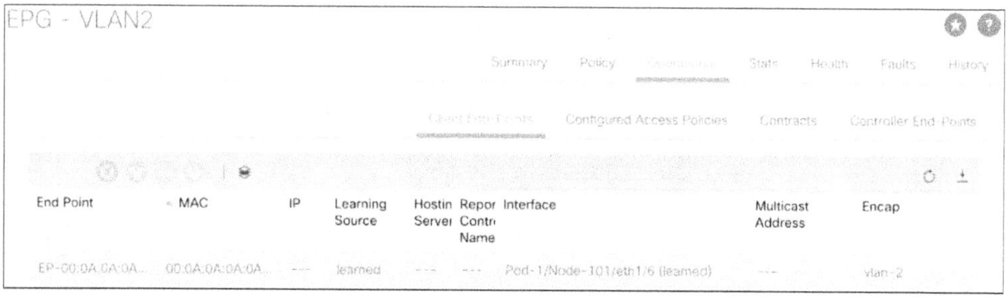

Figure 12-12   *Operational Tab Showing Endpoints for an EPG*

Endpoint Learning in a Layer 3–Enabled Bridge Domain

In the previous section, you learned how learning works for a Layer 2 endpoint. Unless there is a specific requirement for a Layer 2–only segment, most bridge domains are deployed as Layer 3 bridge domains. So what changes in terms of endpoint learning when you enable Layer 3 routing on a bridge domain? For the fabric to act as the default gate-way for servers, an ACI leaf switch needs to know the endpoint's Layer 3 identity, or its IP address. ACI optimizes this by learning the IP address in hardware, similar to the MAC learning process, instead of relying on a control plane protocol like ARP to send an ARP request and process the reply.

In Figure 12-13, WebServer 1 is physically connected to the fabric through a VPC, and a static path has been configured to be a part of EPG *Web*. EPG *Web* is mapped to a Layer 3–enabled BD, BD *Web*.

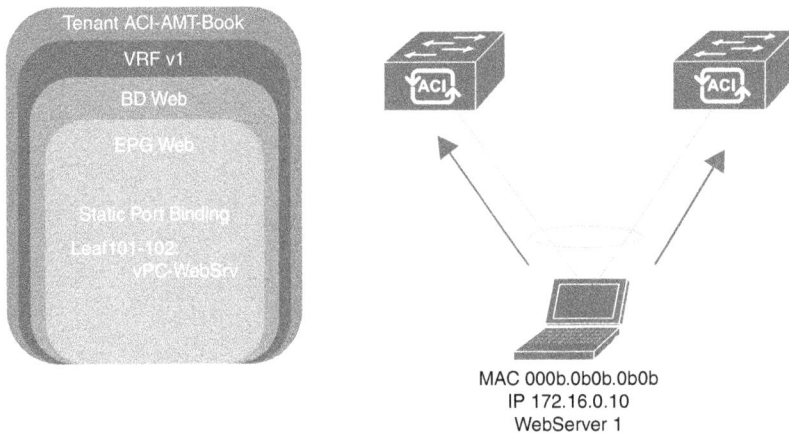

Figure 12-13   *Server 172.16.0.10 Is Connected to a Layer 3–Enabled BD*

If WebServer 1 sends an ARP request for another host within its subnet, the ASIC triggers learning for not only the source MAC address but also the sender IP address. This is again because the ASICs in ACI switches have the ability to inspect the payload of the ARP request and perform learning and forwarding based on it. Figure 12-14 illustrates the learn-ing pipeline for an ARP request that enters the switch via a Layer 3–enabled bridge domain.

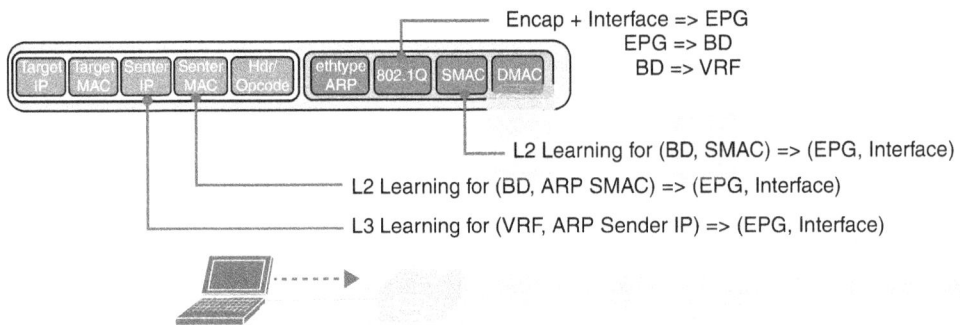

Figure 12-14   *Overview of Layer 3 Learning for an Endpoint Sending an ARP Request*

In Example 12-19, EPM has learned the IP address and MAC address for WebServer 1.

Example 12-19 *Viewing an IP Endpoint from the EPMC Software on the Line Card of a Leaf*

```
leaf101# vsh_lc -c "show system internal epmc endpoint ip 172.16.0.10"
vsh_lc -c "show system internal epmc endpoint ip 172.16.0.10"


MAC : 000b.0b0b.0b0b ::: Num IPs : 1
IP# 0 : 172.16.0.10
Vlan id : 12 ::: Vlan vnid : 10801 ::: BD vnid : 14942176
Encap vlan : 802.1Q/10
VRF name : ACI-AMT-Book:v1  ::: VRF vnid : 2785280
phy if : 0x16000013 ::: tunnel if : 0 ::: Interface : port-channel20
Ref count : 5 ::: sclass : 32775
Timestamp : 01/05/1970 12:04:26.565000
 ::: Learns Src: EPM
EP Flags : local|IP|MAC|sclass|timer|
Aging: Timer-type : HT ::: Timeout-left : 893 ::: Hit-bit : Yes ::: Timer-reset
  count : 0
```

There are two advantages to having the ASIC learn the IP addresses of attached servers through hardware. The first advantage is that ARP does not have to be punted to the CPU for software to inspect it and, through ARP and Adjacency Manager, push this learning back down to hardware. This protects the leaf switch from an ARP storm, where a misbehaving host or networking device causes the ARP Control Plane Policing (CoPP) class or the CPU in-band interface to become congested and impact other hosts attached to any switch that has the L2 segment deployed.

The second advantage is that the Layer 3 identity is instantly learned. This means that if routed traffic comes in destined to the locally attached host, the glean process does not have to be used, and hardware forwarding takes place right away.

Besides ARP, the ACI leaf switch also learns an IP address based on routed IP traffic. That means that if WebServer 1 sends an IP packet toward the router MAC address, the ASIC learns the source IP address as well. This allows the ACI fabric to update its IP-to-MAC bindings immediately, without having to resolve ARP for the endpoint. The pipeline for IP learning based on routed traffic is highlighted in Figure 12-15.

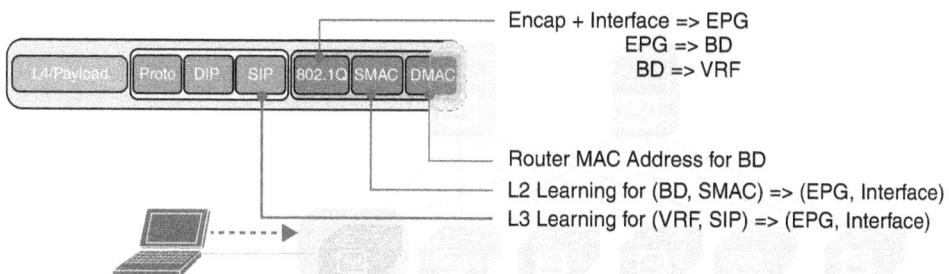

Figure 12-15 *Overview of Layer 3 Learning for an Endpoint Sending Routed Traffic*

In Example 12-20, EPM now has two IP addresses learned. This can happen if the server has a secondary IP address configured that it is using to serve content or a virtual IP address that is owned by a cluster.

Example 12-20 *Multiple IP Addresses Learned Against a Single MAC Address*

```
fab3-leaf101# vsh_lc -c "show system internal epmc endpoint ip 172.16.0.10"
vsh_lc -c "show system internal epmc endpoint ip 172.16.0.10"


MAC : 000b.0b0b.0b0b ::: Num IPs : 2
IP# 0 : 172.16.0.10
IP# 1 : 172.16.0.11
Vlan id : 12 ::: Vlan vnid : 10801 ::: BD vnid : 14942176
Encap vlan : 802.1Q/10
VRF name : ACI-AMT-Book:v1  ::: VRF vnid : 2785280
phy if : 0x16000013 ::: tunnel if : 0 ::: Interface : port-channel20
Ref count : 6 ::: sclass : 32775
Timestamp : 01/05/1970 12:04:26.565000
 ::: Learns Src: EPM
EP Flags : local|IP|MAC|sclass|timer|
Aging: Timer-type : HT ::: Timeout-left : 787 ::: Hit-bit : Yes ::: Timer-reset
  count : 3
```

Example 12-20 shows an EPM entry where two IP addresses are learned on a single MAC address. The ACI leaf switch has the ability to learn 4096 IP addresses per MAC address in ACI Release 3.2, but in Example 12-20, you see that only a single hit bit exists for this endpoint. This is an important fact to be aware of: By default, a single hit-bit timer is used, and if traffic from the MAC address or either IP address is seen, the hit-bit timer is reset, and none of the entries age out. This might not be desirable behavior. If the IP address of the server changes, the leaf switch keeps both entries in hardware until no traffic from the MAC address or the new IP address is seen for longer than the local aging timer. To prevent this issue from happening, you can enable the IP aging policy shown in Figure 12-16 by going to System > System Settings > Endpoint Controls > Ip Aging > Policy.

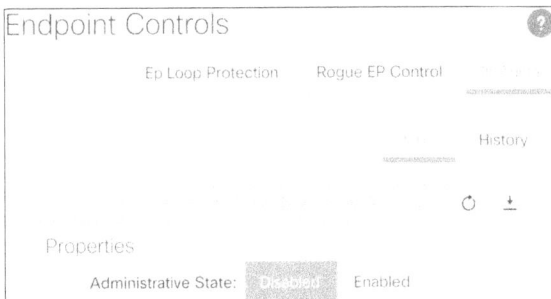

Figure 12-16 *Setting the Administrative State for an IP Aging Policy*

When this policy is changed to Enabled, EPMC keeps a hit bit for each individual IP address learned, as shown in Example 12-21.

Example 12-21 *Endpoint Aging Is Enabled per IP*

```
leaf101# vsh_lc -c "show system internal epmc endpoint ip 172.16.0.10"
vsh_lc -c "show system internal epmc endpoint ip 172.16.0.10"


MAC : 000b.0b0b.0b0b ::: Num IPs : 2
IP# 0 : 172.16.0.10
Aging : Type : HT ::: Timeout-left : 861 ::: Hit : Yes ::: Reset count : 0
IP# 1 : 172.16.0.11
Aging : Type : HT ::: Timeout-left : 861 ::: Hit : Yes ::: Reset count : 0
<Output intentionally omitted>
```

As with Layer 2 learning, the leaf switch uses COOP to update the spine about the locally attached IP addresses. In this example, because the host is attached on a VPC interface, the COOP update to the spine should contain the VPC TEP address. The IP address programming in COOP can be checked by running the **show coop internal info ip-db key** *<VRF VNID> <IP Address>* command on a spine switch, as demonstrated in Example 12-22.

Example 12-22 *Checking COOP State on a Spine for an IP Endpoint*

```
spine201# show coop internal info ip-db key 2785280 172.16.0.10


IP address : 172.16.0.10
Vrf : 2785280
Flags : 0
EP bd vnid : 14942176
EP mac :  00:0B:0B:0B:0B:0B
Publisher Id : 10.0.128.70
Record timestamp : 08 08 2019 14:50:30 613769218
Publish timestamp : 08 08 2019 14:50:30 616445401
Seq No: 0
Remote publish timestamp: 12 31 1969 19:00:00 0
URIB Tunnel Info
Num tunnels : 1
    Tunnel address : 10.0.184.70
    Tunnel ref count : 1
```

10.0.184.70 is the VPC TEP address of Leafs 101 and 102. Notice that the publisher ID is from 10.0.128.70, or the PTEP address of Leaf 101. This is because only one leaf publishes the endpoint to COOP, but the reachability to that endpoint is available via either leaf in the VPC domain.

On top of the COOP update, the leaf sends a notification to the APIC to create an object for the IP address. In the L2 section, **moquery -c fvCEp** is used to see the MO for the endpoint. An attribute for fvCEp is **ip**, but this contains only a single IP address. So how does the ACI object model track IP addresses associated with MAC addresses? A new object exists for endpoint IPs. This is the fvIP object, and it is a child of fvCEp. This means fvIP cannot exist without a MAC address association.

There are situations in which a misbehaving host or an improperly configured router is connected to a bridge domain and sends traffic toward the gateway MAC address with source IP addresses that it does not own. This triggers the ASIC to still learn all these IP addresses, and it could potentially cause an outage. To protect against this, you can configure Limit IP Learning to Subnet. When this feature is configured under the bridge domain settings, EPMC validates every local IP learning instance against the subnets configured under the bridge domain. Figure 12-17 highlights where to configure Limit IP Learning to Subnet. In ACI Release 2.3, this is a default option for any newly created bridge domain, and it is a best practice to configure it.

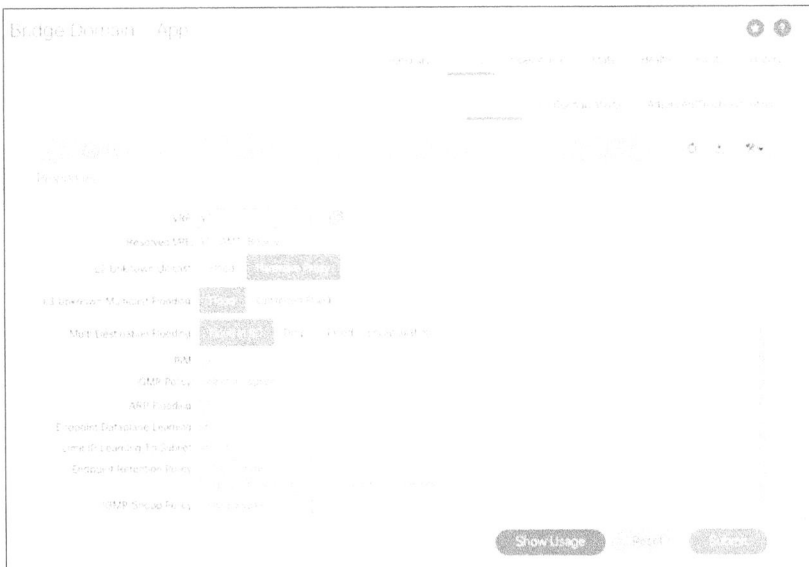

Figure 12-17   *Enabling Limit IP Learning to Subnet on a Bridge Domain*

Fabric Glean

In a traditional network, when a packet is routed, a lookup is done on the destination IP address to see where this packet should be forwarded. If the destination subnet is a directly connected subnet, but ARP is not resolved for the host, the switch punts that unicast packet to the CPU for a glean—which means an ARP request is generated for the host to resolve its location.

In ACI, this process is handled by the spine as well as the leaf. When a packet comes into a leaf and the destination is an address within a bridge domain–defined subnet, it is forwarded to the IPv4/IPv6 proxy on the spines. The spines should have every endpoint that exists inside the fabric in the proxy database, but if the endpoint is silent, it might not be known yet. If that is the case, and the spine fails the proxy lookup, a glean packet is generated and sent to all leaves that have the VRF instance deployed. When leafs get this glean packet, it is punted to the CPU, and an ARP request is sent out all interfaces that have the target BD deployed. Once the host responds to the ARP request, the leaf sends a COOP update to the spines so the endpoint can be installed. Figure 12-18 and the list that follows illustrate this process:

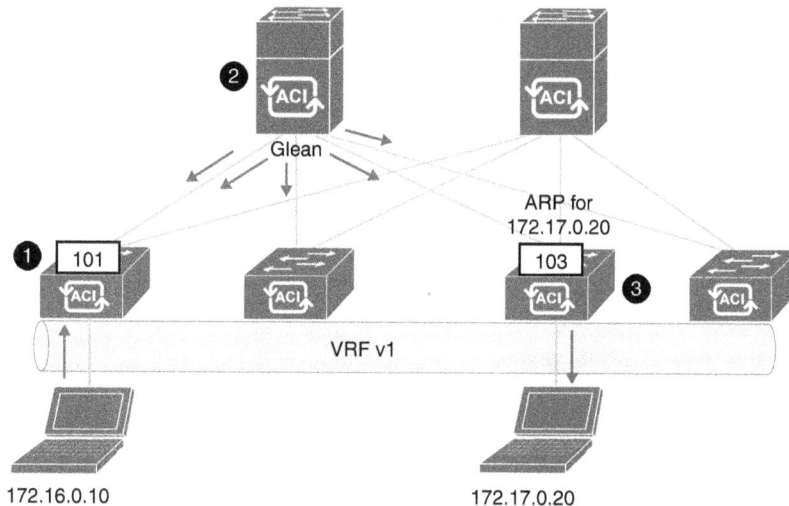

Figure 12-18 *ARP Glean Process*

1. The unicast packet destined to 172.17.0.20 is received on Leaf 101. The route lookup points to the IPv4 proxy.

2. The proxy lookup does not hit an endpoint route. This triggers the ARP glean process, and a multicast packet is sent to all leafs that have the VRF instance deployed.

3. Leaf 103 receives this glean and looks at the destination IP address to determine out of which interfaces to send the ARP request.

Remote Endpoint Learning

You are now familiar with how endpoints are learned locally and distributed to the spines via COOP. What if a packet is received on a fabric port instead of a local interface? Do the ACI leaf switches create entries to depict where an endpoint lives inside the fabric? Of course! Any packet received on the fabric interface has a VXLAN header on it and triggers a remote learn. Remote learning is an important aspect of optimizing policy enforcement and forwarding. If a VXLAN-encapsulated packet is received on the fabric ports of a leaf switch, the leaf does a route lookup to validate that the outer destination IP address is a locally owned address. Typically, this is the PTEP or VTEP address owned by the switch. If so, the ASIC inspects the inner content to make a final forwarding decision and also learn the inner source MAC and/ or IP address of the sending host. Figure 12-19 provides a high-level overview of an outer and inner packet and the key pieces as they relate to learning as well as the learning pipeline for remote learning.

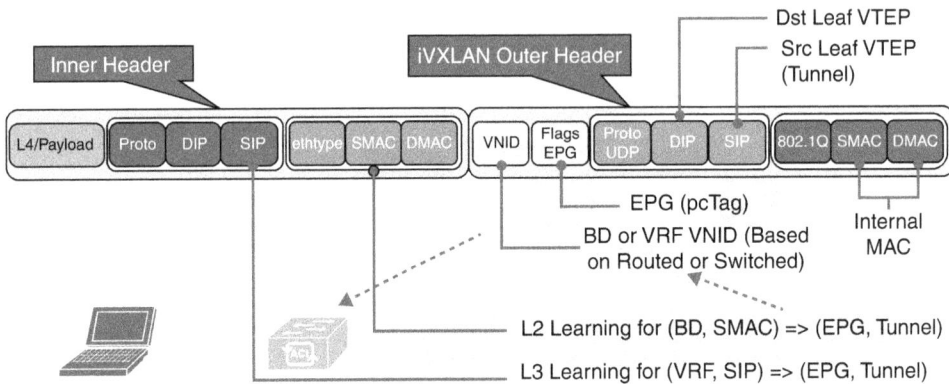

Figure 12-19 *Overview of Remote Learning on a Leaf Switch*

When checking the iBash NX-OS command line, you see that the leaf never shows the MAC address and the IP address for a remote endpoint; it only shows the MAC address or IP address individually. The reason for this is that remote learning is triggered by either a Layer 2 flow where the VXLAN VNID is set to the BD VNID or a routed flow where the VXLAN VNID is always set to the VRF VNID. In Example 12-23, the endpoint information for the app server is located on a remote leaf pair. The VLAN/domain is set to the *ACI-AMT-Book:v1* VRF instance.

Example 12-23 *Remote Learned IP Endpoint*

```
leaf101# show endpoint ip 172.17.0.20
Legend:
 s - arp            H - vtep          V - vpc-attached   p - peer-aged
 R - peer-attached-rl B - bounce       S - static         M - span
 D - bounce-to-proxy O - peer-attached a - local-aged     m - svc-mgr
 L - local          E - shared-service
+---------------------+---------------+-----------------+--------------+-----------+
    VLAN/              Encap           MAC Address       MAC Info/      Interface
    Domain             VLAN            IP Address        IP Info
+---------------------+---------------+-----------------+--------------+-----------+
ACI-AMT-Book:v1                        172.17.0.20                      tunnel30
```

The next step is to verify where this learning came from. There are two common sources: a remote PTEP or a VTEP. To figure out which it is, you first need to understand what Tunnel 30 points to. In Example 12-24, you can see the tunnel status as well as the source

IP address and destination IP address. In this case, the destination IP address 10.0.184.69 represents the tunnel endpoint address of the leaf switch or switches that host 172.17.0.20 is attached to.

Example 12-24   *Tunnel Interface*

```
leaf101# show interface tunnel 30
Tunnel30 is up
    MTU 9000 bytes, BW 0 Kbit
    Transport protocol is in VRF "overlay-1"
    Tunnel protocol/transport is ivxlan
    Tunnel source 10.0.128.70/32 (lo0)
    Tunnel destination 10.0.184.69
<Output intentionally omitted>
```

You can use the **acidiag fnvread** command to view all the PTEP addresses assigned to leaf switches. In Example 12-25, 10.0.184.69 is not listed. This is because the output is only displaying PTEP addresses of the leaf switches.

Example 12-25   *All PTEP Address in Fabric*

```
leaf101# acidiag fnvread
     ID   Pod ID    Name    Serial Number      IP Address   Role    State    Last
                                                                             UpdMsgId

-------------------------------------------------------------------------------------

    101        1   leaf101    FDO202711U6   10.0.128.70/32   leaf    active   0
    102        1   leaf102    FDO202711TH   10.0.128.71/32   leaf    active   0
    103        1   leaf103    FDO2220249E   10.0.128.64/32   leaf    active   0
    104        1   leaf104    FDO221724T9   10.0.128.67/32   leaf    active   0
    201        1   spine201   FOX1919G3BC   10.0.128.65/32   spine   active   0
    202        1   spine202   FDO22090C3J   10.0.128.66/32   spine   active   0
```

In this case, the learning occurred against a VPC VIP of Remote Leafs 103 and 104. To verify the VPC domain that owns IP address 10.0.184.69, check the IS-IS database, as shown in Example 12-26, or the APIC UI, as shown in Figure 12-20.

Example 12-26   *Displaying the VTEP Address and the PTEP Address of the Nodes Advertising Them*

```
leaf101# vsh -c 'show IS-IS database detail vrf overlay-1'  | egrep 10.0.184.69
    TEP Address   :  IPv4          DomainWide AppId 1 [10.0.184.69, 10.0.128.64,
    0.0.0.0]
    IP Internal   :      10.0.184.69/32  Metric : 1    (I,U)
    TEP Address   :  IPv4          DomainWide AppId 1 [10.0.184.69, 10.0.128.67,
    0.0.0.0]
    IP Internal   :      10.0.184.69/32  Metric : 1    (I,U)
```

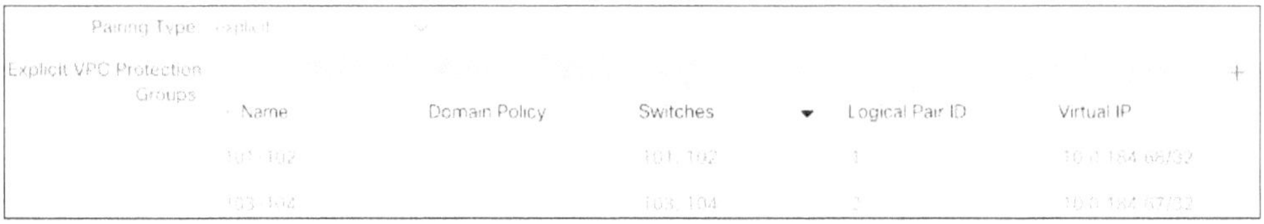

Figure 12-20   *Virtual IP Address Assigned to VPC Pairs*

Keep in mind that IS-IS is isolated to a pod within the fabric. If learning came from a VPC in a different pod, using the UI or object model would be the fastest way to figure out which pair the remote host is attached to.

Note   The MO for a VPC pair and the assigned VIP depends on what pairing type is selected. For explicit pairing, the class is **fabricExplicitGEp**, and for consecutive or reciprocal pairing, the class is **fabricAutoGEp**.

For local Layer 3 learning, Limit IP Learning to Subnet is enabled to prevent the leaf from learning IP addresses that should not be used by hosts in the bridge domain. For remote Layer 3 learning, the VXLAN VNID is always set to the VRF instance, which means validation against the bridge domain cannot be done. To accomplish this functionality throughout a VRF instance, a new feature, Enforce Subnet Check, was introduced. You can enable it under System > System Settings > Fabric Wide Settings (see Figure 12-21). This feature works for any leaf that has a cloud-scale ASIC. When this setting is enabled, the hardware tables have IP learning enabled only for subnets defined under bridge domains. This prevents a misbehaving host from causing the fabric to learn external IP addresses. When this feature is enabled, Limit IP Learning to Subnet is explicitly enabled.

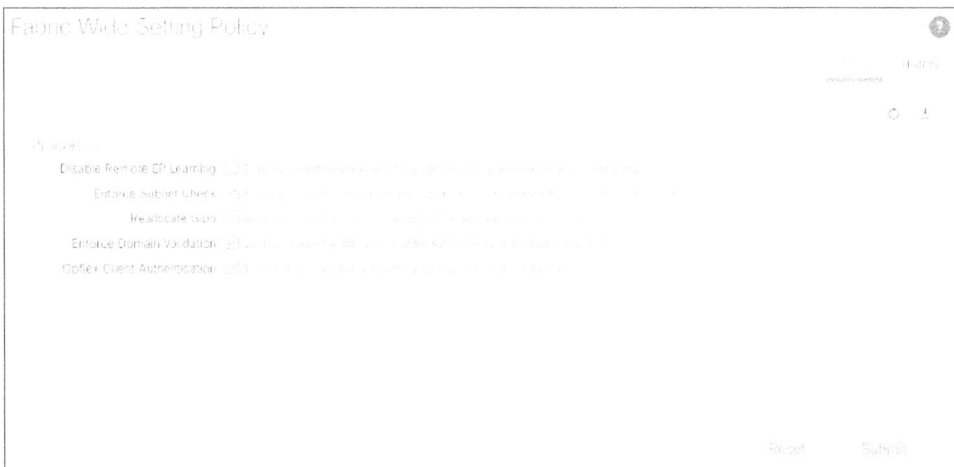

Figure 12-21   *Enabling the Global Subnet Check for All VRF Instances in the Fabric*

To summarize endpoint learning, it is important to remember the following:

- MAC address learning is always triggered.

- Routed traffic or ARP frames trigger IP learning on bridge domains with unicast routing enabled.

- Endpoint learning is synchronized with the spines through COOP.

- Endpoints are added to the management information tree (MIT) on the APIC.

- Remote learning is triggered by iVXLAN-encapsulated traffic.

Endpoint Mobility

Today's data center has to provide network access for a variety of physical and virtual workloads. One major benefit of virtualization is the ability to have a workload move to different physical compute resources as needed. In order for this to work, networks need to support Layer 2 and Layer 3 endpoint identities moving to different physical locations, and they need to update quickly to provide seamless migration and minimal packet loss. You've learned how ACI learns endpoints at Layer 2 and Layer 3 levels. What happens when an endpoint moves to a new location? How does the ACI fabric provide zero packet loss for devices communicating with that server after it moves?

Figure 12-22 shows the topology of two servers communicating with each other in the ACI fabric.

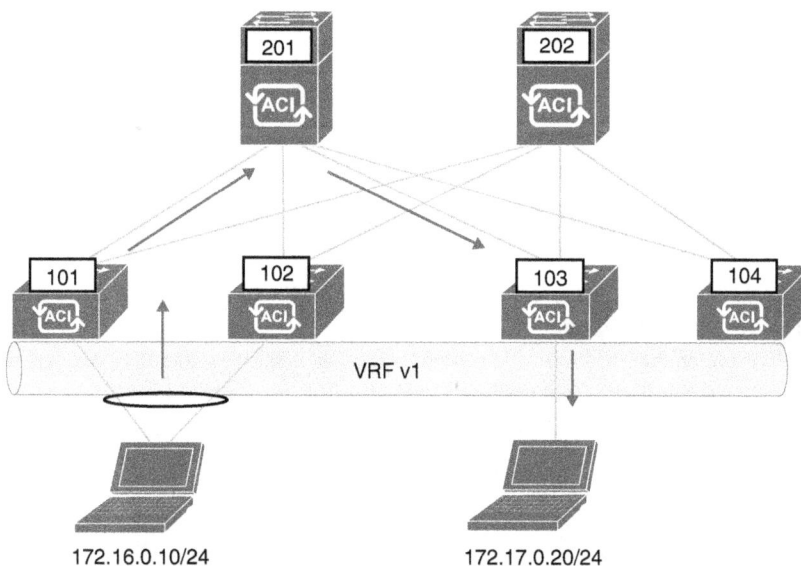

Figure 12-22 *Two Servers Communicating in the ACI Fabric*

In this scenario, traffic is sent from 172.16.0.10 toward the VPC domain 101–102. This traffic should be destined toward the bridge domain anycast MAC address since it is providing default gateway services for the endpoint. Traffic is sent toward Leaf 103, where the destination resides.

Now the 172.17.0.20 host moves from Leaf 103 to Leaf 104. When the host sends an ARP request or a routed frame toward Leaf 104, Leaf 104 updates its endpoint database and also sends a notification to a spine in the form of a COOP update. What's interesting about this COOP update is that the endpoint was previously learned from Leaf 103. Because the spine sees this as a change, it installs a bounce entry on the previous leaf (Leaf 103). This bounce notification is sent in the form of a COOP update from spine to leaf. Figure 12-23 illustrates this process.

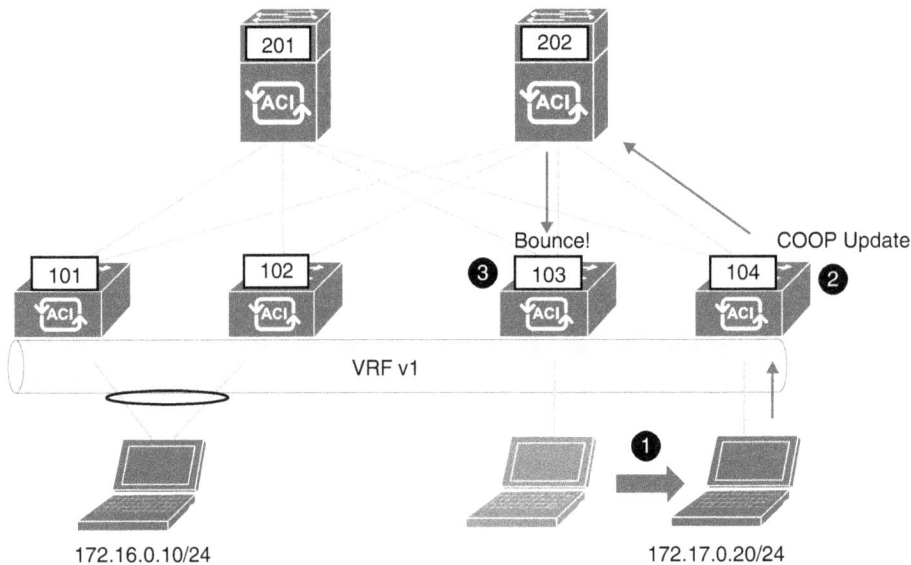

Figure 12-23 *When an Endpoint Moves, the Previous Local Leaf Installs a Bounce Entry*

The reason for the bounce entry is important. In Figure 12-22, you see that 172.16.0.10 is sending traffic to 172.17.0.20 through Leafs 101 and 102. After the endpoint has moved, if a packet has not been received from Leaf 104 destined to Leafs 101 and 102, the remote learning for the endpoint still points to Leaf 103. This means that Leafs 101 and 102 keep sending traffic to Leaf 103. Leaf 103 needs the ability to get the packet to Leaf 104 so that Leaf 104 can create a remote entry pointing to the VPC TEP of VPCs 101 and 102. To achieve this, Leaf 103 bounces the packet back into the fabric and sets the iVXLAN destination IP address to Leaf 104. On top of this, the Exception (E) bit is set in the iVXLAN header. The Exception bit means that if a leaf receives this packet, it cannot send it back into the fabric. This ensures that packets cannot be looped when bounce is in play. Once the remote entry is created on Leaf 104, the return traffic can be sent directly to the VPC TEP of Leafs 101 and 102, and they update the remote entry pointing to Leaf 104. Figure 12-24 illustrates this process.

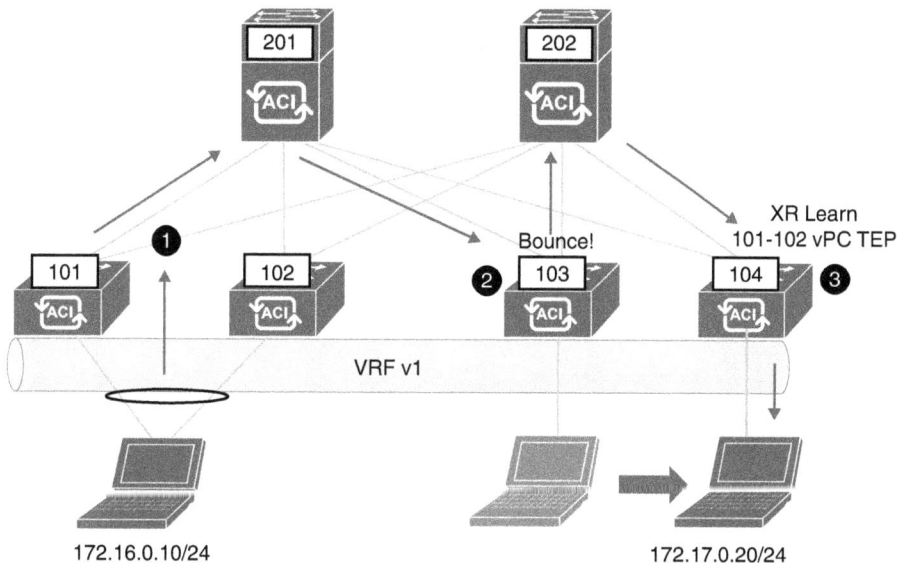

Figure 12-24 *A Packet Is Sent to Leaf 103 but Bounced to Leaf 104*

The bounce timer is configurable at Remote Endpoint Retention Policy under the bridge domain for the MAC address and the VRF instance for IP. The default timer for a bounce entry is 10 minutes.

Anycast Gateway

In order for any network to provide a default gateway, a Layer 3 interface must be configured with an IP address in the host's subnet. Each host in that subnet then has its default gateway configured to point to that address. If the host needs to send traffic to an IP address in another subnet, ARP is resolved for the gateway MAC address, and the unicast frame is sent toward the gateway MAC address. This is how the device that owns the gateway knows it should route the frame.

Traditionally, a network would also rely on some type of gateway redundancy. This is needed in the situation where the device that owns the default gateway goes down. For years, networks have been relying on first-hop redundancy protocols like HSRP and VRRP to handle failover for gateway addresses. However, these protocols, while helpful in ensuring that traffic can still be forwarded during a failover, have some disadvantages. For instance, HSRP requires a minimum of three addresses in the subnet (one address for each of the individual nodes, and a virtual IP address used as the gateway to which the hosts resolve ARP requests). The virtual address is active on one node at a time, and it moves across devices during failover. Furthermore, convergence on failure is always a concern. These protocols use multicast to send heartbeats back and forth. A predefined number of heartbeats needs to be missed before the standby takes over the active role. When the failover happens, there is always a brief amount of time when traffic may be impacted. Finally, traffic that needs to be routed must first be sent to the gateway.

This means that if the gateway is multiple Layer 2 hops away, traffic must be sent on that Layer 2 path before traffic can be routed. Figure 12-25 shows a basic HSRP implementation with a primary and secondary router.

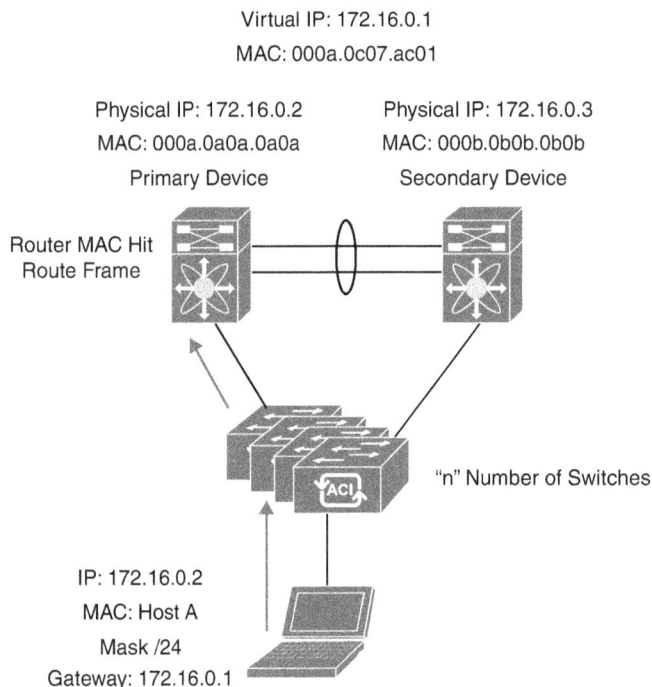

Virtual IP: 172.16.0.1
MAC: 000a.0c07.ac01

Physical IP: 172.16.0.2   Physical IP: 172.16.0.3
MAC: 000a.0a0a.0a0a   MAC: 000b.0b0b.0b0b
Primary Device   Secondary Device

Router MAC Hit
Route Frame

"n" Number of Switches

IP: 172.16.0.2
MAC: Host A
Mask /24
Gateway: 172.16.0.1

Figure 12-25 *Example of Using HSRP in a Traditional Data Center*

Now imagine that a similar approach is implemented in ACI. If two of the leafs act as the gateway for a given bridge domain, then traffic sent from other leafs that is destined for the gateway needs to be switched to the leafs providing gateway functionality. From there, the traffic is routed on to the destination. This can introduce undesirable traffic flows, or hairpinning, as the packet is sent to the gateway first and then returned along the same path toward the destination.

In ACI, routing functionality for endpoints connected in EPGs is handled differently to address the concerns just mentioned. ACI leverages an anycast gateway to provide gateway functionality for devices connected behind a bridge domain. Figure 12-26 shows that all switches have a router mac configured and all are considered active. The key benefits of using an anycast gateway are as follows:

- Only a single address is needed in the subnet.

- The gateway is pushed by the APIC to every leaf in the fabric where the bridge domain is deployed. This ensures that the gateway is always programmed on the ingress leaf to which the servers are connected.

■ Because the address is the same, and always programmed on the leafs, failover is seamless. The leaf is always ready to forward frames destined to the gateway, which provides optimal performance.

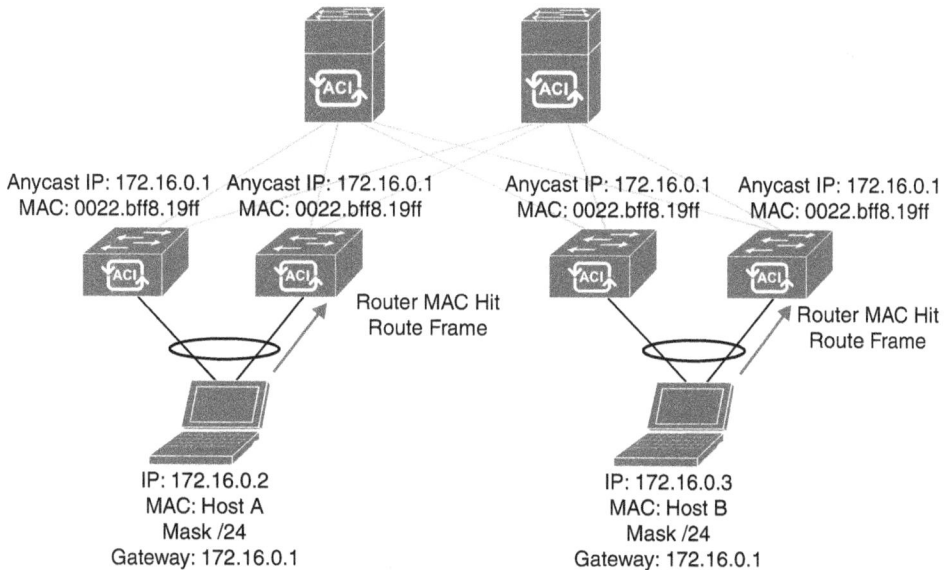

Figure 12-26 *Anycast Gateway Implementation in ACI*

When a subnet is configured under a bridge domain and unicast routing is enabled, the anycast gateway functionality is pushed to the leafs. The APIC evaluates which leafs have the bridge domain configured based on EPG attachment, and then the anycast configuration is automatically pushed to the leaf(s) by the APIC. From an NX-OS software perspective, the gateway is simply an SVI that is enabled on the leaf(s). As traffic enters the leaf, if the destination MAC address is the address configured for the bridge domain, the packet is routed.

Virtual Port Channels in ACI

Virtual port channel (VPC) is a technology that allows for MEC on Nexus switches. In the past, a VPC required a dedicated port channel between the two Nexus switches, and this port channel was used as the peer link. The peer link was used to send control plane traffic between the VPC peers using Cisco Fabric Services over Ethernet (CFSoE) as well as date plane traffic during failure scenarios. A keepalive interface was also required, and it could be the mgmt0 interface or a dedicated Ethernet interface or port channel. Then VPCs could be created toward downstream hosts, switches, and routers. In ACI, the VPC peer link is not required from a date plane perspective, but VPC control messages still need to be exchanged. This is accomplished across the fabric using a TCP connection between the two peers. The keepalive relies on seeing the neighbor in IS-IS. Not having to deploy a physical peer link and keepalive greatly simplifies bringing up VPCs in ACI.

When it comes to endpoint learning, VPC peers synchronize their endpoint databases to ensure full consistency across the VPC domain. One important aspect of these sync messages is that the EPG VNID is used to sync the endpoint information, and if the VNID isn't consistent between the two switches, the sync may fail. To prevent this from happening, it is recommended that you not deploy the same encapsulation from different VLAN pools across a VPC domain. Figure 12-27 illustrates the VPC synchronization process for a VPC-attached endpoint.

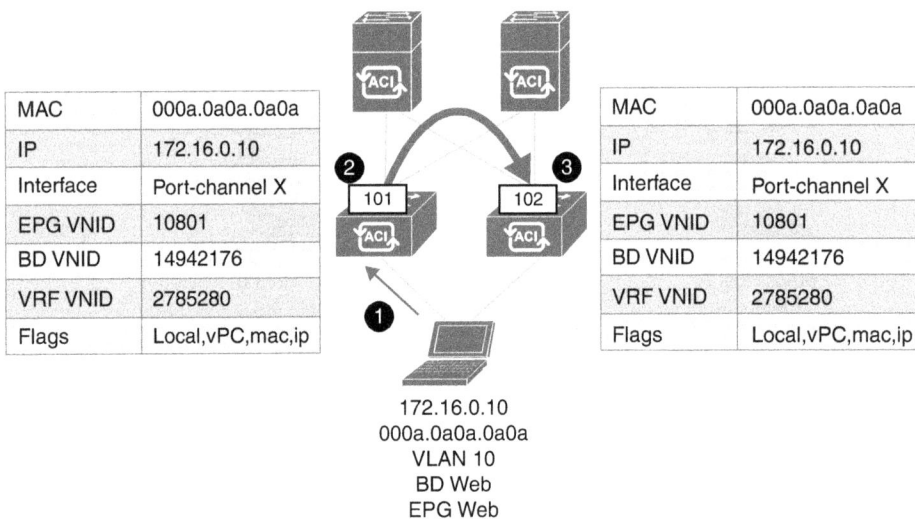

MAC	000a.0a0a.0a0a
IP	172.16.0.10
Interface	Port-channel X
EPG VNID	10801
BD VNID	14942176
VRF VNID	2785280
Flags	Local,vPC,mac,ip

MAC	000a.0a0a.0a0a
IP	172.16.0.10
Interface	Port-channel X
EPG VNID	10801
BD VNID	14942176
VRF VNID	2785280
Flags	Local,vPC,mac,ip

172.16.0.10
000a.0a0a.0a0a
VLAN 10
BD Web
EPG Web

Figure 12-27   *VPC Synchronization Process for a VPC-Attached Endpoint*

Endpoint synchronization does not occur for just VPC-attached endpoints. Single-homed endpoints, or orphan ports, are also synchronized to the VPC peer. This ensures that if traffic needs to be sent to an orphan port on a VPC peer, it can be encapsulated in iVXLAN and unicasted to the peer, rather than having to take the spine proxy. Figure 12-28 illustrates the VPC synchronization process for a single attached endpoint.

When a VPC-attached endpoint sends traffic toward a remote destination, the leaf switches always use a VPC TEP address as the outer source IP address. Both switches advertise reachability for this address, which gives the spines ECMP routes for unicast traffic via both physical switches. When a VPC switch declares its peer no longer reachable, it transitions from using the VPC TEP address to its PTEP address when sending iVXLAN traffic into the fabric. This is also different from traditional NX-OS switches.

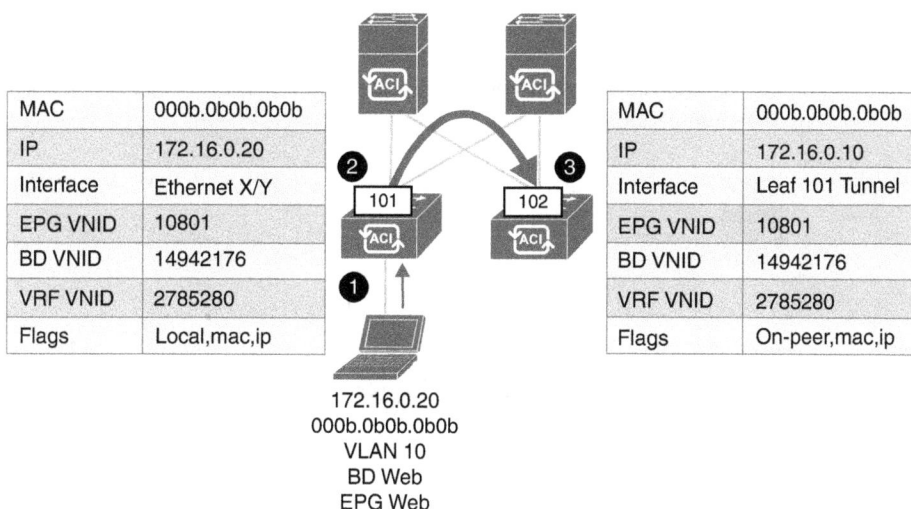

MAC	000b.0b0b.0b0b
IP	172.16.0.20
Interface	Ethernet X/Y
EPG VNID	10801
BD VNID	14942176
VRF VNID	2785280
Flags	Local,mac,ip

MAC	000b.0b0b.0b0b
IP	172.16.0.10
Interface	Leaf 101 Tunnel
EPG VNID	10801
BD VNID	14942176
VRF VNID	2785280
Flags	On-peer,mac,ip

172.16.0.20
000b.0b0b.0b0b
VLAN 10
BD Web
EPG Web

Figure 12-28   *VPC Synchronization Process for a Single Attached Endpoint*

In traditional VPC switches, a concept of a designated forwarder (DF) existed as well. The DF was responsible for sending all multidestination traffic in the transmit direction toward VPC-attached endpoints. In ACI, the DF functionality is not statically defined and is done on a per-packet basis. When a multidestination packet needs to be sent on a VPC toward the server, both switches run a hash against the packet to determine who should forward. The winner replicates a copy of the frame and sends it toward any VPC interface with the bridge domain deployed, as well as to any orphan port. The VPC DF loser only sends a copy toward any orphan port and does not forward it to any VPCs. If only VPCs exist on the loser, the frame is dropped.

Routing in ACI

ACI hides a lot of the complexities typically associated with overlay networks. This section aims to explore the hidden complexities, like what happens in the fabric when L3Outs are configured or how internal subnets can be advertised outside of the fabric. Understanding the complexities that ACI masks will help you understand what the different configuration options change within the internal workings of the fabric.

Static or Dynamic Routes

In your ACI fabric, you are likely to need to access devices outside the subnets defined under the bridge domains. Your ACI fabric might connect to firewalls, your campus network, and potentially an internet- or WAN-facing router. You should advertise subnets that exist in ACI to the external network and also learn the external routes on the leaf switches for full bidirectional communication. To accomplish this, you have to configure an external routed network (L3Out) in your tenant and use a dynamic routing protocol like OSPF, BGP, or EIGRP to exchange routes. When you deploy an L3Out on a leaf switch or a pair of leaf switches, they become border leafs. To illustrate these concepts, in this section we look at routing protocol redistribution on Border Leafs 101 and 102 in the topology shown in Figure 12-29.

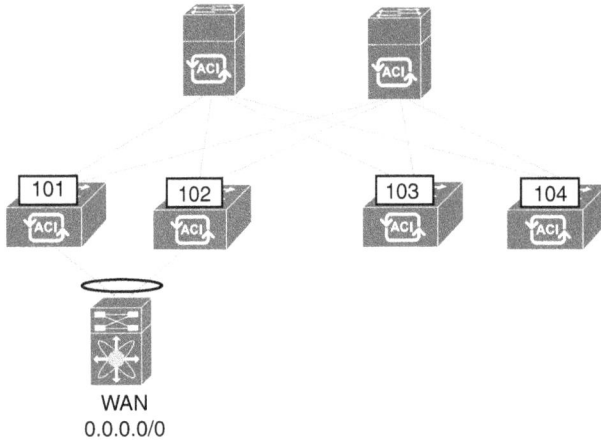

Figure 12-29 *External WAN Router Connected to Fabric*

Leafs 101 and 102 have a VPC configured toward an external router. An SVI exists on both leaf switches, and VLAN 500 is trunked on the VPC toward the external router. Table 12-3 provides a high-level overview of what is currently configured.

Table 12-3 *High-Level Configuration of L3Out*

Parameter	Leaf 101	Leaf 102
VRF	ACI-AMT-Book:v1	ACI-AMT-Book:v1
Router ID	192.168.255.101	192.168.255.102
Encap	Vlan-500	Vlan-500
Peering IP	10.10.100.1/29	10.10.100.2/29
Interface	VPC-9k1	VPC-9k1
Routing protocol	OSPF	OSPF

When deploying an L3Out VLAN on a leaf, the VLAN name is *Tenant:VRF:L3Out-name:Encap VLAN*, as shown in Example 12-27. In Example 12-27, VLAN 14 was deployed for the L3Out. To prevent the ACI leaf switch from learning all source IPs for the routed traffic coming into the fabric, the VLAN is configured in hardware as a BD external VLAN, or BD_EXT_VLAN. A BD_EXT_VLAN is a special type of bridge domain that has hardware-based IP learning disabled and that relies on the traditional ARP/ND process to resolve the MAC address for the next hop. This prevents the leaf from locally learning the IP address—but not on remote leaf switches. For traffic that comes into the fabric from an L3Out, the Don't Learn (DL) bit is set in the iVXLAN header. This bit prevents remote leafs from learning IP addresses that reside outside the fabric.

Example 12-27   *L3Out VLAN Deployed on Leaf 101*

```
leaf101# show vlan id 14 extended

VLAN Name                                    Encap            Ports
---- ------------------------------------  ----------------  ------------------------
14   ACI-AMT-Book:v1:l3out-External-       vxlan-15597457,   Eth1/5, Po14
     Net:vlan-500                          vlan-500


leaf101# vsh_lc -c "show system internal eltmc info vlan 14" | egrep vlan_type
          vlan_type:       BD_EXT_VLAN    : : :       bd_vlan:             14
```

After verifying that the VLAN is deployed properly, you can ensure that the SVIs are programmed as well. In Example 12-28, you can see that 10.10.100.1 is programmed on Leaf 101, and the protocol/link and administrative state are up. If a misconfiguration prevents the IP address from being deployed, a fault is raised. Once the IP address is pushed, the corresponding protocol can peer with the external router.

Example 12-28   *Layer 3 Interface for L3Out*

```
leaf101# show ip interface vlan 14
IP Interface Status for VRF "ACI-AMT-Book:v1"
vlan14, Interface status: protocol-up/link-up/admin-up, iod: 44, mode: external
  IP address: 10.10.100.1, IP subnet: 10.10.100.0/29
  IP broadcast address: 255.255.255.255
  IP primary address route-preference: 1, tag: 0
```

Advertising a bridge domain subnet to an external router requires three steps:

1. The appropriate L3Out needs to be associated to the bridge domain.

2. The subnet needs to be marked as Advertise Externally.

3. A contract association needs to exist between the L3Outs external EPG and the EPG(s) associated with the BD.

What happens at each step, and why is this required? Let's break it down one step at a time. OSPF (or the routing protocol defined on the L3Out) does not advertise BD-defined subnets by default because they are direct/pervasive routes. To have OSPF advertise these routes, they must be redistributed from "external" sources into OSPF through a route map. When associating the L3Out to the BD, this route map—or, more specifically, a prefix list—is created. The route map for the bridge domain and static routes is always called exp-ctx-st-*VRF_VNID*, and it contains two prefix lists: one with an action to deny a specific route tag and another to advertise the BD subnets. In this example, the prefix list is named IPv4-st32773-2785280-exc-int-inferred-export-dst,

where 32773 is the PCTag of the external EPG, and 2785280 is the VNID allocated to
the VRF instance for which the L3Out resides. Example 12-29 and Example 12-30 show
the route map and prefix list.

Example 12-29   *Verifying Route Maps for Redistribution on a VRF Instance for OSPF*

```
leaf101# show ip ospf vrf ACI-AMT-Book:v1
 Routing Process default with ID 192.168.255.101 VRF ACI-AMT-Book:v1
 Stateful High Availability enabled
 Supports only single TOS(TOS0) routes
 Supports opaque LSA
 Table-map using route-map exp-ctx-2785280-deny-external-tag
 Redistributing External Routes from
   static route-map exp-ctx-st-2785280
   direct route-map exp-ctx-st-2785280
   bgp route-map exp-ctx-proto-2785280
   eigrp route-map exp-ctx-proto-2785280
   coop route-map exp-ctx-st-2785280
 Maximum number of non self-generated LSA allowed 20000
    (feature configured but inactive)
    Current number of non self-generated LSA 0
    Threshold for warning message 75%
 Administrative distance 110
 Reference Bandwidth is 40000 Mbps
 SPF throttling delay time of 200.000 msecs,
   SPF throttling hold time of 1000.000 msecs,
   SPF throttling maximum wait time of 5000.000 msecs
 LSA throttling start time of 0.000 msecs,
   LSA throttling hold interval of 5000.000 msecs,
   LSA throttling maximum wait time of 5000.000 msecs
 Minimum LSA arrival 1000.000 msec
 LSA group pacing timer 10 secs
 Maximum paths to destination 8
 Number of external LSAs 0, checksum sum 0x0
 Number of opaque AS LSAs 0, checksum sum 0x0
 Number of areas is 1, 1 normal, 0 stub, 0 nssa
 Number of active areas is 1, 1 normal, 0 stub, 0 nssa
   Area (backbone) (Inactive)
        Area has existed for 00:00:03
        Interfaces in this area: 1 Active interfaces: 1
        Passive interfaces: 0  Loopback interfaces: 0
        SPF calculation has run 2 times
         Last SPF ran for 0.000346s
        Area ranges are
        Area-filter in 'exp-ctx-proto-2785280'
        Number of LSAs: 2, checksum sum 0x0
```

Example 12-30   *Route Map to Redistribute External Routes into OSPF*

```
leaf101# show route-map exp-ctx-st-2785280
route-map exp-ctx-st-2785280, deny, sequence 1
  Match clauses:
    tag: 4294967294
  Set clauses:
route-map exp-ctx-st-2785280, permit, sequence 15801
  Match clauses:
    ip address prefix-lists: IPv4-st32773-2785280-exc-int-inferred-export-dst
    ipv6 address prefix-lists: IPv6-deny-all
  Set clauses:
ileaf101# show ip prefix-list IPv4-st32773-2785280-exc-int-inferred-export-dst
ip prefix-list IPv4-st32773-2785280-exc-int-inferred-export-dst: 2 entries
   seq 1 permit 172.16.0.1/24
```

A second way to advertise subnets is by creating an export route control prefix list in which a specific prefix or an aggregate prefix can be defined to allow a specific range. This is done by creating a route map under the specific L3Out, matching routing policy only and defining a context where the desired subnet with the aggregate flag is matched. When using this option, a custom prefix list is created that is used in both exp-ctx-st and exp-ctx-prot, which is used for transit routing.

The second step is to mark the subnet as Advertise Externally. Why do you have to check this box if the prefix list is updated in step 1? Depending on how you've designed the network, you might have more subnets defined on a BD than just a single prefix. If this is the case and you want to advertise some, but not all, how can you control this? In the route map used by OSPF for static and direct routes, the first sequence is always a rule that blocks the VRF instance route tag 429496794. So if you are using either method to advertise BD routes, checking Advertise Externally removes the route tag, and when using the BD association to advertise the subnet, all prefixes that are part of the BD and marked as Advertise Externally are added to the export prefix list. In Example 12-31, 172.16.2.0/24 is marked as Private to VRF and therefore is tagged with a VRF instance–level tag. When you change this to Advertise Externally, the tag is removed from the pervasive route.

Example 12-31   *Routes Marked as Private to VRF Assigned the Default VRF Instance Tag*

```
leaf101# show ip route 172.16.2.0 vrf  ACI-AMT-Book:v1
IP Route Table for VRF "ACI-AMT-Book:v1"
'*' denotes best ucast next-hop
'**' denotes best mcast next-hop
'[x/y]' denotes [preference/metric]
'%<string>' in via output denotes VRF <string>

172.16.2.0/24, ubest/mbest: 1/0, attached, direct, pervasive
    *via 10.0.184.66%overlay-1, [1/0], 00:59:05, static, tag 4294967294
        recursive next hop: 10.0.184.66/32%overlay-1
```

Note   You can change the VRF instance route tag to another value by navigating to the VRF in the Tenant tab.

The last step is to have a contract association between the external EPG and an EPG associated with the bridge domain that owns the subnet. The APIC doesn't actually push the pervasive BD route until there is a need for the route to exist on that leaf. This means that if no contract exists between an L3Out and an internal subnet, the border leaf does not waste hardware resources on a route that doesn't have a policy that permits traffic. So even if step 1 and step 2 are taken, the route maps are updated, but the route doesn't exist locally on the border leaf, and OSPF can't redistribute a nonexistent route. The only exception to this is if the BD is deployed locally on the border leaf. In this case, the route is present and is advertised, but all traffic from external sources toward the BD is policy dropped.

Learning External Routes in the ACI Fabric

In the previous section, you learned how ACI advertises BD-defined subnets into OSPF, the routing protocol defined on the L3Out. Routes learned from OSPF are inserted into the routing table as OSPF routes, as shown in Example 12-32.

Example 12-32   *0.0.0.0/0 Learned Dynamically from a Peer via OSPF*

```
leaf101# show ip route 0.0.0.0/0 vrf  ACI-AMT-Book:v1
IP Route Table for VRF "ACI-AMT-Book:v1"
'*' denotes best ucast next-hop
'**' denotes best mcast next-hop
'[x/y]' denotes [preference/metric]
'%<string>' in via output denotes VRF <string>

0.0.0.0/0, ubest/mbest: 1/0
    *via 10.10.100.3, vlan14, [110/1], 00:00:45, ospf-default, type-2
```

In order for endpoints on other leaf switches to have connectivity to this route, those leafs need to also install it. From a scalability perspective, it would not be beneficial to peer all compute leafs or non-border leafs using the same routing protocol defined in the L3Out. To address this concern, BGP VPNv4/VPNv6 is used within a pod to share all external prefixes. Within overlay-1, all leaf switches peer with the spines defined as route reflectors in the BGP Route Reflector policy. Example 12-33 shows how you can validate that the BGP sessions are established and peered with the appropriate spines.

Example 12-33   *Checking Spine BGP Neighborships in the Overlay-1 VRF Instance*

```
leaf101# show bgp sessions vrf overlay-1
Total peers 3, established peers 3
ASN 65502
VRF overlay-1, local ASN 65502
peers 2, established peers 2, local router-id 10.0.128.70
State: I-Idle, A-Active, O-Open, E-Established, C-Closing, S-Shutdown


Neighbor        ASN     Flaps LastUpDn|LastRead|LastWrit St Port(L/R)  Notif(S/R)
10.0.128.65     65502 0     01w05d  |never   |never    E  55815/179  0/0
10.0.128.66     65502 0     01w05d  |never   |never    E  44081/179  0/0


leaf101# acidiag fnvread | egrep spine
    201      1      spine201     FOX1919G3BC     10.0.128.65/32    spine
    active   0
    202      1      spine202     FDO22090C3J     10.0.128.66/32    spine
    active   0
```

Within the tenant VRF *ACI-AMT-Book:v1*, BGP is running and redistributing the routes from OSPF into BGP. These routes are tagged with a route distinguisher (RD) and a route target (RT) (see Example 12-34).

Example 12-34   *Checking the BGP Process in a VRF Instance to Determine RD and Export/Import List*

```
leaf101# show bgp process vrf ACI-AMT-Book:v1 | egrep -A 1 "VRF RD|RT"
VRF RD                      : 10.0.128.70:5
VRF EVPN RD                 : 10.0.128.70:5
--
    Export RT list:
        65502:2785280
    Import RT list:
        65502:2785280
```

On the compute leafs, the RT and RD are used to identify which VRF instance the routes should be imported back into and which TEP address is the next hop. Example 12-35 shows the default route that is learned from Leafs 101 and 102 on a VPC. Notice that even though these routes are learned on a VPC port channel, each leaf individually advertises reachability for the prefixes it learns.

Example 12-35 *Viewing the Routing Table on Leaf 103 for a VRF Instance*

```
leaf103# show ip route vrf ACI-AMT-Book:v1
IP Route Table for VRF "ACI-AMT-Book:v1"
'*' denotes best ucast next-hop
'**' denotes best mcast next-hop
'[x/y]' denotes [preference/metric]
'%<string>' in via output denotes VRF <string>

0.0.0.0/0, ubest/mbest: 2/0
    *via 10.0.128.71%overlay-1, [1/0], 01:22:46, bgp-65502, internal, tag 65502
    *via 10.0.128.70%overlay-1, [1/0], 01:22:46, bgp-65502, internal, tag 65502
```

When looking at BGP learned routes on the compute leafs, you see two advertised paths identifying the two border leafs. In addition, you see an extended community that includes the RT as well as a VNID that identifies the VRF instance the route belongs to. Example 12-36 shows the BGP route on Leaf 103.

Example 12-36 *Viewing the BGP Route State on Leaf 103 for a VRF Instance*

```
leaf103# show bgp ipv4 unicast 0.0.0.0/0 vrf ACI-AMT-Book:v1
BGP routing table information for VRF ACI-AMT-Book:v1, address family IPv4 Unicast
BGP routing table entry for 0.0.0.0/0, version 69 dest ptr 0xadb97a50
Paths: (2 available, best #1)
Flags: (0x08001a 00000000) on xmit-list, is in urib, is best urib route, is in HW
  vpn: version 215, (0x100002) on xmit-list
Multipath: eBGP iBGP

  Advertised path-id 1, VPN AF advertised path-id 1
  Path type: internal 0xc0000018 0x40 ref 56506 adv path ref 2, path is valid, is
  best path
          Imported from 10.0.128.70:5:0.0.0.0/0
  AS-Path: NONE, path sourced internal to AS
    10.0.128.70 (metric 3) from 10.0.128.65 (10.0.128.65)
      Origin incomplete, MED 1, localpref 100, weight 0
      Received label 0
      Received path-id 1
      Extcommunity:
          RT:65502:2785280
          VNID:2785280
          CoST:pre-bestpath:162:110
      Originator: 10.0.128.70 Cluster list: 10.0.128.65


VPN AF advertised path-id 2
  Path type: internal 0xc0020018 0x40 ref 56506 adv path ref 1, path is valid, not
  best reason: Router Id, multipath
          Imported from 10.0.128.71:6:0.0.0.0/0
```

```
AS-Path: NONE, path sourced internal to AS
   10.0.128.71 (metric 3) from 10.0.128.65 (10.0.128.65)
     Origin incomplete, MED 1, localpref 100, weight 0
     Received label 0
     Received path-id 1
     Extcommunity:
         RT:65502:2785280
         VNID:2785280
         CoST:pre-bestpath:162:110
     Originator: 10.0.128.71 Cluster list: 10.0.128.65

VRF advertise information:
Path-id 1 not advertised to any peer

VPN AF advertise information:
Path-id 1 not advertised to any peer
Path-id 2 not advertised to any peer
```

Key Topic

Transit Routing

One common routing design in ACI involves multiple external routers connected to the fabric. These could be firewalls, load balancers, or other routers that might provide access to private and public networks. In many cases, these routers need to learn all routes that other external routers are advertising into the fabric. To accomplish this, transit routing needs to be configured. In the previous example, you learned how the fabric redistributes external routes into BGP. In Figure 12-30, a second external router is connected to Leafs 103 and 104, which need to learn all WAN routes.

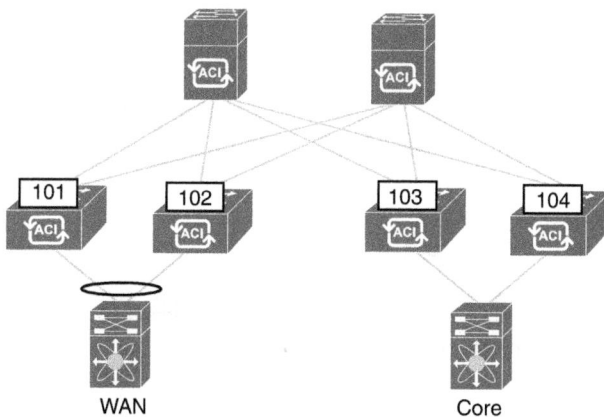

Figure 12-30 *WAN Routes Learned from 101/102 Need to Be Advertised to the Core Router on Leafs 103 and 104*

To accomplish this, you need to configure an Export Route Control Subnet on the core L3Out external EPG. Export Route Control Subnet is a control plane configuration option that creates a route map and allows the export of BGP learned routes (from the WAN L3Out) to the core L3Out. Figure 12-31 shows the configuration of a 0.0.0.0/0 prefix with the aggregate flag set. Aggregate Export is only supported for the 0/0 Export Route Control Subnet, and this advertises all prefixes learned from BGP into the local routing protocol.

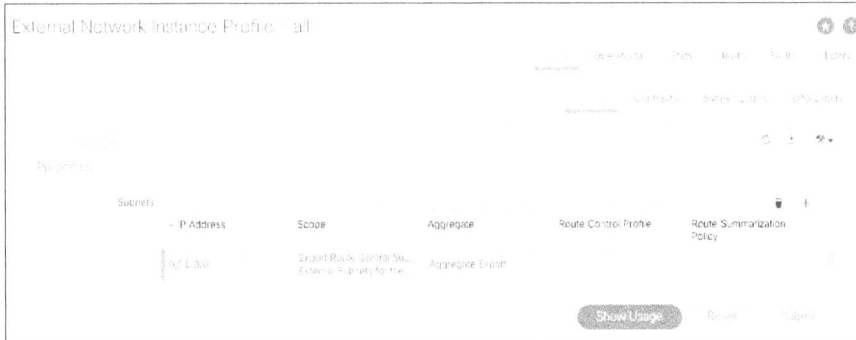

Figure 12-31 *Flags Configured for Transit Routing*

To highlight this, Example 12-37 shows what the Export Route Control Subnet with Aggregate Export does to the OSPF route maps.

Example 12-37 *Viewing the Redistribution Route Map from BGP to OSPF and the Corresponding Prefix List*

```
leaf101# show ip ospf vrf ACI-AMT-Book:v1
Redistributing External Routes from
   static route-map exp-ctx-st-2785280
   direct route-map exp-ctx-st-2785280
   bgp route-map exp-ctx-proto-2785280
   eigrp route-map exp-ctx-proto-2785280
   coop route-map exp-ctx-st-2785280


leaf101# show route-map exp-ctx-proto-2785280
route-map exp-ctx-proto-2785280, permit, sequence 19801
  Match clauses:
    ip address prefix-lists: IPv4-proto32773-2785280-agg-ext-inferred-export-dst
    ipv6 address prefix-lists: IPv6-deny-all
  Set clauses:
    tag 4294967295


leaf101# show ip prefix-list IPv4-proto32773-2785280-agg-ext-inferred-export-dst
ip prefix-list IPv4-proto32773-2785280-agg-ext-inferred-export-dst: 1 entries
   seq 1 permit 0.0.0.0/0 le 32
```

Because 0.0.0.0/0 is configured as Export Route Control Subnet with Aggregate Export, a prefix list permitting anything less than or equal to 0.0.0.0/0 is added to the route map. All these routes are tagged with the VRF instance route tag (4294967295) to prevent the fabric from learning the routes again on a different L3Out and creating a routing loop.

Policy Enforcement

ACI uses endpoint groups to simplify security deployment. You are no longer restricted to individual IP addresses of servers to create access control lists (ACLs). Servers are grouped together, no matter what their IP address, and policy is enforced via the group tag introduced at the beginning of this chapter; this section talks more about how this tag is used. Figure 12-32 shows an overview of the VXLAN bits used to make iVXLAN and EPG policy enforcement work.

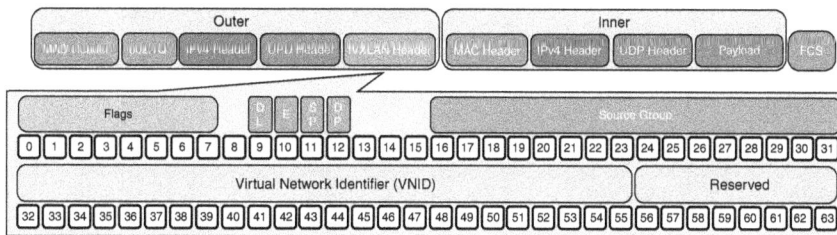

Figure 12-32 *iVXLAN Header Format Containing Source Policy, Destination Policy, and Source Group Bits*

The source group, which can also be referred to as the policy control tag (PCTag), class ID, or source class (sclass), is used to identify the group to which specific traffic belongs. Each EPG is assigned a unique PCTag that can be seen in the UI when navigating to the EPG and viewing the Policy > General tab or navigating to Tenant > Operational > Resource IDs and selecting EPGs or other resources that have group tags assigned to them. Figure 12-33 shows the PCTags assigned to EPGs *Web*, *VLAN2*, and *App*.

Figure 12-33 *Viewing the PCTags Allocated to Different Objects Under a Tenant*

What happens when a contract is placed between EPG *App* and EPG *Web*? The leaf switches program a zoning rule that allows traffic to flow between the two groups of servers. In Example 12-38, you can see how to validate that a contract is pushed as a zoning rule between EPG *App* (the provider) and EPG *Web* (the consumer).

Example 12-38 *Checking Contract Programming on Leaf 101 Between EPG Web and EPG App*

```
leaf101# show zoning-rule scope 2785280 src-epg 32775 dst-epg 16386
Rule ID    SrcEPG    DstEPG    FilterID    operSt    Scope     Action
  Priority

=======    ======    ======    ========    ======    =====     ======
  ========
4129       32775     16386     5           enabled   2785280   log,permit
  fully_qual(7)
4134       32775     16386     9           enabled   2785280   permit
  fully_qual(7)


leaf101# show zoning-filter filter 5
FilterId  Name        EtherT    ArpOpc     Prot      MatchOnlyFrag Stateful
  SFromPort  SToPort    DFromPort  DToPort   Prio       Icmpv4T       Icmpv6T
  TcpRules

========  ==========  ======    =========  =======   ======        =======
  =======    ====       ====       ====      =========  =======       ========
  ========
5         5_0         ip        unspecified icmp      no            no
  unspecified unspecified unspecified unspecified sport    unspecified unspecified
leaf101# show zoning-filter filter 9
FilterId  Name        EtherT    ArpOpc     Prot      MatchOnlyFrag Stateful
  SFromPort  SToPort    DFromPort  DToPort   Prio       Icmpv4T       Icmpv6T
  TcpRules

========  ==========  ======    =========  =======   ======        =======
  =======    ====       ====       ====      =========  =======       ========
  ========
9         9_0         ip        unspecified tcp       no            no
  unspecified unspecified 3260      3260       dport    unspecified unspecified
```

The zoning rules are not specific to a source IP address or a destination IP address. It doesn't matter what the IP address of the server in the EPG is; ACI can enforce ACL-like policy without being concerned about the IP address of the server. To assist in this process, EPM associates an sclass to every endpoint that it learns. Example 12-39 shows the EPM output of a server that belongs to the *Web* EPG. When a forwarding lookup is done, the PCTag is analyzed and, based on the zoning rules, the ASIC determines whether it should drop the traffic.

Example 12-39   *Endpoint with PCTag for Policy Enforcement*

```
leaf101# show system internal epm endpoint ip 172.16.0.10

MAC : 000b.0b0b.0b0b ::: Num IPs : 1
IP# 0 : 172.16.0.10 ::: IP# 0 flags : locally-aged|host-tracked| ::: l3-sw-hit: No
Vlan id : 12 ::: Vlan vnid : 10801 ::: VRF name : ACI-AMT-Book:v1
BD vnid : 14942176 ::: VRF vnid : 2785280
Phy If : 0x16000013 ::: Tunnel If : 0
Interface : port-channel20
Flags : 0x80005c15 ::: sclass : 32775 ::: Ref count : 5
EP Create Timestamp : 08/08/2019 16:30:12.179763
EP Update Timestamp : 08/16/2019 20:52:05.359892
EP Flags : local|vPC|locally-aged|IP|MAC|host-tracked|sclass|timer|

::::
```

One limitation of the source group tag is that it is only 16 bits and would allow for a maximum 65,535 endpoint groups, whereas the VXLAN VNID provides more than 4 million unique segments. To prevent the PCTag from becoming a limitation, it is considered to be VRF instance specific. In Example 12-38, you can see that every zoning rule has a scope. This scope is the VNID of the VRF instance these EPGs belong to; therefore, EPG IDs or PCTags can be reused across different VRF instances.

To enforce policy with devices that exist outside the ACI fabric, external EPGs can be created to map a specific subnet or a set of specific external subnets into a unique external EPG. This is done by creating the external EPG (*l3extInstP*), consuming or providing a contract, and defining a subnet with the External Subnets for the External EPG scope selected. When you do this, the subnet is pushed into hardware with the PCTag of the external EPG. Because a single prefix can be installed with a unique PCTag, the subnet has to be unique within the VRF instance. A special exception exists for the quad-zero network, or::/0, where the PCTag of the external EPG is not associated with the default route in hardware. Instead, the PCTag used is 15 when the default route is used to make a destination lookup; when doing a source lookup, the PCTag is that of the VRF instance and not the external EPG or 15.

On the VRF instance, you can also configure Ingress or Egress Policy Control Enforcement Direction to indicate where external prefixes and zoning rules are changed. With the Egress setting, border leafs have all zoning rules and can enforce policy for traffic going to the external networks. With the Ingress setting, all compute leafs have the policy for all external prefixes and can always enforce policy before sending the packet into the fabric. This eliminates the border leaf from scale concerns as more and more rules are added since they are distributed across the compute leafs.

Shared Services

A shared-service EPG is an EPG that is providing a service to an EPG that is part of another VRF instance. This could be a DHCP and DNS server that all tenants should have access to, or it could be an EPG that provides a backup server that requires high bandwidth where it is undesirable for this traffic to traverse an external router. From a routing perspective, a shared-service EPG requires routes from the provider VRF instance to be leaked into the consumer VRF instances. From a security perspective, zoning rules now need to be applied between two separate scopes (VRF instances). In the previous section, you learned how policy is applied between EPGs within the same VRF instance and how the group ID is locally significant to the VRF instance in which the EPGs reside. This creates a problem for a shared-service EPG because the PCTags can be reused in two different VRF instances. To avoid an issue of duplicate PCTags for shared-service EPGs, PCTag values below 0x4000 (16384) are reserved as shared-service PCTags and are globally unique. This means that an endpoint group that provides a shared service has a PCTag that is never reused within the fabric. Figure 12-34 shows a logical representation of a shared-service EPG EPG (*Backup-Server*) and a consumer EPG (*App*), along with the relevant PCTags.

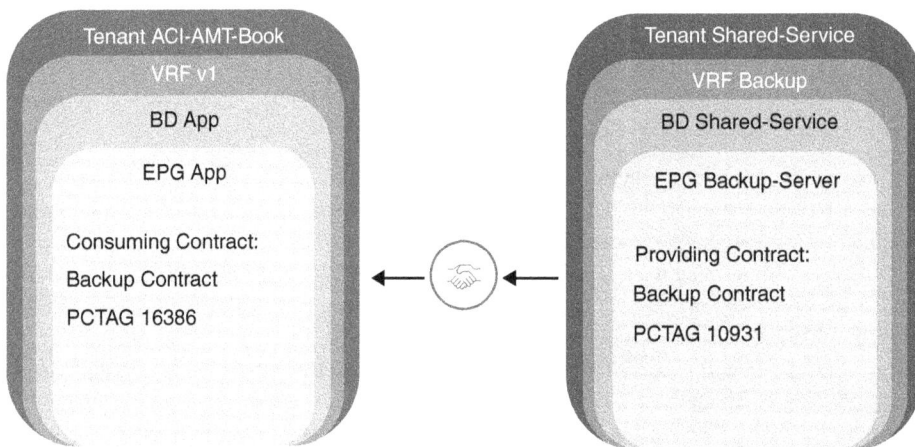

Figure 12-34   *Contract Between Two Tenants and Two Different VRF Instances*

Note   PCTags 0x0 through 0xF are reserved for specific features.

If an iVXLAN-encapsulated packet is routed into the VRF instance *Shared-Service:backup*, the group ID 16386 could have come from any VRF instance and might represent any EPG. It would therefore not be possible to accurately enforce policy in the provider VRF instance. In the consumer VRF instance, though, if a packet comes with PCTag 10931, which is globally unique to the fabric, the leaf switch can enforce policy appropriately. Example 12-40 shows the zoning rule in the consumer VRF (*ACI-AMT-Book:v1*) between the globally unique PCTag and locally significant PCTag for EPG *App*.

Example 12-40 *Zoning Rule Between a Globally Unique PCTag and Locally Significant PCTag*

```
leaf103# show zoning-rule scope 2785280 src-epg 10931 dst-epg 16386
+---------+--------+--------+----------+---------------+--------+--------+------
  +--------+---------------+
| Rule ID | SrcEPG | DstEPG | FilterID |     Dir       | operSt | Scope  | Name |
  Action  |    Priority   |
+---------+--------+--------+----------+---------------+--------+--------+------
  +--------+---------------+
|  4134   | 10931  | 16386  | default  | uni-dir-ignore| enabled| 2785280|      |
 permit   | src_dst_any(9) |
+---------+--------+--------+----------+---------------+--------+--------+------
  +--------+---------------+
```

If traffic originates at EPG *App* and is destined to EPG *Shared-Service*, how does the leaf know what policy to enforce? The only way to give the leaf the intelligence needed to enforce policy is to associate the *Shared-Service* PCTag with the destination route. To make sure this happens, the subnet in the provider EPG must be defined under the EPG itself. When this is configured, the subnet route to the shared service has a PCTag assigned to it. For the *Backup-Server* EPG, the subnet 172.18.3.0/24 is now defined under the EPG, and when the route is leaked into the VRF instance *ACI-AMT-Book*, the route for 172.18.3.0/24 has PCTag 10931, and policy can be enforced in the consumer VRF instance between the source (16386) and destination (10931). Example 12-41 shows an IPv4 route toward a shared service EPG with the PCTag of 10931.

Example 12-41 *Class ID Assigned to a Route with Zoning Rules*

```
leaf103#  vsh -c " show ip route 172.18.3.0 detail vrf ACI-AMT-Book:v1"
IP Route Table for VRF "ACI-AMT-Book:v1"
'*' denotes best ucast next-hop
'**' denotes best mcast next-hop
'[x/y]' denotes [preference/metric]
'%<string>' in via output denotes VRF <string>

172.18.3.0/24, ubest/mbest: 1/0, attached, direct, pervasive
    *via 10.0.184.66%overlay-1, [1/0], 00:01:03, static, tag 4294967294
        recursive next hop: 10.0.184.66/32%overlay-1
        vrf crossing information:  VNID:0x2c0000 ClassId:0x2ab3 Flush#:0x1
leaf103# vsh -c "dec 0x2ab3"
10931
```

```
leaf103# show zoning-rule scope 2785280 src-epg 16386 dst-epg 10931
+---------+--------+--------+----------+--------+---------+---------+------+--------
 +----------------+
| Rule ID | SrcEPG | DstEPG | FilterID | Dir    | operSt  | Scope   | Name | Action
|    Priority     |
+---------+--------+--------+----------+--------+---------+---------+------+--------
 +----------------+
|   4135  | 16386  | 10931  | default  | bi-dir | enabled | 2785280 |      | permit
| src_dst_any(9)  |
+---------+--------+--------+----------+--------+---------+---------+------+--------
 +----------------+
```

To summarize, a shared-service EPG needs to have its subnet defined under the EPG itself so that a policy lookup can be done in the consumer VRF instance. The consumer subnet can still be defined on the bridge domain. In both cases, the subnet has to have Shared Between VRFs selected.

From a routing and forwarding perspective, how does the packet get from VRF instance *ACI-AMT-Book:v1* to the *Shared-Server:backup* VRF instance? The route itself has a VNID rewrite flag set that tells the ASIC to change the VNID before sending the packet to the spine proxy. To see if a route is programmed with a new VNID, check from the VSH command line, as shown in Example 12-42.

Example 12-42   *VNID Rewrite Information for Leaked Routes*

```
leaf103# vsh -c "show ip route 172.18.3.0/24 detail vrf ACI-AMT-Book:v1"
IP Route Table for VRF "ACI-AMT-Book:v1"
'*' denotes best ucast next-hop
'**' denotes best mcast next-hop
'[x/y]' denotes [preference/metric]
'%<string>' in via output denotes VRF <string>

172.18.3.0/24, ubest/mbest: 1/0, attached, direct, pervasive
    *via 10.0.184.66%overlay-1, [1/0], 00:42:16, static, tag 4294967294
         recursive next hop: 10.0.184.66/32%overlay-1
         vrf crossing information:  VNID:0x2c0000 ClassId:0x2ab3 Flush#:0x2
```

Endpoint learning is always disabled when crossing the VRF instance boundary. The leaf ensures that learning is disabled by setting the Don't Learn (DL) bit in the iVXLAN header. For packets that are forwarded to a different VRF instance, the spine proxy is always used to make a forwarding lookup for the destination endpoint location.

Shared L3Outs also use VRF instance VNID rewrite information to send the packet to the appropriate VRF instance. The major difference is that for routes that are outside the fabric, the packet is sent directly to the border leaf instead of to the spine proxy. Such an external route also has a PCTag associated with it that is globally unique. To configure a shared L3Out, the external EPGs have to have the following flags set on the external prefix:

- External Subnets for the External EPG

- Shared Route Control Subnet

- Shared Security Import Subnet

In this case, External Subnets for the External EPG is set so that servers local to the VRF instance have access to the external prefix. Shared Route Control Subnet creates a BGP route map that allows the routes to be leaked into the target VRF instance, and Shared Security Import Subnet is set to give the routes globally unique PCTags. Example 12-43 shows a route leaked from BGP where the next hops are Border Leafs 101 and 102, and the VRF instance VNID maps to the *Shared-Services:L3Out* VRF instance.

Example 12-43   *Leaked Route from Border Leafs 101 and 102*

```
leaf103# vsh -c "show ip route 192.168.8.0/24 detail vrf ACI-AMT-Book:v1"
IP Route Table for VRF "ACI-AMT-Book:v1"
'*' denotes best ucast next-hop
'**' denotes best mcast next-hop
'[x/y]' denotes [preference/metric]
'%<string>' in via output denotes VRF <string>

192.168.8.0/24, ubest/mbest: 2/0
    *via 10.0.128.70%overlay-1, [1/0], 00:12:56, bgp-65502, internal, tag 65502
(mpls-vpn)
        MPLS[0]: Label=0 E=0 TTL=0 S=0 (VPN)
        client-specific data: 2f
        recursive next hop: 10.0.128.70/32%overlay-1
        extended route information: BGP origin AS 65502 BGP peer AS 65502 rw-vnid:
0x228001 table-id: 0x8 rw-mac: 0
    *via 10.0.128.71%overlay-1, [1/0], 00:00:07, bgp-65502, internal, tag 65502
(mpls-vpn)
        MPLS[0]: Label=0 E=0 TTL=0 S=0 (VPN)
        client-specific data: 33
        recursive next hop: 10.0.128.71/32%overlay-1
        extended route information: BGP origin AS 65502 BGP peer AS 65502 rw-vnid:
0x228001 table-id: 0x8 rw-mac: 0
```

To leak these routes from BGP into the target VRF instance, a new BGP route map is created to allow a route to leak only if it is set to Shared Route Control Subnet. An additional route target is added as well to import the routes from the proper VRF instance. Example 12-44 highlights the route map and route target.

Example 12-44 *BGP RT and Route Map/Prefix to Leak Routes*

```
leaf103# show bgp process vrf ACI-AMT-Book:v1 | egrep -A 5 "Import route-map"
    Import route-map 2785280-shared-svc-leak
    Export RT list:
        65502:2785280
    Import RT list:
        65502:2260993
        65502:2785280
leaf103# show route-map 2785280-shared-svc-leak
route-map 2785280-shared-svc-leak, deny, sequence 1
  Match clauses:
    pervasive: 2
  Set clauses:
route-map 2785280-shared-svc-leak, permit, sequence 2
  Match clauses:
    extcommunity  (extcommunity-list filter): 2785280-shared-svc-leak
  Set clauses:
route-map 2785280-shared-svc-leak, permit, sequence 1000
  Match clauses:
    ip address prefix-lists: IPv4-2260993-16386-10932-2785280-shared-svc-leak
    ipv6 address prefix-lists: IPv6-deny-all
  Set clauses:
leaf103# show ip prefix-list IPv4-2260993-16386-10932-2785280-shared-svc-leak
ip prefix-list IPv4-2260993-16386-10932-2785280-shared-svc-leak: 1 entries
    seq 1 permit 192.168.8.0/24
```

Note   The prefix list name includes the VRF instance VNID and external EPG ID, which has Shared Route Control Subnet configured (VNID 2260993 and EPG PCTag 10932), which simplifies troubleshooting when you need to determine why a route is leaked.

L3Out Flags

The external EPG plays an important role in classifying traffic for policy enforcement and also control plane configuration. Table 12-4 summarizes what each flag does.

Table 12-4 *External EPG Flags*

Prefix-Based EPG for Contracts	Function
External Subnets for the External EPG	Classifies traffic sourced from the specific prefix into an external EPG by assigning a PCTag to all traffic coming from this prefix.
Shared Security Import	Used to classify data plane packets for shared/leaked prefixes into external EPG(s) for policy enforcement.

Prefix-Based EPG for Contracts	Function
Route Control	**Function**
Export Route Control	Filters transit routes advertised out of the fabric.
Import Route Control	Used to create route maps that filter which prefixes should be learned from an L3Out. This is only supported for BGP and OSPF.
Shared Route Control	Filters which external routes can be leaked into another VRF instance.
Aggregate Export	Allows prefixes to be aggregated together in the export direction (0/0 or ::/0 only).
Aggregate Import	Allows prefixes to be aggregated together in import direction (0/0 or ::/0 only).
Aggregate Shared Route	Allows prefixes to be aggregated together for shared route control.

Quality of Service (QoS) in ACI

ACI 3.2 supports three user QoS classes that allow an administrator to define queuing characteristics:

- **Bandwidth percentage:** You can reserve a percentage of bandwidth on the egress interface for a specific traffic class. For example, to reserve up to 20% of bandwidth for vMotion traffic even if the interface is congested, a QoS level can be defined with a bandwidth percentage and an EPG, or a contract can be configured with this QoS level set.

- **Weighted round robin:** This scheduling algorithm can be used to schedule packets between the different queues. It takes the bandwidth percentage into account.

- **Strict priority:** This scheduling algorithm can be configured on a QoS level if the requirement is for specific traffic to always be prioritized. An example could be voice traffic or other latency-sensitive traffic going through the ACI fabric.

The fabric tracks these QoS groups by using a class of service (CoS) value in the outer Ethernet header. Besides the three user-definable classes, the fabric has CoS values reserved for internal functions, such as control plane traffic, a best-effort class for SPAN traffic, and a strict priority class for controller communication. QoS Level 3 is the default class. Every packet entering the ACI fabric is placed into this class (unless a custom QoS configuration is used). Table 12-5 shows the reserved fabric QoS groups, with the corresponding function and CoS marking for each one.

Table 12-5   *Fabric QoS Groups and CoS Markings*

QoS Group	3p11.667	CoS Value in iVXLAN
0	Level 3 (default)	0
1	Level 2	1
2	Level 1	2
3	APIC traffic	3
4	SPAN traffic	4
5	Control plane traffic	5
5	iTraceroute traffic	6

If there is traffic to which you need to guarantee bandwidth (NFS, vMotion, backups, and so on), you could consider making Level 2 a QoS class with a bandwidth guarantee and define a percentage. With this configuration, all traffic that should have guaranteed bandwidth can use a contract or a EPG QoS configuration to map the traffic to this level.

Note   If a class has 20% allocated but is using only 1%, another **weighted round robin** class can use the remaining 99%.

If there is traffic that needs to be prioritized no matter what, you can define one class, such as Level 1, to be your strict priority queue.

You can define a QoS configuration in the APIC GUI by navigating to Fabric > Access Policies > Policies > Global > QoS Class. Figure 12-35 shows an example QoS configuration.

In Figure 12-35, Level 1 is a strict priority queue, Level 2 has 20% bandwidth allocated, and Level 3, the default class, also has 20% allocated.

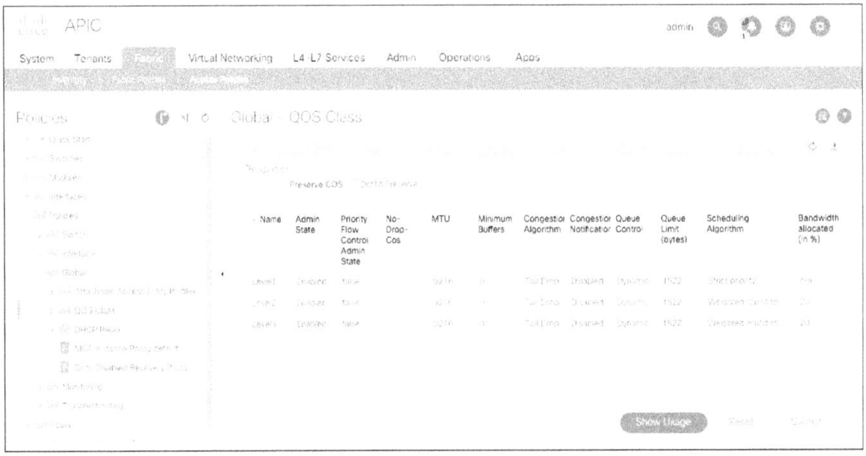

Figure 12-35   *Global QoS Configuration for Levels 1 Through 3*

Externally Set DSCP and CoS Markings

External QoS markings have no impact on classification in ACI unless a custom QoS policy is used to classify based on CoS or DSCP/ToS. There are three ways to classify traffic into a fabric QoS level:

- Place all traffic that is part of an EPG (EPG *QoS*) into a level by assigning the EPG a QoS level.

- Use a custom QoS policy to place traffic into a different service level based on external QoS markings.

- Configure QoS based on a contract (contract *QoS*) by assigning a QoS level to a contract. Traffic that matches that contract gets assigned that QoS level.

EPG QoS

On an EPG, a user can define a QoS class (*fvAEPg.prio*). By default, it is set to Unspecified, which is the same as Level 3 (the default QoS class). This can be changed to Level 1 or Level 2, depending on the requirements and how the levels are configured. All traffic entering the switch on the VLAN or VXLAN ID used to extend this EPG is placed into the configured traffic class. This level is maintained throughout the life of the packet in the ACI fabric. Even if the egress EPG has a different QoS level configured, the initial or ingress-derived QoS value is honored for queuing. The DSCP markings of the tenant traffic are not modified. The CoS value of the tenant traffic is maintained only if the Dot1p preserve configuration is enabled.

Custom QoS Policy

To classify traffic inside the fabric based on external QoS markings, a custom QoS policy can be used. A custom QoS policy works by classifying traffic into a QoS level based on either a DSCP or CoS marking that is received from a connected device. The policy can match either a single DSCP/CoS value or a range of values. A custom QoS policy can also be used to re-mark traffic that matches the criteria to a new DSCP or CoS value.

When configuring a custom QoS policy, the *priority* is the QoS level for which traffic should be placed inside the ACI fabric. To match the traffic, select a DSCP range or CoS range.

Contract QoS

If required, a contract can be used to define the QoS level. If traffic from the *App* EPG to the *Web* EPG is considered critical, for example, a custom QoS level can be defined on the contract, and traffic matching that contract is queued accordingly. To define the QoS level in a contract, expand the subject of the contract and define a QoS priority. Using the contract to define the QoS level allows you to re-mark the traffic as well. One limitation of the contract *QoS* is that the endpoint must be known for queuing inside the fabric to work. If traffic gets sent to the spine proxy for a lookup, because policy cannot be applied on the ingress leaf, no QoS can be applied.

CoS Preservation in ACI

Because ACI uses VXLAN VNIDs to identify the Layer 2 forwarding domain and not VLAN IDs, the 802.1Q header is stripped off the frame before the frame is sent into the fabric. This means the CoS value in the original frame will be lost when the traffic is sent into the fabric. If the requirement is to preserve the CoS value as a frame traverses the ACI fabric, the Dot1p preserve configuration must be enabled. By default, the ingress leaf encodes the external CoS value into the upper, or most significant, DSCP bits of the iVXLAN packet. When Dot1p preserve is enabled, the egress leaf rewrites the CoS bits based on the upper DSCP markings of the packet, ensuring that the CoS value received in the fabric is the CoS value in the frame when it is sent out of the fabric. Table 12-6 shows the mapping of the externally received CoS value to the iVXLAN DSCP value.

Table 12-6 *CoS-to-iVXLAN DSCP Markings*

User CoS	iVXLAN DSCP Marking	Decimal Value
6 (0b110)	0b110xxx	48
3 (0b011)	0b011xxx	24
0 (0b0)	0b0xxx	0

Note The 3 least significant bits represent the CoS value for the fabric QoS group.

iTraceroute Class

One important internal class to understand is the iTraceroute class. iTraceroute is used to identify the path of a packet through the ACI fabric. The use of traceroute policies allows a user to see which way a packet hashes through the fabric even when multiple equal-cost paths are available. Each switch in the fabric has a special TCAM rule to copy (on the spine) and to redirect (on the leaf) all traffic that has an outer CoS value of 6. Based on these CPU-redirected packets, the leaf or spine can send detailed path information back to the originating leaf so the path can be discovered.

QoS and Multi-Pod

ACI writes the CoS value into the outer (iVXLAN) DSCP value at all times. If a packet is sent from a spine in Pod 1 with the DSCP markings set by the ingress leaf, the Inter-Pod Network (IPN) router uses a DSCP-to-CoS table map like the one in Table 12-7 to populate the CoS value in the 802.1Q header as the packet is sent to the remote spine.

Table 12-7 *Default DSCP-to-CoS Map from an IOS Device*

DSCP Value	0	8, 10	16, 18	24, 26	32, 34	40, 46	48	56
CoS Value	0	1	2	3	4	5	6	7

Note   IPN-facing ports are always 802.1Q-enabled subinterfaces. Due to this, CoS is present and can be populated by the IPN router.

If the DSCP value drives a CoS value of 6 through the DSCP-to-CoS table map on the IPN router, the spine treats this as iTraceroute traffic and forwards it to the egress leaf. Because leaf switches redirect all CoS 6 traffic to the CPU, the traffic does not reach its destination. Figure 12-36 and the steps that follow describe this scenario in more detail.

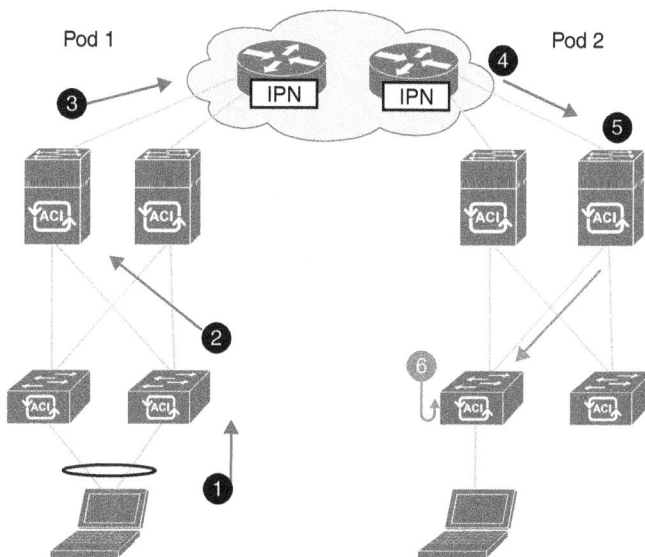

Figure 12-36 *Broken Traffic Flow with CoS 6 Across Multi-pod*

1. A frame is sent into the ACI fabric with a CoS value of 6 and no QoS group configured (default level 3).

2. When the leaf sends the frame encapsulated in iVXLAN into the fabric, the outer DSCP value is set to DSCP value 48, and the outer CoS value is 0 (default level 3 CoS).

3. The spine receives this iVXLAN packet and forwards it toward the IPN.

4. The IPN inspects the DSCP value and inserts the corresponding CoS value when sending to the remote pod.

5. The spine in Pod 2 receives the iVXLAN packet with a CoS value of 6 and a DSCP value of 48. The packet is sent to the leaf based on the outer destination IP address.

6. The leaf receives the packet, and because the outer CoS value is 6, it is redirected to the CPU for iTraceroute functionality instead of being forwarded to the destination host.

To prevent this issue, you can configure the DSCP class-to-CoS translation policy to remap the DSCP value to a QOS group.

DSCP Class-to-CoS Translation Policy

Under tenant *Infra, Policies, Protocol, DSCP class cos Translation policy for L3 traffic*, a CoS-to-DSCP/DSCP-to-CoS mapping can be configured. Before the spines send traffic into the IPN, the DSCP value is rewritten to a user-defined DSCP value based on the outer CoS. Figure 12-37 shows a sample policy.

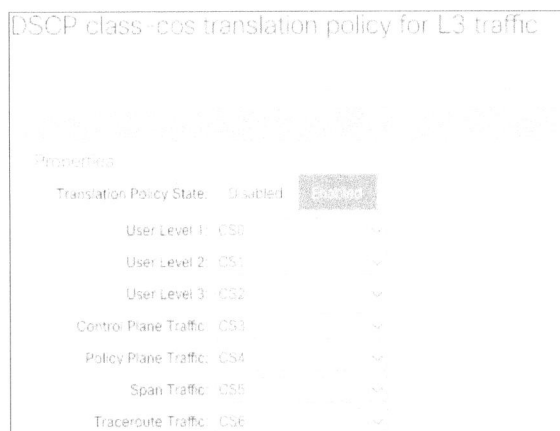

Figure 12-37   *Sample Infra DSCP Class-to-CoS Translation Policy*

Due to the settings in Figure 12-37, user Level 2 traffic is mapped to DSCP value CS2 when sending traffic into the IPN. On the receiving spine, CS2 would be mapped back to an outer CoS value of 2 when sending traffic into the local pod. In this case, if the spine ever sends a packet with CoS 6, the spine rewrites the CoS value when sending it into the fabric/local pod.

Note   In APIC Release 4.0, additional QoS classes are added (4 through 6), and a static mapping is created to map CoS and level to an outer DSCP value, preventing iTraceroute misclassification.

Multi-Pod

Multi-pod was ACI's first feature to allow true multilocation deployment. To accommodate forwarding across an IP network and keep each pod running its own control plane, additional forwarding requirements needed to be added. This section highlights the key differences from a data plane forwarding perspective when multi-pod is in use.

When a multi-pod fabric is deployed, one or more spines at each pod must connect to an IPN switch capable of running OSPF on subinterfaces using VLAN 4 and must support Protocol Independent Multicast (PIM) Bidirectional (Bidir). In order for traffic to traverse a multi-pod fabric, new loopback interfaces were implemented on the spines that connect to the IPN:

- **Control plane TEP (CP-TEP):** When a multi-pod L3Out is created, the router ID defined on the spine node in the logical node profile is chosen as the CP-TEP. The CP-TEP is responsible for establishing a BGP session to each spine in the remote pod. This BGP session is used to advertise endpoint and route information between pods.

- **Data plane TEP, or external TEP (E-TEP):** When multi-pod is configured, each pod is configured with an E-TEP that is chosen by the administrator. This E-TEP acts as the next hop for BGP EVPN and is an anycast address on all spines in a pod that are multi-pod enabled. Furthermore, COOP on the spines uses this as a placeholder for remote endpoints. COOP learns endpoints from BGP, and it points to the ETEP. If a proxy lookup results in the packet needing to be forwarded to the remote spine, based on the ETEP, the packet is sent to the remote pod's external MAC/IPv4/IPv6 proxy TEP.

- **External MAC proxy:** An anycast address is allocated to all multi-pod-enabled spines within a given pod. Each pod has a unique address. Spines in a pod forward traffic to this TEP on the destination pod when a COOP lookup has been performed on a MAC endpoint and this endpoint exists on the destination pod.

- **External IPv4 proxy:** An anycast address is allocated to all multi-pod-enabled spines within a given pod. Each pod has a unique address. Spines in a pod forward traffic to this TEP on the destination pod when a COOP lookup has been performed on an IPv4 endpoint and this endpoint exists on the destination pod.

- **External IPv6 proxy:** An anycast address is allocated to all multi-pod-enabled spines within a given pod. Each pod has a unique address. Spines in a pod forward traffic to this TEP on the destination pod when a COOP lookup has been performed on an IPv6 endpoint and this endpoint exists on the destination pod.

These loopback addresses get advertised into OSPF at each pod, allowing the IPN to learn where each TEP exists and advertise the TEPs to the other pods (see Figure 12-38).

For multicast, the IPN needs to provide a multicast routed infrastructure to allow the forwarding of packets in the bridge domain multicast group. A single spine in a pod is elected authoritative for a BD GIPo range. This means that for each GIPo, one spine in the POD sends an IGMP join to attract the traffic from other pods and also sends the traffic sourced from the local pod on a specific physical interface. If the authoritative spine is reloaded or isolated from the IPN, the other spine can take over for sending or joining specific groups. Figure 12-39 illustrates a multi-pod deployment and the use of authoritative devices.

Spine 1 CP-TEP	1.1.1.1
Spine 2 CP-TEP	2.2.2.2
E-TEP	10.255.1.1
External MAC Proxy	10.0.0.33
External IPV4 Proxy	10.0.0.34
External IPV6 Proxy	10.0.0.35

Spine 1 CP-TEP	3.3.3.3
Spine 2 CP-TEP	4.4.4.4
E-TEP	10.255.2.1
External MAC Proxy	11.0.0.33
External IPV4 Proxy	11.0.0.34
External IPV6 Proxy	11.0.0.35

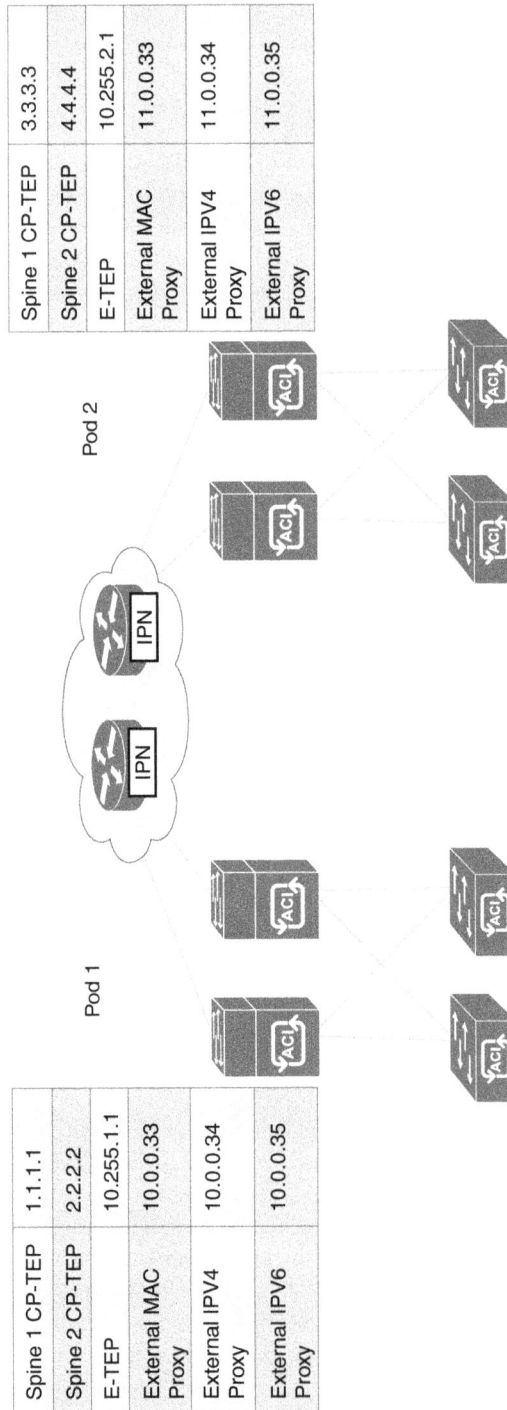

Figure 12-38   *Example of a TEP Addressing Schema Used in a Multi-pod Setup*

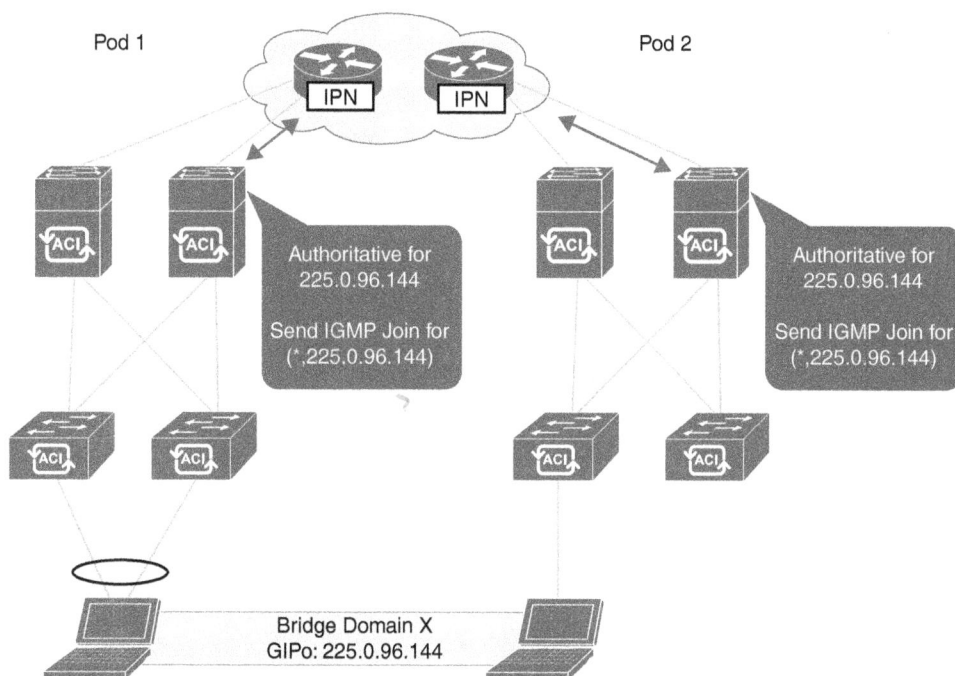

Figure 12-39 *Role of an Authoritative Spine for a BD GIPo*

The IPN must run PIM Bidir for the bridge domain address range. The benefits of PIM Bidir include the following:

- Only the (*, G) entry is installed for a BD route. This is ideal for ACI multi-pod because, otherwise, an (S, G) entry would need to be installed for every leaf that would be sending the multidestination traffic into the IPN. This could have scale impact on the IPN, depending on the number of multicast routes the IPN supports.

- RPF checks are more relaxed when using PIM Bidir. Traffic is always forwarded to the rendezvous point (RP), and thus only the shared tree is used. Because the spines have the capability of changing who is sending and receiving the traffic based on failure scenarios, convergence is improved by using Bidir.

Unlike traditional PIM sparse mode (PIM-SM) Any-Source Multicast (ASM), Bidir PIM does not support the concept of an anycast RP. Bidir PIM redundancy is based on a backup model, or *phantom rendezvous points*. In other words, a single RP handles everything, and in the case of a failure, another RP takes over. This model is achieved by configuring different subnet masks on these loopback addresses for each IPN switch, which allows the use of the longest-prefix-match logic in the routing process. Table 12-8 shows a phantom RP configuration example using the previous topology, where two IPN switches connect two pods.

Key Topic

Table 12-8 *Configuration Example for Phantom RP on Two IPN Routers*

ipn-1	ipn-2
interface loopback1	interface loopback1
description BIDIR Phantom RP	description BIDIR Phantom RP
vrf member MPOD	vrf member MPOD
ip address 192.168.100.1/30	ip address 192.168.100.1/29
ip ospf network point-to-point	ip ospf network point-to-point
ip router ospf IPN area 0.0.0.0	ip router ospf IPN area 0.0.0.0
ip pim sparse-mode	ip pim sparse-mode

When using a dedicated VRF instance to segment the traffic for a multi-pod deployment, configure the static designated RP address (part of the IP subnet previously defined under the loopback interface) under the VRF instance and use the **bidir** configuration keyword at the end of the configuration syntax. Table 12-9 highlights this configuration.

Table 12-9 *Example Configuration for PIM BiDir on Two IPN Routers*

ipn-1	ipn-2
vrf context MPOD	vrf context MPOD
ip pim rp-address 192.168.100.2 group-list 225.0.0.0/8 bidir	ip pim rp-address 192.168.100.2 group-list 225.0.0.0/8 bidir
ip pim rp-address 192.168.100.2 group-list 239.0.0.0/8 bidir	ip pim rp-address 192.168.100.2 group-list 239.0.0.0/8 bidir
ip pim ssm range 232.0.0.0/8	ip pim ssm range 232.0.0.0/8

With this configuration, the route to the RP is preferred via ipn-1 because it has the longest prefix, /30, compared to the /29 configured on ipn-2. If ipn-1 goes down, ipn-2 can take over RP functionality because the /29 becomes the best path for the RP address 192.168.100.2. This is, of course, dependent on each spine having a connection to each IPN. A typical deployment would consist of four IPN switches, with spines in each pod dual connected to two IPNs and the IPNs connected to each other.

In addition, to load balance traffic across multiple RPs, the default fabric multicast GIPo 225.0.0.0/15 can be broken into four different /17 Bidir groups with a different spine as the RP and a backup RP for each group.

Note First-generation Nexus 9000 devices are not supported IPN devices because the Broadcom T2/T2+ ASICs support only a maximum PIM Bidir range of /24.

Another key difference in regard to multi-pod is the concept of *dynamic tunnels*. Up to this point, we've only talked about single pod deployments, where each node within a pod would create an iVXLAN tunnel to all other nodes in the fabric, including the any-cast proxy addresses on the spines. These static tunnels are built when an IS-IS route is learned. With multi-pod, leafs in Pod X may need to communicate to leafs in Pod Y, and thus a tunnel would need to be built between them. However, from a scalability perspective, it's not optimal to statically build tunnels from every device in one pod to every device in another. In addition, IS-IS is localized to a pod, so there needs to be another mechanism to create tunnels between pods. Ideally, tunnels should only be built if there is a traffic flow that requires them. To accomplish this, tunnels are created dynamically between devices in different pods. Dynamic tunnels are created in the following ways:

- When a packet is sent from Pod X to Pod Y, when the egress leaf in Pod Y receives the packet, it copies it to the CPU to generate a tunnel to the source (see Figure 12-40). This ensures that the packet is forwarded out the front panel, but a notification is sent to the CPU to have software create a tunnel.

- A tunnel is created when an external prefix is learned through BGP (for example, if an L3Out exists in Pod 1, but devices in Pod 2 access that L3Out). A dynamic tunnel is built when the BGP route is learned.

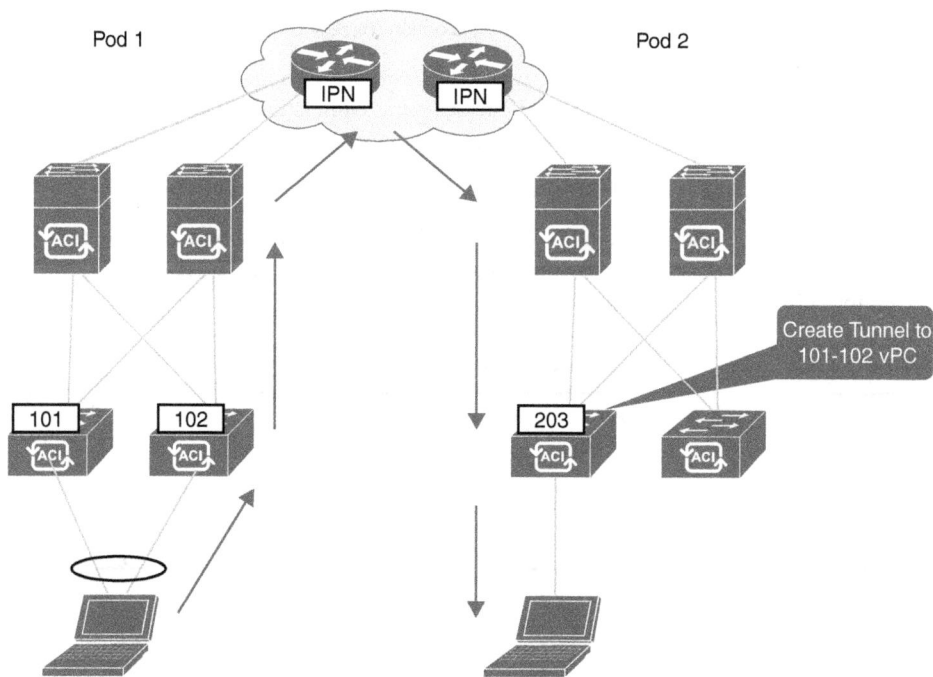

Figure 12-40 *A Dynamic Tunnel Is Created on Leaf 203*

Multi-Site

Multi-site was the next generation of ACI's multi-location strategy after releasing the multi-pod functionality. Multi-site built on the benefits of multi-pod, allowing multiple independent fabrics to have the same policy stretched between them. However, because the fabrics are indeed separate, and the objects and corresponding VNIDs/PCTags are local to each site, special forwarding functionality needed to be implemented for the solution to work.

Multi-site removes the need for the individual external proxy TEPs and instead replaces them with a single TEP: the data plane unicast TEP. When a packet needs to be forwarded to a remote site, the spines and leafs learn about remote endpoints and associate them with the appropriate site's data plane unicast TEP. When spines in a specific site receive an iVXLAN packet destined to this TEP, they do a lookup to see where this EP exists. From there, the packet is forwarded to the leaf switch where the endpoint belongs.

Furthermore, PIM Bidir is no longer required in the inter-site network (ISN) because the spines capable of supporting multi-site can also "head-end replicate" any multidestination frame. This means that instead of flooding the frame in the BD GIPo, a multi-site spine can replicate a unicast copy of the frame and send it to each site that needs to receive it. The original frame is encapsulated in iVXLAN and sent to a unique TEP address allocated to each site: the data plane multicast TEP. When spines in a specific site receive an iVXLAN packet destined to this TEP, they flood the packet on the FTag and GIPo for the bridge domain in the local site.

Multi-site spines can also be connected back-to-back, eliminating the need for an ISN completely if the physical restraints allow it. This can simplify a deployment significantly.

Figure 12-41 shows a typical multi-site deployment and the TEP addresses used.

You can check the unicast and multicast TEP address programming on a spine by running the **show dcimgr repo eteps** command from a multi-site–enabled spine, as shown in Example 12-45.

Example 12-45 *Viewing the Multi-Site Unicast and Date Plane TEP Address on a Spine*

```
spine201# show dcimgr repo eteps

Remote site=2 :
Rem Etep=10.254.6.253/32, is_ucast=yes
Rem Etep=10.254.6.254/32, is_ucast=no
```

Spine 1 CP-TEP	10.254.6.201
Spine 2 CP-TEP	10.254.6.202
E-TEP	10.255.2.1
DP Ucast TEP	10.254.6.253
DP Mcast TEP	10.254.6.254

Site 2

Spine 1 CP-TEP	10.254.5.201
Spine 2 CP-TEP	10.254.5.202
E-TEP	10.255.1.1
DP Ucast TEP	10.254.5.253
DP Mcast TEP	10.254.5.254

Site 1

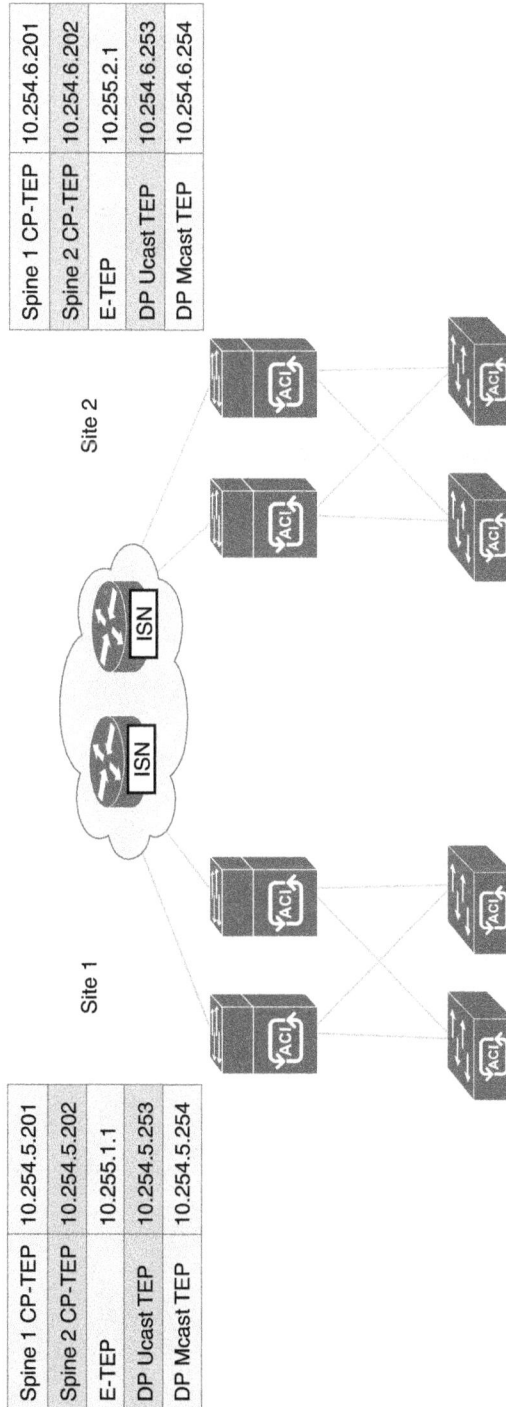

Figure 12-41 *A Typical Multi-Site Deployment and TEP Addressing Scheme*

Finally, because each site is a separate ACI fabric, unique VNIDs and sclass allocations exist. What this means is that if you had devices in two sites that wanted to communicate in a VRF instance, the VRF instance VNID assignment for the VRF instance in each site would be different. How would communication work if the VNID that identifies the segment boundary is different? To overcome this and ensure that workloads can exist and communicate across sites, VNID and sclass translations were implemented.

The ACI multi-site–capable spines maintain a translation table, which allows the spines to map the VNIDs and sclass values of remote sites to locally significant values. Figure 12-42 illustrates a multi-site deployment in which a VRF instance, a BD, and EPGs are stretched between two sites and where VNID/sclass translation will occur.

When a packet is sent between sites, the sending site maintains its local information about the VNID and sclass in the iVXLAN packet. When the receiving site gets the packet, the VNID and sclass are checked and examined against the translation map. The VNID or sclass seen in the packet is considered the remote entry, so before the spine sends the packet into the local site, it replaces the VNID and sclass with the local values. This ensures that proper VNID separation and policy enforcement can occur in the local site. Example 12-46 shows how to verify the VNID and sclass maps on the CLI of a multi-site–enabled spine.

Example 12-46 *Viewing the Multi-Site VRF Instance and sclass Translations on a Spine*

```
spine201# show dcimgr repo vnid-maps
----------------------------------------------------------------
     Remote               |          Local
site  Vrf        Bd       |    Vrf        Bd        Rel-state
----------------------------------------------------------------
  2   2129920             |  2228224                [formed]
  2   2129920   15499164  |  2228224   15368109     [formed]


spine201# show dcimgr repo sclass-maps
-----------------------------------------------------------------
     Remote               |        Local
site  Vrf       PcTag  |  Vrf       PcTag      Rel-state
-----------------------------------------------------------------
  2   2129920   16386|  2228224    49153      [formed]
  2   2129920   16389|  2228224    16392      [formed]
```

VNID	Remote VNID	Local VNID
VRF X	2228224	2129920
BD X	15368109	15499164

EPG	Remote SCLASS	Local SCLASS
EPG X	16386	49153
EPG Y	16389	16392

VNID	Remote VNID	Local VNID
VRF X	2129920	2228224
BD X	15499164	15368109

EPX	Remote SCLASS	Local SCLASS
EPG X	49153	16386
EPG Y	16392	16389

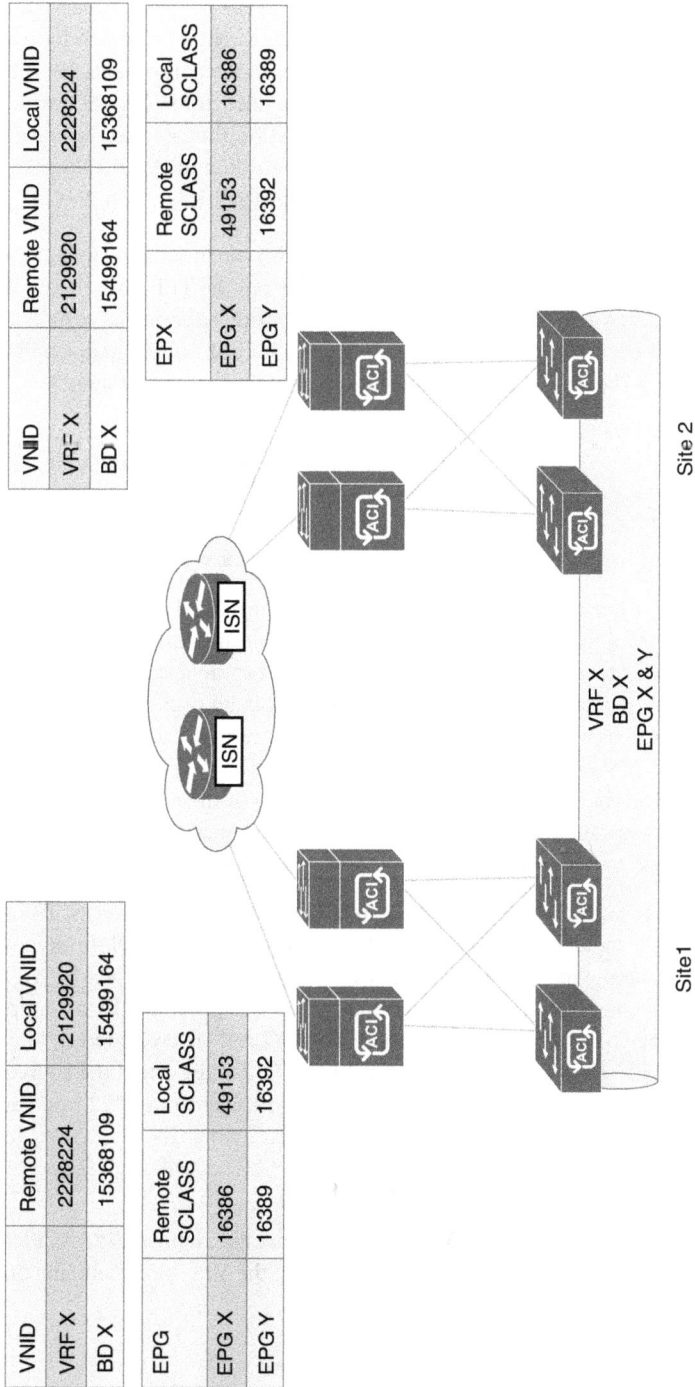

Figure 12-42 *VNID and sclass Translations with Cisco ACI Multi-Site*

Remote Leaf

Remote leafs make it possible to connect a remote data center or branch location to an existing ACI fabric. This is done by connecting at least one pair of leafs to an ISN and allowing IP connectivity back to a main ACI pod. In order for iVXLAN traffic to flow between a pod and remote leafs, TEP addresses must be allocated to the spines in the main pod, as well as to the remote leafs to allow forwarding of iVXLAN packets between them. The TEP addresses that are used in a remote leaf fabric are as follows.

- **Remote leaf data-plane TEP (RL-DP-TEP):** This is an automatically assigned (and unique) IP address for each remote leaf switch from the TEP pool that is allocated to the remote location. VXLAN packets from a remote leaf node are originated using this TEP as the source IP address when the remote leaf nodes are not part of a VPC domain or if the host is single connected to a single remote leaf switch.

- **Remote leaf VPC TEP (RL-VPC-TEP):** This anycast IP address is automatically assigned to the VPC pair of remote leaf nodes from the TEP pool that is allocated to the remote location. All the VXLAN packets sourced from both remote leaf switches are originated from this TEP address if the remote leaf switches are part of a VPC domain and the host is VPC attached to the remote leaf switches.

- **Remote leaf unicast TEP (RL-Ucast-TEP):** This anycast IP address is part of the local TEP pool that is automatically assigned to all the spines in the pod to which the remote leaf switches are being associated. When unicast packets are sent from endpoints connected to the RL nodes to the ACI main pod, VXLAN-encapsulated packets are sent with the destination as the RL-Ucast-TEP address and the source as the RL-DP-TEP or RL-VPC-TEP address. Any spine in the ACI main data center pod can hence receive the traffic, decapsulate it, perform the required L2 or L3 lookup, and re-encapsulate it and forward it to the final destination (a leaf in the local pod or in a separate pod in case of multi-pod fabric deployments).

- **Remote leaf multicast TEP (RL-Mcast-TEP):** This is another anycast IP address that is part of the local TEP pool and is automatically assigned to all the spines in the pod to which the remote leaf switches are being associated. When BUM (Layer 2 broadcast, unknown unicast, and multicast) traffic is generated by an endpoint connected to the remote leaf nodes, packets are VXLAN encapsulated by the RL node and sent with the destination as the RL-Mcast-TEP address and the source as the RL-DP-TEP or RL-VPC-TEP address. Any of the spines in the ACI pod can receive the BUM traffic and forward it inside the fabric.

These TEP addresses are illustrated in Figure 12-43.

Remote leaf switches synchronize VPC endpoints just like regular VPC ACI leafs. However, for orphan-attached hosts on remote leafs, the VPC sync contains the RL-DP-TEP of the leaf where the host attaches.

Leaf 105 RL-DP-TEP	10.100.1.128
Leaf 106 RL-DP-TEP	10.100.2.128
RL-vPC-TEP	10.100.0.96

Remote DC

Anycast RL-Ucast-TEP	10.0.0.36
Anycast RL-Mcast-TEP	10.0.0.37

Pod 1

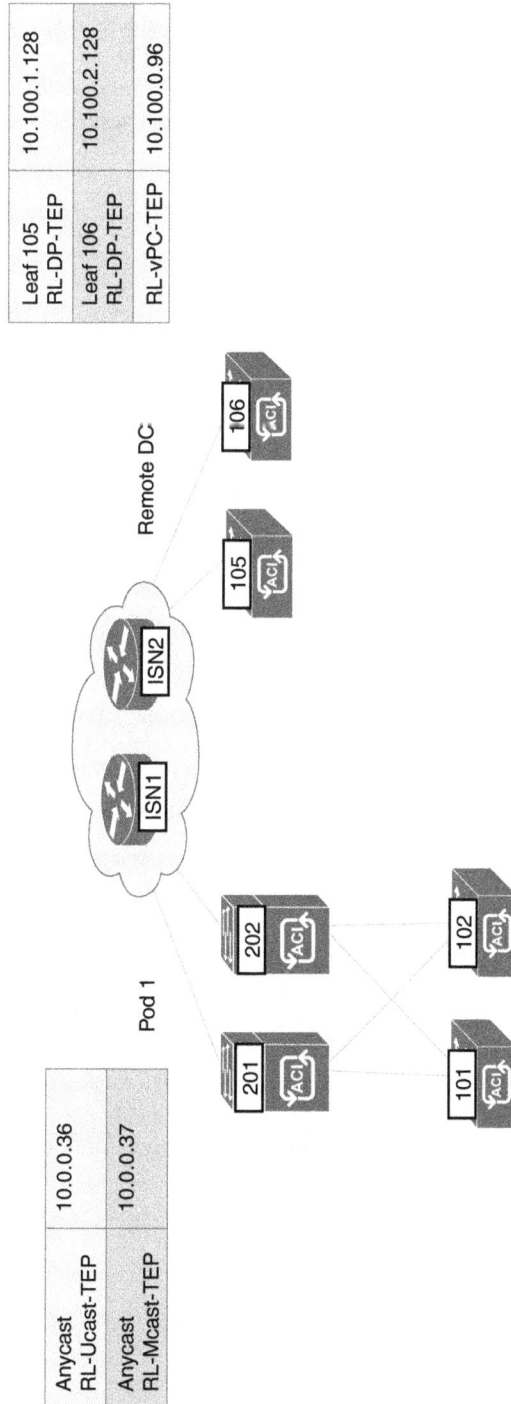

Figure 12-43 *Example TEP Addressing Schema Used in a Remote Leaf Setu*

Forwarding Scenarios

Now that you've learned about ACI forwarding, this section reinforces the concepts learned by reviewing certain scenarios and tracing the life of a packet through each one. Throughout this section, you will study various packet flows that you may see as you gain experience with ACI and see what is happening to a packet as it moves through the ACI fabric.

ARP Flooding

Just like any other networking device, the ACI fabric provides the ability to flood a multidestination frame inside the bridge domain. This is common in deployments where a migration is happening between legacy devices and ACI. Because the legacy devices flood, ACI should act the same way. Figure 12-44 highlights the path of an ARP frame in ACI when the bridge domain is configured to flood ARP. The list that follows explains these highlighted steps in more detail:

1. When 172.16.0.10 sends an ARP request for 172.16.0.11, the frame is received in the ingress leaf, Leaf 101. In this case, the host is sending the frame tagged with VLAN 10. The switch checks to ensure that VLAN 10 is being trunked on the port in which the packet was received. If it is not, the frame is dropped. If it is being trunked on the port in which the packet was received, the frame is classified in the EPG with which the VLAN/port is associated. Because the DST MAC is all f's, the switch needs to flood this frame. If there are other devices in the same bridge domain locally connected to Leaf 101, a copy of this frame is sent on each VLAN/port that is also mapped to the bridge domain, but it is not sent back on the same VLAN/port for which it was received. In addition, a copy of this frame needs to be sent into the fabric in iVXLAN so that other leafs can receive it and perform the same operation.

2. The leaf takes a copy of this ARP request and encapsulates it in iVXLAN. The DST IP is set to the BD GIPo, plus the FTag for which the leaf hashed. In addition, the VNID used is that of the bridge domain because the frame will be flooded in the bridge domain. This sets the L2 boundary for the frame as it moves through the fabric. The sclass is also set to that of the EPG for which the ARP request was received; the source policy/destination policy applied bits is also set because ACI leafs explicitly permit ARP. The spine does a lookup for the DST IP address and sees that it is a multicast address. The last 4 bits are evaluated to determine the FTag, and then the packet is forwarded on the MDT. In this case, only Leaf 103 needs to receive this packet. The outer MAC address info is modified before egressing the packet to Leaf 103.

Outer Header

DST MAC	000d.0d0d.0d0d
SRC MAC	000c.0c0c.0c0c
VLAN	2
SRC IP	Leaf 101 TEP
DST IP	225.1.104.64 + FTAG

iVXLAN Data

VNID	15138760
SCLASS	EPG VLAN10
SP	1
DP	1

DST MAC	ffff.ffff.ffff
SRC MAC	000a.0a0a.0a0a
VLAN	10
Sender IP	172.16.0.10
Target IP	172.16.0.11

DST MAC	ffff.ffff.ffff
SRC MAC	000a.0a0a.0a0a
VLAN	10
Sender IP	172.16.0.10
Target IP	172.16.0.11

VRF v1

EPG VLAN10
Bridge Domain VLAN10
VNID: 15138760
GIPo: 225.1.104.64

172.16.0.10
000a.0a0a.0a0a

172.16.0.11
000b.0b0b.0b0b

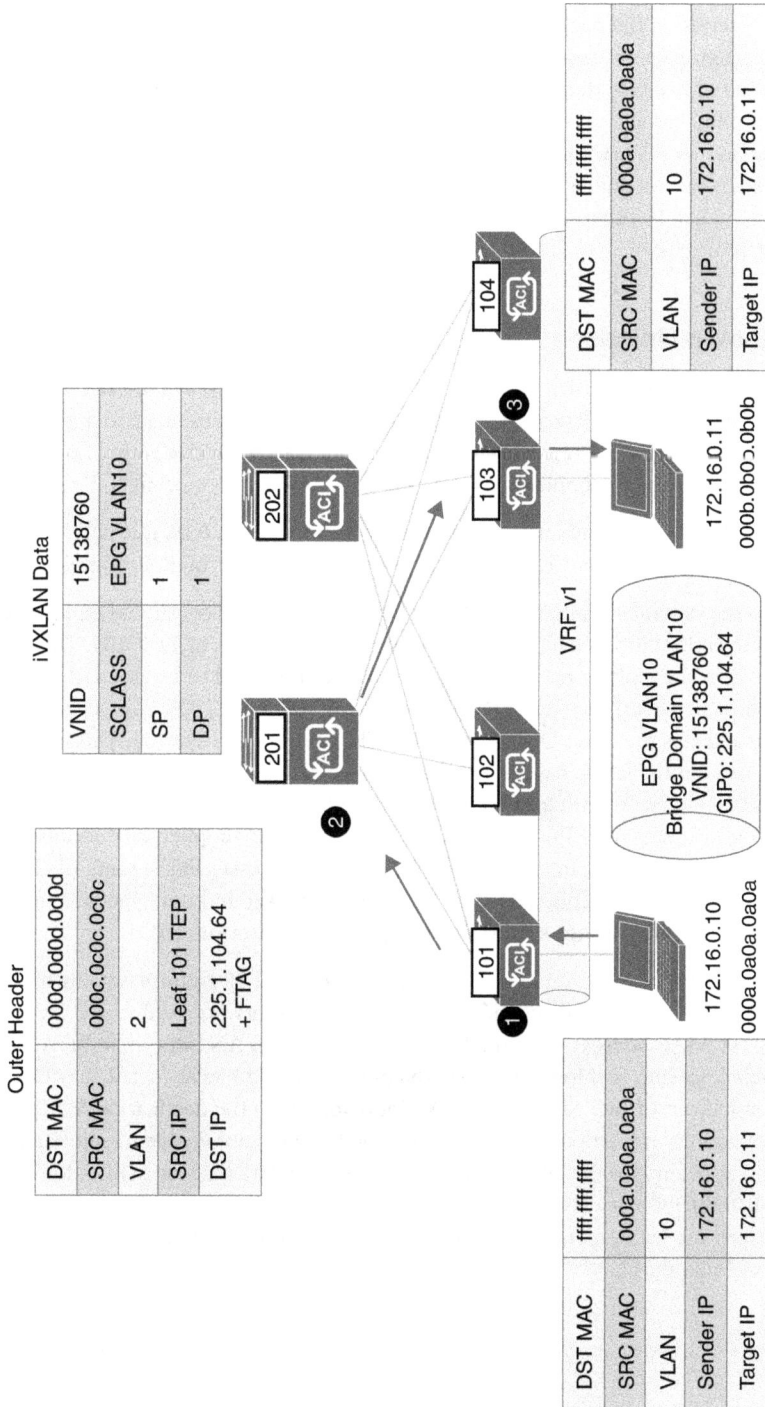

Figure 12-44 *ARP Request Sent in a Bridge Domain with Flooding Enabled*

3. When Leaf 103 receives the frame, a check is performed to see if the BD VNID that was received in the packet exists on the switch. In this case, the BD is deployed, so the packet is de-encapsulated, and the inner content is inspected. No policy lookup is required because the Source Policy and Destination Policy bits are set, hinting that policy has already been enforced in the fabric. The leaf replicates a copy of the frame in every VLAN/port that is associated to the bridge domain. Finally, because the DL bit is not enabled, remote endpoint learning occurs for the MAC address, alerting Leaf 103 that for MAC address 000a.0a0a.0a0a, it exists on the tunnel to Leaf 101.

Layer 2 Known Unicast

In order to understand known Layer 2 unicast, we can use the previous ARP example but now focus on the ARP reply. The ARP reply is a unicast frame sent back to the MAC address of the requester. Figure 12-45 highlights the path of an ARP reply frame in ACI, based on the previous example. The following list provides more detail:

1. When 172.16.0.11 sends the ARP response back to 172.16.0.10, it is unicasted to its MAC address. Ingress VLAN/port checks are run to determine the ingress EPG.

2. From the previous example, you know that the MAC address should be learned as a remote endpoint on Leaf 103 pointing to the TEP address of Leaf 101. This means that when the reply comes into Leaf 103, it does not need to be flooded but rather can be sent directly to the TEP address of Leaf 101. Leaf 103 encapsulates the ARP reply and sets the outer DST IP to be the TEP address of Leaf 101. This is forwarded to a spine in the fabric based on an ECMP hash decision. Each spine in the pod has the same metric, so either of them can be used. Leaf 103 also inserts the BD VNID and the sclass of the EPG VLAN 10 and sets the policy-applied bits because the remote learning programmed the DST and MAC addresses in the same EPG and because it is a ARP reply. The spine receives the packet and only needs to modify the outer MAC address info before egressing the packet to Leaf 101.

3. The packet is received on Leaf 101, and the outer DST IP address is its own TEP. It therefore de-encapsulates the packet and makes a forwarding decision based on the DST MAC address since the VNID set in the iVXLAN data is the BD VNID. A policy lookup is skipped because the policy-applied bits are set. The packet is unicasted out of the leaf on the VLAN/port for which the destination MAC endpoint address is learned. Finally, because the DL bit is not enabled, remote endpoint learning occurs for the MAC address, alerting Leaf 101 that for MAC address 000b.0b0b.0b0b, it exists on the tunnel to Leaf 103. Bidirectional communication between the leafs can now bypass the need to flood the traffic or use the spine proxy lookup.

iVXLAN Data

VNID	15138760
SCLASS	EPG VLAN10
SP	1
DP	1

Outer Header

DST MAC	000d.0d0d.0d0d
SRC MAC	000c.0c0c.0c0c
VLAN	2
SRC IP	Leaf 103 TEP
DST IP	Leaf 101 TEP

DST MAC	000a.0a0a.0a0a
SRC MAC	000b.0b0b.0b0b
VLAN	10
Sender IP	172.16.0.11
Target IP	172.16.0.10

DST MAC	000a.0a0a.0a0a
SRC MAC	000b.0b0b.0b0b
VLAN	10
Sender IP	172.16.0.11
Target IP	172.16.0.10

104

202   2

201

103   1

102

101   3

VRF v1

EPG VLAN10
Bridge Domain VLAN10
VNID: 15138760
GIPo: 225.1.104.64

172.16.0.11
000b.0b0b.0b0b

172.16.0.10
000a.0a0a.0a0a

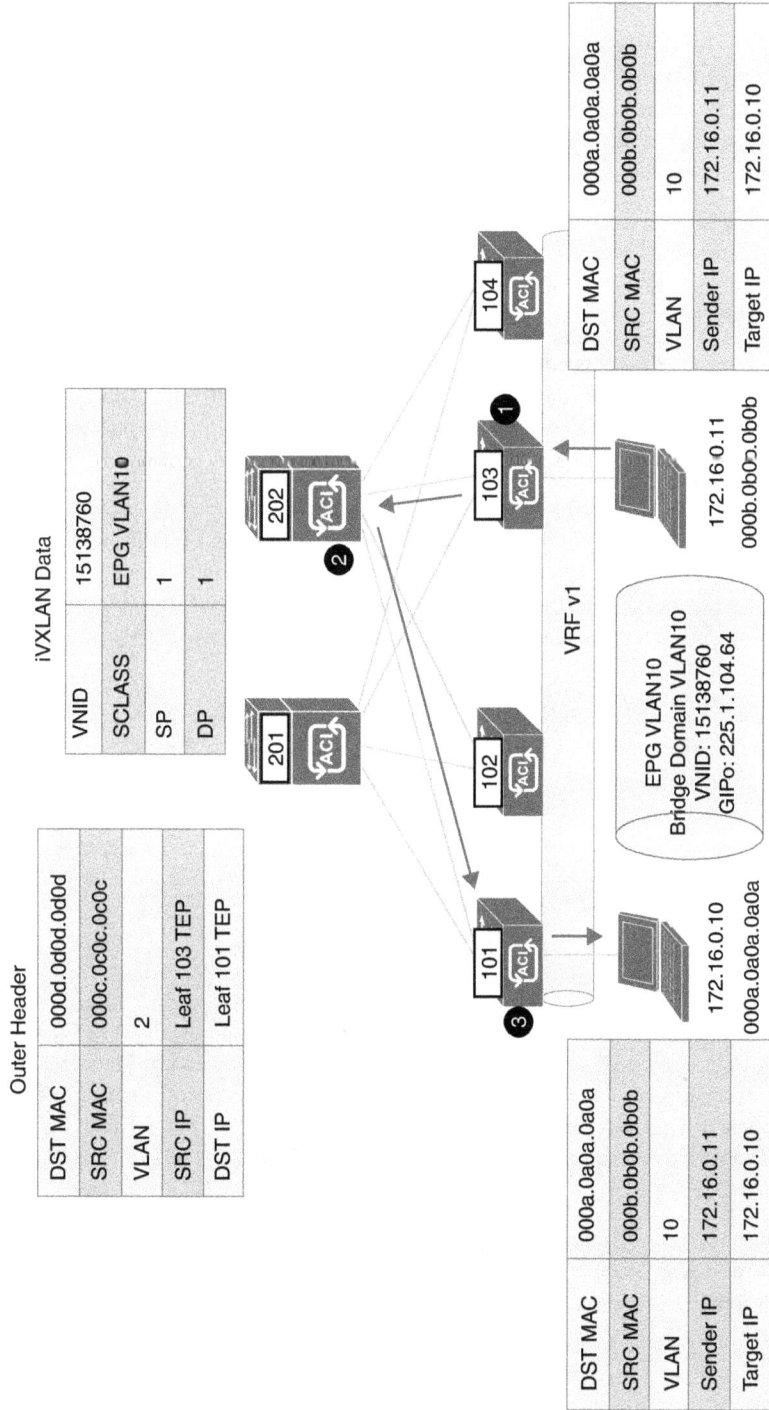

Figure 12-45 *ARP Reply Sent in a Bridge Domain*

ARP Optimization

By default, ARP flooding is not enabled. This means that ARP traffic is unicasted to the leaf where the target IP address resides when the destination is known, and it is sent to the spine proxy when the destination is unknown. This prevents unnecessary flooding of ARP traffic in the fabric. Figure 12-46 shows how ARP optimization works in an ACI fabric, and the list that follows explains in more detail:

1. The ARP frame is received on Leaf 101 from 172.16.0.10. Leaf 101 does an IP lookup for the target IP address 172.16.0.11. If the IP address is known, it is unicasted to the TEP where it resides. When the IP address is not known, the packet is unicasted to the IPv4 proxy instead of being flooded in the bridge domain.

2. The spine receives this packet, de-encapsulates it, and sends it to the fabric modules for a proxy lookup on the target IP address. If the target IP address is not known on the spine, the packet is punted to the CPU to start the ARP glean process. If the IP address is known, a lookup is performed, and the packet is sent back to the line card.

3. When the packet returns from the fabric modules, the line cards know which destination IP address to populate in the iVXLAN header. Based on this, an ECMP hash is done to determine whether the packet should be sent to Leaf 103 or Leaf 104. The Exception bit is also set to ensure that the receiving leaf does not send it back into the fabric for any reason, as the proxy lookup should ensure that it is sent to the correct leaf.

4. Leaf 103 receives the ARP request and does an IP lookup to determine where to send the ARP request locally. An implicit permit rule exists for ARP, and the policy lookup is bypassed. Remote endpoint learning is triggered for the sender's IP address in VRF instance *v1* because the DL bit is not enabled.

Layer 2 Unknown Unicast Proxy

Figure 12-47 illustrates the packet flow for an unknown Layer 2 destination when operating in proxy mode. The following steps provide more detail.

1. When 172.16.0.10 sends a unicast frame to 172.16.0.11, the destination MAC address is 000b.0b0b.0b0b. Leaf 101 does a Layer 2 lookup and does not know where the destination MAC address resides because remote endpoint learning has not happened. This also means that policy cannot be enforced. The frame is encapsulated and sent to the anycast MAC spine proxy TEP with the Policy Enforcement bits set to 0.

2. The spine receives this packet, de-encapsulates it, and sends it to the fabric modules for a proxy lookup. If the MAC address is not known on the spine, the frame is dropped; otherwise, it is sent back to the line card when the lookup has been successful.

iVXLAN Data

VNID	VRF v1 VNID
SCLASS	EPG VLAN10
SP	0
DP	0
DL	0
E	1

Outer Header - Spine Egress

DST MAC	000c.0c0c.0c0c
SRC MAC	000d.0d0d.0d0d
VLAN	2
SRC IP	Leaf 101 TEP
DST IP	Leaf 103 TEP

Outer Header - Spine Ingress

DST MAC	000d.0d0d.0d0d
SRC MAC	000c.0c0c.0c0c
VLAN	2
SRC IP	Leaf 101 TEP
DST IP	Anycast IPV4 Proxy

DST MAC	ffff.ffff.ffff
SRC MAC	000a.0a0a.0a0a
VLAN	10
Sender IP	172.16.0.10
Target IP	172.16.0.11

DST MAC	ffff.ffff.ffff
SRC MAC	000a.0a0a.0a0a
VLAN	10
Sender IP	172.16.0.10
Target IP	172.16.0.11

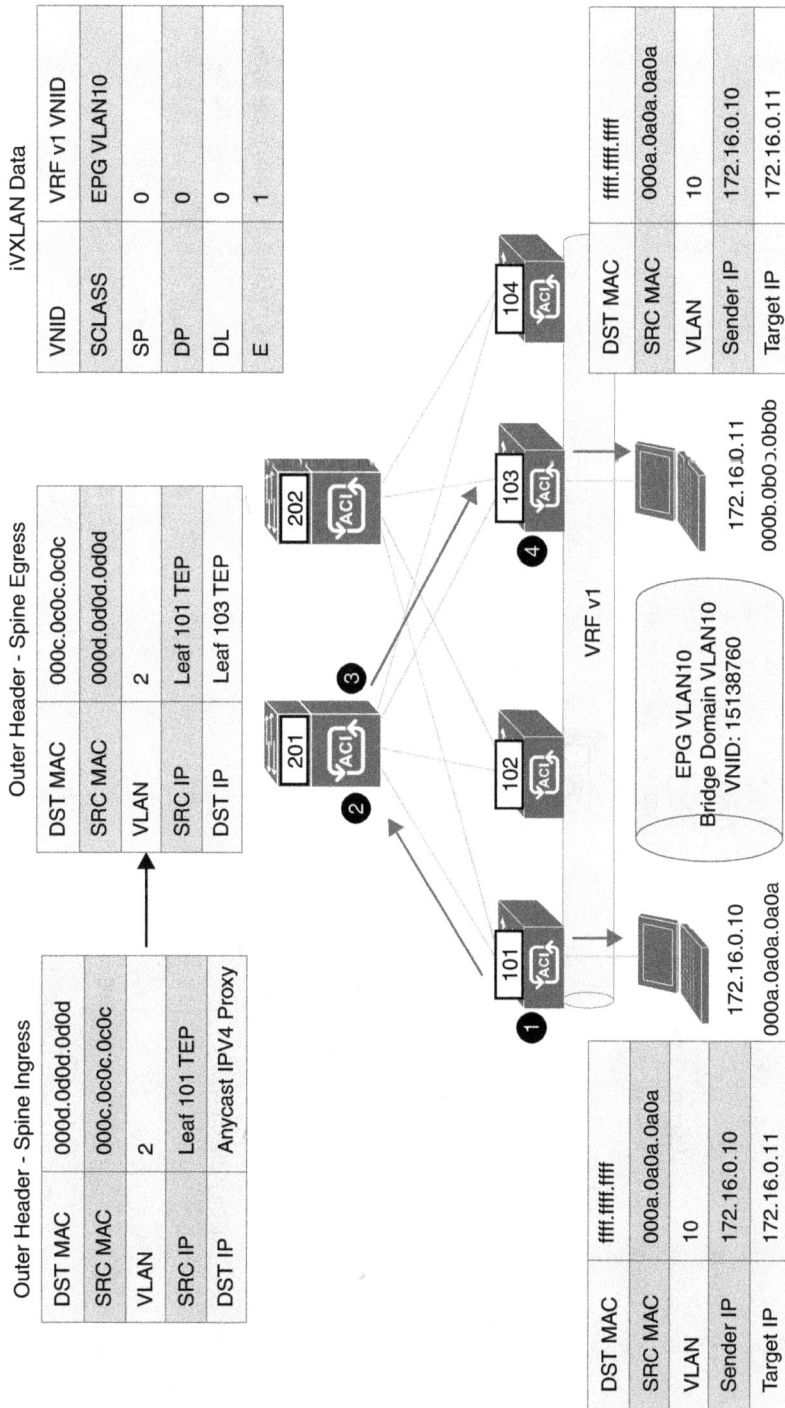

Figure 12-46   *ARP Frame Between Two Hosts with ARP Optimization*

iVXLAN Data

VNID	BD Web VNID
SCLASS	EPG Web1
SP	0
DP	0
DL	0
E	1

Outer Header - Spine Egress

DST MAC	000c.0c0c.0c0c
SRC MAC	000d.0d0d.0d0d
VLAN	2
SRC IP	Leaf 101 TEP
DST IP	Leaf 103 TEP

Outer Header - Spine Ingress

DST MAC	000d.0d0d.0d0d
SRC MAC	000c.0c0c.0c0c
VLAN	2
SRC IP	Leaf 101 TEP
DST IP	Anycast MAC Proxy

DST MAC	000b.0b0b.0b0b
SRC MAC	000a.0a0a.0a0a
VLAN	11
SRC IP	172.16.0.10
DST IP	172.16.0.11

172.16.0.11
000b.0b0b.0b0b
EPG Web2
BD Web

VRF v1

172.16.0.10
000a.0a0a.0a0a
EPG Web1
BD Web

DST MAC	000b.0b0b.0b0b
SRC MAC	000a.0a0a.0a0a
VLAN	10
SRC IP	172.16.0.10
DST IP	172.16.0.11

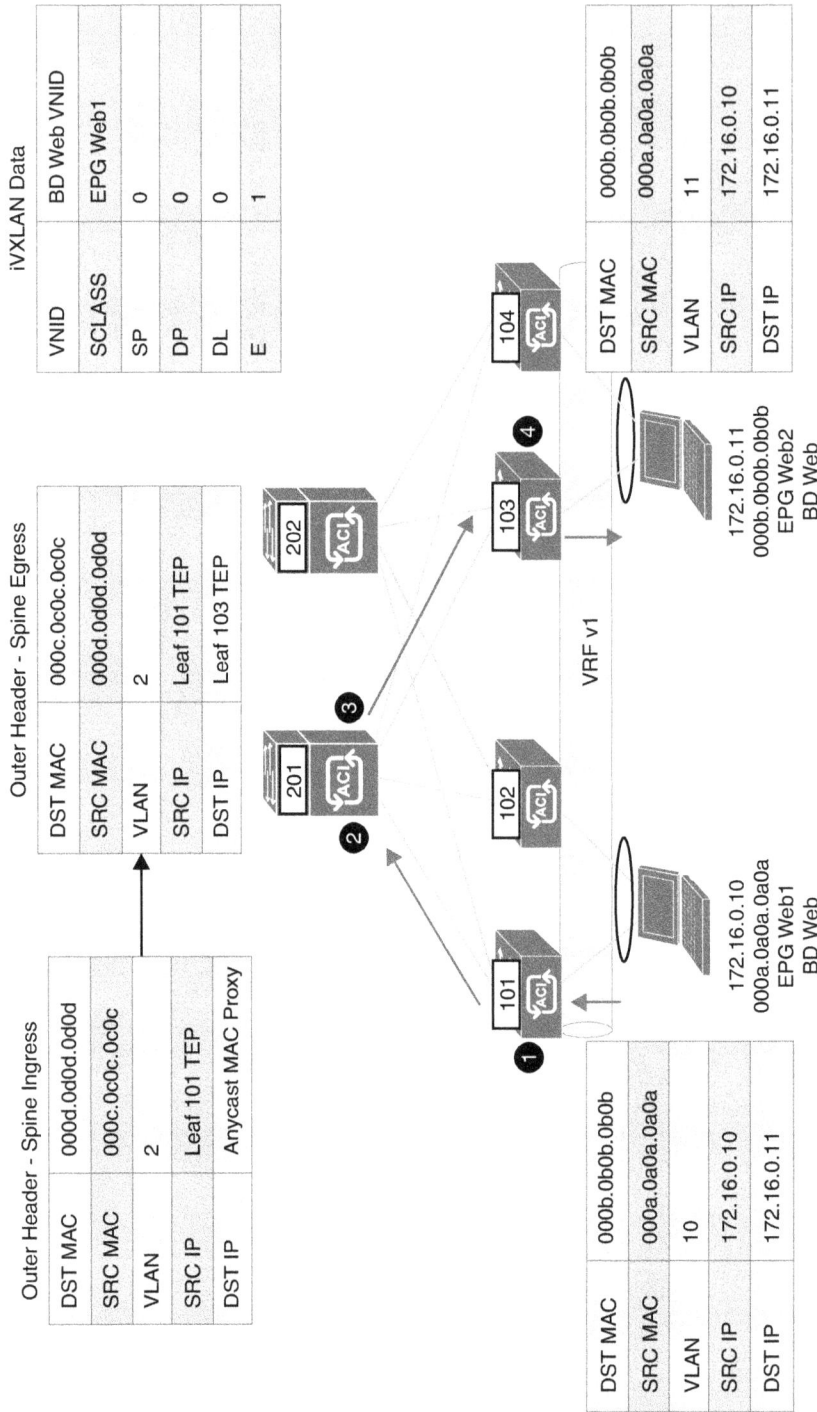

Figure 12-47 *Unknown Layer 2 Unicast Flow with Proxy*

3. When the packet returns from the fabric modules, the line cards know which destination IP address to populate in the iVXLAN header. Based on this, an ECMP hash is done to determine whether the packet should be sent to Leaf 103 or Leaf 104. The Exception bit is also set to ensure that the receiving leaf does not send it back into the fabric for any reason, as the proxy lookup should ensure that it is sent to the correct leaf.

4. Leaf 103 receives this packet and sees that policy has not been applied. Based on the source class in the iVXLAN header and a local hit on the destination MAC address, the leaf can enforce zoning rules and either allow or drop the frame. Remote L2 learning happens on Leaf 103 because the DL bit is not set.

L3 Policy Enforcement When Going to L3Out

By default, a VRF instance is configured in Ingress Policy Enforcement mode. This means that when an EPG has a contract relationship to an L3Out, the contract and policy enforcement is always performed on the compute leaf. This ensures that policy only needs to be pushed where the EPG is deployed and not on the border leaf, which decreases TCAM utilization on the border leaf. The following two examples highlight packet forwarding and policy enforcement between an EPG and an L3Out when the VRF is in Ingress Policy Enforcement mode. Figure 12-48 illustrates a server in EPG *App* communicating with external IP addresses learned via an L3Out. The following steps provide more detail:

1. 172.17.0.20 sends a packet to an external IP address. When this packet is received on Leaf 103 or Leaf 104, because the destination MAC address is the BD MAC address, the switch performs an IP lookup in the VRF instance. If the destination IP address is not learned as an endpoint, the next longest prefix is matched. A route lookup and policy lookup are done to determine where to send this packet. If a contract exists between the internal endpoint and external destination, the leaf sets the policy-enforced bits and sets the destination IP address to either Leaf 101 or Leaf 102 based on an ECMP hash since the route to the destination IP address should be learned via BGP, pointing to either Leaf 101 or Leaf 102. Even though Leafs 101 and 102 are VPCs, the VPC VIP is not used when sending traffic toward an L3Out.

2. The spine receives an encapsulated packet and simply looks at the outer destination IP address to see where to send it.

3. The egress line card rewrites the outer destination MAC address to the leaf MAC address 000c.0c0c.0c0c and leaves the source IP address as the VPC VIP from Leaf 103/104 and the destination IP address of Leaf 101.

4. Border Leaf 101 does a route lookup based on the inner destination IP address and bypasses the policy lookup because the Source Policy and Destination Policy bits are set to 1. In addition, remote learning for the 172.17.0.20 IP address occurs, and the information is installed on the border leaf because the DL bit is not set. If the feature Disable Remote EP Learning is enabled, the border leafs do not learn the endpoint.

iVXLAN Data

VNID	VRF v1 VNID
SCLASS	EPG App
SP	1
DP	1
DL	0
E	0

Outer Header - Spine Ingress

DST MAC	000d.0d0d.0d0d
SRC MAC	000c.0c0c.0c0c
VLAN	2
SRC IP	103-104 vPC TEP
DST IP	101 TEP or 102 TEP

Outer Header - Spine Egress

DST MAC	000c.0c0c.0c0c
SRC MAC	000d.0d0d.0d0d
VLAN	2
SRC IP	103-104 vPC TEP
DST IP	101 TEP or 102 TEP

DST MAC	000b.0b0b.0b0b
SRC MAC	BD App MAC
VLAN	20
SRC IP	172.17.0.20
DST IP	Any

172.17.0.20
000b.0b0b.0b0b
EPG App
BD App

VRF v1

IPV4 Clients
000a.0a0a.0a0a
EPG External-Net/All
VLAN 500

DST MAC	000a.0a0a.0a0a
SRC MAC	L3Out-Core MAC
VLAN	500
SRC IP	172.17.0.20
DST IP	Any

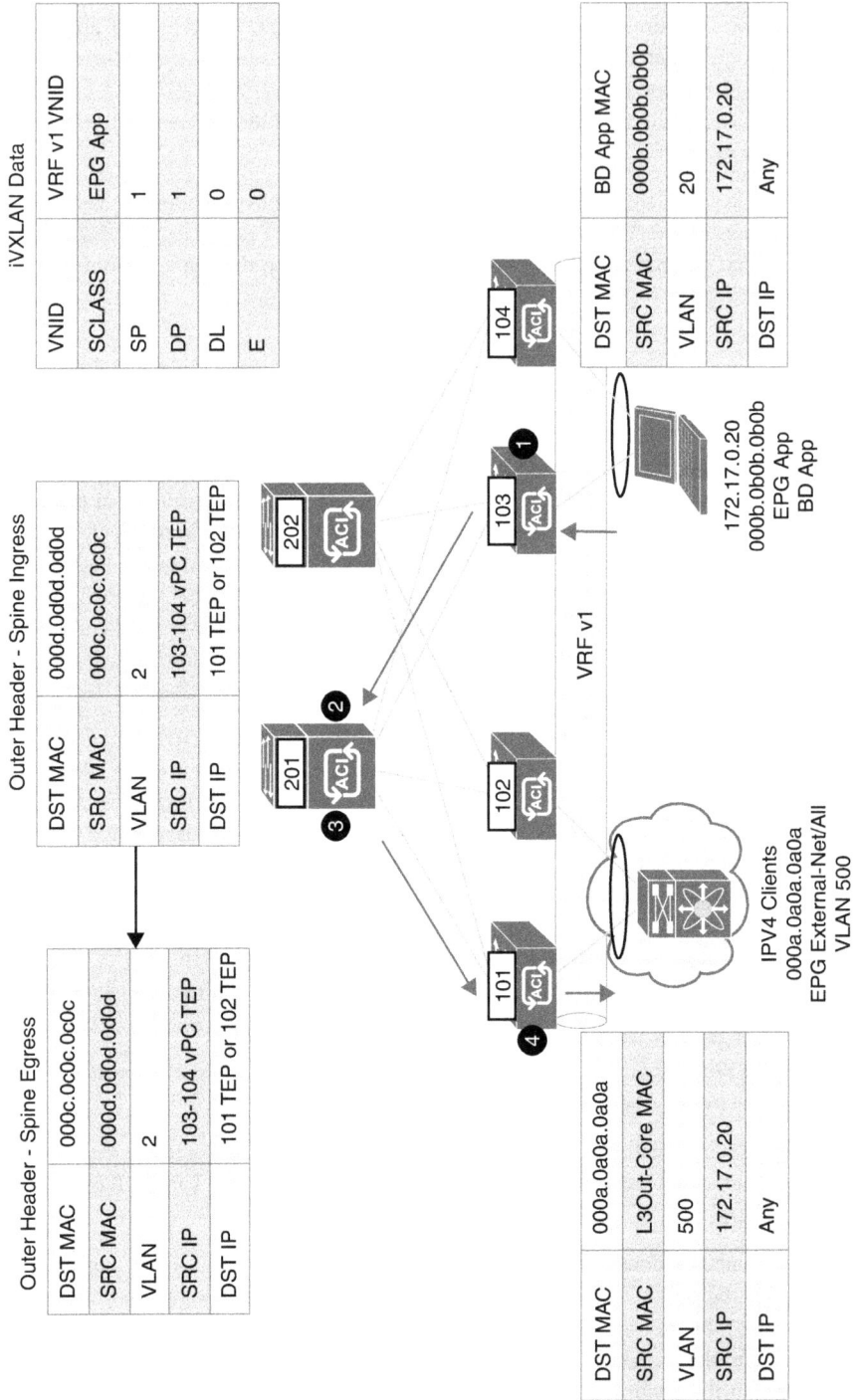

Figure 12-48   *Unicast Packet from the App EPG to L3Out*

L3 Policy Enforcement for External Traffic Coming into the Fabric

Figure 12-49 illustrates the reply direction from the previous example, where the external client connected via the L3Out is communicating to a server in the *App* EPG. The steps that follow provide more detail:

1. A packet is received from an external IP address on a border leaf. Because the VRF instance is in Ingress Enforcement mode, the border leaf does not perform a policy lookup and sets the Source Policy and Destination Policy bits to 0. To prevent the compute leaf from learning the external IP address, the DL bit is set to 1. If the destination endpoint is unknown, the packet is sent to the IP spine proxy.

2. The spine receives the encapsulated packet and does a lookup on the inner destination IP address, using the fabric module.

3. The fabric module returns the packet to the line card, and the destination IP address is set to the VPC VIP for Leafs 103 and 104. The Exception bit is set as well.

4. Leaf 103 receives the packet and sees that the Source Policy and Destination Policy bits are set to 0. Using the PCTag of the L3Out EPG present in the iVXLAN header, a policy lookup is performed to determine whether the packet should be forwarded to the destination endpoint. Finally, because the DL bit is set, no endpoint learning for the source behind the L3Out is done.

Route Leaking/Shared Services

ACI allows an EPG to be accessed by endpoints in different tenants and VRFs. When an EPG is configured to provide services to EPGs in different VRFs, it is called a Shared Service EPG. This section highlights the differences in packet flow when using shared service EPGs.

Consumer to Provider

Figure 12-50 illustrates the packet flow when a shared-service EPG is the destination. EPG *Backup-Server* is the provider of a global contract that is exported and consumed via EPG *App*. The following steps provide more detail:

1. Leaf 103 receives a packet destined to 172.18.3.10, based on the downstream VPC hash. Leaf 103 does not have endpoint learning for the destination IP address. The route to the destination is installed with a next hop of the IPv4 proxy and also has a VNID rewrite flag for the *Provider* VRF instance. When doing a policy lookup, the subnet 172.18.3.0/24 is configured with a global PCTag, and policy can be enforced. This sets the Source Policy and Destination Policy bits. The VNID is changed from VRF instance *v1*'s VNID to the VNID of the *Backup* VRF instance. When using shared services, endpoints are never learned from another VRF instance. Because of this, the DL bit is set, and the packet is forwarded to the spine proxy.

iVXLAN Data

VNID	VRF v1 VNID
SCLASS	EPG External-Net/All
SP	0
DP	0
DL	1
E	1

Outer Header - Spine Egress

DST MAC	000c.0dcd.0c0c
SRC MAC	000d.0d0d.0d0d
VLAN	2
SRC IP	101-102 vPC TEP
DST IP	103-104 vPC TEP

Outer Header - Spine Ingress

DST MAC	000d.0d0d.0d0d
SRC MAC	000c.0c0c.0c0c
VLAN	2
SRC IP	101-102 vPC TEP
DST IP	Anycast IPV4 Proxy

DST MAC	BD App MAC
SRC MAC	000b.0b0b.0b0b
VLAN	20
SRC IP	172.17.0.20
DST IP	Any

172.17.0.20
000b.0b0b.0b0b
EPG App
BD App

VRF v1

IPV4 Clients
000a.0a0a.0a0a
EPG External-Net/All
VLAN 500

DST MAC	L3Out-Core MAC
SRC MAC	000a.0a0a.0a0a
VLAN	500
SRC IP	Any
DST IP	172.17.0.20

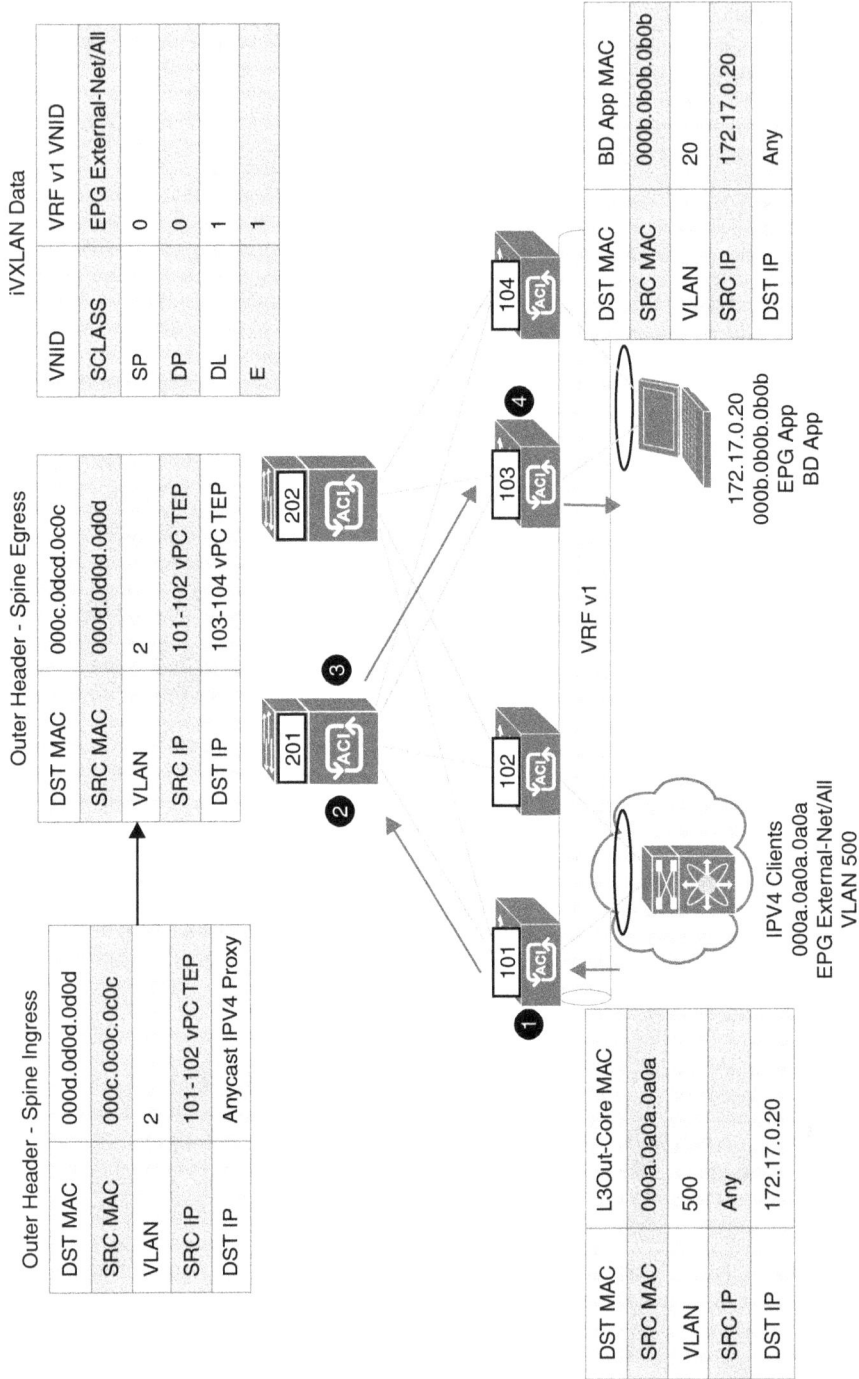

Figure 12-49   *Unicast Packet from L3Out to the App EPG*

iVXLAN Data

VNID	VRF Backup VNID
SCLASS	EPG App
SP	1
DP	1
DL	1
E	1

Outer Header - Spine Ingress

DST MAC	000d.0d0d.0d0d
SRC MAC	000c.0c0c.0c0c
VLAN	2
SRC IP	103-104 vPC TEP
DST IP	Anycast IPV4 Proxy

Outer Header - Spine Egress

DST MAC	000c.0c0c.0c0c
SRC MAC	000d.0d0d.0d0d
VLAN	2
SRC IP	103-104 vPC TEP
DST IP	101-101 vPC TEP

DST MAC	000b.0b0b.0b0b
SRC MAC	
VLAN	20
SRC IP	172.17.0.20
DST IP	172.18.3.10

BD App MAC

DST MAC	000a.0a0a.0a0a
SRC MAC	BD Shared-Service MAC
VLAN	21
SRC IP	172.17.0.20
DST IP	172.18.3.10

172.17.0.20
000b.0b0b.0b0b
EPG App
BD App
VRF v1

172.18.3.10
000a.0a0a.0a0a
EPG Backup-Server
BD Shared-Service
VRF Backup

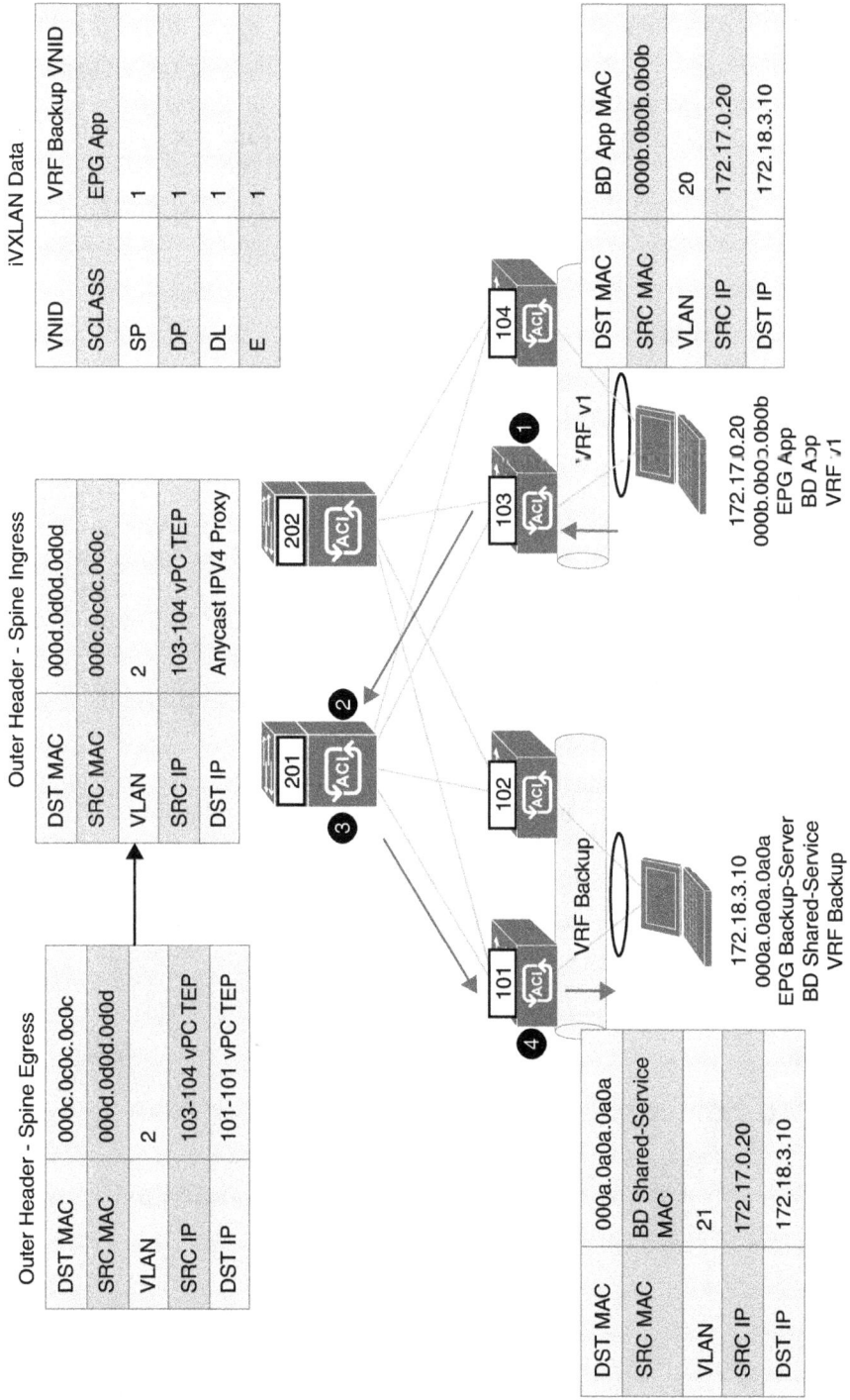

Figure 12-50 *Shared-Service Packet Flow from Consumer to Provider*

2. The packet is received on a spine, de-encapsulated, and sent to the fabric module for a route lookup.

3. The fabric module returns the packet to the line card, and the packet is sent to the egress leaf where the destination IP resides. Because the IP address resides on a VPC, the packet is sent to the VPC VIP of Leafs 101 and 102, and an ECMP hash is run to determine which leaf receives the packet. Leaf 101 is chosen.

4. Leaf 101 forwards this packet without doing a policy lookup because the Source Policy and Destination Policy bits are set.

Provider to Consumer

Figure 12-51 illustrates the packet flow when a shared-service EPG is the source and a regular EPG is the destination. EPG *Backup-Server* is the provider of a global contract that is exported and consumed via EPG *App*. The following steps provide more detail:

1. Leaf 101 receives a packet destined to 172.17.0.20. A route lookup is done and indicates that the VNID needs to be changed to the target (consumer) VRF instance. The PCTag associated with 172.17.0.0/24 is 14, a reserved PCTag that is used when shared services are configured. Policy is not applied, and the Source Policy and Destination Policy bits are set to 0. Because the packet crosses into another VRF instance, the DL bit is set.

2. The spine receives the packet in VRF instance *v1* and does a lookup for the destination IP address on the fabric module.

3. The fabric module returns the packet to the line card, and the packet is sent to the egress leaf where the destination IP resides. Because the IP resides on a VPC, the packet is sent to the VPC VIP of Leafs 103 and 104, and an ECMP hash is run to determine which leaf receives the packet. Leaf 103 is chosen.

4. Leaf 103 receives the packet and does a policy lookup. The PCTag 14 indicates that a source PCTag lookup needs to be performed, and the most specific prefix is 172.18.3.0/24, which has a global PCTag of the shared service EPG. This now allows the leaf to perform a policy lookup.

Multi-Pod Forwarding Examples

Traffic traversing between pods in an ACI fabric uses different logic than intra-pod traffic flows. This section highlights the important differences by following the path of a unicast and multicast packet.

iVXLAN Data

VNID	VRF v1 VNID
SCLASS	EPG Backup-Server
SP	0
DP	0
DL	1
E	1

Outer Header - Spine Egress

DST MAC	000c.0c0c.0c0c
SRC MAC	000d.0d0d.0d0d
VLAN	2
SRC IP	101-102 vPC TEP
DST IP	103-104 vPC TEP

Outer Header - Spine Ingress

DST MAC	000d.0d0d.0d0d
SRC MAC	000c.0c0c.0c0c
VLAN	2
SRC IP	101-102 vPC TEP
DST IP	Anycast IPV4 Proxy

DST MAC	BD App MAC
SRC MAC	000b.0b0b.0b0b
VLAN	20
SRC IP	172.18.3.10
DST IP	172.17.0.20

172.17.0.20
000b.0b0b.0b0b
EPG App
BD App
VRF v1

VRF v1

172.18.3.10
000a.0a0a.0a0a
EPG Backup-Server
BD Shared-Service
VRF Backup

VRF Backup

DST MAC	BD Shared-Service MAC
SRC MAC	000a.0a0a.0a0a
VLAN	21
SRC IP	172.18.3.10
DST IP	172.17.0.20

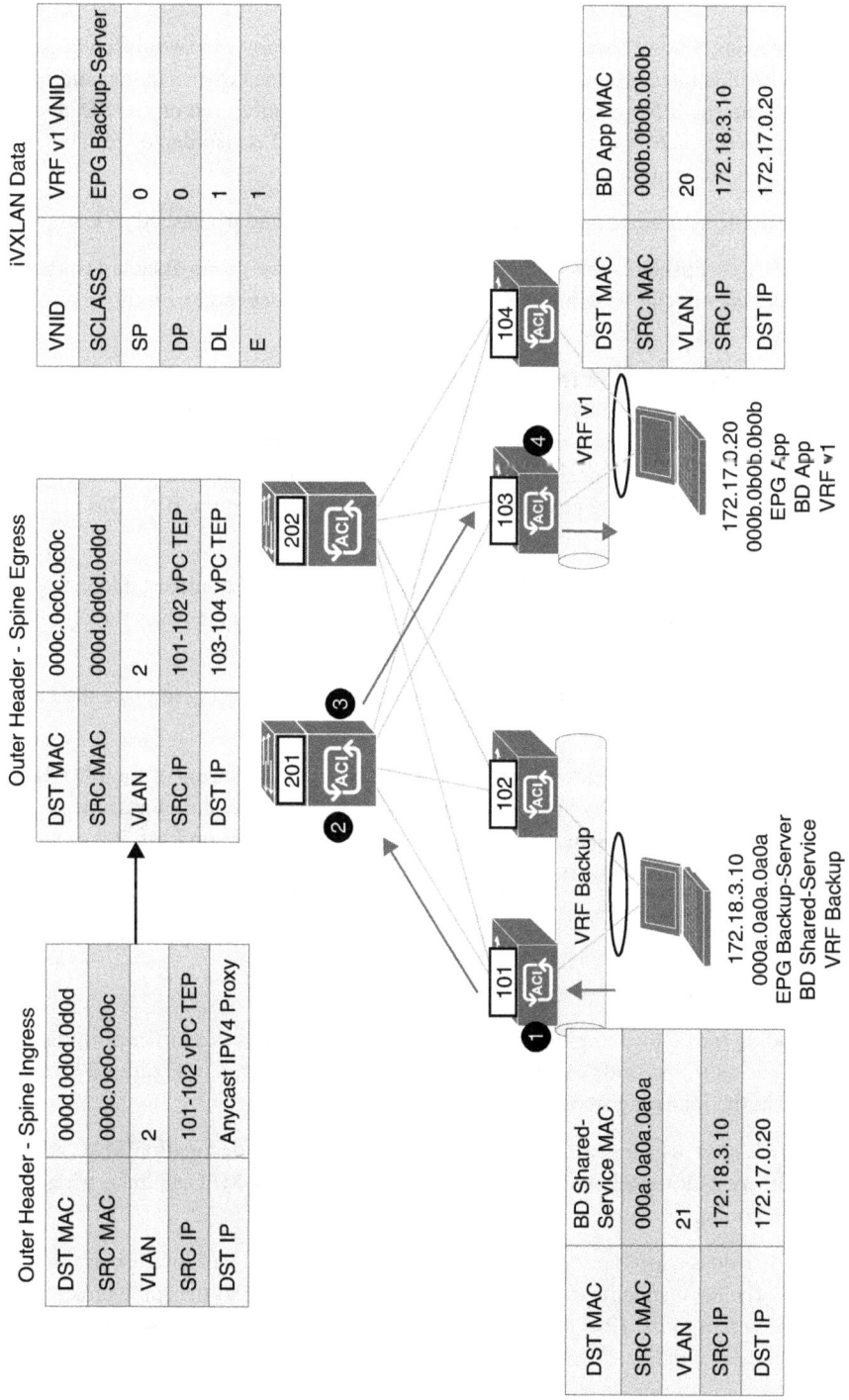

Figure 12-51 *Shared-Service Packet Flow from Provider to Consumer*

ARP Flooding

Multi-pod changes how a packet is forwarded between two hosts in two different pods. Figure 12-52 illustrates primarily what is different on the spines when sending and receiving traffic from the IPN. In Figure 12-52, ARP flooding is configured on the BD, and an ARP packet is sent across the IPN to Leaf 302, where the BD is also deployed. The following steps provide more detail:

1. Host 172.16.0.10 sends an ARP request for 172.16.0.11, and it's hashed to Leaf 101.

2. Leaf 101 encapsulates this frame, sends it to the multicast group assigned to the BD, and encodes an FTag in the 4 least significant bits, depending on the hash of the packet.

3. The spine that is the root for the FTag does not have to be the authoritative spine. In Figure 12-52, Spine 201 is both the FTag root and the authoritative spine for BD VLAN 10, which means it sends the multicast packet into the IPN. The key difference between the pod local multicast packet and the multicast packet sent to the IPN is that the FTag is removed before the packet is sent into the IPN. This limits the number of mroutes that the IPNs need to support.

4. Only the authoritative spine sends an IGMP join for the BD multicast address to the IPN; therefore, only one spine, Spine 402 in this example, receives the multicast packet.

5. Spine 402 runs a hash calculation again to determine which FTag to place the multicast packet in before sending it to the fabric in Pod 2.

6. Leaf 302 receives this packet with an outer destination IP address of the BD GIPo plus the FTag selected by Spine 402. The packet is flooded out all ports that are part of the bridge domain. Remote learning for 172.16.0.10 occurs on Leaf 302 as well, which triggers a dynamic tunnel to be brought up to the VPC VIP of Leafs 101 and 102.

Layer 3 Proxy Flow

When sending traffic to the spine proxy and the endpoint exists in another pod, the spine sends the packet to the pod's external proxy address, as illustrated in Figure 12-53 and described in the following steps:

1. 172.16.0.10 sends a unicast IPv4 packet to 172.17.0.20. The destination MAC address is sent to the destination MAC address of the BD gateway MAC address, triggering a route lookup.

2. Leaf 101 does a lookup for 172.17.0.20 and does not find it as a local or remote endpoint. The most specific route is a pervasive route pointing to the spine proxy, so the packet is sent to the IPv4 proxy on either spine. Since the packet is sent to the proxy, no policy is applied.

Outer Header - Spine Ingress

DST MAC	MCAST
SRC MAC	IPN MAC
VLAN	4
SRC IP	101-102 vPC TEP
DST IP	BD GIPo (FTAG 0)

Outer Header - Spine Egress

DST MAC	MCAST
SRC MAC	000d.0d0d.0d0d
VLAN	2
SRC IP	101-102 vPC TEP
DST IP	BD GIPo + FTAG

DST MAC	ffff.ffff.ffff
SRC MAC	000a.0a0a.0a0a
VLAN	10
Sender IP	172.16.0.10
Target IP	172.16.0.11

Outer Header - Spine Egress

DST MAC	MCAST
SRC MAC	Infra L3Out MAC
VLAN	4
SRC IP	101-102 vPC TEP
DST IP	BD GIPo (FTAG 0)

Outer Header - Spine Ingress

DST MAC	MCAST
SRC MAC	000c.0c0c.0c0c
VLAN	2
SRC IP	101-102 vPC TEP
DST IP	BD GIPo + FTAG

DST MAC	ffff.ffff.ffff
SRC MAC	000a.0a0a.0a0a
VLAN	10
Sender IP	172.16.0.10
Target IP	172.16.0.11

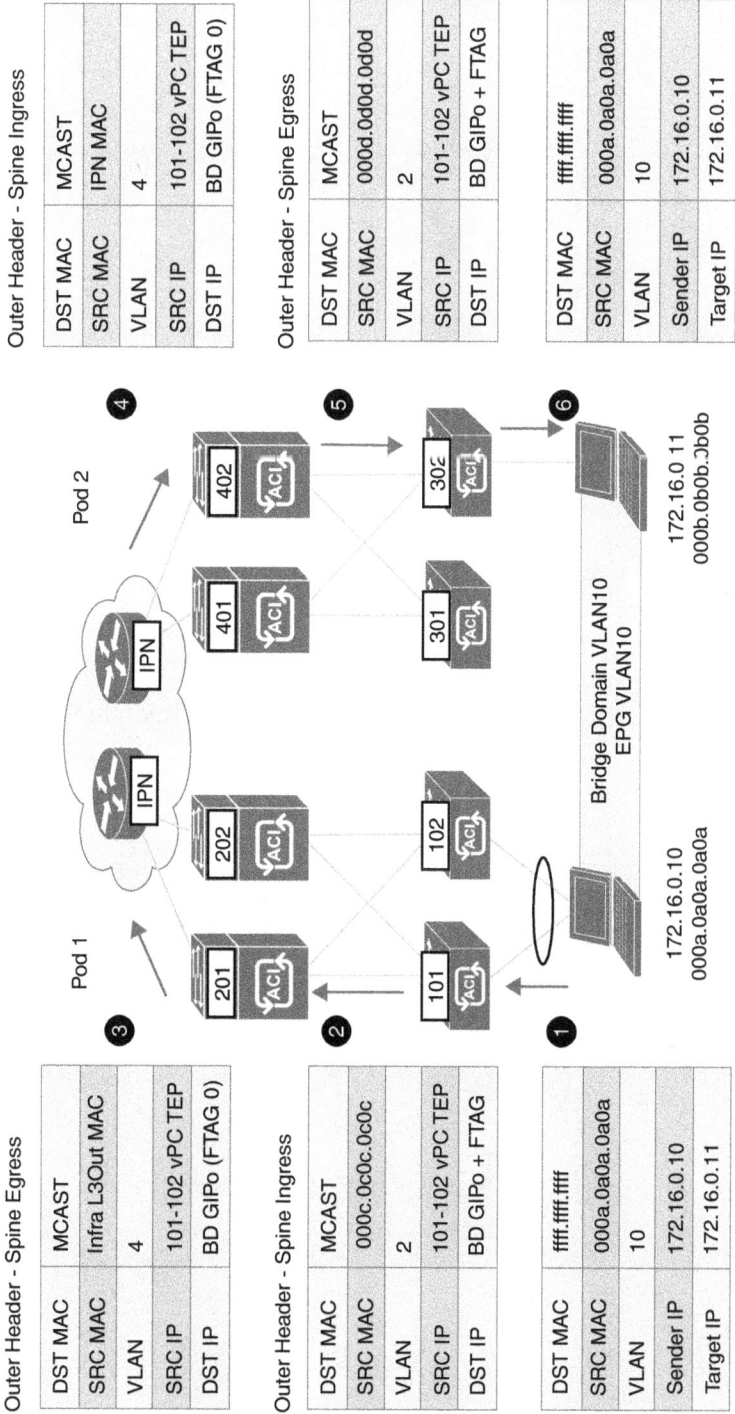

Figure 12-52 *ARP Flooding in Multi-pod*

Outer Header - Spine Ingress

DST MAC	Infra L3Out MAC
SRC MAC	IPN MAC
VLAN	4
SRC IP	101-102 vPC TEP
DST IP	Anycast External IPv4 Proxy Pod 2

Outer Header - Spine Egress

DST MAC	000c.0c0c.0c0c
SRC MAC	000d.0d0d.0d0d
VLAN	2
SRC IP	101-102 vPC TEP
DST IP	Leaf 302 TEP

DST MAC	000b.0b0b.0b0b
SRC MAC	BD App MAC
VLAN	20
SRC IP	172.16.0.10
DST IP	172.17.0.20

Outer Header - Spine Egress

DST MAC	IPN MAC
SRC MAC	Infra L3Out MAC
VLAN	4
SRC IP	101-102 vPC TEP
DST IP	Anycast External IPv4 Proxy Pod 2

Outer Header - Spine Ingress

DST MAC	000d.0d0d.0d0d
SRC MAC	000c.0c0c.0c0c
VLAN	2
SRC IP	101-102 vPC TEP
DST IP	Anycast IPV4 Proxy

DST MAC	BD Web MAC
SRC MAC	000a.0a0a.0a0a
VLAN	10
SRC IP	172.16.0.10
DST IP	172.17.0.20

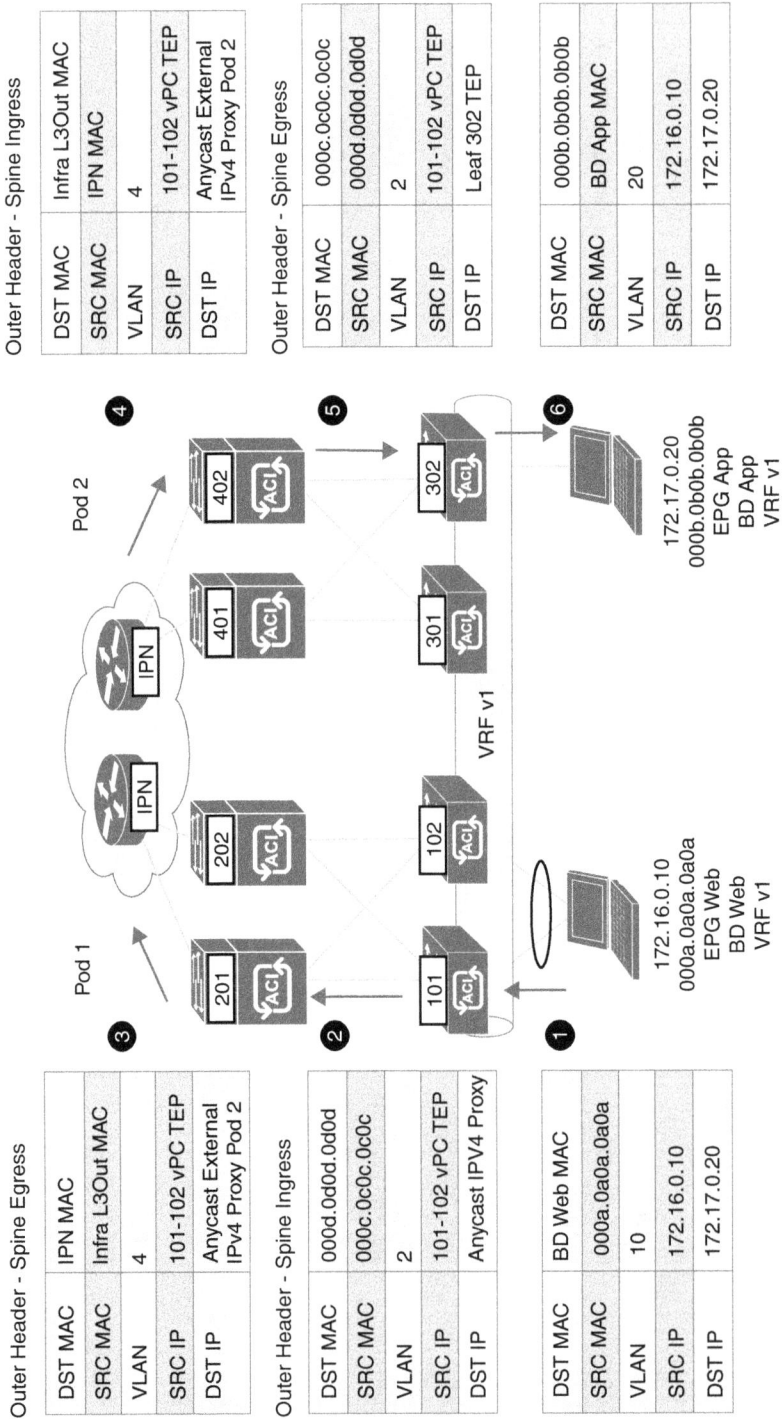

Figure 12-53 *Layer 3 Proxy Flow in Multi-pod*

3. The spine does a lookup on the inner destination IP address and sees that it is learned via the external anycast IPv4 proxy address of Pod 2. A recursive route lookup shows that this packet needs to be sent to the IPN, and the destination MAC address is changed to the IPN MAC address. No other parameters of this packet are modified. The IPN has a route for the external anycast address pointing to both Pod 2 spines.

4. Any of the spines in Pod 2 can receive this packet, based on an ECMP route from the IPN. In this example, Spine 402 receives the packet destined for the external anycast IPv4 address, which triggers a lookup for the inner destination IP address.

5. The lookup points to Leaf 302, and the outer destination IP address is changed to the TEP address of Leaf 302. The packet is sent toward this leaf.

6. Leaf 302 receives the packet destined to its local TEP address, which triggers a lookup on the inner IP address, 172.17.0.20. This endpoint is learned locally, and policy can now be enforced. Remote learning for 172.16.0.10 occurs on Leaf 302 as well, which causes a dynamic tunnel to be brought up to the VPC VIP of Leafs 101 and 102.

Multi-Site Forwarding Examples

Multi-site uses two unicast IP addresses to represent an entire ACI fabric when forwarding traffic between two sites. Multi-site also does VNID and PCTag translation when dataplane packets travel between two different sites. This section illustrates how unicast and multicast packets traverse two sites.

ARP Flooding

Unlike multi-pod, where multicast is used to send flooded traffic between the two pods, multi-site uses head-end replication to send a unicast copy to all sites that require a copy. This is illustrated in Figure 12-54 and described in the steps that follow:

1. Host 172.16.0.10 sends an ARP request for 172.16.0.11.

2. Leaf 101 encapsulates this frame and sends it to the multicast group assigned to the BD and encodes an FTag in the 4 least significant bits, depending on the hash of the packet.

3. Spine 201, the authoritative spine for BD VLAN 10, receives the multicast packet that needs to be sent to Site 2. The outer source IP address is changed to the unicast TEP address of Site 1, and the destination IP address is changed to the data plane multicast TEP address of Site 2. No VNID or sclass rewrite happens. The ISN routers have a route for the Site 2 data plane multicast address via both Spines 201 and 202.

4. Site 2 Spine 202 receives this packet, based on an ECMP hash from the ISN, and changes the sclass and VNID to the local values. The destination IP address is changed to the local BD GIPo plus a hash for which FTag to use.

Outer Header - Spine Ingress (4)

DST MAC	Infra L3Out MAC
SRC MAC	IPN MAC
VLAN	4
SRC IP	Site1 DP Ucast TEP
DST IP	Site2 DP Mcast TEP

Outer Header - Spine Egress (5)

DST MAC	MCAST
SRC MAC	000d.0d0d.0d0d
VLAN	2
SRC IP	Site1 DP Ucast TEP
DST IP	BD GIPo + FTAG

(6)

DST MAC	ffff.ffff.ffff
SRC MAC	000a.0a0a.0a0a
VLAN	10
Sender IP	172.16.0.10
Target IP	172.16.0.11

Outer Header - Spine Egress (3)

DST MAC	IPN MAC
SRC MAC	Infra L3Out MAC
VLAN	4
SRC IP	Site1 DP Ucast TEP
DST IP	Site2 DP Mcast TEP

Outer Header - Spine Ingress (2)

DST MAC	MCAST
SRC MAC	000c.0c0c.0c0c
VLAN	2
SRC IP	101-102 vPC TEP
DST IP	BD GIPo + FTAG

(1)

DST MAC	ffff.ffff.ffff
SRC MAC	000a.0a0a.0a0a
VLAN	10
Sender IP	172.16.0.10
Target IP	172.16.0.11

Site1

Site2

ISN   ISN

201   202   202   201

101   102   102   101

Bridge Domain VLAN10
EPG VLAN10

172.16.0.10
000a.0a0a.0a0a

172.16.0.11
000b.0b0b.0b0b

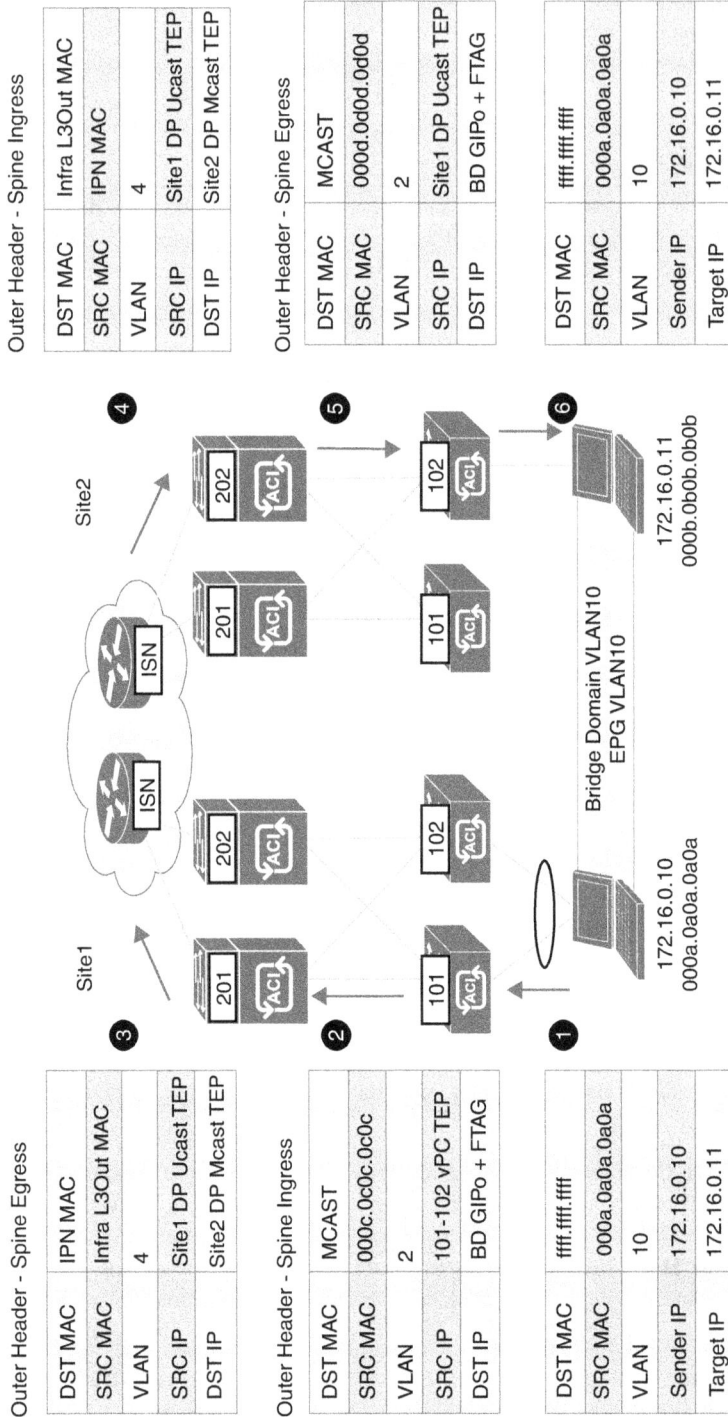

Figure 12-54   *ARP Flooding in Multi-site*

5. The ARP request is now encapsulated in multicast and flooded to all leaves that have this BD deployed. Site 2 Leaf 102 receives this packet.

6. The packet is flooded out all ports that are part of the bridge domain. Site 2 Leaf 102 learns MAC address 000a.0a0a.0a0a via the unicast data plane TEP address of Site 1.

Layer 3 Proxy Flow

In a multi-site proxy flow, the local external data plane TEP address is used as the source, and the destination is the remote unicast data plane TEP address. Figure 12-55 illustrates the packet flow, which is described in more detail in the steps that follow:

1. 172.16.0.10 sends a unicast IPv4 packet to 172.17.0.20. The destination MAC address is set to the destination MAC address of the BD gateway MAC address, triggering a route lookup.

2. Site 1 Leaf 101 does a lookup for 172.17.0.20 and does not find it as a local or remote endpoint. The most specific route is a pervasive route pointing to the spine proxy. The Source Policy and Destination Policy bits are not sent because they are sent to the proxy.

3. The spine does a lookup on the inner destination IP address and sees that it is learned via the Site 2 unicast data plane TEP address. A recursive route lookup shows that this packet needs to be sent to the IPN, and the destination MAC address is changed to the IPN MAC address. No other parameters of this packet are modified. The IPN has a route for the date plane unicast TEP address of Site 2 pointing to either spine in Site 2.

4. Spine 202 receives this packet, and a lookup is done on the inner IP address.

5. The destination address is changed to that of Site 2 Leaf 102, and the sclass and VRF instance VNID is translated to the local values. The outer source IP address is unchanged: It is the date plane unicast TEP of site 1.

6. Remote learning happens on Leaf 102 for 172.16.0.10, pointing to the date plane unicast TEP of Site 1 since the packet was routed on the VRF instance VNID. Policy is applied between the *App* EPG and a PCTag that was created in Site 2 to represent EPG *Web* from Site 1. If policy is allowed, the packet is forwarded to the destination.

Outer Header - Spine Ingress

DST MAC	Infra L3Out MAC
SRC MAC	IPN MAC
VLAN	4
SRC IP	Site1 DP Ucast TEP
DST IP	Site2 UP Ucast TEP

Outer Header - Spine Egress

DST MAC	000c.0c0c.0c0c
SRC MAC	000d.0d0d.0d0d
VLAN	2
SRC IP	Site1 DP Ucast TEP
DST IP	Site2 Leaf 102 TEP

DST MAC	000b.0b0b.0b0b
SRC MAC	BD App MAC
VLAN	20
SRC IP	172.16.0.10
DST IP	172.17.0.20

Outer Header - Spine Egress

DST MAC	IPN MAC
SRC MAC	Infra L3Out MAC
VLAN	4
SRC IP	Site1 DP Ucast TEP
DST IP	Site2 DP Ucast TEP

Outer Header - Spine Ingress

DST MAC	000d.0d0d.0d0d
SRC MAC	000c.0c0c.0c0c
VLAN	2
SRC IP	101-102 vPC TEP
DST IP	Site1 Anycast IPV4 Proxy

DST MAC	BD Web MAC
SRC MAC	000a.0a0a.0a0a
VLAN	10
SRC IP	172.16.0.10
DST IP	172.17.0.20

172.16.0.10
000a.0a0a.0a0a
EPG Web
BD Web
VRF v1

172.17.0.20
000b.0b0b.0b0b
EPG App
BD App
VRF v1

Site 1

Site 2

VRF v1

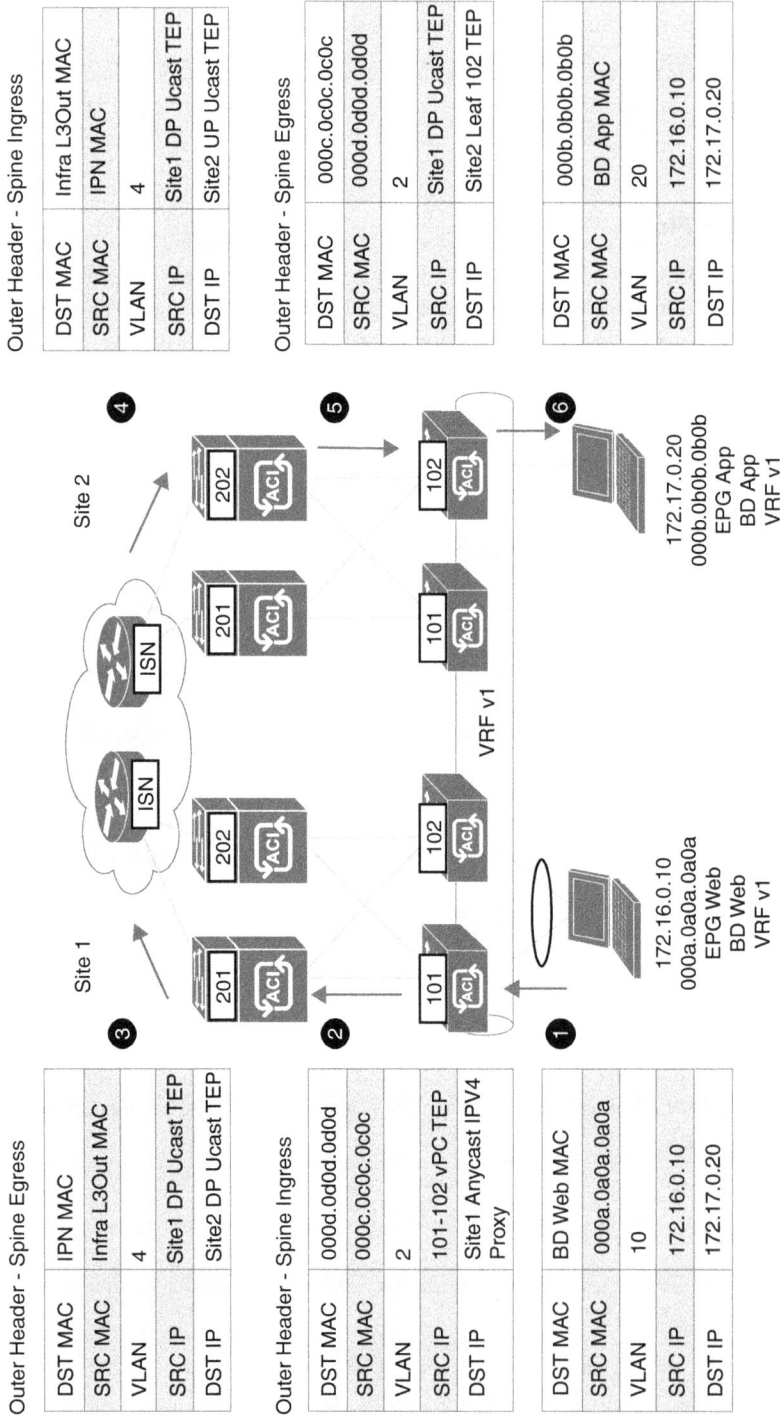

Figure 12-55 *Layer 3 Proxy Flow in Multi-site*

Remote Leaf

Remote leaf forwarding is a mix of multi-pod and multi-site forwarding. This section examines the differences for multi-destination and unicast flows for remote leafs.

ARP Flooding

For multidestination traffic, remote leaf relies on head-end replicating BUM traffic by encapsulating the original frame in a unicast iVXLAN packet. The packet is sent to the anycast RL-Mcast-TEP allocated to the pod where the remote leafs are registered. Figures 12-56 and 12-57 illustrate an ARP request being sent from a host single connected on Remote Leaf 105 and destined to a host in the main pod, as well as the reply. The BD in this example is configured in ARP Flooding mode. The following steps provide more details on ARP flooding between a pod and remote leafs:

1. Host 172.16.0.10 sends an ARP request for 172.16.0.11, and it's received on Leaf 105. Because this is a Layer 2 broadcast packet, it needs to be flooded locally and sent to the spine. The sclass is set to the source class of the *Web* EPG. Because the destination is multicast and ARP, the packet is implicitly allowed.

2. Leaf 105 encapsulates this frame and sends it to RL-Mcast-TEP which is an anycast IP address owned by the spines in the main pod. The VXLAN VNID is sent to the BD VNID.

3. Spine 201 receives the packet based on an ECMP forwarding decision from the ISN and, based on the VXLAN VNID, it remaps the outer unicast IP address to the BD multicast IP address. The packet is now flooded to all leafs that have this BD deployed.

4. Leafs 101 and 102 receive this packet, and the designated forwarder sends the ARP request toward the VPC facing host 172.16.0.10. The designated forwarder is determined based on a per-packet hash. The remote endpoint MAC address is learned from a tunnel pointing to the remote leaf data plane TEP of Leaf 105.

The following steps provide more details on an ARP reply between a remote leaf and the main pod:

1. Host 172.16.0.10 sends a unicast ARP reply back to host 172.16.0.11. The reply is hashed to Leaf 101.

2. Leaf 101 does a unicast lookup in the endpoint database for the MAC address in the bridge domain for which the packet was received. Because an ARP request was sent to Leaf 101 in the previous example, the MAC address is found to be pointing to the RL-DP-TEP of Leaf 105. The packet is encapsulated in iVXLAN sourced from the VPC TEP of Leafs 101 and 102 and destined to the RL-DP-TEP of Leaf 105. The sclass is set to the *Web* EPG, and the VNID is set to that of the bridge domain. Policy is not applied.

3. The spine receives this iVXLAN packet and knows that it is destined to the RL-DP-TEP of Leaf 105. A special rule on the spine causes the source IP address to be rewritten to the spine's anycast RL-Ucast-TEP.

Outer Header - Spine Ingress

DST MAC	Infra L3Out MAC
SRC MAC	ISN MAC
VLAN	4
SRC IP	Leaf 105 RL-DP-TEP
DST IP	RL-Mcast-TEP

Outer Header - Spine Egress

DST MAC	MCAST
SRC MAC	000c.0c0c.0c0c
VLAN	2
SRC IP	Leaf 105 RL-DP-TEP
DST IP	BD GIPo + FTAG

DST MAC	ffff.ffff.ffff
SRC MAC	000b.0b0b.0b0b
VLAN	10
Sender IP	172.16.0.11
Target IP	172.16.0.10

DST MAC	ISN MAC
SRC MAC	Infra L3Out MAC
VLAN	4
SRC IP	Leaf 105 RL-DP-TEP
DST IP	RL-Mcast-TEP

DST MAC	ffff.ffff.ffff
SRC MAC	000b.0b0b.0b0b
VLAN	10
Sender IP	172.16.0.11
Target IP	172.16.0.10

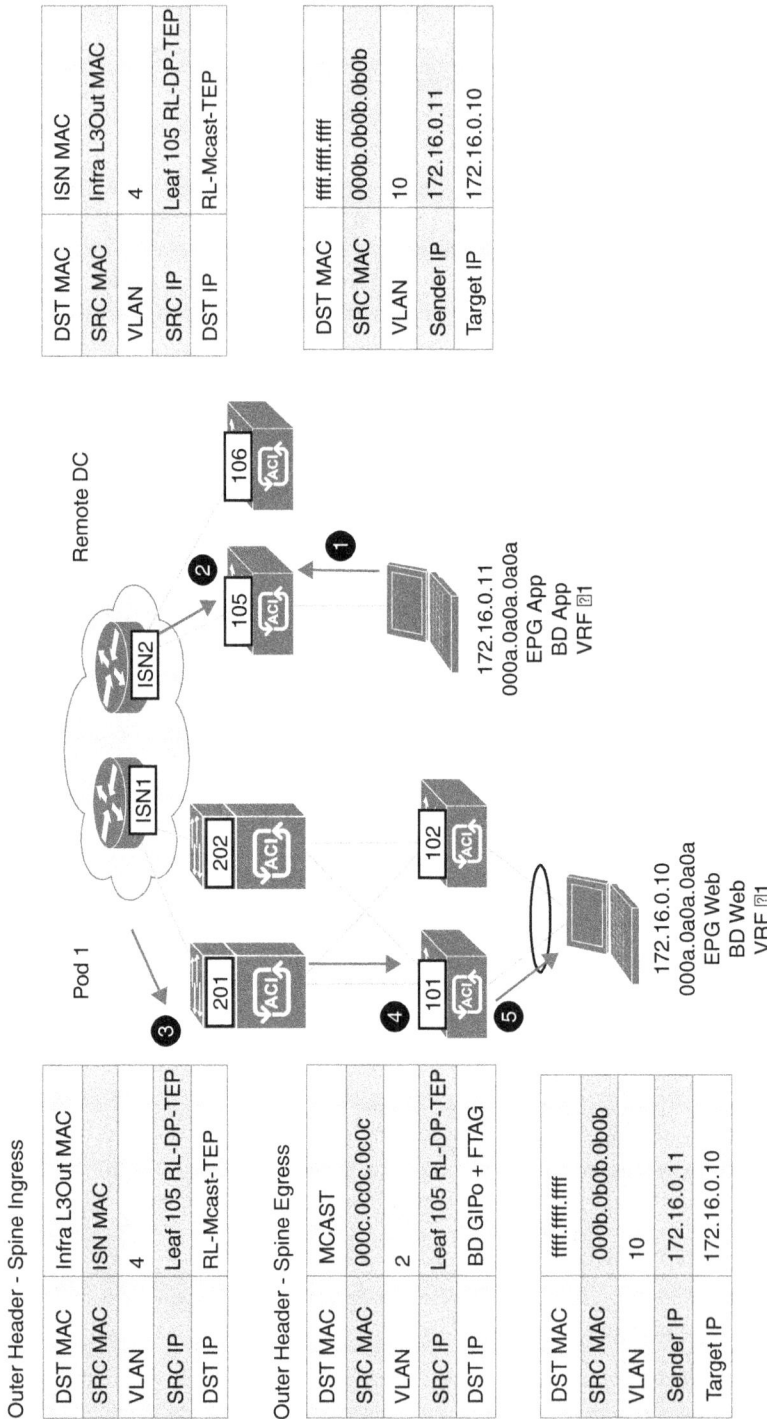

Figure 12-56 *ARP Flooding Between a Pod and Remote Leafs*

Outer Header - Spine Egress

DST MAC	Infra L3Out MAC
SRC MAC	ISN MAC
VLAN	4
SRC IP	RL-Ucast-TEP
DST IP	Leaf 105 RL-DP-TEP

DST MAC	000b.0b0b.0b0b
SRC MAC	000a.0a0a.0a0a
VLAN	10
Sender IP	172.16.0.10
Target IP	172.16.0.11

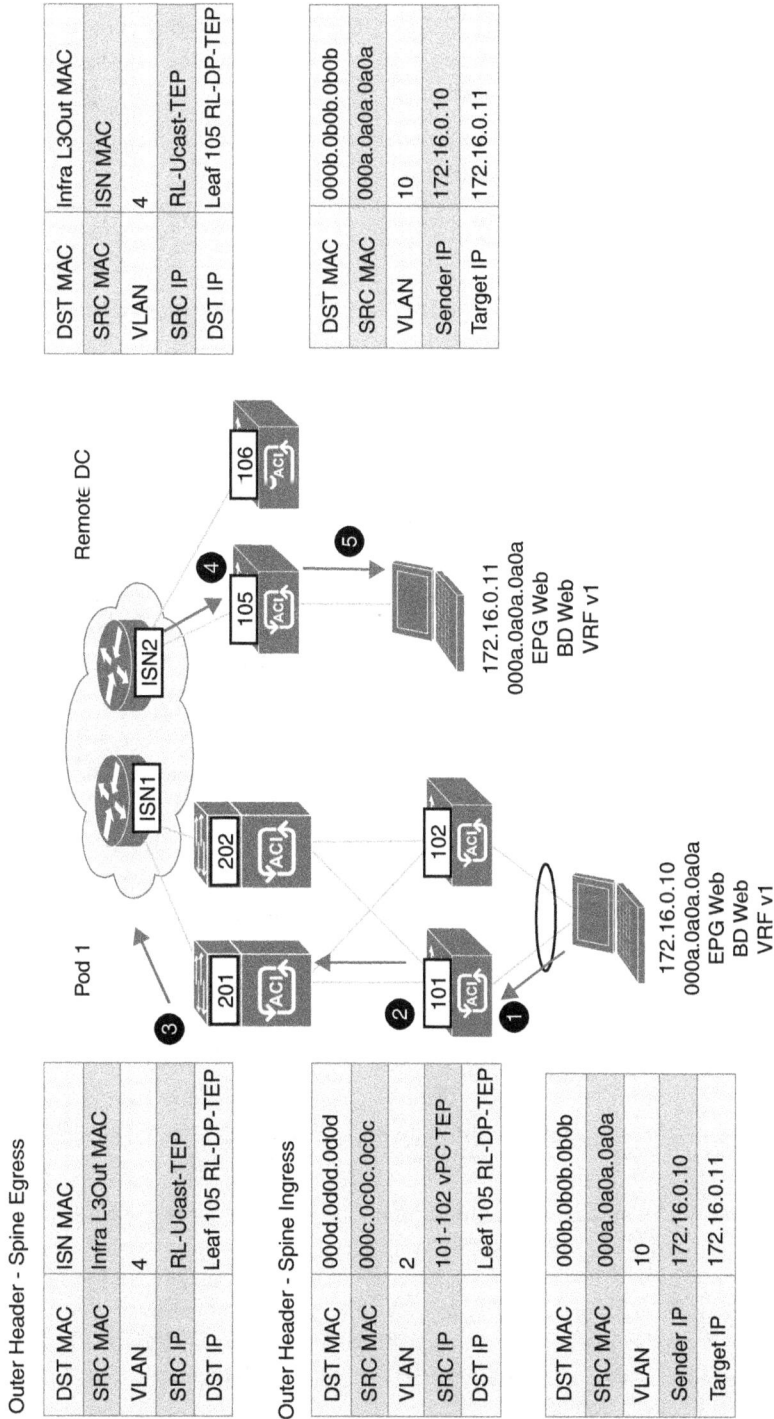

172.16.0.11
000a.0a0a.0a0a
EPG Web
BD Web
VRF v1

172.16.0.10
000a.0a0a.0a0a
EPG Web
BD Web
VRF v1

Outer Header - Spine Egress

DST MAC	ISN MAC
SRC MAC	Infra L3Out MAC
VLAN	4
SRC IP	RL-Ucast-TEP
DST IP	Leaf 105 RL-DP-TEP

Outer Header - Spine Ingress

DST MAC	000d.0d0d.0d0d
SRC MAC	000c.0c0c.0c0c
VLAN	2
SRC IP	101-102 vPC TEP
DST IP	Leaf 105 RL-DP-TEP

DST MAC	000b.0b0b.0b0b
SRC MAC	000a.0a0a.0a0a
VLAN	10
Sender IP	172.16.0.10
Target IP	172.16.0.11

Figure 12-57   *ARP Reply Between a Remote Leaf and the Main Pod*

4. The packet is received on Leaf 105 and de-encapsulated. Remote endpoint learning is triggered for the MAC address 172.16.0.10 pointing to the tunnel for the anycast RL-Ucast-TEP existing on the spines. Policy is applied, and the packet is allowed because the source and destination are in the same EPG.

5. The destination MAC address is learned as a local endpoint in the bridge domain, and the packet is forwarded to 172.16.0.11.

Layer 3 Proxy Flow

For unicast traffic, remote leaf encapsulates the original frame in a unicast iVXLAN packet. The packet is sent to the anycast RL-Ucast-TEP allocated to the pod where the remote leafs are registered. Figures 12-58 and 12-59 illustrate a routed unicast packet being sent from a VPC attached to the host on Remote Leafs 105 and 106. The packet is destined to a host in the main pod, and the host sends a unicast reply. The following steps provide more details on the Layer 3 proxy flow from a remote leaf and the main pod:

1. Host 172.17.0.20 sends a unicast packet toward its gateway MAC address. The destination IP address is 172.16.0.10.

2. The ingress leaf does a route lookup and does not have the IP address learned as an endpoint. The next match is on a pervasive route pointing to the anycast RL-Ucast-TEP that exists on the spines in the main pod. The VXLAN VNID is set to the VRF instance.

3. A single spine receives this packet and does a lookup for the destination endpoint—in this case, Spine 201. Based on the lookup, the outer destination IP address is changed from the remote leaf unicast TEP to the TEP address of the target leaf(s)—in this case, the VPC VIP of Leafs 101 and 102.

4. The egress leaf receives the packet and does a policy lookup based on the outer iVXLAN source class and the class ID of the local endpoint. The packet is allowed because of the contract relationship between the *App* and *Web* EPGs.

5. The packet is forwarded to the destination host.

The following steps provide more details on the Layer 3 reply from the main pod to the remote leaf:

1. Host 172.16.0.10 sends the unicast reply back to host 172.17.0.20. The reply is hashed to Leaf 101.

2. Leaf 101 does a unicast lookup in the endpoint database for the IP address in the VRF instance for which the packet was received. Because a routed unicast packet was sent to Leaf 101 in the previous example, the IP address is found to be pointing to the RL-VPC-TEP of Leafs 105 and 106. The packet is encapsulated in iVXLAN sourced from the VPC TEP of Leafs 101 and 102 and destined to the RL-DP-TEP of Leaf 105. The sclass is sent to the *Web* EPG and the VNID is sent to that of the VRF instance. Policy is not applied.

Outer Header - Spine Ingress

DST MAC	Infra L3Out MAC	ISN MAC
SRC MAC	ISN MAC	Infra L3Out MAC
VLAN	4	4
SRC IP	RL-vPC-TEP	RL-vPC-TEP
DST IP	RL-Ucast-TEP	RL-Ucast-TEP

DST MAC		BD App MAC
SRC MAC		000b.0b0b.0b0b
VLAN		20
SRC IP		172.17.0.20
DST IP		172.16.0.10

Outer Header - Spine Egress

DST MAC	000d.0d0d.0d0d	
SRC MAC	000c.0c0c.0c0c	
VLAN	2	
SRC IP	RL-vPC-TEP	
DST IP	101-102 vPC TEP	

DST MAC	000a.0a0a.0a0a	
SRC MAC	BD Web MAC	
VLAN	10	
SRC IP	172.17.0.20	
DST IP	172.16.0.10	

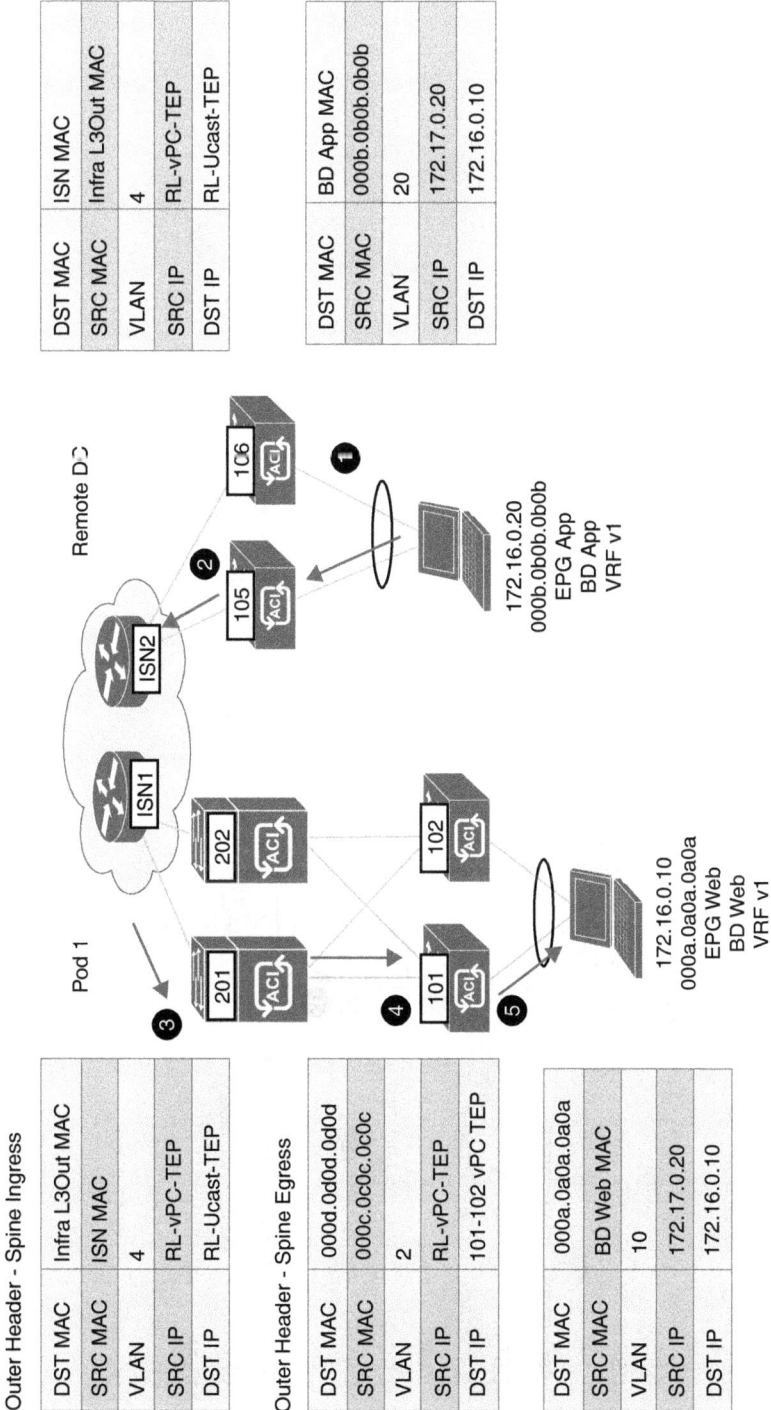

Figure 12-58 *Layer 3 Proxy Flow from a Remote Leaf and the Main Pod*

Outer Header - Spine Egress

DST MAC	Infra L3Out MAC
SRC MAC	ISN MAC
VLAN	4
SRC IP	RL-Ucast-TEP
DST IP	RL-vPC-TEP

DST MAC	000b.0b0b.0b0b
SRC MAC	BD App MAC
VLAN	20
SRC IP	172.16.0.10
DST IP	172.17.0.20

Outer Header - Spine Ingress

DST MAC	000d.0d0d.0d0d
SRC MAC	000c.0c0c.0c0c
VLAN	2
SRC IP	101-102 vPC TEP
DST IP	RL-vPC-TEP

DST MAC	BD Web MAC
SRC MAC	000a.0a0a.0a0a
VLAN	10
SRC IP	172.16.0.10
DST IP	172.17.0.20

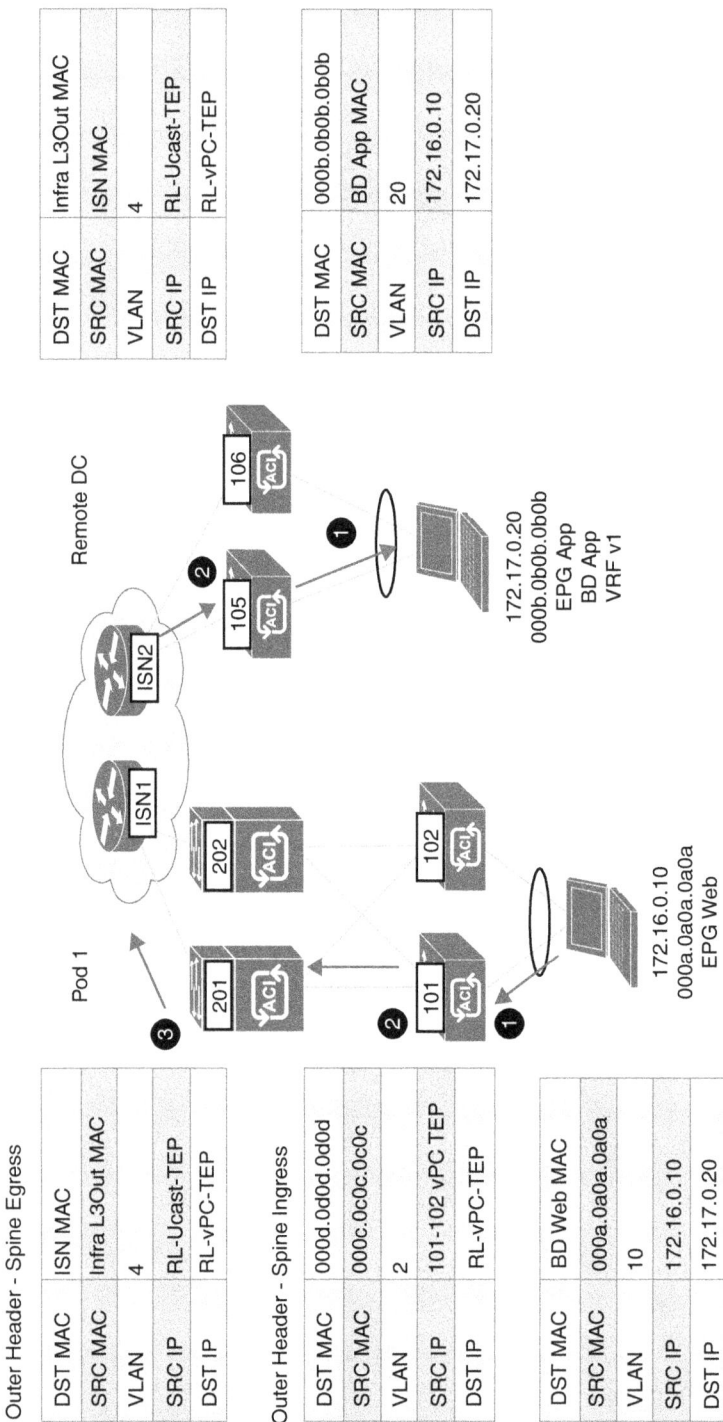

Figure 12-59 *Layer 3 Reply from Main Pod to the Remote Leaf*

3. The spine receives this iVXLAN packet and knows that it is destined to the RL-VPC-TEP of Leafs 105 and 106. A special rule on the spine causes the source IP address to be rewritten to the spine's anycast RL-Ucast-TEP.

4. The packet is received on Leaf 105, based on an ECMP hash from the ISN, and de-encapsulated. The remote leaf does not do remote learning for IPv4/IPv6 addresses, so no remote learning for 172.16.0.10 occurs. Policy is applied based, and the packet is allowed because there is a contract between the *Web* and *App* EPGs.

5. The destination IP address is learned as a local endpoint in the VRF instance, and the packet is forwarded to 172.17.0.20.

Summary

In this chapter, you have learned about ACI forwarding. You should now understand the iVXLAN header, TEP addressing, and routing, and now that you have reviewed various forwarding scenarios, you should feel confident in your ability to understand and trouble-shoot packet forwarding in your ACI deployment.

Review Key Topics

If you are preparing to take the Implementing Cisco Application Centric Infrastructure - Advanced (300-630 DCACIA) exam to attain the Cisco Certified Specialist—ACI Advanced Implementation certification, be sure to review the key topics marked in this chapter as outlined in Table 12-10.

Table 12-10   *Key Topics*

Key Topic Element	Description	Page Number
Section	"High-Level VXLAN Overview" explains how VXLAN and VXlLAN forwarding works in an ACI fabric	613
Section	"Endpoint Learning in ACI" describes how endpoint learning works on a leaf switch	626
Section	"Transit Routing" explains how to verify transit routing route maps and the configuration options	659
Section	"Shared Services" explains how shared services are configured to leak routes between VRFs	664
Section	"Multi-Pod" describes packet forwarding between pods	674
Table 12-8	Describes the required configuration for a multi-pod pim bidir configuration	678
Section	"Multi-Site" describes packet forwarding between sites	703

References

Cisco, "Cisco ACI Remote Leaf Architecture White Paper," Cisco.com

Cisco, "Multi-pod Configuration" white paper, CiscoLive.com

Review Questions

The questions that follow are designed to help you prepare for the Implementing Cisco Application Centric Infrastructure - Advanced (300-630 DCACIA) exam if you are planning on acquiring the Cisco Certified Specialist: ACI Advanced Implementation certification.

1. What underlay routing protocol does ACI use for reachability between TEPs inside a pod?

   a. OSPF

   b. EIGRP

   c. IS-IS

   d. BGP

2. How does multidestination traffic traverse the fabric so that all servers in a bridge domain receive copies of multidestination flooding?

   a. ACI does not support broadcast, unknown unicast, or multicast traffic.

   b. An APIC assigns one of the redundant spines to be the spanning-tree root to ensure that all leaf switches have a loop-free topology.

   c. Multi-destination traffic is not encapsulated but sent over the routed backbone.

   d. IS-IS is used to build loop-free FTags, which are rooted on different spines to allow load balancing while also providing loop-free topologies for multidestination traffic.

   e. FTags are used to encapsulate traffic, and the root is always pinned to one spine for all multidestination traffic.

3. When unicast routing is enabled on a bridge domain, when does ACI learn the IP address of a server? (Choose three.)

   a. When IP traffic is bridged between two servers

   b. When the leaf switch receives IP traffic destined to the router MAC address

   c. When ARP is sent by a device

   d. When it programs the MAC-to-IP binding in hardware

   e. When routed traffic is received via the fabric interfaces

4. What protocol does ACI use within a pod to exchange endpoint information?

   a. BGP EVPN

   b. BGP VPNv4/6

    c. IS-IS

    d. COOP

    e. OSPF

5. Which IP address is used to establish a BGP connection between pods in a multi-pod deployment?

    a. Control Plane TEP (CP-TEP)

    b. Data Plane TEP, or External TEP (E-TEP)

    c. External MAC Proxy

    d. IS-IS

6. From a forwarding perspective, what makes multi-site unique? (Choose three.)

    a. PIM Bidir is used to replicate multicast traffic between sites.

    b. Multi-site sites can be connected back-to-back without going through an IPN router.

    c. Multicast traffic between sites is encapsulated in unicast, eliminating the need for multicast in the IPN router.

    d. Multi-site relies on translating the VNID and SCLASS between sites.

    e. MSO pushes consistent VNID and SCLASS information for MSO-controlled tenants.

7. Which three statements are true about remote leafs? (Choose three.)

    a. Remote leafs do not support L3Outs.

    b. Remote leafs are not connected to ACI spines.

    c. Remote leafs can be controlled by different APIC clusters at the same time.

    d. Remote leafs are pinned to a parent pod.

    e. Remote leafs support VPC.

8. What is the default behavior for ARP forwarding on a bridge domain? (Choose two.)

    a. ARP flooding is not enabled by default.

    b. Leaf switches send proxy ARP responses for known IP addresses.

    c. ARP frames are forwarded to the IPv4 proxy for lookup on the target IP address.

    d. ARP is flooded by default.

    e. ARP is not needed in an ACI fabric.

9. Which of the following are invalid uses of the outer CoS value when traffic traverses the fabric? (Choose two.)

    a. CoS used for the user QoS levels

    b. iTtraceroute

    c. L4–L7 integration

    d. APIC traffic

    e. Policy enforcement

10. How do the ACI leaf switches prevent learning of remote endpoints when traffic is sent between VRF instances?

    a. There is an access control list for each shared route that prevents the learning.

    b. Traffic is sent with the DL bit set in the iVXLAN header when it is routed between VRF instances.

    c. The ACI leaf switches learn remote endpoints when traffic is sent between VRF instances.

    d. A configuration in the Endpoint Manager Client (EPMC) software ignores the learning.

    e. When the route is pushed to the leaf, the object has the Don't Learn attribute set.

Chapter 13

Troubleshooting Techniques

When it comes to ACI, a lot of people fear that all of the ways they would typically troubleshoot certain issues are no longer applicable. With the introduction of a GUI compared to only a CLI, it can be easy to think that most of the tools you had available in a traditional data center network cannot be applied in ACI. In reality, almost every command that can be run on a traditional NX-OS device can also be run on a Nexus 9000 running in ACI mode. Furthermore, the addition of the GUI and API can make it quicker and easier to isolate issues than ever before. This chapter demonstrates various troubleshooting techniques that can be used as you manage, monitor, and troubleshoot your ACI fabric.

This chapter covers the following topics:

- General troubleshooting techniques

- Infrastructure troubleshooting techniques

- How to verify physical- and platform-related issues

- Troubleshooting endpoint connectivity

- Troubleshooting contract related issues

- Embedded Logic Analyzer Module (ELAM)

General Troubleshooting

General troubleshooting involves collecting system logs, process status, and statistical data to diagnose and remediate a problem in order to restore service. ACI provides various methods of troubleshooting using the GUI, the CLI, and APIs, as described in this section.

Faults, Events, and Audits

When an issue pops up, where do you start with your troubleshooting? The APIC controller that centralizes your entry point into the data center makes many tools available to you. Traditionally, network administrators relied on SNMP and syslog to ensure that events were captured and stored in a centralized location. While the ACI fabric supports both of these options, it also stores all event and audit data for the entire fabric locally. In addition, ACI introduced the concept of faults to alert users that something has gone awry in the environment or that a piece of configuration is incomplete.

Faults are a critical component of the ACI fabric, and they widen your visibility at a global level. The first step in troubleshooting any issue is to check whether a fault was raised around the time the issues were reported. When you log in to the APIC GUI, you can see all current faults listed under System > Faults (see Figure 13-1).

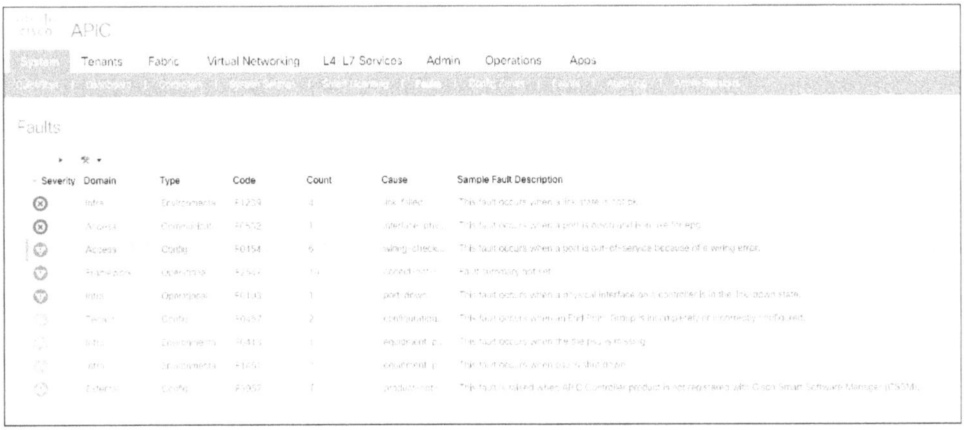

Figure 13-1   *Faults Tab*

Figure 13-1 shows the *faultSummary* MOs, which contain some basic information about faults, including the severity, the code, and how many exist. The faults are broken down by severity from most critical to minor. The Faults tab also shows what object was affected by a fault, provides a description of the issue, and lists the time it was created. You can view this information by double-clicking a fault (see Figure 13-2).

Figure 13-2 shows the *faultInfo* MOs filtered on the fault code selected. This view shows more detailed information about which object is affected, provides a description, and lists when the fault was initially created.

When a fault is raised, there is almost always some type of event or change that triggered it. In the APIC GUI, there is a Troubleshooting tab that displays all changes that were made and all events that occurred within a certain time of the fault being raised. This tab is very helpful in isolating whether a fault was caused by a recent change in the environment. Figure 13-3 shows the Troubleshooting tab.

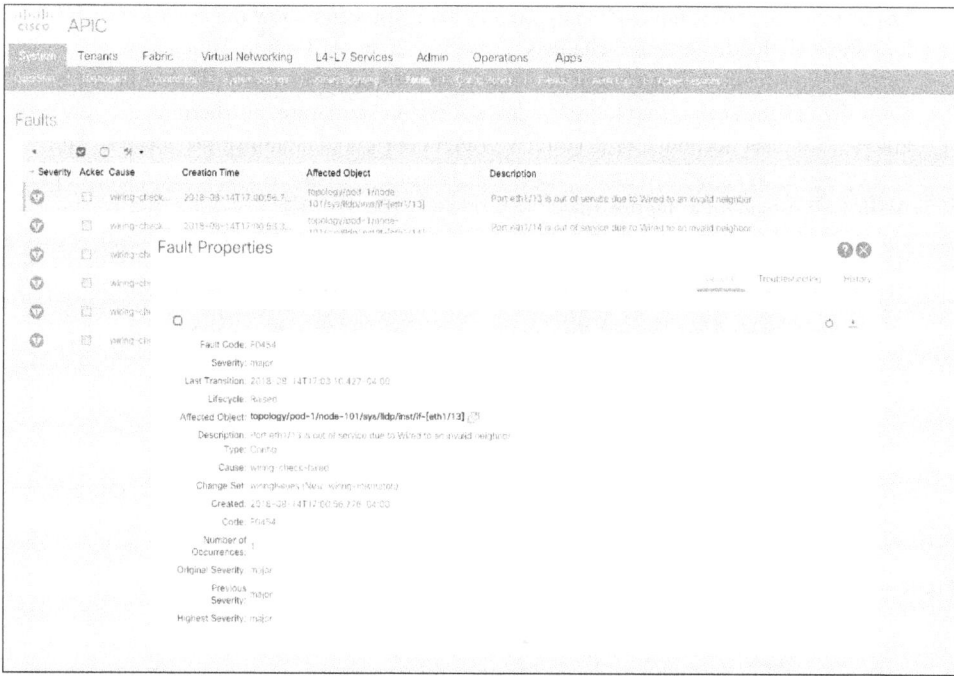

Figure 13-2 *Expanded Fault View*

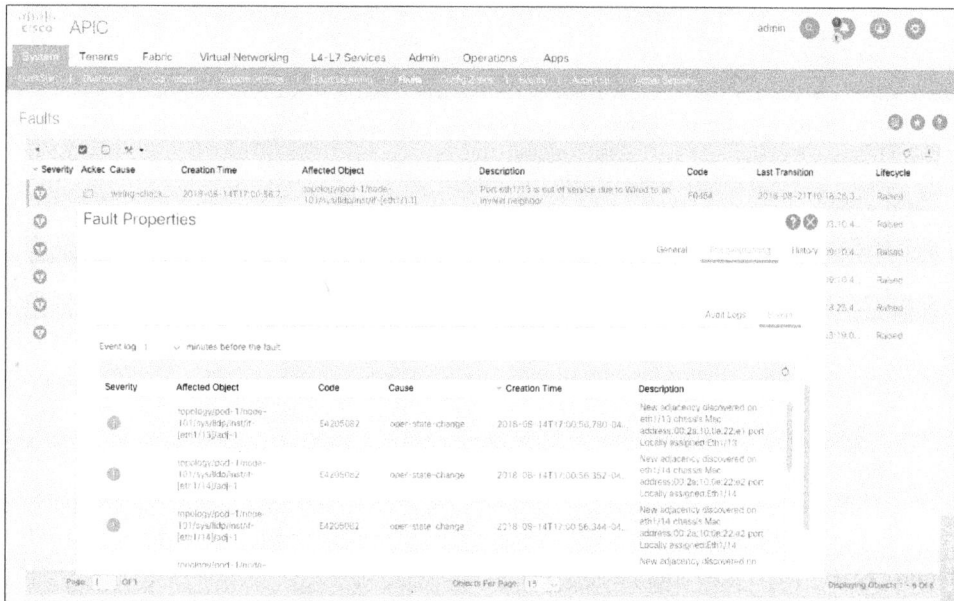

Figure 13-3 *Troubleshooting Tab for a Fault*

Just as you can review faults globally on a system, you can review the audit logs. These logs show all the documented changes that occur in the ACI fabric. When a change is made, the contents of that change are logged and stored as an object. The audit log is equivalent to the accounting log in traditional NX-OS software. Furthermore, if you have unique local user accounts, or if you have AAA configured, administrators can isolate exactly when changes were made and who made them. All audits are listed under System > Audit Log, as shown in Figure 13-4.

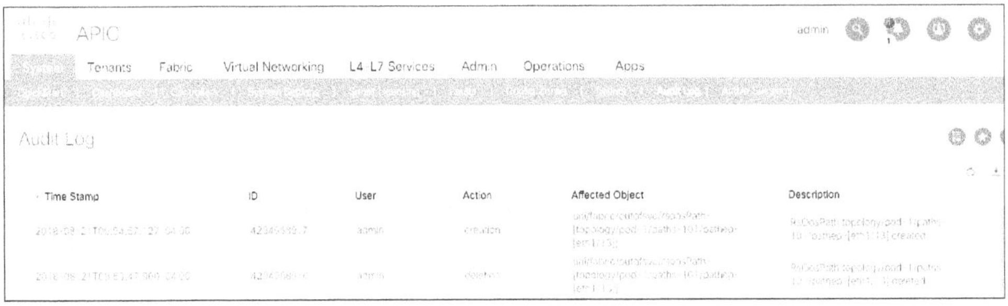

Figure 13-4   *Audit Log Tab*

The audit log lists the affected object, the time a change was made, what exactly changed, and the user who made the change. You can double-click an audit entry to view the specifics of the audit (see Figure 13-5).

Figure 13-5   *Expanded Audit Log View*

The APIC GUI provides an easy way to view every event that has happened on the ACI fabric. Not every change or potential issue is captured in a fault or audit entry. A lot of the time, if a change occurs in the environment but was not specifically caused by a user, information about this change gets propagated as an event. Analyzing events is extremely important when troubleshooting issues because it provides great details about what was happening in the ACI fabric during a time when no user-based changes were made. All events are listed under System > Events, as shown in Figure 13-6.

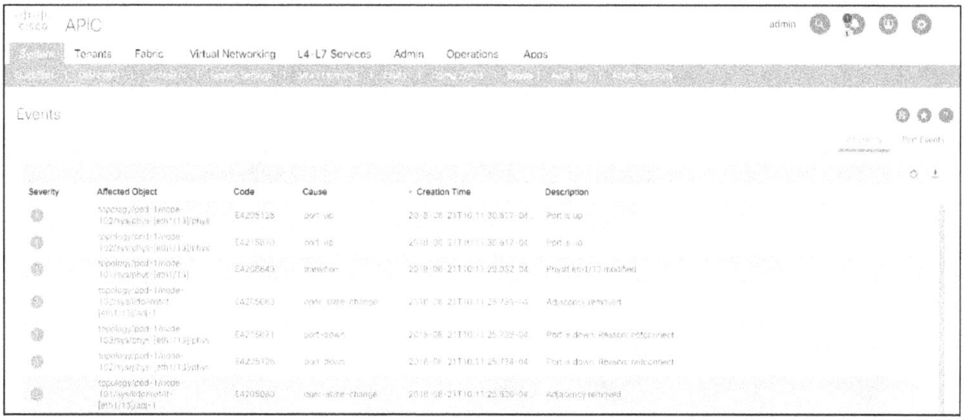

Figure 13-6   *Events Tab*

For each event, the Events tab lists the object that was affected, the time the event was created, a description of the event, and what exactly changed. In the example shown in Figure 13-6, eth1/13 on Leaf 102 was flapping. Events notify the user when links move up and down, and they are stored centrally on the APIC so all events for an entire fabric can be viewed in one place. The user can double-click on an event entry to view the specifics of the event (see Figure 13-7).

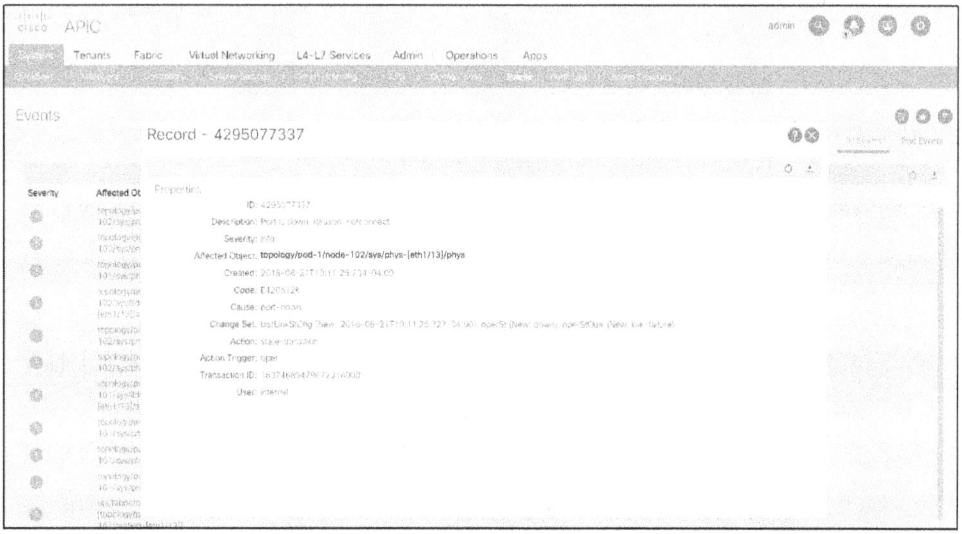

Figure 13-7   *Expanded Event View*

Almost all problems and failures that happen in a network are related to changes. When troubleshooting any issue, be sure to review the faults, audits, and events that have occurred in the timeframe when the issue occurred. Once you have validated that nothing has changed that may be related to the issue you experienced, you can continue to narrow down the issue and investigate in more granular detail.

moquery

While the GUI gives you the ability to view critical data such as faults and events, it's important to understand that the GUI is simply interacting with the REST API that the APIC offers. Some other useful tools can be leveraged when troubleshooting issues, and these tools allow you to interact directly with the API by using the APIC CLI.

moquery, which stands for *managed object query*, is a tool that can be used to query the API and get back nicely formatted data. This tool can be very powerful when you're troubleshooting because you can use it to view any object(s) on the fabric. You can query objects and set many filters to help sort and narrow down the results. **moquery** greatly enhances how you can view and filter changes that may happen in an ACI environment.

In order to run **moquery**, you must pass in an object class to query. You can also pass in other arguments to help filter the results. The following is an example of **moquery** syntax:

moquery -c *<classname>* **-f** *<filters>*

The classnames for faults, events, audits, and health scores are highlighted in Table 13-1.

Table 13-1 *Helpful Classnames for Identifying Changes in an ACI Fabric*

Classname	Description and Purpose
faultInfo	All Current Faults. Query this class to see all faults on the system.
faultInst	Child Object of faultInfo. Query this class to see all faults generated by the APIC controllers.
faultDelegate	Child Object of faultInfo. Query this class to see all faults generated by the fabric switches and external controllers (VMM).
faultRecord	All Historical Fault Data. Query this class to see all faults historically on the system, including faults that have been cleared and retained in the past.
eventRecord	All System Events. Query this class to see all the events that have been raised across the entire fabric.
aaaModLR	All Audit Log Entries. Query this class to see all the audits (changes) that have been raised across the entire fabric.
healthRecord	All Health Score Records. Query this class to see all the health score updates that have been logged in the entire fabric.

Suppose you wanted to review all audits that occurred at a particular time on a specific date. You can query the **aaaModLR** class, which is the class for audit log entries, and you can set a date on your filter. The filter should be set so that it limits results to only audits that were created after the specified time. Example 13-1 shows an example of such a filter.

Example 13-1 *Using moquery to Check Audit Log Entries for a Specific Date and Time*

```
apic1# moquery -c aaaModLR -f 'aaa.ModLR.created>"2018-08-21T10:10"'
Total Objects shown: 9


# aaa.ModLR
id : 4294968921
affected : uni/fabric/outofsvc/rsoosPath-[topology/pod-1/paths-101/pathep-[eth1/13]]
cause : transition
changeSet : lc:blacklist, tDn:topology/pod-1/paths-101/pathep-[eth1/13]
childAction :
clientTag : leaf 101; interface ethernet 1 / 13; shutdown
code : E4211774
created : 2018-08-21T10:10:56.041-04:00
descr : RsOosPath topology/pod-1/paths-101/pathep-[eth1/13] created
dn : subj-[uni/fabric/outofsvc/rsoosPath-[topology/pod-1/paths-101/
  pathep-[eth1/13]]]/mod-4294968921
ind : creation
modTs : never
rn : mod-4294968921
sessionId : k+7KHVxhTTW0t2b5UDijCg==
severity : info
status :
trig : config
txId : 576460752304820775
user : admin


!Output Intentionally Omitted
```

You can get more specific results by adding other options to filter with **moquery**. Say that you want to filter for audit entries that were created in between two times. You know you had an issue in a certain period of time, and you want to narrow down the results to see exactly what happened between those two times. You can continue to add to your filter to accomplish this, as demonstrated in Example 13-2.

Example 13-2   *Using moquery to Check Audit Log Entries Between Two Times*

```
apic1# moquery -c aaaModLR -f 'aaa.ModLR.created>"2018-08-21T10:10"and aaa.ModLR.
  created<"2018-08-21T10:10:58"'
Total Objects shown: 4


# aaa.ModLR
id : 4294968921
affected : uni/fabric/outofsvc/rsoosPath-[topology/pod-1/paths-101/pathep-[eth1/13]]
cause : transition
changeSet : lc:blacklist, tDn:topology/pod-1/paths-101/pathep-[eth1/13]
childAction :
clientTag : leaf 101; interface ethernet 1 / 13; shutdown
code : E4211774
created : 2018-08-21T10:10:56.041-04:00
descr : RsOosPath topology/pod-1/paths-101/pathep-[eth1/13] created
dn : subj-[uni/fabric/outofsvc/rsoosPath-[topology/pod-1/paths-101/
  pathep-[eth1/13]]]/mod-4294968921
ind : creation
modTs : never
rn : mod-4294968921
sessionId : k+7KHVxhTTW0t2b5UDijCg==
severity : info
status :
trig : config
txId : 576460752304820775
user : admin

!Output Intentionally Omitted
```

One thing to consider when using **moquery** is that the more entries you have, the slower the query will be. While **moquery** displays the data in a nice, easy-to-read format, there is a maximum amount of data the command can load. If the total amount of data is too large, it might take a while to load the data, or it might return an error such as "unable to process the query, result dataset is too big". If you face either of these issues, you can break down a single large query into multiple smaller queries, or you can leverage other tools to get the data you need.

iCurl

To get around some of the limitations of **moquery**, you can query the API directly by using iCurl. iCurl supports all the same functionality as **moquery** and returns the data set in an XML or JSON format. This means you can write automation tools to parse the data set on your own. iCurl acts like the traditional **curl** command in Linux, although with iCurl, the current session cookie is passed automatically for authentication. All iCurl requests that are sent to the APIC on port 7777 and to a valid APIC REST API URL are returned with the data set, and you do not need to pass in a token or certificate. Because the APIC REST API supports query filters, you can also pass them as part of the URL for further filtering of the response.

Let's use the same example as before but now run it with iCurl (see Example 13-3). If the data is intended to be viewed on the device, it is best to pipe the command to the JSON parser module that is built into Python on the APIC. This way, you can view the information in a more consumable manner.

Example 13-3 *Using iCurl to Check Audit Log Entries Between Two Times*

```
admin@apic1:~> icurl 'http://localhost:7777/api/class/aaaModLR.json?query-target-
  filter=and(gt(aaaModLR.created,"2018-08-21T10:10")lt(aaaModLR.created,"2018-08-
  21T10:10:58"))' | python -m json.tool
 % Total % Received % Xferd Average Speed   Time Time     Time  Current
 Dload  Upload   Total   Spent    Left Speed
100 2039  100 2039     0     0   73724       0 --:--:-- --:--:-- --:--:-- 75518
{
 "imdata": [
 {
 "aaaModLR": {
 "attributes": {
 "affected": "uni/fabric/outofsvc/rsoosPath-[topology/pod-1/paths-101/
  pathep-[eth1/13]]",
 "cause": "transition",
 "changeSet": "lc:blacklist, tDn:topology/pod-1/paths-101/pathep-[eth1/13]",
 "childAction": "",
 "clientTag": "leaf 101; interface ethernet 1 / 13; shutdown",
 "code": "E4211774",
 "created": "2018-08-21T10:10:56.041-04:00",
 "descr": "RsOosPath topology/pod-1/paths-101/pathep-[eth1/13] created",
 "dn": "subj-[uni/fabric/outofsvc/rsoosPath-[topology/pod-1/paths-101/
  pathep-[eth1/13]]]/mod-4294968921",
 "id": "4294968921",
 "ind": "creation",
 "modTs": "never",
 "sessionId": "k+7KHVxhTTW0t2b5UDijCg==",
 "severity": "info",
 "status": "",
 "trig": "config",
 "txId": "576460752304820775",
 "user": "admin"
 }
 }
 }

!Output Intentionally Omitted
```

The APIC REST API also support *paging*. By default, the maximum number of objects an APIC stores for a particular class is 500,000, and the maximum number of objects that can be returned in a single query is 100,000. Therefore, you need to be specific about which entries you want to collect if there are more than 100,000. You do this by specifying which "page" you want to collect in your query, as demonstrated in Example 13-4.

Example 13-4   *Setting Page Size and Number to Collect Objects*

```
admin@apic1:~>icurl 'http://localhost:7777/api/class/aaaModLR.xml?order-by=
  eventRecord.created|desc&page-size=100000&page=0'
admin@apic1:~>icurl 'http://localhost:7777/api/class/aaaModLR.xml?order-by=
  eventRecord.created|desc&page-size=100000&page=1'
admin@apic1:~>icurl 'http://localhost:7777/api/class/aaaModLR.xml?order-by=
  eventRecord.created|desc&page-size=100000&page=2'
```

This way, you can collect the first 100,000 entries with the first query, the second 100,000 with the second query, and so on. The *desc* in the query means that the objects will be displayed in descending order—that is, most recent changes first.

Visore

iCurl works great if you know the URL syntax for the API query you want to run; however, what if you don't know the format of the URL? How can you easily find out what the syntax should be? The APIC exposes an object navigation browser called *Visore*. Visore is powerful in many ways. It can display object data, and it can be used to create filters and display the URL needed to execute a query. This information can then be used in conjunction with iCurl. Let's again use the example of filtering audit entries but this time using Visore to view the data.

To get to Visore, you navigate to the APIC in a web browser and append /visore.html, as shown here:

```
http(s)://<APIC ADDRESS>/visore.html
```

After logging in, you see an interactive browser where you can filter on a specific class and enter filter arguments. After the input has been entered, you can get the URL used for the exact query by clicking on Display URI of last query link, shown in Figure 13-8.

You can use Visore to view any object in the UI by right-clicking the object and selecting View in Object Store Browser. This is especially helpful when you want to know the classname of an object being viewed in the UI.

These tools can be immensely helpful when you're troubleshooting changes in the environment because they allow you to get very specific about the objects you want to look at and the time ranges you want to view. Once you have isolated a time range where a particular incident occurred, you can view all the changes globally across the fabric in one centralized place. This is where ACI starts to show its true power.

```
APIC Object Store Browser
                                      Filter
Class or DN:  aaaModLR
Property:     created        Op:  >        Val1:  2018-08-21T10:10     Val2:
  Run Query
Display URI of last query

  /api/node/class/aaaModLR.xml?query-target-filter=and(gt(aaaModLR.created,"2018-08-21T10:10"))


Display last response

Total objects shown: 9
                                    aaaModLR                                          ?
  affected    uni/fabric/outofsvc/rsoosPath-[topology/pod-1/paths-101/pathep-[eth1/13]]  ≪ ≥ ▥ ❶ ✪
  cause       transition
  changeSet   lc:blacklist, tDn:topology/pod-1/paths-101/pathep-[eth1/13]  ≪ ≥ ▥ ❶ ✪
  childAction
  clientTag   leaf 101; interface ethernet 1 / 13; shutdown  ≪ ≥ ▥ ❶ ✪
  code        E4211774
  created     2018-08-21T10:10:56.041-04:00
  descr       RsOosPath topology/pod-1/paths-101/pathep-[eth1/13] created  ≪ ≥ ▥ ❶ ✪
  dn          subj-[uni/fabric/outofsvc/rsoosPath-[topology/pod-1/paths-101/pathep-[eth1/13]]]/mod-4294968921  ≪ ≥ ▥ ❶ ✪
  id          4294968921
  ind         creation
  modTs       never
  sessionId   k+7KHVxhTTW0t2b5UDijCg==
  severity    info
  status
  trig        config
  txId        576460752304820775
  user        admin
```

Figure 13-8 *Using Visore to View and Filter Query Parameters*

Infrastructure Troubleshooting

This section cover troubleshooting techniques pertaining to fabric infrastructure, whether the issue is related to APIC cluster health or some other issue related to fabric nodes and their connectivity inside the fabric.

APIC Cluster Troubleshooting

In order for an ACI fabric to remain healthy, the APIC cluster must be able to synchronize at all times. If you have to expand the APIC cluster for any reason or replace an APIC that has failed, it is critical to ensure that they are configured in the correct manner to allow the cluster to maintain a healthy state. If for any reason an APIC in the cluster is not configured properly during the initial setup, it will not be allowed to join the fabric. This section outlines troubleshooting steps for ensuring that the APICs are allowed to be a part of your ACI fabric. Furthermore, it goes over specific steps for validating that APICs have the ability to form a healthy cluster.

To understand why an APIC may not be able to join the fabric, you have to understand the configuration required on an APIC to form a cluster. Table 13-2 outlines the initial setup configuration.

Table 13-2 *Initial Setup Configuration Parameters on an APIC*

Configuration Parameter	Configured the Same Across All Cluster Members?
Fabric Name	Yes
Fabric ID	Yes
Number of Active Controllers (Cluster Size)	Yes
Pod ID	No; reflects the pod ID of the APIC location
Controller ID	No; this is the unique ID for each APIC (1, 2, 3, and so on)
Controller Name	No; this is the hostname of each APIC
TEP Address Pool	Yes
Infra VLAN	Yes
BD Multicast Address Pool	Yes
Out of Band Management Configuration	No

Any of the parameters marked Yes in Table 13-1 must be configured exactly the same on all APICs in the cluster. Failure to configure any one of the fields the same will result in that APIC not being able to join the cluster. Furthermore, during initial installation of the fabric, the parameters will be validated against what is configured on APIC 1. If the parameters on APIC 2 do not match, APIC 2 will not be allowed to join the cluster. APIC 3 will also not be allowed to join until APIC 2 is part of the cluster, even if the parameters on APIC 3 are correct.

Once the APICs are configured and connected to the ACI leaf switches, the APICs and leafs exchange LLDP frames with these key parameters to validate that the configuration is consistent across all members of the cluster. The APICs use an active/standby bond, where the infrastructure VLAN is tagged to do the communication. Figure 13-9 provides a physical topology example for an APIC cluster; in this topology, the solid links are active, and the dotted links are standby.

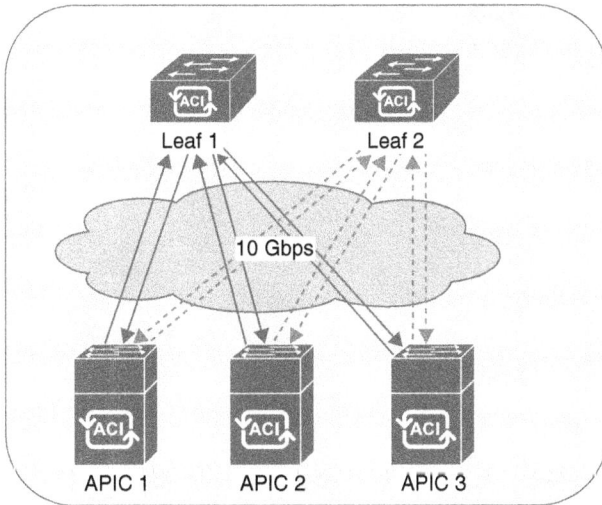

Figure 13-9 *Physical Topology for an APIC Cluster*

The bond used for the infrastructure connectivity is always bond0, where eth2-1 and eth2-2 are assigned to the bond. From both the APIC GUI and the CLI, you can find the active interface in the bond. In the GUI, you can navigate to Controllers > Controller Node-X > Interfaces to see the active interfaces (see Figure 13-10).

Figure 13-10 *Viewing APIC Bond Interfaces in the GUI*

From the CLI, you can view the bond information by viewing the /proc/net/bonding configuration, as demonstrated in Example 13-5.

Example 13-5   *Viewing APIC Bond Interfaces from the CLI*

```
APIC1# cat /proc/net/bonding/bond0
Ethernet Channel Bonding Driver: v3.7.1 (April 27, 2011)


Bonding Mode: fault-tolerance (active-backup)
Primary Slave: None
Currently Active Slave: eth2-1
MII Status: up
MII Polling Interval (ms): 60
Up Delay (ms): 0
Down Delay (ms): 0


Slave Interface: eth2-1
MII Status: up
Speed: 10000 Mbps
Duplex: full
Link Failure Count: 0
Permanent HW addr: 58:f3:9c:5a:42:26
Slave queue ID: 0


Slave Interface: eth2-2
MII Status: up
Speed: 10000 Mbps
Duplex: full
Link Failure Count: 0
Permanent HW addr: 58:f3:9c:5a:42:27
Slave queue ID: 0
```

The APIC provides a built-in utility to view the LLDP frame parameters it is sending and receiving. If for any reason the APIC is not able to join the cluster, you need to check the LLDP frames to ensure that the parameters are correct. This capability is available via the **acidiag** command in the APIC CLI. Example 13-6 shows how to use this tool.

Example 13-6   *Viewing LLDP Frames Sent from an APIC*

```
APIC1# acidiag run lldptool out eth2-1
Chassis ID TLV
     MAC: 58:f3:9c:5a:42:26
Port ID TLV
     MAC: 58:f3:9c:5a:42:26
Time to Live TLV
     120
Port Description TLV
     eth2-1
```

```
System Name TLV
        APIC1
System Description TLV
        topology/pod-1/node-1
Management Address TLV
        IPv4: 10.0.0.1
        Ifindex: 4
<!Intentionally Omitted for Brevity>
Cisco Fabric Name TLV
        Fabric-1
Cisco Appliance Vector TLV
        Id: 1
        IPv4: 10.0.0.1
        UUID: 88e8c4bc-9137-11e8-96c2-774394d6bc51
Cisco Node IP TLV
        IPv4:10.0.0.1
Cisco Port Role TLV
        1
Cisco Infra VLAN TLV
        3091
Cisco Serial Number TLV
        FCHXXXXXXXX
<!Intentionally Omitted for Brevity>
End of LLDPDU TLV
```

The leaf then validates the LLDP frame received with the current database. If any of the required fields have a mismatch, the APIC is not allowed to join the cluster. The leafs have an object to represent the LLDP state of every interface. If an issue is detected, the object is updated to alert the cluster of a wiring issue. This then gets propagated in the form of a fault to alert the user. On each leaf switch where an APIC connects, you can run **moquery** against the **lldpIf** class to check the LLDP state for any issue. You can also add a filter on the query to display only objects that have wiring issues, as demonstrated in Example 13-7.

Example 13-7 *Viewing LLDP Objects on a Leaf for All Interfaces with Wiring Issues*

```
Leaf1# moquery -c lldpIf -f 'lldp.If.wiringIssues!="0"'
# lldp.If
id : eth1/1
adminRxSt : enabled
adminSt : enabled
adminTxSt : enabled
childAction :
descr :
```

```
dn : sys/lldp/inst/if-[eth1/1]
lcOwn : local
mac : 88:F0:31:BC:DF:67
modTs : 2018-08-21T18:51:19.693+00:00
monPolDn : uni/fabric/monfab-default
name :
operRxSt : enabled
operTxSt : enabled
portDesc : topology/pod-1/paths-101/pathep-[eth1/1]
portMode : normal
portVlan : unspecified
rn : if-[eth1/1]
status :
sysDesc : topology/pod-1/node-101
wiringIssues : infra-ip-mismatch
```

There are many reasons an ACI leaf switch might deny an APIC and alert of a wiring issue. Table 13-3 lists the potential errors you might encounter, as well as the causes and remediation steps.

Table 13-3 *List of Potential Wiring Issues with Causes and Remediation Steps*

Wiring Issue Error Message	Cause	Remediation
pod-id-mismatch	The pod ID configured on the APIC does not match the pod ID configured on the connected ACI leaf switches.	Rerun the setup utility for the APIC and correct the pod ID configuration.
fabric-domain-mismatch	The fabric name configured on the APIC does not match the fabric name configured on the connected ACI leaf switches and other APICs in the cluster.	Rerun the setup utility for the APIC and correct the fabric name configuration.
ctrlr-uuid-mismatch	The UUID being received in the LLDP frame of the APIC does not match the current database.	This typically happens when an APIC is replaced or reinstalled but was not decommissioned from the cluster prior to these actions. Decommission the APIC, wait five minutes, and then recommission the APIC to allow it to join the cluster.

Wiring Issue Error Message	Cause	Remediation
wiring-mismatch	Either a leaf is connected to a leaf or a spine is connected to a spine.	In an ACI fabric, if a switch type needs to be connected with the same switch type, LLDP should be disabled, or there will be a wiring mismatch.
infra-vlan-mismatch	The infrastructure VLAN configured on the APIC does not match the infrastructure VLAN configured on the connected ACI leaf switches and other APICs in the cluster.	Rerun the setup utility for the APIC and correct the infrastructure VLAN configuration.
infra-ip-mismatch	The infrastructure TEP pool configured on the APIC does not match the infrastructure TEP pool configured on the connected ACI leaf switches and other APICs in the cluster.	Rerun the setup utility for the APIC and correct the infrastructure TEP pool configuration.
unapproved-ctrlr	The ACI fabric internode secure authentication communications mode is set to Strict, and the controller is not allowed into the fabric.	If the controller has been configured correctly, you can allow the controller into the fabric by changing the mode to Permissive or by commissioning the controller via Unauthorized Controllers.
unapproved-serial number	The serial number used by the APIC is not a trusted serial number.	It is not recommended to allow a device into the fabric with an incorrect serial number.
adjacency-not-detected	The uplink interface on a leaf or the interface on a spine does not see an adjacency.	This could occur because the interface is not up, or LLDP packets are not being received from the peer.

If the leaf ports connecting to the APICs do not have any wiring issues, the *infrastructure VLAN* should get deployed on the leaf interfaces that connect to the APICs. This should allow IP traffic to enter the ACI fabric, which will be used for the cluster communication. If the cluster is not forming, or in any other state besides Fully Fit, you should ensure that you can ping the *bond0.<infra vlan>* interface IP address. This IP address will always be the TEP address pool, where the last octet is the APIC ID. From APIC 1, ensure that you can ping all other APICs in the cluster. This is demonstrated in Example 13-8, where the infrastructure TEP pool is 10.0.0.0/16.

Example 13-8 *Ensuring That APIC 1 Can Ping All APICs in the Cluster*

```
apic1# ping 10.0.0.2
PING 10.0.0.2 (10.0.0.2) 56(84) bytes of data.
64 bytes from 10.0.0.2: icmp_seq=1 ttl=59 time=0.168 ms
64 bytes from 10.0.0.2: icmp_seq=2 ttl=59 time=0.150 ms
64 bytes from 10.0.0.2: icmp_seq=3 ttl=59 time=0.137 ms
64 bytes from 10.0.0.2: icmp_seq=4 ttl=59 time=0.102 ms
--- 10.0.0.2 ping statistics ---
4 packets transmitted, 4 received, 0% packet loss, time 2999ms
rtt min/avg/max/mdev = 0.102/0.139/0.168/0.025 ms

apic1# ping 10.0.0.3
PING 10.0.0.3 (10.0.0.3) 56(84) bytes of data.
64 bytes from 10.0.0.3: icmp_seq=1 ttl=63 time=0.099 ms
64 bytes from 10.0.0.3: icmp_seq=2 ttl=63 time=0.067 ms
64 bytes from 10.0.0.3: icmp_seq=3 ttl=63 time=0.130 ms
64 bytes from 10.0.0.3: icmp_seq=4 ttl=63 time=0.149 ms
--- 10.0.0.3 ping statistics ---
4 packets transmitted, 4 received, 0% packet loss, time 2999ms
rtt min/avg/max/mdev = 0.067/0.111/0.149/0.032 ms
```

Using these tools, you can further isolate why an APIC cluster is not forming or why a single APIC cannot join an existing cluster.

Fabric Node Troubleshooting

Ensuring that the ACI leaf and spine switches remain operational is critical to the overall health of your fabric. However, it's possible that in certain circumstances, devices may become unreachable. This section demonstrates how to troubleshoot when nodes are not reachable in the fabric.

Because an APIC maintains a global database of all nodes in the fabric, you can view the status of each node directly on the APIC. The easiest way to view the state of all nodes is by using the CLI command **acidiag fnvread** on the APIC. This command displays a variety of useful information that you can use to troubleshoot when nodes are not responding. Example 13-9 provides sample output from this command.

Example 13-9 *Using acidiag fnvread on an APIC to View the Fabric Node Status*

```
apic1# acidiag fnvread
 ID   Pod  ID Name  Serial Number  IP Address     Role   State   LastUpdMsgId
 --------------------------------------------------------------------------------
 101  1    leaf101  FDO202711U6    10.0.128.70/32 leaf   active  0
 102  1    leaf102  FDO202711TH    10.0.128.71/32 leaf   active  0
```

```
 103  1    leaf103    SAL1830XLD8    10.0.128.64/32  leaf   inactive  0x10000004efbb0
 201  1    spine201   FOX1919G3BC    10.0.128.65/32  spine  active    0
 202  1    spine202   FDO22090C3J    10.0.128.66/32  spine  active    0


Total 5 nodes
```

Based on this output, you can see that the leaf switch with node ID 103 is not reachable from APIC 1. The output of the command also displays the infrastructure TEP address that is assigned to the leafs. Because you know the TEP IP address of leaf 103, you should run a **ping** test to see if IP connectivity is not working to that leaf, as demonstrated in Example 13-10.

Example 13-10 *ping Test to the TEP Address of Leaf 103 Fails*

```
apic1# ping 10.0.128.64
PING 10.0.128.64 (10.0.128.64) 56(84) bytes of data.

--- 10.0.128.64 ping statistics ---
4 packets transmitted, 0 received, 100% packet loss, time 2999ms
```

The infrastructure TEP routes are advertised via the IS-IS protocol within the fabric. When troubleshooting an issue where a node is inactive, each node must have a valid IS-IS neighborship to the other nodes to which it is connected. If the IS-IS adjacencies are up, the TEP routes should be advertised and distributed throughout the fabric. In this case, the APIC's active interface is connected to Leaf 101. At this point, it is best to validate whether Leaf 101 sees the route to Leaf 103's TEP address in the overlay-1 virtual routing and forwarding (VRF) instance. If it doesn't, the IS-IS adjacency needs to be checked to see if there are valid neighborships. Example 13-11 shows this process.

Example 13-11 *IP Routing Table for the overlay-1 VRF Instance and IS-IS Neighborships on Leaf 101*

```
leaf101# show ip route 10.0.128.64 vrf overlay-1
IP Route Table for VRF "overlay-1"
'*' denotes best ucast next-hop
'**' denotes best mcast next-hop
'[x/y]' denotes [preference/metric]
'%<string>' in via output denotes VRF <string>

Route not found
leaf101# show isis adjacency vrf overlay-1
IS-IS process: isis_infra VRF:overlay-1
IS-IS adjacency database:
System ID SNPA          Level State  Hold Time  Interface
4180.000A.0000 N/A    1      UP 00:01:01 Ethernet1/49.8
4280.000A.0000 N/A    1      UP 00:00:57 Ethernet1/50.7
```

```
leaf101# show lldp neighbors interface ethernet 1/49
Capability codes:
 (R) Router, (B) Bridge, (T) Telephone, (C) DOCSIS Cable Device
 (W) WLAN Access Point, (P) Repeater, (S) Station, (O) Other
Device ID Local Intf    Hold-time Capability  Port ID
spine201 Eth1/49 120        BR          Eth1/36


leaf101# show lldp neighbors interface ethernet 1/50
Capability codes:
 (R) Router, (B) Bridge, (T) Telephone, (C) DOCSIS Cable Device
 (W) WLAN Access Point, (P) Repeater, (S) Station, (O) Other
Device ID Local Intf    Hold-time Capability  Port ID
Spine202 Eth1/50 120        BR          Eth1/1
```

In this case, Leaf 101 sees LLDP neighborships, and the IS-IS adjacency is up to both spines in the ACI pod. The same troubleshooting methodology needs to be applied on the spine switches to validate that IS-IS is being received from Leaf 103 so that the route can be advertised, as demonstrated in Example 13-12.

Example 13-12 *IP Routing Table for the overlay-1 VRF Instance and IS-IS Neighborships on Spine 201*

```
spine201# show ip route 10.0.128.64 vrf overlay-1
IP Route Table for VRF "overlay-1"
'*' denotes best ucast next-hop
'**' denotes best mcast next-hop
'[x/y]' denotes [preference/metric]
'%<string>' in via output denotes VRF <string>


10.0.0.0/16, ubest/mbest: 1/0
 *via , null0, [1/0], 06w00d, static


spine201# show isis adjacency vrf overlay-1
IS-IS process: isis_infra VRF:overlay-1
IS-IS adjacency database:
System ID SNPA         Level State  Hold Time   Interface
4680.000A.0000 N/A    1     UP 00:00:53 Ethernet1/36.37
4780.000A.0000 N/A    1     UP 00:00:55 Ethernet1/33.39


spine201# show lldp neighbors
Capability codes:
 (R) Router, (B) Bridge, (T) Telephone, (C) DOCSIS Cable Device
 (W) WLAN Access Point, (P) Repeater, (S) Station, (O) Other
Device ID Local Intf    Hold-time Capability  Port ID
leaf102 Eth1/33 120        BR          Eth1/49
leaf101 Eth1/36 120        BR          Eth1/49
```

If you inspect the output in Example 13-12, you can see that Spine 201 does not have an LLDP neighborship or an IS-IS adjacency to Leaf 103. Because of this, the only route in the routing table is the TEP address range, which defaults to a null interface because all TEP addresses in the ACI fabric should be advertised in IS-IS and installed as /32 routes in the overlay-1 routing table.

At this point, the physical cabling and device state for Leaf 103 need to be checked. If the cabling is correct, and if the device is currently booted and running ACI software, the leaf should be allowed to registered to the fabric, as long as it has been provisioned. The interfaces on the spine and leaf should be checked for LLDP to ensure that they are seeing each other as neighbors with no wiring issues. If this is the case, IS-IS should come up, and the routes should be advertised.

How to Verify Physical- and Platform-Related Issues

Most people would agree that it takes time and experience to become comfortable troubleshooting issues across multiple different hardware platforms. However, regardless of the differences between devices, a common question is How can I determine whether this device is operating the way it should? Regardless of the device in question, the methodology at a high level does not change much at all. What does change is how you verify it. This section covers physical issues and shows how to validate the platform to ensure that packets are or are not being dropped as they traverse an ACI switch.

Counters

Checking system counters can be helpful in situations where you are experiencing packet loss between devices connected to the ACI fabric.

Before we dive into how to identify drops, it's important that you understand the different "buckets" of drop descriptions for an ACI switch. Drops are typically categorized in the following ways:

- **Buffer drops:** After an ACI switch has performed a lookup on a packet, that packet must pass through a hardware buffer before it can be put on the wire. If there is no buffer space available, the packet is dropped. Buffer drops are almost always caused by congestion on the link, which causes the buffers to fill up.

- **Error drops:** When an ACI switch receives a frame with an incorrect FCS or CRC, this increments an error. These corrupted frames can be dropped and are logged as error drops. When operating at a speed of 10 Gbps or more, corrupted frames can also be forwarded to other ports operating at the same speed due to the nature of cut-through switching.

- **Forward drops:** When an ACI switch receives a frame or packet that fails some type of lookup, the packet is dropped and categorized as a forward drop. Most of the time, these drops are expected, as they could be dropped due to a contract that does not permit them. You will see how to identify if packets are dropped due to contracts in the coming sections of this chapter.

- **Load balancer drops:** In order to optimize scale, multicast addresses assigned to bridge domains can be reused. This is allowed because the unique identifier for an endpoint group (EPG), bridge domain (BD), or VRF instance is the VXLAN identifier assigned to it. It is therefore possible that a leaf may receive traffic from a specific multicast address, but the EPG, BD, or VRF instance that maps to the VXLAN ID is not deployed on that leaf. If this happens, the packet is dropped and marked as a load balancer drop. These drops are expected and do not impact the performance or behavior of the fabric.

When troubleshooting a scenario where there is packet loss, you should check for drops to prove or disprove that the ACI fabric could be at fault. The first step is to identify the connection points for the devices that are seeing packet loss. Once you know where they are connected, you can check the interface(s) for drops. The three main categories of counters can be viewed per interface by attaching to the line card using the **vsh_lc** command and running **show platform internal counters port** *port number*, as demonstrated in Example 13-13.

Example 13-13 *Platform Counters for eth-1/5 on Leaf 101*

```
leaf101# vsh_lc
module-1# show platform internal counters port 5
Stats for port 5
(note: forward drops includes sup redirected packets too)
IF        LPort              Input               Output
                        Packets      Bytes      Packets      Bytes
eth-1/5   5    Total       17672    2730619       10912     2201970
               Unicast         0          0        7901     1921664
               Multicast       0          0        2998      282164
               Flood        3013     284010          23        1564
            Total Drops     14672                      0
            Storm Drops(bytes) 0
            Buffer              0                      0
            Error               0                      0
            Forward         14672
            LB                  0
<!Intentionally Omitted for Brevity>
            Mac RMON
               RX_PKTOK       17780
               RX_PKTTOTAL    17780
               RX_FCS_ERR         0
               RX_ANY_ERR         0
               RX_OCTETSOK  2746396
               RX_OCTETS    2746396
               RX_UCAST           0
               RX_MCAST       17758
               RX_BCAST          22
```

```
RX_PAUSE            0
RX_INRANGEERR       0
RX_UNDERSIZE        0
RX_OVERSIZE         0
RX_FRAGMENT         0
RX_JABBER           0
RX_USER_PAUSE       0
RX_CRCERR           0
RX_TOOLONG          0
RX_VLAN             3068
RX_DISCARD          0
RX_PKT_LT64         0
RX_PKT_64           4955
RX_PKT_65           3061
RX_PKT_128          3811
RX_PKT_256          5845
RX_PKT_512          0
RX_PKT_1024         0
RX_PKT_1519         0
RX_PKT_2048         0
RX_PKT_4096         0
RX_PKT_8192         0
RX_PKT_GT9216       0
TX_PKTOK            11013
TX_PKTTOTAL         11013
TX_FRM_ERROR        0
TX_OCTETSOK         2216686
TX_OCTETS           2216686
TX_UCAST            59
TX_MCAST            10952
TX_BCAST            2
TX_PAUSE            0
TX_USER_PAUSE       0
TX_VLAN             3055
TX_PKT_LT64         0
TX_PKT_64           0
TX_PKT_65           3054
TX_PKT_128          3798
TX_PKT_256          4060
TX_PKT_512          0
TX_PKT_1024         0
TX_PKT_1519         0
TX_PKT_2048         0
TX_PKT_4096         0
TX_PKT_8192         0
TX_PKT_GT9216       0
```

These counters are referred to as the *platform counters*, and hardware is seeing them as packets entering the switch. In addition to the main categories, the platform also breaks down packet statistics for a variety of criteria. These counters are shown under Mac RMON, and they are stored in software, so they can be viewed from the iBash shell. This is where the output of **show interface** gets populated, as shown in Example 13-14.

Example 13-14 *Interface Information for eth-1/5 Viewed from iBash*

```
leaf101# show interface ethernet 1/5
Ethernet1/5 is up
admin state is up, Dedicated Interface
 Belongs to po1
 Hardware: 1000/10000/25000/auto Ethernet, address: 002a.100e.2059
   (bia 002a.100e.2059)
 MTU 9000 bytes, BW 10000000 Kbit, DLY 1 usec
 reliability 255/255, txload 1/255, rxload 1/255
 Encapsulation ARPA, medium is broadcast
 Port mode is trunk
 full-duplex, 10 Gb/s, media type is 10G
 FEC (forward-error-correction) : disable-fec
 Beacon is turned off
 Auto-Negotiation is turned on
 Input flow-control is off, output flow-control is off
 Auto-mdix is turned off
 Rate mode is dedicated
 Switchport monitor is off
 EtherType is 0x8100
 EEE (efficient-ethernet) : n/a
 Last link flapped 07:28:34
 Last clearing of "show interface" counters never
 10 interface resets
 30 seconds input rate 72 bits/sec, 0 packets/sec
 30 seconds output rate 456 bits/sec, 0 packets/sec
 Load-Interval #2: 5 minute (300 seconds)
 input rate 80 bps, 0 pps; output rate 208 bps, 0 pps
 RX
 0 unicast packets 17758 multicast packets 22 broadcast packets
 17780 input packets 2746396 bytes
 0 jumbo packets 0 storm suppression bytes
 0 runts 0 giants  0 CRC 0 no buffer
 0 input error 0 short frame  0 overrun 0 underrun  0 ignored
 0 watchdog 0 bad etype drop 0 bad proto drop  0 if down drop
 0 input with dribble 0 input discard 0 input total drop
 0 Rx pause
 TX
```

```
59 unicast packets 10952 multicast packets 2 broadcast packets
11013 output packets 2216686 bytes
0 jumbo packets
0 output error 0 collision  0 deferred 0 late collision
0 lost carrier 0 no carrier  0 babble 0 output discard 0 output total drops
0 Tx pause
```

So, if you are suspecting a physical layer issue, you can validate whether CRC errors exist on a particular interface by looking at the iBash or platform counters. Because the ACI software is running a more exposed version of the Linux kernel, you can use **grep** and **egrep** to help filter the command, as shown in Example 13-15 and Example 13-16.

Example 13-15   *Viewing CRC Errors via iBash*

```
leaf101# show interface ethernet 1/47 | grep -A 15 RX
 RX
 2128003 unicast packets 0 multicast packets  0 broadcast packets
 2128910 input packets 272500480 bytes
 0 jumbo packets 0 storm suppression bytes
 0 runts 0 giants  907 CRC 0 no buffer
 907 input error 0 short frame 0 overrun  0 underrun 0 ignored
 0 watchdog 0 bad etype drop 0 bad proto drop  0 if down drop
 0 input with dribble 0 input discard 0 input total drop
 0 Rx pause
 TX
 0 unicast packets 96 multicast packets 0 broadcast packets
 96 output packets 8496 bytes
 0 jumbo packets
 0 output error 0 collision  0 deferred 0 late collision
 0 lost carrier 0 no carrier  0 babble 0 output discard 0 output total drops
 0 Tx pause
```

Example 13-16   *Viewing CRC Errors via Platform Counters*

```
leaf101# vsh_lc
module-1# show platform internal counters port 47 | egrep FCS|CRC|ERR
 RX_FCS_ERR         0
 RX_ANY_ERR 907
 RX_INRANGEERR      0
 RX_CRCERR 907
 TX_FRM_ERROR       0
```

Let's say you check the interfaces, and you don't see CRC errors. There might be other types of errors on the port that would indicate an issue. For example, it's possible that an interface might be congested, causing the platform to drop packets due to a buffer drop.

In such a case, you need to check the platform counters for a particular port to see if there are drops incrementing in the buffer category, as shown in Example 13-17.

Example 13-17   *Viewing Buffer Drops via Platform Counters*

```
leaf101# vsh_lc
module-1# show platform internal counters port 6 | egrep eth|Output|Buffer|Packet
IF       LPort                    Input                   Output
                         Packets       Bytes        Packets          Bytes
eth-1/6  6      Total      20233     4120000      159652374    173938042718
                Buffer          0                  52745666
```

Furthermore, if you check the interface from iBash, you can see that the 30-second rate on the port is 9+ Gbps, as shown in Example 13-18. Because the port is only operating at 10 Gbps, the interface is operating at its maximum capable rate, and the platform needs to buffer and might potentially drop frames.

Example 13-18   *Viewing Interface Rate via iBash*

```
leaf101# show interface ethernet 1/6 | grep rate
 30 seconds input rate 0 bits/sec, 0 packets/sec
 30 seconds output rate 9859325232 bits/sec, 880297 packets/sec
 input rate 0 bps, 0 pps; output rate 8359654120 bps, 5793920 pps
```

Manually checking every interface on a switch for errors can be very tedious. When you are troubleshooting, you need quick and easy ways to view counters globally across the fabric. Fortunately, you can leverage the REST API to query the entire fabric for errors, just as you do to review audits. Using **moquery**, you can query the **rmonEtherStats** class and filter on any entry that has a Non 0 CRC counter. This way, you can filter on all ports across the fabric that have errors, as shown in Example 13-19.

Example 13-19   *Using moquery to View CRC Errors Globally Using the API*

```
admin@apic1:~> moquery -c rmonEtherStats -x 'query-target-
   filter=and(ne(rmonEtherStats.cRCAlignErrors,"0"))'
Total Objects shown: 1

# rmon.EtherStats
broadcastPkts : 3
cRCAlignErrors : 907
childAction :
clearTs : 2018-07-11T21:59:15.000-04:00
collisions : 0
dn : topology/pod-1/node-101/sys/phys-[eth1/47]/dbgEtherStats
dropEvents : 0
```

```
fragments : 0
jabbers : 0
modTs : never
multicastPkts : 2693
octets : 2129075492704
oversizePkts : 0
pkts : 19402164374
pkts1024to1518Octets : 0
pkts128to255Octets : 13073564522
pkts256to511Octets : 169
pkts512to1023Octets : 0
pkts64Octets : 3
pkts65to127Octets : 6328599683
rXNoErrors : 19402092220
rn : dbgEtherStats
rxGiantPkts : 0
rxOversizePkts : 0
status :
tXNoErrors : 71247
txGiantPkts : 0
txOversizePkts : 0
undersizePkts : 0
```

Having the ability to understand packet counters in ACI and utilizing the API to filter on counters that can cause problems makes it easier to determine if there is an issue in the fabric.

CPU Packet Captures

In some instances, traffic that enters an ACI switch needs to be processed by the CPU. The following are some examples of this

- ARP frames destined to anycast IP addresses or L3Outs

- ICMP packets destined to anycast IP addresses

- DHCP packets where the BD has a DHCP relay configuration

- IS-IS frames

- BGP, OSPF, or EIGRP packets

If you are troubleshooting an issue that involves using the switch CPU to process a frame or packet and send a response, it is helpful to have some way of validating that the frame is making it to the CPU. In traditional NX-OS, the full Linux Bash shell is not exposed natively by the software. Because of this, NX-OS uses the **ethanalyzer** module to allow the user to capture traffic entering and leaving the CPU. In ACI, the software does expose the Bash shell, so if you want to see traffic on the CPU, you can use **tcpdump** just as you would on any other Linux machine.

The path from ASIC to CPU is laid out as shown in Figure 13-11.

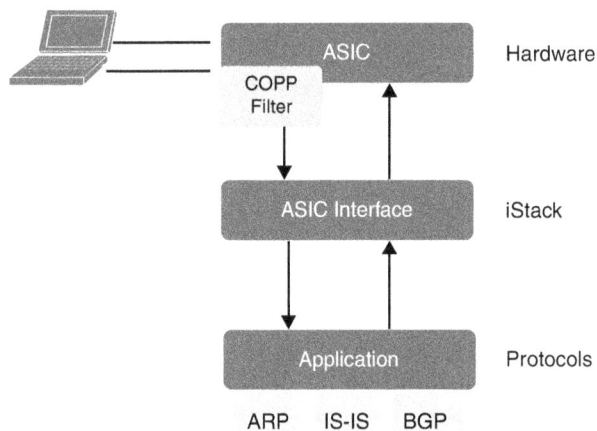

Figure 13-11 *Hardware-to-Software CPU Architecture*

ASIC

As packets enter a switch, TCAM rules determine whether the traffic should be sent to the CPU. Before allowing the traffic to go to the CPU, a hardware rate limiter known as Control Plane Policing (CoPP) validates whether the packets for a certain application are above a certain threshold. If so, the packets are dropped. If the packet does not violate the CoPP filter, the ASIC applies a header to the frame to determine how it gets passed down the CPU stack. This header is used by the ASIC interface to ensure that the packet gets handed to the correct application.

ASIC Interface

The ASIC interface is responsible for grabbing the frame from the ASIC and determining where the packet should go next. As the packet comes in from the ASIC, the headers that were applied are evaluated to determine the following:

- Why was the packet sent to the CPU? This is determined based on the Code value applied in the header.

- On which bridge domain or VRF instance did the packet enter? This is determined by the bd value applied in the header.

This software architecture is known as the *iStack*, and it is important because it allows the switch to validate the packets being sent to the CPU before it gets sent to the specific application. It ensures that the software will be able to process these packets based on the code and bridge domain/VRF in which they were received. The interface name in the software varies depending on the hardware of the device. Table 13-4 highlights the device type and name of the ASIC interface.

Table 13-4 *ASIC Interface Naming Scheme*

Platform	Interface Name
First-generation leaf	knet0 (receive)/knet1 (transmit)
Cloud-scale leaf (EX/FX)	tahoe0 (both send and receive)
Baby spine	tahoe0 (both send and receive)
Modular spine	psdev1.1

Application

The application is the individual process that is responsible for performing a specific function. Each protocol is handled by a different area of the software and, therefore, is defined as a unique application.

Let's say the server team is unable to ping the anycast gateway IP address you have configured under the bridge domain. You can use **tcpdump** to determine if the leaf switch is seeing the ICMP requests and responding to them. However, as the packet gets sent down the stack from the ASIC hardware, it contains a header to help identify the traffic. If you run **tcpdump** on the tahoe0 interface, you just see the raw dump, and it will not be obvious what the headers look like. If you are on a version of ACI from before Release 3.2, you can use **tcpdump2** to decode the headers while looking at packets coming into and going out of tahoe0. The **-Q** flag specifies the direction (in, out, or inout), as shown in Example 13-20.

Example 13-20 *Viewing Packets on tahoe0 by Using tcpdump2*

```
leaf101# tcpdump2 -i tahoe0 -Q inout
tcpdump2: verbose output suppressed, use -v or -vv for full protocol decode
listening on tahoe0, link-type CISCO_IETH (TX header 16 Bytes), capture size 262144
  bytes

13:02:34.676267 This is a RX packet
IETH INFO : SUP_CODE: 7, SRC_PORT: 59, SRC_CHIP: 0, SRC_IDX: 97, SRC_BD: 4612
IP 172.17.0.11 > 172.17.0.1: ICMP echo request, id 11000, seq 8, length 64
13:02:34.676378 This is a TX packet
IETH INFO : SUP_CODE: 40, SRC_PORT: 0, SRC_CHIP: 0, SRC_IDX: 0, SRC_BD: 513
IP 172.17.0.1 > 172.17.0.11: ICMP echo reply, id 11000, seq 8, length 64
```

While the command in Example 13-20 provides a lot of visibility, it does not display exactly what each code means. To enhance this, a tool called **knet_parser** was written to decode the headers and display the output with more information. Starting in ACI Release 3.2, the tool is exposed for use directly on the switch, as shown in Example 13-21.

Example 13-21   *Viewing Packets on tahoe0 Using knet_parser*

```
leaf101# tcpdump -xxvi tahoe0 | knet_parser.py --decoder tahoe


Frame 1
 Time: 10:46:39.975580+00:00
 Header: ieth_extn CPU Receive
 sup_qnum:0x8, sup_code:0x7, istack:ISTACK_SUP_CODE_ICMP(0x7) ← SUP Code is
   displayed
 Header: ieth
 sup_tx:0, ttl_bypass:0, opcode:0x0, bd:0x1204, outer_bd:0x0, dl:0, span:0,
   traceroute:1, tclass:0
 src_idx:0x61, src_chip:0x0, src_port:0x3b, src_is_tunnel:0, src_is_peer:0
 dst_idx:0x0, dst_chip:0x0, dst_port:0x0, dst_is_tunnel:0
 Len: 102
 Eth: 0050.5682.b662 > 0022.bdf8.19ff, len/ethertype:0x8100(802.1q)
 802.1q: vlan:11, cos:0, len/ethertype:0x800(ipv4)
 ipv4: 172.17.0.11 > 172.17.0.1, len:84, ttl:64, id:0x34fe, df:1, mf:0, offset:0x0,
   dscp:0, prot:1(icmp)
 icmp: echo request id:0x10951, seq:0x20


Frame 2
 Time: 10:46:39.975678+00:00
 Header: ieth CPU Transmit
 sup_tx:1, ttl_bypass:0, opcode:0x0, bd:0x201, outer_bd:0x0, dl:0, span:0, tracer-
   oute:0, tclass:5
 src_idx:0x0, src_chip:0x0, src_port:0x0, src_is_tunnel:0, src_is_peer:0
 dst_idx:0x0, dst_chip:0x0, dst_port:0x0, dst_is_tunnel:0
 Len: 98
 Eth: 0022.bdf8.19ff > 0022.bdf8.19ff, len/ethertype:0x800(ipv4)
 ipv4: 172.17.0.1 > 172.17.0.11, len:84, ttl:65, id:0xace7, df:0, mf:0, offset:0x0,
   dscp:0, prot:1(icmp)
 icmp: echo reply id:0x10951, seq:0x20
```

As another example, let's say that a server is unable to resolve ARP to a bridge domain any-cast IP address on the ACI leaf switch. You can apply the logic shown in Example 13-22 and ensure that the ARP request and reply are being seen on the ASIC interface.

Example 13-22   *ARP Request/Reply Validation Through iStack*

```
leaf101# tcpdump -xxvi tahoe0 | knet_parser.py --decoder tahoe
tcpdump: WARNING: tahoe0: no IPv4 address assigned
tcpdump: listening on tahoe0, link-type EN10MB (Ethernet), capture size 65535 bytes


Frame 1
 Time: 11:21:56.243132+00:00
 Header: ieth_extn CPU Receive
 sup_qnum:0x4, sup_code:0x1, istack:ISTACK_SUP_CODE_ARP(0x1)
 Header: ieth
 sup_tx:0, ttl_bypass:0, opcode:0x0, bd:0x1204, outer_bd:0x0, dl:0, span:0, tracer-
  oute:1, tclass:0
 src_idx:0x61, src_chip:0x0, src_port:0x3b, src_is_tunnel:0, src_is_peer:0
 dst_idx:0x0, dst_chip:0x0, dst_port:0x0, dst_is_tunnel:0
 Len: 64
 Eth: 0050.5682.b662 > ffff.ffff.ffff, len/ethertype:0x8100(802.1q)
 802.1q: vlan:11, cos:0, len/ethertype:0x806(arp)
 arp: opcode: request, who-has 172.17.0.1 tell 172.17.0.11, smac:0050.5682.b662,
  dmac:0000.0000.0000, src_ip:172.17.0.11, dst_ip:172.17.0.1


Frame 2
 Time: 11:21:56.244596+00:00
 Header: ieth CPU Transmit
 sup_tx:1, ttl_bypass:0, opcode:0x0, bd:0x201, outer_bd:0x0, dl:0, span:0, tracer-
  oute:0, tclass:5
 src_idx:0x0, src_chip:0x0, src_port:0x0, src_is_tunnel:0, src_is_peer:0
 dst_idx:0x0, dst_chip:0x0, dst_port:0x0, dst_is_tunnel:0
 Len: 60
 Eth: 0022.bdf8.19ff > 0050.5682.b662, len/ethertype:0x806(arp)
 arp: opcode: reply, 172.17.0.1 is-at 0022.bdf8.19ff, smac:0022.bdf8.19ff,
  dmac:0050.5682.b662, src_ip:172.17.0.1, dst_ip:172.17.0.11
```

If for any reason you do not see the packet when you use **tcpdump2** or **knet_parser**, it's possible that it has violated the CoPP Filter policy, and the ASIC is dropping it. You can check whether there are any CoPP violations for all applications by running the command from the vsh_lc shell, as shown in Example 13-23.

Example 13-23   *CoPP Filter Verification on a Leaf CLI*

```
module-1# show system internal aclqos brcm copp entries unit 0
-----------------------------------------------------------
                   INGRESS ENTRIES
-----------------------------------------------------------
Byte Policer
Protocol  CPUQ  PolID  (Sw/HW)  Prio  Rate(Bps)  Burst(Bytes)  GreenBytes  RedBytes
QINQ      51    2      /1       343   4096000    4096000       0           0
HSRP      38    3      /2       207   4096000    2048000       0           0
```

```
LLDP      14     4      /3     339   4096000    4096000     102901764   0
LACP      12     5      /4     330   4096000    4096000     7208576     0
CDP       15     6      /5     322   4096000    4096000     19224718    0
DHCP      25     7      /6     338   4096000    4096000     0           0
ARP       4      24     /23    191   5570560    1392640     1160968     0
<!Intentionally Omitted for Brevity>


-----------------------------------------------------------
                     EGRESS ENTRIES
-----------------------------------------------------------


Packet Policer: Avg pkt size: 3000
Protocol   Type   CPUQ   PolID (Sw/Hw)   Rate(pps)   Burst(pkts)   GreenPkts   RedPkts
bgp        Dyn    18     20    /20        5000        5000          107124      0
cdp        Dyn    15     21    /21        1000        1000          73636       0
glean      Dyn    20     22    /22        100         100           2           0
acllog     Dyn    5      23    /23        500         500           208         0
arp        Dyn    4      28    /28        1360        340           11398       114
```

This output displays each protocol with a measurement. The ingress entries measure the number of bytes, and the egress entries measure the number of packets. In this case, a few ARP packets were dropped due to a filter violation in the packets per second (pps) policer. CoPP in ACI is customizable using a policy. This is configured under Fabric > Access Policies > Policies > Switch > CoPP Leaf or CoPP Spine and supports the following options:

- Default values

- Custom values

- Permissive values

- Intermediate values

- Strict values

Using these tools, you can validate whether an ACI leaf switch is receiving traffic on the CPU for a particular application and generating a response. This is very useful if you think that a particular software feature that requires CPU processing may not be working as expected.

SPAN

You now know how to verify platform counters and view traffic entering and leaving the CPU. What other options do you have to ensure that frames are entering and leaving the ACI switches properly? While counters give you a real-time view of statistics and drops, they do not tell you on a frame-by-frame basis whether a frame entered or left a port. The most reliable way to validate whether a frame left a port is to run a capture on the other end of the link you are troubleshooting. However, if that is not an option, you can configure a SPAN session on the ACI switches to mirror traffic on an ingress/egress basis. There are two types of SPAN sessions you can configure in ACI:

- **Port local SPAN:** This type of SPAN session mirrors all traffic either on ingress or egress or in both directions and sends the traffic to either another physical port on the same switch or via ERSPAN to a remote collection device. This way, the administrator can plug a capture device directly into the switch where the source is configured or rely on remote collection to consolidate the traffic.

- **Tenant SPAN:** This type of SPAN session mirrors all traffic for a given EPG globally across the fabric and sends the traffic via ERSPAN to a remote collection device. The reason ERSPAN is the only supported method for tenant SPAN, versus a port local SPAN, is that the EPG may be deployed across multiple leafs. Each leaf that has the source EPG deployed creates a unique ERSPAN session.

The configuration for SPAN is discussed in Chapter 10, but that chapter does not talk about validating whether the SPAN is working. After configuring SPAN, you can check the status of the SPAN session directly on the node, as shown in Example 13-24.

Example 13-24   *SPAN Session Verification on Leaf 101*

```
leaf101# show monitor session all
 session 1
 ---------------
description : Span session 1
type : erspan
version : 2
oper version : 2
state : up (active)
erspan-id : 1
granularity :
vrf-name : ACI-AMT-Book:v1
acl-name :
ip-ttl : 64
ip-dscp : ip-dscp not specified
destination-ip : 172.17.0.11/32
origin-ip : 1.1.1.101/24
mode : access
source intf :
  rx   :
  tx   :
  both :
source VLANs :
  rx   : 13
  tx   : 13
  both : 13
```

```
filter VLANs : filter not specified
filter L3Outs : filter not specified


 leaf101# show vlan id 13 extended


 VLAN Name Encap          Ports
 ---- -------------------------------- ---------------- ------------------------
 13 ACI-AMT-Book:AMT:Web vlan-10        Eth1/5, Po2
```

Because an EPG is derived based on the VLAN and port for which the traffic is received, the SPAN session represents the EPG using the VLAN in the output. In this example, VLAN 13 maps to the source configured in the SPAN session: EPG Web. Both Rx and Tx traffic is being mirrored to Destination 172.17.0.11.

What happens if the source EPG you are spanning exists on multiple leafs? When traffic from multiple switches gets sent to the same ERSPAN destination, how do you know which leaf sent the SPAN traffic? When configuring the SPAN session, you can specify a prefix other than /32, and the APIC dynamically allocates a unique IP address for each device that creates the SPAN session. This way, the remote ERSPAN device sees traffic coming in from multiple different sources, and each of those sources can be correlated to the leaf that sent it. This is shown in Figure 13-12 and Example 13-25.

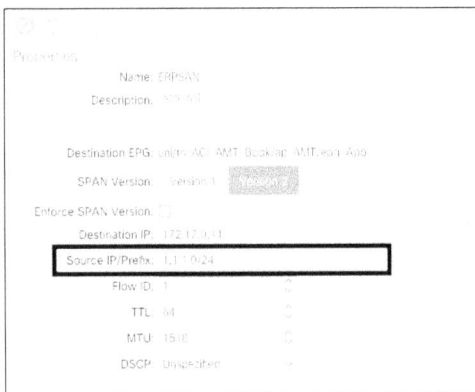

Figure 13-12 *Specifying a Prefix as the Source Gives Each Switch a Unique SPAN Source IP Address*

Example 13-25 *SPAN Session on Leaf 102 Showing a Different IP Address Than Leaf 101*

```
leaf102# show monitor session all
 session 1
 ---------------
description : Span session 1
type : erspan
```

```
version : 2
oper version : 2
state : up (active)
erspan-id : 1
granularity :
vrf-name : ACI-AMT-Book:v1
acl-name :
ip-ttl : 64
ip-dscp : ip-dscp not specified
destination-ip : 172.17.0.11/32
origin-ip : 1.1.1.102/24
mode : access
source intf :
 rx   :
 tx   :
 both :
source VLANs :
 rx   : 17
 tx   : 17
 both : 17
filter VLANs : filter not specified
```

After the SPAN session has been successfully brought up, packets are mirrored based on the filter and sent to the destination specified in the configuration. An administrator can now determine what is being sent and received on the ACI device.

Troubleshooting Endpoint Connectivity

You could argue that the most common cause of packet loss and instability in a data center network is rapid endpoint movement. Typically, this boils down to a MAC flap or, more elaborately, a MAC address that is being learned on more than one physical or logic port within the same VLAN. When this happens, the switch needs to constantly update where it last learned the MAC address, and if it is constantly having to update the location, packet loss is expected. In modern data centers, almost every host relies on some type of load balancing algorithm to disperse the load on a given link, create more bandwidth, and provide redundancy in the event of a failure. When this is not set up properly, the network is exposed to instability.

In ACI, instead of doing MAC learning on a VLAN basis, the flood domain is now the bridge domain. ACI leaf switches learn all MAC addresses in a given bridge domain. Furthermore, as discussed in Chapter 6, "VMM Integration," ACI leaf switches can also learn IP address information from hosts. This allows the leafs to install /32 host routes for optimal routing to endpoints. With this comes not only the possibility of a MAC flap but also the possibility of an IP flap. This section demonstrates how an administrator can check if either of the two types of flaps are being experienced in an environment.

Endpoint Tracker and Log Files

Suppose the server team has added a new server to the environment. The team claims it is using an active/standby load balancing algorithm, so you do not configure a VPC down to this host; instead, you leave it at a normal access port configuration. Shortly after bringing the server online, the server team claims that the connection to the server is extremely intermittent. Figure 13-13 shows the topology used for this example.

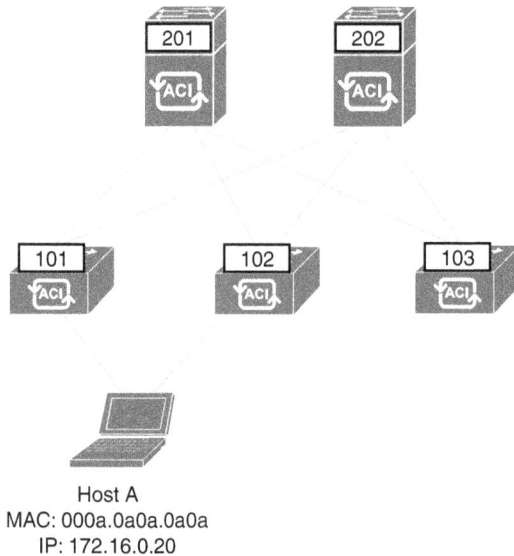

Figure 13-13   *Topology for New Server Added to the ACI Fabric*

Fortunately, Endpoint Tracker can help in this case. Endpoint Tracker allows you to search for an endpoint based on MAC or IP address, and it displays the history of that endpoint. Figure 13-14 shows an example in which Endpoint Tracker is tracking an endpoint moving between eth1/6 on Leafs 101 and 102.

This information gets propagated to the APIC when leaf switches learn about the endpoints. These messages can sometimes be throttled under heavy moves, and in order to go right to the source, you can look at the Endpoint Manager Client (EPMC) logs directly on the leaf. EPMC is the software process that runs on the line card of the leaf. When hardware detects new information, EPMC gets notified, so it can program the hardware and also create a message further up the software stack so the upstream processes such as COOP, as well as the APIC, can be made aware.

The most recent EPMC log file is stored in the /var/sysmgr/tmp_logs directory. If you check the log files for the MAC address, you notice constant movement there as well. A MAC move is triggered when a MAC address is learned on more than one interface in a given bridge domain. Example 13-26 shows how to check the log files to determine if a MAC address is moving.

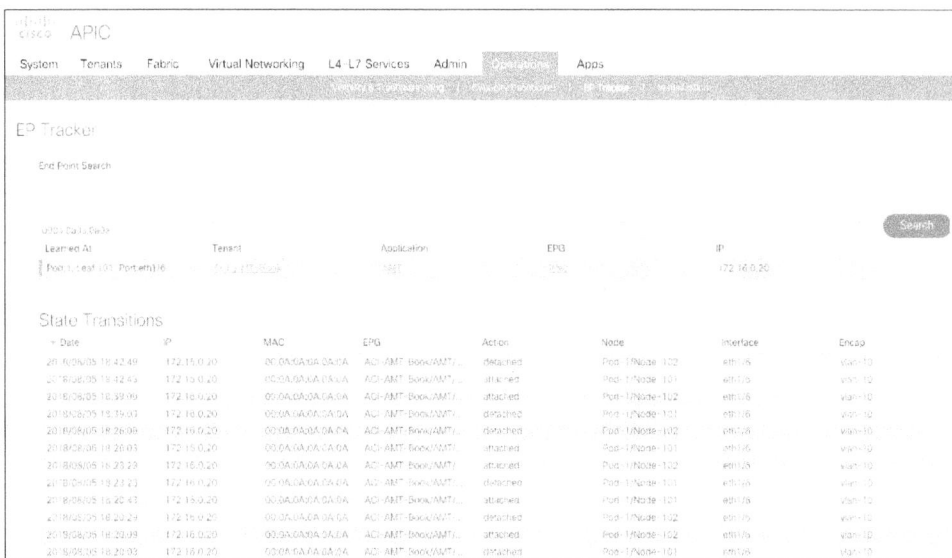

Figure 13-14 *Using Endpoint Tracker to Identify Moves*

Example 13-26 *Using EPMC Log Files to Identify MAC Moves Between a VPC Pair*

```
leaf101# cd /var/sysmgr/tmp_logs/


leaf101# tail -f epmc-trace.txt | grep -A 5 "mac = 000a.0a0a.0a0a"
optype = UPD; mac = 000a.0a0a.0a0a; num_ips = 1
ip[0] = 172.16.0.20; ip_flags =
vlan = 13; epg_vnid = 8201; bd_vnid = 15105996; vrf_vnid = 2981888
ifindex = 0x1a005000; tep_ip_tun_ifindex = 0; sclass = 49154
flags = local|IP|MAC|sclass|timer|
timestamp = 01/03/1970 07:21:55.361099
--
optype = UPD; mac = 000a.0a0a.0a0a; num_ips = 1
ip[0] = 172.16.0.20; ip_flags =
vlan = 13; epg_vnid = 8201; bd_vnid = 15105996; vrf_vnid = 2981888
ifindex = 0x1a005000; tep_ip_tun_ifindex = 0x18010003; sclass = 49154
flags = on-peer|bounce|IP|MAC|sclass|
timestamp = 01/03/1970 07:21:57.117000
--
```

In this case, Leaf 101 and 102 are configured in a VPC, so the log is saying that the MAC address 000a.0a0a.0a0a is moving between a local port and the peer. When it moves to the peer, you also install a bounce entry because traffic could theoretically still be destined to you if other switches have not updated yet. In this case, you see an endpoint constantly moving from a local interface to a remote interface, and the bounce flag is set, so you know this endpoint is unstable. The server team has admitted to its mistake: It configured an active/active bond on the server.

Suppose that the endpoint is not moving between VPC peers but is moving between other switches in the environment. You can still use the EPMC logs to determine where it is moving. In this case, you should look not only at the bounce flags but at the interface on which it is being learned. If it is being learned from a tunnel, you can map back the tunnel interface index to the tunnel IP address to determine the ACI leaf the information is coming from, as shown in Example 13-27.

Example 13-27   *Using EPMC Log Files to Identify MAC Moves Between a Non-VPC Pair*

```
leaf101# cd /var/sysmgr/tmp_logs/
optype = UPD; mac = 000a.0a0a.0a0a; num_ips = 1
ip[0] = 172.16.0.20; ip_flags =
vlan = 13; epg_vnid = 8201; bd_vnid = 15105996; vrf_vnid = 2981888
ifindex = 0x1a005000; tep_ip_tun_ifindex = 0; sclass = 49154
flags = local|IP|MAC|sclass|timer|
timestamp = 01/03/1970 07:59:31.560818
--
optype = UPD; mac = 000a.0a0a.0a0a; num_ips = 1
ip[0] = 172.16.0.20; ip_flags =
vlan = 12; epg_vnid = 15105996; bd_vnid = 15105996; vrf_vnid = 2981888
ifindex = 0; tep_ip_tun_ifindex = 0x18010003; sclass = 0
flags = bounce|IP|MAC|timer|
timestamp = 01/03/1970 07:59:32.459000
--

leaf101# vsh_lc -c "show system internal eltmc info interface ifindex 0x18010003" |
  egrep "interface|Tunnel"
vsh_lc -c "show system internal eltmc info interface ifindex 0x18010003"
 interface: Tunnel3 ::: ifindex:      0x18010003
 Tunnel Index: 0   :::   Tunnel Dst ip:     0xa00d042
 Tunnel Encap: ivxlan    ::: Tunnel VPC Peer: 1
 Tunnel Dst ip str: 10.0.208.66 ::: Tunnel ept: 0x1

leaf101# acidiag fnvread | grep 10.0.208.66
 103 1 leaf103 FDO202711TH 10.0.208.66/32   leaf       active  0
```

In this case, the MAC address is moving between two local leafs: Leaf 101 and Leaf 103. Keep in mind that ACI does IP learning, not just MAC learning. It may therefore be possible that the ACI leaf switches are seeing IP movement rather than MAC movement.

An IP move is triggered when the IP address is learned on more than one interface in a given VRF instance. If this is the case, EPMC logs show which new MAC address the IP address is being learned on, as shown in Example 13-28.

Example 13-28 *Using EPMC Log Files to Identify IP Address Moves*

```
leaf101# cd /var/sysmgr/tmp_logs/
leaf101# tail -f epmc-trace.txt | grep -A 4 172.16.0.20
ip[0] = 172.16.0.20; ip_flags =
vlan = 13; epg_vnid = 8201; bd_vnid = 15105996; vrf_vnid = 2981888
ifindex = 0x1a005000; tep_ip_tun_ifindex = 0; sclass = 49154
flags = local|IP|MAC|sclass|timer|
timestamp = 01/03/1970 08:10:42.860614
[2018 Aug 5 23:14:09.960067494:147254:epmc_process_l3_upd:3311:t] Found ip
    172.16.0.20 in db lookup
[2018 Aug 5 23:14:09.960072043:147255:epmc_process_l3_upd:3521:t] IP 172.16.0.20
    moved from MAC 000b.0b0b.0b0b to MAC 000a.0a0a.0a0a
[2018 Aug 5 23:14:09.960075756:147256:epmc_process_l3_upd:3605:t] Deleting ip
    172.16.0.20
[2018 Aug 5 23:14:09.960128129:147266:epmc_process_l3_upd:3608:t] Adding ip
    172.16.0.20

ip[0] = 172.16.0.20; ip_flags =
vlan = 13; epg_vnid = 8201; bd_vnid = 15105996; vrf_vnid = 2981888
ifindex = 0x1a005000; tep_ip_tun_ifindex = 0x18010003; sclass = 49154
flags = on-peer|bounce|IP|MAC|sclass|
timestamp = 01/03/1970 08:10:44.016000
[2018 Aug 5 23:14:11.160306875:147307:epmc_process_l3_upd:3311:t] Found ip
    172.16.0.20 in db lookup
[2018 Aug 5 23:14:11.160311675:147308:epmc_process_l3_upd:3521:t] IP 172.16.0.20
    moved from MAC 000a.0a0a.0a0a to MAC 000b.0b0b.0b0b
[2018 Aug 5 23:14:11.160314302:147309:epmc_process_l3_upd:3605:t] Deleting ip
    172.16.0.20
[2018 Aug 5 23:14:11.160354788:147315:epmc_process_l3_upd:3608:t] Adding ip
    172.16.0.20
```

Note In ACI Release 4.0 and later, the EPMC logs are binary encoded. Starting in ACI Release 4.2, there is a built-in decoder that allows for easy decoding of the log files. You can apply the logic described earlier to the decoded files(s). You can run the following command to view the most recent logs from the iBash shell:

nxos_binlog_decode *<binary logfile>* **>** *<output filename>*

The following is an example:

nxos_binlog_decode binlog_uuid_472_epmc_vdc_1_sub_1_level_3 >
  /tmp/epmc-trace.txt

Enhanced Endpoint Tracker (EPT) App

Being able to check the log files can be extremely helpful, but in critical situations, you need an easier way to identify moves. While the APIC's built-in Endpoint Tracker is helpful, it has some shortcomings:

▨ If the endpoint no longer exists, you can't search and view the history of the endpoint. This makes it difficult to find the root cause.

▨ Endpoint Tracker events are shown only if they are received on the APIC. By default, events from the leaf switches are throttled before being sent to the APIC to avoid exhausting resources. This means you are likely to miss events when using Endpoint Tracker.

In order to resolve these issues and provide a comprehensive endpoint analysis tool, Cisco developed the Enhanced Endpoint Tracker (EPT) app. The EPT app is available at the Cisco DC App Center, at dcappcenter.cisco.com. EPT subscribes to the Endpoint Manager objects on the leafs, so it can receive all events. Furthermore, it maintains its own database so that even if an endpoint no longer exists, historical data can be retrieved and reviewed. Many other features provided with the app are invaluable in identifying unhealthy endpoints:

▨ Fast searching of endpoints based on MAC or IP address

▨ Detailed events per endpoint, including exact location and move history

▨ Identification of off-subnet endpoints

After installing the EPT app, you can search for any endpoint in your ACI fabric, as illustrated in Figure 13-15.

After selecting an endpoint, you are presented with an abundance of information that you can use to determine the health of that endpoint. You first see a summary of the endpoint, including where it exists physically and the VRF instance and EPG it belongs to. From there, you can view the history of the endpoint, check for move events, and even clear endpoints. Move events are especially helpful because the app details the exact "to" and "from" node/interface for which the move is occurring. For example, an IP address could be moving between two MAC addresses and also between two different interfaces or nodes. EPT can quickly highlight this, as shown in Figure 13-16.

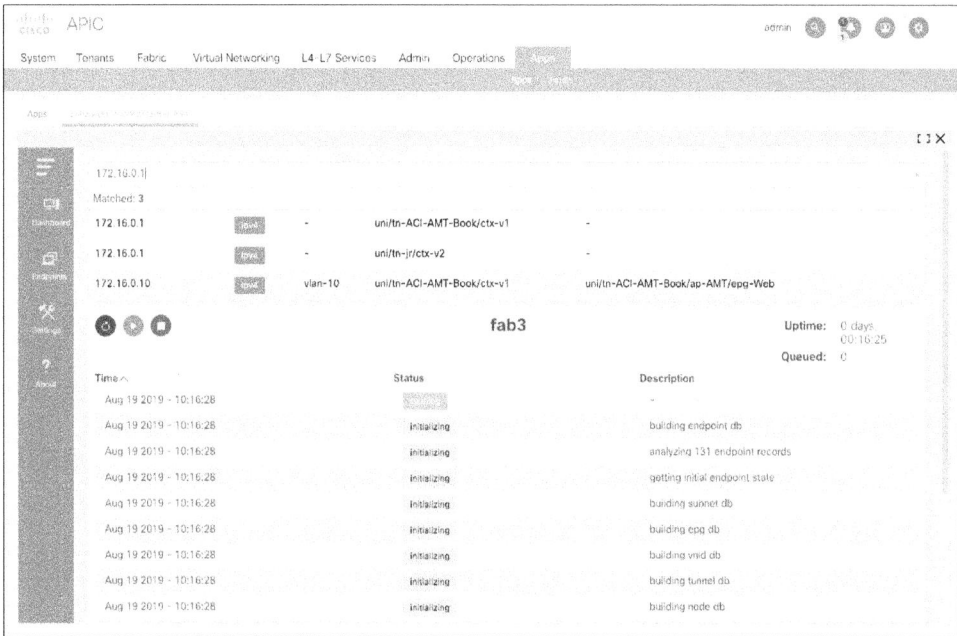

Figure 13-15 *Using EPT to Search for Endpoints*

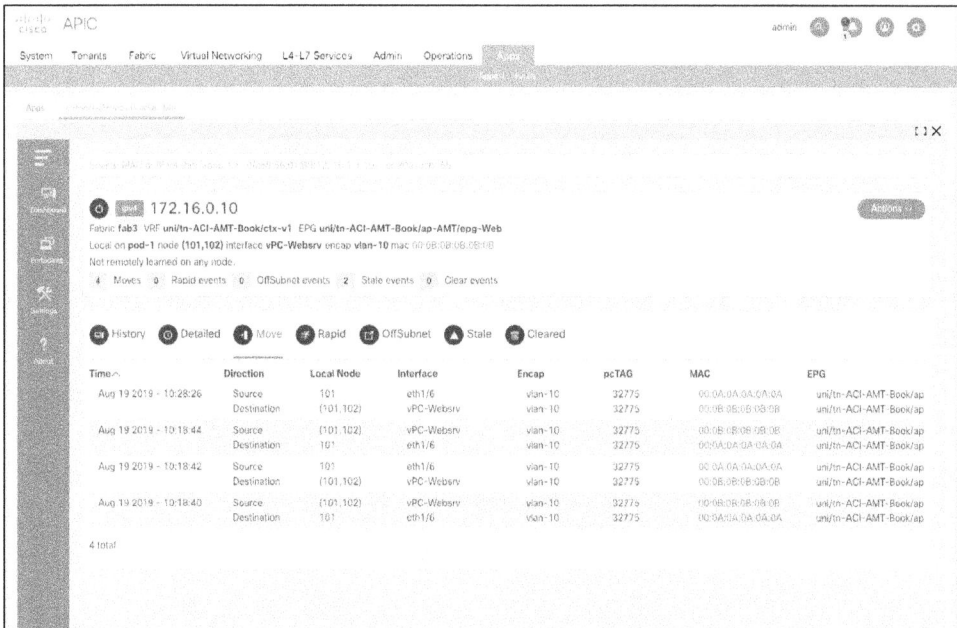

Figure 13-16 *Using Enhanced Endpoint Tracker to Identify Moves*

Rogue Endpoint Detection

In addition to the tools described in the previous sections, the APIC has a feature that can prevent a rapidly moving endpoint from wreaking havoc on the fabric. The feature, called *Rogue Endpoint Detection*, works as follows:

1. If an endpoint (MAC or IP address) moves more than a certain number of times within a detection interval, that endpoint is marked as rogue.

2. When an endpoint is marked as rogue, the endpoint is programmed as static to prevent new local learning about it or updates. In addition, the DL bit is set in the iVXLAN header for any packet sent from this endpoint. This ensures that remote learning is also stopped since the egress leaf will not trigger learning.

3. A fault is raised to alert the administrator.

You configure Rogue Endpoint Detection in the UI under System > System Settings > Endpoint Controls > Rogue EP Control.

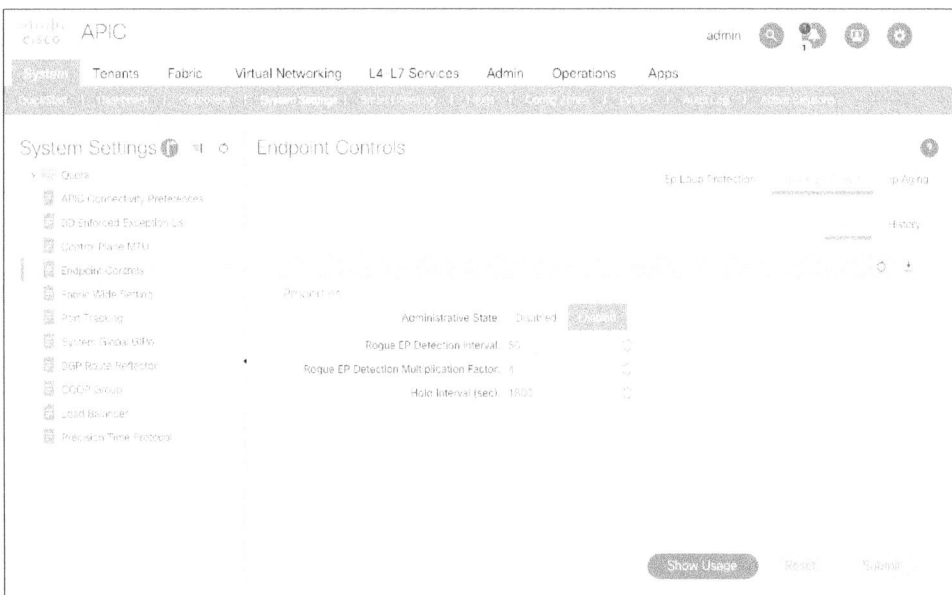

Figure 13-17   *Configuring Rogue Endpoint Detection*

Rogue Endpoint Detection has four configuration options (see Figure 13-17):

- **Administrative State:** Enables or disables the feature globally on the fabric.

- **Rogue EP Detection Interval:** The time period to detect whether an endpoint is rogue.

- **Rogue EP Detection Multiplication Factor:** The number of times an endpoint must move within the detection interval for the endpoint to be marked as rogue.

■ **Hold Interval:** The amount of time, in seconds, before the Rogue flag is removed from the endpoint.

Using the previous example where the EPT provided visibility into the 172.16.0.10 IP address moving between two MAC addresses and switches, the rogue endpoint can also help detect this and block the endpoint from causing further instability. When Rogue Endpoint Detection is enabled, and an endpoint misbehaves, a fault should be raised if the endpoint moved more than the multiplication factor over the detection interval. Figure 13-18 shows an example of a fault that would be raised if an endpoint is marked as rogue.

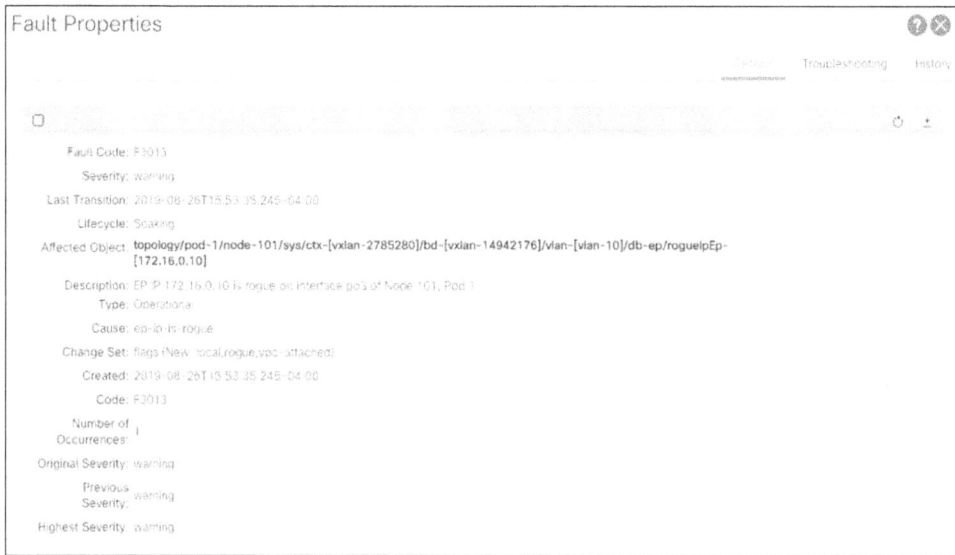

Figure 13-18 *A Fault Is Raised When an Endpoint Is Marked as Rogue*

It's important to note that Rogue Endpoint Detection does not fix the underlying issue related to why the endpoint is moving, but it enables the ACI fabric administrator to protect the fabric from instability, as well as alert the administrator about misconfigured or potentially disruptive devices.

Being able to identify MAC and IP address moves is critical for an ACI administrator. Knowing how to use EPT, how to check the logs for instability, and how to protect the fabric by using Rogue Endpoint Detection will help isolate issues quickly and determine what the potential issue might be.

Troubleshooting Contract-Related Issues

Key Topic

A contract is always configured in a consumer-to-provider relationship. If you were to relate this to a traditional access list, the consumer would be the source, and the provider would be the destination. In addition, contracts in ACI are configured within the realm of a scope and are pushed to the ACI leafs via the APIC as EPGs get deployed. The scope defines the EPGs between which the contract can be applied. You might want a contract to be applied between only EPGs in the same application profile or in the same VRF instance. Or maybe you need a contract to be scoped globally so you can use it between VRF instances and tenants. Regardless of the specifics of the contract, when troubleshooting, it is important to understand how these contracts get pushed to the switch and how the switch uses these contracts when determining if traffic should be forwarded.

As contract relationships are formed, a switch receives programming from the APIC to configure an actrlRule entry. actrlRule represents an ACL or policy that allows traffic from a source EPG to a destination EPG, using a particular filter. In order to best troubleshoot contract-related issues, you need to understand the breakdown of this object. Example 13-29 shows an example of an actrlRule entry.

Example 13-29   *actrlRule Contract Object on APIC*

```
admin@apic1:~> moquery -c actrlRule
scopeId : 2981888
sPcTag : 49154
dPcTag : 16387
fltId : 8
action : permit
actrlCfgFailedBmp :
actrlCfgFailedTs : 00:00:00:00.000
actrlCfgState : 0
childAction :
descr :
direction : uni-dir
dn : topology/pod-1/node-102/sys/actrl/scope-2981888/rule-2981888-s-49154-d-
  16387-f-8
id : 4124
lcOwn : local
markDscp : unspecified
modTs : 2018-08-07T21:09:54.437-04:00
monPolDn : uni/tn-common/monepg-default
name :
nameAlias :
operSt : enabled
operStQual :
prio : fully_qual
qosGrp : unspecified
rn : rule-2981888-s-49154-d-16387-f-8
status :
type : tenant
```

The following important fields determine how a contract will be enforced on an ACI leaf:

- **scopeID:** This is the VRF VXLAN identifier. All contracts are installed on a VRF basis. If contracts are globally scoped, they can provide a shared service between VRF instances, but every VRF instance will have the respective rules installed.

- **sPcTag:** This is the policy control tag (PCTag) of the EPG that is the consumer for the contract.

- **dPcTag:** This is the PCTag of the EPG that is the provider for the contract.

- **fltId:** This is the filter ID. There is a unique ID allocated for each filter.

- **action:** This is what will happen if the traffic matches the rule. Possible settings are permit, deny, and log. (The log setting means the APIC should log packets that meet the rule.)

- **Id:** This is the rule identifier. It is unique for each node in the fabric for which a rule is deployed.

- **operSt:** This the rule that is currently enabled or disabled.

The PCTag for an EPG and the scope ID for a VRF instance are shown directly on the object and can be found by querying the object directly or by viewing the object in the GUI by navigating to any of the following locations (see Figure 13-19 and Figure 13-20):

- Tenants > Tenant > Operational > Resource IDs

- Tenants > Tenant > Application Profile > EPG > Policy

- Tenants > Tenant > Networking > VRF > Policy

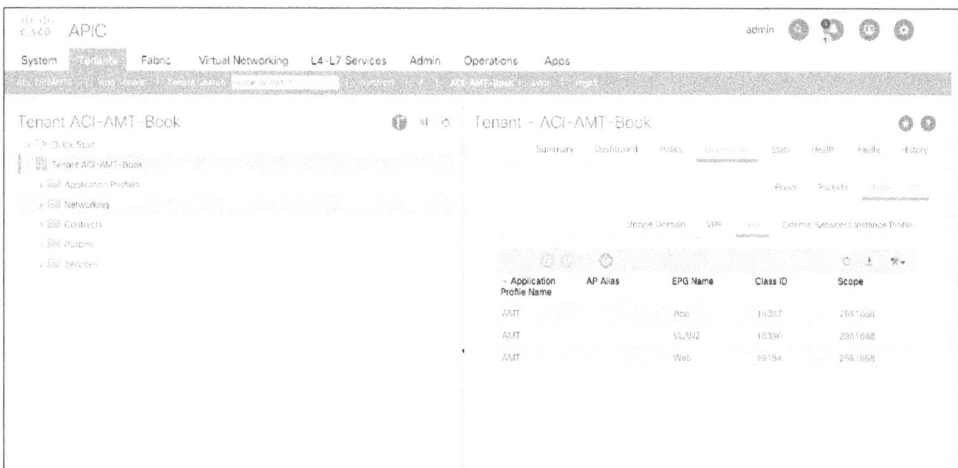

Figure 13-19   *Viewing the PCTag and Scope for Endpoint Groups*

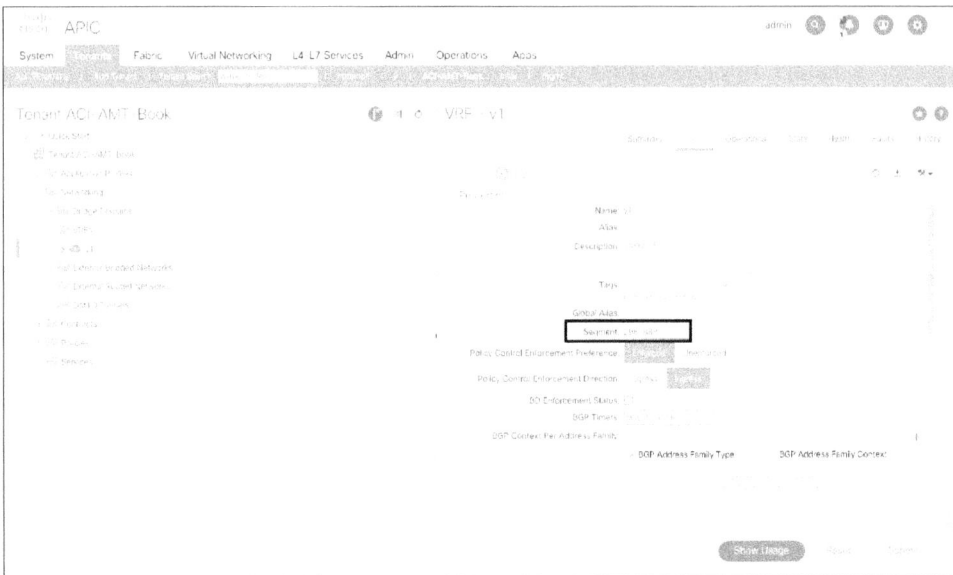

Figure 13-20 *Viewing the Scope ID for a VRF Instance*

When troubleshooting an issue in which you believe contracts are involved, you need to validate that the rules are programmed correctly on the leaf switches. You can check the rules by querying the actrlRule object on the leafs or by running the CLI as shown in Example 13-30.

Example 13-30 *actrlRule Contract Configuration on an ACI Leaf*

```
leaf101# show zoning-rule scope 2981888 src-epg 49154 dst-epg 16387
Rule ID  SrcEPG  DstEPG  FilterID  operSt   Scope   Action      Priority

=======  ======  ======  ========  ======   =====   ======      ========

4124     49154   16387   8         enabled  2981888 log,permit  fully_qual(7)
```

The ACI leaf switches also log stats on a per-rule basis. This is the equivalent of enabling stats per entry for an ACL on an NX-OS device. When you think you are not meeting the correct contract, a useful troubleshooting method is to generate a set number of packets and check the stats, as shown in Example 13-31.

Example 13-31 *actrlRule Stats Information for PCTags 49154 and 16387*

```
leaf101# show system internal policy-mgr stats | grep 49154 | grep 16387
Rule (4121) DN (sys/actrl/scope-2981888/rule-2981888-s-16387-d-49154-f-9) Ingress:
  0, Egress: 0, Pkts: 3000 RevPkts: 0
Rule (4124) DN (sys/actrl/scope-2981888/rule-2981888-s-49154-d-16387-f-8) Ingress:
  0, Egress: 0, Pkts: 3000 RevPkts: 0
```

The stats are read from software, so they are not updated in real time. Allow a few seconds in between sending the packets and running the command to get accurate results.

In order for a contract to be successfully installed in hardware, TCAM resources need to be available. If for any reason the zoning-rule entry is marked as disabled, this means the hardware programming failed when trying to configure the rule. TCAM utilization on a cloud-scale leaf can be validated by executing the command shown in Example 13-32.

Example 13-32   *Viewing Total Policy TCAM Entries on a Cloud-Scale Platform*

```
leaf101# vsh_lc
module-1# show platform internal hal health-stats | grep -A 4 "Policy"
Policy stats:
=============
policy_count  : 63
max_policy_count : 65536
=============--
```

The **max_policy_count** is determined based on the hardware platform that you are using. Refer to the APIC scalability guides at Cisco.com for platform-dependent limits.

The **max_policy_count** numbers are also reflected in the Capacity Dashboard, which shows the total number of policy TCAM entries in relationship to what the platform supports. Be sure to check this dashboard if the rules are disabled. To view the Capacity Dashboard in the APIC GUI, navigate to Operations > Capacity Dashboard, as shown in Figure 13-21.

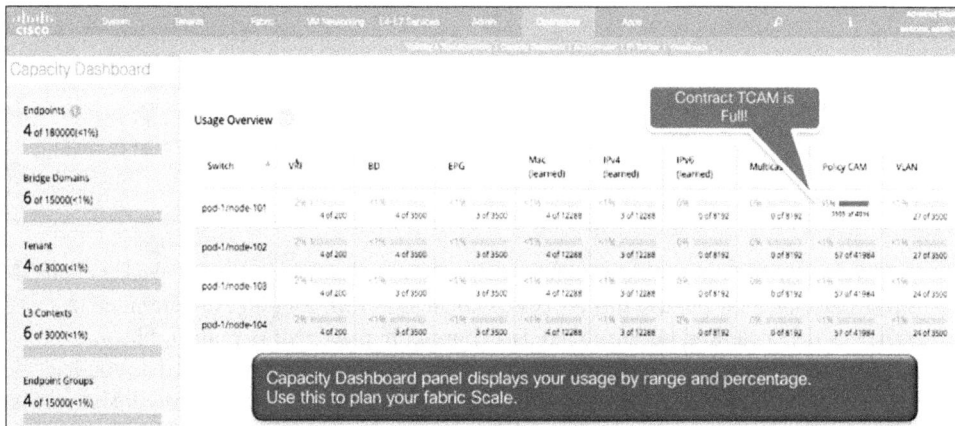

Figure 13-21   *Viewing Total Policy TCAM Entries Using the Capacity Dashboard*

Verifying Policy Deny Drops

The default enforcement mode for a VRF instance is Enforced mode. This means that a contract must exist between two EPGs if the communication is to work. If a valid contract does not exist on the ingress and egress switch in the path of the flow, the packet is dropped because there is always a default deny entry installed for each VRF instance. This default deny entry has the highest priority number, meaning that it will be matched last if there is no other specific policy defined. If the switch cannot match any user-configured contracts, it defaults to meeting the deny rule. If for any reason the switch finds a deny entry, it is logged in software so that it can be viewed locally on the switches and propagated to the APIC.

Users can view flows that have matched a policy deny entry directly on the ACI leaf switches where the devices connect, as demonstrated in Example 13-33. This is very useful when you want to prove that a packet is indeed being dropped due to not having a valid contract configured on the switch. In this example, three different source IP addresses are unable to send ICMP traffic to 172.16.0.20. This is because there is not a valid contract configured on the switch to allow that communication.

Example 13-33   *Viewing Packets That Have Matched a Policy Deny Rule*

```
leaf101# show logging ip access-list internal packet-log deny
[ Wed Aug 8 14:42:14 2018 36248 usecs]: CName: ACI-AMT-Book:v1(VXLAN: 2981888),
  VlanType: FD_VLAN, Vlan-Id: 15, SMac: 0x00505682b662, DMac:0x0022bdf819ff, SIP:
  172.17.0.10, DIP: 172.16.0.20, SPort: 0, DPort: 0, Src Intf: Ethernet1/27, Proto:
  1, PktLen: 98

[ Wed Aug 8 14:42:13 2018 36111 usecs]: CName: ACI-AMT-Book:v1(VXLAN: 2981888),
  VlanType: FD_VLAN, Vlan-Id: 15, SMac: 0x00505682b662, DMac:0x0022bdf819ff, SIP:
  172.17.0.20, DIP: 172.16.0.20, SPort: 0, DPort: 0, Src Intf: Ethernet1/27, Proto:
  1, PktLen: 98

[ Wed Aug 8 14:42:12 2018 36042 usecs]: CName: ACI-AMT-Book:v1(VXLAN: 2981888),
  VlanType: FD_VLAN, Vlan-Id: 15, SMac: 0x00505682b662, DMac:0x0022bdf819ff, SIP:
  172.17.0.30, DIP: 172.16.0.20, SPort: 0, DPort: 0, Src Intf: Ethernet1/27, Proto:
  1, PktLen: 98
```

Alternatively, you can enable a subject within a particular contract to log packets that meet that rule. You can use this process, known as *permit logging*, to determine if traffic is being allowed because there is a contract in place that permits it. In some situations, you might need to troubleshoot why a flow is not being denied as you had expected. Permit logging allows you to validate that a flow is being allowed because it is hitting a particular contract. You can also view this directly on a leaf switch, as shown in Example 13-34.

Example 13-34   *Viewing Packets That Have Matched a Policy Permit Rule*

```
leaf101# show logging ip access-list internal packet-log permit
[ Wed Aug 8 14:52:45 2018 685658 usecs]: CName: ACI-AMT-Book:v1(VXLAN: 2981888),
  VlanType: Unknown, Vlan-Id: 0, SMac: 0x000c0c0c0c0c, DMac:0x000c0c0c0c0c, SIP:
  172.16.0.20, DIP: 172.17.0.11, SPort: 0, DPort: 0, Src Intf: Tunnel15, Proto: 1,
  PktLen: 98


[ Wed Aug 8 14:52:45 2018 685093 usecs]: CName: ACI-AMT-Book:v1(VXLAN: 2981888),
  VlanType: FD_VLAN, Vlan-Id: 15, SMac: 0x00505682b662, DMac:0x0022bdf819ff, SIP:
  172.17..11, DIP: 172.16.100.20, SPort: 0, DPort: 0, Src Intf: Ethernet1/27, Proto:
  1, PktLen: 98
```

You can view all this information globally in the APIC GUI by going to Tenant >
Operational > Flows > L2|L3 Drop or L2|L3 Permit, as demonstrated in Figure 13-22 and
Figure 13-23.

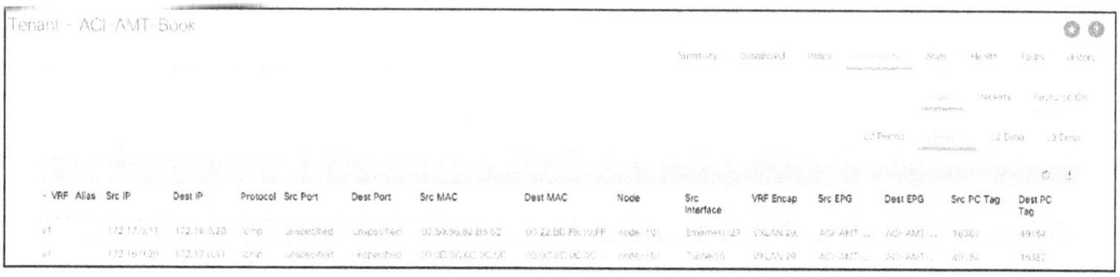

Figure 13-22   *Using the ASIC GUI to View Packets That Have Met a Policy Permit Rule*

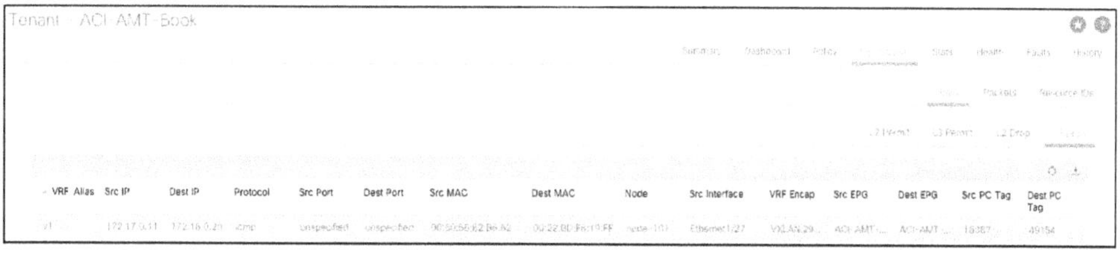

Figure 13-23   *Using the ASIC GUI to View Packets That Have Met a Policy Deny Rule*

Embedded Logic Analyzer Module (ELAM)

As you've seen, being able to identify traffic flow–related issues can be very helpful.
After all, one of the main reasons for purchasing ACI is to have a reliable and optimized
data center network. You've learned how to check for endpoint instability, as well as verify contract drops, but wouldn't it be nice to check at the ASIC level what is happening to
specific packets? Is the ACI switch even receiving the packet? If so, what is it doing with
it? Embedded Logic Analyzer Module (ELAM) was built with exactly this use case in
mind, and TAC engineers use it every day to help isolate traffic flow issues in ACI fabrics

around the globe. Using ELAM, an administrator can set trigger conditions for a single packet and see not only whether the packet was received but also what the forwarding decision is for that packet.

ELAM is built around two basic concepts:

- You need to define what packet parameters to display if a packet is received. This could be inner l2/l3/l4, outer l2/l3/l4, both inner and outer parameters, or something else.

- You need to define a trigger condition. This is what the packet contents should look like, and if received with these contents, you want to show the user what happened.

You might think that ELAM would be straightforward, but due to some of the lower-level complexities of the ASIC, the raw report that is generated if the conditions are met is rather cryptic to read. A lot of the ASIC registers are in hex format, and you need to be very well versed in hex to be able to understand what is happening. For this reason, a Cisco ACI app called ELAM Assistant was created to help demystify some of the ELAM logic and present the administrator with an easy-to-understand, comprehensive analysis. This app is available on the Cisco DC App Center, at dcappcenter.cisco.com. The goal of this section is to demonstrate how the ELAM Assistant app can be instrumental in debugging some packet flow scenarios discussed in this chapter. The topology in Figure 13-24 is used here to highlight how ELAM can be used to capture packets in the fabric.

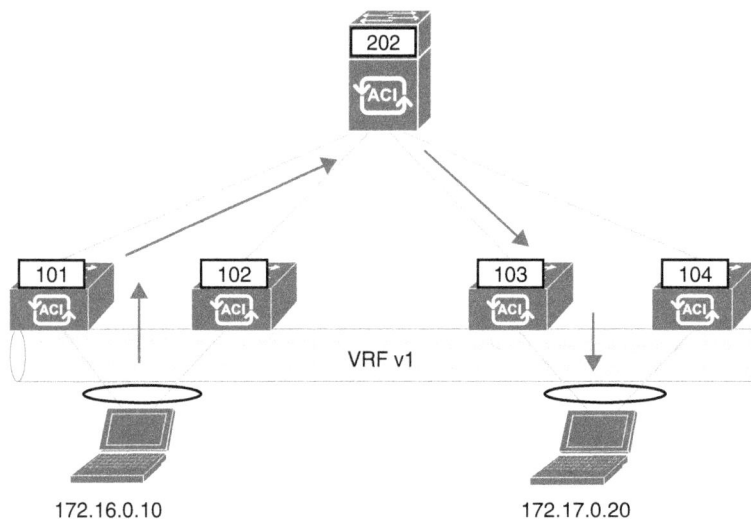

Figure 13-24   *Topology of Web Server Communicating with App Server Using ICMP*

The ELAM Assistant app can help you see what the ACI fabric switches see in regard to packets between a specific source and destination. For example, your server team might tell you that it is having issues reaching the devices using ICMP, a protocol that has been allowed with a contract between the two endpoint groups. This flow is supposed to work, but how can you quickly prove it? Using the ELAM Assistant app, you can add the relevant switches along with the trigger and condition. In this scenario, Leaf 101–104 as well as Spine 202 are added to the ELAM Assistant. Because the packet is expected to be received from the server on Leafs 101 and 102, the direction is set to "from frontport". On the other hand, Leafs 103 and 104 expect this packet to be received from the spine, so the direction is set to "from SPINE". The trigger condition remains the same, defining src ip and dst ip for the two endpoints. Once this is set up, you can click Set to push the ELAM configuration to the defined devices. When all devices are set, you can click Check Trigger to see which devices in the fabric have received this packet, based on the set trigger conditions, as illustrated in Figure 13-25.

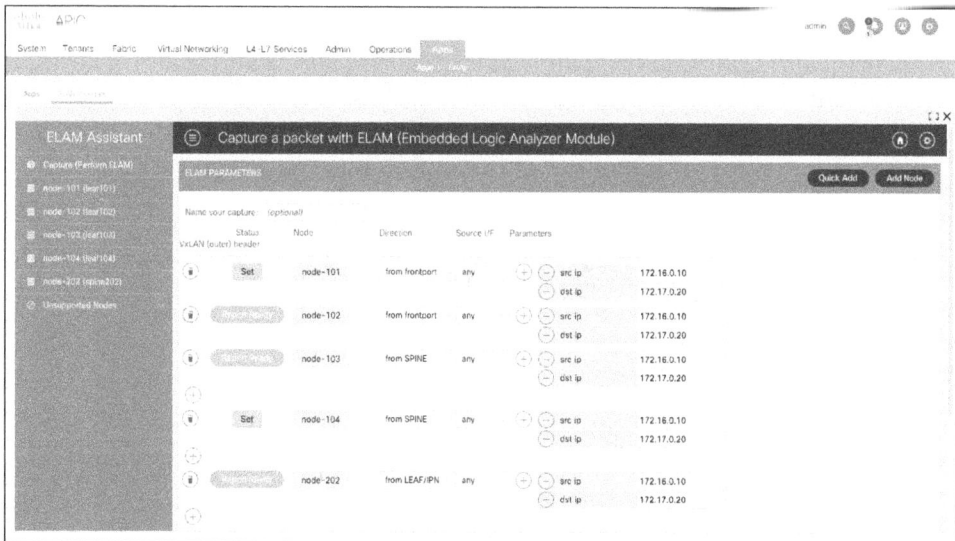

Figure 13-25 *Setting and Checking Triggers Using the ELAM Assistant*

When the ELAM report has been generated, you can click on each node on the left-hand menu to view the report. For example, because the packet was seen on both the expected ingress and egress switches, you can jump directly to the egress leaf to view the report. The report is broken up into two major sections:

■ **Basic Information:** This section shows the packet content, showing the headers, incoming interface, and so on (see Figure 13-26).

■ **Forwarding Result:** This section shows the result or forwarding decision for the packet that the ASIC made (see Figure 13-27).

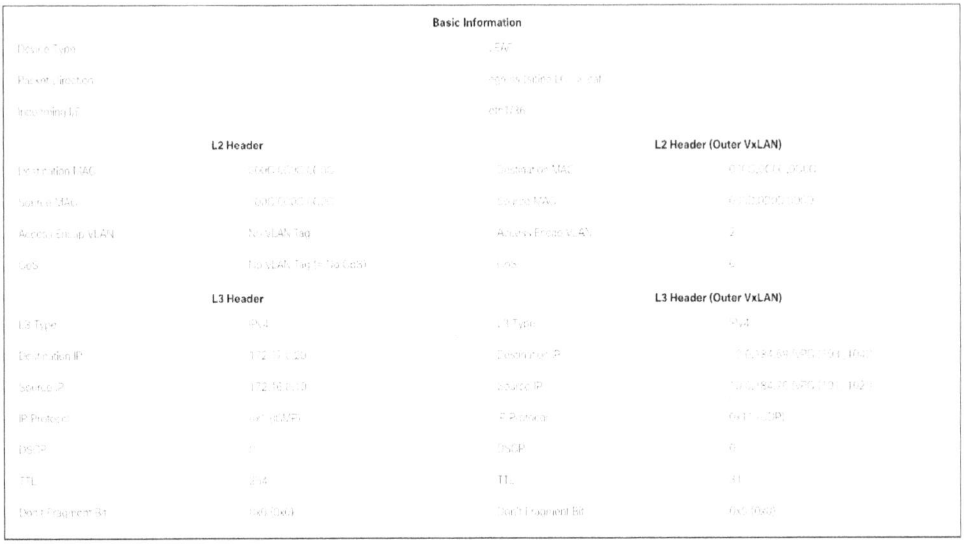

Figure 13-26   *The Basic Information Section of the ELAM Assistant Report*

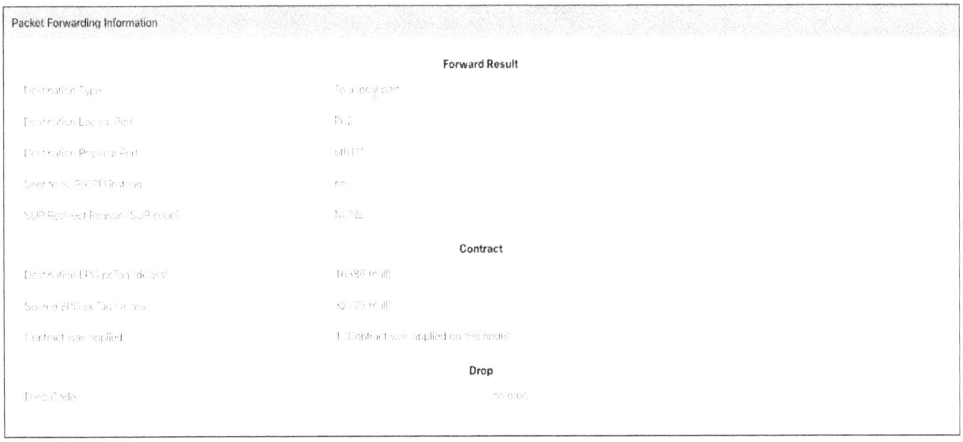

Figure 13-27   *The Forwarding Result Section of the ELAM Assistant Report*

The ELAM report shows an ICMP packet from the source and destination received on Leaf 103. Furthermore, the result is to forward this packet out eth1/1, and the packet is not dropped. The next step would be to set the trigger in the reverse direction to see if the reply packets from 172.17.0.20 destined to 172.16.0.10 are also forwarded correctly in the fabric. If for any reason there is a drop set, the reason should aid in determining why the packet was dropped. Based on this information, necessary configuration changes or isolation steps can be taken to identify and resolve the issue. The ELAM output provides definitive proof about what is happening with the packet.

Summary

As demonstrated in this chapter, ACI offers a powerful and robust set of tools to assist in troubleshooting scenarios. The REST API allows you to send filtered queries to expose issues that might be occurring, and the introduction of a fault and event system alerts you when changes are happening. Furthermore, the switch software exposes many other options for troubleshooting, including the ability to get packet captures, check counters on interfaces and contracts, and dive into logs when endpoints may be moving around. Finally, almost everything that happens on the environment is propagated to the APIC, so it can be viewed graphically and in a single pane of glass.

Review Key Topics

If you are preparing to take the Implementing Cisco Application Centric Infrastructure - Advanced (300-630 DCACIA) exam to attain the Cisco Certified Specialist—ACI Advanced Implementation certification, be sure to review the key topics marked in this chapter as outlined in Table 13-5.

Table 13-5   *Key Topics*

Key Topic Element	Description	Page Number
Section	"How to Verify Physical- and Platform-Related Issues" explains how to validate contract-related issues, which will help when implementing them	737
Section	"Troubleshooting Contract-Related Issues" explains how to validate if packets are being dropped, which helps in understanding packet forwarding.	759

Review Questions

The questions that follow are designed to help you prepare for the Implementing Cisco Application Centric Infrastructure - Advanced (300-630 DCACIA) exam if you are planning on acquiring the Cisco Certified Specialist: ACI Advanced Implementation certification.

1. Which of the following can a user use to interact with the APIC REST API to get relevant data for troubleshooting? (Choose three.)
   a. MOQuery
   b. icurl
   c. APIC UI
   d. Restman
   e. Syslog

2. What initial setup parameters for an APIC may not be unique to each APIC that is being configured? (Choose two.)

  a. TEP address pool

  b. Fabric ID

  c. Controller ID

  d. Pod ID

  e. Number of active controllers

3. What wiring issues could be set on a leaf interface connecting to a controller if there is an APIC cluster misconfiguration? (Choose three.)

  a. ctrlr-uuid-mismatch

  b. pod-mismatch

  c. infra-ip-mismatch

  d. wiring-mismatch

  e. version-mismatch

4. Which are valid drop buckets that packets can be classified in on Cisco ACI leaf switches? (Choose three.)

  a. Buffer drops

  b. CRC drops

  c. Invalid checksum drops

  d. Error drops

  e. Forward drops

5. Which statements are true regarding rogue endpoint detection? (Choose two.)

  a. Rogue endpoint detection only detects MAC moves and not IP moves.

  b. The EP detection interval is not configurable.

  c. When an endpoint is declared rogue, the ACI leaf switch sets the DL bit when forwarding traffic for that endpoint.

  d. A fault is raised when an endpoint is declared rogue.

  e. Rogue endpoint detection fixes the issue on the host that is causing the moves.

6. What attributes are defined on the actrlRule object, which defines a contract rule? (Choose three.)

  a. sPcTag

  b. scopeID

  c. configIssues

  d. fltId

  e. state

7. What does ELAM stand for?

  a. Enhanced Logic ASIC Modifier

  b. Enhanced Logic Analyzer Module

  c. Embedded Logic Analyzer Module

  d. Embedded Logic ASIC Modifier

  e. Embedded Logic ASIC Mask

## Chapter 14

The ACI Visibility & Troubleshooting Tool

This chapter covers the following topics:

- Visibility & Troubleshooting tool overview
- Faults tab
- Drop/Stats tab
- Contracts tab
- Events and Audits tab
- Traceroute tab
- Atomic Counter tab
- Latency tab
- SPAN tab
- Network Insights Resources (NIR) overview

Visibility & Troubleshooting Tool Overview

In Chapter 13, "Troubleshooting Techniques," you learned troubleshooting techniques for a variety of different ACI components. The steps include reviewing relevant faults, audits, and events, as well as contracts and other relevant data. To simplify this process, ACI provides the Visibility & Troubleshooting tool, which automatically compiles data for specific endpoints. The tool is accessible from the Operations tab in the APIC GUI and the NX-OS CLI, and it can be called with the REST API. It is also referred to as the Troubleshooting Wizard (TSW).

To gain quick visibility into traffic flows for two endpoints inside the fabric, a Visibility & Troubleshooting session can be created. ACI supports Visibility & Troubleshooting sessions for both endpoints inside the fabric and endpoints outside ACI. To set up a Visibility & Troubleshooting session using the GUI, follow these simple steps:

Step 1.   Select Operations > Visibility & Troubleshooting tab.

Step 2.   Specify a session name, session type, and targets.

The session is saved and can be viewed again at a later time or accessed by other users. Therefore, when configuring a Visibility & Troubleshooting session, you should use a naming scheme that allows users to understand what endpoints are used during the session. Example 14-1 provides helpful naming schemes.

Example 14-1   *Naming Schemes*

```
Ep172.16.0.10toEp172.17.0.20
    TN-Web-EPG-Server-To-EPG-App-packetLoss
    ExternalUser-to-AD-Authentication_Issues
```

When defining the session type, define the source as the consumer of the service and the destination as the provider of the service. If the destination is in ACI but in a different VRF instance and reachable as through an external routed network, consider the endpoint to be an external IP address in the session type. In this case, two Visibility & Troubleshooting sessions will have to be used: one for the endpoint to the external IP address and one for the external IP address to the endpoint to track communication in both VRF instances and across the relevant leaf switches. When investigating an issue that happened in the past, a custom time window can be defined to limit the faults, events, audits, and statistics to be displayed for only the window specified. If the source or destination is an endpoint within the fabric, it has to be learned, and if the source or destination is external to the fabric, a route has to be present at the time of the configuration of the session.

After you launch the Visibility & Troubleshooting session, you see a topology that reflects how these endpoints connect and which relevant switches and links are used in the fabric to provide connectivity. The Visibility & Troubleshooting tool has a number of tabs: Faults (default view), Drops/Stats, Contracts, Events and Audits, Traceroute, Atomic Counter, Latency, and SPAN. This chapter describes the capabilities of all these tabs and how to use them.

Faults Tab

Figure 14-1 shows the Visibility & Troubleshooting tool.

A Visibility & Troubleshooting session opens to the Faults tab. This tab shows the physical topology interconnecting the endpoints and collects all active faults on the switches as well as fault records. A leaf or spine that has an active fault has an icon next to it, indicating whether the fault is critical, major, minor, or informational.

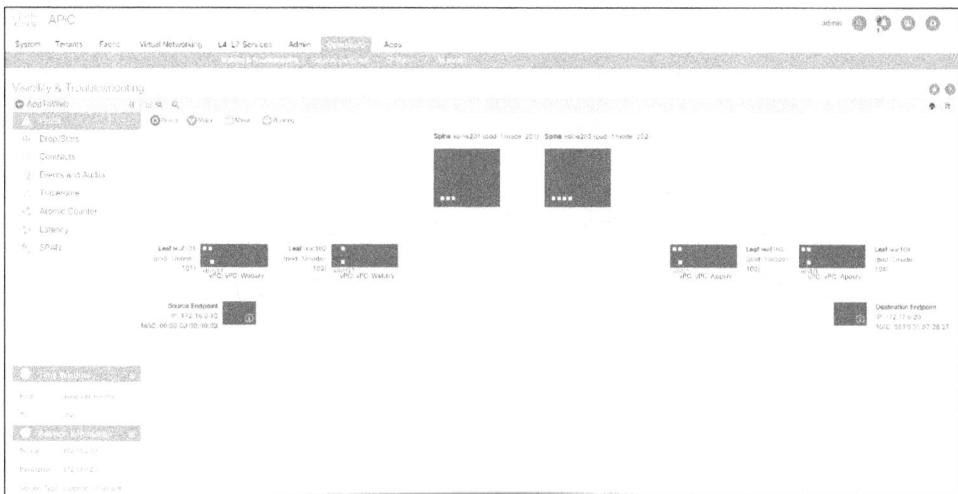

Figure 14-1   *Endpoint to Endpoint Visibility & Troubleshooting Session*

In Figure 14-2, you can see that Leaf 101's uplink to the spine was disconnected. By clicking on node 101 and navigating to the Records tab, you can see the life cycle of Fault 1394, which provides insight into when the interface went down and, if it came back up, at what time the interface transitioned again.

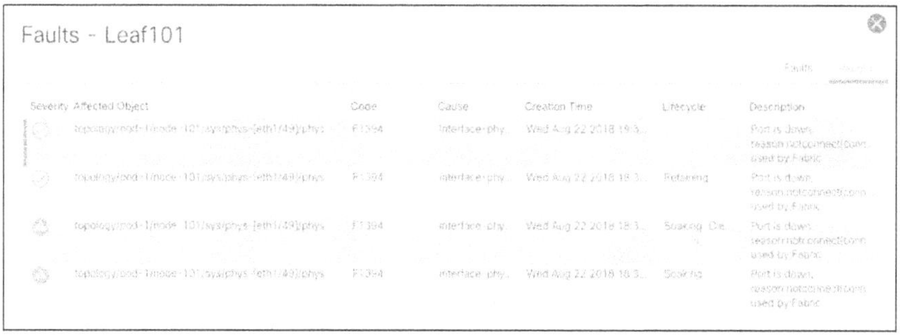

Figure 14-2   *Link Failure in the Visibility & Troubleshooting Tool*

Drop/Stats Tab

Drop stats counters can be misleading on leaf and spine switches because they do not indicate which packet triggered the ASIC to increment a specific drop reason. Chapter 13 discussed the four primary reasons: buffer drops, error drops, forward drops, and load balancer drops. The Drops/Stats tab collects traffic statistics for interfaces involved in connecting the source and destination endpoints, and a network administrator needs to review the drops and determine if they are relevant. The sections that follow describe the most common reasons drop counters might be incrementing and whether these drops should be investigated further.

Ingress/Egress Buffer Drop Packets

Buffer drops are indicative of application issues, slow transfer speeds, or what might seem like latency problems to application owners or users. If buffer drops are seen on the front panel port (facing the server), you should consider adding additional links for the congested device. Also pay close attention to the rate of output of multicast and broadcast packets because those can take up unnecessary bandwidth or be symptomatic of larger problems in the Layer 2 domain (for example, bridging loops, misconfigured endpoints). Starting in ACI Release 4.0, it is possible to see drops on a per-QoS-class basis by using the command **show queuing interface Ethernet X/Y**. If the default class is incrementing, consider using a non-default QoS class on the endpoint group that is experiencing performance issues.

Ingress Error Drop Packets Periodic

Ingress error drop packets increment for FCS errors on the physical port. These typically indicate Layer 1 problems but can be caused by cut-through switching in the fabric. If these errors are incrementing on the uplinks, there is a possibility that they are stomped. Stomping is a process used in cut-through switching to indicate that a packet was corrupted on a different interface but still forwarded into the fabric. You can use the command **vsh_lc -c "show platform internal counters port 24" | egrep "CRC|FCS"**, as shown in Example 14-2, to see if a packet was corrupted on the local link or on a previous leaf or spine.

Example 14-2   *FCS Errors Ingressing on Leaf*

```
Leaf101# vsh_lc -c "show platform internal counters port 24" | egrep "CRC|FCS"
                RX_FCS_ERR              14
                RX_CRCERR                0
```

RX_FCS_ERR increments if the FCS was incorrect on the local link. RX_CRCERR increments if the CRC is the inverse of the FCS; this means a previous bridge along the path stomped this frame, and it was forwarded through the fabric due to cut-through switching.

Storm Control

Storm control is a feature that can be configured on access ports, port channels, and virtual port channels (VPCs). The idea is to limit the amount of traffic that will be flooded in the bridge domain ingressing the specific interface. If the Visibility & Troubleshooting tool detects drops, it reports them based on total bytes dropped for broadcast, unknown unicast, or multicast, as shown in Example 14-3.

Example 14-3 *Storm Control Drops on a Leaf Interface*

```
Leaf101# show interface ethernet 1/24 | grep -A 8 RX
  RX
    738 unicast packets  109 multicast packets  0 broadcast packets
    847 input packets  86815 bytes
    0 jumbo packets  4346 storm suppression bytes
    0 runts  0 giants  0 CRC  0 no buffer
    0 input error  0 short frame  0 overrun  0 underrun  0 ignored
    0 watchdog  0 bad etype drop  0 bad proto drop  0 if down drop
    0 input with dribble  0 input discard 0 input total drop
    0 Rx pause
```

To understand if the flooded traffic is unicast, multicast, or broadcast, you can look at the rmonIfStorm object by navigating the MIT or using **moquery**, as shown in Example 14-4.

Example 14-4 *Storm Control Drop Stats per Class*

```
Leaf101# cat /mit/sys/phys-\[eth1--5\]/dbgIfStorm/summary
# Interface Storm Drop Counters
bcDropBytes  : 0
childAction  :
clearTs      : 2018-08-07T11:40:26.000+00:00
dn           : sys/phys-[eth1/5]/dbgIfStorm
dropBytes    : 0
mcDropBytes  : 0
modTs        : never
rn           : dbgIfStorm
status       :
uucDropBytes : 4346
```

Excessive storm control drops could indicate a bridging loop downstream from the interface that is causing additional flooded traffic. A SPAN session should be used to determine what traffic is being sent into the specific interface and why the ACI leaf is treating it as flooded traffic.

Ingress Forward Drop Packets

The ingress forward drop packets count increments if the forwarding decision of the ASIC is to drop the packets, typically due to contract drops or a data plane policer being configured via the fabric access policies. In Example 14-5 you can see that a data plane policer is enabled on Ethernet 1/24 with the command **show dpp policy**.

Example 14-5 *DPP Policy*

```
Leaf101# show dpp policy
Data Plane Policers


Policer Name    : dppPolicer
Interface       : eth1/24
Direction       : ingress
Layer           : Layer2
Oper State      : enabled
Mode            : bit
Type            : 1R2C
Rate            : 0
Burst           : 2 giga
SharingMode     : dedicated
Conform action  : transmit
Violate action  : drop
```

Drop statistics are easily tracked via the dppIngrDrop5min object, and the cumulative counters can be used to see if the data plane policer is dropping traffic. Because this information is exposed via the API, the network operations team can easily build tools to automatically detect abnormalities or packet drops. The leaf CLI can also be used to query the API using the **moquery** tool, as demonstrated in Example 14-6.

Example 14-6 *Data Plane Policer Drops*

```
Leaf101# moquery -c dppIngrDrop5min | grep Cum
bytesCum        : 21564689
pktsCum         : 0
```

Another common reason forward drops increment has to do with packets that must be processed by the CPU. Examples of such packets are ARP requests, LLDP PDUs, CDP PDUs, and packets from other protocols running on the interface (which is platform dependent and can be different on different hardware versions).

Ingress Load Balancer Drop Packets

The load balancer drop counter typically increments on uplink interfaces when flooded traffic is received on a bridge domain GIPo (with a multicast address assigned to a bridge domain) with a VXLAN ID (VNID) that does not exist on the switch. An example is traffic flooded to the multicast group of the bridge domain but with the VXLAN ID of the EPG. This traffic can include STP BDPUs and certain protocol control messages. If the bridge domain is configured for flooding in the EPG, all flooded traffic will be sent with the VNID of the EPG instead of the VNID of the bridge domain. A bridge domain having multiple EPGs mapped to it can trigger load balancer drops as well. These counters are expected to increment during normal operations of the fabric and do not indicate problems.

Contract Drops Tab

Packets that are not allowed by a contract between two EPGs are logged in the ACI fabric by default. Logging this information on each leaf switch allows a network administrator to see which traffic the leaf switches are discarding. To see if two endpoints are impacted by contract drops, navigate to the Contract Drops tab, shown in Figure 14-3. You can see that packets are discarded between the source and destination defined in the Visibility & Troubleshooting tool, and you can see which Layer 4 protocol and source and destination are dropped by the leaf.

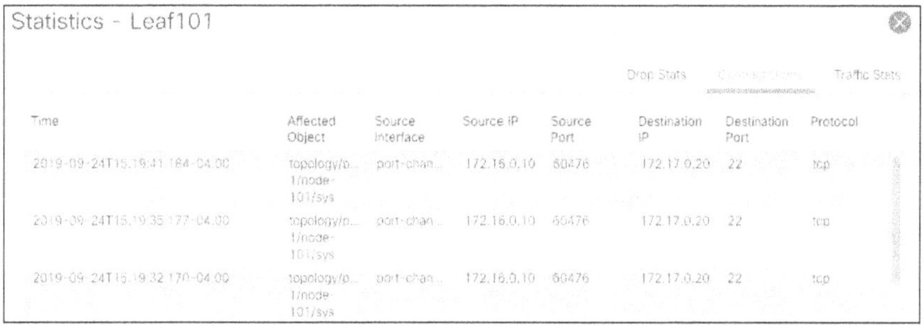

Figure 14-3 *Contract Drops*

Contracts

By default, endpoints in ACI fabric can communicate only if contracts exist. In a complex environment, simply viewing provided or consumed contracts doesn't provide the user information on what filters are programmed between the EPGs or which protocols and ports are allowed in a filter. The Visibility & Troubleshooting tool presents this information, along with traffic statistics on a per-filter basis. With such information, you can easily verify whether, for example, Remote Desktop is allowed via port 3389 or whether the source is sending traffic toward the web service. As Figure 14-4 shows, with per-filter statistics from the Visibility & Troubleshooting tool, you can easily find such information.

If a VRF instance is in Unenforced mode, endpoints within that VRF instance can communicate without contracts.

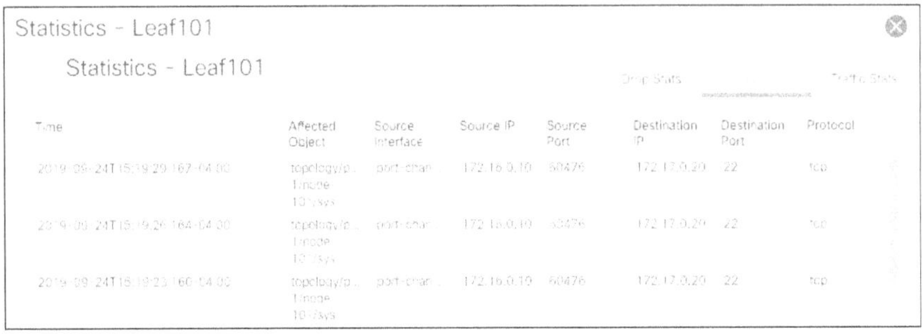

Figure 14-4   *Contract Tab*

The filters are broken down into two separate views. The first view shows what ports are allowed from the source to the destination. The protocol, source ports, and destination ports are defined in the contract between the consumer and provider. The second view, Destination Endpoint to Source Endpoint, shows what port combinations are allowed in the reverse direction. Filters created by bidirectional contracts are noted with the *(rev)* flag, which indicates that they are allowing the reverse direction. The counters refresh automatically every 60 seconds.

By default, two rules always exist in a VRF instance with policy enforcement enabled. The first rule is the Context Implicit rule, which has a Deny, Log action for Filter Implicit. Filter Implicit matches all traffic, much like a contract in which the EtherType is set to unspecified. This rule is used to deny any traffic that doesn't have a contract to permit the traffic between the two endpoints. You can see packets that are denied due to contract violations in the Contract Drops subtab of the Drop/Stats tab.

The second default rule is the BD Allow rule. This contract is used to allow flooded traffic from any endpoint within a BD to all other endpoints. It also uses the Filter Implicit.

Rules that include *any to any, any to EPG,* or *EPG to any* are filters that are pushed due to vzAny being used. vzAny is the name of the object used when contracts are provided or consumed on the VRF level. Using vzAny is a simple way to represent any EPG within a VRF instance as the provider or consumer of a specific contract.

Contract Considerations

Figure 14-5 shows a Visibility & Troubleshooting session between two endpoints in two different EPGs. When you view the Contracts tab, the number of packets you see on the filters is far greater than the number of packets counted via the atomic counter policy discussed later in this chapter. This is because the TCAM entry in hardware counts packets for only source EPG to destination EPG and not for specific endpoints within an EPG. This means that if multiple endpoints exist within an EPG, and they are also actively communicating with other endpoints, the aggregate packet count is presented on the Contracts tab.

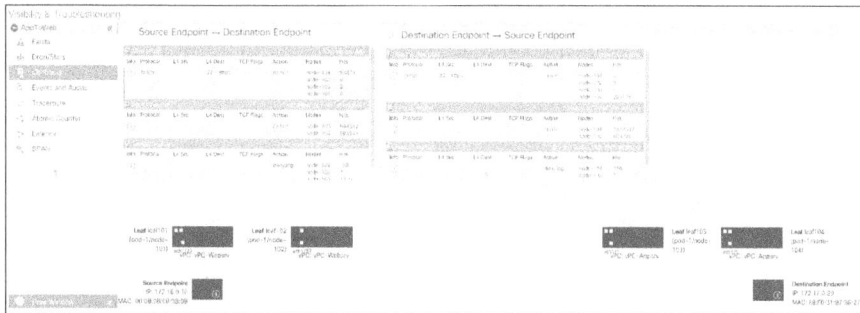

Figure 14-5   *Contract Hits for Two EPGs*

There is another consideration when troubleshooting a flow with an external IP address. If the flow is between a compute leaf and a dedicated border leaf, the contract rules (that is zoning rules) are not pushed to the border leaf if the VRF is in the Ingress Enforcement mode. This means the border leaf cannot collect filter statistics on a per-contract basis, and the user has to rely on statistics from the compute leaf. Figure 14-6 shows an external endpoint communicating through border leafs 101 and 102; the contract stats for those leafs show no hits even though the compute leafs do.

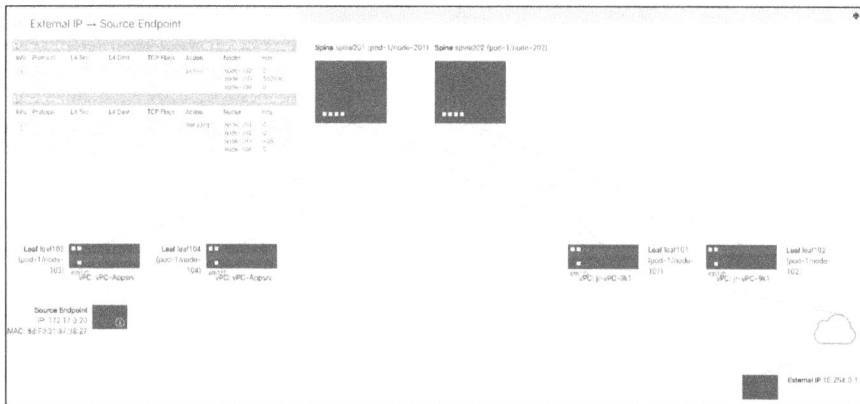

Figure 14-6   *Contract Stats from Two Leafs*

Events and Audits Tab

Like the Faults tab, the Events and Audits tab presents events related to the endpoint, endpoint group, bridge domain, and interfaces used for the traffic flow. In Figure 14-7, you can see transition information by clicking on the endpoint. In this example, you can see that the endpoint detached at time 08:58:05 and attached right afterward. By clicking on the switch to which the endpoint connects (Leaf 101), you can see that an informational event was raised for *excessive-stp-tcn-flush* (see Figure 14-8). Even though ACI does not participate in any version of the Spanning Tree Protocol, the leaf switch still processes BPDUs and looks for whether the TCN flag is set. If TCN is set, ACI flushes all endpoints learned in the encapsulation and relearns them based on traffic patterns that occur afterward.

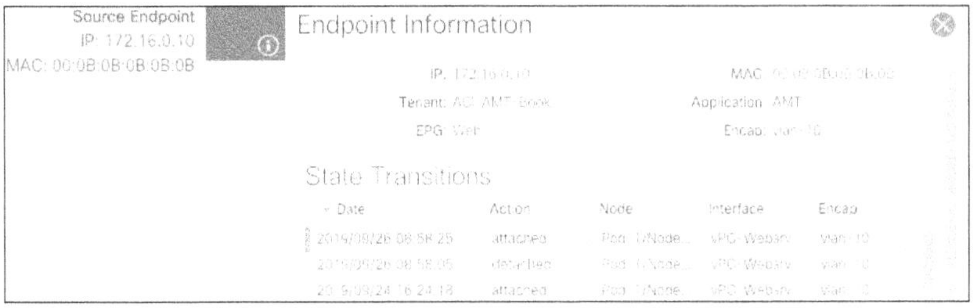

Figure 14-7   *Endpoint State Transitions*

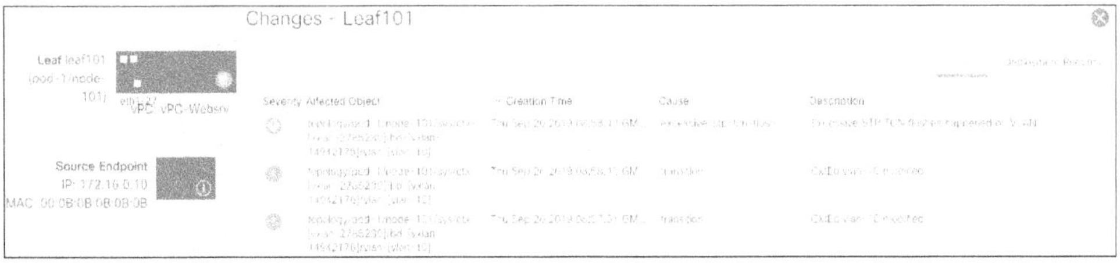

Figure 14-8   *TCN Flush Event on a Leaf*

The Deployment Record subtab shows when a VLAN was programmed. If the endpoint is part of a VMM-enabled EPG and configured for on-demand resolution immediacy, this subtab shows whether the endpoint recently migrated to a new physical interface or whether a configuration for the static path was recently modified. The Visibility & Troubleshooting tool can help you understand what events occurred during a given time to guide troubleshooting.

Traceroute Tab

Today's fabrics pose significant challenges when it comes to network administrators verifying that their fabric is forwarding packets as expected. To simplify this process, ACI provides the iTraceroute tool. iTraceroute can be used to verify forwarding through the fabric for endpoints inside the fabric or even external destinations. iTraceroute works by utilizing the leaf or leaf pair to which the source connects to craft a packet that has the source IP address and destination IP address of the endpoints specified and the protocol chosen by the user. iTraceroute supports ICMP, UDP, and TCP. When using UDP or TCP as the Layer 4 protocol, a source or range of source ports can be specified, as can a destination port or port range. The leaf ASIC decides how to forward this packet as if the source host sent it. This results in the same ECMP hash across the fabric as for traffic sent by the host. The key difference is that the packet is sent into the fabric with a CoS value of 6. All fabric switches use CoS 6 in the outer Layer 2 header as a reserved class for iTraceroute and have an iTraceroute TCAM rule that copies the packet to the CPU while still forwarding it along the regular forwarding pipeline. The spine or leaf that copied the packet to the CPU transmits iTraceroute control plane packets back to the originating leaf with the ingress interface and specific source and destination Layer 4 port information. This is also called an internal traceroute, and it appears as Path Group 0 in the Endpoint to Endpoint Traceroute policy on the Tenant tab. Path Group 1 is considered an external traceroute, and it sends a more traditional traceroute packet, where the TTL of the IP packet is set to 1 and continues to increment up to 31. Because the switch is spoofing the IP address of the source host, a special TCAM rule is created to redirect all data plane traffic (not CoS 6 specific) that matches the traceroute parameters to the CPU. This means that for a short duration, user traffic utilizing the same five tuples of the traceroute session is redirected to the switch CPU for processing.

In the Visibility & Troubleshooting tool, an iTraceroute session can easily be initiated between the source and destination of the session by specifying the protocol to use and a destination port.

After you run an iTraceroute session, the topology diagram shows the path of the packet through the fabric as well as the interface on the leaf switch out of which the packet was forwarded (see Figure 14-9). If the external path fails, you can verify that contracts are configured between the EPGs or captured on the destination host to see if a firewall is dropping the packets.

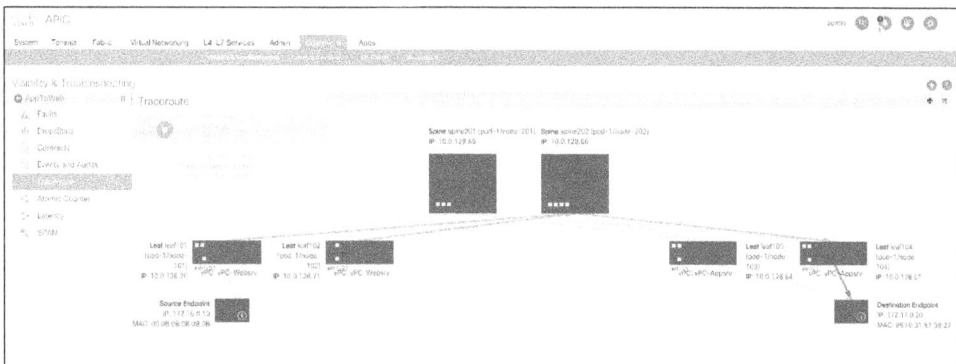

Figure 14-9   *iTraceroute Path Between Two Endpoints*

Note   Each leaf that the source is connected to sends an iTraceroute packet to map the path. This is why the diagram in Figure 14-9 shows Leafs 101 and 102 when going from the source to the destination.

If you need more information, or if you want to understand the exact interface on the spine that the packet took, you can view the Traceroute policy on the Tenant tab. The Visibility & Troubleshooting tool automatically creates a Traceroute policy (under Troubleshooting Policies on the Tenant tab) with the same name as the Visibility &

Troubleshooting session and concatenated with _src_dst or _dst_src. When viewing these sessions, go to the operational tab of the policy, click on the Source Endpoint subtab, and expand the different path groups, as shown in Figure 14-10. Path Group 0 has a Path setting for each uplink that provides a connection to the destination. Path Group 1 shows the routed hops toward the destination. The first IP address shown should always be the bridge domain or EPG-defined gateway IP address.

Figure 14-10   *iTraceroute Session in the Tenant Tab*

Atomic Counter Tab

To help rule out loss within the fabric, you can use an Atomic Counter policy to track packets as they exit the fabric-facing ports on the ingress leaf and traverse the spines to the egress leaf. Using atomic counters is similar to using an access list in standalone NX-OS to count packets, as shown in Example 14-7.

Example 14-7   *Configuration Example for a Traditional NX-OS IP Access List to Count Packets*

```
Nexus7000# show run aclmgr

!Command: show running-config aclmgr
!Time: Thu Aug 16 02:32:55 2018

version 8.1(1)
ip access-list countPackets
  statistics per-entry
  10 permit ip 172.16.0.10/32 172.17.0.20/32
  15 permit ip 172.17.0.20/32 172.16.0.10/32
  20 permit ip any any

Nexus7000# show ip access-lists countPackets

IP access list countPackets
      statistics per-entry
      10 permit ip 172.16.0.10/32 172.17.0.20/32 [match=8]
      15 permit ip 172.17.0.20/32 172.16.0.10/32 [match=9]
      20 permit ip any any [match=18]
```

When you apply countPackets on a switch port or routed port, the ASIC on a standalone Nexus switch counts packets for each entry in the access list, and you can see if a specific packet flow is reaching a port. The shortcoming of this method is that in a complex topology, you will never be able to see if packet loss is occurring because there will always be a time delta between when the command is executed on the source switch and on the destination switch. Figure 14-11 shows two endpoints, EP1 and EP2, that continuously perform data transfers with each other. After you check the access list on Switch 1, you see six packets. If you check Switch 2 shortly afterward, you might see a different number, such as eight packets. At this point, it could be that EP1 transmitted only two more frames, or perhaps it transmitted three or more frames, but some were lost in transit.

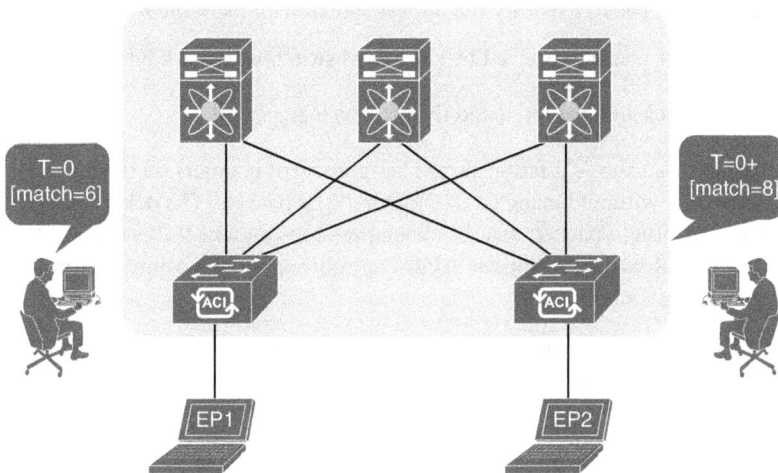

Figure 14-11   *Lack of Atomic Counters*

If a ticket is opened with you, how can you easily confirm that your access switch and core switches are not dropping any packets over a period of minutes, days, hours, or even longer? The ACI fabric can easily provide an answer, thanks to the atomic counters. Atomic counters use the APIC controller to coordinate the marking and counting of packets, and they configure a special TCAM bit on the leaf switches to allow for two different banks of counters. The mark bit (bit 56 in the iVXLAN header) can be set to either 0 or 1, allowing the switches to count packets in either one of the two banks. This allows the fabric to use one bank for active traffic, while allowing all in-flight packets to arrive at their destination before the counters are collected in the currently unused bank. The process works as follows:

Step 1.   The user determines a filter for the traffic of interest.

   a. The APIC configures one TCAM entry for bit 0 and one TCAM entry for bit 1 on the leaf switches to which the endpoints connect.

   b. The APIC notifies all switches to transmit with the mark bit set to 0 for all traffic.

Step 2.   The APIC notifies the switches to clear statistics for the TCAM entry for mark bit 1.

Step 3.   After a defined waiting period, the APIC notifies all switches to start transmitting with the mark bit set to 1.

Step 4.   Statistics for mark bit 0 are cleared.

Step 5.   After 30 seconds, the APIC notifies all switches to use mark bit 0 again.

Step 6.   After a defined waiting period (less than 30 seconds), the APIC collects the following statistics:

- Number of packets sent by the ingress switch with mark bit 1 set
- Number of packets received by the egress switch with mark bit 1 set

Step 7.   Statistics are cleared for bit 1, and the process is repeated.

This technique ensures that the ACI fabric always has consistent counters on the ingress switch and egress switch without having to consider in-flight packets. The delay at step 6 is great enough for all in-flight packets sent by the ingress top-of-rack (ToR) switch to be counted at the egress ToR switch, giving the APIC controller an atomic count of all transmitted data by the user-defined filter.

Atomic counter policies can be set up easily in the Visibility & Troubleshooting tool. Because the fabric has to get in sync with the atomic counters, steps 1 through 7 can cause up to a 90-second delay before accurate statistics can be presented to the user. Figure 14-12 shows the Atomic Counter tab of the Visibility & Troubleshooting tool with the direction of traffic. In this view, Tx counters are what the leaf sent, and Rx counters are what the leaf received. If the spine was dropping packets, the Drop column value would increase. In some cases, such as when traffic is sent to the spine proxy, the atomic counters are not reliable. It is therefore recommended to use on-demand atomic counters for two specific endpoints and not use ongoing atomic counters to identify packet drops. Starting in ACI Release 4.2, flow telemetry can provide even more insights into what packets are being dropped.

Note   You can access the Atomic Counter policy from the Tenant Troubleshooting policies as well.

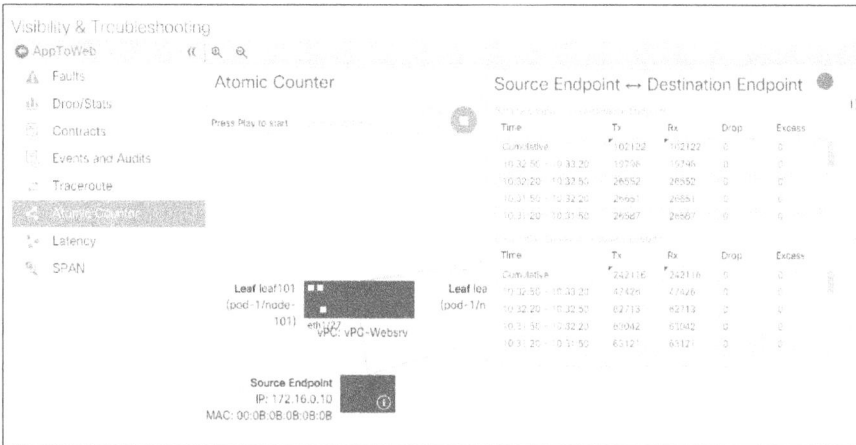

Figure 14-12 *Atomic Counter Tab in the Visibility & Troubleshooting Tool*

Latency Tab

The ACI fabric supports Precision Time Protocol (PTP) without an external master clock in a single-pod deployment. A spine is chosen as the master clock with which all other leafs synchronize. Packets are then tagged with a TTAG header as they traverse the fabric. This allows the receiving switch to measure latency for received packets before it strips the TTAG header off and forwards the data frame to the host.

In a Visibility & Troubleshooting session, latency statistics can be collected, and the cumulative latency statistics as well as the latency statistics over the past 30 seconds can be viewed, as in Figure 14-13. Latency statistics are supported only on switches with cloud-scale ASICs and not on first-generation ACI leaf and spine switches.

Note To enable PTP, go to System > System Setting > Precision Time Protocol.

Figure 14-13 *Latency Statistics from the Visibility & Troubleshooting Tool*

SPAN Tab

The Visibility & Troubleshooting tool can help you isolate connectivity issues with SPAN sessions. This tool makes it easy to configure a number of different types of sessions and to use the topology map to select which interfaces to analyze. All SPAN sessions rely on ERSPAN, so it is important to understand how the source session is used. Figure 14-14 shows the required parameters.

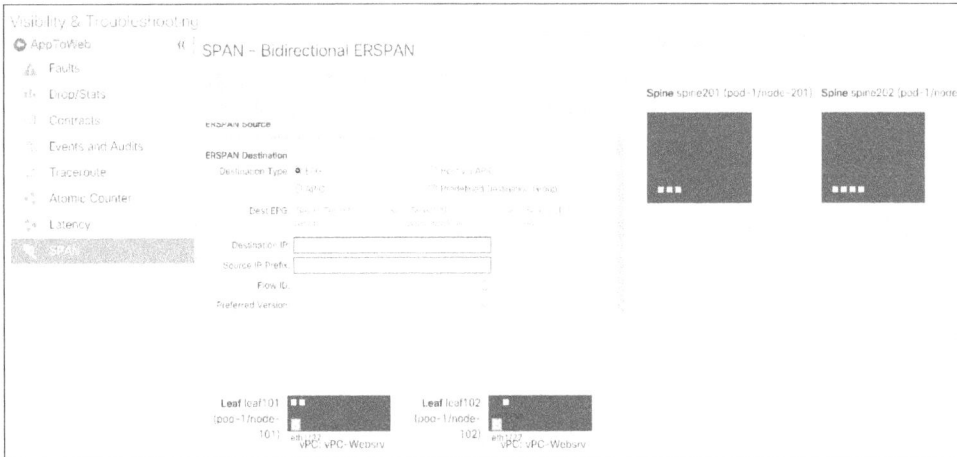

Figure 14-14   *Parameters Needed for SPAN*

An important parameter to understand is the source IP prefix, which provides the fabric a range of source IP addresses to use across the leafs. When configuring a SPAN session on a leaf, the APIC converts the node ID of the leaf to hexadecimal and inserts it as the least significant bits of the source IP prefix configured. To see how this works, let's use 10.0.0.0/8 as the source IP prefix. The hexadecimal value would be 0x0a000000. If the node ID is 101, or 0x65, the source IP address for node 101 is 0x0a000065, or 10.0.0.101, so it is easy to identify where the analyzed ERSPAN packet came from. A second leaf might have a node ID of 300, or 0x12c. This would make the source ERSPAN IP address 10.0.1.44. The ERSPAN flow ID should be a unique value to help identify the mirrored traffic on the destination device if multiple different sessions are coming from the same source IP address. The version of ERSPAN should be set to Version 2, if supported. The first-generation Nexus switches do not support Version 2, but all cloud-scale ASICs support Version 2. The benefit of Version 2 is that the packets are sequenced to simplify the process of following the packet flow in packet capture analyzer software.

For the destination, four types of sessions exist:

- **EPG:** The EPG session is used when the desired destination is a learned endpoint inside the ACI fabric. You need to define the tenant the EPG is in, the application profile the EPG is a part of, and the EPG itself. You can then use the APIC to configure a fabric access SPAN session under Fabric > Access Policies > Policies >

Troubleshooting > SPAN with the correct VRF instance on the leaf switch to use when sending traffic to the destination device.

- **Host via APIC:** This feature uses the APIC as a router to reach the destination. One of the limitations of ERSPAN in ACI is that the destination has to be a learned endpoint inside the fabric. With this feature, the leaf switch sends the traffic to the APIC, and the APIC uses the routing table provided by the OOB or in-band network. For this type of session to work, in-band management needs to be configured. To protect the APIC from excessive inbound traffic, a hardware policer is configured on the leaf facing the APIC to limit the ERSPAN traffic to 10,000 pps.

- **APIC:** This feature works in a similar manner to Host via APIC, but the traffic is captured by the APIC and is made available to the user as a PCAP file to download from the Visibility & Troubleshooting tool. This feature requires in-band management to be set up, and SPAN traffic is rate limited to 10,000 pps.

- **Predefined Destination Group:** If an ERSPAN destination has already been set up under Access Policies, the group can be used by the Visibility & Troubleshooting tool as a destination.

Network Insights Resources (NIR) Overview

When we started the process of writing this book, ACI Release 3.2 was the latest long-lived release, and Release 4.0 was still only on a roadmap. Due to how widely Release 3.2 was deployed, we decided readers would get the most value out of the book if the contents were based on Release 3.2. Since then, Release 4.2 has been deployed—with increased scale, new ToR switches based on the FX2 ASIC, and new features—but overall the fundamentals are still the same.

One tool that has been added that provides revolutionary capability to network monitoring and operations is the Network Insights suite of DCNM and APIC apps. Network Insights Advisor (NIA) provides the latest updates related to the software running on your switches, and Network Insights Resources (NIR) provides software and hardware telemetry to help manage the switches in your network. NIR uses machine learning to help detect anomalies and alert the operator to devices or flows that are different from a previous state or other devices. In this section, we break down the different components of NIR.

Like the Visibility & Troubleshooting tool, NIR uses a time range to provide a snapshot of what occurred during a specified time window. This allows you to focus on only events that happened during a time when a problem occurred. Say that a ticket is opened on Monday for an outage that occurred Saturday night. Traditionally, you would have had to collect all relevant logs from monitoring stations or logs from the switches. With NIR, you just select the timeframe, and all events, flow analytics, and anomalies for the specified time are highlighted to you. Figure 14-15 shows a snapshot of what the time range looks like as well as the anomalies by type.

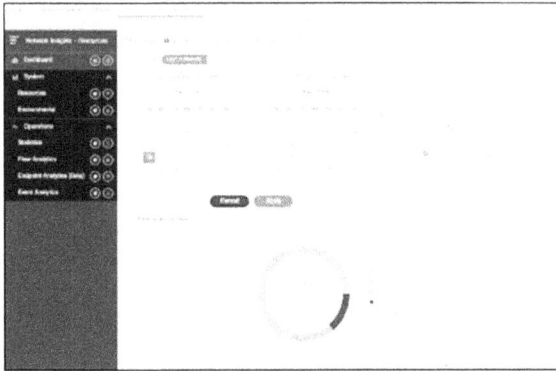

Figure 14-15   *Time Range for NIR and the Anomalies Detected During This Time*

Some of the most important anomalies that NIR provides for you are the Flow Analytics anomalies. Within the NIR app, you can specify prefixes within a VRF instance that you want to troubleshoot, and the ASIC starts to export flows directly to the NIR app to provide visibility into what is happening. This is similar to NetFlow except that with NetFlow, the CPU on the switch is involved in generating the NetFlow packets, and this can cause a significant load on the switch control plane. To prevent the CPU from running at 100% due to NetFlow and no longer processing protocols such as STP and BGP, a control plane policer is used to rate limit the amount of traffic copied to the CPU to generate NetFlow packets. This is an efficient way to protect the CPU but leaves gaps when troubleshooting because not all packets are captured. The Flow Analytics feature in NIR relies on flow tables built into the ASIC that are directly exported from the ASIC to NIR, without going through the CPU. When a flow—defined by source and destination MAC and IP addresses, as well as the L4 protocol and protocol source and destination ports—hits the ASIC, the ASIC checks whether it is known in the flow table (FT), and if not, a new flow is cached. The ASIC then counts the number of bytes and packets for each flow and exports this information in an FT packet toward NIR every second. On top of exporting the flow information, the FT export also contains information on the ingress interface, egress interface, and any drop reason for the specific flow. The following are the three drop reasons that NIR logs:

- **Forward drop:** A forward drop occurs if a route doesn't exist toward the destination or if ARP is not resolved for an adjacency. These drops indicate loss in the data plane, unlike the forward drop counter discussed in Chapter 13.

- **Policy drop:** This drop occurs if a packet was dropped because there was no contract permitting the packet.

- **QoS drop:** This drop occurs when the egress buffer is full and the packet is discarded.

When NIR receives this flow information, it stitches together the data from the other devices in the path and presents a logical topology of the flow, along with any potential drop reason on the devices in this flow. Figure 14-16 shows a working flow, as well as a broken flow. The anomaly shows when a drop reason was first detected and whether it has since cleared. To allow large quantities of flow data to be stored efficiently, NIR combines the flow records received from hardware into larger records representing a longer duration. This allows NIR to store flows for a longer period of time and requires less processing because anomaly detection only needs to occur when more data has been received. In this example, a flow was first detected as being policy dropped at 10:37:59 a.m., which represents the start of the collection chunk.

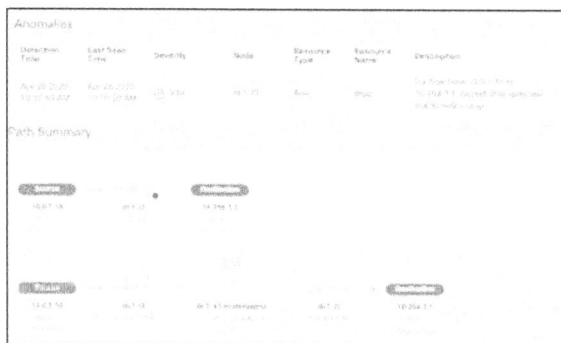

Figure 14-16 *Packet Drop Detected by NIR*

If you use the Event Analytics tab of NIR to narrow in on the detection time of 10:37:59 a.m., you can see that the configuration was changed. You can select a specific time period or a default time period such as 15 minutes, 1 hour, or 6 hours before. Figure 14-17 shows that a configuration of a contract was deleted, and that deletion caused the ASIC to discard packets and record a policy drop.

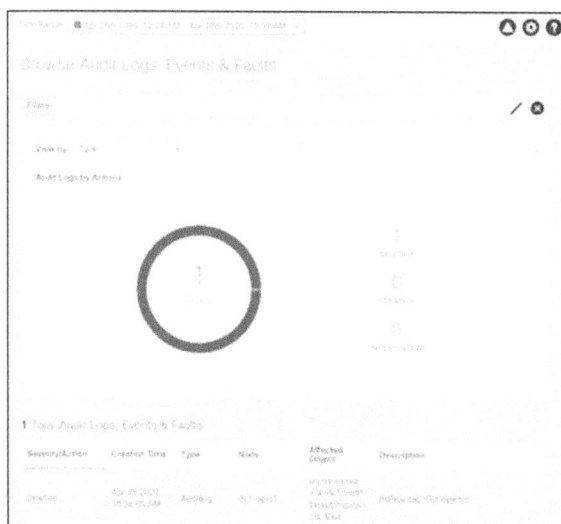

Figure 14-17 *The Audit Log Is Easily Searchable in NIR*

The benefit of having events, audits, and faults in NIR is that it is quickly searchable with customizable filters so that users don't have to use **moquery** or iCurl to get this information. With the Flow Analytics feature in NIR, you can easily isolate issues and quickly find the corresponding network event or audit to reduce the troubleshooting timeframe.

Summary

The Visibility & Troubleshooting tool is a simple but powerful tool that enables network administrators to collect information relevant to a Visibility & Troubleshooting session. It uses the built-in API to collect all objects that contain relevant statistics, faults, and events. It draws a topology to help you visualize the traffic flow you are troubleshooting and allows you to easily configure atomic counter policies, traceroute policies, and SPAN sessions. You can export all this information as a PDF and provide it to TAC or to other team members who are troubleshooting the fabric. NIR goes even further, providing deep visibility into what flows are going through the fabric by utilizing flow telemetry.

Note   There are no Key Topics or Review Questions for this chapter.

Chapter 15

Troubleshooting Use Cases

Hopefully you've enjoyed this book, and you feel your journey through *ACI Advanced Monitoring and Troubleshooting* has been worthwhile. To pull together everything you've learned in this book, this chapter gives you a chance to explore various troubleshooting use cases and situations. It provides real-world examples of issues that have been experienced in the field. Each problem or use case covers a different aspect of the ACI technology. In many cases, the solution can be found by checking faults first. However, in some of these examples, the fault is displayed at the end of the troubleshooting so that deeper isolation techniques can be described for future reference.

This chapter goes through a variety of troubleshooting scenarios for the following topics:

- Fabric discovery

- APIC controllers and clusters

- Management access

- Contracts

- End-host connectivity

- External connectivity

- Leaf and spine connectivity

- VMM domains

- L4–L7 devices

- Multi-pod

- Multi-site

- Programmability

- Multicast

Troubleshooting Fabric Discovery: Leaf Discovery

After setting up a new fabric, you realize that the infrastructure subnet overlaps with some monitoring services used in your environment. Because of this, the APIC routing table prefers the interfaces going to the fabric over the out-of-band interfaces when connecting to these services. In order to resolve this issue, you decide to set up the fabric again, this time using a different infrastructure subnet.

After running the setup script on all three of your APICs, you notice that the switches are not showing up under Fabric Membership. This is preventing you from discovering the switches in the fabric and redeploying the desired configuration. In order to isolate the issue, you check the bond on APIC 1 to see which interface is active, as shown in Example 15-1.

Example 15-1   *Verifying the Active Bond Interface on APIC 1*

```
apic1# cat /proc/net/bonding/bond0
Ethernet Channel Bonding Driver: v3.7.1 (April 27, 2011)

Bonding Mode: fault-tolerance (active-backup)
Primary Slave: None
Currently Active Slave: eth2-1
MII Status: up
MII Polling Interval (ms): 60
Up Delay (ms): 0
Down Delay (ms): 0
Slave Interface: eth2-1
MII Status: up
Speed: 10000 Mbps
Duplex: full
Link Failure Count: 0
Permanent HW addr: 58:f3:9c:5a:42:26
Slave queue ID: 0
Slave Interface: eth2-2
MII Status: up
Speed: 10000 Mbps
Duplex: full
Link Failure Count: 0
Permanent HW addr: 58:f3:9c:5a:42:27
Slave queue ID: 0
```

Based on the output, you know that eth2-1 is the active member. From here, you check whether you are sending and receiving LLDP frames from the connected switch, as this is a requirement for programming the *Infra* VLAN and allowing the DHCP discover packet from the leaf to be received on the APIC. You run the **acidiag run lldptool in eth2-1** command to check whether you are receiving LLDP frames from the connected leaf, as shown in Example 15-2.

Example 15-2 *Verifying LLDP Frames from the Connected Leaf on APIC 1*

```
apic1# acidiag run lldptool in eth2-1
Chassis ID TLV
    MAC: 64:12:25:74:65:49
Port ID TLV
    Local: Eth1/1
Time to Live TLV
    120
Port Description TLV
    topology/pod-1/paths-102/pathep-[eth1/1]
System Name TLV
    Prod-Leaf102
System Description TLV
    topology/pod-1/node-102
System Capabilities TLV
    System capabilities:  Bridge, Router
    Enabled capabilities: Bridge, Router
Management Address TLV
    MAC: 64:12:25:74:65:49
    Ifindex: 83886080
Cisco 4-wire Power-via-MDI TLV
    4-Pair PoE not supported
    Spare pair Detection/Classification not required
    PD Spare pair Desired State: Disabled
    PSE Spare pair Operational State: Disabled
Cisco Port Mode TLV
    0
Cisco Port State TLV
    2
Cisco Serial Number TLV
    SAL1813PBJY
Cisco Model TLV
    N9K-C93128TX
Cisco Firmware Version TLV
    n9000-13.2(5e)
Cisco Node Role TLV
    1
Cisco Infra VLAN TLV
    3091
Cisco Name TLV
    Prod-Leaf102
Cisco Fabric Name TLV
    Prod-Fabric1
```

```
Cisco Node IP TLV
    IPv4:10.0.208.64
Cisco Node ID TLV
    102
Cisco POD ID TLV
    1
Cisco Appliance Vector TLV
    Id: 1
    IPv4: 10.0.0.1
    UUID: 7269dc3c-e157-11e9-9ea0-89c4055bf321
    Id: 2
    IPv4: 10.0.0.2
    UUID: 5895c8ec-e158-11e9-81e1-3bf5402dc3aa
    Id: 3
    IPv4: 10.0.0.3
    UUID: 5d668cda-e158-11e9-a89e-c768499dd00b
End of LLDPDU TLV
```

Based on the LLDP frames being received, it appears that the leaf already has configuration on it. In order for a switch to be discovered in ACI, it must meet the following criteria:

- The switch must be running ACI software. The Cisco Firmware Version TLV information in the LLDP output in Example 15-2 shows that it is running ACI code.

- The switch must be in Discovery mode, which means it must not have any previous configuration on it. This allows the leaf to program the *Infra* VLAN on the ports connecting to the APIC and ensures that the leaf is sending DHCP requests to obtain a valid IP address. Based on the LLDP output in Example 15-2, the switch is not in Discovery mode.

Solution

In order to resolve the issue, you issue the following commands on the leaf connected to eth2-1 on APIC 1 to wipe the configuration and reload:

```
Prod-Leaf102# acidiag touch clean
This command will wipe out the APIC, Proceed? [y/N] y
Prod-Leaf102# reload
This command will reload the chassis, Proceed (y/n)? [n]: y
```

When the switch reloads and comes back online, you can successfully register the device, as shown in Figure 15-1.

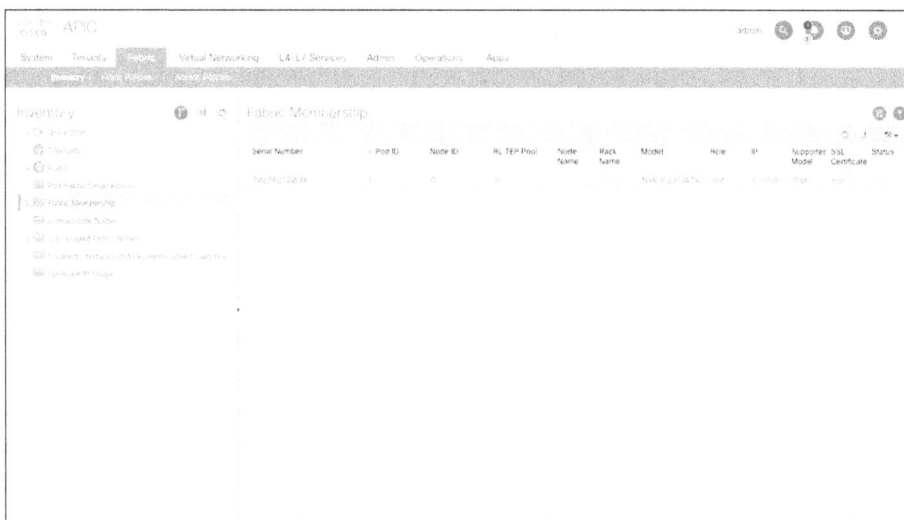

Figure 15-1 *Switch Is Now Ready to Be Registered in APIC*

Troubleshooting APIC Controllers and Clusters: Clustering

Your ACI fabric has been running for some time, but it has been found that APIC 2 is having a hardware-related issue and needs to be replaced. After receiving the replacement unit, you unplug the existing APIC and plug in the new one to the same ports that the old one was connected to. You configure CIMC and finish the initial setup of APIC 2, configuring it identically to the previous APIC. However, after completing the setup script, APIC 2 will not join the cluster, and APIC 1 and APIC 3 see APIC 2 as Unknown and Unavailable, as shown in Figure 15-2.

In order to troubleshoot the issue, you first check whether you have IP connectivity to the APIC from either APIC 1 or APIC 3. You know that the infrastructure address for APIC 2 will always be the second address in the infrastructure subnet, so you issue a **ping** to that address from APIC 1. Example 15-3 shows the result of this test.

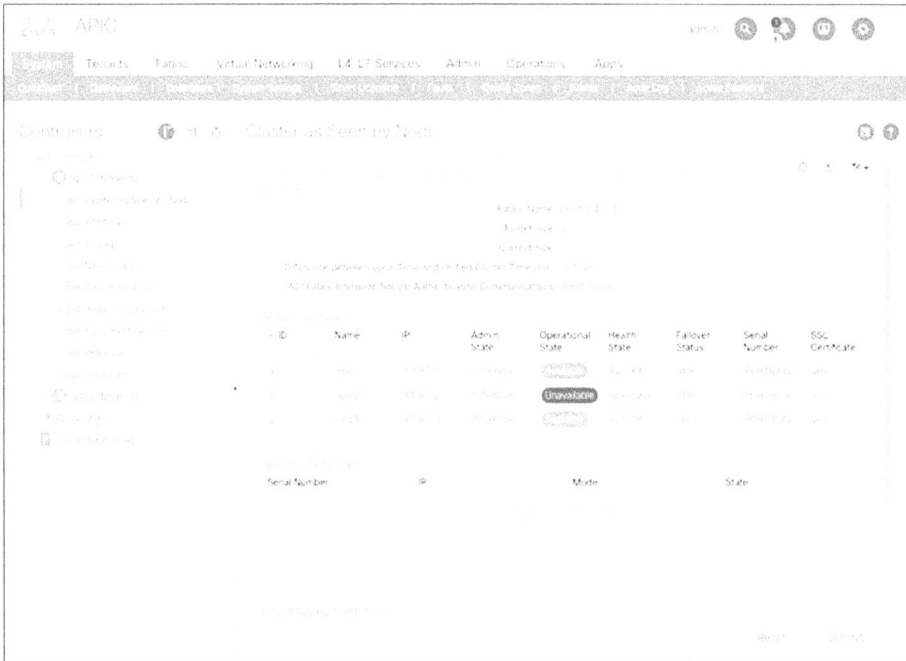

Figure 15-2   *APIC 2 Is Unavailable in the APIC UI*

Example 15-3   *Ping to APIC 2 from APIC 1 Fails*

```
apic1# ping 10.0.0.2
PING 10.0.0.2 (10.0.0.2) 56(84) bytes of data.


--- 10.0.0.2 ping statistics ---
5 packets transmitted, 0 received, 100% packet loss, time 4000ms
```

You know that IP connectivity to APIC 2 is broken from APIC 1. The next thing you check is whether the infrastructure VLAN is programmed on the switch where the APIC connects. You checked LLDP and verified that APIC 2 is plugged into the correct interface, Eth1/3, but the infrastructure VLAN is not programmed on this port, as shown in Example 15-4.

Example 15-4   *Verifying LLDP and Infra VLAN Deployment on Leaf 101*

```
leaf101# show lldp neighbors
Capability codes:
  (R) Router, (B) Bridge, (T) Telephone, (C) DOCSIS Cable Device
  (W) WLAN Access Point, (P) Repeater, (S) Station, (O) Other
Device ID          Local Intf      Hold-time  Capability  Port ID
apic1              Eth1/1          120                     eth2-2
```

```
apic3                   Eth1/2          120                     eth2-2
apic2                   Eth1/3          120                     eth2-2


leaf-101# show vlan extended


VLAN Name                               Encap           Ports
---- -------------------------------    ---------------  ------------------------
10   infra:default                      vxlan-16777209, Eth1/1, Eth1/2
                                        vlan-3091
```

Because LLDP is present, you find it strange that the VLAN is not being deployed on the switch. Referring back to what you learned about clustering in Chapter 13, "Troubleshooting Techniques," you decide to check the *lldpIf* managed objects (MOs) on the leaf for Eth1/3, and you see a wiring issue on the interface, as shown in Example 15-5.

Example 15-5 *Wiring Issue Raised on Eth1/3 of Leaf 101*

```
leaf101# moquery -d sys/lldp/inst/if-[eth1/3]
Total Objects shown: 1


# lldp.If
id           : eth1/3
adminRxSt    : enabled
adminSt      : enabled
adminTxSt    : enabled
childAction  :
descr        :
dn           : sys/lldp/inst/if-[eth1/3]
lcOwn        : local
mac          : 88:F0:31:2B:D7:AD
modTs        : 2019-09-30T15:53:06.107+00:00
monPolDn     : uni/fabric/monfab-default
name         :
operRxSt     : enabled
operTxSt     : enabled
portDesc     : topology/pod-1/paths-101/pathep-[eth1/3]
portMode     : normal
portVlan     : unspecified
rn           : if-[eth1/3]
status       :
sysDesc      : topology/pod-1/node-101
wiringIssues : ctrlr-uuid-mismatch
```

In addition, you see a fault raised in the APIC UI, stating the same information for both leafs connecting to APIC 2, as shown in Figure 15-3.

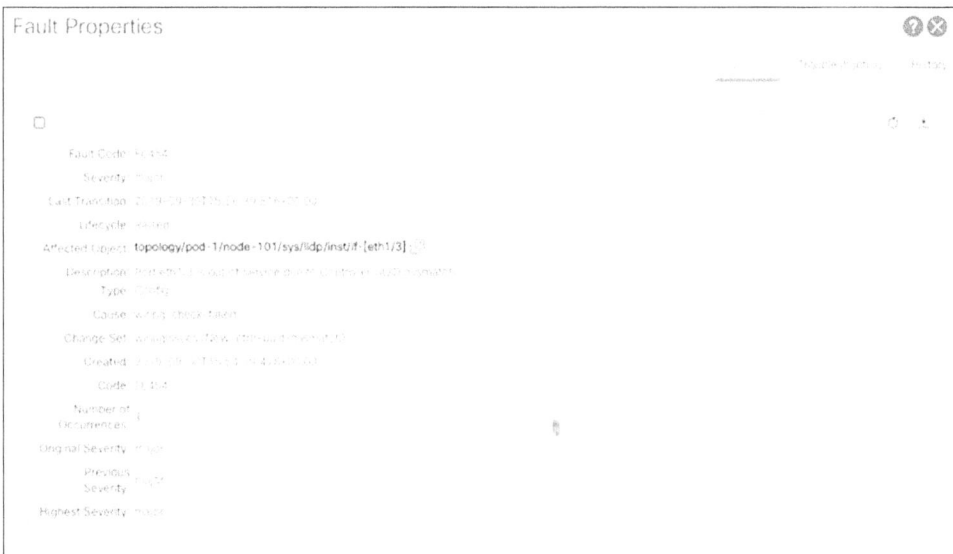

Figure 15-3 *Fault Raised on APIC for a Wiring Issue*

Solution

Before APIC 2 was replaced with a new APIC and before the setup script was run on APIC 2 to configure it with the correct cluster parameters, APIC 2 was not officially decommissioned from the cluster. When a new APIC is connected, a new UUID is configured after the setup is complete. The fabric protects itself from a new controller inserting itself by validating the UUID of the APIC that is clustered to that of the one that is being discovered. In this case, the fabric still has the information of the old APIC in its database, so it's preventing the new one from coming online.

To resolve the issue, you navigate to the cluster members, right-click on APIC 2 from APIC 1, and select Decommission, as shown in Figure 15-4.

It is recommended to wait five minutes before recommissioning the controller, so after five minutes, you right-click on APIC 2 and select Commission. The faults clear, and the APIC is allowed back into the fabric.

For additional remediation steps for various wiring issues, refer to the section "APIC Cluster Troubleshooting" in Chapter 13.

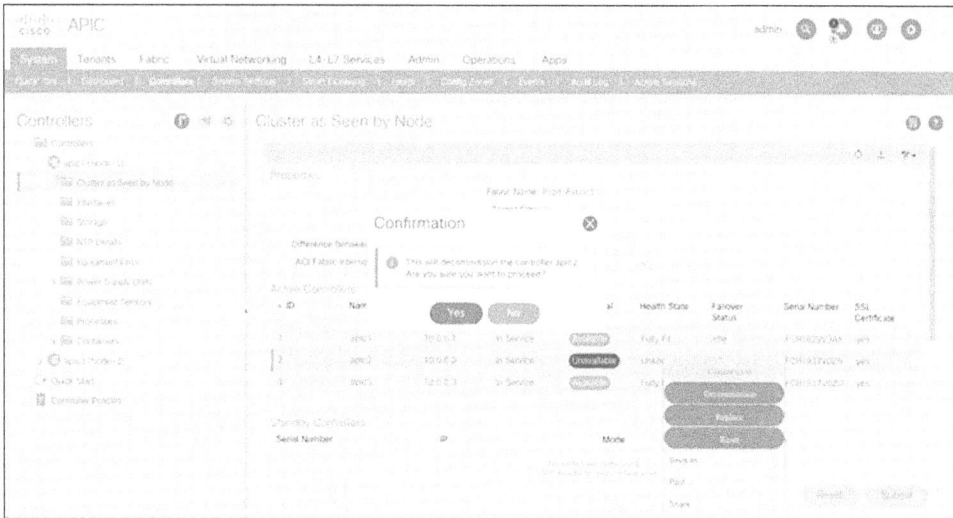

Figure 15-4 *Decommissioning APIC 2 in the APIC UI*

Troubleshooting Management Access: Out-of-Band EPG

After setting up the APIC and discovering the switches, you want to enable SNMP, syslog, and other management protocols. To do this, you decide to configure the out-of-band management EPG and create an out-of-band contract to restrict who can access the APIC. You create an external management network instance profile called *IT_Users*, which contains the 10.254.10.0/24 subnet and consumes the *oobMgmt* contract that you created to restrict access. After doing this, you notice that you can still access the APIC from a laptop on wireless, which falls outside the 10.254.10.0/24 subnet. To begin your investigation, you review your contract configuration and association, as shown in Figure 15-5.

The next step is to test with the switches. You try using SSH to access a switch from your laptop, and the connection fails. Next, you try using SSH to access your management workstation behind the 10.254.10.0/24 subnet and confirm that it works. So far, you've confirmed that the out-of-band contract appears to be working for only the switches but not the APIC. Now you have to determine what is different between your switches and your APIC when it comes to the management EPG. To gain more insight, you right-click on the management EPG and select *Show Usage*. The screen that appears (see Figure 15-6), shows only switches.

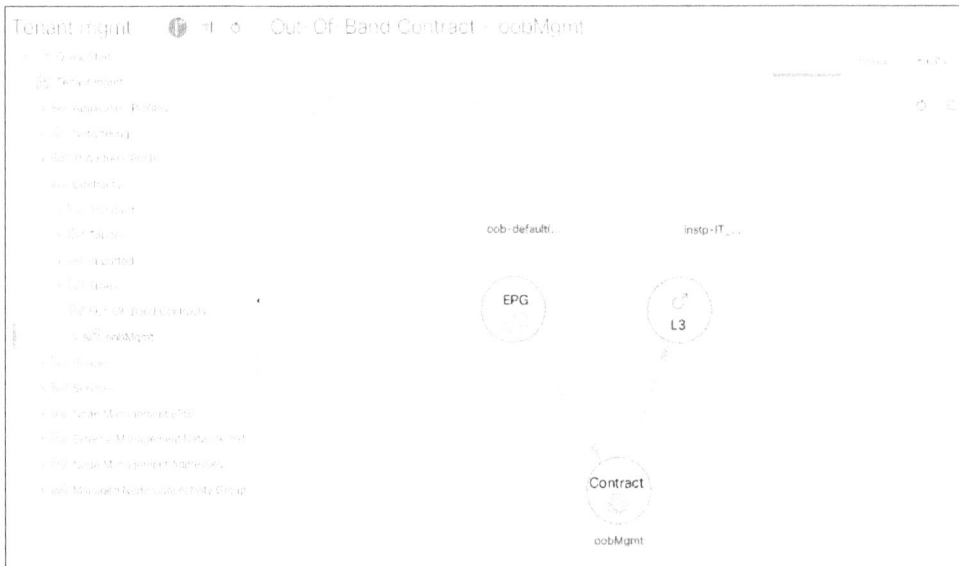

Figure 15-5   oobMgmt *Contract Relationship*

Figure 15-6   *Verifying Policy Usage for the* oobMgmt *Contract*

Why are only switches, and not any of the APICs, in the management EPG? Where are devices placed into a management EPG? This is the node management address configuration. Under Static Node Management Addresses, you've defined the IP address for switches to use and what EPG this IP address belongs to. However, this was never done for the APICs. Therefore, the object model doesn't have the IP configuration of the APIC. The IP configuration was only done during the initial setup wizard, when the underlaying OS was configured, not when the management information tree for ACI was created.

Solution

After you add your APIC to the static node management addresses, the policy model is complete, and an **iptables** configuration can be created and configured on the APICs to block incoming connections on ports that aren't permitted and from sources that aren't allowed. The configuration for APIC 1 is illustrated in Figure 15-7.

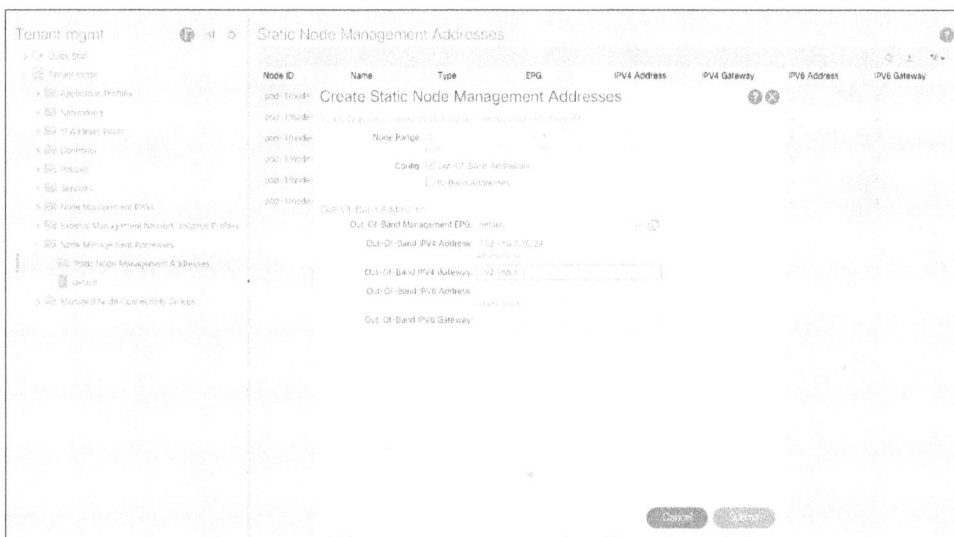

Figure 15-7   *Assigning an Out-of-Band IP Address to APIC 1*

Troubleshooting Contracts: Traffic Not Traversing a Firewall as Expected

You have a AAA server in tenant *Shared-Service*, and a resource in tenant *ACI-AMT-Book* needs access to it. The requirement is that this traffic must flow through a firewall that is connected to the core. To accomplish this, you provide an existing contract called *AAA_ Server* from the AAA EPG in tenant *Shared-Service*. To reach the server in tenant *ACI-AMT-Book*, traffic should go out an L3Out in tenant *Shared-Service*, get routed to the firewall, and come back in the target VRF instance, *ACI-AMT-Book:v1*. Due to the traffic flow, the core L3Out in tenant *ACI-AMT-Book* will be providing the contract *AAA_ Server*, and the *Web* EPG will be consuming it. Figure 15-8 illustrates the topology used.

You run a few tests and confirm that 172.16.0.10 can access 172.18.4.20. When you review the firewall logs, you see no traffic flow logs. Contract *AAA_Server* was defined in tenant *Common*, so to view the contract topology map, you navigate there. Here you confirm that in tenant *Shared-Service*, EPG *AAA_Server* is providing contract *AAA_ Server*, and *Shared-Service-L3OutCore* is consuming it. In tenant *ACI-AMT-Book*, *Internal-Net* is providing the contract, and EPG *App* is consuming it. This is validated in the UI, as shown in Figure 15-9.

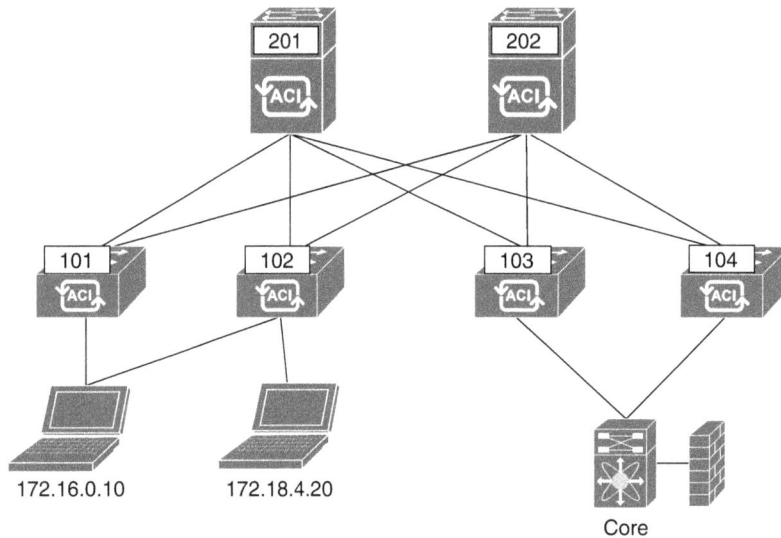

Figure 15-8   *Topology for the Firewall*

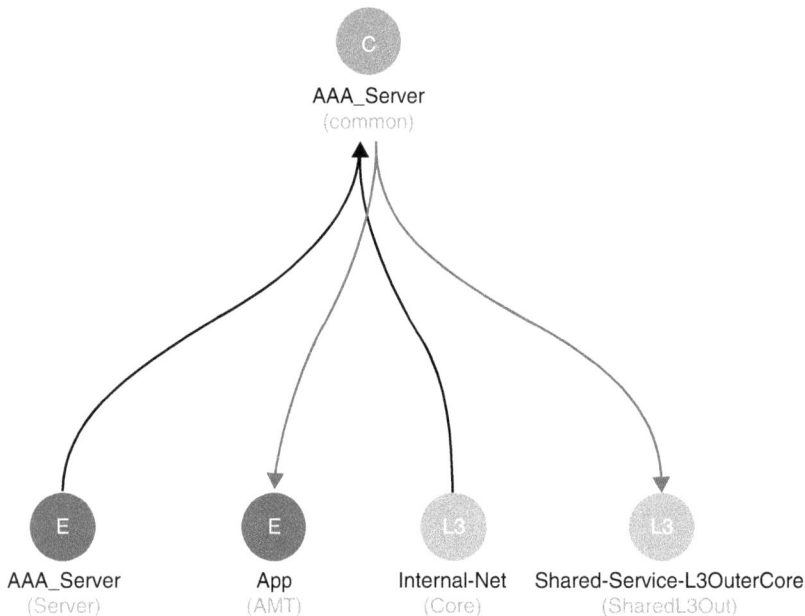

Figure 15-9   *Contract Relationships for Contract* AAA_Server

Here you confirm that in tenant *Shared-Service*, EPG *AAA_Server* is providing contract *AAA_Server*, and *Shared-Service-L3OutCore* is consuming it. In tenant *ACI-AMT-Book*, *Internal-Net* is providing the contract, and EPG *App* is consuming it.

The next stop should be to confirm the routing table, either in software or by using the ELAM app, to see where the packet is going. When running the **show ip route** command (see Example 15-6), you notice that there is a pervasive route pointing to the spine proxy. These routes are only pushed by the APIC when policy exists that requires the specific route.

Example 15-6 *Routing Table of Leaf 103 with a Pervasive Route Pointing to the Spine Proxy*

```
leaf103# show ip route vrf ACI-AMT-Book:v1 172.18.4.0
IP Route Table for VRF "ACI-AMT-Book:v1"
'*' denotes best ucast next-hop
'**' denotes best mcast next-hop
'[x/y]' denotes [preference/metric]
'%<string>' in via output denotes VRF <string>
172.18.4.0/24, ubest/mbest: 1/0, attached, direct, pervasive
    *via 10.0.184.66%overlay-1, [1/0], 00:39:26, static, tag 4294967294
        recursive next hop: 10.0.184.66/32%overlay-1
```

Solution

By taking a closer look at the policy of the contact, you can see that the scope is incorrectly set, as shown in Figure 15-10. Contracts where the scope is set to Global or Tenant can actually leak a route between two VRF instances and cause unexpected traffic flows.

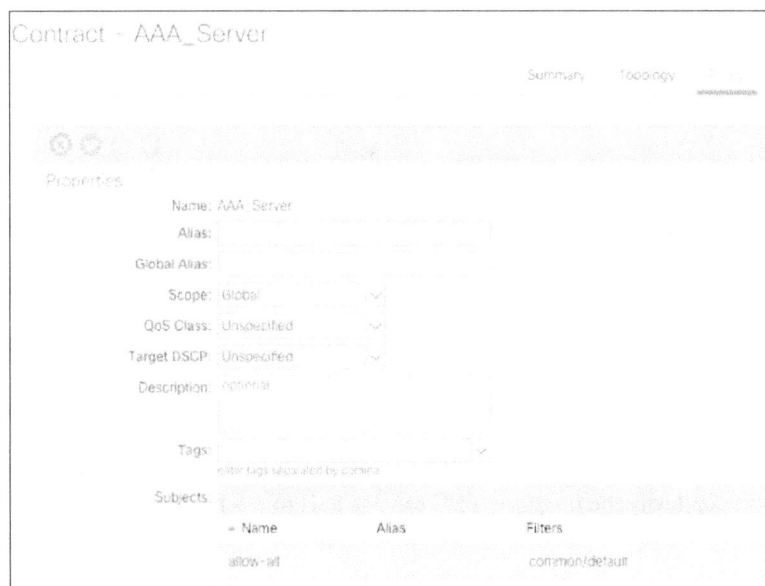

Figure 15-10 *Contract Configuration for Contract AAA_Server*

When using contracts from tenant *Common*, be sure to confirm that the scope is properly set to avoid causing an unexpected traffic path. In this case, the existence of a global contract allows the potential for leaking routes directly instead of having the traffic traverse VRF instances via the external firewall.

Troubleshooting Contracts: Contract Directionality

You've created a new EPG called *JumpBox*, which you use to connect (using SSH) to different servers. In some cases, you need to use SCP to copy files from the jump server to other servers in the VRF instance. Because of this requirement, you've decided to use the *VRF* EPG to provide a contract using port 22. This is often referred to as a *vzAny contract*, based on the object name. In the GUI, the folder is called EPG Collection for the VRF, as shown in Figure 15-11. The contract you create has a single subject called *TCP:22*, and you select Apply Both Directions because you also want to be able to copy files (using SCP) from the JumpBox to other devices. To allow the return traffic to work as well, you select Reverse Filter Ports.

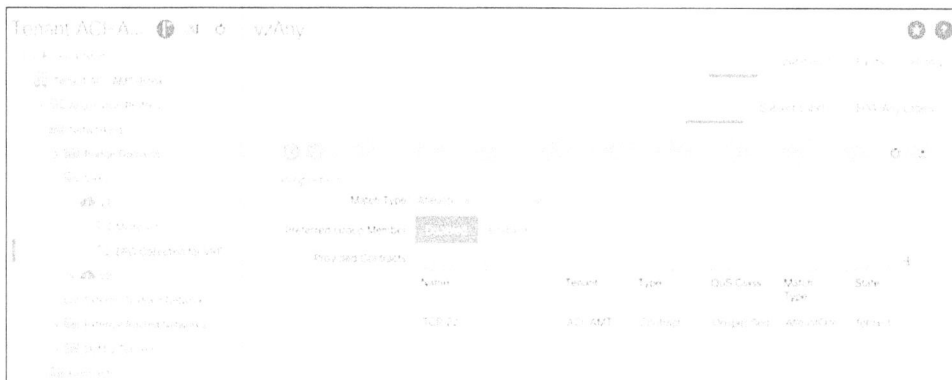

Figure 15-11 *Contract Provided on the VRF Instance*

Contract *TCP:22* is consumed on your new EPG called *JumpBox*. You go to the jump server and open an SCP session to the web server. This works as expected. From the web server, you now try to copy an updated package from the jump server by initiating an SCP session from the web server to the EPG *JumpBox*. The session times out. When you navigate to the Tenant tab to look for contract drops, you see that the flow in question is being dropped, as shown in Figure 15-12.

To further look into this, you log on to the switch CLI to look at the zoning rules. To begin troubleshooting, you check the PCTag assigned to EPG *JumpBox*, which is 16394. You need to understand why the *JumpBox* EPG can use SSH to reach the web server.

In Example 15-7 you can see that EPG *JumpBox* (PCTag 16394) can talk to any EPG (PCTag 0) where the flow matches Filter 19. Filter 19 is what was defined on the APIC to allow destination port 22.

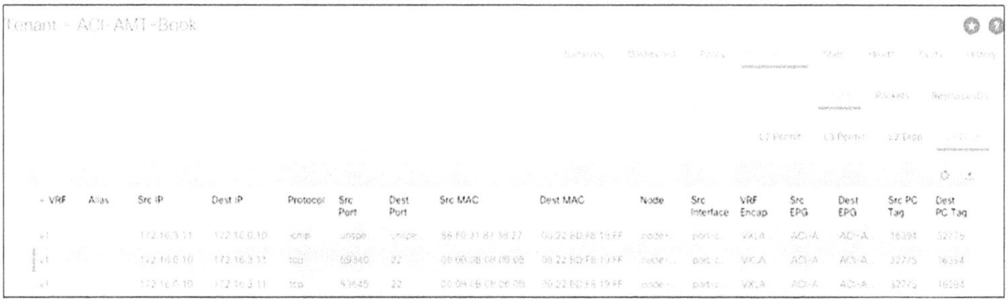

Figure 15-12 *Contract Drops in the Tenant Operational View*

Example 15-7 *Contract Deployment on Leaf 101 for Traffic Sourced from the* JumpBox *EPG*

```
leaf101# show zoning-rule scope 2785280 src-epg 16394
Rule ID    SrcEPG DstEPG  FilterID operSt  Scope   Action    Priority
=======    ====== ======  ======== ======= ======= =======   ========
4158       16394  0        19      enabled 2981888 permit    fully_qual(6)
leaf101# show zoning-filter filter 19
<Snipped for Formatting>
FilterId  Name  EtherT  SFromPort     SToPort       DFromPort     DToPort
========= ====  ======  ===========   ===========   ===========   ===========
19        19_0  ip      unspecified   unspecified   22            22
```

In the reverse direction, PCTag 0 or any EPG is able to communicate with EPG *JumpBox* (PCTag 16394) but using a different filter, Filter 20, as shown in Example 15-8.

Example 15-8 *Contract Deployment on Leaf 101 for Traffic Destined to the* JumpBox *EPG*

```
leaf101# show zoning-rule scope 2785280 dst-epg 16394
Rule ID    SrcEPG DstEPG  FilterID operSt  Scope   Action    Priority
=======    ====== ======  ======== ======= ======= =======   ========
4151       0      16394   19       enabled 2981888 permit    fully_qual(6)
leaf101# show zoning-filter filter 19
<Snipped for Formatting>
FilterId  Name  EtherT  SFromPort     SToPort       DFromPort     DToPort
========= ====  ======  ===========   ===========   ===========   ===========
20        20_0  ip      22            22            unspecified   unspecified
```

Filter 20 just allows source port 22 with any destination port. This is the return traffic of the original traffic flow from EPG *JumpBox* to EPG *Web*. To better understand what happens when using Apply Both Directions and Reverse Filter Ports in hardware, examine Figures 15-13, 15-14, and 15-15.

Apply Both Directions: ☐
Reverse Filter Ports: ☐

Src Port: Unspecified
Dest Port 22

Consumer   Provider

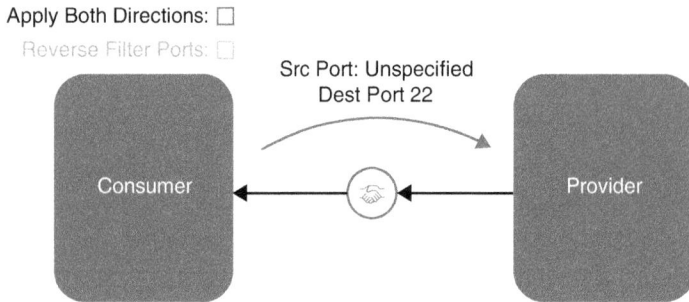

Figure 15-13   *Policy Enforcement Without Apply Both Directions and Reverse Filter Ports*

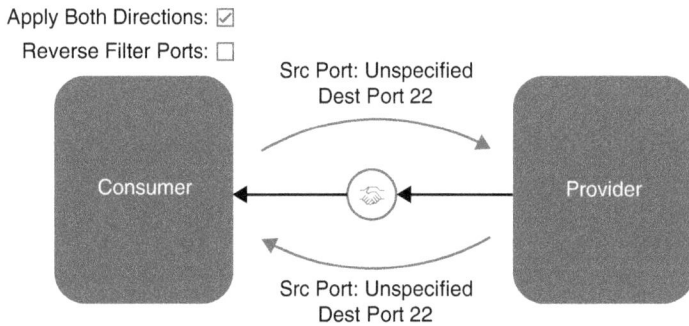

Apply Both Directions: ☑
Reverse Filter Ports: ☐

Src Port: Unspecified
Dest Port 22

Consumer   Provider

Src Port: Unspecified
Dest Port 22

Figure 15-14   *Policy Enforcement With Apply Both Directions and Without Reverse Filter Ports*

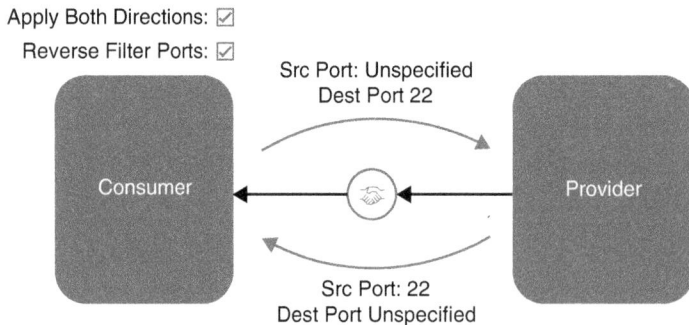

Apply Both Directions: ☑
Reverse Filter Ports: ☑

Src Port: Unspecified
Dest Port 22

Consumer   Provider

Src Port: 22
Dest Port Unspecified

Figure 15-15   *Policy Enforcement with Apply Both Directions and Reverse Filter Ports*

Because of the configuration, no EPG in the VRF instance is able to initiate an SCP connection with the *JumpBox* EPG because there is not a contract in place that allows this source and destination (sourced from unspecified and destined to port 22).

Solution

In order to enable anything in the VRF instance to initiate an SCP connection back to the *JumpBox* EPG, one of two configurations can be deployed:

■ Have both vzAny and the *JumpBox* EPG provide and consume the contract. With vzAny, this is suboptimal because now any EPG can use SSH or SCP to connect to any other EPG in the VRF instance. Providing and consuming the same contract is a better solution when using regular EPGs and not vzAny.

■ Add an additional filter entry to the subject where the source port is 22 and the destination port is unspecified. This allows flow opposite the intended direction.

After adding an additional filter entry, as described in the second option, initiating SCP connections to the *JumpServer* EPG works as intended.

Troubleshooting End Host Connectivity: Layer 2 Traffic Flow Through ACI

The server team has added a new web server to allow for the web cluster to expand. After connecting the machine to the ACI fabric, the server team is unable to communicate with the other server. The team claims that if they initiate a ping to Host A from Host B, the ping times out. This is the first server added to the ACI fabric, as the other server connects to an external switch, which then connects to ACI. After collecting the IP and MAC address information from the server, you are ready to begin troubleshooting, using the topology shown in Figure 15-16.

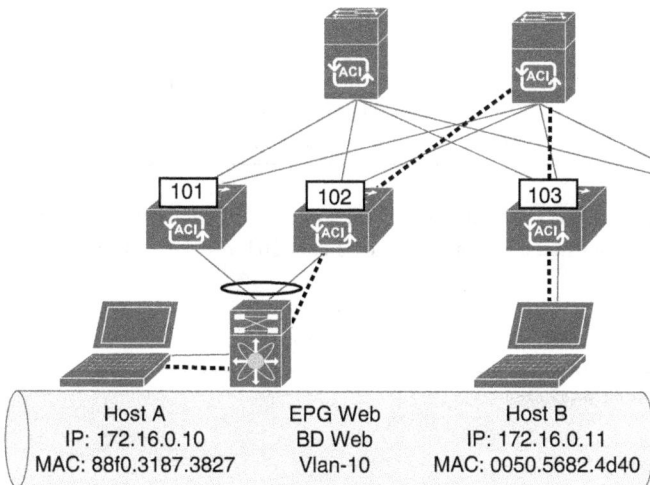

Host A	EPG Web	Host B
IP: 172.16.0.10	BD Web	IP: 172.16.0.11
MAC: 88f0.3187.3827	Vlan-10	MAC: 0050.5682.4d40

Host A Can't Ping Host B

Figure 15-16 *Layer 2 Connectivity for Web Servers*

Before connecting the server, you provision a new EPG called *Web* and a bridge domain called *Web*. The bridge domain has been configured with the following default settings:

- **Unicast Routing:** Enabled

- **Subnet Configured:** No

- **L2 Unknown Unicast:** Proxy

- **ARP Optimization:** Enabled

- **Limit IP Learning to Subnet:** Enabled

Under the EPG, two static path bindings have been added to allow communication to the server as well as the external switch. These bindings have VLAN 10 set to trunk. Because you know you are supposed to have VLAN 10 trunked correctly down to the two locations, the first step would be to validate that the VLAN is correctly programmed on the switch. Example 15-9 demonstrates how to check whether the VLAN is correctly deployed on Leafs 101 and 102.

Example 15-9   *VLAN Deployment on Leafs 101 and 102*

```
leaf101# show vlan extended


 VLAN Name                          Encap            Ports
 ---- ----------------------------- ---------------- ------------------

 16   ACI-AMT-Book:Web              vxlan-16154554   Eth1/5, Po1
 17   ACI-AMT-Book:AMT:Web          vlan-10          Eth1/5, Po1


leaf102# show vlan extended
 VLAN Name                          Encap            Ports
 ---- ----------------------------- ---------------- ------------------

 16   ACI-AMT-Book:Web              vxlan-16154554   Eth1/5, Po1
 17   ACI-AMT-Book:AMT:Web          vlan-10          Eth1/5, Po1
```

The output shows that the VLAN is correctly deployed, so now you can further validate that Host A's MAC address is learned as an endpoint on Leafs 101 and 102, as shown in Example 15-10.

Example 15-10   *Layer 2 Endpoint Verification on Leafs 101 and 102*

```
leaf101# show endpoint mac 88f0.3187.3827
Legend:
 s - arp            O - peer-attached a - local-aged      S - static
 V - vpc-attached   p - peer-aged M - span         L - local
 B - bounce         H - vtep
```

```
+--------------------+---------------+----------------+--------------+-------------+
      VLAN/            Encap           MAC Address      MAC Info/      Interface
      Domain           VLAN            IP Address       IP Info
+--------------------+---------------+----------------+--------------+-------------+
17/ACI-AMT-Book:v1    vlan-10         88f0.3187.3827    LV            po1


leaf102# show endpoint mac 88f0.3187.3827
Legend:
 s - arp          O - peer-attached a - local-aged      S - static
 V - vpc-attached p - peer-aged M - span          L - local
 B - bounce       H - vtep
+--------------------+---------------+----------------+--------------+-------------+
      VLAN/            Encap           MAC Address      MAC Info/      Interface
      Domain           VLAN            IP Address       IP Info
+--------------------+---------------+----------------+--------------+-------------+
17/ACI-AMT-Book:v1    vlan-10         88f0.3187.3827    LV            po1
```

With the VLAN deployed correctly and the endpoint learned on Leafs 101 and 102, the next step would be to check Leaf 103 to ensure that the same applies for Host B. When you check the VLAN deployment on Leaf 103, you notice that the VLAN is missing. If you think the configuration is correct, but it is not being deployed, you should check the EPG to see if there are any faults. If you navigate to Web EPG > Faults, you see a fault raised for the path on Leaf 103, as shown in Figure 15-17.

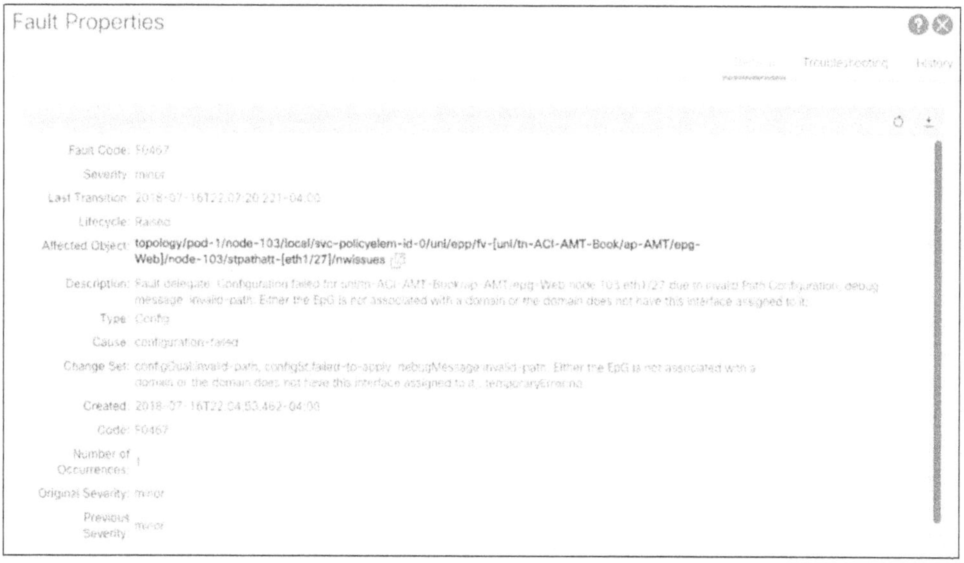

Figure 15-17 *Fault Raised on EPG Web*

Solution

As described in Chapter 5, "End Host and Network Connectivity," for a VLAN to be successfully deployed to an interface, the port you are deploying needs to tie back to a domain. That domain references a VLAN pool that contains one or more VLANs that you wish to deploy on an interface. The error shown in Figure 15-17 explains that the domain you have associated to the EPG does not map back to the interface you have deployed; therefore, the VLAN cannot be configured on this port.

The Troubleshooting tab for the fault can be very useful if you think the configuration was set up correctly. The Troubleshooting tab allows you to look at all changes that were made within a certain time of the fault being raised. If you view it in this case, you see that the attachable access entity profile (AAEP) that was used to associate the domain to the interface was removed, as shown in Figure 15-18.

Figure 15-18   *Troubleshooting Tab for a Fault Raised on EPG* Web

By correcting the configuration as shown in Figure 15-19 and adding the correct AAEP to the interface policy group for the web server, you can see that the fault clears, and the VLAN is successfully pushed to the leaf. This configuration associates the AAEP *WebServers*, which contains the proper domain (*AMT*), with the interface policy group for *WebServers*.

You can now also validate that the endpoint is being learned correctly on Leaf 103, as shown in Example 15-11.

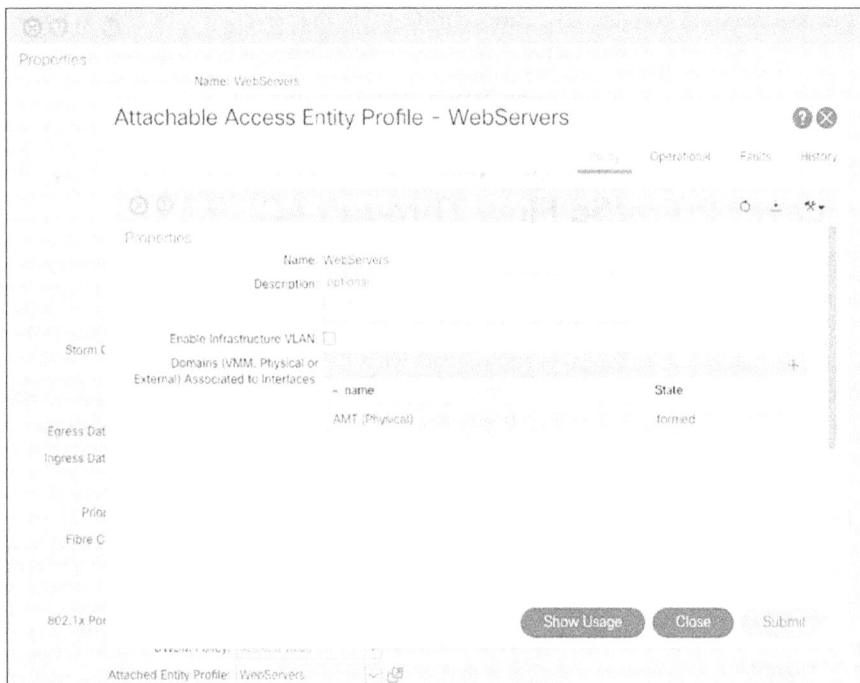

Figure 15-19 *AAEP Configuration for EPG* WebServers

Example 15-11 *VLAN and Endpoint Verification for EPG* WebServers *on Leaf 103*

```
leaf103# show vlan extended

VLAN Name                          Encap Ports
---- ------------------------------ ---------------- ------------------------
17   ACI-AMT-Book:BD1               vxlan-16547722 Eth1/9
18   ACI-AMT-Book:AMT:EPG1          vlan-2 Eth1/9
25   ACI-AMT-Book:Web               vxlan-16154554 Eth1/27
27   ACI-AMT-Book:AMT:Web           vlan-10 Eth1/27


leaf103# show endpoint mac 0050.5682.4d40
Legend:
 s - arp            O - peer-attached a - local-aged     S - static
 V - vpc-attached   p - peer-aged M - span               L - local
 B - bounce         H - vtep
+-------------------+---------------+-----------------+--------------+-------------+
     VLAN/            Encap           MAC Address       MAC Info/      Interface
     Domain           VLAN            IP Address        IP Info
+-------------------+---------------+-----------------+--------------+-------------+
27/ACI-AMT-Book:v1   vlan-10         0050.5682.4d40    L              eth1/27
```

With the configuration corrected, you are confident that the servers will be able to communicate the access policy configuration because the end host connectivity has been resolved.

Troubleshooting External Layer 2 Connectivity: Broken Layer 2 Traffic Flow Through ACI

Despite resolving the fault described in the previous example and correcting the access policy configuration for the server on Leaf 103, the server team is still reporting connectivity issues between the servers. In order to further check what might be happening, you should choose a direction to focus on and validate what the expected packet flow should look like. Because the server team is unable to ping from Host B to Host A, you look to see if Leaf 103 knows where Host A exists. If you check the endpoint database on Leaf 103, you see that it has not learned the MAC address of Host A, as shown in Example 15-12.

Example 15-12 *Host A MAC Address Is Not Learned on Leaf 103*

```
leaf103# show endpoint mac 88f0.3187.3827
Legend:
 s - arp              H - vtep V - vpc-attached     p - peer-aged
 R - peer-attached-rl B - bounce          S - static M - span
 D - bounce-to-proxy  O - peer-attached a - local-aged      L - local
+------------------+---------------+-----------------+--------------+-------------+
      VLAN/            Encap          MAC Address      MAC Info/      Interface
      Domain           VLAN           IP Address       IP Info
+------------------+---------------+-----------------+--------------+-------------+
<EMPTY>
```

In this situation, the switch forwards packets based on the settings configured under the bridge domain. The server team also lets you know that it is unable to resolve ARP to Host A, which it feels is the reason that communication is unsuccessful. With ARP optimization enabled, an ACI leaf forwards ARP frames based on the target IP address in the ARP payload. If the ACI leaf does not know where the IP address of the endpoint exists, it forwards the frame to the IPv4 anycast proxy on either of the spine switches in the pod. However, because Limit IP Learning to Subnet is enabled but there is no subnet defined, the leafs do not learn IP address information for endpoints connected in the bridge domain. Therefore, the spine does not know where to redirect the ARP frame, and a glean cannot be generated by the leaf switches because there is no subnet for which to originate the glean. As a result, the frame is dropped in the ACI fabric. The same would go for unknown unicast traffic as well. If the ACI leaf switch does not know the destination MAC address, by default it sends the frame to the MAC proxy TEP on the spines in the pod. If the host times out or goes silent, the spine does not know of its existence, and the frame is dropped.

Solution 1

When connecting Layer 2 devices in ACI, best practice dictates setting L2 Unknown Unicast to Flood and enabling the ARP Flooding setting, as shown in Figure 15-20. These settings ensure that in situations where a leaf switch has not learned the remote endpoint, traffic can be flooded on the bridge domain, where it will reach the egress leaf(s) and be sent out.

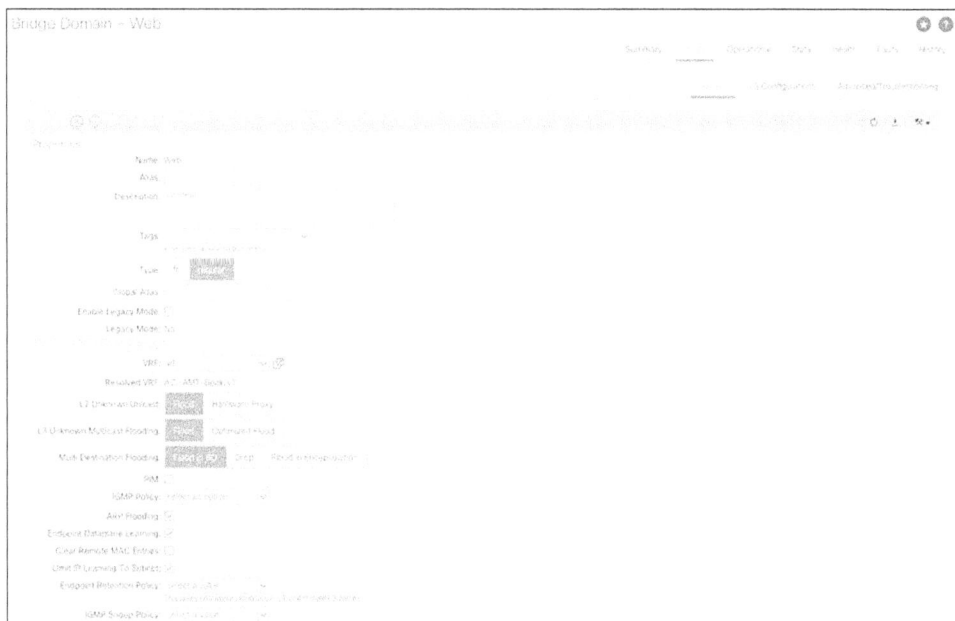

Figure 15-20   *Web BD Should Use L2 Unknown Unicast Flooding and ARP Flooding*

With these settings, the Layer 2 configuration now provides flooding of ARP frames, and the server team is able to communicate with Host A.

Solution 2

Another solution in this scenario would be to add a subnet under the BD. If the intention is to have the gateway on ACI, then this would be required to allow traffic to be routed. If the intention is to have the gateway configured on the external device, an additional IP address in the subnet needs to be allocated to the bridge domain. With the addition of the subnet under ACI, the ACI leaf switches can learn IP address information if it matches the given subnet range, and the leaf can perform host refresh and glean to detect whether hosts are still alive. This resolves the silent host issue if the host is still connected to the network but may not be sending traffic into the ACI fabric. You've decided to add a subnet under the bridge domain to resolve the issue because the intention is to move the routing functionality to ACI in the future.

Troubleshooting External Layer 3 Connectivity: Broken Layer 3 Traffic Flow Through ACI

Now that Layer 2 connectivity is working the way you want for the web servers, a requirement comes in that you need connectivity between web servers and some application servers that the server team is building. For these app servers, the subnet has not been provisioned yet, so the decision is to create the subnet on ACI and have ACI perform the routing functionality for these servers. An L3Out has been provisioned to statically route traffic to the external switch, where it can be sent back into the fabric for any EPGs where the gateway still resides externally. The topology for this flow is illustrated in Figure 15-21.

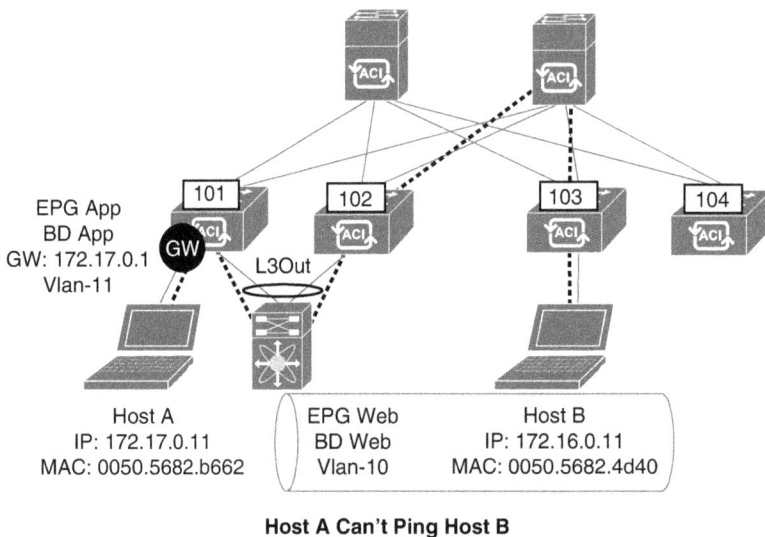

Host A Can't Ping Host B

Figure 15-21 *Layer 3 Connectivity for App and Web Servers*

In addition, a contract has been configured that allows the necessary communication between the *App* EPG and the L3Out, which includes ICMP. After setting this up, the server team notifies you that the app server Host A is not able to ping the web server Host B. The team is, however, able to ping the gateway configured in BD *App*. You need to investigate what is causing the issue.

In this case, Host A is single attached to Leaf 101, so you can begin focusing on Leaf 101. Because the server team has let you know that it can ping the default gateway but not Host B, you need to validate that the route programming looks okay. Example 15-13 demonstrates how to check the routing table on Leaf 101.

Example 15-13 *Routing Table for Route to Host B on Leaf 101*

```
leaf101# show ip route 172.16.0.11 vrf ACI-AMT-Book:v1
IP Route Table for VRF "ACI-AMT-Book:v1"
'*' denotes best ucast next-hop
'**' denotes best mcast next-hop
'[x/y]' denotes [preference/metric]
'%<string>' in via output denotes VRF <string>
0.0.0.0/0, ubest/mbest: 1/0
    *via 10.10.100.3, vlan17, [1/0], 00:03:45, static
```

This looks good. From a routing table perspective, the leaf thinks it should route traffic destined to Host B by using the static default route configured under the L3Out. But even with the route present, the traffic does not work.

If you think back to Chapter 12, "Bits and Bytes of ACI Forwarding," where you learned about the different forwarding paradigms, you know that an ACI leaf does a Layer 3 lookup as follows in the VRF instance in which the frame is received:

■ If the destination IP address is a learned endpoint, the frame is forwarded based on how that endpoint is learned.

■ If no endpoint is learned, the frame is forwarded based on the longest prefix matched route for that destination.

Because you know the route looks okay, you check whether you have learned the destination IP address as an endpoint, as shown in Example 15-14.

Example 15-14 *Remote Endpoint Learned for Host B on Leaf 101*

```
leaf101# show system internal epm endpoint ip 172.16.0.11
MAC : 0000.0000.0000 ::: Num IPs : 1
IP# 0 : 172.16.0.11 ::: IP# 0 flags :
Vlan id : 0 ::: Vlan vnid : 0 ::: VRF name : ACI-AMT-Book:v1
BD vnid : 0 ::: VRF vnid : 2981888
Phy If : 0 ::: Tunnel If : 0x18010003
Interface : Tunnel3
Flags : 0x80004400 ::: sclass : 49154 ::: Ref count : 3
EP Create Timestamp : 07/19/2018 20:02:06.034819
EP Update Timestamp : 07/19/2018 20:07:41.469567
EP Flags : IP|sclass|timer|
:::::
```

You see that you have learned the destination IP address as an endpoint. Why would Leaf 101 have learned this endpoint? This endpoint should only be Layer 2 connected to ACI, as per the earlier requirements. You go back to the previous section, where you configured Layer 2 connectivity for Host B in EPG *Web.* You decided to leave unicast routing enabled on BD *Web*, and added a subnet to perform host refresh. As you know, when unicast routing is enabled, leaf switches learn the IP addresses of endpoints connected in that bridge domain. This also applies for remote endpoint learning, and as endpoints start being learned remotely, the leaf switches always prefer the tunnel where the endpoint is learned versus routing externally.

The design for this traffic flow only requires a contract between the App *EPG* and the L3Out, and because you did not add a contract between the *App* EPG and the *Web* EPG directly, this traffic is not allowed.

Upon further inspection, you notice that there are drops incrementing under the tenant for this flow, so you know the traffic is being dropped because there is no contract that permits this traffic. You can see this by selecting Tenant > Operational > Flows > L3 Drop, as shown in Figure 15-22.

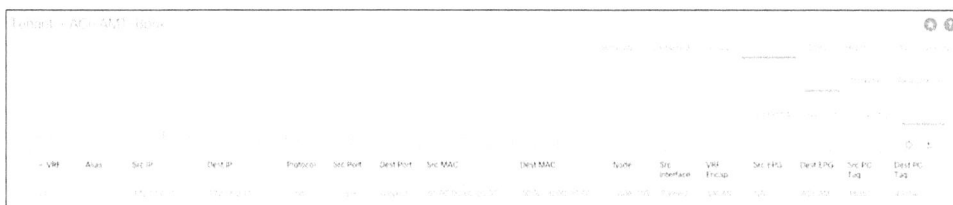

Figure 15-22   *Layer 3 Drop Statistics for Tenant ACI-AMT-Book*

Solution

In order to resolve this issue, you need to review your design for the Layer 2 flow. You had two options to enable Layer 2 connectivity between the two web servers:

- Disable unicast routing and enable ARP flooding and L2 unknown unicast flooding.

- Enable routing and add a subnet to allow for host refreshing and glean.

With the current design, you need to ensure that traffic is sent via the L3Out, so you cannot have the fabric learn IP address information for the servers in EPG *Web* since you have not moved the gateway for the *Web* EPG into ACI yet. In order to prevent IP learning in EPG *Web*, you need to revert to the first option.

After disabling unicast routing and changing to ARP flooding and L2 unknown unicast flooding, the server team tells you that Host A in EPG *App* is able to communicate with Host B in EPG *Web*.

Troubleshooting External Layer 3 Connectivity: Unexpected Layer 3 Traffic Flow Through ACI

You now have a new requirement for the ACI network. The developers need to be able to access the app servers so they can test code and push changes when new vulnerabilities are detected. Developers connect to the network using a different external router than the production external traffic. Because of this, you have configured a new L3Out and assigned the interfaces connecting to the dev external router. The topology in Figure 15-23 is used as reference.

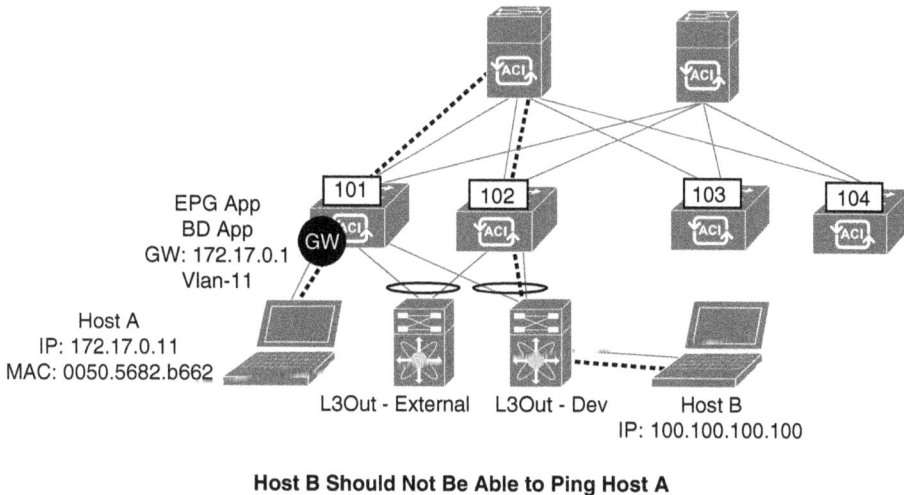

Host B Should Not Be Able to Ping Host A

Figure 15-23   *Layer 3 Connectivity for App Servers and Dev Server*

The security team is very strict about what traffic is allowed through the development environment. The team needs the ACI fabric to only allow the specific ports for the application between EPG *App* and the L3Out toward the dev server. After setting up the new dev L3Out and adding a contract that only allows the ports for the application, the security team calls and says it is able to ping the app servers from the dev network. They need this to be resolved immediately. You need to look at why ICMP is allowed between the *App* EPG and the L3Out for the dev network, despite the contract in place that only allows particular TCP ports.

In this case, it's important to remember how contracts are programmed in regard to L3Outs. Under an L3Out, contracts are configured via external EPGs, where one or more subnets are defined along with one or more contracts. As frames enter the L3Out, policy is enforced based on the prefix that is matched for the external EPG. Because you are applying policy based on IP address, the match occurs for a prefix globally in a VRF instance.

These rules are controlled by the NX-OS process ACLQOS. When a user configures an external EPG and defines prefixes within it, the APIC pushes this configuration to the leaf. The configuration is then pushed into hardware by ACLQOS. Each prefix is assigned the PCTag for the external EPG so that contracts can be applied matching the prefix and, thus, the tag. You can view the prefix configuration for a given VRF instance by finding the VXLAN VNID (segment) for the VRF instance and checking ACLQOS for that VNID, as shown in Figure 15-24 and Example 15-15.

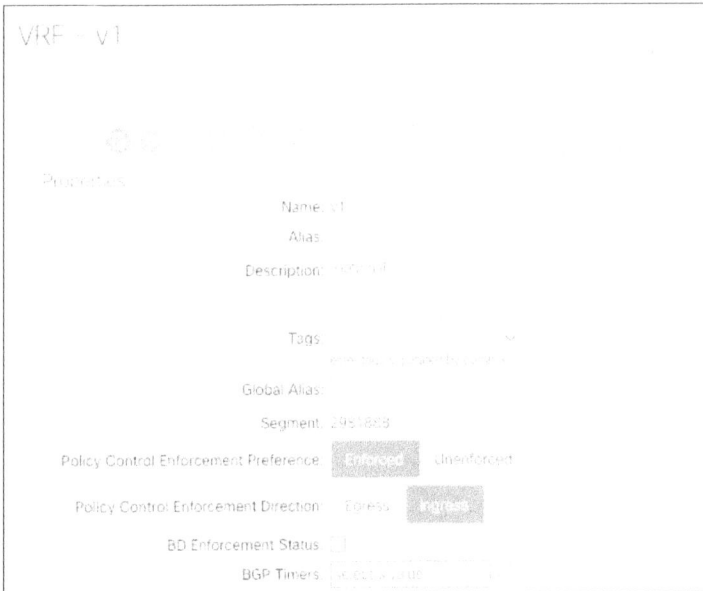

Figure 15-24   *VNID for VRF Instance v1 Within Tenant* ACI-AMT-BOOK

Example 15-15   *IP Prefix Verification Within ACLQOS for a Given VRF Instance on Leaf 101*

```
leaf101# vsh -c "show system internal policy-mgr prefix" | egrep "Vrf|\=|2981888"
Vrf-Vni VRF-Id Table-Id    Table-State  VRF-Name       Addr        Class  Shared Remote
   Complete

======= ====== ========== =========== ============= =========== ===== ====== ======
   ========
2981888 6      0x80000005 Up            ACI-AMT-Book:v1    0::/0    15   False  False
   False
2981888 6      0x5        Up            ACI-AMT-Book:v1 0.0.0.0/0  15   False  False
   False
```

In this case, you can see that only the "any" prefix 0.0.0.0/0 has been configured. This is indeed what has been configured, but what is different is the class or PCTag that has been assigned to this route: 15, or 0xf. This doesn't seem to match what has been allocated for the external EPG defined under the dev L3Out, as shown in Figure 15-25.

In this case, you would expect the subnet (0.0.0.0/0) to get associated with PCTag 16389. However, there is one exception to how prefixes get assigned to the corresponding external EPG PCTag: the all-zeros prefix.

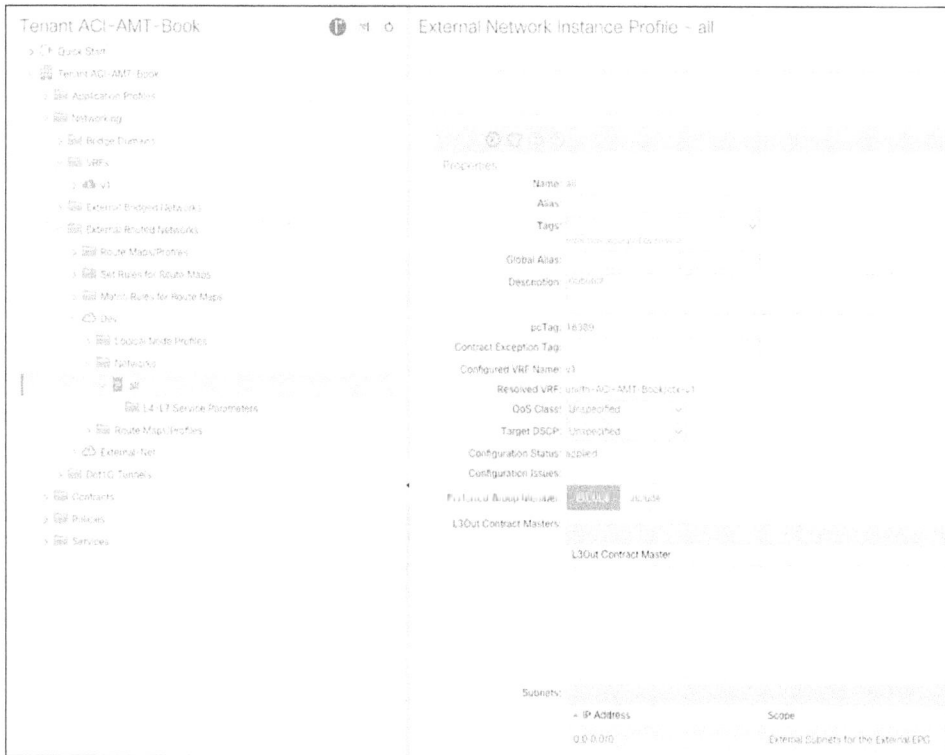

Figure 15-25 *The PCTag for an External EPG in the Cisco APIC UI*

The all-zeros prefix is always allocated the dedicated prefix 15 (0xf) globally within the VRF instance. This means that if any other L3Out that also uses the all-zeros prefix has contracts to an EPG, traffic can be classified using that contract.

In the previous example, you needed to define a contract between the *App* EPG and the L3Outfor *External-Net*. This contract was required to allow traffic to be routed outside the ACI fabric for connectivity to the web servers. The L3Out for *External-Net* was also configured with an all-zeros prefix, and the common/default contract was used to allow all traffic toward the *App* EPG as it came in the L3Out from the external network. Because the all-zeros prefix was defined under multiple L3Outs, traffic is also being classified for the dev L3Out. This is because both L3Outs reside within the same VRF instance, and the prefix 100.100.100.100 falls within 0.0.0.0/0.

You can further validate the filter the switch will use when enforcing policy between the *App* EPG and the VRF instance with the PCTag 15. You do this by checking the zoning-rules on the leaf from iBash, as shown in Example 15-16.

Example 15-16 *Contract and Filter Verification for PCTag 15 on Leaf 101*

```
leaf101# show zoning-rule scope 2981888 dst-epg 15
Rule ID    SrcEPG DstEPG  FilterID operSt  Scope    Action    Priority
=======    ====== ======  ======== ======= =======  =======   ========
4109       0      15      implicit enabled 2981888  deny,log  any_vrf_any_deny(21)
4117       16387  15      default  enabled 2981888  permit    src_dst_any(8)
```

As you can see, all traffic is allowed to communicate between the *App* EPG (PCTag 16387) and any prefix that falls under the all-zeros prefix defined in the VRF instance using the default filter.

Solution

Under a given VRF instance, it is best practice to only define the all-zeros route under one L3Out to prevent traffic from being classified incorrectly. In order to resolve this, you need to remove the all-zeros prefix from the external EPG for development and add a more specific prefix to classify the traffic you want to enforce, as shown in Figure 15-26.

Figure 15-26 *Adding a More Specific Prefix to the External EPG for Development*

After doing this, you now see in ACLQOS that the prefix is directly identified with the PCTag of the external EPG for development, as shown in Example 15-17.

Example 15-17 *Adding a More Specific Prefix to the External EPG for Development*

```
leaf101# vsh -c "show system internal policy-mgr prefix" | egrep "Vrf|\=|2981888"
Vrf-Vni VRF-Id Table-Id Table-State  VRF-Name       Addr    Class  Shared Remote
  Complete

======= === ========== == =============  ============= ==== ==== =====
  ========
2981888  6   0x80000005 Up  ACI-AMT-Book:v1      0::/0        15   False  False
  False
2981888  6   0x5        Up  ACI-AMT-Book:v1    0.0.0.0/0    15   False  False
  False
2981888  6   0x5        Up  ACI-AMT-Book:v1 100.100.100.100/32  16389 False False
  False
```

With this in place, any traffic coming from 100.100.100.100 in that VRF instance is classified using the contract configured under the external EPG for development, which only allows the TCP ports needed for the app servers. You can re-validate the zoning rules on the switch, as shown in Example 15-18.

Example 15-18 *Contract and Filter Verification for PCTag 16389 on Leaf 101*

```
leaf101# show zoning-rule scope 2981888 dst-epg 16387
Rule ID   SrcEPG DstEPG  FilterID operSt  Scope   Action    Priority
=======   ====== ======  ======== ======= ======= =======   ========
4121      16389  16387   8        enabled 2981888 permit    fully_qual(6)


leaf101# show zoning-filter filter 8
<Snipped for Formatting>
FilterId  Name  EtherT  SFromPort    SToPort      DFromPort    DToPort
========= ====  ======  ===========  ===========  ===========  ===========
8         8_0   ip      unspecified  unspecified  3260         3260
```

With this configuration in place, the security team makes you aware that all other traffic is denied from the development network and that it can only connect to the *App* EPG on port 3260 via the development L3Out.

Troubleshooting Leaf and Spine Connectivity: Leaf Issue

Your manager has asked you to troubleshoot an application outage. It's a three-tier application, and users are not able to connect to the front-end web server. You review the network topology where the application is hosted using the ACI fabric (see Figure 15-27).

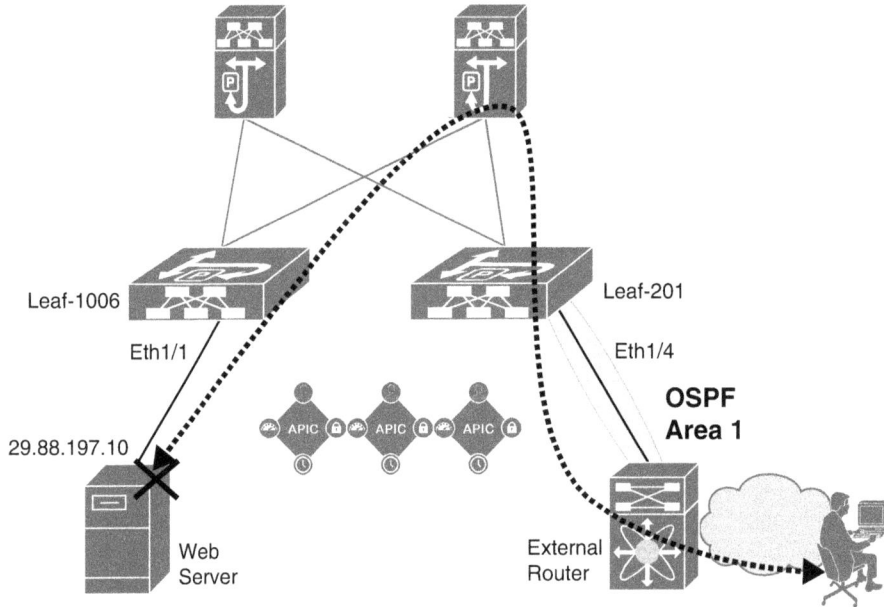

Figure 15-27 *Network Topology Hosting Application*

Solution

To begin troubleshooting the issue, first you should get the IP address of the unreachable web server (in this example, 29.88.197.10). Take this IP address and check to see if
the endpoint IP address is learned in ACI. In order to do this in the APIC GUI, go to
Operations tab > EP Tracker. Type the IP address of the web server in the search bar and
press Enter. Figure 15-28 shows the output.

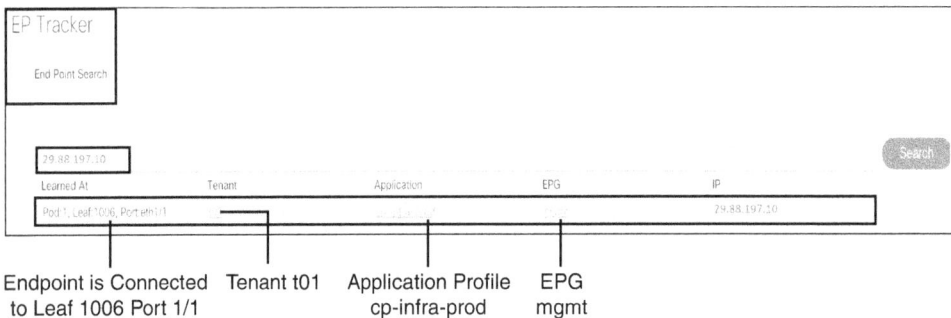

Figure 15-28 *Checking Endpoint Learning in ACI*

You know now that the endpoint is learned in ACI, and the web server is active. Use SSH to access Leaf 1006 to verify that the encapsulation VLAN and anycast gateway are programmed on the switch, as shown in Example 15-19.

Example 15-19   *VLAN and Anycast Gateway Deployment on Leaf 1006*

```
Leaf-1006# show vlan extended


VLAN Name                                   Encap             Ports
---- ------------------------------------  ---------------   -----------------------
28    t01:a-cp-infra-mgmt                   vxlan-15335344    Eth1/1, Eth1/5, Eth1/6,
                                                              Eth1/7, Eth1/8, Po1, Po3
29    t01:cp-infra-prod:mgmt                vlan-1001         Eth1/1, Eth1/5, Eth1/6,
                                                              Eth1/7, Eth1/8, Po1, Po3


Leaf-1006# show ip interface brief vrf t01:standard
IP Interface Status for VRF "t01:standard"(5)
Interface        Address          Interface Status
vlan28           29.88.197.1/27   protocol-up/link-up/admin-up
```

Now check the reachability of the web server from the directly connected leaf:

```
Leaf-1006# iping 29.88.197.10 -V t01:standard
PING 29.88.197.10 (29.88.197.10): 56 data bytes
64 bytes from 29.88.197.10: icmp_seq=0 ttl=63 time=0.756 ms
64 bytes from 29.88.197.10: icmp_seq=1 ttl=63 time=0.375 ms
64 bytes from 29.88.197.10: icmp_seq=2 ttl=63 time=0.551 ms
^C
--- 29.88.197.10 ping statistics ---
3 packets transmitted, 3 packets received, 0.00% packet loss
round-trip min/avg/max = 0.375/0.56/0.756 ms
```

You are now sure that there is nothing wrong with web server reachability from the directly connected Leaf 1006. Because the users are accessing the web server from a remote network external to the ACI fabric, you should now check the connectivity from Border Leaf 201 toward the external router, as shown in Example 15-20.

Example 15-20   *OSPF Neighbor Verification on Leaf 201*

```
Leaf-201# show ip ospf neighbors vrf t01:standard
OSPF Process ID default VRF t01:standard
Total number of neighbors: 1
Neighbor ID      Pri State       Up Time  Address        Interface
39.88.193.129     1 FULL/ -       3w0d     49.88.192.26   Eth1/4
```

You have confirmed that the connectivity from Border Leaf 201 to the external router is fine. Next, you try to ping from Border Leaf 201 to the web server IP address, as shown in Example 15-21.

Example 15-21   *iPing Failing to the Destination*

```
Leaf-201# iping 29.88.197.10 -V t01:standard
PING 29.88.197.10 (29.88.197.10) from 49.88.192.27: 56 data bytes
Request 0 timed out
Request 1 timed out
Request 2 timed out
^C
--- 29.88.197.10 ping statistics ---
4 packets transmitted, 0 packets received, 100.00% packet loss
```

You are not able to ping from Border Leaf 201 to the web server that is plugged in to Leaf 1006. This means there is something wrong in the ACI fabric. You logged in to APIC GUI and checked the system faults. You found that Border Leaf 201 somehow became inactive in the fabric, as shown in Figure 15-29.

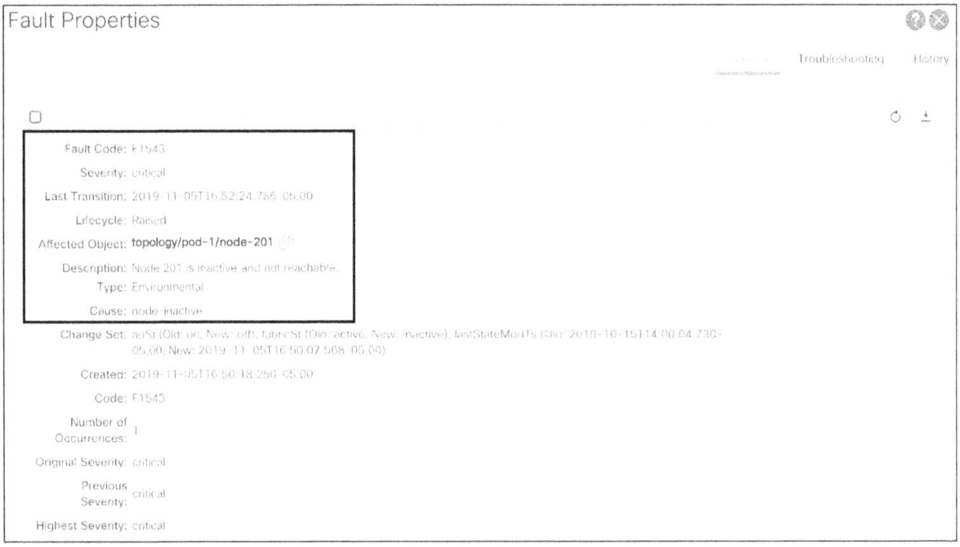

Figure 15-29   *ACI Fault Showing Border Leaf 201 Becoming Inactive*

As you further diagnose the Border Leaf 201 issue, you find that both of the uplinks toward the spines were down due to transceiver errors. You replace the transceivers and bring Border Leaf 201 back to active in the fabric, as shown in Example 15-22.

Example 15-22 *Border Leaf 201 Back to Active State*

```
APIC-1# acidiag fnvread
     ID   Pod ID              Name   Serial Number        IP Address    Role
  State   LastUpdMsgId
-------------------------------------------------------------------------------
  -------------------------
    101       1       Spine-101     FOX2120P68P       10.2.2.76/32    spine
  active    0
    102       1       Spine-102     FOX2126PD4S       10.2.2.77/32    spine
  active    0
    201       1       Leaf-201      FDO212225QJ       10.2.44.65/32   leaf
  active    0
   1006       1       Leaf-1006     FDO21460982       10.2.2.74/32    leaf
  active    0

Total 4 nodes
```

Now, if you try to reach the web server from Border Leaf 201, you should be able to do so, as shown in Example 15-23.

Example 15-23 *Endpoint and Tunnel Verification on Border Leaf 201*

```
Leaf-201# show endpoint ip 29.88.197.10
Legend:
 s - arp              H - vtep            V - vpc-attached    p - peer-aged
 R - peer-attached-rl B - bounce          S - static          M - span
 D - bounce-to-proxy  O - peer-attached   a - local-aged      L - local
+-----------------------------------+---------------+-----------------+-------------
  -+-------------+
     VLAN/                          Encap          MAC Address       MAC Info/
  Interface
     Domain                         VLAN           IP Address        IP Info
+-----------------------------------+---------------+-----------------+-------------
  -+-------------+
t01:standard                                       29.88.197.10
  tunnel25

Leaf-201# show interface tunnel 25
Tunnel25 is up
   MTU 9000 bytes, BW 0 Kbit
   Transport protocol is in VRF "overlay-1"
   Tunnel protocol/transport is ivxlan
   Tunnel source 10.2.44.65/32 (lo0)
   Tunnel destination 10.2.2.74
   Last clearing of "show interface" counters never
```

```
    Tx
    0 packets output, 1 minute output rate 0 packets/sec
    Rx
    0 packets input, 1 minute input rate 0 packets/sec

Leaf-201#
Leaf-201# acidiag fnvread | grep 10.2.44.65
    201        1     Leaf-201       FDO212225QJ      10.2.44.65/32     leaf
  active   0

Leaf-201#
Leaf-201# acidiag fnvread | grep 10.2.2.74
    1006       1     Leaf-1006      FDO21460982      10.2.2.74/32      leaf
  active   0

Leaf-201# iping 29.88.197.10 -V t01:standard
PING 29.88.197.10 (29.88.197.10): 56 data bytes
64 bytes from 29.88.197.10: icmp_seq=0 ttl=63 time=0.756 ms
64 bytes from 29.88.197.10: icmp_seq=1 ttl=63 time=0.375 ms
64 bytes from 29.88.197.10: icmp_seq=2 ttl=63 time=0.551 ms
^C
--- 29.88.197.10 ping statistics ---
3 packets transmitted, 3 packets received, 0.00% packet loss
round-trip min/avg/max = 0.365/0.46/0.654 ms
```

Note   This troubleshooting use case outlines various troubleshooting steps to resolve the issue. However, always remember that if a failure event occurs or someone has made any configuration change that could have destabilized the network, you can check the fault and audit logs to get clues right away.

Troubleshooting VMM Domains: VMM Controller Offline

The server team just installed a new VMware vSphere cluster to deploy production applications. You advise the team to plug the servers in to the ACI fabric so you can use VMM integration with the VMware vDS to help seamlessly map VMware port groups to EPGs in the ACI fabric. However, upon creating the VMM domain, the server administrators advise you that they do not see the vDS that was supposed to be pushed by APIC. When navigating to the VMM domain in the APIC UI, you see the fault shown in Figure 15-30.

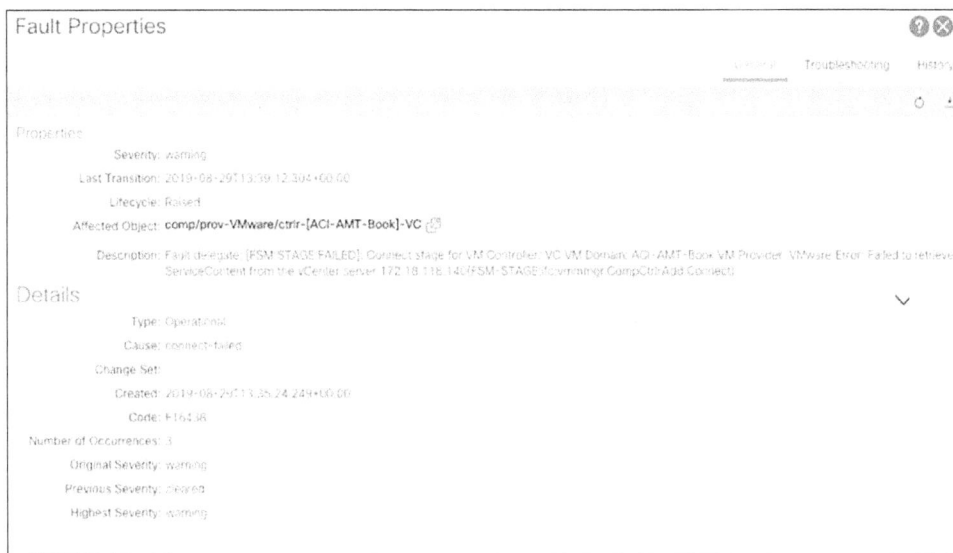

Figure 15-30 *A Fault Raised on the VMM Domain Stating That the APIC Can't Connect to vCenter*

The fault is alerting you that the APIC is unable to connect to vCenter, so it can't pull the inventory and deploy the vDS. You need to check whether the APICs have IP connectivity to the configured vCenter. The APICs form a cluster, but only one APIC is responsible for handling the connection to a VMM domain at a time. This is known as the "shard leader" for a VMM domain. If the shard leader goes down, such as for an upgrade or a replacement, the connection is moved to another available APIC. Because you need to check network connectivity from the APIC to vCenter, you need to locate the shard leader for the VMM domain. This is done on the NX-OS CLI of any APIC by running the **show vmware domain name** *VMM-domain* command, as shown in Example 15-24.

Example 15-24 *Viewing the VMM Domain Configuration and Checking the Shard Leader*

```
apic1# show vmware domain name ACI-AMT-Book
Domain Name                        : ACI-AMT-Book
Virtual Switch Mode                : VMware Distributed Switch
Vlan Domain                        : ACI-AMT-Book (100-150)
Physical Interfaces                :
Number of EPGs                     : 0
Faults by Severity                 : 0, 1, 0, 1
LLDP override                      : no
CDP override                       : no
Channel Mode override              : no
NetFlow Exporter Policy            : no
```

```
vCenters:
Faults: Grouped by severity (Critical, Major, Minor, Warning)
vCenter               Type     Datacenter           Status     ESXs   VMs   Faults
------------------    -------- -------------------- --------   -----  ----- ------
172.18.118.140        vCenter  ACI-AMT-Book         unknown    0      0     0,1,0,1


APIC Owner:
Controller    APIC      Ownership
------------  --------  --------------
VC            apic-1    Leader
VC            apic-2    NonLeader
VC            apic-3    NonLeader


Trunk Portgroups:
Name                                            VLANs
---------------------------------------------   ---------------------------------------
```

Here you can see that APIC 1 is the shard leader for the newly deployed VMM domain.
While APIC 1 is online, all troubleshooting can be performed directly on APIC 1
because it performs the necessary functions for the VMM domain unless it goes offline.
Next, you need to see if APIC 1 has IP connectivity to vCenter by initiating a ping, as
shown in Example 15-25.

Example 15-25 *Checking Shard Leader IP Connectivity to vCenter by Using ping*

```
admin@apic1# ping 172.18.118.140
PING 172.18.118.140 (172.18.118.140) 56(84) bytes of data.
From 10.100.1.10 icmp_seq=1 Destination Host Unreachable
From 10.100.1.10 icmp_seq=2 Destination Host Unreachable
From 10.100.1.10 icmp_seq=3 Destination Host Unreachable
From 10.100.1.10 icmp_seq=4 Destination Host Unreachable
```

Here you can see that you are unable to ping vCenter. vCenter should be reachable via the
OOB network, but the ping request was using the 10.100.1.10 address, which is configured for in-band. In order to see what the Linux routing table looks like on the APIC, you
can run the **route** command from the bash CLI of APIC 1, as shown in Example 15-26.

Example 15-26 *Checking the Routing Table of the APIC Shard Leader*

```
apic1# bash
apic1:~> route
Kernel IP routing table
Destination     Gateway         Genmask          Flags Metric Ref    Use Iface
default         10.100.1.1      0.0.0.0          UG    8      0        0 bond0.10
default         192.168.4.1     0.0.0.0          UG    16     0        0 oobmgmt
10.0.0.0        10.0.0.30       255.255.0.0      UG    0      0        0 bond0.3091
```

10.0.0.30	0.0.0.0	255.255.255.255	UH	0	0	0	bond0.3091
10.0.168.65	10.0.0.30	255.255.255.255	UGH	0	0	0	bond0.3091
10.0.168.66	10.0.0.30	255.255.255.255	UGH	0	0	0	bond0.3091
10.100.1.0	0.0.0.0	255.255.255.0	U	0	0	0	bond0.10
10.100.1.1	0.0.0.0	255.255.255.255	UH	0	0	0	bond0.10
169.254.1.0	0.0.0.0	255.255.255.0	U	0	0	0	teplo-1
169.254.254.0	0.0.0.0	255.255.255.0	U	0	0	0	lxcbr0
172.17.0.0	0.0.0.0	255.255.0.0	U	0	0	0	docker0
192.168.4.0	0.0.0.0	255.255.255.0	U	0	0	0	oobmgmt

Here you see that there are two default routes: one via the in-band interface with a metric of 8, and the other via the out-of-band interface with a metric of 16. Because the in-band interface has a lower metric, that will be the interface used to reach any network outside of what is locally configured.

Solution 1

One solution is to provide network connectivity from the in-band interface of the APIC to vCenter.

Solution 2

Another solution is to change the default APIC connectivity preference to out-of-band versus in-band by navigating to System > System Settings > APIC Connectivity Preferences and selecting ooband.

Note   If other services, such as NTP and syslog, are intended to work using in-band, then you may need to change the configuration of each protocol to explicitly use the in-band EPG. This overwrites the default policy and uses the in-band interface for those protocols.

Troubleshooting VMM Domains: VM Connectivity Issue After Deploying the VMM Domain

Since resolving the previous issue, the APIC has successfully connected to vCenter and pushed a vDS. The server team has added the appropriate hosts behind a UCS B-Series blade chassis to the vDS. The current requirement is to push a port group to vCenter for the *Web* EPG so that new virtualized web servers can inherit the existing policy. However, after mapping the VMM domain to the Web EPG, the server administrators notify you that the VMs are unable to ping the gateway.

When the VMM domain was mapped to the EPG, both Deployment Immediacy and Resolution Immediacy were set to Immediate. To troubleshoot this issue, you navigate to Dynamic EPG Members to see if the VLAN was pushed to the interfaces that connect to the UCS fabric interconnects, but you do not see the paths listed. This means the VLAN that was dynamically allocated for this EPG is not being pushed to the switches and switchports where the UCS fabric interconnects connect.

When deploying using the On-Demand or Immediate setting, a valid LLDP or CDP adjacency must be reported from vCenter for the physical NICs on the host that is added to the APIC managed vDS. To troubleshoot this issue, you look at the faults raised under the VMM domain and notice that there is a fault for being unable to retrieve the adjacency information for a host where the VMs reside, as shown in Figure 15-31.

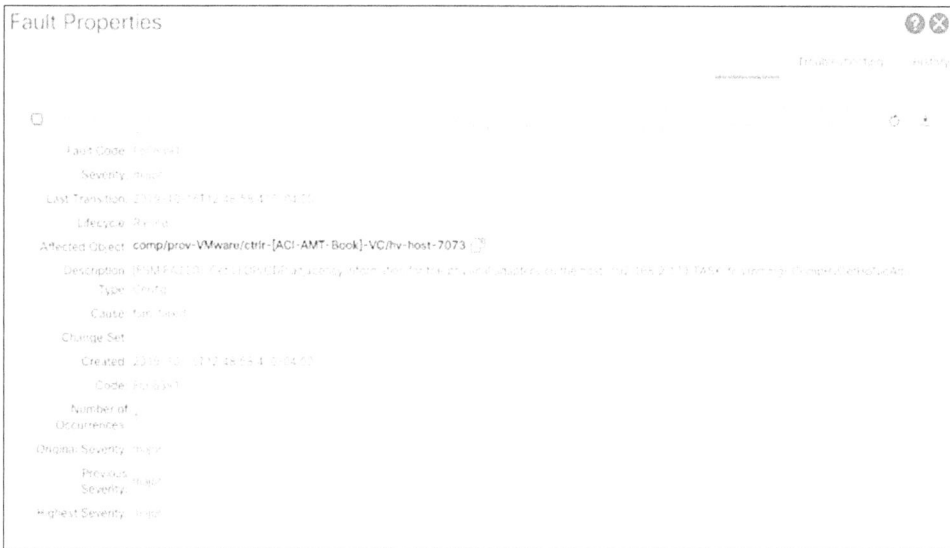

Figure 15-31   *Fault for Missing Adjacency on the ESXi Host*

Because the APIC is unable to retrieve the adjacency information from vCenter, it cannot deploy the dynamic configuration to the switches and ports where the UCS fabric interconnects are connected. Because the fabric interconnects terminate LLDP and CDP on the uplinks and downlinks, it's critical that the UCS domain is configured to send LLDP or CDP, depending on what is desired. In this case, LLDP is configured in the vSwitch policy under the VMM domain. The ultimate goal is to ensure that the discovery protocol pushed to vCenter via the vSwitch policy matches what is being sent and received on the hosts.

Solution 1

The UCS server administrators should enable LLDP under the network control policy for the vNICs on the blades. Once it is enabled, LLDP can be sent and received, allowing the hosts to view a neighbor pointing to the fabric interconnect. The host can then communicate this to vCenter, and the APIC can receive the configuration in the form of an event.

Solution 2

If CDP is the desired protocol, ensure that it is enabled on the UCS domain and change the vSwitch policy so that LLDP is disabled and CDP is enabled. This way, you can push CDP as the discovery protocol on the vDS.

The APIC can then deploy the configuration to switches and ports where the fabric interconnects are connected, based on the neighbor information received from vCenter. Once there is a valid neighbor, the dynamic paths can be seen under Dynamic EPG Members for the EPG, as shown in Figure 15-32.

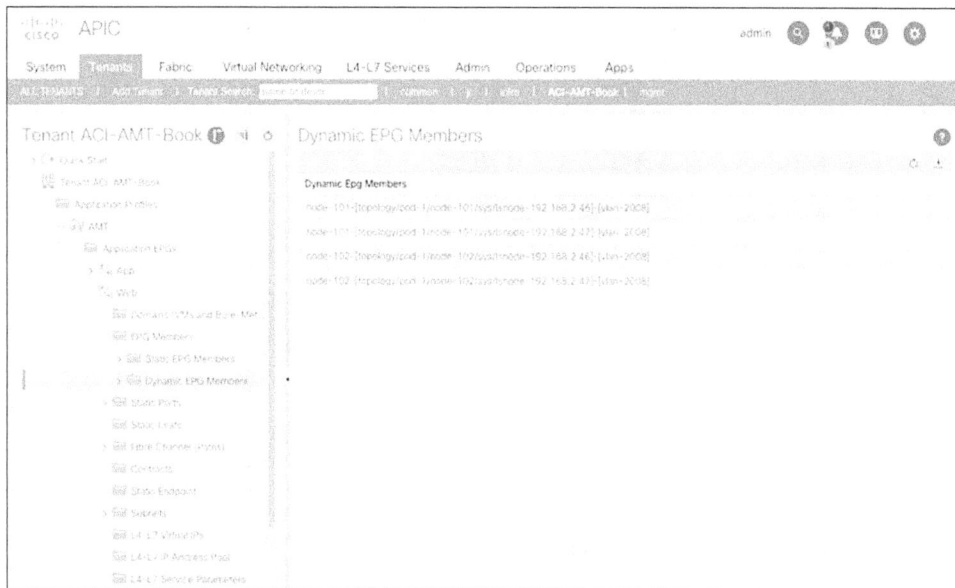

Figure 15-32 *Verifying That Dynamic Paths Are Deployed to the Leafs Connecting to the Fabric Interconnects*

If there are no paths shown in this UI, the adjacency cannot be resolved. This is just an additional way to verify that the correct state has been built in vCenter for the corresponding hosts.

Solution 3

If you don't want the policy to rely on dynamic discovery using LLDP or CDP, you can set Resolution Immediacy on the VMM domain EPG mapping to Pre-Provision to ignore the adjacency requirement and push the VLAN to every switch and interface that is mapped to the AAEP used for the VMM domain. When using Pre-Provision, it is best practice to have a separate AAEP for VMM so that the VLAN is not pushed unnecessarily to interfaces connecting to bare-metal servers or devices providing external Layer 2 or Layer 3 connectivity.

Using either of the three offered solutions, the VLANs can be deployed properly, and the server administrators can notify you that the VMs have connectivity on the network.

Troubleshooting L4–L7: Deploying an L4–L7 Device

Due to business expansion, additional web servers have been deployed to handle the increased load. You decide to insert a policy-based routing (PBR) service graph to intercept traffic and redirect it to the load balancer before it reaches the new web servers. The first step is to connect the load balancer to the fabric so you can configure it directly by creating a static path on an EPG. After configuring the load balancer, you create the L4–L7 device and deploy the service graph template. After doing this, you notice that traffic isn't hitting the load balancer as expected. Figure 15-33 illustrates the topology used.

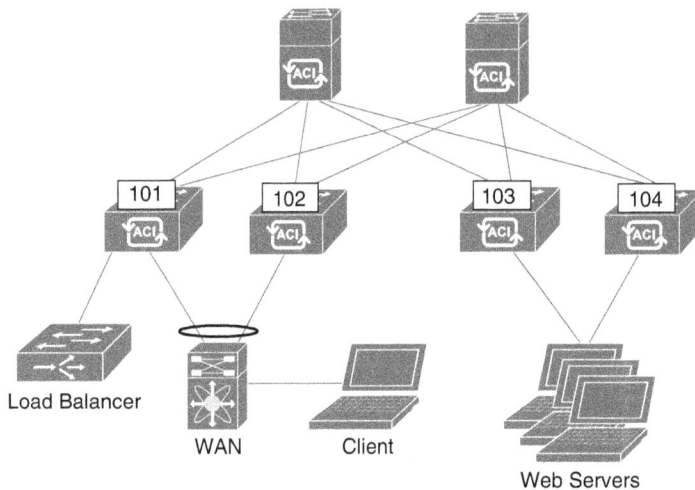

Figure 15-33 *Load Balancer Inserted into Web Traffic Flow*

To begin troubleshooting, you review the L4–L7 deployed graph instance and verify that the right VLANs are deployed on the Ethernet interfaces toward the load balancer. Figure 15-34 shows the view of the deployed service graph instance. You verify that the correct VLANs are configured: VLAN 15 for the outside and VLAN 5 for the inside. From the deployed graph instance, you also see the PCTag assigned to the VLANs. The L4–L7 deployed VLANs are also called *shadow EPGs* because they function like traditional EPGs but are controlled by the service graph.

A quick way to verify whether these VLANs are deployed is by checking the VLANs on the leaf node where the service device is connected. Example 15-27 shows the currently deployed VLANs.

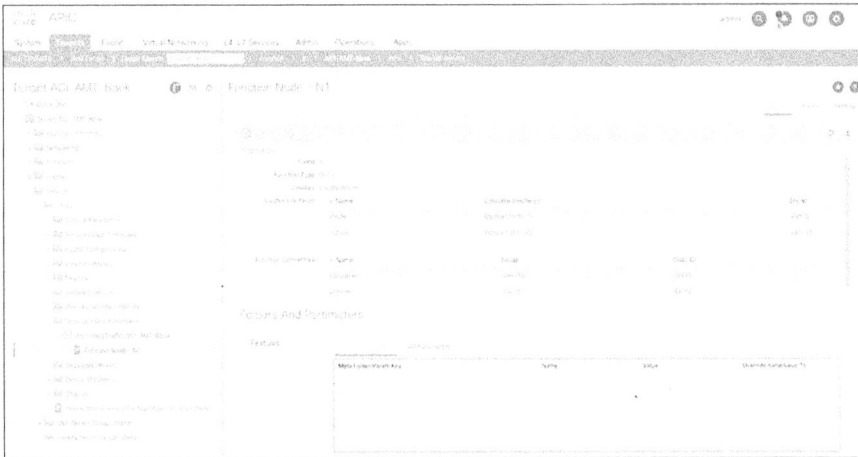

Figure 15-34 *Deployed Service Graph Instance*

Example 15-27 *VLAN Verification on Leaf 101*

```
leaf101# show vlan extended | egrep -A 1 "vlan-5 "
1    ACI-AMT-                        vlan-5        Eth1/21
     Book:LoadBalancerctxv1:inside:
leaf101# show vlan extended | egrep -A 1 "vlan-15 "
 59   ACI-AMT-Book:NetCentric:VLAN15  vlan-15       Eth1/47
```

The VLAN name should always be *Tenant:L4-L7DeviceName+VRF:ClusterInterface Name*. As you can see in Example 15-27, VLAN 5 is deployed properly, but *ACI-AMT-Book:LoadBalancerctxv1:inside* is deployed with VLAN 5, and VLAN 15 is deployed for an EPG named *VLAN15* inside the NetCentric application profile. Based on this output, you determine that the graph did not get deployed properly. The next step should be to look at all faults raised. Given that you don't know where the fault is raised, it is easiest to go to the top-level tenant view and view all faults for the tenant, as shown in Figure 15-35.

Here you can see that fault F0467 is raised; the fault description says that encapsulation is already in use by *ACI-AMT-Book:NetCentric:VLAN15*. This confirms why VLAN 15 wasn't properly deployed as a shadow EPG.

One common issue with service graphs is that the service device interfaces are part of a regular EPG—usually because IP connectivity is required to configure the service device. To resolve this issue, the old static path needs to be deleted so the shadow EPG can be deployed. After making this change, you see that PBR now works, but you are no longer able to use SSH to connect directly to the load balancer to make changes. This indicates a contract issue, and you can confirm it by looking at the packet log or the deny flows in the APIC UI. The service graph does not enable you to access devices inside the shadow EPG.

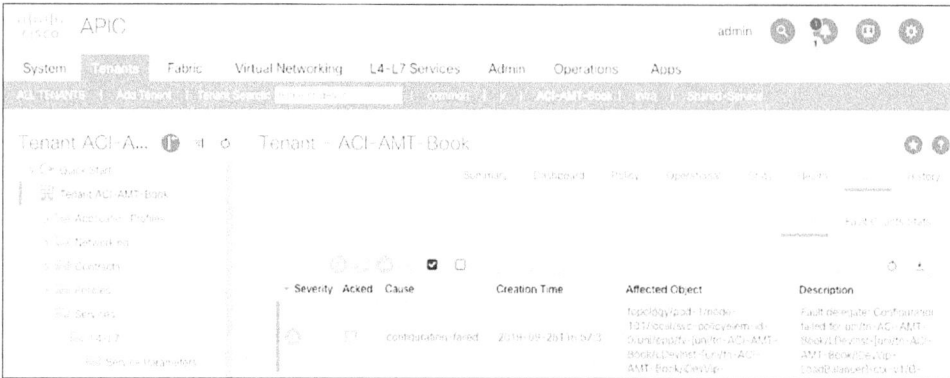

Figure 15-35 *Faults Raised in a Tenant*

Solution

You can update the service graph template to allow Direct Connect, as shown in Figure 15-36. This way, you can create a contract relationship between the consumer or provider EPG and the corresponding shadow EPG.

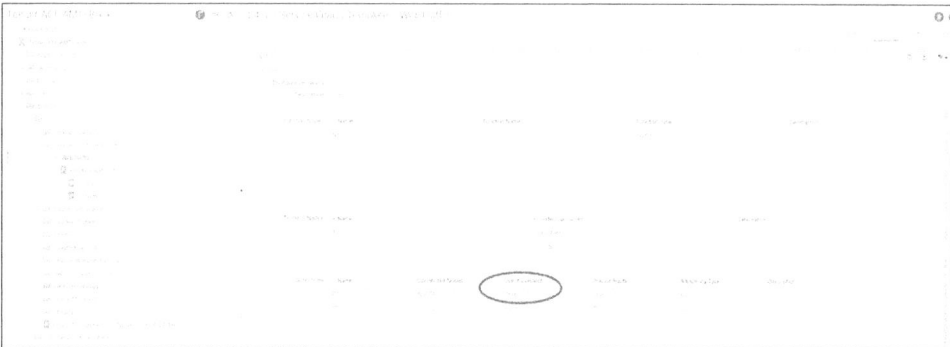

Figure 15-36 *Service Graph Direct Connect*

Troubleshooting L4–L7: Control Protocols Stop Working After Service Graph Deployment

After deploying a new service graph between an EPG and vzAny in the VRF instance, you notice that some control plane protocols, such as CDP, LLDP, and LACP, stop functioning. Servers begin dropping because LACP keeps timing out, and you must move quickly to isolate the issue.

You start by reviewing how the service graph was deployed. The requirement was to have all traffic sourced from EPG *untagged* redirected to a firewall. In order to accommodate this, the service graph was deployed using the EPG as the consumer and vzAny as the provider, as shown in Figure 15-37.

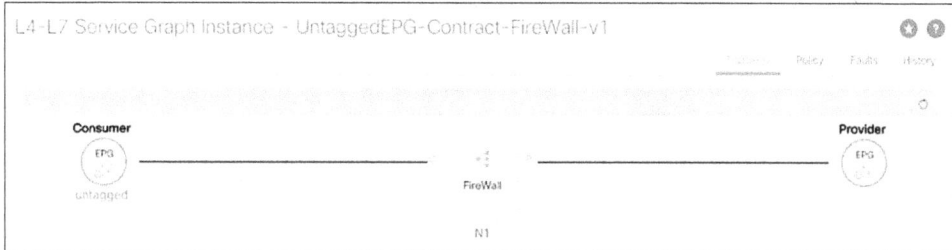

Figure 15-37 *Deployed Graph Instance for Service Graph*

The EPG is named *untagged* because all servers inside this EPG also send traffic without an 802.1Q tag. Control protocols such as LACP also do not include a VLAN tag, so it's possible that the leaf switch could classify these packets in the EPG where the untagged VLAN is deployed.

In order to troubleshoot the issue further, you run **tcpdump** on the *kpm_inb* interface on the leaf where the hosts connect, and you notice that no LACP frames are reaching the CPU, as shown in Example 15-28.

Example 15-28 *tcpdump on kpm_inb Showing No LACP Packets Being Received*

```
leaf101# tcpdump -xxvi kpm_inb ether proto 0x8809
tcpdump: listening on kpm_inb, link-type EN10MB (Ethernet), capture size 65535 bytes
```

You suspect that they might be redirected because of how the service graph is deployed. But how could control protocol frames like LACP frames be redirected? These frames are only Layer 2 and do not include a Layer 3 header, which is what you would expect the match criteria for redirection to be. You decide to take a closer look at the contract that was used to deploy the service graph; see Figure 15-38.

Aha! The contract deployed is using the common/default filter, which matches on all frame types—not just packets with Layer 3 information. Because the service graph was deployed with vzAny as the provider, any packet that gets classified in EPG *untagged* is redirected to the firewall.

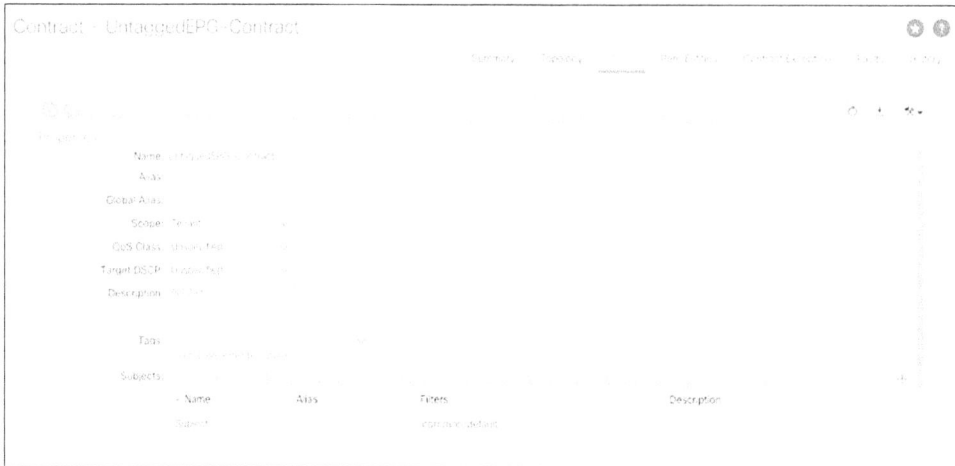

Figure 15-38   *Contract Configuration for the Deployed Service Graph*

Solution

It was only desired to have traffic with an L3 header redirected to the firewall. In order to resolve the issue, you add a new filter to the contract to match only on IP traffic, as shown in Figure 15-39. You then remove the common/default filter from the contract.

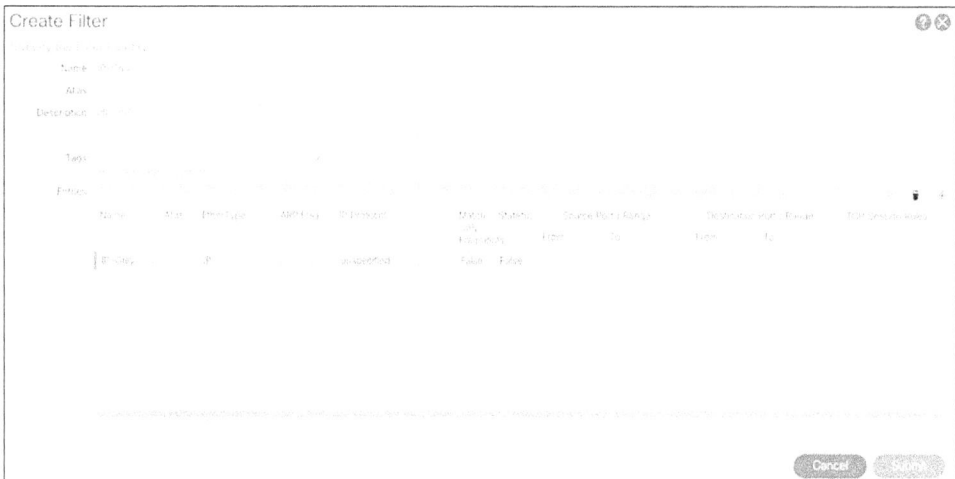

Figure 15-39   *IP-Only Filter to Redirect Only IP Packets to the Firewall*

This way, Layer 2 control plane frames are forwarded to the CPU as normal; they are not redirected to the firewall.

Troubleshooting Multi-Pod: BUM Traffic Not Reaching Remote Pods

Your business is expanding to a new location. You want to extend your ACI fabric to that location to allow for easy integration with your existing environment, and you want a single pane of glass for both locations. You meet all the requirements for deploying multi-pod, so you decide to roll out the deployment by adding the new location as a second pod to your existing ACI fabric.

However, after you add the pod and connect servers at the new location in an existing bridge domain, you find that those servers cannot resolve ARP to servers if they are in different pods. Because servers can always resolve ARP to other servers in the same pod, you are confident that this is an issue with the multi-pod deployment. Figure 15-40 shows the BD stretched across multi-pod.

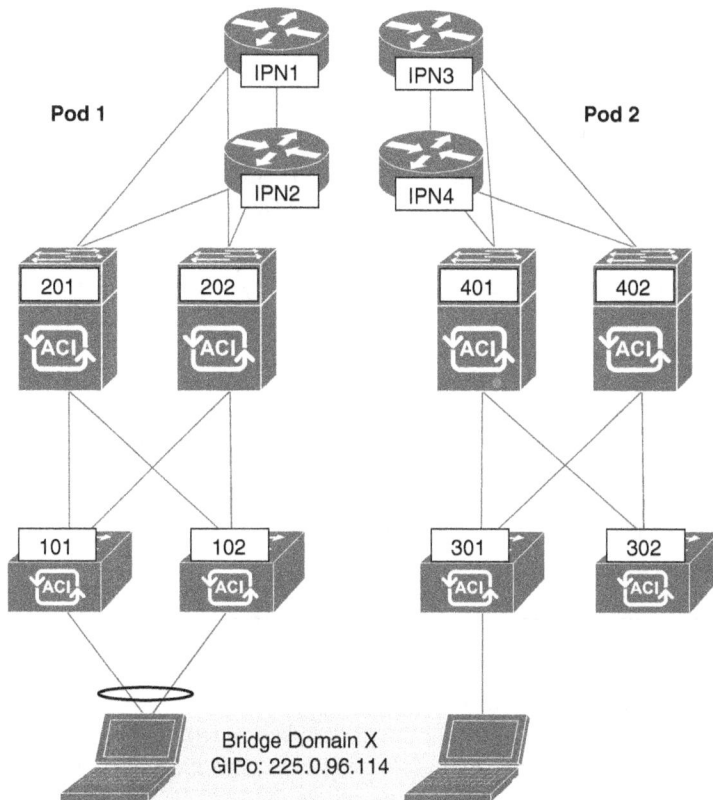

Figure 15-40 *Bridge Domain Stretched Across Pod 1 and Pod 2*

Because you know that only a single spine in each pod will join a group and send traffic for a group, you start by investigating which spine is authoritative for the bridge domain using Group IP outer (GIPo) 225.0.96.144. This can be accomplished by running the **show**

isis internal mcast routes command on a spine iBash CLI and checking if there is an external interface for the route in question. You run the command on Spine 201 and get the output shown in Example 15-29.

Note   In this topology, interfaces Ethernet1/1 and Ethernet1/2 connect to the IPN(s), so running the command and using **grep** for four lines after the match is sufficient. If you had more interfaces connecting to the IPN, you would need to add more lines to the **grep** statement.

Example 15-29   *Checking Spine 201 for a GIPo Route with External Interfaces*

```
pod1-spine201# show isis internal mcast routes | grep -A 4 "225.0.96.144"
GIPo: 225.0.96.144 [TRANSIT]
   OIF List:
     Ethernet1/1.1(External)
     Ethernet1/5.83
     Ethernet1/6.84
```

Based on this, you know that Spine 201 is authoritative for the GIPo and that it is sending traffic for this group toward the IPN on interface Ethernet1/1. This interface connects to IPN1.

The next step would be to check the multicast routing table of the IPNs to ensure that the proper routes are in place to forward the traffic for group 225.0.96.144 between pods. Example 15-30 shows the output of the mroute table on IPN1.

Example 15-30   *mroute Validation on IPN 1*

```
IPN3# show ip mroute 225.0.96.144 vrf IPN
(*, 225.0.96.144/32), bidir, uptime: 00:00:26, igmp ip pim
  Incoming interface: Ethernet1/1.4, RPF nbr: 192.168.1.0
  Outgoing interface list: (count: 2)
     Ethernet1/1.4, uptime: 00:00:26, igmp, (RPF)
```

Here you see that the same interface is listed as incoming and outgoing. The incoming interface should be the interface facing the rendezvous point (RP), or if the RP is local, the incoming interface should be the interface facing the loopback interface where the RP is configured. In this case, the incoming interface is the link connecting to Spine 201 in Pod 1. The spines in ACI do not run PIM, so they are not valid RPFs for the route to the RP.

The IPN thinks the RP is via the spine because of the default OSPF cost. In this topology, the ACI spines are connected at 40 Gbps and have a default OSPF cost of 1. The interfaces between the IPNs are connected at 10 Gbps and have a higher cost due to the lower bandwidth. Because of this, the route to the RP is preferred through the ACI spines.

Solution 1

If the platform supports it, the interfaces between IPNs should have a matching physical speed. This ensures not only that the cost is the same on the link but also that there is a less likely chance of oversubscription.

Solution 2

You can manually set the OSPF cost on the interface connecting the IPN routers by running the **ip ospf cost** *<value>* command on all interfaces. The value can be lowered to 1 to match, or the interfaces that connect to the spine switches can be assigned a higher value to make the route via the spine less preferred.

Troubleshooting Multi-Pod: Remote L3Out Not Reachable

You've added a second pod to your ACI fabric. After configuring a static path for a server attached in Pod 2 to an EPG, you notice that you are unable to ping it from a device in the core router in Pod 1. Contracts are in place between the L3Out and the EPG that allow ICMP. Figure 15-41 provides a high-level overview of the topology.

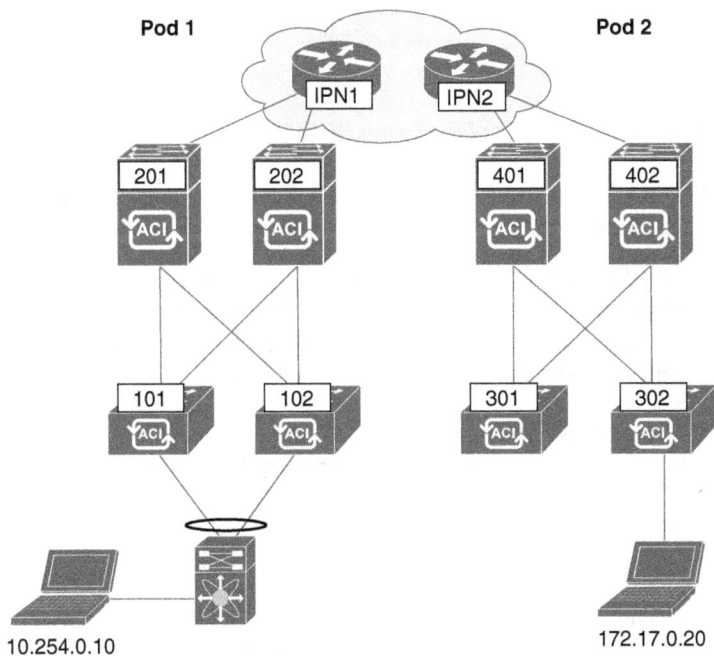

Figure 15-41 *Topology Overview*

When you run **tcpdump** on 172.17.0.20, you see the ICMP requests from 10.254.0.10 come in and replies go out. However, **ping** is showing as timing out from the 10.254.0.10 source. Using ELAM Assistant, you capture the ICMP reply on Leaf 302, and it shows that the packet is dropped, with drop code UC_PC_CFG_TABLE_DROP, as shown in Figure 15-42.

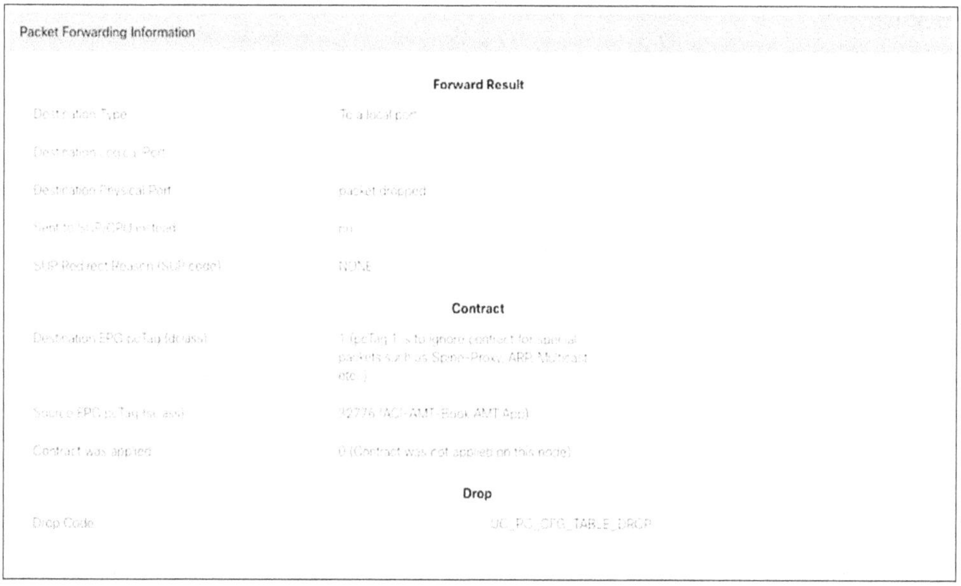

Figure 15-42 *Packet Drop on the Compute Leaf Using ELAM Assistant*

UC_PC_CFG_TABLE_DROP means that there is no route present in the routing table to forward the packet to the destination.

To understand why a route doesn't exist, you go to the leaf CLI and run the **show ip route** command. The odd thing is that only pervasive routes show up, and no BGP learned routes appear. The next step is to see if Leaf 302 has any BGP neighbors by running the **show bgp sessions vrf overlay-1** command, as shown in Example 15-31.

Example 15-31 *No BGP Neighbors Exist on Leaf 302*

```
leaf302# show bgp sessions vrf overlay-1
Total peers 3, established peers 3
ASN 65502
VRF overlay-1, local ASN 65502
peers 0, established peers 0, local router-id 10.0.128.70
State: I-Idle, A-Active, O-Open, E-Established, C-Closing, S-Shutdown


Neighbor        ASN    Flaps LastUpDn|LastRead|LastWrit St Port(L/R)  Notif(S/R)
leaf302#
```

So why don't Leaf 302 and the other leafs in Pod 2 have BGP neighbors? The fabric BGP sessions are established on a per-pod basis. Just like IS-IS, BGP VPNv4 is pod specific, and a unique set of route reflectors must be defined for each pod.

Solution

Under System > System Settings > BGP Route Reflector, you must define a unique set of route reflectors for each pod. Once this is done, the spines take the routes they learn through EPVN from Pod 1 and redistribute them into BGP VPNv4. After you configure the spines in Pod 2 in the route reflector policy, the route learned in Pod 1 is advertised to Pod 2, and Pod 2 spines advertise these routes locally in BGP to the leafs. Example 15-32 shows the route present on the leaf after you add the BGP configuration.

Example 15-32   *Route on Compute Leaf Is Now Reachable via Border Leafs in Pod 1*

```
leaf302# show ip route 10.254.0.10 vrf ACI-AMT-Book:v1
IP Route Table for VRF "ACI-AMT-Book:v1"
'*' denotes best ucast next-hop
'**' denotes best mcast next-hop
'[x/y]' denotes [preference/metric]
'%<string>' in via output denotes VRF <string>


10.254.0.0/16, ubest/mbest: 2/0
    *via 10.0.128.71%overlay-1, [200/1], 00:00:07, bgp-65502, internal, tag 65502
        recursive next hop: 10.0.128.71/32%overlay-1
    *via 10.0.128.70%overlay-1, [200/1], 00:00:07, bgp-65502, internal, tag 65502
        recursive next hop: 10.0.128.70/32%overlay-1
```

Troubleshooting Multi-Site: Using Consistency Checker to Verify State at Each Site

After setting up multi-site and connecting the MSO controller to two different sites, a schema and template are configured to stretch EPGs between sites and allow communication between them. However, a few days after completing the configuration and verifying that the hosts in the respective sites are able to ping each other, a colleague notifies you that communication is down between devices in VLAN 501 in Site 1 and VLAN 502 in Site 2.

In order to begin troubleshooting, you review the configuration that was deployed initially. A single contract called *MSC-ICMP* was used to allow the devices in VLAN 501 and VLAN 502 to ping each other for IP connectivity verification. These APIC policies were configured in MSC under a template called *L3-Stretched*, and the template was associated to both sites.

You check to see if the configuration that is laid out in the MSO controller matches what is pushed individually to each site. In MSO, a built-in consistency checker can validate the configuration at each site and compare it with what is configured in MSO. You navigate to the template and notice in the top-right corner that the state is listed as *unverified*. In order to run the consistency checker, you click on that and choose VERIFY, as shown in Figure 15-43.

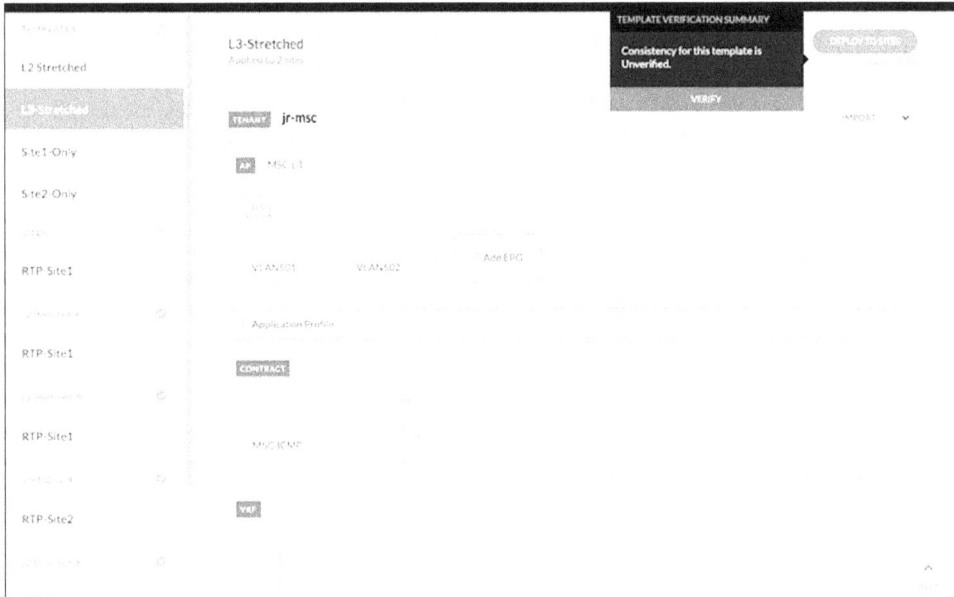

Figure 15-43   *Running a Consistency Check on the Template L3-Stretched*

After running this, you notice in the Site 1 deployment for this template that there is a warning notification. When you click on the deployment, there is a modification symbol under EPG *VLAN502*. If you click on the EPG, you see a warning indicating that modifications made to this EPG in the APIC were not done via the MSO, as shown in Figure 15-44.

Solution

In order to ensure consistency, you want to again push the template configuration to both sites. You go to the template and click on the Deploy to Sites icon to again push the configuration to each site. You then notice that the ping that was previously failing is now working again.

Interested in what changed, you navigate to VLAN 502 in Site 1 via the APIC UI. Under the audit log for VLAN 502, you can see that at the time the configuration was redeployed via MSO, the contract *MSC-ICMP* was re-created, as shown in Figure 15-45. It appears that this contract was removed by another user at the time the issue started happening.

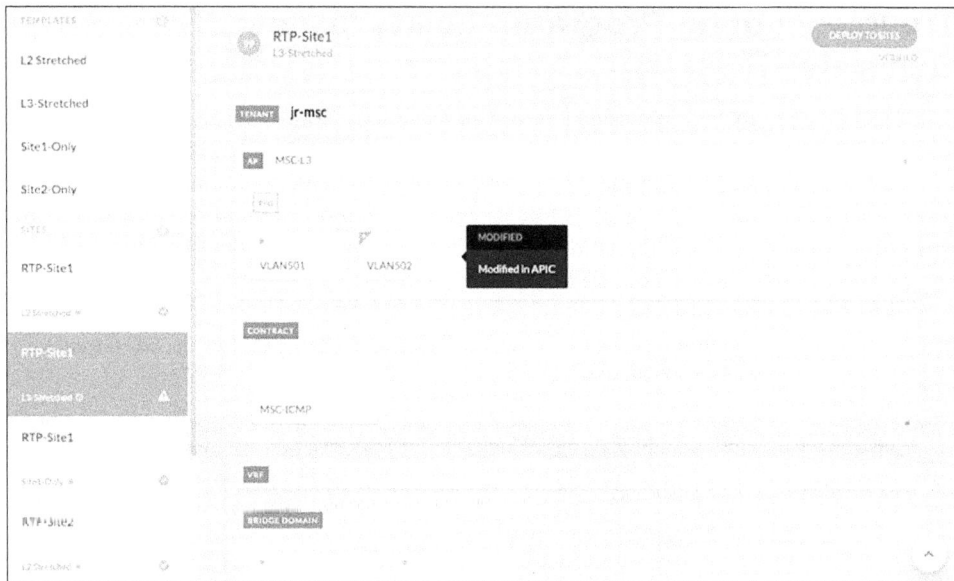

Figure 15-44 *Warning on EPG VLAN 502 That Modifications Were Made via the APIC*

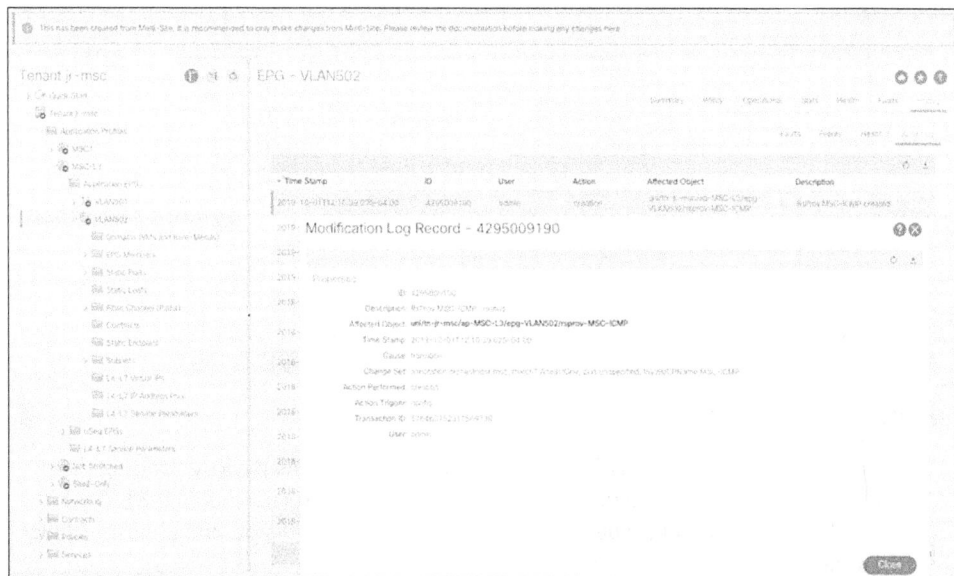

Figure 15-45 *MSC-ICMP Contract Was Re-Created on VLAN 502 in Site 1*

Using the consistency checker in MSO helps ensure that the policy is in sync if changes may have been made outside MSO.

Troubleshooting Programmability Issues: JSON Script Generates Error

You have been asked to provision a tenant by using some sort of programmability. In the near future, you are anticipating an ACI deployment in your data center that requires network provisioning with automation. You have started learning JSON and have created a sample script to validate in a lab before applying it in a production network. You end up with an issue despite calling out the proper JSON syntax through the POSTMAN REST client. An error is generated, as shown in Figure 15-46.

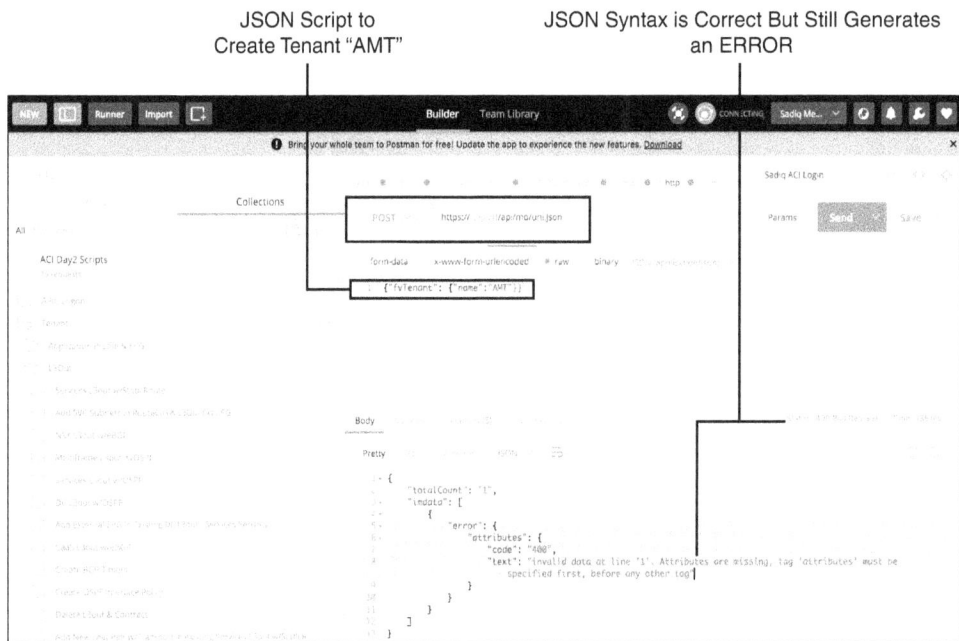

Figure 15-46   *JSON Syntax Error*

Solution

As noted in the error, that **attributes** tag is missing in the JSON payload, causing the script to fail. This is because the APIC controller that provides northbound REST APIs parses the JSON payload inside curly brackets with the object type, and it must include the **attributes** tag, as shown in Figure 15-47.

After you modify the JSON syntax to include the **attributes** tag, the APIC executes the script successfully (status code 200), and the new tenant *AMT* is created, as shown in Figure 15-48.

Added Attributes
Tag in JSON Syntax

APIC Executes the JSON
Script Without Error

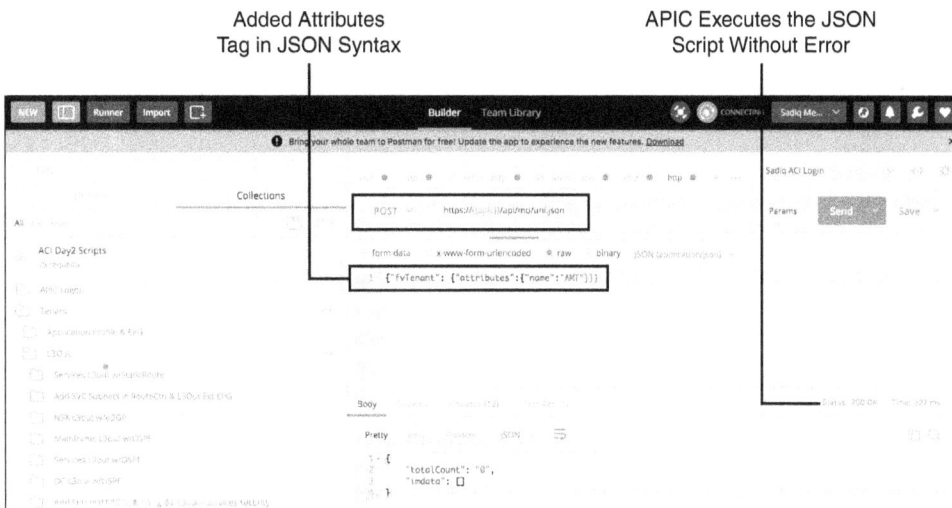

Figure 15-47 *JSON Syntax, Including the attributes Tag*

Tenant AMT is Created

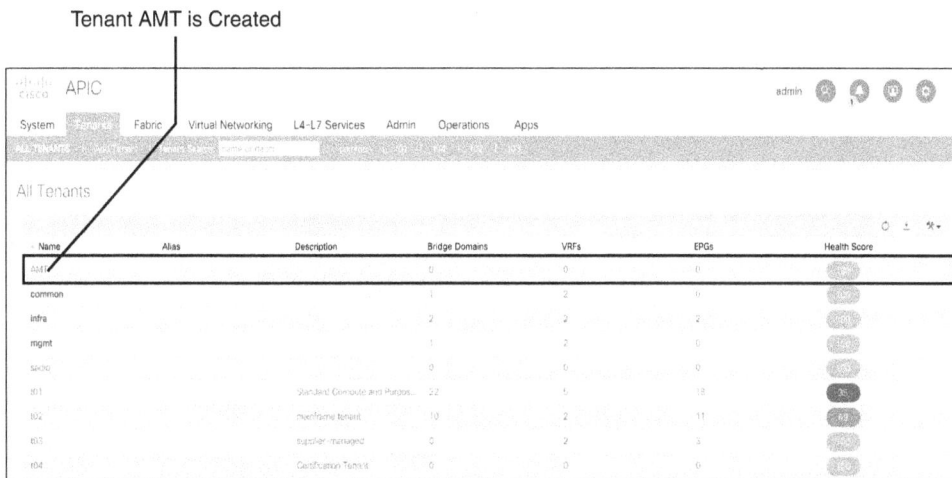

Figure 15-48 *Tenant AMT Created*

You can further verify this through the API Inspector tool in the APIC GUI. This tool is somewhat similar to a packet capture tool that displays each packet flowing through the wire. However, the API Inspector tool displays the API messages that the APIC GUI creates and sends internally to the operating system to execute a task.

To execute the API Inspector tool, you need to log on to the APIC GUI. In the top-right corner, right-click on the circular Help and Tools button and click the Show API Inspector tab to open the API Inspector window. Then you can create a new tenant through the APIC GUI. When this is done, you can switch to the API Inspector window, where you can clearly see in the payload the JSON syntax, including the **attributes** tag that ACI uses to execute the REST call (see Figure 15-49).

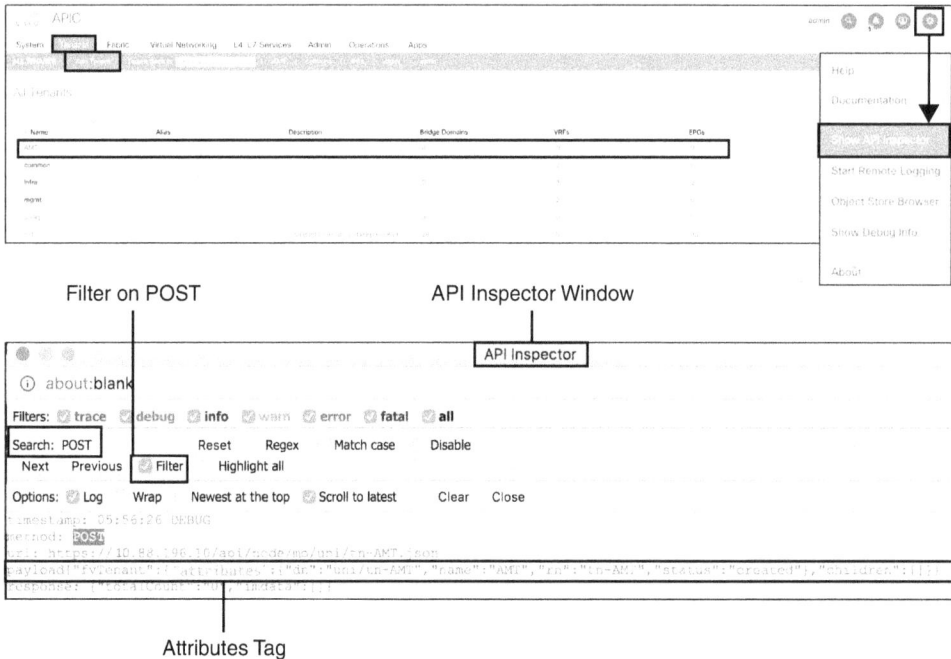

Figure 15-49 *API Inspector Tool*

Troubleshooting Multicast Issues: PIM Sparse Mode Any-Source Multicast (ASM)

Management calls you in because at the CEO's annual employee town-hall meeting, which was supposed to be broadcast through real-time media service, but video streaming did not work. The initial report in the trouble ticket says that the Digital Media Engine (DME) was streaming media content through multicast group 239.80.0.89. This media server has recently been migrated from a legacy network and is now connected to an ACI leaf pair. For decades, your company's network has been enabled to forward multicast traffic by running Protocol Independent Multicast (PIM) Sparse Mode. PIM Sparse Mode Any-Source Multicast (ASM), unlike its counterpart PIM Dense Mode, requires an RP that builds a shortest-path tree between the multicast sender and receiver. The RP (10.100.100.1) is running on your ASR 9000 WAN core router (ASR9K-WAN) outside the ACI fabric. After migrating the DME media server to ACI and connecting to leafs (Leaf-1001 and Leaf-1002), you configured PIM multicast in the fabric, pointing to the external RP (the ASR 9000 WAN core router) by using the Auto-RP feature. The ACI fabric is connected externally to the data center core router (DC-Core) through Border Leaf (BorderLeaf-202). Figure 15-50 shows the network topology enabled with multicast traffic.

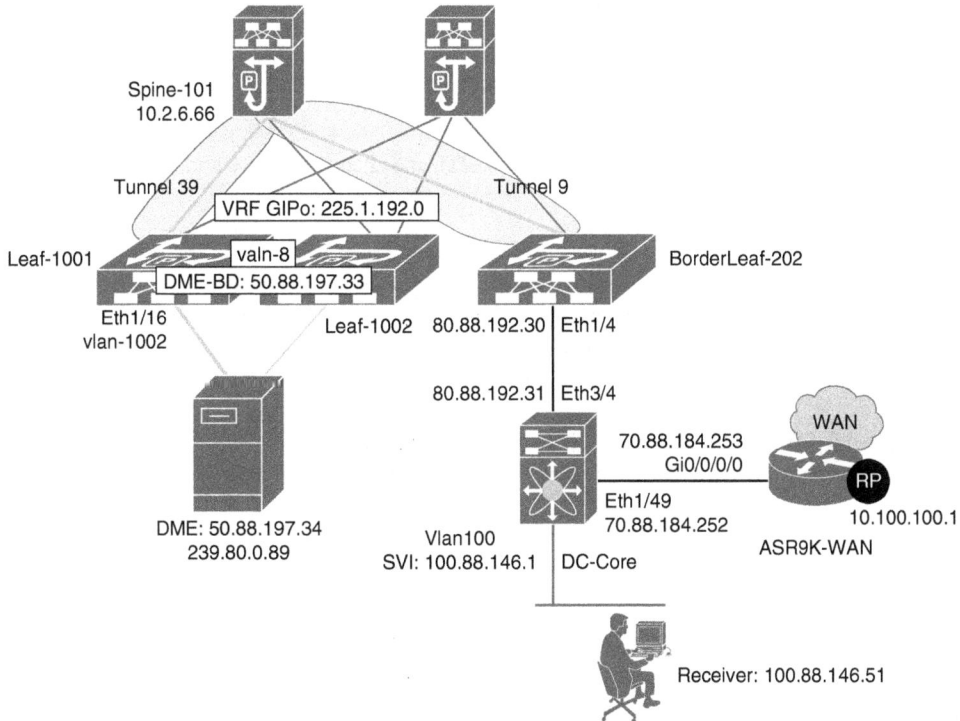

Figure 15-50   *Multicast-Enabled Network Topology*

Solution

To troubleshoot multicast issues using PIM-ASM, you need to consider the following steps:

Step 1.   Find out the multicast source, receiver and RP physical connectivity, and IP addresses.

Step 2.   Ensure that the multicast source, receiver, and RP are IP reachable together through unicast.

Step 3.   Ensure that PIM Sparse Mode is enabled on all the interfaces between multicast source (first-hop router [FHR]), receiver (last-hop router [LHR]), and RP.

Step 4.   Verify that Internet Group Management Protocol (IGMP) Snooping is enabled on the interface connecting to the multicast receiver. (In most switch platform cases, it is already enabled by default.)

A regular multicast flow using PIM Sparse Mode ASM between source and receiver consists of the following:

- The multicast source starts streaming and sends a PIM register message to the RP, using its unicast IP and multicast group addresses (S, G).

- The multicast receiver interested in media streaming sends a PIM join message to the RP, using the multicast group (*, G).

- RP establishes the shortest-path tree (SPT), and then the source and receiver start communicating directly.

You start troubleshooting the issue to determine the root cause. As a first step, you need to ask the application team to provide the IP address of the DME, which in this case is 50.88.197.34. You log in to your APIC via the CLI and run the **show endpoints** command, as shown in Example 15-33. You could also run the EP Tracker tool in the APIC GUI to find out which of the leafs in your fabric have learned the DME IP address.

Example 15-33 *DME IP Address Is Learned on Leaf 1001*

```
apic1# show endpoints ip 50.88.197.34
Legends:
(P):Primary VLAN
(S):Secondary VLAN


Dynamic Endpoints:
Tenant       : t01
Application : cp-infra-prod
AEPg         : services


 End Point MAC     IP Address    Node    Interface   Encap       Multicast Address
 ---------------   -----------   -----   ---------   ---------   --------------
 00:0C:29:B8:34:33  50.88.197.34  1001   eth1/16     vlan-1002   not-applicable

Total Dynamic Endpoints: 1
Total Static Endpoints: 0
```

The command output shows that the DME IP address 50.88.197.34 is learned on Leaf Node 1001 on interface eth1/16 with encapsulation VLAN 1002. After finding out the leaf through which DME is physically connected, you log on to it and try pinging the PIM RP address 10.100.100.1, sourcing from the DME IP subnet anycast gateway address 50.88.197.33, as shown in Example 15-34. The purpose of this is to ensure that the RP is unicast reachable from Leaf 1001, which is the First-Hop Router (FHR) where the DME is connected as multicast source. Example 15-34 shows the multicast RP address reachability from Leaf 1001 via the fabric where DME (multicast source) is connected.

Example 15-34 *RP Address Reachability from Leaf 1001 Sourcing from the DME IP Subnet Gateway*

```
Leaf-1001# show vlan extended

 VLAN Name                                Encap              Ports
 ---- -------------------------------- ---------------- ------------------------
 8    t01:dme-bd                         vxlan-16547722    Eth1/3, Eth1/15, Eth1/16
 9    t01:dme-epg                        vlan-1002         Eth1/3, Eth1/15, Eth1/16

Leaf-1001# show ip interface brief vrf t01:standard | grep vlan8
vlan8         50.88.197.33/27          protocol-up/link-up/admin-up

Leaf-1001# iping 10.100.100.1 -V t01:standard -S 50.88.197.33
PING 10.100.100.1 (10.100.100.1): 56 data bytes
64 bytes from 10.100.100.1: icmp_seq=0 ttl=252 time=1.055 ms
64 bytes from 10.100.100.1: icmp_seq=1 ttl=252 time=1.002 ms
64 bytes from 10.100.100.1: icmp_seq=2 ttl=252 time=1.001 ms
64 bytes from 10.100.100.1: icmp_seq=3 ttl=252 time=1.079 ms
64 bytes from 10.100.100.1: icmp_seq=4 ttl=252 time=0.954 ms


--- 10.100.100.1 ping statistics ---
5 packets transmitted, 5 packets received, 0.00% packet loss
round-trip min/avg/max = 0.954/1.018/1.079 ms
```

In the output shown in Example 15-34, you notice that encapsulation VLAN 1002 is bound to EPG *dme-epg*, which is associated to BD *dme-bd* forwarding on port Eth1/16. You quickly check the status of the anycast gateway of VLAN 8 with IP address 50.88.197.33 and are successful in pinging the RP address 10.100.100.1. Because you sourced the ping using the DME IP subnet anycast gateway address from Leaf 1001 and are successful at reaching the RP address, there is no need to perform this step from Border Leaf 202 or the data center core router.

Next, you check the IP reachability from the multicast receiver by pinging to the multicast source (50.88.197.3) and RP (10.100.100.1) addresses, as shown in Example 15-35. You get the IP address from one of the end users interested in receiving the multicast stream. In this case, it is 100.88.146.51.

Example 15-35 *Multicast Receiver IP Reachability to the Multicast Source and RP*

```
shussa36@eco:~> ip a
1: ens32: <BROADCAST,MULTICAST,UP,LOWER_UP> mtu 1500 qdisc pfifo_fast state UP group
  default qlen 1000
    link/ether 00:50:56:a1:d7:35 brd ff:ff:ff:ff:ff:ff
    inet 100.88.146.51/24 brd 100.88.146.255 scope global ens32
      valid_lft forever preferred_lft forever
```

```
shussa36@eco:~> ping 50.88.197.3
PING 50.88.197.34 (50.88.197.34) 56(84) bytes of data.
64 bytes from 50.88.197.34: icmp_seq=1 ttl=59 time=0.405 ms
64 bytes from 50.88.197.34: icmp_seq=2 ttl=59 time=0.423 ms
64 bytes from 50.88.197.34: icmp_seq=3 ttl=59 time=0.473 ms
64 bytes from 50.88.197.34: icmp_seq=4 ttl=59 time=0.374 ms


--- 50.88.197.34 ping statistics ---
4 packets transmitted, 4 received, 0% packet loss, time 3062ms
rtt min/avg/max/mdev = 0.374/0.418/0.473/0.043 ms

shussa36@eco:~> ping 10.100.100.1
PING 10.100.100.1 (10.100.100.1) 56(84) bytes of data.
64 bytes from 10.100.100.1: icmp_seq=1 ttl=252 time=0.598 ms
64 bytes from 10.100.100.1: icmp_seq=2 ttl=252 time=0.737 ms
64 bytes from 10.100.100.1: icmp_seq=3 ttl=252 time=0.582 ms
64 bytes from 10.100.100.1: icmp_seq=4 ttl=252 time=0.651 ms


--- 10.100.100.1 ping statistics ---
4 packets transmitted, 4 received, 0% packet loss, time 3062ms
rtt min/avg/max/mdev = 0.582/0.642/0.737/0.060 ms
```

Next, you log on to the router running RP and walk through, hop by hop, to verify PIM and RP reachability up to Leaf 1001, where the multicast source DME is connected. Example 15-36 shows the multicast RP and PIM status on the RP.

Example 15-36 *Multicast RP and PIM Status on the RP*

```
RP/0/RSP0/CPU0:ASR9K-WAN# show pim rp mapping
Sun Feb 16 21:52:33.470 UTC
PIM Group-to-RP Mappings
Group(s) 224.0.0.0/4
  RP 10.100.100.1 (?), v2
    Info source: 10.100.100.1 (?), elected via autorp
      Uptime: 6d06h, expires: 00:02:57
Group(s) 224.0.0.0/4
  RP 10.100.100.1 (?), v2
    Info source: 0.0.0.0 (?), elected via config
      Uptime: 6d06h, expires: never


RP/0/RSP0/CPU0:ASR9K-WAN# show pim interface
Sun Feb 16 21:54:21.352 UTC
```

```
PIM interfaces in VRF default
Address          Interface              PIM  Nbr   Hello DR    DR
                                             Count Intvl Prior

10.138.211.1     Loopback0              on   1     30    1     this system
10.100.100.1     Loopback9              on   1     30    1     this system
70.88.184.253    GigabitEthernet0/0/0/0 on   2     30    1     this system
```

Example 15-36 clearly shows that the ASR 9000 WAN core router is acting as the multicast RP with the Auto-RP feature. PIM is enabled on Loopback 0, Loopback 9 (used as the anycast RP address), and the GigabitEthernet0/0/0/0 interface connecting to the data center core router. You should also check to see if the multicast routing table on the RP is showing PIM join messages (*, G) and PIM register messages (S, G), as shown in Example 15-37.

Example 15-37   *Multicast Routing Table on the RP*

```
RP/0/RSP0/CPU0:ASR9K-WAN# show mrib route
Sun Feb 16 21:51:31.729 UTC


IP Multicast Routing Information Base
Entry flags: L - Domain-Local Source, E - External Source to the Domain,
    C - Directly-Connected Check, S - Signal, IA - Inherit Accept,
    IF - Inherit From, D - Drop, ME - MDT Encap, EID - Encap ID,
    MD - MDT Decap, MT - MDT Threshold Crossed, MH - MDT interface handle
    CD - Conditional Decap, MPLS - MPLS Decap, EX - Extranet
    MoFE - MoFRR Enabled, MoFS - MoFRR State, MoFP - MoFRR Primary
    MoFB - MoFRR Backup, RPFID - RPF ID Set, X - VXLAN
Interface flags: F - Forward, A - Accept, IC - Internal Copy,
    NS - Negate Signal, DP - Don't Preserve, SP - Signal Present,
    II - Internal Interest, ID - Internal Disinterest, LI - Local Interest,
    LD - Local Disinterest, DI - Decapsulation Interface
    EI - Encapsulation Interface, MI - MDT Interface, LVIF - MPLS Encap,
    EX - Extranet, A2 - Secondary Accept, MT - MDT Threshold Crossed,
    MA - Data MDT Assigned, LMI - mLDP MDT Interface, TMI - P2MP-TE MDT Interface
    IRMI - IR MDT Interface



(*,224.0.1.39) Flags: S P
  Up: 6d06h
  Outgoing Interface List
    Loopback0 Flags: II LI, Up: 6d06h
    GigabitEthernet0/0/0/0 Flags: LI, Up: 02:53:22
```

```
(10.100.100.1,224.0.1.39) RPF nbr: 10.100.100.1 Flags: RPF
  Up: 6d06h
  Incoming Interface List
    Loopback9 Flags: F A, Up: 6d06h
  Outgoing Interface List
    Loopback0 Flags: F IC, Up: 6d06h
    Loopback9 Flags: F A, Up: 6d06h
    GigabitEthernet0/0/0/0 Flags: F, Up: 6d06h

(*,224.0.1.40) Flags: S P
  Up: 6d06h
  Outgoing Interface List
    Loopback0 Flags: II LI, Up: 6d06h
    GigabitEthernet0/0/0/0 Flags: LI, Up: 01:20:00

(10.100.100.1,224.0.1.40) RPF nbr: 10.100.100.1 Flags: RPF
  Up: 6d06h
  Incoming Interface List
    Loopback9 Flags: F A, Up: 6d06h
  Outgoing Interface List
    Loopback0 Flags: F IC, Up: 6d06h
    Loopback9 Flags: F A, Up: 6d06h
    GigabitEthernet0/0/0/0 Flags: F, Up: 6d06h

(*,232.0.0.0/8) Flags: D P
  Up: 6d06h
```

This does not look good. You notice that the multicast routing table is only showing the (*, G) and (S, G) entries of Auto-RP multicast group 224.0.1.39 and 224.0.1.40; it shows nothing else. There is no PIM join message (*, G) from the multicast receiver, and there is no PIM register message (S, G) from the multicast source on multicast group 239.80.0.89.

You repeat these steps on the next-hop router from the RP, which in this case is the data center core router. Example 15-38 shows the multicast RP and PIM status, along with the multicast routing table on the data center core router.

Example 15-38 *Multicast RP and PIM Status Along with the Multicast Routing Table on the Data Center Core Router*

```
DC-Core# show ip pim rp
PIM RP Status Information for VRF "default"
BSR disabled
Auto-RP RPA: 10.100.100.1, uptime: 3w0d, expires: 00:02:30
BSR RP Candidate policy: None
```

```
BSR RP policy: None
Auto-RP Announce policy: None
Auto-RP Discovery policy: None

RP: 10.100.100.1, (0),
 uptime: 3w0d   priority: 255,
 RP-source: 10.100.100.1 (A),
 group ranges:
 224.0.0.0/4    , expires: 00:02:30 (A)


DC-Core# show ip pim interface brief
PIM Interface Status for VRF "default"
Interface            IP Address       PIM DR Address   Neighbor  Border
                                                       Count     Interface
Vlan100              100.00.116.1     100.00.146.1     1         no
Ethernet1/49         70.88.184.252    70.88.184.252    1         no
Ethernet3/4          80.88.192.30     80.88.192.30     1         no


DC-Core# show ip mroute
IP Multicast Routing Table for VRF "default"
```

You can tell that the data center core router is having no issues reaching the multicast RP. PIM is enabled on all the right interfaces. However, the multicast routing table is showing nothing for the group of interest. There is no PIM join message (*, G) from the multicast receiver. The multicast receiver is connected to a switch on VLAN 100 that is physically connected to the data center core router.

Now you repeat these steps on the next-hop router from the data center core router, which in this case is ACI Border Leaf 202. Example 15-39 shows the multicast RP and PIM status, along with the multicast routing table on ACI Border Leaf 202.

Example 15-39 *Multicast RP and PIM Status Along with the Multicast Routing Table on ACI Border Leaf 202*

```
BorderLeaf-202# show ip pim rp vrf t01:standard

PIM RP Status Information for VRF:"t01:standard"
BSR: Not Operational
Auto-RP RPA: 10.100.100.1/32
RP: 10.100.100.1, uptime: 21:25:04, expires: 00:02:57,
  priority: 0, RP-source: 10.100.100.1 (A), group-map: None, group ranges:
    224.0.0.0/4
```

```
BorderLeaf-202# show ip pim interface brief vrf t01:standard
PIM Interface Status for VRF t01:standard
Interface    IP address          DR address          Neighbor-count  Border-If
tunnel9      90.88.193.132       90.88.193.132/32    0               no
lo3          90.88.193.132/32    90.88.193.132/32    0               no
eth1/4       80.88.192.31/31     80.88.192.31/32     1               no


BorderLeaf-202# show ip mroute vrf t01:standard
IP Multicast Routing Table for VRF "t01:standard"


(*, 232.0.0.0/8), uptime: 3w0d, pim ip
  Incoming interface: Null, RPF nbr: 0.0.0.0
  Outgoing interface list: (count: 0)
```

From Example 15-39, it is observed that ACI Border Leaf 202 is having no issues reaching the multicast RP. PIM is enabled on all the right interfaces. However, the multicast routing table is showing nothing. One other thing you notice is that Border Leaf 202 has PIM enabled on interface tunnel9. You check the details of tunnel9 as shown in Example 15-40.

Example 15-40   *Checking the Details of the tunnel9 Interface*

```
BorderLeaf-202# show interface tunnel 9
Tunnel9 is up
    MTU 9000 bytes, BW 0 Kbit
    Transport protocol is in VRF "t01:standard"
    Tunnel protocol/transport is ivxlan
    Tunnel source 90.88.193.132
    Tunnel destination 225.1.192.0/32
    Last clearing of "show interface" counters never
    Tx
    0 packets output, 1 minute output rate 0 packets/sec
    Rx
    0 packets input, 1 minute input rate 0 packets/sec
```

From the output shown in Example 15-40, you can see that interface tunnel9 is established with source IP address 90.88.193.132 (the Loopback 3 interface) and destination IP address 225.1.192.0 (VRF instance GIPo address), as shown in Figure 15-51.

In ACI, when you enable multicast on the VRF instance, the APIC assigns a unique GIPo address for the VRF instance. In this case, you enabled multicast on the VRF instance *standard*, and APIC assigned the 225.1.192.0 GIPo address.

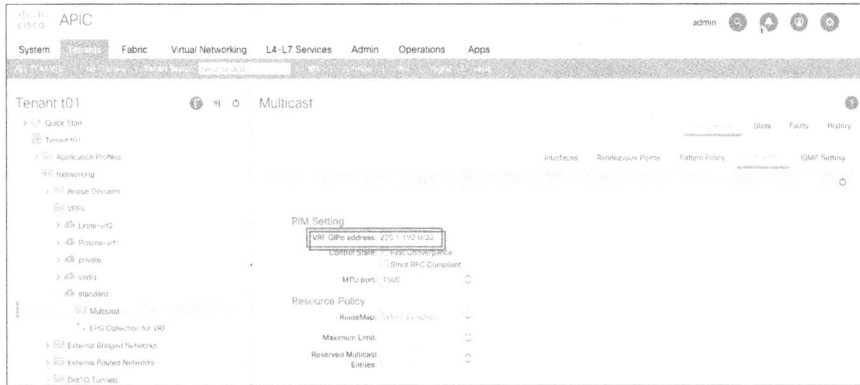

Figure 15-51 *Multicast-Enabled VRF Instance Standard*

Finally, as a last step, you check the RP and PIM status along with multicast routing details on Leaf 1001, which houses the multicast source—the DME streaming video content (see Example 15-41).

Example 15-41 *Multicast RP and PIM Status Along with the Multicast Routing Table on Leaf 1001*

```
Leaf-1001# show ip pim rp vrf t01:standard

PIM RP Status Information for VRF:"t01:standard"
BSR: Not Operational
Auto-RP RPA: 10.100.100.1/32
RP: 10.100.100.1, uptime: 1d5h, expires: 00:02:07,
  priority: 0, RP-source: 10.100.100.1 (A), group-map: None, group ranges:
    224.0.0.0/4
Leaf-1001# show ip pim interface brief vrf t01:standard
PIM Interface Status for VRF t01:standard
Interface    IP address       DR address       Neighbor-count    Border-If
tunnel39     127.0.0.100/32   127.0.0.100/32   1                 no

Leaf-1001# show ip mroute vrf t01:standard
IP Multicast Routing Table for VRF "t01:standard"

(*, 232.0.0.0/8), uptime: 3w0d, pim ip
  Incoming interface: Null, RPF nbr: 0.0.0.0
  Outgoing interface list: (count: 0)
```

From Example 15-41, you can see that Leaf 1001 is having no issues reaching the multicast RP. PIM is enabled on fabric interface tunnel39. However, the multicast routing table is showing nothing. You check the details of tunnel39, as shown in Example 15-42.

Example 15-42 *Checking the Details of the tunnel39 Interface*

```
Leaf-1001# show interface tunnel 39
Tunnel39 is up
    MTU 9000 bytes, BW 0 Kbit
    Transport protocol is in VRF "t01:standard"
    Tunnel protocol/transport is ivxlan
    Tunnel source 127.0.0.100/32
    Tunnel destination 225.1.192.0/32
    Last clearing of "show interface" counters never
    Tx
    0 packets output, 1 minute output rate 0 packets/sec
    Rx
    0 packets input, 1 minute input rate 0 packets/sec
```

Example 15-42 shows that tunnel39 is sourcing from localhost with destination IP address 225.1.192.0 (the VRF instance GIPo address). This means the only missing point in the entire multicast topology is that BD *dme-bd* is not enabled for PIM. To prove this, you need to run the command shown in Example 15-43 in the APIC CLI.

Example 15-43 *Checking PIM Status on BD dme-bd*

```
apic1# show bridge-domain dme-bd detail | grep PIM
PIM Enabled          : no
```

Based on this output, you know that on Leaf 1001 you will not see any PIM register (S, G) entry for multicast group 239.80.0.89, as verified in Example 15-44.

Example 15-44 *Multicast Routing Table on Leaf 1001*

```
Leaf-1001# show ip mroute vrf t01:standard
IP Multicast Routing Table for VRF "t01:standard"

(*, 232.0.0.0/8), uptime: 3w0d, pim ip
  Incoming interface: Null, RPF nbr: 0.0.0.0
  Outgoing interface list: (count: 0)
```

You enable multicast PIM on BD *dme-bd*, as shown in Figure 15-52.

After you enable PIM on BD *dme-bd*, multicast streaming starts working. You check the status of IP multicast on all the routers involved, as illustrated in Example 15-45.

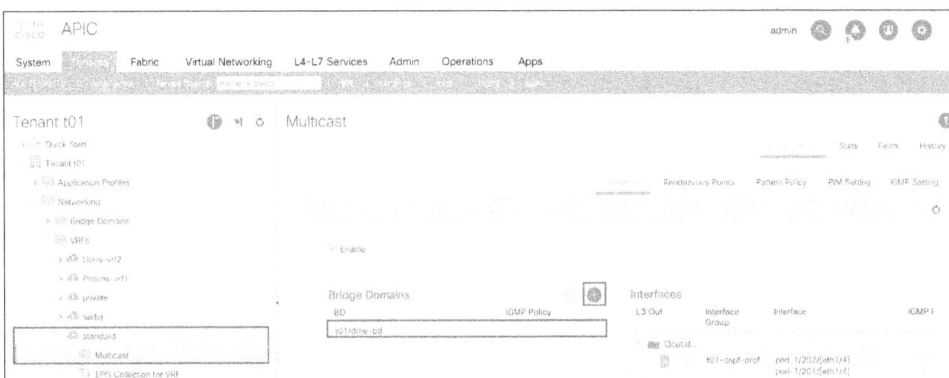

Figure 15-52 *Enabling PIM on BD dme-bd*

Example 15-45 *Checking Multicast Status on All the Routers in the Network Topology*

```
Leaf-1001:
Leaf-1001# show ip pim interface brief vrf t01:standard
PIM Interface Status for VRF t01:standard
Interface      IP address           DR address            Neighbor-count    Border-If
tunnel39       127.0.0.100/32       127.0.0.100/32        1                 no
vlan8          50.88.197.33/27      50.88.197.33/32       0                 no    ← BD SVI


Leaf-1001# show ip mroute vrf t01:standard
IP Multicast Routing Table for VRF "t01:standard"


(*, 224.2.133.134/32), uptime: 00:36:44, igmp ip pim
  Incoming interface: Tunnel39, RPF nbr: 10.2.44.64
  Outgoing interface list: (count: 1)
    Vlan8, uptime: 00:36:44, igmp

(50.88.197.34/32, 224.2.133.134/32), uptime: 00:36:45, ip pim mrib
  Incoming interface: Tunnel39, RPF nbr: 10.2.6.66 (pervasive)
  Outgoing interface list: (count: 1)
    Vlan8, uptime: 00:36:44, mrib

(*, 232.0.0.0/8), uptime: 2w4d, pim ip
  Incoming interface: Null, RPF nbr: 0.0.0.0
  Outgoing interface list: (count: 0)
```

```
(50.88.197.34/32, 239.80.0.89/32), uptime: 00:36:47, ip pim
  Incoming interface: Tunnel39, RPF nbr: 10.2.6.66 (pervasive)        ← Spine1 VTEP
  Outgoing interface list: (count: 0)


BorderLeaf-202:
BorderLeaf-202# show ip mroute vrf t01:standard
IP Multicast Routing Table for VRF "t01:standard"

(*, 224.2.133.134/32), uptime: 3d02h, ngmvpn ip pim
  Incoming interface: Ethernet1/4, RPF nbr: 80.88.192.30
  Outgoing interface list: (count: 1) (Fabric OIF)
    Tunnel9, uptime: 3d02h, ngmvpn

(50.88.197.34/32, 224.2.133.134/32), uptime: 3d02h, pim mrib ip
  Incoming interface: Tunnel9, RPF nbr: 10.2.6.66 (pervasive)
  Outgoing interface list: (count: 1)
    Tunnel9, uptime: 3d02h, mrib, (RPF)

(*, 232.0.0.0/8), uptime: 8w0d, pim ip
  Incoming interface: Null, RPF nbr: 0.0.0.0
  Outgoing interface list: (count: 0)

(50.88.197.34/32, 239.80.0.81/32), uptime: 00:00:54, pim ip ngmvpn
  Incoming interface: Tunnel9, RPF nbr: 10.2.6.66 (pervasive)         ← Spine1 VTEP
  Outgoing interface list: (count: 2) (Fabric OIF)
    Tunnel9, uptime: 00:00:54, ngmvpn, (RPF)
    Ethernet1/4, uptime: 00:00:54, pim             ← Connected to data center core


DC-Core:
DC-Core# show ip mroute

(*, 239.80.0.89/32), uptime: 00:23:28, igmp ip pim
  Incoming interface: Ethernet1/49, RPF nbr: 70.88.184.253  ← Connected to ASR 9000
  WAN
  Outgoing interface list: (count: 1)
    Vlan100, uptime: 00:23:28, igmp  ← Receiver connected and joins IGMP

(50.88.197.34/32, 239.80.0.89/32), uptime: 00:23:28, pim mrib ip
  Incoming interface: Ethernet3/4, RPF nbr: 80.88.192.31  ← Connected to Border Leaf
  202
  Outgoing interface list: (count: 2)
    Ethernet1/49, uptime: 00:23:28, pim  ← Connected to ASR 9000 WAN
    Vlan100, uptime: 00:23:28, mrib  ← Connected to receiver
```

```
DC-Core# show ip igmp groups 239.80.0.89


IGMP Connected Group Membership for VRF "default" - matching  Group "239.80.0.89"
Type: S - Static, D - Dynamic, L - Local, T - SSM Translated, H - Host Proxy
Group Address   Type   Interface   Uptime     Expires    Last Reporter
239.80.0.89     D      Vlan100     01:53:51   00:02:39   100.88.146.51   ← Receiver
  joined multicast group
ASR9K-WAN:
RP/0/RSP0/CPU0:ASR9K-WAN# show mrib route
(*,239.80.0.89) RPF nbr: 10.100.100.1 Flags: C RPF
  Up: 00:22:21
  Incoming Interface List
    Decapstunnel0 Flags: A, Up: 00:22:21
  Outgoing Interface List
    GigabitEthernet0/0/0/0 Flags: F NS, Up: 00:22:21    ← Connected to data center
  core

(50.88.197.34,239.80.0.89) RPF nbr: 10.100.100.1 Flags: L C RPF
  Up: 00:47:46
  Incoming Interface List
    Decapstunnel0 Flags: A, Up: 00:47:46
```

To summarize the solution in this case, you executed the following troubleshooting steps:

Step 1. Ensured that ACI learned the DME media server (multicast source) endpoint 50.88.197.34 on Leaf 1001 eth1/16 (refer to Example 15-33).

Step 2. Verified that the DME media server (multicast source) is associated to EPG *dme-epg* on encapsulation VLAN 1002 with BD *dme-bd*. Checked the connectivity by pinging the DME media server IP address 50.88.197.34 from the ToR ACI leaf (refer to Example 15-34).

Step 3. Checked IP reachability from multicast receiver to the DME media server (multicast source) and to the RP (ASR 9000 WAN core router) (refer to Example 15-35).

Step 4. Logged on to the ASR 9000 WAN core router and checked the RP and PIM interface status (refer to Example 15-36).

Step 5. Verified the multicast routing table on the RP (ASR 9000 WAN core router) (refer to Example 15-37).

Step 6. Logged on to the next-hop router from the RP toward the multicast source, which is the data center core router, and verified the RP, PIM interface status, and multicast routing table (refer to Example 15-38).

Step 7.   Logged on to the next-hop router from the data center core router toward the multicast source, which is ACI Border Leaf 202, and verified the RP, PIM interface status, and multicast routing table (refer to Example 15-39).

Step 8.   Verified that Border Leaf 202 is using the tunnel9 interface sourced from its Loopback 3 IP address 90.88.193.132 and destination by using the VRF instance GIPo address 225.1.192.0. The APIC assigned this GIPo address on the VRF instance when you enabled PIM multicast in ACI on the VRF instance (refer to Figure 15-50 and Example 15-40).

Step 9.   Logged on to the next-hop router from ACI Border Leaf 202, which is ACI Leaf 1001, where the DME media server (multicast source) is connected, and verified the RP and multicast routing table (refer to Example 15-41).

Step 10.   Checked the PIM interface status on ACI Leaf 1001, where the BD *dme-bd* anycast gateway (50.88.197.33/27) resides and found out that it is not enabled with PIM (refer to Example 15-43).

Step 11.   Enabled the PIM interface on BD *dme-bd*, after which multicast started functioning normally (refer to Figure 15-51 and Example 15-45).

Summary

Throughout this book, you have explored the vast areas of ACI, and you should be on your way to becoming proficient in monitoring and troubleshooting an ACI fabric. This chapter demonstrates numerous troubleshooting scenarios that have been seen in the field and provides isolation steps you can follow to identify an issue, as well as remediation steps you can take to fix various issues.

Note   There are no Key Topics or Review Questions for this chapter.

Answers to Chapter Review Questions

Chapter 1

1. A, B, D. ACI brings business agility through rapid deployment of an entire application-hosting infrastructure that includes network, storage, and virtualization. These application infrastructure components are deployed through automation workflows and orchestration techniques, filling gaps between the infrastructure teams that worked in a siloed fashion in the past. ACI supports both bare-metal and virtual compute platforms, with additional ease and benefit in moving virtual machine workloads without compromising application performance. This is explained in the introductory material in Chapter 1.

2. B, D, E. ACI considers network centric and application centric design philosophies while deploying application-hosting infrastructure. It guides you to start with a network centric approach, mapping your traditional network VLANs to EPGs to easily migrate your existing application workloads to ACI. Once all the application workloads are migrated, you can use the more efficient method of the application centric model, using full application logic without bothering about VLAN and network segment allocations and apply security enforcement. You can also use a hybrid model, in which your existing applications workloads are migrated using the network centric model and new applications are deployed using the application centric model. This is explained in the section "ACI Building Blocks" in Chapter 1.

3. B. ACI uses a specific Type-Length-Value (TLV) setting in an LLDP protocol data unit (PDU) to discover fabric nodes. This is explained in the section "Control Plane" in Chapter 1.

4. A, F. ACI uses IS-IS, MP-BGP EVPN, COOP, and OpFlex as control plane protocols and VXLAN as the data plane protocol. VXLAN is used in the data plane to get a large number of application workloads through an extended network segments range. VXLAN uses 24 bits to scale the network segments to roughly 16 million from traditional VLAN-based networks that allow only up to 4096 segments. IS-IS is used

862 Appendix A: Answers to Chapter Review Questions

to build the fabric underlay and distribute VXLAN VTEP addresses inside the fabric. MP-BGP EVPN is used to distribute external routes inside the fabric via border leafs. COOP is a control plane protocol that is used to store endpoint information fabricwide to help optimize traffic forwarding. OpFlex is a Cisco-proprietary protocol used to communicate policy intent from APICs to fabric devices. This is explained in the sections "Control Plane," "Data Plane," and "VXLAN" in Chapter 1.

5. C, E. ACI uses a slightly modified version of the IETF VXLAN protocol. It uses the reserved bits for intelligent forwarding inside the fabric. VXLAN is a Layer 2 overlay scheme that encapsulates MAC addresses into a UDP packet and hence is also called the MAC-in-UDP method. It is commonly used to extend Layer 2 segments between widely dispersed data centers over Layer 3 networks. VXLAN works with 24-bit VXLAN IDs and allows the total number of network segments to scale up to 16 million, whereas the traditional VLAN method uses 12-bit IDs and limits the network segment size to 4096. VXLAN does not require the use of Spanning Tree Protocol as it operates on Layer 3 networks and takes complete advantage of equal-cost multipathing (ECMP) to use all available paths. This is explained in the section "VXLAN" in Chapter 1.

6. A, C, G. In ACI, an application profile is a container to house and organize various application endpoint groups. An EPG is a collection of endpoints that require common policies. Security policies in the form of contracts are applied on EPGs. A bridge domain is a Layer 2 forwarding construct in ACI that can contain a subnet that can be local or advertised externally. Multiple EPGs can be part of a single bridge domain as policies are applied on EPGs and not at Layer 2 (VLAN) or Layer 3 (IP). A tenant is an administrative boundary to securely host multiple organization application-hosting infrastructures. VRF is a Layer 3 forwarding construct to isolate multiple routing domains for security and stability. A contract preferred group allows two or more EPGs to communicate freely as if they were part of the same EPG. EPGs outside the preferred group require a contract to communicate. This is explained in the sections "Tenant," "VRF," "Application Profile," "Endpoint Group," "Contracts," "Bridge Domain," and "External Routed or Bridged Network" in Chapter 1.

Chapter 2

1. A, E. The ACI policy model is a convenient model for building application logic through required policies. These policies are rendered automatically by APICs inside the fabric infrastructure. This is explained in the introductory material of Chapter 2.

2. A, B, D. In ACI, a user interacts with an APIC through the REST API to create and modify objects in the policy model, which ultimately results in the allocation of hardware resources. Configuration is applied through a centralized APIC system to fabric switches. This method ensures consistent changes and avoids human errors. These switches must be registered to the fabric first before they can be configured by an APIC. This is explained in the section "Key Characteristics of the Policy Model" in Chapter 2.

3. C, D. The ACI policy model abstracts the control policy from the configuration in hardware to provide flexibility without disrupting the services. This is explained in the section "Benefits of the Policy Model" in Chapter 2.

4. B, D, F, G. Contracts are used to enforce security policies in ACI. In ACI, contracts are applied on application EPGs to enforce security policies on endpoints, regardless of their Layer 2 or Layer 3 attributes. A contract preferred group allows certain EPGs with full communication within a VRF instance while restricting others through a contract with restrictive filters. A taboo contract allows all traffic but denies certain traffic. It is useful during migration cases. This is explained in the section "Contracts" in Chapter 2.

5. A, C, D, E. Switch policies govern switchwide configurations, which can be grouped together for common functionalities and applied to specific switch nodes. COPP and VPC domain policies are defined under switch policy and in most cases work with the default settings. A switch profile is used to tie a leaf or spine switch to a specific switch policy group. It is recommended to configure a one-to-one mapping between physical switches and the corresponding switch profile. This is explained in the section "Switch Policies" in Chapter 2.

6. B, D, G. Interface policies govern the interface-related policies that are grouped together for common functionality of end-host connectivity. To configure interface policies, first you need to configure policies, and then you include those policies in a policy group, and finally you create a profile with an interface selector and assign a policy group to it. An interface profile associates the Ethernet interfaces through the interface selector and maps it to a switch profile. This is explained in the section "Interface Policies" in Chapter 2.

7. A, B, C. An AAEP restricts admins to access certain VLANs that are part of the domain on a particular interface to avoid overlap. An AAEP is tied to an interface policy group and associated with a domain. If multitenancy is not required, a single AAEP is sufficient for each domain type, such as physical, VMM, External L2, or External L3. This is explained in the section "Attachable Access Entity Profile" in Chapter 2.

Chapter 3

There are no Review Questions for Chapter 3.

Chapter 4

1. B, D, F. Stretch a single ACI fabric to multiple locations by connecting leaf switches in each location through dark fiber to every spine switch in the fabric. A single ACI fabric can be stretched using transit leafs connected through DWDM. ACI fabric with a single APIC cluster can be stretched using transit leafs connected through EoMPLS. This is explained in the section "Single- Versus Multiple-Fabric Design" in Chapter 4.

2. A, B, E. The verified latency between sites is up to 10 milliseconds and distance of up to 500 miles, or 800 kilometers. A single ACI fabric can be stretched between up to three sites. This is explained in the section "Single- Versus Multiple-Fabric Design" in Chapter 4.

3. B, F. ACI fabrics can be connected together using a multi-site design through ISN for applications requiring Layer 2 extension. ACI fabrics can be connected together using a dual-fabric design through DCI (such as OTV) to provide Layer 2 extension for applications. This is explained in the section "Single- Versus Multiple-Fabric Design" in Chapter 4.

4. A, B, E. Multi-pod provides better design resiliency than the stretched fabric using a transit leaf design. It provides fabric scalability for up to 400 leafs. Multi-pod uses separate control plane protocol instances in different pods deployed at different locations. This is explained in the section "Multi-pod" in Chapter 4.

5. B, D, E, F. Spines in each pod are connected to the IPN router with either 40 Gbps or 100 Gbps interfaces. The routing protocol used between spines and IPN routers must be OSPF. PIM Bidir must be enabled in the IPN router. DHCP Relay must be enabled in the IPN router for fabric node registration in other pods. This is explained in the section "Multi-pod" in Chapter 4.

6. B, C. The data plane protocol VXLAN requires a larger MTU size. VXLAN requires an extra 50 bytes in MTU size. This is explained in the section "Multi-pod" in Chapter 4.

7. A, D, E. Cloud-scale spines are required to connect to ISN routers. Spines in each site are connected to the ISN router with either 40 Gbps or 100 Gbps interfaces. The MTU size is required to be increased an additional 50 bytes in the ISN router for VXLAN. This is explained in the section "Multi-site" in Chapter 4.

8. A, D. Migration strategies in a multi-site design include creating brand-new policies in Multi-Site Orchestrator to be deployed at multiple ACI fabric sites and importing existing APIC policies into Multi-Site Orchestrator. This is explained in the section "Multi-site" in Chapter 4.

9. A, C, E, F. Only cloud-scale leaf switches are supported for remote leaf deployments. Only cloud-scale spine switches are supported for IPN connectivity. The ACI fabric expects the DSCP value coming from the remote leaf to the main DC spine over the IPN router to be the same. In a multi-pod fabric deployment, a remote leaf is registered with one specific pod only. This is explained in the section "Remote Leaf" in Chapter 4.

Chapter 5

1. C, D, E. VPC in ACI uses ZeroMQ for control messages. VPC in ACI does not require a physical peer link between leaf switches. An APIC assigns an auto-generated virtual IP address from the system TEP pool for a VPC leaf pair. This is explained in the section "Virtual Port Channel (VPC)" in Chapter 5.

2. B, D, E. Access ports are the end host–facing ports, such as ports for servers, IP storage, switches, routers, and L4/L7 devices. Access ports can be configured as Trunk, Access (802.1P), or Access (untagged). Access (802.1P) sends traffic tagged with VLAN 0, whereas Access (untagged) sends traffic without tagging any VLAN. This is explained in the section "Virtual Port Channel (VPC)" in Chapter 5.

3. A, B, E. In ACI, a clear and meaningful naming standard should be defined and used. There should be one switch profile individually for each leaf switch for access port configuration, and there should be a separate switch profile for each VPC pair configuration. There should be one physical domain per tenant for bare-metal servers, one for virtual compute, and one for external network connectivity. This is explained in the section "Best Practices in Configuring Access Policies" in Chapter 5.

4. A, B, D. A fabric extender (FEX) is a device used to extend switching capability for ease of cable management. There is no support for external router connectivity using L3Outs on FEX ports. A FEX can connect to only a single leaf. This is explained in the section "FEX Connectivity" in Chapter 5.

5. A, C, D. ACI uses the FCoE protocol on leafs to connect to storage devices. In ACI, storage-accessing hosts are connected using an F port, and a SAN switch is connected using an NP port configuration on the same leaf. FCoE traffic in ACI is not forwarded to spine switches. This is explained in the section "Connecting Storage in ACI" in Chapter 5.

6. B, C, E. An external bridge domain helps you extend an entire bridge domain. In ACI, an EPG can be extended to an external bridge network during application server migration. ACI statically maps the traditional VLAN to an EPG to extend a bridge network externally. This is explained in the section "Connecting an External Bridge Network" in Chapter 5.

7. A, B, D. An external routed network is configured under a tenant. External routed network connections support routed interfaces, routed subinterfaces, and SVI interfaces. External routed network connectivity using L3Out configuration supports OSPF, BGP, and EIGRP protocols and static routes. This is explained in the section "Connecting an External Routed Network" in Chapter 5.

8. C, D, E. GOLF is an EVPN-based external routed network connectivity solution for scaling VRF instances. GOLF routers are connected through spines. The OpFlex control plane automates the fabric-facing VRF configuration on a GOLF router. This is explained in the section "GOLF" in Chapter 5.

9. A, B, E. Spine-to-IPN connectivity must be via 40/100 Gbps links. Spine-to-IPN connectivity is configured under the *Infra* tenant, using the OSPF routing protocol only. For remote leaf-to-upstream IPN router connectivity, a QSA adapter is required for 1/10 Gbps connections. This is explained in the section "Network Connectivity Between Pods and Sites" in Chapter 5.

Chapter 6

There are no Review Questions for Chapter 6.

Chapter 7

1. B, D. Service nodes such as firewalls or ADCs can be connected in either Transparent mode or Routed mode using ACI Service Insertion. Service Insertion is configured by creating front-end and back-end EPGs in a sandwich design. This is explained in the section "Service Insertion" in Chapter 7.

2. A, B, C. An ACI service graph, unlike other service insertion techniques, requires the provider and consumer EPGs to communicate through a contract. In a service graph, service nodes are attached using shadow EPGs. Using a service graph, the service nodes do not necessarily need to be the default gateways for application servers. This is explained in the section "Service Graph" in Chapter 7.

3. B, C, D. Managed mode provides a single pane of glass for centralized management of all the L2–L7 configuration and service automation using a Cisco APIC. In Unmanaged mode, the network infrastructure portion of the service graph configuration is carried out by the APIC, and service node configuration is done by non-Cisco service device vendors. With Unmanaged mode, there are no software code alignment restrictions between your ACI infrastructure and service nodes. This is explained in the section "Managed Mode Versus Un-Managed Mode" in Chapter 7.

4. A, C, E. ACI uses service graph technology for speedy deployment of L4–L7 services in a network. A service graph is useful for creating service portals for end users to insert L4–L7 services as they require. An ACI service graph offers three modes of configuration: Managed, Unmanaged, and Hybrid. This is explained in the section "L4–L7 Integration Use Cases" in Chapter 7.

Chapter 8

1. C, E. Automation involves executing configuration changes, collecting statistics, and so on using tools and scripts as a single task on a single device. Orchestration involves executing multiple tasks as a workflow for faster deployment of a business application. Running a script to enable certain ports on network devices is an example of automation, whereas enabling ports on network devices connecting to servers, installing an operating system, and deploying and running an application through a single workflow are examples of orchestration. This is explained in the section "The Difference Between Automation and Orchestration" in Chapter 8.

2. A, D, E. Automation and orchestration techniques help with rapid and consistent configuration changes, bring simplicity with complex application-hosting infrastructure deployments, reduce human error, enable configuration changes on-the-fly, provide service catalog offerings to end users, enable quick recovery of network services during

disasters, and provide overall cost reductions. This is explained in the section "Benefits of Automation and Orchestration" in Chapter 8.

3. B, C, D. With ACI it is possible to make native REST API calls using Extensible Markup Language (XML) or JavaScript Notation (JSON) formats. ACI also offers the option of using a programming language such as Python. Cisco ACI offers the Python Software Development Kit (SDK), also known as Cobra, to make API calls to the APIC without having to post raw XML and JSON format. The other REST API option is the ACI Toolkit, which is essentially a set of Python libraries built on top of the ACI object model that abstracts the model into a simplified version. This is explained in the section "Benefits of Automation and Orchestration" in Chapter 8.

4. B, D, F. REST is a client/server communication method that uses the TCP-based HTTP/HTTPS protocol. ACI uses JSON and XML document formats in native REST API calls. The supported HTTPS methods in ACI are GET, POST, and DELETE. This is explained in the section "REST API" in Chapter 8.

5. A, C, D, G. ACI offers built-in tools that can simplify and help in automating configuration tasks; among them are Visore, Object (Save as), MOQuery via the CLI, and API Inspector. Visore gives you a complete hierarchical view of the management information tree (MIT). Object (Save as) lets you save a particular object configuration on your workstation without showing URL information. MOQuery is a cousin of Visore that provides the same capability of viewing an object in the MIT but working in the CLI only. API Inspector is like a wiretap that gives you the view of API messages. This is explained in the section "Automating Tasks Using Native REST API: JSON and XML" in Chapter 8.

6. C, F, G. Ansible is a data center automation tool that manages application, compute, network, and virtualization. Ansible runs on a computer system called a control node that pushes automation scripts to end devices called managed nodes by using an SSH connection. Ansible is an agentless tool, unlike its competitors Chef and Puppet. This is explained in the section "Automating Tasks Using Ansible" in Chapter 8.

7. A, B, F. UCS Director is a data center automation, orchestration, and monitoring tool that manages the entire application hosting infrastructure. It enables you to build workflows that provide service automation and to publish these workflows in Service Catalog for end users. Using UCS Director, ACI tenant and infrastructure configuration can be automated. This is explained in the section "Orchestration Through UCS Director" in Chapter 8.

Chapter 9

1. A, C, D. A fault is a failure in ACI fabric that is represented by a managed object (MO). A fault code is an alphanumeric string that uniquely identifies the type of fault being raised. The fault life cycle transitions from Soaking to Raised to Clearing. This is explained in the section "Faults and Health Scores" in Chapter 9.

2. B, C, D. Health scores enable you to monitor faults and the general health of the entire ACI fabric. Health scores range from 0 to 100%, with 100% indicating a fully fit and functional ACI fabric. To check the overall fabric health in the APIC GUI, go to System > Dashboard. This is explained in the section "Faults and Health Scores" in Chapter 9.

3. C, D, E. ACI offers built-in tools such as syslog, SNMP, and NetFlow for monitoring the fabric. This is explained in the section "ACI Built-in Monitoring Tools" in Chapter 9.

4. A, C, D. SNMP is a mechanism to manage and monitor computer networks. SNMP in ACI can only perform GET, GET NEXT, GET BULK, and WALK operations. All SNMP protocol versions (v1, v2c, and v3) are supported in ACI. This is explained in the section "SNMP" in Chapter 9.

5. A, B, D. SNMP Traps are generated based on the events or faults that occurred on a managed object (MO). SNMP traps are enabled under access, fabric, and tenant configuration on an APIC. ACI supports 10 trap destination servers. This is explained in the section "SNMP" in Chapter 9.

6. B, C, E. Syslog is a mechanism for collecting and storing system logs. Fault, event, audit, and session logs can be collected and stored locally on an APIC and sent to an external logging server. Faults or events in the ACI fabric can trigger the sending of a syslog message. This is explained in the section "Syslog" in Chapter 9.

7. A, B, E. NetFlow is a protocol used to collect IP traffic information. NetFlow policies are enabled with access and tenant configuration on an APIC. ACI supports only NetFlow Version 9. This is explained in the section "NetFlow" in Chapter 9.

8. A, B, D. NetFlow is used for network monitoring, network usage billing, and forensics. ACI supports only NetFlow Version 9. This is explained in the section "NetFlow" in Chapter 9.

Chapter 10

There are no Review Questions for Chapter 10.

Chapter 11

There are no Review Questions for Chapter 11.

Chapter 12

1. C. In ACI, IS-IS is used as an underlay routing protocol to exchange reachability information about TEP addresses as well as other TEP or IP ranges assigned for different purposes. This is explained in the section "IS-IS, TEP Addressing, and the ACI Underlay" in Chapter 12.

2. D. On top of the unicast routing table, the ACI fabric switches build a multicast distribution tree (MDT) and leverage fabric tags (FTags) on top of IS-IS. IS-IS was the obvious
choice for the ACI underlay because it allows the capability of adding extensions. FTags
are added as an extension to the IS-IS frame and allow the switches to agree on the different paths by which a multidestination frame can flow through the fabric. This allows
for a multidestination forwarding domain that is loop free and provides load sharing
between all available links in the ACI fabric. This is explained in the section "FTAGs and
the MDT" in Chapter 12.

3. B, C, E. If WebServer 1 sends an ARP request for another host within its subnet, the
ASIC triggers learning for not only the source MAC address but also the sender IP
address. This is again because the ASICs in ACI switches have the ability to inspect
the payload of the ARP request and perform learning and forwarding based on it.
Figure 12-14 illustrates the learning pipeline as an ARP request enters a Layer 3–enabled
bridge domain. This is explained in the section "Endpoint Learning in a Layer 3–Enabled
Bridge Domain" in Chapter 12.

4. D. When an endpoint is learned, it needs to be synced to multiple other locations to
ensure proper forwarding throughout the entire fabric. The way this is achieved is by
running a protocol called the Council of Oracle Protocol (COOP). This is explained in
the section "Council of Oracles Protocol" in Chapter 12.

5. A. When a multi-pod L3Out is created, the router ID defined on the spine node in the
logical node profile is chosen as the CP-TEP. The CP-TEP is responsible for establishing
a BGP session to each spine in the remote pod. This BGP session is used to advertise
endpoint and route information between pods. This is explained in the section "Multi-
pod" in Chapter 12.

6. B, C, D. PIM Bidir is no longer required in the inter-site network (ISN) because the
spines capable of supporting multi-site can also "head-end replicate" any multidestination frame. This means that instead of flooding the frame in the BD GIPo, a multi-site
spine can replicate a unicast copy of the frame and send it to each site that needs to
receive it. The original frame is encapsulated in iVXLAN and sent to a unique TEP
address allocated to each site: the data plane multicast TEP. When spines in a specific
site receive an iVXLAN packet destined to this TEP, they flood the packet on the FTag
and GIPo for the bridge domain in the local site. Multi-site spines can also be connected back-to-back, eliminating the need for an ISN completely if the physical restraints
allow it. This can simplify a deployment significantly. Finally, because each site is a
separate ACI fabric, unique VNIDs and sclass allocations exist. What this means is that
if you had devices in two sites that wanted to communicate in a VRF instance, the VRF
instance VNID assignment for the VRF instance in each site would be different. How
would communication work if the VNID that identifies the segment boundary is different? To overcome this and ensure that workloads can exist and communicate across
sites, VNID and sclass translations were implemented. This is explained in the section
"Multi-site" in Chapter 12.

7. B, D, E. Remote makes it possible to connect a remote DC branch to an existing ACI fabric. This is done by connecting at least one pair of leafs to an ISN and allowing IP connectivity back to the main ACI pod. In order for iVXLAN traffic to flow between a pod and remote leafs, TEP addresses must be allocated to the spines in the main pod, as well as to the remote leafs to allow forwarding of iVXLAN packets between them. This is explained in the section "Remote Leaf" in Chapter 12.

8. A, C. By default, ARP flooding is not enabled. This means that ARP traffic will be unicasted to the leaf where the target IP address resides when the destination is known or sent to the spine proxy when it is unknown. This avoids unnecessary flooding of ARP traffic in the fabric. This is explained in the section "Forwarding Scenarios: ARP Optimization" in Chapter 12.

9. C, E. The fabric tracks these QoS groups by using a class of service (CoS) value in the outer Ethernet header. Besides the three user-definable classes, the fabric has CoS values reserved for internal functions, such as control plane traffic, a best-effort class for SPAN traffic, and a strict priority class controller communication. QoS Level 3 is the default class. Every packet entering the ACI fabric is placed into this class (unless a custom QoS configuration is used). This is explained in the section "Quality of Service (QoS)" in ACI in Chapter 12.

10. B. Traffic is sent with the DL bit set in the iVXLAN header when it is routed between VRF instances. This is explained in the "Forwarding Scenarios" section in Chapter 12.

Chapter 13

1. A, B, C. Both MOQuery and icurl are tools you can run on an APIC to query the REST API and get objects back. You can also use the APIC UI because it also queries the REST API and displays it in a GUI. This is explained in the "General Troubleshooting" section in Chapter 13.

2. C, D. The controller ID must be unique to each APIC. Furthermore, the pod ID may be the same, but it also could be different if the APICs exist in different ACI pods. This is explained in the "APIC Cluster Troubleshooting" section in Chapter 13.

3. A, C, D. ctrlr-uuid-mismatch, infra-ip-mismatch, and wiring-mismatch are all valid wiring issues that can be raised on leaf switches. These issues get raised when a leaf detects a configuration parameter on the connected APIC that does not match its configuration, and the APIC is therefore not allowed into the fabric. This is explained in the "APIC Cluster Troubleshooting" section in Chapter 13.

4. A, D, E. The Cisco ACI fabric switches have a few major buckets that packets can be classified in: buffer drops, error drops, forward drops, and LB drops. This is explained in the section "How to Verify Physical and Platform-Related Issues" in Chapter 13.

5. C, D. When an EP is marked rogue, the leaf switch sets the DL bit in the iVXLAN header for any traffic sourced from that endpoint to ensure that other leafs in the fabric also do not learn. Also, a fault is raised about the endpoint that has been marked rogue. This is explained in the section "Troubleshooting Endpoint Connectivity" in Chapter 13.

6. A, B, D. This is explained in the "Troubleshooting Contract-Related Issues" section in Chapter 13.

7. C. ELAM stands for Embedded Logic Analyzer Module. This is explained in the "Embedded Logic Analyzer Module" section in Chapter 13.

Chapter 14

There are no Review Questions for Chapter 14.

Chapter 15

There are no Review Questions for Chapter 15.

Index

www.ingramcontent.com/pod-product-compliance
Lightning Source LLC
Chambersburg PA
CBHW080333220326
41598CB00030B/4492